DATE DUE

			PRINTED IN U.S.A.

Poetry Criticism

Guide to Gale Literary Criticism Series

When you need to review criticism of literary works, these are the Gale series to use:

If the author's death date is:	You should turn to:

After Dec. 31, 1959
(or author is still living)

CONTEMPORARY LITERARY CRITICISM

for example: Jorge Luis Borges, Anthony Burgess,
William Faulkner, Mary Gordon,
Ernest Hemingway, Iris Murdoch

1900 through 1959

TWENTIETH-CENTURY LITERARY CRITICISM

for example: Willa Cather, F. Scott Fitzgerald,
Henry James, Mark Twain, Virginia Woolf

1800 through 1899

NINETEENTH-CENTURY LITERATURE CRITICISM

for example: Fedor Dostoevski, Nathaniel Hawthorne,
George Sand, William Wordsworth

1400 through 1799

LITERATURE CRITICISM FROM 1400 TO 1800
(excluding Shakespeare)

for example: Anne Bradstreet, Daniel Defoe,
Alexander Pope, François Rabelais,
Jonathan Swift, Phillis Wheatley

SHAKESPEAREAN CRITICISM

Shakespeare's plays and poetry

Antiquity through 1399

CLASSICAL AND MEDIEVAL LITERATURE CRITICISM

for example: Dante, Homer, Plato, Sophocles, Vergil,
the Beowulf Poet

Gale also publishes related criticism series:

CHILDREN'S LITERATURE REVIEW

This series covers authors of all eras who have written for the
preschool through high school audience.

SHORT STORY CRITICISM

This series covers the major short fiction writers of all
nationalities and periods of literary history.

POETRY CRITICISM

This series covers poets of all nationalities, movements, and
periods of literary history.

ISSN 1052-4851

R

Poetry Criticism

Excerpts from Criticism of the Works of the Most Significant and Widely Studied Poets of World Literature

VOLUME 2

Robyn V. Young
Editor

 **Gale Research Inc.** • *DETROIT* • *LONDON*

STAFF

Robyn V. Young, *Editor*

Zoran Minderović, Thomas Votteler, *Associate Editors*

Jennifer Brostrom, Cathy Falk, Mary K. Gillis, Ian Goodhall, Elizabeth P. Henry, David Kmenta, Marie Lazzari, Susan Peters, Eric Priehs, David Segal, Bridget Travers, Debra A. Wells, Janet M. Witalec, *Assistant Editors*

Jeanne A. Gough, *Permissions & Production Manager*

Linda M. Pugliese, *Production Supervisor*

Maureen Puhl, Jennifer VanSickle, *Editorial Associates*

Donna Craft, Lorna Mabunda, Paul Lewon, Camille Robinson, Sheila Walencewicz, *Editorial Assistants*

Victoria B. Cariappa, *Research Manager*

Maureen Richards, *Research Supervisor*

Judy L. Gale, Paula Cutcher-Jackson, *Editorial Associates*

Amy Kachele, Robin M. Lupa, Mary Beth McElmeel, Tamara C. Nott, *Editorial Assistants*

Sandra C. Davis, *Permissions Supervisor (Text)*

Josephine M. Keene, Denise M. Singleton, Kimberly F. Smilay, *Permissions Associates*

Maria L. Franklin, Michele M. Lonoconus, Shalice Shah, Nancy K. Sheridan, Rebecca A. Stanko, *Permissions Assistants*

Patricia A. Seefelt, *Permissions Supervisor (Pictures)*

Margaret A. Chamberlain, *Permissions Associate*

Pamela A. Hayes, Keith Reed, *Permissions Assistants*

Mary Beth Trimper, *Production Manager*

Evi Seoud, *Assistant Production Manager*

Arthur Chartow, *Art Director*

Kathleen A. Mouzakis, *Graphic Designer*

C. J. Jonik, *Keyliner*

Contents

Preface

At various points in literary history, poetry has been defined as "jigging veins of rhyming mother wits" (Christopher Marlowe); "the spontaneous overflow of powerful feelings" (William Wordsworth); "the opening and closing of a door, leaving those who look through to guess about what is seen during a moment" (Carl Sandburg); and "a momentary stay against confusion" (Robert Frost). The study of poetry produces a natural curiosity about the political, social, moral, and literary trends of a particular time period and is an essential element of a well-rounded liberal arts curriculum.

Poetry Criticism (PC) was created in response to librarians serving high school, college, and public library patrons who noted an increasing number of requests for critical material on poets. Like its Gale predecessor in genre-oriented studies, *Short Story Criticism (SSC),* which presents material on writers of short fiction, *PC* is designed to provide users with substantial critical excerpts and biographical information on the world's most frequently discussed and studied poets in high school and undergraduate college courses. Each *PC* entry is supplemented by biographical and bibliographical material to help guide the user to a greater understanding of the genre and its creators. Although major poets and movements are covered in such Gale Literary Criticism Series as *Contemporary Literary Criticism (CLC), Twentieth-Century Literary Criticism (TCLC), Nineteenth-Century Literature Criticism (NCLC), Literature Criticism from 1400 to 1800 (LC),* and *Classical and Medieval Literature Criticism (CMLC), PC* offers more focused attention on individual poets than is possible in the broader, survey-oriented entries on writers in these Gale series.

Scope of the Work

In order to reflect the influence of tradition as well as innovation, poets from various nationalities, eras, and movements will be represented in every volume of *PC.* For example, the present volume includes commentary on Robert Browning, one of the most prominent poets of the Victorian era, whose *The Ring and the Book* advanced the art of the dramatic monologue to new levels of technical and psychological sophistication; Claude McKay, the first prominent writer of the Harlem Renaissance, who concentrated on the black working class for his subject matter and for a means of preserving the creativity of the African spirit; Anne Sexton, a member of the often controversial Confessional school of poetry, who wrote highly introspective verse that revealed intimate details of her emotional troubles; and Dylan Thomas, whose lyrical poems, steeped in the lore of his Welsh homeland, became even more celebrated after his premature death. Since many of these poets have inspired a prodigious amount of critical explication, *PC* is necessarily selective, and the editors have chosen the most important published criticism to aid readers and students in their research.

Students, teachers, librarians, and researchers will find that the generous excerpts and supplementary material provided by *PC* supply them with vital information needed to write a term paper on poetic technique, examine a poet's most prominent themes, or lead a poetry discussion group. Twelve to fifteen authors will be analyzed in each volume, and each author entry presents a historical survey of the critical response to that author's work. Some early reviews are included to indicate initial reaction and are often written by the author's contemporaries, while current analyses provide a modern view. The length of an entry is intended to reflect the amount of critical attention that the author has received from critics writing in English and from foreign critics in translation. Critical articles and books that have not been translated into English are excluded. Every attempt has been made to identify and include excerpts from the most significant essays on each author's work. In order to provide these important critical pieces, the editors will sometimes reprint essays that have appeared in previous volumes of Gale's Literary Criticism Series. Such duplication, however, never exceeds fifteen percent of a *PC* volume. Finally, because of space limitations, the reader may find that some important articles are not excerpted. Instead, these pieces may be found in the author's further reading list, with complete bibliographic information followed by a brief descriptive note.

Organization of the Book

A *PC* author entry consists of the following components:

- The **author heading** cites the name under which the author wrote, followed by birth and death dates. If the author wrote consistently under a pseudonym, the pseudonym will be listed in the author heading and his or her legal name given in parentheses on the first line of the biographical and critical introduction. Uncertainty as to a birth or death date is indicated by question marks.

- The **biographical and critical introduction** contains background information designed to introduce a reader to the author and to the critical discussions surrounding his or her work. Parenthetical material following the introduction provides references to other biographical and critical series published by Gale, including *CLC, TCLC, NCLC, LC, CMLC,* and *SSC, Children's Literature Review, Contemporary Authors, Dictionary of Literary Biography,* and *Something about the Author.*

- A **portrait of the author** is included when available. Many entries also contain illustrations of materials pertinent to an author's career, including holographs of manuscript pages, title pages, dust jackets, letters, or representations of important people, places, and events in the author's life.

- The list of **principal works** is chronological by date of first publication and lists the most important works by the author. The first section comprises poetry collections and book-length poems. The second section gives information on other major works by the author. For foreign authors, the editors have provided original foreign-language publication information and have selected what are considered the best and most complete English-language editions of their works.

- The **critical excerpts** are arranged chronologically in each author entry to provide a useful perspective on changes in critical evaluation over the years. All individual titles of poems and poetry collections by the author featured in the entry are printed in boldface type to enable a reader to ascertain without difficulty the works under discussion. For purposes of easier identification, the critic's name and the publication date of the essay are given at the beginning of each piece of criticism. Unsigned criticism is preceded by the title of the journal in which it originally appeared. Publication information (such as publisher names and book prices) and parenthetical numerical references (such as footnotes or page and line references to specific editions of a work) have been deleted at the editor's discretion to provide smoother reading of the text.

- Critical excerpts are prefaced with **explanatory notes** as an additional aid to students and readers using *PC.* The explanatory notes provide several types of useful information, including: the reputation of a critic, the importance of a work of criticism, and the specific type of criticism (biographical, psychoanalytic, historical, etc.).

- Whenever available, **insightful comments from the authors themselves and excerpts from author interviews** are also included. Depending upon the length of such material, an author's commentary may be set within boxes or boldface rules.

- A complete **bibliographical citation,** designed to help the interested reader locate the original essay or book, follows each piece of criticism.

- The **further reading list** appearing at the end of each entry suggests additional materials for study of the author. In some cases it includes essays for which the editors could not obtain reprint rights.

Other Features

- A **cumulative author index** lists all the authors who have appeared in *PC, CLC, TCLC, NCLC, LC, CMLC,* and *SSC,* as well as cross-references to the Gale series *Children's Literature Review, Contemporary Authors, Contemporary Authors New Revision Series, Contemporary Authors Autobiography Series, Dictionary of Literary Biography, Dictionary of Literary Biography Yearbook, Concise Dictionary of American Literary Biography, Something about the Author, Something about the Author Autobiography Series,* and *Yesterday's Authors of Books for Children.* Users will welcome this cumulated index as a useful tool for locating an author within the Literary Criticism Series.

- A **cumulative nationality index** lists all authors featured in *PC* by nationality, followed by the number of the *PC* volume in which the author appears.

- A **cumulative title index** lists in alphabetical order all individual poems, book-length poems, and collection titles contained in the *PC* series. Titles of poetry collections and separately published poems are printed in italics, while titles of individual poems are printed in roman type with quotation marks. Each title is followed by the author's name and the corresponding volume and page number where commentary on the work may be located. English-language translations of original foreign-language titles are cross-referenced to the foreign titles so that all references to discussion of a work are combined in one listing.

A Note to the Reader

When writing papers, students who quote directly from any volume in the Literary Criticism Series may use the following general formats to footnote reprinted criticism. The first example pertains to material drawn from periodicals, the second to material reprinted from books:

[1] David Daiches, "W. H. Auden: The Search for a Public," *Poetry* LIV (June 1939), 148-56; excerpted and reprinted in *Poetry Criticism,* Vol. 1, ed. Robyn V. Young (Detroit: Gale Research, 1990), pp. 7-9.

[2] Pamela J. Annas, *A Disturbance in Mirrors: The Poetry of Sylvia Plath* (Greenwood Press, 1988); excerpted and reprinted in *Poetry Criticism,* Vol. 1, ed. Robyn V. Young (Detroit: Gale Research, 1990), pp. 410-14.

Suggestions Are Welcome

Readers who wish to suggest authors to appear in future volumes, or who have other suggestions, are cordially invited to contact the editors.

Acknowledgments

The editors wish to thank the copyright holders of the excerpted criticism included in this volume, the permissions managers of many book and magazine publishing companies for assisting us in securing reprint rights, and Anthony Bogucki for assistance with copyright research. We are also grateful to the staffs of the Detroit Public Library, Wayne State University Purdy/Kresge Library Complex, and the University of Michigan Libraries for making their resources available to us. Following is a list of the copyright holders who have granted us permission to reprint material in this volume of *PC.* Every effort has been made to trace copyright, but if omissions have been made, please let us know.

COPYRIGHTED EXCERPTS IN *PC,* VOLUME 2, WERE REPRINTED FROM THE FOLLOWING PERIODICALS:

The American Book Review, v. 7, September-October, 1985. © 1985 by *The American Book Review.* Reprinted by permission of the publisher.—*American Poetry,* v. 3, Winter, 1986. © 1986 by Lee Bartlett and Peter White. All rights reserved. Reprinted by permission of the publisher.—*Anglo-Welsh Review,* Spring, 1973.—*Books Abroad,* v. 39, Winter, 1965. Copyright 1965 by the University of Oklahoma Press. Reprinted by permission of the publisher.—*Boston University Journal,* v. XX, Autumn, 1972 for "Stifled Protest: Politics and Poetry in the Work of Rainer Maria Rilke" by Egon Schwarz. Copyright 1972 by the Trustees of Boston University. Reprinted by permission of the author.—*The Centennial Review,* v. XXIII, Summer, 1979 for "Carl Sandburg and the Undetermined Land" by Bernard Duffey. © 1979 by *The Centennial Review.* Reprinted by permission of the publisher and the author.—*CLA Journal,* v. XXII, June, 1979; v. XXXII, March, 1989. Copyright, 1979, 1989 by The College Language Association. Both used by permission of The College Language Association.—*Colby Library Quarterly,* v. X, June, 1973. Reprinted by permission of the publisher.—*Contemporary Literature,* v. 16, Spring, 1975; v. 20, Summer, 1979. © 1975, 1979 by the Board of Regents of the University of Wisconsin System. Both reprinted by permission of The University of Wisconsin Press.—*Critical Quarterly,* v. 7, Spring, 1965 for "Necessity and Freedom: The Poetry of Robert Lowell, Sylvia Plath and Anne Sexton" by A. R. Jones. Reprinted by permission of the author.—*Criticism,* v. XXVIII, Fall, 1986 for "Thomas Gray: Drowning in Human Voices" by Wallace Jackson. Copyright, 1986, Wayne State University Press. Reprinted by permission of the publisher and the author.—*Discourse: A Review of the Liberal Arts,* v. XII, Winter, 1969 for "Rainer Maria Rilke: The Pursuit of the Self" by Karen Elias. © 1969 Concordia College. Reprinted by permission of the author.—*ELH,* v. 47, Fall, 1980. Copyright © 1980 by The Johns Hopkins University Press. All rights reserved. Reprinted by permission of the publisher.—*Encounter,* v. XXXIV, February, 1970. © 1970 by Encounter Ltd. Reprinted by permission of the publisher.—*The Germanic Review,* v. LXIV, Summer, 1989 for "The Mediating Muse: Of Men, Women and the Feminine in the Work of Rainer Maria Rilke" by Kathleen L. Komar. Copyright 1989 by Helen Dwight Reid Educational Foundation. Reprinted by permission of the author.—*Grand Street,* v. 8, Spring, 1989 for "Anna Akhmatova" by Henry Gifford. Copyright © 1989 by Grand Street Publications, Inc. All rights reserved. Reprinted by permission of the publisher and the author—*The Hudson Review,* v. XIII, Summer, 1960. Copyright © 1960, renewed 1988 by The Hudson Review, Inc. Reprinted by permission of the publisher.—*The Massachusetts Review,* v. XIX, Spring, 1978. © 1978./v. IX, Winter, 1968. © 1968. Reprinted from *The Massachusetts Review,* The Massachusetts Review, Inc. by permission.—*Modern Austrian Literature,* v. 15, 1982. © 1982 copyright International Arthur Schnitzler Association 1982. Reprinted by permission of the publisher.—*The Nation,* New York, v. 196, February 23, 1963. Copyright 1963 *The Nation* magazine/The Nation Company, Inc. Reprinted by permission of the publisher.—*New York Herald Tribune Books,* March 6, 1932. Copyright 1932 I.H.T. Corporation./August 23, 1936. Copyright 1936 I.H.T. Corporation. Reprinted by permission of the publisher.—*The New York Times Book Review,* October 24, 1920. Copyright 1920 by The New York Times Company. Reprinted by permission of the publisher.—*Parnassus: Poetry in Review,* v. 11, 1983-84; v. 14, 1987. Copyright © 1984, 1987 Poetry in Review Foundation, NY. Both reprinted by permission of the publisher.—*PHYLON: The Atlanta University Review of Race and Culture,* v. XL, June, 1979. Copyright, 1979, by Atlanta University, Atlanta, GA. Reprinted with permission.—*PMLA,* v. LXXXI, December, 1966. Copyright © 1966 by the Modern Language Association of America. Reprinted by permission of the Modern Language Association of America.—*Poetry,* v. LXXXIX, October, 1956. © 1956 by the Modern Poetry Association./v. CXI, March, 1968 for "Robert Duncan's World" by Paul Zweig. © 1968 by Paul Zweig and the Modern Poetry Association. Reprinted by permission of the Editor of *Poetry* and Georges Borchardt, Inc., for the author./v. LXXXIII, January, 1954 for "Claude McKay's Art" by M. B. Tolson. © 1954 by the Modern Poetry Association. Reprinted by permission of the Editor of *Poetry* and the Literary Estate of the author./v. LXXII, April, 1948 for "Myth and Torment" by Muriel Rukeyser. © 1948, renewed 1976 by the Modern Poetry Association. Reprinted by permission of the Editor of *Poetry* and the Literary Estate of the author./v. XCVI,

COPYRIGHTED EXCERPTS IN *PC,* VOLUME 2, WERE REPRINTED FROM THE FOLLOWING BOOKS:

Authors to Be Featured in *PC,* Volumes 3 and 4

Amiri Baraka, 1934- (American poet, dramatist, essayist, editor, short story writer, novelist, and critic)—An important figure in the development of contemporary African-American letters whose own career has encompassed the Beat movement, black nationalism, and the tenets of Marxist-Leninist philosophy, Baraka writes verse imbued with such concerns as cultural alienation, interracial conflict, and the necessity for social change through revolutionary means.

Hart Crane, 1899-1932 (American poet and essayist)—Often compared to William Blake, Samuel Taylor Coleridge, and Charles Baudelaire, Crane sought salvation through art from the spiritual torment of human existence. His major work, *The Bridge,* has undergone substantial critical reevaluation since its publication in 1930.

Federico García Lorca, 1898-1936 (Spanish poet, dramatist, critic, and essayist)—One of Spain's most important twentieth-century poets, García Lorca combined his knowledge of Spanish and classical literature with folk and gypsy ballads to create an idiom at once traditional, modern, and personal. His verse attests to the beauty and excitement of life experienced close to the natural world.

Pablo Neruda, 1904-1973 (Chilean poet, essayist, short story writer, editor, memoirist, and dramatist)—Awarded the Nobel Prize for Literature in 1971, Neruda is widely regarded as the most important contemporary Latin American poet of the twentieth century. He is remembered for his innovative techniques and influential contributions to major developments in modern poetry, both in his native land and abroad.

Ezra Pound, 1885-1972 (American poet, translator, critic, essayist, editor, and librettist)—Credited with creating some of modern poetry's most enduring and inventive verse, Pound expedited the Modernist period in English and American letters by introducing and elucidating Imagist and Vorticist theories. His experiments with rhythm are often considered the first substantial twentieth-century effort to liberate poetry from iambic patterns.

Arthur Rimbaud, 1854-1891 (French poet)—Rimbaud is regarded as an important forerunner of the Symbolist movement and a major influence on twentieth-century poetry and poetics. His major works, *Les illuminations* and *Une saison en enfer,* demonstrate his contributions to the development of the prose poem and his innovative use of the subconscious as a source of literary inspiration.

Walt Whitman, 1819-1882 (American poet, essayist, novelist, short story writer, journalist, and editor)—One of America's seminal poets, Whitman sought to reach the common people whom he felt were ignored by a literature written for the elite. His masterpiece, *Leaves of Grass,* is a classic in American letters.

William Wordsworth, 1770-1850 (English poet, critic, essayist, and dramatist)—Wordsworth is regarded as a key figure in English literature for his perceptive use of nature as a moral guide, his earnest exploration of philosophical ideas, and for his original poetic theories. His pastoral poems in *Lyrical Ballads* helped initiate the Romantic movement, and his major work, *The Prelude, or Growth of a Poet's Mind,* is considered one of the greatest long poems of the nineteenth century.

Additional Authors to Appear
in Future Volumes

Addison, Joseph 1672-1719
AE (ps. of George William Russell)
1867-1935
Aeschylus 525-546 B.C.
Aiken, Conrad 1889-1973
Akhmadulina, Bella 1937-
Aldington, Richard 1892-1962
Aleixandre, Vicente 1898-1984
Alighieri, Dante 1265-1321
Ammons, A. R. 1926-
Armah, Ayi Kwei 1939-
Ashbery, John 1927-
Barker, George 1913-
Barnes, Djuna 1892-1982
Behn, Aphra 1640?-1689
Bell, Marvin 1937-
Belloc, Hilaire 1870-1953
Benét, Stephen Vincent 1898-1943
Benét, William Rose 1886-1950
"Beowulf Poet" c. 8th cent.
Berry, Wendell 1934-
Berryman, John 1914-1972
Betjeman, Sir John 1906-1984
Bishop, Elizabeth 1911-1979
Bidart, Frank 1939-
Blake, William 1757-1827
Bly, Robert 1926-
Bogan, Louise 1897-1970
Bontemps, Arna 1902-1973
Borges, Jorge Luis 1899-1986
Bradstreet, Anne 1612-1672
Brodsky, Joseph 1940-
Brooke, Rupert 1887-1915
Brooks, Gwendolyn 1917-
Brown, George Mackay 1921-
Brown, Sterling A. 1901-1989
Browning, Elizabeth Barrett 1806-
1861
Brutus, Dennis 1924-
Bunyan, John 1628-1688
Burns, Robert 1759-1796
Byron, George Gordon, Lord Byron
1788-1824
Caedmon d. c. 680
Cardenal, Ernesto 1925-
Carroll, Lewis 1832-1898
Cavafy, C. P. 1863-1933
Césaire, Aimé 1913-
Char, René 1907-
Chaucer, Geoffrey c.1343-1400
Ciardi, John 1916-
Clampitt, Amy 1920-
Clarke, Austin 1896-1974
Coleridge, Samuel Taylor 1772-1834
Corn, Alfred 1943-

Cotter, Joseph Seamon, Sr. 1861-1949
Crane, Stephen 1871-1900
Creeley, Robert 1926-
Cullen, Countee 1903-1946
Cummings, E. E. 1894-1962
Day Lewis, Cecil 1904-1972
De La Mare, Walter 1873-1956
Deutsch, Babette 1895-1982
Dickey, James 1923-
Dodson, Owen 1914-1983
Doolittle, Hilda 1886-1961
Dove, Rita 1952
Dryden, John 1631-1700
Dunbar, Paul Lawrence 1872-1906
Dunn, Douglas 1942-
Dunn, Stephen 1939-
Eberhart, Richard 1904-
Eliot, T. S. 1888-1965
Elytis, Odysseus 1911-
Emerson, Ralph Waldo 1803-1882
Evans, Mari 1923-
Ewart, Gavin 1916-
Forten, Charlotte L. 1837-1914
Gallagher, Tess 1943-
Garrigue, Jean 1914-1972
Gautier, Théophile 1811-1872
"Gawain Poet" fl. 1370
Ghalib, Asadullah Khan 1797-1869
Gibran, Kahlil 1883-1931
Ginsberg, Allen 1926-
Giovanni, Nikki 1943-
Glück, Louise 1943-
Goethe, Johann Wolfgang von 1749-
1832
Goldsmith, Oliver 1728?-1832
Graham, Jorie 1951-
Graves, Robert 1895-1985
Grimké, Angelina Weld 1880-1958
Guest, Edgar A. 1881-1959
Guillén, Jorge 1893-1984
Guillén, Nicolas 1902-1989
Gunn, Thom 1929-
Gustafson, Ralph 1909-
Hacker, Marilyn 1942-
Hagiwara Sakutaro 1886-1942
Hall, Donald 1928-
Hammon, Jupiter 1711?-1800?
Hardy, Thomas 1840-1928
Harper, Frances Ellen Watkins 1825-
1911
Harper, Michael 1938-
Harte, Bret 1836-1902
Hass, Robert 1941-
Hayden, Robert 1913-1980
Heaney, Seamus 1939-

Hecht, Andrew 1923-
Heine, Heinrich 1797-1856
Herbert, George 1593-1633
Herbert, Zbigniew 1924-
Herrick, Robert 1591-1674
Hirsch, Edward 1950-
Hölderlin, Friedrich 1770-1843
Hollander, John 1929-
Homer fl. 9th or 8th cent B.C.
Hooker, Jeremy 1941-
Hopkins, Gerard Manley 1844-1889
Howard, Richard 1929-
Hughes, Ted 1930-
Hugo, Richard 1923-1982
Hugo, Victor 1802-1885
Hulme, T. E. 1883-1917
Hunt, Leigh 1784-1859
Ignatow, David 1914-
Isherwood, Christopher 1904-1986
Ishikawa Takuboku 1886-1912
Jackson, Laura Riding 1901-
Jacobsen, Josephine 1908-
Jarrell, Randall 1914-1965
Jeffers, Robinson 1887-1962
Johnson, James Weldon 1871-1938
Jonson, Ben 1572-1637
Jordan, June 1936-
Justice, Donald 1925-
Kennedy, X. J. 1929-
Kerouac, Jack 1922-1969
Kinnell, Galway 1927-
Kinsella, Thomas 1928-
Kipling, Rudyard 1865-1936
Kizer, Carolyn 1925-
Knight, Etheridge 1931-
Koch, Kenneth 1925-
Kumin, Maxine 1925-
LaFontaine, Jean de 1621-1695
Laforgue, Jules 1860-1887
Lamartine, Alphonse Marie de 1790-
1869
Lamb, Charles 1775-1834
Larkin, Philip 1922-1985
Lawrence, D. H. 1885-1930
Levertov, Denise 1923-
Levine, Philip 1928-
Liberman, Laurence 1935-
Lindsay, Vachel 1879-1931
Longfellow, Henry Wadsworth 1807-
1882
Lorde, Audre 1934-
Lowell, Amy 1874-1925
Lowell, James Russell 1819-1891
Lowell, Robert 1917-1977
Loy, Mina 1882-1966

Lundkvist, Artur 1905-
Lytton, Edward Robert Bulwer 1803-1873
Macaulay, Thomas Babington 1800-1859
MacLeish, Archibald 1892-1982
MacNeice, Louis 1907-1963
Madhubuti, Haki R. 1942-
Mallarme, Stephanie 1842-1898
Malouf, David 1934-
Marlowe, Christopher 1564-1599
Martial 42?-102? A.D.
Marvell, Andrew 1621-1678
McGuckian, Medbh 1950-
Masefield, John 1878-1967
Meredith, George 1828-1909
Meredith, William 1919-
Merrill, James 1926-
Merwin, W. S. 1927-
Miles, Josephine 1911-1985
Millay, Edna St. Vincent 1892-1950
Milosz, Czeslaw 1911-
Milton, John 1608-1674
Montague, John 1929-
Moore, Marianne 1887-1972
Moss, Howard 1922-1987
Murray, Les A. 1938-
Nash, Ogden 1902-1971
Nemerov, Howard 1920-
Neruda, Pablo 1904-1973
Niedecker, Lorine 1903-1970
Nishiwaki Junzaburo 1894-
Nye, Robert 1939-
O'Hara, Frank 1926-1966
O'Hehir, Diana 1922-
Okigbo, Christopher 1932-1967
Olds, Sharon 1942-
Olson, Charles 1910-1970
Olson, Elder 1909-
Ondaatje, Michael 1943-
Ortiz, Simon 1941-
Owen, Wilfred 1893-1918
Pastan, Linda 1932-

Pasternak, Boris 1890-1960
Patchen, Kenneth 1911-1972
Petrarch 1304-1374
Pope, Alexander 1688-1744
Powys, John Cowper 1872-1963
Prokosch, Frederic 1906-
Pushkin, Aleksander 1799-1837
Raine, Craig 1944-
Randall, Dudley 1914-
Ransom, John Crowe 1888-1974
Rexroth, Kenneth 1905-1982
Rich, Adrienne 1929-
Rios, Alberto 1952-
Rodgers, Carolyn M. 1945-
Roethke, Theodore 1908-1963
Rosenthal, M. L. 1917-
Rossetti, Christina 1830-1894
Rossetti, Dante Gabriel 1828-1882
Rothenberg, Jerome 1931-
Rukeyser, Muriel 1913-1980
Sanchez, Sonia 1934-
Sanders, Ed 1939-
Sarton, May 1912-
Sassoon, Siegfried 1886-1967
Schnackenberg, Gjertrud 1953-
Schuyler, James 1923-
Schwartz, Delmore 1913-1966
Scott, Sir Walter 1771-1832
Senghor, Léopold Sédar 1906-
Service, Robert 1874-1958
Shapiro, Karl 1913-
Shelley, Percy Bysshe 1792-1822
Sidney, Sir Philip 1554-1586
Simpson, Louis 1923-
Smart, Christopher 1722-1771
Smith, Dave 1942-
Snodgrass, W. D. 1926-
Snyder, Gary 1930-
Song, Cathy 1955-
Sorrentino, Gilbert 1929-
Soto, Gary 1952-
Soyinka, Wole 1934-
Spender, Stephen 1909-

Spenser, Edmund 1552?-1599
Squires, Radcliffe 1917-
Stafford, William 1914-
Stein, Gertrude 1874-1946
Stevens, Wallace 1879-1955
Strand, Mark 1934-
Swenson, May 1919-1989
Swift, Jonathan 1667-1745
Swinburne, Algernon Charles 1837-1909
Tagore, Sir Rabindranath 1861-1941
Taneda Santoka 1882-1940
Tate, Allen 1899-1979
Tennyson, Alfred, Lord Tennyson 1809-1892
Thoreau, Henry David 1817-1862
Tillinghast, Richard 1940-
Tolson, Melvin B. 1898-1966
Tomlinson, Charles 1927-
Toomer, Jean 1894-1967
Tzara, Tristan 1896-1963
Van Duyn, Mona 1921-
Vergil 70-19 B.C.
Vigny, Alfred de 1797-1863
Wagoner, David 1926-
Wakoski, Diane 1937-
Walcott, Derek 1930-
Warren, Robert Penn 1905-1989
Weiss, Theodore 1916-
Whalen, Philip 1923-
Wheatley, Phillis 1753?-1784
Whittier, John Greenleaf 1807-1892
Wilbur, Richard 1921-
Williams, C. K. 1936-
Williams, Sherley Anne 1944-
Willians, William Carlos 1883-1963
Winters, Yvor 1900-1968
Wright, Charles 1935-
Wright, James 1927-1980
Wright, Jay 1935-
Yeats, William Butler 1865-1939
Zukofsky, Louis 1904-1978

Anna Akhmatova

1888-1966

(Pseudonym of Anna Andreevna Gorenko; also transliterated as Axmatova) Russian poet, translator, and essayist.

Akhmatova is considered one of the finest Russian poets of the twentieth century. A founding member of the Acmeist school, a movement which rejected the mysticism and stylistic obscurity of Symbolism and attempted to restore clarity to poetic language, Akhmatova wrote poetry distinguished by concrete imagery and simple language. Her early volumes contain brief, intimate lyrics that often dramatically present the trials of unhappy love. Akhmatova's most frequent themes include loss, emotional vicissitudes, regret, and the passage of time. Although her *oeuvre* is considered consistently mature, in each successive early volume Akhmatova's tone becomes more weighty and dignified as the effects of the First World War and the Russian Revolution enter her poetic consciousness. She has garnered both popular and critical acclaim for rendering these and other representative experiences in personal terms, creating a unique blend of sonorous traditional rhythms, meters, and forms. Sam Driver acknowledged: "Much of the stir caused by [Akhmatova's poetry] derived precisely from the tension between the very ordinariness of the settings and diction on the one hand and the sophistication in rhythms and sound patterning on the other."

Akhmatova was born Anna Andreevna Gorenko in Odessa, a coastal town off the Black Sea in the Ukraine. She moved with her family at a young age to Tsarskoye Selo, near St. Petersburg, where she was raised. Akhmatova began writing poetry at the age of ten after surviving a mysterious illness that nearly killed her. She became friends with Nikolai Gumilyov, a young poet who later helped form the Acmeist group and became one of its most eloquent spokespersons. Gumilyov and Akhmatova were married in 1910, and she gave birth to a son in 1912. Akhmatova and Gumilyov were not happily married, however, and spent much time apart, finally divorcing in 1918. Akhmatova's early collections of poetry, most notably *Vecher, Chyotki,* and *Belaya staya (The White Flock),* contain lyric self-portraits and personal reflections on love and love's sorrows. As war and revolution spread throughout Russia, Akhmatova wrote of both her own losses and those suffered by all Russian people. By 1917, the year of publication of *The White Flock,* the occasional religious imagery of the earlier volumes predominates as Akhmatova's persona prays for an end to the cataclysms of war.

Akhmatova's next collections, including *Podorozhnik* and *Anno Domini MCMXXI,* drew unfavorable commentary from government officials. Her high status and popularity before the Revolution, her use of death, poverty, and fear of wartime as subject matter, as well as Gumilyov's execution for treason in 1921, put her at odds with the Communist party. An unofficial ban on the publication of her

works went into effect in 1925. Although Akhmatova continued to write poetry, translate verse, and publish critical essays on the Russian poet Alexander Pushkin after the ban went into effect, she did not publish another collection of original verse until *Iz shesti knig* appeared in 1940. In this period of relative silence Akhmatova suffered great personal tragedy, including the loss of many friends to Joseph Stalin's purges and the repeated arrest of her son. Much of Akhmatova's work composed during this period existed for years only in her memory and that of some close associates. These verses, which reflect her anguish over her misfortunes and the changes that time and history had wrought upon her country, were too dangerous to be written down, much less published.

From the beginning of her career through the 1960s, Akhmatova's reputation was based almost solely on the love lyrics she composed in her youth. Since her gradual rehabilitation by the state following the death of Stalin in 1953, a concerted effort has been made to publish the entirety of her works and to incorporate their innovations into her critical standing. Her current reputation rests primarily on two lengthy poem sequences *Rekviem: Tsikl stikhotvorenii (Requiem: A Poem Cycle),* and *Poema bez geroya:*

Triptykh (Poem without a Hero: Triptych). Requiem consists of many short poems that form a quasi-narrative alluding to the Crucifixion. On a more literal level, these poems record Akhmatova's feelings, and by extension, those of many Soviet citizens, who too were notified of the arrest, sentencing, imprisonment and exile of loved ones. Some of the most moving pieces of this cycle concern the fate of those women who waited outside the gates of the state prisons for months on end, hoping to pass some food or clothing to their sons and husbands. *Requiem* is honored for its grave and majestic tone, which stems from Akhmatova's subtle, complex rhythms. John Bayley commented: "In her long poem sequences, Akhmatova uses meters of great robustness and subtlety in the Russian which when transposed into English can often sound all too like Shelley or Poe at their most ebullient. The strong accents and stresses of Russian have a variety and flexibility that iron out a regular beat that would otherwise dominate the more docile English syllables."

A similar phenomenon is present in the challenging poem sequence *Poem without a Hero*. Beginning in 1940, Akhmatova composed and revised this sequence over the course of two decades. *Poem without a Hero* is more elaborately conceived than any of Akhmatova's earlier works and features a cast of masked partygoers—a fictional premise more common to the works of the Symbolists of Akhmatova's youth than to those of the Acmeists. Set in 1913, the poem takes as its catalyst the suicide of a callow young officer after the woman he loves chooses another. Akhmatova invests this incident from her youth with forebodings of the senseless brutality of the war, revolution, and civil strife that successively struck Russia beginning in 1914. Peter France remarked: "In [*Poem without a Hero,* Akhmatova] looks back from the 'high tower of the year 1940' to what has become a remote past, conjuring up images of the dead and seeking to exorcise her own sense of guilt. . . . It is a magnificent achievement."

Considered one of the most accomplished Russian poets of the twentieth century, Akhmatova is also one of the few of her generation to survive to old age. Her early poems earned national acclaim for their accomplished blend of simple, graceful language and complex classical Russian poetic forms. Her tone appropriately somber, her meters majestic, Akhmatova wrote of the terror and grief of wartime as the catastrophes of the twentieth century befell her much-loved homeland. Due to a ban on her works and the persecution of friends and family, Akhmatova was forced to hide or destroy a certain amount of her work, and it has only recently become possible to study the breadth and depth of her achievement.

(For further discussion of Akhmatova's life and career, see *Contemporary Literary Criticism,* Vols. 11, 25; *Contemporary Authors* Vols. 19-20; *Contemporary Authors,* Vols. 25-28, rev. ed. [obituary]; and *Contemporary Authors Permanent Series,* Vol. 1.)

PRINCIPAL WORKS

Vecher   1912
Chyotki   1914

Belaya staya   1917
    [*White Flock,*   1978]
U samovo morya   1921
Podorozhnik   1921
Anno Domini MCMXXI   1923
Forty-Seven Love Songs   1927
Iz shesti knig   1940
Stikhotyoreniya, 1909-1957   1958
Poema bez geroya; Triptykh   1960
    [*Poem without a Hero: Triptych*   1973]
Stikhi, 1909-1960   1961
Collected Poems: 1912-1963   1963
Rekviem: Tsikl stikhotvorenii   1964
Poeziya   1964
Beg Vremeni   1965
Stikhotvoreniia, 1909-1965   1965
Sochineniya.   2 vols. 1965, 1968
Selected Poems   1969
Poems of Akhmatova   1973
Tale without a Hero and Twenty-two Poems by Anna Akhmatova   1973
Requiem and Poem without a Hero   1976
Selected Poems   1976
Way of All the Earth   1979
Poems   1983
Sochineniia v dvukh tomakh.   2 vols. 1986
Poems   1988
Severnye elegii: stikhotvoreniia, poetry, o poetakh   1989
The Complete Poems of Anna Akhmatova.   2 vols. 1990

Ihor Levitsky   (essay date 1965)

[*Levitsky is a professor of Russian and German languages, literature, and culture. In the following excerpt, he examines Akhmatova's poetry in its historical context.*]

At seventy-five, Anna Akhmatova is the last survivor of the Silver Age of Russian poetry. The first two decades of the twentieth century saw a concentration of poetic talent in Russia whose collective achievement was second only to that of Pushkin and his pleiad one hundred years before. Both these movements were closely related to general European literary revivals, the earlier to the Romanticism which had spread from England and Germany, the later to the Symbolism whose beginnings were in the France of the 1880's. Nor were their effects limited to literature: before they had run their course, they had left their mark upon music and the arts as well.

In Russia, the influence of French Symbolism first made itself felt among a group of poets who had rebelled against the sentimental civic poetry then prevalent. They welcomed the assertion of the autonomy of the arts by the French Symbolists. But by 1910 poetry was once more in danger of enslavement by the very themes which had helped liberate it from its earlier bondage. Originally enriched by the broadening of themes to include the worlds of the exotic, the dream, and the supernatural, the language and forms of the new poetry soon were becoming unmanageable. Vagueness and empty rhetoric became the rule. (p. 5)

[The] crisis of Russian Symbolism gave rise to two different movements seeking a way out. There appeared on the one hand the Futurists (Mayakovsky), who, breaking completely with the past, sought to create a "language of the future"; and, on the other hand, those who, while recognizing the need for reform, wanted to remain within the tradition. The latter called themselves "Acmeists," and their aim was to restore the language to its classical perfection; "Gallic" clarity was to replace the "Germanic" obscurity in which the Symbolists had become bogged down. One of the best examples of the application of Acmeist principles is provided by the work of Anna Akhmatova.

Between the years 1912 and 1922, she published five slender volumes of lyrical verse: *Večer* (*Evening,* 1912), **Čětki** (*The Rosary,* 1914), *Belaja staja* (*The White Flock,* 1917), *Podorožnik* (*Buckthorn,* 1921) and, finally, **Anno Domini MCMXXI** (1922). On these is based her reputation as one of the great masters of Russian verse, as well as her perennial popularity with readers both in her homeland and abroad. Neither her reputation nor her popularity seems to have been seriously affected by the severe criticisms to which she has been subjected in the Soviet Union from the point of view of the Communist ideology.

Akhmatova's method in these early works is based on one principle: economy of means. There is not one superfluous word in her poetry. The poems are short; rarely do they exceed three or four stanzas in length. The sentences are short, even verbless, as in:

> Twenty-first. Night. Monday.
> Outlines of the town in mist.

And, compared to the cosmic vaporings that were the fashion in the early years of the century, the subject matter seems extremely limited, too. Nor does Akhmatova celebrate any great achievements or heroic deeds in her poetry. Thus it is not surprising that from the first, the persistent theme of Akhmatova's critics has been her "limited horizon" and the "narrow range of her interests," so that the Soviet critic Surkov in 1961 merely seems to be echoing the critics of fifty years ago.

Is Akhmatova, then, a miniaturist? Not at all. She does not paint pretty little pictures. She is a master craftsman whose art consists in infallibly joining together words in such a way as to insure their greatest possible emotional impact on the reader. Her emotional intensity is the correlate of her brevity. Each of her little poems is charged to the brim with feeling. Compared to her, her symbolist predecessors seem merely grandiloquent, not to say verbose. Her verse is the direct expression, the very substance of emotion, not just a metaphoric rendering of it.

As the late Boris Eichenbaum pointed out long ago, this effect is achieved partly with the aid of techniques borrowed from the novel. Thus, she almost never speaks directly of her feelings; these are indirectly conveyed by descriptions of gestures and movements, as in this famous example from her first book:

> My heart grew chill so helplessly,

> Although my footsteps seemed so light.
> In all my anguish I was drawing
> My left-hand glove upon my right.

> There seemed to be so many steps,
> Although I knew there were but three.
> The breath of autumn in the maples
> Seemed to whisper: "Die with me!

> I have been deceived by fate
> That hath neither faith nor rue."
> And I answered in a whisper:
> "So have I. I'll die with you."

> This is the song of our last meeting.
> I glanced toward the house in the night:
> Only the bedroom lights were burning
> With an uncaring yellow light.

The tone is conversational, the language simple. Many of these poems seem to be addressed to an ever-present, but usually silent partner, a man, whom we know only by his catlike eyes, his favorite black pipe, or by the gloves and riding crop he has forgotten. (pp. 5-6)

The cumulative effect of the five volumes may be compared to that of an epistolary novel, rounded out with a number of diary entries. Out of them emerges an amazingly complete and vivid portrait of the heroine of this "novel in verse." Gradually, we come to know all about her appearance, her dress, her bearing and habits. We witness her bouts with insomnia. We accompany her on her walks and visits, we share with her her most intimate thoughts. We learn about her girlhood and schooldays as we listen to her childhood recollections:

> On the customs floats a faded flag,
> Over the town glides a yellow mist.
> My heart beats slowly under a rag,
> My lips forever remain unkissed.

> To be a little sea-girl again,
> To put soft slippers on naked feet,
> To laugh when dancing under the rain,
> And to sing when running down the street;

> To look from the steps at the dome aflame
> Of the tawny temple of Khersoness,
> Unknowing that, spoiled by luck and fame,
> Hearts are slowly beating to death.

Before our eyes this girl becomes a woman. And what a complex and contradictory creature she is! She falls in love, but love brings her only torment, as she is racked, in turn, by jealousy and remorse. . . . (p. 6)

As if to signalize the arrival of the Muse whose company she seeks more and more often, her conversational language becomes enriched by elements of the elevated style of the Russian classic poets:

> Before the spring there are such days as these:
> The field reposes underneath the snow,
> A merry noise wakes in the leafless trees,
> And warmer, more elated breezes blow.

> You marvel at your body's sudden lightness,
> And hardly recognize your house again;

And that old song you gave up for its triteness,
You sing once more just like a new refrain.

(p. 7)

Who is the heroine of these poems? There is a strong temptation to identify her with Akhmatova, and this is in fact what many readers have done. Many have seen in her early poetry a reflection of her unhappy marriage to the poet Gumilev. But to find this poetry interesting—or uninteresting, for that matter—as the record of the poet's private life, is to miss completely its significance as a work of art, which, as indicated, lies in the perfect union of verse and feeling. As in all great poetry, the feeling then is no longer the feeling of an individual, but is universalized. And, paradoxically, it is universal precisely because it is so completely individual.

Genuine feeling also distinguishes the patriotic verse, which Akhmatova began to write during the First World War, from the common run of such productions. Among her best should be counted the earlier poems in which she refuses to become an exile after the October Revolution, as well as the remarkable poem in which she rejoices that the tragic period of the purges—which affected her personally—found her "not under foreign skies," but with her people. It is ironic, however, that the complete cycle of which the latter is a part was first published abroad last year without the author's knowledge (**Requiem**).

Had Akhmatova never written another line, her place in Russian poetry as an outstanding representative of Acmeism would have been secure. Writing in 1923, Eichenbaum suggested that Akhmatova had carried her style to perfection within the limits of the small form; that the only way for her to grow was to turn to larger forms. It seemed that, if she continued writing in the same vein, her fate would be to repeat the same songs, like Browning's thrush. This is, in fact, what critics have accused her of—and not only in the Soviet Union. It may have been in answer to such criticisms that she wrote: "I have no use for the odes' array / Nor for elegiac ventures. / To me, verse should be inapropos, / Unlike the way it is with people." However that may be, the Soviet critic Zhirmunsky was probably right when he wrote: "Akhmatova is not only the most brilliant representative of the younger generation of poets, but she is endowed with traits that are individual, traits which do not fit completely into the temporary and historical peculiarities of today's poetry." For in the "battle of the poets" the Futurists carried the day; "noisy Moscow" prevailed over "quiet Petersburg." Thereby the way was prepared for another Age of Prose. Thus the Silver Age of Russian poetry recapitulates the history of the Golden Age. (pp. 7-8)

[Of Akhmatova's] work published during the last quarter of a century, the weakest, in this writer's estimation, are the poems that were composed on set themes. But these should be read bearing in mind a sizeable group of excellent poems dealing with the poet's craft, from which it is clear that such a way of writing poetry is quite unnatural to Akhmatova. And she obviously knows it. Her poetry, she continues in the poem whose beginning has been quoted above, grows "like a weed" out of such experiences as

"an angry shout, the smell of fresh tar, the mysterious mold on a wall."

In the background of much of Akhmatova's poetry is the city of Leningrad and its suburb, Detskoe (formerly Tsarskoe) Selo, where she has spent so much of her life, and to which she had already devoted a few early poems. The physical presence of "the dark waters of the Neva," of the canals, the statues in the "moonlit Summer Garden," the Fountain Palace, the Champ de Mars, and of various other places never ceases to delight her and receives loving mention time and again. Dear to Akhmatova are also the city's associations with the two great ages of Russian poetry, Pushkin's and the one in which she herself played such a prominent part. Finally, there are the personal associations—schooldays, "the first kiss," marriage; here, her "sorrowful Muse" first guided her "as though," she says, "I had been blind." (p. 8)

As time goes on—particularly after about 1929—Leningrad, for her, becomes peopled with shadows and reflections. The image of the mirror frequently recurs in her later poetry: "All has vanished into thin smoke, / Died away in the mirrors' depths, / And the song of things irretrievable / The grisly fiddler has struck up."

Thus people die, places change, and memories fade, until finally there comes a day when the long familiar is no longer recognizable; with classic conciseness, Akhmatova has captured this mood in her two **"Northern Elegies"**: "The names of cities change, / The witnesses of events depart, / There is no one to reminisce with, to weep with." And she continues: "And slowly the ghosts leave us, / Whom we no longer summon, / Whose return would terrify us."

Ghosts no longer summoned, however, may return as unbidden guests. And return they do in her longest poem, the **Poem Without a Hero.** It is here that Akhmatova departs most radically from the limpid clarity of her early style. Reading this poem of some six hundred lines is an experience not unlike tackling some of T. S. Eliot's more difficult verse. There is the same wealth of plain and veiled allusions, epigraphs, and quotations (some from English romantic poets). There are also frequent quotations from Akhmatova's own work, sudden transitions, and ingenious lines such as "Esli ne ko mne, tak k komu že?" where the juxtaposition of the three k's is used to convey the narrator's distraught state. But, as in Eliot's case, loss of clarity is compensated by gain in intensity.

The poem seems to have been received with mixed feelings by the poet's old admirers, if we may judge by one of her letters written in 1955 and recently published. Perhaps, as on an earlier occasion many years ago, they "expected more left-hand gloves put on the right." In connection with the **Poem Without a Hero,** she was apparently accused of such things as trying to settle old scores with people now long dead, of writing about things either incomprehensible or uninteresting, and of having, in any case, "betrayed her art."

But Akhmatova refused to be typed. Just as she once caused consternation among those who had thought her safely tagged as "the Sappho of Russia," so, perhaps, she has now offended some who had classified her later poetry as the swan song of Old St. Petersburg.

To this writer it seems that Akhmatova's triptych must be regarded as an act of purgation prompted by a desperate inner need. It remains to be seen whether her attempt to exorcise the ghosts of the past has been successful, whether the waters of the Neva, "along whose legendary embankment the Twentieth Century—the real one, not the calendar one—approaches," have been turned into the waters of Lethe. Thus, at seventy-five, Anna Akhmatova may have crossed the threshhold of a new period of creativity. But even if this is not granted her, her Leningrad poems may yet prove to be, as she says in the last poem of her cycle, **"Secrets of the Trade,"** her "passport to immortality." (pp. 8-9)

Ihor Levitsky, "The Poetry of Anna Akhmatova," in Books Abroad, *Vol. 39, No. 1, Winter, 1965, pp. 5-9.*

Peter France   (essay date 1982)

[*In the following excerpt, France provides a reading of poems selected from throughout Akhmatova's career.*]

> Memory of sun fades in the heart.
> Grass is less green.
> Early snowflakes are fanned by the wind
> Almost unseen.
>
> Narrow canals now flow less freely—
> Water thickens.
> Oh, nothing will ever happen here—
> Nothing, ever!
>
> On the empty sky a willow spreads
> A fretted fan.
> Maybe it's better I did not become
> Your wife.
>
> Memory of sun fades in the heart.
> What then? The gloom?
> Perhaps! In the space of just one night
> Winter can come.

The poem is dated 'Kiev 1911'. But the landscape is not particularly Kievan, it is Akhmatova's own, with canals, snow, grass and willow tree, a landscape of Tsarskoe Selo, the imperial summer residence near Petersburg where she spent most of her youth. And the poem itself, taken from her first collection, has many unmistakable features of her early poetry.

In the first place it has no title. The whole collection is called *Evening* (*Vecher*); the name establishes a tonality which is maintained in this and many other poems. Evening is the time of separation, the end. Neither literally nor figuratively is Akhmatova a poet of the morning; where Pasternak's world, for instance, is freshly and enthusiastically seen, washed clean by rain, hers is more often a place for lament and memory. So much we have from the overall title. The context too is important, for Akhmatova's poems, like those of so many modern Russian poets, are best seen as parts of separate cycles or books. Not that each book necessarily constitutes a 'story'; there is no very obvious progression in *Evening* or in most of Akhmatova's subsequent collections, but rather the re-

lated exploration of a number of central themes and images.

While we may therefore come to the poem with expectations derived from what surrounds it—the immediately preceding poem is one of restrained and guilty despair on parting—we are not given the sort of clear indication that we receive from titles such as Blok's 'The Steps of the Commendatore' or Pasternak's 'Hamlet'. Like most of Akhmatova's poems, this one leaves us much to guess at; it is written round a situation which is not spelled out for us. The first line speaks of oncoming winter—yet it is clearly more than this. We may not at first read the word 'sun' metaphorically, but surrounded as it is by 'memory' and 'heart' it suggests something else besides the description of a season. The something is as yet undefined.

The next five lines all give body to a seasonal reading of the poem; a landscape emerges, sketched in as coolly and briefly as possible. It is felt as a real place, not the imaginary scene of many symbolist poems—and not only is it real, it is fairly ordinary. While retrospectively we may want to invest the descriptive notations with symbolic force, on first reading we will probably not consciously connect the freezing canals with cooling love (the Russian verb fits both contexts). But in line 7 a different, exclamatory voice breaks into the calm description, the tense shifts to the future and there is insistent repetition of key words (*nikogda*, giving 'ever' in English). The eruption of this emotional tone makes us reread what precedes and change our image of the person talking and the emotion carried by the lines. Immediately, in lines 9 and 10, we are returned to the outside world, but now the symbolic charge is easier to perceive. The willow is the tree of mourning, the tree of Desdemona, and its bare branches on the sky are the skeleton of a fan. Then lines 11 and 12 at last give a sort of answer to the question: who is talking and to whom? Two personal pronouns appear, a female 'I' and an unspecified 'you', whom we may perhaps associate with the sun of the first line. What is striking here is again the change of tone: lines 7 and 8 had been exclamatory, but this remark is as prosaic and matter-of-fact as it could be, with the conversational Russian sentence spreading apparently naturally over two lines. The final stanza then takes up the opening words, now enriched with meaning; winter, darkness, night and separation settle on the poem, obliterating even the elegant outlines of the earlier landscape. What we have read is not a poem about parting, or a poem about autumn, but a poem which puts both of these together to suggest a more total decline into dark, cold and immobility.

The experience of reading even such a simple poem as this should be one of discovery. It is very short—only 60 words or so in Russian—and works with light touches. But the few physical details are all such as to suggest a lot beyond themselves. Akhmatova does not need to insist on the connections; she juxtaposes, with sudden shifts of tone and of subject which provoke the reader to explore, to fill in the 'bare-boned fan' and to perceive here the distillation of a whole love story. Little is spoken, but much is heard by the attentive reader.

Sound contributes a great deal to this effect. It is hard to say who is the most untranslatable of Russian poets, but

Akhmatova's reticence and subtlety are arguably more taxing to the translator than the richness of many of her contemporaries. At first sight the poem is formally conventional; the regular stanza form is emphasized by the 'correctness' of the numerous rhymes (sixteen words out of sixty). There is something of the cut gem about much early Akhmatova; we should remember that she was at this time associated with the Acmeist group, who preferred to Symbolist music and indeterminacy the sort of clarity and physicality that they saw exemplified in Théophile Gautier. It is clear however that this is not really a Parnassian poem; the apparent firmness of the form is balanced by a subtle waywardness of rhythm which reminds one more of Verlaine than of Gautier. In the first place the predominantly ternary metre is varied by the use of several trochees, so that the regular beat limps slightly; this, the so-called *dol'nik,* a mild Russian equivalent of Hopkins's 'sprung rhythm', had been pioneered by the Symbolists, Blok in particular. Secondly, a contrast is set up between the long lines and the short ones, which with their rhythmic pattern fall slightly jarringly, preventing any oratorical flow. This is particularly noticeable in the last line—two syllables in the Russian. And thirdly, there is a marked opposition between the firm rhyme scheme and the way in which the low-key sentence: 'Maybe I'm better off as I am, not as your wife' wanders over two lines. In all these respects the form of the poem echoes the fundamental contrast between calmness and anguish which is typical of this collection.

While we may imagine the lived experience behind the laconic suggestion, Akhmatova does not here project a particularly vivid image of herself as woman or as poet. In many of her early poems however she comes nearer to self-dramatization, adopting some of the traditional masks of fiction and poetry. Sometimes, in a way that will strike English-speaking readers as rather Pre-Raphaelite, she and her lover are princess and prince, figures from a sad and beautiful fairy tale. Again, in a version of pastoral, she becomes the country girl and her verse forms imitate those of popular song and poetry. Often she is the *femme fatale,* but often too the sinner gives way to the penitent and the nun. The degree of theatricality varies in these early poems; *Evening* for instance contains a Verlainean **"Masquerade in the Park",** whereas many poems in her third collection, **The White Flock (Belaya staya),** read as direct lyrical cries. Very frequently however the short poem (rarely more than thirty lines) evokes a dramatic scene. Just as the landscape from the previous poem is fairly ordinary, so these scenes are moments from everyday life, neither ethereal nor exotic, but expressing surprisingly complex situations and subtle gradations of feeling. Sometimes it will be a snatch of dialogue between a man and a woman, or else a monologue addressed to a partner who is present and whose actions or reactions have to be read between the lines. Here is an inner monologue written on New Year's Day, 1913, a famous evocation of a scene in the Stray Dog, an intellectual and artistic café which later figures prominently in Akhmatova's *Poem without a Hero* **(Poema bez geroya):**

> We're all revellers here, and harlots,
> A miserable crowd;

On the walls the birds and flowers
Long for distant clouds.

You puff at a black pipe—
Strange the smoke that gathers.
I have put on a narrow skirt
To look even slimmer.

The windows are sealed for good:
What's beyond them, storm or ice?
Like the eyes of a cautious cat
Are your steady eyes.

My heart is aching with grief.
Do I long for death?
But that woman dancing there
Will dance in hell.

There is something here of the form of the poem discussed above, a comparable rhyme scheme and the same abrupt shifts from one image to another. Here too the poem is anchored to a fairly mundane reality (even if this reality had a certain glamour for some readers); there is a sardonic observation of detail, the pipe, the smoke, the decorations on the walls. As in the earlier poem there is a contrast between the apparently cool tone of the centre and the exclamations of the beginning and end, a tension between the particular observed scene and a generalizing view of the world. But in this poem the *dramatis personae* are much more present; if the earlier piece was the indirect presentation of a mood, here we are given a vivid and emotional picture of the hero, the heroine and a surrounding world. Further, there is the suggestion of an unspoken drama of jealousy; what, we wonder, are the relations between the smoker of the pipe, the tight-skirted poet and the hell-bound dancer? We are left to guess—and those in the know may have been able to put names to the faces—but we can have no doubt about the intensity of emotion. Through the rather theatrical presentation comes an image of desolation and damnation which recalls the world of Blok, the world of "The Steps of the Commendatore" which was written only three years before this poem. What is more, Akhmatova's cabaret poem shows something like Blok's nostalgia for other worlds; the birds and flowers yearn for the clouds, as the heroine dreams of a world beyond the sealed windows and pines for something undefined, perhaps the hour of death. Akhmatova may have been associated with the Acmeists, 'those who overcame Symbolism', but one of her masters was the Baudelairean poet Annensky and poems such as this show how far removed she was from those Acemists who called themselves Adamists and set their acceptance of this world against the Symbolist's search for other worlds. Rather than the new-born world of Adam in paradise, she writes of a tired, self-conscious, guilt-racked existence. Her apparently cool realism is belied by her insistence on torment, punishment and death.

It would be wrong of course to suggest that Akhmatova's love lyrics are all agony. There are many poems of light and joy, of tenderness and hope. What they do have in common though, for all their lightness of touch, is a strength and seriousness in the face of experience, which made it possible for the voice of the forsaken and jealous woman to become the voice of the prophet and the mourner. (pp. 55-60)

This powerful, personal voice emerges increasingly in Akhmatova's later poems after the more detached manner of the early lyrics. The war seems to have been a turning point; from 1914 on we find in her poems what Mandelstam called the voice of a Cassandra, prophesying the fate not just of the couple, but of the whole social group, or even the nation. This historical vision is evoked retrospectively in her *Poem without a Hero,* written in 1940, but describing 1913, the end of the old world:

> And always in those icy, stuffy
> Prewar years, so sinful, fateful,
> Lurked a mysterious roar.
> But then the noise was only muffled,
> Then it hardly touched the hearing
> And drowned in Neva's snow.
> As if in the fearful night's mirror
> Man rages madly and refuses
> To recognize his face.
> But still along the famed embankment,
> Real, not as the calendar reckons,
> The twentieth century came.
>
>   (pp. 61-2)

And indeed Anna Akhmatova was not to find life as a poet easy in Soviet Russia. In the first few years after the Revolution she continued to write and publish freely. The collection *Anno Domini,* published in 1921 with a second edition in 1923, continues, as its title suggests, to explore the position of the poet in a changing and often destructive world. The pain, fear and remorse of the love poet are here juxtaposed and sometimes linked with the experiences of her contemporaries and compatriots—she writes of 'we' as well as 'I'. But between 1923 and 1936 she wrote much less; her poetry was increasingly attacked by official opinion as anachronistic and it appears that in 1925 the publication of her work was prohibited by a resolution of the Central Committee of the Communist Party. Much later she returned to favour as a patriotic war poet, but no sooner was the war over than she again fell foul of the authorities; in 1946 she was violently criticized in a speech by Zhdanov and expelled from the Union of Soviet Writers. Only very gradually over the last twenty years has her poetry regained official approval.

Depressing as all this may be, it is not altogether surprising. In an autobiographical note of 1961 she wrote: 'When I wrote them [her poems] I was living to the rhythms which were to be heard in the heroic history of my country', but there is not much of the normal Soviet heroics in her poetry. Take for instance a poem written in 1921 after the terrible years of the Civil War:

> Everything has been sold, soiled and betrayed,
> We have felt the flick of death's black wing,
> Hungry sorrow bites at every heart,—
> Why then do we see light in everything?
>
> By day the town's invaded by the breath
> Of new-found woods of cherry trees,
> At night new constellations stud the depths
> Of the transparent heavens of July.
>
> And the miraculous now comes so close
> To dirty, ruined houses in the city . . .

> Nobody ever knew this happiness
> Now wished upon us by our century.

There is far more brightness in this poem than in many of Akhmatova's post-revolutionary poems, but it can hardly be said to show much sympathy for the aims of the new regime. Revolution is not creation here, but the clearing of an empty space in which perhaps wild flowers will grow; in the darkness the stars can shine. Almost always she wrote less of what had been created than of the human experience, much of it loss and pain, which had accompanied this creation. Early in her own life, suffering from tuberculosis, she had looked death in the face; in later years the many hardships of her existence and the untimely deaths of those close to her bore out the forebodings of her youth and gave her a shared experience with many of her compatriots. The introduction to *Requiem (Rekviem)*, a cycle of poems written between 1935 and 1940 and inspired largely by her son's arrest and imprisonment, tells how in the 1930s, standing in a queue to get information about those who had been arrested, she was asked by a woman if she could write all this down—and answered: 'I can'.

Requiem is a sequence of short poems. Taken together, they make up a fragmentary narrative and lead to a climax which refers directly to the story of the Crucifixion. Taken individually, they are the record of moments in their author's road of suffering, reactions to her son's arrest, sentence, imprisonment and exile. The form and tone of the poems vary, from eloquent protest to something almost

Oil painting of Akhmatova by N.I. Altman, 1914.

like a folk ditty, but all of them are simple and direct, and quite traditional in prosody and vocabulary. Under the stress of pain, Akhmatova has recourse to the time-honoured language of Russian poetry. This can be seen for instance in a poem entitled **"The Sentence" ("Prigovor")**; significantly, the title is omitted in Soviet editions of this poem, where the poems of **Requiem** appear if at all as isolated lyrics rather than as part of a sequence with a very definite historical reference):

> And the stone word fell
> On my still living breast.
> Never mind, I was prepared,
> Somehow I'll cope with it.
>
> I'll have a busy day,
> Turning my heart to stone,
> Stifling memory,
> Learning to live again,—
>
> Or else . . . Summer's hot murmur
> Is like a fair out of doors.
> Long ago I had foreseen
> This bright day, this empty house.

This poem works through the clash of images of life and death (in the form of stone) and the contrast of tones. The first two lines have an ancient solemnity to them. The metaphorical adjective *kamenniy* (stone) is given bodily force by being set against the word *grud'* (breast); the sense hovers between abstraction ('I received bad news') and the suggestion of physical torture. The two lines form a single, eloquent statement, which is contrasted with the more broken rhythm and the casual tone of the third and fourth lines; here there are no metaphors and the language is that of ordinary talk. The final line of this stanza is one foot shorter than every other line in the poem; in literally missing a beat it creates a moment of silence, the silence which seems the only real answer to the situation. Then the matter-of-fact tone continues, listing the work of the day with the bitterly insistent repetition of *nado* (I must). The themes of the first stanza (stone, life and death) reappear—the poet is forcing herself to be calm, but this calmness, the condition of survival, is also death, the death of the soul and of memory (always a central concern of Akhmatova).

The hard, matter-of-fact tone cannot be sustained. In the last stanza, as if to escape from the unspoken hint of madness, there is a sudden lateral movement, an inrush of the life, the heat and rustle of summer. The contrast of the first stanza is now given a new form, the emptiness of the house from which the son has gone is set against the brightness of the natural world—an antithesis given added force by the echoes of sound in its two terms, *svetlyy den'* (bright day) and *opustelyy dom* (empty house). It is one of the most familiar themes of poetry, or indeed of song ('Ye banks and braes o' bonnie Doon'), a lyrical impulse of lament which gives a lie to the 'positive' movement of resignation. The striking, yet subtle shifts of tone and the suggestion of an unspoken passion behind the laconic words are qualities we saw in the early love poems; here they provide a fitting expression for what seems beyond expression.

It was in this way that Akhmatova spoke for the ordinary people of Russia—and again, very effectively, when Leningrad endured its terrible wartime blockade. She loved to write of sonorous bells and her voice was above all the solemn bell of commemoration. 'Memory' is the first word (in the Russian) of the poem at the beginning of this chapter, and from the beginning Akhmatova dwelt on the related themes of passing time, loss, changing emotions, remorse and nostalgia. But naturally these grow increasingly important as the poet lives longer, and lives through a time of 'events which have no parallel'. Her later poetry is dominated by her **Poem without a Hero,** written between 1940 and the time of her death in 1966. Almost all of her later writing is related to this work, feeding into it or branching out from it. The **Poem** itself may perhaps be thought of as Akhmatova's *Doctor Zhivago;* like Pasternak and certain other Russian poets of this century she felt impelled to use longer forms in order to give adequate expression to the historical experience of her generation. In it she looks back from the 'high tower of the year 1940' to what has become a remote past, conjuring up images of the dead and seeking to exorcize her own sense of guilt. Various other levels of time and historical experience are woven into this framework; there are references to the terrors of the 1930s and a long development on Akhmatova's evacuation from Leningrad to Tashkent, with a vision of Russia moving east in defeat and preparing to move back west in victory. It is a magnificent achievement, whose length and complexity would call for a separate essay if one wished to do any justice to them.

What strikes one particularly in **Poem without a Hero** is the way in which thoughts and images of personal memory, guilt and nostalgia are fused with an evocation of larger destinies. The same combination of private and public vision can be seen in many of Akhmatova's late poems, which mostly dwell on the same emotions as the **Poem:** the desire to resurrect the past and escape into it, counterbalanced by a remorseful horror of what this past contains, a fear that the frivolity or sinfulness of this former life (both her own and that of her generation) is in some way to blame for the sufferings of the following decades. Here is a poem of 1940, entitled **"Youth":**

> My young hands signed
> My name on that document
> Among stalls selling flowers
> And the gramophone's clatter
> Under the gas lanterns'
> Oblique tipsy stare.
> I was older than the century
> By exactly ten years.
>
> And the setting sun was shrouded
> With white cherries in mourning
> Scattering a delicate
> Dry and fragrant rain.
> And the clouds were shot through
> With Tsushima's bloody foam,
> And carriages bore smoothly
> The corpses of today.
>
> But now that distant evening
> Would seem to us a carnival,
> Would seem a masquerade,
> A fairy-tale *grand-gala.*

Of that house there remains
Not a brick, that alley's felled,
Those hats and shoes retired
Long ago to the museum.

Who knows the sky's emptiness
Where the tower has fallen?
Who knows the house's quietness
Where the son never came home?
You persist like conscience
Or like air, always with me.
But why demand an answer?
Your witnesses I know:
Incandescent with music
The Pavlovsk station dome,
And the Babolov palace's
White-maned cascade.

We do not know what the document of the second line is, perhaps a real paper in front of the writer, perhaps the symbol of an agreement between people, a love affair, or an individual's pact with a generation. But whatever it is, it leads back into a lost world. Akhmatova suggests this vanished age with an accuracy which has been much admired, and she places herself carefully in it. But the age is not evoked neutrally, nor indeed lovingly; the sinister street lamps could come from Dostoevsky's or Blok's Petersburg. The second stanza, still in the past tense, intensifies the reader's unease; the cherry blossom, white and fragrant, is seen as funereal (death can be white as well as black) and the whiteness of cloud and flowers is tinged with the red of a sunset, that is also the death of an age. Tsushima, a disastrous naval battle in the Russo-Japanese war, sets the poem in 1905, the year of the first Russian revolution. Then, abruptly telescoping time, the last lines of the stanza take up the paradox of the deathly cherry blossom. This is not an elegiac lament, but something more akin to the *danse macabre* (where the living are corpses on leave from death) or perhaps to the vision of Dante which meant so much to Akhmatova and to Mandelstam.

The unreality, indeed the triviality, of this lost world is drummed in by a series of words in the next stanza: carnival, masquerade, fairy-tale, *grand-gala* (in French in the original). From the tower of 1940 the poet and her contemporaries can look back to an age from which they are separated by far more than thirty-five years. Perhaps, as words like *grand-gala* suggest, they can smile in condemnation. But the final part of the poem, set now in the present, stresses the sense of loss. Partly this is the wear and tear of time as Proust shows it in the 'bal masqué' of *Le Temps Retrouvé*—the old fashions now gather dust in museums. But the museums of Soviet Russia are in part places where fragments have been saved from demolition; older Russians are very much aware of the destruction of their cities. The striking image of the void left in the air by a fallen tower seems to hint at more than architectural loss, for the tower is very probably a bell tower, a church tower. The public meaning of the destruction of buildings is made clearer in the lines about the son who never returned—here as in **Requiem** Akhmatova is writing of a personal experience which she shared with millions of Russians.

In this way the poem returns to the private sphere hinted at through the hands and the document of the opening lines. Who is this 'you' who suddenly appears, as in the poem quoted at the beginning of this chapter? Biographical information may suggest various identities. Perhaps it is the son of the previous line, perhaps a man once loved and now dead, perhaps her husband Gumilyov, accused of counter-revolutionary activities, and shot in 1921. Whoever it is, he is presumably connected with the 'document' of line 2, for he has witnesses to testify to some long-gone agreement, and his presence haunts the writer, bringing out obscure feelings of guilt (to whom, for what?) and at the same time, overwhelmingly, of nostalgia, for she closes the poem with images of her pre-revolutionary home, the band at Pavlovsk railway station (also the subject of a fine poem by Mandelstam) and the park of Tsarskoe Selo, sacred to the memory of Pushkin and the scene of so many of her early poems.

The reference to unexplained private events becomes more common in Akhmatova's last poems, short poems written between 1945 and 1965, many of which are very beautiful in their enigmatic simplicity. This is particularly true of **The Wild Rose Flowers (*Shipovnik tsvetyot*)**, a cycle of poems dedicated to Isaiah Berlin. Akhmatova had a fateful meeting with Berlin in 1945, fateful not only because she felt that it helped to provoke the new wave of persecution which she had to endure after 1946, but also because of her continuing communion with this visitor from another world, the world of European culture that might have been hers. In 1956 she felt unable to meet him again out of concern for her son's safety, but this non-meeting gave her strength and formed the subject of several poems in which she seems to be striving through separation for a mystical union. Death is close in some of these poems, but if in **"The Sentence"** there was death in continued life, here there seems to be life in death. Thus in the little poem called **"First Song"** (**"Pervaya pesenka"**) and dated 1956:

Empty the celebrations
Of mysterious non-meeting,
The speeches left unspoken,
The words that have no sound.
The looks that never met
Do not know where to lie,
And only tears are happy
That they can freely flow.
The wild rose close by Moscow
Alas! is part of this . . .
And all this will be given
The name 'immortal love'.

This is a lament, the work of the poet whom Marina Tsvetaeva called the 'muse of tears'. The strongest note is negativity, yet in the midst of the weeping the sudden shift to a wild rose brings brightness into the poem, rather like that of the wild cherry in the poem beginning 'Everything has been sold'. The cycle, we remember, is called **The Wild Rose Flowers.** It is not clear, therefore, whether the last lines should be taken as bitterly ironic, as at first seems to be the case, or as a positive statement of victory in defeat.

Like the last lines of this poem, the final short poem in the cycle also looks not to the past, but to a future time when the present will only be a memory:

And all this will become in time
Like the age of Vespasian,
And this was nothing but a wound
And a little cloud of pain.

These lines are dated 'Rome. Night. 18 December 1964'; they were written in the last years of the poet's life. The 'age of Vespasian' was the time when Jerusalem was destroyed. Here once again private and public experience come together; the individual's suffering is seen in the vast context of human history.

The exploration of time and the preservation of memory are particularly important when changes in society are so great, rapid and painful. Anna Akhmatova responded to the challenge of history. The voice which wept for so many private miseries could also become the voice of a generation, bearing a personal witness to public events. Everywhere in her writings there is a combination of the small and the great, the casual and the ceremonious. She starts from the ordinary detail of life, expressed in ordinary words, quietly, without fuss. In a somewhat Pasternakian poem of 1940 she speaks with delight of the way poems grow like dandelions by the fence out of 'all sorts of rubbish' ('an angry shout', 'the fresh smell of tar', 'a mysterious mildew on the wall',). Such poems, in a world of official grandiloquence, are to be preferred to the 'panoply of odes' and the 'blandishments of elegies'. But this modesty goes naturally with a regal dignity which impressed those who met her; it can still be heard on the recordings she made and can be perceived by the ordinary reader of her poems. She was not afraid of superlatives and loved the sound of noble words; like her idol Pushkin she believed in the dignity of poetry and the power of well-used language:

Gold rusts, the sword rusts in the sheath,
And marble crumbles. Death takes all.
The strongest thing on earth is grief,
The longest-lived the word imperial.

(pp. 63-72)

Peter France, "Anna Akhmatova," in his Poets of Modern Russia, *Cambridge University Press, 1982, pp. 55-72.*

David McDuff   (essay date 1983)

[*In the essay excerpted below, McDuff emphasizes the influence of Russian scholar and poet Innokenty Annensky on Akhmatova's poetic style and themes.*]

Born in 1889 in a Black Sea coastal town, one of five children of a naval engineer [Anna Gorenko] had been taken by her family at the age of eleven months first to Pavlovsk, then to Tsarskoye Selo. When Anna was five, her sister Rika, one year younger than herself, died of tuberculosis. At the age of ten, Anna herself became seriously ill, though the doctors were unable to find the reason for the illness. It was after this illness that she began to write poetry. By the time she was thirteen she had learned French and was already familiar with the poetry of Baudelaire and Verlaine, as well as with that of many of the "Parnassians and *poétes maudits*". . . . At about this time she befriended another young poet, three years older than herself,

Nikolay Gumilyov; Gumilyov had attended the Tsarskoye Selo Men's Academy, where one of his teachers was Innokenty Annensky. Gumilyov, who shared Anna's passion for French Symbolist poetry, fell in love with her, casting her in the role of mermaid and tragic princess as a foil to his own poetic persona of "conquistador" and romantic visionary.

In January 1905 the Gorenkos were shaken by the news of the destruction of the entire Russian fleet by the Japanese at Tsushima. The disaster made a particularly deep impression on Anna; she described it later as "a shock to last one's whole lifetime." At Easter of the same year Gumilyov tried to kill himself in despair at her refusal to take his love for her seriously, and she broke off relations with him. In the summer her parents separated, and she was taken to the south of Russia by her mother. There this fateful year ended for her with the ominous and distant news of the abortive 1905 revolution. It was the year in which for the first time she experienced catastrophe on both a private and a public level and, as she studied for her final-year school exams, she began to write poetry in earnest.

In 1906, Anna Gorenko became Anna Akhmatova. During her lifetime, the poet herself gave several accounts of the events that led up to the choice of this pseudonym. Some aspects of those events remain unclear, however, and they are still surrounded by a certain enigma. The most straightforward version of the story is that Anna's father objected to her using the family name to sign her "decadent" poems, as he feared it might bring it into disrepute. His daughter bowed to this objection, and went in search of a pseudonym. In the end, she chose the family name of her Tatar great grandmother, which was also the name of the last Tatar princes of the Golden Horde. The story may not, however, have been quite as simple as this. Although there is no direct evidence that Annensky, another pseudonymous poet, was in any way directly involved in his pupil's choice of *nom de plume*, certain remarks she made in the course of her life lead one to suppose that this may have in fact been the case. Annensky's significance for Akhmatova's development as a poet cannot be overestimated. His personality and writings together constituted the single most important influence on her poetic art. She considered him her "teacher" in every sense of the word. This is a fact that is sometimes ignored by students of her work, but it is one that repays attention. So strong was the link between these two poets that Akhmatova herself tended only to allude to it, out of a kind of emotional reserve: her poetry is filled with fleeting allusions to Annensky's poems; not surprisingly, her conversation also contained hints and clues that pointed to Annensky's role in her life as an artist. (pp. 55-7)

The year 1910 was a fateful one for Akhmatova. During it she made the first of several pre-World War I visits to Western Europe, and in particular to Paris, where she was to meet, among other people, the then unknown young painter Modigliani. (Two years later, partly as a result of Modigliani's influence, she would visit Northern Italy, where the impression she received from the medieval painting and architecture was, in her own words, "like a dream you remember all your life.")

1910 also saw the release, by the Moscow publishing house *Grif,* of Annensky's posthumous collection *Kiparisovy larets—The Cypress Chest.* Akhmatova recalls coming back to St. Petersburg from Kiev with Gumilyov, whom she had finally consented to marry, in the spring of that year. Together the two poets paid a visit to the Russian Museum. Gumilyov had with him a set of the proofs of *The Cypress Chest.* He gave Akhmatova the poems of his former headmaster to read. She was stunned by them, and read the book right through there and then, in her own words "forgetting everything else in the world." (pp. 57-8)

Akhmatova's poetry proceeds directly from that of Annensky. In one sense her art may be said to represent a completion of Annensky's unfinished labor. Such a claim would be in keeping with a remark made by Akhmatova to Nikita Struve towards the end of her life: "Yes, Innokenty Annensky is an immense (*grandioznyy*) poet, we all came out of him. No one could come out of Blok, he was too complete. . . ." Or again, in a conversation with Lidiya Chukovskaya: "All the poets came out of him: Osip, Pasternak, myself, even Mayakovsky."

Histories of Russian literature generally tend toward the view that modern Russian poetry—and in particular the poetry of the famous "quartet" made up of Akhmatova, Mandelstam, Pasternak, and Tsvetayeva—took its origins in the various literary movements such as Symbolism, Acmeism, and Futurism that flourished in St. Petersburg and Moscow during the early years of this century. Although there is of course some truth in this assertion, it is misleading in that it distracts attention both from the essentially private, individual character of one important element in that poetry, and from the public, general, non-literary character of another of its constituents, an equally important one. The literary squabbling and programism that marked these now largely forgotten guilds and sodalities had in fact rather little to do with the mainstream development of Russian poetry. Much more important to that development was the confrontation between the traditions, literary and non-literary, of the Russian past, and the onslaught of the modern era, with its revolutions, labor camps, and sense of a moral abyss. In Annensky's poetry this conflict is already present in the form of a terrible presentiment sparked by the revolution of 1905. A similar intuition can be found in the poetry of Blok and some of the other symbolists: but nowhere in their poems is it coupled, as it is in Annensky's, with such a profound sense of the cultural and historical past, or with such a burden of guilt and uneasy conscience.

This is, I believe, one of the meanings of Akhmatova's statement that "we all came out of " Annensky. (p. 59)

It is all too easy to read the early work of Akhmatova as "love poetry." Such was the temptation to weave imaginary romances around the poems of *Vecher (Evening)*, *Chyotki (Rosary)*, and *Belaya Staya (White Flock)* that early reviewers and commentators put all kinds of stories and rumors into circulation. The poems were assumed to refer not only to the poet's relations with Gumilyov, but

also to supposed affairs with Aleksandr Blok and even with Tsar Nicholas II. Empty speculation of this kind ran rife among émigré literary circles in the years after the 1917 revolution, and for many years it made a proper assessment of Akhmatova's poetry from this period difficult, if not impossible. Fortunately, the poet was herself able eventually to put to rest most of the wilder rumors—indeed, since the publication of Lidiya Chukovskaya's extensive and valuable memoirs there is little or no room left for such imaginative exercises. While it is true that a small number of the early poems are addressed to Gumilyov, and that others contain references to Knyazev, Nedobrovo, Anrep, and other friends, Akhmatova's purpose is not to provide an open diary of her private emotional life. The *ty* ("thou") of these poems is not an individual human being—it is rather a blending of individual humanity with time, of the concrete and personal with the abstract and impersonal. Akhmatova conducts her conversation with time and destiny as though she were speaking to a being of flesh and blood that may also be something else—a fusion of identities that includes all "I's," one of the [*miriovooi*], the possessors of a myriad of souls, among which their own is lost. As Annensky expresses it at the beginning of his Dostoyevskian poem "The Double": "Not I, and not he, and not you, / And the same as I, yet not the same. . . . "

As in the case of Annensky, it is prose fiction and the condition of fictional characters that suggest themselves as a literary equivalent here. In particular, the techniques of Marcel Proust come to mind: again and again an event, a moment of psychological unease or of emotional nearness, is brought with great clarity before the all-seeing lens of the poet's memory. It is the details of the scene that remain—the people themselves have long since gone their separate ways:

> The final meeting: I stood on the road.
> The house was as dark as shame.
> Only in the bedroom, candles showed
> An indifferent yellow flame.
>   **("The Song of the Final Meeting")**

> How could I forget? He went out, reeling.
> His mouth dreadful, twisted, grim . . .
>   **("I pressed my hands together . . . ")**

In these poems what is important is not so much the actuality of the experience as its historicity, its association with an irrevocably vanished past. Many of the poems are written in the past tense, which accentuates the general sense of loss and muted grief. Even those written in the present tense have a curiously time-locked quality. The fisherman who makes the girl fishers blush belongs to the moment in which he is observed—he will go on fishing there, while the shoals of "fish" (the girls) pass on like the flowing of the river—or of time. The three poems in *Evening* grouped together and devoted to Tsarskoye Selo describe the place not in terms of the present but of the past, first in the form of what appears to be a memory of Annensky ("a soul suffocated / In the delirium before death"), then as a comparison of the poet herself with the statue of Peace in the Yekaterininsky Park (Annensky had also written a poem about this statue), and finally as an imaginary memory of

Pushkin ("Here's where he put his three-cornered hat / And a rumpled book of poems by Parny"). Thus the three poems become, with their backward glance, a part of Tsarskoye Selo itself, sharing in its remembering present.

The function of remembering, of memory, is such an important one in Akhmatova's poetry that it needs special consideration. Pushkin's famous poem "Remembrance," which ends: "I complain bitterly, and shed bitter tears, / But do not wash away the sorry lines" might stand as an epigraph over much of Akhmatova's work. Annensky had already begun to develop this theme in poems such as "Anguish of Remembrance," where the act of remembering becomes identical with the act of creation. Akhmatova makes this creative, individual pursuit of memory into the foundation of her poetic art. For all her apparent concern with relationships and emotional involvements, she speaks out of a condition that is profoundly solitary. It is a solitariness that implies a deeper solidarity than that of love relationships. The woman in these poems is conscious of being unable to fulfill the expectations of men—she is not entirely a being of the here and now: part of her is turned into the face of time. She cannot speak in a voice that is wholly personal; her "I" is fused with other "I" 's in other times and other places. Perhaps she is indeed a mermaid, or a fairytale princess who does not need, cannot respond to earthly affection. At times her sense of unearthliness grows so strong that she appears to herself, in her physical incarnation, as a doll, or a toy:

> And now I have become toylike
> Like my roseate friend cockatoo.

Akhmatova's absorption in memory and the processes of time led her away from any danger of fascination with her personal experience and united her with the wider, shared experience of a public reality. One of the primary aspects of that absorption and that enlarged experience as they express themselves in her poems is the city of St. Petersburg. In many of the early poems, personal, individual time is supplanted by the time of the city. The city's stone architecture absorbs the fates and lives of its individual citizens and projects them toward the condition of art and history:

> My heart sustains its even beat,
> What could the long years give to me?
> Beneath the arch on Gallery Street
> Our shadows will forever be.
> ("Poems about St. Petersburg, II")

Rosary, the collection from which the lines above are quoted, was published in the spring of 1914. The war that broke out later that year was in many ways instrumental in bringing Akhmatova a resolution of the tension she had experienced between the 'public-poetic' and the private aspects of her life. Her marriage to Gumilyov had hardly been a marriage at all, in many respects, since much of their time had been spent apart—Gumilyov in Africa, Akhmatova in Russia. Although in 1912 she had given birth to a son, Lev, she had not continued to look after him herself, but had entrusted him to the care of Gumilyov's mother. By so doing, she considered she had "lost" him. With the outbreak of war, Gumilyov immediately enlisted and went off to the front. Left alone in Slepnyovo, the small estate owned by Gumilyov's parents, Akhmatova

contemplated the onslaught of what later she was to call "The True Twentieth Century."

White Flock, which appeared in 1917 and which contains the poems that give Akhmatova's immediate reactions to the war and to the atmosphere of the period that led up to the 1917 revolution, bears as its epigraph a line from Annensky's sinister poem *Sweetheart* (*Milaya*). This story of a mother who has drowned her child echoes the Gretchen fable in Goethe's *Faust.* Akhmatova develops the theme in her poem **"Where, tall girl, is your gypsy babe"** (**"Gde, vysokaya, tvoy tsyganyonok"**). She reflects that "I was not worthy / To bear the lot of a mother—that bright torture," as she wanders from room to room, looking for her son's cradle.

This acute sense of guilt, grief, and loss was to be reiterated on a very much larger scale in Akhmatova's poems. As Mother Russia began to lose her sons to "The True Twentieth Century," Akhmatova's voice took on a new, tragic note. An intonation of prayer, already present in her earlier work, now became predominant, as personal and public misfortune merged into one. In a poem written in 1916, she says that her first reaction to the news of the outbreak of war was to pray to God and to beg him to destroy her before the first battle. Subsequently this desire for self-immolation became a readiness for self-sacrifice in order to save Russia:

> Give me illness for years on end,
> Shortness of breath, insomnia, fever.
> Take away my child and friend,
> The gift of song, my last believer.
> I pray according to Your rite,
> After many wearisome days,—
> That the storm cloud over Russia might
> Turn white and bask in a glory of rays.

The other important theme of *White Flock* is private friendship and love. It is significant, however, that in addressing those human beings for whom she has particular affection, Akhmatova points away from the context of emotional fulfillment and "happy" love toward a wider, tragic arena, and sometimes toward objects and images that are openly religious in character. The poem **"Statue at Tsarskoye Selo,"** dedicated to Nikolay Nedobrovo, invokes the ponds, autumn leaves, and swans of the Yekaterininsky Park, and the "celebrated girl" with her "unshiveringly crossed legs" who looks out across the pathways from her plinth of "northern stone." Akhmatova says that she feels a "dark fear" as she looks at the statue. "And how could I forgive her," she asks Nedobrovo, "the enthusiasm of your enamoured praise? Look, elegantly naked like that, she's happy to be sad." In another poem, **"When in the gloomiest of capitals"** (**"Kogda v mrachneyshey iz stolits"**), the poet describes how at the time of her flight from St. Petersburg in the summer of 1916— motivated by tuberculosis—the only thing she took with her was the altar cross she had received from her friend Boris Anrep on "the day of betrayal." Feeling guilty because she is unable to love Anrep in the way he loves her, Akhmatova tells him how the cross preserves her from "bitter ravings," and helps her to remember everything— even the "last day," when she left both him and the city.

In these "personal" poems, too, there is the Akhmatovan sacrifice of self, of private identity. It is a sacrifice that involves at once an intensification of pain and a distancing of it. In Akhmatova's poetry, as in that of Dante, the details of individual grief are subsumed by a consciousness of the movements of the spheres, and by a striving to comprehend the Divine will in terms of a moral quest. The 1917 October revolution was experienced by Akhmatova as a catastrophe, a moral disaster—but her love for Russia was far too immense, too absolute for her to be able to turn her back on the calamity. She accepted it as yet another, though colossal, intensification of suffering, another stage in the sacrifice of her nation. Even though it opened the way to the lower circles of Hell, she still believed, like Dante, that the poet can traverse Hell and even redeem it, and that this task is a sacred one:

> When in suicidal anguish
> The nation awaited its German guests
> And the stern spirit of Byzantium
> Had deserted the Russian Church;
> When the capital by the Nevá
> Had forgotten its majesty
> And like a drunken prostitute
> Did not know who would take it next,
> I heard a voice call consolingly.
> It was saying: "Come to me here,
> Leave your remote and sinful country,
> Leave Russia behind forever.
> I will wash your hands of blood
> Take the black shame from your heart
> And cover up with another name
> The pain of insult and defeat."
> But with indifference, peacefully,
> I covered my ears with my palms,
> So that these unworthy words
> Should not sully my mournful spirit.

This poem, with its simplicity of feeling, its directness achieved without the smallest sacrifice of intellectual complexity, and its dark-toned lyrical stoicism, stands like an inscription over the work that Akhmatova was to produce during the next half-century. It marks the inauguration of her later style, which is Dantean, not in any grandiose or "sculptural" sense, but in the sense in which Mandelstam characterized the poetry of Dante: "Imagine a monument made of granite or marble, the symbolic idea of which is not to depict a steed or a horseman, but to reveal the inner structure of granite or marble . . . imagine a monument of granite, erected in honour of granite and in order to reveal its essence. . . . "

In his essay on Akhmatova, published in 1915, Nikolay Nedobrovo had counselled her to follow Pushkin's exhortation to the poet to "go where your secret dreams lead you." This advice served to strengthen within Akhmatova her allegiance to Pushkin's spirit and example, an allegiance already well established by her childhood in Tsarskoye Selo and her apprenticeship to Annensky. The tradition represented by Pushkin was to be of vital importance to her during the years that followed the October revolution. It was thanks to this inspiration that she was able to avoid the twin perils of becoming, as a poet, either exclusively preoccupied with herself or with the upheaval in the outside world. (pp. 60-6)

Nothing could be further removed from the style and spirit of her poetry than the "confessional" mode of versewriting. It was the critic Boris Eykhenbaum who pointed out that the personal, diary-like quality of Akhmatova's poetry is an illustory one: after careful reading, we become aware that these "diary entries" are, in fact, thoroughly impersonal. Their unvarnished concision, their spirituality that is somehow in the world, are the attributes of a poetry that has transcended the illusion of personality and has allied its softly speaking voice to an iron-hard objective knowledge of the limits of the human, a level-headed humility in the face of God's purpose, and a consciousness and understanding of human weakness and frailty. Akhmatova's poems of the revolutionary and immediate postrevolutionary period, published in the collections *Plantain* (1921) and *Anno Domini* (1922) contain no ecstatic or apocalyptic utterances, nor do they represent a withdrawal into the self, into "private life"; what they express above all is grief, and a sense of guilt:

> I called death down on the heads of those I cherished.
> One after the other, their deaths occurred.
> I cannot bear to think how many perished.
> These graves were all predicted by my word.

The event that was uppermost in the poet's consciousness, and conscience, when she wrote these lines was undoubtedly the death of Gumilyov. Akhmatova had divorced her husband in 1918 and had married the Assyriologist Vladimir Shileyko, with whom, however, she had soon parted company, going to live with the composer Artur Lourié and the actress and dancer Olga Sudeykina in a house on the Fontanka. In August 1921, Gumilyov was arrested and shot for his part in an anti-Bolshevik conspiracy. Akhmatova was deeply horrified: her poems began to reflect, for the first time, a creeping sense of fear and dread:

> A sound beyond the wall, muffled yet stark—
> A ghost? A rat? The door? Did I latch it?

With the dread was mingled grief that so many of those whom she had loved and who had loved her—from the young poet Knyazev, who had committed suicide, to Gumilyov himself—had met violent and unnatural deaths. Yet the grief goes beyond even this: it extends into a lament for her entire generation and for the whole of suffering Russia. Love is for Akhmatova, as for Annensky, synonymous with suffering, and in the tragic music of separation, betrayal, fear, and death there is a continued echo of "the bow and the strings":

> As ravens circle above the place
> Where they smell fresh-blooded limbs,
> So my love, with its triumphant face,
> Inflicted its wild hymns.

In the years before the revolution, Akhmatova had built a very considerable literary reputation. Her poems had received wide circulation—she had even become, to some extent, a "popular" poet. After the 1917 revolution, all that began to change. *Plantain* and *Anno Domini* drew hostile criticism from the newly established commissars of the literary left: Akhmatova's poems were felt by them to belong to an age that was past, too exclusively concerned with the problems of personal existence and insufficiently engaged with the themes of "revolutionary" reality. This superficial and blinkered view of her writing was to become all too familiar in the years to come. Matters were not helped by the fact that many of those who had been the poet's most perceptive and sensitive readers were now leaving Russia and going to live in the West. Akhmatova did not follow them. As we have seen, she felt that her place was in Russia, whatever the sufferings she might have to endure there. "I am not with those who have abandoned their land / To be torn apart by its enemies," she wrote at the beginning of a famous poem from *Anno Domini.* In the same poem, however, she professes "eternal sympathy" for the exile, as she does for prisoners, or the sick:

> Dark is your road, wanderer,
> And the foreign bread smells of wormwood.

Indeed, she herself was now to become an exile, although an inner one. The deaths of Nedobrovo (1919), Gumilyov (1921), and Blok (1921) left her feeling isolated, and the hostile comment her books attracted in the new, harsh, and utterly changed political climate meant that she could not hope to continue to publish. The banning order that in 1925 was passed on her in the form of an unofficial Communist Party resolution meant that for the next fifteen years none of her poetry was published in the Soviet Union, and that it was forty years before she was allowed to publish a new book of her own. She was now treated by literary critics and public alike as essentially a voice from the past, and her literary career was considered to be at an end. (pp. 67-9)

In the modern age, [Annensky felt], the poetic word acts as a mediator between the hell of the contemporary *I,* with its consciousness of inescapable loneliness and its mystical terror in face of itself, and the ideal that is implicit in the transcendent miracle of artistic creation. Through the medium of the poetic word, the tortured, isolated *I* becomes aware of other *I*'s, even though its awareness is a broken, fragmented one. In the hints, unfinished sentences, and enigmatic symbols of the new poetry, in its musical suggestiveness, the solitary discovers a solidarity with others like itself. The new poetry, by teaching us to value the word, teaches us also to seek out the *I* of the poet—"not the external, biographical *I* of the writer, but his authentic, incorruptible *I,* the essence of which we can experience as being adequate to our own *I* only in poetry."

Love and respect for the poetic word as an instrument of moral education, as a means of combating the debasement of spirit and language entailed by history's obsession with power and the "useful," and by the individual's involuntary acquiescence in that obsession, are as characteristic of Akhmatova's poetry as they are of Annensky's. In the essay already quoted, Nedobrovo had written of her poems: " . . . that they are constructed on the word may be shown on the example of a poem like the following, which is in no way untypical of *Rosary.*" The poem in question is **"True Tenderness"**:

> There's no confusing true tenderness
> With anything else—it's at rest.
> No good your being so solicitous
> As you drape my furs round my breast.

No good your talking to me
Submissively of first love.
I know those looks, stubborn and hungry,
I know what you're thinking of.

Nedobrovo remarks: "The voice here is so simple and conversational that one may perhaps wonder whether this is poetry at all. But if we read the poem again, we may observe that if all our conversations were like this, it would be enough, in order to exhaust the possibilities of most human relationships, to exchange them for two or three eight-line stanzas—and the result would be a reign of silence."

This concentration and distillation of the colloquial was to remain a fundamental characteristic of Akhmatova's poetry right to the end, even when, later in life, she adopted large-scale forms in order to confront the terrible events of wartime and the darkness of the postwar world. Her refusal to abandon the mode of intimate conversation may be likened to that of Mandelstam, to whom Akhmatova was close during the 1920s and 1930s (their friendship is chronicled in the two volumes of Nadezhda Mandelstam's memoirs), and who in his essay *On the Nature of the Word* (1923) wrote of Annensky as the teacher of "an inner Hellenism, adequate to the spirit of the Russian language, as it were, a domestic Hellenism." Mandelstam's emphasis on the home, on a domestic world outlook, his insistence that

> the happy repository of heaven
> is a lifelong house that you can carry
> anywhere

is very similar to Akhmatova's; both poets were lifelong outcasts and wanderers; neither of them, after childhood, ever really knew a settled existence. Coextensive with the linguistic concern in their poetry is a concern with St. Petersburg as a spiritual home, and an essentially Christian attitude toward people and objects as being ultimately capable of redemption and authenticity.

"I have no use for odic hosts, / The charms of elegiac flights," wrote Akhmatova in a poem of 1940. In the same poem, she gave a thoroughly Annenskian description of the poet's task, derived in part from memories of the lanes and backyards of her Tsarskoye Selo childhood:

> If you but knew the kind of sweepings
> Verses grow from, with no reticence,
> Like weeds—the burdock and the goosefoot,
> The yellow dandelion by the fence.

For all his preoccupation with the intimate lyric, with the "sweepings" of existence, Annensky had at times had recourse to large-scale forms—notably the prose poem and the verse tragedy—and in the last third of her life, Akhmatova, too, addressed the challenge of enlarged formal conceptions. This was in part a response to the massive scale of the catastrophes that had overtaken the world, but it was also an inevitable development of the cyclical character of much of her earlier work. Although Akhmatova did not make use of the *trilistnik,* the miniature tripartite cycle so beloved of Annensky, until very late in her poetic career, the cyclical grouping of poems according to mood, theme, and element was a technique dear to her, and it was by means of it that she was able to approach the building of larger prosodic structures. She had, it is true, taken some steps in this direction as early as 1914, in the autobiographical *poema, By the Seashore;* but it is *Requiem* and the extended poems that make up the central achievement of Akhmatova's later years, and possibly of her art as a whole, the enigmatic and monumental *Poem Without a Hero,* in which the fruits of this endeavor are to be seen. Although these poems, like others of the same period, are still essentially "chamber music," the forms they employ are increasingly symphonic in their grandeur and complexity.

The first great manifestation of Akhmatova's late style, in which a restrained colloquialism is made to convey the mingling of the individual's fate with the events of history, is the cycle *Requiem* which, although it was not published in the West until 1963 (and has never been published in the Soviet Union), consists for the most part of the poems Akhmatova wrote between 1935 and 1940 in response to the arrest and imprisonment of her son, Lev, by the Soviet authorities. The city is still present in these poems, as before, except that now St. Petersburg has been replaced by Leningrad, which is a projection of Russia's past onto its present and of its present onto its past. It is also, in a sense that St. Petersburg is in Annensky's poem, a city of death:

> . . . the hosts of those convicted
> Marched by, mad, tormented throngs,
> And train whistles are restricted
> To singing separation songs.
> The stars of death stood overhead,
> And guiltless Russia, that pariah,
> Writhed under boots, all blood-bespattered,
> And the wheels of many a black maria.

In this requiem for all the women who, like the poet herself, stood in the queues outside the Leningrad prisons, trying to visit their husbands and children, and for all the people who perished in the camps, Akhmatova subordinates her own grief to the public woe. Facing death and madness, talking to them on intimate terms, she leaves behind the realm of the living and approaches the land of the dead. The cycle of poems is conceived as a progress along the stations of the Cross (some of the poems bear titles such as **"The Judgment"** and **"The Crucifixion"**). (pp. 71-4)

These poems are, in the first instance, Akhmatova's own "stations of the Cross." But as the cycle progresses, it acquires an even more profound dimension. The image of the lonely woman waiting at the prison gate is assimilated first to the image of *all* the women, and eventually to the image of Mary Magdalene. The sufferings of the Russian people are identified with the agony of the crucified Christ. Yet nowhere does the writing become abstract or emblematic—the scene is simple, direct, and concrete:

> The choir of angels glorified the mighty hour
> And all the heavens melted into fire.
> To his Father he said: "Why hast thou forsaken
>   me?"
> And to his Mother: "Weep not for me . . . "
>
> Mary sobbed, and beat her breast.
> His favorite disciple stood still as stone.

> But no one dared to cast a glance
> At where the silent Mother stood alone.

The individual, pictorial quality of these scenes is vital: such suffering can only be redeemed in the sacred act of remembrance; the memory of the epoch must not be allowed to fade in people's consciousness, and the poet prays that if ever a monument is raised to her it should be placed not by the sea, or in the park at Tsarskoye Selo, but

> here where for three hundred years I had to
>   wait,
> And still they didn't open that certain gate.

In *Requiem* all the attributes and characteristics of Akhmatova's earlier poetry—the intimate, conversational manner, the struggle with conscience and guilt (at one point in the cycle the poet construes her present sufferings as a punishment for her frivolous girlhood), the brooding presence of the city, the meditation on the themes of love, death, and time, and the concept of poetic inspiration as prayer—fuse together and move forward into a new dimension of transfigured suffering. The nearness of extinction in Leningrad, the city of death, makes the barriers of time irrelevant. What matter now are the absolute, timeless qualities of a grief that has transcended itself and become a monument:

> Let from the lids of bronze, unmoving eyes
> Snow melt and stream like the tears each human
>   cries.

Returning in 1946 to Tsarskoye Selo (it had been renamed "Pushkin" some eight years previously by Stalin), Akhmatova found the town in ruins: "They've burnt my little toy town / And I've no loophole back to the past," begins the poem she wrote as an immediate reaction to her loss. This sense of the door to the past having irrevocably slammed shut had already been confirmed by a number of cataclysmic events, which included the siege of Leningrad in 1941 by the German army, the death of Mandelstam in a labor camp, and Tsvetayeva's suicide. The end of the war saw an intensification of the officially approved campaign against Akhmatova and her work. She was subjected to crude abuse in the press—all hope that she would ever be able to publish seemed to be lost. This, in spite of the fact that during the war she had acted in the most heroic, patriotic manner, broadcasting to the people of Leningrad to give them courage, and dedicating a cycle of poems to the city in its state of siege.

In 1940, aware that a world was coming to an end, Akhmatova had begun to jot down the first sketches of a poem about the eve of the Russian revolution. It was a work she had been thinking about since as early as 1923, when she had made allusion to a long poem she planned to write "in which there is not a single hero." All during 1941, even at the height of the terrible artillery attacks and bombing raids, she continued, weak and ill, to work at this poem. It was to become a characterization in verse of a whole era, conceived as a dialogue of the temporal-historical with the eternal. With its three dedications (to Knyazev / Mandelstam, to Sudeykina, and to Isaiah Berlin, whom Akhmatova had befriended in 1945 when he was a diplomat in Moscow); with its invocation of the year 1913, of the world and Russia as they were on the eve of "The True Twentieth Century," and the poet's friends, surrounded by the shades of the past dressed as mummers; with its intermezzo, bearing an epigraph inspired by T. S. Eliot's *Four Quartets,* "My future is in my past"; and its epilogue, dedicated to the city of Leningrad under siege, the poem presents a complex refracting mirror to the face of history. . . . The mirror that recurs throughout the poem is the eye of conscience: the poet takes upon herself not only her own sins but also the sins of an entire epoch. The personal hell she has traversed is also the hell of man's inhumanity to man. Past, present, and future momentarily coincide, and as they do so, time and history are brought to an end—eternity, in the shape of Russia's mysterious fate, calls through suffering from afar:

> Lowering her dry eyes
> And wringing her hands, Russia
> Walked before me into the East.

In Akhmatova's "**Poem of Memory**," or "Poem of Conscience," as the literary critic A. I. Pavlovsky called it, there is no hero, only the voice of the age and the voice of God. In this work the guilt of an individual past is overcome and expiated in the recognition of a shared, generational suffering, a Way of the Cross that is the same for those of the poet's contemporaries who stayed in Russia, for those who were exiled to Central Asia or Siberia, and for those who went abroad, to the West:

> Some in Tashkent, some in New York,
> And the air of exile has a bitter smack
> Like poisoned wine.

Poem Without A Hero is the expression of a great inner freedom: in it, space and time are transcended, and the threads of the poet's life are brought together in her complete identification with the destiny of her nation and her people. It is also a defiance of the labor camps, of the Terror, a rendering powerless of the evil forces that had laid siege to her own life and the lives of her contemporaries. It is a supreme act of allegiance to the spirit of Russian literary culture and its power of moral education, in particular as that spirit is expressed in the poetry of Derzhavin, Pushkin, and Annensky. And, like the Yekaterininsky Park, which Annensky described in his Pushkin centenary address at Tsarskoye Selo as "the park of memories," it is a public and national monument of enduring beauty.

In the *Poem* an insuperable obstacle to further creation seems to have been overcome, an almost cosmic guilt atoned for. The guilt the poet has felt at the deaths of Knyazev and Gumilyov, at having been spared the fate of Mandelstam, of Tsvetayeva, at being alive at all—all this is lifted in a sudden recognition that she is, after all, an heir to the noble Russian poetic tradition. A poem written in 1958, **"The Heiress,"** describes a walk in the grounds of Tsarskoye Selo in the following terms:

> Among these halls, standing deserted,
> A song was what I seemed to hear.
> Who could have told me in that year
> That this was what I should inherit:
> The swans, the bridges of those times,
> Felitsa, all of her chinoiseries,
> The palaces' ethereal galleries,

> Miraculous beauty of the limes.
> My shadow, even, that fear's wave
> Distorted beyond recognition,
> The hairshirt of the heart's contrition,
> The lilac of beyond the grave.

In the last years of her life, Akhmatova continued to write poetry of undiminished clarity, severity, and grace. By now her fame had penetrated far beyond the boundaries of her native land. Her meeting with Robert Frost in 1962, and her visit to Oxford in 1965, had helped to establish her international reputation as the greatest living Russian poet. Sadly, however, Western translations of her work were still few in number. In 1964, Robert Lowell published his translation (with Olga Carlisle) of *Requiem,* and in 1965 D. M. Thomas offered an English version of the same poem. French, German, and Italian translations were also published at about the same time. It was not until several years after Akhmatova's death in 1966, however, that any substantial account of her work appeared in English translation, the first being Richard McKane's Penguin selection (1969). During the 1970s a relatively large number of translated selections appeared, perhaps the finest of them being Stanley Kunitz' and Max Hayward's *Poems of Akhmatova* (1974). Neither McKane nor Kunitz / Hayward make any consistent attempt to reproduce in their translations the formal, prosodic, and musical qualities of Akhmatova's verse, however, but concentrate primarily on meanings, although Kunitz / Hayward do make an occasional gesture in the direction of rhyme and meter. While these plain but generally accurate versions may be of great assistance to readers with only a partial knowledge of Russian, they—like those of W. Arndt (1976)—are surely intended as an adjunct to the original poems rather than as independent translations (the Kunitz / Hayward versions face the Russian texts). D. M. Thomas' *Way of All the Earth* (1979) makes a more determined move toward the formal attributes of the original poems; some of his versions manage to retain both meaning and structure, and to stand on their own as poems. Others in the volume are weaker, however, and some should simply not have been included at all.

Lyn Coffin's translations of Akhmatova's poetry are the first I have seen to attempt a consistent deployment of rhyme and meter over the whole range of the poet's output. The results come as near, I think, to the sense and form of the originals as may be possible in the English language. In saying this, I do not mean to imply that these versions are by any means perfect; their deficiencies are, however, ones imposed by culture, language, geography, and time, and not by any attempt by the translator to impose her own personality on her subject, or to make Akhmatova more "assimilable" for Western readers. The selection, although relatively short, is a careful one, and covers all periods of Akhmatova's creative life. Among the longer poem sequences and cycles, only a part of *Requiem* is translated, and *Poem Without A Hero* is not represented at all; but there is a fine rendering of the weirdly hermetic **"Midnight Verses"** of 1963, presented in their entirety. The book has an Introduction by the poet Joseph Brodsky [see Further Reading list], who was close to Akhmatova during the last years of her life and whom she helped at the time of his victimization and exile by the Soviet authorities. This concise and powerful essay brings Coffin's translations nearer to Akhmatova's spirit and to the spirit of classical Russian poetry than can be said to be the case with other available translated selections. In particular, it points up just how far from adequate is the type of approach adopted by a translator like Mary Maddock, who in her *Three Russian Women Poets* includes a number of Akhmatova versions that, while they express at least some of the original meaning, are conceived in literary terms so alien to the spirit of the Russian that they miss the essence of the poems altogether. (pp. 75-81)

Writing in 1923 about Innokenty Annensky, Osip Mandelstam expressed himself in the following terms:

> Gumilyov called Annensky a great European poet. It seems to me that when the Europeans find out about him, having meekly educated their generations in the study of the Russian language, just as previous generations were educated in the study of the ancient languages and classical poetry, they will be inspired with fear by the insolence of this regal plunderer, who abducted the dove Eurydice from them and took her to the snows of Russia, who tore the classical shawl from the shoulders of Phaedra and tenderly placed, as befits a Russian poet, an animal skin on an Ovid who was still shivering from cold.

Mandelstam's words might be made equally well to apply to Akhmatova, and to the sense of wonder with which future generations of non-Russians will one day greet her work. (pp. 81-2)

> *David McDuff, "Anna Akhmatova," in* Parnassus: Poetry in Review, *Vol. 11, No. 2, Fall-Winter 1983, Spring-Summer 1984, pp. 51-82.*

Henry Gifford   (essay date 1989)

[*Gifford is an English critic specializing in Russian literature. His works include* The Hero of His Time: A Theme in Russian Literature *(1950) and* The Novel in Russia: From Pushkin to Pasternak *(1964). In the excerpt below, Gifford provides a brief overview of Akhmatova's life and work.*]

[Akhmatova's] first book of poems, **Evening,** came out in 1912. With the second, **Rosary,** in 1914, Akhmatova had gained completely that individual voice, laconic and finely modulated, which won for her a large captive audience. (In course of time, as she proceeded much further, it irked Akhmatova that she had to resist becoming the captive of this audience, reluctant to let her change.) She wrote in these earlier poems about her own situation as a vulnerable but strong-minded young woman, conscious of her effect upon male admirers, and watching herself with the frank recognition of her feelings that Kitty shows during Levin's courtship in *Anna Karenina*. As Mandelstam noted in 1922, when this phase of her art was nearly completed,

> Akhmatova brought to the Russian lyric all the vast complexity and richness of the Russian novel in the nineteenth century. There would

have been no Akhmatova but for Tolstoy with *Anna Karenina,* Turgenev with *A Nest of Gentlefolk,* all Dostoevsky and in part even Leskov. The genesis of Akhmatova lies wholly in Russian prose and not in poetry. Her poetic form, sharply defined and individual, she developed with a backward glance at psychological prose.

This is essentially true, though [Russian poet and scholar Innokenty] Annensky should not be overlooked as a poet with a similar approach, and Russian prose fiction, of course, sprang from Pushkin's poetry even more than from his prose. It was from Annensky that she learned to use prosaic detail for the notation of deeply subjective awareness, and from him too the sudden shift of attention as a new state of feeling, or a new aspect of the situation, is brought into view. Many of her poems in **Rosary** fix the particulars that a novelist would have noted: "the worn rug below the icon," the smile in an admirer's "tranquil eyes / Under the light gold of the lashes," or her feather brushing against the carriage roof in an episode which concludes thus:

> The odor of gasoline and lilac,
> A peacefulness on the alert . . .
> Once more he touched my knees
> With a hand that scarcely trembled.

Here for the first time, as her friend the scholar and critic Zhirmunsky points out, the "hero" in all the poems was a woman. There had been a forerunner, Karolina Pavlova, more than half a century before; but only when Akhmatova appeared, with such assurance, and with "an equivalent center of self" (in George Eliot's phrase) to Annensky or Blok, did the public encounter not a poetess but a woman poet. It would not be long before Tsvetayeva would come to challenge her supremacy in this role, but Akhmatova first entered into the inheritance of a full poetic freedom.

About this inheritance Mandelstam made a telling point when he affirmed the relation of her poetry to folk song. As he says, Akhmatova's was "the purest literary language of her time," but her way with it belonged to the popular tradition of oral poetry, resting on parallelism and startling contrasts. He could hear in her verses the note of the folk lament. This made it possible "to divine in the Russian literary lady of the twentieth century a peasant woman."

Akhmatova always contended that the critic of her work in its initial stage who had shown truly prophetic insight was another close friend, N. V. Nedobrovo. In 1915 he noted not only the virtuosity with which she played syntax against rhythm, but also the firmness and confidence in her tone. He defined her lyrical temperament as "tough rather than too tender, severe rather than tearful," and said very perceptively that she used "the strong armor of words" to save a sensitive nature from destruction. Akhmatova thought it miraculous that so early he should have predicted what lay ahead of her and the steadfastness with which she would meet the difficulties.

Mandelstam a year later spoke of "a sudden change" in her tone to "a hieratic solemnity, a religious simplicity and exultation . . . The voice of renunciation gets stronger in

Caricature of Akhmatova by David Levine, 1984.

Akhmatova's verses, and at the present time her poetry is near to becoming one of the symbols of Russia's grandeur." Those lines were written on the eve of an equally sudden change in the course of Russian history, which would soon make renunciation the rule for Akhmatova and for Mandelstam too. It would postpone until almost the end of a long life the recognition that she had become a national poet speaking for the people who scarcely knew she was among them. (pp. 130-32)

[By 1924, when Akhmatova was banned from publishing in the Soviet Union,] three more books had appeared: *The White Flock* (1917), *Plantain* (1921), and *Anno Domini* (Petrograd 1922, Berlin 1923). It would not be until 1940 that a collection, entitled *From Six Books,* was allowed to come out in Leningrad. For the greater part of those years in the wilderness she lived with the art critic Nikolay Punin: this was an unhappy marriage, when she was once again largely inhibited from writing verse. They shared from 1926 a small apartment with his former wife and infant daughter in a wing of Fontanny Dom, originally the Petersburg palace of the Sheremetev family. The motto inscribed on its gateway, *Deus conservat omnia,* she chose as the main epigraph for *A Poem Without a Hero,* her major preoccupation from 1940 onward. Every Russian poet in those years, if he took his art seriously and guarded its independence, was bound, as Nadezhda Mandelstam has said, to endure at least a period of sterility. This happened to Mandelstam, likewise in disfavor, through the second half of the 1920s. But he was at least enabled to

publish a collection of verse in 1928 and a book of his essays in the same year. Akhmatova, having no outlet and discouraged by Punin, was effectively removed from the community of living writers. Her talent was said to be extinguished; the poetry written before her exclusion no longer deserved a hearing because it failed to confront the real issues of the day.

This was a willful misunderstanding or at the best culpable inattention. Akhmatova always regarded Futurism as destructive of the poetic tradition she valued: its proponents had called, in a notorious phrase, for Pushkin to be thrown overboard from the ship of modernity. Had her critics taken the trouble to look through the three latest volumes (*Anno Domini* in the fuller Berlin edition), they could hardly have missed what is at once clear to those acquainted with her subsequent poetry. Akhmatova already in July 1914 when the First World War broke out (for Russia, 19 July Old Style) had become a poet with a new breadth of vision, even a prophetic power. Her poem written the day after the declaration of war evokes the ominous heatwave and smell of burning in the previous weeks. A crippled passerby utters his prediction, which the censor struck out:

> Fearful times are upon us. Soon
> There will be the crowding of fresh graves.
> Look for famine, earthquake and plague,
> And for eclipse of the stars in heaven.

(pp. 133-34)

Akhmatova's devotion to her country remained unshaken even when, as a lyric of 1921 protests,

> All is plundered, betrayed, sold,

and others were forsaking Russia for exile. It was severely put to the test, and the price would be to accept poverty, solitude and eventually terror. But, as [the Russian poet Joseph] Brodsky has said, she was "a poet of human ties," the strongest of which she felt to be those binding her to the Russian people and their language. Blok's equally intense feeling for Russia had been mystical and exalted, in character with the poet whom she was to call "tragic tenor of the epoch." Akhmatova does not dramatize her instinctive fidelity, which had already shown in the appreciation of natural scenes:

> . . . I yet recall even to aching,
> The meager soil of Tver'.
>
> A crane at the ancient well,
> Above it, clouds like seething milk,
> In the fields creaking gates,
> And the smell of bread, and yearning . . .

(pp. 134-35)

"About the middle of the 1920s," she wrote, "I began very diligently and with great interest to devote myself to the architecture of old Petersburg and a study of the life and work of Pushkin." One of her **"Northern Elegies"** declares in 1945 that her life, its course abruptly changed like a river's, had been deprived of countless opportunities:

> . . . how many skylines of cities
> Could have brought tears to my eyes,

While there is only one city in the world I know
And shall find it fumbling in my sleep . . .

The classical façades of Petersburg, designed often by Italian architects, signified for Akhmatova as for Mandelstam the presence of Europe in Russia. They were the setting for a poetry that upheld the notion of a world culture, the longing for which, according to Mandelstam, formed the essence of Acmeism. In Tsarskoe Selo, Pushkin, Tyutchev and Annensky still could be summoned from the past. Leningrad, for all its beauty and resistance to outward change, held memories that filled her with foreboding. She pointed out to Chukovskaya the windows of the room behind which the Emperor Paul had been strangled; she felt her city to be the inevitable scene for catastrophe: "This cold river, above which there are always heavy clouds, these menacing sunsets, this terrible operatic moon . . . " Such was the nature of Russian history. Yet in the buildings of Leningrad an ideal, the vision of a civilized order swept away, remained before her eyes:

> That city, loved by me from childhood,
> In its December stillness
> This day has appeared to me
> As my squandered inheritance.

But, as Sharon Leiter observes in her illuminating book *Akhmatova's Petersburg* (1983), the poem of 1929 from which this stanza is quoted ends on a promise of resurrection:

> And with a wild freshness and power
> Happiness breathed in my face
> As though a friend long dear
> Had walked with me on to the porch.

(pp. 135-36)

In 1940, when at last a collection of her verse, by no means fully representative, was permitted [to be published in the Soviet Union] and the editors began to make overtures once more, Akhmatova entered upon a new phase of creativity. This was her *annus mirabilis,* and it culminated in the first draft of *A Poem Without a Hero.* Only about half of what she wrote in 1940 could then be published. *Requiem* was so outspoken, so formidable in its tragic power, that only a few intimates could be allowed to hear the poem. Akhmatova was unable to appear in full panoply: at best she was tolerated because of her former reputation, and always a one-sided image was presented—that of a love poet whose later work had made no significant progress. She was praised, grudgingly sometimes, for her craftsmanship. There could be no disputing Akhmatova's popularity when readers were given access to her work; but she did not emerge as the true Akhmatova, matured and made dangerously eloquent by her sufferings.

During the war, nonetheless, some account was taken of her stature. At the beginning of the siege she spoke to her fellow citizens of Leningrad on the radio. In March 1942 *Pravda* carried her short poem **"Courage,"** arousing the people's determination to save their birthright:

> . . . We shall preserve you, Russian speech,
> The great Russian word.
> Free and pure we shall pass you on
> And give you to our grandchildren and deliver
>   from captivity
> For ever!

She wrote this in Tashkent. At the end of September 1941 the Soviet government had seen fit to fly her out of Leningrad together with Shostakovich, whose relations with the régime were no more comfortable than her own. Akhmatova's handful of war poems was published in the press. Her "new-found" patriotism made her once more respectable. Not unlike the Orthodox Church, both Akhmatova and Pasternak could be welcomed to help the war effort, to the extent of writing a few poems generally somewhat below par for either poet. In 1946, when the cold war began and "cosmopolitanism" was denounced, Akhmatova and also Zoshchenko came under heavy fire from Zhdanov, who had taken charge of cultural matters with punitive energy. Akhmatova's situation, after being expelled from the Writers Union, would have broken her altogether, as the same plight did Zoshchenko, but for her own fortitude and the loyalty of her friends.

Samizdat did not come into full swing until the 1960s. She had therefore to rely on the memories of a few chosen friends to preserve her latest poems. She dared not write down *Requiem,* for instance, nor could she ask others to do so. Russian intellectuals, it is well known, possess an amazing faculty for memorizing verse (and even prose in the case of Nadezhda Mandelstam). This incidentally makes for a great strength of Russian poetry, written as it is for the spoken voice. Akhmatova survived physically in those years by translating a wide range of foreign poetry, very often in languages unknown to her such as Korean, when she had to depend upon a crib supplied by an expert. It was a chore she detested, for it usurped the place of her own writing. The new high-risk poems, as we have seen, needed for their preservation the existence of a dozen or so devoted admirers: these were mostly women. Not only did they form a secret repository for her work. There was another vital service they rendered. Among them were extremely sensitive judges of poetry—Lydia Chukovskaya, Tamara Gabbe, Emma Gershstein, to name but three—who provided a necessarily small but active audience. Akhmatova valued their response, and listened to the comments they made. This particularly concerns *A Poem Without a Hero,* over the twenty-two years in which she revised and extended it.

In her introduction to this work, she uses an image that Tamara Gabbe had found to describe what is happening in the poem:

> From the year forty
>   As down from a tower I look on all . . .

She is bidding farewell once again (it had already been done long before), seeming like one who crosses herself and "goes under the dark vaults." The century has now run to forty years, and as Boris Filippov, joint editor of her *Collected Works* in the West, has suggested, Akhmatova's mention of this may hint at the Orthodox ritual of commemorating the dead forty days after their decease. Akhmatova herself, following the epoch, is preparing for death. The year 1940, in the last days of which she began writing the *Poem,* had been for her almost one sustained act of commemoration. The world she had known was finally being destroyed. (pp. 138-40)

When first made aware of her exclusion from Soviet literature, Akhmatova had entered a plea for Lot's wife:

> Her at least my heart will never forget
> Who gave up her life for a single look.

This backward glance, she says in a poem of 1936, Dante had denied himself when leaving for an exile in which he would never forget the city, but even after death still not return there. Zhirmunsky saw in this a reference to the myth of Orpheus, whose looking back lost him Eurydice on the path upward from Hades. In the early days of 1940, Akhmatova wrote **"The Cellar of Memory,"** about the horror of going down, lantern in hand, to a place seldom visited from which return is blocked by a landslip on the stairs. She wants to go home: "But where is my home and where is my reason?"

"For the people of my generation," she noted in some jottings toward an autobiography, ". . . there is nowhere to return." As the elegiac poem on the death of Mikhail Bulgakov in March 1940 had expressed it, hers seemed a desperate position:

> I, half out of my mind,
> I, the hired mourner of ruined days,
> I, smoldering on a slow fire,
> Everything lost, everything forgotten—

how strange that on such a tormented survivor the duty of commemoration should fall. At the close of the year, as a sudden visitant—though it had been foreshadowed by some lines written a few months before about her friend of 1913, the actress Glebova-Sudeykina—there came to her in its first form *A Poem Without a Hero.* (Really, as Tamara Gabbe observed, it has two heroes, time and memory.)

Much of the poem had been structured within a few days. She resumed it in Tashkent, whereupon it seemed to be complete. However, for another twenty years the process of altering, enlarging and fine-tuning the work continued, sometimes to the dismay of her friends as fragments and images familiar to them were discarded, and the expected landfall receded once more. She compared herself to rain penetrating "the narrowest cracks, widening them." Even in the last months of her life she had not quite finished. It dominated her in a strange intermittent way year after year, with long intervals of silence; the many short poems she wrote at the same time are like a flotilla accompanying her majestic flagship.

It is a Petersburg poem, as its subtitle, "A Petersburg Tale," proclaims, set initially in her room under the roof of the Sheremetev palace, and it brings together the city in 1913, the final year of its *belle époque,* and the Leningrad she could imagine twenty-nine years later. . . . However, not only its location makes this a Petersburg poem. Akhmatova has provided a successor to Pushkin's *The Bronze Horseman* and Blok's *The Twelve.* Her city is Pushkin's, and Dostoyevsky's; it stands as a final staging-post of the Petersburg imagination, and Gogol and Andrey Bely are also in some degree represented among her forerunners. And, as with these four writers, the form used is innovative. She has devised her own stanza, on a rising beat, flexible and apt for every tone of the voice,

from epic solemnity to the quiet precision of a personal aside:

> What people call the spring
> I call loneliness.

The verve and dancelike play of association are sustained throughout. **Requiem** is unmatched in her work for its tragic simplicity: it seems to be hewn from a single block, like *Prometheus Bound,* out of her own suffering which reflects the suffering of her people. **A Poem Without a Hero** is more complex. "No torch yet thrown into it," she wrote, "has illuminated it to the depths." More and more aspects were revealed to her as time went on, while she tried to capture what she called its "hidden music."

On New Year's Eve 1940 a prolonged ring at her door brings not the NKVD, fear of which freezes and turns her to stone, but a phantom throng of masked revelers. These are the companions and celebrities of her youth. Marina Tsvetayeva, when they met in June 1941, marveled at her "temerity" in using the worn-out symbolism of "harlequins, columbines, pierrots" from their youth under the shadow of Blok. Others believed that her poem was retrogressive, locked into the by now remote past. This is not so. Akhmatova is elevated above the masquerade—a masquerade as we shall see with tragic implications—surveying it from her tower beset by the fierce winds of the present. She passes judgment, with scorn and severity, and here and there with compassion, on the people of her time and on herself:

> With her who once I was
> In a necklace of black agates
> I have no wish to meet
> Until the last Day of Reckoning . . .

She chooses—rather as Blok had done in *The Twelve*—a tragic incident, an act wanton in its irresponsibility, when a young cavalry officer and minor poet, Vsevolod Knyazev, out of jealousy that a rival is successful with the actress he loves, takes his own life. . . . The seducer whom her follower has resented is unmistakably Blok, "Gabriel or Mephistopheles," in whom Akhmatova discerns all the contradictions of an epoch fascinating to her, yet deservedly doomed. She sought in this poem to present "an apotheosis of the 1910s in all their splendor and weakness."

Chukovskaya, who had taken down all the corrections and additions as they arose, says of the poem:

> I don't know another thing that in extracts to
> such a degree fails to correspond to itself. All its
> fascination is in the relations between the layers
> of memory, between what has "smoldered to ash
> in the depths of mirrors" and the contemporary,
> sober, very real reality.

Akhmatova, the survivor who had been spared the fate of those nearest to her, always kept in mind what others had endured or were yet to endure. As Chukovskaya observed:

> . . . Sounds from *out there,* from the taiga be-
> yond the looking glass, were necessary to the
> poem . . . together with the phantom of de-
> struction by the Mazurian lakes or in the Carpa-
> thians [during the First World War] there was

necessary too the phantom of the concentration camp. So it came in, hurrah for her!

Anna Akhmatova regarded **A Poem Without a Hero** as quite unlike anything else she had written. It seemed to her "very strange" that, whereas normally she had been the sole author, here along "I wrote it all in chorus, together with others, as if by prompting." This does not mean that the voice in her poem, with its oblique statements, and the fine irony in the section where she converses with her puzzled editor (and so with the unenlightened reader), is not the voice of the poet herself. But she was, in the words of the poem, "willing to accept the role of fateful chorus." Into the shaping of this work she had drawn the innermost audience of those friends who could tolerate all her whims and fits of unreasonableness, because they recognized in Akhmatova the representative of the true Russia which she never ceased to believe in. The old age of the poet was marked by a dignity not often witnessed in these days. She had made herself the recorder of a common experience, almost too dreadful to contemplate, unless it could be shown not to have destroyed the humanity that has always shone through the great works of Russian literature. Akhmatova was answerable to Pushkin and to the language he had given as a lifeline. Not to have failed in this charge was her glory. (pp. 141-46)

Henry Gifford, "Anna Akhmatova," in Grand Street, *Vol. 8, No. 3, Spring, 1989, pp. 128-46.*

FURTHER READING

Bayley, John. "Poems with a Heroine." *The New York Review of Books* XXX, Nos. 21 and 22 (19 January 1989): 21-24.
  Compares several English-language translations of Akhmatova's poetry.

Brodsky, Joseph. "Translating Akhmatova." *The New York Review of Books* XX, No. 13 (9 August 1973): 9-11.
  Enumerates the difficulties in translating Russian poetry into English, and in translating Akhmatova in particular.

———. "The Keening Muse." In his *Less than One: Selected Essays,* pp. 34-52. New York: Farrar, Straus and Giroux, 1986.
  Offers insights on Akhmatova's relation to her milieu while asserting her uniqueness.

Chukovsky, Korney. "Akhmatova and Mayakovsky." In *Major Soviet Writers,* edited by Edward J. Brown, pp. 33-53. London: Oxford University Press, 1973.
  Examines Akhmatova's imagery, emphasizing its religious overtones, and compares her dignifed, traditional poetry to that of Vladimir Mayakovsky, a younger contemporary whose poetry expresses the irreverent exuberance of revolutionary Russia.

Driver, Sam [N]. *Anna Akhmatova.* New York: Twayne Publishers, 1972, 162 p.
  Critical biography.

Driver, Sam. "Anna Akhmatova (1889-1966)." In *European Writers: The Twentieth Century,* Vol. X, edited by George Stade, pp. 1521-1542. New York: Charles Scribner's Sons, 1990.
  Compares Akhmatova's early themes and techniques to those exhibited in her later works, particularly *Requiem* and *Poem without a Hero.*

Goldman, Howard A. "Anna Akhmatova's Hamlet: The Immortality of Personality." *Slavic and East European Journal* 22, No. 4 (Winter 1978): 484-93.
  Compares Akhmatova's use of characters from Shakespeare's tragedy *Hamlet* to their appearance in other Russian works, and in the context of Akhmatova's own writings.

Hingley, Ronald. *Nightingale Fever: Russian Poets in Revolution.* New York: Alfred A. Knopf, 1981, 269 p.
  Examines the lives and writings of Akhmatova, Osip Mandelstam, Boris Pasternak, and Marina Tsvetayeva as emblematic of the political and social upheavals in Russia between the outbreak of the two World Wars.

Ketchian, Sonia. *The Poetry of Anna Akhmatova: A Conquest of Time and Space.* Munich: Verlag Otto Sagner, 1986, 225 p.
  Scholarly study of the presence of fire imagery, metempsychosis, and intertextuality in Akhmatova's poetry.

Leiter, Sharon. *Akhmatova's Petersburg.* Philadelphia: University of Pennsylvania Press, 1983, 215 p.
  Traces the evolution of the presence of Akhmatova's hometown in her poetry.

Mandrykina, Ludmilla. "An Unwritten Book: Anna Akhmatova's 'Pages from a Diary'." *Soviet Literature* 6, No. 375 (1979): 101-08.
  Summarizes Akhmatova's private papers held by the State Public Library in Leningrad that outline her unwritten autobiography.

Mihailovich, Vasa D. "The Critical Reception of Anna Akhmatova." *Papers on Language and Literature* V, No. 1 (Winter 1969): 95-111.
  Brief overview of the evolution of Akhmatova's poetic themes and style, along with an evaluation of the critical reception to her work in the Soviet Union.

Ozerov, Lev. "Touches to Akhmatova's Portrait." *Soviet Literature* 6, No. 495 (1989): 155-63.
  Critical homage illustrating Akhmatova's full literary rehabilitation under the Soviet regime of the late 1980s.

Rosslyn, Wendy. *The Prince, the Fool and the Nunnery: The Religious Theme in the Early Poetry of Anna Akhmatova.* Amersham, England: Avebury, 1984, 256 p.
  Examines Akhmatova's early poetry in terms set forth in her poem "Reading Hamlet" in which a woman, rejected by a prince, is instructed to either marry a fool or to join a nunnery.

———. "Theatre, Theatricality and Akhmatova's 'Poema bez geroya'." *Essays in Poetics* 13, No. 1 (April 1988): 89-108.
  Examines theatrical influences in Akhmatova's allusions, rhythms, and structure in *Poem without a Hero.*

Verheul, Kees. "Public Themes in the Poetry of Anna Axmatova." In *Tale without a Hero and Twenty-Two Poems by*

Anna Axmatova, pp. 9-48. The Hague: Mouton Publishers, 1973.

Divides the poems Akhmatova wrote that address public events into those concerning World War I, the revolution and ensuing civil war, the Stalinist terror during the 1930s, and World War II.

Robert Browning

1812-1889

English poet and dramatist.

One of the most prominent poets of the Victorian era, Browning is chiefly remembered for his mastery of the dramatic monologue and for the remarkable diversity and scope of his works. In "Fra Lippo Lippi," "Andrea del Sarto," "The Bishop Orders His Tomb at San Praxed's," and many other well-known poems, as well as in his masterpiece, *The Ring and the Book,* Browning advanced the art of the dramatic monologue to new levels of technical and psychological sophistication. At the same time, his works reflect a versatility of approach and a cosmopolitan range of knowledge that anticipate the eclectic and international character of modern literature. As a highly individual force in the history of English poetry, Browning also made significant innovations in language and versification. For all of these reasons, Browning ranks as an important figure in English literature, one who had a profound influence on numerous twentieth-century poets, including such key figures as Ezra Pound and T. S. Eliot.

Browning was born in the borough of Camberwell in southeast London, where he grew up in a setting of relative affluence. His father, Robert Browning, was a well-read, broad-minded man who worked as a clerk for the Bank of England; his mother, Sarah Anne Wiedemann, was a strict Congregationalist who sought to pass her faith on to her son. Biographers have suggested that his father's cultivated literary tastes—the elder Browning had an extensive library—and his mother's religious devotion had an important influence on Browning's character and writings. Although Browning's home provided an intellectually rich environment, his formal education has been described as erratic. Encouraged to take advantage of his father's collection of books, he read widely as a boy, acquiring an abundant, if unsystematic, knowledge of a wide range of different literatures. He displayed a premature aptitude for poetry, composing his first verses at the age of six, and at ten was sent to Peckam School, where he remained for four years. Because he had not been raised as an Anglican, Browning was barred from attending the major English universities at Oxford and Cambridge, but in 1828 he entered London University. He broke off his studies after less than a year, however, determined to pursue a career as a poet. Due to the income provided him by his parents, with whom he continued to live until 1846, Browning was able to devote his entire energies to his art.

Browning began his literary career in 1833 with the anonymous publication of *Pauline: A Fragment of a Confession.* Because the poem was cast in the form of a self-revelation made to a fictional character named Pauline, many of its first readers interpreted the sentiments expressed as Browning's own. Biographers now speculate that the negative reaction of these readers to what they believed were Browning's thoughts and feelings led the poet to distance him-

self from the characters and emotions portrayed in his subsequent writings by adopting the relatively objective framework offered by dramatic forms of expression. Browning's next work, published in 1835 under the title *Paracelsus,* exemplifies this trend. Based on the life of the Renaissance chemist of the same name, *Paracelsus* is a dramatic monologue detailing a personality that readers could not have confused with Browning's own. The critical reception of *Paracelsus* was largely positive, but *Sordello,* another poem based on a Renaissance subject, met with widespread derision when it appeared in 1840, becoming, according to Philip Drew, a "byword for incomprehensibility." In an effort to regain some measure of the critical reverence that *Sordello* had lost him, Browning initiated in 1841 a series of poems and dramas entitled *Bells and Pomegranates.* Published in pamphlet form, *Bells and Pomegranates*—the last volume of which appeared in 1846—unfortunately did little to repair the damage done to Browning's reputation by *Sordello.*

Despite the overall lack of favorable attention accorded them, Browning's works had illustrious admirers, including Elizabeth Barrett, who was a respected and popular poet. In 1844 she praised Browning in one of her works and received a grateful letter from him in response. The two met the following year, fell in love, and in 1846, ignoring the disapproval of her father, eloped to Italy, where—except for brief intervals—they spent the remainder of their life together. Browning continued to write, publishing the theologically oriented *Christmas Eve and Easter Day* in 1850 and the collection *Men and Women* in 1855. The latter work contains many of his best-known love poems and dramatic monologues, including "One Word More," "Love Among the Ruins," "Fra Lippo Lippi," and "Andrea del Sarto." Although public success still eluded Browning, his works attracted increasing respect from critics, and following Elizabeth's death in 1861, he returned to England, where after a brief period of literary inactivity he began writing again. The appearance in 1864 of *Dramatis Personae,* which contained such important poems as "Rabbi Ben Ezra," "Caliban upon Setebos," and "Abt Vogler," finally brought Browning his first sizable outpouring of critical and popular admiration.

In 1868-69 he published *The Ring and the Book,* a series of twelve dramatic monologues spoken by different characters and based upon the record of an Italian murder case that he had discovered in Florence. Tremendously and immediately popular, *The Ring and the Book* firmly established Browning's reputation in Victorian England. From 1868 on, Browning and Alfred, Lord Tennyson were generally regarded as England's greatest living poets. He remained highly productive, and while much of the poetry he produced between 1869 and his death is not now regarded as his finest, the publication of his *Dramatic Idyls* and other works brought him worldwide fame. In 1880 the Browning Society was established in London for the purpose of paying tribute to and studying his poems, and near the end of his life he was the recipient of various other honors, including a degree from Oxford University and an audience with Queen Victoria. Following his death in 1889 while staying in Venice, he was buried in the Poets' Corner of Westminster Abbey.

Scholars agree that Browning's place in English literature is based to a great extent on his contribution to the poetic genre of the dramatic monologue, the form he adopted for a large proportion of his works. With his topical eclecticism, striking use of language, and stylistic creativity, his ground-breaking accomplishments in this genre constitute the basis of his reputation. Literary historians define the dramatic monologue as a poem in which the speaker's character is gradually disclosed in a dramatic situation through his or her own words. In "Fra Lippo Lippi," for example, the hypocritical nature of the narrator becomes increasingly apparent to the reader as the poem progresses. As the monk speaks, he reveals aspects of his personality of which even he is unaware, while the voice of the poet seems to be absent from the poet altogether. Whether he chose a historical or an imaginary figure, a reliable or an unreliable narrator, Browning evolved the techniques of exposing a character's personality to an unprecedented degree of subtlety and psychological depth. As few previous poets had done, he explored the makeup of the mind, scrutinizing the interior lives of his creations. His characters vary from sophisticated theologians and artists to simple peasant children, spanning a range of per-

sonalities from the pure and innocent to the borderline psychotic. A considerable percentage of Browning's male and female characters, however, display his overriding interest in thwarted or twisted personalities whose lives are scarred by jealousy, lust, or avarice.

In addition to its psychological depth, critics concur that one of the chief strengths of Browning's work is its sheer abundance and variety in terms of subject matter, time, place, and character. His often difficult subjects usually demand intellectual effort from the reader and reflect the enormous breadth of his interests in science, history, art, and music. Browning's primary source of inspiration was Renaissance Italy; its mixture of powerful religion and worldly grandeur, the egotism and brilliance of its leaders, scientists, and artists, and the flourishing of art it brought forth provided him with many of his themes and characters. Nevertheless, his settings range from the Middle Ages to his own epoch, reflecting a diverse assortment of cultures. Browning's poetic diction also shows the influence of many cultures and fields of interest. He introduced a very large and varied vocabulary into his works, using not only colloquial and traditionally unpoetic language, but also obscure and specialized terms drawn from the past or from contemporary science. Rough syntax, contractions, and the rejection of the vague imagery of romantic poetry in favor of more exact and blunt forms of expression also characterizes his writings. Like his use of language, Browning's approach to versification was frequently unconventional. In assessing this facet of his verse, scholars emphasize the variety of his invention—his use of uncommon rhymes and his metrical and stanzaic flexibility.

The critical history of Browning's works initially discloses a pattern of slow recognition followed by enormous popularity and even adulation in the two decades prior to his death. His reputation subsequently underwent a decline, but gradually recovered with the appearance in the 1930s, 1940s, and 1950s of important biographical and critical studies. Browning's early reviewers often complained about the obscurity, incomprehensibility, and awkward language of his works. The long-standing popular impression that Browning's poetry was intellectually difficult and even unintelligible owed its source in large part to *Sordello.* Although he spent nearly twenty-five years following the publication of that work trying to escape from the charge of obscurity, when he did achieve fame with *Dramatis Personae* and *The Ring and the Book,* it was sizable. His late Victorian audience considered Browning a profound philosophical thinker and teacher who had chosen poetry as his medium of expression. Scholars point out that if his contemporaries often continued—after Browning became popular—to regard his poetry as rough-hewn, unnecessarily challenging, and obscure, they found its difficulties justified by what they considered the depth and profundity of his religious faith and optimism.

While modern critics generally agree that the Victorians were mistaken in their conception of Browning as primarily and unhesitatingly optimistic in his outlook on life, the prevailing image of the poet as philosophically buoyant is widely believed to have contributed to the reaction against his works beginning at the turn of the century. In 1900, for example, George Santayana attacked Browning in an essay entitled "The Poetry of Barbarism," establishing the tone for an era that found his mind superficial, his poetic skill crude, and his language verbose. Describing the reasons for Browning's poor reputation throughout much of the first half of the twentieth century, William DeVane, a noted Browning scholar, stated that the poet's outlook on life "seemed incredibly false to generations harried by war and a vast social unrest." Despite this critical disfavor, scholars now recognize that Browning's works had a significant impact on early twentieth-century poets in both England and America, citing in particular the influence of Browning's diction on the poetic language of Ezra Pound and the effect of his dramatic monologues on the pivotal works of T. S. Eliot. In addition to their considerable influence, the value of Browning's works in their own right continues to be reassessed, with critics focusing less on the philosophical aspects of his writings and more on his strengths as a genuinely original artist. While his reputation has never again been as high as it was during his lifetime, few scholars would deny his importance or influence. For his contribution to the development of the dramatic monologue, as well as for his eclecticism, linguistic originality, and stylistic ingenuity, Browning remains a seminal figure in English poetry.

(For further discussion of Browning's life and career, see *Nineteenth-Century Literature Criticism*, Vol. 19; *Yesterday's Authors of Books for Children*, Vol. 1; and *Dictionary of Literary Biography*, Vol. 32.)

PRINCIPAL WORKS

POETRY

Pauline: A Fragment of a Confession   1833
Paracelsus   1835
Sordello   1840
Pippa Passes   1841
Dramatic Lyrics   1842
Dramatic Romances and Lyrics   1845
Christmas Eve and Easter-Day   1850
Men and Women   1855
Dramatis Personae   1864
The Ring and the Book. 4 vols.   1868-69
Balaustion's Adventure, Including a Transcript from Euripedes   1871
Prince Hohenstiel-Schwangau, Savior of Society   1871
Fifine at the Fair   1872
Red Cotton Night-Cap Country; or, Turf and Towers   1873
Inn Album   1875
Pacchiarotto, and Other Poems   1876
La Saisiaz, Two Poets of Crosic   1878
Dramatic Idyls   1879
Dramatic Idyls, second series   1880
Jocoseria   1883
Ferishtah's Fancies   1884
Parleyings with Certain People of Importance in Their Day, to Wit: Bernard de Mandeville, Daniel Bartoli, Chris-

topher Smart, George Budd Doddington, Francis Furini, Gerard de Lairesse, and Charles Avison   1887
Asolando: Fancies and Facts   1889
The Complete Poetical Works of Robert Browning   1915

OTHER MAJOR WORKS

Strafford   (drama)   1837
King Victor and King Charles   (drama)   1842
A Blot in the 'Scutcheon   (drama)   1843
The Return of the Druses   (drama)   1843
Columbe's Birthday   (drama)   1843
Luria, A Soul's Tragedy   (drama)   1846
**An Essay on Percy Bysshe Shelley*   (essay)   1888
The Works of Robert Browning 10 vols.   (poetry, dramas, and translation)   1912
The Complete Works of Robert Browning 5 vols. to date. (poetry, dramas, and essays)   1969-
The Brownings' Correspondence 6 vols. to date   (letters) 1984-

*This work was included in the series *Bells and Pomegranates*, published from 1841 to 1846. Dramatic works in this series are chronologized by date of publication rather than first performance.

**This work was first published in 1852 as an introductory essay in *Letters of Percy Bysshe Shelley*.

W. J. Fox   (essay date 1833)

[*Fox, a family friend, wrote this favorable review of* Pauline. *Originally published in the April edition of* The Monthly Repository, *it became the most positive review the work ever received, and Browning wrote "I shall never write a line without thinking of the source of my first praise."*]

These thoughts have been suggested by the work before us, which, though evidently a hasty and imperfect sketch, has truth and life in it, which gave us the thrill, and laid hold of us with the power, the sensation of which has never yet failed us as a test of genius. Whoever the anonymous author may be, he is a poet. A pretender to science cannot always be safely judged of by a brief publication, for the knowledge of some facts does not imply the knowledge of other facts; but the claimant of poetic honours may generally be appreciated by a few pages, often by a few lines, for if they be poetry, he is a poet. We cannot judge of the house by the brick, but we can judge of the statue of Hercules by its foot. We felt certain of Tennyson, before we saw the book, by a few verses which had straggled into a newspaper; we are not less certain of the author of **Pauline**. . . .

The author cannot expect such a poem as this to be popular, to make 'a hit', to produce a 'sensation.' The public are but slow in recognizing the claims of Tennyson, whom in some respects he resembles; and the common eye scarcely yet discerns among the laurel-crowned, the form of Shelley, who seems (how justly, we stop not now to discuss), to have been the god of his early idolatry. Whatever inspiration may have been upon him from that deity, the mysticism of the original oracles has been happily avoided. And whatever resemblance he may bear to Tennyson (a fellow worshipper probably at the same shrine), he owes nothing of the perhaps inferior melody of his verse to an employment of archaisms which it is difficult to defend from the charge of affectation. But he has not given himself the chance for popularity which Tennyson did, and which it is evident that he easily might have done. . . .

Our limit compels us to pause. Our opinion will be readily inferred from the quantity which we have quoted from a publication of only seventy pages. The chief blemish is a note ascribed to *Pauline,* p. 55; and there are a few passages rather obscure, 'but that's not much.' In recognising a poet we cannot stand upon trifles, nor fret ourselves about such matters. Time enough for that afterwards, when larger works come before us. Archimedes in the bath had many particulars to settle about specific gravities, and Hiero's crown, but he first gave a glorious leap and shouted *Eureka!* (pp. 35-6)

> *W. J. Fox, in an extract in* Browning: The Critical Heritage, *edited by Boyd Litzinger and Donald Smalley, Barnes & Noble, Inc., 1970, pp. 35-6.*

John Forster   (essay date 1842)

[*The following excerpt is taken from a review of* Dramatic Lyrics, *which was originally published in* The Examiner *on November 26, 1842.*]

There was an extremely clever dissertation on Mr. Browning's poems in one of the quarterly reviews the other day, in which *Sordello* was recommended as 'a fine mental exercise.' Something of the sort we had said ourselves, and if poetry were exactly the thing to grind professors of metaphysics on, we should pray to Mr Browning for perpetual *Sordellos.* As it is, we are humble enough and modest enough to be more thankful for *Dramatic Lyrics.* The collection before us is welcome for its own sake, and more welcome for its indication of the poet's continued advance in a right direction. Some of this we saw and thanked him for in his *Victor and Charles,* much more in his delightful *Pippa Passes,* and in the simple and manly strain of some of these *Dramatic Lyrics,* we find proof of the firmer march and steadier control. Mr Browning will win his laurel. We were the first to hail his noble start in *Paracelsus;* [*Strafford* and *Sordello*] did not shake our faith in him; and we shall see him reach the goal.

And is there nothing to object to, then, in the *Dramatic Lyrics*? Oh, plenty—but so much more to *praise*! Readers as well as critics should oftener *remember* Rochester's couplet, which, not having *quoted* this many a day, we will once again repeat.

> It is a meaner part of sense
> To find a fault than taste an excellence!

—and there being many more excellences to be tasted in Mr Browning than faults to be found, we propose just now to follow the advice of Lord Rochester.

It is an honourable distinction of Mr Browning that in whatever he writes, you discover *an idea* of some sort or other. You shall have great difficulty in finding it, when he happens to have the humour of obscurity upon him; and there are many of his wilful humours, in which it shall not be worth the search: but any how there it is. He is never a tagger of verses. There is purpose in all he does. Often there is thought of the profoundest kind, often the most exquisite tenderness, his best passages are full of the best Saxon words, and in the art of versification he must be called a master. It is his surpassing facility in this particular, that now and then plays bewildering pranks with his reader's ear—distracting, dazing, and confusing it, in mazes of complicated harmony. On more happy occasions, the flow with which his lines gush forth into the kind of music most appropriate to the thoughts that prompt them, is to us extremely charming; and for the neatness of his rhymes in his lighter efforts, we think that Butler would have hugged him. In a word, Mr Browning is a genuine poet, and only needs to have less misgiving on the subject himself, to win his readers to as perfect a trust, and an admiration with as little alloy in it, as any of his living brethren of the laurel are able to lay claim to.

The *Lyrics,* as their title imports, are for the most part dramatic: full of the quick turns of feeling, the local truth, and the picturesque force of expression, which the stage so much delights in. The three that open the collection are **"Cavalier Tunes"**; two follow called **"Italy and France,"** apparently designed to show the different estimation of Woman in these different countries: **"Camp and Cloister"** is the title of the next two, the purpose being to illustrate, in the carking monk and careless generous soldier, effects of either training. We have afterwards two on the subject of **"Queen-worship,"** and two of **"Madhouse Cells"**; the rest being matters detached, with stories of their own to tell. **"Artemis Prologuises"** in the stately and sonorous march of the Greek drama: two watched and fated lovers rehearse, **"In a Gondola,"** their love and their voluptuous fancies, with contrasts of dread and pleasure, till the sudden dagger ends the passionate interchange: and in the piece called **"Waring,"** the writer, dramatically assuming the garb of a very commonplace person, seems to regret hugely one of those wonderful friends who are supposed to be able to do everything because they never attempt to do anything. Various is the merit of these various poems: sometimes very grave the faults. But on the whole they confirm what we have said of Mr Browning's genius, and prove that he is fast reclaiming it from the 'vague and formless infinite' of mere metaphysical abstraction. . . . (pp. 82-4)

> *John Forster, in an extract in* Browning: The Critical Heritage, *edited by Boyd Litzinger and Donald Smalley, Barnes & Noble, Inc., 1970, pp. 82-4.*

The North American Review   (essay date 1848)

[*The following excerpt is one of the earliest overviews of Browning's work published in the United States. The anonymous critic concludes his essay by asserting "we will content ourselves with saying that [Browning] has in him the elements of greatness."*]

The first thing that we have to demand of a poet is, that his verses be really alive. Life we look for first, and growth as its necessary consequence and indicator. And it must be an original, not a parasitic life,—a life capable of reproduction. There will be barnacles which glue themselves fast to every intellectual movement of the world, and seem to possess in themselves that power of motion which they truly diminish in that which sustains them and bears them along. But there are also unseen winds which fill the sails, and stars by which the courses are set. The oak, which lies in the good ship's side an inert mass, still lives in the green progeny of its chance-dropped acorns. The same gale which bends the creaking mast of pine sings through the tossing hair of its thousand sons in the far inland. The tree of the mechanic bears only wooden acorns.

Is Robert Browning, then, a poet? Our knowledge of him can date back seven years, and an immortality which has withstood the manifold changes of so long a period can be, as immortalities go, no mushroom. . . . We got our first knowledge of him from two verses of his which we saw quoted in a newspaper, and from that moment took him for granted as a new poet. Since then we have watched him with a constantly deepening interest. Much that seemed obscure and formless in his earlier productions has been interpreted by his later ones. Taken by itself, it might remain obscure and formless still, but it becomes clear and assumes definite shape when considered as only a part of a yet unfinished whole. We perceive running through and knitting together all his poems the homogeneous spirit, gradually becoming assured of itself, of an original mind. We know not what higher praise to bestow on him than to say that his latest poems are his best.

His earlier poems we shall rather choose to consider as parts and illustrations of his poetic life than as poems. We find here the consciousness of wings, the heaven grasped and measured by the aspiring eye, but no sustained flight as yet. These are the poet's justifications of himself to himself, while he was brooding over greater designs. They are the rounds of the ladder by which he has climbed, and more interesting for the direction they indicate than from any intrinsic worth. We would not be considered as undervaluing them. Had he written nothing else, we should allow them as heights attained, and not as mere indications of upward progress. We shall hope presently to show by some extracts, that they are not simply limbs, but are endowed with a genuine and vigorous individual life. But Mr. Browning can afford to do without them. And if he has not yet fully expressed himself, if we can as yet see only the lower half of the statue, we can in some measure foretell the whole. We can partly judge whether there is likely to be in it the simplicity and comprehensiveness, the poise, which indicates the true artist. At least, we will not judge it by its base, however the sculptor's fancy may have wreathed it with graceful or grotesque arabesques, to render it the worthy footstool of his crowning work. Above all, let us divest ourselves of the petty influences of contemporaneousness, and look at it as if it were just unburied from the embalming lava of Pompeii. (pp. 367-69)

Mr. Browning's first published poem was *Paracelsus*. This was followed by *Strafford, a Tragedy*, of which we know only that it was "acted at the Theatre Royal, Covent Garden." We do not need it in order to get a distinct view of his steady poetical growth. Next comes *Sordello*, a Poem; and the list is completed by ***Bells and Pomegranates***, a series of lyrical and dramatic poems published at intervals during the last six years. Were we to estimate *Paracelsus* and *Sordello* separately and externally as individual poems, without taking into consideration their antecedent or consequent internal relations, we should hardly do justice to the author. Viewed by itself, *Sordello* would incline us to think that Mr. Browning had lost in simplicity, clearness, and directness of aim, in compactness and decision of form, and in unity of effect. We may as well say bluntly, that it is totally incomprehensible as a connected whole. It reminds one of Coleridge's epigram on his own Ancient Mariner:

> Your poem must eternal be,
> Dear Sir, it cannot fail;
> For 't is incomprehensible,
> And without head or tail.

It presents itself to us, at first view, as a mere nebulosity, triumphantly defying the eye to concentrate itself on any one point. But if we consider it intently, as possibly having some definite relation to the author's poetic life, we begin to perceive a luminous heart in the midst of the misty whirl, and, indeed, as a natural consequence of it. By dint of patient watchfulness through such telescope as we possess, we have even thought that it might not be wholly incapable of resolution as a system by itself. It is crowded full of images, many of them truly grand. Here and there it opens cloudily, and reveals glimpses of profound thought and conception of character. The sketch of Taurello, the Italian captain of the Middle Ages, drawn rapidly, as with a bit of charcoal on a rough wall, is masterly. Perhaps we should define what is in itself indefinable as well as may be, if we say that we find in *Sordello* the materials of a drama, profuse, but as yet in formless solution, not crystallized firmly round the thread of any precise plot, but capable of it. We will say that it was a fine poem before the author wrote it. In reading it, we have seemed to ourselves to be rambling along some wooded ridge in the tropics. Here gigantic vines clamber at random, hanging strange trees with clusters that seem dipped in and dripping with the sluggish sunshine. Here we break our way through a matted jungle, where, nevertheless, we stumble over giant cactuses in bloom, lolling delighted in the sultry air. Now and then a gap gives us a glimpse of some ravishing distance, with a purple mountain-peak or two, and all the while clouds float over our heads, gorgeous and lurid, which we may consider as whales or camels, just as our Polonian fancy chooses.

A book is often termed obscure and unintelligible by a kind of mental *hypallage*, which exchanges the cases of the critic and the thing criticized. But we honestly believe that *Sordello* is enveloped in mists, of whose begetting we are quite guiltless. It may have a meaning, but, as the logicians say, *a posse ad esse non valet argumentum*. (pp. 369-70)

Having glanced confusedly at *Sordello*, as far as it concerns ourselves, let us try if we can discover that it has any more distinct relation to the author. And here we ought naturally to take it in connection with *Paracelsus.* From this point of view, a natural perspective seems to arrange itself, and a harmony is established between the two otherwise discordant poems. *Paracelsus,* then, appears to us to represent, and to be the outlet of, that early life of the poet which is satisfied with aspiration simply; *Sordello,* that immediately succeeding period when power has become conscious, but exerts itself for the mere pleasure it feels in the free play of its muscles, without any settled purpose. Presently we shall see that it has defined and concentrated itself, and set about the production of solid results. There is not less power; it is only deeper, and does not dissipate itself over so large a surface. The range is not narrower, but choicer. (pp. 371-72)

We cannot leave Mr. Browning without giving one extract of another kind. His humor is as genuine as that of Carlyle, and if his laugh have not the "earthquake" character with which Emerson has so happily labelled the shaggy merriment of that Jean Paul Burns, yet it is always sincere and hearty, and there is a tone of meaning in it which always sets us thinking. . . . Poetry and humor are subject to different laws of art, and it is dangerous to let one encroach upon the province of the other. It may be questioned, whether verse, which is by nature subject to strict law, be the proper vehicle for humor at all. The contrast, to be sure, between the preciseness of the metrical rule and the frolicsome license of the thought, has something humorous in itself. The greater *swing* which is allowed to the humorous poet in rhythm and rhyme, as well as in thought, may be of service to him, and save him from formality in his serious verses. Undoubtedly the success of Hood's "Bridge of Sighs" was due in some degree to the quaintness and point of the measure and the rhyme, the secret of which he had learned in his practice as a humorous versifier. But there is danger that the poet, in allowing full scope to this erratic part of his nature, may be brought in time to value form generally at less than its true worth as an element of art. We have sometimes felt a jar in reading Mr. Browning's lyrical poems, when, just as he has filled us full of quiet delight by some touch of pathos or marble gleam of classical beauty, this exuberant geniality suggests some cognate image of the ludicrous, and turns round to laugh in our faces. This necessity of deferring to form in some shape or other is a natural, and not an ingrafted, quality of human nature. It often, laughably enough, leads men, who have been totally regardless of all higher laws, to cling most pertinaciously and conscientiously to certain purely ceremonial observances. If the English courts should ever dispense with so much of their dignity and decorum as consists in horsehair, we have no doubt that the first rogue who shall be sentenced by a wigless judge will be obstinately convinced of a certain unconstitutionality in the proceeding, and feel himself an injured man, defrauded of the full dignity of the justice enjoyed by his ancestors. (pp. 394-95)

[If] we could be sure that our readers would read Mr. Browning's poems with the respect and attentive study they deserve, what should hinder us from saying that we think him a great poet? However, as the world feels uncomfortably somewhere, it can hardly tell how or why, at hearing people called great, before it can claim a share in

their greatness by erecting to them a monument with a monk-Latin inscription on it which nine tenths of their countrymen cannot construe, and as Mr. Browning must be as yet comparatively a young man, we will content ourselves with saying that he has in him the elements of greatness. To us he appears to have a wider range and greater freedom of movement than any other of the younger English poets. (pp. 399-400)

"Browning's 'Plays and Poems'," in The North American Review, *Vol. LXVI, No. CXXXIX, April, 1848, pp. 357-400.*

The Eclectic Review   (essay date 1849)

[*In the excerpt below, the anonymous critic reviews* Poems *and* Sordello *and discusses the obscure references found in many of Browning's pieces.*]

With no other poet are we acquainted, so inevitably calculated, through the prevailing character of his poetic manifestation, and from the primary conditions of his nature as Poet, to meet with a limited range of sympathy and appreciation, as Robert Browning. Pre-eminently and distinctively, is he to be classed as a poet for the few. Without study, actual *bona-fide* study, his poetry must remain *caviare* to the most intelligent reader. We have encountered literary men, poetic students, who, failing to give this, found themselves utterly unable to make anything of his poetry. And among general readers, though his earliest poem, *Paracelsus,* has been before the public some fourteen years, he still remains, for the most part, an unknown name. Yet, to our mind, this is a great and original poet. One among the greatest who have arisen among us, he seems, since the beginning of the present century; a poet, worthy to claim brotherhood with his contemporary, Alfred Tennyson. In the case of Browning, we do not see how,—he, the while faithfully obeying the impulses of his own genius, it could well have been otherwise with him, than it has been. His poetic genius is essentially recondite; and its expression could be nothing less. In its specific nature, and in its conditions of life, his assuredly, must rank, as a new manifestation of poetic art. (p. 206)

In some quarters, praise has been awarded to Mr. Browning, with no little show of patronage and condescension; with sundry pattings of the back; accompanied by counsel to amendment, in this or that respect. *Such* praise in nowise concerns true merit. In the present instance, it is more than usually inapt. Mr. Browning is in the main, either altogether wrong, or altogether right. For our part, we are inclined to think, Nature herself speaks most plainly, and to most effect, in his actual poetic genius,—such as it is. So far are we from conceiving amendment would follow from his narrowing himself to the capabilities of his readers, we think rather, in those poems, wherein he has striven after the completest definiteness of expression, as in the *Blot in the 'Scutcheon* and some of the other dramas,—the result has been attained by a *sacrifice,* not by an enrichment. Those very poems, such as *Sordello, Pippa Passes,* in respect to which, the loudest complaints of obscurity have been raised, are precisely those, in which the fullest wealth of poetry, the highest creative power, have been realized.

Any reliance, in regard to poetry, on canons of criticism, applicable to purely scientific expression, is, in the last degree, futile and perplexing. The truth of poetry is not the truth of science; not indeed opposed to it; but distinct and independent of it. The truth of Imogen, of Beatrice, of Juliet, of Hamlet, of Lear,—of Homeric manhood,—of the sublime aspiration of the Greek tragedy, or of an Italian Dante,—the truth of our Milton's *Paradise* and of his Satan,—of the blithe, full world of Chaucer,—of a Spenser's dream-shadowing of verities,—is not the truth of mathematic, astronomic, chemic laws. But they are akin: great divisions of actual Truth proceeding from God; bound up alike, with the phenomena of God's nature. The phenomena of humanity, in the largest application of the word, form the province and distinctive prerogative of poetry, of the development of poetic truth. In Browning's own words, occurring amid that noble exposition of his art, in the second canto of *Paracelsus,* which is only surpassed by some among the incidental passages in *Sordello,* on the same topic:

> No thought which ever stirred
> A human breast should be untold; no passions,
> No soft emotions, from the turbulent stir
> Within a heart fed with desires like mine—
> To the last comfort, shutting the tired lids
> Of him who sleeps the sultry noon away
> Beneath the tent-tree by the way-side well.

And thus:

> The lowest hind should not possess a hope,
> A fear, but I'd be by him, saying better
> Than he, *his own heart's language.*

Robert Browning is not one whom we can recommend to the readers of poetry, at their ease: gentlemen who would have their hour's amusement out of their poet. We cannot safely assure such, of finding much, addressing itself to their class. Judging from our own experience, we should doubt whether any could be competent to speak of Browning, till having given him a *second* reading; or fully to estimate him, till after, at least, three readings. For a student of poetry to refuse the amount of labour required for a mastery of the poetic wealth here opened, would be not a little discreditable. Patient study is needed; but no more. Our poet always presupposes an intelligent and thoughtful reader; and herein lies the primary source of difficulty. Almost always, he not only leaves unexplained much that a less bold or abstract poet *would* explain; but also much in the conception of character, to be comprehensively imagined out; or seen at once—taken for granted, as the ground-work for the after-realization of the poet's creative working.

There is, thus far, no positive obscurity in the poet, but only a great demand on the reader. One source of actual obscurity, however, in the poet himself, and the most influential, is his neglect of incident and external material. These, however necessary for the comprehension of the drift of the individual poem, are always hinted at, rather than stated; and that, too, in the loosest way. In *Sordello,* their unravelment constitutes the main difficulty of the

poem. Browning commenced, in fact, his career, in *Paracelsus,* by an avowed sacrifice of the outward constituents of poetic narration, to a more independent and exclusive development of purely mental emotion. And the practice has more or less clung to him, even when external agency is more prominently introduced, than in that poem. In his more recent dramas, however, the unconscious adherence to such practice is to be traced in a very modified degree. The severance of the mental life set forth in the poetic creation, from those outward links connecting it with the actual world, and from those external influences calling it into action, amounts assuredly, in itself, to a factitious result, and is always, more or less, a source of obscurity. At the same time, it is in the development of abstract mental life, that Browning's strength really consists: in its passionately imaginative interpretation; in the clothing of this abstract life, with a new concrete poetic life of its own; after having been cast into *his* 'soul's rich mine,' it 'coming up, crusted o'er with gems;' the external incident meanwhile being shadowed forth, or borne with, but as distant back-ground, or mere skeleton frame-work.

A further cause of obscurity, on a first perusal, is to be found in the remarkable strength and fertility of the poet's associative imagination; leading him to follow out the remotest suggestion which may cross his path. Such tendency is often productive of the greatest difficulty to the reader, who labours under the disadvantages, inseparable from being but the accomplice, not the principal, in the poetic conception. In *Sordello,* this discursive spirit absolutely triumphs, to the dismay, no doubt, of the faint-hearted reader; but with the most splendid poetic fruits.

It may thus be seen, that such shortcoming as exists in Mr. Browning's Expression, springs not from niggardliness but from profusion, of poetic wealth; not from insufficient sight of those ideas within his possession, but from the number and reconditeness of the ideas themselves. The difficulty experienced by the reader springs from the same cause. He has much given him, and in small space; and to all this is to be added, the recondite *manner* of the poet. And herein we arrive at Mr. Browning's most prominent and influential characteristic as a poet. The bent of his genius is eminently and exclusively recondite. This attribute we find to be the inseparable companion of his originality and power. His imagination is peculiarly subtile, and given to refinement; seeing innumerable bearings and aspects of the matter in hand, *not* seen by others. Every incident, topic, event, character, handled by him, is seen from a remote and novel point of view, of which the apprehension is peculiar to the idiosyncrasy of the poet. Sometimes, it is, practically, a mere possibility of mental action, feeling, or thought, in the individual case, which is apprehended; but always a refined inner truth, proper to universal humanity. This attribute of the poet's mind is well exemplified in the case of one of his minor poems —**"The Glove"**—the topic of which is handled after a wholly opposite manner to that of his predecessors. That which by others had been regarded, in accordance with historical tradition, as an action of heartless vanity on the part of the lady in the story, who throws her glove within the lion's cage, to be rescued by her knightly lover, is justified; developed with refined physiologic truth under quite a fresh aspect: as a simple test of idle protestation, a test that was needed, and satisfied to *his* rather than her essential loss. This is recondite, though evidently spontaneously recondite treatment; witnessing, moreover, to that refinement of sympathy with humanity, characteristic of Browning;—a tendency to sympathize with all most needing sympathy, or commonly least encountering it. In the characters themselves embodied by him, his reconditeness of mind is always more or less manifested. These,—whether dreamers, such as *Paracelsus* and *Sordello,* men of action, such as Prince Berthold, the Advocate Valence, Djabal, Luria, are all great refiners in their thinking and action, like the poet himself; though endowed with that full individual variety of manifestation, hindering them from anywise amounting to mere photograph copies of the author's self. This actual self is rarely or never to be caught sight of throughout the whole range of his poetry; so purely objective is it essentially.

The present new and collective edition of Mr. Browning's works, [*Poems,*] contains a singular omission. The longest, most characteristic, every way most important poem—his highest, fullest, poetic flight, *Sordello,* is excluded. . . . The exclusion of *Sordello* can only be accounted for on the supposition, that its author was willing to secure a more extended and actual hearing, by the temporary withdrawal of the poem, which, from its greater inherent difficulties, would most endanger such a hearing. And though to an admirer of Mr. Browning, the present edition looks something like that celebrated enactment of the play of *Hamlet* with the part of Hamlet omitted, we know not but that the plan adopted is the more judicious. We ourselves must confess to having gone through our first reading of *Sordello,* with feelings, for the most part, of unmingled perplexity, occasionally passing into angry despair. Not till we had entered on the second reading, did we begin to apprehend its scope, or unity, or see the exceeding beauty of its parts. But now, in its subtle, yet broadly-marked development of character,—whether drawn at full, as of the dreamy, irresolute aspirer, Sordello himself, or of the showy, prompt, decisive man of action, the warrior Salinguerra—or sketched in brief, at few and slight touches, as of the glorious creature Palma—afar-off shining in the poet's golden shadowing of her beauty, spiritual and material—and of the fervent poet, Eglamour, type of his class; in its consummate wealth of general purely poetic thought, and imaginative beauty, overflooding the whole, the poem stands before us as the most splendid representative conceivable, of all that can be attained by the union, with the purely poetic embodiment of highest thoughtful aspiration—of the fullest luxury of glowing and passionately imaginative vitality. But the involution of conceptions to which the poet's digressiveness of imagination gives rise, is sufficiently productive of obstacles, without a corresponding involution of language. And involved as is the speech, its difficulty would be immeasurably relieved, were a clearer plan of punctuation merely, adopted, in the printing of *Sordello,* than that prevailing in the first edition. When, as in *Sordello* constantly, and sometimes in *Paracelsus,* a period occupies some two or three pages; after journeying on, without once reaching the satisfaction of a full stop for our rescue, or any more efficacious sup-

port than a semicolon, the clearest head will grow dizzy, the most persistent attention slacken.

Commencing with *Sordello,* and thence passing to its younger brother, *Paracelsus;* alike in scope—and though an early, by no means an immature fruit, in general expression simpler, more obviously determinate, but not anywise so pregnant with luxury of beauty and thoughtful wealth; thence proceeding to the noble group of dramas, with their calm, quietly, recondition noble, human heroism; from these, to the indeterminate drama, so original and deep-reaching, of *Pippa Passes,* and "A Soul's Tragedy;" and from these, to the rich suggestive gallery of minor dramatic sketches, including pieces so wondrously rife in deep thought and creative speech, as the "**Madhouse bells,**" "**Pictor Ignotus,**" "**St. Praxed's Church,**" "**The Confessional,**" "**The Last Duchess;**" after running through the entire range, how shall we convey to those unfamiliar with it, any sense of the wealth herein comprised: the large, many-fronted embodiment of human thought, and feeling, and aspiration, the new world of beauty, directly, or suggestively, in it opened up—the significance of life, actual, or dreamed, laid bare before us?

The poet's genius is essentially dramatic, but not in the sense which the word vulgarly bears. Mr. Browning's is mostly the drama of character, not of incident, or scenic effect. Under this aspect, the entire sum of his poetry may be said to be dramatic, though much of it, like so much of Tennyson's, simple *mono*-drama; in which class must be included not only the lyrics, but the entire poem of *Paracelsus.* (pp. 207-11)

Browning develops abstract character at the expense of incident. But it would be a great mistake to imply from this, a general divorcement of incident, and of the outward aspects of humanity, from thought, in his poetry. Bound up with the large human world, is it all. His particular characteristic is this, that whereas others make incident a staple, and thought dependent on *it;* with him, more especially in his earlier and longer poems, incident is subsidiary to thought, introduced, only as elucidatory of the main design, or illustrative of a specific conception. But the outward world *is* there; ever and anon as the given topic of some richly freighted allusion. Exquisite site painting is passing often there in this way; as at the commencement of *Paracelsus,* in the introduction throughout of the "**Sweet Michel,**" and in those glowing pictures of beauty which relieve the continuous fulness of thought of *Sordello,* more especially occurring, and with more salient beauty, throughout the history of Sordello's youth, and in those passages wherein his Princess-love, the superb Palma, occupies a place. So, too, the occasional introduction of external nature, in such frank sincerity,—given so *largely,* and from so elevated a point of view; these slight, yet full revealments, seen to float over the general sum of his poetic working, as a deep, sweet breathing of visible music; a reconciling and fulfilling influence, amid his world of human aspiration, and passion, and striving. Such play of external nature in his poetry, is as that of some Æolian harp amid the high discourse of thoughtful men, heard but at intervals, and then, with fullest beauty, and clearest import.

To the deep thought prevailing throughout Mr. Browning's poetry, we have already sufficiently alluded, in passing. It is to be added, however, that difficulty and apparent obscurity form by no means the universal attendant on this poetic exposition of thought. There are passages and whole poems, of which the meaning and beauty may be transparent to any, and at once. And at least a moiety of his writing, we should judge to be not more distant from the ordinary apprehension than all genuine poetry commonly is.

His mastery over language, and of an essentially poetical language,—condensed, and imaginatively breathing life, is complete; and, for the most part, would seem inborn. It is, in **Paracelsus,** as conspicuous—and in almost equal refinement, as in the latest of his lyrics or dramas. Luxuriant, however, in beauty, as is his subordinate expression, it is the expression of any one of his poems, as a *whole,* which most prominently attracts attention and abides by the memory. For herein is his largeness of imagination most saliently seen; realizing its full effect. His versification, again, is a continuously efficient instrument, a noble servant. It is always,—in whatever measure, strictly individual and characteristic, and of exceeding power and facility—the facility of energy, not of smoothness. It is marked by such license and freedom dangerous only to the poetaster, from merely arbitrary rules, as is proper to the right poet, who is his own lawgiver—following the law of use intelligently, not blindly, only so far as is consistent with the end of this law,—in the first instance proceeding from such as himself. And here, the end of the law is melody, and a meet musical interpretation of the subject-matter of poetic speech. It is this which is to be attained by the versifier, by whatever means. Assuredly, *here,* the end, when actually attained, does justify the means, whatever they may be. The melody of Browning is seldom or never of so finished and heightened a beauty as that of Tennyson. And so, generally, it may be affirmed, he is far from being so consummate an executive artist as his great Brother-poet. (pp. 212-14)

> *"Robert Browning," in* The Eclectic Review, *n.s. Vol. XXVI, July, 1849, pp. 203-14.*

The Massachusetts Review   (essay date 1850)

[*A review of* Poems *and* Christmas-Eve and Easter Day. *Excerpt focuses on the latter work.*]

Christmas-Eve is rainy, but the poet has taken it into his head to attend the service in "Zion Chapel Meeting." We find him shivering in a very moist and uncomfortable porch, rather daunted by the scowls and drippings of the saints, who brush past him, astonished at seeing the scoffer waiting at the gate of their tabernacle:

> From the road, the lanes, or the common,
> In came the flock; the fat weary woman,
> Panting and bewildered, down-clapping
> Her umbrella, with a mighty report,
> Grounded it by me, wry and flapping,
> A wreck of whalebones; then, with a snort,
> Like a startled horse, at the interloper,
> Who humbly knew himself improper,

> But could not shrink up small enough,
> Round to the door, and in,—the gruff
> Hinge's invariable scold,
> Making your very blood run cold.

Each arrival is hit off in admirable style, with his usual eye for individualities and latent humor:

> Then a tall, yellow man, like the penitent thief,
> With his jaw bound up in a handkerchief,
> And eyelids screwed together tight,
> Led himself in by some inner light.

(pp. 377-78)

Concluding quite soon that he had "seen the elephant," he pursued the usual course of extempore naturalists, and left the place. Here the humor deserts the poem, save an occasional glimmer or two, chiefly in a subsequent visit to a Straussian professor at Göttingen. The thought and verse become serious and lofty, while the metre does not change: for Mr. Browning has a very serious object in writing the poem, nothing less than to develop his views of Christian Faith and of Life. We pursue the current, quoting freely without the least remorse, as the book has not yet become frequent here. The same enterprising firm from whom we have received the two handsome volumes above noticed will soon place this also within our reach; and we hope that readers will liberally endorse the taste of those gentlemen.

There was a lull in the rain as he left the chapel, and, as he walks along, he contrasts the serenity of nature with the mephitic atmosphere around the preacher's tripod. There is an analysis of the general sermonic style of Zion Chapel meetings: following which we have a metaphysical discussion of Love and Power. With proper labor, it will be found to contain thoughts worth pondering, and we gain a definite impression of the true, healthy religion of Mr. Browning's nature. His soul rises to God, earnest for the future time when it shall be satiated with His Love. The wind and rain now cease; "the black cloud-barricade was riven," and we have a glorious description of a lunar rainbow, with a fainter one as its counterfoil above it.

> For me, I think I said, 'Appear!
> Good were it to be ever here.
> If Thou wilt, let me build to Thee,
> Service-tabernacles Three;
> Where, forever in Thy presence,
> In ecstatic acquiescence,
> Far alike from thriftless learning
> And ignorance's undiscerning,
> I may worship and remain!'

(pp. 378-79)

With his whole verse, in a fine enthusiasm, he sums up his perception that "too much love there can never be." Out again, borne along in the Vesture's eddy, bound for a visit to a Göttingen professor: so the Christmas lecture of a Straussian is the contrast to the uncritical devotion of the Roman spectacle. A few masterly touches give us the room, the audience, and the professor:

> He pushed back higher his spectacles,
> Let the eyes stream out like lamps from cells,
> And giving his head of hair—a hake
> Of undressed tow, for color and quantity—

One rapid and impatient shake,
(As our own young England adjusts a jaunty tie
When about to impart, on mature digestion,
Some thrilling view of the surplice question,)
—The professor's grave voice, sweet though
    hoarse,
Broke into his Christmas-Eve's discourse.

He finds in reason the foundation for the "Myth of
Christ."

Whether 'twere best opine Christ was,
Or never was at all, or whether
He was and was not, both together,—
It matters little for the name,
So the Idea be left the same.

Upon all these points, we heartily sympathize with Mr.
Browning's acute and racy criticism, and consider that he
has not misrepresented, while dissecting the mythical theory. We are rather surprised, too, to find him so easy and
transparent in this domain. Only a slight difference between us springs up at last, when he seems inclined to exalt
the historical Person above the continual and sufficient
presence of God. But the glow and conviction of his elevating verse indispose us now for any criticism of particular statements.

He begins to feel very tolerant; talks about the value of religion, and the superfluity of sectarianism; hazards the
phrase, "mild indifferentism," and his heart becomes quite
genial in this "lazy glow of benevolence." But the Vesture
is not suited with this, and leaves him alone on the college-
steps, as we think, rather intolerantly, considering that
long ago the same Vesture's hem was touched by such as
needed healing. But let us follow the rather orthodox poet,
who misses his second person of the Trinity, and starts up
in terror, exclaiming:

Needs must there be one way, our chief,
Best way of worship; let me strive
To find it, and, when found, contrive
My fellows also take their share.

If, with his best endeavor, he fails in this, he believes that
God, in his own method, will bring "all wanderers to a single track." On the whole, his reflections are so satisfactory
that they bring back the "flying robe" again, and he feels
like a man who has answered all the fundamental questions of a "council," and has gracious ministerial permission to be ordained. Of a sudden:

at a passionate bound, I sprang
Out of the wandering world of rain,
Into the little chapel again.

He rubs his eyes—the saints have edged away from him,
looking spiritual daggers. And yet, how could he remember all about the sermon, if he had been asleep? So it was,
however; he keeps the orthodoxy of his dream, indulges
in a gentle suspiration for the pope's and professor's salvation, and the **Christmas-Eve** concludes thus:

If any blames me,
Thinking that, merely to touch in brevity,
The topics I dwell on, were unlawful,—
Or, worse, that I trench, with undue levity,
On the bounds of the holy and the awful,

I praise the heart, and pity the head of him,
And refer myself to Thee, instead of him,
Who head and heart alike discernest:
Looking below light speech we utter,
When the frothy spume and frequent sputter
Prove that the soul's depths boil in earnest!
May the truth shine out, stand ever before us!
I put up pencil, and join chorus
To Hepzibah tune, without further apology,
The last five verses of the third section
Of the seventeenth hymn in Whitfield's Collec-
    tion,
To conclude with the Doxology.

Easter-Day commences in the conversational style; the
poet and his imaginary foil discuss the difficulty of being
a Christian. Some fine things are said upon the subject of
faith. For instance, the difficulty of believing is the touchstone of belief:

Could He acquit us, or condemn,
For holding what no hand can loose,
Rejecting when we can't but choose?
As well award the victor's wreath
To whosoever should take breath
Duly each minute while he lived—
Grant heaven, because a man contrived
To see the sunshine every day
He walked forth on the public way.
You must mix some uncertainty
With faith, if you would have faith *be.*

For a while this is the spirit of the conversation; one wishing to "grow smoothly, as a tree," the other declaring that
so the world lives now. Some respectable pursuits are
shown up with light touches of irony—then men find what
evidences of belief they desire:

as is your sort of mind,
So is your sort of search.

A very true thing, said in jest. But the poet assumes the
Divine incarnation in the person of a single history, and
then reminds us of "certain words, broad, plain," which
cannot be explained away:

Announcing this world's gain for loss,
And bidding us reject the same.

The pursuits of the world are finely contrasted with the
spirit of denial. . . . (pp. 380-83)

And so he proves how hard it is to be a Christian, forced
always to ward off the stroke of doubt, "caught upon the
guard" of the better hope. The other speaker awards him
small thanks for this; he already lives in trusting ease, indulging only the "*blind hopes* to spice the meal of life
with." Whereupon, in refutation of worldliness, we have
the relation of another vision. It is a vision of judgment.
This is a noble effort of imagination, pledged to the service
of religious thought,—the verse soars into sublime description, and the pages redden with the fierce hues of this
tremendous vision. The material prodigy of this Easter
judgment passes away, and the scene fills with the presence of God, dealing with the human soul. The poet fixes
his affections upon the world, and thought, and beauty,
and love; in each case, the Spirit declares to him the emptiness of his choice. Love existed in all the other things

which he had enumerated; even his choice of love is somewhat late:

> Now take love!—Well betide
> Thy tardy conscience! Haste to take
> The show of love for the name's sake.

The humbled poet at last resigns every clinging thought
of the world, hoping to find his peace and the favor of the
Spirit in entire renunciation:

> Be all the earth a wilderness!
> Only let me go on, go on,
> Still hoping ever and anon
> To reach, one eve, the better land!
> Then did the Form expand, expand—
> I knew Him through the dread disguise,
> As the whole God within his eyes
> Embraced me.

Easter-Day breaks—"no paradise stands barred to
entry"—spite of dreary moments hope is elastic, and the
poet knows that "mercy every way is infinite."

So cordial is our agreement with the pure spirit of all this,
that we cannot spend a word upon occasional disagree-
ments in theology. Filled with this spirit of religious love,
the reader can return to the power and beauty of this
world, portrayed with such loving sympathy in all the
verse of Mr. Browning, and permit them amid enjoyment
to kindle worship of the unseen world, the kingdom of mu-
nificent correspondences to these partial shows of time.
Thanks to Mr. Browning, we learn from his poem to mingle content with aspiration. We will keep every charm of
earth, every beautiful line that he has added to the treasury of poets, every minute marvel with which God
tempts us to think of the plenitude of heaven. "All partial
beauty" is a pledge of that. The pledge shall not suffice our
mood, yet we cannot refuse to love it now with a tranquil
hope. Nothing of late has so lifted the veil behind our customary routine and feeling, letting in upon them ripples
of glory from the sphere of perfect beauty, as the latter half
of . . . , with its presageful lines, its credible anticipations, its cosmic thought. We forbear to mar the sustained
and solemn grace of the poem by quotations of that which
every man must buy and read. It has the full, vital force
of all the other strokes from the same pen. There is no easy
sentiment for summer afternoons, and reading it is not an
amusement; for that, as the word purports, carries us oftener *away from the muses* than keeps us in their instructive company. Mr. Browning makes our senses all alert;
we cannot listen to him in a reverie, but with self-possessed
faculties. Sometimes even his best images require a salutary effort to clutch them; occasional conceits excepted,
they are not far-fetched, confused and dim, but palpable,
the handle towards the hand, marshalling the fancy the
way it ought to go. This is true of all his works. We think
we can perceive in *Christmas-Eve and Easter-Day* that
Mr. Browning has also gained clearness, without sacrificing a single quality of his genius. Indeed, its power is mate-
rially increased, for his pen serves the thought with a
greater regard for human sympathy. Such lofty beauty
which the many need, is more conformed to the style of
the many, without ever stooping to win by a dilution of
its subtle energies. Is it too much to say that, with this pen

for his sceptre, Mr. Browning can exact the homage of all
hearts? He will permit us to apply to his conceptions of
truth and beauty, what he says of the "chief, best way of
worship":

> let me strive
> To find it, and, when found, contrive
> My fellows also take their share.

We deem that he possesses all the gifts and the exuberant
life needed by the great artist, and he makes us conscious
of a religiousness that can command their services for the
good of men. Give the world a direction towards the good.
Schiller says to the artist: "You have given it this direction, if as a teacher you elevate its thoughts to the necessary and eternal; if, while acting or composing, you transform the necessary and eternal into an object of its impulse. Create the conquering truth in the modest stillness
of your soul, array it in a form of beauty, that not only
thought may pay it homage, but sense lovingly comprehend its presence."

Last words of admiration and gratitude linger on our pen.
We bespeak for every future line of Mr. Browning a cordial welcome here. And it is pleasant to think that he cannot regard the warm, personal friendships he has unconsciously established here, with indifference. We assure him
that he can take his piece entitled **"Time's Revenges,"** and
for "a friend" in the first line read "friends," adapting the
passage to express our ever-increasing regard for the
books he writes.

> Contrive, contrive
> To rouse us, Waring!   Who's alive?
> Our men scarce seem in earnest now;
> Distinguished names!—but 'tis somehow
> As if they played at being names
> Still more distinguished, like the games
> Of children.   Turn our sport to earnest.

(pp. 383-85)

"Browning's Poems," in The Massachusetts
Review, *Vol. III, No. XI, June, 1850, pp. 347-
85.*

The Edinburgh Review   (essay date 1864)

[*The following excerpt is taken from an overview of
Browning's works up to publication of* Dramatis Personae. *The anonymous critic attempts to link many of
Browning's ideas with those of Ralph Waldo Emerson
and Wendell Holmes. The critic ends his essay by concluding that "we do not believe that [Browning's works]
will survive, except as a curiosity and a puzzle."*]

Every reader who glances at Mr. Browning's volumes
however cursorily, must perceive that he is a man of rare
accomplishments, with a singularly original mind capable
of sympathising with a multiplicity of tastes and characters very far removed from every-day experience. We may
regret that he has omitted to draw from those sources of
the sublime, the tender, and the pathetic which will ever
be the most potent means of touching and purifying the
heart, refining the feelings, and elevating the imagination.
We may regret also the habitual neglect of the ordinary
canons of taste and judgment which lamentably diminish-

es the effectiveness of his poetry; but Mr. Browning now lays the work of thirty years before us, and we have but to take it to ourselves and to enjoy it and understand it as well as we can. For it is clear that he has so wedded himself to what is quaint and obscure in his forms of expression and choice of subject, that no change in these is to be hoped for from him; far different in this respect from Mr. Tennyson, whose last volume shows a power of adaptation and a pliability of invention which even his strongest admirers hardly anticipated. His two rustic sketches, "The Grandmother" and "The Northern Farmer," have enriched the language with two scenes of homely and rural life scarcely to be surpassed in truthfulness and simplicity of expression; while his two tales, "Enoch Arden" and "Aylmer's Field," although open to some objection as to the character and construction of the stories, are yet rare triumphs of poetic diction, and in their chastened strength form a very striking contrast with the highly-wrought and fastidious execution of *Locksley Hall* and *Œnone.* On the other hand, there is hardly a fault with which Mr. Browning has ever been charged which is not, in the **Dramatis Personae,** intensified to an extravagant degree. It was said of an eminent lawyer that he wrote his opinions in three different kinds of handwriting—one which he and his clerk could read, another which only he himself could decypher, and a third which neither he or anybody could make out; and into similar categories we are compelled to parcel out the poems of the **Dramatis Personae.**

To form, however, a proper estimate of Mr. Browning as a poet, it would not be fair to dwell exclusively upon this volume, and we shall proceed therefore to pass in review the collected edition of his works as last given to the public. **Paracelsus,** published in 1835, was the first poem by which Mr. Browning became known to the world; its reception was not unfavourable, and this and one or two of Mr. Browning's tragedies may be regarded as the most perfect of his productions, besides being the most ambitious in conception. There is nothing particularly original in the scheme of **Paracelsus;** it depends for its interest, like Faust, René, Manfred, Jacopo Ortis, Oberman, *El mundo diablo,* Festus, and a crowd of lesser known productions, on psychological incidents and transformations—works which have their prototypes in the Book of Job and the Confessions of St. Augustine. The hero of the poem is a shadowy transfiguration of the notorious doctor, alchemist, and quack of the sixteenth century, who filled for a time the chair of physic and surgery at the University of Basle, and began his course by publicly burning in the amphitheatre the works of Galen and Avicenna, and informing his auditory that he was henceforth to hold the monarchy of science; one of his proper names was Bombastus, which from the inflated character of his discourse has passed into modern language, with a signification which will render it immortal. The 'Paracelsus' of Mr. Browning is a very different character, however, from the vain and drunken Swiss empiric, as his drunkenness becomes converted into a sentimental attachment to the wine-cup, and his familiar demons, one of whom was said to reside in the handle of his sword, are kept for the most part unobtrusively behind the scenes. In the first division of the poem, Paracelsus, inspired by the conviction that he has been selected by God for a special mission, determines to go forth

in search of knowledge,—having set before him *knowing* as the great end of achievement. (pp. 538-39)

In the course of his travels he comes to Constantinople, and there pauses for awhile, partly wearied, and partly to sum up the results already attained. While at Constantinople, he falls in with Aprile, an Italian poet, who has failed in the search after love as the end of existence, and dies before Paracelsus of exhaustion and suffering. The seemingly invincible confidence of Paracelsus had already abandoned him before the meeting with Aprile, but a considerable portion of assurance still remains. . . .

This superb egotism melts away, however, before the presence of Aprile, whose desire of love has found vent in a passion for art, which is thus described by Mr. Browning in a passage not unworthy of Keats, though it is disfigured here and there by grotesque and extravagant conceits:

> I would love infinitely, and be loved.
> First: I would carve in stone, or cast in brass,
> The forms of earth. No ancient hunter lifted
> Up to the gods by his renown, no nymph
> Supposed the sweet soul of a woodland tree
> Or sapphirine spirit of a twilight star,
> Should be too hard for me; no shepherd-king
> Regal for his white locks; no youth who stands
> Silent and very calm amid the throng,
> The right hand ever hid beneath his robe,
> Until the tyrant pass; no lawgiver,
> No swan-soft woman rubbed with lucid oils,
> Given by a god for love of her—too hard!
> Every passion sprung from man, conceived by
> man,
> Would I express and clothe it in its right form,
> Or blend with others struggling in one form,
> Or show repressed by an ungainly form. . . .

(pp. 540-41)

Paracelsus had yet, however, other lessons to learn, which are the subject of the Third and Fourth Parts of the poem; he had to come to a due appreciation of the value of the praise and dispraise of his fellow-men, of both of which he had sufficient experience in his professorial chair; and the haughtiness of his nature led him of itself to despise men for the one and to hate them for the other, but in the final scene on his deathbed he sees his error:

> In my own heart love had not been made wise
> To trace love's faint beginnings in mankind,
> To know even hate is but a mask of love's,
> To see a good in evil, and a hope
> In ill-success; to sympathise, be proud
> Of their half-reasons, faint aspirings, dim
> Struggles for truth, their poorest fallacies,
> Their prejudice and fears and cares and doubts;
> Which all touch upon nobleness, despite
> Their error, all tend upwardly though weak,
> Like plants in mines which never saw the sun,
> But dream of him, and guess where he may be,
> And do their best to climb and get to him.
> All this I knew not, and I failed.

He dies in the conviction that men will ultimately recognise his worth. . . . (p. 543)

Paracelsus was evidently written with some consideration for the public, and some fear of the critics before his eyes, which is more than be can asserted of Mr. Browning's next work, *Sordello,* published five years afterwards. This production alone would be amply sufficient to furnish all examples for the 'Theory of the Obscure.' . . . Singularly enough, too, this appears to be the only piece of the collection by the neglect of which Mr. Browning feels aggrieved. In a dedication to one of his French critics, who appears to have arrived at the singular felicity of understanding *Sordello,* Mr. Browning says that the poem was written only for a few, but he counted even on these few caring more for the subject than proved to be the case, and he is still sanguine enough to expect a wider public for *Sordello* than it has yet received.

Sordello is, like *Paracelsus,* a psychological study, the history of the growth of a soul; and the historical decoration is, as Mr. Browning informs us, put in merely by way of background; but, unfortunately, the decorative part is still more hard to comprehend than the crabbed metaphysics and æsthetics which are wrought up into the 'development of 'the soul.' The psychological revolutions and aims of Sordello's mind are so mixed and matted up with an inexplicable knot of tangled and indistinguishable incidents and personages in one of the darkest periods of Italian history, that nothing short of angelic patience is required to make them out at all, and even when the story of 'Sordello's soul' is unravelled from the weeds which adhere to it, there is little interest or novelty discoverable. Like many other poets, he doubts whether song or action should be his aim in life: in the first part of the poem he is constant to song—in the latter portion he forsakes song, takes to action and dies, it is not clear how, under the burden of it.

A single passage will suffice to show the nature of the narrative and the peculiar character of its obscurity, to which we confess that we are unable to give any meaning whatever:

> Heinrich, on this hand, Otho, Barbaross,
> Carrying the three Imperial crowns across,
> Aix' Iron, Milan's Silver, and Rome's Gold—
> While Alexander, Innocent uphold
> On that, each Papal key—but, link on link,
> Why is it neither chain betrays a chink?
> How coalesce the small and great? Alack,
> For one thrust forward, fifty such fall back!
> Do the popes coupled there help Gregory
> Alone? Hark—from the hermit Peter's cry
> At Claremont, down to the first serf that says
> Friedrich's no liege of his while he delays
> Getting the Pope's curse off him! The Crusade—
> Or trick of breeding strength by other aid
> Than strength, is safe. Hark—from the wild harangue
> Of Vimmercato, to the carroch's clang
> Yonder! The League—or trick of turning strength
> Against pernicious strength, is safe at length.

The psychological portions of the poem, in which *Sordello* exhibits a prophetic intimacy with Kantian metaphysics, are plain reading after such passages as the above, and come as a kind of relief; for though, in truth, equally unintelligible, the reader may be beguiled into thinking he understands them. . . . (pp. 544-45)

On the whole, however, this poem is, in our judgment, from its confused and tortuous style of expression, the most illegible production of any time or country. Every kind of obscurity is to be found in it. Infinitives without their particles—suppression of articles definite and indefinite—confusion and suppression of pronouns relative and personal—adjectives pining for their substantives—verbs in an eternal state of suspense for their subjects—elisions of every kind—sentences prematurely killed off by interjections, or cut short in their career by other sentences—parentheses within parentheses—prepositions sometimes entirely divorced from their nouns—*anacoloutha,* and all kinds of abnormal forms of speech for which grammarians have ever invented names—oblique narrations, instead of direct—and puzzling allusions to obscure persons and facts disinterred from Muratori or Tiraboschi, as though they were perfectly familiar to the reader. Indeed, to be compelled to look at a drama through a pair of horn spectacles would be a cheerful pastime compared with the *ennui* of tracing the course of *Sordello* through that veil of obscurity which Mr. Browning's style of composition places between us and his conception. (p. 546)

Even in the *Dramatic Lyrics* some of the best-known pieces are utterly spoiled by Mr. Browning's abhorrence of lucidity. The **"Ride to Aix,"** for example, labours under this fatal defect. The poem is a spirited one, in spite of its quaintnesses, of which it has its full share. For example, if 'Dirck' is 'he' in the first line, why should he not be 'he' in the second? Then why did not Roland's rider put his riding-gear in good order before starting? and Roland must indeed have been a steady roadster if his bit could be chained slacker without interfering with his galloping. All these and other singularities do not hinder the poem from being a very spirited one. But what is fatal to its general success is the impossibility of knowing what all the galloping is about. Some one a few years ago, we observed, was so moved by Roland's achievements as to write to *Notes and Queries* to ask what was the news brought, but the inquiry still remains unanswered. (pp. 549-50)

The fantastic piece, however, with the fantastic title, *Pippa Passes,* is perhaps the best known of all Mr. Browning's dramatic efforts, and deservedly so, for it combines all his peculiar excellences at the same time that it omits some of his characteristic defects. The notion of 'Pippa,' the obscure girl of the silk-mills, exercising, unknown to herself, a good influence over the four little dramas of the piece is pretty enough, notwithstanding that the songs she sings seem little calculated to move the actors of each separate intrigue in the way they do. The verses overheard by Jules the sculptor are an ingenious and appropriate introduction to his story, which leaves him married and determined to be happy with his bride; although he had been befooled into espousing a girl he had never seen before. On the other hand, the criminal amour of Ottima and the German Sebald, which contains a description of a love-scene of questionable decency in a forest, has so uncertain an ending that we cannot tell whether simple suicide, or suicide and murder, or double suicide, or anything of the kind, happens—we only know that Luca Gaddi, the old husband, has been made away with, although he does not seem to have interfered with the happiness of the lovers more than enough to give zest to their illicit intercourse. Luigi goes off on some indefinite errand of assassination, but we are unable to determine whether the strange song which Pippa sings in his hearing had the effect of strengthening or making him waiver in his purpose; and we are quite left in the dark as to what the Monsignore—the most natural character in the piece—means to do after he has circumvented his Intendant and discovers that Pippa is his niece, and the heiress of his brother's property, of which he has arrived to take possession. It is to be regretted, too, that the conception of Pippa's character, which is simple and playful, should be marred by the grotesque rhymes and metaphors which are put into her mouth. Can any one imagine a simple village girl getting out of bed and saying?

> Day!
> Faster and more fast,
> *O'er night's brim, day boils at last;*
> Boils, pure gold, o'er the cloud-cup's brim
> Where spurting and supprest it lay.

The idea of a 'boiling day' is not likely to be associated with the cool breath of a New Year's morn in the mind of any one but a writer straining a metaphor. (pp. 551-52)

The strangest puzzle, however, occurs at the close of the day, where we are entirely at a loss to know what the lark is expected to do:

> Oh, Lark, be day's apostle
> To mavis, merle and throstle,
> Bid them their betters jostle
> From day and its delights!
> But at night, brother Howlet, far over the
>   woods,
> Toll the world to thy chantry;
> Sing to the bats' sleek sisterhoods
> Full complines with gallantry:
> Then, owls and bats, cowls and twats,
> Monks and nuns, in a cloister's moods,
> *Adjourn to the oak-stump pantry!*

We are led by the concluding line to speak of Mr. Browning's passion for doggerel rhymes, which is one of his most striking peculiarities, and one which no estimate of his poetry can omit to take notice of. In a piece like that called the **"Pied Piper of Hamelin,"** a tale written expressly for children, and which, though of a quainter fashion than the **"Ingoldsby Legends,"** is a poem of the same order, we expect to find such rhymes as we meet with in the speech of the rat, the sole survivor of his legion, when describing the peculiar fascination in the tones of the piper's melody, which induced all his brethren to drown themselves in the Weser:

> At the first shrill notes of the pipe,
> I heard a sound as of scraping tripe,
> And putting apples, wondrous ripe,
> Into a cider-press's gripe:
> And a moving away of pickle-tub-boards,
> And a leaving ajar of conserve-cupboards,
> And a drawing the corks of train-oil-flasks,
> And a breaking the hoops of butter-casks;
> And it seemed as if a voice
> (Sweeter far than by harp or by psaltery
> Is breathed) called out, Oh rats, rejoice!
> The world is grown to one vast drysaltery!

> So, munch on, crunch on, take your nuncheon,
> Breakfast, supper, dinner, luncheon!

(pp. 552-53)

Progressing from hence, we find doggerel in Mr. Browning's love verses, doggerel in his artistic poems, and even his professedly religious piece, ***Christmas Eve and Easter Day,*** is written, for a considerable portion, in Hudibrastic doggerel rhyme. Mr. Browning can apparently never resist the fascination of doggerel when it occurs to him. His most popular lyrics are probably the three **"Cavalier Tunes."** In the first of them the jingle of *'Charles'* and *'carles'* caught his ear, and he thought it so good that he has repeated it twice over in three short verses, united with the further rhymes of *parles* and *snarls*—*Charles, carles, parles, Charles, snarls, carles.* These ballads, however, are among Mr. Browning's best; they are very spirited, and have a certain smack of the times about them, although no one could fancy the Cavaliers singing them. No Cavalier ever called himself a 'great-hearted gentleman,' or talked about the 'hot day brightening to blue from its silver gray.' The quaintest specimen, perhaps, of all Mr. Browning's success in doggerel is his description of Nelson:

> Leaning with one shoulder digging,
> Jigging, as it were, and zig-zag-zigging
> Up against the mizen-rigging.

(p. 554)

Mr. Browning's religious feelings and his daring ingenuity of thought and invention have found congenial application in subjects in which a foreknowledge of the Advent of Christ is introduced, as by David in the very fine poem called **"Saul;"** or as dimly known to Karshish, the Arab physician, by hearsay report and by examination of Lazarus; or as just known to **"Cleon,"** the Greek poet and philosopher, who is not certain whether Paulus, 'the barbarian Jew,' 'is not one with him;' or as more fully known to John in the **"Death in the Desert."** All these four poems display a different and remarkable power; and it is to be observed that the daring of the poet has increased with each new attempt in handling the awful theme.

It was a bold undertaking to re-sing the song with which David chased away the evil spirit of Saul; to commence with the celebration of the joys of the shepherd and the reaper—to pass onward through the raptures of manhood and of strength—of the hunter and the warrior—through the praise of exaltation and kingly glory of royalty—finally, to describe the ineffable mercy of the coming of Christ; but the poem has fulfilled its promise more completely than any other of the volumes. It has something like real rhythm in it, and possesses a solemn, and at the same time an easy flow, and is, for Mr. Browning, remarkably clear in expression. The description of Saul, and of the effect of the various portions of David's song upon him, is extremely imposing, and remains upon the imagination. Less praise, however, can, in our opinion, be accorded to the **"Epistle containing the strange Medical Experience of Karshish, the Arab Physician."** The subject is treated with all Mr. Browning's usual subtlety, quaintness, and ingenuity; but it seems to us irreverent in the highest degree to attempt to describe, through Karshish, the demeanour and mode of thought of Lazarus after his three days' experience of the mysterious realms of death. The piece is full of life-like touches—as where the learned leech becomes half ashamed from time to time to dwell much upon the 'case' of a resuscitated man, every quack professing to do as much in these days, and then, while he makes his report to his master in the science, he turns aside to give other more scientific information:—

> Why write of trivial matters, things of price
> Calling at every moment for remark?
> I noticed on the margin of a pool
> Blue-flowering borage, the Aleppo sort,
> Aboundeth, very nitrous.   It is strange!

But these familiar allusions in the person of the Arab physician present a strange contrast to the supernatural element in the poem. The description of Lazarus, and of his three days' experience of the world beyond the grave, is the reverse of natural, and we trace the far-fetched artifices of Mr. Browning's invention in every line. Much more, however, do we object to see St. John on his death-bed made a medium for a writer to philosophise upon the Gospel in Platonic strains, and to add an apocryphal chapter to the New Testament. This latter poem, however, is so obscurely written, that it would puzzle an inquisition of theologians to find any other heresy in it than that of its conception. **"Cleon,"** on the other hand, is kept strictly within the limits of the reverential, and is extremely happy in its invention. It was suggested apparently by the words of St. Paul's address to the Athenians: 'As certain also of your own poets have said,'—indicating that some of these already had had a foretaste of some of the truths of Christianity. Mr. Browning, therefore, exhibits Cleon, the Greek poet and philosopher, writing to his friend Protos 'in his tyranny,' discoursing on man, mind and its destination, the necessity of a future life, and the probability of a revelation; all this while St. Paul was preaching close at hand, whose doctrines, however, he refused to hear. . . . (pp. 555-56)

An equally characteristic class of poems with the above are those which deal with ancient and little-known artists of music and poetry; such as **"Old Pictures in Florence,"** **"Fra Lippo Lippi,"** **"A Toccata of Galuppi's,"** **"Master Hugues of Saxe-Gotha,"** and **"Abt Vogler."** The musical pieces, and that of **"Master Hugues of Saxe-Gotha"** especially, show what an eccentric delight Mr. Browning finds in losing himself utterly in an obscure subject, and how entirely congenial to his own nature is the strange rhapsody of the organist who remains by himself in the old church with the lights expiring one by one, trying to wring out every crotchet of subtle meaning from the over-wrought *fugue* of Master Hugues, and has to grope his way from the loft to the foot of the 'rotten-runged rat-riddled stairs.' The piece called **"Fra Lippo Lippi"** is also a very quaint mixture of strange humour, realistic treatment, and artistic theorising. No other writer could have conceived so strange a character as this wine-bibbing licentious monk and painter, dropping out of the convent-window by night, and caught by the watch while reeling back to his convent, to whom, with sundry snatches of song, he unburdens himself about his own life in particular, and art in general. In **"Andrea del Sarto,"** Mr. Browning has been

less happy, and his piece contrasts unfavourably with the little drama of Alfred de Musset on the same subject—so finely, clearly, and delicately touched, as, indeed, all his pieces are, and full of action and interest. It is, however, in dramatic monologues of this kind that Mr. Browning has achieved the most complete success. He has the faculty of conceiving circumstantially, and sympathising with artist-natures of singular aims and secluded merit. Among such conceptions must also be classed the singular story, the **"Grammarian's Funeral,"** which, in spite of its extreme oddity of thought and imagination, is a noble elegy of one of the indefatigable seekers after learning such as lived shortly after the revival of learning.

To this curious sympathy with exceptional classes and persons we must attribute the excellence of portraiture of all his monks and ecclesiastics, from the monk of the **"Soliloquy of the Spanish Cloister"** to the very confidential **"Bishop Blougram":** the Monsignore in *Pippa Passes* and Ogniben, the Pontifical Legate, in the **"Soul's Tragedy,"** are also equally lifelike. For Mr. Browning's taste for human nature being something of the nature of a taste for rare china or odd old-fashioned weapons, he has, by dint of concentrating all the interest into one character and all the action into one incident, produced some very characteristic studies. It is, however, here not so much the poetry, as the very great condensation of a whole life or a drama into a few lines, which excites the reader's interest; and so artificial a production, where the whole of the speaker's life or character is to be derived from his own words, must always retain something of an air of improbability. In Mr. Tennyson's "St. Simeon Stylites," which, excepting, perhaps, the "Ulysses" of the same writer, is the only analogous poem in the language, the monologue is natural from the very situation of the solitary fanatic; but in the piece called **"My Last Duchess,"** it is very unnatural that the Duke should betray himself so entirely to the envoy who comes to negotiate a new marriage as to let him have the same opportunity of knowing as we have ourselves that his cold austerity and pride had been the death of his late wife; and in the **"Bishop orders his Tomb"** on his death-bed we never lose the peculiar accents of Mr. Browning's quaintness for a moment. It is, for example, Mr. Browning who is speaking through the Bishop's mouth when he says

> And then how I shall lie through centuries,
> And hear the blessed mutter of the mass,
> And see God made and eaten all day long,
> And feel the steady candle-flame, and taste
> Good strong thick stupifying incense smoke!

These lines have a characteristic aptness about them, but no bishop would describe Church ceremonies in this way. Nevertheless, the portrait of the old voluptuous antique-hunting, marble-purloining Roman ecclesiastic is one which cannot fail to strike and to please also to a certain extent; it is a rich example of Mr. Browning's humour in dealing with ecclesiastical subjects, which, however, finds its quaintest expression in the **"Heretic's Tragedy,"**—a Middle-Age Interlude, where the grotesque chuckle of triumph, of self-satisfied, undoubting mediæval intolerance, over the burning of the Grand Master of the Templars at Paris, after two centuries have elapsed, is most characteristically but not pleasingly, rendered in the **"Conceit of Master Gysbrecht."**

The last passage we have quoted leads us to speak of Mr. Browning's descriptive power, which is remarkable. His faculty of word-painting, and of seeing quaint resemblances in dissimilar objects, by some happy touch often vividly calls up a scene before the imagination. In his two Italian sketches, the one called **"Up at a Villa—down in the City, as distinguished by an Italian person of quality,"** and **"The Englishman in Sorrento,"** Mr. Browning's descriptive faculty has produced some pleasant effects. (pp. 557-59)

Another peculiar class of poems forms no small portion of Mr. Browning's first volume, and this may be called the Sophistical,—embodying in rhyme the attempt to make the worse appear the better side. One of the most striking of these is the poem called the **"Glove."** Everybody knows Schiller's ballad on the same subject: how the Knight Delorges on being bidden by his lady to bring up her glove which she had wilfully thrown into the lion's den, leapt, brought it back, and threw it in her face. The ballad is not one of Schiller's best, but Schiller and the world in general have thought the knight to have been in the right. Mr. Browning, however, thinks there is something to be said for the lady, and he has written a poem on the subject. The poem is as ingenious as any of Mr. Browning's, but we doubt if the lady's defence of herself will make many converts, and it is suspicious, to say the least of it, that her excuse is pretty nearly as long as Schiller's whole poem. Perhaps the most successful as well as the most striking of all the poems of this class is that styled **"Holy Cross Day,"**—the day on which, before the present Pontificate, the Jews were compelled to attend on an annual sermon at Rome. It does not, however, begin very promisingly. A Jew is speaking:

> Fee, faw, fum! bubble and squeak!
> Blessedest Thursday's the fat of the week.
> Rumble and tumble, sleek and rough,
> Stinking and savoury, smug and gruff,
> Take the church-road, for the bell's due chime
> Gives us the summons—'t is sermon-time.
>
> Boh, here's Barnabas! Job, that's you?
> Up stumps Solomon—bustling too?
> Shame, man! greedy beyond your years
> To handsel the bishop's shaving shears?
> Fair play's a jewel! leave friends in the lurch?
> Stand on a line ere you start for the church.

The sermon is delivered, and its effect on the Jew audience and the rascally converts, the black sheep of the tribe, is told in the same grotesque but graphic fashion; but the most striking portion of the poem is the Rabbi Ben Ezra's song of death which the unconverted sang in church while obliged to sit there after the Bishop's sermon and meditate on the truths he has been endeavouring to enforce upon them.

"Evelyn Hope" is one of the prettiest of Mr. Browning's love pieces, because it is one of the simplest; though we by no means concur in the exaggerated praises which have been heaped upon it. An elderly student, of about fifty years of age, fell in love with Evelyn Hope, who died at sixteen:

> For God's hand beckoned unawares,
> And the sweet white brow was all of her.
>
> (pp. 560-61)

This, an unjilted lover, consoles himself by placing a leaf in Evelyn Hope's dead hand and persuading himself she will understand all about it when she awakes:

> I loved you, Evelyn, all the while!
>   My heart seemed full as it could hold—
> There was place and to spare for the frank young smile
>   And the red young mouth and the hair's young gold.
> So, hush—I will give you this leaf to keep—
>   See, I shut it inside this sweet cold hand.
> There, that is our secret! go to sleep;
>   You will wake, and remember, and understand.

While on the subject of Mr. Browning's love poems, we must not omit to mention that his lovers are prepared to go lengths in the demonstration of their affection which we hardly like to contemplate. (pp. 561-62)

Among, however, Mr. Browning's inexhaustible variety of poems about lovers—jilted lovers, deserted lovers, quarrelling lovers, forgiving lovers, fortunate lovers, unfortunate lovers, and lovers of every denomination, with their infinite perplexities of love, we come occasionally upon touches as delicate as the following in **"The Lost Mistress,"** where the lover considers how he shall behave towards the lady in future:

> Yes! I will say what mere friends say,
>   Or only a thought stronger;
> I will hold your hand but as long as all may,
>   *Or so very little longer!*
>
> (p. 563)

Having a sincere respect for what we know of Mr. Browning's character, and for his literary industry, we have not sought in the foregoing remarks to disparage or ridicule the efforts of his singular genius; but to enable our readers to form an impartial opinion of his merits or defects from the extracts we have made. Some of them will doubtless think that we have devoted too much of our space to these productions, and will ask, with alarm, whether these are specimens of the latest fashion of English poetry. We confess that it is to ourselves a subject of amazement that poems of so obscure and uninviting a character should find numerous readers, and that successive editions of them should be in demand. Yet this is undoubtedly the case; and far from having reason to complain of neglect, Mr. Browning has a considerable number of admirers in England, and more, we believe, in America. It would seem that in this practical and mechanical age, there is some attraction in wild and extravagant language—some mysterious fascination in obscure half-expressed thoughts. Mr. Browning in truth more nearly resembles the American writers Emerson, Wendell Holmes, and Bigelow, than any poet of our own country. Tried by the standards which have hitherto been supposed to uphold the force and beauty of the English tongue and of English literature, his works are deficient in the qualities we should desire to find them. We do not believe that they will survive, except as a curiosity and a puzzle. But they undoubtedly exercise a certain degree of influence over the taste of the present generation; and on this ground we think they deserve the notice we have bestowed upon them. (p. 565)

"Robert Browning's 'Poems'," in The Edinburgh Review, *Vol. CXX, No. CCXLVI, October, 1864, pp. 537-65.*

Richelieu   (essay date 1868)

[*In this excerpted review of* The Ring and the Book, *the pseudonymous critic defends Browning against his detractors, claiming that here as elsewhere the poet is speaking as a "messenger of truth" to his age. These comments were originally published in the November 28 issue of* Vanity Fair.]

In a few days Mr. Browning will publish another of those great and supposed enigmatical poems at which all *Vanity Fair* stands aghast—not exactly with terror, but with the half-amused, half-puzzled look of the honest country folk who hear for the first time in their lives a Frenchman or a German speaking in his own language. Once more the critics in plush will be heard echoing and re-echoing the verdict of the critics in kid gloves, and while the moustache is gracefully twirled, or the cigar held in suspense, **The Ring and the Book** will be turned over with a patronising air, and in all the sincerity of supercilious wonderment plaintively pronounced 'monstwously cwude in style, and altogether puzzling "to a fella", you know!' There is no help for this sort of thing. It is not Mr. Browning's fortune to stand on a level with the criticism of the present generation. His voice is 'the voice of one crying in the wilderness', and they who dwell in kings' houses will not go out to hear him, and are little likely to be influenced by his teaching.

By particular favour I have seen enough of Mr. Browning's new poem to be quite prepared for a repetition of the old verdict of *Vanity Fair* upon his choice of a subject and his treatment of it; yet I shall venture to speak of this book as one of the most striking lessons ever read by poet or philosopher in the ears of an evil generation. The story is a pitiful one—more pitiful than Hood's "Bridge of Sighs," if that be possible. A young girl of Rome, in those old times which Mr. Browning loves to paint—yet not so remote from the present as his middle-aged dramas—is married to an Italian count, shortly after which she and her father and mother are found murdered by him—nay, he is taken red-handed almost in the very act of butchery, and is eventually executed for the crime. This is the substance of the story found by Mr. Browning in an old 'Book'. How he treats it is to be gathered from his opening apologue of the **Ring**. Some alloy must be mingled with your virgin gold to make it workable, but the goldsmith having finished his design (the 'lilied loveliness' of the ring) the gold is set free from its baser companionship by the last touch of the workman's art. Once more it is pure gold, 'prime nature with an added artistry'. And so understood, the antique goldsmith's ring serves, in the fore-front

of the poem, as a symbol or speaking emblem of the poet's method. Say he has a divine message. How shall he utter it? The story of Guido Franceschini and the babe-like woman he made his bride is the answer.

It is not, therefore, to relate this story with such embellishments as his poetic instinct and sense of artistic beauty might suggest, that Mr. Browning has written. There is a deeply-felt purpose in his work of art, and to accomplish that purpose he has mixed the gold with 'gold's alloy.' We are first told of the tragedy in all its naked ghastliness. Then what 'half Rome' said of it, and what the 'other half.' The motives of the different actors in the drama, and all the little incomplete incidents which go to make up its completeness, are thus vividly realised. We pass them all over, to remark on Mr. Browning's aim, or what may be called the gist of his message in the character of Seer. The handwriting on the wall seems to be this, 'Can evil be done and evil not come of it?' Or this, to vary the expression, 'Is the world ruled by man's cunning devices, or by God's laws?' Or, again, this, 'Can a lie be told, and not make itself manifest, sooner or later, as the work of him who is the father of lies?' Yet, **The Ring and the Book** is not a sermon. It is deeply, intensely, human. It is nevertheless, and for that very reason, a burning protest against the atheistic belief that men and women are the creatures of circumstances. It asserts a Presence in the world, before which every lie, spoken or acted, must wither up, and possibly—nay, most certainly—bring destruction upon those who trust in it.

We picture Dante walking, with sad wide-open eyes, through Purgatory and Hades before he reached the shore of the river across which the loving eyes of Beatrice beamed upon him, and he once more took comfort. So through Vanity Fair and its devious ways, crowded with spectres of men and women as mournful to seeing eyes as those which grieved the heart of the Mantuan bard, we follow the steps of the poet who has been entrusted with this message, and who has already given utterance to it in many like parables. All criticism of Mr. Browning's verse which does not recognise this central fact of his relationship to the age as a messenger of truth seems to me worthless. It is true the good folk in Vanity Fair do not like this sort of thing, and it may be there are times when none of us like it. Belshazzar at high festival has no relish for the mystical handwriting on the wall. It is not always pleasant to be in earnest, and, like Mr. Tennyson's "Lotos-Eaters", we rather enjoy floating down the stream; or like the crew in his glorious "Voyage", we have aims of our own in which it is vexatious to be disturbed. The answer to this objection is that we are not troubled every day, or even every other day, with a great poet's earnest expression of feeling, or with his sense of the living truth of things. No fear that there will not always be space enough in the Fair for vain shows, or, let us say, for harmless mirth and pleasantry. Now and then we may surely pause a moment in the round of ambition or pleasure to hear the Voice of Truth, and to lay up a gracious remembrance for less festive occasions. This, at least, is the kind of appeal which Mr. Browning's new poem makes to the world, be it received how it may. (pp. 284-86)

Richelieu, in an extract in Browning: The Critical Heritage, *edited by Boyd Litzinger and Donald Smalley, Barnes & Noble, Inc., 1970, pp. 284-87.*

[R. W. Buchanan]   (essay date 1869)

[*An appreciative review of Volumes 2, 3, and 4 of* The Ring and the Book. *Buchanan considers Browning's work "the most precious and profound spiritual treasure that England has produced since the days of Shakspeare" [sic].*]

At last, the *opus magnum* of our generation lies before the world—the "ring is rounded"; and we are left in doubt which to admire most, the supremely precious gold of the material or the wondrous beauty of the workmanship. The fascination of [**The Ring and the Book**] is still so strong upon us, our eyes are still so spell-bound by the immortal features of Pompilia (which shine through the troubled mists of the story with almost insufferable beauty), that we feel it difficult to write calmly and without exaggeration; yet we must record at once our conviction, not merely that **The Ring and the Book** is beyond all parallel the supremest poetical achievement of our time, but that it is the most precious and profound spiritual treasure that England has produced since the days of Shakspeare. Its intellectual greatness is as nothing compared with its transcendent spiritual teaching. Day after day it grows into the soul of the reader, until all the outlines of thought are brightened and every mystery of the world becomes more and more softened into human emotion. Once and for ever must critics dismiss the old stale charge that Browning is a mere intellectual giant, difficult of comprehension, hard of assimilation. This great book *is* difficult of comprehension, *is* hard of assimilation; not because it is obscure—every fibre of the thought is clear as day; not because it is intellectual,—and it is intellectual in the highest sense,—but because the capacity to comprehend such a book must be spiritual. . . . The man who tosses it aside because it is "difficult" is simply adopting a subterfuge to hide his moral littleness, not his mental incapacity. It would be unsafe to predict anything concerning a production so many-sided; but we quite believe that its true public lies outside the literary circle, that men of inferior capacity will grow by the aid of it, and that feeble women, once fairly initiated into the mystery, will cling to it as a succour passing all succour save that which is purely religious. Is it not here that we find the supremacy of Shakspeare's greatness? Shakspeare, so far as we have been able to observe, places the basis of his strange power on his appeal to the draff of humanity. He is the delight of men and women by no means brilliant, by no means subtle; while he holds with equal sway the sympathies of the most endowed. A small intellect may reach to the heart of Shakspearean power; not so a small nature. The key to the mystery is spiritual. (p. 399)

We should be grossly exaggerating if we were to aver that Mr. Browning is likely to take equal rank with the supreme genius of the world; only a gallery of pictures like the Shakspearean group could enable him to do that; and, moreover, his very position as an educated modern must necessarily limit his field of workmanship. What we wish to convey is, that Mr. Browning exhibits—to a great extent in all his writings, but particularly in this great work—a wealth of nature and a perfection of spiritual insight which we have been accustomed to find in the pages of Shakspeare, and in those pages only. His fantastic intellectual feats, his verbosity, his power of quaint versification, are quite other matters. The one great and patent fact is, that, with a faculty in our own time at least unparalleled, he manages to create beings of thoroughly human fibre; he is just without judgment, without pre-occupation, to every being so created; and he succeeds, without a single didactic note, in stirring the soul of the spectator with the concentrated emotion and spiritual exaltation which heighten the soul's stature in the finest moments of life itself.

As we have said above, the face which follows us through every path of the story is that of Pompilia, with its changeful and moon-like beauty, its intensely human pain, its heavenly purity and glamour. We have seen no such face elsewhere. It has something of Imogen, of Cordelia, of Juliet; it has something of Dante's Beatrice; but it is unlike all of those—not dearer, but more startling, from the newness of its beauty. From the first moment when the spokesman for the "Other Half Rome" introduces her—

> Little Pompilia, with the patient brow
> And lamentable smile on those poor lips,
> And under the white hospital array
> A flower-like body—

to the moment when the good old Pope, revolving the whole history in his mind, calls her tenderly

> My rose, I gather for the gaze of God!

—from the first to the last, Pompilia haunts the poem with a look of ever-deepening light. Her wretched birth, her miserable life, her cruel murder, gather around her like clouds, only to disperse vapour-like, and reveal again the heavenly whiteness. There is not the slightest attempt to picture her as saintly; she is a poor child, whose saintliness comes of her suffering. So subtle is the spell she has upon us, that we quite forget the horrible pain of her story. Instead of suffering, we are full of exquisite pleasure—boundless in its amount, ineffable in its quality. When, on her sorry death-bed, she is prattling about her child, we weep indeed; not for sorrow—how should sorrow demand such tears?—but for "the pity of it, the pity of it, Iago!" . . .

Extracts can do little for Pompilia: as well chip a hand or foot off a Greek statue. Very noticeable, in her monologue, is the way she touches on the most delicate subjects, fearlessly laying bare the strangest secrecies of matrimonial life, and with so perfect an unconsciousness, so delicate a purity, that these passages are among the sweetest in the poem. But we must leave her to her immortality. She is perfect every way; not a tint of the flesh, not a tone of the soul, escapes us as we read and see.

Only less fine—less fine because he is a man, less fine because his soul's probation is perhaps less perfect—is the priest, Giuseppe Caponsacchi. "Ever with Caponsacchi!" cries Pompilia on her death-bed,

O lover of my life, O soldier-saint!

And our hearts are with him too. He lives before us, with that strong face of his, noticeable for the proud upper lip and brilliant eyes, softened into grave melancholy and listening awe. What a man had he been, shining at ladies' feasts, and composing sonnets and "pieces for music," all in the pale of the Church! In him, as we see him, the animal is somewhat strong, and, prisoned in, pricks the intellect with gall. Little recks he of Madonna until that night at the theatre,

> When I saw enter, stand, and seat herself,
> A lady, young, tall, beautiful, and sad.

Slowly and strangely the sad face grows upon his heart, until that moment when it turns to him appealingly for succour, and when, fearless of any criticism save that of God, he devotes his soul to its service.

> There at the window stood,
> Framed in its black square length, with lamp in
>   hand,
> Pompilia; the same great, grave, grieffull air
> As stands i' the dusk, on altar that I know,
> Left alone with one moonbeam in her cell,
> Our Lady of all Sorrows.

The whole monologue of Caponsacchi is a piece of supreme poetry, steeped in lyrical light. The writer's emotion quite overpowers him, and here, as elsewhere, he must sing. In all literature, perhaps, there is nothing finer than the priest's description of his journey towards Rome with Pompilia, that night she flies from the horror of Guido's house. Every incident lives before us: the first part of the journey, when Pompilia sits spell-bound, and the priest's eyes are fascinated upon her,

> At times she drew a soft sigh—music seemed
> Always to hover just above her lips,
> Not settle,—break a silence music too!—

the breaking dawn,—her first words,—then her sudden query—

> "Have you a mother?" "She died, I was born."
> "A sister then?" "No sister." "Who was it—
> What woman were you used to serve this way,
> Be kind to, till I called you and you came?"

—every look, thought, is conjured up out of the great heart of the lover, until that dark moment when the cat-eyed Guido overtakes them. What we miss in the psychology Pompilia herself supplies. It is saying little to say that we have read nothing finer. We know nothing whatever of like quality.

In a former review we gave a sketch of the general design of the work, explaining that, of the twelve books into which it is divided, ten were to be dramatic monologues, spoken by various persons concerned in or criticizing the Italian tragedy; and the remaining two a prologue and epilogue, spoken in the person of the poet himself. The complete work, therefore, is noticeable for variety of power and extraordinary boldness of design. All the monologues are good in their way, the only ones we could well spare being those of the two counsel, for and against Guido. These, of course, are extraordinarily clever; but cleverness

is a poor quality for a man like Robert Browning to parade. The noblest portions of the book are **"Giuseppe Caponsacchi," "Pompilia,"** and **"The Pope."** The last-named monologue is wonderfully grand—a fitting organ-peal to close such a book of mighty music; and it rather jars upon us, therefore, that we afterwards hear again the guilty scream of Guido. It seems to us, indeed, if we are bound to find fault at all, that we could have well dispensed with about a fourth of the whole work—the two legal speeches and Guido's last speech. To the two former we object on artistic grounds; to the latter, we object merely on account of its extreme and discordant pain. Yet in Guido's speech occurs one of the noblest touches in the whole work—where Guido, on the point of leaving his cell for the place of execution, exclaims—

> Abate,—Cardinal,—Christ,—Maria,—God.
> Pompilia, will you let them murder me?—

thus investing her at the last moment with almost God-like power and pity, in spite of the hatred which overcomes him,—hatred similar in kind, but different in degree, to that which Iscariot may be supposed to have felt for the Master. Nor let us forget to record that the poet, in his bright beneficence, has the lyric note even for Guido. We are made to feel that the "damnable blot" on his soul is only temporary, that the sharp axe will be a rod of mercy, and that the poor, petulant, vicious little Count will brighten betimes, and be saved through the purification of the very passions which have doomed him on earth. No writer that we know, except Shakspeare, could, without clumsy art and sentimental psychology, have made us feel so subtly the divine light issuing at last out of the selfish and utterly ignoble nature of Guido Franceschini.

Fault-finders will discover plenty to carp at in a work so colossal. For ourselves, we are too much moved to think of trifles, and are content to bow in homage, again and again, to what seems to us the highest existing product of modern thought and culture. Before concluding, we should notice one point in which this book differs from the plays of Shakspeare,—*i.e.* it contains, even in some of its superbest passages, a certain infusion of what Mr. Matthew Arnold once called "criticism." So far from this "criticism" being a blot upon the book, it is one of its finest qualities as a modern product. We cannot enlarge upon this point here, though it is one that is sure to be greatly enlarged upon in publications with more space at their command; but we should not conclude without explaining that the work is the more truly worthy to take Shakspearean rank because it contains certain qualities which are quite un-Shakspearean—which, in fact, reflect beautifully the latest reflections of a critical mind on mysterious modern phenomena. (p. 400)

> [*R. W. Buchanan*], *in a review of "The Ring and the Book," in* The Athenaeum, *No. 2160, March 20, 1869, pp. 399-400.*

A. Orr   (essay date 1874)

[*Orr wrote one of the earliest biographies of Browning [see Further Reading list]. In the excerpt below, she of-*

fers an in-depth assessment of Browning's verse up the publication of Fifine at the Fair.]

No writer has aroused in his own time and within his own sphere a more positive interest than Mr. Browning. He has been sincerely loved and cordially disliked. For many persons, both men and women, his works have possessed the support, the sympathy, and the suggestiveness of a secular Gospel; whilst with others they have become a bye-word for ambiguousness of thought and eccentricity of expression. He has been abundantly reviewed in each isolated poem; isolated aspects of his genius have been strongly appreciated and even subtly defined; nevertheless, he has been writing for forty years, and the public are more than ever at issue concerning the fundamental conditions of his creative life; the question is more than ever undecided whether he is what he professes to be, a poet, whose natural expression is verse, or what many believe him to be—a deep, subtle, and imaginative thinker, who has chosen to write in verse. (p. 934)

As a poet, he has had no visible growth; he displays no divisions into youth, manhood, and age; no phases particularly marked by the predominance of an aim, a manner, or a conviction. His genius is supposed to have reached its zenith in *The Ring and the Book,* because nothing he has written before or since has afforded so large an illustration of it, but we have no reason to believe that his writing it when he did, instead of before or afterwards, was due to anything but its external cause; and we might reverse the positions of *Paracelsus* and *Fifine at the Fair,* his first known and his latest original work, without disturbing any preconceived judgment of promise in the one or finality in the other. In their actual relation, each appears in its right place. We see in *Paracelsus* the idealism of a young and lofty intelligence; in *Fifine* the semi-material philosophy which comes of prolonged contact with life; but if *Fifine* had been written when its author was twenty-two, it would have seemed full of the sophistry of a youthful spirit, dazzled by the variety of life, and striving to combine incompatible enjoyments and to reconcile incompatible feelings. And if *Paracelsus* were published now, we should hail in it the final utterance of a mind wearied by its own eccentricities and giving in its solemn adherence to the time-honoured methods of human labour and human love. *Fifine at the Fair* exhibits one sign of a riper genius in the tone of satire which does not spare even itself; but *Paracelsus* bears a still fuller stamp of maturity in its complete refinement of imagery and expression. It shows the touch of a master hand.

We do not mean to assert that during Mr. Browning's long literary career the manner of his inspiration has undergone no change. It has changed so far, that if we compare the first twenty years with the last we shall find emotion predominant in the one period and reflection in the other; but reflection is considered to have acquired a morbid development in *Sordello,* and flashes of intense feeling occur even in the coldest of his later works. The change has been too gradual to draw a boundary line across any moment of his life; and though it is in the nature of things that a change so gradual should be permanent, there is something in Mr. Browning's nature that prevents our feeling

Portrait of Browning by Dante Gabriel Rossetti, 1855.

it as such. It appears too restless to crystallize. (pp. 934-35)

We have said that Mr. Browning's genius had no perceptible growth, because it was full-grown when first presented to the world. This does not imply that it had no period of manifest *becoming;* and there is evidence of such a phase in a fragment called *Pauline,* which became known much later than his other works, but in the last edition of them occupies its proper place at the beginning. The difference of manner and conception which divides it from *Paracelsus* gives the rate of the progress which carried him in three years from the one to the other, whilst the comparative crudeness of the earlier poem affords a curious insight into the yet seething elements of that almost colossal power. We cannot judge how far *Pauline* was a deliberate product of the author's imagination or a spontaneous overflowing of poetic feeling; but this does not affect its relation to his other creations of an equally esoteric kind, and in thought, though not in expression, it is essentially a youthful work. It is the half-delirious self-revealing of a soul maddened by continued introspection, by the irrepressible craving to extend its sphere of consciousness, and by the monstrosities of subjective experience in which this self-magnifying and self-distorting action has involved it. The sufferer tells his story to a woman who loves him, and to whom he has been always more or less worthily attached; and ends by gently raving himself into a rest which is represented as premonitory of death, and in which the image of a perfect human love rises amidst the tumult of the disordered brain, transfusing its chaotic emotions into one soft harmony of life and hope. The same fundamental idea recurs in *Paracelsus,* but in a more subdued and infinitely more objective form. We find there the same consciousness of intellectual power, but with a stronger sense of responsibility; the same restless ambition, but directed towards a more definite and more unselfish end. There is also the same acceptance of love as the one saving reality of life, but the earthly adorer of Pauline has become the exponent of the heaven-born, universal love; and we shall see in one of Mr. Browning's more recent poems how the final expression of these two modes of feeling may be imaginatively resolved into one. *Pauline* is strongly distinguished from its author's subsequent works by an excessive luxuriance of imagery, employed, not as the illustration of a distinct idea, but as the spontaneous embodiment of a complex and intense emotion. It resembles them in its very delicate and powerful rendering of the passion of Love. (pp. 936-37)

The one quality of Mr. Browning's intellectual nature which is at present most universally recognized is its casuistry—his disposition to allow an excessive weight to the incidental conditions of human action, and consequently to employ sliding scales in the measurement of it. The most remarkable evidence of this quality, supplied by his later works, is to be found in **"Prince Hohenstiel-Schwangau."** It is displayed with more audacity in *Fifine at the Fair,* with larger and more sustained effect in *The Ring and the Book.* But *Fifine at the Fair,* though very subjective in treatment, verges too much on the grotesque to be accepted as a genuine reflection of the author's mind; and *The Ring and the Book* represents him as a pleader, but at the same time as a judge. It describes the case under discussion from every possible point of view, but does not describe it as subject to any possible moral doubt. **"Prince Hohenstiel-Schwangau"** is a deliberate attempt on the author's part to defend a cause which he knows to be weak, and as such is a typical specimen, as it is also a favourable one, of his genius for special pleading. It places in full relief the love of opposition which impels him to defend the weaker side, and the love of fairness which always makes him subsume in the defence every argument that may be justly advanced against it; and it also exhibits that double-refracting quality of his mind which can convert a final concession to the one side into an irresistible last word in favour of the other. It is unfortunate that a slight ambiguity in one or two passages obscures the drift of the poem, and disinclines its readers for taking the otherwise small amount of trouble required for its comprehension, for this supposed soliloquy of the ex-Emperor of the French is in every respect a striking expression of the non-pathetic side of its author's genius. Both narrative and argument have a coursing rapidity which rather fatigues the mind, but they are vivid, humorous, and picturesque, carry some serious thought in solution, and leave behind as their residue a distinct dramatic impression of the easy-going Bohemianism which they are intended to depict. Some objection has been taken to the *mise en scène* of the monologue, and the introduction of the Lais of Leicester Square is, indeed, a violation of good taste which could only be accepted on the ground of entire poetic fitness. But there is even more than poetic fitness—there is historic truth in this ideal approximation of the princely exponent of hand-to-mouth existence to its typical embodiment in the lowest social form. (pp. 937-38)

"Bishop Blougram's Apology" is still more sophistical in tone, and though the author represents it in his conclusion as a possible course of argument rather than a just one, it leaves a certain misgiving as to the extent to which he endorses it. It would not be necessary to adduce this monologue in support of the impression conveyed by that of **"Prince Hohenstiel-Schwangau,"** but that it derives a fresh significance from its much earlier date, which proves the co-existence of this casuistic mood with the most poetic phase of its author's imaginative life.

The Bishop excuses himself for having accepted the honours and emoluments of a Church of which he does not fully believe the doctrines, on the plea that disbelief is of its nature as hypothetical as belief, and that it must be not only wise but right to give oneself both temporally and spiritually the benefit of the doubt. He does not say, "My belief is too negative to justify me in renouncing the power for good which I derive from the appearance of belief; or too negative to give me the courage to renounce the good it affords to myself." But he implicitly says, "I am *not* gifted with positive opinions; I *am* gifted with a positive appreciation of the refinements of life and a positive desire for them. I am clearly violating the intentions of Providence if, whilst rejecting a possible truth, I refuse to the one part of my nature that for which I can find no compensation in the other." This palpable confusing of belief with conformity, the higher wisdom with common expediency, worldly profit with spiritual gain, scarcely provokes discussion; and Mr. Browning's concluding lines appear at first sight to value such reasoning at its worth; but we cannot overlook the fact that, while he has put sound objections into the mouth of the Bishop's opponent, he considers the Bishop's unsound arguments to have been a match for them; and the tone of the whole discussion implies at least toleration of the theory that temporal good and spiritual gain are not disparate ideas, but different aspects of one and the same.

There is one poetical passage in this tissue of sophistry, and one true one—that which asserts the frequent shallowness of religious unbelief:

> Just when we are safest, there's a sunset touch,
> A fancy from a flower bell, someone's death,
> A Chorus ending from Euripides,—
> And that's enough for fifty hopes and fears
> As old and new at once as Nature's self,
> To rap and knock and enter in our soul,
> Take hands and dance there, a fantastic ring,
> Round the ancient idol on his base again,—
> The grand Perhaps!

The author takes no account of the many minds in which the disbelief in certain things has assumed the positive character of belief, but his lines are a noble tribute to the tenacity of religious association, even where regret for the displaced idol has no longer power to reinstate it.

If we observe the variety of speculative opinion to which Mr. Browning considers all questions of human conduct to be subject, together with the frequent reference in his works to a Supreme Being in whose will alone lies the absolute solution of such questions, we cannot avoid the inference that the religious sense is far stronger in him than the moral sense. It is evident at least that his mind naturally subordinates the general laws of morality to the specialities of circumstance, and to a feeling of the distinctive position of every human soul. This belief in a special and continuous relation of the human and the divine, or simply in special Providence, is the mainspring of his religious writings, and sceptic as he is, the material mysticism of Low Church Christianity has seldom found amongst its own disciples a more faithful and earnest exponent. But Christianity is based upon a revelation which he does not profess to acknowledge, and whilst the existence and omnipresence of God are proved to him by the nature of things, he recognizes in nature no distinct expression of His will. It is easy, therefore, to conceive that to a mind at once so sensuous and so poetic, so strongly impressed with the connection between the lowest experiences and the highest consciousness of humanity, sanction will appear everywhere stronger than prohibition, and the very belief in a divine ordaining become, in some measure, the equal justification of the varied possibilities of life. Mr. Browning considers all things as good in their way. The more familiar aspects of this idea are illustrated in the Introduction to **The Ring and the Book,** in a passage which gives also some insight into the natural connection between the author's æsthetic impressions of existence and his moral judgments upon it. (pp. 939-41)

Every serious expression of Mr. Browning's casuistry appears to point to some singular union of belief in the subjectivity of all feeling and conviction with that belief in transcendent existence which always implies the recognition of fixed standards of truth; and this double point of view is so frankly assumed in **Fifine at the Fair** as to give to that eminently fantastic poem a philosophic significance which its more serious predecessors do not possess. Its sensualistic conceptions are expressed with the greatest poetic power, but it asserts with equal distinctness the material unity of consciousness and the separate existence of the soul; and though both ideas may be reconciled by a religious theory of creation, Mr. Browning cannot deny that in accepting the one he cuts away all rational foundation from the other. The morality of **Fifine at the Fair** would be even more eccentric than its philosophy, but that its reasonings are neutralized in this direction by the dramatic impulse under which they were carried out; whether or not the author intended it so. The leading figure of the poem is a hard-working social outcast, whom the author had probably seen, and who appears to have suggested to him some idea of the virtues which reside in self-sustainment and of a moral good that may come of immorality, and the whole resolves itself into a series of speculations on the precise mixing of the fruits of experience that may best conduce to the higher nourishment of the soul. These questionings assume the form of a battle within the hero's mind between Fifine, the vagrant, and Elvire, the symbol of domestic love, and unfortunately the one is conceived as an individual, the other only as a type. Elvire is invested in the beginning with enough of the substance of a loving and loveable wife to give prominence to her husband's arguments in favour of an occasional Fifine; but as

the story advances, and its fundamental mood becomes more pronounced, she fades into a pallid embodiment of mild satisfaction and monotonous duty, and by the time Mr. Browning has brought her and her companion back to their villa-door, he cannot resist the delight of making her the subject of a trick which his sense of justice sufficiently disclaims to make him display it in all its heartlessness. His Don Juan proves, in spite of himself, that in individual life disorder does not naturally lead to order, nor a simply erratic fancy rise to the abstractions of universal love.

We should naturally infer, from the temper of Mr. Browning's mind, that the warmth of its affections would belie the indifferentism of its ideas, and we constantly find it to be so. An innate veneration for moral beauty, of which we find scarcely any trace in his philosophizing poems, asserts itself in all those of a more emotional character, and so various is his mode of self-manifestation that the evidence contained in his collective works of his belief in the necessary relativity of judgment is not a whit stronger than their indirect advocacy of courage, devotion, singleness of heart—in short, of all the virtues which are born of conviction. His imagination is keenly alive to every condition of love; but its deepest and most passionate response is always yielded to that form of tenderness which by its disinterested nature most approaches to the received ideal of the Divine. This feeling attains its highest expression in **"Saul,"** where the anthropomorphism so often apparent in the author's conception of God is justified by historic truth and ennobled by a sustained intensity of lyric emotion which has been rarely equalled and probably never surpassed. It is the outpouring of a passionate human friendship gradually raised by its own strength to the presentiment of a divine love manifest in the flesh, and to which in its final ecstasy the very life of nature becomes the throbbing of a mysterious and expectant joy. The love of love is the prevailing inspiration of all such of Mr. Browning's poems as even trench on religious subjects, and it often resolves itself into so earnest a plea for the divine nature and atoning mission of Christ, that we can scarcely retain the conviction that it is his heart, and not his mind, which accepts it. His romance of **Christmas Eve** presents itself as a genuine confession of Christian doctrine, and the poet is at least speaking in his own name, when he judges the German philosopher who has discarded the doctrine as still subject to its hopes and fears. Nevertheless, the poem proves nothing more than a sympathetic adoption of a certain point of view, and a speculative desire to reason it out; and as illogical as we must regard its attack on the consistent non-believer, so unanswerable appears to us the conviction it expresses of the religious uselessness of any conception of Christ falling short of literal belief. **Christmas Eve** is in every respect a striking manifestation of Mr. Browning's muse, for it combines, as does also its companion poem, his most earnest continuousness of thought with his most deliberate abruptness of expression. Its ideas and images succeed each other with the jolting rapidity of categorical enumeration, and though this manner is well calculated to convey the rugged realities of a Dissenter's meeting, it is singularly discordant with the impressions of the abating storm, and of the lunar rainbow, flinging its double arch across

the silent glories of the night; and with the gradual exaltation of soul and sense, in which the speaker finally realizes
the actual presence of Christ.

Mr. Browning is supposed to be taking refuge within the
outer door of a Dissenting Chapel on a rainy evening just
as the service is going to begin. The congregation, recruit-
ed from the slums of the neighbouring town, are hurrying
in one by one. The porch is four feet by two, the mat is
soaked, every new-comer who edges past flings a re-
proachful glance at the intruder; the flame of the one tal-
low candle shoots a fresh grimace at him at every opening
of the door. He thinks he had better go in; but within there
are smells and noises; the priest is all ranting irreverence,
the flock all snuffling self-satisfaction; and in a very short
time he plunges out into the pure air again. Alone, in the
silent night, the spirit of his dream changes: Christ stands
before him; repentant and beseeching he clings to the hem
of His garment, and is wafted first to St. Peter's at Rome,
where religion is smothered in ceremonial, and next to the
lecture-room of a German philosopher, where it is reasoned away by the received methods of historical criticism, and after following through a long course of reflection the successive phases of religious belief, he arrives at
the certainty that, however confused be the vision of
Christ, where His love is, there is the Life, and that the
more direct the revelation of that Love the deeper and
more vital its power,—and he awakens in the chapel,
which he had only left in a dream, with a quickened sense
of the presence among its humble inmates of a transforming spiritual joy, and a more patient appreciation of the
coarse medium of expression through which it finds its
way to their souls.

The originality of the thoughts contained in this poem lies
entirely in their minor developments, which so bare an
outline cannot even suggest; but *Easter Day,* which forms
the sequel to it, is in part the expression of an idea more
entirely Mr. Browning's own—the idea of the religious necessity of doubt. He enters with considerable subtlety into
the difficulties and conditions of belief, and proves, it appears to us with complete success, that an unqualified faith
would defeat its own ends, neutralizing the experiences of
the earthly existence by an overwhelming interest in the
heavenly, and that a state of expectancy equally removed
from the calmness of scientific conviction, and the indifference of scientific disbelief, is the essence of spiritual life.
We follow this doctrine with the more interest from its
congeniality to our prevailing impression of Mr. Browning's mind; we know how dear to his imagination are the
shifting lights, the varied groupings, the curiously blended
contrasts of subjective experience; how habitually it recoils from the rigidity of every external standard of truth;
and in this implied declaration that he adores in the possible Saviour rather the mystery and the message of love
than the revealing of an articulate Will, we see also the reserve under which his most dramatic defence of Christian
orthodoxy must have been conceived. *Easter Day* resolves
itself into a Vision of Judgment, in which the man who has
been blind to the workings of the spirit in the intellect and
in the flesh is threatened with spiritual death; he awakens
to a grateful consciousness that this terrible doom has not

gone out against him, that he may still go through the
world—

> Try, prove, reject, prefer;

still struggle to "effect his warfare."

In speaking of the religious poems, we cannot leave unnoticed **"A Death in the Desert,"** the finest of the *Dramatis
Personæ.* St. John the Evangelist has fled from persecution into a cavern of the desert, and there for sixty days
been at the point of death; but the care of the Disciples has
restored to him for a short space the power of speech, and
in a supreme effort of the expiring soul, he bears witness
to the presence of the revealed Love and to the coming
reign of Doubt, through which its deeper purposes shall
be attained. This slow and solemn extinction of the last living testimony to the mysterious truth already fading beneath the hand of time, brooded over by the silence of the
desert, yet sustained by the tender reverence of those who
watch at the head and feet and on either side of the dying
man, fanning the smouldering life into its last brief outburst of prophetic flame, forms a strangely impressive picture; and some of the lines, in which the poet has expressed
the clairvoyance of approaching death, have a very noble
and pathetic beauty. . . . (pp. 942-45)

Setting aside the points on which it necessarily reflects the
common ideas of Theism, or the common experience of rational minds, it appears to us not only that Mr. Browning's conception of the æsthetic and religious life is essentially imaginative and poetical, but that the analysing tendency which is so disturbing an element in his poetic genius is itself overborne and even conditioned by it; that his
writings, if not always inspired by poetic emotion, are invariably marked by that conception of life which distinguishes a poet from a pure thinker.

A thinker, as such, will always eliminate what is secondary or incidental from his general statement of a case.
With Mr. Browning, thus to simplify a question is to destroy it. The thinker merges the particular in the general;
Mr. Browning only recognizes the general under the conditions of the particular. The thinker sees unity in complexity; Mr. Browning is always haunted by the complexity of unity. It is true that a specious reasoner is often a narrow one, and that an excess of imagination is considered
synonymous with a deficiency of logic. But we cannot im-
pute narrowness of mind to one whose imaginative powers
are coextensive with life; and Mr. Browning's logical subtlety needs no vindication; that it rather works in a circle
than towards any definite issue is the strongest negative
proof of the presence of an opposing activity, and we believe that nothing short of a profound poetic bias could
possess such a power of opposition.

"I remember when Browning entered the drawing-room, with a quick light step; and on learning from me that my father was out, and in fact that nobody was at home but myself, he said: 'It's my birthday to-day; I'll wait till they come in,' and sitting down to the piano, he added: 'If it won't disturb you, I'll play till they do.' . . . He was then slim and dark, and very handsome; and—may I hint it—just a trifle of a dandy, addicted to lemon-coloured kid-gloves and such things: quite 'the glass of fashion and the mould of form.' But full of ambition, eager for success, eager for fame, and, what's more, determined to conquer fame and to achieve success."

—Miss Fox, a family friend, 1890

The dominant impression that all truth is a question of circumstance, and consequently all picturesque force a question of detail, explains Mr. Browning's every peculiarity of form and conception. It explains more or less directly everything that charms us in his writings and everything that repels us. His minutest works no less than the greatest, are each marked by a separate unity of image or idea, but this unity is the result of a multitude of details, no one of which can be isolated or suppressed. He evidently imitates the processes of nature, and strives at unity of effect through variety of means; and the principle is no doubt a sound one; but there is in his department of art a manifest obstacle to its application. He sees as a group of ideas what he can often only express as a series, and however he may endeavour to subordinate the parts to the whole, it is almost impossible that in his argumentative monologues he should always succeed in doing so; we do not think he does always succeed. Every successive reading of these works brings us nearer to their central inspiration, gives greater prominence to their leading idea, a more just subordination to their details; but we do not catch the inspiration at once, and it is natural that the minor facts and thoughts which its warmth has so closely transfused within the author's mind should drag themselves out in ours to a somewhat disjointed length, that the variety of proof should somewhat obscure the thing it is intended to prove. This minute elaboration of his ideas has done much, we are convinced, towards giving to Mr. Browning his reputation for the opposite defect of indistinctness in the statement of them. It is easy to mistake a strain on the attention for a strain on the understanding, and in his case the strain on the attention is the greater that, whilst he never condenses his thoughts, he habitually condenses his expression, and thus conveys to much of his argumentative writing the combined effect of abruptness and length. It is just to admit that, most of all on these occasions he stimulates his reader's mind, lashing it up to its task with the exhilarating energy of a March wind, but the sense of being driv-

en against an obstacle generally remains. We have the wind in our teeth.

From the same intellectual source arises the deeper sense of remoteness which he is so often said to convey. He never employs an ill-defined idea, or a vague or abstruse expression; but his belief in the complexity of apparently simple facts constantly shows itself in the forcing them into new relations, or extracting from them fresh results; and for one person who is capable of following out an abnormal process of thought, and recognizing its individual value and its relative truth, there are a hundred, not wanting in intellectual gifts, to whom it will remain unintelligible or unreal.

Proportionably great is the success of this realistic mode of treatment with all subjects of a pictorial or dramatic nature. The beauties of most of Mr. Browning's minor poems are generally known and appreciated, and it would be difficult to make a just selection from the great number of those which convey an idea, an image, or an emotion, through a succession of minute touches, each in itself a triumph of vivid fancy or incisive observation. The colossal power of *The Ring and the Book* lies less in the exposure of the various lights in which the same action may be regarded by a diversity of minds, than in the author's unlimited imaginative command of the minor circumstances and associations which individualize the same action for different minds. **"Red-cotton Nightcap Country"** exhibits, on a smaller scale, the value of descriptive minutiæ in producing a general effect; and though the poet in this case has had to deal with ready-made personages and events, he retains the credit of having recognized their artistic capabilities and done justice to them. He has not only presented to us the fact that a tragical eruption took place in the midst of an apparently peaceful atmosphere, but by dwelling on the smallest details of its repose he has created the idea of the calm which invites the storm, and the mental stagnation in which passions when once aroused rage unresisted. The story is told in a succession of *genre* pictures, and it is through the realistic accumulation of detail that we gather the ideal force of its catastrophe. In the monologue on the Tower, Mr. Browning has reversed the method, which he pursues with unimportant exceptions throughout the narrative, of presenting its incidents as an ordinary human witness would conceive them; and though we cannot desire to see omitted that part of the poem which contains almost all its pathos and some of its finest poetry, we think that if he had aimed at mere dramatic effect he would have omitted it. He would have left to fancy, speculation, and the balance of probabilities, what real life could explain in no other way; as it is, he has given to Mellerio's death the dramatic force of a prolonged preparation and a sudden fulfillment, but he could not resist the speculative pleasure of retracing its mental as well as its actual antecedents, and writing out the deed in the completed thought, which might impart to it a higher significance. His stand once taken *within* the man's mind, his habitual realism asserts itself, and he shows us by how simple a chain of everyday experience the human spirit may be raised to the white-heat of a supreme emotion. Setting aside the minor question of its perfect artistic consistency, we need only compare this monologue, in which thought, anxious and intense, is slowly quivering into deed, with the finest passages of **"Prince Hohenstiel-Schwangau,"** to feel how necessary is an emotional, and therefore a poetic subject, to the thorough display of Mr. Browning's genius. In no other is it just to itself. Philosophic discussions, which are mainly intended to prove the infinite refrangibility of truth, must sacrifice breadth to subtlety, and the large insight on which they are based has its only adequate expression in the full creativeness of poetic life. It is not as the "idle singer of an empty day," but it is as poet in the deepest sense of the word, that he has stirred the sympathies and stimulated the thought of the men and women of his generation.

It is of course one thing to accept this view of the essential quality of Mr. Browning's inspiration, and another to place him in any known category of poetic art; and the place he claims for himself as dramatic poet is open to dispute if we accept the word Drama in the usual sense of a thing enacted rather than thought out. He has written few plays; in the last, and not least remarkable of these, thought already preponderates over action, and the increasing tendency of his so-called dramatic poems to exhibit character in the condition of motive, excludes them from any definition of dramatic art which implies the presenting it in the form of act; but he is a dramatic writer in this essential respect, that his studies of thought and feeling invariably assume a concrete and individual form, and the reproach which has been so often addressed to him of making his personages, under a slight disguise, so many repetitions of himself, appears to us doubly unfounded. He is always himself, in so far that his mode of conception is recognizable in everything that he writes. But there never was a great artist with whom it was not so. . . . Mr. Browning has, it is true, a verbal language of his own, which is distinct from this finer manifestation of himself; a compound of colloquialisms half eccentric and half familiar, which must be congenial to him, first, because he has created it, and secondly, because he apparently makes opportunities for its employment. It has its strongest expression in parts of *The Ring and the Book,* to which it gives a flavour of mediæval coarseness not always inappropriate, but always unpleasing; and we find it in a modified form wherever he is either arguing or narrating from a point of view which we may imagine to be his own; but he never attributes this language to any person who would be by nature unlikely to use it. It is spoken in *The Ring and the Book* by the Roman lawyer and the Roman gossip, but it is not spoken by Pompilia in the outpourings of her pure young soul; nor by Capon Sacchi as he relates his first meeting with her, and the successive experiences which reveal to him, as in the vision of a dream, the depth, the pathos, and the poetry of life; nor by the Pope, as he ponders in solemn seclusion the precarious chances of human justice and the overwhelming obligations of eternal truth. Mr. Browning does not speak it himself, when he tells us how he stood in the balcony of Casa Guidi on one black summer night, "a busy human sense beneath his feet;" above the silent lightnings "dropping from cloud to cloud," and with his bodily eyes strained towards Arezzo and Rome, and his mental vision towards that long past Christmas Day, saw the course of the Francheschini tragedy unroll before him. To every actor in this

tragedy he has restored his distinctive existence, and not the least individual amongst them is the man in whom he has most strongly caricatured his own caprices of expression—Don Hyacinthus de Archangelis. He is so unpleasantly real, that, whilst we cannot imagine the history of the case as complete without a statement of the legal fictions that were brought to bear upon it, we scarcely understand Mr. Browning's impulse to clothe a mere representative of legal fiction in this very material form. We can only imagine that in his strong appreciation of the natural unfitness of things, he has found a fantastic pleasure in identifying the cause of the saturnine murderer with this kindly-natured old glutton, whose intellect elaborates the iniquities of the defence, whilst his whole consciousness is saturated with the anticipation of dinner, and the thought of the little fat son whose birth-day feast is to be held. The humanity of the characters in *The Ring and the Book* has, in fact, never been questioned, nor could we do more than allude to it in so merely suggestive a survey of the author's works; but we think there is one part of this extraordinary composition the dramatic importance of which has been somewhat overlooked—Count Guido's second speech. We might say its artistic importance, because this expression of the central figure of the poem gives to its widespreading structure a support which nothing else could give it; but it is the triumph of Mr. Browning's dramatic inspiration to have felt that this man alone was talking behind a mask; and that the mask must be torn off; and to have restored even to this villain in the torments of his last hour, in the hope which sickened into despair, and the despair which ran through every phase of rage, scorn, and entreaty, the sympathy which life even in its worst form commands from life. The concluding cry,

"Pompilia, will you let them murder me?"

has an almost terrifying power.

Not only are Mr. Browning's men and women complete after their kind; but as we have already said, he has impressed the fulness of individual character even on his descriptions of isolated mental states. Bishop Blougram has a quite different personality from the Legate Ogniben, though both are easy-going Churchmen, and one probably as convinced as the other that life in the flesh was given us to be enjoyed. Both are distinct from Fra Lippo Lippi, and all are equally so, from the Bishop who is ordering his tomb in St. Praxed's Church. Lippi is the most original of the four, in his mingled candour and cunning, his joyous worship of natural beauty, and his sensuality, as simple and shameless as that of a heathen god. But the last-mentioned Bishop is a mixed product of nature and circumstance, and as such even more powerfully conceived. He is not a genial satirist like the Legate, nor an artistic enthusiast like Lippi, nor a combination of cynic, sophist, and epicurean like Bishop Blougram; but a childish, irascible old man, with a conscience blunted by self-indulgence, and a mind warped by a life-long imprisonment in ceremonial religionism; a scholar, a sensualist, and, in his own narrow way, the greatest Pagan of them all. As Mr. Browning depicts him, he is lying very near his end, curiously imagining that he and his bed-clothes are turning to stone, and he is becoming his own effigy; and as fitful recollections of his past life blend with the thought of death and the presentiment of monumental state, all the luxurious materialism that is in him becomes centred in the details of his tomb. . . . There is something grotesquely pathetic in his petulant entreaties to the sons who inherit his wealth, to impose no stint on that magnificence; above all, not to defraud it of the lump of Lapis-lazuli of which he robbed the Church for that very purpose, and in the final surrender to the inevitable:

> "Well go! I bless ye. Fewer tapers there;
> But in a row; and going turn your backs
> —Ay, like departing altar ministrants,
> And leave me in my Church, the Church for
>   peace,
> That I may watch at leisure if he leers—
> Old Gandolf at me, from his onion stone,
> As still he envied me, so fair she was!"
>
> (pp. 945-51)

To the testimony of the Dramas we may add this fact, that at the age of twenty-two, Mr. Browning conceived from slender historic materials the character and career of Paracelsus—the apostle of natural truth, still hampered by the traditions of a metaphysical and mystical age; his high hopes and crushing disappointment; the lapse into more doubtful striving and more anomalous result; and the death-bed vision which blended the old, fitful gleamings of the secret of universal life into the larger sense of a divine presence throughout creation in which every abortive human endeavour is alike anticipated and subsumed. *Paracelsus* is considered the most transcendental of Mr. Browning's poems. It certainly combines the individuality which with him has so often the effect of abstruseness with a sustained loftiness of poetic conception, and we find in it a faithful reflex of the desire of absolute knowledge and the belief in the possibility of its attainment. . . . [Its] appreciation of the craving for unbounded intellectual life is even less abnormal as expressed by so young a poet, than the tribute it contains to the ideal of human existence which rests upon limitation.

> Power—neither put forth blindly, nor controlled
> Calmly by perfect knowledge; to be used
> At risk, inspired or checked by hope and fear:
> Knowledge—not intuition, but the slow
> Uncertain fruit of an enhancing toil,
> Strengthened by love: love—not serenely pure
> But strong from weakness like a chance-sown
>   plant
> Which, cast on stubborn soil, puts forth changed
>   buds
> And softer strains, unknown in happier climes;
> Love which endures and doubts, and is op-
>   pressed
> And cherished, suffering much and much sus-
>   tained,
> And blind, oft failing, yet believing love,
> A half-enlightened, often chequered trust.
>
> (pp. 963-64)

The one peculiarity of Mr. Browning's verse through which his character of poet is most generally impugned is its frequent want of melody, and his known contempt for melody as distinct from meaning would be sufficient to account for the occasional choice of subjects that excluded

it. But he thus admits the more fully the essential unity of matter and form; and the unmusical character of so much of his poetry is in some degree justified by the fact, that its subjects are in themselves unmusical.

> So I will sing on fast as fancies come;
> Rudely, the verse being as the mood it paints.
>   [*Pauline*]

His actual ruggedness lies far more in the organic conception of his ideas than in the manner of rendering them, whilst his rapid alternations and successions of thought often give the appearance of ruggedness where none is. In beauty or the reverse his style is essentially expressive, and when, as in *Pauline, Paracelsus,* almost all the Dramas, and most of the minor poems, there is an inward harmony to be expressed, it is expressed the more completely for the rejection of all such assistance as mere sound could afford. He has even given to so satirical a poem as **"The Bishop orders his Tomb in St. Praxed's Church,"** a completely melodious rhythm, its satire being borrowed from the simple misapplication of an earnest and pathetic emotion. If he ever appears gratuitously to rebel against the laws of sound it is in his rhymed and not in his blank verse; and there might be truth in the idea that his contempt for the music of mere iteration is excited by the very act of employing it, but that so many of his grandest and sweetest inspirations have been appropriately clothed in rhyme.

There is a passage in *Pauline* in which the speaker describes himself, which accords to so great an extent with the varying impressions produced by Mr. Browning's mind as to present itself as a possible explanation of them. He has deprecated, perhaps unnecessarily, the execution of this poem in an explanatory preface to it, and if he admitted it to contain so much of permanent truth he might more justly deprecate the manner in which it was conceived. But the lines to which we refer have a deliberate emphasis which impresses us with the idea that the young poet was speaking of himself, and that what he said may in some measure have remained true.

> I am made up of an intensest life,
> Of a most clear idea of consciousness
> Of self, distinct from all its qualities,
> From all affections, passions, feelings, powers;
> And thus far it exists, if tracked in all:
> But linked in me, to self-supremacy
> Existing, as a centre to all things,
> Most potent to create and rule and call
> Upon all things to minister to it;
> And to a principle of restlessness
> Which would be all, have, see, know, taste, feel,
>   all—
> This is myself, and I should thus have been
> Though gifted lower than the meanest soul.

Whatever this passage may or may not mean, it can only confirm the one significant fact that a life-long reputation for self-conscious poetic power might have rested unassailed on this the author's very earliest work. (pp. 964-65)

*A. Orr, "Mr. Browning's Place in Literature,"
in* Contemporary Review, *Vol. 23, May, 1874,
pp. 934-65.*

Algernon Charles Swinburne   (letter date 1875)

[A nineteenth-century English poet, dramatist, and critic, Swinburne was renowned during his lifetime for his skill and technical mastery as a lyric poet and is currently regarded as a preeminent symbol of rebellion against the prevailing moral orientation of Victorian aesthetics. In the excerpt below, Swinburne defends Browning against charges of obscurity, deeming his essay "the truest criticism . . . that has appeared on the subject."]

The charge of obscurity is perhaps of all charges the likeliest to impair the fame or to imperil the success of a rising or an established poet. It is as often misapplied by hasty or ignorant criticism as any other on the roll of accusations; and was never misapplied more persistently and perversely than to an eminent writer of our own time. The difficulty found by many in certain of Mr. Browning's works arises from a quality the very reverse of that which produces obscurity properly so called. Obscurity is the natural product of turbid forces and confused ideas; of a feeble and clouded or of a vigorous but unfixed and chaotic intellect. . . . Now if there is any great quality more perceptible than another in Mr. Browning's intellect it is his decisive and incisive faculty of thought, his sureness and intensity of perception, his rapid and trenchant resolution of aim. . . . He is something too much the reverse of obscure; he is too brilliant and subtle for the ready reader of a ready writer to follow with any certainty the track of an intelligence which moves with such incessant rapidity, or even to realize with what spider-like swiftness and sagacity his building spirit leaps and lightens to and fro and backward and forward as it lives along the animated line of its labour, springs from thread to thread and darts from centre to circumference of the glittering and quivering web of living thought woven from the inexhaustible stores of his perception and kindled from the inexhaustible fire of his imagination. He never thinks but at full speed; and the rate of his thought is to that of another man's as the speed of a railway to that of a waggon or the speed of a telegraph to that of a railway. It is hopeless to enjoy the charm or to apprehend the gist of his writings except with a mind thoroughly alert, an attention awake at all points, a spirit open and ready to be kindled by the contact of the writer's. To do justice to any book which deserves any other sort of justice than that of the fire or the waste-paper basket, it is necessary to read it in the fit frame of mind; and the proper mood in which to study for the first time a book of Mr. Browning's is the freshest, clearest, most active mood of the mind in its brightest and keenest hours of work. Read at such a time, and not 'with half-shut eyes falling asleep in a half-dream', it will be found (in [George] Chapman's phrase) 'pervial' enough to any but a sluggish or a sandblind eye; but at no time and in no mood will a really obscure writer be found other than obscure. The difference between the two is the difference between smoke and lightning; and it is far more difficult to pitch the tone of your thought in harmony with that of a foggy thinker than with that of one whose thought is electric in its motion. To the latter we have but to come with an open and pliant spirit, untired and undisturbed by the work or the idleness of the day, and we cannot but receive a vivid and active pleasure in following the swift and fine radiations,

the subtle play and keen vibration of its sleepless fires; and the more steadily we trace their course the more surely do we see that all these forked flashes of fancy and changing lights of thought move unerringly around one centre and strike straight in the end to one point. Only random thinking and random writing produce obscurity; and these are the radical faults of Chapman's style of poetry. We find no obscurity in the lightning, whether it play about the heights of metaphysical speculation or the depths of character and motive; the mind derives as much of vigorous enjoyment from the study by such light of the one as of the other. The action of so bright and swift a spirit gives insight as it were to the eyes and wings to the feet of our own; the reader's apprehension takes fire from the writer's, and he catches from a subtler and more active mind the infection of spiritual interest; so that any candid and clear-headed student finds himself able to follow for the time in fancy the lead of such a thinker with equal satisfaction on any course of thought or argument; when he sets himself to refute Renan through the dying lips of St. John or to try conclusions with Strauss in his own person, and when he flashes at once the whole force of his illumination full upon the inmost thought and mind of the most infamous criminal, a Guido Franceschini or a Louis Bonaparte, compelling the black and obscene abyss of such a spirit to yield up at last the secret of its profoundest sophistries, and let forth the serpent of a soul that lies coiled under all the most intricate and supple reasonings of self-justified and self-conscious crime. And thanks to this very quality of vivid spiritual illumination we are able to see by the light of the author's mind without being compelled to see with his eyes, or with the eyes of the living mask which he assumes for his momentary impersonation of saint or sophist, philosopher or malefactor; without accepting one conclusion, conceding one point, or condoning one crime. It is evident that to produce any such effect requires above all things brightness and decision as well as subtlety and pliancy of genius; and this is the supreme gift and distinctive faculty of Mr. Browning's mind. If indeed there be ever any likelihood of error in his exquisite analysis, he will doubtless be found to err rather through excess of light than through any touch of darkness. . . . (pp. 390-92)

Apart from his gift of moral imagination, Mr. Browning has in the supreme degree the qualities of a great debater or an eminent leading counsel; his finest reasoning has in its expression and development something of the ardour of personal energy and active interest which inflames the argument of a public speaker; we feel, without the reverse regret of Pope, how many a firstrate barrister or parliamentary tactician has been lost in this poet. The enjoyment that his best and most characteristic work affords us is doubtless far other than the delight we derive from the purest and highest forms of the lyric or dramatic art; there is a radical difference between the analyst and the dramatist, the pleader and the prophet; it would be clearly impossible for the subtle tongue which can undertake at once the apology and the anatomy of such motives as may be assumed to impel or to support a 'Prince Hohenstiel-Schwangau' on his ways of thought and action, ever to be touched with the fire which turns to a sword or to a scourge the tongue of a poet to whom it is given to utter as from Patmos or from Sinai the word that fills all the heaven of song with the lightnings and thunders of chastisement. But in place of lyric rapture or dramatic action we may profitably enjoy the unique and incomparable genius of analysis which gives to these special pleadings such marvellous life and interest as no other workman in that kind was ever or will ever again be able to give: we may pursue with the same sense of strenuous delight in a new exercise of intellect and interest the slender and luminous threads of speculation wound up into a clue with so fine a skill and such happy sleight of hand in *Fifine at the Fair* or the sixth book of *Sordello,* where the subtle secret of spiritual weakness in a soul of too various powers and too restless refinement is laid bare with such cunning strength of touch, condemned and consoled with such far-sighted compassion and regret. This last-named poem has been held especially liable to the charge which we have seen to be especially inapplicable to the general work of its author; but although the manner of its construction should not seem defensible, as to me I may confess that it does not, it would be an utter misuse of terms to find in obscurity of thought or language the cause of this perceptible defect. The point of difference was accurately touched by the exquisite critical genius of Coleridge when he defined the style of Persius as 'hard—not obscure:' for this is equally true in the main of the style of *Sordello;* only the hard metal is of a different quality and temper, as the intellect of the English thinker is far wider in its reach, far subtler in its action and its aim, than that of the Roman stoic. The error, if I may take on myself to indicate what I conceive to be the error, of style in *Sordello* is twofold; it is a composite style, an amalgam of irreconcilable materials that naturally refuse to coalesce; and, like a few of the author's minor poems, it is written at least partially in shorthand, which a casual reader is likely to mistake for cipher, and to complain accordingly that the key should be withheld from him. A curious light is thrown on the method of its composition by the avowal put forth in the dedication of a reissue of this poem, that since its first adventure on publicity the writer had added and had cancelled a notable amount of illustrative or explanatory matter, preferring ultimately to leave his work such a poem as the few must like, rather than such as the many might. Against this decision no one has a right to appeal; and there is doubtless much in the work as it stands that all imaginative thinkers and capable students of poetry most assuredly must regard with much more than mere liking; but when the reader is further invited to observe that the sole aim kept in sight, the sole object of interest pursued by the author was the inner study of an individual mind, the occult psychology of a single soul, the personal pathology of a special intelligence, he has a right to suggest that in that case there is too much, and in any other case there is not enough, of external illustration and the byplay of alien actions and passions which now serve only to perplex the scheme they ought to explain. If it was the author's purpose to give to his philosophic poem a background of historic action, to relieve against the broad mass and movement of outer life the solitary process of that inward and spiritual tragedy which was the main occupation of his mind and art, to set the picture of a human spirit in the frame of circumstances within which it may actually have been environed and

beset with offers of help, with threats and temptations, doubts and prospects and chances of the day it had on earth,—if this were his purpose, then surely there is not here enough of such relief to illustrate a design which there is more than enough of it to confuse. But if, as we are now obliged to assume, the author's purpose was studiously and strenuously to restrict within the limits of inner spiritual study the interest and the motive of his work, to concentrate our attention with his own upon the growth and the fortune, the triumph and the failure, the light and the darkness of this one human spirit, the soul of a man of genius fallen upon evil days and elect for great occasions and begirt with strange perplexities, then surely there is here far too much of external distraction and diversion for the reader's mind even to apprehend the issue, much less to comprehend the process, of this inner tragic action. The poem, in short, is like a picture in which the background runs into the foreground, the figures and the landscape confound each other for want of space and keeping, and there is no middle distance discernible at all. It is but a natural corollary to this general error that the body like the spirit of the poem, its form not less than its thought, should halt between two or three diverse ways, and that the style should too often come to the ground between two stools or more; being as it is neither a dramatic nor a narrative style, neither personal nor impersonal, neither lyric nor historic, but at once too much of all these and not enough of any. The result may be to the hasty reader no less repellent than the result of obscurity in thought or in style; but from identity of effect we are not to infer an identity of cause. The best parts of this poem also belong in substance always and sometimes in form to the class of monodramas or soliloquies of the spirit; a form to which the analytic genius of Mr. Browning leads him ever as by instinct to return, and in which alone it finds play for its especial faculties and security against its especial liabilities to error and confusion of styles; a security for want of which his lyric and dramatic writing is apt to be neither dramatic nor lyrical, simply because of the writer's natural and inevitable tendency to analysis, which, by the nature of things as well as by the laws of art, can only explain and express itself either through the method of direct exposition or in the form of elaborate mental monologue. The whole argument of the sixth book is monodramatic; and its counterpart is to be sought in the most dramatic and to me the most delightful passage of equal length in the poem, the magnificent soliloquy of Salinguerra in the fourth book, full of the subtle life and reality and pathos which the author, to speak truth as it seems to me, too generally fails to transfer from monologue into dialogue, to translate into the sensible action and passion of tragedy, or adequately to express in fullness and fitness of lyric form. The finest and most memorable parts of his plays not less than of his poems are almost always reducible in their essence to what I have called monodrama; and if cast into the mono-dramatic form common to all his later writings would have found a better if not a keener expression and left a clearer if not a deeper impression on the mind. . . . Even Chapman, from whom I may be thought to have wandered somewhat far in this inquiry as to what is or is not properly definable as obscurity, has in my judgment a sounder instinct of dramatic dialogue and movement than the illustrious writer who has carved out for himself in the second period of his career a new and better way to the end appointed by nature for the exercise of his highest powers: and Chapman was certainly not re- markable among the great men of his day for the specially dramatic bent of his genius.

I have dwelt thus long on a seemingly irrelevant and dis- cursive inquiry because I could discover no method so fit to explain the nature of the fault I cannot but find in the poet of whom I have to speak, as by contrast of his work with the work of another, upon whom this fault has been wrongly charged by the inaccurate verdict of hasty judges. In answer to these I have shown that the very essence of Mr. Browning's aim and method, as exhibited in the ripest fruits of his intelligence, is such as implies above all other things the possession of a quality the very opposite of ob- scurity—a faculty of spiritual illumination rapid and in- tense and subtle as lightning, which brings to bear upon its central object by way of direct and vivid illustration every symbol and every detail on which its light is flashed in passing. Thus in *Fifine* the illustration derived from a visionary retrospect of Venice, and in *Sordello* the superb and wonderful comparison of the mental action of a man who puts by for a season the memories in which he has indulged for a moment before turning again to the day's work, with that of a fugitive slave who thinks over in a pause of his flight and puts aside for more practical means of revenge the thought of enchantments 'sovereign to plague his enemies', as he buckles himself again to the grim business of escape—these and other such illustrative passages are not more remarkable for the splendour of their imaginative quality than for the aptness of their cun- ning application and the direct light reflected from them on the immediate argument which is penetrated and vivi- fied throughout by the insinuation and exploration of its radiance. (pp. 393-97)

> *Algernon Charles Swinburne, in an extract from a letter to Robert Browning on January 31, 1875, in* Browning: The Critical Heritage, *edited by Boyd Litzinger & Donald Smalley, 1970, pp. 390-97.*

Edward Dowden   (essay date 1887)

[*Dowden was an important nineteenth-century Irish critic who is best known for his Shakespearean criticism. In the excerpt below, first published in June 1887 in the* Fortnightly Review, *Dowden commends Browning's po- etry as an antidote to the spiritual maladies affecting his contemporaries.*]

If Mr. Arnold is the poet of our times who as poet could least resist *la maladie du siècle* in its subtler forms, he whose energy of heart and soul most absolutely rejects and repels its influence is Mr. Browning. To him this world ap- pears to be a palæstra in which we are trained and tested for other lives to come; it is a gymnasium for athletes. Ac- tion, passion, knowledge, beauty, science, art—these are names of some of the means and instruments of our train- ing and education. The vice of vices, according to his ethi- cal creed, is languor of heart, lethargy or faintness of spir- it, with the dimness of vision and feebleness of hand at-

tending such moral enervation. Which of us does not suf- fer now and again from a touch of spiritual paralysis? Mr. Browning's poetry, to describe it in a word, is a galvanic battery for the use of spiritual paralytics. At first the shock and the tingling frightened patients away; now they crowd to the physician and celebrate the cure. Which of us does not need at times that virtue should pass into him from a stronger human soul? To touch the singing robes of the author of **"Rabbi Ben Ezra"** and **"Prospice"** and **"The Grammarian's Funeral,"** is to feel an influx of new strength. We gain from Mr. Browning, each in his degree, some of that moral ardour and spiritual faith and vigour of human sympathy which make interesting to him all the commonplace, confused, and ugly portions of life, those portions of life which, grating too harshly on Mr. Mat- thew Arnold's sensitiveness, disturb his self-possession and trouble his lucidity, causing him often, in his verse, to turn away from this vulgar, distracting world to quiet- ism and solitude, or a refined self-culture that lacks the most masculine qualities of discipline. To preserve those spiritual truths which are most precious to him Mr. Brow- ning does not retreat, like the singer of *In Memoriam,* into the citadel of the heart; rather, an armed combatant, he makes a sortie into the world of worldlings and unbeliev- ers, and from among errors and falsehoods and basenesses and crimes, he captures new truths for the soul. It is not in calm meditation or a mystical quiet that the clearest perception of divine things come to him; it is rather through the struggle of the will, through the strife of pas- sion, and as much through foiled desire and defeated en- deavour as through attainment and success. For asceti- cism, in the sense of that word which signifies a maiming and marring of our complete humanity, Mr. Browning's doctrine of life leaves no place; but if asceticism mean he- roic exercise, the *askesis* of the athlete, the whole of human existence, as he conceives, is designed as a school of strenuous and joyous asceticism. 'Our human impulses towards knowledge, towards beauty, towards love,' it has been well said, 'are reverenced by him as the signs and to- kens of a world not included in that which meets the senses.' Therefore, he must needs welcome the whole ful- ness of earthly beauty, as in itself good, but chiefly pre- cious because it is a pledge and promise of beauty not par- tial and earthly, but in its heavenly plenitude. And how dare he seek to narrow or enfeeble the affections, when in all their errors and their never-satisfied aspirations, he dis- covers evidence of an infinite love, from which they pro- ceed and towards which they tend? Nor would he stifle any high ambition, for it is a wing to the spirit lifting man towards heights of knowledge or passion or power which rise unseen beyond the things of sense, heights on which man hereafter may attain the true fulfilment of his destiny. (pp. 499-500)

> *Edward Dowden, in an extract in* Browning: The Critical Heritage, *edited by Boyd Litz- inger and Donald Smalley, Barnes & Noble, Inc., 1970, pp. 499-500.*

Oscar Wilde   (essay date 1890)

[*Wilde was an Anglo-Irish dramatist, novelist, poet, crit-*

ic, essayist, and short story writer who is identified with the nineteenth-century "art for art's sake" movement. In the excerpt below, Wilde assesses Browning's literary stature, focusing his critique on the poet's language and method of characterization.]

The members of the Browning Society, like the theologians of the Broad Church Party, or the authors of Mr. Walter Scott's Great Writer's Series, seem to me to spend their time in trying to explain their divinity away. Where one had hoped that Browning was a mystic, they have sought to show that he was simply inarticulate. Where one had fancied that he had something to conceal, they have proved that he had but little to reveal. But I speak merely of his incoherent work. Taken as a whole, the man was great. He did not belong to the Olympians, and had all the incompleteness of the Titan. He did not survey, and it was but rarely that he could sing. His work is marred by struggle, violence, and effort, and he passed not from emotion to form, but from thought to chaos. Still, he was great. He has been called a thinker, and was certainly a man who was always thinking, and always thinking aloud; but it was not thought that fascinated him, but rather the processes by which thought moves. It was the machine he loved, not what the machine makes. The method by which the fool arrives at his folly was so dear to him as the ultimate wisdom of the wise. So much, indeed, did the subtle mechanism of mind fascinate him that he despised language, or looked upon it as an incomplete instrument of expression. Rhyme, that exquisite echo which in the Muse's hollow hill creates and answers its own voice; rhyme, which in the hands of a real artist becomes not merely a material element of metrical beauty, but a spiritual element of thought and passion also, waking a new mood, it may be, or stirring a fresh train of ideas, or opening by mere sweetness and suggestion of sound some golden door at which the Imagination itself had knocked in vain; rhyme, which can turn man's utterance to the speech of gods; rhyme, the one chord we have added to the Greek lyre, became in Robert Browning's hands a grotesque, misshapen thing, which made him at times masquerade in poetry as a low comedian, and ride Pegasus too often with his tongue in his cheek. There are moments when he wounds us by monstrous music. . . . Yet, he was great: and though he turned language into ignoble clay, he made from it men and women that live. He is the most Shakespearian creature since Shakespeare. If Shakespeare could sing with myriad lips, Browning could stammer through a thousand months. Even now, as I am speaking, and speaking not against him but for him, there glides through the room the pageant of his persons. There, creeps Fra Lippo Lippi with his cheeks still burning from some girl's hot kiss. There, stands dread Saul with the lordly male-sapphires gleaming in his turban. Mildred Tresham is there, and the Spanish monk, yellow with hatred, and Blougram, and the Rabbi Ben Ezra, and the Bishop of St. Praxed's. The spawn of Setebos gibbers in the corner, and Sebald, hearing Pippa pass by, looks on Ottima's haggard face, and loathes her and his own sin and himself. Pale as the white satin of his doublet, the melancholy king watches with dreamy treacherous eyes too loyal Strafford pass to his doom, and Andrea shudders as he hears the cousin's whistle in the garden, and bids his perfect wife go down.

Yes, Browning was great. And as what will he be remembered? As a poet? Ah, not as a poet! He will be remembered as a writer of fiction, as the most supreme writer of fiction, it may be, that we have ever had. His sense of dramatic situation was unrivalled, and, if he could not answer his own problems, he could at least put problems forth. Considered from the point of view of a creator of character he ranks next to him who made Hamlet. Had he been articulate he might have sat beside him. The only man living who can touch the hem of his garment is George Meredith. Meredith is a prose-Browning, and so is Browning. He used poetry as a medium for writing in prose. (pp. 524-26)

Oscar Wilde, "Oscar Wilde on Browning," in Browning: The Critical Heritage, *edited by Boyd Litzinger and Donald Smalley, 1970, pp. 524-26.*

George Santayana   (essay date 1900)

[*Santayana, who was a Spanish-born philosopher, poet, novelist, and literary critic, made an influential attack on Browning in his 1900 essay "The Poetry of Barbarism." In the following excerpt from that work, Santayana elaborates on his contention that Browning's genius was essentially barbaric in character by underscoring the irrationality and vulgarity of his approach to religious, philosophical, and artistic concerns.*]

If we would do justice to Browning's work as a human document, and at the same time perceive its relation to the rational ideals of the imagination and to that poetry which passes into religion, we must keep, as in the case of Whitman, two things in mind. One is the genuineness of the achievement, the sterling quality of the vision and inspiration; these are their own justification when we approach them from below and regard them as manifesting a more direct or impassioned grasp of experience than is given to mildly blatant, convention-ridden minds. The other thing to remember is the short distance to which this comprehension is carried, its failure to approach any finality, or to achieve a recognition even of the traditional ideals of poetry and religion.

In the case of Walt Whitman such a failure will be generally felt; it is obvious that both his music and his philosophy are those of a barbarian, nay, almost of a savage. Accordingly there is need of dwelling rather on the veracity and simple dignity of his thought and art, on their expression of an order of ideas latent in all better experience. But in the case of Browning it is the success that is obvious to most people. Apart from a certain superficial grotesqueness to which we are soon accustomed, he easily arouses and engages the reader by the pithiness of his phrase, the volume of his passion, the vigour of his moral judgment, the liveliness of his historical fancy. It is obvious that we are in the presence of a great writer, of a great imaginative force, of a master in the expression of emotion. What is perhaps not so obvious, but no less true, is that we are in the presence of a barbaric genius, of a truncated imagination, of a thought and an art inchoate and ill-digested, of a volcanic eruption that tosses itself quite blindly and ineffectually into the sky.

The points of comparison by which this becomes clear are perhaps not in every one's mind, although they are merely the elements of traditional culture, æsthetic and moral. Yet even without reference to ultimate ideals, one may notice in Browning many superficial signs of that deepest of all failures, the failure in rationality and the indifference to perfection. Such a sign is the turgid style, weighty without nobility, pointed without naturalness or precision. Another sign is the "realism" of the personages, who, quite like men and women in actual life, are always displaying traits of character and never attaining character as a whole. Other hints might be found in the structure of the poems, where the dramatic substance does not achieve a dramatic form; in the metaphysical discussion, with its confused prolixity and absence of result; in the moral ideal, where all energies figure without their ultimate purposes; in the religion, which breaks off the expression of this life in the middle, and finds in that suspense an argument for immortality. In all this, and much more that might be recalled, a person coming to Browning with the habits of a cultivated mind might see evidence of some profound incapacity in the poet; but more careful reflection is necessary to understand the nature of this incapacity, its cause, and the peculiar accent which its presence gives to those ideas and impulses which Browning stimulates in us.

There is the more reason for developing this criticism (which might seem needlessly hostile and which time and posterity will doubtless make in their own quiet and decisive fashion) in that Browning did not keep within the sphere of drama and analysis, where he was strong, but allowed his own temperament and opinions to vitiate his representation of life, so that he sometimes turned the expression of a violent passion into the last word of what he thought a religion. He had a didactic vein, a habit of judging the spectacle he evoked and of loading the passions he depicted with his visible sympathy or scorn.

Now a chief support of Browning's popularity is that he is, for many, an initiator into the deeper mysteries of passion, a means of escaping from the moral poverty of their own lives and of feeling the rhythm and compulsion of the general striving. He figures, therefore, distinctly as a prophet, as a bearer of glad tidings, and it is easy for those who hail him as such to imagine that, knowing the labour of life so well, he must know something also of its fruits, and that in giving us the feeling of existence, he is also giving us its meaning. There is serious danger that a mind gathering from his pages the raw materials of truth, the unthreshed harvest of reality, may take him for a philosopher, for a rationaliser of what he describes. Awakening may be mistaken for enlightenment, and the galvanising of torpid sensations and impulses for wisdom. (pp. 161-63)

The great dramatists have seldom dealt with perfectly virtuous characters. The great poets have seldom represented mythologies that would bear scientific criticism. But by an instinct which constituted their greatness they have cast these mixed materials furnished by life into forms congenial to the specific principles of their art, and by this transformation they have made acceptable in the æsthetic sphere things that in the sphere of reality were evil or im-

perfect: in a word, their works have been beautiful as works of art. Or, if their genius exceeded that of the technical poet and rose to prophetic intuition, they have known how to create ideal characters, not possessed, perhaps, of every virtue accidentally needed in this world, but possessed of what is ideally better, of internal greatness and perfection. They have also known how to select and reconstruct their mythology so as to make it a true interpretation of moral life. When we read the maxims of Iago, Falstaff, or Hamlet, we are delighted if the thought strikes us as true, but we are not less delighted if it strikes us as false. These characters are not presented to us in order to enlarge our capacities of passion nor in order to justify themselves as processes of redemption; they are there, clothed in poetry and imbedded in plot, to entertain us with their imaginable feelings and their interesting errors. The poet, without being especially a philosopher, stands by virtue of his superlative genius on the plane of universal reason, far above the passionate experience which he overlooks and on which he reflects; and he raises us for the moment to his own level, to send us back again, if not better endowed for practical life, at least not unacquainted with speculation.

With Browning the case is essentially different. When his heroes are blinded by passion and warped by circumstance, as they almost always are, he does not describe the fact from the vantage-ground of the intellect and invite us to look at it from that point of view. On the contrary, his art is all self-expression or satire. For the most part his hero, like Whitman's, is himself; not appearing, as in the case of the American bard, *in puris naturalibus,* but masked in all sorts of historical and romantic finery. Sometimes, however, the personage, like Guido in **The Ring and the Book** or the "frustrate ghosts" of other poems, is merely a Marsyas, shown flayed and quivering to the greater glory of the poet's ideal Apollo. The impulsive utterances and the crudities of most of the speakers are passionately adopted by the poet as his own. He thus perverts what might have been a triumph of imagination into a failure of reason.

This circumstance has much to do with the fact that Browning, in spite of his extraordinary gift for expressing emotion, has hardly produced works purely and unconditionally delightful. They not only portray passion, which is interesting, but they betray it, which is odious. His art was still in the service of the will. He had not attained, in studying the beauty of things, that detachment of the phenomenon, that love of the form for its own sake, which is the secret of contemplative satisfaction. Therefore, the lamentable accidents of his personality and opinions, in themselves no worse than those of other mortals, passed into his art. He did not seek to elude them: he had no free speculative faculty to dominate them by. Or, to put the same thing differently, he was too much in earnest in his fictions, he threw himself too unreservedly into his creations. His imagination, like the imagination we have in dreams, was merely a vent for personal preoccupations. His art was inspired by purposes less simple and universal than the ends of imagination itself. His play of mind consequently could not be free or pure. The creative impulse could not reach its goal or manifest in any notable degree its own organic ideal.

We may illustrate these assertions by considering Browning's treatment of the passion of love, a passion to which he gives great prominence and in which he finds the highest significance.

Love is depicted by Browning with truth, with vehemence, and with the constant conviction that it is the supreme thing in life. The great variety of occasions in which it appears in his pages and the different degrees of elaboration it receives, leave it always of the same quality—the quality of passion. It never sinks into sensuality; in spite of its frequent extreme crudeness, it is always, in Browning's hands, a passion of the imagination, it is always love. On the other hand it never rises into contemplation: mingled as it may be with friendship, with religion, or with various forms of natural tenderness, it always remains a passion; it always remains a personal impulse, a hypnotisation, with another person for its object or its cause. Kept within these limits it is represented, in a series of powerful sketches, which are for most readers the gems of the Browning gallery, as the last word of experience, the highest phase of human life. (pp. 163-65)

We are not allowed to regard these expressions as the cries of souls blinded by the agony of passion and lust. Browning unmistakably adopts them as expressing his own highest intuitions. He so much admires the strength of this weakness that he does not admit that it is a weakness at all. It is with the strut of self-satisfaction, with the sensation, almost, of muscular Christianity, that he boasts of it through the mouth of one of his heroes, who is explaining to his mistress the motive of his faithful services as a minister of the queen:

> She thinks there was more cause
> In love of power, high fame, pure loyalty?
> Perhaps she fancies men wear out their lives
> Chasing such shades. . . .
> I worked because I want you with my soul.

Readers of the fifth chapter of this volume need not be reminded here of the contrast which this method of understanding love offers to that adopted by the real masters of passion and imagination. They began with that crude emotion with which Browning ends; they lived it down, they exalted it by thought, they extracted the pure gold of it in a long purgation of discipline and suffering. The fierce paroxysm which for him is heaven, was for them the proof that heaven cannot be found on earth, that the value of experience is not in experience itself but in the ideals which it reveals. The intense, voluminous emotion, the sudden, overwhelming self-surrender in which he rests was for them the starting-point of a life of rational worship, of an austere and impersonal religion, by which the fire of love, kindled for a moment by the sight of some creature, was put, as it were, into a censer, to burn incense before every image of the Highest Good. Thus love ceased to be a passion and became the energy of contemplation: it diffused over the universe, natural and ideal, that light of tenderness and that faculty of worship which the passion of love often is first to quicken in a man's breast.

Of this art, recommended by Plato and practised in the Christian Church by all adepts of the spiritual life, Browning knew absolutely nothing. About the object of love he had no misgivings. What could the object be except somebody or other? The important thing was to love intensely and to love often. He remained in the phenomenal sphere: he was a lover of experience; the ideal did not exist for him. No conception could be farther from his thought than the essential conception of any rational philosophy, namely, that feeling is to be treated as raw material for thought, and that the destiny of emotion is to pass into objects which shall contain all its value while losing all its formlessness. This transformation of sense and emotion into objects agreeable to the intellect, into clear ideas and beautiful things, is the natural work of reason; when it has been accomplished very imperfectly, or not at all, we have a barbarous mind, a mind full of chaotic sensations, objectless passions, and undigested ideas. Such a mind Browning's was, to a degree remarkable in one with so rich a heritage of civilisation.

The nineteenth century . . . has nourished the hope of abolishing the past as a force while it studies it as an object; and Browning, with his fondness for a historical stage setting and for the gossip of history, rebelled equally against the Pagan and the Christian discipline. The "Soul" which he trusted in was the barbarous soul, the "Spontaneous Me" of his half-brother Whitman. It was a restless personal impulse, conscious of obscure depths within itself which it fancied to be infinite, and of a certain vague sympathy with wind and cloud and with the universal mutation. It was the soul that might have animated Attila and Alaric when they came down into Italy, a soul not incurious of the tawdriness and corruption of the strange civilisation it beheld, but incapable of understanding its original spirit; a soul maintaining in the presence of that noble, unappreciated ruin all its own lordliness and energy, and all its native vulgarity.

Browning, who had not had the education traditional in his own country, used to say that Italy had been his university. But it was a school for which he was ill prepared, and he did not sit under its best teachers. For the superficial ferment, the worldly passions, and the crimes of the Italian Renaissance he had a keen interest and intelligence. But Italy has been always a civilised country, and beneath the trappings and suits of civilisation which at that particular time it flaunted so gayly, it preserved a civilised heart to which Browning's insight could never penetrate. There subsisted in the best minds a trained imagination and a cogent ideal of virtue. Italy had a religion, and that religion permeated all its life, and was the background without which even its secular art and secular passions would not be truly intelligible. The most commanding and representative, the deepest and most appealing of Italian natures are permeated with this religious inspiration. A Saint Francis, a Dante, a Michael Angelo, breathe hardly anything else. Yet for Browning these men and what they represented may be said not to have existed. He saw, he studied, and he painted a decapitated Italy. His vision could not mount so high as her head.

One of the elements of that higher tradition which Browning was not prepared to imbibe was the idealisation of love. The passion he represents is lava hot from the crater, in no way moulded, smelted, or refined. He had no thought of subjugating impulses into the harmony of reason. He did not master life, but was mastered by it. Accordingly the love he describes has no wings; it issues in nothing. His lovers "extinguish sight and speech, each on each"; sense, as he says elsewhere, drowning soul. The man in the gondola may well boast that he can die; it is the only thing he can properly do. Death is the only solution of a love that is tied to its individual object and inseparable from the alloy of passion and illusion within itself. Browning's hero, because he has loved intensely, says that he has lived; he would be right, if the significance of life were to be measured by the intensity of the feeling it contained, and if intelligence were not the highest form of vitality. But had that hero known how to love better and had he had enough spirit to dominate his love, he might perhaps have been able to carry away the better part of it and to say that he could not die; for one half of himself and of his love would have been dead already and the other half would have been eternal, having fed—

> On death, that feeds on men;
> And death once dead, there's no more dying
> then.

The irrationality of the passions which Browning glorifies, making them the crown of life, is so gross that at times he cannot help perceiving it.

> How perplexed
> Grows belief! Well, this cold clay clod
> Was man's heart:
> Crumble it, and what comes next? Is it God?

Yes, he will tell us. These passions and follies, however desperate in themselves and however vain for the individual, are excellent as parts of the dispensation of Providence. . . . (pp. 166-69)

If we doubt, then, the value of our own experience, even perhaps of our experience of love, we may appeal to the interdependence of goods and evils in the world to assure ourselves that, in view of its consequences elsewhere, this experience was great and important after all. We need not stop to consider this supposed solution, which bristles with contradictions; it would not satisfy Browning himself, if he did not back it up with something more to his purpose, something nearer to warm and transitive feeling. The compensation for our defeats, the answer to our doubts, is not to be found merely in a proof of the essential necessity and perfection of the universe; that would be cold comfort, especially to so uncontemplative a mind. No: that answer, and compensation are to come very soon and very vividly to every private bosom. There is another life, a series of other lives, for this to happen in. (p. 170)

Into this conception of continued life Browning has put, as a collection of further passages might easily show, all the items furnished by fancy or tradition which at the moment satisfied his imagination—new adventures, reunion with friends, and even, after a severe strain and for a short while, a little peace and quiet. The gist of the matter is that we are to live indefinitely, that all our faults can be turned

to good, all our unfinished business settled, and that therefore there is time for anything we like in this world and for all we need in the other. It is in spirit the direct opposite of the philosophic maxim of regarding the end, of taking care to leave a finished life and a perfect character behind us. It is the opposite, also, of the religious *memento mori,* of the warning that the time is short before we go to our account. According to Browning, there is no account: we have an infinite credit. With an unconscious and characteristic mixture of heathen instinct with Christian doctrine, he thinks of the other world as heaven, but of the life to be led there as of the life of Nature.

Aristotle observes that we do not think the business of life worthy of the gods, to whom we can only attribute contemplation; if Browning had had the idea of perfecting and rationalising this life rather than of continuing it indefinitely, he would have followed Aristotle and the Church in this matter. But he had no idea of anything eternal; and so he gave, as he would probably have said, a filling to the empty Christian immortality by making every man busy in it about many things. And to the irrational man, to the boy, it is no unpleasant idea to have an infinite number of days to live through, an infinite number of dinners to eat, with an infinity of fresh fights and new love-affairs, and no end of last rides together.

But it is a mere euphemism to call this perpetual vagrancy a development of the soul. A development means the unfolding of a definite nature, the gradual manifestation of a known idea. A series of phases, like the successive leaps of a water-fall, is no development. And Browning has no idea of an intelligible good which the phases of life might approach and with reference to which they might constitute a progress. His notion is simply that the game of life, the exhilaration of action, is inexhaustible. You may set up your tenpins again after you have bowled them over, and you may keep up the sport for ever. The point is to bring them down as often as possible with a master-stroke and a big bang. That will tend to invigorate in you that self-confidence which in this system passes for faith. But it is unmeaning to call such an exercise heaven, or to talk of being "with God" in such a life, in any sense in which we are not with God already and under all circumstances. Our destiny would rather be, as Browning himself expresses it in a phrase which Attila or Alaric might have composed, "bound dizzily to the wheel of change to slake the thirst of God."

Such an optimism and such a doctrine of immortality can give no justification to experience which it does not already have in its detached parts. Indeed, those dogmas are not the basis of Browning's attitude, not conditions of his satisfaction in living, but rather overflowings of that satisfaction. The present life is presumably a fair average of the whole series of "adventures brave and new" which fall to each man's share; were it not found delightful in itself, there would be no motive for imagining and asserting that it is reproduced *in infinitum.* So too if we did not think that the evil in experience is actually utilised and visibly swallowed up in its good effects, we should hardly venture to think that God could have regarded as a good something which has evil for its condition and which is for that reason profoundly sad and equivocal. But Browning's philosophy of life and habit of imagination do not require the support of any metaphysical theory. His temperament is perfectly self-sufficient and primary; what doctrines he has are suggested by it and are too loose to give it more than a hesitant expression; they are quite powerless to give it any justification which it might lack on its face.

It is the temperament, then, that speaks; we may brush aside as unsubstantial, and even as distorting, the web of arguments and theories which it has spun out of itself. And what does the temperament say? That life is an adventure, not a discipline; that the exercise of energy is the absolute good, irrespective of motives or of consequences. These are the maxims of a frank barbarism; nothing could express better the lust of life, the dogged unwillingness to learn from experience, the contempt for rationality, the carelessness about perfection, the admiration for mere force, in which barbarism always betrays itself. The vague religion which seeks to justify this attitude is really only another outburst of the same irrational impulse.

In Browning this religion takes the name of Christianity, and identifies itself with one or two Christian ideas arbitrarily selected; but at heart it has far more affinity to the worship of Thor or of Odin than to the religion of the Cross. The zest of life becomes a cosmic emotion; we lump the whole together and cry, "Hurrah for the Universe!" A faith which is thus a pure matter of lustiness and inebriation rises and falls, attracts or repels, with the ebb and flow of the mood from which it springs. It is invincible because unseizable; it is as safe from refutation as it is rebellious to embodiment. But it cannot enlighten or correct the passions on which it feeds. Like a servile priest, it flatters them in the name of Heaven. It cloaks irrationality in sanctimony; and its admiration for every bluff folly, being thus justified by a theory, becomes a positive fanaticism, eager to defend any wayward impulse.

Such barbarism of temper and thought could hardly, in a man of Browning's independence and spontaneity, be without its counterpart in his art. When a man's personal religion is passive, as Shakespeare's seems to have been, and is adopted without question or particular interest from the society around him, we may not observe any analogy between it and the free creations of that man's mind. Not so when the religion is created afresh by the private imagination; it is then merely one among many personal works of art, and will naturally bear a family likeness to the others. The same individual temperament, with its limitations and its bias, will appear in the art which has appeared in the religion. And such is the case with Browning. His limitations as a poet are the counterpart of his limitations as a moralist and theologian; only in the poet they are not so regrettable. Philosophy and religion are nothing if not ultimate; it is their business to deal with general principles and final aims. Now it is in the conception of things fundamental and ultimate that Browning is weak; he is strong in the conception of things immediate. The pulse of the emotion, the bobbing up of the thought, the streaming of the reverie—these he can note down with picturesque force or imagine with admirable fecundity.

Yet the limits of such excellence are narrow, for no man can safely go far without the guidance of reason. His long poems have no structure—for that name cannot be given to the singular mechanical division of *The Ring and the Book.* Even his short poems have no completeness, no limpidity. They are little torsos made broken so as to stimulate the reader to the restoration of their missing legs and arms. What is admirable in them is pregnancy of phrase, vividness of passion and sentiment, heaped-up scraps of observation, occasional flashes of light, occasional beauties of versification,—all like

> the quick sharp scratch
> And blue spurt of a lighted match.

There is never anything largely composed in the spirit of pure beauty, nothing devotedly finished, nothing simple and truly just. The poet's mind cannot reach equilibrium; at best he oscillates between opposed extravagances; his final word is still a *boutade,* still an explosion. He has no sustained nobility of style. He affects with the reader a confidential and vulgar manner, so as to be more sincere and to feel more at home. Even in the poems where the effort at impersonality is most successful, the dramatic disguise is usually thrown off in a preface, epilogue or parenthesis. The author likes to remind us of himself by some confidential wink or genial poke in the ribs, by some little interlarded sneer. We get in these tricks of manner a taste of that essential vulgarity, that indifference to purity and distinction, which is latent but pervasive in all the products of this mind. The same disdain of perfection which appears in his ethics appears here in his verse, and impairs its beauty by allowing it to remain too often obscure, affected, and grotesque. (pp. 170-74)

The limits of Browning's art, like the limits of Whitman's, can therefore be understood by considering his mental habit. Both poets had powerful imaginations, but the type of their imaginations was low. In Whitman imagination was limited to marshalling sensations in single file; the embroideries he made around that central line were simple and insignificant. His energy was concentrated on that somewhat animal form of contemplation, of which, for the rest, he was a great, perhaps an unequalled master. Browning rose above that level; with him sensation is usually in the background; he is not particularly a poet of the senses or of ocular vision. His favourite subject-matter is rather the stream of thought and feeling in the mind; he is the poet of soliloquy. Nature and life as they really are, rather than as they may appear to the ignorant and passionate participant in them, lie beyond his range. Even in his best dramas, like *A Blot in the 'Scutcheon* or *Colombe's Birthday,* the interest remains in the experience of the several persons as they explain it to us. The same is the case in *The Ring and the Book,* the conception of which, in twelve monstrous soliloquies, is a striking evidence of the poet's predilection for this form.

The method is, to penetrate by sympathy rather than to portray by intelligence. The most authoritative insight is not the poet's or the spectator's, aroused and enlightened by the spectacle, but the various heroes' own, in their moment of intensest passion. We therefore miss the tragic relief and exaltation, and come away instead with the uncomfortable feeling that an obstinate folly is apparently the most glorious and choiceworthy thing in the world. This is evidently the poet's own illusion, and those who do not happen to share it must feel that if life were really as irrational as he thinks it, it would be not only profoundly discouraging, which it often is, but profoundly disgusting, which it surely is not; for at least it reveals the ideal which it fails to attain.

This ideal Browning never disentangles. For him the crude experience is the only end, the endless struggle the only ideal, and the perturbed "Soul" the only organon of truth. . . . His immersion in the forms of self-consciousness prevents him from dramatising the real relations of men and their thinkings to one another, to Nature, and to destiny. For in order to do so he would have had to view his characters from above (as Cervantes did, for instance), and to see them not merely as they appeared to themselves, but as they appear to reason. This higher attitude, however, was not only beyond Browning's scope, it was positively contrary to his inspiration. Had he reached it, he would no longer have seen the universe through the "Soul," but through the intellect, and he would not have been able to cry, "How the world is made for each one of us!" On the contrary, the "Soul" would have figured only in its true conditions, in all its ignorance and dependence, and also in its essential teachableness, a point against which Browning's barbaric wilfulness particularly rebelled. Rooted in his persuasion that the soul is essentially omnipotent and that to live hard can never be to live wrong, he remained fascinated by the march and method of self-consciousness, and never allowed himself to be weaned from that romantic fatuity by the energy of rational imagination, which prompts us not to regard our ideas as mere filling of a dream, but rather to build on them the conception of permanent objects and overruling principles, such as Nature, society, and the other ideals of reason. A full-grown imagination deals with these things, which do not obey the laws of psychological progression, and cannot be described by the methods of soliloquy.

[We thus see that Browning's sphere, though more subtle and complex than Whitman's, was still elementary. It lay far below the spheres of social and historical reality in which Shakespeare moved; far below the comprehensive and cosmic sphere of every great epic poet. Browning did not even reach the intellectual plane of such contemporary poets as Tennyson and Matthew Arnold, who, whatever may be thought of their powers, did not study consciousness for itself, but for the sake of its meaning and of the objects which it revealed. The best things that come into a man's consciousness are the things that take him out of it—the rational things that are independent of his personal perception and of his personal existence. These he approaches with his reason, and they, in the same measure, endow him with their immortality. But precisely these things—the objects of science and of the constructive imagination—Browning always saw askance, in the outskirts of his field of vision, for his eye was fixed and riveted on the soliloquising Soul. And this Soul being, to his apprehension, irrational, did not give itself over to those permanent objects which might otherwise have occupied it, but ruminated on its own accidental emotions, on its love-

affairs, and on its hopes of going on so ruminating for ever. (pp. 175-77)

In every imaginative sphere the nineteenth century has been an era of chaos, as it has been an era of order and growing organisation in the spheres of science and of industry. An ancient doctrine of the philosophers asserts that to chaos the world must ultimately return. And what is perhaps true of the cycles of cosmic change is certainly true of the revolutions of culture. Nothing lasts for ever: languages, arts, and religions disintegrate with time. Yet the perfecting of such forms is the only criterion of progress; the destruction of them the chief evidence of decay. Perhaps fate intends that we should have, in our imaginative decadence, the consolation of fancying that we are still progressing, and that the disintegration of religion and the arts is bringing us nearer to the protoplasm of sensation and passion. If energy and actuality are all that we care for, chaos is as good as order, and barbarism as good as discipline—better, perhaps, since impulse is not then restrained within any bounds of reason or beauty. But if the powers of the human mind are at any time adequate to the task of digesting experience, clearness and order inevitably supervene. The moulds of thought are imposed upon Nature, and the conviction of a definite truth arises together with the vision of a supreme perfection. It is only at such periods that the human animal vindicates his title of rational. If such an epoch should return, people will no doubt retrace our present gropings with interest and see in them gradual approaches to their own achievement. Whitman and Browning might well figure then as representatives of our time. For the merit of being representative cannot be denied them. The mind of our age, like theirs, is choked with materials, emotional, and inconclusive. They merely aggravate our characteristics, and their success with us is due partly to their own absolute strength and partly to our common weakness. If once, however, this imaginative weakness could be overcome, and a form found for the crude matter of experience, men might look back from the height of a new religion and a new poetry upon the present troubles of the spirit; and perhaps even these things might then be pleasant to remember. (pp. 177-78)

George Santayana, "The Poetry of Barbarism," in his Essays in Literary Criticism, *Charles Scribner's Sons, 1956, pp. 149-78.*

G. K. Chesterton   (essay date 1903)

[*Chesterton was one of England's most prominent and colorful writers during the early twentieth century. Although he is best known today as a detective novelist and essayist, he was also an eminent literary critic. In the following commentary, Chesterton defends Browning against his detractors, emphasising his innovativeness with respect to poetic form and attempting to vindicate the grotesque elements in his work.*]

Mr. William Sharp, in his *Life* of Browning, quotes the remarks of another critic to the following effect: "The poet's processes of thought are scientific in their precision and analysis; the sudden conclusion that he imposes upon them is transcendental and inept."

This is a very fair but a very curious example of the way in which Browning is treated. For what is the state of affairs? A man publishes a series of poems, vigorous, perplexing, and unique. The critics read them, and they decide that he has failed as a poet, but that he is a remarkable philosopher and logician. They then proceed to examine his philosophy, and show with great triumph that it is unphilosophical, and to examine his logic and show with great triumph that it is not logical, but "transcendental and inept." In other words, Browning is first denounced for being a logician and not a poet, and then denounced for insisting on being a poet when they have decided that he is to be a logician. It is just as if a man were to say first that a garden was so neglected that it was only fit for a boys' playground, and then complain of the unsuitability in a boys' playground of rockeries and flower-beds.

As we find, after this manner, that Browning does not act satisfactorily as that which we have decided that he shall be—a logician—it might possibly be worth while to make another attempt to see whether he may not, after all, be more valid than we thought as to what he himself professed to be—a poet. And if we study this seriously and sympathetically, we shall soon come to a conclusion. It is a gross and complete slander upon Browning to say that his processes of thought are scientific in their precision and analysis. They are nothing of the sort; if they were, Browning could not be a good poet. The critic speaks of the conclusions of a poem as "transcendental and inept"; but the conclusions of a poem, if they are not transcendental, must be inept. Do the people who call one of Browning's poems scientific in its analysis realise the meaning of what they say? One is tempted to think that they know a scientific analysis when they see it as little as they know a good poem. The one supreme difference between the scientific method and the artistic method is, roughly speaking, simply this—that a scientific statement means the same thing wherever and whenever it is uttered, and that an artistic statement means something entirely different, according to the relation in which it stands to its surroundings. The remark, let us say, that the whale is a mammal, or the remark that sixteen ounces go to a pound, is equally true, and means exactly the same thing whether we state it at the beginning of a conversation or at the end, whether we print it in a dictionary or chalk it up on a wall. But if we take some phrase commonly used in the art of literature—such a sentence, for the sake of example, as "the dawn was breaking"—the matter is quite different. If the sentence came at the beginning of a short story, it might be a mere descriptive prelude. If it were the last sentence in a short story, it might be poignant with some peculiar irony or triumph. Can any one read Browning's great monologues and not feel that they are built up like a good short story, entirely on this principle of the value of language arising from its arrangement? Take such an example as **"Caliban upon Setebos,"** a wonderful poem designed to describe the way in which a primitive nature may at once be afraid of its gods and yet familiar with them. Caliban in describing his deity starts with a more or less natural and obvious parallel between the deity and himself, carries out the comparison with consistency and an almost revolting simplicity, and ends in a kind of blasphemous extravaganza of anthropomorphism, basing his

conduct not merely on the greatness and wisdom, but also on the manifest weaknesses and stupidities of the Creator of all things. Then suddenly a thunderstorm breaks over Caliban's island, and the profane speculator falls flat upon his face—

> Lo! 'Lieth flat and loveth Setebos!
> 'Maketh his teeth meet through his upper lip,
> Will let those quails fly, will not eat this month
> One little mass of whelks, so he may 'scape!

Surely it would be very difficult to persuade oneself that this thunderstorm would have meant exactly the same thing if it had occurred at the beginning of **"Caliban upon Setebos."** It does not mean the same thing, but something very different; and the deduction from this is the curious fact that Browning is an artist, and that consequently his processes of thought are not "scientific in their precision and analysis."

No criticism of Browning's poems can be vital, none in the face of the poems themselves can be even intelligible which is not based upon the fact that he was successfully or otherwise a conscious and deliberate artist. He may have failed as an artist, though I do not think so; that is quite a different matter. But it is one thing to say that a man through vanity or ignorance has built an ugly cathedral, and quite another to say that he built it in a fit of absence of mind, and did not know whether he was building a lighthouse or a first-class hotel. Browning knew perfectly well what he was doing; and if the reader does not like his art, at least the author did. The general sentiment expressed in the statement that he did not care about form is simply the most ridiculous criticism that could be conceived. It would be far nearer the truth to say that he cared more for form than any other English poet who ever lived. He was always weaving and modelling and inventing new forms. Among all his two hundred to three hundred poems it would scarcely be an exaggeration to say that there are half as many different metres as there are different poems.

The great English poets who are supposed to have cared more for form than Browning did, cared less at least in this sense—that they were content to use old forms so long as they were certain that they had new ideas. Browning, on the other hand, no sooner had a new idea than he tried to make a new form to express it. Wordsworth and Shelley were really original poets; their attitude of thought and feeling marked without doubt certain great changes in literature and philosophy. Nevertheless, the "Ode on the Intimations of Immortality" is a perfectly normal and traditional ode, and "Prometheus Unbound" is a perfectly genuine and traditional Greek lyrical drama. But if we study Browning honestly, nothing will strike us more than that he really created a large number of quite novel and quite admirable artistic forms. It is too often forgotten what and how excellent these were. *The Ring and the Book,* for example, is an illuminating departure in literary method— the method of telling the same story several times and trusting to the variety of human character to turn it into several different and equally interesting stories. *Pippa Passes,* to take another example, is a new and most fruitful form, a series of detached dramas connected only by the presence of one fugitive and isolated figure. The invention of these things is not merely like the writing of a good poem—it is something like the invention of the sonnet or the Gothic arch. The poet who makes them does not merely create himself—he creates other poets. It is so in a degree long past enumeration with regard to Browning's smaller poems. Such a pious and horrible lyric as **"The Heretic's Tragedy,"** for instance, is absolutely original, with its weird and almost bloodcurdling echo verses, mocking echoes indeed—

> And clipt of his wings in Paris square,
> They bring him now to be burned alive.
> [*And wanteth there grace of lute or clavicithern,*
> *ye shall say to confirm him who singeth—*
> We bring John now to be burned alive.

A hundred instances might, of course, be given. Milton's "Sonnet on his Blindness," or Keats' "Ode on a Grecian Urn," are both thoroughly original, but still we can point to other such sonnets and other such odes. But can any one mention any poem of exactly the same structural and literary type as **"Fears and Scruples,"** as **"The Householder,"** as **"House"** or **"Shop,"** as **"Nationality in Drinks,"** as **"Sibrandus Schafnaburgensis,"** as **"My Star,"** as **"A Portrait,"** as any of **"Ferishtah's Fancies,"** as any of the **"Bad Dreams."**

The thing which ought to be said about Browning by those who do not enjoy him is simply that they do not like his form; that they have studied the form, and think it a bad form. If more people said things of this sort, the world of criticism would gain almost unspeakably in clarity and common honesty. Browning put himself before the world as a good poet. Let those who think he failed call him a bad poet, and there will be an end of the matter. There are many styles in art which perfectly competent æsthetic judges cannot endure. For instance, it would be perfectly legitimate for a strict lover of Gothic to say that one of the monstrous rococo altar-pieces in the Belgian churches with bulbous clouds and oaken sun-rays seven feet long, was, in his opinion, ugly. But surely it would be perfectly ridiculous for any one to say that it had no form. A man's actual feelings about it might be better expressed by saying that it had too much. To say that Browning was merely a thinker because you think **"Caliban upon Setebos"** ugly, is precisely as absurd as it would be to call the author of the old Belgian altar-piece a man devoted only to the abstractions of religion. The truth about Browning is not that he was indifferent to technical beauty, but that he invented a particular kind of technical beauty to which any one else is free to be as indifferent as he chooses. (pp. 133-38)

Browning has suffered far more injustice from his admirers than from his opponents, for his admirers have for the most part got hold of the matter, so to speak, by the wrong end. They believe that what is ordinarily called the grotesque style of Browning was a kind of necessity boldly adopted by a great genius in order to express novel and profound ideas. But this is an entire mistake. What is called ugliness was to Browning not in the least a necessary evil, but a quite unnecessary luxury, which he enjoyed for its own sake. For reasons that we shall see presently

in discussing the philosophical use of the grotesque, it did so happen that Browning's grotesque style was very suitable for the expression of his peculiar moral and metaphysical view. But the whole mass of poems will be misunderstood if we do not realise first of all that he had a love of the grotesque of the nature of art for art's sake. Here, for example, is a short distinct poem merely descriptive of one of those elfish German jugs in which it is to be presumed Tokay had been served to him. This is the whole poem, and a very good poem too—

> Up jumped Tokay on our table,
> Like a pigmy castle-warder,
> Dwarfish to see, but stout and able,
> Arms and accoutrements all in order;
> And fierce he looked North, then, wheeling South
> Blew with his bugle a challenge to Drouth,
> Cocked his flap-hat with the tosspot-feather,
> Twisted his thumb in his red moustache,
> Jingled his huge brass spurs together,
> Tightened his waist with its Buda sash,
> And then, with an impudence nought could abash,
> Shrugged his hump-shoulder, to tell the beholder,
> For twenty such knaves he would laugh but the bolder:
> And so, with his sword-hilt gallantly jutting,
> And dexter-hand on his haunch abutting,
> Went the little man, Sir Ausbruch, strutting!

I suppose there are Browning students in existence who would think that this poem contained something pregnant about the Temperance question, or was a marvellously subtle analysis of the romantic movement in Germany. But surely to most of us it is sufficiently apparent that Browning was simply fashioning a ridiculous knick-knack, exactly as if he were actually moulding one of these preposterous German jugs. Now before studying the real character of this Browningesque style, there is one general truth to be recognised about Browning's work. It is this— that it is absolutely necessary to remember that Browning had, like every other poet, his simple and indisputable failures, and that it is one thing to speak of the badness of his artistic failures, and quite another thing to speak of the badness of his artistic aim. Browning's style may be a good style, and yet exhibit many examples of a thoroughly bad use of it. On this point there is indeed a singularly unfair system of judgment used by the public towards the poets. It is very little realised that the vast majority of great poets have written an enormous amount of very bad poetry. The unfortunate Wordsworth is generally supposed to be almost alone in this; but any one who thinks so can scarcely have read a certain number of the minor poems of Byron and Shelley and Tennyson.

Now it is only just to Browning that his more uncouth effusions should not be treated as masterpieces by which he must stand or fall, but treated simply as his failures. It is really true that such a line as

> Irks fear the crop-full bird, frets doubt the maw-
> crammed beast?

is a very ugly and a very bad line. But it is quite equally true that Tennyson's

> And that good man, the clergyman, has told me
>   words of peace,

is a very ugly and a very bad line. But people do not say that this proves that Tennyson was a mere crabbed controversialist and metaphysician. They say that it is a bad example of Tennyson's form; they do not say that it is a good example of Tennyson's indifference to form. Upon the whole, Browning exhibits far fewer instances of this failure in his own style than any other of the great poets, with the exception of one or two like Spenser and Keats, who seem to have a mysterious incapacity for writing bad poetry. But almost all original poets, particularly poets who have invented an artistic style, are subject to one most disastrous habit—the habit of writing imitations of themselves. Every now and then in the works of the noblest classical poets you will come upon passages which read like extracts from an American book of parodies. Swinburne, for example, when he wrote the couplet—

> From the lilies and languors of virtue
> To the raptures and roses of vice,

wrote what is nothing but a bad imitation of himself, an imitation which seems indeed to have the wholly unjust and uncritical object of proving that the Swinburnian melody is a mechanical scheme of initial letters. Or again, Mr. Rudyard Kipling when he wrote the line—

> Or ride with the reckless seraphim on the rim of
>   a red-maned star,

was caricaturing himself in the harshest and least sympathetic spirit of American humour. This tendency is, of course, the result of self-consciousness and theatricality of modern life in which each of us is forced to conceive ourselves as part of a *dramatis personæ* and act perpetually in character. Browning sometimes yielded to this temptation to be a great deal too like himself.

> Will I widen thee out till thou turnest
> From Margaret Minnikin mou' by God's grace,
> To Muckle-mouth Meg in good earnest.

This sort of thing is not to be defended in Browning any more than in Swinburne. But, on the other hand, it is not to be attributed in Swinburne to a momentary exaggeration, and in Browning to a vital æsthetic deficiency. In the case of Swinburne, we all feel that the question is not whether that particular preposterous couplet about lilies and roses redounds to the credit of the Swinburnian style, but whether it would be possible in any other style than the Swinburnian to have written the Hymn to Proserpine. In the same way, the essential issue about Browning as an artist is not whether he, in common with Byron, Wordsworth, Shelley, Tennyson, and Swinburne, sometimes wrote bad poetry, but whether in any other style except Browning's you could have achieved the precise artistic effect which is achieved by such incomparable lyrics as **"The Patriot"** or **"The Laboratory."** The answer must be in the negative, and in that answer lies the whole justification of Browning as an artist.

The question now arises, therefore, what was his concep-

tion of his functions as an artist? We have already agreed that his artistic originality concerned itself chiefly with the serious use of the grotesque. It becomes necessary, therefore, to ask what is the serious use of the grotesque, and what relation does the grotesque bear to the eternal and fundamental elements in life?

One of the most curious things to notice about popular æsthetic criticism is the number of phrases it will be found to use which are intended to express an æsthetic failure, and which express merely an æsthetic variety. Thus, for instance, the traveller will often hear the advice from local lovers of the picturesque, "The scenery round such and such a place has no interest; it is quite flat." . . . Flatness is a sublime quality in certain landscapes, just as rockiness is a sublime quality in others. In the same way there are a great number of phrases commonly used in order to disparage such writers as Browning which do not in fact disparage, but merely describe them. One of the most distinguished of Browning's biographers and critics says of him, for example, "He has never meant to be rugged, but has become so in striving after strength." To say that Browning never tried to be rugged is like saying that Edgar Allan Poe never tried to be gloomy, or that Mr. W. S. Gilbert never tried to be extravagant. The whole issue depends upon whether we realise the simple and essential fact that ruggedness is a mode of art like gloominess or extravagance. Some poems ought to be rugged, just as some poems ought to be smooth. When we see a drift of stormy and fantastic clouds at sunset, we do not say that the cloud is beautiful although it is ragged at the edges. When we see a gnarled and sprawling oak, we do not say that it is fine although it is twisted. When we see a mountain, we do not say that it is impressive although it is rugged, nor do we say apologetically that it never meant to be rugged, but became so in its striving after strength. Now, to say that Browning's poems, artistically considered, are fine although they are rugged, is quite as absurd as to say that a rock, artistically considered, is fine although it is rugged. Ruggedness being an essential quality in the universe, there is that in man which responds to it as to the striking of any other chord of the eternal harmonies. As the children of nature, we are akin not only to the stars and flowers, but also to the toadstools and the monstrous tropical birds. And it is to be repeated as the essential of the question that on this side of our nature we do emphatically love the form of the toadstools, and not merely some complicated botanical and moral lessons which the philosopher may draw from them. For example, just as there is such a thing as a poetical metre being beautifully light or beautifully grave and haunting, so there is such a thing as a poetical metre being beautifully rugged. In the old ballads, for instance, every person of literary taste will be struck by a certain attractiveness in the bold, varying, irregular verse—

> He is either himsel' a devil frae hell,
> Or else his mother a witch maun be;
> I wadna have ridden that wan water
> For a' the gowd in Christentie,

is quite as pleasing to the ear in its own way as

There's a bower of roses by Bendermeer stream,
And the nightingale sings in it all the night long,

is in another way. Browning had an unrivalled ear for this
particular kind of staccato music. The absurd notion that
he had no sense of melody in verse is only possible to people who think that there is no melody in verse which is not
an imitation of Swinburne. To give a satisfactory idea of
Browning's rhythmic originality would be impossible
without quotations more copious than entertaining. But
the essential point has been suggested.

> They were purple of raiment and golden,
> Filled full of thee, fiery with wine,
> Thy lovers in haunts unbeholden,
> In marvellous chambers of thine,

is beautiful language, but not the only sort of beautiful language. This, for instance, has also a tune in it—

> I—"next poet." No, my hearties,
> I nor am, nor fain would be!
> Choose your chiefs and pick your parties,
> Not one soul revolt to me!
>
> (pp. 139-46)

This quick, gallantly stepping measure also has its own
kind of music, and the man who cannot feel it can never
have enjoyed the sound of soldiers marching by. This,
then, roughly is the main fact to remember about Browning's poetical method, or about any one's poetical method—that the question is not whether that method is the
best in the world, but the question whether there are not
certain things which can only be conveyed by that method. It is perfectly true, for instance, that a really lofty and
lucid line of Tennyson, such as—

> Thou wert the highest, yet most human too,

and

> We needs must love the highest when we see it,

would really be made the worse for being translated into
Browning. It would probably become

> High's human; man loves best, best visible,

and would lose its peculiar clarity and dignity and courtly
plainness. But it is quite equally true that any really characteristic fragment of Browning, if it were only the tem-
pestuous scolding of the organist in **"Master Hugues of
Saxe-Gotha"**—

> Hallo, you sacristan, show us a light there!
>   Down it dips, gone like a rocket.
> What, you want, do you, to come unawares,
> Sweeping the church up for first morning-
>   prayers,
> And find a poor devil has ended his cares
> At the foot of your rotten-runged rat-riddled
>   stairs?
>   Do I carry the moon in my pocket?

—it is quite equally true that this outrageous gallop of
rhymes ending with a frantic astronomical image would
lose in energy and spirit if it were written in a conventional
and classical style, and ran—

> What must I deem then that thou dreamest to
>   find

Disjected bones adrift upon the stair
Thou sweepest clean, or that thou deemest that
    I
Pouch in my wallet the vice-regal sun?

Is it not obvious that this statelier version might be excellent poetry of its kind, and yet would be bad exactly in so
far as it was good; that it would lose all the swing, the rush,
the energy of the preposterous and grotesque original? In
fact, we may see how unmanageable is this classical treatment of the essentially absurd in Tennyson himself. The
humorous passages in *The Princess,* though often really
humorous in themselves, always appear forced and feeble
because they have to be restrained by a certain metrical
dignity, and the mere idea of such restraint is incompatible
with humour. If Browning had written the passage which
opens *The Princess,* descriptive of the "larking" of the villagers in the magnate's park, he would have spared us
nothing; he would not have spared us the shrill uneducat-
ed voices and the unburied bottles of ginger beer. He
would have crammed the poem with uncouth similes; he
would have changed the metre a hundred times; he would
have broken into doggerel and into rhapsody; but he
would have left, when all is said and done, as he leaves in
that paltry fragment of the grumbling organist, the impression of a certain eternal human energy. Energy and
joy, the father and the mother of the grotesque, would
have ruled the poem. (pp. 146-48)

To ask why Browning enjoyed this perverse and fantastic
style most would be to go very deep into his spirit indeed,
probably a great deal deeper than it is possible to go. But
it is worth while to suggest tentatively the general function
of the grotesque in art generally and in his art in particular. There is one very curious idea into which we have been
hypnotised by the more eloquent poets, and that is that nature in the sense of what is ordinarily called the country
is a thing entirely stately and beautiful as those terms are
commonly understood. The whole world of the fantastic,
all things top-heavy, lop-sided, and nonsensical are conceived as the work of man, gargoyles, German jugs, Chinese pots, political caricatures, burlesque epics, the pictures of Mr. Aubrey Beardsley and the puns of Robert
Browning. But in truth a part, and a very large part, of the
sanity and power of nature lies in the fact that out of her
comes all this instinct of caricature. Nature may present
itself to the poet too often as consisting of stars and lilies;
but these are not poets who live in the country; they are
men who go to the country for inspiration and could no
more live in the country than they could go to bed in Westminster Abbey. Men who live in the heart of nature, farmers and peasants, know that nature means cows and pigs,
and creatures more humorous than can be found in a
whole sketch-book of Callot. And the element of the grotesque in art, like the element of the grotesque in nature,
means, in the main, energy, the energy which takes its own
forms and goes its own way. Browning's verse, in so far
as it is grotesque, is not complex or artificial; it is natural
and in the legitimate tradition of nature. The verse sprawls
like the trees, dances like the dust; it is ragged like the
thunder-cloud, it is top-heavy, like the toadstool. Energy
which disregards the standard of classical art is in nature
as it is in Browning. The same sense of the uproarious

force in things which makes Browning dwell on the oddity of a fungus or a jellyfish makes him dwell on the oddity of a philosophical idea. Here, for example, we have a random instance from **"The Englishman in Italy"** of the way in which Browning, when he was most Browning, regarded physical nature.

> And pitch down his basket before us,
>   All trembling alive
> With pink and gray jellies, your sea-fruit;
>   You touch the strange lumps,
> And mouths gape there, eyes open, all manner
>   Of horns and of humps,
> Which only the fisher looks grave at.

Nature might mean flowers to Wordsworth and grass to Walt Whitman, but to Browning it really meant such things as these, the monstrosities and living mysteries of the sea. And just as these strange things meant to Browning energy in the physical world, so strange thoughts and strange images meant to him energy in the mental world. (pp. 148-50)

There is another and but slightly different use of the grotesque, but which is definitely valuable in Browning's poetry, and indeed in all poetry. To present a matter in a grotesque manner does certainly tend to touch the nerve of surprise and thus to draw attention to the intrinsically miraculous character of the object itself. It is difficult to give examples of the proper use of grotesqueness without becoming too grotesque. But we should all agree that if St. Paul's Cathedral were suddenly presented to us upside down we should, for the moment, be more surprised at it, and look at it more than we have done all the centuries during which it has rested on its foundations. Now it is the supreme function of the philosopher of the grotesque to make the world stand on its head that people may look at it. If we say "a man is a man" we awaken no sense of the fantastic, however much we ought to, but if we say, in the language of the old satirist, "that man is a two-legged bird, without feathers," the phrase does, for a moment, make us look at man from the outside and give us a thrill in his presence. When the author of the Book of Job insists upon the huge, half-witted, apparently unmeaning magnificence and might of Behemoth, the hippopotamus, he is appealing precisely to this sense of wonder provoked by the grotesque. "Canst thou play with him as with a bird, canst thou bind him for thy maidens?" he says in an admirable passage. The notion of the hippopotamus as a household pet is curiously in the spirit of the humour of Browning.

But when it is clearly understood that Browning's love of the fantastic in style was a perfectly serious artistic love,

Ca Rezzonico in Venice—the villa where Browning died.

when we understand that he enjoyed working in that style, as a Chinese potter might enjoy making dragons, or a mediæval mason making devils, there yet remains something definite which must be laid to his account as a fault. He certainly had a capacity for becoming perfectly childish in his indulgence in ingenuities that have nothing to do with poetry at all, such as puns, and rhymes, and grammatical structures that only just fit into each other like a Chinese puzzle. Probably it was only one of the marks of his singular vitality, curiosity, and interest in details. He was certainly one of those somewhat rare men who are fierily ambitious both in large things and in small. He prided himself on having written **The Ring and the Book,** and he also prided himself on knowing good wine when he tasted it. He prided himself on re-establishing optimism on a new foundation, and it is to be presumed, though it is somewhat difficult to imagine, that he prided himself on such rhymes as the following in **"Pacchiarotto":**

> The wolf, fox, bear, and monkey
> By piping advice in one key—
> That his pipe should play a prelude
> To something heaven-tinged not hell-hued,
> Something not harsh but docile,
> Man-liquid, not man-fossil.

This writing, considered as writing, can only be regarded as a kind of joke, and most probably Browning considered it so himself. It has nothing at all to do with that powerful and symbolic use of the grotesque which may be found in such admirable passages as this from **"Holy Cross Day":**

> Give your first groan—compunction's at work;
> And soft! from a Jew you mount to a Turk.
> Lo! Micah—the self-same beard on chin,
> He was four times already converted in!

This is the serious use of the grotesque. Through it passion and philosophy are as well expressed as through any other medium. But the rhyming frenzy of Browning has no particular relation even to the poems in which it occurs. It is not a dance to any measure; it can only be called the horse-play of literature. It may be noted, for example, as a rather curious fact that the ingenious rhymes are generally only mathematical triumphs, not triumphs of any kind of assonance. **"The Pied Piper of Hamelin,"** a poem written for children, and bound in general to be lucid and readable, ends with a rhyme which it is physically impossible for any one to say:

> And, whether they pipe us free, fróm rats or
>   fróm mice,
> If we've promised them aught, let us keep our
>   promise.

This queer trait in Browning, his inability to keep a kind of demented ingenuity even out of poems in which it was quite inappropriate, is a thing which must be recognised, and recognised all the more because as a whole he was a very perfect artist, and a particularly perfect artist in the use of the grotesque. But everywhere when we go a little below the surface in Browning we find that there was something in him perverse and unusual despite all his working normality and simplicity. His mind was perfectly wholesome, but it was not made exactly like the ordinary

mind. It was like a piece of strong wood with a knot in it. (pp. 151-54)

In the case of what is called Browning's obscurity, the question is somewhat more difficult to handle. Many people have supposed Browning to be profound because he was obscure, and many other people, hardly less mistaken, have supposed him to be obscure because he was profound. He was frequently profound, he was occasionally obscure, but as a matter of fact the two have little or nothing to do with each other. Browning's dark and elliptical mode of speech, like his love of the grotesque, was simply a characteristic of his, a trick of his temperament, and had little or nothing to do with whether what he was expressing was profound or superficial. Suppose, for example, that a person well read in English poetry but unacquainted with Browning's style were earnestly invited to consider the following verse:

> Hobbs hints blue—straight he turtle eats.
>   Nobbs prints blue—claret crowns his cup.
> Nokes outdares Stokes in azure feats—
>   Both gorge. Who fished the murex up?
> What porridge had John Keats?

The individual so confronted would say without hesitation that it must indeed be an abstruse and indescribable thought which could only be conveyed by remarks so completely disconnected. But the point of the matter is that the thought contained in this amazing verse is not abstruse or philosophical at all, but is a perfectly ordinary and straightforward comment, which any one might have made upon an obvious fact of life. The whole verse of course begins to explain itself, if we know the meaning of the word "murex," which is the name of a sea-shell, out of which was made the celebrated blue dye of Tyre. The poet takes this blue dye as a simile for a new fashion in literature, and points out that Hobbs, Nobbs, etc., obtain fame and comfort by merely using the dye from the shell; and adds the perfectly natural comment:

> . . . Who fished the murex up?
> What porridge had John Keats?

So that the verse is not subtle, and was not meant to be subtle, but is a perfectly casual piece of sentiment at the end of a light poem. Browning is not obscure because he has such deep things to say, any more than he is grotesque because he has such new things to say. He is both of these things primarily, because he likes to express himself in a particular manner. The manner is as natural to him as a man's physical voice, and it is abrupt, sketchy, allusive, and full of gaps. Here comes in the fundamental difference between Browning and such a writer as George Meredith, with whom the Philistine satirist would so often in the matter of complexity class him. The works of George Meredith are, as it were, obscure even when we know what they mean. They deal with nameless emotions, fugitive sensations, subconscious certainties and uncertainties, and it really requires a somewhat curious and unfamiliar mode of speech to indicate the presence of these. But the great part of Browning's actual sentiments, and almost all the finest and most literary of them, are perfectly plain and popular and eternal sentiments. Meredith is really a singer producing strange notes and cadences difficult to follow because of the delicate rhythm of the song he sings. Browning is simply a great demagogue, with an impediment in his speech. Or rather, to speak more strictly, Browning is a man whose excitement for the glory of the obvious is so great that his speech becomes disjointed and precipitate: he becomes eccentric through his advocacy of the ordinary, and goes mad for the love of sanity.

If Browning and George Meredith were each describing the same act, they might both be obscure, but their obscurities would be entirely different. Suppose, for instance, they were describing even so prosaic and material an act as a man being knocked downstairs by another man to whom he had given the lie, Meredith's description would refer to something which an ordinary observer would not see, or at least could not describe. It might be a sudden sense of anarchy in the brain of the assaulter, or a stupefaction and stunned serenity in that of the object of the assault. He might write, "Wainwood's 'Men vary in veracity,' brought the baronet's arm up. He felt the doors of his brain burst, and Wainwood a swift rushing of himself through air accompanied with a clarity as of the annihilated." Meredith, in other words, would speak queerly because he was describing queer mental experiences. But Browning might simply be describing the material incident of the man being knocked downstairs, and his description would run:

What then? "You lie" and doormat below stairs
Takes bump from back.

This is not subtlety, but merely a kind of insane swiftness. Browning is not like Meredith, anxious to pause and examine the sensations of the combatants, nor does he become obscure through this anxiety. He is only so anxious to get his man to the bottom of the stairs quickly that he leaves out about half the story.

Many, who could understand that ruggedness might be an artistic quality, would decisively, and in most cases rightly, deny that obscurity could under any conceivable circumstances be an artistic quality. But here again Browning's work requires a somewhat more cautious and sympathetic analysis. There is a certain kind of fascination, a strictly artistic fascination, which arises from a matter being hinted at in such a way as to leave a certain tormenting uncertainty even at the end. It is well sometimes to half understand a poem in the same manner that we half understand the world. One of the deepest and strangest of all human moods, is the mood which will suddenly strike us perhaps in a garden at night, or deep in sloping meadows, the feeling that every flower and leaf has just uttered something stupendously direct and important, and that we have by a prodigy of imbecility not heard or understood it. There is a certain poetic value, and that a genuine one, in this sense of having missed the full meaning of things. There is beauty, not only in wisdom, but in this dazed and dramatic ignorance.

But in truth it is very difficult to keep pace with all the strange and unclassified artistic merits of Browning. He was always trying experiments; sometimes he failed, producing clumsy and irritating metres, top-heavy and overconcentrated thought. Far more often he triumphed, producing a crowd of boldly designed poems, every one of

which taken separately might have founded an artistic school. But whether successful or unsuccessful, he never ceased from his fierce hunt after poetic novelty. He never became a conservative. The last book he published in his lifetime, *Parleyings with Certain People of Importance in their Day,* was a new poem, and more revolutionary than *Paracelsus.* This is the true light in which to regard Browning as an artist. He had determined to leave no spot of the cosmos unadorned by his poetry which he could find it possible to adorn. An admirable example can be found in that splendid poem **"Childe Roland to the Dark Tower Came."** It is the hint of an entirely new and curious type of poetry, the poetry of the shabby and hungry aspect of the earth itself. Daring poets who wished to escape from conventional gardens and orchards had long been in the habit of celebrating the poetry of rugged and gloomy landscapes, but Browning is not content with this. He insists upon celebrating the poetry of mean landscapes. That sense of scrubbiness in nature, as of a man unshaved, had never been conveyed with this enthusiasm and primeval gusto before.

> If there pushed any ragged thistle-stalk
>   Above its mates, the head was chopped; the
>   bents
>   Were jealous else. What made those holes and
>   rents
> In the dock's harsh swarth leaves, bruised as to
>   baulk
> All hope of greenness? 'tis a brute must walk
>   Pashing their life out, with a brute's intents.

This is a perfect realisation of that eerie sentiment which comes upon us, not so often among mountains and waterfalls, as it does on some half-starved common at twilight, or in walking down some grey mean street. It is the song of the beauty of refuse; and Browning was the first to sing it. Oddly enough it has been one of the poems about which most of those pedantic and trivial questions have been asked, which are asked invariably by those who treat Browning as a science instead of a poet, "What does the poem of *Childe Roland* mean?" The only genuine answer to this is, "What does anything mean?" Does the earth mean nothing? Do grey skies and wastes covered with thistles mean nothing? Does an old horse turned out to graze mean nothing? If it does, there is but one further truth to be added—that everything means nothing. (pp. 154-59)

> *G. K. Chesterton, in his* Robert Browning, *The Macmillan Company, 1903, 207 p.*

Stockton Axson   (lecture date 1929)

[*Axson delivered a series of lectures on Browning in March 1929 entitled "Browning: His Times, His Art, His Philosophy." The following excerpt from that series is focused on Browning's relation to the Victorian era. After discussing the poet's differences from his contemporaries, Axson explores Browning's philosophy, praising it as a brave assault on the spiritual problems of the Victorian age.*]

It would be inaccurate to say that there is no "Victorianism" in Browning—there is a great deal—but compared with Tennyson, Dickens, Ruskin, even Carlyle, Thackeray and George Eliot, the Victorianism in Browning is oblique, evasive, indirect, almost ineluctable; not obvious, patent, easily demonstrable as it is in Tennyson. When we are seeking the representative poet of the Victorian Age we turn to Tennyson rather than to Browning. Though Tennyson was somewhat of a recluse, and though Browning was a "man of the world", a "mixer", a most sociable person, mingling, after his wife's death and his temporary withdrawal from Italy, with all sorts and conditions of men and women in England, especially in London, it was Tennyson rather than Browning who fused in poetry most of the obvious things about which English men and women were talking: their politics, their social problems, their religious faith and misgivings, their every-day conceptions of what English people are, should be, or fail to be, their English patriotism and insularity. (pp. 145-46)

In short, Tennyson in the reign of Victoria, like Pope in the age of Anne and the Early Georges, could say better than anybody else the things that many were thinking. Browning, on the other hand, was perplexing most English people of his age, as the Apostle Paul (to whom Browning bore many resemblances) puzzled the fisherman apostle Peter with, as Peter writes, "some things hard to be understood." Tennyson spoke the language of his own time, Browning, the language of a later time. Tennyson was a contemporary; Browning a progenitor. In short, Browning, like many another great man, was a generation or two ahead of his era. (pp. 146-47)

Browning himself had checked, practically halted, his own popularity by overloading much of his poetry with learning too erudite or philosophy too original and involved for the tastes of the Early Victorians. His second important poem, *Paracelsus,* published in 1835, when he was twenty-three years old, had attracted considerable attention from the discerning in England. It came in a "flat" period of English poetry—an eddy, a calm. The great early nineteenth century poetic epoch (the Wordsworth-Byron era) was ended—these earlier poets were either dead (like Coleridge, Scott, Byron, Shelley and Keats), or too old to write with fresh inspiration (Wordsworth and Southey). Tennyson had begun, and the discerning saw that in him a delicately accomplished artist had arrived—but whether the artist would ever discover anything important to say remained to be seen. In *Paracelsus* there was obviously a poet with a great deal to say, and he was saying it in an original and impressive manner. (p. 151)

Then, as if deliberately, Browning set to work to nip his budding fame: by writing a series of plays that did not prove "playable," and by perpetrating such a baffling piece of obscurity as the long poem *Sordello*—a poem which with all its fascinations (and they are many) is still difficult reading. . . . If *Sordello* is difficult now for us who are familiar with Browning's habits of mind and art, his vast learning, introversions of speech, allusions, evasiveness, long parentheses, and all his other idiosyncrasies of matter and manner, including his strange combination of alternating prolixity and condensation, it is not remarkable that the Early Victorians, unaccustomed to his manner and methods, found the poem hopelessly unintelligible.

Even the intellectually elect were baffled by it. It was to be a long time before the author of *Sordello* could win popular favor from the Victorians, but he went doggedly his own way, saying that he had never proposed to write poetry as a substitute for a lazy man's after-dinner cigar or game of dominoes.

This apparent discrepancy between Browning and his age (the discrepancy is only apparent) was due to many things, among them: Browning's attitude toward the public, his attitude toward himself, his attitude toward his art, and his attitude toward what we now call "questions of the day"—the political, economic and social questions which absorbed so much of the thought of thinking people in the first decades of Queen Victoria's reign—the pregnant age of political, economic, industrial and social reform—questions which gave much of the character and color to the work of Tennyson, Ruskin, Dickens, Charles Reade, Charles Kingsley, Matthew Arnold and Mrs. Browning herself—but not Browning.

His attitude toward the public and himself may be dealt with in one category. Browning was so original in his thought and in his manner of expressing his thought that he needed an interpreter, and he declined to be his own interpreter. . . . [He] declined to meet the public on the public's terms; declined to persuade them to understand and like his poetry; declined to lead them gradually to his own mountain tops of thought, feeling and expression; they must climb for themselves without assistance from him. There was his poetry—people could like it or leave it—Browning would not be exalted by their favor or vexed by their neglect. In one respect—in one only—Browning was like his Andrea del Sarto: Andrea, in the poem, tells his wife:

> I, painting from myself and to myself,
> Know what I do, am unmoved by men's blame
> Or their praise either.

So it was with Browning: writing from himself and to himself he pursued his way serenely. Not even his poet-wife . . . could intrude upon his creative moods. (pp. 152-54)

Sometimes when Browning was requested to say what he meant in a designated passage, he would smilingly refer the questioner to the Browning Society. He had a similar attitude of aloofness toward his poetry—in marked contrast with Tennyson's coddling of *his* poetry. When the Browning Society discovered that Browning did not possess printed copies of at least some of his own poems, the Society presented to him a complete set of [his own works] accompanied by a letter recommending them to his attention, as books which contained some good reading matter. Once a lady read to him some lines of poetry, and Browning "slapped his thigh [a characteristic gesture] and said, 'By Jove, that's fine' ". He was enlightened and edified when the lady informed him that the author of the lines was one Robert Browning.

The most eccentric feature of all this is that Browning himself was not at all eccentric—on the contrary a normal sort of person—so normal that . . . many who met him for the first time found it difficult to believe that he was a poet: in dress and manner and conversation he seemed more like a banker or a prosperous merchant. Nevertheless, the fact remains that, after the select success of the early poem *Paracelsus,* Browning for more than thirty years lost favor instead of augmenting it by writing as he pleased instead of studying the public demand and striving to supply it. I do not know that any moral is to be drawn from this. Another and even greater poet, William Shakespeare, studied carefully the popular taste, and met it, and succeeded. But Shakespeare had to make a living by writing, while Robert Browning, a man of independent, moderately comfortable means, could afford to do what he pleased as he pleased to do it.

Not different from this was Browning's attitude toward his art. He wrote nine plays, but none of them has been a really popular success on the stage—notwithstanding extravagant claims to the contrary by some Browning enthusiasts who seem to mistake artistic success for stage success—the latter being a quite tangible thing, ascertainable by statistics of "runs" and box office receipts.

This raises the question . . . why the most dramatic English poet since the age of the Elizabethans did not fit his genius better to a practical stage. One simple answer has already been given, his refusal to study and meet popular demand. Another answer is that he found his true vein, his best medium, in monologue rather than in dialogue. In the dramatic monologue he has few predecessors, shoals of successors, no equals. One of his volumes is called *Dramatic Lyrics*—and that name is emblematic of the character of much of Browning's work—lyric poetry externalized, impersonalized, dramatized. Oscar Wilde said in his *De Profundis,* "I took the drama, the most objective form known to art, and made of it as personal a mode of expression as the lyric or sonnet." Browning might have reversed that statement: I took the lyric, the most subjective form known to art, and made of it as impersonal a mode of expression as the drama. (pp. 154-56)

It is possible, as has been remarked by another, that Browning unconsciously put more of his own personal traits (his reckless courage and his chivalry) into Caponsacchi, the hero-priest of *The Ring and the Book,* than into any other of his characters. But his ideal of poetic creation was the impersonalism of Shakespeare, the dramatic projection of natures and personalities other than his own. Almost truculently, he defied the public to find him, Robert Browning, in his poems. We find this defiance categorically in the poem **"House."** Only rarely does he deliberately express himself, his personality, in his poems: as in the Epilogue to *Asolando; Prospice;* the exquisite concluding lines of the first book of *The Ring and the Book,* the address to his dead wife, beginning

> O lyric Love, half angel and half bird
> And all a wonder and a wild desire;

and in the concluding poem of the volume *Men and Women,* the poem addressed to his living wife, **"One Word More,"** surely one of the devoutest love poems in the language. . . . Add to these things, his first published poem, *Pauline,* and a few of his later poems (notably *La Saisiaz*) and we practically exhaust the personal poems of Browning. The rest, the great mass of them, express fre-

quently passionate convictions and often subtle arguments, but not the personality of Robert Browning. He is a curious combination of intense attachment to ideas and austere detachment from self-revelation. Such, briefly summarized, is his attitude toward his art, an attitude which accentuates his aloofness from his time. Certainly his art is not "Victorian," is distinctly "modern"—twentieth century. One of our "new" American poets (one of the modernists), once said to me, "Browning was the first of us—the first to dramatize a mood."

Finally, there is Browning's attitude toward questions of his day—the problems of the era of reform, the new democracy. He, the most insistent questioner in nineteenth century English poetry, applied few questions to the engrossing matters of political and social reform. He was primarily interested in other things.

Typical Victorian literature was socialized literature, from Carlyle through Kipling. But this dominant note is virtually absent from Browning's poetry. His is an almost unique case of an author, vividly interested in everything about him and yet silent about contemporary actualities. When the creative mood overtook him, he was less responsive to people in their social and political relationships than to people as individuals. . . . His biographer, Mrs. Orr, says: "His politics were, so far as they went, the practical aspect of his religion. Their cardinal doctrine was the liberty of individual growth" [see Further Reading list]. That statement, which has the truth of finality, is strikingly illustrated by a comparison of Browning's sonnet **"Why I am a Liberal"** (published 1885) with several untitled poems by Tennyson (published 1842) on the subject of British liberalism founded in constitutional development. There is one of these stanzas by Tennyson which a preeminent student of constitutional law who rose to be President of the United States never wearied of quoting in support of his position as a conservative progressive—believing that it expressed the essence of political wisdom under orderly (not radical) change:

> A land of settled government,
>   A land of just and old renown,
>   Where Freedom slowly broadens down
> From precedent to precedent.

But what devotee of politics, theoretical or practical, would find any pointed political wisdom in Browning's answer to a questionnaire circulated among prominent men of England in 1885, asking why they were Liberals? The answer is not in terms of politics but in terms of God and the Soul of man—the subjects which most occupied his thinking. In a prefatory note to a reprint of *Sordello* in 1863 he had said that "the stress" was "on the incidents in the development of a soul; little else is worth study."

Victorian literature, in general, by no means neglected "soul." But most of it, that was typical, stressed also the political and social idea: Dickens the Reformer; Carlyle the inquirer into the workings of democracy; Ruskin, with the long shelf of volumes in which he faced about from art to consider questions in economics and social arrangement; Tennyson the inspired interpreter of English liberalism; George Eliot, author of *Felix Holt the Radical;* Charles Kingsley; Charles Reade; Frederick Denison

Maurice; and many others, including Mrs. Browning herself.

The contemporary popularity of the poetry of Elizabeth Barrett Browning and the unpopularity of her husband's poetry throw light on Victorianism and the Brownings. Mrs. Browning was intensely interested in "questions of the day." . . . Her *Aurora Leigh, Casa Guidi Windows, Poems Before Congress* and "The Cry of the Children" are altogether "contemporary" with political and social reform. Consider, for example, "The Cry of the Children" (published 1841). It is the cry of Dickens for reform, of Ruskin against machinery, of Carlyle against the subjugation of the poor, of Dickens' and Tennyson's sentiment—true Victorian sentiment, which in this hard-boiled twentieth century we have come to call sentimentality. It is typically "Victorian" in both its political-social subject and in its treatment of the subject.

None of her husband's poetry is either. In 1841 (before he was married) he had written **Pippa Passes,** a poem about a little mill girl. But there is nothing in this charming dramatic poem about Pippa's economic subjection. It is about her joy as she wanders singing through the village of Asolo on her one holiday in all the year, and the way her singing reaches the hearts, the "souls" of a number of different people, each in a crisis, and turns the destiny of each. It was a new poetic form—not quite dramatic, not quite lyric, a blend of the two—not quite like anything that had been written before, either in matter or manner. It was not "obvious" to people in 1841. But "The Cry of the Children" by Mrs. Browning was entirely obvious to all who were thinking about industrial reforms. It said precisely what many were thinking. Mrs. Browning did not write to "hit the popular taste" any more than did Carlyle. But she was a product of the era which Carlyle, and after him Ruskin, almost created. Robert Browning, "writing from himself and to himself" was not quite of that era. So in 1844-1860 Mrs. Browning was a famous poet, mentioned for the laureateship after the death of Wordsworth in 1850, while Robert Browning was her husband—who also wrote verses. (pp. 156-60)

In talking about Browning and the Victorian Age I have been chiefly occupied with statements of what is *non*-Victorian in the poetry of Browning. Yet, as Percy Hutchison says: "Robert Browning, while in small degree reflecting the purely social aspect of his time and thereby differing essentially from Tennyson, 'dates' even more indelibly than does Tennyson. For the very fount of Browning's compositions was the intellectual rebellion, the aroused intellectual curiosity of his day." The new science and a new philosophy springing out of the new science led some Victorians to doubt and despair, but led Browning to a fresh fervent reaffirmation of God, the Immortality of the Soul, the Freedom of the Will, and an optimism that is gorgeous. Much that was bravest and best in the mental life of the Victorians got its boldest and most dynamic expression in Browning's poetry. Of all Victorians he was the bonniest fighter and certainly the greatest poet: facing the spiritual problems of the Victorian era, and either arguing them out with tenacious logic, or fighting out the

issue with the faith and courage of Paul who met the wild beasts at Ephesus. (pp. 162-63)

• • • • •

It is an inexcusably superficial view which finds an easygoing optimism in Browning's poetry. Lines separated from the body of his poetry may seem chirping and a bit too chirper, such as the familiar lines of Pippa

> God's in his heaven—
> All's right with the world.

Taken *in esse,* it must be remembered that the lines are dramatic, not personal, part of a gladsome song that a little simple-hearted factory girl sings in her joyous rambles on her one holiday of all the year. Taken *in posse,* as an expression of Browning's own faith, they are the conclusion, not the postulate, of a prolonged philosophical process. And whether evil is a negation, an absence of good, as cold is an absence of heat, rest an absence of motion, silence an absence of sound (as Browning's Abt Vogler sees it), it is none the less something to be overcome, and that by valiant fighting. Indolence may be only absence of activity but the indolent man has to make as strong an effort to overcome it as if it were a positive entity. (pp. 186-87)

Browning, speaking through the Pope in **The Ring and the Book** envisages evil as spiritual death, and continual struggle the means whereby evil may be eliminated. In practical living what difference does it make whether the concept of evil is, in the abstract, negative or positive? The conflict is real whether the conflict is with a personal devil or a phantasmagoria such as Shakespeare faced when he wrote *King Lear.*

To assume that Browning reasoned and battled in ignorance or wilful dismissal of the pinch of evil is to disregard Browning's reiterated language, the language not only of his poetry but also of his private correspondence. In a letter dated May 11, 1876, Browning wrote: "I see ever more reason to hold by . . . hope, and that by no means in ignorance of what has been advanced to the contrary." The road to sound optimism is no bower of roses, honeysuckle and sweet jasmine; it is a granite, steep, cobble-strewn trail beset with many difficulties and precipices and crevasses, and a misstep may pitch the pilgrim into perdition.

Browning loved the road precisely because it was not smooth, precisely because he relished a good fight and the glow of fighting. "Am I no a bonny fighter?" exclaims Stevenson's Alan Breck, in the flush of contest. Browning said similar things many times in more recondite language than Alan's.

> It is by no breath,
> Turn of eye, wave of hand, that salvation joins
> issue with death,

exclaims David in Browning's poem **"Saul,"** that is to say by no easy gesture, by no *fiat lux.* Steadily as Milton himself does this nineteenth century optimist Browning welcome battle and scorn easeful ways. (pp. 187-88)

Out of his own heart, mind and experience, he wrote the Epilogue to **Asolando,** speaking for the last time, not as dramatic poet, but as Robert Browning himself; here is the third stanza:

> One who never turned his back, but marched
>   breast forward,
> Never doubted clouds would break,
> Never dreamed, though right were worsted,
>   wrong would triumph,
> Held we fell to rise, are baffled to fight better,
> Sleep to wake. . . .

So much for Browning's optimistic attitude, the optimism of a fighter by temperament; the only sort of optimism that is worth while, the optimism which clearly recognizes that this is a tough old world, in which, among all busy-ness, none is busier than the devil, whether the devil be a person, a principle or a negation. (pp. 189-90)

With regard to the antinomy of God and Nature which perplexed Tennyson, Browning was abrupt, though not always brief. He swept away (in so far as he himself was concerned) the whole idea of beneficent nature, and, apparently without a struggle, abandoned search in Nature for evidence of a loving God. In Nature he saw overwhelming evidence of a God of Power and Knowledge, but no evidence of a God of Love. The evidence of God's love is in man, not in nature—man ready to sacrifice himself for the object of his love. The reasoning is subtle, retraversed in many poems, well condensed in **"Saul."** Reduced to a sentence, it comes simply to this, that postulating God . . . as infinite in power and wisdom and as creator of man, it is illogical to assume that he could have put into man a faculty which he himself does not possess, the faculty of enduring, and often sacrificial love. In other words, Browning reasons back from man to God: the created could not possess a faculty which the Creator had not himself to give his creature.

Browning faces the antinomy of knowledge and faith, with an assertion, like Tennyson's, of the incapacity of knowledge to solve the problem which many people account the most vital of all, man's relationship to God and the individual spirit's survival of death. He was probably more intimately acquainted than was any other English poet of his day with Victorian science. Having the insatiable curiosity of the men of the Renaissance (about whom he knew so much) he was vividly curious about the new science—read widely, even dabbled a little in experimentation. But he was entirely skeptical about the qualifications of science to solve problems of the human spirit. In the poem *La Saisiaz* he questions even the color of grass. We say "green," but comes one who says "red." "Colorblind" we say, but how do we know that? Suppose his is the normal vision, ours the abnormal. Suppose only he and one other inhabited the world—how could the color of grass be determined? Is truth ascertainable by a majority vote? The opinion of today's minority may be the majority opinion tomorrow. It has been so in history. Truth, the truth which saves, comes not through the intellect, but through love, says this most intellectual of the poets. (pp. 190-91)

Progression was Browning's measure of vitality. Not what man is but what man is becoming enlisted his interest. The developmental idea of the new science stirred his dynamic imagination, and led him to philosophical conclusions

which lie at the heart of his thinking. These conclusions were often paradoxical: for instance, his comfort in imperfection. Imperfection is a condition of vital development: where there is growth, there is something to be attained; where there is something to be attained there is obviously something yet unobtained; where there is something unobtained there is incompleteness; where there is incompleteness, there is imperfection; or, to state the paradox in a syllogism:

> the only perfect thing is a thing completed;
> but the only completed thing is a dead thing;
> therefore, the only perfect thing is something
>   dead.

That is argued out in the poem, **"Dis Aliter Visum."**

His paradox of failure is close akin: failure also is a negation, a discrepancy between infinite purpose and finite powers. Because of man's alliance with the infinite he is constantly striving for something beyond his grasp:

> Only I discern
> Infinite passion, and the pain
> Of finite hearts that yearn,

he says in **"Two in the Campagna."** In the *consciousness* of failure, the paradoxical Browning saw the measure of success. Real success is to strive nobly; real failure is not to strive; it is only "apparent failure" when the thing done is less than the thing envisioned; dissatisfaction with the result is only the evidence of the loftiness of the purpose. (pp. 191-92)

Tennyson and Browning accepted the new ideas of science because as thinking men they did not see how they could reject them. But that which Tennyson accepted wistfully, Browning accepted joyously. To his way of thinking the new ideas strengthened rather than weakened the Christian faith. In Paul's epistles Browning had read of the Christian life as a battle, in metaphors which Paul took largely from active struggles: war and fighting wild beasts and athletic contests. And now, in the new science, Browning seemed to learn that this is the law of vitality: struggle, with crown and palm for him who has the courage and endurance to keep fighting. Browning glorified the strenuous life, the life of hopeful fighting. There are several Browning poems (among them *The Inn Album* and **"Apparent Failure"**) in which Browning glimpses hope that God in his mercy will forgive and redeem criminals led by their strenuous activity into wild sins. But repeatedly, in one dramatic form or another, he abandons hope for the slothful, listless, idle, shallow, timid. (p. 193)

[The] poem *La Saisiaz* is one of the most significant in the Browning corpus . . . because it is the last long confessional poem in which he frankly speaks, not dramatically, but as Robert Browning, and utters his own conclusions about the mystery of life and death. . . . Carefully he goes over his old arguments, so familiar to readers of Browning. But bit by bit he abandons arguments and falls back on two intuitions which to him were certainties, God and his own soul. Good and evil, life and death, dissolution and immortality—he reasons about them again, as he had so often reasoned about them. And then he explicitly disavows purpose to solve the problem of evil and God's superintendence in philosophical terms, saying

> I shall "vindicate no ways of God's to man,". . . .
> Traversed heart must tell its story uncommented on.

And again:

> Question, answer, presuppose
> Two points: that the thing itself which questions, answers—is, it knows

• • • • •

> God then, call that—soul and both—the only facts for me.

Do we get the point? Robert Browning, now sixty-eight years old, confronted by the crashing fact of death, definitely rehearsed his old arguments and retreated to intuitive faith for the only answer for him, Robert Browning. Alexander Pope, the shallow logician, had undertaken to "vindicate the ways of God to man." John Milton, the learned theologian, had undertaken in a philosophical poem, *Paradise Lost,* to "justify the ways of God to men." But Robert Browning, Pope's superior as a logician, Milton's equal in theology and learning, will neither "vindicate" nor "justify" the mystery of Providence. He accepts, and in his acceptance, he is reassured. Browning concludes his long years of scrutiny, not in a theodicy, but in a reaffirmation of his personal faith in God and the indestructibility of the soul. Not what God means in this vast universe, but what God means to him, Robert Browning, and to all believing souls, is the sum and substance of it all.

A lame and impotent conclusion of the long years of inquiry by the most inquiring mind in nineteenth century English poetry? Perhaps so, if you think science and logic can prove anything about the reality of God and the human spirit. Not so, if you believe they can prove nothing whatever. (pp. 195-97)

"[The subjective poet struggles towards] not what man sees, but what God sees— the *Ideas* of Plato, seeds of creation lying burningly on the Divine Hand. . . . Not with the combination of humanity in action, but with the primal elements of humanity he has to do; and he digs where he stands,—preferring to seek them in his own soul as the nearest reflex of that absolute Mind, according to the intuitions of which he desires to perceive and speak."

—Robert Browning, 1851

People sometimes complain that . . . Browning wrote so much about things morbid and ugly. Browning loved the

beautiful and often wrote of it. But a world garlanded in orange-blossoms is not all the world. And Browning, the all-curious, wanted to see all of it. He wanted to proclaim the beauty of life while facing its ugliness. It requires courage to do that. In the dim and hushed solemnity of the cathedral, under its vaulted arches, splashed with prismatic colors from its stained-glass windows, when the organ is pealing and the surpliced choir lifts on high the anthem, with the incense in our nostrils, before our adoring eyes the symbols of sacrificial cross and victorious crown, amid the bowed worshippers and the sonorous ritual—here it is not hard to believe in God. But can we leave the cathedral and go into the alley, see the cripple in his rags, the lazar in his sores, hear the harlot's curses, and the drunkard's ravings—can we do this and still believe in God? If we cannot, we don't believe in Him very much. Browning really did believe in God. Not an absentee God, remote, concealed somewhere behind his tent of blue sky, but an always present God. Not an inert God, but a vitalizing God. And he believed that in strenuous living of the life of the spirit, in sympathetic living with his fellow men, he was linking himself with God's own spirit.

Browning's spirit is more important than his reasoning. His arguments may not convince the reason, but his courage is infectious. The reasons he gives for his optimism are the least important things about his optimism. His arguments are only the corollary of his instinct, and instinct is personal. Not God in the universe, but God in the spirit of the individual is Browning's real theme. His spirit tingled with the spirit of God. And for us his spirit is a challenge, to turn failure into victory, doubt into faith, weakness into strength. It is a challenge to be brave, to keep on fighting, believing, hoping, recuperating. He was glad because he believed that he and you and I are engaged in a great adventure, the outcome of which depends chiefly upon our courage for the adventure. (pp. 198-99)

Stockton Axson, "Browning: His Times, His Art, His Philosophy," in The Rice Institute Pamphlet, *Vol. XVII, No. 4, October, 1931, pp. 145-99.*

F. R. G. Duckworth   (essay date 1932)

[In the following excerpt, Duckworth attempts to trace personal elements in Browning's poetry by employing sections taken from letters and criticism written by Elizabeth Barrett Browning.]

Browning's attitude towards those who pretended to discover in his poems a key to his personal feelings and thoughts is described at some length, but in rather obscure language, by Mrs. Orr in her biography. It seems to come to this, that he resented the attempt to read him into his poems as impertinent or irrelevant. But his protest did not, and, in the nature of things, could not, carry much weight with his critics either in his own lifetime or later. Furnivall spoke with violence of Browning's habit of hiding himself behind his characters, "whose necks," said he, "I for one should like to wring." In our own day two critics have made comments on this dramatisation. One of them describes the dramatis personæ as the poet's own fancy-dress ball; the other speaks of his masquerade. The problem has not been very fully discussed by his critics, and a further examination of it will yield some curious results.

Certain things which Browning himself said about his own poetry in his letters to Elizabeth Barrett appear to have been neglected by those of his biographers and critics whose works appeared after 1898, the date of the publication of the *Love Letters.* In her first letter to Robert Browning, Elizabeth Barrett had invited him to criticise her poetry and had expressed her admiration of his work. To this he replies (in what was only his second letter to her):

> Your poetry must be, cannot but be, infinitely more to me than mine to you—for you *do* what I always wanted, hoped to do, and seem only now likely to do for the first time. You speak out, *you,*—I only make men and women speak—give you truth broken into prismatic hues, and fear the pure white light, even if it is in me, but I am going to try.

And he fears that since now he must learn to do without the company of the men and women of his creation, he will find it bleak work, "this talking to the wind (for I have begun)." To this she replies: "I have been guilty of wishing that you would give the public a poem unassociated directly or indirectly with the stage, for a trial on the popular heart. I reverence the drama, but—" Then he tells her she knows nothing of him yet. "Is it true," she answers, "that I know so 'little' of you? And is it true, as others say, that the productions of an artist do not partake of his real nature. . . . ? It is *not* true to my mind." Browning will not accept this. "What I have printed gives no knowledge of me. . . . I have never begun, even, what I hope I was born to begin and end—'R. B.—a poem.' "

He is going to "try to speak out"—to give out the "pure white light." Indeed, he has already begun the new attempt—the attempt to produce something non-dramatic. This is all in the letters of January and February 1845. What of Browning's work was at that time in hand? *Luria* and *A Soul's Tragedy*—both dramas. He cannot be referring to either of them. Was something in hand then which has never reached the light of day?

Whatever the answer to that question, the important fact is that Browning had determined, apparently, before he had begun his correspondence with Elizabeth Barrett, to launch out into a new kind of poetry. Now, it might be argued that in the first ardours of love—when the contacts are being made and two souls are burning to take each other's measure—it is absurd to attach too much importance to the actual words said. These are not times when the lover sees either himself or his mistress in the right perspective. "You do not know me," cries the lover—for what lover has not? "I am a more mysterious being than you think me." There are two answers to this argument. First, it is by no means certain that Browning was at this stage in love with Elizabeth Barrett, whom he had never seen. Secondly, even if one admits that the scene was set and the lights turned on for that romantic affair, which was already in anticipation upsetting the rhythms of the poets' souls, yet allusions to this coming change—or rather to this intended change in Browning's work—keep on

recurring in the correspondence long past the point at which the unconscious tendency of a lover to make himself mysterious in the eyes of the beloved is passed. It is more than a year after the first interchange of letters, it is in April of 1846, after the last of the **Bells and Pomegranates** had been published, that there occurs in one of Browning's letters this most significant passage. In it Browning is explaining that he looks upon *Luria* and *The Soul's Tragedy* as failures. They have failed, because his heart had not been in the writing of them. And how had that come about? It had come about through his meeting her: this had seemed to him like a deliverance from prison, from his old ways of conceiving and writing, and had revealed to him a new and greater way. How could he, seeing this promise of a better kind of poetry, take interest in the final stages of producing poems which belonged to the old and limited kind? (pp. 183-86)

But what did the dawn bring? What comes next after *Luria* and *The Soul's Tragedy?* Nothing until, in 1850, **Christmas Eve and Easter Day.** Are these what the *Love Letters* foreshadow? At first sight there is some reason to think that this may be so. Neither poem appears to be an attempt to present a character. The speakers in them do not live in our imaginations as do Fra Lippo Lippi or even the narrator in *The Flight of the Duchess,* and there is nothing in the title to suggest a dramatic intention in either poem. But beyond this and far more important than this there is fairly strong evidence that at least **Christmas Eve**—the earlier written of the two—is based upon an interchange of ideas which we find in the *Love Letters.* It does not appear to have been remarked that the nucleus of **Christmas Eve** is contained in one of Elizabeth Barrett's letters (15th August, 1846):

> I felt unwilling, for my own part, to put on any of the liveries of the sects. The truth, as God sees it, must be something so different from these opinions about truth. . . . I believe in what is divine and floats at highest, in all these different theologies—and because the really Divine draws together souls, and tends so to a unity, I could pray anywhere and with all sorts of worshippers, from the Sistine chapel to Mr. Fox's, those kneeling and those standing. Wherever you go, in all religious societies, there is a little to revolt, and a good deal to bear with—but it is not otherwise in the world without; and, *within,* you are especially reminded that God has to be more patient than yourself after all. Still you go quickest there, where your sympathies are least ruffled and disturbed—and I like, beyond comparison best, the simplicity of the dissenters . . . the unwritten prayer . . . the sacraments administered quickly and without charlatanism! and the principle of a church as they hold it, *I* hold it too. . . . Well, there is enough to dissent from among the dissenters . . . you feel moreover bigotry and ignorance pressing on you on all sides, till you gasp for breath like one strangled.

There is hardly a phrase in this which could not be paralleled by some phrase in **Christmas Eve.** Browning's reply to this must also be noted:

> Dearest, I know your very meaning in what you

said of religion, and responded to it with my whole soul—what you express now is for us both . . . those are my own feelings, my convictions beside—instinct confirmed by reason. Look at that injunction to 'love God with all the heart and soul and strength'—and then imagine yourself bidding any faculty, that arises towards the love of him, be still! If in a meeting house, with the blank white walls, and a simple doctrinal exposition—all the senses should turn (from where they lie neglected) to all that sunshine in the Sistine with its music and painting, which would lift them at once to Heaven,—why should you not go forth?—to return just as quickly, when they are nourished into a luxuriance that extinguishes, what is called, Reason's pale wavering light, lamp or whatever it is—for I have got into a confusion with thinking of our convolvuluses that climb and tangle round the rose-trees—which might be lamps or tapers!

Let it be considered that Browning had come to believe that this change in his poetic work, determined upon and even begun (in an experimental way perhaps) before he met Elizabeth Barrett, was now closely bound up with their joint lives; that *she* was to help and confirm and encourage him in this new way. The new way was the way of self-expression. And here in this particular question of religious ritual there were convictions which they shared in common—Browning says so himself. Moreover, they are convictions upon matters which both he and she considered to be of the profoundest significance and weightiest moment. What more natural, then—indeed, what more inevitable—than that such convictions should form the theme of the first of the poems in the new style?

These arguments seem difficult to controvert. Let us ask what arguments there are on the other side. There is Browning's own declaration, repeated over and over again after his wife's death, that *all* his work is dramatic except a few of the later poems. That he could have forgotten *Christmas Eve* is impossible: that he made a mental exception of it seems equally impossible—no motive could be imagined for such an attitude. There is also Mrs. Browning's statement about *Easter Day:* "I have complained of the *asceticism* in the second part, but he said it was 'one side of the question.' Don't think he has taken to the cilix—indeed, he has not—but it is his way to *see* things as passionately as other people *feel* them. . . ." If, then, *Easter Day* is not the expression of Browning's feeling, it is difficult to think that *Christmas Eve* so entirely differed from it in character, especially as the second poem is explicitly linked up with the first. Lastly, although the passages quoted from the *Love Letters* are certainly the nucleus of *Christmas Eve,* there is one most important difference. Elizabeth Barrett declares (and we must remember that Browning said he wholly and entirely shared her views): "I felt unwilling to put on any of the liveries of the sects." Browning, in his answer, protests against the view—which is the view of the dissenters, one presumes, in the little chapel in *Christmas Eve*—that *any* faculty that arises towards the love of God should be repressed. On the other hand, the speaker in *Christmas Eve,* having seen the dissenting chapel and been repelled by all that is ignorant and crude in that ritual, having also in a vision seen the

Christmas Eve Mass in Saint Peter's and been present at the Göttingen professor's lecture, finds that he must make his choice—that he cannot stay indefinitely outside the enclosure of some doctrine, that he must put on the livery of some sect. Therefore he chooses the dissenters' chapel:

> Meantime, in the still recurring fear
>   Lest myself, at unawares, be found,
>   While attacking the choice of my neighbours
>   round,
> With none of my own made—I choose here.

Now, we know from the biographies and from Browning's own letters that, in fact, Browning did not make a choice, that he never put on the livery of any sect. So far did he go in this way, that the question was for long disputed whether he was an orthodox Christian—or a Christian in any permissible sense of the word.

The speculation may be indulged in, whether Browning, when he began to write *Christmas Eve,* had every intention of speaking out, but that something more powerful than that intention interfered and prevented the purpose being achieved, so that in the end these two poems represent not his own convictions but three points of view—with one of which, we now know, he was more in sympathy than with the other two. Evidently, it will be of the first importance to inquire what was this something which frustrated his serious and often avowed intention. The inquiry is not easy, and it is only undertaken because it is germane to the main purpose of the present chapter, which is to exhibit in Browning's work the nature and results of a certain conflict.

A point, the significance of which will be developed later on, may here be accorded particular notice—and that is the confusion of thought in which Browning became involved in working out the simile of Reason's pale wavering light, convolvuluses, rose-trees, lamps and tapers.

Perhaps the best way in which to attack our present problem will be to recall the poems in which Browning did avowedly speak in the first person. Applying, then, the strictest tests, we find that there is only one such poem, *La Saisiaz,* which it will be worth while examining. Of the others, "One Word More" is admittedly a poem standing apart and not to be judged as characteristic; and the two poems in the *Pacchiarotto* volume, in which he is speaking in person, merely amount to the statement that his poems are not keys with which to unlock his heart. Incidentally, it is of interest that *La Saisiaz* bears a date only two years later than the warning issued in *Pacchiarotto.* Of *La Saisiaz* it may first be remarked that no one nowadays reads it for its own sake. The narrative and more purely descriptive part of it deserve, perhaps, more attention than they are likely to receive now or hereafter. Browning winds his way into his theme more rapidly and certainly than in many of his later poems. The whole thing moves easily enough up to the point at which he begins to attack his central problem, the evidence of personal survival of bodily death.

> Life thus owned unhappy, is there supplemental
>   happiness
> Possible and probable in life to come? or must
>   we count

Life a curse and not a blessing, summed up in its
    whole amount
Help and hindrance, joy and sorrow?
           Why should I want courage here?
I will ask and have an answer—with no favour,
    with no fear,—
From myself.

But from that point the course of the argument is terribly
involved and difficult to a degree not exceeded in any other
poem of Browning's except, perhaps, **Sordello.** The very
core of the whole argumentation of the poem—the paragraph beginning

What though fancy scarce may grapple with the
    complex and immense
—"His own world for every mortal" . . . —

will only yield its secret after not one but many most careful readings. And the difficulties are not due to vague or
obscure historical allusions, but to the wavering thread of
thoughts carried precariously through labyrinthine parentheses and through thickets of qualifying clauses. And to
what shrine does this clue lead us? To what white light
which we may be glad to exchange for the "prismatic
hues" of his dramatic poems? To no white light at all, and
to no hue which has not been discernible in those other
poems. Nearly all the main thoughts are to be found in
other poems—in **"Mr. Sludge the Medium," in "Saul,"**
"A Death in the Desert," *Easter Day,* **"The Pope," "Fi-**
fine at the Fair" and **"Francis Furini."** All that is left peculiar to this poem is the special insistence on the idea that
we can hope, and no more than hope, for a future existence, and that to be certain of it would be in our present
state no help to us, but a hindrance. (pp. 187-93)

What, then, does *La Saisiaz* seem to tell us? Not, it may
be urged, that Browning himself *never* knew when he was
writing dramatically and when he was not. Nor does it
prove that Browning had no personal convictions or ideas
of his own—that there was no "white light" in him. Indeed, it can hardly he held to give us any help in answering
the question what it was that prevented him from writing
"R. B.—a poem." It does, however, suggest that when
Browning attempted the non-dramatic, it took him no farther than the dramatic. *La Saisiaz,* as we said above, reflects the prismatic hues of many of the dramatic poems,
but in no sense does it combine them into a white light.
If it had done so, then, in spite of its obscurity, it would
be one of the best known and, if not most read, then at
least most quoted of his poems.

In what way, then, are we precluded from inferring that
there was no white light in Browning? If it was there, why
could he not unveil it for us? "White light" is a useful metaphor of Browning's own invention. He contrasts it with
the prismatic hues of his own dramatic poetry—"I only
make men and women speak—give you truth broken into
prismatic hues." This can only mean that the white light
is the absolute truth or the whole of truth, and that again
is something which, as a philosopher would say, unifies,
or co-ordinates, or is a synthesis of, our whole experience.
But Browning was not first and foremost a philosopher—
it is important to keep that fact well in view at this point.
The philosopher in his pursuit of truth employs a dialec-

tic—an analytic logic; his labour is ratiocination. The poet
relies on intuition and on visions. He leaps or flies across
the abyss while the philosopher is laboriously laying the
foundations of a bridge. Or, to use a different metaphor,
he has heaven opened to him in a vision. How far he succeeds in making us also see that vision depends upon two
things—the adequacy of his medium and the distinctness
and clarity of his own seeing eye. And so far as Browning
has in any instance or in any degree failed, it has been
usual to attribute failure to the inadequacy of his medium—that is, of human language. It is not impossible, however, that he did not always manage to see very clearly
what it was he desired to convey. And that may have been,
as he himself hints, because he could not endure to face
the central incandescence of that revealment. Certainly he
desired to see, and to make others see, the world irradiated
with that light—the light that shone within himself. Because it shone within himself, therefore, to impart the light
would be to express himself—it would be to achieve the
work for which he hoped and believed he was born—"R.
B.—a poem." But it was never written.

Let us notice that though the poem was never written, the
unity never achieved, the white light never transferred in
full radiance to his page, that is not to say that Browning
had no hint at all of what the poem might be if it ever
should come to be written. The metaphor of prismatic
hues breaks down at this point, therefore, since from them
alone no one could gather any hint at all of the whiteness
of white light. The metaphor being abandoned, we are
committed, if we are to proceed with this inquiry, to nothing less formidable than a study of the psychology of the
poetic act. Adequately conducted, it would extend far beyond the limits of the present book. Even narrowed down
to the strictest limits compatible with any measurable result, it remains most difficult, and happens to be one in
which we have very little evidence from which to work.
The poets, who alone could give evidence, have been reticent. They are not, as a rule, given to an examination of
their own states of mind in moments of creation. However,
it so happens that Browning himself in his Preface to the
spurious *Letters of Shelley,* published in 1851, has given
us a hint. From his own poems (improbable as it may seem
at first sight) we can deduce something, and lastly we have
something in Wordsworth and in Keats which should be
of use.

What Browning has to say in the Preface does very little
more than confirm what was said just now—that the poet
apprehends his truth in a vision. The subjective poet, says
Browning, struggles towards "Not what man sees, but
what God sees—the *Ideas* of Plato, seeds of creation lying
burningly on the Divine Hand. . . . Not with the combination of humanity in action, but with the primal elements
of humanity he has to do; and he digs where he stands,—
preferring to seek them in his own soul as the nearest reflex of that absolute Mind, according to the intuitions of
which he desires to perceive and speak." The predominating metaphors here are of vision and light. From Wordsworth, who more than any other of the great poets was interested in the becoming of his poems, we may quote this
from *The Prelude* (Book I):

The Poet, gentle creature as he is,
Hath, like the Lover, his unruly times;
His fits when he is neither sick nor well,
Though no distress be near him but his own
Unmanageable thoughts: his mind best pleased,
While she as duteous as the mother dove
Sits brooding, lives not always to that end,
But like the innocent bird, hath goadings on
That drive her as in trouble through the
    groves . . .

The point there which calls for particular notice is the fit of restlessness which comes over the poet from time to time—a goading on (what in fashionable jargon would now be called "an urge") towards some unknown goal. However well trained for his flight Wordsworth might think himself, yet when it came to choosing a theme, all went awry. For if he chose a historic theme, that might be merely because he mistook—

Proud spring-tide swellings for a regular
    sea, . . .

Besides restlessness, there is something else that hampers the poet. He must come to his act of creative contemplation in a mood of complete humility, simplicity, sincerity. He must, in short, make an act of entire self-surrender. It might be a mystic who had written those lines. (pp. 193-97)

And Keats knew well the "unruly times" of the poet— "After working day by day at writing, I have a swimming in my head, and feel all the effects of a mental debauch, lowness of spirits, anxiety to go on, without the power to do so." Finally, he also believed that the poet must be passive and must make a complete surrender of himself—"It struck me what quality went to form a man of achievement, especially in literature. . . . I mean *Negative Capability,* that is, when a man is capable of being in uncertainties, mysteries, doubts, without any irritable reaching after fact and reason." And again: "Let us not go hurrying about and collecting honey, bee-like buzzing here and there for knowledge of what is to be arrived at; but let us open our leaves like a flower and be passive and receptive." Finally, just these words: "The poetical character has no self—it is everything and nothing."

We know that Browning, like Wordsworth and Keats, had his "unruly times . . . his fits when he was neither sick nor well," and that he felt those goadings on that drove him "as in trouble through the groves." Elizabeth Barrett Browning writes in one of her letters:

Robert waits for an inclination, works by fits and starts—he can't do otherwise he says. Then reading hurts him. . . . The consequence of which is that he wants occupation and that active occupation is salvation to him with his irritable nerves, saves him from ruminating bitter cud, and from the process which I call beating his dear head against the wall till it is bruised, simply because he sees a fly there, magnified by his own two eyes almost indefinitely into some Saurian monster.

And so she was glad when he took to clay modelling and to sculpture. We know from Mrs. Orr that his nervous ex-

citability was such that, when he called upon a friend, he often wondered whether he would be able to make his way into the drawing-room. Perhaps here we may find a special significance in these lines from **"The Guardian Angel"**:

If this was ever granted, I would rest
    My head beneath thine, while thy healing
        hands
Close-covered both my eyes beside thy breast,
    Pressing the brain, which too much thought
        expands,
Back to its proper size again, and smoothing
Distortion down till every nerve had soothing,
    And all lay quiet, happy and suppressed.

How soon all worldly wrong would be repaired!
    I think how I should view the earth and skies
And sea, when once again my brow was bared
    After thy healing, with such different eyes.

Incidentally, this is one of the few earlier poems in which Browning is speaking avowedly for himself.

Turmoil and restlessness are very clearly pictured here, in those interludes, at least, between the actual times of poetic creation. But in those times themselves Browning seems to have found himself beset with even greater difficulties than Wordsworth. For difficult as was the entry into the viewless realm of poesy, once there he still found himself a prey to his own intrusive emotions. He feared the white light. At this point we may fitly recall certain passages in his poetry, already quoted in previous chapters, in which he dwells upon the danger to mortal man of having his human sight exposed to this light. Those passages occur, it will be remembered, in **"Bishop Blougram's Apology,"** **"A Death in the Desert"** and **"Karshish,"** and because the idea is put into the mouths of three individuals so widely different as the worldly Roman prelate, Saint John the Divine and an Arabian medical student, it may legitimately be ascribed to Browning himself. Certainly his attempts to confront the white light were accompanied by great distress of mind, and there is a special set of associations not grasped by all readers in the beginning of the Invocation of the first part of *The Ring and the Book:*

Boldest of hearts that ever braved the sun
Took sanctuary within the holier blue
And sang a kindred soul out to his face. . . .

In *Paracelsus* and in *Sordello* we find allusions to the psychology of the poetic act. Aprile, the poet in *Paracelsus,* has failed because he did not learn to temper love with wisdom. He says:

I could not curb
My yearnings to possess at once the full
Enjoyment, but neglected all the means
Of realizing even the frailest joy.

And his own endeavour in poetry he sums up in these words:

Last, having thus revealed all I could love,
Having received all love bestowed on it,
I would die: preserving so throughout my course
God full on me as I was full on men.

He could not bring himself to understand in time that the task being so great and the time so brief, he could only accomplish a part of his aim. But for our present purpose it is even more important to notice the restlessness and bedazzlement which possessed him in his moments of poetic vision:

> Dazzled by shapes that filled its lengths with
>   light,
> Shapes clustered there to rule thee, not obey,
> That will not wait thy summons, will not rise
> Singly, nor when thy practised eye and hand
> Can well transfer their loveliness, but crowd
> By thee for ever, bright to thy despair? . . .

It may be argued that Aprile is a dramatic creation, and that we have no right to assume that Browning is picturing his own state of mind. That Aprile is to some extent a dramatic creation need not be disputed, but that there were common features in his experience and in Browning's is demonstrable. Compare the first of the three quotations above with this passage from a letter to Elizabeth Barrett—"But this is very foolish . . . and is part of an older—indeed primitive body of mine, which I shall never get rid of, of desiring to do nothing when I cannot do all, seeing nothing, getting, enjoying nothing, when there is no seeing and getting and enjoying *wholly.*" Moreover, there is a strong probability that a poet—especially a poet of twenty-three—in describing the psychology of another poet, whether a real poet or a figment of his own imagination, will to some extent consciously and to a greater extent unconsciously draw upon his own experiences.

In Sordello we have another poet who desired to get and enjoy everything at once, and who was, in a sense, the victim of his own imagination. And since the poem to which he gave his name is to yield much material for what follows—that is to say, for the remaining part of our inquiry into the poetic psychology of Browning—it is necessary to consider in this case also how far the poem is autobiographical and how far truly dramatic. What have Sordello and his creator in common? We have already mentioned the desire to get and to enjoy everything all at once. Next there is this, that just as in *Sordello* the spirit was allowed with its infinite power to work destructively upon the weak and limited flesh, so we know from the *Love Letters* how even in his early manhood Browning suffered in his physical constitution from the effects of high nervous tension and the excitability and restlessness of the poet's creative act. Again, in *Sordello* Browning was making a huge effort to work out a new style—almost a new poetic language. Of this there is complete evidence in the biographies. The poet Sordello had this aim also among others, and the passage in which the aim is set out contains some of the soundest criticism ever made by a poet. Not only is the criticism worth reading on that account, but also because it is a presage, in 1840, of certain doctrines which in this day critics and poets regard as characteristically modern. The new language which Sordello tried to create failed—

> Because perceptions whole, like that he sought
> To clothe, reject so pure a work of thought
> As language: thought may take perception's
>   place
> But hardly co-exist in any case,
> Being its mere presentment—of the whole

> By parts, the simultaneous and the sole
> By the successive and the many. Lacks
> The crowd perception? painfully it tacks
> Thought to thought, which Sordello, needing
>   such,
> Has rent perception into: it's to clutch
> And reconstruct—his office to diffuse,
> Destroy . . .

Elsewhere in the poem, in a curious passage in which, so to speak, Browning himself peeps out from behind the mask he is wearing, we have evidence that Sordello's conception of the function of poetry in its final or most perfect development is also Browning's conception. In this development the poet becomes "Dramatist, or, so to call him, Analyst" (to quote the heading of page 419 in Vol. III of the 1863 edition):

> Once more I cast external things away,
> And natures composite so decompose
> That . . . Why, he writes *Sordello!*

The inverted commas enclose Sordello's words—the rest is Browning's comment.

Other evidence of community of thought and experience between Browning and Sordello may be found in the fact that Sordello has ascribed to him many thoughts ascribed also to others of Browning's creations, which may for that reason be considered as characteristic of their creator. More valid is the identity of Sordello's thoughts with thoughts expressed in *La Saisiaz,* since in the latter poem Browning is avowedly speaking *in propria persona.* We may therefore set side by side this passage from *Sordello* (Sordello himself is speaking)—

> Forget
> Vain ordinances, I have an appeal—
> I feel, am what I feel, know what I feel;
> So much is truth to me—

in which we have an expression in the briefest possible form of that subjective idealism which Professor Henry Jones recognised as the characteristic Browning metaphysic, with these lines from *La Saisiaz:*

> I have questioned and am answered. Question,
>   answer presuppose
> Two points: that the thing itself which questions,
>   answers,—is, it knows;
>
>   . . . . .
>
> Knowledge stands on my experience: all outside
>   its narrow hem,
> Free surmise may sport and welcome! Pleasures,
>   pains affect mankind
> Just as they affect myself? Why, here's my
>   neighbour, colour blind,
> Eyes like mine to all appearance: "Green as
>   grass" do I affirm?
> "Red as grass" he contradicts me: which employs the proper term?

From such evidence of community of thought between Sordello and Aprile and Browning on this and that specific point, we may guess at a wider range of community of experience—including all those ideas and emotions which in their case accompanied or constituted the poetic act.

Let us once more consider what were the special characteristics of this experience. The first feature to be noted was a certain restlessness which arose from an unsatisfied desire to seize and to enjoy at once all forms of beauty revealed to the poet. Neither Aprile nor Sordello is a being half-angel and half-bird that fronts the sun and sings a kindred soul out to his face. They are more like moths that dash at the light and dash away in contracting or expanding spirals until their wings are singed and they die—desiring the white light and yet terrified by it. In Sordello the idea of the disruptive power of spirit forcing itself on the too-weak flesh is cardinal to the whole poem. And here it is not impossible that we have given to us, in a different metaphor, the same idea which Paracelsus embodies of the poet baffled and finally ruined in his attempt to possess the whole of beauty at once. That similarity in the conceptions can be exhibited in the following way. There is obviously a sense in which we may talk of spirit and the beauty in which spirit manifests itself as one and the same thing. In that case it is probably immaterial whether we speak of the poet's destruction being caused by the spirit trying to force itself in all the extent of its power and beauty and in one moment upon the inadequate and limited human being, or of that human being with all the inadequacies and limitations of the world of time and space in which he has his existence attempting in one moment or act to achieve and hold all beauty and power.

Aprile could not restrain himself from this vain and self-destructive aim any more than the moth can restrain itself from flying into the candle. Sordello, indeed, when it was too late, learnt the lesson of restraint, the means of sacrificing some part of the ineffable vision of power and bliss. Only love can reconcile the poet to this act of restraint and sacrifice. That is the love of humanity which Shelley—the strongest influence in Browning's time of adolescence—had made a leading theme in his poetry. We know from Browning's letters and from his biographers that to help, strengthen and comfort humanity was considered by him to be the poet's highest aim or office. He must not and cannot remain in the far region of incommunicable dreams of bliss. To help on his fellows he must be able to communicate, and if beauty in its entirety and power is not to be communicated, he must content himself with revealing only some part of it, with lifting just a corner of the curtain. And the method which Browning chose was the method of revealing so much of this spectacle of power and beauty as could be seen at work in the minds of a character or set of characters—in their minds or their imaginary utterances.

That, then, might be one explanation of the adoption of the dramatic style or treatment—that it is a deliberate self-limitation or sacrifice by the poet. But there is another explanation towards which most of the preceding discussion of the problem in this chapter will seem to have been leading, that fear or, short of fear, trouble, turmoil, confusion may have deterred the poet from facing the light—the central and informing influence in his poetic vision. And without any attempt to derogate from Browning's motives, we may remark that when he is discussing with Elizabeth Barrett his plans for the future, his intention of speaking out, and the causes which have led him to make his work

dramatic, he does not speak of a deliberate self-limitation, and he announces his intention of following her example and allowing the white light to shine out. It was not love of humanity which had hitherto caused him to veil that light—or it was only at times and in part that his motive had been this.

Let us once again for a moment divest the discussion of the metaphors of light. We have already suggested that, interpreted in the language of logic, this seeing of the white light of ultimate truth amounts to a co-ordination, a harmonisation of the poet's experience—it is the attainment of that unity which the mystic assigns as the essential character of the Supreme Being. It was this co-ordination or unification of his experience, not, indeed, by means of the logician's dialectic but by means of the poet's intuition or vision, which seemed so difficult a task to Browning. Every movement which he made in this direction seemed to be inhibited. He stumbled and tripped. The effects show themselves in his style. He knew that *Sordello* was obscure, and he attempted to re-write it. The attempt failed, and he consoled himself by reflecting that while it was easy enough to express certain things or facts, such as "bricks and mortar," the ideas of Sordello came near transcending the powers of language. It might be laid down as a general rule that the obscurity of Browning is in proportion to the earnestness of his attempt to achieve, by intuition, a synthesis of his most intimate thoughts—as in the concluding parts of *Fifine at the Fair*, in *La Saisiaz*, in *Easter Day*, in **"Jochanan Hakkadosh,"** in **"Francis Furini"** and so forth. Poems like *Pacchiarotto* are difficult for a different reason—namely, that Browning is deliberately indulging in freaks of language. And Aprile and Sordello may to this extent, if no further, be projections of their creator's own self, that as in their case, so in his, strenuous concentration of the mind upon the ultimate problems of life had a definitely harmful effect upon the physical constitution.

But all this is not to deny that he had his moments, though not frequent, in which the scattered and conflicting elements of experience were co-ordinated and unified—moments, if we prefer the language, of vision. They are to be found in **"Saul,"** in **"Rabbi Ben Ezra,"** in **"Abt Vogler,"** in **"The Last Ride Together."** . . . In the main, however, he found himself bound to accept as a condition of his work a certain dissipation of his experience. To return to his own metaphors, he had to take light not from its source but as reflected and refracted from this object or that. He consoled himself with this knowledge,

> Yet my poor spark had for its source the sun,

even though it was rarely that he could direct upon that source "the great looks which compel light from its fount."

So far, in considering the psychology of the poetic act as exhibited in Browning, we have been concerned with showing that certain inhibitions were at work here. The question inevitably arises at this point—"What were these inhibitions?" The word "inhibition" at once suggests some theory of the kind put forward by psycho-analysts. And it seems that such theories have already been brought to bear upon Browning, inasmuch as someone has suggested that **"By the Fireside"** shows upon analysis clearest evidence that Browning was jealous of the success of his wife's poetry and hated her for it! One can also imagine that **Sordello** might be taken as a proof that Browning suffered from an inferiority complex. Such methods of dealing with the problem raised in this chapter must be left to others. To the question—of what nature was the inhibition from which Browning suffered, no satisfactory answer can be suggested by the present writer. He will travel thus far with the psycho-analysts as to say that there were powerful forces at work in the man which never succeeded in finding their appropriate outlet. And it is also not impossible that **Sordello** affords evidence that Browning was so far ahead of his age as to have come within a hair's breadth of this modern way of stating his own trouble. The idea of the spirit, timeless and out of space, destroying the poet's limited and temporal bodily constitution in an attempt to express itself comes extraordinarily close to the more modern idea of primitive instincts and desires thrusting themselves into the conscious life of a man and ruining him, body and mind. But the similarity must not be exaggerated. Browning's "soul" eternal and free is a very different notion from the modern "libido." (pp. 197-209)

The attempt has been made to suggest that certain inconsistencies and anomalies in Browning result from a deep-seated conflict in his mind. The warring elements could be described as either the poet and the bourgeois, or as the mystic and the poet of action. The poet of action works within the realms of time and space, since these are necessary conditions of action. For him, action has value in itself; and since attainment is the death of action, he likes to think of attainment as perpetually deferred. Again, he believes in the value of the individual and the concrete, the creatures of time and space. Nothing that can happen to the individual soul is alien to him—he is full of "eager mundane curiosity." Over against him stands the contemplative poet whose thought wings itself beyond the realms of time and space, who can see each minute sealed with the mark of the infinite and eternal because the infinite and eternal include and swallow up the finite and the temporal. In his eyes nothing that has happened of good or beautiful can perish, because it is stored up for ever in the repository of the eternal. This assurance he has from God, revealed not by the unaided reason but in a moment of direct communication, since "God has a few of us whom he whispers in the ear." The mood and the language are not restless and vari-coloured, but quiet and contemplative—not inert, but tense.

But the contemplative appears more rarely than the poet of action. The reason seems to be that, when Browning tried to rise above the realm of action into the realm of contemplation, the effort produced in him a turmoil and distress of a particular kind. The contemplative was eager to rise to those regions of vision, but the poet of action pulled him back. Or, to try a different picture, Browning figures like a child in a fairy story who has been promised that he shall be allowed to enter paradise on this one condition, that he will suppress his curiosity and his desires and quietly watch all that passes before him. Any movement on his part will blur and finally destroy that paradisi-

acal prospect. But, try as he may, he cannot suppress himself. The light of that supreme vision hurts his eyes—all the beautiful things he sees stir an irresistible desire to clutch and possess: he springs forward to grasp them—and the charm is broken—he finds himself back on earth again among his men and women. The white light which shone for a brief instant is quenched.

In his earlier years this feeling of conflict and distress which accompanied the poetic act produced definite physical repercussions—a physical restlessness, headaches, neuralgia—which he tried to cure by vigorous exercise. In later life the conflict may have become less severe—through what causes cannot exactly be known. The shock of his wife's death might be expected to produce violent reactions. However this may be, after the finishing of **The Ring and the Book** there grew up a sort of dullness and dryness at the very core of his poetry. Another effect of the conflict would be a tendency to shut off his poetry from the rest of his life. In some measure, though probably not in great measure, there may have been a reluctance to admit strangers into a workshop which he had never quite succeeded in ordering properly. What he said himself was that his poetry was an affair between him and his God, not meaning thereby that it was a matter too sacred and intimate to be divulged to the curious vulgar, but that no one could help him in it any more than it is given to any man to save his neighbour's soul. But his account of the situation may be incomplete, and it may have been that he unconsciously shrank from reviving the restlessness and turmoil of the poetic moment.

The dissociation of his poetry would also tend to make him in outward life, as he mixed with his fellows, more a man of the world, more, even, of the bourgeois. . . . We know it was difficult for Archbishop Benson . . . , for he writes in his diary for 3rd May, 1884: "R. Browning introduced himself to me because I had quoted him in my speech. He looks strangely to me if he does really live his poems."

It is probable that he came nearer to a reconciliation of the two sides of his nature during his married life than at any other time: and this also is the period of his greatest work. His wife fostered in him the belief that he could rise above limited and partial expressions of the truth to a steady and embracing view of the whole of truth. But to such a point he never, in fact, did rise. Every now and again he caught a glimpse of that Promised Land, but it is hardly too much to say that he died upon Pisgah. Here may be found the true reason why he cannot be classed with the very greatest of poets—with the Wordsworth of the *Immortality* Ode and *Tintern Abbey* and with the Keats of the *Odes* and the *Sonnets*. But that short of the very greatest names he is yet great—and greater than most of us take him for—that would not be very difficult to establish, even if in the process it became necessary (as it pretty certainly would) to discard large masses of that work to which nothing except a kind of excited restlessness was always driving him. And it will be necessary for anyone who might desire to do him better justice than he has yet received not to blame him for the mistakes and short-sightedness of his previous critics—mid-Victorian, late-Victorian or late-Georgian. It is not likely that any critic of to-day or to-morrow will have to struggle against the tendency to condemn him as a subverter of morals. Nor yet shall we ever again come to think of him as a mighty champion of established doctrines standing between us and ruin, though perhaps we shall recognise in the man himself, when times are propitious for such a view, a courage, nobility and constancy, a generosity and power of sympathy too rare in this present day. We may come to think of him as a poet who struggled bravely to gain an insight into the hidden soul of things—fought his way towards a light that by turns eluded and blinded him. And, meanwhile, what a world he created may some day be again revealed even to the most intelligent of us—its colour, its abundance of life, its palpitating vigour, its movement that goes glorying in its own rapidity and strength. When we look below outward things in that world, we may come to see some of our own troubles and pleasures, our own most modern doubts and certainties, faithfully mirrored or forecast with a marvellous accuracy. (pp. 209-13)

> *F. R. G. Duckworth, in his* Browning: Background and Conflict, *E. P. Dutton & Co., Inc., 1932, 217 p.*

Kenneth L. Knickerbocker   (essay date 1959)

[Knickerbocker refutes the arguments made by George Santayana [see essay dated 1900] point by point.]

One who tries to assess the modern appraisal of Browning is aware of a vast horizontal wagging of heads and a reproving dental click of tongues. On the pages of magazines and books are scrawled the legend: "Browning go home." The poet once accounted deep and subtle has become a man of straw with an empty head. Every poet, as the generations pass, moves more or less violently up and down the scale of critical popularity, and Browning, one suspects, has been pushed as near oblivion as he is likely to go.

The near-oblivion is testified to by many critics. One, a reviewer of Roma J. King's *The Bow and the Lyre,* wrote early in 1958: "Certainly Browning's reputation needs at this point all the help it can get." Writing also this year, an editor of a new batch of Browning letters observes: "It must be admitted that the hundredth anniversary of *Men and Women* . . . finds [Browning] with fewer readers than at any time in the last fifty years." This reviewer and this editor are convinced that the icon of the Browning societies has been pretty well smashed. They are no doubt right, as we shall see.

Professor Boyd Litzinger in his excellent dissertation, *Robert Browning's Reputation as a Thinker, 1889-1955,* has made available, among other things, a highly convenient collection of critical remarks concerning Browning. Here are a few of the judgments culled from Professor Litzinger's findings for the years 1950-55. Browning is "intellectually unsatisfying"; along with Tennyson, he is "fundamentally . . . dishonest" [John Heath-Stubbs]. Another critic: "he was not a thinker at all . . . compared with Tennyson or Arnold or Newman, he was philosophically illiterate" [Richard Altick]. And still another: "So

inferior a mind and spirit as Browning's could not provide the impulse needed to bring back into poetry the adult intelligence" [F. R. Leavis]. And besides all these, we have Mrs. Betty Miller. Dr. Litzinger describes her method as follows: "Wielding her evidence as though it were a flat-edged palette knife, Mrs. Miller scrapes assiduously away at past portraits of Browning until at the end of her labors we are given a scarred painting of Browning as an insecure, incompetent mamma's boy who in one sense was a failure at everything, including his roles as suitor and father."

It is clear that Browning is being kept alive by adverse criticism; if, of late, only favorable views of Browning were to be counted, the poet of the *Ring and the Book* could indeed be reckoned virtually dead. The fact that he can still provoke reams of critical animosity shows, one supposes, a curious vitality.

Even in these days, Browning has mustered a few defenders, notably Professor Roma J. King and some others. In a paper called "A Tentative Apology for Browning," I set forth a few words in Browning's behalf. The present paper is really a second installment of the "Tentative Apology," a paper which singled out for examination Professor Richard Altick's provocative article, "The Private Life of Robert Browning." How effective in general my paper was, I do not know, but I suspect that those who already felt as I do continued to feel that way and that those who were of an opposite opinion persisted in their wrongheadedness. In the latter category is, naturally, Professor Altick, who informed me in a letter dated December 29, 1956: "the point of view expressed in my article remains unaffected."

Having failed with a living scholar, I now try my hand on a dead one: the eminent Spanish philosopher and teacher, George Santayana. It may be that on some heavenly eminence, Browning and Santayana have had it out by now; yet, it is hardly conceivable that these two opposites are occupying the same limbo. If both have been granted their visions of the heavenly scene, then Browning may be imagined in any of a number of postures, Santayana in only one. Browning may be cantering through eternity on that famous last ride; or he may be enjoying an extended moment in his wife's arms; or he may be welcoming celestial rebuffs along with Rabbi Ben Ezra; or he may be back on earth in some other form (possibly as Ezra Pound). Browning looked to the infinite as a place of infinite possibilities. Santayana, on the other hand, expected to spend his eternity contemplating a cosmic navel; he would be at one with the One.

But I have run a bit ahead of myself. Why choose Santayana as a critic of Browning who deserves special attention? Professor Litzinger in his aforementioned dissertation gave a good deal of attention to Santayana's "The Poetry of Barbarism" [see excerpt dated 1900] and in part justified this procedure by remarking: "As far as I can tell, none of Browning's admirers has ever made an attempt to put into print an adequate answer to Santayana's charges." Even if Dr. Litzinger himself had wanted to defend Browning—and I believe he did not—it was no part of his job to offer a special plea for the subject of his study.

Since no one else has been tempted to encounter Santayana, and since this seems to imply that he must be devastatingly right, instead of merely devastating, I have taken on the task, without reluctance but with plenty of trepidation.

One may assume that "The Poetry of Barbarism," even though it was printed more than a half-century ago, is an important element in any modern appraisal of Browning. Echoes of this essay, acknowledged and unacknowledged, are audible in many later criticisms of Browning. It is clear, therefore, that if one hopes to get anywhere with a defense of Browning, one must take into account arguments presented in "The Poetry of Barbarism."

Santayana is a formidable figure, full of subtleties and certainties. Fortunately, he is not full of the jargon of philosophy. He writes with grace. Indeed, no small part of his persuasiveness comes from his emotional and non-ascetic style. For a philosopher, however, he is perhaps too prone to depend upon meagerly supported generalizations as an aid to argument.

The more one reads of and about Santayana, the more one is convinced that Browning would have delighted in composing a special plea for him, say under the title, "The Philosopher's Apology." The substance of such a poem could be derived in part from "The Poetry of Barbarism," which is a prose rationalization, a fine soliloquy in which the author, vastly disturbed by the spectacle of Whitman and Browning, attempts to dispose of these flies in the transcendental ointment.

I confess unhappily that I know Santayana far less well than I think I know Browning. Nevertheless, I have culled from the Spanish philosopher many remarks which suggest, I think, that his attitude towards Browning was inevitable, that indeed a vibrant Browning did not have a chance when measured against the narrow criterion invented by this curiously austere critic.

I have two rather large contentions to support: one, that Browning would have been a poorer poet if he had conformed fully to Santayana's expectations of a poet; and, two, that Browning would have been a somewhat poorer poet if he had been as lacking in totality as Santayana erroneously says that he is. To put this another way: Santayana's expectations of a poet and of poetry—though repeatedly said to be based upon reason—are unreasonable; furthermore, the lack of totality charged to Browning is, in fact, chargeable to Santayana who took from Browning only what he needed to support his position and let the rest go.

Under my first large contention, I should like to examine three points: first, Santayana's definition of poetry and where that definition leaves poets and poetry in general and Browning in particular; second, Santayana's emphasis on *idealization* and the curious esthetic judgments which result from such an emphasis; and, third, Santayana's instinctive dislike of optimism and the effect this distaste had upon his attitude towards Browning. So far as Browning is concerned, Santayana's even reading him is similar to the spectacle of sour John Knox carried "to the playhouse at Paris, Vienna, or Munich." Not that Santayana was a puritan. He was far from that, but energy did disturb

him. For some reason, nevertheless, he was set down—or for some reason sat down—before the lively spectacle of Browning and was shocked at all the exuberance. (pp. 1-4)

Basic to Santayana's approach to poetry is this statement: "Religion and poetry are identical in essence, and differ merely in the way in which they are attached to practical affairs." This fiat commits the philosopher-critic to a point of view which squeezes from top poetic ranks most of the world's poets, including Shakespeare. Indeed, it is the sort of dictum which, like the dramatic rules of the eighteenth century, ignores effect and produces a judgment such as this; "Those of us . . . who feel that the most important thing in life is the lesson of it, and its relation to its own ideal, . . . can hardly find in Shakespeare all that the highest poet could give." Because, then, Shakespeare—according to Santayana—was without a religion, he was also lacking in the essence of poetry.

Santayana in considering the merits of Goethe, Lucretius, and Dante admits that "If it were a question of the relative pleasure a man might get from each poet in turn, this pleasure would differ according to the man's temperament, his period of life, the language he knew best, and the doctrine that was most familiar to him." Pleasure, however, is not the point. "Goethe is the poet of life; Lucretius the poet of nature; Dante the poet of salvation." Goethe lacks totality, and Lucretius comes nearer to having it. Dante, however, goes far beyond both; he has "spiritual mastery of . . . life, and a perfect knowledge of good and evil." But Santayana concludes that a poet truly great at all points would have to be a combination of Lucretius, Dante, and Goethe. "This supreme poet," he admits, "is in limbo still."

Yet, it is apparent that Dante came nearest to Santayana's poetic ideal. Dante saw Beatrice and idealized her. Here Santayana makes a key observation, "The child of seven whom Dante saw at the Florentine feast was, if you will, a reality. As such she is profoundly unimportant." So Beatrice as a reality was "profoundly unimportant." If this is true, does Santayana mean that Dante could have created an ideal Beatrice without having seen the real Beatrice? Or does he mean that just any Italian girl would have served just as well? Whatever he may mean, it is evident that to him the poet who merely *realizes* is inferior to the poet who *idealizes*. The love, therefore, of Robert Browning for Elizabeth Barrett—a love which combined reasonably well the real and the ideal—would simply baffle Santayana. Without idealization, the philosopher insists, happiness "is not found,—no, never,—in spite of what we may think when we are first in love." Man must idealize or be forever corroded by the bitter reality of a specific woman. One begins to see that Santayana is not really going to sympathize with, perhaps not even understand, such lines as these from **"By the Fireside":**

> Oh moment, one and infinite!
>   The water slips o'er stock and stone;
> The West is tender, hardly bright:
>   How grey at once is the evening grown—
> One star, its chrysolite!
>
> We two stood there with never a third,
>   But each by each, as each knew well:

The sights we saw and the sounds we heard,
    The light and the shades made up a spell
Till the trouble grew and stirred.

Oh, the little more, and how much it is!
    And the little less, and what worlds away!
How a second shall quicken content to bliss,
    Or a breath suspend the blood's best play,
And life be a proof of this!

Perhaps these lines represent a "barbaric yawp." Perhaps to Browning, the reality of Elizabeth Barrett should have been "profoundly unimportant," instead, as seems to be true, the most profoundly important influence in his life and in his conception of an after-life. Perhaps Browning should have bounded up the staircase in the house on Wimpole Street, looked intensely for a moment on the reality, and then trudged off to a lifetime of idealization. I should imagine, however, that the Beatrice of Dante's imagining simply did for the gloomy Italian what the vibrant reality of the lady of Wimpole Street did for a gloomless Browning.

In the lines just quoted from **"By the Fireside,"** Browning indulges in a form of idealization. So far as external beauty is concerned—if we are to trust the photographs of Mrs. Browning—this may have been a stern test of Browning's powers of imagination. He managed, however, to live very well with the reality and the ideal combined. Dante, on the other hand, took a wife and at the same time retained Beatrice as the mistress of his soul. Santayana acknowledges this dual relationship as possibly a "species of infidelity"—not to the wife, but to the mistress. In any event, Dante did not find much discernible happiness in his situation, surely less than Browning found in his. What kind of advantage, then, accrues to the idealizer? A feeling of superiority, of being above it all? Does the idealizer say to himself: "This life is nasty and short; my imagination at least can set me aside from the ordinary run of mortals and lift me into the pure and the eternal"?

That Santayana may have so reasoned seems probable. Edmund Wilson in an essay on the correspondence of Harold J. Laski and Chief Justice Holmes observes: "There is a brilliant remark about Santayana in a letter of 1924 [from Laski to Holmes]: 'In a general way [Santayana's] thinking more than that of other philosophers coincides with mine. But he has a patronizing tone—as of one who saw through himself but didn't expect others to.' " As we shall see in a moment, the patronizing tone to which Laski refers is most evident in "The Poetry of Barbarism." Indeed, the tone is part of the argument, a device intended to silence reply.

Santayana's lofty view of life may be valid but then, again, it may not. In any event, no poet should be required to subscribe to such a view—and few poets have. When Santayana condemns Browning for revelling in reality, he is condemning him for accentuating the very thing which gives his poetry—indeed, any poetry—its essential power. (pp. 4-6)

Santayana tells us in "The Poetry of Barbarism" how far Browning fell short of the ideal. It is here that the patronizing tone observed by Laski becomes painfully evident. The philosopher-critic uses time-honored devices to dis-

arm anyone who might be sympathetic with Browning. Says he: "a person coming to Browning with *the habits of a cultivated mind* might see evidence of some profound incapacity in the poet." And elsewhere he adds, "no poet is so undisciplined that he will not find many readers, if he finds readers at all, less disciplined than himself." In short, cultivated, disciplined readers do not approve Browning, uncultivated, capricious readers do. This may be so, but it is not difficult to concoct a counter-statement: "A person coming to Browning with a free and open mind, unfettered by pre-conceptions, might see evidence of a profound and various capacity in the poet and less incapacity than, as a human being, he was entitled to."

I suppose most of us do not want to be classified as uncultivated and still less to be identified as barbarians. A barbarian Santayana defines as "the man who regards his passions as their own excuse for being; who does not domesticate them either by understanding their cause or by conceiving their ideal goal." I am afraid this definition gets us precisely nowhere. Santayana had no more notion or understanding of the *cause* of passions than had Browning or any other finite creature. He implies that we have passions in order to domesticate them, just as, I suppose, we have tigers in order to make tabby cats of them. If Santayana does not know the cause of passions, neither does he know their ideal goal. He implies that we have passions so that we may absolutely quench them by a perpetual curfew.

The subjection of the passions may be man's chief task, and if all men strove hard to douse their desires, a generation of saints might be the result. One suspects that as the saints came marching in, poetry would go marching out. At precisely this point, however, Santayana would disagree. In his essay on "Platonic Love" he makes it clear that Dante is great partly because he idealized his love for Beatrice. As Santayana interprets the situation, the Italian poet had a wife for ordinary purposes, but he retained Beatrice—or what his imagination made of her—for his ideal. Not only Dante, but Guido Cavalcanti understood love through having a Giovanna as the counterpart of Dante's Beatrice. Even the poetry of Michael Angelo is worth study because in it the great artist—and relatively poor poet—seems to sympathize with the Platonic ideal. And, finally, Lorenzo de' Medici is a poet worth noting because he sometimes rises "to the purest sphere of tragedy and religion."

Santayana's test, then, of the essence of great poetry is simple: great poems involving love will never center on a specific being as the object of love but will always idealize the object out of anything but a faint resemblance to the reality. Herein, Browning failed. "Readers of the fifth chapter of this volume [the chapter on "Platonic Love"] need not be reminded here," says Santayana, "of the contrast" which Browning's method of understanding love "offers to that adopted by *the real masters of passion and imagination.*" The "real masters of passion and imagination," then, are Dante, Guido Cavalcanti, Michael Angelo, and Lorenzo de' Medici.

As we have seen, the one thing these four men had in common was the same willingness to idealize, a willingness deriving, at least in part, from a poetic vogue similar in effect to that which provided a formula for Elizabethan sonneteering. Idealizing poetry may indeed be great, but it has at least one fault: it is inescapably monotonous. No matter how the love poems start, they must all end the same way: Beatrice, Giovanna, Elizabeth Barrett, Juliet, Lady Macbeth and Grace Kelly when rendered by the idealizing imagination all come out as indistinguishable from one another. It seems to me that any poet who subscribed to the rules of Platonic love would write one love poem and be done.

Browning wrote many love poems, some of them similar to others but most of them distinct, unique creations. He surely followed no vogue, submitted himself to no formula. His characters are as diverse as life. Ottima and Pompilia, Lucrezia and Phene, Constance and Mildred, the Duchess of Ferrara and Cristina, the Countess Gismond and Porphyria, the mistress of the Bishop of St. Praxed and the lady of "Time's Revenges," Evelyn Hope and James Lee's wife—can one seriously wish that the poet, through idealization, had substituted himself, first for the lovers of these women and then for the readers? (pp. 6-8)

Platonic love as interpreted and evangelized by Santayana apparently is restricted to males. It is like the neat arrangements of knight errantry with ladies needing to be saved and knights available to save them. Platonic love implies that women need to be idealized (they may, of course) and men should find their greatest satisfaction in performing this service. The service, however, does not benefit any particular woman but allegedly does wonderful things for the man.

If Santayana was disturbed by Browning's devotion to reality, he was, no doubt, even more baffled by the poet's speculations concerning evil. In an essay called "Obiter Scripta," he drops this remark: "Of all systems an optimistic system is the most oppressive. Would it not be a bitter mockery if, in the words of Bradley, this were the best of possible worlds, and everything in it a necessary evil?" It is easy to parry this observation and Browning could have parried it by asking: "Would it not be a bitter oddity if this were the worst of possible worlds and everything in it an unnecessary evil?" Could there be a worse world than one in which evil has no purpose, not even the purpose of "silence implying sound"?

As we have seen, to Santayana poetry and religion are identical. The function of poetry, he says, is "to draw from reality materials for an image of the ideal to which reality ought to conform, and to make us citizens by anticipation, in the world we crave."

At this point, I come to my second large contention: that Browning would have been a somewhat poorer poet if he had indeed been as lacking in totality as Santayana contends, if he had completely ignored idealization, ecstasies, and the possibility on occasion of being made a citizen "by anticipation, in the world we crave." But Browning is not to be fairly caught here, only unfairly by ignoring an important segment of his works.

In **"How It Strikes a Contemporary"** it is more than hinted that the poet's duty lies in

Doing the King's works all the dim day long,

and in being essentially God's spy. Lines in the poem **"Amphibian,"** which precede *Fifine at the Fair,* recognize poetry as a substitute for heaven.

> Emancipate through passion
>   And thought, with sea for sky,
> We substitute, in a fashion,
>   For heaven,—poetry.

And later, with reference to "the spirit-sort," the poem continues:

> Whatever they are, we seem:
>   Imagine the thing they know;
> All deeds they do, we dream;
>   Can heaven be else but so?

It is clear that Browning does not refuse to recognize the affinity of poetry and religion, but one notes at once to what Santayana would object in the lines just quoted. Says the philosopher in his essay on "Understanding, Imagination, and Mysticism": "the specific and the finite, I feel, are odious; let me therefore aspire to see, reason and judge in no specific or finite manner—that is, not to see, reason or judge at all. So I shall be like the Infinite, nay I shall become one with the Infinite and (marvellous thought!) one with the One." When Browning refers to the "spirit-sort" as "they," he simply misses Santayana's idea of heaven. It could as well be concluded, however, that Santayana does unavoidably "see, reason [and] judge"—and nowhere better than in the passage just quoted—and that through seeing and reasoning with quite finite capacities he judges that to be one with the One would be better than to be a discrete spirit among many discrete spirits. Browning judges otherwise. Nirvana may be a quite lovely and blissful state; it certainly is an irresponsible one, and it may be that the mystic's ecstasy is largely a sense of union with cosmic irresponsibility. The point I believe to be true, however, is this: that Browning did not emphasize what Santayana emphasizes proves little concerning Browning's powers as a poet and not much about the superiority of Santayana's powers as a philosopher.

Curiously enough Santayana, completely absorbed in Browning's barbarism, gives no credit to the poet for recognizing the part a mystical experience may have in producing temporary happiness—that is, in releasing an individual from this world's seeming. Yet Abt Vogler lives briefly in a mystical, musical experience and sees in it "the finger of God." He holds onto the experience as long as he can, with confidence that

> All we have willed or hoped or dreamed of good
>   shall exist;
> Not its semblance, but itself.

But life does not proceed in an ecstasy. Its normal concern is "the C Major of this life." Santayana does not mention **"Abt Vogler,"** but he should have, for he says in prose what Browning, through Abt Vogler, has said in poetry: "Thus mysticism, although a principle of dissolution, carries with it the safeguard that it can never be consistently applied. We reach it only in exceptional moments of intuition, from which we descend to our pots and pans with habits and instincts virtually unimpaired. Life goes on;

virtues and affections endure, none the worse, the mystic feels, for that slight film of unreality which envelops them in a mind not unacquainted with ecstasy." Abt Vogler, one notes, was reconciled to finding a resting place in the "C Major of this life"; Santayana uses the homelier figure of descending "to our pots and pans." One notes further that Browning was concerned with the virtues and affections (also the vices and the hatreds) which endure with or without the intrusion of ecstatic experience. He clearly was not unacquainted with the claims of mysticism and, by and large, his poems are not—as Santayana says they are—"aimless in their vehemence and [mere] ebullitions of lustiness in adventurous and profoundly ungoverned souls." (pp. 8-10)

One observes that Santayana, in describing his own creative purposes, describes at the same time Browning's method. Yet, the philosopher says that the poet's method is wrong, for "his art is all self-expression or satire . . . his hero . . . is himself." In any ultimate sense, of course, every creative artist must be his own hero and his own villain. What Santayana means is that Santayana is a proper hero and that Browning is not. Essentially Santayana is of the East, Browning of the West. To the philosopher, life quickly became curiously savorless, a complexity to be spurned, to hide from eventually in the shadows of the Eternal City. To the other, life was a wonder, a self-justifying delight, the one complex evidence of God's meaning for man. Santayana's views are exclusive, Browning's inclusive—even to the point of embracing some of Santayana's pet speculations.

Browning will survive. The modern attitude will shift back to the reasonable estimate of him as an ever-curious explorer of the human scene, a wayfaring poet who refused to avert his gaze from the world as it is. (pp. 10-11)

> *Kenneth L. Knickerbocker, "Robert Browning: A Modern Appraisal," in* Tennessee Studies in Literature, *Vol. IV, 1959, pp. 1-11.*

Robert Langbaum   (essay date 1966)

[*Langbaum's main critical concern has been to reestablish a vital connection between the literature of the nineteenth and twentieth centuries, to "connect romanticism with the so-called reactions against it." In his best-known work,* The Poetry of Experience: The Dramatic Monologue in Modern Literary Tradition (1957), *Langbaum makes a distinction between an older, ordered "poetry of experience" in which the imagination and the writing process itself help to shape the meaning of the poem. In the excerpt below, Langbaum explores Browning's use of myth.*]

To ask about Browning's use of myth is to ask two questions. The first is whether Browning believed in using—as Arnold did in *Sohrab* and *Merope,* and Tennyson did in the *Idylls*—the grand old enduring subjects that have come down to us in the literary tradition. The answer to the first question is no. Browning agreed with Miss Barrett, when she said in that often-quoted letter to him: "I am inclined to think that we want new *forms,* as well as thoughts. The old gods are dethroned. Why should we go back to the antique moulds, classical moulds, as they are so improperly called?" Browning himself said as much and more when, at the end of his life, he dealt, in **"Parleying With Gerard de Lairesse,"** with the question of how far the Greeks ought to be used as models for modern art. We have gone beyond the Greeks, he concluded, in religion and in moral and psychological insight. Modern poets should not, therefore, pour new wine into old bottles. They should no longer

> Dream afresh old godlike shapes,
> Recapture ancient fable that escapes,
> Push back reality, repeople earth
> With vanished falseness, recognize no worth
> In fact new-born unless 't is rendered back
> Pallid by fancy, as the western rack
> Of fading cloud bequeaths the lake some gleam
> Of its gone glory!

We should not ignore reality in favor of old subjects from mythology. Nor should we render modern facts poetical by decorating them with outworn mythological allusions.

On the issue raised by Arnold in the "Preface" to his *Poems* of 1853—the issue as to which subjects are better for modern poetry, the grand, enduring subjects or subjects drawn from modern life—Browning stood against Arnold and with the modern realists. It is true that Browning himself almost always used subjects drawn from the past. But he used them as history rather than myth. This explains his taste for little-known characters and incidents out of the past. For such characters and incidents have clearly not come down to us through the literary tradition. We can believe in the factuality of characters and incidents whose existence is authenticated even though they are no longer remembered. The forgotten historical character is the very opposite of the mythical character whose historical existence is doubtful even though he is vividly 'remembered.'

The historical attitude suggests that the past was as confused and unglamorous as the present. The historical attitude is also interested in tracing change—in showing how different were the ideas and values of the past from ours, in showing that the past was itself in the process of change. Yet the historical change is apparent because we can measure it against a recognizably continuous human or psychological reality. This again is opposite to the mythical attitude, which idealizes the past in order to set it up as a permanent criterion of value. At the same time, the mythical attitude makes the people of the past seem different from us, larger, sometimes superhuman. It is the past as permanent criterion that Arnold had in mind in the "Preface." In his very use of the past, then, Browning disagreed with Arnold. And he disagreed, too, on that other important issue of the "Preface"—Arnold's attack on internal drama, on the idea that modern poetry ought to treat, in Browning's phrase, "the incidents in the development of a soul."

On the issues raised by Arnold in the "Preface" and elsewhere, Browning was mainly right. For it is surely a weakness in Arnold's critical position that, while he could see art as dependent on the power of both the man and the moment, he should have supposed that the masterwork of one historical moment could or should have the virtues of the masterwork of another historical moment. Browning, on the other hand, was wrong in not understanding the importance of an action or of some external mechanism for portraying an internal state. Browning's poems fail just to the extent that his characters describe and analyze their thoughts and emotions, without any vividly apparent external reason for doing so. Browning was interested in talking about both history and psychology, and his problem as an artist was to find a means for doing so. Now a *mythos* or action, properly understood, is a way of accomplishing this end. For the kind of action we call mythical, just because it does not imitate a strictly external reality, is the kind that can speak with one voice of both internal and external reality. The problem is to use myth or the mythical method without archaizing—to use them in a distinctively modern way.

We have here a criterion for understanding the course of Browning's development and for assessing his work. For while he failed in *Paracelsus* and *Sordello* to reconcile internal and external reality, the two are successfully brought together in the best dramatic monologues. In *Paracelsus,* Browning fails because he has pushed offstage just those historical events that might have given outline and interest to his obscure historical character. What we get through a long poem is a continuing high-pitched reaction to we hardly know what; and we find ourselves longing for those vulgar events that Browning was so proud to have excluded.

In his long labors over *Sordello,* however, Browning apparently wrestled with the problem of reconciling internal and external reality. As DeVane has shown in his *Browning Handbook,* [see Further Reading list] *Sordello* was written in four different periods, in each of which Browning took a quite different view of his subject. In the first version, Browning treated his obscure historical character in the manner of *Paracelsus*—he gave us the history of a soul. In the second version, he made Sordello a man of action, a warrior and lover, thus showing Sordello's impact on the world around him. In the third version, he neglected Sordello himself and concentrated on the historical events of the period. In the fourth version, he rounded out his plot by making Sordello the champion of the masses and Salinguerra's son. The four Sordellos, which are imposed one upon the other, never do add up to a single *Sordello.*

It is just the elements of the first three *Sordellos* that are brought together in the best dramatic monologues. They are not brought together by plot—if by plot we mean a complete action, the kind that ties all the threads together and therefore seems to modern writers, especially novelists, who judge by the criteria of realism to offer too neat a rationalization of the material. But the three elements are nonetheless brought together by an action—a direction of the speaker's energies outward. It is because the speaker is not trying to tell the truth about himself, but is trying to accomplish something or make an impression, that he actually does reveal himself truly. This is the way characters reveal themselves in drama.

As in drama, the speaker has outline because we see him

not, as we see Paracelsus, in a confiding relation; we see him rather in a conflicting relation with another person. And we get, therefore, through the contrast, a sense of how he looks from the outside. The speaker also has outline because his fundamental human energies are clothed in the predilections peculiar to his age—as in **"The Bishop Orders His Tomb,"** where the Italian Renaissance bishop manifests his competitiveness and desire for immortality by ordering for himself a more expensive tomb than his rival's. A whole way of seeing, thinking, and feeling is manifested through that aim; so that we get, through one action, the man and the age, the man as he looks to others and himself, the outer and the inner reality. The action is, however, incomplete. That is the price Browning pays for using a realistic action; for the characteristically realistic action is the slice-of-life.

His best dramatic monologues entitle Browning to his rank among the two or three best Victorian poets. But is he also—as he certainly aimed to be—one of the great poets of English literature? In trying to answer, we have to admit that even in his best volume, **Men and Women,** Browning was tempted—in dramatic monologues like **"Cleon"** and **"Bishop Blougram"**—to slip back to the analytic, discursive style of the earlier, the *Paracelsus* period. And we know how, in the later dramatic monologues—in **"Mr. Sludge," "Prince Hohenstiel-Schwangau," "Fifine"**—he did slip back, without even the lyric fire of the *Paracelsus* period.

We have also to admit that even his very best dramatic monologues remain, after all, only splendid vignettes—"prismatic hues," as he himself called them. They do not add up to what Browning called "the pure white light," the total vision of life that the greatest poets give us, and that Browning from the start—from the time of *Sordello*—intended to give us. **The Ring and the Book,** of course, is Browning's climactic attempt to give us a total vision of life. He brings several dramatic monologues, several points of view together, in order to collapse the "prismatic hues" into "the pure white light"—in order to make explicit what is implicit in all the dramatic monologues, that the relative is an index to the absolute, that the relative is our way of apprehending the absolute.

This brings us to the second question about Browning's use of myth, the question that arises from our experience of Yeats, Eliot, and Joyce. In reviewing *Ulysses* for *The Dial* of November 1923, Eliot argues that Joyce is not as people think a "prophet of chaos," but that he has given us the materials of modern disorder and shown us how to impose order upon them. He has done this by what Eliot calls "the mythical method." Eliot is referring to the continuous parallel between the trivial and apparently meaningless events of Joyce's novel and the events in the *Odyssey.* . . . With the mythical method, the modern writer can render the disordered surface of modern life, while showing how nevertheless the mythical patterns inevitably reassert themselves at the unconscious roots of existence. This is the method Eliot himself uses in *The Waste Land.*

Now the whole point of *The Ring and the Book* was to pull out of a forgotten and sordid old Roman murder case the

Christian scheme of sin and redemption. Having himself, in an experience of illumination, seen through to the *truth* of the case, Browning's artistic strategy for conveying that truth was to restore *The Old Yellow Book* in which he had found the documents of the case. He wanted to give us the experience of reading the raw documents, to give us the jumbled real-life surface of the case and yet make us see through the facts—the facts so peculiar to the place and time—an eternal pattern. This is something like what Eliot says Joyce does.

Something, but not quite. For the case, as Browning renders it, does not really present a surface of ambivalence; and the pattern is rather too explicitly a moral pattern. We feel, as a result, that we are getting not absolute truth, but Browning's notions about absolute truth. **The Ring and the Book,** therefore, in spite of the many great things in it, does not in the end quite come off. Browning is more convincing in the best dramatic monologues, where he gives us truth as simply a relative manifestation that points somehow to the absolute. How? Through the fundamental human energy of the speaker, that seems to lead back to an unconscious ground of existence where all energies merge and are justified.

It is out of this unconscious ground that myths, according to twentieth-century theory, arise. And there remains, in **The Ring and the Book,** a pattern which is in Eliot's sense mythical because underlying. I mean the pattern of the Andromeda-Perseus myth and its Christian analogue, the myth of St. George and the dragon. We know that Browning's imagination was dominated, throughout his career, by the image of the beautiful Andromeda, chained naked to the rock, waiting helplessly for the serpent to come out of the sea to devour her, but waiting also—though she does not consciously know this—for Perseus to descend miraculously—to "come," as Browning puts it in **Pauline,** "in thunder from the stars"—to rescue her. The combination of sexual and spiritual ramifications gives the image its strength and validity.

The Andromeda-St. George myth connected Browning's life and art, giving him, as only myths can, what Yeats called "unity of being." In the greatest event of his life, he repeated the mythical pattern by rescuing Miss Barrett. And there is no doubt that he recognized the same mythical pattern when he read in *The Old Yellow Book* about Caponsacchi's rescue of Pompilia. He even changed the date of the rescue to make it fall on St. George's Day. It was because Browning was able to assimilate the murder case to the myth that **The Ring and the Book** is at once a very personal and a very impersonal poem.

There are many references throughout **The Ring and the Book** to the Andromeda-St. George myth, and it is used rather as the vegetation myth is used in *The Waste Land.* We are made to see a continuity between the pagan and Christian versions of the same myth. And all the characters seem inevitably to have some memory of the myth—though the debased characters remember it in a debased form; while the cynical characters, who see Caponsacchi's rescue as an abduction, turn the myth into its obverse, the myth of Helen and Paris. Nevertheless, the references re-

main only references—mythological allusions to illustrate points that are really being made discursively.

The Ring and the Book is an important poem, because it moves in the right direction. It moves away from myth as overt subject matter; yet it goes so far as to bring back the mythical pattern—not the particular events and characters of the Andromeda story, but the pattern—as inherent in the very structure of the mind, in what we would nowadays call the unconscious. **The Ring and the Book** does the same thing for the Christian pattern of sin and redemption—bringing Christian virtue alive again out of what Miss Barrett, in the letter I have quoted, calls "this low ground," and through circumstances, like Caponsacchi's abduction of Pompilia, which would seem the reverse of virtuous. The fact that Miss Barrett goes on, after inveighing against subjects drawn from classical mythology, to say that "Christianity is a worthy *myth,* and poetically acceptable," shows that she and Browning were against the classical mythology of the official literary tradition, because it projects obsolete meanings we only pretend to believe in as a literary game. It is because Browning did not go far enough in his use of mythical pattern, did not allow the meaning of his poem to rest in the pattern, that he considered that myths could grow obsolete.

Browning's idea of progress would seem to prevent a complete reliance on mythical pattern. For Yeats, the symbols and myths are permanent, and the ideas about them change. But for Browning, the myths change; myths are the progressively changing symbolic language for the same continuing idea. In **"Parleying With Charles Avison,"** Browning takes off from the idea, expressed forty years earlier in a letter to Miss Barrett, that " 'in Music, the Beau Ideal changes every thirty years'." Music, like Avison's, of a generation or two ago, seems so obsolete; yet the thing music talks about remains the same, and it requires only a few technical adjustments to translate from an old to a new musical idiom. We need the ever-changing idioms to startle us over and over again into ever new apprehensions of the old truth. (pp. 575-78)

In defending himself in a letter to Ruskin against Ruskin's charge of obscurity, Browning explains that the poetry or effect of simultaneity lies precisely in the jumps that the reader is forced to make for himself.

> I *know* that I don't make out my conception by my language, all poetry being a putting the infinite within the finite. You would have me paint it all plain out, which can't be; but by various artifices I try to make shift with touches and bits of outlines which *succeed* if they bear the conception from me to you. You ought, I think, to keep pace with the thought tripping from ledge to ledge of my "glaciers," as you call them; not stand poking your alpenstock into the holes, and demonstrating that no foot could have stood there;—suppose it sprang over there? In *prose* you may criticise so—because that is the absolute representation of portions of truth, what chronicling is to history—but in asking for more *ultimates* you must accept less *mediates,* nor expect that a Druid stone-circle will be traced for you with as few breaks to the eye as the North

Crescent and South Crescent that go together so
cleverly in many a suburb.

And he says of a poem of his: "Is the jump too much
there? The whole is all but a simultaneous feeling with
me."

Browning sketches out what has come to be the dominant
twentieth-century theory about poetry—that it makes its
effect through the association in the reader's mind of disparate elements, and that this process of association leads
to the recognition, in what has been presented successively, of static pattern. The recognition is often in the twentieth century called "epiphany." It is the recognition of
what Hopkins calls the "inscape" of the object in poetry.

The difference between Browning and Hopkins is that
Hopkins dislocates language in order to make his *image*
more palpable—to make us feel the force of the bird's
soaring in "The Windhover," and the even greater force
of its falling movement. The meaning emerges as paradox,
and then only by implication—the implication that the active and passive life are equally intense, that Christ triumphed through failure. Browning, on the other hand,
tries to achieve the effect of simultaneity through discursive thought itself. That is why Browning is hardly ever
at his best where he is obscure; while Hopkins is often at
his best where he is obscure. Hopkins goes farther than
Browning in symbolizing and myth-making.

Yet if you can get certain knotty passages of Browning sufficiently well in mind to leap playfully from idea to idea
with the swiftness and freedom of Browning's mind, you
actually start a process of association that turns the discursive thought into poetry. Swinburne gives the best description of the pleasure to be derived from the discursive
Browning. In comparing Browning with a really obscure
poet like Chapman, Swinburne denies that Browning is
obscure at all. For obscurity is the product of a confused
and chaotic intellect; whereas

> if there is any great quality more perceptible
> than another in Mr. Browning's intellect it is his
> decisive and incisive faculty of thought, his sure-
> ness and intensity of perception, his rapid and
> trenchant resolution of aim. . . . He is some-
> thing too much the reverse of obscure; he is too
> brilliant and subtle for the ready reader of a
> ready writer to follow with any certainty the
> track of an intelligence which moves with such
> incessant rapidity, or even to realize with what
> spider-like swiftness and sagacity his building
> spirit leaps and lightens to and fro and backward
> and forward as it lives along the animated line
> of its labour, springs from thread to thread and
> darts from centre to circumference of the glitter-
> ing and quivering web of living thought woven
> from the inexhaustible stores of his perception
> and kindled from the inexhaustible fire of his
> imagination. . . . It is hopeless to enjoy the
> charm or to apprehend the gist of his writings
> except with a mind thoroughly alert, an atten-
> tion awake at all points.

To return, then, to our two questions about Browning and
myth, we might say that Browning defined his realism precisely through opposition to myths as overt subject matter.

He was, however, feeling his way to the twentieth-century
development, through realism and psychology, to a psychological use of myth. In rejecting myth in **"Parleying
With Gerard de Lairesse,"** Browning asks whether he
would do better to tell two stories—to repeat the old myth
through realistically apprehended modern circumstances,
repeat the myth of Dryope plucking the lotus blossoms
through the story of an English girl plucking "fruit not
fabulous" but "Apple of English homesteads." "Advantage would it prove or detriment / If I saw double?."

It is through just such double vision that twentieth-
century writers have returned to myth. Browning's phrase
recalls Blake's distinction between single vision, which is
Newton's way of seeing facts as just facts, and double vision, which is the capacity to read facts symbolically. "Oh,
we can fancy too!" Browning continues,

> but somehow fact
> Has got to—say, not so much push aside
> Fancy, as to declare its place supplied
> By fact unseen but no less fact the same,
> Which mind bids sense accept.

We have here the modern distinction, derived from Coleridge, between neoclassical fancy and romantic or modern
imagination. The neoclassicist went on using the old
myths, not because he believed in them, but because they
were decorative and poetical. The modern artist, instead,
insists on the truth of his mythical vision . . . because it
evolves out of direct perception of the facts. The modern
artist creates his own myths and symbols by bringing to
the sensuous apprehension of reality the whole mind or
imagination.

This is the essence of modern symbolist theory. (pp. 579-
80)

In **"Daniel Bartoli,"** Browning rejects a kind of symbolism quite different from the modern—the kind set forth
in Bartoli's *Dei Simboli Trasportati al Morale*, where the
seventeenth-century Jesuit historian does two things
Browning does not like. Bartoli repeats implausible legends, and uses them to teach moral lessons; whereas for
Browning "historical fact had," as DeVane puts it, "a
righteousness of its own." Bartoli is represented as telling
an absurdly miraculous legend of a female saint, in order
that Browning may, by way of contrast, tell a story from
a memoir, in which a real girl, acting in plausible circumstances, shows herself to be a saint in a far more important
sense than Bartoli's Saint Scholastica. (pp. 580-81)

In **"Francis Furini"**—the parleying that makes the most
complete statement of symbolist doctrine—Browning defends the nude in painting, by showing that the nude figure is more symbolic than the clothed figure, and symbolic
precisely of soul. The artist agonizes

> to adumbrate, trace in dust
> That marvel which we dream the firmament
> Copies in star-device when fancies stray
> Outlining, orb by orb, Andromeda—
> God's best of beauteous and magnificent
> Revealed to earth—the naked female form.

The artists who see most clearly God's purpose—to dispense "all gifts / To soul through sense"—are those who

"bid us love alone / The type untampered with [i.e., the archetype], the naked star!"

In symbolism, there is no high or low; symbolism demonstrates that we can know the so-called high only by knowing the so-called low. There you have the error of the Darwinians—and it is no digression for Browning to associate them with the prudish enemies of the nude—who think that their knowledge of man's low origin negates his spirituality. Once we see that the large subject of **"Furini"** is symbolism, then the attack on the Darwinians has even more cogency, and Browning's depreciation of man's cognitive faculties has more philosophical justification than DeVane makes out. We can see how Browning's relativism leads to symbolism when, in criticizing in a letter of 1881 the Darwinian idea that evolution is ungoverned by intelligence, Browning says that "time and space" are "purely conceptions of our own, wholly inapplicable to intelligence of another kind."

The Darwinians do not realize, Browning implies in **"Furini,"** that their theory is itself, by its hierarchical arrangement of nature, an anthropomorphizing symbol system based on intuition of a perfection from which all nature can be scaled downward. The Darwinians, who take an abstract view of nature, looking downward from the top, see only what is lacking. An artist like Furini, instead, who takes his stand within nature, can through loving penetration of a particular living thing uncover "Marvel at hiding under marvel, pluck / Veil after veil from Nature," and thus see the living thing as pointing upward, as symbolizing the whole perfect scheme. (p. 581)

In the **Parleyings**—which is Browning's intellectual autobiography and the most complete statement of his credo—Browning answers the problems of his time by suggesting that we change the nature of the questions we put to the universe, that we turn upon all aspects of life double rather than single vision. Had Browning been able to realize such doctrine in his art, had he been able to make his fragmentary glimpses of life symbolic of the whole, of an absolute vision, he would have broken through to the modern mythical method. He would have broken through to a final clarity of vision and style and been one of the great poets of English literature. As it is, he is a poet of enduring interest—partly because his very faults show that he was turning analytic thought against itself, that he understood what had to be done.

I would like to conclude, however, by mentioning a few poems in which Browning does use, and with great success, the modern mythical method. The first is the famous **Childe Roland,** where the meaning is not extractable but is simply *in* the pattern of movement. Although the poem dramatizes a reference in a well-known play to a well-known figure, it hardly deals with one of Arnold's grand, enduring subjects. Browning has made the poem his own private myth.

The second is a major work. Yet it is undeservedly overlooked in courses on, and discussions of, Browning. I refer to **Balaustion's Adventure,** in which the Greek girl Balaustion retells Euripides' *Alcestis* as translated by Browning. Balaustion is fresh, gentle, sweet, compassion-

ate. She has what Browning thought of as the very best qualities of nineteenth-century sensibility; so that, in filtering Euripides' play through her, Browning makes us feel how modern in its sensibility the play is, and how modern Euripides is. He makes us understand why, in **The Ring and the Book,** the Pope says that Euripides was a Christian before the advent of the Christian era. For without giving the *Alcestis* a Christian construction—and it is a good thing that Balaustion herself is a contemporary of Euripides—Browning makes us feel, through his rendition, that any person has a Christian heart who understands that love is a greater force than death.

Published in 1871, **Balaustion's Adventure** was written directly after **The Ring and the Book.** I certainly agree with DeVane, in the *Browning Handbook,* that **Balaustion's Adventure** ought to be considered as closing—which is to say as within—Browning's best period. It is actually more successful than **The Ring and the Book** in achieving what it sets out to do. If I hesitate to rank it above or even with **The Ring and the Book,** it is only because the poem is after all mainly Euripides. Yet I am not sure this matters. We probably ought to understand the poem as we understand Ezra Pound's translations—as a creative appropriation of ancient material, a way of giving an ancient poet a historical consciousness he himself could not have had. Eliot said of Pound that he "is much more modern, in my opinion, when he deals with Italy and Provence, than when he deals with modern life." This way of being modern is what Eliot means by the mythical method.

Eliot means something quite different from that use of established classical mythology so expertly traced by Douglas Bush in *Mythology and the Romantic Tradition.* Bush is mainly right when he says that "Browning was not a poet of mythological imagination; the few moments in which he seems to deserve that name only emphasize his normal character as a novelist in verse." I demur, however, when Bush gives as evidence the fact that in Browning's Greek poems "the Greece he presents is a mixture of the completely real and the completely unreal. Whatever solid properties can be seen or touched are Greek; the psychological motives he evolves are usually not Greek." The modern mythical method challenges and re-establishes mythical pattern precisely through realism and through psychology in the modern sense; though the poem will indeed be novelistic where mythical pattern is not re-established. That is the difference between the novelistic **Ring and the Book,** where the re-establishment of mythical pattern is only incidental, and the Greek **Balaustion,** where it is central.

The Ring and the Book and **Balaustion** employ the mythical method from opposite sides. For we start in **Balaustion** with the myth or pattern, and the narrator undertakes to make it real—to describe for us, as she says, the human expressions beneath the masks of the mythical characters. The myth of Alcestis is another version of the Andromeda-Perseus myth; Heracles, who brings back Alcestis from the dead, is even a descendant of Perseus. The thing Balaustion does is to draw out, through her comments on Euripides' tragicomedy, the underlying tragicomic pattern—the pattern of impasse and miracle—that is at the heart of Browning's view of the world and of his Christian faith.

Heracles' entrance into the play is beautifully interpreted by Balaustion. Left to themselves, human motives and the logic of events have led to an impasse; Alcestis must die and there is no help for it. But then, suddenly, there breaks upon the scene "that great interrupting voice." There is certainly a Christian analogue in the fact that the appearance of the god is heralded (a touch not really in Euripides) by his voice. "Sudden into the midst of sorrow," says Balaustion,

> leapt
> Along with the gay cheer of that great voice,
> Hope, joy, salvation: Herakles was here!
> Himself, o' the threshold, sent his voice on first
> To herald all that human and divine
> I' the weary happy face of him,—half God,
> Half man, which made the god-part God the
> more.

It is because Heracles was a man that we can see as miraculous his willingness to labor for men for no reason other than his love—that he can, in other words, symbolize Divinity.

The movement is assimilated to the pattern of death and rebirth in the vegetation cycle. When Heracles goes gaily off to bring back Alcestis from the dead, Balaustion comments:

> I think this is the authentic sign and seal
> Of Godship, that it ever waxes glad,
> And more glad, until gladness blossoms, bursts
> Into a rage to suffer for mankind,
> And recommence at sorrow:

just as, Balaustion continues, the flower is willing, at the height of its bloom, to drop its seed—

> once more die into the ground,
> Taste cold and darkness and oblivion there:
> And thence rise, tree-like grow through pain to
> joy,
> More joy and most joy,—do man good again.

The same cyclical pattern governs the moral and spiritual life of each individual. After Alcestis' husband Admetus has said everything except the truth—that he ought not to have allowed Alcestis to die for him—after Admetus has told all the lies: after, in Balaustion's metaphor, "the last of bubbles broke" leaving the surface "placid"—then "up swam / To the surface the drowned truth, in dreadful change." The metaphor describes perfectly the psychological movement of the best dramatic monologues—where it is after the speaker has told all his lies, that inadvertently, and as if of its own accord, the truth rises to the surface. Only here we see how the deepest psychology leads back to a mythical pattern that is itself imbedded in the very order of things.

We see in the tragicomic pattern of impasse and miracle the meaning behind the Andromeda myth. The miracle in the *Alcestis* is, as Browning interprets it, the transformation of Admetus' consciousness. It is when Admetus—who feared death as the worst of evils—suddenly *sees* "how dear is death, / How loveable the dead are" that Al-

cestis is restored to him as the external sign of the internal transformation. The same thing happens in **Childe Roland,** where a transformation of consciousness makes the dark tower appear and turns all the facts that spell defeat into victory. The logic of events leads to winter; *spring* is the miracle. Transformation of consciousness is the way through the impasse logic leads to! This is Browning's understanding of the Incarnation, the descent of Divinity into human life.

Such collapsing of diverse events into a single pattern is at the heart of the mythical method. An interest in **Balaustion** might lead to revaluation of certain other neglected poems—of, for example, that strange and difficult late lyric, **"Numpholeptos."** "Numpholeptos" is like **"Andrea del Sarto,"** in its Tennysonian echoes (echoes here of "Tithonus"), in its sustained contrast between images of silver and gold, and in the speaker's final choice of continued enslavement to the lady against whom he has said so much. The comparison helps us see that the lady of **"Numpholeptos"** is another kind of Lucrezia, one who torments by being all too idealistic and sexlessly pure. The comparison helps us see that the case here is still psychological. But the psychology is in **"Numpholeptos"** projected through a peculiarly modern penetration of mythical figures, the nymph and nymphenraptured lover, who are themselves seen as emerging out of natural phenomena—the cold radiance of the moon: and the white light that is refracted through the dust of earth into warm hues that, like the man of the poem, go forth only to return and die into their origin in the white light.

An interest in Balaustion might suggest that Browning did, after all, go farther than I have indicated toward projecting a total vision of life. **Balaustion** should certainly make us pay attention to the beautiful little lyric on spring with which Browning, in **"Parleying With Gerard de Lairesse,"** concludes his argument against the use of classical mythology. This is, he says, the modern poet's way of making rhyme. The lyric, through a precise rendition of spring flowers, suggests all that the myths tell us about death and rebirth. Christianity, Browning implies, makes such realism possible, by confirming our deepest intuition that the vegetation cycle is, indeed, symbolic of our fate after death. **"Numpholeptos"** and the lyric on spring work from opposite directions—the first from the archetype to the human situation or seen fact, the second from the seen fact to the "fact unseen but no less fact the same." They both, however, employ double vision, and thus show how realism and psychology lead to the distinctively modern recovery of symbol and myth. (pp. 582-84)

> *Robert Langbaum, "Browning and the Question of Myth," in* PMLA, *Vol. LXXXI, No. 7, December, 1966, pp. 575-84.* *[This essay was published in a slightly revised form in Langbaum's* The Word from Below, *University of Wisconsin Press, 1987.]*

Harold Bloom   (essay date 1979)

[*Bloom, an American critic and editor, is best known as the formulator of "revisionism," a controversial theory of literary creation based on the concept that all poets are subject to the influence of earlier poets and that, to develop individual voices, they attempt to overcome this influence through a deliberate process of "creative correction," which Bloom calls "misreading." In the following excerpt, Bloom considers the difficulties and rewards of reading Browning's poetry, which he characterizes as a complex rhetorical field in which "every self is a picnic of selves, every text a tropological entrapment."*]

> A tower that crowns a country. But alas,
> The soul now climbs it just to perish there!
> For thence we have discovered ('Tis no dream—
> We know this, which we had not else perceived)
> That there's a world of capability
> For joy, spread round about us, meant for us,
> Inviting; and still the soul craves all. . . .

This is Browning's Cleon, describing what Shelley had called "thought's crowned powers," the aesthetic dilemma of an elite beyond religion. That dilemma was not Browning's own, as a man, but in some ways it was his, as a poet. Yet it is cited here as the inevitable dilemma of Browning's reader, and so as an epigraph to an introductory discussion of the difficulties of reading one of the strongest and most perplexing poets in the English language.

Of all the problematic elements in Browning's poetry, what increasingly seems the central challenge to a reader is the peculiar nature of Browning's rhetorical stance. No poet has evidenced more than Browning so intense a will-to-power over the interpretation of his own poems. The reader rides through the Browning country with the poet always bouncing along at his side compulsively overinterpreting everything, very much in the manner of his own Childe Roland, who thus usurps the reader's share. Browning as self-interpreter has to be both welcomed and resisted, and he makes the resistance very difficult. Such resistance, though, may be Browning's greatest gift to his attentive reader. The Sublime, as Longinus formulated it, exists to compel readers to forsake easy pleasures in favor of more strenuous satisfactions, and Browning, like his master Shelley, crucially extends the possibilities of a modern Sublime. (pp. 1-2)

To read Browning well we need to cope with his poetry's heightened rhetorical self-awareness, its constant consciousness that it *is* rhetoric, a personal system of tropes, as well as a persuasive rhetoric, an art that must play at transcendence. Browning is read very badly when that apparent and deeply moving transcendence is too easily accepted, as Browning in his social or public self tended to accept it. But Browning teaches his more strenuous readers not only the Sublime necessities of defense against his poems' self-interpretations, but also a healthy suspicion that poet and reader alike are rhetorical systems of many selves, rather than any single or separate self. Here I think is the true center in reading Browning. The problems of rhetoric—of our being incapable of knowing what is literal and what figurative where all, in a sense, is figurative—and of psychology—is there a self that is not trope or an effect of verbal persuasion?—begin to be seen as one dilemma.

If Browning did not share this dilemma with all poets and their readers, then he would not be representative or even intelligible. However, his particular strength, which insures his permanent place in the canon, is that he appropriated the dilemma for his time with a singular possessiveness. An informed reader, brooding upon the rhetorical limits of interpretability, and upon the labyrinthine evasions of self-identity, will think very quickly of Browning when these problematic matters rise in the context of English poetic tradition. Browning's strength, like Milton's or Wordsworth's, is finally a strength of usurpation, in which a vast literary space is made to vacate its prior occupancy so as to permit a new formulation of the unresolvable dilemmas that themselves constitute poetry.

A number of the traditional issues that vex Browning criticism can be reoriented if we see them as burdens of rhetorical stance, when that stance itself determines Browning's psychopoetics. The dramatic monologue is revealed to be neither dramatic nor a monologue but rather a barely disguised High Romantic crisis lyric, in which antithetical voices contend for an illusory because only momentary mastery. The frequently grotesque diction appears a reaction formation away from Shelleyan verbal harmony, which means that the grotesquerie becomes a pure irony, a bitter digression away from meaning itself. The violent thematicism of Browning, including his exuberance in declaring a highly personalized evangelical belief in Christ, becomes something dangerously close to a thematics of violence, in which fervor of declaration far surpasses in importance the supposed spiritual content of the declaration. The notorious optimism begins to look rather acosmic and atemporal, so that the hope celebrated is much less Pauline than it is Gnostic. The faith demystifies as a Gnostic elitist knowledge of Browning's own divine spark, which turns out to be prior to and higher than the natural creation. Most bewilderingly, the love that Browning exalts becomes suspect, not because of its manifest Oedipal intensity, but because something in it is very close to a solipsistic transport, to a wholly self-delighting joy. He is a great lover—but primarily of himself, or rather of his multitude of antithetical selves.

The Browning I describe is hardly recognizable from much if not most of the criticism devoted to him, but few other poets have inspired so much inadequate criticism. Only Whitman and Dickinson among the major nineteenth-century poets seem to me as badly misrepresented as Browning has been. The prime fault of course is Browning's own, and so I return to his will-to-power over the interpretation of his own texts.

Hans Jonas remarks of the Gnostics that they delighted in "the intoxication of unprecedentedness," a poetic intoxication in which Browning, Whitman, and Dickinson share. Borges, with Gnostic irony, has pointed to Browning as one of the precursors of Kafka, an insight worthy of exploration. Against the Bible and Plato, the Gnostics refused the dialectics of sublimation and substitution, the Christian and Classical wisdom of the Second Chance. Like the Gnostics, Browning is interested in evasion rather than substitution, and does not wish to learn even the Wordsworthian version of the wisdom of the Second

Chance. The "sober coloring" of a belated vision had no deep appeal to Browning, though he exemplifies it beautifully in the character and section of *The Ring and the Book* called "The Pope." The fire celebrated in the **"Prologue"** to his final volume, *Asolando: Fancies and Facts,* is the Gnostic fire of the First Chance, now "lost from the naked world." Browning appeals to "the purged ear," and a Voice rather clearly his own, at its most stentorian, proclaims: "God is it who transcends." "God" here is an hyperbole for poetic strength, which is Browning's violent and obsessive subject, whether in the overtly Shelleyan long poems that began his career or in the ostensibly dramatic romances, monologues, and lyrics of his more profoundly Shelleyan maturity.

Browning praised Shelley above all for

> his simultaneous perception of Power and Love in the absolute, and of Beauty and Good in the concrete, while he throws, from his poet's station between both, swifter, subtler, and more numerous films for the connection of each with each, than have been thrown by any modern artificer. . . .

Perhaps Browning's truest swerve away from this strong interpretation of Shelley, was an uncanny refusal to distinguish between Power and Love in the absolute, since for Browning both were forms of his own poetic self-recognition. What is Bishop Blougram but the strong poet taunting the weak critic?

> If I'm a Shakespeare, let the well alone;
> Why should I try to be what now I am?
> If I'm no Shakespeare, as too probable,—
> His power and consciousness and self-delight
> And all we want in common . . .
>
>   . . .
>
> We want the same things, Shakespeare and my-
>   self,
> And what I want, I have: he, gifted more,
> Could fancy he too had them when he
>   liked. . . .

The reader who believes that the bishop means chair and wine by "what I want" is indeed another silent Mr. Gigadibs, who believes he sees "two points in Hamlet's soul / Unseized by the Germans yet." Sometimes Browning simply drops the mask and declares his precise agon:

> For—see your cellarage!
>   There are four big butts of Milton's brew.
> How comes it you make old drips and drops
> Do duty, and there devotion stops?
> Leave such an abyss of malt and hops
>   Embellied in butts which bungs still glue?
> You hate your bard! A fig for your rage!
> Free him from cellarage!
>
> 'Tis said I brew stiff drink,
>   But the deuce a flavour of grape is there.
> Hardly a May-go-down, 'tis just
> A sort of a gruff Go-down-it-must—
> No Merry-go-down, no gracious gust
>   Commingles the racy with Springtide's rare!
> "What wonder," say you "that we cough, and
>   blink
> At Autumn's heady drink?"

The strength of Browning's poetry is thus professedly an intoxication of belatedness, "Autumn's heady drink," and the weak reader's rage against both Milton and Browning is due to a weak head that doubts its own capacity. Browning's splendidly outrageous aggressivity is not so much latent as it is concealed in his more characteristic poems. Even in the charming and good-natured self-idealization of **"Fra Lippo Lippi,"** where Browning loves his monologist as himself, the appetite for a literal immortality is unabated. Poetic divination, in Browning, returns to its primal function, to keep the poet always alive: "Oh, oh, It makes me mad to see what men shall do / And we in our graves!" (pp. 2-6)

Yeats remarked that he had feared always Browning's influence upon him. In a deep sense, Yeats was right, not only because of the shared Shelleyan ancestry, but because of the shared Gnosticism, though the esoteric religion was quite overt in Yeats. Browning does all he can to evade what Yeats (following Nietzsche) named as the *antithetical* quest in Shelley, the drive beyond nature to a nihilistic annihilation that is the poetic will's ultimate revenge against time's "it was." But the evasion was only half-hearted:

> For I intend to get to God,
>   For 'tis to God I speed so fast,
> For in God's breast, my own abode,
>   Those shoals of dazzling glory, passed,
> I lay my spirit down at last.
>   I lie where I have always lain,
> God smiles as he has always smiled. . . .

True that this is Johannes Agricola the Antinomian, chanting in his madhouse cell, but no reader would dispute such exuberance if he substituted the Gnostic alien god, the Abyss, for the "God" of these lines. Make the substitution and Johannes Agricola may be permitted to speak for another Browning-self or soul-side, and for the entire *antithetical* tradition. (pp. 7-8)

Browning's visionary is arguing against Cerinthus and other early Gnostics, but the argument is more Gnostic than Christian (which may have been Browning's shrewd unconscious reading of the Fourth Gospel). To be present from the first, at the origins, is to have priority over nature and history, and involves denying one's own belatedness, which is thus equated with weakness, while a return to earliness is strength. To do the deed and judge it at the same time is to impose interpretation, one's will-to-power over both text and the text of life. Browning is most uncanny as a poet when two or more of his selves contend within a poem to interpret that poem, a struggle that brings forth his greatest yet most problematic achievements, including **"A Toccata of Galuppi's," "By the Fireside," "Master Hugues of Saxe-Gotha," "Love Among the Ruins," "The Heretic's Tragedy," "Andrea del Sarto," "Abt Vogler," "Caliban Upon Setebos," "Numpholeptos," "Pan and Luna," "Flute-Music, with an Accompaniment,"** and **"Childe Roland to the Dark Tower Came."** These dozen poems alone would establish Browning's permanent importance, but I have space here only to glance briefly again at **"Childe Roland,"** which is a text that never lets go of a reader once it has found you. The poem may well be the definitive proof-text for the modern Sublime, more uncanny than Kafka, stronger than Yeats at his most uncompromising.

Browning's Roland descends ultimately from the Marlovian-Shakespearean hero-villain, by way of Milton's Satan and the High Romantic metamorphoses of Satan. Tennyson's Ulysses has something of the same complex ancestry, but he is less Jacobean than Roland, who like Webster's Lodovico in *The White Devil* could say he had limned his own night-piece, and it was his best. Roland is a savagely reductive interpreter whom the wary reader must resist, until at its close the poem so opens out that the reader suddenly wants Roland to interpret more, only to discover that the Childe is done with interpretation. The reader is left with the uncanny, which means with the self in Browning that finds both his aim and his origin in the Sublime, unlike the remorselessly reductive self that has spoken most of the poem.

The ogreless Dark Tower, where the quester must confront himself and his dead precursors, to "fail" at least as heroically as they have failed before him, is a composite trope for poetry if not for the Sublime poem itself. Indeed, the figuration is so suggestive that the Dark Tower can be read as the mental dilemma or *aporia* that Browning's reader faces in the poem. The Dark Tower is the black hole in the Browning cosmos, where Power and Love become one only through a supremely negative moment, in which loss of the self and loss of the fulness of the present pay the high price of achieved vision. . . . (pp. 8-9)

After a life spent training for the vision of the Dark Tower, you do not see it until burningly it comes on you all at once. How do we interpret the shock of "This was the place!" when we have learned to resist every one of Roland's earlier interpretations? Is it that we, like Roland, have overprepared the event, in Pound's fine phrasing? Roland is overtrained, which means that he suffers an acute consciousness of belatedness. We are overanxious not to be gulled by his reductiveness, which means that we suffer an acute consciousness that we have selves of our own to defend. In the Sublime agon between Roland and the reader, Browning stands aside, even at the very end, not because he is an "objective" as opposed to antithetical poet, but because he respects the *aporia* of the Dark Tower. Poetry is part of what the Gnostics called the Kenoma or cosmic and temporal emptiness, and not part of the Pleroma, the fulness of presence that is acosmic and atemporal. The Pleroma is always absent, for it inheres in the Abyss, the true, alien God who is cut off from nature and history.

The name of that alien God in Roland's country is Shelley's trumpet of a prophecy, which enters by way of another precursor, the boy-poet Chatterton, whose poetry provides the slug-horn that is sounded:

> There they stood, ranged along the hillside, met
>   To view the last of me, a living frame
>   For one more picture! in a sheet of flame
> I saw them and I knew them all. And yet
> Dauntless the slug-horn to my lips I set,

And blew. "Childe Roland to the Dark Tower came."

The picture is Browning's, the frame or context is given by the living but contradictory presence, where there can be no presence, of the precursors: Shelley, Chatterton, Keats, Tasso, who lived and died in Yeats's Condition of Fire, Roland's "sheet of flame." Browning as man and poet died old, but his anxiety seems to have been that his poethood *could* have died young, when he forswore the atheist Shelley in order to win back the approving love of his evangelical mother. Roland's equivocal triumph achieves the Sublime, and helps guarantee Browning's poetic survival.

Roland sees and knows, like Keats's intelligences which are at once atoms of perception and God. What he sees and knows are the heroic precursors who are met to see *him,* but who cannot know him, as presumably his readers can. Roland's knowledge ought to daunt him, and yet against it he sets the trumpet of his prophecy. His will is thus set in revenge against time's: "It was," but we do not know the content of his prophecy. After a full stop, and not a colon, comes the poem's final statement, which is at once its Shakespearean title and epigraph. Either the entire poem begins again, in a closed cycle like Blake's *The Mental Traveller,* or else Roland proclaims his story's inevitable lack of closure. What seems clear is that Roland is not performing his own poem, in direct contrast to Shelley at the close of the *Ode to the West Wind,* where the words to be scattered among mankind are the text of the *Ode.*

It is after all the many-selved Browning who is undaunted by belatedness, by the dilemmas of poetic language, and by his own struggle for authority as against both precursors and readers. Poetic self-confidence delights us when we are persuaded that it can sustain itself, that it has usurped imaginative space and has forced its way into the canon. Again we are in the Sublime of Longinus, as the reader becomes one with the power he apprehends. The danger of sublimity is that the pit of the bathetic suddenly can open anywhere, and Browning (who wrote much too much) sometimes pulls us down with him. This hardly matters, where we are given so large a company of splendid self-deceivers and even more splendid deceivers of others, of all but the wariest readers. Browning, more than Yeats or Stevens, more than his disciple Pound or his secret student Eliot, is the last of the old High line, as in the audacious rhetorical gesture that concludes his magnificent, unread **"Pan and Luna"**:

> . . . The myth
> Explain who may! Let all else go, I keep
> —As of a ruin just a monolith—
> Thus much, one verse of five words, each a boon:
> Arcadia, night, a cloud, Pan, and the moon.

(pp. 10-12)

Harold Bloom, "Introduction: Reading Browning," in Robert Browning: A Collection of Critical Essays, *edited by Harold Bloom and Adrienne Munich, Prentice-Hall, Inc., 1979, pp. 1-12.*

Clyde de L. Ryals   (essay date 1982)

[*Ryals examines Browning's use of irony, tracing his technique back to the eighteenth century German poets, particularly August Wilhelm and Friedrich Schlegel, Novalis, and Ludwig Tieck.*]

When one focuses intently on a literary figure, it is difficult not to overvalue him: one justifies one's work by insisting on the greatness of the subject of that work. Well aware of my own bias I nevertheless maintain that Robert Browning is the most daring English poet of the nineteenth century and that he came near to perfection of what he dared. His achievement, I believe, sets him among the most innovative poets in English. (p. 23)

It has long been a commonplace of Browning scholarship to trace the poet's literary lineage from the English Romantics, especially Shelley. But once we question this bit of conventional wisdom we realize that almost no poet could be less like Shelley—or Wordsworth or Byron. For Browning does not offer a vision of the world redeemed, as does Shelley, or of the world devoid of values, as Byron so often does. On the contrary, with Browning it is not a question of either/or; rather, it is a matter of both/and. More than any of his immediate predecessors and contemporaries Browning is able to hold a view of the world in which the most contradictory statements to be made about it are alike true. In a word, Browning is an ironist—the supreme ironist among English poets of the nineteenth century. (pp. 23-4)

The kind of irony Browning adopted was not the old rhetorical irony which had a polemical aim. It was instead more nearly like the romantic irony of the German writers of the end of the eighteenth century—the Schlegels, Novalis, Tieck—which had its home in philosophy and was metaphysical and aesthetic. As Friedrich Schlegel said in *Lyceum Fragment* No. 108, romantic irony "originates in the union of a sense of an art of living and a scientific intellect, in the meeting of accomplished natural philosophy and accomplished philosophy of art. It contains and incites a feeling of the insoluble conflict of the absolute and the relative. . . . " Like God, the ironist is both in and out of his creation—immanent and transcendent, subjective and objective. It is not without aesthetic implications that the Incarnation became the basic mythic pattern of Browning's poetry. (pp. 24-5)

From the beginning we find Browning attempting to break away from his Romantic inheritance. *Pauline* (1833), a lyric "confession," as its subtitle proclaims, is nevertheless, according to Browning's prefatory note to the 1868

The Poet's Corner of Westminster Abbey, where Browning was buried.

edition, "dramatic in principle" and thus is the poet's first attempt to attain scope and diversity within an essentially lyric mode. The speaker of *Pauline* is realized by us dramatically in that we learn about him as much from how he tells of himself as from what he actually says. And although we are invited to sympathize with him, it is difficult to lend him our sympathy because of the emotional extravagances of his utterance. Hence the reason for many readers' difficulty with the poem: we are presented with a speaker who does not command our sympathy yet cannot be ignored. Browning had not yet learned how to individualize character to the extent that he could elicit our sympathetic interest in foolish or even despicable speakers.

Moreover, even though the speaker believes that he can bid farewell to Shelley (apostrophized as "Sun-Treader"), to Romantic ideals, and to the lyric mode, we discover that he retains a very Romantic notion of the poet's role. Pauline has convinced him that "a perfect bard was one / Who shadowed out the stages of all life," which is to say that he is now willing to deal in verse with the general life instead of the personal emotion. But he retains the Romantic idea of the bard as priest and prophet who from his overview of life will disclose secrets about man and nature unrevealed to ordinary men.

It appears that the events narrated in *Pauline* are reflections of Browning's own experience, and because of that fact many readers have understood the poem as the poet's own confession. Browning seems to have realized that this intended dramatic confession might be mistaken for his own, and to distance the poem from himself—and incidentally to cast in doubt the idea of the poet as bard—he enclosed it within a framework which signals us that *Pauline* should be read as something objective and distinct from the poet's own personality. The headnote in Latin, the motto in French, the affixed dates at the beginning and end, the long note in French signed by Pauline—all these invite us to read *Pauline* as a fictional edition.

Editing is of course a way of distancing experience. And the fiction of editing allowed the young Browning a technical means of distancing story from narration, of making the lyric and subjective more dramatic and impersonal. Moreover, the fiction of editing allowed the poet to be, like God, both immanent and transcendent, both in and out of his work.

In the last analysis, this rudimentary attempt at a fictional edition—what Pauline as editor speaks of in a note as a "sketch" of a new genre—permitted the young poet to find a solution to his Romantic desire, adumbrated in the confession, to arrive at the supreme point of view of the Absolute. "I cannot chain my soul," the speaker says;

> it will not rest
> In its clay prison; this most narrow sphere—
> It has strange powers, and feelings, and desires,
> Which I cannot account for, nor explain,
> But which I stifle not, being bound to trust
> *All* feelings equally—to hear *all* sides:
> Yet I cannot indulge them. . . .

Obviously no life can indulge such a desire to view an object or an event from all sides, not sequentially, but simultaneously, to have in effect the last word. Only God, as Author and Judge, can assume this stance: "And what is that I hunger for but God?" asks the speaker. God is, Browning was to write in *Paracelsus,* "The PERFECT POET, / Who in his person acts his own creations." But might not other authors, imperfect poets, emulate the Divine if they also became judges? As editors, who in effect are judges, might they not have the final word? The fictional edition would then be a strategy in satisfying the Romantic urge to "be all, have, see, know, taste, feel, all" while admitting all the time that such a desire, outside art, is utterly impossible of fulfillment. Already, at age twenty-one, Robert Browning was well on his way towards a pronounced ironic view of life; it but remained for him to discover the forms which would best allow him to indulge it.

Paracelsus (1835), Browning's next work, seems to be cast in the form of a five-act play, but the poet specifically warns in the foreword that it is "a poem, not a drama." And certainly any effort to view it as a drama, as almost all Browning's critics do, must necessarily result in misvaluation. What we find is five important moments in the life of the protagonist in which he examines and reveals his inner life and is brought by his utterance at each moment to new insights allowing him to act. These moments of crisis are instants of lyrical intensity presented discontinuously; joining them together must be the work of the reader. As Browning said in the Preface, it is a "difficult form" which depends "on the intelligence and sympathy of the reader for its success—indeed were my scenes stars it must be his co-operating fancy which, supplying all chasms, shall connect the scattered lights into one constellation—a Lyre or a Crown." In effect, the five parts are—in spite of the fact that there are other characters who are not mere auditors, as in *Pauline*—like five monologues offered as a narrative of the protagonist's life. The pattern of the poem is ironic in that false attainment results from true aspiration in Scenes I and II and true attainment stems from false aspiration in Scenes IV and V.

Paracelsus is the first of Browning's many historical characters. . . . Born at the end of the fifteenth century, Paracelsus lived in an age of transition, in many respects resembling Browning's own. Humanism was emphasizing the importance of life in this world, science was providing a material explanation for phenomena formerly conceived as of supernatural origin, theology and religious practice were undergoing radical change—all alluded to in the several references to Erasmus, Paracelsus' own scientific research, and Martin Luther. In other words, Paracelsus lives in a time when self-definition is no longer a given, when the soul has become problematic. *Paracelsus,* more plainly than *Pauline,* is a poem in which, to quote the preface to the 1863 edition of *Sordello,* the poet's "stress lay on the incidents in the development of a soul."

Browning's hero fancies that he can realize his essential self only by knowing all that is to be known. Denying all help from friends or sages of earlier times, Paracelsus sets off on his quest for total knowledge. Failing in his quest, he encounters a young poet who too has sought an absolute—to "love infinitely, and be loved"—and hence has not put to use the talents he possesses. Because he could not reproduce "lovingly" in his art all the beauty and joy of the world, he has produced nothing. Aprile in his dying moments discovers that "God is the PERFECT POET" who alone can experience absolute love and beauty. But Paracelsus is unmindful of the vision vouchsafed to and related by Aprile, and abjuring the desire to know infinitely, he vows to seek infinite love. On this second quest he of course meets with no more success than on the first, and only in the last scene, in his dying hour, is he granted an understanding of the necessary limits on earthly love and knowledge.

In the last part, Paracelsus, like Aprile in Scene II, learns that his earlier quest had been ill-conceived because it had been founded on the idea of a static universe. Since "progress is / The law of life," both Paracelsus and Aprile had been deluded from the start. Aprile had wanted to record in art every aspect of reality; Paracelsus had wished to know the total creation; and each had despised his achievement because it had not attained completeness. Just before they died, each learned that the meaning, the "power" and "love," for which each had sought lies in the incompleteness of the process, learned in other words that failing to attain the goal each had sought was in part the way of attaining the power and love proper to human life. In their quests for the perfect they had overlooked the value of the imperfect in an evolving universe in which every new stage of advance modifies the past. Man's "half-reasons, faint aspirings, struggles / Dimly for truth" are "all ambitious, upward tending," and in a dynamic universe will go on forever, one stage leading to another which in turn is to be transcended. The insight permitted Paracelsus is that success is failure and failure is success enough: life is not having and resting, but being and becoming.

Although the revelation granted to Paracelsus is presented as a paradox, it nevertheless is meant to stand as final truth. And this works against the ironic arrangement of the parts and also Paracelsus' own discovery that all explanatory systems are inadequate because language can never be sufficiently refined to deal with ultimate truth. At this point Browning apparently was not yet ready to forgo

formal closure, even though it was at variance with the ideas presented in the work.

The irony in both *Pauline* and *Paracelsus* is largely a matter of form—and elementary at that. The completion of *Paracelsus,* however, with its enunciation in Part V of the doctrine of becoming, provided Browning with a philosophical basis for his irony which allowed him to enlarge his conception of it to cosmic scope. For in a state of becoming, the principle of contradiction is not applicable: anything can be both itself and not itself at any specific moment, it being in the process of becoming something else. Once Browning accepted the idea of progress with its attendant idea that being is also becoming—that *a* is both *a* and not *a*—then the way was opened to the kind of irony which is to be seen not so much as a form of irony or as a device but as a way of presenting it, really the dramatization of irony. Many of the implications of such an irony were set down by Friederich Schlegel, some of whose works Browning may have known directly or, more likely, as mediated through Carlyle. It was, however, an Englishman who probably delineated for the young poet the dramatic possibilities of irony as a cosmic view. Writing on the irony of Sophocles in 1833, Connop Thirlwall observed that in the *Antigone,* Sophocles impartially presented two equal and opposite points of view and, expanding on this, remarked that irony may reside in the attitude of an ironic observer or, more precisely, in the situation observed. . . . (pp. 25-9)

The relationship of word and thing, veil and truth, body and soul . . . is given extended study in Browning's next poem. *Sordello* (1840) is well known, by title at least, as a difficult poem. It becomes more penetrable, however, when one recognizes it as one of the supreme examples of ironic art. For the poem has as its chief subject the impossibility of writing the kind of poem its author would like to write and yet is, at the same time, a brilliant example of the type of art to which he aspires. To borrow the paradox of *Paracelsus,* its failure is also its success.

Let us first consider what Schlegel called the ironist's recognition "of the impossibility and necessity of total communication." Like his Sordello, Browning would say it "All at once." Yet language is linear: a poem is a text to be inspected one word at a time, in a given sequence, while perception—and by perception Browning means abstract perception or idea or character as well as visual perception pure and simple—is simultaneous: that is, all the elements that contribute to a perception are grasped at once. Sordello finds that "perceptions whole, like that he sought / To clothe, reject so pure a work of thought / As language: Thought may take Perception's place / But hardly co-exist in any case, / Being its mere presentment—of the Whole / By Parts, the Simultaneous and the Sole / By the successive and the Many." This being the case, how may any verbal work of art achieve simultaneity? Sordello finds that it cannot, and so, unable to express his "whole dream," he gives up poetry entirely.

The poet, on the other hand, continues, both in his own voice and as the narrator of the poem, to write; and he learns, at the end of Book III, what Sordello learns in Book V—namely, that language is a social enterprise, poetry a dialogic art. Where Romantic bards sing to themselves—"All poetry is of the nature of soliloquy," said J. S. Mill in "What Is Poetry?" (1833), carrying Romantic theory to its logical conclusion—Browning's poet would engage his audience in the enterprise and demand, as Browning himself had in the Preface to *Paracelsus,* that the audience join in the construction of the poem. This may well be why Browning chose for his hero a poet-troubadour, one whose art depends on interaction with his audience. The form of such a work would depend on its language, "brother's speech," a language of sparseness and suggestiveness:

> a single touch more may enhance,
> A touch less turn to insignificance
> Those structures' symmetry the Past has
>   strewed
> Your world with, once so bare: leave the mere
>   rude
> Explicit details, 'tis but brother's speech
> We need, speech where an accent's change gives
>   each
> The other's soul—no speech to understand
> By former audience—need was then to expand,
> Expatiate—hardly were they brothers! true—
> Nor I lament my less remove from you,
> Nor reconstruct what stands already: ends
> Accomplished turn to means: my art intends
> New structure from the ancient.

But even this new kind of poetry, although it will allow more to be expressed than ever before, will prove inadequate to deal not only with all human experience but also with what the poet himself wants to say: the poet "must stoop contented to express / No tithe of what's to say—the vehicle / Never sufficient."

Fully aware of the impossibility of total communication, Browning nevertheless has his go at "saying it all at once." As the narrator tells us in the beginning, a poet who would set forth "unexampled themes" and embody "quite new men" must be present in his work as well as absent from it, or, as he says in Book III, the poet works "as a god [who] may glide / Out of the world he fills, and leave it mute / For myriad ages as we men compute, / Returning into it without a break / O' the consciousness." The creations of such a poet are characterized both by fixity and looseness, enclosure and open-endedness. Thus the ironic poet is both like Eglamor, who sought to apprehend experience as "his own forever, to be fixed / In rhyme, the beautiful, forever," and also like Sordello, who penetrates to the perception that in all "true works" there is more energy than form can totally encompass. This is why the narrator of the poem can dismiss and yet at the end embrace Eglamor and plead for and still condemn Sordello as artists; for the poet of *Sordello* is both a poet of closure and

of openness, one whose "art intends / New structure from the ancient." Hence *Sordello* is organized on an epic pattern, the present action broken by a long flashback (in the first three books) to explain how the present moment of crisis (in the last three books) is reached. The first half of the poem covers thirty years in the life of the eponymous hero; the second half, three days. The details are realistic, historically accurate, and copious; in addition there is not one dangling motive. The verse form is rhymed couplets. In brief, the poem is carefully structured, the basic organization being temporal and sequential. Yet at the same time the poem *seems* disorganized, formless, the effect of the whole being one of unreality, of fantasy rather than history. The narrator even goes out of his way to contradict himself, such as his assurance in Book V that Eglamor has totally disappeared from history and in Book VI that Eglamor lives on. Sordello dies, a failure as a poet and as a man of action: "a sorry farce / Such life is, after all;" yet the narrator invites our interest in and sympathy for him throughout the poem and even goes out of his way to speak on Sordello's behalf. The narrative is frankly unsatisfactory as plot. The language of the verse is highly colored, and the imagery runs the gamut from the delicately beautiful to the harsh and grotesque. There is a systematic derangement of tense, frequent ambiguity of referent, and highly elliptical syntax. The apparent organization of the poem, which seeks to concentrate its entire length into a single moment of simultaneous perception, is therefore largely spatial and nonsequential.

Being both linear *and* circular, sequential *and* nonsequential, *Sordello* is Browning's attempt at a poem which is both text and song, embodied in print and constrained by linearity but defying the rules of grammar and the expectations of logic. *Sordello* is, as I have said, a perfect example of the ironist's art, in that it shows how irony cannot accommodate itself to anything which seeks to limit it, how it wishes to be everywhere, to be all, or not to be, and how the ironist must be a comedian or buffoon who makes sport of himself, his reader, and his work. As Friederich Schlegel observed, in true ironic works "there lives a real transcendental buffoonery. Their interior is permeated by the mood which surveys everything and rises above everything limited, even above the poet's own art, virtue, and genius; and their exterior form by the histrionic style of an ordinary good Italian buffo." In *Sordello,* Browning tries to "say it all at once" with the ironist's full recognition of the impossibility of such utterance. If, as Aprile discovered, only God is the perfect poet, then no mortal, even though he mimics in his art God's ability to be immanent and transcendent, can be a "whole and perfect Poet." *Sordello* marks Browning's full disavowal of all Romantic notions of the bard.

Such a complex, playful work must almost inevitably strike the public as opaque and frivolous; and as all the world knows, this was exactly the fate of *Sordello.* To this very day *Sordello* remains undervalued, although Browning was surely right in considering it among his three or four most important works. . . . (pp. 33-6)

"Robert is peculiar in his ways of work as
a poet. I have struggled a little with him
on this point—for I don't think him
right—that is to say, it wouldn't be right
for me—and I heard the other day that it
wouldn't be right for Tennyson. Tennyson
is a regular worker, shuts himself up daily
for so many hours. And we are generally
so made that a regular hour is good, even
for so uncertain an influence as
mesmerism. But Robert waits for an
inclination—works by fits and starts—he
can't do otherwise he says. Then reading
hurts him. As long as I have known him
he has not been able to read long at a
time—he can do it now better than in the
beginning of time. The consequence of
which is that he wants occupation and that
an active occupation is salvation to him
with his irritable nerves, saves him from
ruminating bitter cud, and from the
process which I call beating his dear head
against the wall till it is bruised, simply
because he sees a fly there, magnified by
his own two eyes almost indefinitely into
some Saurian monster. He has an
enormous superfluity of vital energy, and
if it isn't employed, it strikes its fangs into
him."

—Elizabeth Barrett Browning, 1861

[The two pamphlets *Dramatic Lyrics* (1842) and *Dramatic Romances and Lyrics* (1845) contain] some of Browning's finest monologues. . . . Previously he had been able to reveal psychological conflict only in the form of the confessional soliloquy, as in *Pauline,* or in narrative, as in *Sordello.* Acting on his knowledge, most plainly set forth in *Sordello,* that point of view determines one's notions of truth and that one's sense of self necessitates special pleading, Browning hit on a form which would allow him to present the impetus to action from one angle of vision and at a special moment when a speaker would most likely reveal himself and this motivation. Hence it would be a "dramatic lyric," a song portraying conflict. With its opportunities for the representation of casuistries and sophistries, of tangled logic and torturous language as means of arriving at a position which justifies an intended or past action, the form would be a splendid vehicle for the ironist.

We see this to be almost obviously the case with **"My Last Duchess."** There is no compulsion upon the duke to reveal—to, of all people, the envoy from a prospective duchess—how he came to do away with his previous duchess. Yet at a moment when he is swept up into song he tells all and, furthermore, attempts to justify it. We the readers see, just as undoubtedly the envoy sees, that there can be no justification for the murder (if that is what it is) of a

kind young lady whose only apparent error was that she was not sufficiently haughty to be (in the duke's mind) Duchess of Ferrara; yet at the same time we perceive—as presumably does the envoy, for he makes no demur—that the duke is a fascinating character, bigger than life and disdainful of the merely ordinary. With admirable irony Browning succeeds in giving us—and causing us to hold—two conflicting views of the same individual. And that is not all: making every attempt to locate the poem in time and place and thus force us to to accept it as the utterance of someone other than the poet, Browning in the end calls attention to the poem as a poem when he has the duke refer to Neptune, "Taming a sea-horse, thought a rarity / Which Claus of Innsbruch cast in bronze for me." In that passage we are invited to see the statue as a summarizing symbol of the speaker, this not by the duke himself but the poet, who remains in his work in spite of all disclaimers in the Advertisement to *Dramatic Lyrics* that the utterances in these poems are those "of so many imaginary persons, not mine." The ironic mode of the dramatic monologue thus allowed Browning the mutually enriching interaction of the objective and the subjective, the dramatic and the lyric modes.

Although there are superb pieces in *Dramatic Lyrics* and *Dramatic Romances and Lyrics,* only one other monologue has the ironic richness of **"My Last Duchess." "The Bishop Orders His Tomb at St. Praxed's,"** from the latter collection, engenders the same tension between sympathy and judgment. The bishop has obviously broken almost every rule of conduct imposed by the Church upon her clergy; yet, so much caught up in the secular spirit of the Renaissance, he deludes himself that he has earned the right to a magnificent tomb in a choice spot in his own church. As readers we know full well how defective a cleric he has been and condemn him for his failure, but at the same time we are impressed by his exquisite taste and, further, pity him because he knows that his sons will bury him in a tomb of only "gritstone, a-crumble." The poem is not, however, merely the bishop's monologue. The poet intrudes into it by making the utterance a sermon on the text "Vanity, saith the preacher, vanity," which is the first line of the monologue. The poem thus becomes an exemplum preached by the bishop who, not incidentally, throughout the monologue constantly lapses into a homiletic style simply out of habit: the preacher proves his text, unknowingly, by the revelation of his character; his plea for sympathy becomes a literary form—a sermon—which stands in judgment of him. A poet can hardly go further in achieving so subtly in the work of art itself those reflections of the work of art which characterize the highest irony. (pp. 38-9)

[Browning's work of his] married years and that appearing soon after is generally regarded as his very best. And surely no one who loves literature can but love the monologues of *Men and Women* (1855) and *Dramatis Personae* (1864). Yet for the admirer of Browning's irony and radical formal innovations, seeing all things through the eyes of Elizabeth Barrett Browning had its limitations. In the first place, Mrs. Browning demanded of poetry that everything be spelled out—no loose ends, no parts unlinked by logical copula, no requirement that the reader employ his "co-operating fancy." . . . In the second place, Mrs. Browning wanted the "meaning" of the poem to be as clear as its form. As Browning wrote (13 Jan. 1845), she spoke out, while he only made men and women speak. Hereafter he would address himself more directly to the moral concerns of his fellow men, would bear in mind his "mission of humanity" (25 Feb. 1846).

I do not mean to imply that the great monologues of the fifties and sixties are reducible to their moral content, but I do say that they have more moral design upon the reader than do the earlier poems. **"Cleon," "Karshish," "Childe Roland," "Abt Vogler," "A Death in the Desert," "Caliban,"** to name only some of the best—all are concerned with the communication of some moral or religious message. Admittedly there are ironies galore—Cleon and Karshish do not embrace the Christian answer to their problems which lies so readily at hand, Roland meets with both success and defeat in finding the tower, Abt Vogler accidentally discovers an image of heaven which he cannot recapture in soberer mood and which he doubts may have occurred—but they are ironies which point always to some moral. Even those monologues specifically concerned with art—**"Fra Lippo Lippi"** and **"Andrea del Sarto,"** to me the most excellent of the monologues of this period—even they are designed to communicate something about the morality of art. There is never any question about their "meaning." Browning had reoriented his art to the point where he was ready and willing to assume the bardic mantle, something he had continually disavowed earlier, although this new idea of the bard involved not being *overheard* (as J. S. Mill said all true poetry should be) but heard directly. Speaking in **"One Word More"** in his own voice and out of his own experience of unappreciation, Browning tells of the poet who like Moses is both looked up to for guidance and deprecated for it. It is a wearying business, but "Never dares the man put off the prophet."

I have spoken only of the best poems of the fifties and sixties. If I were to speak of others—***Christmas Eve and Easter Day,*** **"Respectability," "Rabbi ben Ezra," "Gold Hair,"** the "Epilogue" to ***Dramatis Personae***—I could make an even clearer case for the reorientation of Browning's art towards a religio-moral aesthetic. The demand that poets address themselves to the immediate religious and moral needs of their society was of course in the air throughout the forties and fifties—witness what happened to Tennyson—but in the case of Browning, who in Florence was living at quite a remove from his native country, the demand that he suppress the "frivolous" irony of his earlier verse was evidently formidably reinforced by his wife. I say this because the verse written after and not immediately influenced by Elizabeth's death is of a different nature. It is different in that the old sense of irony returns, never so wonderfully zanily as in the case of ***Sordello,*** but boldly and paradoxically nevertheless. It is different too in that Browning gives up working mainly with one form, the dramatic monologue, and begins again the formal experimentation of the ironist who, aware of the principle of becoming and the inadequacy of any form to serve for more than one occasion, must always be seeking for new vehicles to embody new ideas.

The first fruit of his new artistic freedom was ***The Ring and the Book.*** For years it has been customary to speak of this long poem as the culmination of Browning's art. If by "culmination" one means that it is the finest of his works, then I cannot quarrel with such an assessment, although I am inclined to put ***Sordello*** and the ***Parleyings*** on the same level. But if by "culmination" is meant the logical outcome of his earlier verse, as seems to be the case, then I must argue most vehemently against any such notion. For ***The Ring and the Book*** is very little like the poems of the 1850s and the sixties. To be sure, most of it is a series of dramatic monologues and some of them seem to have a moral design upon the reader, but it is also a great work of ironic art, a narrative which mixes genres and ultimately undercuts the moral statements made by the monologists. There are wonderful characters in it who exist, almost like the Duke of Ferrara, for the sake of the characters themselves—those of the second, third, and fourth books, for example, even Guido himself, a study first of covert then of open villainy; and there are characters who, splendid in themselves, are nevertheless designed to have a moral effect upon us. What could be more affecting than the monologues of Caponsacchi, Pompilia, and, as the authorative voice, the Pope? But then we read the twelfth and last book, which calls into question everything that has gone before. For in it the poet, apparently speaking in his own voice, tells us that all these "pleadings and counter-pleadings" have been just so many words. Even the Pope, who has pronounced the innocence of Caponsacchi and Pompilia and who has claimed to evolve the final truth (a claim which most critics have accepted)—even the Pope's soliloquy is called into question in the last book. It is not that he lies; rather, it is simply that he may not have spoken the full truth, for the simple reason that, even in soliloquy, he has an axe to grind, must justify himself to himself. The narrator says, "our human speech is naught, / Our human testimony false, our fame / And human estimation words and wind." Only art, "wherein man nowise speaks to men," may tell a truth because it aims for ideal significance by pretending to be nothing other than itself. As I understand ***The Ring and the Book,*** it is not the culmination of Browning's work but a transitional poem re-introducing radically ironic notions of art.

Since, as I noted at the beginning of this essay, I have already written at some length on Browning's poetry after ***The Ring and the Book,*** I have chosen to use most of the space allotted me to discuss the poet's earlier work. In what follows hereafter I shall hastily try to indicate how in his later years Browning returns to something like the style and mode of the poetry prior to his marriage. Once again the poetry becomes daringly innovative. ***Balaustion's Adventure*** (1871) stretches the dramatic monologue to formal lengths unenvisioned even in the writing of ***The Ring and the Book:*** it contains a whole version of a play by Euripides, with the strong implication that Balaustion, the simple girl from Rhodes, has seen more in the material than has Euripides and that she in her innocence has discovered the evolving nature of deity in the phenomenal world. **"Prince Hohenstiel-Schwangau"** (1871), perhaps the most misunderstood of Browning's later poems, presents the case of a voluptuary talking to himself who seems to be a reasoning man speaking to a courtesan. *Fifine at the Fair* (1872), the poem which Browning called the most "metaphysical" he had written since *Sordello,* presents seventy-two ways (or thereabouts) of looking at and justifying adultery—all of them wrong. *Red Cotton Night-Cap Country* (1873), a first-person narrative, gives all the evidence why a manic-depressive has a religious impulse to do the impossible and why he is both right and wrong. *Aristophanes' Apology* (1875) carries the dramatic monologue to the breaking point: it contains, *inter alia,* a debate between Aristophanes and Balaustion about the relative merits of Euripides and Aristophanes, comedy, tragedy, and tragi-comedy, a transcription of the Euripidean *Herakles,* and finally a seeming vindication of Euripides *and* applause of Aristophanes—all within one monologue. In such poems Browning tried, as he had in *Sordello,* to concentrate a vast amount of time and space into a prolonged but single moment of simultaneous perception, attempting, as Aristophanes envisions a future poet doing, "to take in every side at once, / And not successively." The last of the long poems of the 1870s, *The Inn Album,* is a narrative composed of eight dramatic scenes in which the melodramatic action becomes the text of the album at the inn ironically hailed as a "salubrious spot" of "calm acclivity." These six long poems in a highly ironic mode deserve more recognition as belonging among Browning's greatest achievements.

For a dozen years thereafter Browning turned to shorter works. Although they represent experiments with new forms—the idyl, for example—and examine from an ironic stance the function of evil as a contribution to ultimate good, by and large they are less interesting than the long poems of the period 1871 to 75. It may be that Browning was acting out in person his own sense of irony. Everyone knows how Browning loved to dine out and be taken not for a poet but for a successful financier, how Henry James thought that the man he met in society could not possibly be Robert Browning the poet. During the later seventies and early eighties Browning lived his irony as he had never before been able to do.

In his penultimate work, *Parleyings with Certain People of Importance in Their Day* (1887), Browning achieves a masterpiece of ironic art. He summons from the past a group of artists, satirists, moralists, politicians, philosophers, musicians, all of whom had a certain influence on the poet's early life, and then proceeds by means of a parleying with some contemporary figure to justify why these men of the past, insignificant though they may now be, have had a salutary effect on the poet's development even though their views may be outmoded or wrong. Thus with a kind of double vision the poet sets into motion a process of dialectic in which he is and is not present, one which he can sit back and enjoy. The main subject of each parleying is the nature of fact and fancy; and the answer, if indeed answer it is, is that fact either cannot exist "unfancifully" or is worthless unless imaginatively apprehended by fancy. For the ironist the parleying is an ideal form in that it allows the author to be both immanent and transcendent and, further, while advancing claims to philosophical seriousness, does not pretend to be anything other than a work of art.

In his last volume, *Asolando* (1890), there is a poem which may be taken as a summarizing statement of Browning's essentially ironic view of the world. In **"Development"** the poet speaks of how he had first learned of the *Iliad* from his father: from re-enactment in play of the siege of Troy, to reading of it in Pope's translation, finally to studying it in the Greek original: each phase of his acquaintance with Homer was suited to the proper stage of his development. By the time he reached young manhood he was so well acquainted with Homer that concerning the facts of the blind poet's life he was convinced "nothing remains to know." But then came the German "Higher Criticism" which proceeded to show that there had never been a Troy and, worse, "No actual Homer, no authenticated text, / No warrant for the fiction I, as fact, / Had treasured in my heart and soul so long." He should have not been surprised because he should have known that, in an evolving universe, nothing remains static. Yet today, in spite of this new knowledge, which he of course accepts, he will nevertheless guard in his soul's shrine the reality of Helen, Hector, Achilles, Ulysses, and the rest; in the life of the imagination he will retain "fact's essence freed and fixed / From accidental fancy's guardian sheath." It is irony which permits, in Friederich Schlegel's words, this "clear consciousness of an eternal agility, of the infinitely abundant chaos." It is irony which allows for the provisional negation of the "serious" or "objective" character of the external world and, correlatively, for the provisional affirmation of the creative omnipotence of the thinking subject; it is irony which, after the poet's declaration that "No dream's worth waking," returns us in the end to the world of quotidian reality where it is "boys' way" to soil a book "with bread and milk," "crumple, dogs-ear and deface." If there has been any "development," it is only that the gray-haired man doesn't disfigure a book.

From the time of *Paracelsus,* Browning had held firmly to what many regard as mindless optimism. As he relates in **"Reverie,"** the last poem of *Asolando* excepting the "Epilogue,"

> Even as the world its life,
>   So have I lived my own—
> Power seen with Love at strife,
>   That sure, this dimly shown,
>   —Good rare and evil rife.

Yet he has clung to the faith that eventually wrong will be righted. "Why faith?"

>   but to lift the load,
>   To leaven the lump, where lies
> Mind prostrate through knowledge owed
>   To the loveless Power it tries
>   To withstand, how vain!

We may speak of this as willed faith, but correctly we must name it irony, that philosophical and aesthetic mode (to borrow from Leo Capel's introduction to his translation of Kierkegaard's *The Concept of Irony*) aspiring to ideal significance whose meaning is contradictory, whose structure is dialectical, whose medium is the language of reflection, and whose style is antithetical.

No other Victorian poet is so thoroughly ironic in his view of the world or in the presentation of that view in his art.

Among the early Victorians we have to go to Carlyle, mainly *Sartor Resartus* (written almost directly under the influence of the German romantic ironists), to find work similar to those "transcendental buffooneries" of Browning, yet Carlyle was unable or unwilling to sustain his irony for very long and so in the later 1830s lapsed into the prophet. Dickens was clearly working towards a thorough-going irony in *Bleak House,* yet he never developed it in his later works. What happened to both Carlyle and Dickens was what happened to Browning during his middle period, the twenty years from 1846 to 1866: they failed to maintain the double vision of the ironist. Browning however recaptured his old way of seeing and, with a remarkable outburst of energy, returned to the ironic mode in his later works.

Browning remained aware of the conflict between the old religious and the new positivist world-views and, more importantly, of the impossibility on his part to take either side or bring them into accord. In this respect he was not unlike, say, Matthew Arnold, who was well aware of wandering between two worlds. He was different from Arnold not in recognizing these conflicts but, in a large body of his work, presenting them ironically so as to transcend them. It was his irony that allowed Browning, unlike most of his contemporaries, to rise above mere argument or special pleading for this or that cause. It was his irony that permitted him to be among the least topical of English poets and yet simultaneously to be among the most fully grounded in the life of his time. In sum, it was his irony that makes him one of the most innovative and enduringly influential poets in English. (pp. 40-6)

> *Clyde de L. Ryals, "Browning's Irony," in* The Victorian Experience: The Poets, *edited by Richard A. Levine, Ohio University Press, 1982, pp. 23-46.*

FURTHER READING

Arms, George. " 'Childe Roland' and 'Sir Galahad'," *College English* 6, No. 5 (February 1945): 258-62.
> An explication of the similarities and differences between Browning's and Alfred, Lord Tennyson's treatment of the Holy Grail legend in "Childe Roland to the Dark Tower Came" and "Sir Galahad."

Auerbach, Nina. "Robert Browning's Last Word." *Victorian Poetry* 22, No. 2 (Summer 1984): 161-73.
> Argues that Browning disagreed with his wife Elizabeth's poetics, ultimately appropriating material from her poem *Aurora Leigh* and "butcher[ing] it in *The Ring and the Book*."

Bloom, Harold, and Munich, Adrienne, eds. *Robert Browning: A Collection of Critical Essays.* Twentieth Century Views, edited by Maynard Mack. Englewood Cliffs, N.J.: Prentice-Hall, A Spectrum Book, 1979, 207p.
> Includes commentary by such noted critics as John Hollander, Harold Bloom, and Robert Langbaum.

Broughton, Leslie Nathan; Northup, Clark Sutherland; and Pearsall, Robert. *Robert Browning: A Bibliography, 1830-1950.* Cornell Studies in English, edited by Charles W. Jones, Francis E. Mineka, and William M. Sale, Jr., Vol. XXXIX, Ithaca, N.Y.: Cornell University Press, 1953, 446p.
> Considered a primary reference tool in Browning studies. The authors supply detailed, comprehensive information concerning writings by and about Browning for period indicated.

Browning Institute Studies: An Annual of Victorian Literary and Cultural History I- (1973-).
> Annual periodical. Each issue carries scholarly essays on Browning's canon and on the works of such contemporaries as Matthew Arnold, George Eliot, and Alfred, Lord Tennyson.

DeVane, William Clyde. *A Browning Handbook.* 2d ed. New York: Appleton-Century Crofts, 1955, 594p.
> An invaluable aid to Browning studies. DeVane devotes a section of his *Handbook* to each of Browning's publication, describing the work and providing information on such topics as composition and publication dates and contemporary reaction to the volume.

Erickson, Lee. *Robert Browning: His Poetry and His Audiences.* Ithaca, N.Y.: Cornell University Press, 1984, 287p.
> Book-length study in which author attempts "to offer readings of Browning's poetry that analyze his characters' relationship with their audiences." Erickson's examination of Browning's work is "placed within the context of his biography, and especially of his love for Elizabeth—how Browning sought an audience for his poetry, found one in Elizabeth Barrett, and lost one when she died."

Drew, Philip, ed. *Robert Browning: A Collection of Critical Essays.* London: Methuen & Co. Ltd, 1966, 278p.
> Collects essays on Browning by such critics as Henry James, William C. DeVane, John Stuart Mill, and Richard D. Altick.

Fuson, Benjamin Willis. *Browning and His Predecessors in the Dramatic Monolog.* State University of Iowa Humanistic Studies, edited by Franklin H. Potter, Vol. VIII. Iowa City: State University of Iowa, 1948, 96p.
> Refutes the notion that Browning invented the dramatic monologue, citing a long history of such contemporaries in English literature.

Gosse, Edmund. *Robert Browning: Personalia.* London: T. Fisher Unwin, 1890, 96p.
> Features a reprint of "The Early Career of Robert Browning, 1812-1846," a literary and biographical sketch based on interviews that Gosse conducted with Browning.

Greer, Louise. *Browning and America.* Chapel Hill: University of North Carolina Press, 1952, 355p.
> Covers such subjects as Browning's associations with Americans and the progress of his popularity and critical reputation in the United States.

Griffin, W. Hall, and Minchin, Harry Christopher. *The Life of Robert Browning.* New York: Macmillan Co., 1912, 342p.
> Considered the standard biography of Browning.

Honan, Park. *Browning's Characters: A Study in Poetic Tech-*

nique. 1961. Reprint. Hamden, Conn.: Archon Books, 1969, 327p.

> Examines Browning's poems and dramas in the context of character portrayal, maintaining that such an investigation reveals the "complexity, intensity, and unity of his best dramatic verse."

Jones, A. R. "Robert Browning and the Dramatic Monologue: The Impersonal Art." *Critical Quarterly* 9, No. 4, (Winter 1967): 301-38.

> An assessment of Browning's dramatic verse.

Khattab, Ezzat Abdulmajeed. *The Critical Reception of Browning's "The Ring and the Book," 1868-1889 and 1951-1968.* Salzburg Studies in English Literature: Romantic Reassessment, edited by James Hogg, Vol. 66, Salzburg: Institut für Englische Sprache und Literatur, Universitat Salzburg, 1977, 214p.

> Surveys and compares the response of Victorian and modern critics on *The Ring and the Book*.

Lounsbury, Thomas R. *The Early Literary Career of Robert Browning.* London: T. Fisher Unwin, 1912, 205p.

> A series of lectures exploring Browning's modern critical reputation. Lounsbury focuses on the reception given to *Pauline, Paracelsus, Strafford, Sordello,* and *Bells and Pomegranates.*

Nettleship, John T. *Robert Browning: Essays and Thoughts.* London: J. Lane, 1909, 454p.

> Traces Browning's artistic development.

Orr, Mrs. Sutherland. *Life and Letters of Robert Browning.* Rev. ed. Boston: Houghton, Mifflin, and Co., 1908, 431p.

> An important early biography. This edition, which was originally published in 1891, includes material revised and rewritten by Frederic G. Kenyon.

————. *A Handbook to the Works of Robert Browning.* 6th ed. 1892. Reprint. New York: Kraus Reprint Co., 1969, 420p.

> An early reference book on Browning, largely descriptive in nature.

Pound, Ezra. *Literary Essays of Ezra Pound.* Edited by T. S. Eliot. New York: A New Directions Book, 1968, 464p.

> Contains scattered references to Browning, including a passage in the essay "T. S. Eliot" praising the dramatic monologue form used in *Men and Women* as the "most vital form" in Victorian poetry.

Ryals, Clyde de L. *Browning's Later Poetry, 1871-1889.* Ithaca, N.Y.: Cornell University Press, 1975, 262p.

> Underscores the artistic integrity of Browning's later works, focusing on his commitment to discovering new formal methods for expressing his vision of reality.

Sessions, Ina Beth. "The Dramatic Monologue." *PMLA* LXII, No. 2 (June 1947): 503-16.

> Brief critical discussion of Browning's dramatic monologues, including "My Last Duchess," "Count Gismond," and "A Woman's Last Word."

Swinburne, Algernon Charles. Letter to John Nichol. In his *The Swinburne Letters: 1854-1869,* Vol. 1, edited by Cecil Y. Long, pp. 100-01. New Haven, Conn.: Yale University Press, 1959.

> Acknowledges the excellence of "Mr. Sludge," "The Medium," and "Caliban upon Setebos." On previous occasions Swinburne had denounced Browning's poetry.

Robert Duncan

1919-1988

(Born Edward Howard Duncan; also wrote under the pseudonym Robert Edward Symmes) American poet, essayist, editor, playwright, and author of children's books.

Duncan is regarded as an important contemporary American poet who has been linked at various times with the Black Mountain School, the San Francisco Renaissance, and the Beat Movement. Many critics also note that his style of verse has affinities with Romanticism. Duncan's poetry combines his knowledge of such disciplines as history, mythology, mysticism, and literature with personal observations and emotions. The experimental form of Duncan's verse reflects his belief that composing a poem is a spontaneous act and that the poet need not revise nor formally structure his work. Duncan's poetic output, which he has termed a "collage," encompasses disparate themes throughout an ongoing creative process that he views as an extension of the vast tradition of poetry.

Duncan's poetics were formed by the events of his early life. His mother died during his birth, leaving his father, a day-laborer, to care for him. Six months later, Duncan was adopted by a couple who selected him on the basis of his astrological configuration. Their respect for the occult in general, and especially their belief in reincarnation and other concepts from Hinduism, was a lasting and important influence on his poetic vision. Encouraged by a high school English teacher who saw poetry as an essential means of sustaining spiritual vigor, Duncan chose his vocation while still in his teens. He was an active figure from the 1930s to the 1950s in the literary communities of San Francisco, the East Coast, and North Carolina's Black Mountain College. The poems in his earliest works, collected in *The First Decade: Selected Poems, 1940-1950* and *Derivations: Selected Poems, 1950-1956,* concern homoerotic themes veiled in medieval allusions. Reflecting myriad influences, these poems display the wide range of Duncan's interests and learning.

In 1956, Duncan taught at Black Mountain College, which was administered by the poet Charles Olson. Duncan is often credited, along with Olson and Robert Creeley, as a leading practitioner of "projective" or "open field" verse. In this type of poetry, the poet's emotional and intellectual energy is transmitted directly and spontaneously, with lines determined by natural pauses for breathing. Some critics believe that Duncan carried this process farther than did Olson, defining the poem as an open field without boundaries of any kind. A Duncan poem, accordingly, resembles a collage in which materials from diverse sources accumulate in a series of organic digressions. This eclectic and allusive nature of much of Duncan's verse has prompted charges of obscurity and even incomprehensibility. Duncan's champions, however, maintain that his poetry is a bold attempt to distill the mysterious essence of nature and creativity.

Duncan's first major volume, *The Opening of the Field,* announces his use of Black Mountain aesthetic principles. The volume's opening poem, "Often I Am Permitted to Return to a Meadow," exemplifies Duncan's belief that the poet is a shamanistic figure deeply affected by the external world. This book also presents the first poems in a sequence entitled "The Structure of Rime," one of Duncan's several ongoing series of prose poems. Referred to by Duncan as "trance projections," this sequence is intended to convey poetic theory within the practice of composition. In his next collection, *Roots and Branches,* Duncan employs more elegant language in order to distance himself from mundane experience and to ennoble the art of poetry. Several poems in this work explore the border between physical and transcendent realities.

The poems in *Bending the Bow* concern social and political issues of the 1960s. This volume contains the first of Duncan's "Passages," another open-ended sequence that differs from "The Structure of Rime" by its unhindered expanse of subject matter. In these poems, Duncan liberally intersperses quotes from and allusions to other sources as well as his own works. The overt political nature of *Bending the Bow* is evidenced in the poem "Up-Rising" ("Passage 25"), which attacks the American government's involvement in the Vietnam War. After the publication of *Bending the Bow* in 1968, Duncan announced he would not publish a major collection for another fifteen years. During this hiatus he hoped to produce process-oriented poems instead of the "overcomposed" poems he wrote when he thought in terms of writing a book. In his next major volume, *Ground Work: Before the War*, Duncan again explores his topics through poetic sequences and collage patterns. Duncan received the National Poetry Award for *Ground Work: Before the War*. The consistency of Duncan's verse led Geoffrey O'Brien to comment: "The single-mindedness of [Duncan's] life's work shows itself in the confident energy of every line; in an era when poets exercise their 'craft' and 'control' with defensive restraint, *Ground Work* exhilarates by its utterly uncautious raid on the sublime." *Ground Work II: In the Dark,* which contains poems written between 1976 and 1984, indicates Duncan's declining health through its overriding concern with the interrelation between life and death.

Duncan's esteemed reputation in the poetry community derives from his mastery of several verse forms, his attempt to make poetry a vehicle for religious and metaphysical insight, and his ability to synthesize diverse influences into an original vision. Duncan was instrumental in propagating "open field" verse, in which the form of a poem emerges from the subject matter rather than from arbitrary, premeditated structures. Largely responsible for the establishment of San Francisco as the spiritual center of contemporary American poetry, Duncan has left a significant contribution to American literature through the body of his writings and through the many poets who have been influenced by the theory behind his poetics.

(For further discussion of Duncan's life and career, see *Contemporary Literary Criticism,* Vols. 1, 2, 4, 7, 15, 41, 55; *Contemporary Authors,* Vols. 9-12, rev. ed., Vol. 124 [obituary]; *Contemporary Authors New Revision Series,* Vol. 28; and *Dictionary of Literary Biography,* Vols. 5, 16.)

PRINCIPAL WORKS

POETRY

Heavenly City, Earthly City   1947
Medieval Scenes   1950
Caesar's Gate: Poems, 1949-1950   1955
Letters   1958
Selected Poems   1959
The Opening of the Field   1960; revised edition, 1973
Roots and Branches   1964
Writing Writing   1964
Of the War: Passages 22-27   1966
The Years as Catches: First Poems, 1939-1946   1966
Bending the Bow   1968
The First Decade: Selected Poems, 1940-1950   1968
Derivations: Selected Poems, 1950-1956   1968
Tribunals: Passages 31-35   1970
A Seventeenth Century Suite   1973
The Venice Poem   1975
Ground Work: Before the War   1984
Ground Work II: In the Dark   1987

OTHER MAJOR WORKS

The Sweetness and Greatness of Dante's "Divine Comedy,"
   1265-1965   (essays)   1965
The Truth & Life of Myth: An Essay in Essential Autobiography   (essay)   1968
Fictive Certainties: Five Essays in Essential Autobiography
   (essays)   1985

Muriel Rukeyser   (essay date 1948)

[*An American poet, critic, and translator, Rukeyser was respected for verse that addressed social, psychological, and political issues. In the following excerpt, she favorably reviews* Heavenly City, Earthly City.]

The irresistible qualities of this first book of poems are myth and torment. I have had the fortune to see the full manuscript of which **Heavenly City, Earthly City** is one part: I know that the "promise" of this book is answered. Here are the poems of one year, 1946, when the poet was twenty-seven. They acknowledge their origins—frankly, in statement, in their allusive vocabulary, and (in the fuller manuscript, which I hope will soon be published) by absorbing these origins.

The statement gives the range. Duncan says, "I owe much in the development of my poetics to the works of Wyatt and Surrey, to *The Temple* of George Herbert, to the work of such moderns as Wallace Stevens, D. H. Lawrence, the Spender translation of Rilke's *Duino Elegies,* and Edith Sitwell's *Street Songs.* In my psychological concept I am indebted to Sigmund Freud, Karl Barth, and particularly to *Dark Night of the Soul* by the 16th century St. John of the Cross."

The scene is San Francisco Bay, where Duncan lives and was born. He brings to this bay of hills the older myths: Orpheus, Prometheus. They are here, with the sea leopards, the rocks, the city, the "turbulent Pacific." (pp. 48-9)

I have heard one poet say of this poet: "Intellectual torment, sexual confusion." And a publisher says of him: "He lacks what Winters calls 'moral fibre.'" Duncan printed an article last year in *Politics,* and the echoes have not faded. Now two touchstones of American sentimental reactions are, I think, the names of communism and homosexuality; signals to the unsure for fear-trigger responses that will be identical, whatever the subject that releases them. (And we have also Mother, Food, Women, Negroes, Jews, Poetry—and several others you can name.) Robert Duncan, writing of one of these, will have the "sentimental" response, and I am sure that, as an artist, he will deal with it. The torment of these poems goes, at the poems' best, beyond subject, as it must. In the held rhyme of the first poem "I listen in the shade to one I love" he prepares the ear, the imagination, for the repeated notes of later lines. And now, as the book begins, the words and figures gather, alert and musical: "Christ-crossed" (crisscrossed), the parallel between the image of love and Zeno's endless race, and the passages—in "Sleep is a deep and many voiced flood":

> Now,
> watching over your loved form where it lies
> admitted to life's death-sounding, sleep . . .

Some of it is rhetoric, yes it is; but Duncan begins to go past this. Some of it sinks in its decoration; but the best emerges. (pp. 49-50)

Grace, dance movements, enter these poems. In **"An Elegiac Fragment,"** beginning "The women in the many-chambered dawn." you will come upon the lines

> There is an innocence in women
> that asks me, asks me;
> it is some hidden thing they are
> before which I am innocent.
> It is some knowledge of innocence.
> Their breasts lie undercover.
> Like deer in the shadow of foliage,
> they breathe deeply and wait;
> and the hunter, innocent and terrible,
> enters love's forest.

This poem leads to the Portraits, to the one beginning "Jimenez in the golden company." The music which Duncan compels is clear in this single line, with its pattern of sound dropping three times to the "-en," and the word "in" pointing to the rest.

But the personal statements are stronger than anything else in the book—the "radiant joy," the culpable cries of grief, and

> If only my sense of your passion
> could flow back and fill you

and

> I am a most fleshly man, and see
> in your body what stirs my spirit.
> And my spirit is intimate of my hand,
> intimate of my breast and heart . . .
> I am a most fleshly fire, and yearn
> for your body to replenish my flame.
> I would embrace you and name myself
> anew in your flesh.

The praise of the sun in these poems is partly the old same praise that is everywhere; it is also local, Californian; it also reflects the work of poets, Wallace Stevens, and Edith Sitwell's great book that reached our spirits with discovery. The ape, the gold, some of those terms of hers, that vocabulary of hers which she has turned into a philosophy, they are here; they are one beginning for Robert Duncan. He has struck past his apparent flaws; I think he has found his own voice, and among the Miller-haunted writers of this coast, he is building the scene into poems, making experiment, music, debt, into a personal and widening art. (pp. 50-1)

Muriel Rukeyser, "Myth and Torment," in Poetry, *Vol. LXXII, No. 1, April, 1948, pp. 48-51.*

Frederick Eckman   (essay date 1956)

[*Eckman is an American poet and critic. In the following excerpt, he views* Caesar's Gate *as a partially successful work marred by Duncan's mysticism and excessive mannerism.*]

When Robert Duncan speaks in a *persona* like that of **"Processionals, II"** [in *Caesar's Gate*] with its precise rhythms and carefully withheld irony, he is an attractive poet. . . . (p. 62)

But as soon as he turns prophet or sibyl, scrawling out large, shadowy gestures of mysticism, Duncan is neither appealing nor convincing. He has taken over many of Kenneth Patchen's weird apocalyptic devices: prose-poems scribbled in black crayon, arrows, underlines, outcry and apostrophe, splashy surrealist photo-collages. All these are signs of the would-be daemonic poet—not the real article, who is impelled as powerfully toward rigid form as the quasi-daemonic is driven away from it. Poe, Rimbaud, Crane, Thomas, were experimental only insofar as their unorthodox visions demanded it; otherwise they hungered after the only thing durable enough to save them: form. Duncan, like Patchen, is a rhetorician, a fact that becomes painfully evident upon reading the preface to the book. Here is its opening paragraph:

> *HELL.* Dante says accurately that it is a forfeiting of the goods of the intellect. How far can there be a poetry of hell, out of hell? It is all that is not terror: the nostalgias, sophistications, self-debasements here that are voice of a soul-shriveling, the ironies of mediocrity. To this point I came, willingly demoralized, to pray for grief, or for sleep, for the tides of blood, for the worm to turn.

When the rhetoric wears out, one is left with a weary post-Eliotic whine, as in **"He Has a Good Time There"**:

> Ridiculous, the butterfly
> —avatar of the serious worm—
> he lights upon the merde of Art;
> that swish old relique, self-enamourd
> fly-by-night, he hovers
> among the cafe tables.

Duncan's own devices—the omission of unstressed *e*'s in weak participles (*burnd, stirrd, gaspd, calld*), his fondness for exclamation, and his lapses into French—are less strategies than compulsions or mere mannerisms. Of the six poets [reviewed] here, Duncan risks most by way of experimentation—and, in the end, loses most; because his experiments never proceed from necessity so much as from a superficial desire for differentness. *Caesar's Gate* is the only volume of the six reviewed here that intends to be a *book,* with its own unity and dramatic structure; but Duncan is successful only in isolated poems and parts of poems, when he is being a poet and not a mystic. (p. 63)

Frederick Eckman, in a review of "Caesar's Gate," in Poetry, *Vol. LXXXIX, No. 1, October, 1956, pp. 52-63.*

A. R. Ammons (essay date 1960)

[*Ammons, an American poet and critic, is regarded as a significant contributor to the Emersonian Transcendentalist tradition of poetry. In the following excerpt, Ammons notes that Duncan's immoderate explanation of his own verse detracts from the potentially outstanding work in* Selected Poems.]

[Duncan] is a conscious artist, able to tie up or absorb his loose ends into his method, to incapacitate possible opposition by incorporating it. That is the defensive attitude. On the offensive, Duncan is also capable: he drives a spearhead to the heart (Cortes to the person of Montezuma). That is, Mr. Duncan has taken up the central order-disorder position from which he can regard all being, if he likes, or only selected, representative parts of being. His poems [in **Selected Poems**] are illustrations, objectifications of the interchange between order and disorder, accompanied by the appropriate emotions, which are more nearly suggested than realized, of amazement and love at the sight of perfect order, awe and fear at the possibilities of new forms (sometimes monstrous) arising from disorder, and grief at the processes of decay, disintegration, and return. Art—specifically, poetry—is a part of this large concern, and references to poetry or to the poet occur in nearly every poem. Duncan's relationship to poetry, to the creation of form, becomes the symbol of order and change operating in all aspects of reality.

What that relationship is can best be suggested by thinking of Mr. Duncan as a ballet teacher. He stands at the bar, before a wall-size mirror, assumes a stance, and explains both his image and the emotions that should be evoked: "Note the configuration of that hand. That means disdain. Now, this thigh-line, *on stage,* will suggest emotional agility." Etc. The imaginative students probably get through the machinery of the emotion occasionally to the actual, on-stage emotion. But Mr. Duncan never goes on stage. He analyzes and reports the materials of the experience as well as the reactions to the materials. (p. 53)

I do not find anything supremely good or his own in Duncan's technique. The early poems are paragraphic in stanza pattern and mostly (often, loosely) metrical:

> Our little Death from which we daily
> do survive, it seems tonight
> the very tide of life itself
> upon whose surface we toss,
> unwilling to submit, like two swimmers
> eager for rest but eager too for each other.

The last line shows how, even among archaisms, Mr. Duncan can suddenly say something wonderful. But the movement through this book is toward a more nearly phrasal rhythm, with much freer (and, paradoxically, tighter) visual patterns. . . . (p. 54)

Practically every influence on our time is represented in Duncan's work. This, from **"The Banners,"** looks like Yeats:

> The days before awakenings, dark ages,
> are long with hours for the poets' tapestry.
> The unicorn of gold and swan-white threads
> nuzzles the sleeping virgin in the park.

Above their heads the signet of the Prince
is woven, elaborate blood-red signature.

Add Freud, Joyce, Jung, Frazer, Stevens, et al. There are several small matters of syntax, spelling and neologism which I leave to the possibility that Mr. Duncan has a bigger dictionary than I.

Every *possibility* of the outstanding poet exists in this work: development of the poem's total form (as opposed to a few flashy lines), excellent sonant quality and movement, conservation of statement, and intensity of rendered image, and a commanding point of view. It is because Mr. Duncan is already an accomplished poet that I ask more of him: more immediate experience, less comment and explanation. (pp. 54-5)

> *A. R. Ammons, in a review of "Selected Poems," in* Poetry, *Vol. XCVI, No. 1, April, 1960, pp. 52-55.*

Albert J. Gelpi (essay date 1967)

[*Gelpi is an American critic who has written critical studies on Emily Dickinson and Adrienne Rich. In the following excerpt, he praises* Roots and Branches *as superior examples of poems about the poetic process and comments on Duncan's use of myth.*]

Robert Duncan's **Roots and Branches** confirms his important presence in contemporary poetry. He belongs in that long and various line of American vatic poets which arose from Emerson and first expressed itself fully in Whitman. Duncan's remarks about the practice of poetry say a great deal of his individual conception of his role as poet. "I make poetry . . . to exercise my faculties at large"; "unwittingly we achieve our form" in life and in art, and so poetry is "the inevitable use" we make of language to discover to ourselves as well as to our readers "what we are becoming." The emerging form is the vital link between life and art; for "to form is to transform, is a magic then, and . . . a metaphor is not a literary device but an actual meaning arising from, operating in, and leading us to realize the co-inherence of being in being." Thus "we perceive forms because there are correspondences," and in a real sense the poem is "an occult document," "a rite," "magic," whose "open composition" must mirror the individual in the realization of this correspondence.

It is a difficult and often painful process because the individual is caught in the toils of his double nature as both carnal (sexual) and visionary. The poems aim at articulating the coming to recognition of the unity under the seeming duality of body and soul, and the crowning moment is the total fulfillment of the individual through an integration of passion and exaltation in Love, when the body is transfigured by the activity of spirit. Duncan's poetry is involuted and idiosyncratic; since it attempts to express the awareness of coming to awareness, the movement transpires almost completely in his own mind. The reason that his poetry is so difficult is that he is pushing language to the perimeters of what is communicable; he has to find words to say the unsayable, images which convey in recog-

nizable terms, terms that we can share, the dynamic dawning of an utterly private revelation.

How can he find language adequate to this theme? In his
previous volume, *The Opening of the Field,* Duncan tried
to solve the problem often by projecting a personal mythology that is more mystifying than communicative, and
the problem persists on occasion in this book too, as in a
"theosophical" play called **"Adam's Way."** If the symbols
are not fleshed out, they remain phantasies in Duncan's
mind, and at his most subjective he seems to be playing
games with the figments of his own imagination. However,
sometimes, as in **"Osiris and Set"** and **"Cyparissus,"** he
can reconstruct myth to his own meaning with vivid immediacy. And sometimes—often enough to make him one
of the most electric poets writing in America today—he
is able to body forth his subjective state in words and images so that we are made to participate in the very movement of consciousness as it finds itself in the whole scale
of being. **"Variations on Two Dicta of William Blake,"**
"Now the Record Now Record," "A Set of Romantic
Hymns," "A Part-Sequence for Change" (to name a few
of my favorites) are remarkably achieved poems—as is the
title poem [**"Roots and Branches"**]:

> Sail Monarchs, rising and falling
> orange merchants in spring's flowery markets!
> messengers of March in warm currents of news
>   floating,
>   flitting into areas of aroma,
> tracing out of air unseen roots and branches of
>   sense
>   I share in thought,
> filaments woven and broken where the world
>   might light
>   casual certainties of me. There are
>
>   echoes of what I am in what you perform
> this morning. How you perfect my spirit!
>   almost restore
> an imaginary tree of the living in all its doctrines
>   by fluttering about,
> intent and easy as you are, the profusion of you!
> awakening transports of an inner view of things.

Here nature signifies the terms for describing the life of the
mind. And yet although art emerges organically from living, it also, paradoxically, has an essential relation with
dying as well. For in Duncan's poems if the experience of
Love, which is the triumph of life, is also the triumph over
death, that transcendence still does not shatter the temporal wheel; the contention of Eros and Thanatos opens up
again, and in some sense Thanatos will win. So art becomes not just the definition of the triumph of Love over
Death but it becomes besides the recording against Death
of that triumph, as in **"Nel Mezzo del Cammin di Nostra**
Vita" the Watts Tower is both the expression of and the
monument to Simon Rodilla. True as it is that organic art
grows from the roots and branches of life, the poem once
achieved ceases growing and is fixed in death; yet it is true
too that our only chance against the vicissitudes of time
is to make experience die into art. In **"What Happened"**
Duncan speaks of "the troth that poetry keeps with the
grave."

This dilemma makes the artistic process and the nature of

the aesthetic object so basic a concern that they frequently
become the subject of the poem. In **"A New Poem"** Duncan poses the question to himself succinctly. Is Poetry the
boat in which we sail the lake—designed and directed,
ship-shape, water-tight—or is Poetry the unfathomable
lake itself over which we make our mysterious way by instinct? In other words, is Poetry the man-made convey-
ance or is it that unknown reservoir, the source and end
of being, through which language tries to negotiate a voyage to name the unnameable? If Poetry is the poem, then
it is finally fulfilled and fixed (and dead) in the accomplished form. However, if Poetry is the unfolding experience for which the poem is a mere shadow, then Poetry
is life itself, and the poet's tongue must never be still. His
job is never complete, no matter how many poems he has
completed. In fact, his function as poet returns him to life
again and again. He must keep telling because he keeps ex-
periencing, and he must continue to render a record of the
successive moments of process. These poems do exactly
that: their fluid but achieved forms mark stages of a progressive evolution. (pp. 1030-32)

> *Albert J. Gelpi, "The Uses of Language," in*
> The Southern Review, *Louisiana State Uni-*
> *versity, Vol. III, No. 4, Autumn, 1967, pp.*
> *1024-35.*

Paul Zweig (essay date 1968)

[*Zweig, an American critic and poet, wrote the acclaimed critical biography* Walt Whitman: The Making
of the Poet *(1984). In the following excerpt, Zweig provides a generally unfavorable review of* The Years as
Catches *and* Of the War, *finding much of Duncan's
verse inordinately rhetorical while also noting flashes of
brilliant insight.*]

Robert Duncan's poetry resembles a vast landscape of rhetorical trees and animals. Bodies larger than life float and
contort themselves, without ever quite touching the
ground. Each body is a kaleidoscope, a heaven of interior
animals and the hero of this visionary landscape is the
poet. He floats in a world of his own making, travelling
tirelessly among these creatures and faces projected out of
his own inner life.

Duncan's confidence in the imagination is boundless. The
only drama he acknowledges is that of contrary images;
languages that make war on each other:

> In the groves of Africa from their natural won-
>   der
> the wildebeest, zebra, the okapi, the elephant,
> have entered the marvelous. No greater marvel-
>   ous
> know I than the mind's
> natural jungle.

"An African Elegy" descends from these lines into "the
mind's natural jungle". It is a convincing adventure, and
the poem is one of Duncan's best; perhaps because the
"marvelous", here, is sharpened by a sense of melancholy,
a solitude which reappears in the poem like a leitmotif:

> I am waiting this winter for the more complete
>   blackout

for the negro armies in the eucalyptus, for the
        cities
laid open and the cold in the love-light, for
        hounds
women and birds to go back to their forests and
        leave us
our solitude.

The Years As Catches contains a selection of Duncan's
early work—1939 to 1946—and many of its poems are
among the most interesting he has done. There is a poetry
of praise in the early work which reaches beyond the self-
involved rhetoric of the seer. At their best, these are poems
about the world:

The green world moves around me, birds, the
        still pools,
disturbed only by rain, left after rain, stilld,
coold under the branches alive with mosquitoes.
Shadblow and lilac. The air is blue. The air
is white, because the shad have come up the river
bearing in their bellies the pockets of roe like
        sand,
and the delicate trunks of their trees
reach into a cluster of torn flowers.

Even in these early poems, however, Duncan cannot resist
the impulse of his language. Words beget words. His confidence in the imagination turns to self-indulgence, an endless ribbon of eloquence flowing out of his "jungle" and
finally diluting it. Rarely is Duncan's imagination anchored in a true bodily intensity, as in the passages I have
quoted. Elsewhere, the skin of his vision floats out; it becomes a vast, eloquent surface, but the body has been left
behind; the body rots out of sight somewhere, beneath the
airy spaces of the poem which seems to be talking about
it. *The Years As Catches* gives a sense of Duncan's imagination which is still accurate: a mixture of unique lyrical
insight and vapid self-indulgence; alternations of visionary
intelligence, and the all-too-frequent abdications of that
intelligence. (pp. 402-03)

Of the War contains Duncan's **"The Up Rising,"** one of
the finest political poems to have been written during the
past years. The language of **"The Up Rising"** is galvanized
with an ominous power which increases from stanza to
stanza, as the poet describes how "men wake to see that
they are used like things spent in a great potlatch, this
Texas barbeque / of Asia, Africa, and all the Americas".
There is a terror of recognition in Duncan's description of

the all-American boy in the cockpit
loosing his flow of napalm, below in the
        jungles
        "and life at all or sign of life" his target,
drawing now
        not with crayons in his secret room
the burning of homes and the torture of mothers
        and fathers and children.

Many of us could learn from Duncan's ability, in this
poem, to entangle the terrors of our public world, of our
war and violence, into the intense privacy of the emotions,
where poetry is fashioned. (pp. 404-05)

Robert Duncan presents his reader with a problem: that
of threading his way through forests of inflated trees, in
order to come upon those moments of insight which are

remarkable, and which make Duncan the curiously irre-
placeable poet he is. (p. 405)

Paul Zweig, "Robert Duncan's World," in Po-
*etry, Vol. CXI, No. 6, March, 1968, pp. 402-
05.*

Laurence Lieberman   (essay date 1969)

[*Lieberman, an American poet and critic, belongs to no
critical school of thought, relying instead on personal
criteria for determining poetic worth. In the following
excerpt, he observes that Duncan's engagement with political issues in* Bending the Bow *has rejuvenated his
work after several years of intensely private verse. This
review was reprinted in Lieberman's book* Unassigned
Frequencies: American Poetry in Review *(1977).*]

Robert Duncan's struggle in [**Bending the Bow**] to over-
haul his technical apparatus to make it able to accommodate political denunciation may be likened to Yeats's
metamorphosis in *Responsibilities,* the volume in which he
explicitly set out to bury his allegiances to "old mythologies" and to intensify reality in his work. In the effort to
demythologize his medium, Duncan is undertaking a similarly exhaustive labor of self-effacement and self-renewal.
Duncan has desperately needed for many years to retrieve
his poetry from the incantatory monologue of private reverie and myth, and to initiate a return to subjects of public
consequence. In the years since the publication of his best
volume, *The Opening of the Field,* Duncan appears to
have succumbed more and more to debilitating preciosi-
ties of mannerism, mostly derived from the poetry of Ezra
Pound: abbreviated spelling, philological queries, overt
pedantic scholarship. This defect of artificiality sinks to a
new low of self-consciousness in the poem **"Spelling,"**
which humorlessly explicates stylized misspelling in the
manner of a gloss to an Old English text.

The Opening of the Field had announced the birth of a
surpassingly individual talent: a poet of mysticism, visionary terror, and high romance. Duncan's work is outstanding among his contemporaries' in having rehabilitated
from three hundred years of relative disuse and stagnation
the emblem—not the image, or the symbol—as the central
vehicle of the poem's drama. Duncan's emblems are populated by flaring presences, who, like crucified angels, blaz-
ingly dance out of the "black pit" of blindness, and into
"the beginnings of love". But in his recent books he has
produced numerous exercises—lacking all vividness—
while he waits for the return of his demon. These many
autotelic performances are like prayers to the absent spirits urging their return: they may serve, for us, as a record
of soul-priming, the readying of fallow poetic ground for
the next major theme, whenever it may strike.

Such a theme is the Viet Nam War. In the best new poems,
"Up Rising," "Transgressing the Real," "The Soldiers,"
Duncan's new esthetics of political engagement embodies
his outrage in the most viable, grotesque emblems he has
produced in any poetry: "The Grand Poker Table", where
"the hydra" (heads of State), "shuffling cards, beyond
number", gambles away the lives of thousands; Lyndon
Johnson's "Texas barbecue", a gargantuan super-feast

"swelled with the votes of millions" of pampered, overfed, innocently criminal Americans, "good people in the suburbs turning the / savory meat over the charcoal burners and heaping their barbecue / plates with more than they can eat." It may well be that these agonizingly Dantesque, emblematic hymns point ahead to a full resurgence of Duncan's demonic genius. (pp. 43-4)

Laurence Lieberman, "A Confluence of Poets," in Poetry, *Vol. CXIV, No. 1, April, 1969, pp. 40-58.*

Ronald Hayman   (essay date 1970)

[*An English biographer and critic, Hayman has written critically respected biographies on such literary figures as Franz Kafka, Friedrich Nietzsche, and Jean-Paul Sartre. In the following excerpt, Hayman presents a laudatory review of* The First Decade *and* Derivations, *praising Duncan's masterly tone of voice and keen attention to detail.*]

Duncan's metaphysical premises may be quite unacceptable to us but, as with Yeats, they do not invalidate the poetry. He has always believed in a transcendent reality and in a "continuity of spirit in the universe." The whole of creation is charged with meaning. . . .

In his early poems [in *The First Decade*], the Miltonic cadences and the habit of straining after absolutes take the edge off his directness. But the authoritative tone of voice and the sensitivity to detail combine to compel our attention, even when he is adopting an orphic stance, as in **"An Apollonian Elegy."** Though he is less economical with words than he became later, he depended on verbs rather than on adjectives, achieving great muscularity and flexibility. In **"Heavenly City, Earthly City"** his mind throbs painfully with longings for eternity and the pain leaves a clear residue in the rhythms. He has quoted Ezra Pound as saying "I believe in technique as the test of a man's sincerity"; the proof of Robert Duncan's sincerity is the relationship he has achieved between the pulse of the sensation and the pulse of the line.

"The Venice Poem" (1948) represents an important turning point in his development. The language varies effectively between the elegiac and the colloquial. The visual perceptions become sharper, the rhythms more incisive, and there is a greater precision in the shaping of the lines. But above all it is a feat of structure. Othello's Venice swims behind the Venice that Duncan observes and the whole poem (conscious of itself looking) resembles a series of reflecting surfaces angled in on each other. But nothing remains static and the movement probes into the nature of the processes that are constantly at work in us and on us. (p. 84)

Like a self-destroying machine, the poem works its way forwards into a total collapse. There are five despairing stanzas in the coda which all end with the Beckett-like line "I am barely able to go on." The substance of the stanzas justifies the refrain but the ensuing sequence, in which the poem picks itself off the ground to enact the birth of a baby, is less successful. The affirmative note seems *voulu*.

The First Decade ends with two poems inspired by the Korean War and *Derivations* begins with a third, **"An Essay on War."** A poem still in the process of being written is compared with a war still in the process of being fought. The form and language change as the questions it asks go deeper. Like **"The Venice Poem"** it drives itself to a standstill and twice it breaks down into prose. But the poetry, self-conscious but well able to make each of its own movements meaningful, revives itself with the intensity of its own efforts to make itself go on, trying to make sense of its efforts to make sense of experience that makes no sense.

In the long run, Olson's influence was to prove fruitful for Duncan but *Derivations* is taken up mainly with the prose poems, the "Letters" and the imitations of Gertrude Stein he wrote between 1951 and 1955, which are less interesting than either his earlier or his later work. He went through a severe spiritual crisis in San Francisco in 1956, during which it was almost impossible for him to write verse but the (prose) letters he wrote to himself are fascinating and moving. It is also interesting in **"For a Muse Meant"** to watch him hovering over each pause in his verse, keeping himself enjoyably in suspense about what was going to come next. The poetry is in the process. But what we now need is a selection or better still a collection—of his verse between 1956 and 1969. It is in this period that all his best work has been done. (pp. 84-5)

Ronald Hayman, "The City & the House," in Encounter, *Vol. XXXIV, No. 2, February, 1970, pp. 84-91.*

Gilbert Sorrentino   (essay date 1970)

[*A distinguished poet and experimental novelist, Sorrentino is also regarded as an insightful critic whose essays on lesser-known or neglected Black Mountain poets has generated wider interest in these writers. In the following excerpt, Sorrentino praises* The First Decade, Derivations, *and* Roots and Branches, *noting Duncan's development into an important and powerful poet.*]

Reading Robert Duncan's three books—two new [*The First Decade: Selected Poems, 1940-1950* and *Derivations: Selected Poems, 1950-1956*] and one reissued [*Roots and Branches*]—we have the opportunity to chart the development of a master. It is strange that, as I have mentioned, this mastery has been so often treated as "experiment". Duncan himself says, "I am not an experimentalist or an inventor, but a derivative poet", on the back cover of *Roots and Branches,* yet the flap of *Derivations* says, "This second volume covers his most experimental and prolific period." And there have been many critics and reviewers who, faced with what is clearly the work of a richly gifted man, admit this work with the qualification that it is experimental. This is a subtly derogatory word and may be taken to be a euphemism for that work which cannot be called "serious". Let me go into this a little bit. Had Duncan focused his poetics on poems like **"The Venice Poem** and **"An Essay at War"**—that is, continued to write in this luminous vein, a brilliant and single vision, I submit that he would have been accorded all the honors the literary establishment could afford. Perhaps not all the honors, but a meaty bone or two. But he went from these remarkable poems to a total confrontation with the poem as an instrument whereby the poet is relieved: he stands outside of himself. The Stein imitations and *Writing Writing* develop the problem, if you will, of reality as itself and reality as it is created in the poem: they make a specific statement so that the poem is constructed as a province apart, and wherein the imagination revealed in the structure of the poem is real. The imagination is real. Williams said that "only the imagination is real", which statement does not mean, it seems to me, that the imagination can extend itself beyond the ongoing language given the poet to work with. That is, simile as "artistic" ornament is still a form of verbal garbage whereby the poem is dirtied, no matter the poet's insistence on the simile as a figure that carries his imaginative thought. If the imagination is to be real in the poem, that is, if the words themselves are real, and not counters for reality—well, then the poet has his work cut out for him. "Losing ourselves in the otherness of what is written", Duncan says. Because, contemporary propaganda notwithstanding, the poem is not a tool but a manifestation of the poet's imagination that is absolutely real, and, as it is composed, it becomes an "otherness". It is no longer ours, but it is an artifact. Unfortunately for metaphysics, politics, and religion, it *is* an artifact, it is itself, an otherness. (pp. 114-15)

The Stein imitations, which have been justly celebrated, are not only remarkably successful as a *tour de force,* they complement the poems of *Writing Writing* and of *Letters* (also included, in full, in *Derivations*) in their insistence on the word within the poem as final poetic reality. In *Letters,* the poet says, "As we start the sentence we notice that birds are flying thru it; phrases are disturbd where these wings and calls flock; wings are a wind, featherd, a beating of the air in passage or a word, the word 'word,' hovers, sailing before dropping down the empty shafts of sense toward. . . ." The explanation of the poem is the poem, it sets up its resonances in its own structure, it arranges its correspondences. It is worth noting that the teaching of Jack Spicer seems, in the poems of *Derivations,* to be most clear.

I see in the exquisite beauty of Duncan's work the configuration of the true poet who has wrought it. A man who at first fought doggedly with that work so that it would make sense of, and bring some order to, his life; but the development of this work admits a graph of surrender to the fact that the writing of poems brings order to, and makes sense of—only the poem. As the poet himself writes in a note on *The First Decade,* quoting his own **"The Venice Poem,"** "Never in living / but here, here, / all felt things are / permitted to speak." Confronted by this sublime intransigence, what else can a rhymester do but call this work experimental? Duncan is in service and bondage to The Art of Poetry, so that his very career is an affront to those who conceive of this art as a "part of" their lives. We look for Duncan in his poems, where else? (p. 115)

In *Roots and Branches,* Duncan writes:

> —the poet's voice, a whole beauty of the man
> Olson,
>   lifting us up into

> where the disturbance is, where the words
>   awaken
> sensory chains between being and being,

stating, here, that "disturbance" is a quality of the poem necessary to its success. The poem, as it exists between poet and reader, as it is alive in both the writing and the reading, is, in fact, a disturbance, one that awakens us, or irritates us into attention. It disturbs and allows us release from our tired and tried ways of seeing: so that the language itself is a way of seeing, is sight itself. I think that for Duncan there is no understanding or recognition of the real unless it can be so seen in the language of the poem. This book, *Roots and Branches,* along with the one published previously to it, *The Opening of the Field,* display the great power of the poet, a full use of those materials tested in fire in the poems written between 1949 and 1956. The poems show a strength and beauty which place them among the major literature of this time. (p. 116)

> *Gilbert Sorrentino, "Black Mountaineering," in* Poetry, *Vol. CXVI, No. 2, May, 1970, pp. 110-20.*

Jonathan Galassi   (essay date 1973)

[*Galassi is an American critic, poet, and editor. In the following excerpt, he lauds Duncan for his skillful blending of contemporary events with metaphysics and myth in* Tribunals: Passages 31-35.]

Let the line surpass your uses. This injunction from Pound is Robert Duncan's watchword in *Tribunals,* parts 31 to 35 of a longer work entitled *Passages.* His association with Pound and the poem's title itself point to essential differences in method and intent between Duncan and younger writers aiming at a more popular strain of speech. Duncan attempts a synthesis of the fragmentary modern consciousness, "the isolated satyr each man is", into the stream of history. The work is symbolized in his versification. Short broken lines abounding in halting repetition and oxymoron slowly metamorphose into complex organic periods. Duncan relies on a transcendental vision for his idea of order: "there was a covenant made that we call the Age of Gold, the Ancestral design, / and this alone governs what endures." This abstract mythology embraces the dichotomies and oppositions of the physical world. The Poet, a holy pariah conscious of his mission "To unglue the tight-up esthetics", speaks a "Language beyond Speech". And yet Duncan's poem is as deeply grounded in contemporary events as it is in metaphysics and myth. . . . Duncan's achievement is to have provided an accessible theoretical context, a coherent ordering of seemingly irreconcilable aspects of the modern experience. *Tribunals* is consciously and consistently difficult, too difficult to be dealt with fairly here. The reader may not share Duncan's idealism, but at least he leaves the poem with more than an introduction to the poet's idiosyncrasies. Because Duncan alludes to an external and communal, if not common, body of knowledge, we can bring our intelligence to bear on the problems posed in the poem and come away with an inkling of how they may be managed.

Duncan does not write in an "open idiom". Where the younger generation is unassuming, quotidian, and rambling, he is prophetic, abstract, structured, and he takes himself and his task very seriously. But because his poem concerns itself with objectively shared experience, it yields the patient reader more in its own rarefied way than a tautological surrealism ever will, no matter how "simply" expressed. (pp. 347-48)

Jonathan Galassi, "An Open Idiom," in Poetry, *Vol. CXXI, No. 6, March, 1973, pp. 343-48.*

A. K. Weatherhead   (essay date 1975)

[*Weatherhead is an English critic and author of the study* The Edge of the Image: Marianne Moore, William Carlos Williams, and Some Other Poets *(1967). In the following excerpt, Weatherhead comments on the collage-like structure of Duncan's poems in* Bending the Bow.]

In the introduction to **Bending the Bow,** Duncan speaks of poems as spatial objects; the poem is not, for instance, a stream of consciousness, "but an area of composition in which I work with whatever comes into it." Or there is this, in the same introduction:

> . . . parts [of the poem] belonging to the architecture not only by the fittings . . . by what comes one after another as we read, but by the resonances in the time of the whole in the reader's mind, each part as it is conceived as a member of every other part, having, as in a mobile, an interchange of roles, by the creation of forms within forms as we remember.

A series of poems entitled **Passages** which commence in **Bending the Bow** are to be thought of largely as collages. In the poems of this series it is interesting to notice how often spatial terms are countered or at least coupled with those suggesting the temporal or linear development of the poem or with terms of music. For example, in **"At the Loom: Passages 2,"** the poet describes how in the "old ways" of poetry, "the stuff / vanishes upon the air, / line after line thrown." He calls for another method, "Let there be the clack of the shuttle flying / forward and back, forward and / back . . . " which suggests a movement countering the conventional forward progress of a poem bound by its proper temporal conditions, a movement associated here with the creation of a spatial design. (pp. 165-66)

"Bending the Bow," the title poem of its volume, is a fabric in which terms of space and time are subtly in counterpoint with one another. The poem opens with the contrast between reality and dream, which latter, as Duncan suggests elsewhere, may indeed be the greater reality: "We've our business to attend Day's duties, / bend back the bow in dreams as we may." A note to the poem directs us to Fragment 51 of Heraclitus, part of which runs, "there is a connexion working in both directions, as in the bow and the lyre." And G. S. Kirk's *Heraclitus,* mentioned in the notes, observes the phenomenon alluded to in the opening lines of the poem, that if a bow is sufficiently bent back it will take on the shape of the lyre. The bow of day's duties,

associated with space, becomes the lyre of dreams, associated with song, and hence time. As the poem proceeds, bow and lyre and terms of area and time sequence are juxtaposed: dreams "flow" in time and are a "current"; day's duties are "surfaces"—of the table, of the crockery, of the "whole / composition." (Duncan remarks elsewhere, "Rilke said that these things / tables, chairs, beds, houses / were vessels in which men might find and store humanity.") Later in the poem are other lines where shadows in space and notes in time come together:

> You stand behind the where-I-am.
> The deep tones and shadows I will call a woman.
> The quick high notes . . . You are a girl there too,
>   having something of sister and of wife

which exemplify other alternative realities that are to be permitted to remain in tension. As a whole the poem is a choreography of counterpointing realities, shifting across the stage. It closes by bringing bow and lyre together:

> and I would play Orpheus for you again,
>
>   recall the arrow or song
>   to the trembling daylight
>   from which it sprang.

The significant feature, however, is not the space and time terms in the content but the overall shape of the whole poem which defies, as far as it may, temporal development and settles for an architecture which may be compared with that of some of the old medieval cathedrals, in which no dominating overall plan determines the relationship of parts, which may be walked around, surveyed, one may say, as "sea bord seen by men sailing" and admired *seriatim* for the glory of God, but not conceived of as a whole. No one specimen of the **Passages** poems can be called typical; but the unstructured development in **"The Architecture: Passages 9"** will serve to illustrate Duncan's procedure, partly because the prose passage with which it opens, from Gustave Stickley, *Craftsman Homes* (1909), offers prescriptions for a room that might be extended to prescribe for a poem:

> " . . . it must have recesses. There is a great charm in a room broken up in plan, where that slight feeling of mystery is given to it which arises when you cannot see the whole room from any one place . . . when there is always something around the corner." (Spaced periods, Duncan's)

There follow images of light and of music. Then:

> from the bookcases   the glimmering titles
>   arrayd   keys
> Hesiod . Heraklitus . *The Secret Books of the Egyptian Gnostics* . . .

The list of books is interrupted by the continuation of the passage from Stickley, which in turn is interrupted for a list of more books. Then come two lines juxtaposing images of music to those of the room: "I was reading while the music playd / curld up among the ornamental cushions"; and then a continuation of Stickley, prescribing prominence of the staircase in a house "because it forms a link between the social part of the house and the upper regions." This quotation is broken off to give way to images relating to the garden, some quotations from Truman Michelson, *The Owl Sacred Pack of the Fox Indians,* and images of the poet reading in the lamplight. The last line of the poem concludes the broken off passage from Stickley: "which belong to the inner and individual part of the family life."

There are some manifest relationships between parts of the collage—between, say, the architecture of the house and that of the human being, the body and the mind of the poet reading. But one should be careful not to assault the poem with the old expectations of thematic coherence and overall unity. Nor, similarly, does the poem permit the sustaining of a melodic line. I suspect that one of the principles back of the **Passages** poems is that though melody is present it must be controlled by space, as the lyre by the bow. In **"Wine: Passages 12"** it seems as if the music gets off on its own and carries all before it into a lyrical utterance:

> thick perfumes of those lost flowers,
>   mimosas of those afternoons?
> Where are the fairy colors of long-gone suns
>   bedded down?
>   *"Je vois longtemps*
> *la mélancolique lessive d'ors*
>   *du couchant."*

But on the whole a poem's tendency to be melodic is inhibited by the poet's insistence on an opposing principle: that it aspire to the condition of the collage.

What are the implications in Duncan of a poem being as much like a collage as a poem can be? First of all, it is a collage with no single dominant feature. In these poems, Duncan is avoiding the central thing, the single meaning; these are poems without souls, only bodily parts. In his study of Gérard de Nerval, Duncan characteristically takes delight in the plurality of designation in the opening lines of *El Desdichado,* terms taken by Nerval from his sources, says Duncan, "in order to form a community of meanings." In a poem of his own he may open parentheses four or five times without closing them, decoying us like a mother mocking-bird away from any sense of a central thought in the poem. In such a collage poem there is the field and there are individual images within it of which no single configuration forms *the* subject, each poem being only an extension of a primordial reality behind all things. (pp. 166-69)

The open poem attempts to be spatial. It reserves entrance for the extraordinary, the irrational, and the completely unsought to come insinuating or crowding in. The closed poem on the other hand works in linear time and a form that eliminates the detail irrelevant to its logic or its narrative. Duncan is repelled by excluding form:

> We domesticate, civilize, idealize, characterize, humanize ourselves and all that is "ours"; taking identity in what we can command. This house commands a view of the valley. Great ceremonies, rituals, paradigms, pentacles, perspectives, strive to bring into the command of a little room titanic or demonic powers, to define time and space, to give primordial form—the process of reality to which cosmos and life belong—a con-

ventional form. In periods of greatest panic, such as the eighteenth century following the nightmare religious enthusiasms and wars of the seventeenth, the form tolerable to convention can shrink to a tennis court. But there remains the deepest drive of the artist, a yearning to participate in the primordial reality that challenges the boundaries of convention and the purposes of pedagogy again and again.

>   (*Truth of Life and Myth*)

It is a beautiful passage; it enlists our sympathy and gives us a "commanding" perspective from which to view the works of those, artists or others, who seek or have sought power by the use of conventional forms, contracting the world to one kind or another of tennis court—a governing doctrine, a fixed intractable organization, a formula, or a form. And although as a basis of poetic strategy it precludes action, as we shall see, it is understandable that the open poem, open to every nuance of a reality of which the bounds are unknown, is the proper vehicle for Duncan. One can hardly conceive of him settling for a kind of unity that would exclude anything at all, though other poets with visions have made their accommodations, and truth to be truth need not be naked.

One singularly ugly part of contemporary experience, the Viet Nam war, left Duncan disgusted and angered. But his poetry turns to it repeatedly as the tongue seeks out a canker in the mouth; for even this horror is a part of the Grand Symphony. The perpetrators of this evil he condemns; and one realizes that, in his terms, these men from whose faces "Satan looks forth" have resorted to their activities because they have seen too narrowly; they have reduced reality to a small canvas where a single motif is permitted to become huge and disproportionate and to dominate the whole field: "that our Nation save face," for example. Men have organized their policies and taken actions—actions that prodigiously injure the world—according to the kind of limited and exclusive view that Duncan distrusts utterly. And the collage with no central motif or single dominating figure in it obliquely reflects that distrust: the poet's eye goes beyond the narrow pragmatism of leaders.

But to return to the passage quoted above: as a basis for strategy these prescriptions against narrowness preclude all action, not just evil. And in doing so they separate Duncan from the exercise of his own fine lyric gift. In the open collage poem the mind consciously and passively meditates among phenomena, is open to all aspects of truth, and excludes nothing that the spirit purveys; but in the lyric it must act unselfconsciously, cutting, selecting and appropriating what is demanded by the melody on the one hand, and the expression of the mood on the other, assuming most often a strict form, closed to what for its limited purposes is irrelevant, and not saying too much. The lyric is the product of a kind of action that momentarily excludes the rest of the world. As a species of music it naturally depends on time sequence, the medium that the collage poems attempt to break down. Duncan can write lyric poetry in which idea, feeling, and melody fuse into a linear unified statement with no self-conscious qualifications or deliberate dissonances. (pp. 172-73)

It is possible that he shares with some earlier and older poets the sense that complete and exclusive commitment to the simple, single feeling that lyric demands is not possible for those who bear the burden that broad social and political awareness confers. Blake, Shelley, and Yeats were not so inhibited: in the full consciousness, vivid enough, of social and political evil, they wrote their lyrics. They were also men of action, in some cases single-minded and precipitant. And accordingly they had no scruple in taking the exclusive kind of action that is demanded in the creation of a lyric. The predicament of Duncan, on the other hand, seems to be that of a number of poets of the thirties, C. Day Lewis and Stephen Spender, for example, who, conscious of the poverty and hunger in the economic distress of the times, the impotent suffering of the poor, the violence of the powerful, were assailed by a sense of irresponsibility in writing the lyric when so much of the rest of the world made such great appeals to their consciences. (pp. 173-74)

Duncan may be compared with these poets inasmuch as he will not write the perfect lyric, but must corrupt the linear melody for the strategy of the collage, break up thematic unity with elements recalcitrant and untamed, and bring in contemporary horrors. As a poet he is a scholar gypsy, accepting but not bound by old wisdom, open to vision and impulse, eschewing preconceived form, precluded from the action of the lyric, nourishing a strong sense of music in poems controlled by a sense of their existence in space. (p. 174)

> A. K. Weatherhead, "Robert Duncan and the Lyric," in Contemporary Literature, *Vol. 16, No. 2, Spring, 1975, pp. 163-74.*

Nathaniel Mackey (essay date 1980)

[*In the following excerpt, Mackey analyzes "The Continent" and discusses how Duncan differs from poets with whom he is commonly associated, particularly William Carlos Williams.*]

["The Continent"] is the concluding piece in *Roots and Branches,* the book Duncan designates as a return to what he calls a rhetoric of Romantic elevation, a mode incorporating the rhapsodic, the elegiac, the fabulous and so forth, "the high Edith Sitwell manner" of which his conversion to Olson's poetics had made him feel ashamed. . . . One of the factors making for his embarrassment would of course have been the impact upon the Black Mountain movement of Williams' insistence on the use of an American vernacular, of down-to-earth diction and of everyday patterns of speech. Duncan's impatience with Williams' " 'American' thing or speech," which he elsewhere in *The H. D. Book* calls "Williams' regular-guy voice," has a lot to do with the threat it posed to his more rhetorical bent. His sense of shame, that is, tends to mingle with a sense of defiance, just as he tends to be both inclusive and contentious at the same time. . . . The poems in *Medieval Scenes,* as the title suggests, revel "with vengeance" in precisely what Williams could rail against as anachronistic diction and outmoded lore.

I'm not sure Duncan ever really, even temporarily, left the rhetoric behind, but the poem in *Roots and Branches* which most overtly expresses his sense of having done so, and of thereby having it as something to which he could now return, is the one called **"Returning to the Rhetoric of an Early Mode."** The poem's celebration of the greenness of an earth and a foliage-, flower- and fruit-bearing tree which are both in fact its rhetorical flourish ("the abundance, / the verdant rhetorical," "green panic," "all verdant thought"), is intended, I think, to be recalled by the invocation of the "mother of the Lady Verdure" in **"The Continent."** Here's the first stanza of **"Returning to the Rhetoric of an Early Mode":**

> If I think of my element, it is not of fire,
> of ember and ash, but of earth,
> nor of man's travail and burden
> to work in the dirt, but of the abundance,
> the verdant rhetorical. Servant of the green,
> the Gardener of the Hesperides returns,
> sometime no more than pompos of the poem,
> a claim I made on some modal prince
> I thought I had seen so real he was mine
> received in the music-magic of Sitwell or of Ste-
>   vens,
> robed round in sound, rich as a tree
> in full foliage of metaphor, flower and fruit.

Here's how **"The Continent"** begins:

> Under-
> earth currents, Gaia, Hannahanna,
> mother of the Lady Verdure
> all dresst in green
> her leafy graces, in margins
>
> the writ illumined, wreathed round
> with pomegranate
> split for in-betweens of jeweld hive
> red seed upon red seed,
> ripe peach, pear, apple cut
> to show the core,
>
> vine tendril into talon curls,
> faces in the fruit occur.

Though the line here is considerably more stripped down than that of **"Returning. . . "** and its manner less rhetorical in that its thrust is more pictographic than declarative, its picture of plenitude, of cornucopic abundance, and its musicality hark back to the earlier poem. While **"The Continent"** isn't a rhetorical poem in the sense in which **"Returning . . . "** and the early poems in *The Years As Catches* are, it does have to do with and seeks to celebrate the dream-swollen world the more overtly rhetorical poems bear witness to.

"The Continent" appears to be an attempt to include within the boundaries of the same poem both the fable- or myth-world of the earlier rhetoric and a here-and-now colloquialness worthy of Williams. One encounters the slanginess or hipness of "In Iowa they do not dig / the swarming locale," the ungrammatical Americanness of "They do not remember the body of / them waters" and the folksiness of "it's a caution / to see their faring." It's as though Duncan had set out, again with a vengeance perhaps, to make use of specifically American forms of speech. Much of the poem could in fact be called "a funny

play around Williams," as Williams' work is pretty blatantly alluded to at various points. Just as the phrase
which brings section I of the poem to a close, "against the
/ run to the mythic sea, the fabulous," recalls the title of
Book IV of *Paterson,* "The Run to the Sea," the opening
lines of section II, with their description of Earth as "murmurer," bring to mind the phrase "Earth, the chatterer,"
also from *Paterson.* Similarly, the final stanza of section
II—

> I'm not so old but I can put
> the thought away, my foot
> before my foot,
> climbing the hill as if for rime
> my teeth are gnashing, and again
> the thought returns
> that we conquer life itself to live,
> survive what we are.

not only suggests, with the phrase "my foot / before my
foot," Williams' figure of walking or of dancing, throughout *Paterson* or in a poem like "Heel & Toe to the End,"
as a manner of speaking of poetic meter, but with its last
three lines both echoes ("the thought returns") and answers the following lines from *Paterson:*

> The thought returns: Why have I not
> but for imagined beauty where there is none
> or none available, long since
> put myself deliberately in the way of death?

The line midway through section II, "a sparrow smasht
upon the sidewalk," alludes to Williams' poem "The Sparrow," and the first few lines of section III continue with
the allusion. Williams describes the flattened bird as:

> a wisp of feathers
> flattened to the pavement,
> wings spread symmetrically
>   as if in flight,
> the head gone,
>   the black escutcheon of the breast
>   undecipherable,
> an effigy of a sparrow,
>   a dried wafer only

From which Duncan derives:

> The head crusht sideways, the wings
>   spread out
> as if embracing the sidewalk, too close
>   for shadow,
> the immediate!

(pp. 599-603)

But what exactly is Duncan doing with these allusions and
derivations? It seems to me that he's doing a number of
things: celebrating, having fun with and even correcting
or reclaiming Williams. The extent to which these allusions focus on *Paterson,* the work in which, as Duncan argues in *The H. D. Book,* Williams the dreamer of the
world-poem triumphs over Williams the feet-on-the-
ground American realist, suggests an effort to recover Williams from the widely-held sense of him as the down-to-
earth, no-nonsense "regular-guy" of American poetry.
Duncan's answer at the end of section II to Williams'
question "Why have I not . . . put myself . . . in the way
of death?" echoes his own assertion in **"Apprehensions,"**

one of the earlier poems in **Roots and Branches:** "To survive we conquer life or must find / dream or vision." **"Apprehensions,"** a poem upon which **"The Continent"** in several ways relies, opens with the line "To open Night's eye
that sleeps in what we know by Day," a line which not
only says a lot about Duncan's intentions but also explains
the phrase *day's eye* and the recurrence of the words *day*
and *sun.* Section III of **"The Continent,"** that is, allies Williams' demotic aspirations, his desire to be "of the people,"
with a daylit or sunlit sense of things, with a reality principle ("a day's eye" or "what we know by Day") which mili-
tates against dream, against vision, against "the fabulous"—against the "Night's eye" Duncan's rhetoric
serves. The crushed sparrow, brought down to the ground
and no longer capable of flight, symbolizes a shadowless
and depthless immediacy of perception, while the exclamation "the immediate!" recalls Williams' use of that term
to suggest a peculiarly American approach to things. . . .
(pp. 603-04)

As we've seen however, Duncan's most approving sense
of Williams dissociates him from "the great beast," from
any one-sidedly sunlit or daylit version of the world and
from his self-declared " 'American' thing." He sees him
as a fellow "artist of the margin" and this marginality is
a part of what he applauds. . . . Yet **"The Continent"** is
a poem which does resort to the theme of an American
ethic, though it does so only by way of Duncan's holding
himself apart from that ethic. In fact, he holds himself
apart or "of the margin" exactly on the basis of what, in
large part owing to Williams, has become a pet obsession
for many American poets—the idea of locality. Looking
"east, east, east" from his birthplace and homeground, the
San Francisco Bay area, he writes of middle America:

> The mid-Western mind
> differs in essentials
> —another time zone.
> In Iowa they do not dig
> the swarming locale, this port of
> recall. There's no
> Buddhist temple in the mid-West town.

Against the heartland insularity of the mid-West Duncan
poses "the swarming locale," the cosmopolitan heterogeneity of San Francisco, an international port. Some such
cult of "the immediate!" as Williams would view as typically American and to which section III of the poem alludes gets presented here as a case of American-Adamic
amnesia. The mid-West's lack of use for "this port of / recall," after being implicated in a spiritual isolationism
which has no use for Buddhism, is elaborated upon in the
lines which follow:

> Earth drains down the Old Man River and runs
>   out
> in swamps and shallows of the Caribbean.
>
> They do not remember the body of
>   them waters
> but stand with feet upon the ground
>   against the
> run to the mythic sea, the fabulous.

Here then is that characteristically "American" feet-on-
the-ground aversion to the myth-world to which Duncan's

rhetoric inclines, an aversion to "the mythic sea" suggestive of Williams' cry, "The sea is not our home. (Williams goes on to use the phrase "the nostalgic sea," which further agrees with Duncan's sense of the disdain for "the body of them waters" as a suppression of memory. The sea is a much-encountered symbol for the "collective unconscious" or some global "race-memory" in the literature of psychology.)

Duncan returns to the association of San Francisco with what could be called an oceanic sense in section IV of the poem, doing so in lines which are highly reminiscent of and probably indebted to Olson's myth of "Pacific man":

> . . . Here
> our West's the Orient,
> our continent the sea.

In the concluding chapter of *Call Me Ishmael,* which was for Olson what *In The American Grain* was for Williams—an "historical grammar," call it, of the poetics of his American myth—Olson writes:

> . . . the Pacific gives the sense of immensity. She is HEART SEA, twin and rival of the HEARTLAND. The Pacific is, for an American, the Plains repeated, a 20th century Great West. . . . With the Pacific opens the NEW HISTORY. . . . The movement into it during the 19th century, of which Melville was a part, makes the third great shift. Melville felt the movement as American. He understood that America completes her West only on the coast of Asia.

Taking Ulysses, to whom he says Homer gave "the central quality of the men to come: *search, the individual responsible to himself,*" as the prototype of Western man, Olson argues that while Homer's Ulysses corresponds to the Mediterranean-centered phase of Western history and Dante's to the Atlantic-centered phase, the death of Melville's Ahab represents the death of the individualist ethic and ushers in its replacement by that of "the NEW HISTORY" and of "Pacific man":

> The third and final odyssey was Ahab's. The Atlantic crossed, the new land America known, the dream's death lay around the Horn, where West returned to East. The Pacific is the end of the UNKNOWN which Homer's and Dante's Ulysses opened men's eyes to. END of individual responsible only to himself. Ahab is full stop.

Olson strongly implies not only a communal ethic as characteristic of "Pacific man" (playing on *pacific*'s alternate meaning of "peaceful"), but also, taking off on Frederick Jackson Turner's famous thesis, an exploration of inner space—what the Buddhist temple in **"The Continent"** stands for—as his "West," his new frontier. Duncan, likewise alluding to Turner, as well as to the Continentalist movement of the 1840s, converts geographic fact into poetic shorthand and asserts that the continent to be crossed in our time is "the mythic sea," a neglected or repressed interiority, the psychic realm.

It's not hard to see how the sense of San Francisco as a hub of international influences, the Golden Gate to the Pacific and to the Orient, etc., alongside Olson's view of the

new communalism of "Pacific man," accords with and supports the idea of a world-poem. **"The Continent"** makes additional reference to this idea by way of the use Duncan makes of Alfred Wegener's and Tuzo Wilson's theory of continental drift. Wegener, a German meteorologist, first put forth the theory in 1912, arguing that 200 million years ago all the continents of the world were joined together as a single supercontinent. He suggested that due to forces having to do with the rotation of the earth this land mass broke apart, opening up the Atlantic and Indian oceans. The novelty of his hypothesis was its contention that if masses of earth could move vertically in response to vertical pressures they must also be able to move laterally. Most physicists at that time found the mechanics of Wegener's proposal unlikely, but fifteen or so years ago Tuzo Wilson put together a variety of evidence supporting while somewhat modifying Wegener's theory. The disruption and migration of continents could be explained by the behavior of what are called convection currents. These, the "under-earth currents" at the beginning of **"The Continent,"** conduct heat up from the earth's core by way of its mantle, moving laterally as well as up and down. Using these with other findings, Wilson argues "that about 150 million years ago, in mid-Mesozoic time, all the continents were joined in one land mass and that there was only one great ocean." Duncan thus writes in section VI of **"The Continent,"** echoing Wilson:

> . . . There is only
> the one continent, the one sea

The Wilson-reconstructed map of the world at the time of Pangaia (Wegener's name for the supercontinent), which later appears on the cover of Olson's *Maximus Poems IV, V, VI,* serves in Duncan's mind as a symbol of world Unity and of the global inclusiveness of the world-poem.

Section V is the poem's most exemplary enactment of the world-poem idea. The universalist ethic at the core of this idea, epitomized by such statements as Pound's famous assertion that "all times are contemporaneous to the mind," dictates the sort of imaginative participation in and sense of solidarity with so-called primitive beliefs one finds in lines like:

> Gaia! Time's mother too
> must wear guises,
> hop on one leg
> and hide her head in a hut,
> dance with the rest among the maskt guys.

Here, like the now pretty much extinct Carib Indians—who whenever there was an earthquake said, "The Earth-Mother dances!"—Duncan characterizes the phenomenon of "under-earth" dislocations, of which earthquakes and, on a much larger scale, continental drift are two dramatic manifestations, as a ritual dance in which the Earth—Time's, which is to say Kronos', mother in ancient myth—herself takes part. (The passage also resonates with a possibly "local" reference to San Francisco's quake-prone history.) Such passages as this put into practice the conviction Duncan states in *The H. D. Book:* "We go now to the once-called primitive—to the bush man, the child, or the ape—not to read what we were but what we are." The three stanzas which follow this passage, written, they themselves tell us, on the day before Easter, give a small inkling of the global reach of the Resurrection myth, "the dream of everyone, everywhere," as it were:

> It's still Saturday
> before Easter
> and Love's hero lies
> in the nest of our time.
>
> In Banyalbufar the little doll of the Virgin
> once more meets the sorrowing procession,
> the black-clad walkers
> before the green of April, and looks upon
> His corpse they carry forth
> to meet her.
> Effeminized, the soul is Sleeping Beauty
> or Snow White who waits
> for Sunday's kiss to wake her.

The geographical distance between San Francisco and Banyalbufar collapses, as does the vertical or hierarchical distance between the presumed height or depth of the Archetypal (Resurrection) and the presumed lowliness or shallowness of the fairy tale (Sleeping Beauty, Snow White). Within the crucible, so to speak, of Duncan's inclusionist alchemy, scientific theory, aboriginal belief, religious myth, children's lore and so forth are all melted down and flow together as one ongoing dream of "the Cosmos as Creation and Man as Creative Spirit." This melting down allows him the opening lines of section VI:

> There is only the one time.
> There is only the one god.

Beginning with the third line of section VI, the poem returns to Williams and his " 'American' thing," having by now provided the context by which that "thing" is to be revised. In Book III of *Paterson*, Williams likens the poetic imagination to a cleansing fire. The fire which destroyed the Paterson Library near the turn of the century serves as a metaphor for an Adamic contempt for tradition, the "defiance of authority" he declares beauty to be. The figure of a burning page accordingly mirrors the creative/deconstructive workings of the poet's mind as it confronts the past:

> The night was made day by the flames, flames
> on which he fed—grubbing the page
>   (the burning page)
> like a worm—for enlightenment

Duncan takes over this figure in the lines:

> There's only the one promise
>
> and from its flame
> the margins of the page flare forth.
> There's only the one page,
>
> the rest remains
> in ashes. . . .

In so doing, he deprives Williams' impulse towards renewal of its self-declared "Americanness." The Adamic wish for a return to the beginning of things or for a new beginning, whether symbolized by Christ's or Osiris' resurrection, the "discovery" of the New World, Sleeping Beauty's awakening or whatever, is "the one promise," "the dream of everyone, everywhere," which unites the world. It can-

not be laid claim to as the private property of any nation, sect or other such group. Very much in the tradition of humanity's centuries-old dream of renewal, Williams' "Americanness," its aversion to "the mythic sea" notwithstanding, is itself a myth—and not a particularly new one at that. (pp. 604-10)

A certain amount of repetition, of variation on certain images, themes and turns-of-phrase is to be encountered in the work of almost every poet. Duncan's work, however, makes use of reverberation to a degree uncommon enough to establish it as a deliberate, self-conscious maneuver on Duncan's part. By dissolving the boundaries between poems, by having his poems echo one another so insistently, Duncan puts aside the notion of the discrete, self-contained poem in favor of the field concept, a concept which wants to suggest or give inklings of an ineffable simultaneity or synchronicity, the "one event" or "one time" the world ultimately is. Duncan has pointed out that for him the field concept is synonymous with the idea of eternity, and the fact that in the Tree diagram of the Kabbalistic tradition the complement of the sefirah *Nezah,* or Eternity, is *Hod,* or Reverberation, would appear to ratify his use of dispersiveness, of reverberation, to suggest a coherence which transcends sequential, which is to say temporal, divisions. The reverberations are like the experience of *déjà vu,* "something in which time is suddenly revealed to be other than it is." The paradox, the *discordia concors,* again, is that dispersiveness is used to suggest coherence, recurrence or reverberation (time repeating itself) to suggest the eternal, the illusoriness of time. Insofar as the poem has to do with this transcendental, paradox-inducing coherence, its title refers to the "continent of feeling beyond our feeling" of **"Apprehensions,"** of which Pangaia remains a suitable symbol.

The paradoxicality here has to do with the fact that a hierarchical view of the universe is being put forth. The fragmentariness in which the world-poem reveals is a token of the fact that the Unity to which it alludes is taken to be not-of-this-world, unattainable here, and that any pretense of having achieved such coherence, any work which fails to let its fragmentariness show, is viewed as hubristic. The fragmentariness of the world-poem partakes of the humility which befits any earthly act. Yet this humility, like that of prayer, is an upward-reaching one, and the attribution of Unity to a necessarily *higher* realm may be differently stated so as to attribute a fallenness or (where we have to do with convection currents, earthquakes and such) a faultedness to the terrestrial plane. The latent or lurking theme of a Fall accounts for one aspect of **"The Continent"** with which I've yet to deal, certain lines of an ominous or portentous nature. These lines bring into the poem the apocalyptic theme encountered in the sections of *The H. D. Book* which have to do with the world-poem. In these sections Duncan characterizes the 20th century as a time of great crisis, the most dramatic sign of which being the two World Wars. The communalism of the world-poem emerges as a dialectical response to the manifest disunity of a world at war, while one of its themes is the apocalyptic portent of that disunity. . . . (pp. 614-15)

The apocalyptic portent, while understated, is unmistakably present in **"The Continent."** This portent takes the form of certain undertones (or, more appropriate to this particular poem, undercurrents) which cast a shadow of doom over what are otherwise hopeful themes, those of Unity and Resurrection. At the beginning of section II, for example, the first of the three words used to characterize Earth, *murther,* despite its similarity in sound to *mother,* is actually a dialect variant of *murder.* The word which follows, *murmurer,* seems to be ominously referred back to in section IV where the "pang" made "in the heart of things" might very well be a murmur. . . . And the third work, *demurrer,* given the ring of the courtroom one of its meanings carries, suggests judgement and retribution, while its meaning of "one who objects or takes exception" casts Earth in the role of spoiler. Likewise, at the beginning of section IV the shear-waters, small soot-black birds related to the storm petrel and the albatross and thought to forebode calamitous weather, can be said to be harbingers of some disruption:

> These figures: a snake-coil of water,
>   a bird-wheel in the sky,
> to the great wheel of sooty shear-waters
>   passing north
> counter-clockwise as far as the
>   horizon
> between shore and the islands
>
> make their announcement
> in the heart of things. . . .

In section V, as we've seen, the world is pictured awaiting Easter Sunday's "kiss" of Resurrection, a new dawning of Love:

> Time zone by time zone
> across the continent dawn so comes
> breaking the shell of flowers
> a wave
> Earth makes in turning
> a crest
> against tomorrow breaks.

The "wave / Earth makes in turning" recalls the tidal wave attendant upon the birth of Aphrodite, and while the "time zone by time zone" advance of dawn makes one think of Earth's "turning" as her daily rotation, the fact that earthquakes are the cause of tidal waves suggests that this "turning" is the "dance"—Duncan's way of referring to a quake—she does in stanza three. Finally, the last two lines of the poem, with their image of Pangaia's rifting, put the finishing touch on an apocalyptic mood in which revival or renewal is anticipated, though overshadowed by the prospects of an initiatory catastrophe. The promise of "the green of April," that is, carries with it the warning which comes of Duncan's observation in *The Opening of the Field* that "death is prerequisite to the growth of grass."

These portents are the thematic complement of the poetics' insistence on openness, non-containment or disclosure, an insistence which can itself be termed apocalyptic, given the derivation of the term from the Greek verb meaning "to uncover." On another level, these portents, coming as they do in the final poem in *Roots and Branches,* anticipate "the great theme of War" to which Duncan,

inspired and outraged by U.S. aggression in Vietnam, turns in *Bending the Bow,* the volume which follows *Roots and Branches.* In the poems having to do with the Vietnam War the critique of American Adamism we see subtly at work in **"The Continent"** finds a less literary occasion and becomes considerably more explicit:

> . . . this secret entity of America's hatred of
> Europe, of Africa, of
> Asia,
> the deep hatred for the old world that had driven
> generations of
> America out of itself . . .

R. W. B. Lewis in his study *The American Adam* refers to the opponents of the Adamists, whom he calls the party of Hope, as the party of Memory. Duncan's "conservatism," his emphasis on the respect owed the past by the present, the old world by the new, puts him solidly in this latter group. In 1967 at a seminar on "Parable, Myth and Language" Duncan spoke of being "overtaken by myth," the myth of Christ in particular, in a way which relates both to this critique of the United States and to what in **"The Continent"** is called a "run to the mythic sea":

> My experience as a poet is that my reality depends on the reality of Christ. It's very clear in my work. I wasn't born and raised a Christian. When I spoke of myth overtaking you, I began to see that I will have to incur some of the rather grievous difficulties that poets who are overtaken by the myth of Christ have. Poetry is an effort to protect yourself against these things overtaking you. I think America will have no redemption until it suffers what all of humanity suffers. I think we have to come into an abyss of human suffering and share what, as a matter of fact, all of humanity shares. All this I see entirely in the figure of Christ as if it were overtaking me. . . .

The "coming of all men into one fate" taught by this myth of Christ is the coming of all men into "rather grievous difficulties," and the wave which "time zone by time zone" overtakes the world on the day of Christ's Resurrection in **"The Continent"** portends exactly that. While the "one promise" to which the world-poem aspires is redemption or renewal, the "one fate" it portends is the achievement of that renewal through duress and suffering, indeed holocaust: "and from its flame / the margins of the page flare forth." The being overtaken by myth, what Duncan means by "the / run to the mythic sea" in **"The Continent"** and by "the rush, the being carried away" in **"Returning to the Rhetoric of an Early Mode,"** is both a remembering and a paying of dues to a tradition of ordeal, the communality of "what all of humanity suffers." (pp. 615-17)

Nathaniel Mackey, "The World-Poem in Microcosm: Robert Duncan's 'The Continent'," in ELH, *Vol. 47, No. 3, Fall, 1980, pp. 595-618.*

Ron Silliman   (essay date 1985)

[*Silliman is an American poet and critic. In the following excerpt, he provides a favorable review of* Ground

Work: Before the War, *commenting on Duncan's use of language and theosophy and his treatment of death and the role of the individual.*]

> I have in mind a poetry that will frame the
> willingness of the heart and deliver it over to the
> arrest of Time, a sentence as if there could stand
>   some
> solidity most spacial in its intent against the
>   drifts
> and appearances that arise and fall away in time
>   from
> the crude events of physical space. The Mind
>   alone
> holds the consequence of the erection to be true,
>   so
> that Desire and Imagination usurp the place of
>   the
> Invisible Throne.

"The Structure of Rime XXVIII,"
"In Memoriam Wallace Stevens"

This doctrine, which has been central to Robert Duncan's poetics for more than forty years, has never before been so visibly the dominant element as it is in this gathering of poems composed between the years 1968 and 1974. As such, this first volume of **Ground Work** (a second has already been completed) is the purest exposition of Duncan's primary concerns available. To his many longtime readers, this is a publication of major, if not unparalleled, importance. And yet, for precisely the same reason, **Ground Work** may be the most impenetrable text conceivable for any new reader attempting to make an entrance into this formidable body of writing. To those who have found his earlier books indulgent, arcane or obscure, this one . . . is the perfect object for flinging at a wall in total exasperation. In short, **Ground Work** is an ideal example of Robert Duncan.

What distinguishes it from his earlier "major" collections, **The Opening of the Field** (1960), **Roots and Branches** (1964) or **Bending the Bow** (1968), is how this dominant theme shuts out, finally, all others. What this theme is, exactly, proves somewhat more difficult to say: it is not simply that it is, or might be, Time, the Mind, the Heart, the Ideal, the Absolute, the Ineffable or the Other, but rather that words relate to It (as "It" is sometimes called) metonymically, but not denotatively. It is that which is shared by every word, regardless of dialect, so that each term is a manifestation or example, a relation that, in itself, renders each incapable of naming the whole. Not surprisingly, there are moments in **Ground Work** as virtually absent of "content" as anything ever written by Clark Coolidge or Bruce Andrews. Yet this unnameable theme is not simply language, which is also only an example or aspect.

Nonetheless, language, in the sense of that ultimate structure of possibility from which each national language, dialect and idiolect must descend, offers us at least a partial model of what it might be that has for so long concerned Duncan, and now, apparently, all but consumed him. What is most critical about this *langue,* an "innate capacity" in Noam Chomsky's view, is that it does not exist in any one given place. One cannot examine it under lock and key somewhere in France. Yet, barring major disability, it is something shared by all persons. It is that through

which we experience much, if not all, of our own subjectivity, our identity, and without which the possibility of any intersubjectivity would be problematic indeed. Language, viewed thus, is not so much personal as it is *transpersonal:*

> It must be
> completely under command, not
> self-moved (these études
> like Dante's odes,
> having their own ease
> I feel and rule that understand
> I've but to follow thru, do
> what their evolving likeness will
> prove in me, engrosst
> in every freedom allowed, draw close)
>
>   and measured,
> not out of measure; the words proposed
>   to the edge of meaning
> and not beyond it, justified,
> having their sense so in the sound of it
>   demanded of me, I hear
> "our" tongue, no other
>   I did not know in the bone of me
>
> the marrow music ever I contrived
> this "harmony of musical connection"
>
>   rime supplies
>
>   my own
>
> true tone where, reader,
>
> you and I must try
>
> the truth that Nature means in me.

("Dante Études, Book Two": "On
Obedience")

This command comes not from the writer (and certainly not from the writer's ego), whose "rule" is not to lead, but "to follow." Such a position may well be no more than a restatement of negative capability, and obviously shares more than a little with Jack Spicer's Cocteau-derived model of the poet as radio or medium. But what separates Duncan so radically from his ancestors or peers is the degree to which he insists that that which "comes thru" be understood as a message, i.e., intentional. Language (and that of which language is but an aspect or manifestation) represents not simply innate capacity, an amorphous, passive, even entropic swamplike thing, but rather an active, willful intelligence, an Overmind of which each individual intelligence, animal or otherwise, is but a fragment. . . .

This is all deeply spiritual stuff—which is exactly how Duncan, a theosophist by both upbringing and inclination, understands it. A synthesis of mysticisms, theosophy anticipated all of the more recent attempts at the integration of Eastern and Western intellectual and cultural traditions. . . . Critically for a poet such as Duncan, who is far more well-rounded in his reading than, say, either a Pound or an Olson, theosophy offers an approach which is not given to excluding one tradition in favor of another and which, when confronted with new information, instinctively is driven to incorporate, rather than reject, the data, seeking always to generate an ever greater unity. It is this vision of an overriding and thoroughly conscious (if not especially human) Oneness at the heart of all that is matter, and all that is not, which fundamentally motivates the poetics of Robert Duncan.

This perspective has always situated him in a curious position with regard to the other major Projectivists. Like Olson and Creeley, Duncan's poetry is grounded in a critique of consciousness, particularly that of the romantic individual, the subject of subjectivity which is our major inheritance from the humanist tradition. Yet Duncan's concern extends beyond the tracing out of the fragmentary and discontinuous presence of the Self toward an embracing of that which, for him, connects (and legitimizes) the existence of so many partial and incomplete individuals. Nowhere is this distinction more evident than in the place and use of sound in the poem. Almost as if to point out that the mythology which has grown up around the Black Mountain poets is nothing more than a distortive reduction, sound in Duncan's poems has never been equated with voice. Even if the reader here were to skip over the remarkable preferatory "Some Notes on Notation," the rhetorical structure of the very first stanza of the opening **"Achille's Song,"**

> I do not know more than the Sea tells me,
> told me long ago, or I overheard Her
>   telling distant roar upon the sands,
>   waves of meaning in the cradle of whose
>   sounding and resounding power I
> slept

is certain to slow the cadence below that of "normal" speech. By no coincidence whatsoever, the passage itself is about the function of sound, presented here as being both meaningful and inhuman. The poet's body, that vehicle through which the field of sound is converted in the system of Olson's early poetics into individual voice, is, for Duncan, turned away from the reader and toward that originating Tone instead. . . . (p. 10)

For Duncan, the cadences of the body lead, like all else, away from the individual, toward that "deeper rhythm." Thus, in the etude cited earlier, words are conceived of as "having their sense so in the sound of it / demanded of me." This meaning, this demand, exists prior to the arrival of the poet's writing, whose task instead is but to "hear / 'our' tongue, no other / I did not know in the bone of me." The body (the actual life of the poet) serves only to provide access to this "marrow music." The long sequence of **"Dante Études,"** which occupies as much space in *Ground Work* as all of the new excerpts from "Passages" combined, leads inescapably to the most un-Olsonian of conclusions, **"And a Wisdom As Such,"**

>   a loosening
> of energies and every gain! For good.
> A rushing-in place of "God", if it be!
>
> Open out like a rose
> that can no longer keep its center closed
> but, practicing for Death, lets go,
>
> let's go. . . .

This moment of ultimate acquiescence both echoes and alters the italicized key refrain of **"Passages 36"** (*"Let it go. Let it go. / Grief's its proper mode."*), which is also the central poem of the book's other major series, **"A Seventeenth Century Suite."** If such a welcoming of death is unthinkable in Olson, it is nonetheless hardly an instance of nihilism here. The poet is but a fragment and what matters is the whole. Wisdom, which for Duncan means an acceptance of a meaning greater than the possible knowledge of any individual, is the point at which the system coheres. Yet, precisely because Duncan's critique of consciousness has gone beyond that of the romantic subject, he does not mistake, as Pound did, that larger unity with one that must be reflected in the text. Far from being the postmodernist that writers such as George Butterick have claimed him to be, Duncan is making an argument against postmodernism, as such.

AUTHOR'S COMMENTARY

There is not a phase of our experience that is meaningless, not a phrase of our communication that is meaningless. We do not make things meaningful, but in our making we work towards an awareness of meaning; poetry reveals itself to us as we obey the orders that appear in our work. In writing I do not organize words but follow my consciousness of—but it is also a desire that goes towards—orders in the play of forms and meanings toward poetic form. This play is like the play of actors upon a stage. Becoming conscious, becoming aware of the order of what is happening is the full responsibility of the poet. The poem that always seems to us such a highly organized event is in its very individuality ("idiocy" the classical Greek would have said), in its uniqueness, crude indeed compared with the subtlety of organization which in the range of contemporary linguistic analysis the study of syntax, morphology, etymology, psychology reveals in the language at large from which the poem is derived. The materials of the poem—the vowels and consonants—are already structured in their resonance, we have only to listen and to cooperate with the music we hear. The storehouse of human experience in words is resonant too, and we have but to listen to the reverberations of our first thought in the reservoir of communal meanings to strike such depths as touch upon the center of man's nature.

(essay date 1966)

This, I think, explains many of the more puzzling aspects of *Ground Work.* Duncan's insistence, in the preface, that silences function for him "as phrases, units in the measure, charged with meaning," is not, for example, because the absence of voice (or print) is the moment at which the limits of the signifier become perceptible, as would be the case with Charles Bernstein, but rather because it is in silence, and white space, that the articulation of the poet and the pulse of that "deeper rhythm" are identical, with no need for any word to serve as a metonym or translation of that "felt tone." Silence, in this sense, is the privileged voice in the book.

Time itself undergoes a similar transformation. One of the most immediately startling aspects of *Ground Work* lies in its sharp turn away from the topicality of *Bending the Bow.* There are few poems in this nearly two hundred page volume which invoke current history in anything like the way it was brought in play by **"Passages 13," "Passages 21," "Passages 25," "Passages 26," "Passages 27"** or **"Passages 29"**—and the primary examples, **"Before the Judgement," "Passages 35 (Tribunals)"** and **"Santa Cruz Propositions,"** occur in tandem, virtually an island in a sea of metaphysics. This return to the rhetorically timeless mode of his earlier books is itself explicated by **"Passages 36,"** a poem which is not historical so much as it is about historicity, where the refrain, composed by the poet in his sleep, "was about the end of an old friendship" with that most topical of writers, Denise Levertov. Rejecting here anything like Creeley's theory of correspondences, the problem of the particular is, for Duncan, that each instance is, again, merely a metonym for a larger Truth, capital T, whose fundamental reality lies precisely in its status beyond, or outside of time.

Thus the critical aspect of the book's title rests in time's presentation there. As Gary Burnett has noted, each of Duncan's major collections has foregrounded the figure of origin in its name. "The War" of the subtitle, as Butterick points out, is itself identified in the preface of ***Bending the Bow:***

> We enter again and again the last days of our
>   own
> history, for everywhere living productive forms
>   in
>   the
> evolution of forms fail, weaken, or grow
>   monstrous,
> destroying the terms of their existence. We do
>   not
>   mean
> an empire; a war then, as if to hold all China or
>   the
> ancient sea at bay, breaks out at a boundary we
>   name
> *ours.* It is a boundary beyond our understanding.

This boundary ("again and again") is not that of the history of events, but between the actual and the eternal, between the individual and Duncan's theosophic vision of a higher order. Time, in this view, has but two states: Timelessness, and that which comes before.

Accordingly, the central poems in ***Ground Work*** are those which have been most often discounted by the book's reviewers, **"A Seventeenth Century Suite"** and **"Dante Études."** Ron Loewinsohn called them "the worst offenders" of "a windy, abstract rhetoric," while Butterick finds value in "two or three" of the etudes (there are 40), maintaining a pointed silence concerning the suite. Yet these two sequences constitute fully one-third of the volume. Their archaisms, hardly a new device in Duncan's poetic vocabulary, serve precisely to *violate time.*

To say that he wishes to demonstrate the currency which might be found, say, in Dante is accurate only up to a point. The larger unity for which Duncan is arguing must itself obliterate the specificity of instances, as such. Context, far from being the controlling aspect of meaning, must be unmasked as an illusion. Thus the model for language in the Stevens elegy cited at the beginning of this review is "most spacial," contrasted first "against the drifts and appearances" of time, but also outside of "the crude events of physical space."

It is the exception, in Duncan's elaboration of the figure Fire in two poems "derived" from Robert Southwell's "The Burning Babe," which best demonstrates the rule. The original, published in 1595, offers a vision in which "Love is the fire" and "The mettall . . . are mens defiled souls." The first of Duncan's responses follows this conceit to comment upon his own "stubborn residue" of envy and "black jealousy,"—nonetheless noting that this heat "is no more than an image in Poetry." The second reverses the dynamics entirely, the fire being that of literal napalm burning the "broil flesh" of Vietnamese children. Here flame is material, a signifier "exceeding what we would *know*," beyond our capacity for horror. This is *the one* moment in ***Ground Work*** in which Duncan shrinks from his essential idealism:

> I cannot imagine, gazing upon
>   photographs
>   of these young girls, the mind
> transcending what's been done to
>   them.

Yet it is the imagination whose weakness is faulted in these lines. The limit seen here is not that of a greater unity, but of the individual's ability to conceive of it.

In much the same way, carping about Duncan's faults as a writer misses the point. To treat these poems, as the dual interwoven series of **"Passages"** and **"The Structure of Rime"** should remind us, as if they were individual works is to ignore precisely that dimension in which Duncan places (literally) the deepest faith, and where he invests his fullest energy. This book is not a discrete series, but rather occasions of a larger Poetry which Duncan has been "given" to write. This is why, so often, the areas of his worst indulgences are often precisely those of his greatest strengths.

It is the violation of the temporal which underlies his most notorious strategy here: the decision not to publish a book for fifteen years after the appearance of ***Bending the Bow.*** This, it should be noted, he accomplished only by failing to acknowledge the publication of ***Tribunals*** by Black Sparrow and the etudes under the title *Dante* in the Curriculum of the Soul series of the Institute for Further Studies. Given that New Directions is virtually the archetype of the independent publisher in the United States, this sleight-of-hand, placing the press above its peers, is more irritating than effective. Oddly, it seems also to have served just the opposite of its intended result. Rather than raising Duncan out of history, *beyond time,* his absence from any widely-distributed perfect-bound form for so long has only intensified his identification as a poet of the Sixties, much more so than is the case, say, with John Ashbery. This collection, published a decade after its composition, and whose primary topical references are to the Vietnam War and the Santa Cruz mass murders committed by John Lindley Frazier over 17 years ago, can only serve to deepen the impression. If one is to take issue with Duncan's metaphysics, the best evidence may well be the history of ***Ground Work*** itself. (pp. 11-12, 23)

Ron Silliman, "Waves of Meaning," in The American Book Review, *Vol. 7, No. 6, September-October, 1985, pp. 10-12, 23.*

Thomas Gardner   (essay date 1986)

[*In the following excerpt, Gardner lauds* Ground Work: Before the War *and links Duncan to Walt Whitman as a poet who identifies the self with the "world as an evolving whole."*]

Robert Duncan's *Ground Work: Before the War,* his first full collection since 1968, is an attempt, in the poet's words, "To speak my mind, / unfold the secrets of the heart." As such—as a work committed to "enact[ing] my being" or shaping "that / shifting definition I am"—it shares its aims with most recent American poetry. What makes this new work so powerful—makes it, to my mind, one of the most important books of the last ten years—is the manner in which, following Whitman, Duncan links that unfolding self ("open[ing] out radiant and singing petals from itself ") to the world surrounding him. Like Whitman, Duncan sees that world as an evolving whole—a form of forms, gradually creating itself at the level of individual events. "I see Creation as a process of evolution of forms," he writes in an essay, "and these forms in turn as arising and surviving in a ground of individual variations and mutations where the multiplicity is not superfluous but the necessary condition of potential functions." Each individual variation, then—each of "the scenes and deeds in which Man has illustrated his nature," for example—is an essential aspect of that yet-to-be-completed design, linked, if one could see the whole, to all other parts of the design: "each part in every other having, if we could see it, its condition—its opposite or contender, and its satisfaction or twin." What this means for a poet intent on creating a self in his work—and here Duncan again echoes Whitman—is that his deepest sense of identity comes only in understanding, as fully as possible, his own unique place, his own possible connections, within that whole. . . . What Duncan does in *Ground Work* is attempt to define himself by "imagining" his place as a single "pivot" of the unfolding "story we belong to"—working out his place in the ground "beyond us," as the title suggests, and thereby "releas[ing] full my man's share of the stars' / majesty thwarted."

He is prodded to do so—forced, perhaps, would be the better word—by the "discord" of our involvement in Vietnam, an event which, reluctantly acknowledged as part of the story he belongs to, shatters his old ordering and forces him to attempt to imagine a greater whole, and thus a fuller version of himself, in which that discord would also be an essential part. As the book's subtitle suggests, and as the dates given for a majority of the poems (1968-74) confirm, Duncan stands, in this work, "before the war," acknowledging "an empty space of Asia that crept into me" and attempting to imagine a whole in which this "immediate percept is / to be justified." Vietnam functions as a painful but necessary disordering: "This is the creative strife Heraclitus praised, breaking up, away from what you know how to do into something you don't know, breaking up the orders I belong to in order to come into

alien orders, marches upon a larger order." Both catastrophe and release, an "undoing"—as this volume suggests—still being responded to today, the war is the source of the richly-inventive self-unfoldings of these poems: "Angry, confused, . . . the workers are released from the old order into the Great Work beyond their understanding. They must go beyond the bounds of their art."

The early poems here, quite dark, look forward, at the same time, to such an expansion of identity:

> Something has wreckt the world I am in
>
> I think I have wreckt
>   the world I am in.
> It is beautiful. From my wreckage
>   this world returns
> to restore me, overcomes its identity in me.
>   **("A Song from the Structures of Rime
>   Ringing as the Poet Paul Celan
>   Sings")**

The first struggle is simply to face the discordant element—and in doing so, permit it to dissolve the old order. **"Passages 36"** says this very clearly:

> I know but part of it and that but distantly,
> a catastrophe in another place, another time,
>   the mind addresses
> and would erect within itself itself
>   as Viet Nam, itself as Bangladesh,
> itself exacting revenge and suffering revenge,
>   itself the Court and before the Court

Addressing what had seemed distant, acknowledging the work of war as a work of man and thus, to his created world, potentially part of "itself," Duncan must make something ("erect" something) with that new knowledge. In many of the early poems of this volume, the task seems almost overwhelming. Reading farther in **"Passages 36"**:

>   For a moment,
>
> ephemeral, we keep
> alive in the deepening shame of Man,
>
>   this room where we are, this house,
>   this garden, this home
>   our art would make
>   in what is threatened from within.
>
> House made of the changing of the light;
> House made of darkness
>   in which the stars again
>   appear to view;

The fragile household these poems seek to establish is, of course, only a momentary uniting of what seemed discordant (light and the darkness)—and yet, responding to one remaking the changing world, it is at the same time a living aspect of the creation's unfolding.

The stars referred to in several of the poems I've quoted from, returning to sight with the coming of darkness, can be said to be those already established works of man, those "essential parts of the story we belong to," which the destruction of the old order has permitted the poet to see once again. As **"Passages 31"** has it, extending Jacob Boehme's distinction between the individual spirit and the eternal stars, they are potential deep sources in establishing a new household:

> Yet the quality of the stars
> *reigneth* in the spirit; tho the spirit can
> and may raise or drown itself
>   in its own qualities, or take its life
> in the influence of the stars, as it pleaseth.
>   For it is free. It has got for its own
> the qualities it has in itself, its own
>
>   plot or myth, its feel
>   of what belongs to it

Those established forms awaken the poet; in taking life in them, in plotting a series of engagements with them, he vastly extends the world he belongs to and so opens a way to reorder what seems discordant. So, for example, Hermes appears in one of these poems, offering the solitary Odysseus a means of managing Circe's darkness:

>   "Where are you going?" I askt,
> "You are so alone my own life
> which was eternal and self-contained
> opens up vast breaches of promise in the
> thought of you you know nothing of."

And so, in **"Passages 35,"** taken aback by his outrage at the daily count of our wartime atrocities ("wrapt in the stench of vegetable rot, / destroyed forests and fields, / and from villages the putrid dead"), Duncan remembers Dante, facing a similar hell, and guided by his ancestor Virgil:

> Discontent with that first draft. Where one's
>   own
>   hatred enters Hell gets out of hand.
>
> Again and again Virgil ever standing by Dante
>   must caution him. In Malebolge
>
> where the deep violation begins,
>
> *Mentr'io laggiù fissamente mirava,*
> *lo duca mio, dicendo "Guarda, guarda"*

Like Dante, he allows himself, throughout this volume, to take warning and direction from those he acknowledges, in this same poem, as "ancestors of the household we keep even in adversity, figures who,

>   their bodies a like grace, a music, their
> minds a joy,
>   abundant,
>   foliate, fanciful in its flowering,
>
> come into these orders as they have ever come,
> stand,
>   as ever, where they are acknowledged,
> against the works of unworthy men, unfeeling
>   judgments, and
>   cruel deeds.

As he takes his life in these abundant presences, then—acknowledges or "tunes himself" to those with whom he shares resonance—he both sketches in a more extensive outline of his deepest sense of identity and, seeking to order those forms in "a harmony / large enough to account for conflict," works out an unfolding of the design beyond him:

> The individual man
> having his nature and truth
>   outlined
> in relation to groups
> appropriate to his household
>
>   his own
>   ideogram
>
>   a tuning in
>
> on What Is and seeks harmonies in his
>   district
>   **("The Individual Man")**

If in his understanding of self creation Duncan stands as a contemporary extension of Whitman, the "abundant, foliate" figures he draws from mark him, at the same time, as our most ambitious contemporary descendant of Ezra Pound. Even a partial listing indicates that Duncan takes his life in Pound's creators rather than Whitman's drivers: Carlyle, Hesiod, Dickens, Blake, Schrödinger, Dante, Pindar, Zukofsky, Jonson, Brancusi, Sir Walter Ralegh, John Adams, Carl Sauer, Thom Gunn—stars in this volume's remarkably diverse set of constellations. What is distinctly Duncan's, however—and to my reading distinctly non-Poundian in its openness—is Duncan's manner of embracing these figures. Each new identification arouses him, opening up new directions in his thought and providing the language to explore those hints. He writes, for example, in the preface to an extended sequence of derivations from Dante that, "I draw my 'own' thought in reading Dante as from a well-spring." Each of these explorations, richly varied as they are, follows a similar pattern in which Duncan starts by speaking the words of his sources, then gradually rewords the words into the context of his own troubled world, at the same time reworking (rewording) himself by tracing out the hints and directions these new words necessarily smuggle into his world. We are witness to a self-definition based on a "constant exchange," one of these poems has it, a movement into and out of these sources, enriching both. (pp. 90-4)

> *Thomas Gardner, in a review of "Ground Work: Before the War," in* American Poetry, *Vol. 3, No. 2, Winter, 1986, pp. 90-5.*

Thom Gunn   (essay date 1988)

[*An English poet and critic who has lived in California since 1954, Gunn combines a respect for traditional poetic forms with an interest in popular topics. In the following excerpt, he asserts that* Ground Work II: In the Dark *continues Duncan's career-long attempt to examine the spectrum of "spontaneous imagination," a project Gunn regards as ambitious as Walt Whitman's and Ezra Pound's.*]

[Robert Duncan] tells us, in "The Self in Postmodern Poetry",

> What I would point out in my work as one of its underlying currents is the weaving of a figure unweaving, an art of unsaying what it says, of saying what it would not say. I want to catch myself out.

It is this current that accounts for the most exciting, and the most exasperating, of Duncan's writing: for he trusts his spontaneity so completely that he encourages it to *trip up* his conscious intentions.

Yet there is room for both those intentions and the tripping up within the larger project, which started in the book of 1960 and was continued through *Roots and Branches* (1964), *Bending the Bow* (1968), *Ground Work: Before the war* (1984) and, now, *Ground Work II: In the dark.* The project might be characterized as an attempt to explore the entire field of a spontaneous imagination. His ambition, in fact, is fully as great as Whitman's or Pound's: he too wants to include everything he can in the great single poem of his collected work. The risk of inclusiveness is inflation, and he accepted that risk: certainly some of the poetry is inflated, as it is in Whitman and in Pound too, quite simply because, though you may want to include everything in your poem, you cannot write with equal force about everything (unless you are Dante or Shakespeare). But the attempt is heroic, and for all that is inflated or occulted there still remains a large amount of poetry that is fully rewarding and that would not exist without the foolhardy heroism.

In 1972 Duncan announced that he did not intend to issue another collection of his work until fifteen years had passed since *Bending the Bow.* The fifteen years stretched into sixteen, and in February 1984 he suffered a complete kidney collapse. After this date he composed only one two-page poem, an eerie account of his illness, and lived his last four years essentially as a posthumous poet, still talking volubly and on occasion brilliantly (as is testified to by published interviews), but unable to concentrate long enough to read anything more demanding than the short stories of Kipling and the *Oz* books (he who had devoured books, as he once said, "gluttonously"), let alone write either poetry or prose. Later that year he published *Ground Work: Before the war,* which as one of his most accurate commentators, Ken Irby, has noted, consists of poetry written between 1968 and 1975. The succeeding collection, *Ground Work II: In the dark,* therefore consists of poems written in 1976-84 and, since two of those years were unexpectedly barren, is probably only half as long as he had hoped it would be.

One reviewer, Tom Clark, has said "it's indeed hard *not* to read this book as a journal of holy dying", but Duncan did not know he was dying until he wrote the last poem, **"After a Long Illness".** Nevertheless, his health must have been secretly deteriorating during the years of composition, and there is far more about the subjects of death and disease in this collection than in any of the others. It is not for nothing that its subtitle is *In the dark,* for a major theme is the interpenetration of life and death.

There are both serial groups and individual poems here which count among his best. Such a serial group, "An Alternate Life", makes a fitting opening to the collection, for it exemplifies the peculiarities and strengths of Duncan in all their mutual involvement. Here we may appreciate the full adventure of entering the process of a Duncan composition, fifteen pages of it, energetic yet tentative, assertive yet self-revising, opportunistic yet receptive, taking place

as it does in some area between directionless flux and rigid authorial control. It is about his having fallen in love during a visit to Australia and deals with his return to his household in San Francisco and his lover of many years. We may mark the fact that "household" is a word always associated in Duncan's work with his firmest values: it is not quite the same as "marriage", suggesting rather something "home-made", something built up bit by bit between the foundations and roof-beams of the physical house, individual, specific, improvised. These last three terms also apply to the whole work: Duncan follows the unpredictable currents of feeling, avoiding no awkwardness or inconsistency to make them seem smoother. He sees himself as ridiculous at one point ("An old man's hand fumbles at the young man's crotch"), but passes no judgment on the two others involved. And the poet of open form is also open in the sense of being frank—if this is about a form of adultery, it is not found with that hypocrisy which is adultery's customary companion.

Hypocrisy would give shape and order to this implied story of adultery; alibis, after all, tend to have classical and tightly knit plots. It is precisely the lack of such a plot that makes the work's overall structure obscure on early readings: nothing is closed off, nothing gets decided; there are no renunciations as there are no condemnations. Duncan moves, either physically or emotionally, between alternates, alternate *you*s, alternate *he*s, alternate hemispheres, alternate lives, alternate seasons. His problem, of course, is in fitting enough contents for two lives into "the one life I am leading". The situation is desperately commonplace, and one of its most commonplace features is that the influence is greatest of whatever place he is currently in: "O daily actual life", he says back home, "I am // deep in your thrall."

Commonplace language for a commonplace situation, the reader might remark of that last phrase. Duncan would say so too. "Deep in your thrall" exemplifies the kind of risk he is prepared to take, with language as with structure; it is lushly Romantic, certainly time-worn, if only from its endurance at least through the nineteenth century into the movies and songs of our own. Duncan both *means* it and is aware of its time-worness, aware the emotion giving rise to it is both nineteenth-century Romantic and twentieth-century Hollywood. I insist on his disconcerting awareness, which is heightened by the variety of other modes of speech here, one of which is the self-scrutinizing language of wit, the cool perception of paradox. When "news comes from the South", he sees it as "gifts from another time I / most hold in losing". The letter from Australia in his hand, he holds that other life "in" losing it, that is, both *while* and *by* losing it. He almost relishes the neatness of the paradox, his tone is so far outside the conscious self-indulgence of the earlier phrase.

The "hero of possibility" necessarily takes such things as his subject-matter, but this is a book written "in the dark", and so we come to the magnificently eloquent poem **"Styx"**, and the river where the apparently endless mingling streams of human possibility come to stasis. **"Styx"** is organized as description; but every physical detail in it speaks to the death which will close off this collection:

And a tenth part of bright clear Okeanos his circulations—mists, rains, sheets, sheathes—lies in poisonous depths, the black water. "Circulations" is another loaded word for Duncan. It is in their circulation that not only ocean but blood and song remain vital: and the water of Styx is the *un*circulating stillness that we originate from and also "thirst for" (as the last line tells us) "in dreams we dread". Once more the undeclared war, in which we thirst and dread at the same time, is brilliantly evoked, and with the later poem **"In Blood's Domaine"** he openly enters the conflict once more.

"In Blood's Domaine" starts by naming "the Angel Syphilis in the circle of Signators"—and other deadly angels are to follow: Cancer, Tuberculosis, Leukaemia. Perhaps the word Signators recalls Pound's "Regents" of Canto LI (and Duncan seems to be confirming that allusion by, after Pound, introducing the monster Geryon farther on in the poem): like the Regents, the Signators are emblematic functionaries self-appointed to act as a check on human thriving. The difference is that Pound's figures stand for evil, being the Regents of Usury, but Duncan's Signators are beyond good and evil—the spirochetes of syphilis may be seen as embodiments of a life as justified, as daring, and as divine as that of the sparrows pecking on the rhinoceros or of the human beings perched on the globe. They are "attendants of lives raging within life". Is the word Signators then in some way a reference to the DNA code—a suggestion that the signatures of disease are joined with our own so that their lives are transmitted with ours, inextricably "attendant" on all of us?

I should point out that Duncan is not being sentimental or fanciful, the ultimate humanitarian standing up for the rights of syphilitic spirochetes, but is simply affirming the rather traditional belief that the destructive impulse, the pursuit of death, the will to war, must all be acknowledged as necessary balance to what we see as the positive and productive tendencies of life, which are in fact defined by the presence of such counter-tendencies. Perhaps it is the intervention of Freud that takes him so far from the late Romantic optimism of Emerson. "Link by link I can disown no link of this chain from my conscience", he says in recognizing even the Hitler within himself, and through such language looking forward to those other chains in the yet unwritten poem, the last of the book, in which he describes his kidneys as "cloggd with light chains". He is terrified, he is dismayed, even as he contemplates the grandeur of the Angels. He cannot help but acknowledge their strength and their enduring presence within their opposites: "Hel shines in the very word *Health* // as *Ill* in the Divine Will shines."

It is worth pausing over the style of this last line. "Hel" (like "thot" for "thought" and other words elsewhere) suggests Miltonic spelling. This, the capital initials, the inverted word order, and the exalted language all point to a prophetic mode which, in its loftiness and assurance of tone, is not common among the poets we take seriously in the second half of the twentieth century. Such a mode is not invariable in his mature books, but it constantly recurs: and much of Duncan's unusualness for a new reader comes from his unfamiliar readiness to take what I have

called the high road. Historically it has become less used only recently, since poets started to move away from the grand style. Most of us have in recent years taken a very low road indeed, finding our virtues in understatement and our safety in irony; we are tentative and evasive; we disown passion or we clothe it in indirection. Duncan by contrast makes claims for the importance of poetry that are both Poundian and Shelleyan (perhaps Dantean as well): in doing so he holds himself responsible for deep feeling, whether public or personal, without the qualification of irony, and adopts the voice of the seer or the bard even to the extent of giving an archaic cast to his speech. It is time to suggest, then, that we pay more attention to the work of a man whose aims and accomplishments have been larger than those of the run of contemporary poets, though assuredly the kind of ambition implied is not stylish on either side of the Atlantic. (pp. 1299-1300)

> *Thom Gunn, "Containing Multitudes," in* The Times Literary Supplement, *No. 4469, November 25-December 1, 1988, pp. 1299-1300.*

Mark Andrew Johnson   (essay date 1988)

[*In the following excerpt from his critical study* Robert Duncan, *Johnson interprets major poems from* The Opening of the Field.]

[*The Opening of the Field*] opens with the poem that establishes the controlling images of field, play, flowers, fire, boundary, and permission, **"Often I Am Permitted to Return to a Meadow."** Duncan's recurring dream of a reconciled world is evoked in five masterful sentences. That world is his and not his, a made place and an eternal pasture. Paradox is not irony, of course, but rather a circumvention of logical reasoning in an attempt to enter a different way of thinking. That different way of thinking's Platonic roots are revealed when we are told that this made place is "created by light / wherefrom the shadows that are forms fall."

These forms or "architectures" are actually likenesses of "the First Beloved." The field of the poem, which the poet is permitted to enter—often, but not as a matter of his will alone—presents "flowers [which] are flames lit to the Lady." Such an intermixture of flame and flower will recur, or rime, in key passages of the book, and indeed close it, at the end of **"Food for Fire, Food for Thought."**

What is the significance of flaming flowers? The children's game is "ring a round of roses," the medieval chant to ward off the plague inverted to a game—"ashes, ashes, all fall down." But this metaphor is central in Duncan's poetics: blossoming is followed by decay, destruction inevitably follows upon realization and is superseded in its turn by renewal. Dust returns to dust inevitably, but this is a fertilizing decay from which new life, phoenixlike, arises.

The field is the major figure of the book, proposing the poem as an area of activity rather than as a static object. The poem's movement is spatial, multidirectional rather than linear. The poet enters this poem as a matter of permission, but must be an active participant, prepared for the opportunity. The field, then, is "not mine, but is a made place, / / that is mine." The locus of the field is immaterial, in both senses: it does not matter where the poet (or reader) may physically be, and it is not matter but spirit. Thus the Platonic overtones of the field's being "created by light / wherefrom the shadows that are forms fall."

In an act of faith ("as if"), the poet accepts as a "given property of the mind / that certain bounds hold against chaos." The poems seem to delineate boundaries or fields of order against chaos, but only seem, because in the larger view Duncan has of poetry and the universe, chaos or disorder are parts of a larger order. The real boundary of this poem, then, is between a state of awareness and its absence. Delineating that boundary, or more fundamentally recognizing the difference, is the responsibility of the poet. In the "disturbance of words within words," the poet's poems are constructs, architectures, flowers which turn into "flames lit to the Lady." The limits and definitions of physical reality must give way before the reality of the visionary imagination. Paradoxes, fairy tales, children's games are not evasions but ways of entry, supralogical confrontations with "what is." Duncan firmly stands in the romantic tradition, which he has identified as "the intellectual adventure of not knowing." In his poetry, then, he will constantly interrogate boundaries, question assumptions, disrupt even the melodies of his own poems in order to participate in the dance, the play of the poem.

In doing so, he demands of his reader a certain tolerance of uncertainty. This opening poem is playful but abrupt, almost orphic. Its title is its first line, and the opening lines must be read, retraced and reread, forcing the reader to reenact the circling and countercircling of the children's game. As he told one interviewer, "I don't have problems with how does it begin, how does it close, because the true form of the thing exists in re-reading it, and re-reading it, and re-reading it." The form of this poem, like that of the book, will be *playful, tentative, improvisatory, shadowy*. It is a bound against chaos that invites chaos in as part of the whole—which it is. Duncan delights in tongue-twisting alliteration and ambiguous punctuation, so an unsympathetic reader should be forewarned. But such a reader is also invited. A poem is supposed to be delightful, after all, and the adventure or game attracts us. Duncan demands a great deal of attention to sound, rhythm, and, of course, sense. Attentive readers are rewarded with delight, and with an intellectual adventure.

Developing throughout the book, these images culminate in the final poem of the book, **"Food for Fire, Food for Thought,"** in which Duncan self-consciously comments on the paradox of a last poem in an open poetics: "This is what I wanted for the last poem, / a loosening of conventions and return to open form." The attempt to define or limit is frustrating and necessarily ongoing rather than definitive, but the activity is the poet's preoccupation: "We trace faces in clouds: they drift apart, / palaces of air—the sun dying down / sets them on fire." Fire is the concluding image, again transformed into a flower, as an "unlikely heat / at the edge of our belief bud[s] forth." In these two poems and those in between, Duncan explores the shifting borderlines between essence and form, childhood and adulthood, flame and flower. Like Leonardo, he

sees "figures that were stains upon a wall" as he operates "at the edge of belief." (pp. 65-7)

The major convention for Duncan is "rime," a concept far more comprehensive than simple end-rhyme, and is informed by his view of the cosmos as a whole. As he told interviewer Howard Mesch:

> Rime, or meter, which is the same word in English, is simply a sense of measure being present. And while measure may be like a ruler—12 marks, and all of them equal—a measure actually means you're feeling something did happen before or did not happen before. Any sense of resemblance or any sense of disresemblance indicates the presence of rime. It was taken before, of course, to mean that you have MOON, JUNE. . . . My composition is dependent on how much I feel I am knowing whether something has occurred within an area before. . . . We won't guarantee when it's going to happen. A conventional poem guarantees when it's going to happen, and that's its most important guarantee. When we are no longer centered on convention you have to be aware all the time.

Rime is not only a matter of sound, but also of image, emotion, and thought.

Both fire and flower rime, for instance, in the alliterative *f*s and *r*s, but more importantly in their corresponding visual beauty and in their being loci of energy. Both are ephemeral, consuming themselves as they bud or flicker forth. Their identity is reflected in the "green flame" of the opening lines (which again include the title):

> Food for fire, food for thought,
>   good wood
> that all fiery youth burst forth from winter,
>   go to sleep in the poem.
> Who will remember thy green flame,
>   Thy dream's amber?

Language itself then enters the rime as the theme of permission is again proposed: "Language obeyd flares tongues in obscure matter." The Pentecostal imagery is intentional, as the poet's obedience to the inspiration of the poem brings forth blessings of creative and destructive fire.

The next eleven lines juxtapose images of shadowy figures that the artist and reader must see and join in play. "We trace faces in clouds: they drift apart, / palaces of air" mingles direct and eye rime as the next line echoes the flaming clouds of **"Poem Beginning with a Line by Pindar."** Runes appear on the sandy sea shore and in stains upon a wall. For the attentive onlooker, permission ("let") to play follows: "Let the apparitions contain in the ground / play as they will." Apprehension, entry into the magical field, awaits anyone sensitive enough to see the significant rimes.

The speaker confuses and then identifies the fragrance of a branch with the sound of its burning on the hearth. More than a simple confusion of the senses (synaesthesia), this is an assertion of identity, of the oneness of the universe, and of its openness to the apprehensive poet. More references to fire and flower than can be summarily explicated follow, to the book's closing lines:

> We are close enough to childhood, so easily purged
> of whatever we thought we were to be,
>
> flamey threads of firstness go out from your touch.
>
> Flickers of unlikely heat
> at the edge of our belief bud forth.

Returning to the children's ring a round of roses of the book's first poem, these lines return as well to childhood innocence and faith, "easily" purging our adult preconceptions with "flamey threads of firstness." At the very boundaries of consciousness and rationality, an unlikely belief can bud forth in flame. Even a sensitive paraphrase must be accompanied by an alertness to the ideas of the poem and its attention to rimes of sound and image. This book is major contemporary poetry because its parts so successfully cohere and because it engages us in its vision of oneness and faith. (pp. 67-9)

Perhaps the single most important poem in this book is **"Poem Beginning with a Line by Pindar."** Generated by the misreading of a line from the first Pythian Ode, this four-part poem exemplifies most of the qualities—thematic and technical—of Robert Duncan's mature poetry. An apparent jumble at first reading, the Pindar poem is a collage of allusion, sound, and images that rime internally and that reverberate throughout *The Opening of the Field: "The light foot hears you and the brightness begins / god-step at the margins of thought, / quick adulterous tread at the heart."* In the synaesthesia of the first line, several key motifs appear. The foot-step-tread recurs throughout the poem, as do the themes of darkness and light and of adultery and love.

Their first occasion is Goya's painting *Cupid and Psyche,* the lovers whose tale as recounted in Apuleius's *Golden Ass* also informs part 3 of this poem. Cupid is not the chubby little archer of the Valentine card, but Eros, physical love, in fact a *daimon* or intermediate being between the gods and mortals. Love, then, is a power that can bind the human soul (psyche) to the gods. In the tale, briefly, Psyche's great beauty caused even the worship of Venus to be neglected. The angry goddess sent her son, Cupid, to punish Psyche, but he fell in love with her and made her his wife, though visiting her only at night and forbidding her to look upon him. Her curiosity overwhelmed her, but when she saw him in all his glory by lamplight, she was so startled that she spilled hot oil on his shoulder. He angrily flew away, and she set out on a journey to find him. She eventually surrendered to Venus in despair and was scourged and given four impossible tasks. With the aid of several miraculous interventions she accomplished them and was reunited with Cupid as an immortal. In her quest, Psyche is a figure of the poet, with Eros as the god-poem.

Duncan's poem calls to our attention the details of the painting, particularly the copper light falling upon Cupid's body, which provides illumination or knowledge even as it imposes separation from the loved one. A brief look at only one stanza serves to highlight Duncan's use of sound:

> A bronze of yearning, a rose that burns
> the tips of their bodies, lips,
> ends of fingers, nipples. He is not wingd.
> His thighs are flesh, are clouds
> lit by the sun in its going down,
> hot luminescence at the loins of the visible.

In the "loosening of conventions" that he advocates, Duncan employs a subtler use of sound than mere heavy end-rime. In the first three lines here, "bronze" is echoed by "burns" which also rimes with "yearning," "tips" rimes with "lips" and is heard again in "nipples," and "fingers" sets up "wingd." Despite the near-rime of "clouds" and "down," lines four through six are more subtle in their aural pleasures. The high frontal vowel of "thighs" shifts to the low frontal "clouds," "lit" evokes the tips and lips of line two and begins the sequence of short vowels (including six short *i*s) which, along with the alliterative *l*s, dominate the final two lines. Psyche's powerful sexual longings for Cupid, Eros, are rendered in a very physically appealing poetry for which we have no precise system of notation. Similarly, Cupid's thighs, seen in the painting as clouds lit by a setting sun, will appear again in section 4 of this poem and (as we have seen) in the book's final poem. More such rimes are in this book than can be enumerated, but they add, quite literally immeasurably, to the delights of reading this book.

In the Pindar poem's second section, the lovers' passion is proposed as an eternal magic, never to grow old. This thought turns the verse toward its predecessors, to "the old poets" and "their unaltering wrongness that has style, / their variable truth." The specific poets he has in mind include Walt Whitman, William Carlos Williams, Charles Olson (to whom section 3 is dedicated), and Ezra Pound.

The phrase "their variable truth" alludes to Williams, whose "variable foot" was an innovative poetic convention. The poem mentions "a stroke"—moving us from Goya's brush stroke to Williams's own stroke, *aphasia,* which had recently crippled him and especially affected his speech. That speech is parodied in the following lines, which open with a pun on the term aphasia itself:

> . . . A phase so minute,
> only a part of the word in-jerrd.
>
> *The Thundermakers descend,*
>
> damerging a nuv. A nerb.
> The present dented of the U
> nighted stayd. States. The heavy clod?
> Cloud. Invades the brain. What
> if lilacs last in *this* dooryard bloomd?

"The Thundermakers descend," apparently a continuation of Pindar's ode, fits quite well here. Not only are Williams and the other "thundermakers" physically and inevitably declining, but the verb calls to mind Williams's "The Descent" from *Paterson,* book 2, itself a masterful display of his variable foot and a testimony to the inevitable rightness of the design. Further, Duncan's imitation of Williams's aphasic speech introduces a diatribe against current American policies in an appropriately punning

way—the U. S. is presently dented and benighted, clouded with clods, its leadership since 1865 in sharp contrast to Whitman's beloved Lincoln:

> Hoover, Roosevelt, Truman, Eisenhower—
> where among these did the power reside
> that moves the heart? What flower of the nation
> bride-sweet broke to the whole rapture?
> Hoover, Coolidge, Harding, Wilson
> hear the factories of human misery turning out
>   commodities.
> For whom are the holy matins of the heart ring-
>   ing?
> Noble men in the quiet of morning hear
> Indians singing the continent's violent requiem.
> Harding, Wilson, Taft, Roosevelt,
> idiots fumbling at the bride's door,
> hear the cries of men in meaningless debt and
>   war.
> Where among these did the spirit reside
> that restores the land to productive order?
> McKinley, Cleveland, Harrison, Arthur,
> Garfield, Hayes, Grant, Johnson,
> dwell in the roots of the heart's rancor.
> How sad "amid lanes and through old woods"
>   echoes Whitman's love for Lincoln!

The sound rime of the first three lines underlines the disparity between the flower of the nation and the spiritual power to move the heart and the dented present of President Eisenhower, himself a recent stroke victim. Just as the clod/cloud that invades the brain recalls by contrast the sun-lit cloud-like thighs of Eros, the bride-sweet flower of the nation with idiots fumbling at her door only emphasizes the distance from Psyche. The agonizing question, "Where among these did the spirit reside / that restores the land to productive order?" and the brief quotation from "Lilacs," section 5, delineate the central contrast between fruitful love and ravishing sex.

Even as the poem attests to the continuity of Duncan's poetic tradition—indeed as it enacts that continuity—it laments the disruption of values that makes poetry and life itself such a struggle for contemporary man. The individual suffers in the context of a society's "meaningless debt and war": "I too / that am a nation sustain the damage / where smokes of continual ravage / obscure the flame."

Whitman's "glorious mistake," represented in two lines quoted from the 1855 preface, is only that his ideal vision of America ("The theme is creative and has vista") and its poet ("He is the president of regulation") is not actual, is not true in terms of historical realities. This poet, nonetheless, must strive "to meet a natural measure."

Section 3, dedicated to Charles Olson, unites the earlier sections' concerns with earlier poets and the story of Eros and Psyche, linking them in turn to the idea of the poet as quester or hero. Venus, Cupid's mother, charged Psyche with four "impossible tasks," completion of which would prove Psyche worthy of a divine mate. The first was to sort seeds Venus had scattered—

> Psyche's tasks—the sorting of seeds
> wheat barley oats poppy coriander
> anise beans lentils peas —every grain
>   in its right place

> before nightfall.

The alignment of the seeds, in the "natural measure" called for in the final phrase of section 2, subtly echoes Whitman's catalogs of facts in *Leaves of Grass* or Emerson's "Hamatreya." The soul must also encounter danger ("must weep / and come near upon death") and must not open Proserpina's box. Thinking to capture the secret of beauty for herself, Psyche is overcome by Melancholy and enters a deadly sleep. In *The Truth and Life of Myth,* Duncan's comments about sleep, will, and poetry illuminate these lines: "dreaming, the Romantics had realized, was involuntary Poetry. The grace of the poem, the voice, comes from a will that strives to waken us from our own personal will or to put that will to sleep." Such a submission, however, is more than a simple surrender. "But that angel of the event of the poem gives the poet both a permission and a challenge. The poet waking from waking takes up the challenge of the voice of the poem and wrestles against sleep, bringing all the watchful craft and learned art into the striving form in order that that much recognition and admission enter into the event. He strives to waken to the will of the poem, even as the poem strives to waken that will."

As much as we may be dismayed by Psyche's curiosity, which after all got her into trouble in the first place, we recognize her all too human behavior. The extension of her plight to that of the poet is artful—

> These are the old tasks.
> You've heard them before.
>
> They must be impossible. Psyche
> must despair, be brought to her
>   insect instructor;
> must obey the counsels of the green reed;
> saved from suicide by a tower speaking,
>   must follow to the letter
>   freakish instructions.

Following such freakish instructions to the letter, the poet can enter the field of the poem. Like Psyche, Ezra Pound at Pisa was helped by ants, and the poem interpolates several brief allusions—most italicized—to the Pisan cantos, especially numbers 74, 76, 82, and 83.

These lines are interrupted by the question "Who? / let the light into the dark? began / the many movements of the passion?". Like Psyche again, the poet, or any questing hero, illuminates our situation whether we want it or not, and begins the passion. Whereas "West / from east men push," the hero "struggles east / widdershins to free the dawn." One of the few arcane words in this difficult poem, *widdershins* can be understood in its context, and means moving in a direction opposite to the usual, especially in a direction contrary to the apparent course of the sun. Considered unlucky, such motion is irresistible, nonetheless—the hero "must struggle alone toward the pyres of Day." The battle of darkness against the light is now on a far more ominous plane than that of the book's first poem, with its game, with its secret circle and its "dream of the grass blowing / east against the source of the sun

> The light that is Love
> rushes on toward passion. It verges upon dark.

Duncan at Point Lobos.

Roses and blood flood the clouds.
Solitary first riders advance into legend.

Eros, desire itself, informs the quest and impels it into the margins of light and dark. Rimes, both aural and thematic, recall Cupid's thighs as clouds. Neither moral nor amoral, such a quest is necessary and even legendary. The mention of legend introduces a few heavily allusive lines about the West: "Its vistas painters saw / in diffuse light, in melancholy," quickly drawing together Whitman's vistas, Goya's diffuse light, and Psyche's melancholy. The poem then returns to the Cupid and Psyche story, but now explicitly identifies Psyche's longing and travail with the poet's own.

The fourth section ties directly to the third. Where the third ends "Cupidinous Death! / that will not take no for an answer," the fourth begins "Oh yes!" The ominous, adulterous tread at the margin of thought reappears in the footfall of "the boundary walker." A parenthetical explanation does not really explain to the uninitiated that Duncan and friends lived in a cabin on Maverick Road in Woodstock, New York, in 1949. As the snow on the roof melted, it sounded as though a giant were circling the cabin. "That foot," a poetic foot perhaps, "informed / by the weight of all things / that can be elusive" must be attended to, just as the poem was generated by an attention to a mistake in reading Pindar. Even at that, what results is "no more than a nearness to the mind / of a single image."

The poem repeats its affirmation ("Oh yes!") of "this / most dear," a "catalyst force" that brings the sensitive person's attention to bear, and further rimes with the poem's opening lines: "Who is there? O, light the light!". Cupid's apprehension, his avoidance of the light, rimes with Ezra Pound's eager anticipation of the dawn in his

prison cage. In the face of the light, opponents fall back. Cupid, or "Lust gives way. The Moon gives way. / Night gives way," and, in a telling pun that illuminates the poem's own progress, "Minutely, the Day gains." Light and love again verge upon the dark.

Unfortunately, the knowledge gained proves to be bitter. Psyche sees her beloved, but in that instant loses him. Similarly, our inexorable advance into self-consciousness causes us to lose that very innocence of which we are now conscious. In lines again calling to mind the opening poem of the book, Duncan powerfully evokes this bitter loss:

> She saw the body of her beloved
>   dismembered in waking . . . or was it
> in sight? *Finders Keepers* we sang
>   when we were children or were taught to sing
> before our histories began and we began
>   who were beloved our animal life
> toward the Beloved, sworn to be Keepers.

A prose passage disrupts the poem completely, and comments on its method. "Pindar's art, the editors tell us, was not a statue but a mosaic, and accumulation of metaphor." The Pindar poem is itself such a mosaic, a collage of pieces of literature, history, fable, and autobiography, which informs and directs the poem. From "everywhere,"

> the information flows
>   that is yearning. A line of Pindar
> moves from the area of my lamp
>   toward morning.
>
> In the dawn that is nowhere
>   I have seen the willful children
>
> clockwise and counter-clockwise turning.

"Information" is a pun: data, but form-giving data, flows into the poem. The poet's desire merges with Psyche's yearning, as his lamp and hers merge into the dawn, while the willful children play out their widdershins dance. (pp. 70-8)

The Opening of the Field also introduces Duncan's **"The Structure of Rime,"** the first of several continuing long poems. That is, while individual poems of the set are complete, the set itself has not stopped. Duncan has several such poems, [including **"Passages"**]. . . . (p. 81)

A primary fact the reader must keep in mind when considering these sets is that Duncan's work is polysemous. As complex as **"The Structure of Rime"** and **"Passages"** are, they are never self-contained units, but rather exist also as parts of the books in which they appear. Thus the first **"Structure of Rime"** is directly linked to the immediately preceding poem, **"The Law I Love Is Major Mover,"** in its imagery of the poet wrestling with the poem as Jacob wrestled with the angel. The eleventh one relates more directly to the three following poems, also not part of **"The Structure of Rime"** but forming a separate constellation of their own dealing with such central Duncan themes as boundaries and the ongoing process of destruction and renewal.

As a set of related poems, **"The Structure of Rime"** does display some identifying characteristics: most, though not all, are in prose; they all deal directly with the nature of poetic language and form; and they contain what Duncan has called "the persons of the language." The first thirteen sections of **"The Structure of Rime"** appear in *The Opening of the Field* (14 through 21 are in *Roots and Branches;* 22 through 26 in *Bending the Bow;* 27 and 28 in *Ground Work*). "Rime," as we have seen, means far more than similar end sound, and rather is a sense of correspondence. In **"The Structure of Rime II,"** the poet asks, "What of the Structure of Rime?" and is told, *"An absolute scale of resemblance and disresemblance establishes measures that are music in the actual world."* This absolute or all-pervasive scale incorporates discord or opposition as well as similarity ("resemblance and disresemblance") and operates in the actual world rather than as an ideal form. Its pursuit amounts to a "beautiful compulsion," at once longed for and feared.

The first poem of the series tells us, "Writing is first a search in obedience." The poet apostrophizes the sentence—itself ambiguously a construction of words and a judgment against the poet ("a law of words")—asserting, "O Lasting Sentence, / sentence after sentence I make in your image. In the feet that measure the dance of my pages I hear cosmic intoxications of the man I will be," only to be reproved by the voice of the poem for being "a fierce destroyer of images," one who "vomit[s] images into the place of the Law!" The interrogation of the nature of poetic form continues in every poem of the sequence. (pp. 81-2)

Rime itself results, because it "falls in the outbreakings of speech as the Character falls in the act wherefrom life springs, footfalls in Noise which we do not hear but see as Rose pushd up from the stem of our longing." Poetry is as sure as a genetically encoded message. As we again experience poetry synaesthetically—this time we see the footfall's noise, whereas in the Pindar poem the light foot heard—the sexual urge of the poem, most evident in the image of the Rose just cited, is chilled in the final line, Glélé's response: *"I am the Rose."* Fear and desire, apprehension as an act of knowing and as gut level fear, come together in a poetry that is indeed a "stranger to tranquility." (p. 83)

Mark Andrew Johnson, in his Robert Duncan, *Twayne Publishers, 1988, 155 p.*

Norman Finkelstein   (essay date 1988)

[*In the following excerpt from his critical study* The Utopian Moment in Contemporary American Poetry, *Finkelstein identifies the utopian nature of Duncan's verse as relating to creativity and tradition as well as to political matters. The critic also compares Duncan's poetic approach to that of the poet's friend Jack Spicer.*]

If the sublime comes to be regarded as an increasingly less viable mode of poetic discourse in New York in the Fifties and Sixties, then an attempt to revive it takes place at the same time across the country in Berkeley. Robert Duncan stands at the center of the so-called San Francisco Renaissance; and along with such firmly established figures as Charles Olson and Allen Ginsberg, he represents a deliberate return to the poet's vatic role, based on an unprece-

dented synthesis of Romantic and Modernist strategies. Duncan in particular has declared himself derivative in his craft, thus affording himself "permission" to create the frequently outrageous totalities that mark his poetry as one of the most ambitious bodies of work in our time. For Duncan's poetic is totalizing; to an even greater extent than Pound or Olson, he seeks to in-form the "orders" or "scales" of reality in an open-ended tapestry or collage of language. In this regard, he operates in exact antithesis to [John] Ashbery and [Frank] O'Hara: he seeks to establish, or rather, prove, that the interrelated networks of material, psychological, and spiritual realities are all coordinated hierarchies that function under the force of universal Law. Rather than level modes of perception, value systems and forms of knowledge, Duncan would place them all within their proper contexts, so that an awareness of overarching Form allows the reader to perceive a previously hidden totality. Poetry, of course, is the most significant medium for such a process; hence the poet holds a privileged place within the orders of language. Duncan's thought is transparently utopian in regard to matters of creativity and tradition, as well as in relation to immediate political concerns; and while sometimes problematic in its applications, its insistence on infinite human potential within a communal identity is, as Oppen would say, "ennobling." As Duncan declares in **"Orders,"**

> There is no
>
> good a man has in his own things except
>
> it be in the community of every thing;
>
> no nature he has
>
> but in his nature hidden in the heart of the
> living
>
> in the great household.

Duncan's insistent metaphors are often so compelling that they seem to obviate criticism, and therefore it is important to observe that at the same time Duncan's totalizing project is getting under way, a related but in some ways radically dissimilar poetic is being formulated by his old friend—and critic—Jack Spicer. Cranky, admonitory, haunted, Spicer's work presents as unified a poetic as Duncan's, but carefully avoids the sweeping gestures of order and coherence that have become the distinguishing mark of even the most open of Duncan's poetic fields. Spicer's sincere distrust of the totalizing impulse in both Romantic and Modernist poetry leads him to a poetic of disruption and difference, of radical otherness and possession, in which the poet is far less the willing spokesman for the sublime than its unsuspecting victim. Whereas Duncan celebrates the "Lasting Sentence" in his *Structure of Rime,* Spicer warns us, in *The Heads of the Town Up to the Aether,* that "words / Turn mysteriously against those who use them." In fact, it could be argued that Duncan and Spicer draw upon the same poetic precursors and philosophical systems and create complementary views of the poetic act. For Duncan, Romantic myth-making and theosophical doctrine combine with Modernist explorations of history, anthropology and phenomenology to confirm Yeats's old dictum that "The things below are as the things above." For Spicer the Romantics' demonic subjectivity, the dualities of the gnostics and the Modernists' fragmentation of lyric and narrative all yield the equally Yeatsian notion that "there is a deep enmity between a man and his destiny."

Both poets then are certainly dedicated to reviving a vision of the sublime; and both share, however doubtfully, in poetry's utopian propensity. Like Ashbery in "These Lacustrine Cities," Spicer offers a highly condensed and elliptical retelling of the dialectic of civilization and poetry in the "Textbook of Poetry" section of *The Heads of the Town:*

> the city that we create in our bartalk or in our
>   fuss
> and fury about each other is in an utterly mixed
>   and
> mirrored way an image of the city. A return
>   from exile.

Spicer has Dante's exile from Florence in mind, but must also be conscious of the **"Heavenly City, Earthly City"** envisioned by Duncan more than ten years before:

> In the moment of song—earthly radiant
> city of poetry—that golden light
> consumes in its focus a world I have sufferd,
> the darkend city of my perishable age.

And although Spicer doubts, as Duncan himself comes to doubt, that the utopian city or the new Arcady could be built among the Bohemian poets of San Francisco, both poets maintain that we must, as Spicer says,

> Hold to the future. With firm hands. The future
>   of
> each afterlife, of each ghost, of each word that
>   is
> about to be mentioned.

Because both poets pay great attention to "each word that is about to be mentioned," it can be said that the very notion of futurity in their work is closely related to the models of poetic inspiration to which they constantly refer. Spicer and Duncan are two of the leading practitioners among contemporary poets of poetry as poetics, which is to say that they attain that high level of self-consciousness necessary to relate their work as individuals to the ongoing activity of poetry as a historical continuum. One such moment of recognition occurs in the first letter to Lorca in Jack Spicer's *After Lorca* (1957), that disquieting book in which Spicer attempts to remake himself into the poet he wishes to be. He does so by giving himself up to the *daimon* (as Yeats would call him) or *duende* (as Lorca himself would call him), and thus speaks with an authority he previously lacked. He assumes a traditional stance, and with wonderful irony speaks of tradition itself:

> In my last letter [though this is the first letter
> Spicer writes] I spoke of the tradition. The fools
> that read these letters will think by this we mean
> what tradition seems to have meant lately—an
> historical patchwork (whether made up of Eliza-
> bethan quotations, guide books of the poet's
> home town, or obscure hints of obscure bits of
> magic published by Pantheon) which is used to
> cover up the nakedness of the bare word. Tradi-

tion means much more than that. It means generations of different poets in different countries patiently telling the same story, writing the same poem, gaining and losing something with each transformation—but, of course, never really losing anything. This has nothing to do with calmness, classicism, temperament, or anything else. Invention is merely the enemy of poetry.

Spicer's vision of generations of poets is one of the most recent formulations of a venerable idea. Among poets writing in English, its spokesmen have included such major (and diverse) figures as Shelley, Yeats, Pound and Eliot, all of whom would agree that poets are always "writing the same poem," with invention always "the enemy of poetry."

Much the same is true for Duncan in *The Truth & Life of Myth:*

> Myth, for Dante, for Shakespeare, for Milton,
> was the poet-lore handed down in the tradition
> from poet to poet. It was the very matter of Poet-
> ry, the nature of the divine world as poets had
> testified to it; the poetic piety of each poet, his
> acknowledgement of what he had found true Po-
> etry, worked to conserve that matter. And, for
> each, there was in the form of their work—the
> literary vision, the play of actors upon the stage,
> and the didactic epic—a kind of magic, for back
> of these forms we surmise distant origins in the
> rituals toward ecstasy of earliest Man.

Tradition here is a source of primal empowerment: it can provide the individual poet with a transpersonal, communal authority that will allow him to articulate his own contribution to the ongoing matter of the historical work. Duncan's open fields (***Passages, The Structure of Rime,*** etc.) and Spicer's "books" can both be seen as attempts to find contemporary correlatives to the historically appropriate forms of a Dante, a Shakespeare, a Milton. They seek to respond to the demands of the moment, knowing full well that in doing so, they intuitively respond to the movement of history as one moment opens on to the next. . . . (pp. 62-5)

Although both poets wish to open their poems to the incoming future . . . , there remains the crucial difference between them that we have already cited: the difference between the mage and the medium, the domestic householder and the barroom heckler, the Logos and the Lowghost. In a revealing passage from *The Truth & Life of Myth,* Duncan explains one of his models for inspiration and composition:

> Speaking of a thing I call upon its name, and the
> Name takes over from me the story I would tell,
> if I let the dimmest realization of that power
> enter here. But the myth we are telling is the
> myth of the power of the Word. The Word, as
> we refer to It, undoes all the bounds of semantics
> we would draw in Its creative need to realize Its
> true Self. It takes over. Its desire would take over
> and seem to put out or to drown the individual
> reality—lonely invisible and consumed flame in
> the roaring light of the Sun—but Its creativity
> moves in all the realities and can only realize It-

self in the Flesh, in the incarnation of concrete
and mortal Form.

Significantly, Duncan *lets* the power enter and begin its
work; mutuality and reciprocity are established between
the individual and the Word. "Things," i.e., material reality, move the poet; such inspiration establishes the connection between consciousness and the otherwise distant sublime. The sense of continuity that Duncan is able to establish in his poetry, the totality of effort that encompasses
even the most diverse content, may be traced back to his
personal sense of confidence as expressed in this idea of inspiration. For Duncan, the world will respond to the responsive poet ("the Poet on Guard," as he calls him in an
early poem); and even in the midst of the most severe personal or political crisis, apprehensions of universal order
inevitably appear. . . . (p. 66)

[The] art of collage as practiced by Duncan and Spicer is
most purely the art of the possible. Rather than consoli-
date temporal and spatial relations into self-sufficient
worlds, they insist that the very notion of self-sufficiency
is impossible, given the means by which their poetry
comes into existence. No single meaning, however complex or ambiguous, can be sufficient; the text's polysemous
nature not only summons other meanings, but other texts
as well. As Duncan declares:

> and only in the imagination of the Whole
> the immediate percept is
>   to be justified—Imagining
>   this
>   pivot of a totality
>   having
>   no total thing in us, we so
>   live beyond ourselves
>
>   —and in this   unitive.

But if we reverse Duncan's declaration, it remains to be
seen whether "the immediate percept" justifies "the imagination of the Whole." Again and again in the reading of
both poets, certain more or less discrete poems and fragments impose themselves upon the imagination: the work
is not of a piece in its actual execution, and textual boundaries insist upon being drawn. *Language,* for example, is
simply not as strong as *The Heads of the Town* or *The Holy
Grail;* despite the evocative force of individual poems, the
play of correspondences seems too diffuse; and one is
forced to concede that Spicer needed the concentration of
his "obsessions" in order to take dictation most successfully. And in all of Duncan's volumes, including the recent
Ground Work, certain individual poems, no matter how
complex within themselves or related to accompanying
pieces, provide the greatest satisfaction. When Duncan's
work is anthologized, it is **"Often I Am Permitted To Return To A Meadow," "This Place Rumor To Have Been
Sodom"** or **"A Poem Beginning With A Line By Pindar"**
(from *The Opening of the Field*) or **"My Mother Would
Be A Falconress"** (from *Bending the Bow*) that editors select; and it is worth considering that Spicer's work has not
been adequately represented in anthologies because editors have yet to learn that one of his single, cohesive books
is the best demonstration of his genius. Is it only in principle, then, that the work as grand collage can be defended?

Unfortunately, there is no simple response to such a question. If it is naive, given the nature of Duncan's or Spicer's
enterprise, to simply "analyze" an individual poem, it is
likewise naive to simply accept the paralyzing binary opposition between scrupulous New Critical interpretation
of "well wrought urns" and dizzying Postmodern proclamations of intertextuality and open form. The open /
closed dichotomy which so bedevils the critics in their dis-
courses on such poetry seems to bother the poets to a
much smaller extent. If one is really composing in accordance with the "content under hand" (the phrase is
Charles Olson's), then the poem must follow the contours
of thought and feeling: form of any sort cannot be pre-
scribed, but will reveal itself to the reader as both necessary and appropriate. This is what Duncan means when
he speaks of the "Form of Forms," "the wholeness of a
poem in which all of its parts are redeemed as meaning."

Consider Duncan's recent **"Circulation of the Song."** This
magnificent poem, which appears at the end of *Ground
Work,* is notable for its unusually self-sustained form, consistency of tone and voice, and completed (rather than
fragmentary) syntax. It is built upon a clearly delineated
stanza structure and makes use of a relatively limited and
accessible set of literary allusions and references. It is a
particularly striking contrast to the other major efforts in
Ground Work, such as **"Poems from the Margins of Thom
Gunn's *Moly,*" "A Seventeenth Century Suite"** and
"Dante Etudes," all of which are derivations and rework-
ings of freely acknowledged precursor texts; or the *Tribunals* sections of *Passages,* which, like earlier sections of
that poem, make extensive use of quotation, allusion and
spatialized fields of reference. The subtitle of **"Circulations of the Song"** is simply "After Jalai Al-Din Rumi,"
though Rumi's presence in the poem is totally subsumed
by Duncan's own persistent, and by now easily identified
tone. What's more, the poem is much less overtly self-
reflexive than most of Duncan's mature work: although it
does speak to questions of its own inspiration and composition, it is equally concerned with the connections between the poet's religious beliefs, his long-standing relationship to his lover, and his sense of himself as he grows
old. Like the deeply moving **"My Mother Would Be A
Falconress,"** its rich lyric diction may be correlated to a
largely interior, subjective project which Duncan often
calls "essential autobiography." In short, it is, at least on
the surface, a far more conventional, "bounded" poem
than Duncan is wont to write.

Yet **"Circulations of the Song"** confirms every important
idea that Duncan has developed in regard to his poetic
practice, and renews the utopian sense of openness and
possibility that makes his best work so important:

> I am like a line cast out
>   into a melodic unfolding beyond itself
>   a mind hovering ecstatic
>   above a mouth in which the heart rises
>   pouring itself into liquid and fiery speech
>   for the sake of a rime not yet arrived
>   containing again and again resonant arrivals.

Here the poet is both a subjective force of ecstatic inspiration and an objective vehicle for that inspiration, whose
words are perpetual preparations for "a rime not yet ar-

rived," a poetry of pure futurity. But this ecstatic awareness is tempered by Duncan's increasing certainty of his
own mortality. Thus the *He* of the poem, the dark homosexual Eros who consecrates the poet's marriage to his
lover, is also a god of death; and the fulfillment of the sexual relationship is a premonition of that final fulfillment:

> How has your face
> aged over these years to keep company with
>   mine?
> ever anew as I waken endearing.   Each night
>   in the exchange of touch and speech blessing,
>
> prepared thruout for rest.   Is it not
> as if He were almost here?   as if we were
>
> already at rest?

Physical beauty and the confidence of youth likewise pass
into such knowledge:

> For a moment did Beauty pass over my face?
> I did not have to reach for *your* beauty.
> Radiant, it entirely flowd out and thru me.

Because of this, Duncan's relationship to his muse is all
the more fierce and perilous:

> Again you have instructed me to let go,
> to hold to this falling,   this
>   letting myself go.
> I will succumb entirely to your intention.
>
>   *Contend with me!*
> you demand. And I am surrounded by wingd
>   confusions. *He*
> is everywhere,   nowhere
>   now where I am.
>
> In every irreality there is Promise.
>   But there
> where I am not   *He*   really is.
>
>   In Whose Presence
> it is as if I had a new name.

This passage is yet another restatement of one of Duncan's
central myths, Jacob's wrestling with the angel, which
permeates both his poetry (*The Opening of the Field*) and
criticism (*The Truth & Life of Myth*). This poetic fiction,
or "irreality," is especially full of hope. The erotic physical
contact with the divinely beautiful and the linguistic revelation that follows in Jacob's being renamed Israel have
always attracted Duncan, but now the stakes are higher:
as he ages he must give himself over more completely to
struggle, confusion, and the intention of the Absolute. For
Duncan such contention has always been equated with
composition, and the shaping of the present poem comes
to vindicate his faith. Yet this does not entail a merely personal expression of religious belief, or even the confirmation of the poet's metaphysical grounding of aesthetic doctrine. As Duncan concludes:

> In the Grand Assemblage of Lives,
>   the Great Assembly-House,
> this Identity, this Ever-Presence, arranged
>   rank for rank, person for person, each from
>   its own
> sent out from what we were to another place
>   now in the constant exchange
>   renderd true.

What begins as personal revelation is made into a concrete
universal, not to be asserted in abstraction, but to be re-
enacted in lived experience—including the encounter with
linguistic form. (pp. 70-3)

> *Norman Finkelstein, "The New Arcady," in
> his* The Utopian Moment in Contemporary
> American Poetry, *Bucknell University Press,
> 1988, pp. 62-95.*

FURTHER READING

American Poetry 6, No. 1 (Fall 1988).
  Special issue devoted to Duncan.

Bertholf, Robert J. "Robert Duncan: Blake's Contemporary
Voice." In *William Blake and the Moderns,* edited by
Bertholf and Annette S. Levitt, pp. 92-110. Albany: State
University of New York Press, 1982.
  Explores the influence of Blake on Duncan and their
  "spiritual affinities." Also compares their poetic treat-
  ment of Jesus Christ, Eros, memory, war, innocence,
  freedom, and the self.

Brien, Dolores Elise. "Robert Duncan: A Poet in the Whit-
man-Emerson Tradition." *Centennial Review* 19, No. 4 (Fall
1975): 308-16.
  Analyzes the importance of Walt Whitman and Ralph
  Waldo Emerson on Duncan's poetry as manifested in
  such themes as love, self, God, the body, the creative
  process, and the role of poetry in society.

Gutierrez, Donald. "The Beautiful Place in the Mind: Robert
Duncan's 'Often I Am Permitted to Return to a Meadow.'"
American Poetry 6, No. 1 (Fall 1988): 25-30.
  Explication of "Often I Am Permitted to Return to a
  Meadow."

Ironwood 11, No. 2 (Fall 1983).
  Special issue devoted to Duncan. Includes poetry and
  prose by the author as well as essays by Hugh Kenner,
  Hayden Carruth, Michael Davidson, and others.

Kamenetz, Rodger. "Realms of Being: An Interview with
Robert Duncan." *Southern Review* n. s. 21, No. 1 (January
1985): 5-25.
  Includes Duncan's views on the influence of Jewish mystical texts and tradition on *Letters* and *The Opening of
  the Field* as well as comments on language, law, his parents' religion, and the relationship between his art and
  life.

Levertov, Denise. "A Memoir and a Critical Tribute." In
Contemporary Poets: Modern Critical Views, edited by Harold
Bloom, pp. 57-83. New York: Chelsea House Publishers,
1986.
  Personal recollection of Levertov's friendship with Duncan, his role in the development of her poetry, and her
  thoughts on his work.

Meachen, Clive. "Robert Duncan: 'To Complete His

Mind.' " In *Modern American Poetry,* edited by R. W. (Herbie) Butterfield, pp. 204-17. London: Vision Press Limited and Totowa, N. J.: Barnes & Noble Books, 1984.

> Discusses the open and inclusive nature of Duncan's poetry as well as his treatment of apocalypse, God, and rebirth.

Nelson, Carey. "Between Openness and Loss: Form and Dissolution in Robert Duncan's Aesthetic." In *Our Last First Poets: Vision and History in Contemporary American Poetry,* pp. 97-144. Urbana: University of Illinois Press, 1981.

> Detailed analysis of Duncan's theory of open form as well as several of his themes, including loss, sexuality, religion, history, language, and war.

Nelson, Rudolph L. "Edge of the Transcendent: The Poetry of Levertov and Duncan." *Southwest Review* LIV, No. 2 (Spring 1969): 188-202.

> Compares Duncan and Levertov's theories of organic form and their views of transcendence.

Rosenthal, M. L. "The 'Projectivist' Movement: Robert Duncan." In his *The New Poets: American and British Poetry Since World War II,* pp. 174-84. New York: Oxford University Press, 1967.

> Analyzes *The Opening of the Field* and *Roots and Branches* and extols Duncan as the most naturally gifted of the Black Mountain poets.

Sagetrieb 4, Nos. 2/3 (Fall and Winter 1985).

> Special issue devoted to Duncan. Includes verse, prose, and letters to poet William Everson by Duncan as well as essays by George F. Butterick, Thomas Gardner, Norman Finkelstein, and others.

Wheaton, Bruce. "Bound to Be Present: Memory and Imagined Space in the Work of Robert Duncan." In *The Green American Tradition,* edited by H. Daniel Peck, pp. 228-44. Baton Rouge: Louisiana State University Press, 1989.

> Assesses the role of memory in Duncan's poetry.

Thomas Gray

1716-1771

English poet and essayist.

Gray is considered one of the most influential English poets of the mid-eighteenth century. Although his poetic canon is small—throughout his lifetime he wrote less than one thousand lines of verse—Gray was a major transitional figure between the sensibility and classical perfection of the Augustans and the emotional reverberation of the Romantics. While the influence of the Augustans is manifested in Gray's concentration on complicated metrical schemes and intellectual ideals, he was in fact a precursor to the Romantic movement because of his sensitive and empathetic portrayal of the common man. Nowhere is this more evident than in his "Elegy Written in a Country Churchyard," Gray's most famous work and one of the most beloved poems in English literature. While Gray wrote a number of odes, among them "Ode on a Distant Prospect of Eton College" and "Ode on the Spring," it is the language of the "Elegy" that has infused modern colloquial speech more than any other piece of English literature that contains so few consecutive lines. Alfred, Lord Tennyson recapitulates the "Elegy's" universal appeal by declaring it contains "divine truisms that make us weep."

Born in Cornhill, England, Gray was the son of a milliner and her husband, a respected scrivener. Although the family was fairly prosperous, Gray's father was a morose and violent man who at times abused his wife unmercifully. There is uncertainty as to whether Gray's parents separated, but it is well-documented that it was arranged for Gray to attend Eton College when he was eight years old so that he could be properly educated. A studious and solitary boy, Gray formed intimate friendships with only three other students: Thomas Ashton, Horace Walpole, and Richard West. They proclaimed themselves the "Quadruple Alliance" and were were given to precocious conversation on life and literature. West and Walpole figured significantly in Gray's literary development and later in his poetic career, which blossomed during Gray's four years at Cambridge. While at Cambridge, Gray attracted attention as an accomplished writer of Latin verse, even though he left in 1738 without taking a degree. Shortly thereafter, Gray joined Walpole on an extended tour of Europe but in 1741 they quarreled violently, the cause of their differences still a matter of speculation, and the two parted company until their reconciliation in 1745.

After returning to England alone, Gray postponed his reinstatement to Cambridge for two years, spending the interval with his mother, now a widow, at the house she had recently taken in rustic Stoke Poges, Buckinghamshire. Here, in 1742, Gray composed his first major poem, "Ode on the Spring," which he unknowingly sent to Richard West on the day of the latter's unexpected death at age twenty-six. Gray's bereavement only served to enhance his creative activity; his level of production at this time was

so intense that it was seldom to be repeated during his lifetime. During the next three months Gray wrote "Ode on a Distant Prospect of Eton College," "Hymn to Adversity," and "Sonnet on the Death of Richard West." This scurried activity prompted Edmund Gosse to write that it was when Gray was the most melancholy that he experienced his "periods of greatest vitality." Gray also turned from Latin to English as his primary poetic medium at this time. Although he worked intermittently on "Elegy Written in a Country Churchyard," which was not published until 1751, it is speculated that Gray began this poem as early as 1742, when he was still living in Stoke Poges in close proximity of the inspirational "ivy-covered spires" of the local church.

Gray soon returned to Cambridge however, and settled into the life of a university scholar after being awarded a Bachelor of Civil Law degree in 1743. He resided at the college for the better part of his life, but was never a fellow and never took part in tutoring, lecturing or other academic duties. He occasionally spent time away from Cambridge, either visiting his mother in Stoke Poges, studying at the newly opened British Museum, or journeying to the Lake District and Scotland. Throughout his life Gray quietly pursued his studies, taking advantage of the intellectual amenities of the university setting. Classical literature, medieval history, painting, architecture, Celtic and Norse mythology, and botany were only a few of his interests. "Perhaps he was the most learned man in Europe," wrote Gray's contemporary, William J. Temple. Scarcely anything remains to attest to his profound and varied scholarship, apart from a vast accumulation of notes and letters, but Gray enjoyed his academic pursuits immensely, finding great pleasure in knowledge and discovery despite the lack of any developed work or critical recognition. Of the importance of his studies, Gray wrote, "To be employed is to be happy," and "to find oneself in business is the great art of life." It was during this time of intense personal scholarship that Gray was elected Regius Professor of Modern History at Cambridge, an office he held until his death in 1771.

"Gray wrote at the very beginning of a certain literary epoch of which we, perhaps, stand at the very end," wrote G. K. Chesterton in 1932. "He represented that softening of the Classic which slowly turned into the Romantic." Gray's "Elegy Written in a Country Churchyard" represents more than any other work during Gray's time the elements of the intuitive, the emotional, and the metaphysical which, when introduced, were in direct opposition to the established tenets of English neo-classical literature. From the onset, Gray's technical accomplishments were impressive, but what set him apart from his contemporaries were his evocative descriptions of the sights around him and his ability to spark a catharsis of mood and feeling in his readers. Some critics have suggested that while Gray's earliest poems, among them "Ode on the Spring" and "Hymn to Adversity," are intensely personal and represent an impassioned response to life and death, his later poems are emotionally distant in comparison. This development, critics suggest, may have been due in part to Gray's precarious position as a bridge between two conflicting poetic movements. As Matthew Arnold states, "Gray, a born poet, fell upon the age of prose. . . . [With] the qualities of mind and soul of a genuine poet, [Gray] was isolated in his century."

Despite Gray's sometimes antithetical poetic voice, his "Elegy Written in a Country Churchyard" is still considered a classic in English poetry. In this poem, Gray gave expression to the thoughts that were buried deep in the English consciousness of the eighteenth century—thoughts about history and tradition, the Anglican religion, and the tranquility of English landscapes and village life. Even Samuel Johnson, Gray's harshest critic, found the "Elegy" rich "with the images which find a mirrour in every mind, and with sentiments to which every bosom returns." While this poem brought Gray immediate critical and popular acclaim and was frequently reprinted throughout his lifetime, it was almost published in a disreputable magazine without Gray's sanction. If it had not been for Walpole's intervention, the initial publication of the "Elegy" may have been radically modified, lessening the impact of the poem. Controversy also surrounds the last four stanzas of this work, the portion commonly called "The Epitaph." When first published, critics were discontented with its lack of harmony in comparison to

the rest of the poem, but Gray, in due course, made some drastic alterations. While various commentators have speculated on the purpose and origin of these last four stanzas, the process of the "Elegy's" composition will always remain uncertain.

The success of the "Elegy" focused critical attention on Gray for the rest of his life, leading to close scrutiny of his subsequent works. "The Progress of Poesy" and "The Bard" were his efforts to imitate the stazaic structure of the Greek poet Pindar. In the first ode, Gray set himself to glorify the poet's calling; and he did so with an exhaltation and allusiveness that render many of the passages difficult. "The Bard," the second in Gray's *Odes,* portrays a traditional episode during the final subjugation of Wales by English forces. Although Gray demonstrated that he was widely versed in English history, these odes, on the whole, were not well-received and he was accused of being obscure in his attempt to write not for the world but for his fellow poets. While the *Odes* were widely read and discussed, they were not understood or appreciated by the general readership or highly respected by literary authorities. In the midst of this critical controversy, with some critics praising the significance of the *Odes* and others freely parodying them, documentation shows that Gray was unconcerned with public displeasure. In a letter written to his friend the Reverend James Brown, Gray justifies his concentration on classical allusion and imagery: "The odes in question . . . were meant to be vocal to the intelligent alone."

From the time of his first publication to the present day, Gray's poetry has had as many admirers as detractors. Although scholars continue to praise the "Elegy" as a brilliant piece of verse, they also puzzle over the inconsistancies in theme and approach that riddled the rest of Gray's poetic output. Yet it is almost unanimous among critics that in the "Elegy" Gray broke new ground in concepts and attitudes by tapping into the pulse of the common man with great insight and passion. To the neo-classicists, Gray's statement that "any fool may write a most valuable book by chance, if he will only tell us what he heard and saw with veracity" would appear impetuous and incognizant, but it is the very veracity in Gray's work that has established his place in literary history as the author of one of the most exquisite poems in English literature.

(For further discussion of Gray's life and career, see *Literature Criticism from 1400 to 1800,* Vol. 4.)

PRINCIPAL WORKS

POETRY

Ode on a Distant Prospect of Eton College   1747
*"Ode on the Death of a Favourite Cat, Drowned in a Tub of Gold Fishes"   1748
*"Ode on the Spring"   1748
An Elegy Wrote in a Country Church Yard   1751; also published as *Elegy Written in a Country Churchyard,* 1834
Designs by Mr. R. Bentley for Six Poems by Mr. T. Gray 1753

OTHER MAJOR WORKS

*Both poems were first published in *A Collection of Poems by Several Hands,* 1748.

**This volume contains what are commonly called Gray's Pindaric odes: "The Bard" and "The Progress of Poesy."

***Published in the journal *Universal Magazine.*

Oliver Goldsmith   (essay date 1757)

[*An English poet, novelist, dramatist, and critic, Goldsmith was one of the most important writers of the Augustan Age. He distinguished himself during his lifetime as the author of two major literary works:* The Vicar of Wakefield *(1766), a novel which pioneered the utilization of the protagonist as narrator; and* She Stoops to Conquer *(1773), a drama written in reaction to the tradition of sentimental and moral comedy. In the following excerpt, Goldsmith examines Gray's Pindaric Odes and while finding value in their classical form and imagery, he suggests that Gray return to the subject of his "Elegy Written in a Country Churchyard;" that of the English experience. "Study the people," Goldsmith retorts, and adapt your works to the "dispositions of [your] countrymen."*]

As this publication seems designed for those who have formed their taste by the models of antiquity, the generality of Readers cannot be supposed adequate Judges of its merit; nor will [Thomas Gray], it is presumed, be greatly disappointed if he finds them backward in commending a performance not entirely suited to their apprehensions. We cannot, however, without some regret behold those talents so capable of giving pleasure to all, exerted in efforts that, at best, can amuse only the few; we cannot behold this rising Poet seeking fame among the learned, without hinting to him the same advice that Isocrates used to give his Scholars, *Study the People.* This study it is that

has conducted the great Masters of antiquity up to immortality. Pindar himself, of whom our modern Lyrist is an imitator, appears entirely guided by it. He adapted his works exactly to the dispositions of his countrymen. Irregular enthusiastic, and quick in transition,—he wrote for a people inconstant, of warm imaginations, and exquisite sensibility. He chose the most popular subjects, and all his allusions are to customs well known, in his days, to the meanest person.

His English Imitator wants those advantages. [Gray] speaks to a people not easily impressed with new ideas; extremely tenacious of the old; with difficulty warmed; and as slowly cooling again.—How unsuited then to our national character is that species of poetry which rises upon us with unexpected flights! Where we must hastily catch the thought, or it flies from us; and, in short, where the Reader must largely partake of the Poet's enthusiasm, in order to taste his beauties. To carry the parallel a little farther; the Greek Poet wrote in a language the most proper that can be imagined for this species of composition; lofty, harmonious, and never needing rhyme to heighten the numbers. But, for us, several unsuccessful experiments seem to prove that the English cannot have Odes in blank Verse; while, on the other hand, a natural imperfection attends those which are composed in irregular rhymes:—the similar sound often recurring where it is not expected, and not being found where it is, creates no small confusion to the Reader,—who, as we have not seldom observed, beginning in all the solemnity of poetic elocution, is by frequent disappointments of the rhyme, at last obliged to drawl out the uncomplying numbers into disagreeable prose.

It is, by no means, our design to detract from the merit of our Author's present attempt: we would only intimate, that an English Poet,—one whom the Muse has *mark'd for her own,* could produce a more luxuriant bloom of flowers, by cultivating such as are natives of the soil, than by endeavouring to force the exotics of another climate: or, to speak without a metaphor, such a genius as Mr. Gray might give greater pleasure, and acquire a larger portion of fame, if, instead of being an imitator, he did justice to his talents, and ventured to be more an original. These two Odes, it must be confessed, breath much of the spirit of Pindar, but then they have caught the seeming obscurity, the sudden transition, and hazardous epithet, of his mighty master; all which, though evidently intended for beauties, will, probably, be regarded as blemishes, by the generality of his Readers. (pp. 239-40)

In conformity to the antients, these Odes consist of the *Strophe, Antistrophe,* and *Epode,* which, in each Ode, are thrice repeated. The Strophes have a correspondent resemblance in their stricture and numbers: and the Antistrophe and Epode also bear the same similitude. The Poet seems, in the first Ode particularly, to design the Epode as a complete air to the Strophe and Antistrophe, which have more the appearance of Recitative. There was a necessity for these divisions among the antients, for they served as directions to the dancer and musician; but we see no reason why they should be continued among the moderns; for, instead of assisting, they will but perplex the Musician, as our music requires a more frequent transition from the Air to the Recitative than could agree with the simplicity of the antients.

The first of these Poems celebrates the Lyric Muse. It seems the most laboured performance of the two, but yet we think its merit is not equal to that of the second. It seems to want that regularity of plan upon which the second is founded; and though it abounds with images that strike, yet, unlike the second, it contains none that are affecting. (p. 240)

The second Ode is founded on a tradition current in Wales, that Edward the first, when he compleated the conquest of that country, ordered all the Bards that fell into his hands to be put to death. The Author seems to have taken the hint of this subject from the fifteenth Ode of the first book of Horace [see excerpt above]. Our Poet introduces the only surviving Bard of that country in concert with the spirits of his murdered brethren, as prophetically denouncing woes upon the Conqueror and his posterity. The circumstances of grief and horror in which the Bard is represented, those of terror in the preparation of the votive web, and the mystic obscurity with which the prophecies are delivered, will give as much pleasure to those who relish this species of composition, as anything that has hitherto appeared in our language, the Odes of Dryden himself not excepted. (p. 242)

> *Oliver Goldsmith, in an originally unsigned essay titled "Gray's 'Odes'," in* The Monthly Review, *London, Vol. XVII, September, 1757, pp. 239-43.*

Samuel Johnson   (essay date 1781)

[*A remarkably versatile and distinguished man of letters, Johnson was the major English literary figure of the second half of the eighteenth century. His monumental* A Dictionary of the English Language *(1755) standardized for the first time English spelling and pronunciation while his moralistic criticism strongly influenced contemporary tastes. Perhaps the foremost principle in Johnson's critical theory was that a work must be evaluated chiefly on its ability to both entertain and instruct the reader. In the following excerpt, he disparages the language and thought of Gray's poetry but reserves unqualified praise for the "Elegy."*]

Gray's poetry is now to be considered, and I hope not to be looked on as an enemy to his name if I confess that I contemplate it with less pleasure than his life.

His **"Ode on Spring"** has something poetical, both in the language and the thought; but the language is too luxuriant, and the thoughts have nothing new. There has of late arisen a practice of giving to adjectives, derived from substantives, the termination of participles, such as the *cultured* plain, the *daisied* bank; but I was sorry to see, in the lines of a scholar like Gray, 'the *honied* Spring.' The morality is natural, but too stale; the conclusion is pretty.

The poem ["**Ode on the Death of a Favourite Cat**"] was doubtless by its author considered as a trifle, but it is not a happy trifle. In the first stanza 'the azure flowers that blow' shew resolutely a rhyme is sometimes made when

it cannot easily be found. Selima, the Cat, is called a nymph, with some violence both to language and sense; but there is good use made of it when it is done; for of the two lines,

> What female heart can gold despise?

> What cat's averse to fish?

the first relates merely to the nymph, and the second only to the cat. The sixth stanza contains a melancholy truth, that 'a favourite has no friend,' but the last ends in a pointed sentence of no relation to the purpose; if what glistered had been 'gold,' the cat would not have gone into the water; and, if she had, would not less have been drowned.

The **"Prospect of Eton College"** suggests nothing to Gray which every beholder does not equally think and feel. His supplication to father Thames, to tell him who drives the hoop or tosses the ball, is useless and puerile. Father Thames has no better means of knowing than himself. His epithet 'buxom health' is not elegant; he seems not to understand the word. Gray thought his language more poetical as it was more remote from common use: finding in Dryden 'honey redolent of Spring,' an expression that reaches the utmost limits of our language, Gray drove it a little more beyond common apprehension, by making 'gales' to be 'redolent of joy and youth.'

Of the **"Ode on Adversity"** the hint was at first taken from 'O Diva, gratum quæ regis Antium'; but Gray has excelled his original by the variety of his sentiments and by their moral application. Of this piece, at once poetical and rational, I will not by slight objections violate the dignity.

My process has now brought me to the 'Wonderful Wonder of Wonders,' the two Sister Odes; by which, though either vulgar ignorance or common sense at first universally rejected them, many have been since persuaded to think themselves delighted. I am one of those that are willing to be pleased, and therefore would gladly find the meaning of the first stanza of **"The Progress of Poetry."**

Gray seems in his rapture to confound the images of 'spreading sound' and 'running water.' A 'stream of musick' may be allowed; but where does Musick, however 'smooth and strong,' after having visited the 'verdant vales,' 'rowl down the steep amain,' so as that 'rocks and nodding groves rebellow to the roar'? If this be said of Musick, it is nonsense; if it be said of Water, it is nothing to the purpose.

The second stanza, exhibiting Mars's car and Jove's eagle, is unworthy of further notice. Criticism disdains to chase a schoolboy to his common-places.

To the third it may likewise be objected that it is drawn from Mythology, though such as may be more easily assimilated to real life. 'Idalia's velvet-green' has something of cant. An epithet or metaphor drawn from Nature ennobles Art; an epithet or metaphor drawn from Art degrades Nature. Gray is too fond of words arbitrarily compounded. 'Many-twinkling' was formerly censured as not analogical; we may say *many-spotted*, but scarcely *many-spotting*. This stanza, however, has something pleasing.

Of the second ternary of stanzas the first endeavours to tell something, and would have told it had it not been crossed by Hyperion; the second describes well enough the universal prevalence of poetry, but I am afraid that the conclusion will not rise from the premises. The caverns of the North and the plains of Chili are not the residences of 'Glory' and 'generous Shame.' But that Poetry and Virtue go always together is an opinion so pleasing that I can forgive him who resolves to think it true.

The third stanza sounds big with Delphi, and Egean, and Ilissus, and Meander, and 'hallowed fountain' and 'solemn sound'; but in all Gray's odes there is a kind of cumbrous splendour which we wish away. His position is at last false: in the time of Dante and Petrarch, from whom he derives our first school of poetry, Italy was overrun by 'tyrant power' and 'coward vice'; nor was our state much better when we first borrowed the Italian arts.

Of the third ternary the first gives a mythological birth of Shakespeare. What is said of that mighty genius is true; but it is not said happily: the real effects of this poetical power are put out of sight by the pomp of machinery. Where truth is sufficient to fill the mind, fiction is worse than useless; the counterfeit debases the genuine.

His account of Milton's blindness, if we suppose it caused by study in the formation of his poem, a supposition surely allowable, is poetically true, and happily imagined. But the 'car' of Dryden, with his 'two coursers,' has nothing in it peculiar; it is a car in which any other rider may be placed.

"The Bard" appears at the first view to be, as Algarotti and others have remarked, an imitation of the prophecy of Nereus. Algarotti thinks it superior to its original, and, if preference depends only on the imagery and animation of the two poems, his judgement is right. There is in **"The Bard"** more force, more thought, and more variety. But to copy is less than to invent, and the copy has been unhappily produced at a wrong time. The fiction of Horace was to the Romans credible; but its revival disgusts us with apparent and unconquerable falsehood. (pp. 433-38)

To select a singular event, and swell it to a giant's bulk by fabulous appendages of spectres and predictions, has little difficulty, for he that forsakes the probable may always find the marvellous. And it has little use: we are affected only as we believe; we are improved only as we find something to be imitated or declined. I do not see that **"The Bard"** promotes any truth, moral or political.

His stanzas are too long, especially his epodes; the ode is finished before the ear has learned its measures, and consequently before it can receive pleasure from their consonance and recurrence.

Of the first stanza the abrupt beginning has been celebrated; but technical beauties can give praise only to the inventor. It is in the power of any man to rush abruptly upon his subject, that has read the ballad of *Johnny Armstrong,*

     Is there ever a man in all Scotland—

The initial resemblances, or alliterations, 'ruin,' 'ruthless,' 'helm nor hauberk,' are below the grandeur of a poem that endeavours at sublimity.

In the second stanza the Bard is well described; but in the third we have the puerilities of obsolete mythology. When we are told that Cadwallo 'hush'd the stormy main,' and that Modred 'made huge Plinlimmon bow his cloud-top'd head,' attention recoils from the repetition of a tale that, even when it was first heard, was heard with scorn.

The 'weaving' of the 'winding sheet' he borrowed, as he owns, from the northern Bards; but their texture, however, was very properly the work of female powers, as the art of spinning the thread of life in another mythology. Theft is always dangerous; Gray has made weavers of his slaughtered bards by a fiction outrageous and incongruous. They are then called upon to 'Weave the warp, and weave the woof,' perhaps with no great propriety; for it is by crossing the woof with the warp that men weave the web or piece; and the first line was dearly bought by the admission of its wretched correspondent, 'Give ample room and verge enough.' He has, however, no other line as bad.

The third stanza of the second ternary is commended, I think, beyond its merit. The personification is indistinct. Thirst and Hunger are not alike, and their features, to make the imagery perfect, should have been discriminated. We are told, in the same stanza, how 'towers' are 'fed.' But I will no longer look for particular faults; yet let it be observed that the ode might have been concluded with an action of better example: but suicide is always to be had without expence of thought.

These odes are marked by glittering accumulations of ungraceful ornaments: they strike, rather than please; the images are magnified by affectation; the language is laboured into harshness. The mind of the writer seems to work with unnatural violence. 'Double, double, toil and trouble.' He has a kind of strutting dignity, and is tall by walking on tiptoe. His art and his struggle are too visible, and there is too little appearance of ease and nature.

To say that he has no beauties would be unjust: a man like him, of great learning and great industry, could not but produce something valuable. When he pleases least, it can only be said that a good design was ill directed.

His translations of Northern and Welsh Poetry deserve praise: the imagery is preserved, perhaps often improved; but the language is unlike the language of other poets.

In the character of his **"Elegy"** I rejoice to concur with the common reader; for by the common sense of readers uncorrupted with literary prejudices, after all the refinements of subtility and the dogmatism of learning, must be finally decided all claim to poetical honours. The **"Church-yard"** abounds with images which find a mirrour in every mind, and with sentiments to which every bosom returns an echo. The four stanzas beginning 'Yet even these bones' are to me original: I have never seen the notions in any other place; yet he that reads them here persuades himself that he has always felt them. Had Gray written often thus it had been vain to blame, and useless to praise him. (pp. 438-42)

     Samuel Johnson, "Gray," in his Lives of the English Poets, *Vol. III, edited by* George

Birkbeck Hill, *1905. Reprint by Octagon Books, Inc., 1967, pp. 421-43.*

J. Aikin   (essay date 1804)

[*The following excerpt is taken from a collection of letters Aikin wrote to a young woman named Mary. He details what he considered the virtuous elements of Gray's verse, namely the diversity of subject and manner, and the poet's talent for uniting description with moral reflection.*]

The *Odes* of Gray are pieces of great diversity both with respect to subject and manner. The **"Ode on Spring,"** and that **"On a distant Prospect of Eton College,"** unite description with moral reflection. In the first of these the imagery has little novelty, but is dressed in all the splendour and elegance of poetical diction. You will remark the happy choice of picturesque epithets in such instances as *"peopled* air," *"busy* murmur," *"honied* spring," . . . in which a whole train of ideas is excited in the mind by a single word. The second is new in its subject, and the picture it draws of the amusements and character of the puerile age is very interesting. Yet the concluding imagery of the friends of vice and misfortune, watching in ambush to seize the thoughtless victims on their entrance into life, presents one of the gloomiest views of human kind that the imagination ever formed.

The author's melancholy cast of thought appears with more dignity and moral instruction in his **"Hymn to Adversity,"** which, if not one of the most splendid, is perhaps the most finished of his compositions. The sombre colouring, relieved with the brighter touches of benevolence, admirably harmonizes with the subject.

I do not mean to make remarks on all Gray's smaller pieces; but his **"Fatal Sisters,"** from the Norse tongue, is worthy of observation, not only for the new vein of mythological imagery which it and the subsequent piece open, but on account of its measure. This consists of stanzas of four lines, each composed of seven syllables, long and short alternately. If its effect upon your ear resembles that upon mine, you will feel it to possess extraordinary spirit and animation, and to be singularly fitted for subjects of warmth and action.

The two Pindaric Odes of this writer are the productions which have principally contributed to his eminence among lyric poets. The term *pindaric,* originally derived from the name of the celebrated Greek poet, had been assumed by [Abraham] Cowley and others to denote compositions which were characterized by nothing but their irregularity. This character extended not only to their subjects, but to their versification, which consisted of verses of every length and modulation, forming unequal stanzas, without any return or repetition of the same measures. But this laxity was found not to be justified by classical example, which, in its correct models, provided regular returns of similarly constructed stanzas. On this plan Gray has framed the versification of his two odes; and upon examination you will find in each the mechanism of a ternary of stanzas trebly repeated in corresponding order. Whether much is gained by this artifice in point of harmony, you

will judge from your own perceptions: to me, I own, the return seems too distant to produce the intended effect; and in reading, I am unable to take in more than the melody of the current stanza. The measures, however, considered separately, are extremely melodious, and in general well adapted to the sense. Probably the English language does not afford examples of sweeter and richer modulation.

The Greek motto prefixed to the first of these odes, **"The Progress of Poesy,"** implies that it was addressed to the intelligent alone; and indeed a familiarity with ancient learning greater than falls to the lot of most readers. . . . [Even] critics have misunderstood it, and scholars have read it with indifference. The truth is, that no poem can be interesting without an express subject perspicuously treated; and that obscure allusions and shadowy images can make no strong and durable impression on the mind. The proper theme of this piece is lost in glittering allegory, and the illustrations are too scanty and too slightly touched to answer their purpose.

The **"Bard"** has gained more popularity, because it begins with presenting to the imagination a distinct historical picture of great force and sublimity, and such as might be transferred to canvas with striking effect. The figure of the prophetic poet on his rock, the "long array" of Edward winding down the side of Snowdon, the awe-struck and alarmed chieftains, are conceived in a truly grand style. The subsequent sketches from English history, though touched with the obscurity of prediction, yet present images sufficiently distinct, when aided by the previous knowledge of the reader. There is, however, too much of enigma in the lines hinting at the future race of English poets, nor does their introduction seem well suited to the awful situation of the speaker. A poet of more invention, too, would have avoided the sameness of alluding to Shakespeare and Milton at the close of both his odes. A greater fault appears to me the fiction of the *magical web,* borrowed from the Scandinavian superstition. It has no proper place in the costume of a Welsh bard; and (what is a greater incongruity) the weaving is only imaginary, since the Bard's fellow-labourers are spirits of the dead: it could not, therefore, upon any supposition, operate as a *cause* of the disastrous events which are depicted. Yet this notion is clearly implied by the lines

> Now, Brothers, bending o'er th' accursed loom
> Stamp we our vengeance deep, and ratify his
>   doom.

A poet has a right to assume any system of supernatural machinery he pleases, as if it were a real mode of operation, provided he be consistent in the use of it. But it was Gray's talent to gather from all parts of his multifarious reading, images, and even expressions, that struck him as poetical, which he inserted in his compositions, sometimes with happy effect, sometimes with little attention to propriety. Thus, in this poem, borrowing Milton's noble comparison of Satan's great standard to a "meteor streaming to the wind," he applies it to the "beard and hoary hair" of the bard; where it is altogether extravagant.

The work of this poet which readers of all classes have most concurred in admiring is his **"Elegy in a Country**

Church-Yard.'' No performance of the elegiac kind can compare with it either in splendour or in dignity. Not a line flows negligently: not an epithet is applied at random. Sensible objects are represented with every picturesque accompaniment, and sentiments are impressed with all the force of glowing and pointed diction. The general strain of thinking is such as meets the assent of every feeling and cultivated mind. It consists of those reflections upon human life which inspire a soothing melancholy, and peculiarly accord with that serious and elevated mood in which true poetry is most relished. There are, however, some obscure passages; and the connexion of the thoughts is not always manifest. It may also be questioned whether a good effect is produced by calling off the attention from the real fortunes and characters of the inhabitants of a village, to those of the imaginary poet with whose epitaph the piece concludes. There seems no reason why we should be introduced to him at all, unless curiosity were to be better gratified concerning him; and his address to himself, (''For thee, who mindful of th' unhonour'd dead,'') with the subsequent account of his own death, strangely confuses the reader's imagination. Notwithstanding these defects, however, this poem has merited that extraordinary popularity which has been testified by innumerable imitations, parodies, and translations into ancient and modern languages. Its success affords a remarkable proof of the power of poetry, which, by the charm of melodious verse and splendid diction, could raise so much admiration and interest from so slender a fund.

The fragments of great undertakings to be met with in Gray's works show that nature had not been bountiful to him in the faculties requisite for a poet of the first class, and that his vein, when not supplied from the stores of memory, was soon exhausted: for it would be too indulgent to suppose that he *could* have finished these designs in the spirit with which he commenced them. The finest of these, the **"Essay on the Alliance of Education and Government,"** is a noble specimen of heroic poetry; but it is evident that he had lavished away the most picturesque ideas belonging to his subject, and had run his fancy out of breath. (pp. 185-93)

> *J. Aikin, "Letter XIV," in his* Letters to a Young Lady on a Course of English Poetry, *1804. Reprint by Hopkins and Seymour, 1806, pp. 184-98.*

Matthew Arnold   (essay date 1880)

[*Arnold was one of the most important English critics of the nineteenth century. Although he was also a poet and, more significantly, a commentator on the social and moral life in England, Arnold was essentially and apologist for literary criticism. He argued that the major purpose of the critic was to inform and liberate the public at large, and to prepare the way—through the fostering of ideas and information—for his or her country's next creative epoch. Arnold's critical methodology called for the rejection of both the personal estimate and the historical estimate of art; the first assumes the value of something based on the subjective criteria; the second distorts the value of a creative work by overemphasizing its influ-*

ence on historical development. Instead he advocated—though often failed to achieve it in his own writing—the "real estimate" of the created object, which demands that the critic judge a work of art according to its own qualities, in and out of itself, apart from the influence of history and the limitations of the subjective experience. In the following excerpt from an essay originally published in 1880, Arnold addresses the issue of brevity of Gray's poetic canon, using as a refrain James Brown's statement that Gray "never spoke out."]

He never spoke out. In these four words is contained the whole history of Gray, both as a man and as a poet. The words fell naturally, and as it were by chance, from their writer's pen; but let us dwell upon them, and press into their meaning, for in following it we shall come to understand Gray.

He was in his fifty-fifth year when he died, and he lived in ease and leisure, yet a few pages hold all his poetry; *he never spoke out* in poetry. Still, the reputation which he has achieved by his few pages is extremely high. True, Johnson speaks of him with coldness and disparagement. Gray disliked Johnson, and refused to make his acquaintance; one might fancy that Johnson wrote with some irritation from this cause. But Johnson was not by nature fitted to do justice to Gray and to his poetry; this by itself is a sufficient explanation of the deficiencies of his criticism of Gray. We may add a further explanation of them which is supplied by Mr. Cole's papers. 'When Johnson was publishing his *Life of Gray,*' says Mr. Cole, 'I gave him several anecdotes, *but he was very anxious as soon as possible to get to the end of his labours.*' Johnson was not naturally in sympathy with Gray, whose life he had to write, and when he wrote it he was in a hurry besides. He did Gray injustice, but even Johnson's authority failed to make injustice, in this case, prevail. Lord Macaulay calls the *Life of Gray* the worst of Johnson's *Lives,* and it had found many censurers before Macaulay. Gray's poetical reputation grew and flourished in spite of it [see excerpt dated 1781]. (pp. 70-1)

The immense vogue of Pope and of his style of versification had at first prevented the frank reception of Gray by the readers of poetry. The **"Elegy"** pleased; it could not but please: but Gray's poetry, on the whole, astonished his contemporaries at first more than it pleased them; it was so unfamiliar, so unlike the sort of poetry in vogue. It made its way, however, after his death, with the public as well as with the few; and Gray's second biographer, Mitford, remarks that 'the works which were either neglected or ridiculed by their contemporaries have now raised Gray and Collins to the rank of our two greatest lyric poets.' Their reputation was established, at any rate, and stood extremely high, even if they were not popularly read. Johnson's disparagement of Gray was called 'petulant,' and severely blamed. Beattie, at the end of the eighteenth century, writing to Sir William Forbes, says: 'Of all the English poets of this age Mr. Gray is most admired, and I think with justice.' Cowper writes: 'I have been reading Gray's works, and think him the only poet since Shakespeare entitled to the character of sublime. Perhaps you will remember that I once had a different opinion of him. I was prejudiced.' Adam Smith says: 'Gray joins to the sublimity of Milton the elegance and harmony of Pope; and nothing is wanting to render him, perhaps, the first poet in the English language, but to have written a little more.' And, to come nearer to our own times, Sir James Mackintosh speaks of Gray thus: 'Of all English poets he was the most finished artist. He attained the highest degree of splendour of which poetical style seemed to be capable.'

In a poet of such magnitude, how shall we explain his scantiness of production? Shall we explain it by saying that to make of Gray a poet of this magnitude is absurd; that his genius and resources were small, and that his production, therefore, was small also, but that the popularity of a single piece, the **"Elegy,"**—a popularity due in great measure to the subject,—created for Gray a reputation to which he has really no right? He himself was not deceived by the favour shown to the **"Elegy."** 'Gray told me with a good deal of acrimony,' writes Dr. Gregory, 'that the **"Elegy"** owed its popularity entirely to the subject, and that the public would have received it as well if it had been written in prose.' This is too much to say; the **"Elegy"** is a beautiful poem, and in admiring it the public showed a true feeling for poetry. But it is true that the **"Elegy"** owed much of its success to its subject, and that it has received a too unmeasured and unbounded praise.

Gray himself, however, maintained that the **"Elegy"** was not his best work in poetry, and he was right. High as is the praise due to the **"Elegy"**, it is yet true that in other productions of Gray he exhibits poetical qualities even higher than those exhibited in the **"Elegy"**. He deserves, therefore, his extremely high reputation as a poet, although his critics and the public may not always have praised him with perfect judgment. We are brought back, then, to the question: How, in a poet so really considerable, are we to explain his scantiness of production? (pp. 71-4)

The reason, the indubitable reason as I cannot but think it, I have already given elsewhere. Gray, a born poet, fell upon an age of prose. He fell upon an age whose task was such as to call forth in general men's powers of understanding, wit and cleverness, rather than their deepest powers of mind and soul. As regards literary production, the task of the eighteenth century in England was not the poetic interpretation of the world, its task was to create a plain, clear, straight-forward, efficient prose. Poetry obeyed the bent of mind requisite for the due fulfilment of this task of the century. It was intellectual, argumentative, ingenious; not seeing things in their truth and beauty, not interpretative. Gray, with the qualities of mind and soul of a genuine poet, was isolated in his century. Maintaining and fortifying them by lofty studies, he yet could not fully educe and enjoy them; the want of a genial atmosphere, the failure of sympathy in his contemporaries, were too great. . . . Coming when he did, and endowed as he was, he was a man born out of date, a man whose full spiritual flowering was impossible. The same thing is to be said of his great contemporary, Butler, the author of the *Analogy*. In the sphere of religion, which touches that of poetry, Butler was impelled by the endowment of his nature to strive for a profound and adequate conception of religious

things, which was not pursued by his contemporaries, and which at that time, and in that atmosphere of mind, was not fully attainable. Hence, in Butler too, a dissatisfaction, a weariness, as in Gray; 'great labour and weariness, great disappointment, pain and even vexation of mind.' A sort of spiritual east wind was at that time blowing; neither Butler nor Gray could flower. They *never spoke out.* (pp. 91-4)

Gray's production was scanty, and scanty, as we have seen, it could not but be. Even what he produced is not always pure in diction, true in evolution. Still, with whatever drawbacks, he is alone, or almost alone (for Collins has something of the like merit) in his age. Gray said himself that 'the style he aimed at was extreme conciseness of expression, yet pure, perspicuous, and musical.' Compared, not with the work of the great masters of the golden ages of poetry, but with the poetry of his own contemporaries in general, Gray's may be said to have reached, in style, the excellence at which he aimed; while the evolution also of such a piece as his **"Progress of Poesy"** must be accounted not less noble and sound than its style. (pp. 98-9)

> *Matthew Arnold, "Thomas Gray," in his Essays in Criticism, second series, The Macmillan Company, 1924, pp. 69-99.*

Grace Harriet Macurdy   (essay date 1910)

[*In the following excerpt, originally a paper read before the fourth annual meeting of the Classical Association of the Atlantic States in New York City on April 23, 1910, Macurdy reappraises the influence of Gray's scholarship on his poetry.*]

The poet Gray was accounted by his friends the most learned man of his time. If omniscience was not his foible, it was acknowledged as his possession, with the exception of mathematics, his ignorance of which he deplored. One does not need profound learning in order to recognize him as the scholar-poet, and to one who has an acquaintance with the great works of ancient and modern literature, every line of Gray is reminiscent of some earlier poet. Yet with all this erudition he has written one thing which is perhaps the best known short single poem "In the world, written between Milton and Wordsworth". I here quote Edmund Gosse, Gray's latest biographer, who says again "The **'Elegy'** may be looked upon as the typical piece of English verse, our poem of poems". The "exquisite felicities", as Gosse loves to call them, of this poem and of the last part of the **"Ode on a Distant Prospect of Eton College"** have become in the interchange of daily speech as fully common property as the usual Shakespearean quotations. In this respect, as Gosse says, the poems have suffered from an excess of popularity.

Yet with all his learning and with all his recognition by the *vulgus profanum* of the unlettered, Gray has still not had Sappho's good fortune in becoming a poet beloved of poets. Gosse is far from right when he maintains that Swinburne is the only writer of authority since the death of Johnson who has ventured to depreciate Gray's poetry. Birkbeck Hill has assembled in his notes on Johnson's *Life of Gray* the adverse criticisms of many a fellow craftsman which support the harsh verdict of "The Great Bear" [Gray's name for Samuel Johnson] himself. Coleridge, for example, finds his poems "frigid and artificial". Carlyle calls them a "laborious mosaic through the hard, stiff lineaments of which little life or true grace could be expected to look". Hazlitt finds his Pindaric odes stately and pedantic, a kind of methodical borrowed frenzy. Wordsworth says that he "failed as a poet not because he took too much pains, but because his pains were of the wrong sort". "He wrote English verse", says Wordsworth, "as his brother Eton school-boys wrote Latin, filching a phrase now from one author and now from another. I do not profess to be a person of very various reading; nevertheless, if I were to pluck out of Gray's tail all the feathers which I know belong elsewhere, he would be left bare indeed".

Wordsworth's harsh description, it cannot be denied, sets forth the method which Gray consciously or unconsciously pursued. But his genius has made the results great and noble poetry. A remark of his in a letter to Horace Walpole is of great significance. He writes "I send you a bit of a thing for two reasons; first because it is one of your favorite's, Mr. M. Green; and next because I would do justice; the thought on which my second Ode turns is manifestly stole from thence. Not that I knew it at the time, but having seen this many years before, to be sure it imprinted itself on my memory and, forgetting the author, I took it for my own". (p. 58)

At the present time it is a very usual thing to say about Gray that he is Greek in his poetic art. Gosse finds that he is Simonidean in his gift of pure cold song and Palgrave writes that he is "reminded of Sophocles or Pindar by Gray's splendid odes". This judgment appears to me peculiarly inapt and a somewhat close study of the sources of Gray's poetic thought and phrasing confirms me in the belief that Gray is influenced by the Latin literature far more than by the Greek and that in his English verse as in his Latin his great masters are Vergil, Horace and Lucretius. His contemporary, William Collins, has the Greek feeling in his directness and sincerity. Comparing him with Gray Swinburne says "as a lyric poet Gray is unworthy to sit at the feet of Collins". But Collins with all his points of contact with Gray stands alone in the eighteenth century. Gray's qualities, whether you call them "exquisite felicities" with Gosse or "cumbrous splendors" and "rhetorical elaborations" with Johnson and Swinburne, are characteristic of that century and eminently Latin. . . . The great English sources of his style among his predecessors are Milton and Pope. It is sometimes difficult to decide whether he has got his classical phrases at first-hand or through the medium of their poetry.

Gosse finds that Gray first shows his Greek quality in the **"Ode to Adversity"**. "Perhaps the fragments of such lyrists as Simonides", Gosse writes, "gave Gray the hint of this pure and cold manner of writing. The shadowy personages of allegory throng around us and we are not certain that we distinguish them from one another". "These shadowy personages of allegory", however, are borrowed from Horace's "Ode to Fortune" or suggested by that Ode, and Gray's use of them is reminiscent of Horace and

Vergil rather than of the Greek lyric poets. Simonides has nothing like this. Gray's poem, also, owes its inception and some of its best lines to an English translation of a Graeco-Roman ode of the reign of Hadrian, written by a Cretan Greek, Mesomedes, who was music-master at the Roman court of Hadrian and Marcus Antoninus. This Greek ode was long attributed to Dionysius, but was vindicated for Mesomedes by Burette in the *Histoire de l'academie des inscriptions et belles lettres* (1729). Mesomedes, according to notices of him in Eusebius and Jerome, was a protegé of Hadrian and wrote a eulogy of Antinous. Antoninus raised a tomb to him, though according to Julius he had at one time in a fit of economy reduced his salary. Of his hymns three have come down with their musical notation, namely, "To the Muse," "To the Sun", "To Nemesis".

Although Gray in a prefatory note states that his **"Ode to Adversity"** was suggested by Dionysius's "Ode to Nemesis," his indebtedness to the translation has been, I believe, entirely overlooked. . . . (pp. 58-9)

This translation, which misses the meaning of the Greek in several places and overtranslates it in others, has in spite of the droning monotony of the meter a certain dignity of phrase. Neither the Greek hymn of Mesomedes nor the Reverend James Merrick's translation of it is in any sense great poetry. But we owe to them ultimately Wordsworth's great "Ode to Duty", which in the opinion of Swinburne and many others outranks the "Ode to Immortality".

Gray has transformed the verses

> Thou whose adamantine rein
> Curbs the arrogant and vain

into

> Bound in thine adamantine chain
> The proud are taught to taste of pain.

The next line

> And purple tyrants vainly groan

is adapted from Horace's "Ode to Fortune"

> purpurei metuunt tyranni.

From Horace he also gets the material for his fourth stanza

> Scared at thy frown terrific fly
> Self-pleasing Folly's idle brood,
> Wild Laughter, Noise, and thoughtless Joy,
> And leave us leisure to be good.
> Light they disperse and with them go
> The summer friend, the flatt'ring foe;
> By vain Prosperity received
> To her they vow their truth and are again believed.
>
> (p. 59)

The best stanza is the last and far outdoes Horace with his prayer for Caesar's preservation and his irrelevant pessimism:

> Thy form benign, oh goddess, wear,
> Thy milder influence impart,
> Thy philosophic train be there

> To soften, not to wound my heart.
> The generous spark extinct revive,
> Teach me to love and to forgive,
> Exact mine own defects to scan,
> What others are to feel, and know myself a man.

To this we owe those wonderful lines of the "Ode to Duty":

> Stern Lawgiver! but thou dost wear
> The Godhead's most benignant grace,
> Nor know we anything so fair
> As is the smile upon thy face.
> Flowers laugh before thee in their beds
> And fragrance in thy footing treads.
> Thou dost preserve the stars from wrong
> And the most ancient heavens
> Through thee are fresh and strong.

Since by Wordsworth's own confession this perfect ode of his is modelled on Gray's ode, we may well wonder at Wordsworth's gibe about the feathers that could be plucked from Gray, leaving him so bare. To pluck this perfect poem from Wordsworth because he has taken form, meter, and tone from Gray would be no more unfair than to condemn Gray, as Wordsworth has done, for filching, to use Wordsworth's odious word. If there is filching in the case of either poet, both are, as Swinburne called Milton, "celestial thieves" and repay to the world a thousandfold what they have taken from their brother-poets. Wordsworth in his Ode reaches a height of perfection that is as great as that of Sophocles or Aeschylus and greater for us because the poem is freed from mythology, with no alien Zeus or goddess Dike or Moira. . . . The ode of Mesomedes has reminiscences of Aeschylean thought and phrase, slight though it is. But Gray's **"Ode to Adversity"** is not Aeschylean in feeling; rather it is a sententious and allegorical poem in the Latin style of Horace, ennobled and raised above the moralizing of that cheerful worldling by the Vergilian sense of tears in human things, which is so marked in the work of Gray. (p. 60)

A study of the two Pindaric Odes also shows affiliation with Latin authors rather than Greek. True, in the **"Progress of Poetry"**, there is a fine translation of Pindar's first Pythian, but the lines that follow are full of reminiscences of the Latin poets Horace, Vergil, and Catullus. The **"Bard"**, though called a Pindaric Ode, has no parallel in Pindar, and Dr. Johnson, following Algarotti, attributed it to Horace 1.15, the prophecy of Nereus. The correctness of this was admitted by Gray, who writes: "The Review I have read and admire it, particularly the observation that the **'Bard'** is taken from *Pastor quum traheret,* and the advice to be more original". (p. 61)

[The] pursuit of the elements which go to make up the wonderful mosaic of Gray's style increases our wonder at his enormous learning, his mastery of the great literatures of his own times, as well as those of Greece and Rome, and at his high poetic gift which could fuse into a stately and beautiful whole what he had gathered from so many sources. Professor Woodberry has lately said of Gray that his work reminds him "most often of the minor craftsmanship of the Greek artisans who made of common clay for common use the images and funeral urns; such seems to

me", he says, "to be the material of the poems, but in form how perfect they are, both for grace and dignity". The figure seems to me not to fit the art of Gray, who worked not with humble material, but with the splendid phrases of his great predecessors. That with this method he avoids being ornate and overladen is a marvel due to the exquisite refinement of his poetic nature. "I love a little finery", Gray said on the occasion of finding the jonquils and jessamine-powdered wig of a certain Lord too fine even for him. But his own poetic splendors are not spoiled by the fineries of literature fashionable in his century. His *curiosa felicitas* of taste and phrase has saved him in that path of imitation of the world-great poets, where so many have failed. Professor Woodberry has lately called him a minor poet. That is not the rank to give the author of the **"Elegy",** whose "divine truisms" express for learned and unlearned alike the great and inevitable thought of life. It is not the rank for the poet of whom his severe critic the poet Swinburne has said "As an elegiac poet, Gray holds for all ages to come his unassailable and sovereign position". (pp. 61-2)

Grace Harriet Macurdy, "The Classical Element in Gray's Poetry," in The Classical Weekly, *Vol. IV, No. 8, December 3, 1910, pp. 58-62.*

Title page of the first edition of Gray's "Elegy," 1751.

The Times Literary Supplement   (essay date 1933)

[*In the following excerpt, the anonymous critic attempts to demystify Gray's "Elegy" by reevaluating its importance in a period of English poetry that was considered to be "sterile, dry, and deserted."*]

No poem has paid for its popularity so continuously and so highly as Gray's **"Elegy."** That popularity began when Horace Walpole, to whom the poem as a whole was first sent, showed it round to friends. Copies were taken, and one of these fell into the hands of the *Magazine of Magazines.* The news that it was about to appear there forced Gray to get Walpole to publish it for him, the quarto of Dodsley (February 15, 1751) beating the *Magazine of Magazines* by one day. Seven editions appeared before the close of 1752. Imitations, translations, parodies followed so plentifully that the literary historian might be driven to allowing the Elegy-à-la-Gray the prominence of a genre to itself. Everybody knows the **"Elegy,"** many know much of it by heart. It became the poem of schools and examinations, of teachers, preachers and moralists, politicians, Everyman. Its public history shows Gray to have become what in another connexion, adapting his words from Pope, he phrased as "a mere poet, a fetcher and carryer of singsong." People who think they know nothing of poetry beyond a speech or two from Shakespeare, know Gray's **"Elegy,"** that poem which one's mother transcribed as a schoolgirl in swelling copperplate and still preserves unchipped and awful in the only cabinet in her memory. Gray has become the safest, least startling of poets. The **"Elegy"** of all his poems has suffered most of all—that and the ending of the Eton College Ode. If one is to criticize it, the glass dome which covers it over must be broken deliberately.

The **"Elegy"** has been unfortunate in another way. It belongs to that period of English poetry, the mid-eighteenth century, which most people believe to be sterile, dry and deserted. This was the period of personifications and apostrophes, of "poetic diction," the period when the theory that the general was of more importance than the particular had led to emptiness of content. It is thought of as a period of brown Gothic ruins, one when external nature might have been a collection of dusty wool embroideries and "horrid" chasms for all the poets saw in it. There is truth in this view but not the whole of the truth. As far as the **"Elegy"** is concerned it is worth while granting the truth of this view in order to understand those places where Gray is of his time (and often admirably so) and, more importantly, those places where Gray is departing from the accepted standards of contemporary taste, "speaking out" for all Matthew Arnold's essay [see excerpt dated 1880].

A critic of the **"Elegy"** then, must break through the plate-glass remove which divides the **"Elegy"** from his touching it, and must then examine it without prejudice against its period. The **"Elegy"** belongs to that troop of graveyard poems which began with Thomas Parnell's "Night-Piece on Death." Dodsley put the **"Elegy"** beautifully in its place when he provided its title-page and headline with a band of ornament which showed spade, mattock, skull, hour-glass gleaming white on a ground of black ink—a common ornament of funeral verses and one suited to the Parnellian meditation. The **"Elegy"** henceforward became the recognized examplar for graveyard meditators. Moreover, the furniture of the **"Elegy"** is of its time. It has a tower, and the tower is ivy-mantled, which means that it is at least beginning to crumble. It has a swain—and a hoary-headed one at that. There are abstract nouns created into persons by the easy wand of a capital letter—Ambition, Honour, Grandeur, Flattery, Memory. Syntactically, the poem has marks of its time: one or two rhetorical questions ("Can storied urn . . . ?") and one apostrophe ("ye Proud"). There is stilted diction, or what after Keats and Shelley we feel to be stilted diction: "incense-breathing Morn," "fond breast," "children . . . lisp their sire's return." Some of the phrases, though not actually "diction"—that is, words derived from Milton and used without the fiery renewal brought off by the great poetic borrowers—some of the phrases read dustily: "pleasing anxious being," for instance, which though an admirable summary has for some reason dated.

Then the personification. When a poetic idea has had such popularity among a number of respectable poets and some good poets, it is advisable to attempt the task of justifying, condoning, or explaining it. Personification in the eighteenth century was part of the fashion for rococo. It was felt to be necessary to poetry. Cœlebs in Hannah More's book remarks that "In Mason's English Garden . . . Alcander's precepts would have been cold, had there been no personification." Undoubtedly, personification was used too much, and used too much by bad poets. But one must distinguish when personifiction is used well and when used badly. Speaking generally, personification is badly used when either the abstract noun remains stuck and inanimate after its coronation with the capital, or when, though it comes alive—that is, does something—it does something unworthy or not sufficiently important, either for itself or for the poem. Personification is well used when the animated abstract does something significant (verb) or is given a significant attribute (adjective). Collins's ode "The Passions," provides examples of every grade of good and bad personifications.

Before blaming Gray or any other poet for personifying, one must see first of all whether he was intending to personify or not. One has to remember that writers in the eighteenth century had not begun to restrict capitals to proper names as the nineteenth century learned to do. Capital letters in the eighteenth century were sprinkled over manuscripts and printed pages, and some fell on abstract nouns with no intention of animating them. In the lines

> If chance by lonely Contemplation led
> Some kindred Spirit shall enquire thy Fate,

"Contemplation" need not be considered as a person any more than "reason" would be in the common phrase "reason leads me to suppose." And in these lines

> The Threats of Pain and Ruin to despise,
> To scatter Plenty o'er a smiling Land,

There "Plenty" cannot possibly be a "heavenly Maid" or any other person. One must, therefore, restrict personifications to abstract nouns that do something which, without being persons, they could not do. Further, one must remember that all poets have personified to some extent.

When one turns to the **"Elegy"** to look for personifications that are personifications, one is struck by their unobtrusiveness. The **"Elegy"** has nothing so bold and merely melodramatic as Collins's

> . . . *Vengeance,* in the lurid Air,
> Lifts her red Arm, expos'd and bare.

One finds that the personifications in the **"Elegy"** are dramatic, that is, they serve a meaning which does not concern themselves. They are actors giving up their potential individuality in order to play their part in the life of somebody else. In the **"Hymn to Adversity"** one does not feel this. The personifications there are given epithets which claim the reader's examination. Only two of the ten certain or probable personifications in the **"Elegy"** are given the distracting momentary prominence of an epithet: "Chill Penury" and "Fair Science." The other eight control verbs, but those verbs do not point backwards, reflexively, to characteristic actions of their own. They point forward and away to the object affected by their action.

> . . . Melancholy mark'd him for her own.

That does not tell you anything characteristic about melancholy. It tells you how melancholy affected the young man whose epitaph you are reading. Indeed, it tells you how *being melancholy* affected him. And so with the others. Gray's personifications, in this poem at least, are so pure as to be virtually not personifications at all. It is surprising to find Gray using personification, in an age which was wild with it . . .

Then there is the mid-eighteenth-century vision of external nature, usually worded in accordance with the fashion for poetic diction. The purest taste can discover perhaps two instances of this in the **"Elegy"**: the molesting of the owl's "ancient solitary Reign" and the "incense-breathing Morn." The first of these is not very difficult to accept as poetry, but the image implied in "Reign" is rather too gilded and rococo. "Incense-breathing Morn" comes out of Milton. In Book IX. of *Paradise Lost* there is the phrase:

> . . . humid flowers, that breath'd
> Their morning incense.

In Milton the image is proper, the flowers are part of the "silent praise" that Eden and its "sacred light" is offering to the Creator. Pope, who borrowed the image before Gray, uses it for the same purpose as Milton. . . . Gray takes over the idea, though he does not take over the justification. Incense, to the Western mind at least, means a gloomy, hot, indoor smell, the last to be thought of in a morning that can be supposed to be giving a "breezy Call." Gray's line is as bad meaning as it is bad sound—with its donkey cacophony of "ee" and "aw":

> The breezy Call of incense-breathing Morn.

But those two instances apart, the **"Elegy"** is free from the conventional way of seeing and stating external nature.

When one has said all this, made all historical allowances,

what remains? One finds that one has scarcely touched the poem. Moreover, its virtues are overwhelmingly freed. Some of those virtues are doubly worth having when they can be seen as uncommon ones for their age, virtues running counter to accepted taste. There is the "nature poetry" to begin with. When this is examined as if it had never been read before, never learned by heart in a hot classroom on a June afternoon, it is remarkably true and fine, and comparable to the best painting of the English school. The poem, like **"Il Penseroso,"** begins with evening and ends with morning. The lines on evening (apart perhaps from the owl's reign) are as right as any other evening in English poetry. They are as right, for instance, as the "black vesper's pageants" which Antony interpreted to Eros, or as the more luminous and upland evening of Collins. Gray's lines have been echoed too much by bad poets for their meaning to be as new and clean now as in 1751. But the word "holds," now as then, means what it says:

> And all the Air a solemn Stillness holds.

It is part of the calm solidity which Gray always sensed at the right moments in external nature. And the lines following that one:

> Save where the Beetle wheels his droning Flight,
> Or drowsy Tinkleings lull the distant Folds,

these are all hearing in near and distant spaces, no sight—the wheeling of the beetle is the parabola of its drone rather than of its visible body. Sight is restricted to the glimmering landscape, with its tower and moon, everything else is heard rather than seen. When this is said in part analysis there remains the synthesized aura of the whole and that inexhaustibly solitary, sombre line, equating the external darkness with the darkness in the poet's mind:

> And leaves the World to Darkness & to me.

When one turns to the morning that closes the poem proper one finds a surprisingly contrasted beauty:

> Oft have we seen him at the Peep of Dawn
> Brushing with hasty Steps the Dews away
> To meet the Sun upon the upland Lawn

and so on. Nothing could be less of its period than this. There is nothing here that Wordsworth could have seen more purely. The morning of the first two stanzas of "The Leechgatherer" is more fully realized, but not more satisfying. In Gray the morning is part of a running piece of narrative. And yet everything is there among the monosyllables, and perhaps this swift concentration is the harder thing to bring off. The misted grey in the lee of the hill, the small splashings of wet stalks and leaves, and then the wide light on the upland lawn: these are things which the poets of the nineteenth century go all out for.

There were times when Gray's feeling for such things was too strong for his immediate sense of form. This passage, the old man's outdoor biography of the poet, was fuller in the earlier stages of writing. Gray must have been carried away, and carried away to some purpose. Two stanzas, extant in various forms, were dropped after consideration, and perhaps after heart-bleeding, they are so lovely in themselves.

Him have we seen the Green-wood Side along,
While o'er the Heath we hied, our Labours done,
Oft as the Woodlark piped her farewell Song
With whistfull Eyes pursue the setting Sun. . . .

There scatter'd oft the earliest of the ye Year
By Hands unseen are Showers of Vi'lets found
The Redbreast loves to build and warble there,
And little Footsteps lightly print the Ground.

The details here are exact and non-general. Without the exquisite and protracted evidence of the manuscript notes and drawings in his Linnæus, there is enough evidence in the poetry to make Gray historically memorable as a naturalist. He loved particulars. His liking for the exactly right word is one mark of this. There is the "nodding beech That wreathes its old fantastic Roots so high" (a departure from the general that Gray was brought to task for), there are "those rugged Elms," the "droning" flight of the beetle, the swallow's nest in a "straw-built" shed. The particulars are important.

Gray took particulars when he wanted them, but he knew that the general had equal virtues for other effects. The design of the **"Elegy"** is intentionally built on general lines. And rightly so, since it was planned to cover a large common tract of human experience and sentiment. Building on general lines does not necessarily mean that the lines do not enclose solid material. To succeed, a general poem must represent in lucid and spacious summary a tranquilized tract of human emotion, of human knowledge, of truth. The tract of knowledge and experience covered by the **"Elegy"** is as wide as that of any of Gray's four large poems, which is wide indeed. In the final paragraph of his fault-finding [*Life of Gray*] Dr. Johnson made large amends with a perfect appraisal of this quality in the **"Elegy."**

The absence of all ornament from the metrical scheme, the sureness of sound, the even pentameters are all due to this same need for the general. The pentameter is a metre which readily gapes if it is not being fed. Gray fills it serenely. The sense of music comes from Milton and centres round the vowels which must be various and full. The same vowel falling on two consecutive stresses, unless there is local reason, almost amounts to a cacophony. By these standards most of the lines of the **"Elegy"** could not have fallen more smoothly and finely. But by the same laws Gray left the **"Elegy"** less than perfect. The line about the incense-breathing morn has already been spoken of. And there is a larger defect. Among the thirty lines from 62 to 92 there are eighteen rime-words with the diphthong "i." Apart from this the poem covers a large and varied area of verbal music. The variety within the slow rhythms can be measured by comparing the slowest stanzas (*e.g.,* the first) with the most running (*e.g.,* the "Peep of Dawn" stanza).

With this in mind, one can note the flaws in the progression of the poem. As syntax the **"Elegy"** is not so successful as it is as music. Gray seems to have found progression of thought a supreme difficulty. A *précis* of the **"Elegy"** could be made but it would not be found shapely enough for prose. The ideas do not always grow out of each other, or, if they do that, are not always quite on the right scale.

The development is admirably firm and homogeneous up to line 76. Then it begins to weaken. Lines 94-98 do not even make grammar. The three manuscripts and the text as finally published . . . indicate Gray's troubles over this passage:

For thee, who mindful of th' unhonour'd Dead
Dost in these Lines their artless Tale relate,
If chance by lonely Contemplation led
Some kindred Spirit shall enquire thy Fate;
Haply some hoary-headed Swain may say . . .

"Chance" here must be understood as meaning "perchance." But the syntax is very faulty. "For thee" and "thy Fate" should read "Of thee" and "the Fate" in the strict and respectable interests of grammar. But these "emendations" would leave the passage in other ways clumsier than ever. The dulling popularity of the poem, if it has obscured its virtues, has also obscured faults such as these. The reader surrenders himself to the slow iambs and ceases to ask for the virtues of sound prose, which is a pity, of course. One need not accuse Gray of counting on his music to cover defects in his meaning. One must remember that he was averse from publishing. He had only spent eight years or so on the poem. Given another year, that stanza might have been stroked into perfection. (pp. 501-02)

> *"Gray's Elegy," in* The Times Literary Supplement, *No. 1643, July 27, 1933, pp. 501-02.*

Lord David Cecil   (essay date 1945)

[*Cecil, an English editor and academic, was the author of* Two Quiet Lives: Dorothy Osborne, Thomas Gray *(1945) and* Modern Verse in English, 1900-1950 *(1958). In the following excerpt, originally a lecture delivered on March 21, 1945, Cecil provides a psychoanalytical interpretation of Gray's works, concentrating on the elements of the poet's personality which caused his verse to lack "imaginative heat."*]

Appreciation of an author, if it is to be profitable, involves more than just making a list of his excellences, taking the reader on a personally-conducted tour, as it were, of his subject's works, stopping to point out outstanding beauties. The critic should interpret as well as exhibit, perceive the relation between particular works in such a way as to discover the general character of the personality that produced them, and to analyse the special compound of talent and temperament which gives his writing its individuality. With Gray, this is hard. For one thing, his work is so diverse that it is not easy to see it as the expression of a single personality. It is odd that this should be so; for he wrote very little. There are not more than a dozen or so of his memorable poems. But among this dozen we find light verse and serious verse, reflective and dramatic, a sonnet on the death of a friend, and an ode composed to celebrate the installation of a chancellor of Cambridge University. Further, Gray's poems are composed in a highly conventionalized form which obscures the direct revelation of their author's personality. His figure is separated from us by a veil of literary good manners which blurs its edges and subdues its colour.

All the same, personality and figure are there all right, if we train our eyes to look carefully. The good manners are Gray's special brand of good manners; whether he is being light or serious, personal or public, Gray shows himself as much an individual as Blake or Byron. What, then, is his individuality? As might be expected from the diversity of its expression, it is complex, combining unexpected elements. The first that strikes the critic is the academic. Gray is an outstanding example of the professional man of learning who happened by a chance gift of fortune to be also a poetic artist. No one has ever lived a more intensely academic life. (pp. 43-4)

[Gray was] a typical eighteenth-century scholar-artist with a peculiarly intense response to the imaginative appeal of the past and whose pervading temper was a sober melancholy. His memorable poems—for some are mere craftsman's exercises—are the characteristic expression of such a man. They divide themselves into two or three categories, in accordance with the different aspects of his complex nature. His three long odes are inspired by the historical and aesthetic strain in him. That on the **"Installation of the Duke of Grafton as Chancellor of Cambridge"** was, it is true, originally designed as an occasional piece. But in it Gray takes advantage of the occasion to show us in what particular way Cambridge did appeal to his own imagination. As might be expected, this is historical. . . . **"The Bard"** gives Gray's historical imagination greater scope. The last of the Druids prophesies to Edward I the misfortunes that are to overtake his line: in a sort of murky magnificence, names and events heavy with romantic and historic associations pass in pageant before us. **"The Progress of Poesy"** is less historical, more aesthetic. Though in the second part Gray traces the development of poetic art from Greece to Rome and from Rome to England, this historical motive is made subsidiary to an exposition of what the author considers to be the place of poetry in human life. Like Keats's "Ode on a Grecian Urn," the **"Progress of Poesy"** is a meditation about the fundamental significance of art. Not at all the same sort of meditation though. The difference between the Augustan and Romantic attitude to life could not appear more vividly than in the difference between these two poems. There is nothing mystical about Gray's view, no transcendental vision of art as an expression of ultimate spiritual reality, where Truth is the same as Beauty and Beauty the same as Truth. (pp. 49-50)

The second category of Gray's poems deals with his personal relation to life: his impressions of experience and the conclusions he drew from them. In one poem, indeed—the sonnet on the death of his friend West—he draws no conclusion: the poem is a simple sigh of lamentation. But, in all the other expressions of this phase of work sentiment leads to reflection and reflection to a moral. The Eton College Ode shows Gray surveying the scenes of his youth and observing the unthinking happiness of childhood through the eyes of a disillusioned maturity. With a sad irony he draws his conclusion:

> Where ignorance is bliss, 'tis folly to be wise.

The **"Ode on the Spring"** is inspired by the spectacle of a fine day in early spring, with the buds hastening to open and the insects busily humming. How like the activities of the world of men! says Gray, and hardly more ephemeral. But once more irony steps in—Who is he to condemn? It is true he has chosen to be spectator rather than actor: but he is no wiser than the actors and perhaps enjoys himself less. The unfinished **"Ode on Vicissitude"** points yet another moral. Though life is a chequer-work of good and ill, sad and happy, we ought not to repine: perhaps without the sadness we should enjoy the intervals of happiness less than we do. The Adversity Ode is sterner in tone. Adversity is a trial sent by God to school us to virtue, if we are strong enough to profit by it. Finally there is the **"Elegy."** Here the sight of the graveyard stirs the poet to meditate on the life of man in relation to its inevitable end. Death, he perceives, dwarfs human differences. There is not much to choose between the great and the humble, once they are in the grave. It may be that there never was; it may be that in the obscure graveyard lie persons who but for untoward circumstances would have been as famous as Milton and Hampden. The thought, however, does not sadden him; if circumstances prevented them achieving great fame, circumstances also saved them from committing great crimes. (pp. 50-1)

This group of poems is all concerned with the same thing, the relation of a sensitive contemplative spirit to the throng, mysterious, tragic, transient world into which he finds himself thrown. For all their formality of phrase, they are consistently and intensely personal.

There remains the brief and brilliant category of Gray's satirical and humorous verse—**"The Long Story," "The Ode on a Cat," "Hymn to Ignorance,"** and the **"Impromptu on Lord Holland's House."** Now and again in these poems, more particularly in **"The Long Story,"** Gray the historian shows his hand; while they all display his scholarly sense of finish. Mainly, however, they reveal Gray the man of the world—Gray the admirer of Pope and the friend of Walpole. In the best eighteenth-century manner he uses his taste and his learning to add wit and grace to the amenities of social life. But they are none the less characteristic for that. As much as pindaric or elegy they contribute essential features to our mental portrait of their author.

Gray's mode of expression is as typical of him as is his choice of themes. His style is pre-eminently an academic style, studied, traditional, highly finished. His standard of finish, indeed, was so high as sometimes to be frustrating. He could take years to complete a brief poem. During the process he sent round fragments to his friends for their advice. Like Mr. James Joyce, though not so publicly, Gray was given to issuing his work while 'in progress.' Sometimes it remained for ever in this unreposeful condition. He never managed to get the **"Ode on Vicissitude"** finished at all. His choice of forms, too, is a scholar's choice. Sedulously he goes to the best authors for models. He writes the Pindaric Ode—making a more careful attempt than his predecessors had, exactly to follow Pindar—the Horatian Ode, the classical sonnet, and the orthodox elegy, leading up to its final formal epitaph. His diction is a consciously poetic affair; an artificial diction, deliberately created to be an appropriate vehicle for lofty poetry.

'The language of the age,' he stated as an axiom, 'is never the language of poetry.' Certainly his own language was not that of his age—or of any other, for that matter. It is an elaborate compound of the language of those authors whom he most admired: Horace and Virgil, Pope and Dryden, above all, Milton. . . . Sometimes the influence of one of these poets predominates, sometimes of another, according to which Gray thinks is the best in the kind of verse he is attempting. He follows Pope in satire, Dryden in declamation, Milton in elegiac and picturesque passages. It was from Milton, incidentally, he learnt the evocative power of proper names:

> Cold is Cadwallo's tongue,
> That hush'd the stormy main:
> Brave Urien sleeps upon his craggy bed:
> Mountains, ye mourn in vain
> Modred, whose magic song
> Made huge Plinlimmon bow his cloud-top'd
>   head.

Nor does he just imitate other authors. He openly quotes them. The Pindaric Odes especially are whispering galleries, murmurous with echoes of dead poets' voices—Shakespeare's, Spenser's, Cowley's. Sometimes he will lift a whole passage; the image of Jove's eagle in the second stanza of **"The Progress of Poesy"** is transplanted from Pindar's First Pythian. Sometimes he will adapt a phrase: 'ruddy drops that warm my heart' in **"The Bard"** is a modification of the 'ruddy drops that visit my sad heart' in *Julius Caesar.* Once again, Gray curiously reminds us of a modern author. This device of imbedding other people's phrases in his verse anticipates Mr. T. S. Eliot. Gray's purpose, however, is very different. The quoted phrase is not there to point an ironical contrast as with Mr. Eliot; rather it is inserted to stir the reader's imagination by the literary associations which it evokes. Conscious, as Gray is, of poetry developing in historic process, he wishes to enhance the effect of his own lines by setting astir in the mind memories of those great poets of whom he feels himself the heir.

The trouble about such devices is that they limit the scope of the poem's appeal. Gray's pindarics, like Mr. Eliot's *Waste Land,* can be fully appreciated only by highly educated readers. Indeed, Gray's education was not altogether an advantage to him as a writer. At times his poetry is so clogged with learning as to be obscure. **"The Bard"** and **"The Progress of Poesy"** are crowded with allusions that need notes to explain them. While we are painstakingly looking at the notes, our emotional response to the poem grows chilly. (pp. 51-3)

It is another defect of Gray's academic method—and, it may be added, of his academic temperament—that it involved a certain lack of imaginative heat. Scholars are seldom fiery spirits: Gray's poems are, compared with those of Burns let us say, a touch tepid. (pp. 53-4)

Indeed Gray's head is stronger than his fancy or his passions. Always we are aware in his work of the conscious intellect, planning and pruning: seldom does his inspiration take wing to sweep him up into that empyrean where feeling and thought are one. The words clothe the idea beautifully and aptly and in a garment that could only have been devised by a person of the most refined taste and

the highest culture. But they clothe it, they do not embody it. For that absolute union of thought and word which is the mark of the very highest poetry of all, we look to Gray in vain. He had not that intensity of inspiration; and, anyway, education had developed his critical spirit too strongly for him to be able completely to let himself go. His poetry, in fact, illustrates perfectly the characteristic limitations of the academic spirit.

But it also reveals, in the highest degree, its characteristic merits. Always it is disciplined by his intellect and refined by his taste. The matter is rational; Gray never talks nonsense; each poem is logically designed, with a beginning, a middle, and an end. Every line and every phrase has its contribution to make to the general effect; so that the whole gives one that particular satisfaction that comes from seeing a problem completely resolved. Even the best lines . . . are better in their context than when they are lifted from it. Moreover, though Gray fails to achieve the highest triumphs of expression, he maintains a consistently high level of style—better than some greater men do. No doubt it is a style that takes getting used to: artificial styles always do. We must accustom ourselves to the tropes and the antitheses, the abstractions, classical allusions and grandiose periphrases which are his habitual mode of utterance. They are as much a part of it as the garlands and trophies which ornament a piece of baroque architecture; for Gray lived in the baroque period and shared its taste. A poem like **"The Progress of Poesy"** is like nothing so much as some big decorative painting of the period in which, posed gracefully on an amber-coloured cloud, allegorical figures representing the arts and the passions offer ceremonious homage to the goddesses of Poetry or Beauty. . . . (pp. 54-5)

And it is executed with a similar virtuosity. Gray attempts the most complex and difficult metres. His work is thickly embroidered with image and epigram. But the images and epigrams are appropriate. Every cadence is both musical in itself and an apt echo of the sense:

> Say, has he giv'n in vain the heav'nly Muse?
> Night, and all her sickly dews,
> Her Spectres wan, and Birds of boding cry,
> He gives to range the dreary sky:
> Till down the eastern cliffs afar
> Hyperion's march they spy, and glittering shafts
>   of war.

I am quoting from **"The Progress of Poesy"**: for it is in these Pindaric Odes that Gray's virtuosity appears most conspicuously. They are not, however, his most successful works. For in them he is dealing with subject-matter which does reveal his limitations. This is especially true of **"The Bard."** Here Gray tries to write dramatically; he addresses us in the person of a medieval druid about to commit suicide. Such a role does not suit him. Gray was excited by reading about druids; but he was not at all like a druid himself. Nor had he the kind of imagination convincingly to impersonate one. He tried very hard—'I felt myself the Bard,' he said—but, alas, the result of all his efforts was only a stagey, if stylish, example of eighteenth-century rhetoric, elaborately decked up with the ornaments of a Strawberry Hill Mock-Gothic. In **"The Progress of Poesy"** Gray wisely refrains from any attempt at impersonation and the result is far more successful. Indeed, in its way, the poem is a triumph. But a triumph of style rather than substance. The pleasure we get from the work is that given by watching a master-craftsman magnificently displaying his skill in an exercise on a given conventional theme.

No—Gray writes best when he does not try a lofty flight of imagination but, with his feet planted firmly on the earth, comments lightly or gravely on the world he himself knew. Here, once more, he is typical of his period. Eighteenth-century writers are, most of them, not so much concerned with the inward and spiritual as with the social and moral aspects of existence—less with man the solitary soul in relation to the ideal and the visionary, than with man the social animal in relation to the people and the age in which he finds himself. For all he lived a life of retirement, Gray is no exception to his contemporaries. The region of romance and art in which he liked to take refuge was to him a place of pleasant distraction, not the home of a deeper spiritual life, as it was for Blake, for instance. Even when in the **"Ode on the Spring"** he contrasts his own inactive existence with that of his fellows, his eye is on them; his interest is to see how his life relates to theirs. And the thoughts stirred in him by his contemplations here, as also in his Eton ode, are of the straightforward kind which they could understand. So might any thoughtful person feel on a spring day, or when revisiting their old school. What Johnson said of **"The Elegy in a Country Churchyard"** is equally true of Gray's other elegiac pieces. 'They abound with sentiments to which every bosom returns an echo.' Indeed Gray's relative lack of originality made him peculiarly able to speak for the common run of mankind. But he spoke for them in words they could not have found for themselves. Poetry, says Pope, should be 'what oft was thought but ne'er so well expressed.' This is not true of all poetry. But it is true of Gray's. The fact that he was an exquisite artist made it possible for him to express the commonplace with an eloquence and a nobility that turn it into immortal poetry. Moreover, his vision is deepened and enriched by his historic sense. His meditations in the churchyard acquire a monumental quality, because they seem to refer to it at any time during its immemorial history: his reflections on his Eton schooldays gain universality from the fact that he perceives his own sojourn there as only an episode in the School's life, and his personal emotions about it as the recurrent emotion of generations of Etonians.

These reflective poems, too, are more moving than the Pindaric Odes. No wonder: they were the product of the deepest emotional crisis of his life. The Pindarics were written in his tranquil middle age; these other poems, all except the **"Elegy,"** in the later months of 1742; and the **"Elegy,"** composed a few years later, is a final comment on the same phase of his experience. Two events produced this phase. Gray's prospects were very dark; poverty was forcing him back to take up life at Cambridge at a moment when he felt a strong reaction against it: and the pair of friends who were his chief source of happiness were during this time lost to him. He quarrelled with Walpole, and West died. Under the combined stress of these misfortunes his emotional agitation rose to a pitch which found vent

in an unprecedented outburst of poetic activity. Even when inspired by such an impulse, the result is not exactly passionate: but it is heartfelt. The sentiment it expresses has its birth in the very foundations of the poet's nature; it is distilled from the experience of a lifetime. Let me quote the sonnet on the death of West:

> In vain to me the smileing Mornings shine,
> And redning Phœbus lifts his golden Fire:
> The Birds in vain their amorous Descant joyn;
> Or chearful Fields resume their green Attire:
> These Ears, alas! for other Notes repine,
> A different Object do these Eyes require.
> My lonely Anguish melts no Heart, but mine;
> And in my Breast the imperfect Joys expire.
> Yet Morning smiles the busy Race to chear,
> And new-born Pleasure brings to happier Men:
> The Fields to all their wonted Tribute bear:
> To warm their little Loves the Birds complain:
> I fruitless mourn to him, that cannot hear,
> And weep the more because I weep in vain.

Is not this poignant? Once more, you will remark, its effect is intensified by what I can only call Gray's commonplaceness. It is interesting in this connexion to compare it with a more famous lamentation over the dead, with *Lycidas*. Poetically, of course, it is of a lower order. Gray had nothing like Milton's imaginative and verbal genius. All the same, and just because Gray was not so original a genius, his poem does something that Milton's does not. It expresses exactly what the average person does feel when someone he loves dies. (pp. 55-8)

Gray's formality acts as a filter of good-mannered reticence through which his private grief comes to us, purged of any taint of sentimentality or exhibitionism, and with a pathos that seems all the more genuine because it is unemphasized:

> I fruitless mourn to him, that cannot hear,
> And weep the more because I weep in vain.

In lines like these, as in the more famous **"Elegy,"** the two dominant strains in Gray serve each to strengthen the effect of the other. The fastidious artist and the eighteenth-century gentleman combine to produce something that is in its way both perfect and profound.

Equally perfect and from similar causes is Gray's lighter verse. . . . He is never pedantic, he jests with the elegant ease of a man of fashion. But the solid foundation of scholarly taste, which underlies everything he writes, gives his most frivolous improvisation distinction. Nor do those characteristics of his style which sometimes impede our appreciation of his other work trouble us here. In light verse it does not matter if we are aware of the intellectual process at work. It is right in comedy that the head should rule the heart and fancy. As for Gray's baroque conventionalities of phrase, these, when introduced, as it were, with a smile, enhance his wit by a delightful ironical stylishness:

> The hapless Nymph with wonder saw:
> A whisker first and then a claw,
> With many an ardent wish,
> She stretch'd in vain to reach the prize.
> What female heart can gold despise?
> What Cat's averse to fish?

'The Cat,' says Dr. Johnson caustically, 'is called a nymph, with some violence both to language and sense.' Perhaps she is. Nevertheless—and one can dare to say so aloud now Dr. Johnson is no longer with us—the effect is charming.

Gray has two masterpieces in this lighter vein; these lines on the Cat, and those on the artificial ruins put up by Lord Holland at Kingsgate. The [**"Ode on the Death of a favourite Cat, Drowned in a Tub of Gold Fishes"**] is the more exquisite, in its own brief way as enchanting a mixture of wit and prettiness as *The Rape of the Lock* itself. But the bitter brilliance of the other shows that, had he chosen, Gray could equally have rivalled Pope as a satirist in the grand manner. . . . (pp. 58-9)

Horace Walpole said that 'humour was Gray's natural and original turn, that he never wrote anything easily but things of Humour.' In view of these poems, it is hard to disagree with him. Nowhere else does Gray's virtuosity seem so effortless; nowhere else does he write with the same spontaneity and gusto. For once Gray seems to be sailing with the wind behind him the whole way. Of all his work, his light verse appears the most inspired.

How far this means that it is also the most precious is a different problem. A very big one too: it opens the whole question as to whether comic art can of its nature be equal in significance to grave art, whether the humorist's view of things is always, comparatively speaking, a superficial view. This takes us into deep waters; too deep to be fathomed in the brief close of a discourse like the present. But the issue is, I suggest, a more doubtful one than those earnest personages, the professional critics of literature, appear for the most part to think. (pp. 59-60)

> *Lord David Cecil, "The Poetry of Thomas Gray," in* Proceedings of the British Academy, *Vol. XXXI, 1945, pp. 43-60.*

D. S. Bland   (essay date 1948)

[*In the following excerpt, Bland refutes the commonly-held belief that Gray was the "harbinger of Romanticism," stating that there is nothing worthwhile in Gray's poetry other than Augustan-like "economy and unity."*]

Histories of English literature are now so much in the habit of telling us that Gray is 'a harbinger of Romanticism' that one may reasonably ask whether this opinion is not hardening into a critical convention through unquestioning repetition. This uneasy doubt is emphasized when the literary history view is put alongside a statement by Adam Smith (a contemporary of Gray who was a literary critic before he turned to political economy) that the poet 'joined to the sublimity of Milton the elegance and harmony of Pope'. Here is a complete divergence of opinion, at any rate, which invites investigation. Who is in a better position to judge: the contemporary, or the modern critic who has the whole perspective of the second half of the eighteenth century before him? The modern critic will maintain in his own defence that if the sublimity of Milton (the self-disciplined Milton of *Paradise Lost*, presumably,

not the sensuous and romantically inclined Milton of *Lycidas*) and the elegance and harmony of Pope are to be found in Gray's work, then it is difficult to account, for instance, for Goldsmith's protest against the 'blank verse and Pindaric Odes, choruses, anapaests and iambics, alliterative care and happy negligence', which he found in the poetry of the mid-eighteenth century, a protest which, if not specifically directed against Gray's own Pindaric Odes, is at least directed against what was a growing practice of the time (in which Gray played no negligible part), a practice which later critics have seen as a straw in the wind blowing in the direction of Romanticism. (p. 169)

The critic who attempts to reconcile or to account for the differences between the literary history view of Gray and the implications of Adam Smith's opinion is faced with the fact that Gray's diction and polish, the social assurance and dainty elegance of the [**"Ode on the Death of a Favourite Cat"**], proclaim him an Augustan, while his love of nature, his 'Leucocholy' and his egoism seem to point to affinities with the Romantics. But his egoism and his melancholy are matters of temperament rather than of poetry. The Romantic poet can claim no monopoly of the 'romantic' temperament. And the love of nature is evident not so much in Gray's poetry as in his letters. It is to these that critics, seeking to enrol Gray in the ranks of the Romantics, must turn to justify their case. Thus W. Macneile Dixon, in *An Apology for the Arts,* speaking of the enlargement of sensibility that occurred in the second half of the eighteenth century, and including **"The Progress of Poetry," "The Bard"** and **"The Descent of Odin"** in that movement, continues:

> But the effects of the revolution in taste were not confined to poetry, or even to literature in general. If we turn to Gray's Letters and Journals we shall find sentences breathing new and surprising sentiments.

But the temptation to use Gray's letters in this way must be resisted. With many poets, reference to their letters, journals, table-talk and so on often provides valuable corroborative evidence for an assessment of their poetry. But with Gray, more often than not, the evidence is all the other way. In assessing Gray's achievement as a poet, and in deciding whether that achievement can be hailed as the dawn of Romanticism, therefore, it is necessary to distinguish between the poet and the letter-writer. Extra-poetic evidence may legitimately be used to corroborate poetry, but it cannot be made to do duty for what a writer fails to express in his poetry itself. An example of illegitimate use of such evidence occurs in Lytton Strachey's *English Letter Writers,* chapter v. Strachey claims that in his love of nature Gray 'was one of the earliest precursors of the school of Wordsworth', and quotes the following passage from one of Gray's letters in support of his view:

> As I advanced, the crags seemed to close in, but discovered a narrow entrance turning to the left between them. I followed my guide a few paces, and lo, the hills opened again into no large space, and then all further way is barred by a stream, that at the height of above fifty feet gushes from a hole in the rock, and spreading in large sheets over its broken front, dashes down from steep to

steep and then rattles away in a torrent down the valley. The rock on the left rises perpendicular with stubbed yew trees and shrubs starting from its side to the height of at least three hundred feet; but those are not the things; it is that to the right under which you stand to see the fall that forms the principal horror of the place. From its very base it begins to slope forward over you in a black and solid mass, without any crevice in its surface, and overshadows half the area below with its dreadful canopy . . . The gloomy and uncomfortable day well suited the savage aspect of the place, and made it still more formidable.

It is true that the scene itself here described is one which might have acted on the imagination of Wordsworth. De Quincey, a self-confessed Wordsworthian, has left evidence in his *Recollections of the Lake Poets* that he *was* moved by a sight similar to this.

Amongst the fragments of rock which lie in the confusion of a ruin on each side of the road, one there is which exceeds the rest in height, and which, in shape, presents a very close resemblance to a church . . . This mimic church has a peculiarly fine effect in this wild situation, which leaves so far below the tumults of this world: the phantom church, by suggesting the phantom and evanescent image of a congregation, where never congregation met; of the pealing organ, where never sound was heard except the wild natural notes, or else of the wind rushing through the mighty gates of the everlasting rocks—in this way the fanciful image that accompanies the traveller on his road for half a mile or more, serves to bring out the antagonistic feeling of intense and awful solitude, which is the natural and presiding sentiment—the *religio loci*—that broods for ever over the romantic pass.

It is true, too, that the last sentence of the passage from Gray's letter seems to echo in anticipation the moving lines of *Kubla Khan:*

A savage place! as holy and enchanted
As e'er beneath a waning moon was haunted
By woman wailing for her demon lover!

But is the interest in nature displayed in Gray's letter that which, in fact, we associate with the Romantic school as a whole, a love of nature in and for herself, or even with the Wordsworthian view? For all its apparent resemblance, Gray's letter does not display the feelings which are displayed in De Quincey's description. His mimic church is in a *wild* situation, above *the tumults of the world.* Man is not normally present, nor is his presence required. Indeed, his absence is emphasized by the very suggestion of the *phantom* congregation and music, while the solitude arouses *antagonistic* feelings at the indifference to man which the scene displays. But in Gray's use of 'horror', 'dreadful' and 'uncomfortable' human feelings are far more intimately involved. Gray's feeling for nature, that is to say, accurate though his observation may be, is the 'picturesque' feeling which tends to look on nature as a decorative setting for man. Even the emphasis on the 'horror' of the scene provides little more than an emotional titillation, the general effect of which is pleasurable. Gray,

one feels, is gratified at the feelings which the scene arouses rather than genuinely awestruck; to come so far and to have the emotions so appropriately worked on is a matter for congratulation. . . . The cult of the picturesque acts on its devotees with the force of a convention, and Gray's feelings by the waterfall are those which the cult expects in the presence of 'the sublime'. If there is more than this in Gray's letter, it is that general attraction towards the 'romantic' elements of life which has never been far below the surface of English art even in its most 'classical' phases, a romanticism which is best seen in the graphic arts, and which is most obvious in literature, therefore, when it deals, as in this letter, with the visible appearances of the world.

Does all this mean, then, that Gray is not so much of a Romantic forerunner as he has sometimes been made out to be? Has the attention paid to him by critics looking for the genesis of the English Romantic movement been no more than misplaced enthusiasm for a poet who is, after all, an Augustan who can claim Milton and Pope as his begetters? Is Adam Smith's judgment a sound one?

Any answer to these questions must take into account Gray's small output as a poet, although the temptation to say that he has had more attention paid to him than his scanty achievement warrants must be resisted. Arnold (who used the evidence of Gray's letters correctly, that is, to point to the discrepancy between his temperament and his poetic achievement) appears to have been tempted in this way in the early pages of his essay on Gray. At least, he raises a doubt in the reader's mind whether Gray merits the high praise given him by his contemporaries. . . . Arnold returns, however, to the answer he has already adumbrated in the essay on *The Study of Poetry,* that the eighteenth century was a century of prose, when the poetry produced served the ends of prose. Gray's poetry, therefore, 'for want of a genial atmosphere', failed to express all that he had in him to express. 'He never spoke out'. Finally, Arnold pushes his argument to the view that though Gray himself never spoke out, his poetry *stands* out against the work of his contemporaries. 'He is alone, or almost alone (for Collins has something of the like merit) in his age' [see excerpt dated 1880]. (pp. 170-73)

That Gray's poetry, in spite of his small output, stands out against this contemporary mediocrity will not be disputed. But is the contrast one of degree, or one of kind? Gray's poetry, some critics have suggested, is both restricted in output and in contrast to that of his contemporaries because he stands at the turn of the tide which after him will flow strongly in the direction of Romanticism. But Gray himself is in slack water, 'lackeying the varying tide', and is therefore a poet of divided allegiance. This comes near the truth, but the real answer is that however temperamentally inclined Gray may be towards the new spirit, he cannot free himself from the pressure of his age with any degree of success. Not only must we distinguish between Gray the letter writer and Gray the poet (for the feeling we get from his prose descriptions of nature is not that we get from his poetry), but we must also distinguish between levels in his poetry. At his best he is an Augustan and when he does break with his age he fails as a poet.

Only an unregulated enthusiasm, however, could claim for even his best work the sublimity of Milton, though his learning approached in depth and diversity that of Milton. . . . But with all this intellectual equipment which Milton himself might have envied, Gray lacked the power and the assiduity to make it issue in his verse; and though he regarded Milton as one of his masters, he seems to have assimilated little of what Milton could teach the sympathetic apprentice. Now and again, a phrase like 'substantial night' (**"The Descent of Odin"**) or 'blasted with excess of light' (**"The Progress of Poesy"**) brings an echo of *Paradise Lost* or *Samson Agonistes.* (p. 74)

Gray, it is true, can manage the ode with something of the mastery of Milton (or of Dryden). Certainly he is better at it than Collins. The ode, as written by many English poets, runs the dangers of all free verse. Lacking the control of the regular stanza and sometimes of rhyme as well, it requires the stiffening of a well-ordered poetic logic, expressing itself in controlled variations of the rhythm, if it is not to be inchoate. This is the fate of many of the odes of Collins, who is often uncertain of what he means to say. Gray always knows what he wants to say and says it firmly. This in itself argues an Augustan clarity, but even so Gray is a long way from the mastery of Dryden and Pope, for a reason which, because it was consciously held, militated against the possibility of his writing any really great poetry. For Gray (and in this he is completely of the eighteenth century) regarded poetry as an accomplishment rather than as an art. Temple declared that Gray 'could not bear to be considered himself merely as a man of letters; and though without birth, or fortune, or station, his desire was to be looked upon as a private independent gentleman, who read for his amusement'. The words of his young friend Bonstetten, 'Gray was the ideal of a gentleman', suggest that he achieved this desire. He would have had little sympathy with 'the young of both sexes' for whom, as Wordsworth said, 'poetry is, like love, a passion', while the excess evident in Keats's 'I find I cannot exist without poetry' is quite foreign to Gray's nature. His attraction towards poetry is self-controlled; his impulse to create is measured. 'I will be candid and avow to you', he writes to Horace Walpole, 'that till fourscore and upward, whenever the humour takes me, I will write; because I like it, and because I like myself better when I do so'. This is a long way from Keats's "I had become all in a Tremble from not having written anything of late—the Sonnet overleaf did me some good. I slept the better last night for it'. The age of Gray was an age in which the practice of poetry was the mark of a man of culture. When this is so, poetry runs the risk of declining into a merely mechanical talent for verse making. (pp. 175-76)

Reason and judgment alone, though they may prevent a poet from falling into the temptation of excess, do not necessarily make for fecundity of ideas. And reason and judgment Gray undoubtedly possessed, along with an Augustan polish, but only on two occasions did they help him to write poems which, although they differ greatly in feeling and intention (but not so greatly in tone), must both be ranked very high. The **"Ode on the Death of a Favourite Cat"** is poetry for the same reason that the *Rape of the Lock* is poetry, in the vividness, lightness and economy

of its satire. As for the **"Elegy in a Country Churchyard"**, it is as certain of a continuing place in English poetry as any poem is, though its universal popularity is based more on its subject matter than on its poetic qualities, as Gray himself recognized. 'His "Churchyard Elegy" . . . he told me with a good deal of acrimony', wrote Dr. Gregory to Dr. Beattie, 'owed its popularity entirely to the subject, and that the public would have received it as well if it had been written in prose'. Poets are notoriously bad judges of their own work, of course, but Gray is undoubtedly right here. In popular appeal the **"Elegy"** is probably rivalled only by the *Rubaiyat,* and to read it for the first time is like reading a dictionary of familiar quotations.

(It may be noted in passing that the immediate popularity of the **"Elegy"** was not only due to the fact that its subject was commonplace, but also to the fact that the poem was, at the time of its composition, a *fashionable* one. The titles alone of several of the contemporary poems given above suggest that melancholy was a fashionable attitude of mind between 1730 and 1750. Their contents amply confirm the suggestion. But this strain of melancholy is not the Romantic *mal du siècle.* That is a personal emotion. The melancholy of Gray and his contemporaries is turned outward upon the lot of humanity in general. Gray contemplates the fate of the personages in the **"Elegy"** with-

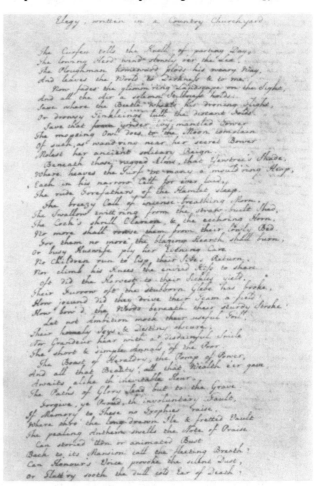

A section of Gray's handwritten manuscript of the "Elegy."

out feeling personally involved in it, and he is not so much interested in the subject for its own sake as for the treatment to which it lends itself. The impersonal tone to which this attitude leads is enhanced by the borrowing of many of the thoughts and expressions from previous writers, and by the rational construction, the even pace, the logical correctness of the poem. Gray's approach to poetry, then, as exemplified by the **"Elegy"**, is by way of the Augustan road of judgment rather than by that of the imagination.)

'The **"Churchyard"** ', said Dr. Johnson, 'abounds with images which find a mirror in every mind, and with sentiments to which every bosom returns an echo' [see excerpt dated 1781]. This is no fault, of course. The greatest poetic subjects, love, death, beauty and its evanescence, and so on, are the greatest commonplaces of life, and the meaning of the most moving poetry is often trite (the word is not used in a pejorative sense) when analysed into its prose equivalents. What the successful poet does is to rediscover the great commonplaces for himself and to modify them by living himself into them, and by elevating them from transcripts of reality into symbols. This is what Gray has done in the **"Elegy"**, and his symbols are presented with a sonority and a stateliness of rhythm that exactly suit his serious intention. The poem has all the assurance of the best Augustan verse in knowing exactly where it is going. (pp. 176-77)

It would seem, then, that although Gray's letters display an interest in nature, that interest is not quite that which we find in the Romantics themselves, and further, that Gray conceived it to be no part of his poetic purpose to embody that interest in his verse. And though his letters are written in the most charming language, he remained true in his poems to his own doctrine that 'the language of the age is never the language of poetry'. This alone sets Gray at the opposite pole from Wordsworth, who (however much he may have failed to put his theory into practice) started from the assumption that the language of poetry should be 'a selection of the language really used by men', and specifically mentions Gray as being 'at the head of those who, by their reasonings, have attempted to widen the space of separation betwixt Prose and Metrical composition, and was more than any other man curiously elaborate in the structure of his own poetic diction'. (p. 179)

Setting aside his interest in nature, then, as an interest which does not come over into his poetry in any preponderating degree, can it be said that the antiquarian interest displayed in Gray's Norse and Celtic poems is a link attaching him to the Romantics? It is true that this interest, in other writers, led, through the Gothic novel, to the work of Scott, but it is an interest which Gray and these other writers share with many of their contemporaries who have no claim to be called harbingers of Romanticism. Only in so far as this interest subserves the cult of the picturesque, and only in so far as that cult may be said to herald the coming of Romanticism, can it be said that Gray is a forerunner of that school of poetry. But the link is a frail one, and it might be argued that Pope constructing his grotto at Twickenham was doing as much in this respect as Gray in **"The Bard"** and **"The Descent of Odin"**. If we *must* look for a progenitor of the Romantic

movement among the poets of the mid-eighteenth century, then Collins (whom Gray, significantly enough, failed to appreciate) has a greater claim on our attention than Gray, not only because he was writing an *Ode on the Popular Superstitions of the Highlands of Scotland,* with its significant sub-title, 'considered as the subject of poetry', at the same time as Gray was composing the **"Elegy"**, but because of his subsequent influence, not solely on the greatest among the Romantic poets, but on those who more nearly represent the average literary taste of the time, such as Leigh Hunt, whose first volume of *Juvenilia* and many subsequent verses are strongly reminiscent of Collins.

To conclude. There is little that is either remarkable or new in Gray's poetry. There is little that is remarkable except its comparative excellence in an age of mediocrity, and that excellence is Augustan in its proportion, economy and unity. Where these things are lacking, as they are in **"The Progress of Poesy"** (though even here *the attitude towards poetry* which Gray displays is Augustan) their absence cannot be excused on the grounds that they have given place to other excellencies of a new age of poetry. There is little that is new, since Gray succeeds in that part of his work where he is writing not in the new Romantic way but in the old Augustan way against which the Romantics revolted. Where Gray himself is in revolt against the tradition of his age (though revolt is perhaps too strong a word to apply to him) his poetry suffers from the uncertainty of his position. If Milton feared that he would fail as an epic poet through being born in 'an age too late', Gray fails as a would-be Romantic through being born in an age too soon. (pp. 179-80)

> *D. S. Bland, "Gray and the Spirit of Romanticism," in* The Cambridge Journal, *Vol. II, No. 3, December, 1948, pp. 169-80.*

Robert Pattison   (essay date 1978)

[*In the following excerpt, Pattison discusses how Gray's philosophy of rationalism is apparent in "Ode on a Distant Prospect of Eton College."*]

[The Augustan] age sought to make wit and judgment a single phenomenon and strove to eliminate the troubling distinction between words and things, so that one would replicate the other, [and so] in their imagery the Augustans tried to combine the mythic and the matter-of-fact. . . . This dualism works on the same principle as the heroic couplet: the two halves are painfully distinct, but taken together, give a third sense which, without infringing on either of its parts, almost seems like a third member subliminally inserted in the couplet form. Children lent themselves handsomely to this type of image-making; their matter-of-factness had been, from antiquity, established through indifference, yet Christian dogma gave to them mythic overtones of Eden, of the Fall, of man's free will and salvation. Gray's **"Ode on a Distant Prospect of Eton College"** (1742) demonstrates the way in which the Augustans developed the actual and the mythic aspects of the child in a single image, which, in form if not substance, was bequeathed to the romantics, the Victorians, and our own era.

In Marvell's poems on youth the poet sets himself at a remove from the child which gives his wit and perception a freedom not to be found in the meditational poets, while at the same time emphasizing the distance between the fallen artist and his paradisical subject. In Gray this distance is raised to the level of a conceit. "Distant" is not only the key word of the title, but an idea carefully nourished throughout the first stanza and the poem as a whole:

> Ye distant spires, ye antique towers
> That crown the watry glade,
> Where grateful Science still adores
> Her HENRY'S holy Shade;
> And ye, that from the stately brow
> Of WINDSOR'S heights th' expanse below
> Of grove, of lawn, of mead survey,
> Whose turf, whose shade, whose flowers among
> Wanders the hoary Thames along
> His silver-winding way.

There are numerous distances here—the physical distance of the poet from what he observes (which is a theme of the **"Elegy"** as well), the historical distance of present from past, the distance of court and convention from natural simplicity (reflected even in the capitalization), and behind the rest, the distance of the writer from himself, which is the distance between childhood and maturity, between Eton and the prospect overlooking it, and between Eden and our world.

The poem revolves around this sense of distance, using the child figure as its focal point:

> Ah happy hills, ah pleasing shade,
> Ah fields belov'd in vain,
> Where once my careless childhood stray'd,
> A stranger yet to pain!
> I feel the gales, that from ye blow,
> A momentary bliss bestow,
> As waving fresh their gladsome wing,
> My weary soul they seem to soothe,
> And, redolent of joy and youth,
> To breathe a second spring.

Gray is in many ways the poetic disciple of Locke. . . . and part of the sense of distance in the "Ode" can be traced to an empirical impulse to achieve understanding through what Locke called the "art and pains" of a distant perspective: "The understanding, like the eye, whilst it makes us see and perceive all other things, takes no notice of itself; and it requires art and pains to set it at a distance and make it its own object."

In Gray, however, the "art and pains" are not seen simply in the context of attaining a higher wisdom. They become the melancholy torment which is the penalty paid by man for civilization. In the "Ode," the understanding makes the adult conscious that he is civilized, and to be civilized is to be doomed. . . . Throughout the [**"Ode on a Distant Prospect of Eton College"**] adulthood is used as a metaphor of the "baleful," fallen condition of civilization; it is a doomed state. Childhood, on the other hand, becomes a vehicle for investigating the original condition of society and ascertaining the fundamentals of man's role within

civilization. The young Etonians, traditionally the future pillars of English society and civilization, make the image of childhood in the "Ode" even more pointedly about the relationship between "doom," civilized life, and the original state which necessitates them both.

Gray uses the child figure to express his belief that the rational state of adulthood is not only the highest evolution of the human species, as Locke would have it, but a condition in which man must be painfully conscious of his fallen nature. In this sense, children are "little victims"; their understanding is still undeveloped, and hence, like Aristotle's children, they cannot fully participate in the benefits of civilization. But at the same time, Gray's children are spared the terrifying consciousness of the world's doomed state and their own. The child is caught in a paradox: to be a man, he must accept this painful knowledge, while to try to remain a child is to fail to meet one's human potential. Some of Gray's Etonians, "bold adventurers," are aware of living inside this paradox, and for them it produces "a fearful joy" as they live out their childhood:

> While some on earnest business bent
> Their murm'ring labours ply
> 'Gainst graver hours, that bring constraint
> To sweeten liberty:
> Some bold adventurers disdain
> The limits of their little reign,
> And unknown regions dare descry:
> Still as they run they look behind,
> They hear a voice in every wind,
> And snatch a fearful joy.

The first four lines of the stanza give us the picture of youth aiming at adulthood, "graver hours" whose liberty is constraint filled with "earnest business" and "labours." Then three lines give us the "bold adventurers," who are conscious of an "unknown region." The final three lines give us the conflict inevitable when the first two ideas are brought together, finely expressed in the oxymoron, "a fearful joy."

If anyone doubts that Gray's emotions are all ranged on the side of childhood as he has pictured it, the next stanza eliminates the doubt:

> Gay hope is theirs by fancy fed,
> Less pleasing when possest;
> The tear forgot as soon as shed,
> The sunshine of the breast:
> Theirs buxom health of rosy hue,
> Wild wit, invention ever-new,
> And lively chear of vigour born;
> The thoughtless day, the easy night,
> The spirits pure, the slumbers light,
> That fly th' approach of morn.

Throughout the "Ode," Gray is suspended between an exuberant romanticism (this last stanza, by itself, might have come directly from Wordsworth) and a careful, melancholy empiricism derived from Locke.

With Locke, Gray rejects Inate Ideas. The Etonians are "thoughtless"; their minds are *tabulae rasae* awaiting the imprint of understanding, which the poet at his remove already possesses. But in neither Gray nor Locke does the rejection of Innate Ideas imply a rejection of all things innate, which in effect would have been to reject the concept of Original Sin on which so much Christian—and especially Protestant—dogma rests. In the *Essay* Locke says: "Nature, I confess, has put into man a desire of happiness and an aversion to misery: these indeed are innate practical principles which (as practical principles ought) *do* continue constantly to operate and influence all our actions without ceasing: these may be observed in all persons and all ages, steady and universal; but these are *inclinations of the appetite* to good, not impressions of truth on the understanding. I deny not that there are natural tendencies imprinted on the minds of men." But where Locke regarded these "inclinations of the appetite" as an animal function unworthy of detailed discussion and placed understanding in the forefront of his philosophy as that which "sets man above the rest of sensible beings, and gives him all the advantages and dominion which he has over them," Gray found both beauty and importance in thoughtless appetite. The "gay hope," "the tear forgot as soon as shed," the "buxom health of rosy hue"—these are for Gray pleasures which are an end in themselves and which represent an important counterbalance to "the Ministers of human fate" attendant on adulthood. Further, for Gray the appetite not only predates the understanding but also overwhelms it. The last stanza of the "Ode" sets out something very much like the romantic idea of natural joy, but is unable to find any transcendence in the concept:

> To each his suff 'rings: all are men,
> Condemn'd alike to groan,
> The tender for another's pain;
> Th' unfeeling for his own.
> Yet ah! why should they know their fate?
> Since sorrow never comes too late,
> And happiness too swiftly flies.
> Thought would destroy their paradise.
> No more; where ignorance is bliss,
> 'Tis folly to be wise.

The Augustan sense of life's folly pervades these lines, but the Augustans looked to Locke and understanding to save them as another age had looked to grace. Gray had no part of this: "Thought would destroy their paradise"; "ignorance is bliss." And yet he was still no romantic. What separates Gray from the romantics and gives his poetry its particular poignancy is his feeling that adulthood is an inevitable though unwelcome condition and that nature is a painful place in which men are not only outcasts from Paradise but possess no means of transcendence within fallen nature. Childhood is for Gray a medium through which the poet can look to gain perspective on man's fallen place in a fallen world and gauge the extent of the corruption in which he is involved. Moreover, this corruption comes with the development of that faculty which Locke had considered as the means of rational happiness, the understanding.

Gray himself prefixed the "Ode" with a particularly melancholy line from Menander which highlights his attitude in the poem: . . . "I am a man; sufficient reason to be miserable." But Menander spoke of being *human,* whereas Gray uses the line to mean, "I am an *adult;* sufficient reason to be miserable." By contrast, the child figure in Gray represents the human happiness possible before the under-

standing develops, bringing with it the unhappy organization of humanity into civilization. . . . (pp. 30-7)

> *Robert Pattison, "The Preromantic English Tradition," in his* The Child Figure in English Literature, *The University of Georgia Press, 1978, pp. 21-46.*

Wallace Jackson   (essay date 1986)

[*An American critic and professor of English, Jackson is noted for his contributions to the scholarship of Alexander Pope and John Dryden. In his work, Jackson attempts an intertextual methodology, a tactic not commonly practiced in eighteenth-century studies where biographical and historical modes dominate. In the following excerpt, Jackson refutes the common critical assessment that Gray was a poet whose verse was dominated by two antithetical voices, stating that Gray's dualism can be resolved through a variety of critical strategies.*]

What may we learn from what has been written about Thomas Gray's poetry and how may we escape from the perspective it has imposed upon us? On the face of it even the most influential and insightful criticism seems strangely repetitive, as though bound to a model that forces antithesis, variations on a theme. Gray was unhappily separated from his age or from the deeper sources of his power; his voice was divided against itself and he lost the essential imaginative integrity of his own being. From the publication in 1757 of the notorious Pindarics, **"The Progress of Poesy"** and **"The Bard,"** criticism has spoken its uneasiness. Here was a man who was to be the first poet of the age, yet who dwindled into fastidious protest against publication and into infrequent creativity. The initial charge has always remained foremost. Why did the poet who wrote the **"Elegy"** write two such unaffecting and coldly remote works as those? What, then, had happened to the man who imagined the **"Elegy,"** that poem abounding "with sentiments to which every bosom returns an echo"? Insofar as Johnson's brief, even perfunctory, life of Gray takes up the issue of his poetry, it does so in terms of explicit opposition. The **"Elegy,"** in a brief and well-remembered concluding paragraph, is established as the delight of the "common reader," even as the Pindarics are antithetically rejected as his despair. W. P. Jones's modern survey of the contemporary reception of the odes confirms the judgment: they were "unintelligible, or at least unacceptable, to the average reader." (p. 361)

Gray is either or seems to be oddly flawed, divided against himself; such a view requires then confirmation or correction. If division is present in the poetry, it is so as a symptom of his relation to an uncongenial age, or the result of his own unfulfilled sexuality, and is manifested in a language dominated by two antithetical voices, which may be resolved into some sort of unity through various critical strategies. Even should it turn out to be the case that Gray was obsessed with conflicts ("life's incessant and intolerable presentation of opposites") not "capable of poetic resolution," it yet remains true that in many of his poems "form and content are triumphantly interfused, the subject is frequently the universal plight of mankind, the statement peculiarly personal." This accolade accompanies a marriage, a restoration of equilibrium with which the scene closes upon Thomas Gray, now the conquerer of his own dualisms and at peace with himself. (pp. 363-64)

Yet who and where are the redemptive voices and will they speak to me? In the **"Ode on Vicissitude,"** "Yesterday . . . Mute was the music of the air." Today ("Now the golden Morn aloft . . . wooes the tardy spring, / Till April starts, and calls around"), voice is the invoked "presence" in the ode. Awakened it compels other voices ("The birds his [April's] presence greet: / But chief the sky-lark warbles high / His trembling thrilling ecstacy"). To invoke voice is also to invoke the memory of its absence ("Mute"), as well as its capacity to accuse, indict, and speak the unspecified guilt, as in the **"Ode to Adversity"** ("With thundering voice and threatening mien"). From the beginning, in Gray's canon, there is a special alertness to what is voiced. The implied ironic deflationary speakers at the close of the **"Ode on the Spring"** impugn the youth who repudiates pleasure: "Methinks I hear in accents low / The sportive kind reply: / Poor moralist! and what are thou? / A solitary fly!" Antithetical voice is almost always a creation of (a projection of, and thereby an ambivalence within) primary voice. In the **"Elegy,"** "some hoary-headed swain may say." In **"A Long Story"** an unidentified voice impatiently interrupts the narrative ("Your history wither are you spinning? / Can you do nothing but describe?"). Subsequently the poet in the poem speaks his own apologia and is forgiven his propensity to scribble by the Viscountess who invites him to dinner. **"A Long Story"** is an intentional fragment; the mock self-justificatory mode determining its progress is obviously affiliated with other less playful modes of apology. Far more solemnly, for example, the **"Elegy"** offers its own excuse for the poet ("Large was his bounty and his soul sincere"), as does of course **"The Progress of Poesy,"** locating Gray himself as the end and goal of Poesy's enforced pilgrimage. In the **"Descent of Odin"** the hero makes his way to the underworld, awakening the "prophetic maid," and requiring that she foretell the future, the death of Hoder by Odin's son. Odin conjures the maid with "runic rhyme," the "thrilling verse that wakes the dead." The journey to voice in the **"Descent"** is only a variation of the related journey in the **"Elegy,"** for the churchyard is yet a place of speaking ("Ev'n from the tomb the voice of Nature cries"), but equally a place where the power of voice is mocked and denied: "Can Honour's voice provoke the silent dust, / Or Flattery soothe the dull cold ear of Death?" Yet to what purpose is speaking if voice is betrayed by time? The question catches up the vocal chorus of Gray's many voices and underscores the entire quest that comprises the paratactically narrated myth of journey within the canon. There is always the tendency to dismiss transmitted (voiced) knowledge ("Ah tell them they are men!") in the melancholic pessimist, concluding the Eton ode: "Yet ah! why should they know their fate?" The power to become self-creative, to find the way back to originary voice, is rejected in the inevitable enactments or remembrances of suffering, the "groan" that at the close of the Eton ode displaces voice or substitutes for it. Or there is the most famous occasion where voicelessness is justified as another example of the law, Nature's edict, the result

of which is the diminished and paradoxical thing, "Some mute inglorious Milton." Every common reader intuits the churchyard as the center of Gray's imagination, the place where he pauses in the midst of passage to insist that the vast negative absolute of death renders voice impotent:

> The breezy call of incense-breathing morn,
> The swallow's twittering from the straw-built
>   shed,
> The cock's shrill clarion or the echoing horn,
> No more shall ruse them from their lowly bed.

All the authority that elegy enables him to summon is marshalled against the power of voice, as though the vanity of voice and the deep humanity of it are barely audible antagonists among the tombs.

Understood in this way, the **"Elegy"** is an extended meditation on what voice can or cannot accomplish. The legacy passed from generation to generation, from poet to "kindred spirit," is the commemorative word itself, and the self is contextualized ("Their name, their years, spelt by the unlettered muse") within other texts ("And many a holy text around she strews, / That teach the rustic moralist to die"). The **"Elegy"** is surely Gray's most subversive poem, restricting and limiting the power of voice while universalizing the need to speak. All the dead are predecessor voices. The poet's way is, literally and figuratively, toward those forebears, precursors who had voices, even if not those of Pindar or Shakespeare, Dryden or Milton. The kindred spirit is there to receive the legacy of voice, to make of it what he will or can, for the inheritance is the common fate of those who are and are not poets.

"He spoke," begins the penultimate line of **"The Bard."** The entire poem has been a prophetic speaking, the authoritative summoning for Edward of futurity, and the Bard's voice is confirmed as oracular utterance. Such speaking affirms both the truth and cost of voice. What curious kindredness haunts the relation between the poet of the **"Elegy"** and the seer of **"The Bard"**? Each poem leads to the death of voice, as though its exercise compels its cessation. The **"Elegy"** chronicles village legend, "village Hampdens," "guiltless Cromwells." **"The Bard"** writes unborn history. Taken together, the speaking in each poem seems to comprehend opposed modes of human activity, as though the **"Elegy"** is an alternative text to **"The Bard,"** and **"The Bard"** a soliloquy within the high heroic pageant of historical drama. Is this the way Gray would make his epic, constitute the polarities of his vision by antithetical addresses which define the range and scope of his poetic speaking? His own version of knowledge enormous becomes, then, a received and cumulative wisdom derived from various distant envisionings, the recovery in the **"Elegy"** of precedent lives, the revelation in **"The Bard"** of futurity.

Yet there runs through all of this the self-conscious mockery implicit in the plaint of the drowning Selima [in **"Ode on the Death of a Favourite Cat"**]: "Eight times emerging from the flood / She mewed to every watery god, / Some speedy aid to send." It may be just one more case of voice unheard, prayer unanswered. Are Selima's mewings a parody of poetic invocation, a self-deflationary response to the particular poetic act that characterizes the poet Gray?

On the other hand, the recovery of voice is widely recognized as the special archaeology of poets in the middle and later years of the Eighteenth Century. It is the one certain and shared enterprise, of which Chattertonian and Macphersonian ventriloquism is merely one phrase, oracularity (as in **"The Bard"**) another. Blake's Piper and Bard, the various dissonantal voices of *Innocence* and *Experience,* define—not to say satirize—the problematics of voice itself. What Blake brings to the subject is pluralistic and dialogical. Voice is composed in opposition to other voices, reconstituted in the interplay between contrasting voices. The relation becomes choral and choric, itself a commentary on, or critique of, the adequacy of voice. Gray's disillusioned speaker of the [**"Ode on a Distant Prospect of Eton College"**] is thus in retrospect a voice of Experience; the rationalizing philosopher of mutability in the **"Ode on Vicissitude"** another such spokesman for restraint and limitation, the optimism of a mechanical view of temporality. Blake's *Songs,* so regarded, are satires of authoritative voice, the numen or nominated power that presides over the multiple voices that make up the *Songs of Innocence and of Experience.* The daemonology of mid-eighteenth-century verse modulates between the invocation of the poetical character and, say, the hobgoblin spookiness of Collins's ode on highland superstitions. In Gray the range is from Selima's desperate and forlorn speaking, to inattentive feline gods, to the spectral Medusan presence of Adversity, the strong figure and voice of harsh universal law.

The range includes the journey to graveyard voices, the distant way taken to precursor poets, even the attentive listening to Margaret, Countess of Richmond and Derby, mother of Henry VII, as she leans, like a Blakean Piper "From her golden cloud" and speaks her welcome to the Duke of Grafton, newly installed as Chancellor of Cambridge and the occasion for Gray's late **"Ode for Music."** Such summoning and listening may have a relation to the *tradition.* There must be a difference between widely assimilated poetic influence, as in Pope's poetry, wherein voice is allusively deployed, and the petitioning of voice that so amply fills Gray's pages. More so than Pope, Gray reflects the poet's uncertain claim to voice; his own poetry is vocal to a few or, in its alternative churchyard mode, voice is a " 'Muttering [of] wayward fancies,' " an incoherence presumably vocal to none.

"A Long Story" reproduces a similar poetic mumble ("Yet something he was heard to mutter, / How in the park beneath an old-tree / . . . 'He once or twice had penned a sonnet' ") and loses "500 stanzas" after the Viscountess condescends to " 'Speak to a commoner and poet!' " In one way or another voice is private or, as in **"A Long Story,"** simply lost. The distant way is thus not only back to an originary voice, but outward to an audience that may be, as the reception of the two Pindaric odes so fully demonstrated, largely baffled by the voices they hear. To be so isolated between voice and audience seems the familiar fate of mid-eighteenth-century poets. In Gray the problem is especially acute, and unlike Chatterton or Macpherson he does not choose a voice that assumes particular priority. He becomes instead a petitioner of voices, the ode itself, as Paul Fry observes, finding its motive in

invocation, "a purposeful calling in rather than a calling out." "The poet who can prolong presence . . . has 'taken on,' strictly speaking, the identity he has striven for." "I felt myself the Bard," said Gray.

The taking on of a strong identity correlates to the escape from a weak one. These self-identifications may be, as Northrop Frye long ago remarked, either manic or bizarre, but they require pilgrimages, journeys to voice, and they arise from the initial malady of displaced voice from which all mid-century speaking seems to suffer. Thus the *journey to,* the immediate function of *way* in Gray's poems, is explicable in terms of the necessity to find the voice that is always to be appropriated or always abandoned: "He spoke, and headlong from the mountain's height / Deep in the roaring tide he plunged to endless night." The self merges with inchoate sound (the mighty sound of waters, the very source of voice), enters the endless night of bardic or churchyard death. These poems are all elegies for the poets who speak them, memorials of heroic or contemplative speaking, acknowledgments of the fate of voice. (pp. 366-70)

I want to propose now that many of Gray's poems may be comprehended under the head of progress pieces. The historical and geographical movements delineated in the eighteenth-century progress poem blend in his work with the movement of spiritual autobiography, and the "public" and "private" ways of progress are enacted before the reader as separate and yet merged actions in which man and men participate. **"The Progress of Poesy"** ends with Thomas Gray. Historical movement is traced by the man writing the poem to the same man who is now the immediate goal of history, the agent upon whom it closes. Thomas Gray, man and poet, is derived from history; there is no other way of explaining or accounting for him. He originates in the distant logic of Poesy's westward movement, and the vast aggregation of events, the momentous causes of Poesy's flight, lead to him. This is not simply an occasion for the egotistical sublime; it is an apologia for the self derived from a myth of progress, a figuration of journey, however much Johnson may find the logic of Poesy's course merely a pleasing fiction. Behind the poet Gray are not only Dryden and Milton, Shakespeare and Pindar. There are also Venus and Cybele, Jove and Hyperion. They are as much "ministers of human fate" as are Misfortune, Anger, Shame, et al. of the [**"Ode on a Distant Prospect of Eton College"**]. They are all creatures and creations of the mind mindful of time, forms of history's making by which the imagination marks human progress. They may even be the forms out of which history is constituted. Such phantoms and realities ground human identity in various knowable objectifications, renderings of the self's sense of itself and of the myths it creates and inhabits so as to further know itself. To the imagination Venus is only an alternative figure to Love, an alternative to allegoresis. Gray keeps grounding the self in what it knows. The Bard's projected history is only another variation of this kind of perception, dependent upon our knowledge of the veracity of his historical prophecy. What does Edward I know of those future persons? Who to him could be the " 'She-wolf of France' " or " 'The bristled Boar' "? As she-wolf and boar such entities are the figurations of an historical identity that is not literal, a transformation of fact into figure, of history into metaphor. Gray figures, then, the forms inhabiting time; it is his version of plenitude.

The self knowing itself knows history, which means that it knows the stages of its real and imagined progress (they are ultimately the same). It means also that it knows what can only be called metahistory, the personifications that arise from the mind's sense of its location in time. It means also that it knows the myths in which it is inevitably captured, contextualized. Such ways of knowing comprise the textuality of Gray's poems, an allusive and referential structure, densely layered, in which the self, public and private, always and simultaneously exits. The progress poem offered Gray just this sort of generic openness, a *kind* that could "explain" or dramatize historical change but could equally incorporate what was, strictly speaking, beyond or outside the province of history (as are, for example, the agents of prosopopoeia). Miner refers to Dryden's *The Hind and the Panther,* remarking: ". . . it can best be described as a historical structure infused and controlled by typological elements suggestive both of matters beyond history and of areas in which history is not the proper mode of regarding human experience." History as public myth is only limitedly "the proper mode."

Prosopopoeia and myth are public and private in different ways, expressive of the self 's sense of its own daemons and its own gods, and also of what is general, collective, and the common property of a civilization. The **"Elegy"** elegizes everyone and no one. It is the only major poem of its kind in English precipitated by no death. Lives, like poesy, move westward, though occasioned by no political or moral motive, but only by the fact of mortality itself. In his early discussion of the progress piece in the Eighteenth Century, R. H. Griffith speaks of "the conception of history [that] passes from that of a pageant of independent, unconnected scenes to that of a pageant dominated by a principle of continuity, of cause and effect, with each scene alternating its role as effect and cause." Something of this sort is apparent in **"The Bard"** and **"The Progress of Poesy,"** but something less logically formal, less causally sequential, is equally evident in other of Gray's poems. Origin, meaning cause, is hid, though not uncommonly invoked by the poet. "With what song, Goddess," asks Gray of Nature in **"De Principiis Cogitandi,"** "shall I speak of you, the dearest offspring of Heaven, and of your origin?" The poem is itself another occasion of progress, dominated by metaphors of movement and motion: "Moreover, on every side, wherever the field of awareness extends, the companions of diverse pleasures, an idle crowd, are borne

The country churchyard in Stoke Poges, Buckinghamshire. Gray's tomb is seen close to the church, between the two large windows.

along, and the forms of pain, terrible to behold, which darken every doorway."

Characters as various as the poet of the **"Elegy"** and Milton of the **"Ode for Music"** roam across the landscape at the same time of day and with presumably the same companions. " 'Oft have we seen him at the peep of dawn / 'Brushing with hasty steps the dews away / 'To meet the sun upon the upland lawn.' " Milton is comparably self-described: " 'Oft at the blush of dawn / 'I trod your level lawn, / 'Oft wooed the gleam of Cynthia silver-bright / 'In cloisters dim, far from the haunts of Folly, / 'With Freedom by my side, and soft-eyed Melancholy.' " The poet and Milton are similar figures in transit; that they are not going anywhere in particular does not matter. Excursion is a mere synecdoche, a notation of journey.

"I felt myself the Bard," said Gray of himself during the writing of that poem. Yet he is also the musing, melancholic poet of the **"Elegy,"** the prosopopoeically companioned, otherwise solitary, Milton. Such self-similitudes are the recurrent investitures of the self (public and private), alternative and yet like forms of identity, fictions of the self in incompleted narratives, forms of passage. The audacious Milton of **"The Progress of Poesy"** is yet another solitary voyager: "He passed the flaming bounds of place and time." In **"Luna Habitabilis"** Gray's muse tells "of the first colonist emigrating to the moon. . . . As once Columbus sailed across the watery plains of an unknown sea to see the lands of Zephyr, new realms." (pp. 372-74)

Should we now look to those familiar antitheses that have comprised the canonical interpretation of Gray and recompose them within the textuality of progress itself? The journey is historical and biographical, cultural and individual. Such an engagement with time seeks its own structuration, seeks, one might argue, to escape the local and personal, yet to inform the general and public with the "I" that is a part (even when unspecified) of all the imagined journeys on which Gray's personae are embarked. It is useless to call such adventures "pre-romantic," yet they no more belong to those "psychological self-identifications," manic and bizarre, on which Frye long ago founded his notion of "Sensibility." The tradition here is almost as old as Wordsworth's hills. It is found in the journeying soul of Chaucer's pilgrims and Bunyan's Pilgrim. Gray brings it up to date, by which I mean he finds alternative poetic forms for it in elegy and fills those with the mind's consciousness of its own being as historical and individual entity, derived from the flow of time and to be returned to that movement.

His poetry is one of various resurrections, of voice but also of vanished ages, of village dead, of childhood, all of which occur as an effort to assume mastery over what has suffered closure and now requires revisiting and assimilation into the meditative self. In the **"Hymn to Ignorance"** the "sacred age" of Ignorance is petitioned mockingly to return again and "bring the buried ages back to view." In the **"Hymn"** and in the "Eton College Ode" childhood and the darkness of ignorance are equivalent moments in the history of consciousness. They exist as compatible events of origin, distant stages in the history of the race and of the self, and the occasion of summoning them is

predicated, ironically or not, on the assumption that they have something to say. Ignorance is a "soft salutary power!" that the poet "adore[s]." "Oh say, successful," he implores, "dost thou still oppose / Thy leaden aegis 'gainst our ancient foes?" But: "Oh say—she hears me not." In the Eton ode, Father Thames is summoned: "Say, Father Thames, for thou hast seen," but he does not speak. What voice there is exists as the insinuation of futurity, another muffled prophetic speaking, which the children of Eton hear: a "voice in every wind." The quasi-autobiographical locales, Eton and Cambridge, suggest on Gray's part a return to origin, a desire to solicit sources that remain partially or wholly mute.

To write in this way is to belong to an age, to the greater rising awareness of the self as historical and individual presence that concentrates our focus on Gray as poet and historian. To see him in this way raises legitimate questions about the scope of a vision he clearly does not control in the usual sense of writing it out, seeing it through. But it does indicate something of what he sees and what is to be seen in his poetry, the turn to what Fredric Bogel rightly calls "the literary order of time itself" in the second half of the Eighteenth Century. Gray's place in this "turn" is in the effort to create a figure for time's progress and man's location within it, while simultaneously evoking those voices that have sounded throughout it, disputing or rationalizing the logic and law of its judgments. This is the large-scale subject Gray largely evaded, leaving in its place the fragments, those surviving notations that are his poems and tell us much of what he did perceive and what he could not. (pp. 375-76)

Wallace Jackson, "Thomas Gray: Drowning in Human Voices," in Criticism, *Vol. XXVIII, No. 4, Fall, 1986, pp. 361-77.*

FURTHER READING

Bateson, F. W. "Gray's 'Elegy' Reconsidered." In his *English Poetry: A Critical Introduction,* pp. 181-93. New York: Longmans, Green and Co., 1950.

> Response to Cleanth Brooks's essay on Gray in his *The Well Wrought Urn* [see below]. While agreeing with a number of Brooks's arguments, Bateson also purports that Brooks excluded the social and historical factors that influenced Gray's poetry.

Brooks, Cleanth. "Gray's Storied Urn." In his *The Well Wrought Urn: Studies in the Structure of Poetry,* pp. 105-23. New York: Reynal & Hitchcock, 1947.

> Detailed explication of "Elegy Written in a Country Churchyard," contrasting the simplicity of the poem's subject with the sublety of its structure.

Chesterton, G. K. "On Mr. Thomas Gray." In his *All I Survey,* pp. 144-55. Freeport, NY: Books For Libraries Press, Inc., 1932.

> Speculates how Gray came to write his "Elegy" and also attempts to place Gray in literary history.

Coleridge, Samuel Taylor. *Biographia Literaria,* edited by J. Showcross, pp. 43-68. Oxford: Oxford University Press, 1907.

Response to William Wordsworth's negative assessment of Gray's use of language.

"The Bicentenary of Gray." *Cornhill Magazine* XLII, No. 247 (January 1917): 98-106.

Address given by the Dean of Norwich on the occasion of the bicentenary of Gray's birth. Analyzes the societal and literary elements which influenced Gray to write the two Pindaric Odes.

"A Review of 'Poems by Mr. Gray.' " *The Critical Review,* XXV (May 1768): 368-71.

Praises the strength of Gray's verse and examines three poems not previously published: "The Fatal Sisters," "The Defense of Odin," and "The Triumph of Odin."

Drew, D. L. "Gray's Elegy and the Classics." *The Classical Weekly* XIX, No. 14 (1 February 1926): 109-11.

Analyzes the classical elements in Gray's "Elegy Written in a Country Churchyard" by comparing this work to Vergil's "Elegy with Georgics."

Dyson, A. E. "The Ambivalence of Gray's Elegy." *Essays in Literature* VII, No. 3 (July 1957): 257-61.

Explores the contradictory elements in Gray's "Elegy," specifically Gray's presentation of the common man as a victim to be pitied.

Ellis, Frank Hale. "Gray's Elegy: The Biographical Problem in Literary Criticism." *Publications of the Modern Language Association of America* LXVI, No. 6 (December 1951): 971-1008.

Refutes the common charge that Gray's "Elegy" is essentially an autobiographical document.

"Strictures on Gray Discussed." *The Gentleman's Magazine* 52 (January 1782): 19-21.

Letter to the Editor in response to Samuel Johnson's negative assessment of Gray in his *Lives of the English Poets* [see excerpt dated 1781].

Hazlitt, William. "On Swift, Young, Gray, Collins, Etc." In his *Lectures on the English Poets,* pp. 160-89. New York: Oxford University Press, 1818.

Favorable overview of Gray's poetic canon.

Hillis, Frederick W. and Bloom, Harold. "Gray's Elegy Reconsidered." In their *From Sensibility to Romanticism: Essays Presented to Frederick A. Pottle,* pp. 139-169. New York: Oxford University Press, 1965.

Detailed explication concerning the structural and thematic elements of Gray's "Elegy."

Hutchings, W. "Syntax of Death: Instability in Gray's 'Elegy Written in a Country Churchyard.' " *Studies in Philology* LXXXI, No. 4 (Fall 1984): 496-514.

Linguistic analysis of the imagery in Gray's "Elegy" which transforms the subject of death to the object of the poem.

Kuist, James. M. "The Conclusion of Gray's Elegy." *The South Atlantic Quarterly* LXX, No. 1 (Spring 1971): 203-14.

Examines the controversy surrounding the chronology and strength of the conclusion of Gray's "Elegy."

"A Review of 'Odes by Mr. Gray.' " *The Literary Magazine* 2, No. XVII (15 October/September 1857): 422-26.

Reviews Gray's Pindaric Odes, condemning their obscurity and classical complexity.

"Defence of Gray." *The Monthly Anthology* 6, No. 2 (February 1809): 95-8.

Detailed reaction to Samuel Johnson's indictment of Gray's poetic canon, specifically "The Bard."

Rogers, Pat. "Sensibility." In his *The Augustan Vision,* pp. 133-144. New York: Harper and Row Publishers, Inc., Barnes & Noble, 1974.

Examines the Augustan influences of a number of Gray's works, including "The Bard" and "The Progress of Poesy."

Spacks, Patricia Meyer. "Thomas Gray: Action and Image." In her *The Poetry of Vision: Five Eighteenth Century Poets,* pp. 90-118. Cambridge: Harvard University Press, 1967.

Survey of Gray's poetry in which Spacks provides in-depth interpretations of "Ode on the Spring," "Ode on a Distant Prospect of Eton College," and "Sonnet on the Death of Mr. Richard West."

Stockdale, Percival. *An Inquiry Into the Nature, and Genuine Laws of Poetry Including a Particular Defence of the Writing and Genius of Mr. Pope* 1788. Reprint. New York: Garland Publishing, Inc., 1970 pp. 94-124.

Praises Gray's "Elegy," stating it "does honor to the English nation," but criticizes the Pindaric Odes because of their uninteresting characters.

Wordsworth, William. "Preface to 'Lyrical Ballads.' " In his *The Prelude, with a Selection from The Shorter Poem, The Sonnets, The Recluse, The Excursion, and Three Essays on the Art of Poetry,* edited by Carlos Baker, pp. 1-32. New York: Holt, Rinehart and Winston, 1948.

Faults the prosaic elements of Gray's verse, using the "Sonnet on the Death of Mr. Richard West" to illustrate his argument.

A. E. Housman

1859-1936

(Full name: Alfred Edward Housman) English poet, critic, essayist, translator, and editor.

Housman was among the most renowned classicists of his time, but it is his poetry that continues to generate both critical recognition and controversy. Although Housman's creative output consisted of three slim volumes, his first collection, *A Shropshire Lad,* has become one of the most celebrated and best-selling books of verse in the English language and has secured his standing in literary history as a great but thematically restrained poet. A. F. Allison's observation is representative of the critical debate that surrounds much of Housman's poetry: "Housman offered in the name of poetry much that was false and petty and perverse, but he gave a little that was exquisite." Only recently have critics begun to reassess Housman's literary achievements to determine why so few of his contemporaries enjoy an analogous level of popularity.

Housman was born in Fockbury in the county of Worcestershire, England, within sight of the Shropshire hills, a place that he would later allegorize in his poems. Housman was the eldest of seven children in a family that would produce a famous dramatist, Housman's younger brother, Laurence, and a novelist and short story writer, his sister Clemence. He attended Bromsgrove School, a notable institution that emphasized Greek and Latin studies, where he worked diligently and developed a talent for precise translation that would later earn him a reputation as a formidable classical scholar. Despite his academic success, Housman's childhood was not a happy one. In addition to being a small and frail boy who did not easily form congenial friendships, Housman also had to confront the death of his mother when he was twelve years old. This tragedy affected him profoundly and set into motion the slow erosion of his religious faith. Years later, Housman wrote that he "became a deist at thirteen and an atheist at twenty-one." This religious disillusionment was reflected in his poetry in the form of stoic despair and a fatalistic view of life.

Housman entered Oxford University in 1877. He continued to immerse himself in his favorite subjects, Latin and Greek, and also helped to found *Ye Round Table,* an undergraduate magazine featuring humorous verse and satire. Housman's contributions to this publication demonstrate not only his wit, but his talent for nonsense verse, which he kept well-concealed in later years even as his critics were condemning his poetry for being stark and humorless. While at first excelling in his work at Oxford, Housman later inexplicably failed his examinations in 1881 and did not earn his degree until 1892, when he was made professor of Latin at University College in London. The cause for Housman's failure was for many years a subject of speculation among critics and biographers. Today it is known from Housman's diaries that the reason

for his failure at Oxford was at least partially caused by his hopelessness over his relationship with a young science student named Moses Jackson. The realization of his own homosexuality and the eventual rejection by Jackson embittered Housman. He became a repressed and melancholy recluse who later declined all honors he was offered, including the poet laureateship of England and the Order of Merit, one of the most prestigious distinctions bestowed by the British government. Housman scholars contend that other than the death of his mother, this rebuff by Jackson was the most determinative event of Housman's life.

It was shortly after the crisis at Oxford that Housman wrote all of *A Shropshire Lad.* His declaration that "I have seldom written poetry unless I was rather out of health" seems to substantiate the opinion that emotional trauma greatly influenced his work. Such poems as "Shake Hands We Shall Never Be Friends, All's Over," and "Because I Liked You Better" make direct reference to his relationship with Jackson, although Housman did not allow them to be published during his lifetime. While Housman wrote an ironic poem on the occasion of Oscar Wilde's imprisonment for homosexual acts, stating in part that "they're taking him to prison for the colour of his hair," he nonetheless was an extremely proper and reserved Victorian gentleman and dreaded the opprobrium associated with homosexuality. Some critics have related this repression of Housman's sexual identity to his preoccupation with form and organization.

In *A Shropshire Lad,* Housman adopted the persona of a young Shropshire yeoman, whom he called Terence Hearsay, in order to distance himself from the autobiographical aspects of his work. This technique has caused some commentators to charge that Housman never developed his themes of unrequited love, the oblivion of death, and idealized military life beyond the emotional and intellectual capabilities of his rustic personae. Two well-known poems contained in this volume, "To an Athlete Dying Young" and "When I Was One-and-Twenty," concentrate solely on the loss of youthful dreams and the isolation of adolescence. The thematic limitations of *A Shropshire Lad* and the lack of emotional development led Cyril Conolly to state that "many of Housman's poems are of a triteness of technique equalled only by the banality of thought." However, other critics praise the economy of Housman's verse and his expertise with the pastoral tradition. Most of the poems included in *A Shropshire Lad* are short, sometimes not more than one stanza in length, and written in the four-line ballad style with rhyming alternate lines. According to many critics, this stylistic symmetry demands great discipline and sophistication and in this sense Housman's poems rival the classics in their mastery of conciseness and sublety. Concentrating on the stylistic elements of his verse, H. P. Collins justifies Housman's thematic limitations by declaring that "the greatest poetry does not need complex emotions."

Housman's subsequent collection, *Last Poems,* appeared twenty-six years after the first publication of *A Shropshire Lad,* leading some critics to speculate on the reticence of Housman's poetic talent. While this volume was also praised for its fine craftsmanship, it was noted by many reviewers that the themes presented in this volume were mere continuances of those expounded upon in *A Shropshire Lad.* This did not prevent *Last Poems,* which included "Epithalamium," a piece commemorating the wedding of Moses Jackson, and "Hell Gate," which chronicles a successful rebellion against the forces of death, from becoming quite popular among the general readership. *More Poems,* published posthumously by Housman's brother, Laurence, was also a popular success, but since most of the poems included had been omitted from the previous volumes by Housman himself, it is generally considered an inferior body of work.

Housman's famous lecture at Cambridge University, entitled *The Name and Nature of Poetry,* represents the only statement that Housman ever made about his personal theories of poetry. Housman cited Shakespeare's songs, Heinrich Heine's poetry, and the Scottish border ballads as his major poetic influences. Metrically, his poems stand midway between the lyric and the quatrain form of the ballad, while thematically, the influence of Shakespeare is apparent in Housman's dismissal of the theological and emphasis on everything mortal. Dramatic irony and sur-

prise endings are important elements in the work of Heine, and Housman uses them in much the same fashion as the German poet. While critics contend that Housman's comments offer important insights into the motivations behind his own verse, they also speculate that Housman intended to be deliberately vague and misleading to provoke controversy. In a review of the published lecture, Ezra Pound reflected the general reaction of the Cambridge audience by noting the "surprising and sudden limits of (Housman's) cognizance." However, Housman prefaced his lecture with the statement that although he would be attempting to delve into the characteristics of poetry, he was not by nature a critic and preferred instead the discipline of writing verse.

Housman continues to be a popular and frequently read poet despite the fact that since the initial publication of his verse, his work has been intermittently praised and rebuffed for what has been called its "obvious limitations." While his overriding morbidity of theme is often described as tedious and adolescent, Housman's open investigations of the mysteries of death and the dual nature of humankind have earned him acknowledgment as a precursor to the development of modern poetry. Stephen Spender attempts to identify the subtle duality sometimes displayed in Housman's poetry and the elements which make his poetry unusually satisfying: "At his best, Housman is a poet of great force and passion whose music is quite unforced, combining sensuousness with a cold discipline." Whatever Housman's limitations, his poems, by virtue of their emotional force and classical beauty, continue to attract attention and praise.

(For further discussion of Housman's life and career, see *Twentieth-Century Literary Criticism,* Vols. 1, 10; *Contemporary Authors,* Vols. 104, 125; and *Dictionary of Literary Biography,* Vol. 19.)

PRINCIPAL WORKS

POETRY

A Shropshire Lad   1896
Last Poems   1922
More Poems   1936
Additional Poems   1937
The Collected Poems of A. E. Housman   1939
The Manuscript Poems of A. E. Housman   1955
The Complete Poems of A. E. Housman   1959

OTHER MAJOR WORKS

The Name and Nature of Poetry   (criticism)   1933
A. E. Housman: Selected Prose   (essays and criticism)   1961
The Letters of A. E. Housman   (letters)   1970

William Archer   (essay date 1898)

[*A Scottish critic, translator, journalist, and dramatist, Archer was the author of more than twenty books, in-*

cluding A Plea for a Rational World-Order *(1912) and* On Dreams *(1935). The following excerpt is from one of the first reviews of* A Shropshire Lad, *in which Archer praises Housman's simplicity and use of common speech while meditating on the complexities of life and death.*]

[A. E. Housman's book, *A Shropshire Lad,*] is a very small one. It contains some sixty brief lyrics, occupying less than one hundred pages in all. You may read it in half-an-hour—but there are things in it you will scarce forget in a lifetime. It tingles with an original, fascinating, melancholy vitality.

Mr. Housman writes, for the most part, under the guise of "A Shropshire Lad"—the rustic namefather of his book. But this is evidently a mere mask. Mr. Housman is no Shropshire Burns singing at his plough. He is a man of culture. He moves in his rustic garb with no clodhopper's gait, but with the ease of an athlete; and I think he has an Elzevir classic in the pocket of his smock frock. But it is not Theocritus, not the Georgics or the Eclogues; I rather take it to be Lucretius. Never was there less of a "pastoral" poet, in the artificial, Italian-Elizabethan sense of the word. The Shropshire of Mr. Housman is no Arcadia, no Sicily, still less a courtly pleasaunce people with beribboned nymphs and swains. It is as real, as tragic, as the Wessex of Mr. Hardy. The genius, or rather the spirit, of the two writers is not dissimilar. Both have the same rapturous realisation, the same bitter resentment, of life. To both Nature is an exquisitely seductive, inexorably malign enchantress. "Life's Ironies" might be the common title of Mr. Hardy's long series of novels and Mr. Housman's little book of verse. And both have the same taste for clothing life's ironies in the bucolic attire of an English county.

Mr. Housman's strong and stern temperament finds expression in curiously simple, original, and expressive verse. In deference to his rustic mask, and probably to something fundamental in his talent as well, he attempts no metrical arabesques, no verbal enamelling. With scarcely an exception, his metres are of the homeliest; yet, in their little variations, their suspensions, their tremulous cadences, we recognise the touch of the born metrist. Mr. Housman's chief technical strength, however, lies in the directness and terseness of his style. There is nerve and fibre in every line he writes, and of superfluous tissue not a trace. He says what he wants to say, not what his measure dictates, or his rhyme; and his words seem to fall into their places with a predestinate fitness which (inconsistent as it may seem) gives us in every second stanza a little shock of pleasurable surprise. His diction and his methods are absolutely his own. He echoes no one, borrows no one's technical devices. If he reminds us of any other poet, it is (now and then) of Heine; yet he is English of the English. We divine his culture in the very simplicity of his style; but . . . we find no direct evidence of his ever having read another English poet. His verse might quite well be the glorified offspring of the most unsophisticated popular poetry—the chap-book ballad or the rustic stave.

Mr. Housman has three main topics: a stoical pessimism; a dogged rather than an exultant patriotism; and what I may perhaps call a wistful cynicism. His pessimism he formulates again and again.

> The world has still
> Much good, but much less good than ill;
> And while the sun and moon endure,
> Luck's a chance, but trouble's sure.
>
> (pp. 263-65)

In a remarkable poem called **"The Welch Marches"** he seems to give an ethnological reason for this sombre strain in his temperament. At Shrewsbury, he says (in a splendid stanza):

> The flag of morn in conqueror's state
> Enters at the English gate:
> The vanquished eve, as night prevails,
> Bleeds upon the road to Wales.
>
> * * * *
>
> When Severn down to Buildwas ran
> Coloured with the death of man,
> Couched upon her brother's grave
> The Saxon got me on the slave.
>
> * * * *
>
> In my heart it has not died,
> The war that sleeps on Severn side;
> They cease not fighting, east and west,
> On the marches of my breast.

Whatever its origin, whether it proceed from the subjection of the Celt to the Teuton, or from some more modern source, Mr. Housman's melancholy is inveterate and not to be shaken off. But there is nothing whining about it. Rather, it is bracing, invigorating. (pp. 265-66)

To show how Mr. Housman can touch his worldweariness to absolute beauty, I quote, before leaving this subject, a poem so delicate that even the tenderest breath of praise would only shake off some of its bloom: . . .

> In valleys of springs and rivers,
>   By Ony and Teme and Clun,
> The country for easy livers,
>   The quietest under the sun,
>
> We still had sorrows to lighten,
>   One could not be always glad,
> And lads knew trouble at Knighton
>   When I was a Knighton lad.
>
> By bridges that Thames runs under,
>   In London, the town built ill,
> 'Tis sure small matter for wonder
>   If sorrow is with one still.
>
> And if as a lad grows older
>   The troubles he bears are more,
> He carries his griefs on a shoulder
>   That handselled them long ago.
>
> Where shall one halt to deliver
>   This luggage I'd lief set down?
> Not Thames, not Teme is the river,
>   Nor London nor Knighton the town:
>
> 'Tis a long way further than Knighton,
>   A quieter place than Clun,
> Where doomsday may thunder and lighten,
>   And little 'twill matter to one.

The English language is appreciably the richer for such work as this.

Mr. Housman's patriotism, as it appears in *A Shropshire Lad,* is local rather than national or imperial. His soldiers fight, not so much for the glory of England, as for the credit of Shropshire. Of the joys of battle he tells us little enough. He accepts war as the destiny of a stubborn fighting race, and as a safety-valve for energies that might find a still more noxious outlet in peace. He sings of the sacred bond of comradeship, and, like Mr. Kipling, he has a good deal to say of the price we pay for Empire in blood and tears. (pp. 267-68)

Perhaps the most characteristic . . . of all his military pieces, . . . **"The Day of Battle"**:

> Far I hear the bugle blow
> To call me where I would not go,
> And the guns begin the song,
> 'Soldier, fly or stay for long.'
>
> Comrade, if to turn and fly
> Made a soldier never die,
> Fly I would, for who would not?
> 'Tis sure no pleasure to be shot.
>
> But since the man that runs away
> Lives to die another day,
> And cowards' funerals, when they come,
> Are not wept so well at home,
>
> Therefore, though the best is bad,
> Stand and do the best, my lad;
> Stand and fight and see your slain,
> And take the bullet in your brain.

The third element in Mr. Housman's inspiration is what I have roughly called a wistful cynicism. He dwells, not harshly, but rather with compassion, upon the mutability of human feeling, the ease with which the dead are forgot, the anguish of love unrequited, and the danger that long life may mean slow degradation. Among the crowd at Ludlow Fair, he wishes that those who are destined to die young, "to carry back bright to the coiner the mintage of man," could bear some mark about them so that they might be honoured and envied. (p. 268)

By far the best of the group is a dialogue between a dead man and his living friend, the gist of which lies in the friend's last answer:

> Yes, lad, I lie easy,
>   I lie as lads would choose;
> I cheer a dead man's sweetheart,
>   Never ask me whose. . . .

In a few of Mr. Housman's poems, however, there is no touch of that bitterness of feeling which I have named, or misnamed, cynicism. **"Bredon Hill"** seems to me almost unrivalled in its delicate, unemphatic pathos. . . . (p. 269)

It is long since we have caught just this note in English verse—the note of intense feeling uttering itself in language of unadorned precision, uncontorted truth. Mr. Housman is a vernacular poet, if ever there was one. He employs scarcely a word that is not understood of the people, and current on their lips. For this very reason, some readers who have come to regard decoration, and even contortion, as of the essence of poetry, may need time to acquire the taste for Mr. Housman's simplicity. But if he is vernacular, he is also classical in the best sense of the word. His simplicity is not that of weakness, but of strength and skill. He eschews extrinsic and factitious ornament because he knows how to attain beauty without it. It is good to mirror a thing in figures, but it is at least as good to express the thing itself in its essence, always provided, of course, that the method be that of poetic synthesis, not of scientific analysis. Mr. Housman has this talent in a very high degree; and cognate and complementary to it is his remarkable gift of reticence—of aposiopesis, if I may wrest the term from its rhetorical sense and apply it to poetry. He will often say more by a cunning silence than many another poet by pages of speech. That is how he has contrived to get into this tiny volume so much of the very essence and savour of life. (p. 271)

William Archer, "A Shropshire Poet," in The Fortnightly Review, *n.s. Vol. 44, No. 380, August, 1898, pp. 263-71.*

J. B. Priestley   (essay date 1922)

[*A highly prolific English writer, Priestley is the author of numerous popular novels that depict the lives of the middle class. In this respect, Priestley has often been likened to Charles Dickens, a comparison he dislikes. His most notable critical work is* Literature and Western Man *(1960), a survey of Western literature from the invention of movable type through the mid-twentieth century. In the following excerpt, Priestley examines Housman's use of measure and meter in* A Shropshire Lad. *Although he calls Housman's metrical framework simple and conventional, Priestley goes on to purport that the collection is written with the "cadence of our common human speech which no ear can help recognizing and no heart can reject."*]

There are no intricate measures in *A Shropshire Lad,* and it is clear that [Housman] relies very little upon the charm of metre. The new volume repeats the favourite measures of the old one, and shows that the poet has not taste for metrical experiments. He is fond of the octosyllabic line and ballad measure in its simplest form. Here and there he makes clever use of a five-line stanza, which is a striking variation on the old Short Measure, the first and third lines being unrhymed and having each a redundant syllable, the second, fourth, and fifth lines rhyming together. This peculiar metrical structure gives to the fifth line of the stanza the air of being an afterthought, which is made to add considerably to the poignant force of the verses in which it is used:

> They tolled the one bell only,
>   Groom there was none to see,
> The mourners followed after,
>   And so to church went she,
>   And would not wait for me.

But throughout *A Shropshire Lad* the poet's appeal does not depend upon a highly elaborate and cunning arrangement of vowel sounds and so forth. I am writing of a poet and not a mere dauber in words, and I do not mean for one instant to imply that he has no skill in the manipulation of vowel sounds and in other technical devices. In the verse quoted above—to take the nearest example—the two "o" sounds echoing down the verse from the first line, like the chime of the bell, show us that he knows what he is about. But he is not one of our masters of verbal music. Those rapturous, infinitely beguiling phrases that linger about the ear for ever are not for him. But, nevertheless, even here he has accomplished something that not only increases our admiration but makes his work a fruitful study for other poets. In his moments of passionate stress he has given us, within that terse and finely tempered style of his, the true ring and cadence of ordinary natural speech. . . . Another poet of our time, Mr. W. B. Yeats, has always laboured and on the whole successfully, to give his style a similar directness and naturalness, but at the same time he has always pursued a delicate research of his own into the endless possibilities of stressed language, so that all his best poems move to lovely little tunes of his own, which must be caught before the peculiar beauty of his work can be appreciated. . . . But this lovely personal music is not to be found in *A Shropshire Lad;* in its place, within the simple metrical framework, is that cadence of our common human speech which no ear can help recognising and no heart can reject. Take it at its very simplest:

> We still had sorrows to lighten—
> One could not always be glad;
> And lads knew trouble at Knighton
> When I was a Knighton lad. . . .

Now, that is apparently as plain and straightforward as prose, but, print it as you like, you cannot make it into prose; if you simply say the lines you must sing them, and if, on the other hand, you begin by singing them your voice must inevitably fall into their natural affecting cadence. It is this that makes his mournful folk seem to cry from the heart, as few others do in the poetry of our time. And though *A Shropshire Lad* has had such a great influence, though traces of that influence can be discovered in all manner of unlikely places in contemporary verse, I know only one or two of our younger poets who have been able to reproduce this curious characteristic. But perhaps too many of them are now more concerned with the look of a poem on the printed page than with their reader's ear. (pp. 182-83)

> *J. B. Priestley, "The Poetry of A. E. Housman," in* The London Mercury, *Vol. VII, No. 38, December, 1922, pp. 171-84.*

William Rose Benét   (essay date 1923)

[*Benét was an American poet, editor, and novelist. Among his works are his Pulitzer Prize-winning autobiographical novel in verse,* The Dust Which Is God *(1941), and* The Oxford Anthology of American Literature *(1956), which he edited in collaboration with Norman Holmes Pearson. In the following excerpt, Benét examines both the technique and emotional power behind Housman's* Last Poems. *He finds Housman's style powerful and impressive in its classic simplicity, but*

maintains it is impossible to identify the source of Housman's peculiar but effective point of view because, at that time, little was known about the circumstances that shaped Housman's life and attitudes.]

A. E. Housman published in the late nineties some sixty poems which reflected the spirit of the close of his century, though they were of a grain that set them immediately apart from the characteristic work of that period. Now, in our own time, after long silence, he issues his *Last Poems,* and strangely enough they fall in very well with the spirit of our own time. At least they are "good medicine" for our time; even though it is not too brash of us to assert beyond their general conclusion that it is still worth while building, worth while enjoying and striving while we live.

Yet Housman also says that. We shall see this presently.

Few realize that Housman was thirty-seven years old when *A Shropshire Lad* was published, and that now he is about sixty-four years old. When he remarks in his tiny foreword: "It is not likely that I shall ever be impelled to write much more. I can no longer expect to be revisited by the continuous excitement under which in the early months of 1895 I wrote the greater part of my other book, nor indeed could I well sustain it if it came", there is a mild irony in the statement. Housman has, indeed, completed his "century"—if we take the word in the sense that cricketers use it when any cricketer amasses one hundred runs. Housman has written a few over one hundred poems, and on these hundred or so poems, many of them most brief, his whole reputation rests.

Now if I were to add one letter to the word "century", making it "centaury", from the Greek *Kentaureion,* in that word you would have the essence of his gift to our age; for centaury is the name of a herb said to have been used medicinally by the centaur Chiron, the instructor of the young heroes. And as Chiron was to the youth of his day, in his stoicism, sad wisdom, and the virtues of his magic herb, so is Housman to the younger poets of our own.

We find in him knowledge of the flesh and, through the flesh, knowledge of the spirit. Each leaf of his books astringently medicines. (pp. 83-4)

Examining *Last Poems* more closely we find, quite naturally, less about young love in it, as much again, about battle. There is also Housman's obsession with the idea of the gallows. Oftener, it seems to me, in the songs of the first book "the feather pate of folly" bore "the falling sky". Once indeed, out of more sombre pages, flashed the talaria of Hermes, flickering the presence of the god of eternal youth. . . . (p. 84)

In execution I find *Last Poems* little, if at all, inferior to *A Shropshire Lad.* There is, perhaps, nothing quite so perfect in its poignancy as was that first cry of youth, **"When I was one-and-twenty"**. Yet the work in *Last Poems* is again admirably compact, admirably reticent, often admirably melodious. Again many lines, many verses, deeply imprint the memory. It had seemed, when one first read in the first book **"Farewell to barn and stack and tree"**, that never again could a man render so perfectly the atmosphere of mortal tragedy. But, in *Last Poems* we have **"Eight O'Clock"**, stark fatality, perfectly presented in eight lines. We have also the bitterly moving poem just before it, **"The Culprit"**, which could not possibly be bettered in expression. And in **"The rain, it streams on stone and hillock"** is what seems, to me at least, about the truest transcript of a man's grief for a fellow man that has ever been versified. It is intolerably searching in its recognition of the casuistry of human sorrow, in its setting of the lips and lifting of the chin—till the last verse leaps out with sudden terrible eloquence.

In **"West and away the wheels of darkness roll"** is a most original image, springing from a more scientifically accurate view of the world in space than most poets have taken:

> But over sea and continent from sight
> Safe to the Indies has the earth conveyed
> The vast and moon-eclipsing cone of night,
> Her towering foolscap of eternal shade.

Such is the deftness of Housman's technique. (pp. 84-5)

His poem **"The laws of God, the laws of man"** is like to become a new testament for free thinkers. **"Hell Gate"**, the longest poem in *Last Poems,* reveals fiery dramatic imagination. **"Lancer"** may be excerpted from to illustrate the power of his irony. It epitomizes by inference both the glamour and the waste of war.

> For round me the men will be lying
> That learned me the way to behave,
> And showed me the business of dying:
> *Oh who would not sleep with the brave?*
>
> They ask and there is not an answer;
> Says I, I will 'list for a lancer,
> *Oh who would not sleep with the brave?*

One triumph of technique impresses as it has always impressed. A. E. Housman is one of the few living poets who knows how and just where to end a poem. His terminations are remarkably effective. His gifts of condensation, elimination, and intimation contribute to this.

> For so the game is ended
> That should not have begun.
> My father and my mother
> They had a likely son,
> And I have none.

Technique accomplishes it, but the effectiveness of the poem springs more deeply from the power of the emotion behind it. All the poet's gifts would prove void were it not for the intensity of a point of view to which all his poems are but footnotes. . . .

Of the influences and circumstances that sharpened Housman's point of view we know but little. . . . We have read of him as an odd and "cranky" personality, a recluse and a crabbed scholar—we can weigh the obsessions of his mind, calculate from the form and tone of his work its peculiar strains and stresses. But the intimate man remains a mystery.

If the permanence of poetry be in proportion to the intelligent emotion it evokes, Housman's poetry should certainly endure. His style is wholly his own. He is master of a certain kind of strict expression. And he is still, in many ways, the noblest Roman of them all. (p. 85)

William Rose Benét, in a review of "Last Poems," in The Bookman, *New York, Vol. LVII, No. 1, March, 1923, pp. 83-5.*

J. F. Macdonald   (essay date 1923)

[*In the following excerpt, Macdonald analyzes the characteristics of Housman's poetry that make it uniquely his own. After discussing such elements as theme, temperament, and meter, Macdonald attempts to refute charges that Housman is a minor poet.*]

What kind of verse would a competent critic expect Housman to write, if one make the incredible assumption of such a critic ignorant of his poetry but familiar with his prose? He might expect, no doubt, poems distinguished by their clearness and directness, by felicity in choice of word and turn of phrase, by a touch of satire, perhaps even of bitterness, and by firm stressed musical rhythm. But I cannot imagine even a supercritic predicting *A Shropshire Lad.* It was as new and fresh a note in English poetry as Coleridge's *Love* or *The rime of the Ancient Mariner.* Yet its theme was an old one, the joy and beauty of life in springtime dimmed by the shadow of swift-coming death. . . . In *A Shropshire Lad* it centres about the figures of the soldier, of rural lovers, of hapless lads who were hanged or did themselves to death, and the still more hapless lad who left the country with its homely comforters for the bitter struggle of London. (p. 119)

Rather to Housman's own surprise, I think, the world has accepted *A Shropshire Lad.* It has not, of course, had the amazing vogue of Omar Khayam but it has steadily grown in favor and influence until it has quietly taken its place as one of the minor classics of our literature. Its sale must have been very considerable. There were seven new editions or reprints in the decade after it was first published and I don't know how many since in England and America. There is something curious in this growth of Housman's reputation. He himself kept out of the public eye and the professional critics practically ignored him. . . . And yet one had only to mention *A Shropshire Lad* in any group of poetry lovers to see eyes light up and hear favorite bits lovingly quoted.

After more than a quarter of a century Housman last October published another little volume which he resolutely calls *Last Poems.* It has been received with favor in every quarter from a friendly cartoon in *Punch* to a laudatory review in *The Times.* The reviewers, of course, are not agreed about the exact points in which *Last Poems* fall short of or surpass *A Shropshire Lad.* Most of them, however, declare that, so far as metre and rhythm are concerned, the later book merely repeats the few simple measures of the earlier one. The anonymous reviewer in *The Times,* Mr. Priestley in *The London Mercury,* and S. M. Ellis in *The Fortnightly Review,* are in substantial agreement. Let Mr. Priestley speak for all: 'There are no intricate measures in *A Shropshire Lad,* and it is clear that its author relies very little upon the charm of metre. The new volume repeats the favourite measures of the old one, and shows that the poet has no taste for metrical experiments' [see excerpt dated 1922]. (pp. 122-23)

My head goes round. Is this generation of reviewers deaf, or do they never read poetry aloud? Housman once protested in reviewing a new edition of Ovid: 'It is hard to write without bitterness of the loss of time inflicted on an intelligent student by editors who cannot even be trusted to hand down the discoveries which their betters have made.' Change 'editors' to 'reviewers' and the protest holds. (p. 124)

'The new volume repeats the favourite measures of the old one, and shows that the poet has no taste for metrical experiments,' says Mr. Priestley. Here are the facts. Housman uses 21 different measures in the 63 poems in *A Shropshire Lad.* Only 9 of these measures recur once or oftener in the 41 lyrics that make up the **Last Poems.** Two of these are used in 5 poems, one in 3, one in 2, and five in 1 each. No less than 18 new measures are introduced. Let me put this another way. In the 63 poems there are 21 different measures; in the 41 there are 27. In the 104 poems that form the two little volumes, there are 39 different measures, 28 of which are used only once. It is true that two measures used 22 times in *A Shropshire Lad* occur 10 times between them in **Last Poems,** but it is an amazing deduction from this fact that 'the poet has no taste for metrical experiments.' Where else in English poetry, except possibly in Thomas Campion's *Books of Airs,* can one find so great a variety of measures in 104 consecutive poems?

It is quite true that Housman is fond of the octosyllabic; about one-third of all the lines in the two volumes are octosyllabic. But he has few poems wholly in octosyllabic verse. To be exact there are 13 in *A Shropshire Lad* and only 2 in **Last Poems.** All but one of these are written in couplets, or in quatrains of two couplets. Moreover, the octosyllabic lines in **Last Poems** are outnumbered by both six syllable and seven syllable lines. It is interesting to note that he has only one poem in decasyllabics, and only two others in which there are any lines of ten syllables. All three of these are in the new volume.

The range of his metre is very great, the lines varying from four to fifteen syllables in length. Still more remarkable is the amount and the subtlety of variation within a single stanza, and the almost uncanny felicity with which the stresses of the metrical pattern coincide with the normal accents of the sentence. Let anyone who has an ear for poetry read even this one stanza and judge of Housman's control of metre and of the reliance he places on its charm:

> The chestnut casts his flambeaux, and the flow-
> ers
> Stream from the hawthorn on the wind away,
> The doors clap to, the pane is blind with show-
> ers.
> Pass me the can, lad; there's an end of May.

How perfectly that 'clap to' echoes the bang of the door slamming shut; how admirably the young man's disgust at his spoilt walking trip is voiced in the closing line. And then the magic of

> Stream from the hawthorn on the wind away

A manuscript page from Last Poems.

—why one can see the blossoms grow dim in the distance with the dying cadence of that unbroken line. But enough of metre for a moment—those who have ears need no persuasion and those who have none are deaf to it. (pp. 124-26)

A great minor poet—is that to be the judgement finally passed on Housman by our classifying age? Even if it is he may be in good company. Some time ago a casual statement in a manual on Greek literature almost took my breath away. 'Among the Greek minor poets', it began, 'Pindar and Sappho'—. Pindar and Sappho—who wouldn't covet their companionship on the slopes of Mount Parnassus? Is Burns a minor poet? Is Gray or Blake? What is the test? No one imagines Housman with his two slender volumes of lyrics should take rank with Shakespeare and Homer, with Dante and Vergil. No, nor with Browning and Wordsworth, or Shelley and Keats. These men in sheer bulk, in range and breadth are altogether beyond him. A minor poet—yes, if you like, but one who writes genuine poetry. (pp. 127-28)

In the little preface to **Last Poems** Housman says, 'I can no longer expect to be revisited by the continuous excitement under which in the early months of 1895 I wrote the greater part of my other book, nor indeed could I well sustain it if it came. . . . About a quarter of this matter belongs to the April of the present year, but most of it dates between 1895 and 1910.' If the inspiration has been fitful since that wonderful spring, it has been none the less genuine. *Last Poems* fully sustains the high reputation won by *A Shropshire Lad*. It has almost everywhere the note of intense feeling expressed in language of absolute precision, and of such great simplicity that it is almost vernacular. . . . It is noteworthy too that the language is everywhere concrete. The famous adjectives that Milton used in stating the essential qualities of poetry are peculiarly fitted to describe these poems of Housman—'simple, sensuous, passionate.'

The old figures of *A Shropshire Lad* reappear, with the exception of the rival lovers, but spring has changed to autumn, or rather the thought of autumn colours the poet's vision of spring. The earlier lyrics are remarkable for the vivid colors Housman delights in—gold, silver, scarlet, red, azure, and the white of snow, and the cherry and hawthorn bloom. In *Last Poems* the dark, the grey of mists, black and russets and tans predominate. Instead of the spring sun we have the rains of autumn. The whole landscape is darker. Moreover, the twenty odd flowers, white and gold and blue, are replaced by a bare half-dozen, most of them of duller shade. The difference in color between the two volumes is very marked. *A Shropshire Lad,* too, has almost everywhere the air of morning in its descriptive passages; *Last Poems* have the shades of evening or the gloom of night. Further, there is something almost sinister in these later mornings. Instead of the drum-beat of **"Reveille"**

> Up, lad, up, 'tis late for lying:
> Hear the drums of morning play;
> Hark, the empty highways crying
> Who'll beyond the hills away?

we have the half humorous protest

> Yonder see the morning blink:
> The sun is up and up must I,
> To wash and dress and eat and drink
> And look at things and talk and think
> And work, and God knows why.

(pp. 130-31)

One sometimes feels in reading the poems of Thomas Hardy that their diction is that of scientific prose. It conveys nothing beyond the regular and precise dictionary meaning of the words. But Housman even in his barest and most realistic poems uses words that suggest more than they state. The two brief poems, **"The Culprit"** and **"Eight O'Clock"** could hardly be less decorated than they are. There are just two adjectives in the seven stanzas and the words are of the simplest. Yet note the effect.

"The Culprit"

* * * * *

> My mother and my father
> Out of the light they lie;
> The warrant would not find them,
> And here 'tis only I
> Shall hang so high.

* * * * *

> For so the game is ended
> That should not have begun.
> My father and my mother
> They had a likely son,
> And I have none.

"Eight O'Clock"

> He stood, and heard the steeple
> Sprinkle the quarters on the morning town.
> One, two, three, four, to market-place and people
> It tossed them down.
>
> Strapped, noosed, nighing his hour,
> He stood and counted them and cursed his luck;
> And then the clock collected in the tower
> Its strength, and struck.

What is it that grips our heart-strings here? No doubt there is something that defies analysis, but this thought of a family with 'a likely son' dying out in failure and disgrace brings a lump in the throat. The pity of his end! And how bitter it is to die on this bright and bustling morning as the chimes toss down the quarters to the busy market-place. The premonitory whirr before the first stroke of the hour falls and with it the trap-door under the doomed man, seemed to the tense nerves of the poet a conscious effort of the old clock to brace itself for the moment of horror when it struck. For sheer artistry in making metre enforce the thought these two stanzas would be hard to match. Yet this is the author that Mr. Priestley says 'relies very little upon the charm of metre.'

A good deal has been said in recent reviews of *Last Poems* about Housman's pessimism. On this side of the Atlantic, at least, pessimist is just one degree below bolshevist as a term of abuse. We dislike the fact, indeed we shut our eyes to the fact, that in this world every religion, every culture, that stood the test of long years had in it a core of stoicism by which it endured even if it couldn't rejoice and triumph. And we are prone to confuse stoicism with pessimism. Galsworthy has a sketch in *A Commentary* of an old deep sea fisherman lamed by accident and reduced to a precarious livelihood won by selling pennyworths of groundsel for canaries. 'In the crowded highway, beside his basket, he stood, leaning on his twisted stick, with his tired, steadfast face—a ragged statue to the great, unconscious human virtue, the most hopeful and inspiring of all things on earth, Courage without Hope.' In Housman the virtue is a conscious one—he has no illusions about what the future holds for him. In **"The Oracles"** he tells us how the ancient voices are dumb but the heart of man still answers and how from that oracle he heard the priestess shrieking

> That she and I should surely die and never live again.

He answers doggedly

> Oh priestess, what you cry is clear, and sound good sense I think it;
> But let the screaming echoes rest, and froth your mouth no more.

'Tis true there's better booze than brine, but he
   that drowns must drink it;
And oh, my lass, the news is news that men have
   heard before.

And then with only italics to indicate that the next lines
are quoted he gives the substance of the message brought
to Leonidas at Thermopylae by an excited messenger:

The King with half the East at heel is marched
   from lands of morning;
Their fighters drink the rivers up, their shafts be-
   night the air,
And he that stands will die for nought, and
   home there's no returning.
The Spartans on the sea-wet rock sat down and
   combed their hair.

One need hardly point out the inference; what the Spartans did we also can do.

But the doing is not easy and Housman makes no attempt
to delude either us or himself about the inevitable end.
This is what gives the profound pathos to **"When summer's end is nighing"** in *Last Poems.* The youth who delighted to climb the highest hill and watch the glow fade
out of the western sky, now turns in middle age to the shelter of his room and the glow of his lamp to shut out the
night and the thought of night. . . . Moreover, nature has
ceased to comfort as she did in the days of *A Shropshire
Lad.* Then he felt her sympathetic comradeship:

In my own shire if I was sad,
Homely comforters I had:
The earth, because my heart was sore,
Sorrowed for the son she bore.

But now he realizes that his old faith in nature was only
a spell cast over him by that enchantress,

For nature, heartless, witless nature,
Will neither care nor know
What stranger's feet may find the meadow
And trespass there and go,
Nor ask amid the dews of morning
If they are mine or no.

The one faith that burns clear in his poems from first to
last is trust in friendship. Over and over this is
voiced. . . . Friendship is the theme of **"Hell Gate"**, the
most remarkable and most original poem in the new volume. A lad pacing sadly across the 'uncoloured plain' with
his dark conductor sees in the shadow beneath the towering wall in the distance a spark stir to and fro. Though he
says not a word the sombre guide answers his unspoken
question,

At hell gate the damned in turn
Pace for sentinel and burn,

As they approach, the sentry vaguely reminds him of a
sentry in an earthly corps. When Sin and Death, warders
of the gate, rose to give entrance to their lord and father,
then

The portress foul to see
Lifted up her eyes on me
Smiling, and I made reply:
'Met again, my lass,' said I.
Then the sentry turned his head,
Looked, and knew me, and was Ned.

Even at the gate of hell, friendship triumphs. Ned strad-
dles in revolt across the entry and with his musket from
hell's arsenal shoots down his king.

And the hollowness of hell
Sounded as its master fell.

The two friends take the backward track in silence:

Once we listened and looked back;
But the city, dusk and mute,
Slept, and there was no pursuit.

This brief summary gives no conception of the cumulative
effect of the incidents in the poem or of its weird Dantesque power of description. I do not know anything just
like it in English. But through it all the passion of friendship is the shaping force.

It is the pity of having to leave one's friends that makes
the poem he chooses to close his *Last Poems* so wistful
and pathetic. He tells how he used to play the flute for
country dances [but now]

The lofty shade advances
I fetch my flute and play:
Come, lads, and learn the dances
And praise the tune to-day.
To-morrow, more's the pity
Away we both must hie,
To air the ditty,
And to earth I.

It is superfluous, almost impertinent, to call attention to
the sigh of regret and resignation in those closing lines. It
is the very spirit of Gray's *Elegy* in twentieth century
form.

Whether Housman plays the flute I do not know, but his
choice of it seems peculiarly appropriate. For his verse has
the very tones of that instrument, clear, mellow, piercing,
with something added of the undertones one catches in old
folk songs. It appeals to lovers of poetry whether they be
unread or as cultured as Housman himself. His poems in
their restraint, their simplicity, their clear outlines are essentially Greek; in their pathos, their poignancy, their
tremulous sensibility, they are Celtic and Romantic.

Housman, indeed, is the poet of a temperament. It nar-
rows his range while it deepens his intensity. To an increasing number he makes a peculiar appeal. Nature has
not proved the consoler that Wordsworth found her and
that Arnold expected she would more and more become.
Most of our poets of to-day—that is those of them who
think at all—have fallen back on a dogged stoicism and
an intense joy in whatever glimpse of beauty may be
caught as we journey on what Housman in one of his rare
moments of bitterness calls our 'long fool's errand to the
grave.' And so Housman's thought is to-day in what Arnold calls 'the main stream of ideas.' Whether this explains his influence I am not sure—it may in part—but I
am sure that with the exception of Thomas Hardy, no living English poet has had such an effect on the work of his
fellow-craftsmen. (pp. 131-37)

J. F. Macdonald, "The Poetry of A. E. Hous-

man," in Queen's Quarterly, *Vol. XXXI, No. 2, October-December, 1923, pp. 114-37.*

H. P. Collins (essay date 1925)

[*In the following excerpt, Collins calls Housman a "poet of genre" and argues that his subjectivity and personal treatment of themes result from Housman's choice of a rustic persona, and not from his lack of sophistication or emotional breadth.*]

The author of **The Shropshire Lad** has recently issued, after an interval of twenty-six years, his second and final collection of poetry under the title **Last Poems.** Professor Housman is a poet of large utterance, and he has an emotional intensity, finely controlled, which scarcely three of his contemporaries have surpassed. He has thought fit to create, he declares, only at moments of keen personal experience. **The Shropshire Lad** was a first fine careless rapture which he does not hope to renew. But the quality of these few later pieces is unchanged. He is the poet of a *genre;* he has therefore a vicarious method of self-realization which gives him a more *objective* power. (p. 67)

The most remarkable thing to be noticed about Mr. Housman is that when he wrote **The Shropshire Lad** he was rather ahead of his age; to-day, in producing poetry of a similar nature, he is a little in the wake of things; but he is also *nearer* to the general thinking mind than he was in the 'nineties. In other words, his natural vision has a prophetic quality. Bearing this in mind, let us examine more particular points: the literary method and the peculiar transposition of attitude that distinguish him.

Take first **The Shropshire Lad,** since it is pure *genre* poetry; consider how far it is personative and how far subjective, personal. All the themes are elemental. All the language is that in everyday use. The emotional attitude is so untouched with the subtleties of culture that we must suppose it is deliberately simplified. This means that the poet first imposes on himself a restraint akin to that involved in the use of dramatic structure; though not actually dramatic.

Once more, let us remember: the greatest poetry does not need complex emotions. The thoughts of the Shropshire lad are not the thoughts, even by poetic licence, of an ordinary peasant; they are the thoughts of a poet whom one pretends to have the upbringing and outlook of a country boy. So the rustic, elemental world that is the subject of contemplation is viewed, in consistency, as a world complete in itself. There is no adjustment, no relation to the exterior, wider realities of the universe of educated apprehension. . . . The Shropshire lad speaks of things as he feels them: Mr. Housman does not stand behind him to tell us how else they might have been felt.

This is an uncommon thing in modern literature: the lowly protagonist recounting a tale in the first person is not familiar in recent fiction, and under older traditions he was never free from the interpositions of his creator. . . . Mr. Housman, as a poet, is quite unique in this respect; he can make his countryman give us back any experience without a trace of inconsistency. In qualification it may be said that the Shropshire lad is not a detached creation but the embodiment of Mr. Housman's own temperament at a lower range of culture and experience. But that does not affect the achievement; is probably, rather, a condition of it; making the purely lyrical attitude possible.

How far—since this question must touch the quality and scope of his vision—is Mr. Housman faithful to his whole experience, and how far does he limit himself to the spiritual (as apart from the cultural and social) experience possible in a peasant? Does he, under the necessity of excluding subtle experience, 'unsight the seen'? Is it possible to do so and still be a sincere poet; that is, a poet?

It is certain that very much is 'seen' by Mr. Housman that could not reasonably be brought within the expression of a rustic spokesman. But is the spiritual essence of these perceptions, apart from the intellectual setting that relates them and might be needed to symbolize them in a more sophisticated way, attributable to a simple mind?

No true poet, none who has the authenticity that is written large upon Mr. Housman's work, denies his own full, emotional experience. 'It is not possible.' But he can restrict himself in the language, the range of equivalence, through which he liberates these perceptions, and thus does he bring them into dramatic character. Sophisticated poetry—and the highest poetry must be that—is the subtle relation of simple intuitions: in simplifying poetry one symbolizes and correlates the same intuitions more slowly, as it were; shutting off from one's stock of experience derivative and allusive imagery and the more sophisticated properties of language. The poetry may be strengthened in consequence, or it may be weakened. Usually in the case of the poets who can face at all such deliberate restriction as is needed in *genre* poetry, the quality of the poetry is deepened, because concentrated, and its range is narrowed. In view of one or two pieces in the **Last Poems,** it seems that Mr. Housman's **Shropshire Lad** had enabled him to accentuate the unity and sincerity of his thought, and has cut him off from very little that is valuable to his particular receptiveness.

The pervading note of Mr. Housman's assertion is a peculiarly barren scepticism. To this state of joyless indifference—it is neither fear nor tedium of life, but something that seems far less pregnant—every fragment of experience that he sets down, in the end returns. Towards the close of the Victorian epoch, when literature was still steeped in the habit of religious certitude, such a negation of any purpose beneath the scheme of things was wholly unfamiliar. Mr. Housman, though we may not easily recognize it to-day, did enter the literary arena in his homely Shropshire guise as the originator of a new poetical philosophy. He was apart equally from the daring, exuberant, shallow paganism of Swinburne and from the grave, profound, subtly moral atheism of Thomas Hardy. For the joy of mortal life as life he gave us only the exaltation of despair; for the earnest, questioning revolt against the witless arbitration of our destiny he substituted a brutal defiance:

> Oh, never fear man, nought's to dread
> Look not left nor right:
> In all the endless road you tread
> There's nothing but the night.

> . . . malt does more than Milton can
> To justify God's ways to man,
> Ale, man, ale's the stuff to drink
> For fellows whom it hurts to think:
> Look into the pewter pot
> To see the world as the world's not. . . .
> Heigho, the tale was all a lie;
> The world, it was the old world yet. . . .
> Luck's a chance, but trouble's sure,
> I'd face it as a wise man would,
> And train for ill and not for good.

This particular aspect of Mr. Housman's thought does not, in the nature of things, inspire his highest poetry. More impressive, in its restraint, is his half-stoical attitude towards beauty. Mr. Housman is timorous, not of life in any aspect, but of that joy in beauty which exalts and vivifies the feelings until they become a menace. Hence the fierce refutation of that solace which the sweetness of nature and of primal things offers to the sensitive mind; his perception of sheer beauty is persistently blotted, in these earlier poems especially, by the contrasting presence of sordidness, shame and death; peace is only admitted as a retrospect or a hopeless dream. Of that unrest which men miscall delight, Mr. Housman is entirely sceptical; joy—the adventitious bloom of life, as Aristotle saw it—is to him at best a narcotic; it is not a moral condition. The sense of moral effort may add intensity to our defiance of the injurious gods; but the fruits of goodness are dust and ashes in our mouths.

This seems like a philosophy of moral desperation; yet it is the essence of Mr. Housman that something valid does remain. It lies partly in his realization that an elusive, purposeless beauty touches such a philosophy as his more closely than rational, inherent, elevating beauty ever could. The reader is always aware of this, and it tinges every shade of emotion that is evoked. . . . (pp. 68-74)

The beauty that touches Mr. Housman's verse—to define it further by a series of negations—is not sensuous and physical; nor is it personal and difficult by its nature to communicate, in the mystic's way; nor is it transcendental, abstract. Rather it is simple; flames from the clash of tragic contrast between happiness and its eternal foiling. (p. 74)

Mr. Housman has not the sustained breadth of comprehension that makes the great poet; to set against this he makes no attempt, seemingly does not desire, to write 'out of Time'—or to escape from his own place in Time. There is in his work no negative quality, no vain revulsion of spirit; in his language no superfluity, no lack of discipline and self-sufficiency. His æsthetic response to life is always direct; though a certain indiscriminateness as to what is valuable to poetry has accentuated in him a limitation best described as an occasional, local poverty of sensibility, by contrast with Mr. Hardy's all-embracing sympathy. To those who feel, with much justice, that Mr. Housman's poetry is of the earth earthy, it must be opposed that what he can presumably do best he does indeed; in this he is unlike nearly all the others, who, whatever they may attempt, do nothing.

As for the **Last Poems,** though the voice of criticism has been, for all its shrillness, rather half-hearted, there can be no question of retrogression; they are deeper, more varied, and not less spontaneous than those of **The Shropshire Lad.** In "The West" Mr. Housman's deepest idiosyncrasy is finely and memorably revealed, and **"Hell Gate"** is an experiment of novel and broadened significance. The **Last Poems,** . . . are simply less of a sensation than the earlier volume, relative to a more sophisticated and sceptical atmosphere in religion and moral acquiescence. (pp. 76-7)

> *H. P. Collins, "A. E. Housman," in his* Modern Poetry, 1925. *Reprint by The Folcroft Press, 1970, pp. 67-77.*

AUTHOR'S COMMENTARY

Poetry indeed seems to me more physical than intellectual. A year or two ago, in common with others, I received from America a request that I would define poetry. I replied that I could no more define poetry than a terrier can define a rat, but that I thought we both recognised the object by the symptoms which it provokes in us. One of these symptoms was described in connexion with another object by Eliphaz the Temanite: 'A spirit passed before my face: the hair of my flesh stood up.' Experience has taught me, when I am shaving of a morning, to keep watch over my thoughts, because, if a line of poetry strays into my memory, my skin bristles so that the razor ceases to act. This particular symptom is accompanied by a shiver down the spine; there is another which consists in a constriction of the throat and a precipitation of water to the eyes; and there is a third which I can only describe by borrowing a phrase from one of Keats's last letters, where he says, speaking of Fanny Brawne, 'everything that reminds me of her goes through me like a spear.' The seat of this sensation is the pit of the stomach. . . .

I think that the production of poetry, in its first stage, is less an active than a passive and involuntary process; and if I were obliged, not to define poetry, but to name the class of things to which it belongs, I should call it a secretion; whether a natural secretion, like turpentine in the fir, or a morbid secretion, like the pearl in the oyster. I think that my own case, though I may not deal with the material so cleverly as the oyster does, is the latter; because I have seldom written poetry unless I was rather out of health, and the experience, though pleasurable, was generally agitating and exhausting.

(lecture date 1933)

Guy Boas   (essay date 1936)

[*Boas was an English writer, educator, editor, and critic. In the following excerpt, he attempts to identify the distinctive elements of Housman's poetry by delving into Housman's religious ideology. Boas purports that Housman's position is daring and independent because while other poets presume to judge men, Housman "presumes to judge God."*]

The appearance of **More Poems** by A. E. Housman, selected by his brother, Mr. Laurence Housman, and post-humously published by the author's 'permission, not by his wish', is a literary event. The new volume does little to belie the title of the previous **Last Poems** as almost all the verse in the new book was composed before **Last Poems** was published. It does, however, contradict the spirit of the author's foreword to **Last Poems** which discouraged us from expecting more. If the new book does not contain much equal to the finest quality in the previous ones, it is nevertheless throughout the authentic vintage; the work of a poet who has been successfully parodied but never successfully imitated: and it sets us thinking afresh of Housman's art.

In one way Housman's poetry is not difficult to assess. We have only to take down three small volumes from the shelf, and most of what they contain it is hardly necessary to re-read since so many of the poems have already stuck fast in the memory of every one who has an ear for the music of words. That, however, is the only easy thing about the business: all else is paradoxical, bewitching, uneasy.

Here is a poet with seemingly an equal zest for life and for the grave, filled equally with admiration for the soldier and with mockery for his trade, who yearns for more than the psalmist's span for loving the 'loveliest of trees', yet who yearns passionately to 'sleep again', who salutes every beauty of nature, the stars, the hills, the 'April elm', the flambeaux of the chestnut, the 'thymy wold', the 'trefoiled grass', the 'Christmas field', sunrise, sunset, and the Wain, with a sensitive admiration equal to that of the most passionate lover of creation, but who arraigns the Creator as a 'brute and blackguard', and can offer youth no more consoling nor edifying advice than to 'shoulder the sky, my lad, and drink your ale'.

Youth. Here the paradox reaches its climax. Who can doubt as he reads either volume that as the caustic scholar-poet watched, both in the earlier and the later of his two spasms of poetic inspiration, the 'lads' born and doomed to serve the Queen and then the King, to save the former for thirteen pence and the latter—together with 'the sum of things'—'for pay', his heart for once was free from bitterness, but for the thought of what unkind fates were in likely store for these splendid beings. (pp. 210-11)

A poet does not differ from other men except in degree of sensibility and intuition. But in the measure in which in these he does differ, his unescapable mission, whether he knows, acknowledges, likes it, or not, is to teach us, not necessarily what life should be—the province of the preacher—but what life can be, and what life is.

> What, still alive at twenty-two,
> A fine upstanding lad like you?

The Cambridge parody is deadly to the point. Revolt against life, disillusioned acceptance of duty as the least culpable and slow passage to the grave, an instant plucking-out of offending eye, and ending of life itself when the soul is sick, at best a weary acceptance of the Queen's shilling and of the comfort of ale pending the ultimate deliverance, this is all—apparently—the poet has to offer in way of testament to the lads he loves so well. He is uneasy and

tries to escape responsibility. We are all in the same boat, and he is responsible neither for the bark nor the voyage. 'The laws of God, the laws of men': he made neither; let them keep them themselves, he will not be party to a contract he has never subscribed to:

> I, a stranger and afraid
> In a world I never made.

And *what* a world! A world in which, however, many seeds are sown,

> The stinging nettle only
>   Will still be found to stand:
> The numberless, the lonely,
>   The thronger of the land,
>   The leaf that hurts the hand.

The poet will not be responsible for himself under these conditions, let alone for others. He would willingly fly to Saturn or to Mercury, and if he does comply with celestial or human decrees, it is only because God and man are strong, and he has no option.

As a message it will not do. The very individuality of the standpoint is part of the secret of the intense interest which Housman arouses. No one has written like Housman, not only because no one has been compounded of just that admixture of chemicals which produced from this 'oyster' its 'secretion', but because no one else, not even Donne or Webster, has wished or dared to take up so independent a position. Other poets have presumed to judge men, including the kings of the earth. Housman presumes to judge God—and to find him wanting. However vague and pantheistic most poets' conception may be of God, Spirit of the Universe, Spirit of Beauty, Reality, Life-Force, call it what they will, they are at pains to put men in harmony with the same God with whom they find themselves in sympathy. The profound sensation of hopeless negation which Housman's poetry produces comes from the fact that he will admit no God, no Reality, no spirit with whom he can find communion, and he is therefore powerless to help others either to vision or to peace. All that he can do, as was said of the Russian realistic novelists, is 'to see life as it is and proceed to make it a great deal worse'. . . . (pp. 211-13)

Nothing which the splendid intellect, the superb literary economy, the word-magic, the crystal lucidity, the great simple beauty of the poems may do to bind us in affection, admiration, envy, and gratitude to Housman's poetic art, should blind us to the elementary fact that his moral is wrong from top to bottom. Wrong, not because we disagree with it, but because it is non-existent. However much enjoyment the poems afford, at the end we have learnt from them no more of the meaning of life and nature than when we began; all that we have been told is that our gifted instructor cannot make head or tail of the lesson himself. (p. 213)

A mind of piercing clarity, a poet—that is, a maker—who expresses himself with classical lucidity can throughout 152 perfectly wrought poems make nothing whatever of the cosmos and of philosophy except negative confusion and doubt. The poems of Housman are compositions which decompose everything except themselves. Granite-like in form and expression they are hewn and stand, but the thoughts they contain and provoke whirl in kaleidoscopic commotion.

Three themes predominate, beating recurrent alarm like tocsins, Soldiership, Love, and the Gallows.

War has been derided elsewhere, but the satire of *Troilus and Cressida* or *Arms and the Man* is a velvet compliment compared with the bite of Housman's teeth. God will save the Queen, never fear, provided we beget children as suitable for cannon-fodder as the last. Sure, I must strap on my sword that will not save, and I must be brave. Why? Because the heroic triumphs of my military ancestors inspire me to victory? No. There is a reason, but a very different reason from that:

> What evil luck soever
>   For me remains in store,
> 'Tis sure much finer fellows
>   Have fared much worse before.

Who is the 'happy warrior' in Housman, that every man in arms should wish to be? The answer is simple and insistent: there are soldiers beyond the reach of the sergeant and of the enemy's missiles, who have no need of the admiration of the lasses or of treating by a friend, who have only the smallest space of ground which they need, though they cannot defend it. . . . Soldiership, for all its glamour and activity, is connected in the mind with death, but Love, which alone can make terms with the Destroyer, which peoples the world with energy, warding off the last silence with song and the last blackness and blankness with colour and romance—surely the poet can surrender on this subject to joy, and forget for once the curtain-fall. Not so Housman, who watches lovers like an undertaker—is it wistfully, sympathetically, or triumphantly, knowing that in the end he shall have his fee?

> Lovers lying two and two
>   Ask not whom they sleep beside,
> And the bridegroom all night through
>   Never turns him to the bride.

Abstain even from Love, unless you wish to go even sooner than otherwise to destruction: it can do you no good by preserving or recreating life which should never have been, while it may do you infinite injury in making what is bad worse:

> His folly has not fellow
>   Beneath the blue of day
> That gives to man or woman
>   His heart and soul away. . . .

And so, by swift and easy stages, we come to preoccupation with the rope.

> And bacon's not the only thing
> That's cured by hanging on a string.

Again the Cambridge parody epitomizes that obsession with the hangman which Wilde in the course of one poem depicted ineffaceably, but which haunts Housman's verses throughout.

> Strapped, noosed, nighing his hour,
>   He stood and counted them and cursed his
>   luck;
> And then the clock collected in the tower
>   Its strength, and struck.

This **"Eight O'Clock"** is mere onomatopoeic horror; Grand Guignol played with finest literary craft. Far more terrible is **"The Culprit,"** in which both victim and poet are conscious to the last, conscious not only of one grim episode, but of all the tragedy and horror, looking before and after, which philosophy extracts from every such tragedy. Should man be born of woman if he may suffer so? Should man beget man, if this may be the end? . . . Father Time in Hardy's *Fude* did what he did 'because we are too many'. To Housman one on the globe is too many; at least he can hang himself.

Scrambling out of this charnel house, and throwing off these cerements before we are suffocated, let us try to solve this problem of a poet who, living to a ripe old age, in comfortable circumstances, popular in his small output of poetry beyond all his more fertile contemporaries, combined so much intellectual energy with so much morbidity, and won wide popularity by singing songs of suicide.

'Beauty is truth, truth beauty.' If Keats's dictum were as true as it sounds inevitable, it would explain Housman's secret. For what Housman says is true, though only partly true, because he writes as though catastrophe is typical, which it is not. Whatever Keats may have meant—which has never been exactly determined—it is certain that much which is beautiful is not true. It would perhaps be just to say that what Housman said was true, and how he said it was beautiful, but no healthy or sane mind could accept his subject-matter as beauty. The beauty of his poetry therefore is dependent not on matter but on form, which is a shallow beauty compared with the unfathomable depths of Homer or Dante or Shakespeare, where beauty of style is born not of outward verbal felicity but of inward spirit, beautiful to the core.

What then is specially notable in Housman's style, which plays so great, too great, a part in his art? The style is that of a poet who has passed through every phase of romantic ornament and emerged satisfied with nothing but economy, bleak and massive, the economy of Lear's 'Pray you, undo this button'. Prose-writers too, as Ruskin, have passed through opulence to this thrift, but it is remarkable in Housman's case that the last phrase is also the first. . . . The main characteristics of his economy are obvious; the profusion of monosyllables, the preponderance of short Saxon words, the classical simplicity and lucidity of expression, the rhymes so easy and antitheses so inevitable that they are unnoticed. These characteristics are frequently concentrated into four lines:

> So here I'll watch the night and wait
>   To see the morning shine,
> When he will hear the stroke of eight
>   And not the stroke of nine.

But neither poet nor financier ever achieved fortune by economy only, and it is interesting to try and detect how it is that from this ultra-simple wording such captivating music sounds, frequently rich in effect and persistently grand.

To probe the secret we must think of music proper. How is it that Mozart with almost childlike simplicity of notation and orchestration opens the gates of Heaven which remain shut to so many composers who have brought every complication of modern orchestration into prodigious play? There are two styles in which a great artist may express himself greatly, the complicated and the simple. Neither style is greater nor less than the other, but the artist to succeed in the complicated style must be as great as a Wagner: if he is less, his work may be interesting but will not be great. . . . That greatness which instead of triviality produces the grand style is inherent in the poet's spirit, and, while the achievement is evident, the cause, being spiritual, cannot be analysed. We can only fall back on Matthew Arnold's touchstone of specimens. If we compare lines from Housman with Arnold's specimens, with

> In la sua volontade é nostra pace

or

> And courage never to submit or yield
> And what is else not to be overcome

Housman is inferior neither in simplicity nor in force.

> We want the moon, but we shall get no more.

. . . .

> The troubles of our proud and angry dust
> Are from eternity, and shall not fail.

And yet from the broad open effect of Dante's and Milton's great sentences there is, to the sensitive ear, a difference: the music of Dante and Milton is at one with the objective music of the universe: Housman is as simple, but with the simplicity of an individual, sophisticated soul, who rather than joining in the universal chorus pipes a questioning obligato to the main theme. (pp. 213-17)

Returning to the subject-matter of the poems, we have noted that Love, War, and the Gallows work their havoc throughout the poet's pages; but against what background? If it were only against the bare walls of the condemned cell, the withered and blasted battlefield, or the garish haunts of prostitution, what a world of nightmare would it be! But this is no more so than in Thomas Hardy. In Housman as in Hardy the Devil dances in country lanes and meadows, warmed by God's sun, freshened by God's rain, decorated by trees and flowers, watched at night by the stars, wrapped in the beauty of winter's snow, and called every spring to new raptures of life and to the profusion of nature's glory. No optimistic poet has ever loved the beauty of nature more sincerely than Housman, and perhaps it is the genuineness and intensity of this affection coupled with his crystal clear vision and interpretation of the lovely details of nature's workshop and paint-box which act as an antiseptic to the gloom of his philosophy and dilute the poison in his cup. (p. 218)

The story of the lovers of Bredon Hill is a typical Housman tragedy, yet those who know the rhyme of their fate by heart may well ponder when they recall the poem whether it is the dead lady and the heart-broken swain that really stick in the memory, or whether it is the picture of the 'coloured counties' and 'the larks so high'. So many poetic weddings have been thwarted or destroyed by Fate that another more or less adds little to the untimely death of the Miller's daughter of Allan Water, but there is nothing in the old ballad or in any similar threnody which comes into the mind quite like the 'coloured counties', as for oneself one surveys them from high ground on a summer day. However distorted may be the picture of human thought and passion in these poems, the picture of nature's activity is foursquare both with truth and beauty. Whether it is a set piece:

> The night goes out and under
> With all its train forlorn;
> Hues in the east assemble
> And cocks crow up the morn.

or whether it is a detail, 'the skylit water', 'the leafless timber', 'the cloudled shadows', the poet's testimony is flawless. Men and women may tear their hearts and souls to pieces among the flowers of Paradise, but when the actors are all corpses the lovely scenery remains untorn. It is a fearful notion that had Housman continued to write into the days of massive airfleets, even the fair body of nature could no longer have seemed to him secure: not only would courageous and honest men have been born for no better fate than the sword, but nature would generate her orchards and forests only to be demolished by high explosives, and her coloured counties only to be withered by poison gas. It may well be that so the poet thought before he died, but it is perhaps a relief that having presented us with a world sombre enough already he did not add to it one of nightmare which may not occur, and which, if it does, had better pass unrecorded in the language of Helicon:

> Comrade, look not on the west.

Though Housman outlived Thomas Hardy, the gloomy questioning world in revolt against sugared complacency, which seared Hardy's soul and moulded his philosophy, did the same for Housman. 'It is a question', writes Hardy in *The Return of the Native,* 'if the exclusive reign of orthodox beauty is not approaching its last quarter. The new Vale of Tempe may be a gaunt waste in Thule.' Tennyson's Vale of Tempe turns in Housman to the gaunt waste in Thule. They are both beautiful not because they are kindred beauty, but because many now see beauty—even prefer it—in a landscape from which admirers of *Crossing the Bar* turn in disgust.

Yet there is a still more personal clue, and of singular value. Hardy, for all his lifelong contest with Heaven, lies buried in the Abbey, and whether or not this would have been his own wish, the instinct of his countrymen to lay him there is generally accepted as right. Nine years before his death, Housman wrote . . . "For my Funeral," which was duly sung in Trinity College Chapel before his burial:

> O thou that from thy mansion
> Through time and place to roam,
> Dost send abroad thy children,
> And then dost call them home,
>
> That men and tribes and nations
> And all thy hand hath made
> May shelter them from sunshine
> In thine eternal shade:

> We now to peace and darkness
>   And earth and thee restore
> Thy creature that thou madest
>   And wilt cast forth no more.

So then it was the poet's belief that some one made him, sent him out, and called him home. No atheism here. But theism is no guarantee of a benevolent God, and what nature does the poet recognize in the God whom these lines acknowledge? 'And wilt cast forth no more.' In the two harsh monosyllables 'cast forth' the clue is surely given. From peace and to peace we are called, but during the interim of our worldly activity we are in every sense cast forth, and, though we keep faith even to the Cross, who can repress the cry 'My God, my God, why hast thou forsaken me?'?

Even the poet himself had a twinge of conscience, and tried to explain himself: but it is significant that the explanation was only published posthumously 'by his permission, not by his wish'.

> They say my verse is sad: no wonder;
>   Its narrow measure spans
> Tears of eternity, and sorrow
>   Not mine, but man's.
>
> This is for all ill-treated fellows
>   Unborn and unbegot,
> For them to read when they're in trouble
>   And I am not.

So then it was all altruism, was it? Creeds destroyed, illusions shattered, the very heavens derided, not because of any personal grudge or grievance but to benefit and comfort the other tortured fellows. Never, surely, has there been a more dubious method of philanthropy or a more unconvincing profession of humanitarianism, weighted down by the mighty ambiguity of 'And I am not'.

Nothing is more unbecoming than to pity a man of genius, to say how much nicer it would have been if he had been otherwise, which probably means that he would not have been a genius at all. If Housman had been endowed with the faith of the Vicar of Wakefield, we should not possess his poems, and the world would be the poorer and we no wiser. Yet there is nothing impertinent in pointing out that whatever pleasure poems such as Housman's give, however much they may teach us of literary art, they serve as little more of a guide to life than would be served by an exclusive tour of cemeteries, derelict battlefields, mortuaries, and prisons. The greatest of all artists have made no sermons as they wrote, but Shakespeare, and Bach, and Velázquez, by showing us the whole of life, its glory as well as it grime, its joy and comedy as well as its tragedy, preach without need of text, and proclaim God without mentioning him.

Housman, in common with all pessimists, draws a false picture, because, if it is false to say that all's well with the world, it is equally false to say that all's ill. Things no more always go wrong than they go right: many a soldier has saved the Queen with no thought of pay-day in his mind; many a soul that has been sick, refusing to end itself, has become sound again; and the mintage which many an old

man has carried back to the coiner is brighter than that of the lads who will never be old. (pp. 218-21)

Guy Boas, "The Poetry of A. E. Housman," in
English, *Vol. I, No. 3, 1936, pp. 210-22.*

The Times Literary Supplement   (essay date 1936)

[*In the following excerpt, the anonymous reviewer compares Housman's* More Poems *to his two previous collections. While the critic finds merit in this volume, he does maintain that in many ways the themes and stylistic elements are mere continuances of those found in* A Shropshire Lad *and* Last Poems. *What makes* More Poems *worthwhile, the critic purports, is that it reveals Housman's emotions more than any of his other works.*]

A fuller knowledge of Housman may be gained from **More Poems.** This book has been eagerly awaited. For Housman has probably a wider public than any modern poet, a public which comprises not only those who admire him as an artist uniting a supreme felicity with a power of moving the emotions never excelled by any English lyric poet, but also many un-literary persons who, stirred by the emotions of youth, or by the recollection of it, are pleased to find their own feelings simply and musically expressed. . . . It must at once be said that the collection is not, as a whole, as fine as either of the earlier volumes, and that even its highest peaks are not quite as high as some that Housman reached before. Further, Mr. Laurence Housman, in his natural (and admitted) zeal to ensure that his brother's admirers shall lose nothing that they might enjoy, has printed several poems . . . which, on any standard, should have been excluded.

Most of those pieces in **More Poems** which had been composed before the publication of his earlier volumes were omitted by their author, we surmise, for two very different reasons: some because they were too like, and a few because they were too unlike, his other poems. A score or so of these poems, it is interesting to learn, belong to the "Terence" series and were written when **A Shropshire Lad** was written; and of most of these, and of some others, it may be said that they are neither better nor worse than "the average of his published works." The lover of Housman would not be surprised, either by their character or by their quality. . . . (p. 845)

No one, we have been told, ever wished *Paradise Lost* a line longer; many have wished **A Shropshire Lad** longer by many lines, and now their wish has been fulfilled. What a strange mixture of old and new delight is provided, for instance, by the following:

> I lay me down and slumber
>   And every morn revive.
> Whose is the night-long breathing
>   That keeps me man alive?
>
> When I was off to dreamland
>   And left my limbs forgot,
> Who stayed at home to mind them,
>   And breathed when I did not?
>
> I waste my time in talking,
>   No heed at all takes he,

My kind and foolish comrade
    That breathes all night for me.

Elsewhere, after two inferior stanzas, come lines of a supreme and characteristic beauty:

The stinging nettle only
    Will still be found to stand:
The numberless, the lonely,
    The thronger of the land,
    The leaf that hurts the hand.

It thrives, come sun, come showers,
    Blow east, blow west, it springs;
It peoples towns, and towers
    Above the courts of Kings,
    And touch it and it stings.

There are in this book a score of such lyrics, and their beauty will profoundly move those who care for poetry. Yet it is not difficult to guess the reasons which compelled Housman to exclude them from his own collections: even the best of them are, after all, little more than echoes of things he had done before. For Housman, like many another poet, had a repetitive mind; he repeated both theme and phrase; even the artifice of his verse, though it is never transparent, is sometimes betrayed by the recurrence, within quite a small compass, of some alliterative or other device. . . . (pp. 845-46)

This repetitiveness, if not in itself a defect, is a feature which Housman evidently did not wish to mark too noticeably the small body of verse which he was to leave behind him.

Certainly this tendency to iteration contributes to the marked peculiarity of his poems; and it is no doubt this very peculiarity—its utter unlikeness to any other poetry, its utter and consistent likeness to itself—that makes his poetry to some readers quite intolerable, to others attractive in a way in which no other poetry attracts them, and makes it impossible for either to explain their attitude towards it. Another element in this peculiarity is a stiltedness, an affectation in his diction, which stamps many phrases as indubitably his, though they cannot be paralleled elsewhere in his work: "the *primal fault*"; "they blaze, but *none regard*"; "Tell me of *runes to grave*" in *More Poems*; "Thews that lie and cumber Sunlit pallets never thrive"; "There flowers no balm to sain him" in *A Shropshire Lad*—such phrases sufficiently explain why some persons find it difficult to read his work with pleasure. More readers, however, are repelled by ever-recurring phrases like "for aye," by frequent references to the grave and to the field of battle, and by that hardened offender, with its kindred colloquialisms, "my lad." It is the use of phrases such as these, with all that their use implies, that alienates the majority of Housman's detractors; and Professor Garrod once took him publicly to task for his "false pastoralism," his *dramatis personae* of chaps and fellows, his apparatus of footballs and scaffolds and bullets, and his treatment of earth itself as nothing but a graveyard. . . .

His poems are of three fairly distinguishable kinds: those inspired by emotions arising from man's relations with his fellow-men, those inspired by the contemplation of human destiny, and those inspired by external nature. It is only the first kind that affords scope for the bucolic convention. No trace of it mars those poems in which man is set alone against the background of his destiny—though the unfaltering despair with which the poet confronts and defies his fate sometimes leads those who do not share his attitude to suspect that his fortitude consists merely in the maintenance of a pose. The record of his life and personality lends no colour to the suspicion; and if ever any cry came from the heart it is heard in his lines "Be still, my soul, be still." . . .

Nor is there any affectation in the love displayed in his nature-poems for the countryside:

Tell me not here, it needs not saying,
    What tunes the enchantress plays
In aftermaths of soft September
    Or under blanching mays,
For she and I were long acquainted
    And I knew all her ways.

The poems on these themes—and they include some of his loveliest and most moving work—are completely innocent of the idiom with which Housman's name is generally associated; neither the setting nor the phraseology is open to the criticism of belonging merely to a stock-in-trade.

Let us go to the opposite extreme and take a poem which exhibits all that Housman's critics rightly reprehend—the unabashed sentimentalism, the melodrama, the meretricious metrical effect, the diction at once colloquial and stilted, the inattention to harmony which, though never silencing it, sometimes gave a queer metallic ring—the ring of an epigram, not of a song—to the music of his verse:

I did not lose my heart in summer's even,
    When roses to the moonrise burst apart;
When plumes were underfoot and lead was flying,
    In blood and smoke and flame I lost my heart.

I lost it to a soldier and a foeman,
    A chap that did not kill me, but he tried;
That took the sabre straight and took it striking,
    And laughed and kissed his hand to me and died.

What a pity that the editor did not invoke the prerogative which he says he has exercised elsewhere in the book and omit the second stanza! Standing alone, the first stanza has an effectiveness which the second seems to caricature. And this is but one example of a taint which recurs at several points in Housman's published verse, and is apt to vitiate his poems about the young men who walk out with Rose Harland, and fasten their hands upon their hearts, if they have not drowned their sorrows in the ale of Ludlow—the taint, in a word, of self-dramatization.

How far self-dramatization enters into all writing of lyric poetry is a question which may be left to the aestheticians; it may be that the fault in Housman was not that he dramatized himself, but that he did not dramatize himself successfully. At all events, some projection of his personality was necessary to him; and although it cannot be doubted that the emotions expressed in his verse were genuine and deeply felt, and although it must remain for ever uncertain what actual experiences evoked them, it is at least plain that in order to transmute his feelings about persons into poetry he had to invent a world, a series of incidents, and a character at once himself and not himself. This need to dramatize himself resulted, one must believe, from a lack in his own life—the lack of those emotional "contacts" from which he shrank—from his inability to expose himself to any other person, from his refusal to be lured "into the labyrinth of another's being" or to allow another to see into the secrecy of his own. . . .

The lyric impulse craves for an occasion, that it may have matter and form for its fulfilment; a mere state of feeling, in particular the dead level of frustrated emotion, is rarely enough to start unaided in the conscious or the subconscious being the process which ends in a poem. The poet needs an incident, a person, a situation—at all events, a contact. It was just this that Housman, in order to write poems expressing the emotions arising out of personal relationships, had to supply in imagination; and, if it came easiest to him to supply it in a highly artificial setting, it must be remembered that his emotions were evidently of a kind for which English poetry does not provide a very ready means of expression. . . .

This, then, is the source of Housman's bucolic convention: a lack of particular emotional occasions, and a difficulty in expressing directly the emotions that he felt. But it must not be forgotten that Housman several times dispensed with that convention even when writing poems of the affections, and several of his most moving poems are the result:

> If truth in hearts that perish
>   Could move the powers on high,
> I think the love I bear you
>   Should make you not to die . . .
>
> This long, this sure-set liking,
>   This boundless will to please,
> —Oh, you should live for ever
>   If there were help in these—

that is the expression of an emotion which, whether experienced in fact or in imagination, has not been dressed up for the occasion of print; the poet is speaking in the first person, and with his own voice, undisguised.

More Poems is particularly interesting in that it reveals more clearly than anything yet published Housman's undisguised emotions. A few words in the Preface warn us how little of his verse must be taken to be "autobiographical," and indicate clearly enough the two or three poems in this book to which that name can truly be applied. It is not rash to suggest that most of them had been written before *A Shropshire Lad,* at least before *Last Poems,* was published. If so, Housman's reason for excluding them was precisely the opposite to that which caused the exclusion of the poems belonging to the "Terence" series: they were not too like, but too unlike, the other published poems; if they had stood side by side with them, the contrast in manner, in tone, would have been apparent, and would have damaged the effect of both. . . .

[Those] who say that *More Poems* is merely a collection of echoes of Housman's already published work have failed to recognize a difference which throws light on something that is fundamental in him, both as a poet and as a man. (p. 846)

> *"A. E. Housman: More Poems and a Memoir," in* The Times Literary Supplement, *No. 1812, October 24, 1936, pp. 845-46.*

Eda Lou Walton   (essay date 1936)

[*An educator and editor, Walton is the author of* The City Day *(1929) and* This Generation *(1940). In the following excerpt, Walton praises Housman's* More Poems *for its universality and classic simplicity.*]

Housman is dead; he who without wit or metaphysics saw death clearly has undergone it. In his will he stated that his brother Laurence might print such poems as he thought good. We have, therefore, in [*More Poems*] forty-eight . . . poems which are worthy of the poet, though some have not quite the simple, dramatic perfection of those Housman himself printed. His own funeral poem and many others now belong, as Housman does, to the world; they are the product of one of the finest "minor" poetic talents in English literature. Housman's request to his brother to destroy his notebooks on poetic ideas and his workshop material results in a terrible loss to all students of poetry. Notes on a craft as perfect as Housman's would have been invaluable. We are left with only one example, printed in this book, of two versions of a poem, but this single example indicates how Housman rid himself of the characteristic romanticism and personal emotionalism common to the other poets of his period.

Housman, it must be remembered, knew the impact of modern despair as early as 1895, the year of his greatest poetic output. This is the period of decadent romanticism during which Dowson wrote of passion as a drug to stimulate and to kill, Kipling and Henley hymned physical activity as reason for living, and many poets turned Catholic. Thirty years before our modern poets announced the death of an era, Housman wrote of it. While Yeats wrapped himself in the cloak of Irish myth and legend, Housman faced reality and found it tragic. He was of his own times in that he focused on individual tragedy but of our times in his bitterness against injustice, his hatred of war and empire. And he alone of the poets of his era depersonalized his philosophy and emotions so that they, and his poems, became "not mine, but man's."

To speak of these new poems of Housman's is to speak of his poetry in general. Most of them date with *Shropshire Lad* and the *Last Poems.* Housman presents the modern knight, common man, fighting his last battle against too much self-knowledge, fighting with his "sword that will not save," pride and courage. His form is an adaptation of ballad and bucolic lyric, medieval and classical forms shaped to the simple, impersonal lyric which gives the essence of a story and an emotion. In words of one syllable Housman asserts the paradox of life—that the human will is immediately negated by a man's taking thought. The closing lines of poem after poem illustrate this. Here are two examples from his recent book:

> The head that I shall dream of
> That will not dream of me
>
> Thy creature that thou madest
> And wilt cast forth no more

Such dramatic reversals as conclude Housman's poems—"our eyes are in the places where we shall never be"—indicate this poet's irrevocable belief that man's own sense of time and death must deny him—once youth and its illusions of physical delight are past—any reason for living save the will to endure.

There are, as Kenneth Burke once remarked, nuclei of emotions and ideas fused in any poet's writing and from these a poet's characteristic images and symbols emerge. The finer the poet the fewer, most probably, his essential responses, for in the fine poet emotions and ideas form clusters which determine a point of view or a philosophy. Housman illustrates this perfectly. His visual scene is Shropshire, its moor and mountain, town and steeple, barn and stack, a background simple and universal enough to be named and not elaborately described, a country small enough to seem typical of any provincial setting wherein man takes thought concerning his own life and the life of others. His fundamental belief is that man's own awareness of decay and death is tragic. It follows therefore that youth, less aware, is alone happy, that suicide is justifiable if willed, that love may momentarily blind one to an inevitable defeat in life. And Housman's symbols—youth in sport, youth in love, the soldier in the fight of life, the mature man thinking about time and its harvest—all emerge from his philosophy. But because Housman's poetry is rather more classic than romantic, his scene and his essential drama and its characteristics are presented simply and universally, in inevitably correct and direct statement, so that his poetry—even when the first person pronoun is used—seems impersonal and applicable to every man. This is why every clear and perfect line of his, every poem with its dramatic close, is remembered.

> *Eda Lou Walton, "Not Mine, but Man's," in*
> The Nation, *New York, Vol. 143, No. 19, November 7, 1936, p. 552.*

Conrad Aiken   (essay date 1936)

[*An American poet, essayist, critic, short story writer, and editor, Aiken was the author of such critical works as* Notes on Contemporary Poetry (1919) *and* A Reviewer's ABC: Collected Criticism (1958). *Aiken was one of the first critics to level the often repeated charge that Housman's poetry is adolescent in outlook. Aiken also maintains that the celebrated simplicity of Housman's lyrics may be a result of his devotion to the classical form. This essay first appeared only three weeks after Housman's death, and Aiken's ill timing and insensitivity in publishing such a harsh indictment provoked normally moderate critics to condemn him as a publicity seeker.*]

The **Last Poems** of Housman have now been succeeded by

More Poems, chosen from among the completed verses which he left behind him at his death, and thus the total number of lyrics given to the world by this most reticent and self-denying of poets grows to the total of one hundred and fifty-three; but one can say at once that it is an addition which does not change, that the addition of the third volume, like the addition of the second, extends slightly, if at all, the range, does not alter the character, and that the three books are really one, are really **The Shropshire Lad.** It is more or less true that the third collection is very slightly inferior to the second, just as the second was very slightly inferior to the first. The thinnesses and barenesses are more noticeable, the repetitions of theme and tone more staring, the genuine felicities are certainly fewer. Nor are there whole poems, as many of them, which attain to quite the cool completeness of the best in **The Shropshire Lad**. . . .

That [Housman] is limited, no one in his senses would deny. The actual range, when one stops to consider it, is extraordinarily narrow, and the perhaps too-well-disposed critic wonders whether he is not wish-thinking in supposing that many of Housman's restrictions were self-restrictions. It is one thing—one may say—to be limited, another to *impose* limitations on oneself; and somehow or other the myth has grown up that Housman's limitedness, like the smallness of his output, was the result of an iron discipline and restraint, a process of selection and elimination at a very high degree of tension, and that the product was accordingly, *ipso facto,* severely and beautifully classic. Housman himself did a good deal to encourage the growth of this notion. . . .

Moreover, an idea got abroad, whether with his own imprimatur or not, that one reason for the extreme smallness of his output was that the intensity of the effort, as of the "inspiration," for even the tiniest and most fragile of his verses, was too exhausting for him, could not more than occasionally be endured, an idea only partially offset by a sister rumor that it was really beer which was his inspiration—the often-celebrated "pot" of the poems. Just the same, it is permissible perhaps to question whether the narrowness of the range and the smallness of the output were not actually implicit in the nature of Housman's talent, and imposed from within rather than from without; and to question in parallel fashion whether the often-praised "classic" perfection and severity of his style might not more justly, now and then, be termed pseudo-classic.

And that, for better or worse, and at the risk of being considered guilty of something perilously like *lèse majesté*, the present reviewer has always thought, and still thinks, thinks more than ever after a rereading of the three little books. It is idle to deny the charm, the grace, the dexterity, the neatness, whether of form or thought, just as it is idle to deny the wistful and brave individuality which everywhere shows in these poems; but it seems equally idle to deny that the classic should be made of sterner and deeper stuff than this, and that if it is not to be profounder, then it must at least be more richly and variously wrought.

And even taken at its best, the texture of Housman's verse tends to be thin. Nor is this wholly a matter of choice. Simplicity is aimed at, to be sure, but there is always, also, a little *more* simplicity than was aimed at, and this looks as if it arose from the fact that Housman's sensory equipment for poetry was definitely somewhat arid. The range of mere perception is very narrow indeed—it is a world in which the grass is green and the sheep are white, as simple a world as that of W. H. Davies, for example, but with almost nothing of Davies' sudden felicities of observation or quick aptnesses of statement. Housman conventionalizes, and that would be all right if the conventionalization were itself more interesting; but for this reader at least the constant reliance on a pretty threadbare and perhaps deliberately anachronistic kind of martial imagery, joined with a bucolic imagery just as deliberately "quaint" or "homely," becomes in the end both barren and defrauding.

That one should cease to believe might not matter, provided the *playing* at poetry, the playing at profundity or skepticism, were itself more richly and ingeniously managed; but this Housman only seldom achieved. The result is a charming but incomplete and essentially adolescent poetry—the questionings and despairs and loyalties are alike adolescent, and so are the thoughts and the bravenesses and the nostalgic gayeties; and what makes it sometimes worse is one's suspicion that this adolescent note, this boyishness, is a calculated thing, a calculated falsetto. . . .

But no, that is perhaps being too hard on a very fine poet, and to overdo our point that at least a part of Housman's charm grew from his very limitations. Greatness? No. Epigrammatic, lovely, light-colored, youthfully charming above all. . . . (p. 51)

> *Conrad Aiken, "A. E. Housman," in* The New Republic, *Vol. LXXXIX, No. 1145, November 11, 1936, pp. 51-2.*

Stephen Spender   (essay date 1940)

[*Spender is an English writer who rose to prominence during the 1930s as a Marxist lyric poet and as an associate of W. H. Auden, Christopher Isherwood, C. Day Lewis, and Louis MacNeice. Like many other artists and intellectuals of his generation, Spender became disillusioned with socialism after World War II, and although he occasionally makes use of political and social issues in his work, he is more often concerned with aspects of self-knowledge and depth of personal feeling. Since World War II, Spender's stature as a perceptive literary critic has grown. In the following excerpt, Spender examines the merit of the poems included in* The Collected Poems of A. E. Housman. *Spender contends that the new poems in this volume are nothing but repetitions of Housman's earlier verse and do not do justice to the poet's passion or discipline.*]

[There are] one hundred and seventy-five poems, and three short translations of Greek Choruses [in *The Collected Poems of A. E. Housman*]. Of these, seventy poems were not published during the poet's lifetime, and one may guess that he would certainly have wished the greater number of his posthumously published poems to have been suppressed. (p. 295)

The posthumous poems are interesting, but on the whole they do him a disservice, because although they contain beautiful lines, and even whole poems as good as many he wrote, they say in a cruder form, which sometimes amounts almost to parody, what he had said before, and they do the one thing which Housman must have wanted to avoid doing—heighten the reader's curiosity about the biographical background to his poetry.

If one starts thinking of Housman's poems in this way, one can go on trimming and paring away poems around a fairly well-defined core which one might call the Essential Housman, of perhaps less than fifty poems, in which Housman really says all he has to say. The remainder of the poems are slight, or attempts to say something which he conveyed better in other poems, or else introductory ornaments, like the opening poems in *A Shropshire Lad* and *Last Poems.*

At his best, Housman is a poet of great force and passion whose music is quite unforced, combining sensuousness with a cold discipline which gives the poetry an almost anonymous quality of being something said rightly, rather than something said by someone. . . . (pp. 295-96)

Housman wrote some great poetry if not great poems and no criticism can lessen the value of certain lines and whole poems which have an independent rightness and certainty which is beyond comment. All criticism can do is to attempt to define the range of his poetry, and say whether the pessimistic philosophy which he advances repeatedly in poem after poem is an adequate attitude towards life.

Housman's poems have properties as defined as the machinery of diabolism in Baudelaire: the countryside of Western England, the lads who are brave and true, the references to the ancient world, the stilted and firmly established imperialism. Within this environment, there springs a poetry which has three main sources of inspiration: a frustrated love, a passion for justice, equally frustrated, and the view that life is misery and that man is only happy when he is safely under the ground.

Ultimately, the whole of Housman's pessimism and sense of injustice springs from the idea of frustrated love:

> He, standing hushed, a pace or two apart,
>   Among the bluebells of the listless plain,
> Thinks and remembers how he cleansed his
>   heart
> And washed his hands in innocence in vain.

The young, the straight, the true, the brave, gain nothing from their virtue; they are shot just the same, and the world is so vile a place that they are happiest dead: "Let us endure an hour and see injustice done." . . . (pp. 296-97)

If one compares Housman's love poems with those of Donne, one sees how inadequate his rejection of love and hence life is. In Donne we feel that the poet has tasted deeply of life, and that while he is still tasting it, it turns to ashes. In Housman, we feel that he had a youthful disappointment on which he constructed an edifice of personal despair and bitterness which lasted a lifetime. For Housman himself this disappointment may have been tragic, but it is not valid as a judgement by which the whole of life, or even the life of the senses can be condemned. The effect of Donne's poetry is to make one feel that life is haunted by the sense of death and guilt; the effect of Housman's, after one has reached a certain age, merely to make one feel very sorry for Housman.

The nature of Housman's disappointment is revealed in these lines:

> Because I liked you better
>   Than suits a man to say,
> It irked you, and I promised
>   To throw the thought away.
>
> To put the world between us
>   We parted, stiff and dry;
> "Goodbye," said you, "forget me".
>   "I will, no fear," said I.
>
> If here, where clover whitens
>   The dead man's knoll, you pass,
> And no tall flower to meet you
>   Starts in the trefoiled grass,
>
> Halt by the headstone naming
>   The heart no longer stirred
> And say the lad that loved you
>   Was one that kept his word.

The idea of death simply as a negation of life is very strong in Housman. The idea of the city that is not, the young man who is not, the lover who is not,

> The pale, the perished nation
>   That never see the sun,

recurs again and again in this purely negative form. For him there is just life and not-life. Death, as he points out in one of his poems, is the same as not having been born.

Death the negation of life, ill the negation of good, injustice the negation of justice, everything in Housman's poetry exists side by side in a pure and undiluted form, with the balance, of course, always on the side of the bad, because there is bound to be more death, more evil, more injustice in the world at any given moment than the reverse. . . . His puritanism is of a kind which is always very close to death not in a religious sense, like Donne or the Elizabethans, but in a pseudo-scientific sense, like Aldous Huxley's novels, simply because there is so much death and corruption about. But this means that life too ceases to be positive and becomes merely a feeble little effort to pretend, with cricket balls, footballs, sex, Shropshire, etc., that it is worth doing, when to the honest man it must be evident that nothing positive has any virtue because of the immense surplus of what is not which denies and frustrates it the whole time.

Housman once compared himself with T. E. Lawrence. One of the qualities he must have shared with that other great scholar—though he did not indulge it to the same extent—is surely a shrinking from publicity combined with an almost violently censured tendency towards exhibitionism. Both Housman and Lawrence throw out a kind of double legend which is probably the shadow of a double personality. The one legend is of a severe, puritanical, repressed, passionately single-minded, integrated personality, one who has looked evil fearlessly in the eyes, is master of his destiny. The other legend, of which Lawrence and

Housman both disclaim all responsibility, is of a mysterious and withdrawn personality, who not only has a secret clue to his passional life, but to whom also something has definitely happened at some period in his life which will not happen again. . . . One side of Housman censured the posthumously published poems; but the other side scored a victory in writing them at all; moreover this second Housman managed to insert numerous dark hints to puzzle generations of Wykehamists in **Last Poems,** and even in **The Shropshire Lad** itself.

Why are there two sides to Housman's poetry? I think it may be that Housman recognized the inadequacy of his philosophy of life, and wished to reinforce it with special pleading in defence of his own personal situation. This opens out another possibility: that he might have thrown aside the role of repression altogether and written a poetry which explored his own personality. But this would have involved accepting far more of life than he was willing to accept. (pp. 298-300)

> *Stephen Spender, "The Essential Housman,"*
> in Horizon, *London, Vol. 1, No. 4, April, 1940,*
> *pp. 295-301.*

John Peale Bishop   (essay date 1940)

[*As a West Virginian-born poet, Bishop is often associated with such Southern Renaissance authors as Allen Tate and Robert Penn Warren, though Bishop's verse is not significantly concerned with Southern themes or subjects. Competent and formalistic, Bishop is usually regarded as an exemplary minor American poet. He has also published short stories, a novel, and critical essays. In the following excerpt, Bishop addresses the issue of Housman's homosexuality and how his pursuit of fulfillment influenced the emotional despair so often portrayed in his poetry. Bishop purports that because Housman was unable to confront his sexuality directly due to the mores of his time, his poetry often lacked definition and clarity of thought.*]

Now that the **Collected Poems** are out, we have all we shall ever know of A. E. Housman's poetry. The long silence that followed **A Shropshire Lad** was broken by Housman himself in 1922, when he brought out his **Last Poems** while, as he said, he was still there to see them through the press. He died in 1936. And later that same year **More Poems** were published by Laurence Housman, who after a little decided that he could, without violating the wish of his older brother that nothing be printed after his death that was not up to the average level of what had already appeared, produce twenty-eight **Additional Poems.** Their number is now thirty-three, three of them rescued from old magazines, two from the poet's papers. To these have been appended three translations from the Greek, made long ago for an anthology of odes from the Greek dramatists. The remaining manuscripts and notes have been destroyed. The way in which Housman's poetry has been published is marked throughout by his passion for distinction, his craving to be famous, his equally strong and perverse dislike of being known.

Moses Jackson

The posthumous poems will not much change the estimation in which Housman has been held. They are work worthy of that proud mind. The **Additional Poems,** while they increase the sum of his poetry, add no poetic quality that was not there before. This they could hardly do, for it is apparent from the list of dates, incomplete as it is, which Laurence Housman has allowed to be included in the present volume, that they were composed along with the poems we already know. Some of them are contemporaneous with **A Shropshire Lad**; the latest, as far as anyone knows, is from 1925. What they do is to let us see the poet plain. Now that we have his poetry whole, we know what his personal plight was, and that is bound to affect our reading of all the poems. To know "Oh who is that young sinner with the handcuffs on his wrist?" is to know something that we should have known all along about those culprits of **A Shropshire Lad.** We have known and long known those hanged boys who hear the stroke of eight from the clock in the tower on the market place and never hear the stroke of nine. We know now for what crime all of them have been condemned. We have known when the noose went round their necks, but not whose head stood above the rope. They have many names and all have one name. Their features are not beyond recognition. The head is A. E. Housman's.

Romantic poetry as Housman received it was in need of correction. He corrected it. The romantic conflict of man against society, of man against immutable laws is still there, but presented by a man who had the classic craftsman's respect both for himself and his craft. The form is concise and accurate; but for all their lightness, his poems never lose the sense of earth, for all their grace, they are tough enough to sustain a considerable irony. The limits within which Housman was able to feel at all were strict, but within them he felt intensely, and both strictness and intensity are in his verse. (pp. 144-45)

The passion for truth was in Housman. He could, in his poetry, condemn himself as contemporary opinion—in the very year *A Shropshire Lad* was written—had condemned Wilde. When almost all others had abandoned him, Housman sent Wilde a copy of *A Shropshire Lad* to prison; Wilde's answer was *A Ballad of Reading Gaol.* But it was not only an account of the poet that Housman had to consider prison; there was someone else, whom he had known more closely, confined. His death is recorded in *The Isle of Portland.* Housman could go beyond imprisonment; not once, but many times, he sent his culprit straight to the scaffold. For whatever was will and conscience in Housman was conservative. It was on will that his career was founded and it was continued with a conscience as scrupulous as it was churlish, so that he could end, Kennedy Professor of Latin at Cambridge, all honors at his disposal and all declined. He was quite ready, if not willing, in his career as in his style, to conform outwardly to convention. For both career and style are masks. (pp. 145-46)

No matter where we open Housman's poems, we are almost sure to be struck with how young are those who suffer in them, how brief and sure their suffering, its course predictable, since all has been known before:

> These, in the day when heaven was falling,
>   The hour when earth's foundations fled,
> Followed their mercenary calling
>   And took their wages and are dead.
>
> Their shoulders held the sky suspended;
>   They stood, and earth's foundations stay;
> What God abandoned, these defended,
>   And saved the sum of things for pay.

Whatever the occasion that gave rise to them, these moving lines can scarcely be read without bringing to mind the part played by the professional soldiers of the British Army in the retreat from Mons. They are called, however, simply **"Epitaph on an Army of Mercenaries,"** and as they stand are as applicable to the soldiers of some desperate and remote army in some forgotten war of antiquity as they are to the men of 1914. Here, a particular situation has produced a tragic emotion; whatever is lacking we can supply, so that the event behind the lines is adequate to the emotion. But this is not always so in Housman. If—to follow Joyce's excellent and convenient definitions—pity is present in poetry whenever what is grave and constant in human sufferings is united with the human sufferer; terror, whenever what is grave and constant in human sufferings is united with the secret cause; then pity and terror should scarcely be lacking from anything that Housman wrote. And pity and terror do not lack in this noble and completely successful poem. And yet, in Housman's poetry as a whole something is lacking. Despite an apparent clarity such that almost any poem seems ready to deliver its meaning at once, there is always something that is not clear, something not brought into the open, something that is left in doubt. Housman knew very well what he was doing. He could always put himself in the reader's place. You must, he wrote his brother, "consider how, and at what stage, that man of sorrows is to find out what it is all about. You are behind the scenes and know all the data; but he knows only what you tell him." What Housman told the reader is clear. But there is much that he would not, and while he lived could not, tell him. Of the suffering we have no doubt, but something it seems has been suppressed that it is essential to know of the particular situation of the human sufferer. There is an emotion here that is unaccounted for. (pp. 147-49)

Death has its attraction, and it is possible for a poet to put it in a moral framework so that we know, not only how strong it is, but its motivation. Yeats has done it, not once, but many times. But in Housman we move so rapidly from the personal situation to an impersonal despair that we cannot but feel that something has been left out. What has been left out is his personal plight, which did not find a perfect solution in poetry and probably could not, so long as no place could be found for it in any moral scheme of which Housman's mind could approve. The facts are clear; the meaning is not. "Even when poetry has a meaning, as it usually has, it may be inadvisable to draw it out," Housman wrote. "Perfect understanding will sometimes extinguish pleasure."

It is possible that Housman did not want his meaning drawn out; but about that I am not certain. Perfect understanding of his poems depends upon knowledge of his personal plight, for until that is known, the emotion must seem in excess of its object. Now that we know from the posthumous poems what that plight was, all slips into place. The despair is explained; the scholar's abandonment of Propertius for Manilius; the reticence that at last seemed to fix his mouth in a perpetual snarl; the churlish silence which made the poet who had written the poems which above all others in our time have been loved into the least lovely of men. There is point to his philosophy. And we are at last in a position to understand the special pathos of *A Shropshire Lad.*

What Housman did in *A Shropshire Lad* was not to create an object of desire. That he had found, presumably in London, and none can doubt the intensity, the reality, the impossibility of his love. What he did was to make himself into a proper lover, or at least into one of an appropriate age, and to create in a country called Shropshire conditions where that love—without ceasing to be what it was—could come into its own. He became young, but with such a youth as he had never known. The hands which for almost twenty years had scarcely left their Greek and Latin texts, were put to the plow. He was a young yeoman, complete with an ancestry which Housman made up, perhaps without knowing it, since he seems presently to have persuaded himself that it was his own. The heart of the

youth was his, the temper was his own, and, what is most remarkable, the voice he found for him had the vibration of very youth.

The country of *A Shropshire Lad* is so created that it is with surprise that we learn, not only that Housman was not native to Shropshire, but that he had seldom been there. But once we begin to think about it, we see, not only that no such countryside exists in England, but that there could have been none like it in the last century. It is a country that belongs to the dead. What was important to Housman about Shropshire was that it lay on the western horizon of the Worcestershire in which his own boyhood was passed. The West has long been in popular imagination where the dead dwell, and, at the very time that Housman was writing, English soldiers did not die—they went West. . . . It is the underworld. And to Housman with his mind on the classical poets, it is probable that the West is identified, not only with their underworld of the nerveless dead, but also with a classical world, long dead, in which loves such as his would not have found all the laws of God and man against them:

> Look not in my eyes, for fear
> They mirror true the sight I see,
> And there you find your face too clear
> And love it and be lost like me.
> One the long night through must lie
> Spent in star-defeated sighs,
> But why should you as well as I
> Perish? gaze not in my eyes.

If we love at all, it is because our bodies, if not we, anticipate death for us. But in this poem of Housman's it is to be noticed that the loved one can, like the lover, love himself and that if he should once be attainted by that desire, he would perish. In the two lovers identity of desire is possible, but the identification of love with death is prompt and precise. Just as in *A la Recherche du Temps Perdu,* Proust's narrator has never such conviction of completely possessing Albertine as when he sits motionless by her side and looks at her lost in sleep, so, in Housman's poetry, there is no complete consummation of desire until the lad he loves lies dead. The body that lust demanded must be all bone and contemplation before he is finished with fear and condemnation. Even then, Housman cannot delude himself into believing that any love, least of all a love like his, can long survive on the contemplative satisfactions of the grave. (pp. 149-52)

What we should know from our own responses to Housman's poetry, if we have not already learned it more explicitly from Proust's prose, is that such desire as his, while it differs from others in its object, is most painfully distinguished from them by the brevity of time in which it is possible, even as unrequited desire. The youth's garland is always briefer than a girl's. And it is this constant presence and inescapable pressure of time that constitutes the special poignancy of Housman's poetry.

But if his personal plight is responsible for much of the poignancy of the emotions that went to the making of Housman's poetry, it also placed serious limitations on his emotions. And what nature had not limited, Housman himself thwarted. He is the poet of the end of an age in

England and he is the best poet that could be produced at the end, as he is probably, in England, the purest poet of the whole age. His range is small. We have only to look largely at poetry to see that there is an honesty, a humanity, that simply is not in Housman, any more than it was in the world that made him. What was left in that world was enough for him to perceive how impossible is the achievement of all desire, how vain the search for honor and happiness, and yet what pathos, what beauty, what grandeur even, man releases in their vain pursuit. (p. 153)

> *John Peale Bishop, "The Poetry of A. E. Housman," in* Poetry, *Vol. LVI, No. 111, June, 1940, pp. 144-53.*

Morton Dauwen Zabel   (essay date 1940)

[*Zabel is a poet, critic, and prominent scholar who was influential in increasing the study of American literature in South America. During the mid-1940s, he held the only official professorship on American literature in Latin America, and wrote two influential American literary histories in Portuguese and Spanish. In the following excerpt, Zabel examines the contradictory elements of Housman's verse, specifically the lack of thematic development in the midst of the admirable and genuine versification of his poetry.*]

Silence is the initial condition of Housman's poetry, as it was the token of a painful diminution of personality that befell him at the outset of adult life. His verse was set from the beginning, by an almost violent mandate, in a fixed and deliberate mold. It offers no characteristic modern pattern of growth, experiment, and discovery. . . . His distance from the great poets of tragedy or pessimism—agonized, rebellious, impressionable—is great: not only from Baudelaire, Verlaine, and Villon, for whom he expressed a distaste, or from Heine, whose continuous influence brought so little of the German's critical wit and exhilaration into his lyrics, or from Arnold and Hardy, whom he admired above all his contemporaries, but from Pascal and Leopardi, those two stricken witnesses of the dark abyss and the frightening heavens, whom he "studied with admiration" and whose anguished vision and starlit shudders are sometimes caught in his own finest songs. Beyond any of these brothers in darkness [Housman] stifled his agony before the mystery and fatality of life. His lyrics speak from the threshold of silence itself. Had their discipline become as absolute as the one he imposed on his practical emotions, his poems would have receded wholly into the reserve that marked Housman's outward character.

That discipline was as final as any poet, short of the defeat of his gifts, could make it. Housman's first problem as a lyrist was to perfect a form and language exactly expressive of the extreme mandate of will he imposed on his sensibility. He once admitted Heine, Shakespeare's songs, and the Border ballads as his models but was "surprised" at the imputation of Latin and Greek influences. But these cannot be slighted. Housman's whole temper, recognizing its suspension between an active poetic impulse and a willed surrender of it, between an instinctive fervor for life and a tragic denial of its value, sharpens toward irony, seeks resolution in the ambiguity of epigram, and tends to

express the ingrowth of its forces and the tension of its faculties in a salient virtue of the Latin lyric style—its integrity of structure, its verbal and tonal unity, its delicate stasis of form. What it gave him—as did the Elizabethans, among whom he once called Jonson his master—were the interlocking balances and inversions of phrase, the distributed reference in nouns and pronouns, the hovering ambiguity of particles, the reflexive dependence of verbs and subjects that give his stanzas their tightness and pith. Had he coerced a purely modern and explicit English into these structures he would have produced a language continuously—instead of intermittently—stilted. But here one of his strongest sympathies came to his rescue—his love of folk speech. The aphoristic tang and irony of peasant idiom, grafted to the sophistication of the Horatian style, relaxed his temper, freed it from formulated stiffness and cliché, and gave Housman his true and single medium as a poet—a verse style marked by a subtle irony of tragic suggestion, a tensile integrity of phrasing, a sense of haunting human appeals playing against the grim inexorability of law. In that medium, rising above the inertness of a formula and the desperate repression of his impulses, he wrote his finest poems.

These, now that his work stands complete, no longer appear in some of his most quoted lyrics, those that cast his thought into the inflexibly didactic form that is always the bane of a negative temperament. The lesser Housman, the one most vulnerable to parody, imitation, and personal attack, is seen wherever his lyric style hardens into such inflexibility and his pessimism into the hortatory despair that becomes by inversion sentimental. Originally, it appears, Housman had an extremely uncertain taste in words and meters. He was fond of the singsong lilt or chant used in rather tawdry and superficial poems like **"Atys, The Land of Biscay,"** and **"Far known to sea and shore."** Of **"Atys"** ("Lydians, lords of Hermus river, Sifters of the golden loam") he once said that he was so fond of the rhythm that he always doubted the merit of any poem in which he succumbed to its attraction. He came to guard himself from that music as he guarded his emotional impulses from the appeals of common life and friendship. At both ends of his narrow lyric range, as at both ends of his emotional character, he exercised a ruthless vigilance: here from the spontaneity of feelings that had to be canceled, there from the violence of a censorship so strong that it could end not merely in silence but in emotional paralysis and the logic of suicide. Recoiling from instinctive music or feeling, he produced poems of an opposite extreme: of a deadly and inverted romanticism, of a pessimism so imperative and bare of realistic qualities that they produce a repellent travesty of his talent. Here the Latinized concentration bristles with guards to emotion, and starkness of vision becomes as cloying as the lines in which he rings changes on the ale, the lads, the night, the noose, and the gallows to the point of comic surfeit. It appears at its worst in **"Think no more, lad," "The Welsh Marches," "Say, lads, have you things to do," "Others I am not the first," "The laws of God," "Yonder see the morning blink," "The Immortal Part,"** and **"The Culprit."** The authentic part of his talent demanded escape from confines as laming as these, and it is only when he gives some voice to the instinctive delight of his senses, to memories of lost youth, or to responses to nature, that he arrives at the finer sincerity of **"With rue my heart,"** **"On Wenlock Edge," "Far in a western brookland,"** and **"The Merry Guide."** He succeeds best of all when the repressed emotion becomes externalized, released from an iron-clad vigilance, adopts a dramatic mask or situation, and so takes on the life and pathos of genuine lyric realism: when, in Bredon Hill, Hughley Steeple, **"Is my team plowing," "To an athlete," "I to my perils," "In valleys green and still,"** and **"With seed the sowers scatter,"** he resolves the hostilities of his nature to their finest delicacy and harmony, avoids both the curt asperity and the occasional Aeschylean pomp of which he was capable, and contributes exquisite poems to the English lyric tradition.

They succeed, moreover, in revealing and relaxing the enigmatic nature of the man who wrote them and in dissolving the contradiction that gave him his quality as a character. They make credible the tyrant of Latin texts who could flay rivals or sycophants alive, yet who led a life of painful loneliness and who, given evidences of affection, described their effect as "almost overwhelming"; the solitary who called himself a Cyrenaic but who favored Epicureans above Stoics; the critic who disliked democracy and defended slavery but who protested the tyranny of the laws of God and man and pleaded for the felon taken to prison "for the color of his hair"; the man who enjoyed bitterness and kept notebooks carefully indexing his vituperations but who saw himself in T. E. Lawrence's words as stricken by "a craving to be liked—so strong and nervous that . . . the terror of failure in an effort so important made me shrink from trying"; the recluse who was contemptuous of comfort and flattery but who told a young American admirer, "Certainly I have never regretted the publication of my poems. The reputation which they brought me, though it gives me no lively pleasure, is something like a mattress interposed between me and the hard ground."

He was complex obviously and an eccentric certainly, a personality of laming deficiencies and self-persecuting logic; a lyric artist of the most limited order. He lends himself almost naively to J. Bronowski's attack (in "The Poet's Defense") as a victim of inverted sentiment from whose "welter of standards" little emerges but a cancelation of feelings almost antiphonal in regularity and as a self-belittler who took evasive refuge in negations of life, of emotion, of the nature and meaning of poetry itself. Housman's admirers have done him the disservice of blind adulation; his detractors, with the added cooperation of his own perverseness and inconsistency of temperament, will go to inevitable extremes. There are even severer measures of his stature. The cry of despair has sounded in modern poetry, as in ancient, with an anguish but also with an illumination that Housman seldom or never attains. (pp. 684-85)

Yet as we now see Housman in his full stature, as the obscurity of his temperament begins to wane, so also the exacerbation of his emotion and his evasion of responsible feeling begin to take on the alleviation of what at its best becomes a subtle and ennobling lyric dignity, a mastery of selfhood and of style that surmounts the imposed denials

of his life and the implacable tragedy he saw there but, having seen and faced it, refused to disguise from himself. What that tragedy was is too much a part of the complex of his nature and his poems to bear crude expression, but this much he makes unmistakable: it was his realization that he was destined to live a life deprived of human love. . . . Whatever irresolution exists in [**The Collected Poems of A. E. Housman**] is a reflection of the contradiction imposed on his faculties by nature itself; the pervading frustration resulted from an intelligence that permitted no blinkers before the fact. But concealed in Housman's nature, masked by his forbidding exterior and his scholarly isolation, existed the true stuff of the poet, once free and impulsive but surviving even its later curtailment, and he was strong enough to make of that conflict the strength and charm of his poems. The science and realism that permit us to see the errors or defects of men also impose the responsibility of understanding them. Outside his poems Housman made that understanding difficult enough, and even inside his verse the slightest comparison with Baudelaire and Hopkins, Yeats and Rilke, immediately gives the measure of his lower station. Yet if he ate of the shadow so long that he became something of the shadow of a man, he at least refused to lapse into sullen silence over the whole wretched business of existence. His endurance was the sign of his character, and the lyrics he wrested from grief and discipline are the mark of his true, if minor, genius. (pp. 685-86)

> *Morton Dauwen Zabel, "The Whole of Housman," in* The Nation, *New York, Vol. 150, No. 22, June 1, 1940, pp. 684-86.*

Tom Burns Haber   (essay date 1948)

[*An American professor of English and humanities, Haber is a reputable Housman scholar whose works include* The Making of the Shropshire Lad *(1966) and* A. E. Housman *(1967). In the following excerpt, Haber provides a formalistic analysis of Housman's verse, suggesting that Housman's true genius did not lie in "the meaning of his poems but rather in the form and rhythm of his lyrics."*]

A. E. Housman is one of those unfortunate poets who pass into literature over-burdened with a message. The earliest reviewers of *A Shropshire Lad* discovered and announced it; it was found again in *Last Poems,* and in one way or another many commentators on Housman's collected verse have been busy with his message. Comparatively few have had much to say about his poetry.

This preoccupation with one minor phase of Housman is not surprising for it is undeniable that his world of ideas, though small, is interesting. In this fact lies the secret of the poet's appeal to the lettered and to the unlettered. The layman admires Housman for his clear, candid reappraisals of the old, old delights and miseries of the human heart. (During the past few years Housman has had what may be called a mild revival as a result of his popularity in soldiers' barracks—and hospitals). As for the scholar, he finds in Housman's new-garbed philosophy endless provocation for the pursuit of sources, influences, analogues, and other recondite matters that have their special attraction for the academic mind.

I have said that comparatively few critics of Housman have been concerned with his poetry. Oddly enough, hardly any attention has been paid to his poetic ear. This neglect is surprising, for Housman's claim to fame rests entirely upon his poetry, and, more than any other literature, poetry must be read aloud if it (with its message) is to be comprehended. How any given poem makes its impact on the mind of a qualified reader is a very complex process, which has never been properly understood. The final explanation may be forthcoming from the musicologists. In the meantime I shall hazard a guess that more important than has been supposed is the cooperation required of the reader's ear and his organs of speech. By them poetry is brought into life and its meaning received into the mind. Hearing the sounds of a line of verse as they come from our own lips will aid us immeasurably in understanding the ideas behind those sounds. The effort or ease with which a line is translated from print into hearing will make us aware of subtle meanings stored within it. . . . (pp. 257-58)

It needs to be said of Housman's poetry, as it will undeniably be said of two models he greatly admired—the lyrics of Heine and the old English Ballads that silent reading leaves half the magic mute on the page; much of the meaning, too. Anyone returning to *Last Poems,* for example, will reap a full reward only from an oral reading, and I mean by this that the reader and the reaper will not be two different persons.

At this point it may be objected that an oral reading of Housman awakens certain rhythms and accents which had better be left lying in the toneless placidity of print. Housman *does* like downright thumping rhyme, and he has a strong leaning toward the iambus. But, admitting that Housman's metrical limits are somewhat straightened, an inquiring reader may discover that they have not been fully explored. A careful reconsideration of Housman's feeling for sound will reveal new sources of delight in his poetry.

Possibly too much has been made of Housman's devotion to iambic tetrameter. Even the unassisted eye running through his poems will pick up many variations of rhythm and meter. One variation indeed—trochaic verse—had so great an appeal to the poet that, according to his brother Laurence, one poem written in this style, **"Atys,"** was rejected both from *A Shropshire Lad* and *Last Poems* because the self-suspicious author "always doubted the merit of any poem in which he had succumbed to its attraction." He did succumb frequently for there are few pages of Housman that do not contain some trochaic verses. (pp. 258-59)

Feminine endings, a natural feature of the trochaic line, appear in Housman's earliest verse: not only in the first-composed lyrics of *A Shropshire Lad* but also in his *juvenilia.* . . . The first four verses of this early poem set a pattern which the maturing poet remembered and returned to:

> Breathe, my lute, beneath my fingers
>   One regretful breath,
> One lament for life that lingers
>   Round the doors of death.

This pattern of feminine rhymes in the odd-numbered verses of a quatrain Housman was later to find abundantly in Heine's poetry. It is significant that Housman's use of this measure is almost invariably intended to announce an *Abschied* theme, which, one might say, resides intrinsically in the lingering, falling accents of the very sounds. (pp. 260-61)

As one listens thoughtfully to his own reading of the lyrics of *Last Poems,* it is impossible to miss what Housman is trying to communicate in the feminine endings of his verses. These deftly rung cadences sound most beautifully in the three concluding pieces of that volume. The pattern for [**"When summer's end is nighing"**] is shown in this stanza:

> They came and were and are not
>   And come no more anew;
> And all the years and seasons
>   That ever can ensue
> Must now be worse and few.

The next poem brings out more clearly the antiphonal questions and affirmations of the odd- and even-numbered lines:

> Possess, as I possessed a season,
>   The countries I resign,
> Where over elmy plains the highway
>   Would mount the hills and shine,
> And full of shade the pillared forest
>   Would murmur and be mine.

But the symphonic beauty of the movement in which the poet was working attained its complete expression in the next and final lyric, where it is full-voiced and perfect, like the closing movement of a Beethoven concerto. Here, joining four times in each stanza, the feminine and masculine accents—the one retreating and reluctant, the other dominant and inexorable—convey equally with the words the sense of death embracing life and overcoming it:

> The lofty shade advances,
>   I fetch my flute and play:
> Come, lads, and learn the dances
>   And praise the tune today.
> Tomorrow, more's the pity,
>   Away we both must hie,
> To air the ditty,
>   And to earth I.

The testimony of one's active speech organs and his receptive ear will show that Housman is a master of the art of onomatopeia. The understanding reader here, like the poet, *nascitur non fit.* Let me therefore cite some examples with only the briefest comment; first some on the edge of silence:

> Halts on the bridge to hearken
>   How soft the poplars sigh

> My soul that lingers sighing
>   About the glimmering weirs

> Its rainy-sounding silver leaves
> And the darkness hushes wide.

Here the quiet sounds suggest more complex ideas:

> The bluebells in the azured wood
> Her waving silver-tufted wand
> It nods and curtseys and recovers.
>
> (pp. 261-63)

Here the sounds are bolder:

> Drumming like a noise in dreams
> —humming hive of dreams
> While the hive of hell within
> Sent abroad a seething hum
> Tempest tread the oakwood under.

Feel the plodding, relentless weight of this line.

> Nothing: too near at hand,
> Planing the figured sand,
> Effacing clean and fast
> Cities not built to last.
>
> (p. 263)

Sometimes Housman's echoic verses bring to life the sounds the condemned criminal hears:

> And sharp the link of life will snap
> —gallows used to clank

> And then the clock collected in the tower
> Its strength, and struck.

The clock in this poem sounds the death hour to the prisoner. The sound of *clock collected* is a series of metallic clicks, the grinding of the gears and drivers; then falls the hard final line, accenting like doom two of the heaviest words in our speech.

Bell sounds and the chime of tower clocks must have had a deep fascination for Housman, for his poetry often echoes them. **"Eight O'Clock"** (the poem from which the last quotation was made) might have been in Housman's mind when in his lecture, *The Name and Nature of Poetry,* he referred to some of his poems which, contrary to his usual methods of composition, cost him more than ordinary trouble. Before the word *tossed* was fixed upon in line four, he had tested *loosed, split, cast, told, dealt,* and *pitched.* (p. 264)

Housman's best-known bell poem is **"Bredon Hill."** The clang and boom of bells come to the ear in every stanza:

> In summertime on Bredon
>   The bells they sound so clear;
> Round both the shires they ring them
>   In steeples far and near,
>   A happy noise to hear.

To the reader listening closely to his own interpretation of this poem, after two or three stanzas, line two marks the stroke of the clapper, line four the echo, line five the fading after-chime. The first line of the sixth stanza is as perfect in its concord of vowels and consonants as Tennyson's famous "mellow lin-lan-lone of evening bells." (pp. 264-65)

Sound, being the primitive element in language, contains within itself the nebulae of human emotions: vague, shifting, indefinable. Certain sounds and rhythms seem expressive of lightness and joy; others mean dread and heaviness. Such sounds by themselves make a kind of inarticulate speech which arouses about the same responses in all listeners. The radio has made us acutely aware of these inherent meanings in various sounds: unpleasantness and warning in the sound of a fog-horn; the challenge to alertness in a rooster's crow; ennui or boredom in the slow ticking of a clock. When sounds become parts of words and articulate speech is thus established, the elemental quality of sound becomes less important to the sophisticated ear. But it does not disappear entirely. If we pause to examine our casual speech, we find abundant proof of our ancient apprehension of certain sonic values. The testimony of dictionaries is in this same direction: words beginning with the sounds in *sl* tend to fall into one field of meaning; many words that begin with *gr* have to do with another. A series of words containing sibilants opens up mental vistas in one direction; gutturals, another; and so forth.

The poet is an inheritor of these dual values of sound and sense. As an inheritor he is bound by certain restrictions: he cannot write an elegiac poem in anapestic trimeter; if his *métier* is blank verse, the Muse will not grant him to aspire to the height of lyrical excellence. But in the interplay between the sound and meaning of words there is room for almost infinite variety. In the little room of two consecutive lines of [**"My dreams are a field afar"**] of *More Poems* Housman illustrates something of this variety:

> But they, when I forgot and ran,
>   Remembered and remain.

In line one, the tongue finds no rest among the varied vowel sounds. There is no alliteration. This sonic effect is perfectly in accord with the looseness and dispersion which the line means. Contrast the stability of line two, fixed by its close assonance and the double alliteration in the two verbs. (pp. 265-66)

As Housman was warming to his theme in *The Name and Nature of Poetry,* he glanced almost longingly at an alternate subject: "The Artifice of Versification." Had he chosen to devote his Leslie Stephen lecture to that subject, he would have made this paper—and a good many abler ones—unnecessary. Versification, so Housman hinted, "has underlying it a set of facts which are unknown to most of those who practice it; and their success, when they succeed, is owing to instinctive tact and a natural goodness of ear." (p. 268)

If Housman had brought his wit and learning to bear on "The Artifice (observer that he will not say *Art*) of Versification," we might well have spared, we say, some emendations of Martial or Euripides. Certainly his lucid, tempered mind would have produced something precious both to poets and to lesser men. As it is, the unfinished window in Aladdin's tower must so remain.

But within sight and easy hearing of that tower, there is room for smaller edifices, one of which should be dedicated to Housman's skill in the technic of sound. There each would read to himself the lyrics of this modern singer— read them through the sensual ear to the spirit and discover that for this poet, as for all great lyricists, sound was not the mere handmaiden of sense but an intimate and equal companion. (p. 269)

Tom Burns Haber, "Housman's Poetic Ear," in Poet Lore, *Vol. LIV, No. 3, Autumn, 1948, pp. 257-69.*

Michael Macklem (essay date 1952)

[*A Canadian publisher, professor of English, and editor, Macklem is the author of* The Anatomy of the World: Relations between Natural and Moral Law from Donne to Pope *(1958). In the following excerpt, Macklem maintains that only by understanding Housman's use of the classical pastoral elegy is the reader able to unify and appreciate the random elements of his verse.*]

Housman's devotion to the classics has generally been thought an unfortunate digression from his poetry, and his ostensible disregard for the latter a typically British affectation. Edmund Wilson took a step in the right direction by looking for a parallel between the poetry and the classical scholarship, but his conclusion, that the inconsequentiality of the scholarship is reflected in the poetry, does not deserve attention. His final comment—"his achievement has been merely to state memorably certain melancholy commonplaces of human existence without any real presentation of that existence as we live it through . . . One can only come the same painful cropper over and over again and draw from it the same painful moral"—though it has a partial truth, illustrates the limitations of Wilson's treatment rather than those of Housman's poetry. I shall examine here a number of the themes of Housman's poetry with the purpose of defining his central attitudes to the "commonplaces of human existence". This, I suggest, will lead to an appreciation of the intimate nature of the relationship between the values, for Housman, of the classics and those of the poetry, and will broaden and deepen the meanings of the poetry itself.

The informing mood of *A Shropshire Lad,* and likewise of *Last Poems* and *More Poems,* is one of anguish, an anguish closely connected with a sense of time. This appears, in one of its forms, as a sense of loss for the past and as nostalgic recollection.

Into my heart an air that kills
    From yon far country blows:
What are those blue remembered hills,
    What spires, what farms are those?

This is the land of content, which is lost and cannot come again. The same mood and idea recur in more obvious ways in Housman's treatment of love and friendship:

With rue my heart is laden
    For golden friends I had,
For many a rose-lipt maiden
    And many a lightfoot lad.

By brooks too broad for leaping
    The lightfoot boys are laid;
The rose-lipt girls are sleeping
    In fields where roses fade.

Here the central theme of mutability is stated at its simplest—so simply and blandly, indeed, that it illustrates what truth there is in Wilson's view that Housman deals in the trite and commonplace. Here the control of nostalgia which created the poetic tension in **"Into my Heart an Air that Kills"**, is lacking. Concentration is so weakened that Housman allows himself embarrassing epithets like 'rose-lipt' and 'lightfoot'.

A sense of the transience of the present accompanies the sense of loss for the past. This, in the widest terms, is the subject of most of Housman's poetry. As such, it takes both simple and descriptive, and complex and symbolic forms. In **"Loveliest of Trees"** the sense of the ephemerality of the moment cuts across the joyful experience of beauty:

Loveliest of trees, the cherry now . . .

The final word, 'now', controls the line, being emphasised by its position and rhyme. The stanza continues by describing the beauty of the bloom and the woodland ride. In this way, the poem forces on our awareness two ideas at the same time: the image of beauty and the knowledge of mutability. The second stanza, which opens with heavy emphasis on 'Now', states directly what the first stanza implies:

Now, of my threescore years and ten,
Twenty will not come again . . .

The final stanza gives the active response: to enjoy the moment before it has passed:

About the woodlands I will go
To see the cherry hung with snow.

In **"Oh See How Thick the Goldcup Flowers"**, the same facts of change and decay produce an urgent invitation to love, set against the backdrop of "the hours / That never are told again". This desire to enjoy the moment while the moment lasts is characteristic. It is given most direct expression in **"Think no More, Lad; Laugh, be Jolly"** . . . .

Often the idea of ephemerality is simply stated, and left without a positive response in moral action. This is the case in **"To an Athlete Dying Young"**, where Housman uses a narrative rather than a descriptive technique, without great success, and in **"Bredon Hill"**, which is built around the contrast between the ringing of wedding bells and the tolling of the funeral bell, and which, like most of the poems about love, lacks passion and personal intensity. In the love-poems the theme generally follows a simple pattern: time, decay, and death destroy love; love is a good in itself and the pathos of its loss derives at once from its beauty and its transience. In **"The Sigh that Heaves the Grasses"**, **"The Half-moon Westers Low, my Love"** (both in *Last Poems*), and in **"Along the Field as We Came by"**, from *A Shropshire Lad,* the treatment is rather obvious. The central images are the united lovers and the grave, and the poetry, often loose in texture, is again neither personal nor passionate. The war-poems illustrate the same theme: the loss of the moment of joy. They celebrate the self-sacrifice of youth—the sacrifice of the moment, beauty, the cherry-tree, the girl—to duty. Their pathos lies precisely in the value of the moment of youth and life, and its loss in death.

> Far and near and low and louder
> On the roads of earth go by,
> Dear to friends and food for powder,
> Soldiers marching, all to die.

But this conviction is not constant. Many poems (which may be late) grow out of the feeling that belief in the joy and worth of the moment is an illusion. . . . This idea, that life is not worth living, the moment not worth enjoying, informs a large number of the lyrics in *A Shropshire Lad.* It appears first in the seventh, **"When Smoke Stood up from Ludlow"**. Ploughing becomes a symbol of the uselessness of effort. . . . And in **"Illic Jacet"**, the moment of joy with the rose-lipt maiden has become an eternity of 'content' in death: "A sleeper content to repose . . . / He lies with the sweetheart he chose." In **"If it Chance your Eye Offend you"** the emotions compelling the desire for death are expressed with still greater concentration and effect. . . . The sickness of the soul, the offence which life commits against man, is given wonderfully dense, fluid, and complex expression in **"Be Still, my Soul, be Still"**. The poem ends with the question, "Oh, why did I awake? when shall I sleep again?" The next begins, "Think no more, lad; laugh, be jolly: / Why should man make haste to die?"

This debate between life and death, between the value of the moment and its vanity, comes to a tense focus in **"When I Watch the Living Meet"**. In the "house of flesh" the "heats of hate and lust" are strong; in the "house of dust" the peace of nothingness ("the nation that is not") overcomes hatred and sorrow in the long sojourn of death.

> There revenges are forgot,
> And the hater hates no more.

But the peace of death annihilates love as well as hatred. The last stanza is cutting in its pathos:

> Lovers lying two and two
>   Ask not whom they sleep beside,
> And the bridegroom all night through
>   Never turns him to the bride.

At times, the rejection of life proceeds from repudiation of the worth of life itself, as in the two poems on the vanity of labour, in **"Be Still, my Soul"**, in which we must "endure an hour" to "see injustice done", and in the lines on lust and hatred in **"When I Watch the Living Meet"**. But oftener it proceeds from a sense of the transience of the moment and of life itself, the emotions of despair in this case issuing directly from an appreciation, not of the vanity, but of the value of life, and at the same time of its transience. This explains the emphasis on youth, when the joy of the moment is most intense, and on its shortness and its loss. It also explains the frequent use of love as a traditional symbol at once of the intensity and the brevity of happiness. Looked at from this point of view, Housman's poetry forms a unit of emotional, if not intellectual, logic. It begins with a vivid response to the sensuous joy of the moment, expressed in the symbols of love, friendship, spring, and, above all, youth. At the same time, it is cut across by a sense of the transience of life, suggested in images of the loss of love and friendship, winter and death.

This contrast between the joy of life and its transience is the source of Housman's elegiac theme. His use of it re-

lates him directly to the elegiac tradition of poetry and, in a particularly intimate way, to its classical forms. Furthermore, his treatment of elegiac material is distinctively pastoral—so much is clear, to go no farther, from the title of *A Shropshire Lad.* As such, his poetry appears as a contemporary modification of the traditional form of pastoral elegy. This fact is important because Housman thus indicates his own outlook in relation to the classical and Christian treatments of the same themes. (pp. 39-45)

In the classical form of the pastoral elegy . . . , the mood is that of personal grief, but the poet's grief is generalized into a sympathetic response to the universal facts of change and death. The fact of human death is set beside images of natural rebirth in spring, to combine the poetry of death (elegy) with the poetry of life (pastoral). The pastoral elegiac theme is taken, essentially, from the contrast between the immortality of nature and the mortality of man, between the natural cycle of rebirth and the finality of human death. (pp. 45-6)

In Housman's poetry we have recognised a modern version of pastoral elegy, seen in the spring of the year and in the youth of man. Especially interesting in Housman is the way in which he deals with the meanings attached to spring in the Christian tradition of pastoral elegy, and works out for himself a restatement of the pastoral elegiac theme in relation to its classical and Christian versions which is symptomatic of the contemporary attitude to Christian dogma.

"Easter Hymn" is crucial. The two stanzas provide opposite alternatives. The first:

> If in that Syrian garden, ages slain,
> You sleep, and know not you are dead in vain,
>
> . . . .
>
> Sleep well and see no morning, son of man.

The second:

> But if, the grave rent and the stone rolled by,
> At the right hand of majesty on high
> You sit . . .
>
> . . . .
>
> Bow hither out of heaven and see and save.

There is no explicit choice, but the implication is negative, that Christ is "ages slain" in a Syrian garden; at best, if He sits "at the right hand of majesty on high", He watches the fires of hate and lust He "died to quench" unmoved. Easter is emptied of its symbolic meaning, its promise of resurrection, and spring, the season and natural counterpart of Easter, is cut off from its spiritual connections.

The theme of Easter reappears in **"Loveliest of Trees"**, in which the cherry is "wearing white for Eastertide". Yet the cherry is a symbol, not of eternity, but of ephemerality. The irony centres in the fact that the cherry wears white, like the altar of the Church, but signifies the nearness of death, not the certainty of resurrection and life. The symbol of Easter is handled in the same way in **"The Lent Lily"**. The season is spring, the spring of the primrose and the daffodil "under thorn and bramble". The imagery, intense and evocative, is focussed on

> . . . the Lenten lily
> That has not long to stay
> And dies on Easter day.

Easter is entirely detached from the elements of permanence and eternal life. Its Christian meaning is reversed. Easter means not suffering in life on earth (Good Friday) redeemed and relieved by resurrection to eternal life, but brief beauty and joy in life and then sudden and eternal death. The moral conclusion is the same as in **"Loveliest of Trees"** and **"Think no More, Lad"**.

The theme of spring extends the narrower theme of Easter. In **"Bredon Hill"** the meaning is conveyed by the contrast between spring, love, and marriage, and winter, death, and burial. But the relation between them established in Christian pastoral clegy is reversed: winter is no longer the suffering of life before the joy of resurrection, but eternal death after the joy of life; spring is no longer resurrection after death, but the brief moment of life to be ended by death. This complicated working out of the loss of faith in spring as a symbol of resurrection leads into the large number of poems which deal with the theme of spring more simply. These, in the fashion of classical pastoral elegy, contrast the rebirth of spring with human change and death. That is the characteristic irony of Housman's poetry: the juxtaposition of the fullness of life in the beauty of youth and spring with the certainty of its loss in death. This is the context of **"Loveliest of Trees"** and **"Oh See How Thick the Goldcup Flowers"**, with their desperate seizure of the moment of joy; of the pathos of **"To an Athlete Dying Young"**, in which the explicitly elegiac treatment is suggestive of classical forms; of the nobility and heroism of war-poems like **"On the Idle Hill of Summer"**, of the sense of loss in the love-poems, of the urgency to enjoy, to "think no more", to "laugh, be jolly".

In the setting of classical culture pastoral elegy had been a means of expressing sorrow for the shortness of life. The form became a complex of conventions, but the formal conventions unite to express a single idea: the beauty and joy of life as contrasted with its transience. The mood of pathos, irony, or sorrow thus set up is deepened by contrasting the shortness of human life and the finality of death with the rebirth of spring in nature.

The outlook and attitude of classical pastoral elegy had been conditioned by the religious attitude of classical culture. It was inevitable, therefore, that, in the Christian period, pastoral elegy would assume a different meaning. In Christian belief, death is not final but is the prelude to spiritual rebirth. The classical contrast between the finality of human death and the renewal of nature in spring is therefore transcended, in Christian pastoral elegy, and spring is used as a symbol of the spiritual rebirth of man. Pastoral elegy becomes joyful.

In Housman, the meaning of spring is once more reversed. Winter, as man's exile on earth, is no longer followed by spring, as eternal rebirth, but rather, spring, as joy on earth, is followed by winter, as eternal death. This return to the classical treatment of the pastoral elegiac theme and

to the classical outlook which underlay it, shows up, in the first place, the disintegration of faith in the central symbols of Christianity. But more than that, examination of Housman's use of pastoral elegiac material in its relation to classical and Christian treatments, discloses some of the deepest meanings in his poetry. It connects the poetry with the classical scholarship. It unifies the random 'commonplaces' of his verse and gives it a logical texture. It brings into focus his preoccupation with youth and love, joy and beauty, war and death, and shows the connection between them. It clarifies the recurrent symbols of Easter, youth, spring, flowers, and winter. It gives his poetry a coherence and a strength of meaning, an intelligence and an emotional control that it has not been supposed to have. By explaining the meaning of traditional symbols and by pointing to Housman's distinctive use of them, it reveals in full, for our consideration, the view of life which Housman used his poetry to express. (pp. 49-52)

> *Michael Macklem, "The Elegiac Theme in Housman," in* Queen's Quarterly, *Vol. LIX, No. 1, Spring, 1952, pp. 39-52.*

John Wain   (essay date 1957)

[*Wain is one of the most prolific English authors of contemporary fiction and poetry. He is also recognized as a significant twentieth-century critic. Central to his critical stance is his belief that in order to judge the quality of a piece of literature, the critic must make a moral as well as an imaginative judgment. In the following excerpt, which was originally published in his* Preliminary Essays (1957), *Wain argues that Housman's poetry suffered because of its academic tone. According to Wain, Housman "merely assimilated the poet in him to the professor" and never rose above the atmosphere that "fosters habit and repetition."*]

I have been expecting—but not, so far, seeing—a resurgence of interest in Housman; if not as a poet, then at least as a case-history. After all, he was, in his day, almost alone in facing a problem which is nowadays faced by quite a number of people: the problem of how to combine the two functions of poet and professor. If we read "literary artist of any kind" for "poet," and "academic teacher of any kind" for "professor," we have a situation that is very much of our time; both in England and America, the universities are coming to provide a shelter for writers which saves them from having to be schoolteachers or ad men— though there is still no tendency, in this country at any rate, for a university to employ a poet *because* he is a poet. He gets the job first, in the normal way, and then shyly produces his poems. (p. 26)

Housman side-stepped these problems, partly by luck and partly by giving in to them. When I say "luck," I mean that his extraordinary talent for emending Latin texts brought him, in early middle life, a Cambridge chair which seems to have involved no very arduous duties. When I say "giving in" I mean that Housman made no attempt to do two things at once. He merely assimilated the poet in him to the professor. The smallness of his output, the narrowness of his range, the elaborate pains he took to safeguard the text from misprints (as if he were one of his own dead authors), are all academic characteristics. So was his inability, or refusal, to develop, to admit any new light, to *move* in any direction.

I must elaborate this last point a little. Housman's major faults as a poet—the things that kept him a *minor* poet—are (*a*) the immature and commonplace nature of his subject-matter, all self-pity and grumbling; (*b*) the lack of any development. Although he wrote poems over a period of some forty years, it is oddly true that if one shuffled them, and had only internal evidence to go by, one would never recover the original order. That is why I feel justified in discussing him among "Victorian" poets, in spite of his going on writing until well into my own lifetime. The last poems he wrote are no different from the first; that is, they exhibit faults (*a*) and (*b*) above.

Now this is such an extraordinary thing—for after all it is human to develop, and we usually do so whether we wish to or not—that one has to ask the reason for it. I have already called it an *academic* characteristic; and, unfortunately, the evidence seems to bear me out. There is something about the academic atmosphere that fosters habit, repetition, getting set in one's ways. Everything is so permanent. Perhaps all institutions do this; certainly the Army and the Church have both been accused of it. And of course a professor is like a colonel or an archdeacon in one respect: most of his work consists of doing the same thing over and over again. When Housman had finished taking one class through Propertius, there would be another waiting to begin. When he had edited one piece by Manilius, he started on another one just like it.

Now Housman can hardly be blamed for succumbing to this petrification. If it is true that even the strongest minds go down, how could he resist? For his was not, in any broad sense, a strong mind. His stock of ideas was tiny, his human responsiveness, after early life, almost nil; his general intelligence, poor. (Cite *one* interesting remark that Housman made on any general topic.) His getting himself ploughed in Greats was good strategy; it enabled him to claim not to have been trying; and there is no evidence that he would have done well if he *had* tried. Philosophy was obviously alien ground to him. If the tendency of Cambridge was to shut him off from life, it must be said that he collaborated to the full. He spared no pains to turn himself into the solitary, life-resisting, formidable figure of the anecdotes. The banked-up fires exploded in two directions only; his poems, and his savage baiting of other scholars who did not conform to his standards of accuracy. (pp. 27-8)

These remarks may seem merely provoking, but I think they can be proved. After all, a very gifted poet *can* be a stupid man; his stupidity will keep him a minor poet, but it will not spoil his gift. And a great classical scholar can be stupid too, off his own ground. Bentley, who is usually named as Housman's only superior, has left us detailed proof of his imbecility, in his emendations of *Paradise Lost*. What, then, is the moral?

The moral is, if you are going to be an academic poet, *be stupid*. Dig in, refuse to grow, and cultivate your most specialized talent. Then both sides will respect you. Housman

was fantastically overpraised, in his lifetime and since, by his fellow academics, because he offers a justification of the donnish way of life. But for the young writer, employed at a university, he is the *memento mori*. The dead hand of academicism, which kills everything it touches, lay heavily on his exquisite gift. He rejected life, and life certainly had its own back on his poetry, which never gets free of a certain triviality, a certain pettiness and lack of emotional breadth. (pp. 28-9)

> *John Wain, "Housman," in* A. E. Housman: A Collection of Critical Essays, *edited by Christopher Ricks, Prentice-Hall, Inc., 1968, pp. 26-31.*

Christopher Ricks (essay date 1968)

[*An English editor and professor, Ricks is the author of a number of critical essays. In the following introduction to his* A. E. Housman: A Collection of Critical Essays, *Ricks attempts to identify the elements that make Housman "a poet about whom poets write poems," despite the fact he is often described as an "adolescent" poet.*]

The poems of A. E. Housman disrupt all the usual allegiances. Edith Sitwell can join with F. R. Leavis, George Meredith, and Hugh Kenner in disapproval of the author of *A Shropshire Lad,* while William Empson can concur with H. W. Garrod, John Sparrow, and G. K. Chesterton—who, with numerical oddity, called Housman "one of the one or two great classic poets of our time." W. B. Yeats expressed a grudging admiration: "*A Shropshire Lad* is worthy of its fame, but a mile further and all had been marsh." It was left to T. S. Eliot to perform his accustomed feat of balancing. His review of *The Name and Nature of Poetry* (a review which Dr. Leavis called an "ambiguous piece of correctness") is respectful, distant, and the equivocal work of Old Possum:

> Observation leads me to believe that different poets may compose in very different ways; my experience (for what that is worth) leads me to believe that Mr. Housman is recounting the authentic processes of a real poet. "I have seldom," he says, "written poetry unless I was rather out of health." I believe that I understand that sentence. If I do, it is a guarantee—if any guarantee of that nature is wanted—of the quality of Mr. Housman's poetry.

The quality of Housman's poetry, acknowledged by Mr. Eliot, is no longer assured of recognition. The force that was once felt in *A Shropshire Lad* was not always purely acknowledged in straight literary criticism—it was acknowledged in some bizarre and nonliterary ways, as . . . [Grant Richards'] anecdote about Housman makes clear:

> He also told me that Clarence Darrow, the U.S.A. lawyer, insisted on coming to Cambridge to him as he had got off so many possible murderers by quoting poems out of *A Shropshire Lad* in support of his arguments: he showed Housman reports which bore this out. In particular **"The Culprit"** (which, incidentally, is in *Last Poems*) had been useful. The poem reads:

But fetch the county kerchief;
    And noose me in the knot,
    And I will rot.

But the "country kerchief" in Mr. Darrow's mouth had become the "County Sheriff"— "Fetch the County Sheriff, &c"! . . .

It is a curious tribute to his poems, though it is one about which he is likely to have been of two minds. [Housman] was not the sort of man who is unequivocally opposed to capital punishment, and he believed that "Revenge is a valuable passion, and the only sure pillar on which justice rests." (pp. 1-2)

Without being too credulous about poet-critics, we might nevertheless believe that Housman's claim on our attention is manifest in the attention he has elicited from other poets. Housman is a poet about whom poets write poems—W. H. Auden, Ezra Pound, Kingsley Amis (and Witter Bynner, E. H. W. Meyerstein, and Paul Engle). Some of the most appreciative criticism on Housman is by Randall Jarrell, Richard Wilbur, Robert Graves, and William Empson. Other poets—John Crowe Ransom, John Peale Bishop, Stephen Spender, John Wain—may have had severe reservations about the value of Housman's poems, but for each of them Housman was a poet worth applying one's mind to.

The point would not much matter if there weren't the widespread idea that Housman's poems are nothing more than the literature of those who don't really care about literature. Maiden aunts and old-world dons are thought to be "fond of" Housman, as they are fond of detective stories. So there hangs about Housman's reputation a fatal combination of the musty and the bright-eyed, as of elaborate bindings at school prize-givings. What better gift (at once cultural and innocuous) than *The Rubáiyát of Omar Khayyám* or ***A Shropshire Lad*** or the poems of Kahlil Gibran? . . .

It is true that Housman's work sometimes pays a price for the wide appeal that it seeks—Housman sometimes makes a poem too instantly palatable. (Not that this is a worse fault than the determined unpalatability of some present-day verse.) Like Edna St. Vincent Millay, and John Betjeman, Housman is the kind of poet easily overrated by the middlebrow many, and easily underrated by the highbrow few. (p. 3)

One hope of the present collection is to disentangle Housman from the jealous embrace of a certain kind of admirer. Just as Jane Austen is too good a writer to be left to "The Janeites," so in the 1960's Housman needs to be protected against some of his friends. In 1929 H. W. Garrod could begin a lecture on Housman: "I have confessed before to a fondness for the poetry of Fellows of colleges." Even those with a soft spot for donnishness and nostalgia may feel that, with friends like Garrod, Housman's poems don't need enemies.

But popularity—and in particular popularity with those who are unpopular—is only one of the things that needlessly come between Housman and a certain kind of modern reader. "Adolescent": that is the word used with quite different valuations by critics as different as R. P. Black-

mur, George Orwell, Conrad Aiken, W. H. Auden, and Hugh Kenner. What exactly do we mean by "adolescent," and is it simply a pejorative word? These are precisely the issues which some of the critics here have felt obliged to consider. (p. 4)

The mistaken assumption has been that "adolescent" poems are what adolescents enjoy. The opposite is the case. They are what yesterday's adolescents enjoyed. Mr. Eliot tells us that he was "intoxicated by Shelley's poetry at the age of fifteen, and now finds it almost unreadable"— and what effect was that remark sure to have on fifteen-year-olds? No self-respecting adolescent is likely to give his time to literature that his elders describe as written for, or appealing to, the likes of him. None of us likes to be thought of as "the likes of." It is true that poets like Housman and Shelley have in the past had a potent appeal to the young—but that was mainly because their claims and concerns seemed vividly adult. But once the appeal to the young is bruited abroad, the whirligig of time brings in its revenges, and the young are quick to move on. That Housman is a poet of adolescence, Mr. Auden truly remarks, shouldn't mean "that nobody over the age of twenty-one can or should enjoy reading him." But the actual situation is harshly the opposite: it is only those *over* twenty-one who read Housman or Shelley (by choice), since for the young the poems of Housman and Shelley have been too brutally stamped "for the young." The problem for those who wish to get Housman's poems a fair hearing is now the opposite of what it used to be. When George Orwell said, "Such poems might have been written expressly for adolescents," he pointed directly—though silently—at the reason why the average age of Housman's admirers is in danger of getting higher every year. (p. 5)

Christopher Ricks, in an introduction to A. E. Housman: A Collection of Critical Essays, *edited by Christopher Ricks, Prentice-Hall, Inc., 1968, pp. 1-10.*

William R. Brashear   (essay date 1969)

[*In the following excerpt, Brashear purports that despite his obvious failings, Housman may be a greater poet than has previously been acknowledged. While the critic admits that "trouble," or what he terms "something that in a positive way makes life more difficult," is a predominant and oftentimes tedious theme throughout Housman's poetic canon, he also states that Housman is redeemed by his genius.*]

Housman has had few serious advocates, and the easy answer may be that he has not merited many. In an ironic sense he has found the "peace and darkness" for which he so persistently yearned. But there may be factors other than or in addition to the intrinsic quality of his work that have prevented him from coming into his own. He may be a greater poet than anyone cares to believe. He may, indeed, on occasion reach a profundity we would rather ignore. No one would argue that he is not a small figure compared to Tennyson, and his despair, which as with Tennyson is the biggest part of him, is of correspondingly diminished stature. It cannot, however, be shrugged off. It has, when fully apprehended, a unique starkness and power. I qualify this statement advisedly, for it is entirely possible that Housman is seldom largely apprehended even by his most ardent devotees, who, often themselves cynics, see and like him most either as the puerile malcontent or the sardonic commentator. They see much less than the full Housman, a poet vitally and not happily committed to the starkest hopelessness. . . . (pp. 81-2)

Housman himself is largely responsible for the narrow reading of his poems. For the Shropshire pose is at once effective and misleading. It tends to draw attention too much to the "local" (and not simply geographically so) complaints of a melancholic and sensitive youth, complaints too generally represented by that key word in Housman, "trouble," and its less often employed variants, "grief" and "ill." "Trouble" is indeed the principal theme throughout Housman's poetry as he himself attests in the verse that prefaces the final volume, *More Poems:*

> This is for all ill-treated fellows
> Unborn and unbegot,
> For them to read when they're in trouble
> And I am not.

But in Housman's poems the various meanings of trouble extend over a vast scope. In many instances it means just what we ordinarily take it for—something undesirable, something painful, something that in a positive way makes life more difficult. A young man's life, whether he be a Knighton or London lad, is filled with this kind of trouble, which finds in "grief" and "ill" its rough equivalents. (pp. 82-3)

And, after all, what are these troubles? The poems in which the general terms (trouble, grief, ill) appear usually remain silent as to the particulars, but there are plenty of poems, most numerous in *A Shropshire Lad,* that do deal with specific complaints. Most frequently appearing are those of unrequited passion, unfaithfulness (or death) of the beloved, the thinning of old friendships, and the waste of young manhood by war. In vaguer moods it is plain and simple "bad luck." . . . (p. 83)

On the whole these poems are not among his greatest, though often well-turned and eminently successful in the achievement of their limited effects. But these effects are over-indulged. While some of these poems possess a high degree of coherence, they lack congruence; the tonal or attitudinal emphasis often goes beyond acceptable bounds. There is relatively too much to do about a too little or common complaint. They are the work of a diminutive Housman. The author's preoccupations strike one as unwholesome and immature. (p. 84)

For "trouble," as used by Housman, can embrace far more than these particular ills or the generality which is the sum or resultant of the particulars. It is sometimes, and I think not always fortunately so, made to stand for the unhappy fact of life itself as apprehended through Housman's intense and hopeless vision. In this sense it is neither good nor ill, right nor wrong, but a poignant apprehension of the nothingness (at once ultimate and imminent) of all, distinguished from traditional nihilism by a quality of life or aliveness which persists—a vibrant anguish. It is, in its broadest extension, the agony of dying consciousness ap-

prehending intuitively and directly its own sound and fury. It is in this wider, cosmic sense that we encounter the term in **"On Wenlock Edge the wood's in trouble."** Conscious life is here an agitation, a disturbance, a wind that blows through succeeding generations of dying individuals and races:

> There, like the wind through woods in riot,
> Through him the gale of life blew high;
> The tree of man was never quiet:
> Then 'twas the Roman, now 'tis I.

> The gale, it plies the saplings double,
> It blows so hard, 'twill soon be gone:
> To-day the Roman and his trouble
> Are ashes under Uricon.

A somewhat different conception of the metaphorical "gale" is carried over into the more personal context of the next poem in the *Shropshire* sequence:

> From far, from eve and morning
> And yon twelve-winded sky,
> The stuff of life to knit me
> Blew hither: here am I.

Here the "stuff of life" is something distinguishable from the wind itself. But we can turn back now to Housman's introduction to *More Poems:*

> For them to read when they're in trouble
> And I am not.

This takes on this broader significance: for them to read when they're *alive* and I have ceased to be alive, when the gale blows through them and no longer through me. And, if the pun may be excused, this is the "trouble" encountered in Housman's most imposing work.

These poems of cosmic anguish, or the best of them, are generally short, often no more than two to four quatrains, or the equivalent. They otherwise follow, with some exceptions, a similar pattern of metaphorical development from a local or confined perception to a vast, all-encompassing imaginative apprehension that startles with its sweep and starkness. Housman was, before all else, a master of simple metaphorical extension through which he accomplishes an immediate, often disquieting leap from the local to the cosmic, bypassing, for better and for worse, the intermediate stations, the levels of meaning and complexities that constitute the enriching substance for most major poets. (pp. 84-5)

The view of life [Housman's poetry enforces] may be taken to be a gross over-simplification, but this is, after all, Housman's position. He is indeed simple-minded, in a sense, and this is most apparent when we try to compare him with Eliot or Yeats or other modern poets. But, on the other hand, suppose he is right. Suppose everything is just this simple—just this vacant, and that all our elaborate effort at constructing meanings, significations, and values is so much whistling in the dark. His poems, I submit, are convincing on this point—in a manner and to a degree that they seem to transgress some deeper, instinctive rule of sportsmanship. We can perhaps complain that Housman is not playing the game—of human survival—and is betraying first principles that even the most decadent and recalcitrant of his contemporaries and successors have never questioned. Our humanistic inclinations cry "foul," and there is the temptation to throw out the accusation of puerility again. But for what Housman is saying in these poems maturity has no answer—except, perhaps, that it ought not to be said. Rather than puerile, then, these poems are subversive—not politically, or socially, or even philosophically, but in a deeper sense. (pp. 87-8)

Housman himself was petrified by his own vision. He had no power to resist what he saw, and in this regard he differs radically from Tennyson, who is redeemed by his "vitalism," by the persisting struggle of the "living will" against the dark despair it cannot dissolve. Housman has not only abandoned all hope, but also all will. His surrender amounts to an affront to humanity—even more so to yeomanry:

> Lie down, lie down, young yeoman;
>   What use to rise and rise?
> Rise man a thousand mornings
>   Yet down at last he lies,
>   And then the man is wise.

Yet there is something more than this in Housman, something that to a measure does redeem him; and this is the genuine and unmitigated anguish that emerges in the imaginative realization of his starkest visions. Although most of his poems are framed in detachment, even cynicism, in his best and most serious work the impact runs quite counter to the apparent design. Of course, many of his lesser poems are purely cynical, or something like cynical, and for one conditioned to look at Housman in this light most of his poems can be accommodated to this kind of reading. But to read him this way entirely is to miss a great deal. For in his best poems his imagination overcomes his composure (which may explain why they often result in more than they promise). In his diminutive work he may evoke a kind of perverse pleasure in cheering "a dead man's sweetheart," but this attitude, whatever the conscious intention may be, does not carry through in such poems as **"Now hollow fires"** or **"With rue my heart is laden."** Yet, interestingly, I believe that it *is* possible to read most of these more serious poems either way, depending on where the emphasis is placed, and even, and perhaps best, both ways together. **"Now hollow fires"** again a good example. The disparity between the detached and casual stance and the ultimate imaginative realization contributes something to the poems' impact. (pp. 88-9)

> *William R. Brashear, "The Trouble with Housman," in* Victorian Poetry, *Vol. VII, No. 2, Summer, 1969, pp. 81-90.*

John W. Stevenson   (essay date 1972)

[*A noted Housman scholar, Stevenson is the author of* The Pastoral Setting in the Poetry of A. E. Housman *(1956) and* Arcadia Re-Settled: Pastoral Poetry and Romantic Theory *(1967). In the following excerpt, Stevenson explores the juxtapostion of Housman's style and sense of irony. He suggests that Housman's "ironic pose," or meticulous attention to style, is a device which*

prevents the poet from being swept away by emotion or confusion.]

The achievement of Housman's style is not so much in its traditional structure—Housman is no innovator—but the ritual of performance, the "ceremony of innocence" confronting the world, in which he finds the means to celebrate an attitude almost aristocratic in its restraint and quiet assurance. Moreover, one can perceive in the pastoral setting, the economy of language, the colloquial tone, and the rusticity of the "lad" of the poems the fulfillment of Wordsworth's theory and a basis for Housman's modernity.

Housman's technique is an attempt to impose order, to give concreteness to a subjective, often romanticized theme. One is aware in the poetry of a firm control which permits no roughness or carelessness. The final performance discloses an emotional and intellectual discipline strenuously sought for and deliberately shaped.

What little criticism exists about Housman's style concerns itself almost solely with the external shape, and the repeated judgment is that the poetry is "mechanical" or adopts a few characteristics and repetitive devices; the effect is a manufactured form. Edwin Muir, for example, sees the style as repetitive, a formula which "tends to become threadbare." Dame Edith Sitwell echoes Muir in describing the style as mechanical: the style, she writes, exposes a threadbare texture without "passionate upheaval under the line." A more recent Housman critic, Mr. Norman Marlow, suggests that the poet "had not a creative mind," that his "architectonic faculty was weak." Such judgments sometimes overlook the relationship between structure and theme, or think of technique as wholly instrumental—or want to separate the dancer from the dance. But style is the poet's response to his theme because having something to say he must say it within a form which he as poet controls. The matter depends wholly on manner. He is not just "expressing" himself; he is giving expression to a form. He can write poetry without worrying about being a *poet*. That is, the style is intimately welded to the subject matter (it works because it is natural, is not self-consciously "literary" or contrived; the effort does not show) because this is the poet's responsibility; he has to bring the subject within his grasp and give it substance. In the end, no matter whether the same form or subject has been used before, the poet has to make them his own.

Ritual or ceremony grows threadbare and mechanical (lacks "passionate upheaval") when the form becomes idiosyncratic or private, that is, when form becomes merely manner pretentiously displayed. . . . Housman's shaping of the texture, his craftsmanship, is achieved in the knowledge of the relation between style and theme, a knowledge which he describes symbolically through an image of labor as both man's curse and man's achievement—Housman's rendering of Yeats's "great-rooted blossomer":

> The olive in its orchard
>   Should now be rooted sure,
> To cast abroad its branches
>   And flourish and endure.
>
> Aloft amid the trenches
>   Its dressers dug and died

The olive in its orchard
　Should prosper and abide.

Close should the fruit be clustered
　And light the leaf should wave,
So deep the root is planted
　In the corrupting grave.

(*Additional Poems,* ["The Olive in its
Orchard"])

If Housman's style "abides" it is due in large measure to his ability to suppress his personality within the form, to extinguish the private emotion in the public performance, "so deep the root is planted." He is not carried away by the emotion of his subject, but rather controls the emotions within the requirements of the form. Certainly nothing new animates his themes; what is new is the manner in which he expresses the themes and yet is able to express them through traditional stanza forms. He stands aside and lets the style become the mask by which he celebrates the ceremony of man's condition—the blight man was born for. Hence, the Shropshire setting, the rustic lad, the striving for the colloquial tone: the Kennedy Professor of Latin knew nothing of these country parts; he uses the setting to extinguish his personality in order to achieve the bardic tone of anonymity, to recapture what Mr. Richard Ellmann, writing of Yeats's style, describes as the "traditionally authoritative manner of the poet." The bardic position is always public (the ceremonial voice), and this stance is what Housman strives for in his poetry in order to hold in tension the double view of both innocence and experience. . . . (pp. 45-7)

Another device of Housman's technique is his directness, his chariness of modifiers, his sparing use of metaphor so that the dramatic meaning of his lyrics is almost always straightforward. His manuscript *Notebooks* support his working always for this direct, unencumbered effect. He said, of course, in *The Name and Nature of Poetry* that simile and metaphors are "things inessential to poetry"; but he was talking about poetic diction (explicitly, the conceit of seventeenth-century metaphysicals) and what should rightly be called poetry. Moreover, he thought most eighteenth-century poetry unpoetic because the poets tried to write what they thought was the opposite of prose: "They devised for the purpose what was called 'a correct and splendid diction'." The nineteenth century, he added, established its own poetic "lingo," and by the seventies and eighties poets imitated a preconceived poetic diction, "imitative and sapless; its leading characteristic was a stale and faded prettiness." Housman's concern for diction grows out of his concept of poetry as "more physical than intellectual." One should attend to poetry for its sound, for a kind of electric charge which sets off a series of imaginative responses. Thus, the meaning of a poem is secondary to its primary function of appealing to the senses. His insistence that poetry is essentially physical accounts perhaps for his own exclusive use of the lyric form. (p. 49)

In his poetry Housman reaches always for a purely lyric effect, an effect, he writes, originating in "some region deeper than the mind" but subsequently controlled and la-

"CURIOSITIES OF LITERATURE."

The Muse. "OH, ALFRED, WE HAVE MISSED YOU! MY LAD! MY SHROPSHIRE LAD!"

Caricature of Housman by Bert Thomas, 1922.

bored after. The result is the only mask that can conclusively be attributed to him, the mask that is his style: the thing that as far as the poetry is concerned *is* Housman, an achievement that is at once his labor and his public ceremony.

At the same time, Housman's poetry is a mask for his deep sense of integrity, his preoccupation with perfection. How reconcile this ideal with the human condition? Perhaps the only reconciliation possible is through an attention to a strict form, for within a structure that is self-contained one can at least sustain the disinterested pose, can give a meaning that, perceived physically, is pleasurable in the sense of rightness. The added unreality of setting and incident takes on the larger vision found only in symbolic action. The situation of the poems is not an escape measure or adolescent nostalgia; the lads in their twenties are perceived as more than one-dimensional, are, in fact, a way of pointing up a dramatic relation between the setting and the theme. The ideal of the lyric is to achieve a heightened effect, a response to experience that is partly intuitive and partly elemental.

Housman's use of irony is basic to his general theme of man's mortality, of man's confrontation with the promise of fulfilment and the fact of failure. Indeed, his choice of the lad, non-hero that he is, at the moment of fulfilment and death is not only a type of paradox but also the symbol of that kind of revelation which can be perceived only in the knowledge of this discovery, a moral discovery that comes only to the innocent. To this kind of paradox there needed to be fashioned as pure a form, as felicitious a language as could sustain the complexity of the theme, just as Housman's use of a pastoral setting suggests a further appearance of simplicity. What happens often with this sharp contrast is a self-conscious irony or histrionic effect especially in a final line or twist that is not fully prepared for dramatically—that is, an over-straining for understatement. Perhaps this characteristic in some of the poems can be explained as the result of the economy of diction which often precludes the use of a more complex and dramatically developed metaphor.

On the other hand, Housman uses understatement with dramatic effect and as a metaphoric device in his use of nouns as verbs to carry the whole weight of the metaphor: for example, the second line of **"To an Athlete Dying Young"** renders the public response to the personal victory of the local hero in the sharp image of "The time you won your town the race / We *chaired* you through the market place" (*A Shropshire Lad*). The same sharp and dramatic effect is found in other examples: "The long cloud and the single pine / *Sentinel* the ending line" (*Last Poems,* ["The West"]); and in "But fetch the country kerchief / And *noose* me in the knot" (*Last Poems,* ["The Night My Father Got Me"]). . . . (pp. 51-2)

A frequent device of Housman's style is his reliance on personification as a figurative means of dramatizing the incongruities of the poem's situation. William Empson has pointed out in a brief analysis of *Last Poems,* ["The Sigh That Leaves the Grasses"], the trick of Housman's method. "The whole point," he writes of this poem, "is to deny the Pathetic Fallacy, [though] its method is to assume [it] as a matter of course."

> The diamond tears adorning
>   Thy low mound on the lea,
> Those are the tears of morning,
>   That weeps, but not for thee.

Nature, Mr. Empson adds, "may weep for pains reassuringly similar to those of humanity, whether consciously or not, or actually for those of man though not of one individual. That the dew might not be tears at all the poetry cannot imagine, and this clash conveys with great pathos and force a sense that the position of man in the world is extraordinary, hard even to conceive." One has to read Housman's irony, then, in his method as well as in his subject; as Empson makes clear, the irony is misleading for the poet hides facts he pretends to accept.

The ironic pose then suggests the style as a mask for the poet. How seriously are we to take his metaphoric statements? The personification seems on the surface to be used as a way of soliciting the comfort of nature, when in fact it is used to reject a too facile acceptance, and to set up the tone of wry amusement and detached wisdom. The pose is a device for not giving way to the passion of the moment or being swept away into confusion; it insists on

maintaining the form at all costs (the "good breeding"), yet having it charged with the emotions of the experience. Accordingly, Housman's style is a pose, a mask for his awareness of maintaining an aristocratic belief in the outward appearance of inner conviction, a sense of seeing in the incongruities of experience a way of fashioning a form that is fastidious, that eschews the ornate and the baroque for the formal and traditional.

For this reason the poetry reveals a unity and achieves a performance that gradually unfolds as each angle of the theme is explored and perceived. The dramatic effect is fully achieved in the larger ironic revelation of the knowledge of the simple. How can these rustics know so much? Speak with such wisdom and wit? The answer is found in just this contrast between style and theme: in the guise of rustic or innocent the poet can hide his feelings by a scrupulous attention to form. The resulting incongruity produces both the startled delight and the shock of discovery. The awful reality of man's mortality and his seduction by death is rendered in the only acceptable manner possible, for style as ceremony and as ritual gives the only meaning, through its attention to form. . . . (pp. 52-3)

John W. Stevenson, "The Ceremony of Housman's Style," in Victorian Poetry, *Vol. 10, No. 1, Spring, 1972, pp. 45-55.*

Gordon B. Lea   (essay date 1973)

[*In the following excerpt, Lea asserts that many critics, including William Brashear (see excerpt dated 1969), have underestimated the dualities found in Housman's verse and have failed to see that Housman has created an "illuminating paradox" in which to investigate the relationship between life and death.*]

In his discussion of "trouble" in the poetry of A. E. Housman, William R. Brashear speaks of the "unmitigated anguish" of the poet's vision [see excerpt dated 1969]. But his explanation ignores an important aspect of Housman's art—namely, Housman's use of irony. For ironies and dualities, verbal, formal, thematic, and situational, seem always to underlie Housman's pejoristic world view, especially in *A Shropshire Lad.* These engaging discrepancies occasionally accentuate the bleakness of Housman's vision, but more frequently they relieve it, and, as a result, a poetry whose sentiments ought to depress us actually delights us. It is perhaps a failure to understand these extraordinary contrarieties that prompts some critics to condemn the Shropshire cycle for what they consider are its inconsistencies. A careful study of *A Shropshire Lad* reveals that Housman has created an illuminating paradox, the purpose of which is essentially didactic.

One of the most pronounced ironies involves Housman's antitheism, which is frequently vocalized in diction, phrases, and cadences either directly from, or highly reminiscent of, the King James Bible. Norman Marlow details many of these allusions and explains that they function to make Housman's verse seem timeless. But the tonal authority with which the anti-Christian theme is invested, as a result of Housman's employing these Biblical echoes, is also worth noting. These allusions make his world view more persuasive to the Christian, especially the Anglican reader, either consciously or subliminally. Ironically, the Bible, the revealed "Word," is employed to undercut "the Word" as well as to indict God himself.

A few examples illustrate the success of this technique. **"1887"** challenges the claim of the British national anthem by arguing that not God but British soldiers protect and maintain the monarchy. That these selflessly dedicated patriots are mocked and cheated by the sentiments expressed in the anthem is evident in Housman's use of a phrase with which Christ was assailed on the Cross. Housman's soldiers are "saviours" who do not return home because "themselves they could not save" (Mark 15:31). The same Biblical incident is recalled by **"The Carpenter's Son,"** in which a Shropshire felon, moments before his execution, commands his friends to learn from his experience. Bitterly, he urges them to be shrewder than he, in order to enjoy a less indecent end. And he adds, "Live, lads, and I will die," an ironic upending of Jesus' claim that He died so that mankind might live eternally. Housman's sacrificial lamb also employs a phrase that brings to mind a central New Testament metaphor: "Walk henceforth in other ways," he says, and thus his listeners are asked to avoid "the Way" recommended and represented by Christ (John 14:6). (pp. 71-2)

The most suggestive of these New Testament reverberations is found in **"I hoed and trenched and weeded,"** which ends the Shropshire cycle. Here, Housman calls on Jesus' Parable of the Sower (Mark 4), for Terence, likening his poems to flowers that will yield seed, says

> Some seed the birds devour,
>   And some the season mars,
> But here and there will flower,
>   The solitary stars.

In the New Testament, the seed is Christ's gospel. Is Housman's *A Shropshire Lad,* then, a new gospel, one not of hope but of despair? (p. 73)

There exist other contrarieties, but these meliorate rather than reinforce Housman's anti-Christian world view. Not the least fascinating of these is Housman's musicality. The poetry dramatizes that life is an agony and God an oppressor, but it does so to a music that is distractingly light and melodious, a music that often functions as an ironic descant to the bleak sentiments and painful experiences it accompanies. In short, sound at times appears to belie theme. This incongruity is pronounced in **"When I was one and twenty,"** which deals with the pain of young love. In this piece, the price paid for temporary bliss is clear— "endless rue." But sound acts as a counterpoint to theme. Agile iambic trimeter lines (line one, three, five, and seven in each of the two eight-line stanzas contain an extra syllable), predominance of short vowel sounds, and monosyllabic diction (of the ninety words in the poem, seventy-six are monosyllables) combine merrily to undermine the sadness of the speaker, a rejected or abandoned lover.

Musicality modifies meaning in other *Shropshire Lad* pieces. **"It nods and curtseys and recovers"** is about man's mortality but the melody celebrates the vitality of the nettle, a symbol for nature, and nature is not subject to death.

Sound and sense are also at odds in one of Housman's most poignant treatments of the isolation that accompanies old age, **"With rue my heart is laden."** The melody of this dramatic lyric is lively, vibrant, especially in the first quatrain. The discrepancy is fitting because it is the loss of this very vitality that the piece commemorates. And Housman's attempt to "harmonise" the world's sadness is equally successful in **"Into my heart an air that kills,"** one of the exile poems. Here, melodiousness qualifies theme, for the poem is about separation from beloved places and people. The irony that results is effective, for two emotions are blended: the joy, the sweetness, associated with the past, and the pain, the bitterness, that marks that separation and the speaker's recognition that return is impossible. The musicality also accentuates the figure in the first line, for memory is an "air" in two senses: a gentle breeze and a light bitter-sweet melody.

The sometimes startling discrepancy between matter and manner in much of Housman is, then, particularly fascinating. In effect, the music bemuses, captivates, entrances. Expressions of the darkest despair are musically tempered and, as a result, seem less hopeless and, not insignificantly, more memorable. Housman's bitter-sweet lines have a stubborn way of staying with us. And we are not so much depressed by the poet's matter as we are invigorated by his manner.

There are other ironies. In many *Shropshire Lad* pieces that apparently celebrate life, vitality, Housman weaves subtly disturbing references to imminent death. **"Loveliest of trees, the cherry now,"** for instance, ostensibly celebrates the beauty of nature in the spring, but the exquisite loveliness of the cherry blossom, and the joy the young speaker derives from that loveliness, are evanescent. The allusion to Easter, the mention of the speaker's "threescore year and ten," and the reference to snow introduce the chill of death.

The same disturbing combination is achieved in other *Shropshire Lad* poems. **"The Lent Lily," "The Merry Guide,"** and **"Say, lad, have you things to do?"** seem to celebrate life, but death is ominously present, perhaps because in Housman, a pastoral poet, nature, itself perpetual, is a constant reminder of the brevity of man's temporal stay. What is more, in Housman's verse, spring, traditionally the season of birth and regeneration, produces the most poignant indications of man's mortality. Occasionally, nature may seem to sympathize with man, may seem even to suffer from the same blight. Flowers and plants, the seasons, the years—each and all may appear, at times, to be death struck. But in truth they are not. Their vitality is eternal.

Ironically, however, death, which is literally inescapable in Housman's poetry, is not necessarily a curse. Indeed, there are indications that death can be desirable, and few modern poets dramatize so persuasively the appeal of non-being. **"To an Athlete Dying Young," "The lads in their hundreds," "The Immortal Part,"** and **"Be still, my soul, be still"**—these and other poems imply that life is a cruel and punitive dispossession, a curse, and that oblivion, non-being, is preferable. In these poems, death is the only sure refuge from the "trouble" that is life.

But is the choice that simple? Housman's *A Shropshire Lad* suggests that it is not, for those poems that seem to laud death, particularly early death, simultaneously pay tribute to life. In **"Is my team ploughing,"** a colloquy between a dead man and his living friend, the dead man sleeps in a good "bed," safely tucked away from life's troubles, but he manifests a burning interest in life. The condition of his horses, the sound of their jingling harness, the state of his land, the local soccer games, whether his friend has a mistress—these are the activities to which the dead man refers. In this poem as in others in Housman's cycle, life is vital, active, whereas death is monotonous, passive.

Housman's paradox is intriguing and disturbing. Death brings peace, surcease of life's anguish. It may even be a victory in man's endless battle against an oppressive deity. But it is a Pyrrhic victory because it is paralysis. Housman never permits us to forget that "blood's a rover" and "clay lies still." This conflict between the different appeals of being and non-being is at the heart of Housman's *A Shropshire Lad,* but it is perhaps most lucidly dramatized in **"Oh fair enough are sky and plain."** Death by drowning promises the speaker an idyllic existence, fairer, purer, quieter, and more serene than any found on earth, for death is a becalmed reflection of nature the speaker sees in the water. But the youth's other self, his non-self, as it were, gazes at him from the surface of the water enviously. Real life is as appealing to him as death's promise is to the speaker. Neither "lad" is at peace.

Housman also engages in verbal irony, particularly multiple meanings, plurisignification, and puns. In **"It nods and curtseys and recovers,"** the dead man over whom the nettle performs its taunting measure is both a lover *in* the grave and a lover *of* the grave, a death-lover. Similarly, in **"To an Athlete Dying Young,"** the dead athlete is "smart" in that he is both shrewd and quick, and the term "cut" in the lines "Eyes the shady night has shut / Cannot see the record cut" means both *recorded* and *broken.* And when Terence Hearsay refers to the "smack" of his poetic brew, he means two things: the bitter taste and the painful impact. (pp. 73-6)

These, then are some of the engaging contrarieties threaded through Housman's Shropshire cycle, and most mitigate Housman's apparently hopeless view of the human condition. The crowning irony in the collection, however, is revealed in **" 'Terence, this is stupid stuff,' "** which constitutes a frame. Here, Housman, through Terence Hearsay, indicates his overall intention in *A Shropshire Lad.* This poem intimates that, in order to bear life's "troubles," one must recognize, first, that such tribulations are inescapable and, second, that they are universal rather than particular. Only then can some semblance of peace be achieved—the kind of contentment Terence manifests eating "victuals" and drinking his Ludlow draught. The poetry may seem, as Terence's complaining Shropshire critic insists, mere "moping melancholy," and, worse, a means of rhyming "friends to death before their time." But its real purpose is to train Terence's listeners for temporal "ills" that are ubiquitous and unavoidable. "The world has still / Much good," says the Shropshire poet, "but much less good than ill." Thus, the Shropshire

cycle is essentially didactic. It urges man to "train for ill." The following poem, **"I hoed and trenched and weeded,"** which ends the cycle, reinforces Housman's didacticism. Here, Terence voices his hope that the Shropshire poems will prepare future generations of "lads" to face and withstand life's "troubles." That the underlying vision will be resisted, especially in Housman's own time, is clearly signalled, for the poems, "flowers," are "brought . . . home unheeded" from the market, and some, planted as seeds, will perish. Like men, perhaps, poetic insights can be destroyed. But a few poems, "solitary stars," will remain after Terence's death, and other "luckless lads" will wear them.

In effect, then, Housman's *A Shropshire Lad* is an indirect plea for recognition, acceptance, and endurance. But what, ultimately, helps man bear his troubles, endure his ills? Ironically, that which never fails to remind man of his mortality, nature and art, will constitute a refuge from the agony of being and the paralysis of non-being. Nature and art, both of which are timeless, immortal, will sustain and befriend man **"In the dark and cloudy day."** Nature is, after all, beautiful in its own right, and, in respect to art, it is a statue that causes the Shropshire exile in **"Loitering with a vacant eye"** to accept life manfully. Man's tribulations are relatively short, the statue seems to imply, whereas it must bear its ill forever. Poetry, another art form, will also assist. Terence's "stuff " may not be as tasty as ale, nor will it befuddle the brain, but it will sustain "heart and head," and, perhaps more important, it will help man build up a resistance to the poison that is life. (pp. 77-8)

Of course, one needs to be very cautious about attributing these views to Housman. They are essentially Terence's. But Terence is indubitably an exemplar in *A Shropshire Lad:* he observes, experiences, records, and educates, and, as a result, he endures. Through him, we perceive that awareness, acceptance, and endurance are possible. His vision may shatter our hopes and illusions, but it also decreases our fears. He teaches us that one can achieve self-respect, genuine self-respect, without expecting any recompense in this or the next world. What is more, Terence teaches us that one can attempt wryly to laugh at, even to sing about, the injustice that is life, as so many of Housman's Shropshire speakers do. But we cannot forget, I think, that they laugh and sing in order not to weep. (p. 79)

Gordon B. Lea, "Ironies and Dualities in 'A Shropshire Lad'," in Colby Library Quarterly, *Series X, No. 2, June, 1973, pp. 71-9.*

B. J. Leggett   (essay date 1976)

[In the following excerpt, Leggett refutes the charge made by many critics that the philosophy expressed in Housman's poems is adolescent. Leggett views Housman's use of the Shropshire Lad persona as a device similar to that outlined in W. B. Yeats's theory of the mask. He suggests that a fundamental, yet unrecognized duality in Housman's work is the split between poet and persona. He goes on to argue that one cannot assume that statements Housman makes in the poems where he em-

*ploys this poetic persona are accurate reflections of the
poet's own beliefs.*]

One indication of Housman's singular position in the tradition of British poetry at the turn of the century may be seen in his commentators' preoccupation with the nature of his verse. More perhaps than any other poet of his generation Housman has prompted questions of classification and definition in regard to a small body of poetry which does not fit easily into any school or movement. For the critics of the thirties it was primarily a question of classicism versus romanticism. . . . Yet despite numerous . . . efforts to articulate the special character of Housman's verse, one must agree with Christopher Ricks's observation that we are still "hard put to say why we like or dislike his poems." It is the very nature of his poetry which remains in question.

Housman, we know from his statements in *The Name and Nature of Poetry,* had little sympathy with the efforts of criticism to label and define what was for him a personal and human response, and there is something to be said for his concern that the tendency of criticism in his time was to confuse the provinces of literature and science. But he was obviously not opposed to the more humanistic branch of literary criticism, typified in the nineteenth century by his favorite critic, Matthew Arnold, and his primary objection to twentieth-century criticism was centered on its attempt to substitute empirical truth for informed opinion and good taste. Housman's cautious position on the limits of the intellect in the appraisal of poetry voiced in *The Name and Nature of Poetry* should serve to remind the commentator how tentative and even capricious his own pronouncements may be, and the tone of tentative inquiry befitting an admirer of Housman and Arnold is the tone I wish to take here. (pp. 325-26)

The theory articulated in *The Name and Nature of Poetry* can provide some help for an approach to Housman's verse if we do not allow it to take us too far. At the very least it can give us some sense of Housman's conception of the tradition out of which he was writing. That is not enough, finally, but it does afford a base from which to proceed. That tradition, as Housman defined it, suggests that we should expect to encounter a poetry of feeling in the manner of the Romantics, although not necessarily in the Romantic style. It suggests further that we should not expect to find anything approaching the formulation of a philosophical world-view or the exposition of ideas, since Housman was convinced that his verse made its appeal not to the intellect but "to something in man which is obscure and latent, something older than the present organisation of his nature."

The opposition between intellect and emotion is central to Housman's own conception of poetry, and in his effort to define the essential nature of poetry he took great pains to show that the intellect is not the seat of aesthetic appreciation. "There is," he says, "a conception of poetry which is not fulfilled by pure language and liquid versification, with the simple and so to speak colourless pleasure which they afford, but involves the presence in them of something which moves and touches in a special and recognizable way." . . . (pp. 327-28)

I am convinced that Housman's commentators have gone astray in pursuing the philosophy of his poetry, just as Housman believed Wordsworth's admirers were misdirected in concentrating on his philosophy of nature. In both cases we are confronted with a sense of the world which is beyond (or below) the intellect. That is, the poetry does not lend itself readily to philosophical schema or systemization. Further, Housman's poems are not frequently concerned with anything more than dramatizing the moment in which insight occurs. It is a commonplace of Housman criticism that he kept writing the same poem, and that poem most frequently is a means of placing the persona in a situation in which some vague sense of his condition is realized. The structures, the strategies of the poems, moreover, serve most often to convey the shock of recognition, the moment of insight. (pp. 328-29)

One may . . . note, in examining the best known of Housman's poems, the types of situations in which Housman involves his persona. A celebration of the fifty years that God has saved the Queen serves to remind him of the soldiers buried in foreign fields who shared the work with God, giving him a momentary glimpse of the mortality on which the permanence of the race is founded. A walk through the woods at Eastertide to observe the cherry in bloom produces a sudden intimation of mortality. The lad at two-and-twenty exclaims, of the transience of love, "And oh, 'tis true, 'tis true." A storm on Wenlock Edge, the site of an ancient Roman city, leads to the knowledge that "Then 'twas the Roman, now 'tis I." An athlete dying young, a funeral observed from Bredon Hill, the sounds of the soldiers' tread, the imagined last hour of a murderer who hangs at the stroke of nine—these are the occasions for the innocent's confrontation with the alien world of time and death.

But it is the manner in which Housman conveys to us the significance of the discovery that provides the force of many of his best poems. At times the poem depends on the paradox or irony of **"To an Athlete Dying Young"** or **"1887,"** so much admired by the New Critics at the expense of the body of his verse. But he may also employ more subtle means in which no daring metaphors or metaphysical conceits are evident. Consider, for example, one of the most straightforward of the poems of *A Shropshire Lad,* **"Loveliest of Trees,"** which has been generally admired. The tone of the poem clearly depends on the point of view of the naive persona, his essential innocence, and even his inability to articulate with any sophistication what he has discovered. His attitude is difficult to characterize, for it is not governed by pessimism or bitterness at his human state; Housman seems interested only in the persona's discovery of his own mortality, and the poem is structured in such a manner as to make that discovery its central element. The poem depends to a great extent on a curious but obscure relationship between the sight of the cherry in bloom at Eastertide and a sense of human limitation. The first stanza concentrates wholly on the description of the cherry, "wearing white for Eastertide," and the second stanza on the persona's realization of his mortality. The causal connection between the two experiences is left unstated. Perhaps it is not capable of discursive statement. The lad's calculation of his threescore years and then is handled in an almost neutral manner, with no betrayal of emotion:

> Now, of my threescore years and ten,
> Twenty will not come again,
> And take from seventy springs a score,
> It only leaves me fifty more.

There is more attention to arithmetic than to feeling here, much in the manner of Frost's "Stopping by Woods on a Snowy Evening," where the persona seems more involved with the owner of the woods and the horse than with the consequences of his experience. But in both cases the effect is the same. The poet escapes the danger of a maudlin treatment of a commonplace experience by the neutrality of tone and the attention to detail. John Ciardi has spoken of the duplicity of Frost's method, and the term is applicable here. In both cases, the force of the poem is greater than the occasion or the accumulation of details would seem to warrant. The opposite effect is sentimentality, a constant threat for poets like Frost and Housman who deal in potentially melodramatic situations.

The understatement of the last stanza provides an instance of Housman's characteristic treatment of the consequences of insight:

> And since to look at things in bloom
> Fifty springs are little room,
> About the woodlands I will go
> To see the cherry hung with snow.

The details of the stanza carry a significance hardly warranted by the commonplace sentiment they express or the bland language in which they are couched, and that is due almost entirely to the fact that they are now weighted by the persona's intuitive sense of his own mortality, introduced in stanza two. "Things in bloom" now suggest something of the vitality of life which has become more precious. The limitations of life are condensed into the almost trite phrase "little room," and the sense of death which now colors all living things is conveyed by the single description of the white blossoms of the cherry, "hung with snow." It is an effect which relies on what is unsaid, comparable to the similar conclusion of Frost's poem, "And miles to go before I sleep," although Frost's line seems almost heavy-handed in comparison. The poem relies also on its progressive structure and on metaphor and allusion, all of which warrant further discussion, but at the moment I should like to pursue the thematics of a poetry of insight, especially as it involves the problems of character and point of view.

It would be misleading to state that the point of view adopted by the persona in **"Loveliest of Trees"** is typical of that of the majority of Housman's poems. His reaction to the discoveries he makes in poem after poem varies from renewed vitality to melancholy. What remains constant is, however, the degree to which the poems depend for their effect on the character of the persona, his ability to voice afresh sentiments which in the mouth of a more sophisticated speaker would appear trite. Housman avoids the dangers of the trite, the sentimental, by separating himself from his poems through a created character, whereas a poet like Frost pretends actually to be the homely rustic speaker that the poem demands, a role Frost apparently found congenial to his public life as a poet. Housman's poetics are not elaborate enough to allow for Yeats's theory of the mask, but the result of the split between poet and persona produces a similar situation. His solution to the problems of personality and personae which Yeats spent a lifetime working out was simply to create the fiction of the Shropshire lad, substituting for the voice of the learned classical scholar whose reticence was almost legendary that of the rustic innocent. . . . The persona thus becomes a kind of Yeatsian mask or anti-self, the opposite of all that the poet represents in his private life. The resulting tone, carefully cultivated, controls Housman's verse so pervasively that it has been tempting to blur the distinction between the personalities of poet and speaker. Such a crucial distinction has, of course, been an element of modern criticism for the past forty years, yet Housman criticism gives evidence that the formalist principle of the separation of poet and persona has been more often observed in theory than in practice.

The nature of the persona we may expect to encounter in Housman's verse—initially the innocent confronted with the alien world, later the exile seeking to recapture his lost innocence—has been described in some detail. There is, moreover, the question of the persona's change throughout the sequence of *A Shropshire Lad*—he is certainly not a static character. But that is a related issue which I have attempted to treat elsewhere. I should like to examine here another aspect of the persona, the effect of his presence in the poem as a whole. That is, what does Housman's art gain or lose by his use of the pastoral mask? It is a question which can be answered only by examination of individual poems, for the persona's presence is felt more strongly in some poems than in others. Housman rarely drops the mask, but sometimes it is crucial; at other times it seems only a habit of composition.

To look first at an instance in which the character and point of view of the speaker are decisive in determining the form of the poem, we may consider Lyric XXX of *A Shropshire Lad*, **"Others, I am not the first."** The poem has received little attention; it contains none of the obvious designs of irony or metaphor which would attract the notice of the formalists, and I suspect it would be set down as a relative failure by many, for its tone approaches that of **"Could man be drunk for ever,"** a poem Cleanth Brooks condemns for its theatrical gestures and sentimentality. There *is* a kind of theatricality in **"Others, I am not the first,"** but one must be cautious in ascribing it to the poem as a whole, as opposed to its persona, who is presented as a young man dealing with his first taste of the desire and guilt which are the fruits of experience. His attempt to order his feelings and to relieve their intensity comprises the strategy of the poem. . . . The theme of private versus shared experience achieves a curious effect in the poem, for the speaker's determination to console himself with the knowledge that his feelings have been shared by other men serves only to reinforce the sense of their privacy. In the same way, the mental process, the argument of the poem, is continually undermined by its physical details. The fear and desire which contend in the reins, the seat of the passions, are stronger ultimately than the intellect, and they render the argument of the poem ineffectual. It is, in fact, an argument that cuts both ways; the attempt to escape the consequences of experience leads to the further revelation that such experience is the inescapable lot of the condition of man.

The poem is not quite as simple as it appears in paraphrase, but some measure of its complexity can be maintained only through the separation of persona and poet. The persona's response to his situation is obviously inadequate, as he casts about for ways to find release from his strong feelings. He reasons that he is no different from other men; he tries to take comfort in the thought that men die. But the poem as a whole, the poet's response to the experience, contrives to undermine the persona's strategy, as the poem reveals the weakness of his rationalizations by its concentration on the physical symptoms of his fear and desire. The poem reveals the inadequacy of the intellect, the domination of the feelings; and the conventional response of commentators to poems such as this—that Housman is advocating death as a release from the pain of life—misses the point for the very reason that it blurs the distinction between poet and speaker.

To label Housman's point of view adolescent, as has been frequently done, is to assume that he shares the innocence of the persona, but the effect of many poems depends on the exposure of such naiveté. **"Is My Team Ploughing,"** for example, is constructed on the contrast between the knowledge, shared by the reader and poet, that life is transient, and the innocence maintained by a young man who has died believing that his girl and his best friend remain unchanged. . . . There is, of course, no possibility of confusion here between the two points of view, since Housman has the youth speaking from the grave, but in poems such as **"The Recruit"** and **"Oh see how thick the goldcup flowers"** the point is made in less obvious ways. In **"The Recruit"** the sentiments of the persona are denied by the poem itself. He assures a young soldier that he will be long remembered in his home shire while the poem as a whole suggests the opposite. In **"Oh see how thick the goldcup flowers"** the naiveté of the speaker is exploited in a seduction scene in which his expectations are dashed and his argument is turned against him. (pp. 329-34)

It is clear that Housman uses his lyrics to explore the obscure and unnamed feelings which give man a sense of his human state and that he treats the feelings as somehow prior to the intellect. The thesis of *The Name and Nature of Poetry*—that poetry is not of the intellect and that the intellect may hinder its production and retard its appreciation—whatever its value as a statement about art, is certainly a clue to Housman's method as an artist. It offers one explanation for his attraction to the sort of rustic persona who can express his passions without being able to account for them, and whose efforts to rationalize his situation are pitiably inadequate. (p. 334)

What Housman gains in his use of the Shropshire lad fiction may be further noted in observing that many of the most admired effects of his poems—the daring conceits, the paradoxes—are merely extensions of the point of view created through the innocent persona. To select one example, **"The night is freezing fast"** (*Last Poems*) has been praised for its brilliant use of metaphor and handling of tone. Both may be traced to the speaker Housman has created for the occasion of the poem. It is the speaker's memory of his dead friend and the schoolboy attitude he adopts which dictate the tone of the poem:

> The night is freezing fast,
>   To-morrow comes December;
>   And winterfalls of old
>   Are with me from the past;
>   And chiefly I remember
>   How Dick would hate the cold.
>
> Fall, winter, fall; for he
>   Prompt hand and headpiece clever,
>   Has woven a winter robe,
>   And made of earth and sea
>   His overcoat for ever,
>   And wears the turning globe.

One is reminded here of Wordsworth's "A Slumber Did My Spirit Seal," with its similar images of Lucy "Rolled round in earth's diurnal course, / With rocks, and stones, and trees." There is, however, one crucial difference. Wordsworth's persona views Lucy's return to nature as a tragic loss: "No motion has she now, no force; / She neither hears nor sees." He is the bereaved lover whose love had blinded him to Lucy's earthly nature. . . . The final image of his beloved helplessly spun by the forces of the earth reinforces his sudden recognition of the reality of death which his illusion of love's permanence had denied him. Housman's young speaker, on the other hand, seems incapable of that sort of recognition. He views Dick's death as a clever strategy for outwitting the cold. Rather than becoming the helpless victim of the impersonal turning globe, Dick is seen as triumphing over the misery of life. He has at last escaped the cold by making the earth his "overcoat for ever." In spite of the jesting tone, or perhaps because of it, the speaker's attitude toward death is essentially naive. It might be compared to that taken by Wordsworth's persona before he awoke to death's finality. Housman's speaker sees death only in terms of life. It is as if Dick, like Lucy, could not feel the touch of death. He attributes to Dick a will and a purpose which are obviously based on the memory of his personality when he was still alive: "Prompt hand and headpiece clever." Dick was a clever man, and his wit has finally paid off. In contrast to Wordsworth's persona, the speaker of **"The night is freezing fast"** displays no sense of the loss involved in death, but it is important to note that the poem, as opposed to the persona, does suggest such a loss. As Brooks notes, the gay tone "actually renders the sense of grief not less but more intense." He attributes this result to the fact that the tone is characteristic of the dead youth, and that may be a part of it. But what is more important in accounting for the paradoxical effect the poem achieves is the split between the persona's attitude and the attitude of the poem as a whole. The insufficiency of the persona's view of death is revealed in the same manner that the rhetoric of the funeral sermon is negated by the motionless corpse. We receive a sense of what death entails in a way that the speaker cannot. It is a curious and complex device, since it involves the assertion of two contradictory attitudes—gaiety and grief, triumph and defeat. The poem reveals perfectly how non-discursive elements may deny what, discursively, the persona asserts. (pp. 335-36)

The tension between the innocence of the persona and the sophistication of the poet is evident in many of his most successful poems. It is, however, a difficult tension to sustain, and Housman is not always successful with it. When he fails, the resulting tone gives the impression that it is the poet himself whose attitude is hopelessly childish and inadequate, and it is true that in some instances Housman found his poetic mask too congenial, so that he was unable to separate himself sufficiently from the Shropshire lad. Since his persona was, in Housman's words, "an imaginary figure with something of my temperament and view of life," it was perhaps too easy to blur the distinction. It might be argued, in fact, that the statement just quoted gives evidence that there was no distinction, but that is to confuse life and art, ideas with their expression. . . . Although we may have all shared, at times, the emotions expressed by Housman's persona, we would not ordinarily express them in the manner in which they are expressed by the rustic, and if we did create an "imaginary figure" to give vent to our emotions, we would no longer simply be expressing feeling but creating a fiction which would necessarily modify the feelings.

Readers who object to the "philosophy" of Housman's poetry are, in reality, objecting to the mode in which a view of life is being expressed, and they fail to take into account the narrative technique which Housman first employed for the poems of *A Shropshire Lad* and which carried over into the whole body of his poetry. To state the case in the most direct manner, if the feelings expressed in Housman's poetry seem to us adolescent, that is precisely because they are placed in the mouth of an adolescent. To insist on this point is not, however, to justify fully Housman's device of employing the rustic as his speaker. While it is the means by which he achieved his characteristic successes, it also imposes a severe limitation on his poetry. It is primarily responsible for the limited range of his verse and its sameness of tone. What is missing in Housman is the range of voices and attitudes that we find in a poet like Yeats, and Yeats's status as a major poet owes a great deal to the fact that he was able to overcome, through his own self-criticism and through the system constructed about his theories of self and mask, the complex problems involved in the relationship between poet and persona.

Housman seems to have been uninterested in exploring such critical problems. . . . He subscribed to the Romantic notion that the peculiar function of poetry was "to transfuse emotion—not to transmit thought but to set up in the reader's sense a vibration corresponding to what was felt by the writer." Holding such a belief, he was naturally drawn to devices and techniques which would enable him to deal with the deepest and most elementary human feelings, and his choice of the innocent as persona allowed him to explore a range of feelings revolving around man's first discovery of the world in which he finds himself. He owes much of his success as a poet to the manner in which he was able to exploit the relationship between poet and persona, but his status as a minor poet is also due in some measure to the restrictions imposed on his poetry by the nature of his persona. (pp. 337-39)

B. J. Leggett, "The Poetry of Insight: Persona and Point of View in Housman," in Victorian Poetry, *Vol. 14, No. 4, Winter, 1976, pp. 325-39.*

Robert K. Martin   (essay date 1984)

[*Martin is a Canadian professor of English who has written* The Homosexual Tradition in American Poetry *(1979). Of his work, Martin states that it "has taken its present form from a growing awareness of the need to speak out of my own experience as a gay man who can still hope to find significance through the creation of a viable artistic tradition." In the following excerpt, Martin explores the two ways in which Housman responds to his homosexuality and how these responses are reflected in his verse. While many critics often address the whole of Housman's work as a single entity, Martin believes that* A Shropshire Lad *and* Last Poems *represent two very different presentations of self.*]

Asked about his use of place, A. E. Housman replied drily, "My Shropshire, like the Cambridge of Lycidas, is not exactly a real place." The remark is suggestive in several ways. It serves to remind us of *A Shropshire Lad*'s status as fiction, its qualities of invention and imagination as ways of transforming experience into art. If the "Shropshire" of the poem is not really Shropshire, neither is the speaker of most of the poems, Terence Hearsay, Housman himself. At the same time Housman's comment seems to invite us to read *A Shropshire Lad* at least partly in the light of Milton's monody. To do so is to understand much of the structure of Housman's work, the transformation of the "uncouth swain" into the "lad" of the later poem, but also to see how *Lycidas,* with its Christian reassurance, becomes an ironic model for Housman's Stoic or antitheist elegy.

In the popular imagination the poems of *A Shropshire Lad* are often seen as pastoral lyrics singing the praises of innocent rural life and the loves of lads and lasses. In fact, however, the book is a series of dramatic monologues depicting a fallen pastoral. The world they portray is as cruel as Frost's rural New England—Frost is in fact one of Housman's most important spiritual and poetic descendants. The speaker gives us a panoramic view of Shropshire as a world dominated by guilt and death. And yet, paradoxically, the poems triumph over the world they record: the lads die, but the love they inspire gives rise to the poems which preserve that love in a way that life is incapable of. *A Shropshire Lad* is a book which begins in death and concludes in an eternal life of shared art and love.

A Shropshire Lad was indeed a deeply personal work, the poetic consequence of Housman's love for Moses Jackson and his recognition of the impossibility of fulfilling that love in life. Housman found an adequate means of rendering his love only through the effective exclusion of the personal self from the poems. Housman's invention of a rural uncouth persona was not merely an indication of his indebtedness to a poetic tradition; it was the means by which he could make his suffering into the material of art and hence surmount it. The Shropshire lad is Housman's objective correlative for his own sense of loss.

This process, which I have termed Housman's "strategy of survival," is most clearly indicated in the penultimate poem of the collection, the only one in which the speaker is specifically identified as Terence. Terence replies to accusations that his poetry (which we have just read, of course) is "stupid stuff" by explaining that his poems are not merely "a tune to dance to." If poetry is an escape from thought, then its place can well be taken by ale. But, following the liquor analogy, his brew is "sour," for it has been distilled "in a weary land," "Out of a stem that scored the hand." In his first explanation of his poetry, the speaker appears to justify it in terms of reality: if his poetry is grim, it is because life is grim as well (it has, in his words, "much less good than ill"). (p. 14)

The pain of the poems is also mithridatic; it is designed to introduce a controlled amount of pain in order that the reader may be inured against an even larger dose. By this analogy, Housman reveals his own strategy of control and distance. The king survives because he has trained his body to respond to poison; the knowledge of poison has made him strong. So, we are to understand, it is with these poems: they are also ways of learning to survive, not through escape from pain but through the ability to take the pain in small doses. As therapy for the reader, they build an immunity that may enable him to overcome adversity; as therapy for the author, they are an index of the ability of pain to heal itself, by a kind of burning-out process.

It should be remembered that the speaker in this poem is Terence—but Terence in his guise as poet, even if still the unsophisticated poet of Ludlow. The poem is thus Terence's poetics, or Housman's poetics as spoken through Terence. For Terence is integral precisely to the strategy that Housman describes in this poem. It was through the creation of a less sophisticated, cruder self that Housman could give voice to his pain while still retaining an element of control. The shepherd's lament became Housman's way of channeling, and hence mastering, his own mourning. Those who met Housman were often surprised to find such an unsympathetic, cold person, not at all like the warm-hearted voice of the poems. What they seem not to have understood is the extraordinary inner tension that led to the creation of two different public identities, the cruelly correct classics scholar, and the lively, vulgar lad. Housman seems to have had no way of bringing them together. (pp. 14-15)

The idea that art preserves by transforming love from the transitory realm of the real into the eternal world of the imagination was not unique to Housman, of course, although it is one of his most persistent themes. There is perhaps no more important source for this concept as expressed in Housman's poetry than in Shakespeare's sonnets, such as sonnet 18, with its lines,

> But thy eternal summer shall not fade
> Nor lose possession of that fair thou owest;
> Nor shall Death brag thou wander'st in his
>   shade,

When in eternal lines to Time thou growest:
> So long as men can breathe or eyes can see,
> So long lives this and this gives life to thee.

Housman's most famous single poem, **"To an Athlete Dying Young,"** is one of a number of his poems which touch on this theme. It must be remembered that the poem is based on Pindar's Olympian Odes and that, like them, it celebrates the beauty and grace of the athlete at the moment of his perfection. It is therefore inaccurate to think of Housman's elegaic poems in terms of the world-weariness and *amour de l'impossible* of the poets of the [1890s]: for their mourning is always countered by an assurance of a compensating life, never certainly in the Christian terms of *Lycidas* but often in the aesthetic terms of Shakespeare.

"To an Athlete Dying Young" is structured around the figure of the laurel, which, as Housman knew, was used for the wreath of the victorious athlete and for the poet. Although the laurel in the poem refers explicitly only to the athlete's crown, the poem's full meaning depends upon an understanding of its unstated other reference. For the poem itself is the laurel wreath bestowed on the young man, and it is the wreath which guarantees a life beyond death. In the third stanza, the speaker praises the youth:

> Smart lad, to slip betimes away
> From fields where glory does not stay
> And early though the laurel grows
> It withers quicker than the rose.

In the natural world, indicated by the "fields where glory does not stay," nothing is permanent, all life leads to death. The laurel grows "early" because the beauty of the youth achieves its peak, according to the Greek ideal of beauty, in late adolescence. But that beauty dies equally quickly, and indeed "withers quicker than the rose," the emblem of feminine beauty as well as of short flowering.

The final stanza returns to the figure of the laurel, now transformed from an emblem of early death into one of permanent life:

> And round that early-laurelled head
> Will flock to gaze the strengthless dead,
> And find unwithered on its curls
> The garland briefer than a girl's.

The irony of this transformation, that this garland which is "briefer than a girl's" should be still "unwithered," is the poet's assertion of the permanence of art (and memory). For although the athlete is presumably dead, he is always imagined in the poem's terms as alive (indeed the title sees him only "dying," not dead): the imperatives of stanza 6 "set" and "hold" suggest his continued activity, while it is the others who are now "the strengthless dead." He remains alive because he wears a laurel that will not wither, a garland of words, in fact the very poem we are now reading and in that act gazing once more on that "early-laurelled head." Thus the poem's last line, "The garland briefer than a girl's," accomplishes an ironic triumph, since its very brevity is what enables it to survive; so too the line suggests the love for a young man, although destined for an early death, prevails over death in a way that the rose garland of heterosexual love cannot. Like most pederastic poems of this period, Housman's **"To an Athlete Dying Young"** suggests that it is the purity of boy-love which preserves it from time and mortality. (pp. 15-16)

If the fundamental strategy of *A Shropshire Lad* is the attempt to overcome pain by controlling it, Housman's second (and final) collection of poems, *Last Poems,* proposes a very different strategy. These are poems of rebellion, poems that clearly affirm life over death. For whatever reason, Housman appears no longer to have found necessary the strategies that made *A Shropshire Lad* possible. Most of the poems appear still to be written in the voice of Terence (although there are striking exceptions such as the **"Epithalamium,"** which Housman wrote for Moses Jackson's wedding), but the dominant elegaic tone is gone. Indeed the first poem sets the tone for the volume by insisting on a refusal of death. Housman was in his 60's when the book was published, and so one might have anticipated poems which looked toward the end. Instead the book is dominated by its *carpe diem* theme; the presence of death makes life all the more valuable. In the initial poem, **"The West,"** the speaker acknowledges the appeal of death, troped variously as the West, the sea, and "our native land." If there is still no reason to deny that all life will terminate in death, yet there is no reason to succumb to its beguilements. The reason for the change is clear in the poem: the presence of the comrade who "stride for stride, / Paces silent at my side." The word "lad" is used twice in the poem, both times in association with the desire for death, while the living figure is referred to four times as "comrade." The use of these terms in this way appears to signal a shift from the pederastic mode to the Whitmanic mode. There is a strong sense of a newfound equality that matches the determination to accept life, to "Plant your heel on earth and stand." Since death will mean an end to love, the call of the poems is to life. . . .
 (p. 16)

One of the best known poems from this collection, **"The chestnut casts his flambeaux,"** is indicative of the change in attitude. The poem's sense of loss through time is carefully controlled by the ironic voice. His plaints may be those of a slightly drunk Terence, but the anger is now present along with the self-pity, particularly in the curse against "Whatever brute and blackguard made the world." It is a cry like that in *Atlanta in Calydon,* against a malevolent god. Shorn of hope for an afterlife, man in these poems has only the possibility of assuming human responsibilities, those which require him to do his work as best he can. The Stoic philosophy of the poem is slightly undercut by the final phrase, "and drink your ale," but it remains nonetheless essential to Housman's attempt to delineate a world without god. He seeks no consolations, but indeed uses the confrontation with evil and absence as the occasion for spiritual growth. Man is . . . "a stranger and afraid / In a world [he] never made."

Although Housman's rejection of Christianity appears to have occurred fairly early in his life (it became final around 1880-1881) and although it is in any case not unlike that of Swinburne in its angry phase or Arnold in its milder moments, in this particular poem Housman seems to draw a connection between his "criminality" and his atheism. It is important to recall the crimes and criminals of *A Shropshire Lad,* and to suggest that they may be, more than realistic portrayal, the metaphor for Housman's own situation as a sexual criminal, an awareness heightened for him, of course, by the Wilde trial. In the earlier volume the representation of his own sexuality as crime remained at the level of metaphor; it requires a knowledge of biography to guess that Maurice's murderer in *A Shropshire Lad* may represent to some extent Housman's own outlawed status as a homosexual. In *Last Poems,* however, the feelings of anger are much closer to the surface. "Let them mind their own affairs," the speaker declares, or "look the other way." . . .

The most significant manifestation of the "revolutionary" Housman is **"Hell Gate,"** in which he turns again to the model of Milton; but the Milton called upon here is not the pastoral elegist of *Lycidas* but the epic poet of *Paradise Lost*—and that poem is reimagined in a Romantic way. The speaker reaches Hell, only to find that the sentry guarding the gate is an old soldier friend named Ned. Greeting his old friend, the sentry is now transformed into a "flaming mutineer" who kills the master of Hell, and the act of cosmic rebellion leaves the two friends alone, about to begin "the backward way." The expulsion from the Garden becomes the escape from Hell, the revolt against God becomes the revolt against Satan, and the original couple, Adam and Eve, are radically recast as a "pair of friends." The poem is astonishing in its vision of human rebellion against an unjust world. That injustice is no longer some vague notion of Fate, but is, in this collection of poems, specifically seen as the attempt by God and man to impose "foreign laws" to make men "dance as they desire." The poem's role as a trope of homosexual revolt is seen not only in the final emblem of the two friends, but also in the repeated references to the "plain," recalling the Cities of the Plain, and the reference to the moment when the two rebels "looked back," recalling Lot's wife. "There was," however, the poem concludes, "no pursuit." It has been argued the poem is the only one to achieve a "return to the pastoral world" and deals with "the redemption of the fallen world by the innocent world of the past." Although the friends go back, it is back from death to life, not from experience to innocence. There is no suggestion that the pastoral can be restored. The sentry may be an old friend from Shropshire, as it were, but he is a far different figure from the lads of the earlier book. **"Hell Gate"** is the poem in which Housman imagines that love may conquer death, that man need not accept the fear of damnation, and that evil is vanquished by a transformation of the lad into "the soldier at my side." It is Housman's vision of a triumphant humanity, joined by what Whitman would have called "manly love." . . .

The death of both the individual and the art that he creates leads Housman to a celebration of life, "learn the dances / And praise the tune to-day." Terence refused the call for a dance tune in the penultimate poem of *A Shropshire Lad;* the speaker's concluding image of himself as the flautist in *Last Poems* suggests the distance that has been travelled. Evil is no longer administered as antidote to even greater evil; instead it is confronted and vanquished.

In that sense only is the pastoral recaptured at the end of *Last Poems.* The pipes of Pan call forth a new, invigorated, and sensual music that arises from experience while still retaining the vigor of innocence. No longer seeking strategies of survival through distance from the self, Housman left as his *Last Poems,* a new strategy of anger, rebellion, and the joy that might come if only Hell were vanquished. (p. 17)

> Robert K. Martin, "A. E. Housman's Two Strategies: 'A Shropshire Lad' and 'Last Poems'," in The Victorian Newsletter, *No. 66, Fall, 1984, pp. 14-17.*

John W. Stevenson   (essay date 1986)

[*In the following excerpt, Stevenson, a noted Housman scholar, offers an explanation for Housman's continuing popularity.*]

One poet whose work makes a small stay against neglect is A. E. Housman. Housman never has been a fashionable poet, nor one taken very seriously in the academy, yet he continues to maintain an audience, and his reputation remains steady. Curiously, here in the closing decades of the twentieth century, he is still read—and in spite of his minor status.

Housman's little book **A Shropshire Lad** appeared at the close of the nineteenth century (1896) when, as at the close of the twentieth, no living major voices were present: Tennyson, Browning, Arnold were dead, as now are Eliot, Frost, Yeats, Stevens. And, as now, so in 1896 a hundred separate voices combined for special recognition, espoused a new aesthetic, took up new theories of art. What about those contemporaries of Housman who are now rarely read, if read at all: those sometime decadent voices whose vision never grew wider than the limits of their own self-imitation: Ernest Dowson, Lionel Johnson, John Davidson, William Watson (whose poem "Wordsworth's Grave" Housman called "one of the precious things in English literature"), Alice Meynell, Arthur Symons, Richard Le Gallienne, John Gray, William Archer, Henry Newbolt—most of whom in the waning years of the twentieth century arouse no more curiosity than a curiosity about antimacassars?

And what of **A Shropshire Lad?** Since 1896 there have been over ninety editions, the most recent published in 1983. One obvious answer is that Housman continues to be read—but by whom? If you except general anthologies published to introduce literature courses, Housman is certainly not read in the academy. And yet for many nonprofessionals—for that common reader—Housman continues to be of interest. . . . (pp. 613-14)

The poems persist, and many of them endure in the consciousness of readers who are not especially readers of poetry. I keep wondering what that appeal is. Is it that Housman calls up in us a memory of a time long past, a time of innocent waywardness? Or a place we can no longer recover? (p. 614)

Housman created a distinctive figure—the image of a restive innocent finding an early death, or disillusioned in love, or cut off from his native land—and the condition and the waywardness of Housman's lad appealed to the city dweller. Modern man came to the city to find the promise of progress, to make a name and a living in the concrete surroundings of urban commerce, but he found he could no longer recover the golden friends of his youth—no longer recapture the rose-lipped maidens. He could no longer travel the happy highways where he would not come again. The Shropshire voice spoke to some far longing in the soul of modern man, and it spoke in a language that carried this endemic memory.

Housman's special staying power also lies in his fashioning within traditional poetic forms a distinctive and original voice. He said things in a "poetic" way that were not necessarily "literary." He thought in quatrains and in the smaller lyric forms. He wrote for those who found in his poetry a line and a rhythm they could quote on special occasions. (pp. 614-15)

People want on these particular occasions the ritual of verse, especially for those occasions when they talk about the past and their memory of themselves in that past:

> Here, on the level sand,
> Between the sea and land,
> What shall I build or write
> Against the fall of night?
>
> *More Poems*

And they can quote Housman, for the ceremony of his style satisfies their sense of how poetry should sound.

Housman himself was by profession and temperament an urban man, and nothing in his background explains the creation of the Shropshire lad and his country setting—that is, nothing in his private or public life explains the distance between the reserved and solitary Cambridge don and the lad of the poems. The critics of Housman shy away from this curious anomaly, shy away (with some few exceptions) even from writing about the poetry itself. The history of Housman criticism is almost wholly a history of finding the mystery of the man in his poetry as if it were a key to the private world of the creator of the Shropshire lad. The theme of disillusionment found in many of the lyrics ("The troubles of our proud and angry dust / Are from eternity, and shall not fail") is then attributed to Housman's sexual health, his failure in Greats at Oxford, the so-called trauma of his mother's death when Housman was very young, his affection for an undergraduate friend named Moses Jackson, and so on. Such preoccupation with Housman's private life is not the reason for his continuing appeal. (pp. 615-16)

The circumstances of this life are curious: an academic whose range was narrow, whose view of the world was provincial and hidden. He is a puzzle, and over the years a great many people worried about that puzzle and looked to his poetry for a key. I think they look in vain. That common reader who now reads Housman looks at the poetry because this same reader, like many of us, leads a provincial and limited life, stays for the most part in one place, resists radical change, and seeks comfort in the memory of a time and a place—and finds then in Housman's lyrics a fleeting memory of that past steadfastness and belongingness. And perhaps because Housman understood the everydayness of routine that sometimes drowns the spirit. . . . (pp. 616-17)

Housman always followed traditional forms. He published his poems, however, when poetry was moving away from the cadences and structures of these traditional forms, and simultaneously shifting away from a wider and more general audience. Moreover poetry was growing more specialized and becoming the province of academic critics as well as the modern poet's own preoccupation with private experience and experimentation. And if the audience for poetry was shrinking, so too the general reader, now a specialist in his own vocation, was turning from literature to the wider marketplace for his reading: self-help psychology, tracts for self-improvement, and the self-generating powers of positive thinking. In poetry, as in the marketplace, solipsism won the day.

Nevertheless Housman's poetry stood as a holding action against the emerging modernism. And for no other reason than that his poetry echoed in its language and structures the perennial themes of lyric poetry—themes wholly different from the more self-conscious themes of modern art. Rather than indulging in private and personal emotion in his poems, Housman establishes and maintains the distance necessary for the reader to respond to the small drama of the lyric. His control of the structure of a poem is such that we can immediately say: "That is a Housman poem." But rarely do we say: "That is Housman speaking." And for those public occasions (for example, in Isak Dinesen's *Out of Africa,* the Baroness Blixen turns to Housman's **"To an Athlete Dying Young"** for a funeral elegy) and for private reflection the lines return because they are often memorable. (pp. 617-18)

Housman died in 1936, and fifty years have passed since his death. Of this kind of permanence he once observed: "If a man, fifty or 100 years after his death, is still remembered and accounted a great man, there is a presumption in his favor which no living man can claim." I make no claims for Housman himself as a great man, but his poetry is still remembered and endures the passage of time, as many other poets who followed him do not—those others who moved into narrower bounds and limited their audience to those more knowledgeable and more self-consciously attuned to the specialties of art.

Is it that the common reader has found himself left out? I keep thinking this reader found in Housman's poetry the voice and the language he remembered when he thought of poetry. I wonder if Housman may have sensed both this loss and this need, for in the epigraph of **Last Poems** he wrote a simple farewell:

> We'll to the woods no more
> The laurels all are cut,
> The bowers are bare . . .
> That once the Muses wore . . .

But the holding action was a stay against the coming changes of art, and his poetry stayed, continues to stay. It is a presumption in his favor, one that few of his contemporaries have earned. (pp. 618-19)

John W. Stevenson, "Revaluation: The Dura-

bility of Housman's Poetry," in The Sewanee Review, *Vol. XCIV, No. 4, Fall, 1986, pp. 613-19.*

FURTHER READING

Adelman, Seymour. "He Didn't Like Us, but We Liked Him: A Book Collector's A. E. Housman." *The New York Times Book Review* (14 September 1986): 3.
> Introduction to the exhibition catalog of the author's private collection of Housman's letters, first editions, and manuscripts displayed at the Pierport Morgan Library, New York City, in 1986.

Auden, W. H. "Jehovah Housman and Satan Housman." *New Verse,* No. 28 (January 1938): 16-17.
> Brief review of Laurence Housman's biography, *A. E. Housman.* Examines the influence of the contradictory elements of Housman's character on his verse.

Blackmur, R. P. "The Composition in Nine Poets: 1937." In his *The Expense of Greatness,* pp. 199-223. Glouchester, Mass.: Peter Smith, 1958.
> Discusses Housman's limitations in regards to imagery and complexity of theme.

Brooks, Cleanth. "The Whole of Housman." *The Kenyon Review* III, No. 1 (Winter 1941): 105-09.
> Discusses the elements of despair which possess Housman's young soldiers, shepherds, and athletes.

Gottcent, John H. "Housman and the Handling of Allusion." *Four Decades of Poetry* 1, No. 4 (July 1977): 264-70.
> Examines the numerous ways Housman uses allusion to invoke a certain mood or atmosphere in his poetry.

Gwynn, Stephen. "The Poetry of A. E. Housman." *The Dalhousie Review* III, No. 4 (January 1924): 431-37.
> Discusses the various themes that permeate Housman's poetry: suicide, tragic love, revolt, and the idealized soldier.

Haber, Tom Burns. "The Spirit of the Perverse in A. E. Housman." *The South Atlantic Quarterly* XL, No. 4 (October 1941): 368-78.
> Discusses the development and purpose of Housman's perversity, including his concentration on premature death.

———. "A. E. Housman's Downward Eye." *The Journal of English and Germanic Philology* LIII, No. 3 (July 1954): 306-18.
> Relates the events of Housman's youth and early manhood to the emotional elements found in his verse.

Mandel, Jerome. "Housman's Insane Narrators." *Victorian Poetry* 26, No. 4 (Winter 1988): 403-12.
> Demonstrates that Housman's narrators are often unreliable, irrational, and unable to distinguish between illusion and reality.

Plomer, William. "The Land of Lost Content." *The Listener* LXI, No. 1565 (26 March 1959): 545-46.

Examines the ambiguities contained in Housman's poetry by interpreting various events of Housman's life.

Ransom, John Crane. "Hancy and Gall." *The Southern Review* VI (Summer 1940): 2-48.
Compares the language, irony, and celebration of mortality found in the poetry of Housman and Thomas Hardy.

Reynolds, Judith. "Housman's Humor." *Western Humanities Review* XXII, No. 2 (Spring 1968): 161-64.
Explores the nature of Housman's humor through the examination of his nonsense verse and personal letters.

Stevenson, John W. "The Pastoral Setting in the Poetry of A. E. Housman." *The South Atlantic Quarterly* LV (1956): 487-500.
Examines the relationship between Housman's classical scholarship and his poetry.

————. "The Martyr as Innocent: Housman's Lonely Lad." *The South Atlantic Quarterly* LVII (1958): 68-85.
Discusses Housman's use of the rustic persona as a symbol of the progress of man from youth to maturity.

Sweeney, Francis. "The Ethics of A. E. Housman." *Thought: Fordham University Quarterly* XX, No. 76 (March 1945): 117-25.

Examines the influence of Housman's religious ideology, specifically "his unbelief in God's existence," on his verse.

"The Classical Side of Housman." *The Times Literary Supplement,* No. 3701 (9 February 1973): 137-38.
Relates Housman's classical scholarship to the highly intellectual elements of his poetry.

Walcutt, Charles Child. "Housman and the Empire: An Analysis of '1887'." *College English* 5, No. 5 (February 1944): 255-58.
Analyzes the themes, imagery, and irony found in Housman's "1887."

Whitridge, Arnold. "Vigny and Housman: A Study in Pessimism." *The American Scholar* 10, No. 2 (Spring 1941): 156-69.

Examines the pessimism that pervades the poetry of Housman and Alfred de Vigny and attempts to explain how such pessimism can ultimately lead to a deeper sense of optimism.

Wilcox, Louise Collier. "Some Recent Poetry." *The North American Review* 182 (1906): 757-58.
Early review of *A Shropshire Lad* upon its first publication in the United States.

Claude McKay

1889-1948

(Born Festus Claudius McKay; also wrote under the pseudonym Eli Edwards) Jamaican-born American poet, novelist, short story writer, journalist, essayist, and autobiographer.

McKay is a seminal poet of the Harlem Renaissance, a prominent literary movement of the 1920s during which African-Americans garnered unprecedented artistic and intellectual recognition. His work ranged from dialect verse celebrating peasant life in Jamaica to militant poems challenging white supremacy in the United States. More than any other black writer of his time, McKay managed to convert anger and social protest into poems of lasting value. The publication of his most popular poem "If We Must Die" in 1919, though not overtly racial, was a shout of defiance and a proclamation of the unbreakable spirit and courage of the oppressed black individual, and is considered to have provided a major impetus behind the Harlem Renaissance and the civil rights movement immediately following World War I. In all his works, McKay searched among the common folk for a distinctive black identity, and for a means of preserving the African spirit and creativity in an alienating world.

McKay was born in the hills of Jamaica to peasant farmers whose sense of racial pride greatly affected him in his youth. His father was instrumental in reinforcing this pride through folktales, as well as through stories of McKay's African grandfather's enslavement. From these accounts of his grandfather's experiences with white men, McKay acquired an early distrust for whites. Under the tutelage of his brother, a schoolteacher and avowed agnostic, McKay was imbued with his elder sibling's freethinking philosophies. In 1907 McKay left his rural home to apprentice as a woodworker in Brown's Town, where he met Walter Jekyll, an English linguist and specialist in Jamaican folklore. In addition to furthering McKay's interest in English poetry, Jekyll introduced McKay to the British masters—including John Milton, Alexander Pope, and Percy Bysshe Shelley—and also encouraged McKay to write verse in his native dialect. In 1909 McKay moved to Kingston, Jamaica's capital city, where he later served as a constable. His native town of Sunny Ville had been predominantly populated by blacks, but in substantially white Kingston the caste society, which placed blacks below mulattoes and whites, revealed to McKay alienating and degrading aspects of city life. McKay's first exposure to overt racism contributed toward his allegiance to the working class and to peasant life, wherein the black individual was not directly discriminated against by controlling races.

With Jekyll's assistance McKay published his first volumes of poetry, *Songs of Jamaica* and *Constab Ballads,* in 1912, both of which contain lyrical verse written in Jamaican vernacular. In the same year his first poems were pub-

lished, McKay traveled to the United States to study agriculture. In 1914, after attending Tuskegee Institute in Alabama and Kansas State College, McKay decided to abandon his studies and move to New York City. By 1917, McKay established literary and political ties with the left-wing society of Greenwich Village through his associations with Frank Harris, editor of *Pearson's Magazine* in which his militant poem "To the White Fiends" appeared, and Max Eastman, editor of the Communist journal *The Liberator.* Upon the initial publication of "If We Must Die" in *The Liberator,* McKay commenced two years of travel and work abroad. In London he worked on the socialist periodical *Workers' Dreadnought,* and in 1920 he published his third collection, *Spring in New Hampshire, and Other Poems.* McKay returned to the United States in 1921 and involved himself in various social causes, and the following year his most highly acclaimed poetry volume, *Harlem Shadows,* appeared. Shortly after the publication of this collection, McKay left America for twelve years, traveling first to Moscow to attend the Fourth Congress of the Communist Party.

Extolled as a great American poet among the Russian populace, McKay soon grew disenchanted with the Communist Party when it became apparent he would have to subjugate his art to political propaganda. In 1923 McKay moved to Paris, and later journeyed to Germany, North Africa, Spain, and to the south of France. During the years 1923 to 1934, when he returned to the United States, McKay concentrated his efforts on writing fiction, completing three novels as well as a collection of short stories. All but the novel *Home to Harlem,* which became the first best seller by a black writer, were almost wholly neglected by the reading public as the Depression diminished interest in Harlem Renaissance literature. Once back in Harlem, he published his autobiography in an attempt to bolster his financial and literary status. Following the publication of this work, McKay developed an interest in Roman Catholicism and became active in Harlem's Friendship House, a Catholic community center. Through his religious conversion and work at the Friendship House, he wrote *Harlem: Negro Metropolis,* an historical essay collection that failed to spark much interest. By the mid-1940s his health had deteriorated and, after enduring several illnesses, McKay died of heart failure in Chicago.

McKay's first collection of verse heralded him as an authentic and unique voice in poetry. Poems in *Songs of Jamaica* depict a universal and optimistic portrait of provincial life, though some pieces address such topics as racial prejudice and poverty. McKay employed Jamaican dialect in a similar fashion as had Scottish Romantic poet Robert Burns utilized common language to create lyrical verse celebrating nature and the peasant's bond to the soil. Unlike other black poets who employed vernacular with pitying or humorous intent, McKay's use of dialect exalts the lives of his characters in a realistic manner, as in "Quashie to Buccra" in which the peasant speaker conveys the beauty of his harvest goods. Commenting on *Songs of Jamaica,* James Weldon Johnson noted that "[the dialect poems] are free from both the minstrel and plantation traditions, free from exaggerated sweetness and wholesomeness; they are veritable impressions of Negro life in Jamaica."

The setting in *Constab Ballads* shifted from the countryside to the city, and poems in this book express a heightened sense of social protest. Drawing upon his experiences as a constable, McKay's central thematic concern is to delineate a contrast between provincial and urban life. Jean Wagner maintained that "[the city] acquires in the racial context a symbolic importance. . . . The city, presented as the antithesis of the land, is consequently the enemy of the black man also." In the city McKay observed that the black peasant was subject to oppression from whites, mulattoes, and urbanized blacks, who, in positions of authority, exploited their power. In the autobiographical lyric "The Heart of a Constab," McKay deplores the fact that his circumstances in the city alienate him from the land and his peasant people. The militant tone of *Constab Ballads* is perhaps best exemplified in "The Apple Woman's Complaint," in which a woman bitterly decries the injustice of being told she can't sell her apples in the street, leaving theft her only other option for survival. In reference to this work, Wagner concluded that "[the poem] heralded what will be McKay's stance in his American poems. Of all the Jamaican poems, 'The Apple Woman's Complaint' is the most bitter, violent, and militant."

McKay reached his zenith as a poet with the publication of *Harlem Shadows,* a collection that "clearly pointed to the incipient Renaissance," according to George E. Kent. Comprised of new poems in addition to works previously published in periodicals and in the volume *Spring in New Hampshire, and Other Poems,* works in *Harlem Shadows* are characteristically constructed in conventional forms, most notably the sonnet. Evident in these poems is the conflict McKay faced as a black poet writing within a tradition espoused by whites, a dilemma which manifested itself in a sense of double consciousness that W. E. B. DuBois had outlined in his *The Souls of Black Folk* in 1903. McKay expressed this conflict in his own words when he wrote: "A Negro writer feeling the urge to write faithfully about the people he knows from real experiences and impartial observation is caught in a dilemma . . . between this group and his own artistic conscientiousness." While maintaining a sense of universality that denied judgement of merit based on race, McKay sought a vital identity for the black individual, and his poems overtly reflect his origins. In "The Tropics of New York," for example, the speaker of the poem—a West Indian living in New York City—conveys the alienation experienced by many people cut off from their homeland, yet, by evoking lush, tropical imagery, he highlights the unique sorrow of an estranged West Indian.

In addition to poems expressing a romantic longing for his island homeland, *Harlem Shadows* offers McKay's most militant and race-conscious verse. McKay included his best known work "If We Must Die" in this volume, a sonnet he had excluded from *Spring in New Hampshire* to avoid reference to "color." This piece was originally composed in response to the racial violence that occurred throughout America during the summer of 1919. Although the poem expresses universal feelings of rebellion and anger of the oppressed fighting against a dominant enemy, many people interpreted it as a warlike cry by black radicals. Stephen H. Bronz maintains that "['If We Must Die'] was written to apply to an extreme situation; such desperate fighting need be resorted to only when 'the mad and hungry dogs' are at one's very heels, as McKay felt was the case in 1919." As an example of the work's appeal across ethnic and racial lines, British Prime Minister Winston Churchill recited the poem in an emotional speech before the House of Commons in response to Nazi Germany's threat of invasion during World War II. McKay's militancy has been variously interpreted, notwithstanding, Wagner contends that a significant theme in McKay's work is hatred and that "among all black poets, [McKay] is *par excellence* the poet of hate." Hatred, however, is employed not in the service of destructive aims, but rather as a vehicle of change, as in the sonnet "The White City," which calls upon hatred to vitalize oppressed spirits.

Also evident in *Harlem Shadows* is McKay's response to the vogue of African primitivism popularized in the early twentieth century. In the ironic poem "The Harlem Dancer," McKay addresses the myth of the Noble Savage wherein devotees of African exoticism often ignored racial discrimination and the difficulties of cultural dualism among African-Americans. Originally published in 1917 in *The Seven Arts,* "The Harlem Dancer" is perhaps the earliest poetic work to present Harlem's nightlife as its subject matter. Analyzed by several critics as an allegory of the prostitution of African-American art, the poem characterizes an exotic dancer's proud indifference to her audience, highlighting the superficial appreciation that the predominantly white audience holds for the woman's beauty.

At the time of his death, McKay was in the process of collecting old verse and writing new poems to be published in a fifth volume. This collection, *Selected Poems,* published posthumously in 1953, is notable for the religious verse written in his later years. John Hillyer Condit posited that McKay strove throughout his life and with his literary works for unity, despite his fierce sense of individualism. Remarking on McKay's conversion to Roman Catholicism after many years of agnosticism, Condit states that "in the Church, McKay found that sense of wholeness very important to him, and without the surrender of his individuality." Critics cite such sonnets as "The Pagan Isms" and "Truth," in which McKay turns to God for a means of ascertaining a higher knowledge and a final synthesis to the black individual's cultural dualism, as evidence that the poet ultimately achieved unity within himself by turning to God. While these poems lack the rebellious tone of his earlier work, they address issues of racism and social change nonetheless.

McKay's literary accomplishments in poetry, prose, and nonfiction are acclaimed as pioneering efforts by a black artist who influenced writers subsequent to the Harlem Renaissance. His work not only inspired such Francophone poets as Aimé Césaire and Léopold Sédar Senghor, whose verse espoused tenets of *négritude,* a movement begun in the 1930s that also sought to reclaim African cultural heritage, but also writers of the Black Arts Movement, which flourished during the 1960s through such acclaimed poets as Amiri Baraka (LeRoi Jones) and Haki R. Madhubuti (Don L. Lee). McKay's poetic forms were thought to be too conventional and limiting for the density of his themes; however, in recent years he has been praised for the intensity and ardor of his poetry and for his ability to convert social protest into art.

(For further discussion of McKay's life and career, see *Twentieth-Century Literary Criticism,* Vol. 7; *Contemporary Authors,* Vols. 104, 124; and *Dictionary of Literary Biography,* Vols. 4, 45, 51. See also the "Harlem Renaissance" entry in *Twentieth-Century Literary Criticism,* Vol. 26.)

PRINCIPAL WORKS

POETRY

Constab Ballads   1912
Songs of Jamaica   1912
Spring in New Hampshire, and Other Poems   1920
Harlem Shadows: The Poems of Claude McKay   1922
Selected Poems   1953
The Dialect Poetry of Claude McKay   1972

The Passion of Claude McKay: Selected Poetry and Prose, 1912-1948   1973

OTHER MAJOR WORKS

Home to Harlem   (novel)   1928
Banjo: A Story Without a Plot   (novel)   1929
Gingertown   (short stories)   1932
Banana Bottom   (novel)   1933
A Long Way from Home   (autobiography)   1937
Harlem: Negro Metropolis   (nonfiction)   1940
Trial by Lynching: Stories about Negro Life in North America   (short stories)   1977
My Green Hills of Jamaica, and Five Jamaican Short Stories   (essays and short stories)   1979
The Negroes in America   (nonfiction)   1979

Louise Townsend Nicholl   (essay date 1922)

[An American poet, editor, and critic, Nicholl is regarded as a religious poet whose verse attains an ethereal quality. In the following excerpt, Nicholl offers an appreciative review of McKay's poetry collection Harlem Shadows.*]*

There is a terrible simplicity, an unconscious pride and lifting of the head, about the poems of this negro poet— the first poems of a negro, as Max Eastman says in his introduction, which are interesting not simply because [Claude McKay] is a negro but because he is also a poet. Something of the nobility which honesty and courage make, something sad and stark and utter, is about these poems which deal with his hatred of the white race which has oppressed his own, with his love of beauty, with the lusts of his flesh, with the gnawing grief for his mother who died ten years ago. Of her he writes

> Reg wished me to go with him to the field,
> I paused because I did not want to go;
> But in her quiet way she made me yield
> Reluctantly, for she was breathing low.
> Her hand she lifted slowly from her lap
> And, smiling sadly in the old sweet way,
> She pointed to the nail where hung my cap.
> Her eyes said: I shall last another day.

Most obvious in the book are the conflicts which pull him many ways, more conflicts than even the usual poet has, and which may make of him a better poet than the usual. There is not only the fear which all artists have of losing human joys and living through their art, the strange and inconsistent yearning to be ordinary and as others are; but there is also the racial struggle between a burning hatred of the white race, and a keen, young, zestful attraction by it, by the life, the achievements, the knowledge, it has to offer. Life and art would be unbearable for this young negro poet, where it not for the cooling loveliness of his own lyricism, and the relaxation of an occasional humorous, though still sad, detachment which makes him able to write verses like **"Alfonso," "Dressing to Wait at Table,"** and **"On the Road,"** concerned with colored waiters in a swaying, hot, and crowded dining car. Even **"The**

Lynching" becomes more bearable because he is able to face it, describe it exactly as it is. Poets are compensated for their over-burden of feeling by their power to get relief. When a race, like a person, gets too conscious, it must speak. This man, "darkly-rebel," avid for freedom and liberation of every kind, possessed with the desire to help his people, has done for them here what will in the long run help them most—freed them out of dumbness; out of dark life into its recreation, art, which is a lighter, truer, more relieving thing.

He has not yet found his medium, I think. He says himself:

AUTHOR'S COMMENTARY

When the work of a Negro writer wins recognition it creates two widely separate bodies of opinion, one easily recognizable by the average reader as general and the other limited to Negroes and therefore racial. . . .

This peculiar racial opinion constitutes a kind of censorship of what is printed about the Negro. No doubt it had its origin in the laudable efforts of intelligent Negro groups to protect their race from the slander of its detractors after Emancipation, and grew until it crystallized into racial consciousness. The pity is that these leaders of racial opinion should also be in the position of sole arbiters of intellectual and artistic things within the Negro world. For although they may be excellent persons worthy of all respect and eminently right in their purpose, they often do not distinguish between the task of propaganda and the work of art. . . .

My own experience has been amazing. Before I published *Home to Harlem* I was known to the Negro public as the writer of the hortatory poem **"If We Must Die."** This poem was written during the time of the Chicago race riots. . . .

The poem was an outgrowth of the intense emotional experience I was living through (no doubt with thousands of other Negroes) in those days. It appeared in the radical magazine the *Liberator,* and was widely reprinted in the Negro press. . . .

"If We Must Die" immediately won popularity among Aframericans, but the tone of the Negro critics was apologetic. To them a poem that voiced the deep-rooted instinct of self-preservation seemed merely a daring piece of impertinence. . . .

They seem afraid of the revelation of bitterness in Negro life. But it may as well be owned, and frankly by those who know the inside and heart of Negro life, that the Negro, and especially the Aframerican, has bitterness in him in spite of his joyous exterior. And the more educated he is in these times the more he is likely to have. . . .

It matters not so much that one has had an experience of bitterness, but rather how one has developed out of it. To ask the Negro to render up his bitterness is asking him to part with his soul. For out of his bitterness he has bloomed and created his spirituals and blues and conserved his racial attributes—his humor and ripe laughter and particular rhythm of life.

(essay date 1932)

O word I love to sing! thou art too tender
For all the passions agitating me;
For all my bitterness thou art too tender,
I cannot pour my red soul into thee.

O haunting melody! thou art too slender,
Too fragile like a globe of crystal glass;
For all my stormy thoughts thou art too slender,
The burden from my bosom will not pass.

There is the feeling that, in spite of the easiness and inevitability of these regular forms, he will some day break away from them, get darkly rebel about prescriptions for lines as about other things, and have his fling at something all his own: although it is also quite certain that he will come back in the end to regularity, when he has made himself independent of it and can use it from conviction and choice, not from necessity.

There is a faint, piquant tinge and flavor of what we love as quaint and different, and have come to expect, in colored people's talk; sometimes this is conscious, in descriptive, reminiscent poems, and very rarely it is unconscious, when a strange, spontaneous little line like "But soon again the risky ways I tread" slips out. Who else would say "the risky ways"?

But far more important than any of the traces which mark him colored, any of the conflicts which mark him individual, are the simple clearness, the freshness, the new exactness, the occasional startling loveliness, which mark him poet. (pp. 16-18)

There is no one perfect poem in the book, but still one thinks already eagerly about his second book. He has one poem **"To a Poet,"** beginning, "There is a lovely noise about your name." Its last stanza brings us very close to the man who is, even more essentially than a colored man or a rebel, a poet:

But the rare lonely spirits, even mine,
Who love the immortal music of all days,
Will see the glory of your trailing line,
The bedded beauty of your haunting lays.

(p. 18)

Louise Townsend Nicholl, "A Negro Poet," in The Measure, *No. 17, July, 1922, pp. 16-18.*

M. B. Tolson   (essay date 1954)

[*Tolson was an American poet, journalist, and dramatist who is best known for his complex, challenging poetry. In his most famous collection of verse,* Harlem Gallery *(1965), Tolson employed both standard and black English to illuminate the lives of African-Americans and to examine the role of the black artist in mainstream society. In the following excerpt taken from a review of* Selected Poems, *Tolson lauds the universality of McKay's verse.*]

During the last world war, Sir Winston Churchill snatched Claude McKay's poem, **"If We Must Die,"** from the closet of the Harlem Renaissance, and paraded in it before the House of Commons, as if it were the talismanic uniform of His Majesty's field marshal.

The double signature of the role would not have gone undeciphered by the full-blooded African poet who could avouch, in spite of apartheid: "I have never regarded myself as a 'Negro' poet. I have always felt that my gift of song was something bigger than the narrow limits of any people and its problems." (p. 287)

Professor Dewey, in his preface to [*Selected Poems*], singles out a line from the lyric, **"North and South"**: "A wonder to life's common places clings." The quotation revitalizes Yeats' observation that poets of the new idiom were "full of the unsatisfied hunger for the commonplace," since no manna fell, supposedly, from either the Temple or the Capitol. In this tradition, then, and out of a heterogeneity of experiences with an underlying unity, Claude McKay, as wheelwright, constable, agriculturist, porter, longshoreman, waiter, vagabond, rebel, and penitent, created his best poems.

Contrived seemingly as the plot of the Hardyesque is the triangle of a poet mythicized by Harlem, feted by Moscow, and haloed by Rome. His sensibility quick with image and idea, McKay explores the plurality of his world, inward and outward. He can etch, with a Dantean simplicity terrifying in detail, a picture of himself as surgeon in the grotto of the self.

> I plucked my soul out of its secret place,
> And held it to the mirror of my eye,
> To see it like a star against the sky,
> A twitching body quivering in space. . . .

McKay likes to explore the axis of day and night when he holds the looking glass to his ego, his race, his moment, his milieu; and sometimes what he sees shocks him, as in the case of his beloved Africa, bereft of her ancient honor and arrogance and glory, and he cries: "Thou art the harlot, now thy time is done, / Of all the mighty nations of the sun."

Although his odyssey took him into Temple and Capitol, his poems are without ideological vestiges. McKay's verse has interludes during which his "memory bears engraved the high-walled Kremlin" or his soul tingles in Tetuan from "Filigree marvels from Koranic lines." Often he cannot stay till dawn in a caravansary; some bedeviling urge drives him toward the rain of fluid rock. He is aware that his passions are "saturated with brine," and, leaving the crystal glass of lyricism, he can only cry, "O tender word! O melody so slender!"

McKay, like his contemporaries of the Negro Renaissance, was unaffected by the New Poetry and Criticism. The logic of facts proves Mr. [Allen] Tate's observation that this literary ghetto-ism "too often limited the Negro poet to a provincial mediocrity," from which he is just now escaping. Thus, in that era of ethnic mutation, McKay's radicalism was in content—not in form: the grammar of *The Souls of Black Folk* [by W. E. B. DuBois] demanded the seven league boots of the "huge Moor."

The Negro poet of the 20's and 30's broke the mold of the Dialect School and the Booker T. Washington Compromise. For the first time he stood upon a peak in Darien, but he was not silent. Like the Greeks of Professor Gilbert Murray, he had stumbled upon "the invention of habit breaking." It is aphoristic that he gave the "huge Moor" and Desdemona a shotgun wedding, minus the ceremony "Traditional, with all its symbols / Ancient as the metaphors in dreams" for the poet-rebel, whether in content or form, travels *his* hypotenuse and not the right angle, toward *his* reality.

In his most famous poem, Claude McKay's [**"If We Must Die"**] reaches beyond this time and that place.

> If we must die, let us not die like hogs
> Hunted and penned in an inglorious spot,
> While round us bark the mad and hungry dogs,
> Making their mock at our accursed lot.
> If we must die, O let us nobly die,
> So that our precious blood may not be shed
> In vain; then even the monsters we defy
> Shall be constrained to honor us though dead!
> O kinsmen! we must meet the common foe!
> Though far outnumbered let us show us brave,
> And for their thousand blows deal one death-
>   blow!
> What though before us lies the open grave?
> Like men we'll face the murderous, cowardly
>   pack,
> Pressed to the wall, dying, but fighting back!

The mood of McKay's "must" is grammatical, psychological, and philosophical. The simile, "like hogs," packs both rhetorical and dialectical implication, as foreshadowed in the words "let us not die." The theme, ignobleness versus nobleness in man's tragedy, escapes, in this poem, from the abstract and the didactic into the reality of the imagination. McKay insures the catholicity of his theme in two ways: he does not reveal the ethnic identity of his protagonist, nor does he hog-tie the free will of the attacked by the imposition of an affirmative decision. This, then, is the poem, above all others in the *Selected Poems,* which, in the holocaustal year 1919, signalized Claude McKay as the symbol of the New Negro and the Harlem Renaissance. The poem is a pillar of fire by night in many lands. (pp. 287-90)

> *M. B. Tolson, "Claude McKay's Art," in* Poetry, *Vol. LXXXIII, No. 4, January, 1954, pp. 287-90.*

Jean Wagner   (essay date 1962)

[*Wagner was a French author and critic who specialized in American slang and dialects. His* Les Poètes Nègres des Etats-Unis *(1962), which was translated into English in 1973, is regarded as one of the most authoritative and innovative sources available for the study of African-American poets. In the following excerpt taken from this work, Wagner presents an extensive overview of McKay's poetry to analyze stylistic and thematic devices.*]

Many Negro Renaissance intellectuals never looked on Claude McKay as being one of themselves, in the first place because he belonged to an older generation and was already thirty at the end of World War I. They also had a slight tendency to regard as an interloper this Jamaican immigrant who arrived in Harlem one fine day after having earned his living in countless ways. Moreover, he preferred the company of the far left to the elegant surroundings of the drawing room. While the Renaissance was in full swing in America, Claude McKay was traveling in Europe and North Africa, and thus was rather cut off from Harlem, which in the meantime had become the center of the black world. Finally, his selfwilled character with its violence and intransigence, and his passionate denunciations of his friends as well as of his enemies in the two races, often gained for him the reputation of being an unsociable person and a rebel.

With all his faults, however—and sometimes because of the virtues inherent in these very faults, but above all because of his outstanding gifts as a poet—he remains beyond a doubt the immediate forerunner and one of the leading forces of the Renaissance, the man without whom it could never have achieved what it did. His contribution served as a corrective and lent added stature. To the frivolities of the chaotic existence that was all the rage, and to the Harlem primitivism of which he soon had had enough, McKay opposed the solid qualities of his Jamaican heritage, the sureness and perspicacity of his judgment, and his desire for inner progress and ennoblement. Showing no self-indulgence, he instinctively sought the discipline of the sonnet. Exigent also vis-à-vis his ethnic brothers, he invited them to abandon the various forms of dead-end particularism in which they were wasting their racial pride, and he urged them to set out along with him on the high road that alone leads to the discovery of authentic values. (pp. 197-98)

The two collections [of poetry] published in Jamaica in 1912 constitute a diptych of McKay's experience in his native island. The first, *Songs of Jamaica,* is a sort of highly colored epitome of the years of childhood and young manhood spent in the mountains, where he listened to Nature's great voice and shared the life of the black peasantry. Often in direct opposition to these first poems are those of *Constab Ballads,* which reveal the disillusionment and pessimism the poet felt when plunged into the life of the capital. These first two volumes are already marked by a sharpness of vision, an inborn realism, and a freshness which provide a pleasing contrast with the conventionality which, at this same time, prevails among the black poets of the United States.

Not the least original aspect of these seventy-eight poems is the rough but picturesque Jamaican dialect in which most of them are written, and of which they constitute the earliest poetic use. Thus we are far removed from the dialect of the [Paul Laurence] Dunbar school, which was taken over from the whites who had concocted it in order to maintain the stereotype of black inferiority and to limit blacks more surely to the role of buffoons under orders to entertain the master race. An instrument of oppression when handled by white writers, the dialect became an avowal of subservience in its use by Dunbar, most of whose readers were whites. . . . [In the case of McKay's dialect] everything is entirely and authentically Negro. It all comes directly from the people and is rooted in the soil, alike the phonology, often flavored with a delightful exoticism, and the rather summary morphology; the typically fantastic placing of the tonic accent and the somewhat ru-

dimentary syntax, seldom in accord with the Queen's English; and, finally, the often unexpectedly roughhewn words and images, which originate in the hard-working folk's immediate contact with a soil reluctant to part with its riches. (pp. 204-05)

Every bit as much as their language, it is the poetic quality of these works that links them genuinely to the people for whom they were written. It was no mere rhetorical flourish when McKay entitled his first collection *Songs of Jamaica.* For six poems, he adds in an appendix melodies which he composed. The songs and ballads he did not set to music are so rhythmical that a musical accompaniment could easily be provided. (p. 205)

How close the bond of sympathy was between McKay and the people is manifested also by the realism with which he characterizes the black Jamaican peasant. . . . McKay's portraits at once transcend the limits which . . . inevitably weighed on American Negro dialect and forced it to sound only the registers of humor and pathos. In any case, there is no humor to be found here, nor will it play any part in the later work. . . . Unlike the character portraits usually associated with American Negro dialect, these portraits are the actual incarnation of a whole people's racial pride.

All in all, McKay's characterization of the Jamaican peasant is substantially that of the peasant anywhere in the world: deeply attached to his plot of land, over which he labors with an atavistic skill; and unsparing of himself, yet seemingly condemned to unalleviated poverty, since there is always someone to snatch the fruits of his labor. He owes his pride to the sense of work well done, and has no feeling of inferiority vis-à-vis the whites whom, when the occasion arises, he will address in the bluntest terms. (p. 206)

[McKay's critique of society becomes urgent in poems] where the responsibilities of the whites are categorically stated. They have organized the economic life of the island so as to profit from the resources that nature had destined for the blacks. That is the force of the following lines, in which the poet apostrophizes his native island:

> You hab all t'ings fe mek life bles',
> But buccra 'poil de whole
> Wid gove'mint an' all de res'
> Fe worry naygur soul.

"Two-an'-Six," a poem that runs to 136 lines, speaks out against the catastrophic effect of such an economy on the life of the peasants, who are plunged into bitter poverty by a drop in sugar prices. One Saturday morning at cockcrow, while the stars are still in the sky, everybody is already astir to make ready the products that Cous' Sun is going to take to the fair in the neighboring town—in a borrowed cart, McKay notes—and while on his way

> . . . he's thinkin' in him min'
> Of de dear ones lef' behin'
> Of de loved though ailin' wife,
> Darlin' treasure of his life,
> An' de picknies, six in all,
> Whose 'nuff burdens 'pon him fall:
> Seben lovin' ones in need,

Seben hungry mouths fe feed;
On deir wants he thinks alone,
Neber dreamin' of his own,
But gwin' on wid joyful face
Till him re'ch de market-place.
Sugar bears no price te-day,
Though it is de mont' o' May.

(pp. 207-08)

Here, with penetrating realism, McKay disdains to make a racial issue of his critique. Not once is the white man named. The poet lets the facts speak for themselves and, though it is clear that he is attacking white avariciousness, the reproach is situated nevertheless in the economic and social domain. (p. 209)

While **"Two-an'-Six"** says nothing of the whites, **"Hard Times,"** on the contrary, strikingly portrays the moneyed idleness of the white men and the harsh life led by the black peasant, with not the least prospect of shaking off his poverty. (p. 210)

All these poems, nevertheless, end on a note of faith in the future. In **"Two-an'-Six,"** Sun's discouragement is dispelled by the loving, consoling words uttered by his wife:

An' de shadow lef' him face,
An' him felt an inward peace
As he blessed his better part
For her sweet an' gentle heart.

In **"Hard Times,"** it is faith in Providence that resounds in the last stanza:

I won't gib up, I won't say die,
    For all de time is hard;

Aldough de wul' soon en', I'll try
My wutless best as time goes by,
    An' trust on in me Gahd.

All in all, health, vigor, and self-assurance make up the impression left by this portrait of the black Jamaican peasant, whose age-old practical virtues and wisdom have not been sapped by his material poverty. Thus the optimism that McKay discovers in this rural milieu is derived, in the first place, from extant moral values. But there are racial reasons also. For it is highly significant that all these country folks are blacks, excluding the mulattoes whom McKay implicitly rejects as all too eager to see in their white ancestry a justification for disdaining the blacks. Finally, the real values that constitute the superiority of the black peasant reside in his closeness to the soil of Jamaica. One can scarcely overstress the importance of this element in McKay's trinitarian symbolism, which associates the good with the black race and the soil. (pp. 210-11)

[McKay's] roots in the soil of his native island are amazingly deep and lasting. These roots make him one with the soil. Through them he draws in his nourishment; the island's enchanting scenes call forth his earliest verses, and no one will ever rival him in praise for the mildness of its climate, the vividness of its colors, the luxuriance of its vegetation, or the coolness of its streams. (p. 211)

But uniting the black man and the earth is a more intimate, subtle relationship, a secret harmony as it were, and simply to name the familiar scenes is enough to arouse in the poet's sensibilities a physical resonance, to send a tremor through his frame:

Loved Clarendon hills,
Dear Clarendon hills,
Oh! I feel de chills,
Yes, I feel de chills
Coursin' t'rough me frame
When I call your name.

Thus the union of the poet and his land is consummated in a romantic ecstasy. This correspondence between Nature and the poet is indeed "the organic exaltation produced by physical agents" or the recollection of them, "the joy of all the senses in contact with the world" which Cazamian analyzed, many years ago, in the English Romantics. Like them, McKay felt constantly drawn to nature and sensed the need to become totally merged in it. The emotion it aroused in him transcended by far the exclusively aesthetic plane. For Nature is an ever renewed source of strength, and instinctively he returned to commune with it. (pp. 212-13)

The earth is the whole man. He had already proclaimed this before he had turned twenty, and he realized it all the more clearly after he had left it and experienced enormous disillusionment in contact with the city, whose inhabitants he looked on as rootless, in the most concrete sense of the word:

Fool! I hated my precious birthright,
Scorning what had made my father a man.

He attributed to his native soil, the nurturer, all the strength of his character and his poetic vigor. . . . (p. 214)

Between the black man and the earth there is a total identification. When, vexed by the city, he returns to his mountains, he will see in this return not only a reunion with the earth, but with his people also:

But I'll leave it, my people, an' come back to
    you,
    I'll flee from de grief an' turmoil;
I'll leave it, though flow'rs should line my path
    yet,
    An' come back to you an' de soil.

Thus the racial values he associates with the soil also help to tinge his feeling for nature, and in his mind he conceives nature and the city as mutually exclusive forces. (pp. 214-15)

Hatred of the city is one of the principal motifs in McKay's Jamaican poems, and the American poems will offer variations on the same theme. In Dunbar's work one could already note some aversion toward urban civilization, but this was only sporadic, and the motivation behind it was entirely different. Dunbar was sensitive, above all, to the ravages wrought by industrialization which, as it spread ever wider, made men's lives ugly and polluted the air they breathed. . . .

But with McKay the theme is not merely more amply treated; it acquires in the racial context a symbolic importance not found in Dunbar. The city, presented as the antithesis of the land, is consequently the enemy of the black man also. (p. 215)

[In McKay's *Constab Ballads,* the] city symbolizes an evil that is multiple. In part it finds expression in the traditional ways but also, and especially, it adopts other forms that are significant in the racial context.

We will not linger long over the former, which for the most part illustrate the corrupting power of the city, on which McKay superimposes his keen awareness of the corruption rampant among the police. (p. 217)

The police are also reputed to be a tool in the hands of the whites for oppressing the blacks. This is the lament of the apple woman in **"The Apple Woman's Complaint,"** when the police forbid her to sell her wares in the street. If she is not allowed to ply her modest trade honestly, she will have to live by stealing, and in either case she will be at odds with the police, who in any event live at her expense. From this poem we cite only those passages that present the attitude of the police as having originated in hatred of the blacks:

> Black nigger wukin' laka cow
> An' wipin' sweat-drops from his brow,
> Dough him is dyin' sake o' need,

McKay in his constable uniform, circa 1911.

P'lice an' dem headman boun' fe feed.

. . . .

> Deheadman fe de town police
> Mind neber know a little peace,
> 'Cep' when him an' him heartless ban'
> Hab sufferin' nigger in dem han'.

. . . .

> We hab fe barter out we soul
> To lib' t'rough dis ungodly wul';—
> O massa Jesus! don't you see
> How police is oppressin' we?

The vehemence of this protest against oppression, here placed in the mouth of the apple woman, and the boundless despair of the last stanza, are in violent contrast with the cold objectivity of the social critique voiced in the rural poems of *Songs of Jamaica.* It heralds what will be McKay's stance in his American poems. Of all the Jamaican poems, **"The Apple Woman's Complaint"** is the most bitter, violent, and militant. Thus it serves to make entirely plain the changes that city residence brought about in McKay. (pp. 217-18)

[McKay's] American poems give vent to his racial pride with a forcefulness he had never exhibited before. This outburst is so authentic, and so much in keeping with his own fiery, passionate temperament, that little influence need be attributed to the stimulus he could have found elsewhere in the paeans to race that were being sounded by his compatriot [Marcus] Garvey. Furthermore, as he faced the onslaught of white insolence, his pride grew in militancy without losing any of its nobility:

> Your door is shut against my tightened face,
> And I am sharp as steel with discontent;
> But I possess the courage and the grace
> To bear my anger *proudly* and unbent.
>   [**"The White House"**] . . .

As this pride is strengthened and tested by adversity, he raises racial consciousness to the aesthetic plane. One would almost be tempted to affirm that the poet is inaugurating a hedonism of color, when one beholds how with a supremely refined sensuality he savors the heady joy of his blackness, gaining awareness of it amidst a community that tortures him, but to which he feels superior in every fiber of his being. . . . (p. 223)

No one ever expressed with such a wealth of nuances the opposing eddies that swirl in a mind in search of equilibrium amid stupidly hostile surroundings. This attempt at introspective insight clearly demonstrates how racial pride can act as a redemptive force.

Yet it must meet a rude challenge when, gloriously garbed, the poet's sworn enemy, the White City, displays the whole spectrum of her seductive wiles in order to win him over and ruin him:

> For one brief moment rare like wine
> The gracious city swept across the line;
> Oblivious of the colour of my skin,
> Forgetting that I was an alien guest,
> She bent to me, my hostile heart to win,
> Caught me in passion to her pillowy breast;
> The great, proud city, seized with a strange love,

Bowed down for one flame hour my pride to
    prove.
                                          ["The City's Love"]
                                                    (p. 224)

To no lesser degree than the intoxication of being black,
Claude McKay learned in America how intoxicating it is
to hate. He vents his joy in **"The White City"**:

> I will not toy with it nor bend an inch.
> Deep in the secret chambers of my heart
> I muse my life-long hate, and without flinch
> I bear it nobly as I live my part.
> My being would be a skeleton, a shell,
> If this dark passion that fills my every mood,
> And makes my heaven in the white world's hell,
> Did not forever feed me vital blood.
> I see the mighty city through a mist—
> The strident trains that speed the goaded mass,
> The poles and spires and towers vapor-kissed,
> The fortressed port through which the great
>   ships pass,
> The tides, the wharves, the dens I contemplate,
> Are sweet like wanton loves because I hate.

Hatred has acquired quite a power of transfiguration. It
becomes the favored theme of the poet's song, for it alone
can make his surroundings bearable. (pp. 224-25)

It was once declared that hatred is not a poetic emotion.
If this act of exclusion were to be acquiesced in, it would
oblige us to find no poetic merit whatever in Claude
McKay's most striking poems since he, among all black
poets, is *par excellence* the poet of hate. This, when situated in its racial context, has a very special characteristic.
As **"The White City"** so clearly shows, it is the actual prerequisite for his survival, since it transmutes into a paradise the base inferno of the white world. It is a sort of antidote secreted throughout his being and which prevents the
White City from emptying him of his substance—were it
not for this fostering flood of hatred, which constantly
provides him with fresh energies, he would be reduced by
the city to the level of a skeleton, of a sea creature's abandoned shell. Hatred is the compensatory factor that assures the equilibrium of his personality, allowing him to
adapt himself adequately to his environment. (pp. 225-26)

McKay's hatred, as John Dewey has so well put it, "is
clean; never mean nor spiteful." This is no suppurating,
latent affliction that forms an ulcer. It might more accurately be compared to the red-hot iron that cauterizes and
disinfects. In the following lines, which certainly have
nothing morbid about them, the poet expresses the same
thought:

> There is a searing hate within my soul,
> A hate that only kin can feel for kin,
> A hate that makes me vigorous and whole,
> And spurs me on increasingly to win.

McKay is fond of employing, as he does with great precision, this image of an inner flame to convey the ardor of
the lyric inspiration that urges all his being onward to liberation. The purifying effect of this flame must be stressed:
note the adjective "searing," with its host of surgical implications. On the other hand, this inner flame raises to the

melting point all the alloyed metals that make up his steel-
hard temperament:

> And I am fire, swift to flame and burn,
> Melting with elements high overhead.

                                                    (pp. 226-27)

His own hatred is thus an antidote that enables him to
fight, on an equal footing, against the hatred that burns in
the oppressor; the racial struggle becomes a fiery furnace
in which flame confronts hostile flame. This is the meaning of the sonnet entitled **"Baptism"**:

> Into the furnace let me go alone;
> Stay you without in terror of the heat.
> I will go naked in—for thus 'tis sweet—
> Into the weird depths of the hottest zone,
> I will not quiver in the frailest bone,
> You will not note a flicker of defeat;
> My heart shall tremble not its fate to meet,
> My mouth give utterance to any moan.
> The yawning oven spits forth fiery spears;
> Red aspish tongues shout wordlessly my name.
> Desire destroys, consumes my mortal fears,
> Transforming me into a shape of flame.
> I will come out, back to your world of tears,
> A stronger soul within a finer frame.

The last two lines once again stress the transforming
power of the fire of hatred, and the sonnet expresses the
poet's ultimate goal, which is to take on his shoulders,
when he emerges from this baptism of fire, the burden of
all his race. (pp. 227-28)

[With the publication of **"If We Must Die,"** McKay be-
came] the incarnation of the new spirit and the spokesman
for a whole people at last resolved to witness no longer,
in resignation and submissiveness, the massacre of its own
brothers at the hands of the enraged white mob, but to return blow for blow and, if necessary, to die. With the possible exception of James Weldon Johnson's "Negro National Hymn" ["Lift Every Voice and Sing"], no poem by
any black poet has been so frequently cited and extolled.
(p. 229)

The welcome accorded this sonnet is also due, in part, to
its being one of those poems in which McKay's poetic gift
reaches beyond the circumstances of the day to attain the
universal. Along with the will to resistance of black Americans that it expresses, it voices also the will of oppressed
peoples of every age who, whatever their race and wherever their region, are fighting with their backs against the
wall to win their freedom. Some twenty-five years after its
initial publication, **"If We Must Die"** was reprinted in an
English anthology at a time when England, alone and with
its back to the wall, was withstanding the onslaught of the
Luftwaffe. And the text of the poem was discovered in
1944 on the body of a young white American soldier who
had been killed in action.

It is important, at this juncture in our examination of
McKay's hatred, to try to determine against what, exactly,
his hatred was directed. One might, indeed, choose to regard him as a last-ditch defender of Negro culture, filled
with a global detestation of America and the Western culture for which, in his eyes, it stood. This interpretation of

his cultural attitude has actually found supporters. (p. 230)

McKay appears to have expressed all the complexity of his real feelings about America in the sonnet entitled **"America"**:

> Although she feeds me bread of bitterness,
> And sinks into my throat her tiger's tooth,
> Stealing my breath of life, I will confess
> I love this cultured hell that tests my youth!
> Her vigor flows like tides into my blood,
> Giving me strength erect against her hate,
> Her bigness sweeps my being like a flood.

What is predominant here, and basic also, is his love for America, whose strength acts on the poet like a stimulant. The other half of the picture, the hatred that America has for blacks, does not obliterate the poet's love for it. McKay's hatred does not mean a rejection of America; it is a reproach directed against the country's inability to reconcile discriminatory practices with egalitarian democratic doctrines. In the last analysis, what he hates is not America, but evil. An unpublished sonnet makes this explicit:

> I stripped down harshly to the naked core
> Of hatred based on the essential wrong.

We know that the essential evil is the division between man and man, the white man's hatred and contempt for his fellow man, and the exploitation of black by white. In the "civilized hell" of America, evil adopts the most varied guises. But a natural defense reaction leads McKay to note those in particular which deny the black man's humanity. The metaphors often depict America as a kind of vampire seeking to deprive the victim of his substance and to leave him a mere shell or skeleton. America becomes, for instance, a tiger, his striped coat representing the stripes of the American flag, who seizes his prey by the throat and nourishes himself on the blood. . . . (pp. 231-32)

In another poem, **"Birds of Prey,"** whites are depicted as birds darkening the sky with their wings, then swooping down on their victims to gorge themselves on the hearts. . . . (p. 232)

Blood and heart quite assuredly have a symbolic value in these poems, which denounce the depersonalization of the black man and his exploitation by society's rulers, who glut themselves on his financial and artistic substance. But this carnage also requires a more literal interpretation, so that the poems may be understood as a condemnation of lynching, like the sonnet **"The Lynching,"** where McKay speaks more openly.

At times, too, McKay succeeds in utilizing a less violent mode to chant the horrors of racial discrimination. **"The Barrier"** is a delightful poem which, in a manner that is partly light and partly serious, considers the interdict prohibiting any love between a black man and a white woman. It is reminiscent of those trials that judged a man's intentions when, in the Deep South, blacks used to be convicted of the "visual rape" of a southern white beauty:

> I must not gaze at them although
>   Your eyes are dawning day;
> I must not watch you as you go
>   Your sun-illumined way;
>
> I hear but I must never heed
>   The fascinating note,
> Which, fluting like a river reed,
>   Comes from your trembling throat;
>
> I must not see upon your face
>   Love's softly glowing spark;
> For there's the barrier of race,
>   You're fair and I am dark.

(pp. 232-33)

Though McKay may justifiably be called the poet of hatred and rebellion, his real personality would be seriously misrepresented if one were to treat him as an out-and-out rebel. Without meaning to do so, Richard Wright undoubtedly slights McKay in his nobility by asserting of him: "To state that Claude McKay is a rebel is to understate it; his rebellion is a way of life." To adopt this point of view is to overlook the remarkable selfmastery that McKay could summon up, and to neglect the personal purification and, when all is considered, the moral elevation that McKay believed he could derive from his hate.

It is, indeed, admirable that in his case hatred and rebellion did not become, as they might have, a vehicle lurching onward without reins or brakes. Even when he revels in his hate, he does not wallow in it, and in the midst of the hurricane he retains his control:

> Peace, O my rebel heart!. . . .

(p. 235)

He simply does not look on hatred as an end in itself. It is but a stage on the path that ends in the divine charity, for which its purifying action prepares the way. Understood thus, McKay's hatred is a holy anger the manifestation of which occurs only in entire clarity of mind, as did the divine anger directed against the deleterious hypocrisy of the Pharisees, or against the merchants who had made of the temple a "den of thieves." Ultimately, what sets a limit to hatred is the spiritual. Such is the message of the sonnet **"To the White Fiends,"** in which God compels hatred to stop on the brink of murder, directing it to a higher goal:

> Think you I am not fiend and savage too?
> Think you I could not arm me with a gun
> And shoot down ten of you for every one
> Of my black brothers murdered, burnt by you?
> Be not deceived, for every deed you do
> I could match—out-match: am I not Afric's son,
> Black of that black land where black deeds are
>   done?
> But the Almighty from the darkness drew
> My soul and said: Even thou shalt be a light
> Awhile to burn on the benighted earth,
> Thy dusky face I set among the white
> For thee to prove thyself of higher worth;
> Before the world is swallowed up in night,
> To show thy little lamp: go forth, go forth!

Thus, far from being a "way of life," McKay's hatred undergoes a sublimation that induces it to consume itself. In its place comes a tranquillity that is not indifference, but a deepening and internalization of racial feeling. (pp. 235-36)

In McKay's work, the feeling for nature occupies almost as important a place as racial feeling. . . . Unlike Countee Cullen or Langston Hughes, who never vibrated in unison with nature (which usually remains a mere concept for them), McKay brings to it the understanding and sympathy of a person who grew up in it and whose rare sensitivity brought him to an authentic integration with it. In *Harlem Shadows,* the nature poems make up nearly one-third of the volume. The languorous sweetness of their lyricism is like a cool breeze from the Isles, introducing a note of most welcome tranquility into the militant fierceness of the poems of rebellion. (p. 236)

It can be seen that McKay's feeling for nature has no autonomous existence. Since it is linked with the racial symbolism of the earth and remains closely subordinated to it, seen from this point of view it most often amounts to the enunciation of a sense of belonging.

Its expressive value, because of this role, falls together with that of the African theme as treated by many poets of the Negro Renaissance. For them, Africa is the land still unpolluted by the inhuman machine outlook of the white man, hungry to enslave his fellow men. But for them—those who are unable to identify with America, the land that treats them inhumanely—Africa is the substitute land where they can seek their roots; Africa is the mother with whom, in the place of stepmotherly America which has rejected them, they try to form an *a posteriori* bond of relationship.

McKay is totally unconcerned with these substitute values. For he comes from a land where blacks are in the majority, where he struck roots both tenacious and extraordinarily deep, a land with which his identification was perfect, if one allows for the extraterritorial status he imposed on the city of Kingston. He has no need to go all the way to Africa to find the palm trees to which he can compare the black girls. Jamaica is his Africa, and its exoticism is a genuine exoticism, not a dream escape to some substitute fatherland the need for which springs from a feeling of frustration.

It is not surprising, therefore, that he keeps the African theme within much more modest limits than the other Renaissance poets, whose feeling of unqualified admiration for Africa he does not share. The whole body of his work contains scarcely more than half a dozen poems devoted to Africa, and not one of them can be considered an apologia. (pp. 238-39)

In **"Outcast,"** it is again the sense of being captive in the white man's empire that occupies the poet's mind, rather than any feeling of solidarity with Africa. Nevertheless, this second factor emerges with greater clarity here than in any other poem by McKay. But he is less intent on affirming his link with Africa than in regretting that the elements forming this link have been lost or forgotten. . . . He must be taken to express his kinship with the blacks of the United States, whose spokesman he has become, and to state the truth, as suggested by the poem's title, that

he himself has been rejected by the white American majority. These two ingredients are more obvious than any putative avowal of genuine solidarity with Africa. (p. 242)

Thus if McKay is a forerunner of the Negro Renaissance, this is not due to his vision of Africa. The genuine quality of his Jamaican exoticism had immunized him against the heady African mirage, and his ability to stand resolute against its seductions attests, in the last resort, the cohesiveness and equilibrium of his personality.

McKay has left us only a few poems dealing with Harlem, the "Mecca of the Negro Renaissance." His 1922 volume, though entitled *Harlem Shadows,* has but two poems on the theme, the title poem and **"The Harlem Dancer."** (p. 243)

Yet, though for these reasons he can scarely be called the poet of Harlem, at least he has the merit of being the first to introduce Harlem into Negro poetry. For in December, 1917, **"The Harlem Dancer"** appeared in *The Seven Arts,* and **"Harlem Shadows"** was included in **Spring in New Hampshire** (1920). Earlier than Langston Hughes, it is Claude McKay who provided the first annotations on the frivolous night life that, until the 1929 crash, would enable Harlem to prosper. These poems might also be said to constitute the first poetic documents on the reactions of the black man borne to the urban centers by the tide of the Great Migration.

"Harlem Shadows" is a poem in a minor key on the prostitutes that urban civilization, with its lack of humanity, had thrown onto the Harlem sidewalks. The poem is reminiscent of those that McKay, in the 1912 volumes, had devoted to the moral debacle of two country girls as a result of their going to live in Kingston. But **"Harlem Shadows"** is an innovation in the sense that McKay attributes a primordial importance to the prostitutes' color (blackening them further by referring to them as shadows) and makes their downfall symbolic of the whole race's. In each case, the blame is implicitly allotted to racial oppression. This biased suggestion deviates significantly from McKay's usually realistic, objective manner, and one would have expected him to treat these prostitutes as victims of the city rather than as slaves of the master race. This deference to racial propaganda spoils the end of the poem, which otherwise would have been very much to the point:

> Ah, stern harsh world, that in the wretched way
> Of poverty, dishonor and disgrace,
> Has pushed the timid little feet of clay,
> The sacred brown feet of my fallen race!
> Ah, heart of me, the weary, weary feet
> In Harlem wandering from street to street.
>
> (p. 244)

"The Harlem Dancer" plunges us into the atmosphere of one of the countless night spots that sprang up in Harlem after World War I. This sonnet raises the problem of another sort of prostitution, that of Negro art to popular (mainly white) demands. White people appear in the sonnet as drunken spectators who gobble up with their eyes the form of a naked black dancer. Between the young whites, in search of venal pleasures, and the nobility of the black beauty, the comparison is to the advantage of the latter. She appears before us in all the pride of a tall palm tree swaying majestically in the wind, yet she is an uprooted palm tree, torn from a kindlier country where she has left her soul. Her natural grace and beauty contrast with the artificial setting into which she has been transplanted, and her forced smile cannot hide her longing for her native land. Underneath the exoticism of detail, we once again come upon a thesis greatly favored by McKay and the Negro Renaissance, maintaining that the white world, more often than was generally believed, was a setting unfit to receive all that blacks have to offer it. (pp. 244-45)

One may establish a parallel between **"The Harlem Dancer"** and another sonnet, **"Negro Spiritual,"** which, though leaving Harlem unmentioned, considers this same problem of the exploitation of Negro art by whites. In this magnificent sonnet, McKay gives particularly fortunate expression to all the glorious, grievous overtones awakened in the black soul when hearing spirituals sung. But the primitive natural beauty of these songs of the slaves' cruelly tested existence is doubly betrayed with an orchestration that falsifies the songs and in the setting of a too artificially beautiful auditorium. There they strike a false note, as did the almost feline grace of the black dancer in the decadent atmosphere of the Harlem joint. Between Negro art and the blundering receptivity of the white artlover lies the abyss of "an alien spirit." McKay condemns this attitude adopted by whites, since they approach Negro art with the mentality of slaveowners. All they have in mind is to find diversion in this art, just as they used to make buffoons out of the slaves they owned. (p. 245)

Poets have often been attracted by the theme of black dancers. Dunbar . . . has left us entertaining portrayals of evenings spent dancing the quadrille with, in his day, the added savor of forbidden fruit. Jazz, in its turn, will soon find its true poet in Langston Hughes. Thus it need not surprise us that McKay also should have chosen to see in the liberation of the dance, as in the spontaneity and the subtle rhythms of the dancers, an especially revealing manifestation of the "immortal spirit" of his race, since here one could note the urge to expand, to express oneself, to free oneself, instincts that in daily life had to be kept in check at every instant.

But whereas Dunbar and Hughes let themselves be swept away by the vortex of the dance, McKay remained the detached observer, though sensing the emotion that radiated from the dancers to him. His view is an external one; a space remains between him and the crowd of dancers and allows him no identification with them. . . . It can be sensed that McKay experiences a measure of despair vis-à-vis the tragedy of this superficial response of a whole race to the oppression and contempt by which it is victimized.

This is, we believe, another manifestation of McKay's reserved attitude when confronted by the folk temperament, with which he never felt entirely at ease. Other elements that lead us to the same conclusion are the total absence of humor throughout his poetry and his preference for such classical poetic forms as the sonnet. Spirituals, blues, and jazz, whose popular forms were taken over by Langston Hughes, Sterling Brown, and many other poets, have no place in McKay's poetic work. In this connection, it is

necessary to correct the mistaken view propounded by Henry Lüdeke (no doubt on the basis of uncertain information) that in **Harlem Shadows** the rhythms were "strongly influenced by popular poetry, above all the spirituals." Quite the contrary, McKay must have had a background awareness that the popular forms and outlook could become, as has in reality often occurred, an excuse for avoiding personal reflection, and so would have been only another sort of escapism for the poet. Thus, while he defends Negro art against the deformations that whites inflicted on it, he defended it no less vigorously against those Negroes who were tempted to ask of it something that it could not provide: a soul. . . . [In] Harlem he could now see to what a degree this culture was emptied of substance the moment it lost contact with the soil, which alone could give it life, and was transported to the city, which in McKay's eyes had ever been a corrupting influence. In a word, he judged Negro popular culture, as he had encountered it in America, to be incapable of fulfilling his need for an authentic spiritual life. (pp. 246-47)

[McKay], with his nonconformist temperament, was repelled by the idea of adhering to traditions that took the place of individual reflection. His religious poetry is the expression of an inner growth, and his discovery of God the result of his individual search for truth. From a more general vantage-point, his poetic opus may be considered as the account of a vast attempt at a synthesis between the antagonistic elements of the black world and the Western world warring within him. There can be no denying that McKay, like every black exiled in a white milieu, was for a long time a divided man, so that it is possible to speak of his cultural dualism. But he never acquiesced in being torn apart by this dichotomy. His whole being urged him to find unity. The critique to which he subjected the antinomies deprived them, little by little, of their contingencies and laid bare their authentic values. In Jamaica, he affirmed the primacy of the soil and contrasted it with the inanity of the dream, cherished by the mulattoes, of a heightened social status. He rejected the mirage of Africa as a source of racial pride, looking on it as merely pathetic. He shunned the nationalism of a Garvey, whom he regarded as a charlatan, and while he defended Negro folklore against whites, who would have denatured it, he nevertheless could not find spiritual sustenance in it. On the other hand, it was his natural instinct to evaluate the possibilities of spiritual advancement offered by Western, Christian culture, but there too he perceived the corroding evil that sowed hatred between men. In his dialogue with the West, conducted through the medium of his hatred, this emotion was slowly filtered of its dross as he came to grasp the necessity of raising himself above it. Unless the individual is engaged in a ceaseless effort to transcend himself, no victory over hatred will ever be possible. Neither rationalism nor Communism could provide the higher principle capable of reconciling the conflicting theses of his cultural eclecticism. At long last he discovered this principle within himself, and at the same time he discovered God. Thus his spiritual itinerary is an account of the internalization of his racial feeling.

"I was always religious-minded as some of my pagan

poems attest. But I never had any faith in revealed religion." (pp. 248-49)

[McKay's] skepticism, which was aroused by rationalist influences, signifies an estrangement from the church rather than from God. It would seem equally likely that this estrangement was motivated by certain practices or pastoral attitudes on the part of the Anglican clergy. . . .

Be that as it may, the poet's critique of what we shall call the official faith soon led him to become his own spiritual advisor. This imbues him with a taste for that upward movement of the soul that a victory over his passions represents, and it accustoms him to view progress as a continual upgrading of the individual through self-transcendence, which alone makes existence worthwhile "in an empty world." These are the qualities of soul that McKay brings to the spiritual enrichment of black poetry, as his voice blends in with those of the American black poets. (p. 251)

His fundamental expectation in turning to God, and the object of the prayers he addresses to Him, is the light of truth. . . . That this is the ultimate objective of his spiritual quest is confirmed by the sonnet **"Truth,"** written shortly before he died:

> Lord, shall I find it in Thy Holy Church,
> Or must I give it up as something dead,
> Forever lost, no matter where I search,
> Like dinosaurs within their ancient bed?
> I found it not in years of Unbelief,
> In science stirring life like budding trees,
> In Revolution like a dazzling thief—
> Oh, shall I find it on my bended knees?
> But what is Truth? So Pilate asked Thee, Lord,
> So long ago when Thou wert manifest,
> As the Eternal and Incarnate Word,
> Chosen of God and by Him singly blest;
> In this vast world of lies and hate and greed,
> Upon my knees, Oh Lord, for Truth I plead.

His prayer will be granted, and divine illumination will bring him to recognize at last that the "essential evil" he had spent his life hunting down and fighting is not outside, but within him. To track down injustice and oppression by hating America is to fight against shadows. The basic evil is hate itself, and that is what he must hate. It is hate that wrecks unity, setting men one against the other, and the individual against himself. But it is the farthest point to which the pagan doctrines can lead one. God alone can lead a man further on and conquer hate itself:

> Around me roar and crash the pagan isms
> To which most of my life was consecrate,
> Betrayed by evil men and torn by schisms
> For they were built on nothing more than hate!
> I cannot live my life without the faith
> Where new sensations like a fawn will leap,
> But old enthusiasms like a wraith
> Haunt me awake and haunt me when I sleep.
> And so to God I go to make my peace.

(pp. 256-57)

Jean Wagner, "Claude McKay," in his Black Poets of the United States: From Paul Laurence Dunbar to Langston Hughes, *translated*

by Kenneth Douglas, University of Illinois Press, 1973, pp. 197-257.

Helen Pyne Timothy   (essay date 1975)

[*In the following excerpt, Pyne Timothy, citing events from McKay's peasant background, American and European experiences, and socialist enterprises, posits that a central thematic concern in McKay's poetry is "the survival of the individual black in Western civilization."*]

The concern for [McKay's] race could only be expressed through his writings: and throughout these we are presented with themes which reveal McKay's responses to many facets of black life. Bernard Shaw when he met Claude McKay in 1919 remarked 'it must be tragic for a sensitive Negro to be an artist'. Indeed, McKay's life and work portray to a painful degree just this sensitivity to some of the problems which contributed to the appalling dilemma which life itself presented for the black man, whether he was based in colonial Africa, in America or in Europe. Some of the issues to which he repeatedly responded were those of Jamaican nationalism, the maltreatment of the Afro-American, the viability of communism as a solution to the race problem, the values of miscegenation and segregation. But these public issues were always seen from the viewpoint of the individual. The great issue for McKay was simply the survival of the individual black in western civilization.

It is customary to counterpoise the Jamaican period of McKay's life against the later American and European years of hardship, bitterness and loneliness. Within this dichotomy, the Jamaican years are seen as representing a structured pattern of peasant values within which McKay, demonstrating the security of total understanding, found a sense of peace which informed both the artist and his output. This coherency and wholeness gave him the capability of producing literary works which had the serenity of art. The bitter and fragmented American experiences are thought to have engendered the militancy which made his work propagandistic.

But a careful study of McKay's work reveals that even in his earliest dialect poetry, written as a young man in Jamaica, there is some intent which could be called propagandistic. His two volumes of dialect poetry appeared in 1912 when McKay was just twenty-three years old. At this time he was under the definitive influence of Dr. Walter Jekyll, the eccentric Englishman who encouraged his reading and his poetic instinct. But Jekyll was 'unconsciously biased against what he felt was propaganda'. Hence it is likely that McKay in writing his early poetry would have eschewed the use of propaganda in his verse. Yet in McKay's dialect poetry there is an intention at the deep level which is not merely sentimental and romantic, but which is clearly social and political. Such a meaning emerges in the poem **"Quashie to Buccra"** for example, where a peasant speaking to the white man says:

> You tase'e petater an' you say it sweet,
> But you no' know how hard we wuk fe' it;

You want a basketful fe quattiewut,
'Cause you no know how 'tiff de bush fe cut.

The militant tone here is masked by the stanzaic form of
the poem and by the lyrical movement which is imparted
both by the form and by the informal rhythm of the Jamaican dialect: and the young McKay vitiates his social militancy when at the end he succumbs to romanticism:

Yet still de hardship always melt away
Wheneber it come roun' to reapin' day.

But it is true that the political tone of these works is far
less apparent than the author's interest in the basic concerns of the life of the ordinary Jamaican peasant.
Through McKay, and in his own authentic speaking
voice, the Jamaican creole, the peasant parades the
rhythm of his day-to-day life. All aspects of his attitudes
and beliefs, his cultural habits are represented: **"Little
Jim"** has his sore toe healed with a blue stone, and the little girl in **"Fetchin' Water"** is memorable as she struggles
uphill with her gourd.

These vignettes of rural life are interesting and authentic.
Atmosphere is created by the actual natural beauty of the
Clarendon hills. Here is the rich, unchanging tapestry of
nature which had such a powerful influence on McKay's
imagination and which seemed to have represented the
fertility of all life on the island. Yet inescapably, some of
the special qualities which characterized the later McKay
are there. He always asserted the importance of authenticity of setting for his literary works and attempted to maintain the expression of black life in the different levels of
language which were appropriate to different characters.

These linguistic attempts ratify the notion of McKay's
iconoclasm. It is in fact remarkable that McKay should
have published a book of dialect poetry in 1912. The spoken language of the peasants in Jamaica was then and still
is considered by the intelligentsia as ignorant, broken English. It has never been considered a proper vehicle for serious, intelligent or learned conversation and is rarely
written except with humorous intent or for the provision
of local colour. McKay, the son of peasants, saw that his
environment could be seriously treated in the formal mode
of poetry using the language of blacks. This apprehension
demonstrated qualities he never lost: the tremendous sense
of poise and confidence which he had in himself and in the
black race in general, and his determination to advocate
the preservation of their culture and their diversity.

The later stances of McKay on other public issues are further apparent in the dialect poetry. In *A Long Way From
Home* and, fictionally, in *Banjo* McKay articulates his intense dislike for the effects of colonialism as seen in France
and Morocco, and especially for the individual who was
the petty British official, that type who was 'over bearing
to common persons and crawling to superiors'. The colonial British subject was always a common person, always
exposed to the unsympathetic, often cruel and brutal arm
of government. Certainly McKay seems to have thought
that the colonial situation put the government out of touch
with the true aims, desires, and beliefs of the common
man. In a poem like **"My Native Land, My Home"** nationalistic ideas about the place of the blacks in the world

are interwoven with complaints of the everlasting petty ir-
ritations of the colonial government:

Jamaica is de nigger's place
No mind whe' some declare!
Although dem call we "no-land race,"
I know we home is here.

(pp. 15-18)

McKay's basic sympathy with the peasants and his antipathy towards officialdom, the arm of colonial administra-
tion as represented in his island, made him unable to remain in the Police Force of Jamaica. Some of his poetry,
published in **Constab Ballads** (1912) while he was a policeman, is amusing in that he interprets the common people's
complaints against the police: their interference in the
peasant's attempts to obtain a livelihood, their use of their
position to exploit women. But what made McKay most
unhappy as a policeman seemed to have been the realization that he could not serve the government and also serve
his people. This dilemma is movingly expressed in **"The
Heart of a Constab"** where he reveals that his position has
estranged him from his people and has engendered hatred
between him as the official, and them the peasants. Here
it is clear that McKay, unlike most educated colonial
blacks who consciously sought to distance themselves
from the illiterate mass, deliberately set out to reimmerse
himself in the ordinary mainstream of black endeavour.

It is interesting to note that once McKay had emigrated,
his loneliness and nostalgia reduced the social intent of
those examples of his poetry which dealt with Jamaica.
The tropical riot of nature, the freshness and serenity of
his beloved **"Snake River"** provided oases of pleasure
when, in memory, he revisited them while living in the
greyness, harshness, the concrete and steel of New York
City. Having left Jamaica he abandoned dialect poetry. As
he told Frank Harris, he had come to America not merely
to educate himself but also to find a bigger audience.
Hence those poems which he wrote about Jamaica from
the American scene were written in standard English.
They proved more interesting to literate Jamaica, and in
fact his poem **"Flame Heart"** is perhaps the best-known
example of his work there. The social and political ambivalence of life in Jamaica have been distilled by the loneliness of the years of exile. Only the happiness, the meaningful rhythms of rural life remain forever and with love imprinted on his memory.

But the American experience brought into McKay's poetry all the anger and frustration, the boiling emotionalism
with which his sensitive spirit continually responded to his
position as a black man. He said that as a writer he carried
'a poem in his heart, and a story in his head' and he clearly
used his poetry to express the spectrum of all the emotional responses which American life pulled out of him. In
general terms it may be said that, apart from the lovely,
lyrical, warm poems of the **Songs for Jamaica**, many of
the other poems are militant, concerned with the place of
the black man in white society, overwhelmed by the burning necessity of a response to the social situation in which
McKay finds himself. In **"To the White Fiends"** for example, McKay begins:

> Think you I am not fiend and savage too?
> Think you I could not arm me with a gun
> And shoot down ten of you for every one
> Of my black brothers murdered, burnt by you?

Poems like the above, the famous **"If We Must Die"** and **"The Lynching"** all express McKay's rage, particularly in response to the post-World War I lynching of blacks in the Southern United States, and the general brutality white society directed against blacks.

Sometimes, however, McKay's response to America showed not militancy, but a delicate tenderness and melancholy for the plight of 'the Negro' in America. **"Outcast"** expresses this mood. Its final couplet declares:

> For I was born, far from my native clime,
> Under the white man's menace, out of time.

Occasionally, also, the poet seems burdened by the responsibility of expressing these powerful emotions, not merely for himself, but also for his race. He poignantly reveals this in **"O Word I Love to Sing"** where he seems to consider the medium of poetry 'too slender / Too fragile like a globe of crystal glass' to ' . . . render / My hatred for the foe of me and mine.'

Poems like the above demonstrate that it would be a mistake to think of the Afro-American McKay only as the poet of militancy and turbulent emotion. He also expresses his joy in the vigorous, stimulating struggle for existence which occurs in New York, his admiration for the beauty of some member of his race whose sudden vision has perhaps pierced his imagination, or his celebration of some meaningful romantic entanglement. All of these aspects of his poetry are interesting, and all bear the stamp of the identity of the author as a black man.

The dates of McKay's poetic expression in the post-Jamaican period are not readily established. Apparently he wrote poetry throughout his life. But much of the material in the **Selected Poems** belongs to the early years in Harlem (and the period to 1928). His association with Frank Harris and Max Eastman between the years 1919 and 1922 is well known. Harris, as editor of *Pearson's Magazine,* the radical publication, and Eastman, then in charge of the Communist *Liberator,* both encouraged McKay's writing of poetry and gave him the opportunity to publish his work. During this period the literary circles in the U.S. were aware of him as a good (if militant) poet and an effective columnist who always used his pen to write on 'the Negro question'. His commitment to the expression of what he considered the 'true position of the Negro in America' led to a quarrel with his co-editor on the *Liberator* and McKay resigned. During this period he also went to England where he worked with Sylvia Pankhurst on the communist paper, *Workers Dreadnought.* At this time McKay considered himself an 'international socialist' because he apparently felt that communism represented a path through which the black worker could make significant social progress. (pp. 18-20)

But it was clear even in 1922 that McKay as a socialist was something of a maverick. He seems to have cherished a highly romantic notion in which he saw 'communism liberating millions of city folk to go back to the land' . . . . As his poetry had revealed, McKay was interested in na-

tionalism and socialism but only from the viewpoint of progress for the black man. Communism was not an abstract concept equally applicable to all workers and in which he fully believed. (p. 21)

McKay's experiences in Western Europe were firmly contrasted with the attitude of the Russian intellectual and peasant when, in 1922, he attended the Fourth Congress of the Third Communist International in Moscow. McKay, although thinking himself a socialist, was not then a member of the American Communist Party, and seemed to have viewed Russian communism from a highly individualist perspective. While being feted by the officials of the party, he spent most of his spare time among writers who were anti-Bolshevist. While he was discussing 'the Negro problem' and attempting to persuade the leaders to include 'the Negro worker' as a special group within the international workers' movement, he was writing to Max Eastman:

> Do you think any fool could think that with the revolutionary overturn in Russia all class, national and racial differences would disappear as if by magic?

It is clear that even as early as 1922 McKay would not see communism as providing a salvation for 'the Negro' in any quick or easy way. And he would not, he thought, totally embrace a revolutionary political system unless it could offer to the whole of the black race, trapped within the system of the United States and Western Europe, a way through which their social and economic positions could be improved. (p. 22)

[McKay] had always pursued an iconoclastic, even solitary, way of life. Yet this personal isolation did not dull his understanding of the importance of group interaction among blacks. He saw clearly that only within the group could the black personality truly flower; that only the black man's understanding of himself and of his people could lead to a thorough integration of the black personality. He was concerned that the divisiveness caused by the minority status of blacks in Europe and in America would seriously scatter individuals, warp values, divide the group, and lead to the loss of human understanding, spirituality and warmth, those redeeming qualities which had contributed to the survival of blacks as a race.

As a man and as an artist, therefore, he had remained faithful to the task which he had set himself, to mirror and express his individual conscience, and the consciousness of his race. (p. 28)

> *Helen Pyne Timothy, "Claude McKay: Individualism and Group Consciousness," in* A Celebration of Black and African Writing, *edited by Bruce King and Kolawole Ogungbesan, Ahmadu Bello University Press, 1975, pp. 15-29.*

John Hillyer Condit   (essay date 1979)

[In the excerpt below, Condit examines the apparent imbalance between McKay's movement toward universalism and his strong individualism, maintaining that

*McKay's favorite verse form, the sonnet, typifies the uni-
fication of imbalance.*]

In his *The Passion of Claude McKay,* Wayne Cooper provides McKay's readers and critics with a most salutary ad-
monition. "McKay transcends any one decade or movement. His literary significance can be understood only
within the full context of his life and career."

Yet, more easily said than done! As Melvin B. Tolson observed, "Contrived seemingly as the plot of the Hardyesque is the triangle of a poet mythicized by Harlem,
feted by Moscow, and haloed by Rome" [see excerpt dated
1954]. Small wonder, then, that critics whose sympathies
seem to lie mainly along one side of such a triangle would
have difficulty perceiving the whole figure. (p. 350)

"I suppose I have a poet's right to imagine
a great modern Negro leader. At least I
would like to celebrate him in a monument
of verse. For I have nothing to give but
my singing. All my life I have been a
troubadour wanderer, nourishing myself
mainly on the poetry of existence."
—Claude McKay, 1937

Had all but heeded Cooper's warning to place McKay
"within the full context of his life and career," this critical
discord might not have been so rife. Along with Cooper,
only Tolson seems fully to have recognized that "out of
a heterogeneity of experience with an underlying unity,
Claude McKay . . . created his best poems."

This underlying unity transcending any one decade or
movement is precisely what I hope to identify and then use
in the discussion of several McKay sonnets. For I wholeheartedly agree with Cooper that throughout the many vicissitudes in McKay's life and literary career "the man's
basic humanism and his great personal integrity stand
out."

Indeed, by expanding the term "humanism" to "universalism" and by slightly altering the phrase "great personal
integrity" to "proud individuality," I believe Cooper's accolade can be made to yield the essence of the unity underlying McKay's life and art. Virtually at any given moment
or in any given work, Claude McKay was striving to balance his universalism with his proud individuality.

On the one hand, McKay possessed an insistent urge toward wholeness, a need to merge with any larger unit of
which he deemed himself a part. At the same time, his
fierce pride would not permit him to embrace any universe
that did not accept him at his full worth. I will contend
that Claude McKay sought as a man and a poet to resolve
his universality and individuality on as transcendent a
plane as possible. (p. 351)

When young McKay left the country hills [of Jamaica]
and arrived in Kingston, he encountered for the first time

barriers between himself and a wholeness which welcomed all individual worth. Unlike the mother, play-
mates, neighbors, and nature of his hilltop homeland,
Kingston made distinctions which set city folk against
country folk, mulattoes against blacks, rich against poor.

In the face of such discrimination, McKay used his poetry
to reaffirm his black rural origin and the wholeness it represented to him. He also refused to accept the categories
thrust upon him when he took a job as constable, but instead extended in his verse his "most improper sympathy"
to "wrongdoers." (pp. 353-54)

Discernible in the free-thinking Darwinism espoused by
McKay at this time is a desire to ascribe these upsetting
experiences to some universal design. Jamaican inequality
seemed more the result of a class system than of direct racial oppression, and upward mobility for blacks was possible. Also, the Jamaican black had been taught of his rights
as a British citizen. Thus McKay reacted to this general
state of affairs with a romantic pessimism.

McKay next sought to relate to an even larger, more hostile world. He left Jamaica for the United States "to find
a bigger audience" for his poetry and avoid isolation
"from the great currents of life." The year was 1912;
McKay met "race hatred in its most virulent form." This
phenomenon proved too devastating to his need for wholeness for any rationalization through some combination of
romantic pessimism and social Darwinism. Unable either
to accept alienation or renounce his proud sense of identity, McKay made manifest his urge toward wholeness in
both his burning hatred for the men and institutions which
excluded him and his support of a new international order
which promised to obliterate all invidious distinctions. (p.
354)

Through this hatred McKay could feel a part of his new
world, even assert kinship to his foes, without surrender-
ing an iota of identity. . . .

Hatred, however, did not long, by itself, satisfy McKay's
urge to wholeness. He needed, as he stated in **"To the
White Fiends,"** to prove himself "of higher worth."

The evidence seems clear that McKay's attraction to socialism and the ideals of the Russian revolution lay in the
hopes they stirred for a truly just international brotherhood of man. . . .

In 1922, McKay attended the Fourth Congress of the
Communist Party, in Russia. (p. 355)

During his stay in Russia, McKay particularly thrilled to
the "unique mixture of Eastern and Western cultures"
and the polyglot populace. He was even more taken with
his reception by the Russian masses: "It was so beautifully
naïve; for them I was only a black member of the world
of humanity." At last, it would seem, his urge to wholeness had found satisfaction.

Such was not the case. McKay's disenchantment with
Marxism had already begun. He was discovering an inveterate racism lurking in far too many American and European socialists and communists. Besides, he increasingly

realized that to toe the party line would entail the sacrifice of artistic integrity: "I could never be a disciplined member of any Communist Party, for I was born to be a poet." (pp. 355-56)

McKay's own final thrust toward wholeness resulted in his baptism into the Catholic Church on October 11, 1944, in Chicago. It is true enough, as James R. Giles asserts, that McKay, previous to this event, had been isolated by his political and artistic stances and enervated by extremely poor health. Surely though, much more was involved in his conversion than the "personal gratitude" to the Church for succoring him in his illness and the resentment toward those political and artistic acquaintances who misunderstood and abandoned him [see Further Reading list]. Nor was the conversion "a complete reversal of his former beliefs" as Cooper holds. McKay's turn to Catholicism was too much a part of his life pattern to constitute either a compromise or a reversal.

The respect for "the dignity of the individual and the oneness of all humanity" which McKay discovered in Catholic Spain was exactly the quality he had experienced during his rural Jamaican boyhood and had hoped to recapture through involvement with **"The Pagan Isms."** As McKay, shortly before his death, wrote to Max Eastman, "I still like to think of people with wonder and love as I did as a boy in Jamaica and the Catholic Church with its discipline and traditions and understanding of human nature is helping me a lot." In the Church, McKay found that sense of wholeness very important to him, and without the surrender of his individuality. (p. 357)

Melvin B. Tolson provides us with this succinct evaluation of McKay's contribution to the development of black American poetry: "Thus, in that era of ethnic mutation, McKay's radicalism was in content—not form. . . . " Tolson refers, of course, to the fact that, excluding two volumes in Jamaican dialect, McKay's poetry was cast in traditional verse forms. The question then arises as to why a poet whose content of "despair, anger, alienation, and rebellion," according to Cooper, "marked a new important departure in American literature," would rest content with the conventional verse forms of a culture he considered racist.

For Tolson, it was quite enough for McKay to have pio-

neered in breaking the mold "of Dialect School and Booker T. Washington Compromise." For Giles, "The extreme traditionalism of his poetry" can be accounted for by "McKay's Jamaican education and reading," both being "based firmly upon the major British poets." These explanations have merit, but neither, I feel, does full justice to McKay as a poet nor brings us to a complete understanding of McKay's choice to use traditional verse forms. To achieve these goals, we must again recall Wayne Cooper's advice and view McKay's poetry "within the full context of his life and career."

As Giles indicates above, there was another world to which McKay was exposed as a boy besides that of rural Jamaica. "The direction of our schooling was, of course, English," McKay later wrote. "And it was so successful that we believed we were little black Britons." Through that schooling and in the library of his mentor, Mr. Walter Jekyll, McKay early became acquainted with the world of traditional English verse. Given his poetic calling and his urge to unity, it is hardly surprising he should seek his place in that world.

Although temporarily deflected by Walter Jekyll toward writing verse in Jamaican dialect, McKay's original poetic orientation was soon renewed by the following incident:

> I had read my dialect poems before many of these poetry societies before and the members used to say "Well, he's very nice and pretty, you know, but he's not a real poet as Browning and Byron and Tennyson are poets." I used to think I would show them something. Someday I would write poetry in straight English and amaze and confound them.

We have already seen how barriers to any world to which McKay felt he rightfully belonged would only increase his determination. Not surprisingly, then, he remained true to this adolescent vow.

Throughout his life, McKay continued to relate to basically this same poetic world. His adult views echoed his youthful position: " . . . it [black art] must be compared with the white man's achievement and judged by the same standards."

In McKay's chosen poetic universe, his "favorite mode of expression" was the sonnet. This predilection can be partly explained by the challenge inherent in a demanding verse form practiced by many of the greatest English poets. Mastering the sonnet would be irrefutable proof that he too was "a real poet." Still, I believe other equally important factors were involved. (pp. 357-59)

[McKay cited] the "discipline and tradition" of the Catholic Church as among its foremost attractions. In the poetic domain, the sonnet emphatically provides these same two qualities. Indeed, one may well wonder if any other verse form could have contained what McKay himself, in his poem **"O Word I Love to Sing,"** feared were "passions" too bitter for "words" and "melody" to convey. McKay might have realized that the strong sense of structure afforded by the demanding nature of the sonnet's metrical pattern and rhyme scheme would allow him to be his most passionate self without running amok.

McKay and Max Eastman in Moscow, 1922.

Also, Paul Fussell, Jr., has stated that "the poet who understands the sonnet form is the one who has developed an instinct for exploiting the principle of imbalance." McKay's most prevalent theme might be said to consist of the imbalance between the unity he craved and the alienation he so frequently experienced. In my opinion, McKay's sonnets often skillfully exploit this congruence between the sonnet form and his most typical theme.

Now "the principle of imbalance" in the sonnet depends, according to Fussell, upon "the convention of the turn." It is there "we are presented . . . with a logical or emotional shift by which the speaker enables himself to take a new or altered or enlarged view of his subject." The imbalance results because the turn traditionally occurs not at the middle of the fourteen lines, but rather at the start of the closing sestet in a Petrarchan sonnet or at the beginning of the final couplet in a Shakespearean sonnet. Sometimes, the influence of the earlier Petrarchan convention on the Shakespearean sonnet results in "a slight turn" at the beginning or within the final quatrain. In all instances, the normal pattern builds up pressure through the larger opening portion of the sonnet and then releases it one way or another over the remaining lines.

A particularly effective employment of the traditional turn takes place in McKay's best known sonnet, **"If We Must Die."**

> If we must die, let it not be like hogs
> Hunted and penned in an inglorious spot,
> While round us bark the mad and hungry dogs,
> Making their mock at our accursed lot.
> If we must die, O let us nobly die,
> So that our precious blood may not be shed
>   In vain; then even the monsters we defy
> Shall be constrained to honor us though dead!
> O kinsmen! we must meet the common foe!
> Though far outnumbered let us show us brave,
> And for their thousand blows deal one death-
>   blow!
> What though before us lies the open grave?
> Like men we'll face the murderous, cowardly
>   pack,
> Pressed to the wall, dying, but fighting back!

The form of **"If We Must Die"** is that of the Shakespearean sonnet with a Petrarchan-influenced slight turn at the beginning of line nine. The slight turn is signaled by the phrase "O kinsmen!" which shifts the exhortation onto a higher plane of unified and active resistance. The closing couplet, therefore, instead of bearing the entire responsibility of the sonnet's resolution, serves more as a "finishing kick" to the last six lines. The effect is further intensified by the variation in the iambic pattern which occurs in the last line: "/ dȳ iňg / bŭt / fīght / iňg bāck. /" The two adjacent unaccented syllables cause greater emphasis to fall on "fight."

All this added force may well be required to counter the back-to-the-wall pressure generated over the first eight lines. Certainly the principle of imbalance proves appropriate to the subject matter—a contest, unequal in numbers, but resolved through an assertion of unified, transcendent nobility by those outnumbered.

In **"If We Must Die"** the urge to wholeness achieves satisfaction through unification in a noble and transcendent defiance. In a later sonnet, **"The Pagan Isms,"** the movement is again toward wholeness, but this time toward the "perfect way of life" to be found in acceptance of "God's plan."

> Around me roar and crash the pagan isms
> To which most of my life was consecrate,
> Betrayed by evil men and torn by schisms
> For they were built on nothing more than hate!
> I cannot live my life without the faith
> Where new sensations like a fawn will leap,
> But old enthusiams like a wraith,
> Haunt me awake and haunt me when I sleep.
>
> And so to God I go to make my peace,
> Where black nor white can follow to betray.
> My pent-up heart to Him I will release
> And surely He will show the perfect way
> Of life. For He will lead me and no man
> Can violate or circumvent His plan.

Here again, we find the rhyme scheme of a Shakespearean sonnet, but the space between lines eight and nine plus the definite turn at the beginning of line nine suggest the Petrarchan sonnet form. This might strike some as a case of what Paul Fussell calls "structural schizophrenia." I, however, believe it to be an even stronger and more innovative utilization of the closing couplet as a final thrust toward unity than in **"If We Must Die."**

As noted, **"The Pagan Isms"** turns unequivocally with the "And" which introduces line nine after the break. Here the leap is made from a life consecrated to the pagan isms across the abyss to a life placed in God's hands.

The last two lines prove especially effective in reinforcing this theme. The thirteenth line seems abbreviated since the previous line has not been end-stopped and "intrudes" for a full foot ("Of life"). Then line thirteen itself is run-on into the last line. The net result is that the reader passes quickly over "man" and comes heavily to rest on the already doubly accented "His plan." The closing couplet's rhyming pair, "man" and "plan," are thus joined in a manner contrasting the weakness of the first with the strength of the second. This recapitulates and reinforces the movement toward wholeness, which constitutes the sonnet's theme.

Within this verse form's inherent discipline and tradition, McKay's sonnets sometimes take even greater liberties to communicate his very personal and often revolutionary themes. For instance, **"On the Road"** executes what might be termed a "double turn."

> Roar of the rushing train fearfully rocking,
> Impatient people jammed in line for food,
> The rasping noise of cars together knocking,
> And worried waiters, some in ugly mood,
> Crowding into the choking pantry hole
> To call out dishes for each angry glutton
> Exasperated grown beyond control,
> From waiting for his soup or fish or mutton.
> At last the station's reached, the engine stops;
> For bags and wraps the red-caps circle round;
> From off the step the passenger lightly hops,
> And seeks his cab or tram-car homeward bound;

The waiters pass out weary, listless, glum,
To spend their tips on harlots, cards and rum.

Through the opening eight lines, the irritation and frustration felt by the waiters builds as the train trip lengthens. Then, at the beginning of line nine, with the phrase "At last," the sonnet turns as the train arrives in the station, bringing release. But only for the passengers! In the closing couplet, the sonnet unexpectedly turns again and sends the waiters to a leisure as depressing and deadening as their work. Long and heavy vowel and consonant sounds accent this second turn, the effect culminating in the "um" rhyme of the closing couplet. The urge to wholeness makes its presence felt through being so unexpectedly denied both formally and thematically.

Still more daring and personal turns can be seen in the three sonnets **"Africa," "Outcast,"** and **"The Castaways."** In them, the turn moves from a state of actual or potential wholeness to one of decline or alienation. This reversal in pattern leaves the reader, along with the poetic voice, unfulfilled. The sonnet form in these works bends even more to the black experience. (pp. 359-63)

Claude McKay was much more of a conscious poetic craftsman than critics such as James Giles and especially David Littlejohn would lead one to believe. When Alain Locke changed the title of the sonnet, **"The White House,"** for inclusion in an anthology, McKay responded:

> If you understand how an artist feels about *the* word that he chooses above other words to use— if you know that artistic creation is the most delicate of all creative things—if you want to pit against how a craftsman, a goldsmith, an engraver, might feel about someone changing his design—then you'll understand how I feel about **"The White House."**

It is exactly this too frequently slighted craftsmanship that I have tried to illustrate in the above sonnets.

One may legitimately wish along with Giles that "McKay had attempted some of the innovations in black form and language that dominate Hughes's poetry and McKay's own fiction." Yet one may also feel Giles and others make the very mistake in evaluating McKay that Giles himself warns against—"to minimize what he did accomplish."

McKay's poetic achievement involved more than the radical content which even Giles acknowledges "represented a necessary and new direction for Afro-American poetry." McKay also handled the traditional sonnet form in an innovative, effective manner. His variations ranged, as we have seen, from subtle to bold, and all were responsive to his urge toward wholeness and the black experience as he knew it. Surely, then, Littlejohn is not correct when he criticizes McKay because "there is nothing new or experimental about his efforts."

McKay's greatest contribution to Afro-American verse, however, was his example of universalism and personal integrity. He realized that, as Melvin Tolson states in *Harlem Gallery,*

> . . . the Color line, as well as the Party line,
> splits an artist's identity.

McKay's urge to wholeness could not tolerate such a split. As a result, we are forced to see his career and his poetry as a unique whole if we would understand them. (pp. 363-64)

> *John Hillyer Condit, "An Urge Toward Wholeness: Claude McKay and his Sonnets," in CLA Journal, Vol. XXII, No. 4, June, 1979, pp. 350-64.*

William H. Hansell   (essay date 1979)

[*In the following excerpt, Hansell appraises several poems contained in McKay's early verse collections* Songs of Jamaica *and* Constab Ballads, *discerning four thematic categories which would become subject matter in his later works.*]

The early volumes, *Songs of Jamaica* and *Constab Ballads,* are important for the insight they give into formative influences on McKay and as an introduction to nearly all the themes which would constitute his major concerns thereafter. Often sentimental, for the most part the poems are genre studies of peasant life, both rural and urban. Twenty years after leaving Jamaica McKay wrote what he felt he had accomplished: "I . . . captured the spirit of the Jamaica peasant in verse, reproducing their primitive joys, their loves and hates, their work and play, their dialect." (p. 123)

Both *Songs of Jamaica* and *Constab Ballads* reveal the young poet, still not twenty, writing in various conventional lyric forms. Walter Jekyll, a white Jamaican who made a sort of protegé of McKay and wrote an introduction for *Songs of Jamaica,* commented that the dialect of black Jamaicans had been accruately reproduced by McKay. The poems can be fitted into four categories: poems on commonplace settings and activities, love poems, poems portraying the peasant mind, and poems with racial or social themes.

Poems in the first category attempt to convey responses to commonplace things or to capture commonplace occurrences. All of them are in dialect. . . . There is no hint of protest in these poems, even though the poems on the police barracks and on the virtues of "ol' time cultivation" provided convenient opportunities.

The love poems briefly to be considered here, like nearly all his love poems of this period, are also in dialect and are free of any criticism of race or society. Except for the dialect and the setting they could concern lovers anywhere. The narrator in **"To Bennie,"** absent for some time, must send back reassurances of his undying love. In **"My Pretty Dan,"** a woman declares her love for the

> Prettiest of naygur . . . my dear police,
> We'll lub forever, an' our lub won't cease.
>
> (pp. 123-24)

Difficulties in love are the same as those written of anywhere. **"Taken Aback"** records a girl's anger when a lover behaves irresponsibly; another poem laments a lover's departure (**"Lub O' Mine"**); and **"Heartless Rhoda"** presents a girl who sneers at her lover's insistence that love can be permanent, when her own inclinations suggest to her that a capricious "Fate," inscrutable and inconstant, rules all things. For her, or him, to talk of forever is a mockery.

Somewhat less conventional than the love poems and a great deal more interesting insofar as they provide insights into the attitudes of Negro Jamaicans, are those poems which portray the peasant mind. Over twenty years after leaving Jamaica, McKay himself made an interesting comment on his break from "peasant patterns" of thought and behavior:

> It was not until I was forced down among the rough body of the great serving class of Negroes that I got to know my Aframerica. . . . their spontaneous ways of acting on and living for the moment, the physical and sensuous delights, the loose freedom in contrast to the definite peasant pattern by which I had been raised . . . cut me finally adrift from the fixed moorings my mind had been led to respect, but to which my heart had never held.

McKay, then, clearly believed his own break from the "peasant pattern" came after his arrival in Harlem, where he sought to commit himself to "the loose freedom" of Afro-Americans. (pp. 124-25)

The poems grouped here under the category of the peasant mind shed some light on the nature of the "fixed moorings." They reveal quite definitely the peasant's sense of living best when closest to home and to nature. A homesick man, for example, regrets that he has nothing to guide or please him while absent and can take cheer only from the thought of eventually returning (**"To Clarendon Hills and H.A.H."**). **"Mother Dear"** portrays a woman of dignity and courage dying. Although she is urged to listen to the parson at her side, it is the natural, commonplace sounds and activities which hold her attention. Those who have left home, though not the island of Jamaica, and live "among strange folks in a strange lan'," as in **"My Mountain Home,"** exemplify the effects of estrangement. The narrator laments the loss of simple pleasures and the seeming inappropriateness of native values in the new environment. The poem concludes with a vow to return home; and perhaps the "relief" the narrator finally achieves, which is not otherwise explained, is simply his sense that the separation will not be permanent. What he will return to are simple joys, freedom, and trust in life. Similarly, other poems present individuals who have left rural areas for the cities, bewailing the loss of suitable guides to conduct. (p. 125)

These individuals getting their first experience of town life lament the feeling, however brief, that their native values have no application in the new place. They begin to "distrust" their beliefs the more they experience the shallow and frivolous world they discover away from home. On the other hand, the return home is enough to revive their faith, as, for example, in **"The Hermit."** Several other poems illustrate that the travellers are restored to their native values by returning to the place of their birth. The escape from the preoccupations of the town, from "life's pleasures an' de greed of pelf," finds them once again responding to the earlier influences. Thus, **"The Hermit"**

portrays a man restored to his native values by the simple process of returning to a familiar milieu. The expatriate, then, seems to mourn constantly for the home he left behind. He dreams of it and of the values which are closest to his heart, values that in the new place are almost lost. Momentary relief is found in dreams or visions of returning home; but the actual return apparently allows the wanderer to resume his former ways. In poems McKay wrote after leaving Jamaica, this sense of the restorative powers of the image or vision of his native home as a source of solace and inspiration became increasingly important; for in many of the later poems the imagined return has almost the same emotionally restorative effects as in these early poems.

McKay portrays a great many specific aspects of the life in Jamaica as he knew it, the "peasant pattern," which was the source and preserver of the native values. **"Dat Dirty Rum"** brings out a puritan strain in peasant attitudes which McKay seems to approve. Rum, the poem says, ruins boys for anything they might dream of doing. There is no qualification, and all the blame falls on the drinker. Continuing in this vein, **"Out of Debt"** celebrates frugality and self-restraint. It depicts a family sacrificing presents and treats at Christmas in order to escape the burden of debt their imprudent neighbors fall into. These virtues of temperance, frugality, self-restraint, industry, and economy are the ones McKay evidently believed were natural to Jamaican peasants. However, once the break with their rural patterns had been made, the peasants, as McKay depicts them in **Constab Ballads,** seem to have quickly succumbed to the dissipation and vice prevalent in the new urban milieu. For most of them the only way virtue and wholesomeness could be restored was by returning to their homes.

A particular brand of "resignation" is also characteristic of the peasant life McKay portrays. There is an essential determinism in the peasant's acceptance of whatever circumstances confront him. In a half-humorous, half-pathetic poem recounting a boy's response to a severely injured toe, which will prevent him from participating in common games and pastimes and from doing his usual work, we see the boy solace himself with the thought that he at least did not lose the entire toe (**"Little Jim"**). (pp. 126-27)

A poem, **"Whe' Fe Do?"** (roughly, "What Should One Do?") is one of McKay's longest attempts to dramatize the nature of the peasant's world. The narrator complains that the world is full of pains, backbreaking work, little pleasure, and much disappointment, especially the black man's world; nevertheless, he seems to see justice, or some meaning in all this. Urging his listener to make the best of it, he concedes that to advance in life, one must suffer, work, and hope to improve the race—even if no good comes of it. That this desperate condition should be endured with slight hope of change and song on the lips, tells us something of the nature of those songs:

> And though de wul' is full o' wrong,
> Dat caan' prevent we sing we song
> All de day as we wuk along—
>   Whe' else fe do?

The last three stanzas of **"Whe' Fe Do?"** demonstrate quite clearly the ambivalences in the peasant's view of life. Drawn into sharp contrast are the beliefs in hard work and progress as opposed to the deterministic sense that all the effort may be for nothing. Several of McKay's poems depicting peasant life elaborate further on the view that life is a painful burden, full of "swap an' bite, an' haul an' pull. . . ." (p. 127)

"Heart Stirrings" suggests that at least there is an element of choice, of freedom, in deciding one's worldly fate. In a monologue addressed to a boy, the narrator tells him of the harshness of life. He is told that since appearances are not trustworthy he must be very careful of whom he selects as models. To choose wrongly leads surely to grief. Good examples, however, are hard to find because life is mysterious; people who seem happy—two white people are cited—often are not. The child is reminded of a seemingly prosperous man whom debt drove to sudden suicide and of a distinguished woman who in fact pines constantly for a lover she will never have. The narrator himself has chosen unwisely and is constantly tormented, yet has no real advice to give. All the child has been told is that appearances often deceive and that he should resign himself to whatever comes. Here, again, McKay emphasizes the uncertainty which pervades peasant life. One's most carefully thought out decisions, and one's best intentions, may result in wrong or inadequate actions. **"To E. M. E."** is probably even more pessimistic. The narrator expresses astonishment that anyone can take pleasure from life or think that the narrator does. All his seeming joy is grief, nothing gives pleasure, not song or dance, eating or sleeping. Death is the only escape.

Many of McKay's early poems are written in the first person, and several of these poems treat of a poet's experiences. In most of them it is not demonstrable that McKay is portraying himself; yet in **"Kite Flying"** there seems to be good reason for arguing that McKay's personal attitudes are being expressed. The poem offers an escape from worldly problems, but does not seem to reveal, if it was ever intended to, an imaginative resource of Jamaican peasants in general. The experience seems too special to be commonplace. Unlike nearly all the other poems, McKay uses only a little dialect, and there seems to be no reason for it where he does use it. The poet is speaking here it seems as a poet. The kite, at first realistically presented, becomes a symbol of the narrator's aspirations, of his desire to escape a disillusioning world:

> Just to soar away like you,
>   Rising to a happier sphere
> Deep within yon skies of blue,
>   Far from all de strife an' care.
> . . .
> Higher fly, my pretty kite,
>   Higher, ever higher;
> Draw me with you to your height
>   Out the earthly mire.

Poems with racial or social themes form a category used for the purpose of bringing together other poems which come closest to specific protest and poems which suggest McKay's early racial or social attitudes. **"My Soldier Lad,"** for example, relates a black girl's love for a white soldier-musician; and it tells of her particular pleasure in the envy all the other girls feel. The girl is not in any way attacked in the poem for believing a white lover makes the other girls envious; neither is it hinted that the poet feels she is right to believe she possesses something all black Jamaicans desire: a white partner. Perhaps McKay wanted primarily to portray these lovers simply as evidence that such interracial love occurred. Perhaps too he thought there should be more such relationships; but there is no evidence in this poem to demonstrate that he was critical of the girl, the soldier, or the conditions that brought them together. (pp. 127-29)

Racial relations, however, often created problems McKay dealt with in various ways. **"Quashie to Buccra"** (*buccra* means white man) is a monologue in which a field hand good-humoredly undertakes to explain to a white man that life on a farm is no bed of roses and that a great amount of labor is necessary to make the fields yield abundantly. In another poem, **"Fetchin' Water,"** whites touring the countryside are described as being very pleased at the grace and strength of the girls balancing water jars on their heads, but they fail utterly to appreciate the gruelling labor. The problem black Jamaicans have conforming to English ways is partially shown in **"Jim at Sixteen."** The boy in the poem had fallen into bad ways because he resisted standing "under no rule" (under any rule); so now he is in jail. The boy is repentant because he had publicly disgraced his family, not because he broke English laws. He vows to return to proper native behavior. . . .

McKay does not call much attention, on the whole, to the conflict between native and colonial values. In *Songs of Jamaica* there is not a single poem in which someone is punished for adhering to native or peasant customs in violation of civil law. There are, on the other hand, poems which criticize the harshness of punishments administered under the law; and there are poems criticizing the rigidity of some laws. The right of the government to punish and to restrict, however, is never questioned by McKay in these early works. (p. 129)

A somewhat more definite criticism of white-black relations is made in **"Pleading,"** essentially a love poem. A man asking his girl to return to him states that the "Squire's" son's interest in her is simply a "whim." The man implies the white planter's son could not possibly have serious intentions; yet his attack on the squire's son seems to serve more as an instance of the extremes to which frustrated lovers will go than as a comment on the sexual exploitation of Jamaican peasants by white overseers. The bereft lover is portrayed as bitter, angry, revengeful, willing, in short, to use any means to regain her love. **"De Dog Rose"** similarly portrays a black girl who sheds a lover of her own race and settles down in the "great-house," *i.e.,* the plantation house, with a white man. The poem's chief concern is not race but ideas about the duration of love. The girl comments contemptuously on her former lover's belief in love's permanence, renounces all her pledges to him, and is last described settled in the plantation house with "her baby son." If measured from a romantic perspective, her new ideas about love are cynical. McKay could of course be suggesting that in breaking with her social background she has had to abandon its values as well, though such an interpretation is not at all demanded by the terms of the poem.

Two poems are even less equivocal in criticizing whites, who in "A Country Girl" are shown as presenting a bad example, and in "A Midnight Woman to the Bobby" as treacherous and unreliable. The "country girl" has fled to the city and taken up evil ways; she is probably a prostitute. Though homesick and saddened by her fall from virtue, she cannot leave the city, despite its admittedly evil atmosphere; for it also provides variety, excitement, and a kind of anonymity. When her lover says he will forgive her "sin," she becomes defensive at first, then positively snobbish:

> . . . after all, many girls richer than me,
> Pretty white girlies of better degree,
> Live as I do, an' are happy an' gay
> Then why should not I be as happy as they?

In the second poem, a vice-hardened woman being arrested by a bobby insults and badgers him, calls him a hillbilly and mocks his official status. He may be working for the white man now, she says, but soon enough they'll get rid of him just as they have so many others. Whites, colonizers, confer the mere resemblance of power and authority; whites are treacherous. The themes are very militant and constitute McKay's recognition that some black Jamaicans distrusted whites and were contemptuous of blacks who served them. Having been a policeman, McKay could have had first-hand experience of such hostility. Nonetheless, it is doubtful that he was using the woman as a spokesman for his own attitudes, or even to represent those of the majority of black Jamaicans. The woman is portrayed as vindictive and immoral, furious at being arrested by someone she feels superior to. Her attack on white authority is mild when compared to the abuse she heaps on the policeman's rural background, which as McKay portrays it, has been only superficially influenced by white men.

Far more numerous than the above derogatory poems are poems portraying the positive gain resulting from the peasant's association with whites. "Cudjoe Fresh from de Lecture" is a monologue in which a Jamaican semi-literate recounts the essential points of a white man's lecture on science, particularly on evolution and its religious significance. The narrator is very pleased to learn that all men evolved from monkeys, for clearly, then, he feels, there is some kind of equality among men. This doctrine confirms his belief that black Jamaicans, although they do not share the wealth and powers of whites, are essentially equal as human beings. Black skin, as the lecturer stated, was not a sign of natural inferiority. The narrator also reports with some pleasure that the theory of evolution provides a more satisfactory explanation of the origins of mankind than does the parson's talk about man's creation out of a handful of clay. Finally, the narrator no longer feels burdened by the problem of understanding how life could be so full of pain and sorrow and death if the universe were actually the creation of a good and loving God.

Although the lecturer said that men exist by accident of birth, and that worldly conditions remain essentially un-

changed—things will never get any better—the narrator still brings away a certain optimistic sense that the material conditions of life have been improved. "Cudjoe Fresh from de Lecture" also portrays the black Jamaican's willingness to accept rational and scientific interpretations of the universe. Implicity criticizing social and political inequalities, it nonetheless emphasizes that assimilation into Western society, even though still on a very limited basis, in many respects has been a positive gain for blacks. McKay himself, much later in his career, after he had repeatedly attacked racial conditions in America, nonetheless was an outspoken critic of Marcus Garvey's back-to-Africa movement. Afro-Americans, McKay insisted, were more Western than African, and what they needed was someone to unite them here, and lead them here—or wherever they were—to unity, freedom, and equality.

These early poems on white-black relations indicate that McKay was aware of problems between the races; but his belief that the race was fortunate to have been brought to Jamaica makes it plain that for him the good outweighed the evil. Misunderstandings between the races there were, but he also clearly believed interracial understanding and love were possible.

The last small group of poems from *Songs of Jamaica* brings together poems which overtly deal with Jamaica and England. "My Native Land, My Home," for example, is conventional and uninspired in its patriotic sentiments; but it is atypical in its anti-British sentiments. The narrator of the poem evidently is a peasant, markedly nationalistic and anticolonial. His nativism is openly expressed in his declaration that Jamaica truly belongs to the black inhabitants:

> Jamaica is de nigger's place,
> No mind whe' declare. . . .

(Again, of course, this use of an epithet ordinarily regarded as derogatory raises questions as to McKay's intentions. As in other poems, it seems to be used here without ironic or derogatory connotations.) The narrator next states his belief, or "hope," that all of Jamaica's sons love their country enough to make whatever sacrifices might be necessary in its defense. Following this, Jamaica's abundant natural wealth and generosity to immigrants are praised.

"My Native Land, My Home" contains overt criticism of the imposition by whites of a government whose policies almost cancel Jamaica's seemingly limitless potential for happiness. How much this reflects McKay's view is difficult to assess. He was a policeman. He did declare that African blacks benefitted by being brought to technologically advanced countries. His intention in expressing such criticism, then, may have been simply to record the opinion of those black peasants who believed they had not benefitted from the opportunities provided by Western culture, or who as yet failed to understand and take advantage of that culture. Both intentions would fit McKay's larger ambition, his desire to portray the whole range of Jamaican life as he knew it. (pp. 130-32)

McKay's autobiography, *A Long Way From Home,* clearly reveals that his ideas and feelings concerning England underwent considerable modification after he had lived there briefly. He came to believe that racism was built into the English social system and he was very depressed by the scars industrialization inflicted on the landscape. In his autobiography, McKay explains that his intense admiration for England ended, at least in part, because of what he saw there on his first visit. In London he "felt entirely out of sympathy with the environment" and with ' "chimney factories pouring smoke" '—a quotation from one of his own early poems. But before travelling to England, the young McKay praised "Old England" almost without qualification.

Much of his praise in the poem **"Old England"** specifically refers to familiar tourist landmarks: St. Paul's Cathedral, Westminster Abbey, and Queen Victoria's tomb. Milton, Shakespeare, Wordsworth, and Gray are the four poets, "great souls," whose graves he designates as those he would especially like to visit. One cannot tell from this poem what significance any one, or all, of these poets had for McKay, apart, that is, from their prominence among English poets. There is an allusion in the poem to the "ancient" chair of England's kings which is not quite as vague with respect to the personal significance it had for McKay. He is mildly censorious of the older, absolute monarchy and describes it as a "vanity." The poem then states a definite preference for the constitutional monarchy represented by Queen Victoria. (p. 133)

Between *Songs of Jamaica* and *Constab Ballads* there are several obvious similarities. With the exception of a few poems, both are written in dialect, both deal primarily with lower-class individuals, and both express the same attitudes towards life. Poems in *Constab Ballads,* of which at least two appeared in *Songs of Jamaica,* tend to be longer than those in the earlier collection. One narrator who appears frequently in the *Ballads* speaks for McKay himself. Like McKay, he is a rural boy who has come to the city as a constable; but the surest evidence that McKay's own attitudes are being stated in the poems comes from his preface to the book. In it, McKay comments upon his experience as a constable, candidly declares his belief that he (along with other "blacks") was "somewhat impatient of discipline," and reveals that his personal inclination "to make peace" between criminals and victims was often stronger than his duty to strictly enforce the law. Although he believed some reforms among the "sub-officers" was needed, McKay states that on the whole the policeman's life is "admirable."

The major difference between the two books is revealed through the change in setting. The *Constab Ballads* are "town" poems. Most of them are set in a town or city, perhaps Kingston, and nearly all present narrators who came from back country or agricultural regions. Formally, there is no clear-cut advance either in stylistic or imaginative qualities, though the poems are somewhat more varied than those in the first collection.

Two poems establish that the basic attitudes towards life expressed in *Songs of Jamaica* are also expressed in *Constab Ballads.* **"Bennie's Departure,"** essentially a lament for a friend who has resigned from the constabulary, reiterates an idea found in several poems in *Songs of Jamaica.*

Life is described as generally lacking in pleasure, and those joys which are available usually survive only a short time. The chief consolations, this poem states, are friendship and love. This inconstancy in men and nature is concisely expressed in another poem, **"Consolation,"** in which men seem the playthings of cruel gods. (pp. 134-35)

On the positive side, McKay wrote favorably of the drill and comradeship (**"De Route March"**), of the admiration of women and the excitement of a day on the rifle range (**"Fire Practice"**), of the security and monetary rewards (**"Fe Me Sal"**), and even of the "grand" funeral given a recruit who died (**"Second-Class Constable Alston"**). Considering the number of poems in which McKay celebrates the pleasures of comradeship, they would appear for him the most attractive feature of a "bobby's" life. . . .

In **"Flat-Foot Drill,"** McKay focuses on the more rugged and demanding aspects of the semi-military life, by showing the harassment recruits are subjected to by drill instructors. In the preface to the collection, he ambivalently describes his overall response to that life. On the one hand, he states that it was "admirable" or could have been, if not for the behavior and attitudes of the lower ranking officers.

> As constituted by the authorities the Force is admirable, and it only remains for the men themselves, and especially the sub-officers, to make it what it should be, a harmonious band of brothers.

On the other hand, elsewhere in the preface, McKay states that his own temperament, and perhaps that of all black Jamaicans, is unsuited to the discipline required. Moreover, his own temperament, as he says, made the life less suited to him than to others of his race.

> I am, by temperament, unadaptive; by which I mean that it is not in me to conform cheerfully to uncongenial usages. We blacks are all somewhat impatient of discipline, and to the natural impatience of my race there was added, in my particular case, a peculiar sensitiveness which made certain forms of discipline irksome, and a fierce hatred of injustice. Not that I ever openly rebelled; but the rebellion was in my heart. . . .
>
> (p. 135)

Notwithstanding his frequent portrayal of the desirable aspects of life as a bobby, McKay's feelings about the disadvantages of life on the force at times became so intensely negative that he could portray it as a life of "unmixed pain" (**"Comrades Four"**) and upon his release from the force he wrote a poem the title of which, **"Free,"** all but tells the story of his great relief and joy to be able to return home to his "loved Clarendon hills."

As McKay saw it, in important ways the life of a bobby was painfully complicated. It was often necessary to mistreat and thus to become one of the enemies of the very people he had hoped to serve. **"The Heart of a Constab"** expresses the dilemma:

> 'Tis grievous to think dat, while toilin' on here,
>   My people won't love me again,

My people, my people, me owna black skin,—
De wretched t'ought gives me such pain.

The poem includes a pledge to leave the service and rejoin his people.

As **"The Heart of a Constab"** reveals, McKay evidently was more concerned with racial conflicts in the *Constab Ballads* than in *Songs of Jamaica;* and in two poems racial conflict is a major element. **"Me Whoppin' Big-Tree Boy"** concerns a boy who cuts and sells wood, and who rebels at the unfair and overbearing attitude of his Syrian boss. The narrator in the poem is almost beside himself with joy on seeing the young man's rebellion. Another Syrian, in **"Pay-Day,"** is sarcastically described as among the most persistent of those who prey on the recently paid bobbies. It is interesting to note that McKay's harshest criticism in the early works is aimed at Syrians rather than at the British. Whether he believed the Syrians more guilty of racial and economic exploitation of black Jamaicans than the British, however, cannot be determined from these early books.

McKay depicts the difficulties created for a policeman who would rather make peace than strictly enforce the law in **"The Bobby to the Sneering Lady."** An officer, the narrator of the poem, asks a white woman not to report him for his refusal to arrest a servant girl. The weeping girl has already been whipped, which is punishment enough, the bobby insists, for her crime. "The sneering lady" accuses him of being just another corrupt officer, siding with the criminal rather than the victim. This conflict will not reduce to simple racial confrontation, for the bobby wants to be a good officer and wants to be respected; moreover, the woman's distrust and contempt for policemen is not restricted to black officers.

Actually, the bulk of the criticism of the force in *Constab Ballads* is directed at the conduct and practices themselves. **"The Malingerer"** laments the extra labor and expense thrown onto the shoulders of the responsible officers by shiftless comrades. In a vein which McKay would develop more fully in poems written years after he had left Jamaica, **"Bumming"** denounces some bobbies for soliciting drinks from intimidated civilians and contemptuous tourists. McKay expresses sympathy for the fact that bobbies are paid so little; but he insists that whatever the excuses or reasons, personal pride should prevent them from degrading themselves. The following excerpt contains what is possibly McKay's harshest and most direct criticism of white superior officers:

Our trouble is dat those above
Do oftentimes oppress;
But we'll laugh at or pity dem,
Or hate dem mo' or less.

It is at least possible, of course, that the reference to "those above" is not to white superiors—the highest ranking officers—but to black non-commissioned officers. A non-commissioned officer in **"A Recruit on the Corpy,"** for example, fails to perform his own duties and commits certain immoral acts. If his subordinates refuse to turn over the money he needs for alcohol, he submits false charges against them. No other poem, however, captures the crim-

inal milieu of the bobby better than **"Pay-Day."** As the bobbies receive their pay, a crowd of loan sharks, prostitutes, other creditors, and people who feel one or another bobby has cheated them crowd around. The few bobbies who manage to keep some money from this mob seem to spend what remains on rum. (pp. 136-37)

Implicit in all the criticism of the bobby's life is a criticism of town life itself, because each time an alternative or escape is suggested it is always in the form of a return to rural Jamaica. (p. 137)

The celebrations of country life in *Constab Ballads* mark a sharp contrast to all but a few of the most enthusiastic poems on a bobby's life and duties. Life in the hills or on farms in the small backwoods settlements is portrayed as immensely better, being replete with various pleasures, but it is not a paradise; McKay had to age a few more years and travel thousands of miles before the truly idealized portraits of Jamaica begin to emerge.

A boy dying away from home is portrayed, in **"Last Words of the Dying Recruit,"** as vividly recalling favorite plants and flowers, and imagining that his dead mother has come to ease his suffering. The memory of rural life solaces, and it revives a condition in which envy and strife between men is rarely seen and in which life itself is freer and more beautiful. That is part of the picture painted in **"To W. G. G."** Another equally important aspect of the life presented in **"To W. G. G."** is that man is subject to capricious powers beyond his control. Although even this country life is not perfect, it is the best that man can achieve. (p. 138)

What value is there in examining McKay's early dialect verse? The verse itself is almost doggerel; the love poems are at best merely conventional in expressing the pleasures and pains of lovers. Most of his other poems are simple portraits of a land and people dear to the author. The tropical settings and the peasant attitudes were satisfying to him in nearly every way, and he admired the peasants' stoic acceptance, their capacity for discovering redeeming aspects in all situations. He could also praise (as in **"Cudjoe Fresh from de Lecture"**) their slow absorption of more "advanced" ideas. Science and technology were very new to them; yet they could envision promises of improved conditions and to some extent accept explanations of the universe, the origins of life, and the nature of man which did not conform to the teachings of religion. The real value, however, of the early poems is that they clearly show that McKay did not learn protest by being the victim of American racism. Before he had come to the United States he had protested against injustice, the cruelty of man, the misunderstandings that ignorance could engender, and the evils of deprivation. For the general disharmonies, he blamed fate; for specific evils, he put the primary responsibility on individuals. (p. 138-39)

William H. Hansell, "Some Themes in the Jamaican Poetry of Claude McKay," in PHYLON: The Atlanta University Review of Race and Culture, *Vol. XL, No. 2, June, 1979, pp. 123-39.*

Geta J. LeSeur   (essay date 1989)

[In the following excerpt, LeSeur discusses McKay's romanticism.]

When McKay says [in his autobiography *A Long Way from Home*] that he used [Robert] Burns as a model, he is also suggesting a silent rebellion on the part of a West Indian youth. When he wrote poetry in the Jamaican Scottish dialect, he used Burns' Scottish dialect as a model. His first poems published in the dialect were **Songs of Jamaica** (1912) and **Constab Ballads** (1912). This was only the beginning of the sturdy independence and faithful affection he was to exercise throughout his life and writing career.

Allegiances and coalitions were goals visualized by Claude McKay. They are present in his autobiography, as a specific statement of purpose, and in his verse. Although a radical, he was a conservative poet, for his verse forms were traditional. The sonnet was his favorite, and he actually wrote most of his poems on the time-honored subjects of love and nature. Regardless of the fact that the writing tradition adopted by McKay was that of the romantic "movement" from his school days in Jamaica, it was not until he came to the United States in 1912 at age twenty-three that his best poetry-writing began. Max Eastman, his lifelong friend and editor of the *Liberator,* which he coedited, later said this of him:

> It was not until he came to the United States that Claude McKay began to confront the deepest feelings in his heart and realize that a delicate syllabic music could not alone express them. Here his imagination awoke, and the colored imagery that is the language of all deep passion began to appear in his poetry.
>
> (p. 297)

McKay has said that, of the English models and schools of writing he has been associated with, it is the classicists and romantics that he admires, but he owes "allegiance to no master." He adds that he has used only that which he considered to be the best of the poets of all ages. The language used in his poetry was that derived from the Jamaican dialect, archaic words, and figures of speech, which are then reshaped to suit his specific purposes. The introductory pages ("Author's Word") to **Harlem Shadows** has been cited repeatedly by scholars, critics, and McKay's readers to justify or support theories regarding his poetry. The important information given in that short essay is that McKay thinks the traditional should work best on "lawless and revolutionary passions and words, "so as to give the feeling of the "highest degree of spontaneity and freedom." "For me," he says, "there is more quiet delight in 'The golden moon of heaven' than in 'The terra-cotta disc of cloud land.' " The last quoted line here is ironically from a poem by one of the best-known Harlem Renaissance poets, Langston Hughes.

It is no accident that Claude McKay felt uncomfortable with the poetry and lifestyle of the New Negro Movement of the 1920s. He was never really a part of that whole milieu. He disagreed with their involvement with "art for art's sake" and with their being self-appointed messiahs to uplift the privileged few. Theirs was a tightly knit circle which excluded many. Because McKay's tendencies were

more akin to the European tradition and experience, he was a misfit at a time when blackness was being celebrated. First, McKay's reading was Byron, Shelley, Keats, and the late Victorians. Secondly, his friends, personal and literary, were the whites in New York's suburbs and its downtown Greenwich Village. Thirdly, he was older than most of the Renaissance writers—Hughes, [Countee] Cullen, [Jean] Toomer, and others. And fourthly, he lived in Europe during most of the key Renaissance years. Consequently, for these reasons and more, he was, as Frank Harris of *Pearson's Magazine* noted, "an oddity, . . . a noble black poet with romantic intentions."

McKay felt a great tension between black content and traditional white form, and this, for him, was perhaps the hardest problem to solve. He grappled with the two as to where the thrust of his writing should be. He had been praised for producing poems which gave no hint of color. . . . The problem became a personal one of how to keep his allegiance to the British models—whose poetry he truly felt and knew well—and be a black poet emotionally. Writing poetry was not difficult for him, but what was difficult was the personae in conflict, the paradox of self which mars some of the poems.

Consequently, while McKay constantly preferred to keep the West Indian identity and the British training, he was conscious that nothing could change the fact that he was a writer who also happened to be a Negro. When told to mask his identity, and when in his novel *Banana Bottom* (1933) certain words were changed into "Britishisms," he became extremely angry and replied to his publishers and friends in this way:

> Of all the poets I admire, major and minor, Byron, Shelley, Keats, Blake, Burns, Whitman, Heine, Baudelaire, Verlaire and Rimbaud and the rest—it seemed to me that when I read them—in their poetry I could feel their race, their class, their roots in the soil, growing into plants, spreading and forming the background against which they were silhouetted. I could not feel the reality of them without that. So likewise I could not realize myself writing without that conviction.

Again, the problem of allegiance and coalition were sur-

The outskirts of Sunny Ville, Jamaica, McKay's birthplace.

faced to deal with these constant attempts to subjugate color to content. The natural and the creative became problematic also. McKay, regardless of all the places to which he traveled, realized that the artist's faith had to be in his origins, a patriotism as one might find in Whitman's America and in Yeats' Ireland. Furthermore, McKay's best poetry and prose were about Jamaica; as for him, the artist being inseparable from his roots would be an alien thought. (pp. 298-300)

The poetry looks romantically to Jamaica and prophetically to blackness. His prophecy for Jamaica as an independent, Third World nation, for example, was fulfilled in the last two decades. *Spring in New Hampshire* (1920) and *Selected Poems* (1953) have in them mostly nostalgic lyrics about Jamaica and songs celebrating nature, and they reflect those themes found in the nineteenth-century Romantics.

McKay's romanticism exhibits itself in several ways but primarily in his writing and lifestyle. His literary heroes were writers of conventional works, the sonnet his favorite mode of expression, but some of his poems are done in freer style. An example of the combination of Jamaican remembrance and celebration of nature in the less conventional style is **"Flame-Heart."**

> So much I have forgotten in ten years,
> So much in ten brief years! I have forgot
> What time the purple apples come to juice,
> And what month brings the shy forget-me-not.
> I have forgot the special, startling season
> Of the pimento's flowering and fruiting;
> What time of year the ground doves drown the fields
> And fill the noonday with their curious fluting.
> I have forgotten much, but still remember
> The poinsetta's red, blood-red, in warm December.

(pp. 300-01)

In **"The Spanish Needle"** McKay uses a more conventional pattern to write about a very common and wild weed in Jamaica by the same name. It is a plant much like a dandelion in America, but the language and tone which he uses in the poem make the Spanish needle become a regal plant; thus the common and everyday in the hands of a romantic like McKay becomes uncommon. The following verses of that poem show the endearment which he feels for the ordinary:

> Lovely dainty Spanish needle
> With your yellow flower and white,
> Dew bedecked and softly sweeping,
> Do you think of me to-night?
>
> Shadowed by the spreading mango,
> Nodding o'er the rippling stream,
> Tell me, dear plant of my childhood,
> Do you of the exile dream?
>
> Do you see me by the brook's side
> Catching crayfish 'neath the stone,
> As you did the day you whispered:
> Leave the harmless dears alone? . . .

This poem is very much in the romantic tradition of Shelley and Keats and is probably one of the few poems by McKay that every Jamaican schoolchild must recite "by heart." **"Home-Thoughts"** is one of his better poems with the homeland theme:

> Oh something just now must be happening there!
> That suddenly and quiveringly here,
> Amid the city's noises, I must think
> Of mangoes leaning o'er the river's brink,
> And dexterous Davie climbing high above,
> The gold fruits ebon-speckled to remove,
> And toss them quickly in the tangled mass.
> Of wis-wis twisted round the guinea grass;
> And Cyril coming through the bramble-track
> A Prize bunch of bananas on his back;
> ....
> This is no daytime dream, there's something in it,
> Oh something's happening there this very minute!

The use of local words like *mango, wis-wis, guinea grass, bramble track, purple apple, ground dove, pimento, ping-wing, rose apple, poinsetta,* and *banana* in **"Flame-Heart,"** **"The Spanish Needle,"** and **"Home-Thoughts"** are entire images in themselves, and even without notes to explain their meanings and connotations, the mood, tone and theme of the poems are obvious. These poems all go back to the West Indian scene, and in them are found the similar conflicts and opposing attractions which plagued McKay throughout his lifetime. In them, also, joy and sorrow are accepted with the stoic indifference which was part of the romantic passion.

"The Snow Fairy," **"Spring in New Hampshire,"** and **"After the Winter"** use the same American seasonal landscape as their background. They too are good, have a simplicity of diction and tone, and are full of longing and passion, but they by no means compare with the lilting, spontaneous yet deep emotion of **"Tropics in New York."** In comparing a few lines from **"Spring in New Hampshire"** with **"The Tropics in New York,"** one can see that the differences are very obvious, not only because of the subject, but because of McKay's involvement with the places closest to his heart:

> Too green the springing April grass,
> Too blue the silver-speckled sky,
> For me to linger here, alas,
> While happy winds go laughing by,
> Wasting the golden hours indoors,
> Washing windows and scrubbing floors.

The weariness and tedium of scrubbing floors in spring is felt, while outdoors the enjoyment of nature passes. Rather than being happy in nature, there is sorrow because the speaker is physically removed from it but is mentally aware of its presence. He is a prisoner of circumstance. **"The Tropics in New York"** finds the speaker a prisoner also in a foreign country, but the nostalgia, though sorrowful, is much more lyrical, and he seems closer to this subject, and the poem is richer:

> Bananas ripe and green, and ginger-root,
> Cocoa in pods and alligator pears,
> And tangerines and Mangoes and grape fruit,
> Fit for the highest prize at parish fairs,

Set in the window, bringing memories
Of fruit-trees laden by low-singing rills,
And dewy dawns, and mystical blue skies
In benediction over nun-like hills.

My eyes grew dim, and I could no more gaze;
A wave of longing through my body swept,
And, hungry for the old, familiar ways,
I turned aside and bowed my head and wept.

McKay obviously is the speaker in this poem, although he speaks for the hundreds of West Indians who became exiles away from their homeland primarily because of economic and dilplomatic reasons. The poem, therefore, does have a oneness of feeling about it. The alienation felt is one of time and distance, and the consequence and helplessness is clearly felt in the last three lines. The progression is from glorious song to despair. It is one of his most moving poems on this theme, and the experience, as in **"If We Must Die,"** is the universal black experience. (pp. 301-04)

[McKay] seemed to have done his best work when he maintained a distance between himself and his subject. This in itself was not true of all romantic writers, but it is true of the romantic spirit for nostalgia, mysticism and fascination. About life McKay wrote to Eastman (28 July 1919):

> . . . life fascinates me in its passions. It may survive when everything else is dead and fused into it. I revere all those spirits who in their little (bit?) way are helping the life force to attain its wonderful and beautiful communication.

In the same letter he says, "I love your life more than your poetry, more than your personality. This is my attitude toward all artists."

It is apparent that McKay believes strongly in the nationality, personal identity, and uniqueness that each writer brings to his art. It is that special uniqueness which makes each one different and reinforces the sturdy independence of each human's nature. It was in Europe and elsewhere that he missed America most and in America that he reminisced about Jamaica consistently.

All poetry, McKay thought, should be judged by its own merits, not by categories of race and nationality. The double standard was something which he opposed, and this too was carried over into his lifestyle. Because he was a "foreign" Negro with white friends, the reality of racial prejudice and the embarrassing moments he experienced from whites and blacks left him torn. He wanted to be accepted, but the pain which nonacceptance brought others plagued him. He was not accepted by the blacks of the Harlem Renaissance group, and his friends were the white literati, not the black "Niggerati," as he called them. It is no wonder, then, that the romantic modes and distances worked best for McKay. Some of the most personal poems are about those experiences such as **"To the White Fiends"** and **"The White House."** The militancy and anger are there and very uncompromising. Regardless of this, it was the realm of "literary truth" with which McKay was most preoccupied. He spoke of and "defined" it in a letter to Eastman:

> I think that if the intellectual idea of literary

truth were analyzed, it would prove at bottom to be nothing more than "a wise saying" or a "beautiful phrase" delivered in a unique and startling manner—an addition to the sum of the universal wisdom of mankind. Such a wisdom exists telling of the passions, the folly and the sagacity, success and failure, pain and joy of life. It existed long before modern science and I believe it will continue to exist as vigorous and independent as ever as long as humanity retains the facilities of feeling, thinking—the inexhaustible source of which great and authentic literature springs whether it is cerebral or sentimental, realistic or romantic.

The essence of McKay's romanticism was not only in his poetry, but in the life he lived, the places he visited, and the people and ideas he encountered. His daily vocabulary was very interestingly sprinkled with romantic asides, as was his autobiography, *A Long Way from Home,* and his letters to Max Eastman of *The Liberator.* . . . It is obvious that McKay was completely immersed in a romantic style of life very similar to that of some of his British models and contemporaries. A vocabulary interspersed with words carrying the romantic notion means that he consciously draws attention to where his allegiances to nature, life, and self lie. All of these coalesced to create poetry which said yes to life by its explicit philosophy.

Claude McKay has been called "Jamaica's Bobbie Burns," although he gave up that citizenship some twenty-eight years later. The land of his birth, Jamaica, about which he wrote his best prose, verse, and lyrics, still claims him as its citizen. The comparison with the Scottish Burns is by no means superficial, however, as there are many similarities in their writing and points-of-view. The romantics—Keats, Shelley, Wordsworth, Whitman, and Yeats—were also his literary heroes, because of the content of their works and the lifestyles which they led. It was, and still is, unusual to have a black man writing in the mode of the romantics, using their themes, subject matter, and meter. The two natures of self and art, of allegiance and coalition, were things for which McKay worked throughout his life and career. Regardless of his thoroughly British orientation, emotionally and literarily he never forgot his blackness. For a modern poet, the sonnet was his favorite form, and he wrote most of his poems on the time-honored subjects of love and nature. The universality of his romanticism and poetry surpasses color or time lines. (pp. 305-08)

> *Geta J. LeSeur, "Claude McKay's Romanticism," in CLA Journal, Vol. XXXII, No. 3, March, 1989, pp. 296-308.*

FURTHER READING

Bronz, Stephen H. "Claude McKay." In his *Roots of Negro Racial Consciousness, The 1920s: Three Renaissance Authors,* pp. 66-89. New York: Libra Publishers, 1964.
Biographical and critical survey of McKay.

Collier, Eugenia W. "The Four-Way Dilemma of Claude McKay." *CLA Journal* XV, No. 3 (March 1972): 345-53.

Analysis of McKay's poetry with respect to four distinct crises he faced as a black writer. Collier suggests that McKay's poetry was affected by a series of dilemmas peculiar to black people in America.

Cooper, Wayne [F]. "Claude McKay and the New Negro of the 1920s." *PHYLON: The Atlanta University Review of Race and Culture* 25, No. 3 (Fall 1964): 297-306.

Discussion of McKay during the Harlem Renaissance. Cooper concludes that McKay will be best remembered for his poetry wherein he expressed "the New Negro's determination to protect his human dignity, his cultural worth, and his right to a decent life."

Cooper, Wayne F. *Claude McKay: Rebel Sojourner in the Harlem Renaissance.* Baton Rouge: Louisiana State University Press, 1987, 441 p.

Comprehensive biography.

Elimimian, Isaac I. "Theme and Technique in Claude McKay's Poetry." *CLA Journal* XXV, No. 2 (December 1981): 203-11.

Discusses themes on race, politics, love, and religion within the traditional forms of McKay's poetry.

Emanuel, James A., and Gross, Theodore L., eds. *Dark Symphony: Negro Literature in America.* New York: The Free Press, 1968, 604 p.

Brief biographical and critical survey of McKay's life and works, supplemented by reprints of nine well known poems.

Giles, James R. *Claude McKay.* Boston: Twayne Publishers, 1976, 170 p.

Critical biography.

Hansell, William H. "Jamaica in the Poems of Claude McKay." *Studies in Black Literature* 7, No. 3 (Autumn 1976): 6-9.

Examines such elements in McKay's Jamaican poems as love, innocence, beauty, and a sense of community as reflexive of the poet's idealized vision of his homeland. Hansell posits that the island represents to McKay "an inspirational symbol for all Negroes of a place and condition where life could be different from what they typically experienced."

Kent, George E. "The Soulful Way of Claude McKay." In his *Blackness and the Adventure of Western Culture,* pp. 36-52. Chicago: Third World Press, 1972.

Presents McKay's personal and artistic achievements as pioneering efforts toward developing an inherent group consciousness among black people in Occidental culture.

Lee, Robert A. "On Claude McKay's 'If We Must Die'." *CLA Journal* XVIII, No. 2 (December 1974): 216-21.

Close reading of McKay's poem "If We Must Die" that focuses on delineating a unique racial perspective in the work.

Pyne-Timothy, Helen. "Perceptions of the Black Woman in the Work of Claude McKay." *CLA Journal* XIX, No. 2 (December 1975): 152-64.

Studies facets of McKay's female characters, discerning a common role among women to provide psychological and economic support for the men in their lives. Pyne-Timothy further contends that McKay portrays two kinds of female characters: survivors and victims.

Redding, J. Saunders. "Emergence of the New Negro." In his *To Make a Poet Black,* pp. 93-125. College Park, Md.: McGrath Publishing Co., 1939.

Historical perspective of African-American writers during the Harlem Renaissance, characterizing McKay as a seminal new Negro poet whose poems demonstrate "the proud defiance and independence that were the very heart of the new Negro movement."

Story, Ralph D. "Patronage and the Harlem Renaissance: You Get What You Pay For." *CLA Journal* XXXII, No. 3 (March 1989): 284-95.

Explores issues of white patronage among Harlem Renaissance writers, depicting McKay's associations with radical leftist patrons as, in some ways, atypical of the movement.

Ovid

43 B.C. - c. 18 A.D.

(Full name: Publius Ovidius Naso) Roman poet.

Ovid is widely recognized as one of the greatest poets of classical Rome and his works are among some of the most influential in European literature. The dominant theme of his poetry is love, which he celebrates in such works as the *Amores* (*Loves*), the *Heroides* (*Heroines*), the *Ars amatoria* (*The Art of Love*), and the *Metamorphoses*. Irreverent, playful, and sensuous, Ovid is considered a master Latin stylist whose technical accomplishments permanently enriched the language. The epic *Metamorphoses,* long recognized as his masterpiece, describes the loves—and transformations—of characters from classical mythology, providing masterful and accessible renditions of ancient tales. That work has inspired generations of writers and artists, including Chrétien de Troyes, Dante Alighieri, Geoffrey Chaucer, Titian, Edmund Spenser, William Shakespeare, John Milton, Johann Wolfgang van Goethe, T. S. Eliot, and Ezra Pound with its vivid depictions of the humanity inherent in both mortals and gods.

Ovid was born in Sulmo (modern Sulmona) into a prosperous family of the equestrian order. The *equites,* or knights, were the second class of Roman society and supported the status quo of the ruling senatorial elite. Sent to Rome to study rhetoric under the foremost rhetoricians of the time in preparation for a legal career, Ovid distinguished himself as a student but ultimately chose the vocation of a poet. His poetical genius gained him admission to the circle around the statesman and literary patron Messalla, and he quickly became a favorite of the Roman elite, who delighted in his poetic tributes to the art of love. Here Ovid met the other leading poets of the day, including Propertius and Horace.

While a member of Messalla's circle Ovid published his love poetry, including the *Loves,* the *Heroines, The Art of Love,* the *Remedia amoris* (*The Remedies of Love*), and *Medicamina faciei femineae* (*On Taking Care of a Woman's Face*). All highlight Ovid's keen insight into the feminine psyche and his genuine understanding of human nature. Ovid's first work, the *Loves,* appeared originally in five volumes around 20 B.C. and by 1 A.D. was re-released in a shorter three-book edition, which is the only version extant today. The *Loves* consists of a series of elegies about the narrator's love affair with a woman named Corinna; the name, critics have suggested, refers not to a real person, but is rather a fictional composite. The majority of the poems are lightly humorous in tone, except for the elegy on the poet Tibullus, and all display Ovid's consummate handling of the elegiac meter. The *Heroines* is generally regarded as Ovid's second endeavor, although some evidence suggests a later date. This work takes the form of love letters addressed by such mythological females as Penelope, Medea, and Dido to their absent husbands or lovers. Here Ovid highlights his profound knowledge of my-

thology and shares his insight into feminine psychology by creating clever, rhetorical dramatic soliloquies of unhappy love, which breathed new life into an almost exhausted Greek genre. *The Art of Love* was published around 1 B.C. and instantly caused a sensation. A didactic poem on the art of seduction and intrigue, *The Art of Love* parodies conventional love poetry and didactic verse while offering vivid portrayals of contemporary Roman society. As this poem implicitly ridiculed the conservative moralism of the Augustan regime, Ovid hastened to compose a recantation, *The Remedies of Love,* but critics have found the work rather acerbic as well. *On Taking Care of a Woman's Face,* of which about one hundred lines survive, contains formulas for care of the female complexion and is generally included in collections of Ovid's love poetry.

In 8 A.D. the emperor Augustus banished Ovid, then Rome's most popular poet, to Tomis on the Black Sea (now Constanta, Romania) under somewhat peculiar and still unexplained circumstances. The poet was tried for high treason in the Emperor's private court, and his sentence was pronounced directly by Augustus. Ovid's books were subsequently removed from public libraries, but he lost neither his citizenship nor property, nor was he forbidden to communicate with his friends or wife, as was normal in such cases. Ovid claimed that a poem and an indiscretion (*carmen et* error) had caused his exile. The poem Ovid referred to was most likely *The Art of Love,* which had been in circulation for about eight years, and the indiscretion may have been Ovid's links with Augustus's licentious granddaughter Julia, who was exiled the same year for adultery, and possibly for her political ambitions. On the eve of his exile Ovid was composing the *Fasti* (*Calendar*) and the *Metamorphoses*. The *Calendar* is a description of the Roman religious year in which he traces the various festivals to their legendary origins. Intended as a paean to Rome, Ovid's poem contains, as Edward John Kenney wrote, an excess of flattery and standard patriotism "for which the undoubted brilliance of the narrative passages does not atone." Today, the *Calendar* is particularly interesting as an anthropological account of Roman religious lore.

The *Metamorphoses* is, critics and readers agree, undeniably Ovid's masterpiece. As Ezra Pound declared, "I assert that a great treasure of verity exists for mankind in Ovid and in the subject matter of Ovid's long poem." A repository of mythological and legendary tales that has been mined by generations of artists and writers, it remains today one of the most accessible sources of Greek myth. A poem in fifteen books of hexameter verse covering tales of transformation from the creation to the apotheosis of Julius Caesar, the *Metamorphoses* is much more than the sum of its parts. While epic in scope, the work's meter, tone, and subject are quite unlike Rome's imperial epic, Vergil's *Aeneid*. Drawn from Greek mythology, Roman folklore, and Mesopotamian sources, the stories constituting the *Metamorphoses* are all linked by a common motif—transformation. According to Kenney, the importance of this theme is "more apparent than real. The essential theme of the poem is passion, and this gives it more unity than all the ingenious linking and framing devices the poet uses." By using this passion to portray the gods in human terms, Ovid produces perhaps his most lasting legacy; the shift of myth from the realm of the religious to the aesthetic and imaginative.

Ovid's works written while in exile include the *Tristia* (*Lamentations* or *Sorrows*) and the *Epistulae ex Ponto* (*Letters from the Black Sea*). *Lamentations* is a series of elegiac letters to unnamed friends—Ovid at this point was *persona non grata* and dangerous to be associated with—bemoaning the harshness of his punishment and his desire for clemency. One letter is an elaborate apology and is often interpreted as an autobiographical statement. These were written from 8-12 A.D. and published shortly thereafter. *Letters from the Black Sea* is similar to the *Lamentations* except now Ovid's friends are identified and his hopes that his banishment will be rescinded are centered on Germanicus, the adopted son of Augustus's successor, Tiberius. Ovid's pleas of clemency in the *Lamentations* and *Letters from the Black Sea* were in vain, however; Tiberius did not repeal Ovid's sentence, and he died in Tomis sometime in 17 or 18 A.D.

Ovid's banishment and the removal of his works from public access did nothing to diminish his popularity, which can be attested to by the appearance of quotes from *The Art of Love* in graffiti at Pompeii. While Quintillian and both the Senecas admonished Ovid for his lack of control and irreverent tone in his verse, other Latin writers freely emulated Ovidian poetic technique. In Medieval times, commentators and translators revised his poems into allegories by purging their erotic content in accordance with Christian doctrine. Nonetheless, Ovid was honored as a learned poet, and Dante places Ovid with the great pagan poets (Vergil, Homer, Horace, and Lucan) in the Fourth Canto of his *Inferno*. In the fourteenth century, which has been called the *aetas Ovidiana* (age of Ovid), Ovid was revered by such writers as Geoffrey Chaucer and John Gower.

Ovid's works were frequently translated into English in the mid-sixteenth and early seventeenth centuries and his critical reputation increased. Opinions varied, however: Arthur Golding's translation of the *Metamorphoses* in 1567 became immensely popular, going through six printings during Shakespeare's lifetime, while Christopher Marlowe's free adaption of the *Loves,* published in 1597 as *The Elegies,* was publicly burnt in 1599. Modern criticism retained this ambivalent attitude toward Ovid. While some critics regard Ovid as a frivolous and superficial poet, comparing him unfavorably to Vergil, others laud his mastery of poetic form, narrative skill, and extraordinary grasp of the human, particularly feminine, psyche. Literary historians view Ovid as a seminal poet whose works provided medieval writers with a wealth of literary symbols and ideas. For example, the stories and concepts in the *Metamorphoses, Loves,* and *Heroines,* as interpreted by the troubadours, helped form the concept of courtly love, which played an important role in the genesis of Arthurian literature.

Ovid himself characterized his poetic accomplishment as immortal in a prophetic statement which was fully validated by the enduring Ovidian tradition in European literature. "My work is complete," he writes at the end of the *Metamorphoses*. "A work which neither Jove's anger, nor fire nor sword shall destroy, nor yet the gnawing tooth of time. That day which has power over nothing but my body may, when it pleases put an end to my uncertain span of years. Yet with my better part I shall soar, undying, far above the stars, and my name will be imperishable. Wherever Roman power extends over the lands Rome has subdued, people will read my verses. If there be any truth in poets' prophecies, I shall live to all eternity, immortalized by fame."

PRINCIPAL ENGLISH TRANSLATIONS

Metamorphoses   (translated by Arthur Golding)   1567
The Elegies (Amores)   (translated by Christopher Marlowe)   1597
Ovid's Metamorphosis, Englished, Mythologiz'd, and Represented in Figures   (translated by George Sandys)   1632

John Dryden (essay date 1680)

[*Regarded by many as the father of modern English poetry and criticism, Dryden dominated literary life in England during the last four decades of the seventeenth century. By deliberately and comprehensively refining the English language in all his works, he developed an expressive, universal diction which has had immense impact on the development of speech and writing in Great Britain and North America. Recognized as a prolific and accomplished dramatist, Dryden also wrote a number of satiric poems and critical works, some of which are acknowledged as his greatest literary achievements. In his critical works, particularly* Of Dramatic Poesy *(1668), Dryden effectively originated the extended form of objective, practical analysis that has come to characterize most modern criticism. In the following excerpt from the preface to his 1680 translation of Ovid's* Heroides, *here known as the* Epistles, *Dryden praises the classical poet's skill in presenting "natural emotion" and claims that "they are generally granted to be the most perfect pieces of Ovid."*]

The Life of Ovid being already written in our language, before the translation of his ***Metamorphoses,*** I will not presume so far upon myself, to think I can add any thing to Mr. Sandys his undertaking. The English reader may there be satisfied, that he flourished in the reign of Augustus Cæsar; that he was extracted from an ancient family of Roman knights; that he was born to the inheritance of a splendid fortune; that he was designed to the study of the Law, and had made considerable progress in it, before he quitted that profession, for this of Poetry, to which he was more naturally formed. The cause of his banishment is unknown; because he was himself unwilling further to provoke the Emperor, by ascribing it to any other reason than what was pretended by Augustus, which was, the las-

civiousness of his ***Elegies,*** and his ***Art of Love.*** 'Tis true, they are not to be excused in the severity of manners, as being able to corrupt a larger Empire, if there were any, than that of Rome; yet this may be said in behalf of Ovid, that no man has ever treated the passion of love with so much delicacy of thought, and of expression, or searched into the nature of it more philosophically than he. (pp. 230-31)

If the imitation of Nature be the business of a poet, I know no author, who can justly be compared with ours, especially in the description of the passions. And to prove this, I shall need no other judges than the generality of his readers: for, all passions being inborn with us, we are almost equally judges when we are concerned in the representation of them. Now I will appeal to any man, who has read this poet, whether he finds not the natural emotion of the same passion in himself, which the poet describes in his feigned persons? His thoughts, which are the pictures and results of those passions, are generally such as naturally arise from those disorderly motions of our spirits. Yet, not to speak too partially in his behalf, I will confess, that the copiousness of his wit was such, that he often writ too pointedly for his subject, and made his persons speak more eloquently than the violence of their passion would admit: so that he is frequently witty out of season; leaving the imitation of Nature, and the cooler dictates of his judgement, for the false applause of Fancy. Yet he seems to have found out this imperfection in his riper age; for why else should he complain that his ***Metamorphoses*** was left unfinished? Nothing sure can be added to the wit of that poem, or of the rest; but many things ought to have been retrenched, which I suppose would have been the business of his age, if his misfortunes had not come too fast upon him. But take him uncorrected, as he is transmitted to us, and it must be acknowledged, in spite of his Dutch friends, the commentators, even of Julius Scaliger himself, that Seneca's censure will stand good against him; *Nescivit quod bene cessit relinquere:* he never knew how to give over, when he had done well; but, continually varying the same sense an hundred ways, and taking up in another place what he had more than enough inculcated before, he sometimes cloys his readers, instead of satisfying them; and gives occasion to his translators, who dare not cover him, to blush at the nakedness of their father. This, then, is the allay of Ovid's writings, which is sufficiently recompensed by his other excellences: nay, this very fault is not without its beauties; for the most severe censor cannot but be pleased with the prodigality of his wit, though at the same time he could have wished that the master of it had been a better manager. Every thing which he does becomes him, and if sometimes he appears too gay, yet there is a secret gracefulness of youth which accompanies his writings, though the staidness and sobriety of age be wanting. In the most material part, which is the conduct, 'tis certain, that he seldom has miscarried; for if his ***Elegies*** be compared with those of Tibullus and Propertius, his contemporaries, it will be found that those poets seldom designed before they writ; and though the language of Tibullus be more polished, and the learning of Propertius, especially in his Fourth Book, more set out to ostentation; yet their common practice was to look no further before them than the next line; whence it will inevitably follow, that they can drive to no certain point, but ramble from one subject to another, and conclude with somewhat, which is not of a piece with their beginning:—

> Purpureus late qui splendeat, unus et alter
> Assuitur pannus . . .

as Horace says; though the verses are golden, they are but patched into the garment. But our Poet has always the goal in his eye, which directs him in his race; some beautiful design, which he first establishes, and then contrives the means, which will naturally conduct it to his end. This will be evident to judicious readers in this work of his **Epistles,** of which somewhat, at least in general, will be expected.

The title of them in our late editions is **Epistolæ Heroidum,** the **Letters of the Heroines.** But Heinsius has judged more truly, that the inscription of our author was barely **Epistles;** which he concludes from his cited verses, where Ovid asserts this work as his own invention, and not borrowed from the Greeks, whom (as the masters of their learning) the Romans usually did imitate. But it appears not from their writings, that any of the Grecians ever touched upon this way, which our poet therefore justly has vindicated to himself. I quarrel not at the word *Heroidum,* because it is used by Ovid in his **Art of Love—**

> Jupiter ad veteres supplex *Heroidas* ibat.

But sure he could not be guilty of such an oversight, to call his work by the name of **Heroines,** when there are divers men, or heroes, as namely Paris, Leander, and Acontius, joined in it. Except Sabinus, who writ some answers to Ovid's **Letters,**

> (Quam celer e toto rediit meus orbe Sabinus,)

I remember not any of the Romans who have treated this subject, save only Propertius, and that but once, in his Epistle of *Arethusa to Lycotas,* which is written so near the style of Ovid, that it seems to be but an imitation; and therefore ought not to defraud our poet of the glory of his invention.

Concerning this work of the **Epistles,** I shall content myself to observe these few particulars: first, that they are generally granted to be the most perfect pieces of Ovid, and that the style of them is tenderly passionate and courtly; two properties well agreeing with the persons, which were heroines, and lovers. Yet where the characters were lower, as in Œnone and Hero, he has kept close to Nature, in drawing his images after a country life, though perhaps he has Romanized his Grecian dames too much, and made them speak, sometimes, as if they had been born in the city of Rome, and under the Empire of Augustus. There seems to be no great variety in the particular subjects which he has chosen; most of the **Epistles** being written from ladies, who were forsaken by their lovers: which is the reason that many of the same thoughts come back upon us in divers letters: but of the general character of women, which is modesty, he has taken a most becoming care; for his amorous expressions go no further than virtue may allow, and therefore may be read, as he intended them, by matrons without a blush. (pp. 233-36)

John Dryden, "Preface to Ovid's Epistles," in his Essays, *edited by W. P. Ker, Russell & Russell, 1961, pp. 230-43.*

Hermann Fränkel   (essay date 1945)

[*Fränkel is a noted classicist whose* Dichtung und Philosophie des frühen Griechentums *(1951;* Early Greek Poetry and Philosophy) *is considered a landmark in Greek literary studies. In an excerpt from his 1945 work,* Ovid: A Poet between Two Worlds, *he discusses Ovid's* Amores, *finding both love and poetry as presented by the poet to be indicative of a higher level of meaning where they "can satisfy man's finer thoughts and nobler sentiments."*]

After young Ovid had made his [career] choice, he looked up with more veneration than ever to the great masters of Roman verse who were still living. He was eager to make their personal acquaintance and to hear them recite their own poems. But they were soon to leave the scene. Of those men whom we are accustomed to call the poets of the Augustan age, Ovid was by far the youngest. He was only twenty-four years old when Vergil and Tibullus died, in 19 B.C. On the death of Tibullus he wrote an elegy which bears testimony to the most sympathetic intimacy with Tibullus' writings. Sometime after 15 B.C., Propertius passed away, and in 8 B.C., Horace.

Very soon Ovid established his own reputation as a writer of elegy. He did not have to wait for fame until his first book was published and on sale in the bookshops. At the time, it was the custom to have the manuscripts of single poems circulate among those who were interested, and to recite to a group of invited guests a number of one's own compositions as soon as they had been put into their final shape. Ovid started giving recitations, as he tells us, after "he had had his beard trimmed once or twice." Valerius Messalla Corvinus, a man of high rank and a friend of the Muses, recognized Ovid's talent and encouraged him to make his work public. The first collection of poems he published bore the title **Amores** and was in five books. We possess the second edition, which the author had reduced to three volumes by eliminating material he thought less valuable. The number of elegies is fifty or fifty-one. Most of the **Amores** seems to have been written while he was in his twenties.

When we open a book of love poetry, we expect to find in it the expression of that particular author's individual experiences. A Roman collection of erotic elegies is broader in scope and less closely bound to reality. No doubt the Roman writer would actually be in love with someone when he composed a love poem, and he would speak as if he were, at the moment of his writing, involved in the situation he describes; yet his ambition was to ignore the accidental limitations of his own personal adventures. He was trying to picture, not one person's emotions, but any true lover's love. His subject was **The Story of Love,** and that, after all, is what the title **Amores** means. The **Story** is told by Ovid in terms of various specific experiences, real or imaginary, of the author. Not only was the poet entitled to improve on the crude facts; it was beside the point to ask how much of what he said was actually true as long as all of it was potentially true; not even strict consistency throughout the book was required. By a number of concrete examples the poet tried to present a comprehensive image of what a young man's existence is like when it is dominated by a passionate attachment. Of the lover's existence he would draw an ideal picture which boldly challenged comparison with the lives of nonlovers. (pp. 10-11)

The main assumption of the poet is this: Love is no mere incidental event, flavoring an otherwise normal life; it is a preoccupation which molds the whole being of its victim into a new and specific shape and places him, as it were, in a new and peculiar sphere apart from the rest of mankind, with a different horizon, climate, and atmosphere. The kind of love the Roman elegists have in mind is neither purely sensual nor predominantly sentimental; rather, they glorify a passionate state of mind which fails to discriminate between the two sides. The lovers, of course, are not married to one another, nor do they want to formalize their friendship; a proposal of marriage has no place in this kind of poetry or in this romantic frame of mind. A marriage, as a rule, was preceded in Rome not by a courtship but by negotiations between the respective families; and the contentment of domestic and family life would never be admitted as a subject for literary treatment. Thus the lovers in the elegies are united by no legal ties, and their relationship is dependent on their affection alone. Society did not object to irregular connections of that sort, as far as the young man was concerned; and the young woman would supposedly not belong to society, but be free to follow her inclination. The lady is assumed to live by herself or with some other man of her choice; beyond that, her position is left rather indefinite. It is made plain, however, that the concerns of the heart rather than material considerations ought to determine her attitude toward the admirer. He would, it is true, try to brighten her life with such presents as he could afford; this, however, was an accessory only. No doubt there were in Rome very many independent young women to answer the specifications, and with one or another of them a union would be formed which, after all, was not to last forever and yet gave the attractive prospect of a more than momentary engrossment for both the partners. It is axiomatic for Ovid that the woman should be on an equal footing with the man and should be looking for the same kind of benefits from their association; a fundamental divergence of objectives would spoil everything for him.

The atmosphere of Ovid's *Amores* is by no means blissfully entrancing and balmy with May-day fragrance; rather, the emotional weather is brisk and subject to moody shifts like April storms and sunshine. *The Story of Love* consists of a series of dramatic incidents and crises, and more especially so since the relationship is not on a secure and permanent basis. Hope and fear sway hither and thither the mind of the adventurous lover, and he does not want to miss the thrills of either hope or fear. Continually he is haunted by jealousy, and yet his pleasure is heightened by the constant threat of a rival, real or imaginary. The existence of an eager competitor proves that his mistress is desirable, and his own successes are the more valuable as they are precarious. Nothing is stable and final. The lover will sometimes swear eternal allegiance to his lady and

perhaps at the moment actually mean what he says, but in fact there is no bond which cannot be severed, just as there is no break which cannot be mended.

This erratic state of affairs is reflected in the incoherent character of a work like Ovid's *Amores.* There is little continuity in the volumes of Roman erotic poetry, and scholars who have tried to piece together the history of one individual affair have lost their labor. The order in which the elegies are arranged is willful and confusing, and it is an exception when one poem begins where the previous one left off. Each elegy is to be seen in its own light, and taken all together they give a composite picture of a lover's life and world. In twelve of Ovid's elegies the lady is given the pseudonym Corinna; but even in one of those twelve it is made abundantly clear that no one woman was able to monopolize the poet's attentions. It also happened that Ovid was unable to make up his mind which one of two lovely girls he preferred, with the result that he devoted himself to both with equal ardor. All that can be expected is that there was one to occupy the first place in his heart for most of the time, and she was presumably identical with the so-called Corinna. Thus the situation became never quite dull and stationary, and the man as well as the woman offered their partner ample opportunities for jealousy. Exuberance rated more highly than loyalty.

The modern reader, however historically minded, is likely to have moments when he frowns on that sort of exuberance and feels that, even if people did indulge in such practices, there was no need to waste good poetry on them. It may therefore be remarked in passing that a Roman young man of feeling had little choice in his quest for a worthy pursuit to employ his leisure. Where should he look for something to engage his youthful enthusiasm? He belonged to a nation which was none too imaginative and was not given to spiritual, theoretical, and impractical pursuits; and he was a member of a snobbish and prejudiced society. Roman religion made no appeal to the emotions; it was more of an institution than an inspiration. Not a few people at that time were won over to Oriental beliefs and cults which gave a more satisfactory outlet to fervid piety; but fervid piety was outlandish and wholly against the spirit of Roman traditions. There was, of course, philosophy which tried to appeal both to the heart and the intellect. But the philosophies of the age were past their fresh and creative stage; all schools were annoyingly contentious; their teachings had an air of quaint unreality; and, worst of all for our young man, they opposed any and all strong emotions and professed to lead their adepts to a calm and mellow serenity. There might have been science and scholarship; but the Romans had a natural gift for only two special fields: antiquarian history and the development, if not the theory, of law. Furthermore, the idea seemed insufferable that a better-class Roman should bend all his energies to research for its own sake. He was not supposed to do more than round out his general education and equip himself with a smattering of the current views and theories; or, at most, make a hobby of reading or writing books on material already familiar to experts. There was art; but if one wished to retain his standing in the world of fashion he could indulge in a passionate artistic interest only by collecting expensive objects or feverishly building mansions and villas, two lines which for an obvious reason were not open to the average young man. There was the wide-open world to be explored; and one could, and did, travel and see the old centers of civilization. There was literature. The study of literature and the writing of poetry, indeed, were taken up by many Romans of the time, young and old, with almost fanatical zest. And there were, finally, friendship and its far more emotional counterpart, love. Love and literature were combined in Roman erotic poetry. Here then was a field of literature congenial to the typical young Roman because it originated from personal experience and pointed the way to practical experience; just as, on a very different level, a mature statesman would be engrossed in books of history because he had his hand in the making of history.

Love as an autonomous occupation is frequently contrasted by Ovid to other pursuits. . . . War with its strenuous exertions is the direct opposite of love with its languid sentimentality; nevertheless, that truism challenged ingenuity to invent reasons why they should not rather be considered as similar. Once, in the elation of his first triumph over Corinna's heart, Ovid makes a clever remark to the effect that love is a kind of one man's war upon the enemy in which teamwork is out of the question and chance plays no part; which is a facetious way of saying that love is a very personal kind of activity. There, it is each man for himself, and the effort, the achievement, the prize, and the glory are all his own. In earnest, of course, Ovid would never match himself against a soldier. His tender heart abhorred the cruelty of war, and his liberal mind despised the sordid greed which animated most professional soldiers. Doubly odious were ruthless soldiering and base avarice to Ovid when they desecrated the sublime sphere of love. As a horrible example for everything love should not be, Ovid once pictures his lady in the arms of a soldier. As he puts it, the intruder had made a fortune by hiring out his body for the loot to be gained in war; and the poet's mistress had yielded to that man in the same mercenary spirit. In this connection, Ovid again rehearses the worldly pursuits of mankind: bloody war; trespassing in ships on the ocean; stirring up the soil with the plow; and the other occupations that human ingenuity devised and perfected to the debasement of the human soul, all of them motivated or corrupted by avarice. Wealth alone, he says, gives access to the senate, and it is wealth which lifts a man to equestrian rank and invests him with the authority of a judge. "Be it so; let them lay their grasping hands upon everything, let them sway elections and lawsuits, if only they leave one thing—it is all we ask—to the poor man." In another characteristic elegy, a slight lack of delicacy on the lady's part is enough to make the excitable lover complain in bitter indignation. "You ask why I have changed? 'Tis because you demand gifts from me." Chafing, he explains that he used to love her body and soul; but now the blemish on her character has tarnished the brilliance of her beauty, so that it dazzles him no more; his madness is over, his mind once again clear and sober. (We wonder how coolheaded he may be with his offended feelings.) Then he proceeds to lecture his mistress as if she had actually begun to sell, instead of giving, him her favors. The lecture goes on for a long time (too long a time, in fact),

until the poet suddenly relents (this is typical of Ovid) and says:

> There is no harm, of course, in demanding a reward from a rich man. . . .
> But the poor pays with his service, his devotion, and his loyalty.
> Let each man give his mistress what he happens to possess.
> A deserving woman can also be celebrated in poetry.
> That endowment is mine; I make known her whom I select.
> Dresses will rend, jewels and gold will crumble; but the glory which poetry bestows will live on through time.

This sententious prophecy would have made a resounding finale, in good conventional style, for the elegy; but Ovid adds a gentle postscript, as it were:

> It is not my giving but your demand which hurts and repels me.
> You ask for a thing, and I refuse; cease to want it, and I shall give.

The comprehending lover is ready for a liberal compromise; he will soon make up for his diatribe with a surprise gift.

These examples show how the spirit of love, as conceived by Ovid, sets up its own code of propriety, and how it enjoys the fight for its own preservation, waging a jolly war on enemies both from without and within. There are many things the lover has to contend or put up with, but I shall not, and indeed should not care to, offer a complete list of them.

In Ovid's erotic elegies the struggling passion is dramatically depicted with all its reasonings and imaginings. Some of the lover's notions change with his moods; others are inherent to his condition. Invariably he will feel that the concerns of the heart are of prime importance and that everything else must give way to them. He tries to ignore any facts that contradict his sentiment. Out of his own emotions and what they reveal and demand, the lover builds an exclusive system in which he wishes and labors to believe; all the rest of knowledge and experience is pushed back out of sight, to a secondary plane of reality, shadowy and unsubstantial by comparison.

As a consequence, in this poetry delusion and self-deception are considered as meritorious whenever they satisfy the feeling and invigorate the emotion. "I often mistake what could be for what is," says Ovid, boasting no doubt of the independence of his active mind. The possibility to which he is referring in the context makes the anguish of a pathetic situation more poignant and more personal for him. Another time, he indulges in jealous suspicions which are obviously unfounded. While trying to convict his mistress of a breach of faith, he sadly overrates the stringency of his arguments; but his gratuitous reproaches show how highly he treasures the integrity of their association. In his heart of hearts, however, he knows very well her profound devotion to him, and with a delightful couplet he half recants his incriminations. More frequently, breezy imagination travels in the opposite direction, looking for pleasant dreams to blot out unwelcome realities. More than once Ovid tells his mistress to dissemble and steadfastly deny whatever transgression she may have committed. One elegy begins with this couplet:

> I own that your beauty gives you the right to sin;
>   but I refuse to have the wretched truth forced
>   upon me.

Thus the poet exhorts his lady to develop a double personality; he wants her to appear modest under ordinary circumstances, and only in the most private moments of their relationship to cast off all her reserve. Her frank admission of faithlessness has given him a cruel shock:

> I am out of my mind and dying, whenever you
>   confess to have sinned,
>   and the blood in my veins flows cold.
> That makes me love, makes me hate—in vain,
>   for I cannot help loving;
>   it makes me yearn to be dead—but together
>   with you.
> I shall not ask questions, nor search into that
>   which you are hiding. Deceit I shall accept as
>   a bounty.

These forceful lines are unusual, penetrating as they do deep into a maze of strange and painful emotions. The poet sees no way out of it except by embracing the part of a dupe. In default of what he really craves for, he invites thoughtful cant.

Time and again we find Ovid bent on concealing from his own eyes a disagreeable fact; but he also sees to it that the cloak is transparent. The bitter-sweet passion of love, as he conceived it, fed upon the incongruity between things as they are and as they ought to be. There is some degree of realism, after all, in a game where you know that an illusion is an illusion.

The make-believe in Ovid's erotic verse frees the lover's soul and allows his sentiments to range far and wide, deep and high, unhampered. But there is no artificial disguise; the lovers are not garbed in a pastoral costume or put into fictitious pastoral surroundings. The ladies are represented as real ladies of real Rome, and yet the poet's love invests them, in earnest or in sport, with extraordinary qualities and powers. In an ecstasy of veneration he deifies his mistress, or ranks her with the divine beings because like the almighty gods she can make or mar his happiness. In fact, the goddess in the flesh can do more for him than the dubious beings in faraway heaven. Ovid once prays to Venus to give him victory over the heart of his fair neighbor on the circus bench, and he pretends to have seen the image of the deity nod assent; immediately, however, he asks the lady personally to confirm the promise:

> May Venus pardon me: you will be a greater
>   goddess.

(pp. 24-31)

[Elsewhere] he says that "beauty possesses a divine majesty" (*forma numen habet*), so that the gods themselves bow to its authority and ignore a girl's false oath, if she is pretty enough.

Poetry likewise is considered as divine:

> We poets are called sacred and favorites of the
>   gods;
>   some even believe that we possess divine
>   power.

We are quoting from the poem on the death of Tibullus, the revered master of erotic elegy. When Tibullus' body was burned on the pyre, Ovid was shocked by the experience that death was permitted profanely to lay his "dark hands" upon the prophet of the Muses.

To write poetry means, among other things, to transform reality, lifting it to a level where it can satisfy man's finer thoughts and nobler sentiments. Love performs a similar feat by means of a similar inspired madness. Small wonder, then, that Ovid wove his poetry and his love into one and the same texture. He indicates that he would enter on an amorous affair with an artist's eye on converting it into verse. Seen in this light, erotic poetry was more realistic and substantial than either drama or epic; here alone, the author composed his own life and lived his own verse. It was, however, a universal dogma that drama and epic, with their lofty and virile themes, ranked far above erotic verse. Ovid had no reason to question this view so far as style and treatment were concerned; his talent did not tend toward sustained grandeur, and it was the most natural thing for him to keep his *Amores* on a moderate level, with only momentary excursions into the sublime. On the other hand, he was convinced that the emotional experiences of people of feeling, as exemplified in his own person, deserved to be represented in poetry just as well as the fables of myth, the figments of legend, or the exploits of the great; and he happened to be a past master in giving voice to the events going on in the human soul. Thus he must have resented the tenet that erotic poetry was the lowest variety of the art, undignified and inconsequential. In his many utterings on the objectives and merits of his erotic elegiacs, he wavered between an apologetic attitude and a defiant one, or else hid his confusion behind playful irony. Now he would submit to the general view, and now scoff at the idea of his writing elevated hexameters about the legendary war between the gods and the giants. I was describing that cosmic battle, he says, and in my verse was brandishing Jupiter's thunderbolt, when my mistress locked me out; immediately I dropped the bolt and forgot Jupiter:

> Forgive me, O Jove, but your weapon availed me
>   nothing,
>   for the thunderbolt of a locked door is more
>   formidable than yours.

> So I took up once more my own weapons, blandishment and elegy:
>   mild words softened the hard door.

This kind of poetry, then, was practical; its ingratiating charm helped the lover to persuade a woman, and its glory held out for her the coveted honor of being made known all over the world. And passion, in turn, provided the writer with congenial subjects and with the proper frame of mind for composing his spirited verse; it had aroused his talent. . . . (pp. 31-3)

Although not given to theoretical reasoning, Ovid saw clearly some essential facts of his own calling. He understood that poetry lives on its own plane of reality and that we commit a blunder when we confuse the different planes. He also saw that our ideals are not to be found in life as it is, but are to be projected by us into our individual lives. And indeed, the higher we set our human standards, the more we must create what we shall worship. To that truth Ovid was to give the final and consummate expression in the Pygmalion story of the *Metamorphoses*. . . .

We have referred to the *Metamorphoses* . . . for several reasons. First, we would indicate the consistency of Ovid's thinking all through the different periods of his life. Secondly, we wanted to show that we have not been exaggerating the significance of the ideas implied in his erotic elegies. If Ovid later followed up one or another of those ideas and developed its full import, then we can conclude that the sportive play of his earliest work also has a more serious side. And lastly, it may be interesting to throw a fleeting glance at the finished form of a thought while we are still studying its first emergence and still remember the conditions under which it arose. The *Amores* gives a vivid picture of the decadence of Ovid's age, and it shows how the poet, far from being a radical reformer, enjoyed and promoted those trends which could make life more tenderly emotional. But he did more than merely select what he wanted and ignore the rest. With loving zeal he embellished whatever seemed defective, and substituted fine illusions for offensive facts. Pygmalion, as Ovid will tell his tale in the *Metamorphoses,* was shocked into creative idealism by the depravity he witnessed in actual life. The ferment of disintegration set free all sorts of forces; and some of them were, after all, constructive and progressive. (p. 35)

Hermann Fränkel, in his Ovid: A Poet Between Two Worlds, *1945. Reprint by University of California Press, 1956, 282 p.*

Moses Hadas (essay date 1952)

[*Hadas was a distinguished American scholar whose many works, including* A History of Greek Literature *(1950),* A History of Latin Literature *(1952), and* Hellenistic Culture: Fusion and Diffusion *(1959), range over the entire field of classical literature. In the following excerpt from the second-named work, Hadas gives an overview of Ovid's verse, stressing the author's storytelling ability and wit while affirming that "nothing in him is immoral unless the absence of moralizing is immoral."*]

Readers who demand of a poet moral instruction or inspiration will find Ovid completely frivolous; critics who choose to disregard the "tyranny of the subject" would regard him as almost the only pure artist in Latin literature. In none does verse seem so natural an idiom; none devoted his verse so singly to providing the kind of pleasure which it is the function of literature to provide. Literary pleasure Ovid has offered with generous abundance to the countries of Europe, whose literatures he has enriched more potently than any other Latin poet has done. But puritan Europe (like puritan Rome) has been a little uneasy in conscience at receiving pleasure unsalted with edification. It has looked mainly to the *Metamorphoses*, which could be es-

teemed as a useful handbook of ancient mythology, whose deities it was no longer blasphemous to smile at, and there have been attempts to construe the amoral *Amores* as an allegory recommending the pursuit of Mistress Wisdom. But Ovid is not prurient; he aims not to titillate but to entertain, he does not leer but smile. Nothing in him is immoral unless absence of moralizing is immoral. Amoral he may be, but that is the proper posture for a professed expert, and none can deny that Ovid was indeed an expert in a realm of no small importance in our world—the ways of the species woman. Of this subject no Roman shows profounder understanding, and no Roman has shown greater skill in the art of telling a story. With great finesse and great perception, and sometimes with highly literate and agile fooling, Ovid creates a mimic world for the delectation of readers able to refract some part of his own mercurial wit. (p. 201)

Of Ovid's extant works those published before his banishment are *Amores, Heroides,* and the series comprising *Ars amatoria, Remedium amoris, Medicina faciei.* The *Metamorphoses* were completed but not corrected, and the *Fasti* doubtless begun. In exile he wrote the *Tristia,* and the *Epistles from Pontus,* the *Halieuticon,* and the *Ibis.* Ovid speaks of having burnt some of his works, and he surely wrote more than the ample volume we possess, but the only non-extant work of which we have positive knowledge that it survived him is his tragedy on *Medea.* Of this Quintilian says: "That work seems to me to demonstrate how great Ovid's achievements might be if he had preferred to rule his genius rather than indulge it." It was Quintilian also who called Ovid "overfond of his own genius." The genius, admirable or not, appeared in full stature in Ovid's early youth and continued with force but slightly abated to his death.

Ovid's earliest elegies are included in the *Amores,* which, he tells us in the introductory epigram, were originally in five books and are now reduced to three; certain poems may have been omitted for prudential considerations. Tibullus' Delia probably was real, Propertius' Cynthia was almost as certainly a real woman though skeptics have suspected she might be a literary figment. In the case of Ovid's Corinna there can be no doubt, on the one hand, that she is synthetic, and on the other that the experiences out of which she was created were real. Such a poem as *Amores* I.5 may be cited as evidence:

> In summer's heat and mid-time of the day,
> To rest my limbs upon a bed I lay.
> One window shut, the other open stood,
> Which gave such light as twinkles in a wood,
> Like twilight glimpse at setting of the sun,
> Or night being past, and yet not day begun;
> Such light to shamefast maidens must be shown,
> Where they may sport and seem to be unknown.
> Then came Corinna in a long loose gown,
> Her white neck hid with tresses hanging down,
> Resembling fair Semiramis going to bed,
> Or Lais of a thousand lovers sped.
> I snatched her gown, being thin, the harm was small,
> Yet strived she to be covered therewithal.
> And striving thus as one that would be chaste,
> Betrayed herself and yielded at the last.

Stark naked as she stood before mine eye,
No one wen in her body could I spy.
What arms and shoulders did I touch and see!
How apt her breasts were to be pressed by me!
How smooth a belly under her waist saw I!
How large a leg, and what a lusty thigh!
To leave the rest, all liked me passing well;
I clinged her naked body, down she fell.
Judge you the rest; being tired, she bade me kiss,
Jove send me more such afternoons as this.
                                    —Christopher Marlowe

What sets Ovid's elegies apart from his predecessors' is not only their greater ebullience and wit but their versatile variety. The others require a rather special taste or special introduction; Ovid's poems can be enjoyed by anyone who can enjoy Palgrave's *Golden Treasury.* An indication of the contents of the forty-nine elegies which comprise the three books will illustrate Ovid's variety, and at the same time both his debt to his predecessors and his anticipations of his own later work. (pp. 204-05)

Next in order are the *Heroides,* a series of imaginary letters from women of the heroic or legendary age to their absent heroes. All the women grieve for the separation, but the circumstances and the character of each heroine are different, so that the letters are by no means repetitious. The *Heroides* may be regarded as Ovid's most representative work; they illustrate his very great skill as a storyteller, his intimate understanding of types of female character, his ever-present and all enveloping wit. It is just that the *Heroides* should have proved perhaps the most popular of Ovid's works. The notion of a fictitious letter had been used by Propertius; Ovid's innovation was in limiting his correspondents to the remote past, thus providing free scope for the narrative art which we see more fully presented in the *Metamorphoses.* (p. 209)

The great attraction in all the letters is their dramatic quality. Each is a tragedy in miniature, containing all that the reader (as contrasted with the spectator) seeks. Though the pattern remains constant, actually there is at least as much variety in incident and, more important, character delineation as there is in Plautus' or Terence's adaptations of New Comedy. Ariadne, Oenone, Dejanira, Hypsipyle, and Dido have all been deserted, but each is a different woman, and their circumstances are different. Medea is burdened not only by Jason's desertion but by the weight of remorse for her own crimes. Phaedra is the victim of an illicit but irresistible passion. Penelope, Laodamia, and Hermione have suffered no wrong from their husbands but have their individual reasons for appealing to them. Briseis complains of another's violence and can charge her correspondent only with supineness. Like the dramatist too, Ovid is detached from his creatures. They, not he, speak; he stands apart with his audience, stage-managing his performance and permeating it with his wit to afford easiest comprehension and greatest delight.

The tongue-in-cheek quality of the didactic series on love is apparent in its first member, *Medicina faciei,* or "Face Lotions," of which only some hundred lines are extant. In what looks like a parody of Vergil's *Georgics* Ovid declares that cultivation improves the various sorts of agricultural produce; cultivation can similarly improve that great re-

source of womankind, the face—though Ovid makes decent acknowledgement of the importance of good manners and amiability. (p. 211)

He then proceeds to give very knowledgeable advice on how, by means of design and color, to make the most of good points and conceal blemishes, on the uses of tears, a graceful gait, accomplishments in music, literature, and games, on how to make and exploit the acquaintance of men, how to rouse and retain their interest, and, lastly, on how to give and derive the greatest pleasure.

Except for the latter rubric—and the exception is due only to our different notions of propriety—Ovid's well-bred decency removes all offense from even his most questionable matter. Only a prurient or an oafish mind could degrade his charm to pruriency or oafishness. Much of the depreciation which the *Art of Love* has suffered at the hands of moralists is due to the wrong assumption that a Victorian social order obtained in ancient Rome; either, then, the women the poet envisages must be professional courtesans, or else Ovid was encouraging the seduction of respectable maids and matrons. Actually neither class is in question; what Ovid has in mind are freedwomen or women who had entered the legally recognized and respectable but less constraining form of marriage known as *usus.* It is true enough that the spirit of the book is directly contrary to the spirit of the Augustan reforms looking towards the elevation of conventional family life and the increase of population; but Ovid is not suborning crime nor advocating general debauchery. And since *das ewig Weibliche* is the exclusive domain of neither Rosie O'Grady nor the Colonel's lady, much may be learned from the shrewd and observant professor of love. So far from being a salacious book the *Art of Love* may actually be recommended to the young on some such terms as Plautus' *Truculentus* or the *Book of Proverbs.* The poem is a minor masterpiece.

It is not too much to call the *Metamorphoses* a major masterpiece. It has no lofty program, and none of Lucretius' intensity or Vergil's exaltation, but it is a highly artistic and thoroughly adult handling of one of the world's richest legacies of stories. Judged by the gauge of direct and seminal influence, European literature and art would be poorer for the loss of the *Metamorphoses* than for the loss of Homer. What Ovid accomplishes in the *Metamorphoses* is the linking together into one artistically harmonious whole of all the stories of classical mythology. The link is the element of transformation (which is the meaning of *metamorphoses*), and Ovid traverses the entire range, from the dawn of creation, when chaos was transformed into the orderly universe, down to his own age, when the soul of Julius Caesar was transformed to a star and set in the heavens among the immortals. Every important myth is at least touched upon, and though the stories differ widely in time and place there is no break in the sequence of the narrative. It is in his transitions that the poet shows his consummate skill. For passing from cycle to cycle every thread of connection is exploited, and where none exist some ingenious transition is adroitly contrived. The wonderland of fantasy is continuous, one magic enticement growing naturally out of another, not a series of disparate museum rooms. The closest Alexandrian model we know of are the *Aitiai* of Callimachus, but these, like Propertius' aetiological poems, were disparate pieces. The framework for other great collections of individual tales— the *Decameron, Canterbury Tales, Arabian Nights,* Don Juan—is more plausible because more naturalistic. Ovid's framework makes no concession to naturalism but is pure artifice. Artifice, indeed, is the key to the Ovidian mood. Homer presumably believed in the historicity of his tale and expected his auditors to believe it. Callimachus obviously did not believe in his, but wrote as if he expected his readers to believe in them. Ovid makes no pretense of literal belief and is addressing people on the same side of his fence. His work is pure play, seriously conceived and respected as such. But this is not to say that he is oblivious to all truth: it is only for the archaeological truth that Ovid invites to suspension of disbelief; of the perennial human truths he is an acute observer and effective expositor. Aristotle's dictum in the *Poetics* to the effect that poetry is truer than history is as perfectly applicable to the *Metamorphoses* as to Greek tragedy. Whether the actual events transpired as set forth is of no consequence; but given such events the loves and hates and ambitions of men and women would so manifest themselves. The *Metamorphoses* are truer than the handbooks from which Ovid derived his tales in the same way as Shakespeare's plays are truer than his sources.

In all respects the *Metamorphoses* present Ovid at the height of his power. It was completed when he was fifty, just before he went into exile. He says (*Tristia*) that he burned his own copy out of disgust with poetry or because the work was rough and unfinished; this may suggest his own high aims for the work. He himself had no doubts of its immortality, as his Epilogue shows; this is a modernization of Golding's version, which Shakespeare read:

> Now have I brought a work to end which neither
>   Jove's fierce wrath,
> Nor sword, nor fire, nor fretting age with all the
>   force it hath
> Are able to abolish quite. Let come that fatal
>   hour
> Which, saving of this brittle flesh, hath over me
>   no power,
> And at his pleasure make an end of my uncertain
>   time;
> Yet shall the better part of me assured be to
>   climb
> Aloft above the starry sky; and all the world
>   shall never
> Be able for to quench my name; for look! how
>   far so ever
> The Roman Empire by the right of conquest
>   shall extend,
> So far shall all folk read this work; and time
>   without all end,
> If poets as by prophecy about the truth may aim,
> My life shall everlastingly be lengthened still by
>   fame.

The fifteen books of the *Metamorphoses,* in nearly twelve thousand hexameter lines, contain some two hundred fifty myths. Ovid's meter is rapid, his Latin easy, though he seems to have coined some two hundred words, especially compounds. These enable him to obtain clever effects, in matching sound to sense. He makes frequent and effective use of epigrams and antitheses. Translation naturally loses or cheapens the effect of such devices as *Consiliis non curribus utere nostris,* "Take my counsel, not my car" ("The Sun to Phaethon"), but they are effective in the Latin and communicate the right note of ironic playfulness. A half-ironic playfulness also eases the pantheist doctrine which underlies the book. This is reflected in the account of creation in Book I and reverted to in an account of the Pythagorean theory of transmigration in Book 15, which gives a kind of philosophic authority to the idea of metamorphosis. Pythagoras (an odd figure in the *dramatis personae* of the *Metamorphoses*) delivers a long discourse on vegetarianism and the cycle of generation on which the system depends. Mind circulates eternally, and at what is called death passes quickly from man to beast, and beast to man:

> All things do change; but nothing sure doth perish. This same sprite
> Doth fleet, and frisking here and there doth swiftly take his flight
> From one place to another place, and ent'reth every wight,
> Removing out of man to beast, and out of beast to man;
> But yet it never perisheth nor never perish can.
> And even as supple wax with ease receiveth figures strange,
> And keeps not aye one shape, nor bides assured aye from change,
> And yet continueth always wax in substance; so I say
> The soul is aye the selfsame thing it was, and yet astray
> It fleeteth into sundry shapes. . . .
> In all the world there is not that that standeth at a stay.
> Things ebb and flow, and every shape is made to pass away.
> The time itself continually is fleeting like a brook,
> For neither brook nor lightsome time can tarry still. But look!
> As every wave drives other forth, and that that comes behind
> Both thrusteth and is thrust itself, even so the times by kind
> Do fly and follow both at once, and evermore renew,
> For that that was before is left, and straight there doth ensue
> Another that was never erst.
>
>   —Arthur Golding

Space cannot be spared for citing a more typical story from the *Metamorphoses,* nor is it necessary to do so, for every reader of English literature, though he may not be aware of it, has acquaintance with the book; all that need be said is that the copies are seldom superior to the original.

In the *Metamorphoses* the note of Roman imperial patriotism is struck at many passages besides the concluding section on Julius Caesar. Ovid's specific contribution to the institutional literature of Rome is his *Fasti,* a poetical calendar in elegiac verse. The poem is didactic, but its form and spirit are unique in Latin literature and Ovid's own. Only six of the projected twelve books were completed when Ovid was banished. The original dedication to Augustus is retained at 2.3-18. These books, partially revised by Ovid and with a new dedication to Germanicus, were published after his death. The last six books were too fragmentary to be published, though citations from them occur. The plan devoted a single book to each month of the year; what we have covers the months from January through June. Under each month the material is arranged in three divisions—astronomical, historical, and religious; the risings and settings of constellations are set forth, together with remarks on the weather; legendary and historical events connected with specific dates are described; and festivals and religious rites are recorded with minute detail. Ovid's astronomy is vague and inaccurate; his technical information he derived from an astronomical calendar prepared for his use by his friend Clodius Tuscus, but like other Roman works on astronomy this was taken from the Greek without allowances being made for differences of time and place and with confusion of the real and apparent risings and settings at sunrise and sunset. It is in the antiquarian portion of his work that Ovid is most interested and has most to contribute. In the historical portion there is little (except the dubious dating by month and day) that is not to be found in the first decade of Livy, but the stories of Lucretia or of the Sabine women are told with Ovid's usual economy and light grace. But for religious antiquities Ovid's *Fasti* is a first-class source. Only Varro as he is represented in St. Augustine throws the same kind of light on popular observances and beliefs, but where Varro's interest is scholarly Ovid's is human. If his explanation of a religious custom is not always satisfactory to the historian of religion, it is good enough for the student of popular beliefs and practices. . . .

The *Fasti* is something of the same kind of index to the life and interests of the Romans as is a personal calendar to the life and interests of the individual; and the mythological pictures with which this calendar is adorned are far superior to those provided by beer or insurance companies.

When Evander's mother offers her son encouragement, she says (*Fasti*), *Omne solum forti patria est, ut piscibus aequor,* "To a man of stout heart any soil is his country, like the sea to fish." But in his exile at Tomis on the Black Sea Ovid himself was a fish out of water. The five books of *Tristia* and the four books of *Epistles from Pontus* are filled with complaints, sometimes descending to self-pity, and with supplications for reinstatement, sometimes descending to servility. But the brightness of the versification is untarnished and the Ovidian wit still flashes. The *Tristia* is a collection of elegies, in the form of letters, consisting chiefly of laments upon his exile. The first of the five books was written in the course of the journey but finished off at Tomis and dispatched from there. As in all the books (except the second, which is a continuous essay), the first and last poems are prologue and epilogue and were written last; the remainder seem to stand in the order of their composition. The prologue poem sends the book off to Rome, poorly bound as befits its exiled author, and apologizes for its halting inspiration as being due to suffer-

ing. The author hardly dares hope that anyone will introduce the book to the emperor's presence. The book's elder brothers, the *Ars amatoria,* are spoken of as murderers of their sire, whose altered shape might now place him in the *Metamorphoses.* The second poem, actually the first of the series, was written during a storm at sea while Ovid was en route to Tomis. He has kind thoughts for his wife, who does not know that peril of drowning has been heaped on his punishment. His sentence was deserved, but his guilt was involuntary. The third poem is a moving description of Ovid's last night in Rome:

> Ah! when I think of that last fatal eve
> When all the joys of Rome I had to leave,
> When I recall that cruel, cruel hour
> E'en now adown my cheeks the tear-drops pour
>
>   . . . . .
>
> And 'twas my task to choose the serving train
> Who should attend my exile o'er the main.
> But my poor heart was numbed with long delay,
> I could not think nor count each passing day,
> No gold had I prepared, no raiment for the way.
>
> Of all my friends but one or two had come
> To say farewell ere I should leave my home.
> My loving wife with cruel grief distressed
> Clasped me still mourning to her mourning breast.
>
>   . . . . .
>
> Women and men and even children weep
> And every corner seemed its tears to keep.
> In truth, if we may match the small and great
> So Troy appeared when at the open gate
> The Greeks came storming in and Ilion knew her fate.
>
>   —F. A. Wright
>   (pp. 215-21)

As the letters proceed, the note of pessimism appears to deepen. The concluding poem of the fourth book, addressed to posterity, is of special interest . . . for its autobiographical details. The last poem of all offers his wife the consolation of the immortality which his poetry has vouchsafed her and praises her constancy.

Letters of the same sort make up the four books of the *Epistles from Pontus,* except that here, as Ovid himself says, the recipients are addressed by name:

> This work is not less sad than that which I sent before—in theme the same, in title different, and each epistle reveals the recipient without concealing his name.
>
>   —A. L. Wheeler

The great event upon which Ovid set his hopes was the celebration of Tiberius' Pannonian triumph in A.D. 13, but Tiberius proved as adamant as Augustus. Ovid apparently concluded that direct appeal to friends might be more effective and, apparently obtaining the permission of his correspondents (3.6 seems to refer to one who refused permission), published the collection of the first three books of the *Epistles,* with prologue 1.1 and epilogue at 3.9, both addressed to Brutus. In 3.7 he finally resigns himself, with a degree of fortitude:

> Words fail me to make the same request so many times; and at last it shames me that my idle prayers are endless. You are all weary of my monotonous verses, and my request you have learned by heart, I think. What message my letter bears you know already, although the wax has not been broken from its bonds. So let me change the purport of my writing that my course be not so often against the hurrying stream.
>
> For my good hopes of you, pardon me, my friends: of such error now there shall be an end. Nor will I be called a trouble to my wife who in sooth is as true to me as she is timid and backward in her efforts. This also, Naso, thou shalt bear, and thou hast borne worse things; no burden can affect thee now.

> —A. L. Wheeler

After the death of Augustus in A.D. 14 Ovid wrote a panegyric on the emperor and even composed a glorification of Caesar in the Getic language. But Tiberius could not be swayed. The poems of the fourth and last book give evidence of the poet's despairing resignation. Here as in all the poems written in exile, the main themes are concern for the deterioration and constraint of his Muse and complaints of his barbarous environment.

In his famous literary feud with Apollonius of Rhodes Callimachus' heaviest artillery was his (lost) *Ibis,* named for a foul scavenger bird. In *Tristia* 4.9 Ovid had threatened to make some unnamed enemy immortal with his pen, and his *Ibis* (650 lines), an imitation rather than a paraphrase of Callimachus' poem, is apparently the fulfilment of the threat. In the opening verses Ovid declares that in the previous fifty years of his life (which dates the poem to the early period of his exile) he had never written a line injurious to anyone but himself. The unidentifiable culprit, we gather, was a one-time friend who calumniated the poet and his wife and tried to enrich himself by confiscating their property. Every imprecation recorded in history or legend is hurled at the enemy in a profusion that would be even more shocking if somewhat labored learning did not remove some of the sting. For the figures out of the past that he cites Ovid uses patronymics rather than their familiar names, and he alludes to their stories by obscure periphrases. At the breathless end of his catalogue of curses the poet asks the gods to multiply their number and promises that he will yet reveal the dastard's name.

The last in the list of Ovid's genuine works is the fragmentary and uncompleted *Halieutica* (132 lines), a treatise on fishing. The subject had been treated by Greek writers and was a favorite in Rome, whose epicures prized exotic fish above all dainties. Ovid's interest and information were doubtless due to his residence in the Black Sea fishing port. The first part of the poem deals with means of defense with which nature has endowed all creatures (not fish alone), and the second tells where various species of fish are to be found. Lost works of Ovid of which we have knowledge, besides the *Medea* and the panegyrics on Augustus in Latin and Getic of which mention has been made, are a *Gigantomachy* (never completed), an *Epitha-*

lamium for Fabius Maximus, epigrams, an elegy on Messalla, and a poem on the triumph of Tiberius in A.D. 13. (pp. 223-24)

> *Moses Hadas, "Ovid," in his* A History of Latin Literature, *Columbia University Press, 1952, pp. 201-26.*

Michael Grant   (essay date 1954)

[*Grant is a distinguished English classical scholar, translator, and editor known for his eminently readable studies of the classical world, especially Rome. His numerous writings encompass a large variety of topics and include* The Ancient Mediterranean *(1969),* The Jews in the Roman World *(1973),* Caesar *(1974),* Jesus: An Historian's Review of the Gospels *(1977), and* The History of Rome *(1978). In the following excerpt, Grant briefly explores Ovid's works in the context of Roman elegy, claiming that "much of his work belongs to a new era, and is of a new character."*]

Ovid is the light of the middle and later years of Augustus. He was younger than the other leading elegists, and long outlived them. Much of his work belongs to a new era, and is of a new character. Virgil's *Aeneid* and Horace's *Secular Hymn* had not long been published when Roman society began to feel the inevitable reaction against their exalted imperialism. Love elegy had not long reached its summit under Propertius when a more blasé 'golden youth' began to feel a distaste for his strong expression of strong personal feeling—while equally deprecating the 'hearty', masculine double standard of feminine values displayed by Horace.

Ovid, like so many of his forerunners, was not a Roman; he came from Sulmo (Sulmona) in central Italy. But his father was a gentleman who gave him a fashionable Roman upbringing, and Ovid grew up to be the perfect representative of the less serious, more sophisticated smart society which now flourished at the capital. His diction reflects the new fashions of rhetorical education which he had experienced. Ovid's language moves rapidly, lightly and brilliantly. It unites perfectly with the elegiac metre. But this metre underwent a new interpretation at the hand of Ovid, in accordance with his talent and the spirit of the age. It became a more polished and refined medium than it had ever been before. Tibullus had pointed the path away from the passion and morbidity of Propertius. But with Ovid the flight becomes faster and lighter still, and there is little real seriousness left. He himself personifies the Elegiac Muse, no longer as 'tearful' according to the most familiar tradition, but as flippant and 'festive'. He develops this metre into a medium suited for the rapid production of satisfyingly neat effects of no very great profundity.

So a new era began, and was recognised to have begun, when soon after 16 B.C., Ovid published the first edition of his *Loves* (*Amores*). At this time, Horace was setting his final signature to the literary lyric by the preparation of his last *Odes.* The love-elegies of Propertius and Tibullus had been known for more than a decade. Ovid's *Amores* are love-poems too, as their title indicates; but they are love-poetry of quite a new sort. Ovid is not a poet of serious love. To him, love is as frivolous a subject as it is to Horace. But Ovid, unlike Horace, has the Alexandrian absorption in female psychology; Ovid understands the woman's point of view. He 'possessed a . . . gift of sympathetic understanding often perceptible behind the gloss, the glitter, and the cynicism of his society verse. A friend and a guide, he wants to emancipate the fair sex from dullness and squalor' [Ronald Syme].

The heroine of Ovid's verse is 'Corinna'. Twenty years later he said that people were still asking who she was. Perhaps she never existed. This is not subjective love-poetry, about passions felt by Ovid himself. In case we did not notice this, he tells us so. The **Amores** introduce us to the light-hearted Ovidian world, and to the new, quick version of the elegiac metre which perfectly reflects it. Only occasionally does Ovid show us what more he could have done if he had wanted to. He is moving when he writes of the death of Tibullus who had been his friend. More often his regrets contain an element of mockery or humour—as when he upbraids the tablets on which he had written an unfortunate love-letter:

> To these my love I foolishly committed,
> And then with sweet words to my mistress fitted.
> More fitly had they wrangling bonds contained
> From barbarous lips of some attorney strained.
> Among day-books and bills they had lain better,
> In which the merchant wails his bankrupt debtor.

Ovid's second endeavour was called the **Heroides** ('heroines', i.e. legendary women). This is a collection of poetic letters. He himself describes them to us as letters (*epistulae*), recalling that Horace's first poetic *Epistles* were published a few years earlier. Most of these 'letters' of Ovid are ostensibly addressed by mythical ladies to their absent husbands or lovers. Unhappy love is the theme of the **Heroides.** Menander's Greek plays of the Athenian New Comedy had contained a love interest, but it is Ovid who handed down this permanently appealing theme to medieval and modern literature. His women's plaints are rhetorical and ingenious. They are presented with great vividness and modernity. Yet for literary purposes they are placed in the legendary epoch. This element of fantasy is an incentive to romance and adventurous excitement. It lends itself to an imaginative, lively vein, which foreshadows the romantics.

But Ovid often has his tongue in his cheek; and, even when he has not, this is not real, earnest love-poetry. The poet is almost feminine in his sensitiveness to his heroines, yet in writing of their passion he himself remains wholly dispassionate. He regards their psychological performances observantly and sympathetically, but with clinical objectivity. This interpretation of elegy was something new. So was Ovid's handling of the traditional myths. Quite gone is the reverence, the antique atmosphere with which Virgil had surrounded many old legends. Ovid's mythical heroines are entirely modernised, brought right up to date. They are, but for their names, ladies of the contemporary fashionable world.

They delighted the Middle Ages, and fostered the idea of knightly love—at times the letters were even believed to be real. They also delighted the Renaissance. Immediately after the invention of printing, editions of the **Heroides** were published in rapid succession: the first was printed at Rome in 1471, and there was a Venice edition twenty years later. An English translation appeared in 1567; and fifteen years later these poems engaged the attention of Christopher Marlowe, whose versions, however, were publicly burnt by order of the Church in 1599.

After the **Heroides,** Ovid hit on the idea of making fun—at one and the same time—of the love-elegy, of moralists, and of 'didactic' instructive poetry in general. He had already written in this vein **On Painting the Face (Medicamina Faciei).** Soon after 1 B.C., he published his **Art of Love (Ars Amatoria).** It pretends to treat of love didactically, as a science, and does so with a cynicism that is not typically Roman. At the same time this picture of Ovid as Professor of Love contains some of his maturest thoughts on life—for instance 'if you want to be loved, be lovable'. Macaulay described the **Ars Amatoria** as Ovid's best poem; and Goethe's *Roman Elegies* (1795) are prefaced by a motto from it, fittingly enough since Goethe knew Ovid better than he knew any other poet. In the intervals of ironic pedantry, the **Ars Amatoria** reverts to Ovid's prime talent of telling stories—to which his scintillating versification perfectly lent itself. These stories have won the fancy of many fine artists. Titian's 'Ariadne on Naxos' is said to be based, not on Catullus' famous poem on that subject, but on the version in Ovid's **Ars Amatoria.**

However, at the time of its publication, this poem flew against traditional respectability, and against the efforts of Augustus to revive the morals of Roman society. There was disapproval. Ovid himself bears witness to this by writing a conciliatory sequel, **The Cures of Love (Remedia Amoris).** But this is too flippant to have reconciled any critics. Ovid did not at first experience imperial sanctions. But later, in A.D. 8, he was suddenly banished to a remote semi-barbarous frontier-post of the Empire, Tomis (Constanta in Roumania). During the remaining nine years of his life, including three under Augustus' successor Tiberius, he was never granted permission to return.

He himself describes the causes of his exile as two, 'a poem and a mistake'. The poem was presumably the **Art of Love,** but that had been published for quite a long time—perhaps eight years—before this bolt came from the blue. The 'mistake' was clearly regarded as the more serious reason for his downfall.

> The cause of this, too much to most revealed,
> Must be for ever by myself concealed.

But Ovid suggests that he saw something he should not have seen. Now in A.D. 8, the year of Ovid's exile, it was disclosed that the emperor's grand-daughter Julia was involved in personal scandals. The emperor, with his official policy of moral improvement, did not tolerate this subversive activity in his own house; and she was disgraced—as her mother had been for similar reasons ten years earlier. Perhaps Ovid, banished in the same year, had seen misconduct by her, regarded as of political significance, which he ought to have reported.

For a townsman and a metropolitan like Ovid, the fate was a terrible one. At the time when it descended upon him, two important works were well under way. The *Metamorphoses,* in hexameters, were nearly ready. The *Fasti,* a calendar of the Roman year in elegiac verse, were about half finished; six out of the twelve books were complete. Ovid, having tried mock-didactic elegy in the *Ars Amatoria,* was now using the same metre for didactic that is more serious—though nothing written by Ovid can be wholly serious for long. This poetic calendar includes descriptions of festivals, religious rites, legends and historical events. The origins and antique customs of Rome were a time-hallowed subject for poetry, going back to Ennius. Ovid discusses them in something of the spirit of the Alexandrian master Callimachus, whose most famous poem had been his *Causes (Aitia)*. The precedents of Callimachus and Ennius had likewise helped to inspire Virgil's talent for the antiquarian folk-lore of Italy.

But those three, the Greek and the two Romans, had written in hexameters. The earliest surviving elegiac poetry dealing with such archaeological topics is from the hand of Propertius. In his later years, disappointed in love and encouraged by Maecenas, he had turned increasingly to the antiquities of Rome—but had retained his own elegiac metre, thus creating a new elegiac *genre* which Ovid now adapts to his own uses in the *Fasti.* Propertius had shown a profound insight into the romance of the legends, handling them with a power worthy of Virgil; Ovid is, rather,

Daphne transforms into a laurel tree to escape the unwanted amorous attentions of the god Apollo in this sculpture of a scene from the Metamorphoses *by Bernini.*

inclined to use these myths as a piquant source-book for his special gifts, including, now, an increased dexterity and neatness in his interpretation of the elegiac couplet.

Thus Ovid, too, became a national patriotic poet. He himself remarks what a strange thought this was. But it was evidently not enough for the emperor; or it was too late. It was sadly ironical that the patriotic *Fasti* should have been in progress when the order for his exile arrived. The poem was published, as far as it went, only after his death, with a dedication—added by him in his exile—to the heir presumptive Germanicus.

Ovid continued to write elegiac poetry from Tomis; and to express his grief at his banishment he had recourse to the epistolary form which he had used to such effect in the *Heroides.* The first collection published after his exile consisted of five books of *Lamentations (Tristia),* and they were followed by the *Letters from the Black Sea (Epistulae ex Ponto).* There is also the *Ibis,* a vigorous curse, and the *Nux,* a nut-tree's lamentation about the stones thrown at it. All these naturally lack the gaiety of earlier work, and Ovid grovels humiliatingly to the great. But the poems are of value for their personal and biographical indications; and his skill in handling the elegiac couplet is unimpaired.

His version of this couplet—not those of Catullus and Propertius—served as the model for successive generations. Rome never produced a rival to Ovid, though there are flashes of beauty in the elegies—four centuries later—of the last 'classical' poets, Ausonius and Claudian. (pp. 223-29)

> *Michael Grant, "Horace, Ovid and After," in his* Roman Literature, *Cambridge at the University Press, 1954, pp. 205-54.*

Mary M. Innes   (essay date 1955)

[*In the excerpt below, Innes examines some aspects of Ovid's style, skill, and ingenuity in the* Metamorphoses, *finding the work "full of the freshness and charm of a world newly born."*]

Among all the writings of Latin authors, few have appealed to a wider public or had more effect on later literature than the *Metamorphoses* of Ovid. In this work, the poet has gathered together a rich assortment of tales, which have one element in common: they all deal with transformations. He tells us of chaos changed into ordered harmony, of animals turned to stone, of men and women who become trees or animals, stones or stars. With this slender unity of theme, he has produced a poem of fifteen books, which holds the reader's attention to the end. The telling of stories must have been one of the earliest forms of entertainment, but it has lost none of its fascination, and in the *Metamorphoses* Ovid reveals himself as a prince of story-tellers. The tales he has to offer are not new: he has collected them from the pages of the Greek poets whose works formed an essential part of the education of every Roman, from previous anthologies of Greek myths, from Latin folk-lore, and even from further afield, from Babylon and the East. But he has infused new life into the old

stories, retailing them with the inimitable grace and practised ease of one who knows well how to hold his audience.
The result is a treasure-house of myth and legend, which
was read with delight in his own day, and has continued
to charm succeeding generations, providing a source from
which the whole of western European literature has derived inspiration. And yet this poem, coloured with rhetoric, it is true, but full of the freshness and charm of a world
newly born, is the work of one who was, at the same time,
among the most sophisticated of Latin writers. (p. 9)

His first published works were the *Amores,* a collection of
shorter poems, weaving different variations on the basic
theme suggested by the title. They followed closely in the
tradition set by earlier elegiac poets, though the sincerity
of Ovid's passion for the lady Corinna, and even her existence, may be doubted. Numerous allusions in the poems
show him to be, as one would expect, already widely acquainted with mythology, and ready to embellish his
verses with reminiscences of the classical tales. It is in the
Heroides, however, which followed soon after, that he
first uses stories of earlier, legendary, lovers as material for
his own poetry, giving a new vitality to the ancient myths.
These letters in verse, supposedly written by deserted ladies to the lovers who have abandoned them, led naturally
to his next production, the *Ars Amatoria,* a handbook on
the subject of love. Whatever criticisms it may have
aroused, the *Art of Love,* as it is usually called, does undoubtedly convey a fascinating picture of contemporary
Rome, and the daily life of its gay pleasure-loving society.
In the course of this poem, Ovid occasionally digresses
from his main theme to tell at length one of the old myths
which has some relevance to his argument, or has been
suggested to him by the context. In these passages his skill
as a story-teller is already clearly revealed: they stand out
from the rest as delightful cameos, instinct with a freshness and sympathy that contrasts notably with the polished cynicism of the rest. The pleasure which he obviously derived from relating the stories of Daedalus and Icarus, Cephalus and Procris, Theseus and Ariadne, all of
which are retold in the *Metamorphoses,* may well have
suggested the idea of a longer poem in which he could exercise his narrative gift on such themes exclusively. In any
case, the *Art of Love* was a tour-de-force which could not
be repeated: he published the *Remedies of Love,* to provide an antidote for his own prescriptions, but after that
it was necessary to find some other medium for his restless
genius.

It was probably at this time that he experimented in a
more ambitious field, and composed his tragedy, the
Medea, which was highly praised in antiquity, but has unfortunately not survived. It would have been interesting
to compare it with the treatment of the same theme in the
Metamorphoses. But, however successful it was, Ovid apparently decided against continuing in this branch of literature.

His next production was the *Metamorphoses* itself. For
this he abandoned the elegiac couplet, and employed the
hexameter line throughout. From its metre and its
length—fifteen books in all—it can claim to be regarded
as Ovid's essay in epic verse, and it is so regarded by Quin-

tilian. Others have denied its right to be considered as an
epic, for it can scarcely be said to possess the underlying
unity that should characterize such verse. However,
thanks to Ovid's unfailing dexterity, the work is so cleverly constructed that the reader is led on from one story to
the next, without being conscious of any lack of cohesion.
The poem has a certain chronological framework, beginning with the transformation of chaos into an ordered universe, then ranging at length through Greek mythology to
the Trojan war and the escape of Aeneas to Italy. This
leads to a synopsis of early Roman kings and so, with rather a rapid bound, to the transformation of Julius Caesar
into a star, for the greater glory of his adopted son, the emperor Augustus with whose praises the poem ends.

But it was in vain that Ovid paid his tribute to Augustus.
Before the *Metamorphoses* had received its final polish,
while the *Fasti,* a poem on the Roman calendar, was only
half-done (for he had characteristically begun on this before the completion of his previous work) Ovid was suddenly expelled from Rome, on some charge that was never
made explicit, and ordered to live a life of exile at Tomis
on the Black Sea coast. We have the poet's word for it that
he had been guilty only of an indiscretion, not a crime, but
for the rest we can only speculate. In a final burst of melodrama, before leaving Rome, he flung his *Metamorphoses*
in the fire, declaring it as yet unfit for publication. No
doubt he had Virgil in mind, who died before his epic was
completed; but, without being uncharitable, we may feel
sure that this gesture was not intended to be final, that
Ovid knew there were other copies of his work in circulation, and that he had not any real intention of destroying
the poem.

From his exile he continued to write, pouring out polished
verse, appealing for pardon, describing the horrors of the
land to which he had been exiled, its barbarity and icy
chill, deploring the constant threats of war, and again appealing for a reprieve. But the years went on, and the pardon he sought was never granted. There are signs that he
became more reconciled to his lot, and varied the laments
of the *Tristia* and the *Epistulae ex Ponto* by writing a
poem on the fishes of the Black Sea, and even attempting
a poem in the Getic language. But he never ceased to
speak longingly of Rome, even when his hopes of return
gradually faded and disappeared. In A.D. 17 Ovid died,
still an exile in Tomis. His fame, however, was securely
founded: his own proud boast in the closing lines of the
Metamorphoses has been supremely justified.

When the general plan of the *Metamorphoses* had suggested itself to Ovid, there was no lack of material for him
to use. All the best-known myths could be found in the
works of Homer, or of the Greek dramatists, with which
he would naturally be familiar from his schooldays. Moreover, the idea of collecting such tales into omnibus volumes was one that had already appealed to poets of the
Hellenistic age. We know of such a compilation, the
Ornithogonia, assigned to one Boios, which dealt with the
transformation of men into birds, and Nicander of Colo-
phon had been responsible for another collection, which
Ovid probably used. In Rome itself, Ovid's friend and contemporary, Aemilius Macer, had translated the *Ornitho-*

gonia, and the Greek Parthenius, tutor to Virgil and Tiberius, had produced a work entitled *Metamorphoses.* It is impossible to say how much Ovid may have derived from these earlier writings, but there is no doubt that, both in its scope, embracing some two hundred and fifty stories, and in the elegance of style and treatment, Ovid's *Metamorphoses* is unique. The narrative skill which the poet possessed was employed to weave his tales into one vast and elaborate tapestry—an appropriate metaphor, for the pictorial effect of Ovid's writing is sometimes almost overwhelming.

After the usual epic invocation of heaven's aid, Ovid launches straightway into an account of the origin of the world from a chaotic mass of elements, and describes their transformation into an ordered whole. We are then told of the four ages of the world, transmuted from gold to silver, then to bronze, and finally to iron. In this last age, all manner of wickedness appeared: there is therefore full scope for the story-teller. An age that is too peaceful and law-abiding makes dull reading, after a while. Jupiter himself reports to the gods the first transformation of man to beast, the punishment inflicted on Lycaon for his wickedness. The father of gods and men then announces his intention to destroy the entire human race. Afraid of fire, he sends the flood, strangely similar to that described in the Old Testament, but saves Deucalion and Pyrrha to repeople the earth. From that point the poem sweeps steadily on with never a break or hesitation. Apollo appears and slays the Python, then falls in love with Daphne, and the amorous adventures of the gods have begun. They continue throughout the next five books, and the first half of the sixth. Then it is the turn of the heroes of ancient Greece, Jason and Theseus and their like, till we come at length to the Trojan war and so, through Aeneas, to the ancient tales of Italy and of the Roman kings. The last and most glorious metamorphosis of all, in a Roman's eyes, is that of Julius Caesar into a star, in order that the father of Augustus may be no mere mortal. And so, with a panegyric on the emperor, the poet ends: having, as he set out to do, spun a thread of continuous narrative from the beginning of the world down to his own times.

Apart, however, from this continuous narrative, Ovid has a host of ingenious devices for introducing his stories. Sometimes one character recounts an anecdote for the benefit of the company, the daughters of Minyas while away the time as they spin by telling each other stories, broken-hearted Orpheus fills a whole book with his repertoire of songs, the Muses have a contest with the daughters of Pierus, which ends in the transformation of those presumptuous sisters. This contest enables Ovid to include the touching tale of Ceres and Proserpine, which he puts into the mouth of Calliope. Without some such excuse, it has no place in a record of transformations, even if the poet seeks to justify himself by recording changes that befell some of the minor characters.

The skill with which he links his tales is no less admirable than the variety of their presentation. There is no obvious connexion, in many cases, but Ovid is never at a loss. A character in one legend suggests another incident in which he was concerned, the name of a tree or flower, some chance remark, will serve to recall another story. No connexion is too slight, and yet there are few that seem forced. Nowadays the *Metamorphoses* is commonly read only in selections, and of course it lends itself admirably to such selective treatment. But it is only when the poem is read as a whole that one can fully appreciate Ovid's achievement. The work gives at least an illusion of unity, and he has managed to produce a semblance of cohesion between incidents where there is no necessary dramatic link.

The same gods are, of course, introduced over and over again, and have no sooner finished with one adventure than they become involved in the next. Jupiter is the chief menace to nymphs and mortal maidens, but Apollo and Mercury are not far behind. These are not by any means gods to be reverenced: but even Homer had at times failed to take the Olympians seriously, and we can hardly blame an Augustan poet for his attitude. If the deities show themselves distressingly susceptible to human faults and frailties, it is just because of these failings that Ovid makes them seem so alive, and gives such verisimilitude to his world of fancy. Jove can, on occasion, be majestic, but for the most part gods and men are treated in the same way, as actors in a universal drama, where Destiny is the only overriding force.

In his previous works Ovid, speaking in his own person, had had a reputation to maintain as a witty and cynical man of the world; in the *Metamorphoses,* a purely narrative poem, he can abandon this standpoint and reveal, not only insight, but a sympathetic insight into human emotions. As he had done in the *Heroides,* he portrays again pity and fear, tenderness and love, the first stirrings of passion, the turbulent jealousy of scorned love, with a faithfulness which no modern psychologist could surpass. His knowledge of human nature, so devastatingly employed in the *Art of Love,* is here used with kindlier intent. In the same way, the satirical wit of the earlier poem is replaced by a gentler kind of humour, such as is seen in the whimsical description of Jupiter changed into a bull for the carrying off of Europe, in the account of Polyphemus decking himself out to attract Galetea, or again in the delightful picture of Baucis and Philemon. He can even be whimsical at his own expense when, in describing Perseus' first glimpse of Andromeda, he almost makes his hero stand still in astonishment, but remembers in time that this would be fatal for one winging his way through the air.

The danger of monotony is avoided, partly by a variation of pace, and partly by changes in the tone of the poem. By lingering over some stories, passing over others briefly, or merely alluding to them in passing, Ovid prevents the feeling that this is a mere mythological handbook. Thus, when he makes the daughters of Minyas consider and reject so many tales, he is able to give us a brief acquaintance with a whole series of metamorphoses which he does not propose to treat at length. Again, when one particular myth has already received full treatment in some other Latin poem, he tends to pass over it rapidly. So we have only a short account of the desertion of Ariadne, which Ovid himself, in the *Art of Love,* and Catullus before him, had already described. The story of Iphigenia, told with such pathos by Lucretius, is given quite a different emphasis: the actual sacrifice is dismissed in one or two lines. The wanderings of Aeneas, familiar from the *Aeneid,* are only touched upon, and that same hero is hurried through the underworld with almost unseemly haste. This is not, of course, universally true: where a story appealed to him particularly, he was not deterred from telling it again. An instance that springs to mind is the tale of Orpheus and Eurydice, which is given in detail, though Virgil had already recounted it in the *Georgics.* The story of Procris and Cephalus, and that of Daedalus and Icarus, both of which had been introduced into the *Art of Love,* are related again at considerable length in the *Metamorphoses.* Lengthy too, and less pleasant reading, are the orgies of horrors in Ovid's descriptions of battle scenes. Like Lucan after him, he leaves nothing to the imagination. On the whole, however, there is a skillful blending of detailed and less detailed narrative, and of stories of different lengths.

Nor is there any lack of variety in tone and style. It has been said that Ovid felt a sustained effort in the grand manner to be beyond him: hence his rejection of the heroic epic in favour of a more intimate variety. None the less he can, when occasion demands, rise to a really noble tone. The first book, in the description of the world's creation, is solemn and dignified, and can bear comparison with any epic verse. The same is true of much of the philosophy in the fifteenth book. There is grandeur in his description of the North wind, lyric ecstasy in the invocation of Bacchus: while passages calling for gentler and more subdued treatment find him ready with an easy flow of musical verse.

It must be admitted, however, that at times his rhetorical training becomes rather obtrusive. We see it in his love of catalogues, admittedly a feature of epic, but carried to quite incredible lengths by Ovid. One has only to think of the list of hounds which tore Actaeon apart, the trees that crowd into a shade round Orpheus, the mountain peaks set alight by Phaethon, the lovesong of Polyphemus, to realize how far he carried this trick, which strikes a modern reader as somewhat tedious. He also shows a fondness for stock themes, where he seems to invite comparison with earlier poets. An instance of this is to be found in his description of the Golden Age, a favourite subject of Augustan authors: another is his account of the plague which carried off the subjects of King Aeacus, and calls to mind the passages in Virgil and Lucretius, dealing with the same topic. The long speech of Pythagoras in the fifteenth book may be taken to be Ovid's answer to philosophical poetry, challenging the Epicurean philosophy of Lucretius, but it has a rather subtle application to the theme of the *Metamorphoses* itself. The main doctrine of the Pythagoreans, metempsychosis, taught that the soul migrated from one body to another, even from humans into animals, and this might seem to lend a kind of justification to the transformations that Ovid has been describing in the previous books. This idea is never made explicit: stress is laid not so much on the transmigration of souls, as on the vegetarianism that it entails. None the less the constant state of flux and the changing forms that Pythagoras describes may well have seemed to Ovid to lend colour to the changes he himself recorded. His education in rhetoric makes itself felt most forcibly, however, in the set speeches which he puts into the mouths of his characters, whenever opportunity offers. In times of stress his heroines, debating with themselves possible courses of action, do so with all the accomplished tricks of style which an experienced orator might use. Medea and Byblis, Myrrha and Scylla and the rest, show every sign of having studied profitably in the schools of Rome; so carefully do they weigh up balanced arguments on both sides, presenting the alternatives as persuasively as possible, indulging in rhetorical questions and antitheses, before committing themselves to the course of action which they have obviously been intending to pursue from the start. The most elaborate example of a debate is, however, a more legitimate one, the contest between Ajax and Ulysses, to determine the fate of Achilles' arms: a theme which we learn from Juvenal was a stock subject of debate in the rhetorical schools.

Before leaving our consideration of the *Metamorphoses,* it is worth while to notice how much is contributed to the poem by Ovid's appreciation of the beauties of nature. Ovid as a nature poet is somewhat unexpected, but in the setting of the stories, no less than in their personages, he delights to exercise his vivid imagination and, by his words, conjure up a clear and detailed picture of the scenes of the various adventures. There is no suggestion that he, any more than most classical poets, was concerned to describe the actual landscape with which he was himself familiar, in Italy, Sicily, or Greece. The settings for these conventional tales are themselves conventional: a cave in some secluded glade, a bay of the sea, a mountain overhanging the waters—in each case his artist's eye sees the whole picture, and gives it reality by stressing just the kind of detail that would naturally be noticed. The stream so clear that its pebbles can be counted, the still pool hidden among shady trees, the beach where the sand is of just the right texture for walking, these are places we all know, and yet there is a magic about them too, so that his woodlands and his limpid pools are eminently fit to be peopled by nymphs and rustic deities. This shows yet another side of Ovid's talent, and pastoral poetry could and did derive much from the pages of the *Metamorphoses.* No less effective are the more specialized descriptions of places which, though we are never likely to see them, are made real to us by the poet's words. We have only to think of the house of Envy, where all is slime and rottenness, the hungry haunts of Famine, the whispering home from which Rumour sees and hears and exaggerates news from all the world, the drowsy cave of Sleep, to realize the liveliness of the poet's fancy, and his outstanding descriptive talent. (pp. 10-18)

Mary M. Innes, in an introduction to The Metamorphoses of Ovid *by Publius Ovidius Naso, translated by Mary M. Innes, Penguin Books, 1955, pp. 9-25.*

Gilbert Highet   (essay date 1955)

[*A Scottish-born classical scholar, writer, critic, and translator, Highet complemented his highly regarded scholarly work with efforts to popularize great literature, particularly the Greek and Roman classics. His writings, which discuss topics in several areas of the humanities, include* The Classical Tradition *(1949),* The Art of

Teaching *(1950), and* The Anatomy of Satire *(1962). In the following excerpt taken from a 1955 essay, Highet praises the "enormous wealth and variety of stories" in the* Metamorphoses *and discerns their archetypical nature.*]

One of the most famous and most amusing books in the whole of European literature got off to a very bad start. Its author was condemned to exile for life before it was published. He burned his manuscript in agony and despair. But fortunately some of his friends had copies, and they got it published for him. It was an instantaneous success, and has been read and enjoyed by hundreds of thousands of people ever since. It was one of William Shakespeare's favorite books, and gave him lots of ideas. The French philosopher Montaigne said that when he was a little boy of seven or eight he used to hide in order to read it without being disturbed. The stern Milton and the still sterner Dante were both devoted to it. It has provided subjects for dozens and dozens of artists, from Botticelli to Picasso. It is a delightful imaginative poem about miracles, by the Roman poet Ovid.

Its official title is **The Metamorphoses,** which means **The Transformations.** In plan, it is a history of the world from creation down to the death of Julius Caesar—or rather of all the miracles, and in particular all the miraculous changes of form, which happened during those long centuries. But most of the time, as we read it, we are scarcely conscious of the plan; we see the poem simply as a long and fascinating string of surrealist stories, fantastic legends—some beautiful and sad, some grotesquely comic, some harsh and horrible, but all easy to read and hard to forget. And furthermore, all are told by a man who was a master storyteller as well as a skillful poet. Practically every tale he relates is as impossible as the *Arabian Nights.* His legends appeal not to the cool, reasoning, logical mind, but to the daring and creative imagination; not to our sense of reality, but to our subconscious, which prefers the strangest things to the most ordinary, the impossible to the everyday, fiction to fact.

Fortunately, this is one of the classical poems which have been really well translated. There is a good brisk eighteenth-century version in couplets, 'by divers hands'; and quite recently the American poet Rolfe Humphries has published a gay, brisk, and epigrammatic rendering in modern English. . . . By the way, the first large English book written in America was a translation of the poem by George Sandys, the treasurer of the Virginia Company: it appeared in 1626, and was much admired.

The best thing in the poem is its enormous wealth and variety of stories. Many of the legends which have become an essential part of our Western literature and thought were first told by Ovid, or were best told by Ovid. It was he, for instance, who dug up the story (virtually unknown before his time) of the two Babylonian lovers who could speak to each other only through a narrow chink in the wall dividing their houses. They arranged a secret meeting outside the city at midnight. The girl reached the meeting place first. As she waited, she saw a lion which had been out killing cattle. In terror, she ran off and hid. The lion found her scarf on the ground, and with its bloody teeth chewed it and tore it. Soon afterward, the young man arrived . . . to find his sweetheart's scarf lying on the ground covered with blood and surrounded by the tracks of a wild beast. In despair he killed himself with his own sword. Then, as the body turned cold, the girl returned. She kissed his dead lips. She saw the veil and the sword; she understood; and, rather than be separated from him by the wall of mortality, she used the sword upon herself. That is the tale of Pyramus and Thisbe. It was adapted from Ovid to become one of the first poems in the whole of French literature, and something of its pathos and its desperation went into the story of Romeo and Juliet.

There was a miraculous transformation connected with that legend, as with all Ovid's tales, but it was a small and unimportant one. The two lovers died under a mulberry tree; their blood stained its berries, and ever since then the mulberry tree has had dark blood-red fruit. (White mulberries were a later importation from the Far East.) Sometimes in Ovid's tales the human interest is paramount and the miracle is subsidiary; sometimes the miracle itself is the center of interest and is deeply symbolic.

Such is the adventure of King Midas, who was offered a miraculous gift by a divinity—a gift of power. He chose it himself. He asked that everything he touched should turn to gold. The power was conferred on him; but he had forgotten that he must eat and drink. The food changed to solid metal when it touched his lips; the wine as it entered his mouth became liquid gold. Likely to die of thirst and starvation, he could only ask the same divinity to take back the gift and restore him to humanity. Such, too, is the sad story of Orpheus, whose young wife died suddenly. He went to the underworld to find her. There he made such exquisite music that the King of the Dead allowed him to take Eurydice back to life, provided only that he did not look on her face before they reached the upper world. But he was in love, he was anxious about the sad silent shape which followed him on the long climb, he turned to reassure himself—and this time he lost her forever. And there is the story of Narcissus, the handsome youth who fell in love with his own reflection in the water and pined away, gazing at it, until nothing was left except a flower with a drooping head looking into the forest pool. Then there is the terrible story of Tereus and his outrage on his wife's sister Philomela, and his wife's ferocious revenge; there is the tale of the first men to fly through the air, Daedalus and Icarus; and the wild adventures of Hercules, and Medea, and a dozen other legendary figures.

What is important about stories such as these is that they do not appear to be merely inventions. They appear to be symbols of profound psychological truths which cannot be properly expressed through logical utterance. For example, the story of Pyramus and Thisbe—which is so like the story of Romeo and Juliet and the story of Tristan and Isolde and many others—appears to symbolize some strange connection between violent love and violent death (not death through cruelty, but death through devotion and self-immolation); and also some hidden link between ardent young love and utter self-forgetfulness; and much more which we can feel, but can hardly discuss except in poetry and music.

The meaning of the myths and miracles goes deeper yet. The Swiss psychologist Jung could write a marvelous commentary on the whole of Ovid's poem, both on its central theme and on every one of its separate myths. Jung tells us that in the unconscious mind—not of any single extraordinary individual, but rather of all humanity—there are many patterns through which we interpret the world and ourselves. These patterns, he believes, are just as universal and necessary to us as the structure of our eyes or the dexterity of our fingers. One set of these patterns he calls the Archetypes of Transformation. They appear in dreams. They appear in situations which particularly impress us and in which we participate (for instance, certain religious and social rituals such as initiation ceremonies). They appear in recurrent themes of drama, fiction and myth—such as the long and partially subterranean journey, the quest for a magical or divine talisman, the ordeal in which a soul is tested by hostile or supernatural powers, and the miraculous transformation. In dreams or visions shaped by these archetypal patterns we may see ourselves being transformed, or we may watch strange metamorphoses in process: a tree altering its shape and nature; a human being changing into an animal; a mysterious bird speaking intelligible words. These (says Jung) are not merely confused and meaningless fantasies produced by a brain which is sick or exhausted; and the legends in which they appear are not merely ingenious distortions of reality designed to amuse and to astonish. They are symbols of psychical growth. They are descriptions of what we experience as we explore our own subconscious—that task on which we all, whether we know it or not, are continuously engaged. And (I think I should venture to add) they are interpretations of some of the great emotional and mystical experiences through which all of us must pass. Therefore, it is because these legends—eccentric or absurd as they may superficially seem to be—reflect truly universal human experiences that they have survived for so long, fascinated so many poets and provided subjects for so many artists and musicians.

The stories are the important thing in Ovid's poem. It is a one-volume manual of Greek and Roman mythology. However, it has been enjoyed for a number of other reasons too. Ovid was a brilliant psychologist, at least as far as women are concerned, and his book contains several astonishing monologues in which women, tense with love and despair, analyze their own feelings and try to overcome their conflicts. He did not care much about philosophy, but he knew much more about it than the average writer does today; so he gave a surprising amount of space to the teaching of that mysterious figure Pythagoras, and worked in an exposition of his doctrine of transmigration and his treatment of the paradox of change within permanence. And, strangest of all, during the Middle Ages Ovid himself was thought of as a great authority on cosmology, because, while the standard account of the creation of the world was of course to be found in Genesis, Ovid at the opening of his poem gave a much more detailed description of the process, which was scarcely ever in direct conflict with Scripture and often appeared to supplement it, even explaining some of the things the Bible leaves unexplained. Like Vergil, he was thought to be one of the few pagan poets who had been partially inspired by the spirit of true religion. I do not for a moment believe he was; but then, if you are a skillful technician, you can convince most people that you are sincere.

And he was a skillful technician, a smooth and consummate craftsman: he was the Mozart, or at least the Rossini, of Latin poetry. He began writing verse when he was only twelve years old, and his first book was a tremendous success when he was about twenty-two. *The Metamorphoses* is one of the easiest and most pleasant of the Roman classics to read—it ought to be taught in schools and colleges before the youngsters approach the somber and thoughtful Vergil—and its lightness and rapidity are not accident, but the result of practiced art and long experience. Rolfe Humphries's translation is not quite so melodious as the original Latin, but it has nearly all of Ovid's liveliness and speed. Here is his version of the climax of the famous tale about the first men who flew. Daedalus, wisest of inventors, the man who built the Labyrinth, was imprisoned on the island of Crete: so he constructed wings for himself and his son Icarus, and escaped on them. Off the two flew, through the middle air.

> Far off, far down, some fisherman is watching
> As the rod dips and trembles over the water,
> Some shepherd rests his weight upon his crook,
> Some ploughman on the handles of the plough-
>   share,
> And all look up, in absolute amazement,
> At those air-borne above. They must be gods!
>   . . .And the boy
> Thought *This is wonderful!* and left his father,
> Soared higher, higher, drawn to the vast heaven
> Nearer the sun, and the wax that held the wings
> Melted in that fierce heat, and the bare arms
> Beat up and down in air, and lacking oarage
> Took hold of nothing. *Father!* he cried, and
>   *Father!*
> Until the blue sea hushed him, the dark water
> Men call the Icarian now. And Daedalus,
> Father no more, called 'Icarus, where are you?
> Where are you, Icarus? Tell me where to find
>   you!'
> And saw the wings on the waves, and cursed his
>   talents.

Good poetry—as light as the feathers which bore up the two fliers. Ovid himself had a disastrous fall: he soared too high, and crashed down, and cursed his talents. Yet the work of his ebullient imagination survived, and is still flying on through the upper air of myth and poetry. (pp. 264-70)

> *Gilbert Highet, "Ovid's 'Metamorphoses': The Book of Miracles," in his* The Power of Poetry, *Oxford University Press, 1960, pp. 264-70.*

Horace Gregory (essay date 1958)

[*In the following excerpt, Gregory emphasizes the importance of the* Metamorphoses *to modern readers.*]

The Metamorphoses or *Transformations* of Ovid was completed at Rome in the year 8 A.D. which also was the year that the Emperor Augustus sent its author into retirement far away from Rome. Lucretius's great work *De*

Rerum Natura, On the Nature of Things had ended with the year of his death in 55 B.C., and in 19 B.C., the year of Virgil's death, that poet's epic, the *Aeneid,* celebrating Rome's heritage from Troy, came to its conclusion. It can be said that *The Metamorphoses,* written at the beginning of the Christian era, was the last long-sustained major work of a great age in Latin poetry—and it was also evidence of a peculiarly Italian genius which places it at a middle distance away from the *Aeneid,* since it was not a true and heroic epic, toward the novellas of Bandello and the lyricism of Petrarch. In English literature *The Metamorphoses* (and here Ovid became "the poet's poet") held sustained appeal for Chaucer, Spenser, Shakespeare, Chapman (whose famous version of Homer's epics shows debts to Ovid), Dryden, Swift. Pope knew his Ovid: though his incident in "Eloisa to Abelard" is medieval, his Eloisa is an Ovidian heroine; her confessions of love, her complaints, her raptures are in the Ovidian manner:

> To sounds of heav'nly harps she dies away,
> And melts in visions of eternal day.
> Far other dreams my erring soul employ,
> Far other raptures of unholy joy.

In these lines rather than in his translations from the ninth and fourteenth books of *The Metamorphoses,* Pope's readings in Ovid caught fire and showed his debt to Ovid's nearly flawless understanding of women in love.

The nineteenth century, even among its poets, lost contact with *The Metamorphoses,* or rather, *The Metamorphoses* showed aspects of mythology as well as of human conduct that the age did not care to advertise. An extremely un-Italian Victorian Olympus came into view. It had been introduced by Lord Elgin's marbles shipped from Greece to London. Pictorially and in sculpture the nymphs and goddesses became ideal English girls, represented in dreamy yet modest poses by Sir Frederic Leighton; they looked freshly bathed, well-fed, and nearly sexless. If the *Aeneid* did not represent a Greek Olympian order, its nobility, its pathos showed a Roman kind of moral order that would not lead the well-educated Latin schoolboy astray. Meanwhile *The Metamorphoses* was not unread, but placed on a high shelf, almost out of reach, alongside Suetonius's *Lives of the Caesars.* In schools Suetonius was regarded as a dubious gossip—he did not speak too well of Julius's nephew, Octavian Augustus. *The Metamorphoses* was read as the work of a "capricious" poet, one who was irreverent, decidedly un-Olympian, and at times immoral. He was no longer "the poet's poet," but belonged to readers who were looking for a collection of "naughty" stories. As studies in classical literature declined, it had become easier to discard Ovid in favor of Horace and Virgil; Ovid had lost the prestige he had held for so many hundreds of years.

There is no doubt that the twentieth century has begun to rediscover *The Metamorphoses.* Something of its original importance is beginning to be understood. Its collection of myths (once called "fables" by Dryden and by Pope) has taken on fresh colour and richness, for some of the transformations retold by Ovid are pre-Homeric as well as post-Homeric in their origins, drifting through the memories of Mediterranean peasants as well as scholars,

and contemporary anthropologists are finding new meanings in Ovid's "fables" and miracles. How far anthropologists are willing to trust a poet, I do not know, but Schliemann's trust in Homer opened a new chapter in archæological research, and historians found an actual Troy to burn. The only warning that an anthropologist needs is never to read too many literal meanings into an Ovidian story, for the importance of the poet's truth is almost never factual. In Book XV of *The Metamorphoses* Ovid telescoped the battlefields of Philippi and Pharsalus into a single reference, superimposing one upon the other. Keats' famous error in mistaking Cortez for Balboa in his sonnet "On First Looking into Chapman's Homer" does not invalidate the essential truth of the poem. The very "realms of gold" that Keats wrote of in the sonnet came as much from Chapman's reading of Ovid as of Homer, probably more so. These kinds of poetic truth are fusions of poetic imagination which transcend literal facts and historical incident.

We may take for granted that readers of Freud, Brill, and Jung will find much to rediscover in *The Metamorphoses.* Their attraction to it is the same that brought it so forcefully to John Dryden's attention who went to *The Metamorphoses* to study the "passions," and with an attitude as critical as any living psychiatrist. He asked a question: "Would any man, who is ready to die for love, describe his passion like Narcissus? Would he think of *inopem me copia fecit,* and a dozen more such expressions . . . signifying all the same thing?" He concludes that Ovid at times is too lighthearted, far too witty—but he ignores Ovid's desire to show the ridiculous futility, the terror of Narcissus' all-conquering self-love. Able as Dryden was in reproducing the smoothness of Ovid's lines, there was much in Ovid that his cold eye rejected. His temperament was ill-suited to the contradictory display of the "passions" that Ovid gave him. Therefore he limited his version of *The Metamorphoses* to a translation of Book I and what he considered choice passages from others. Yet the attraction of Ovid's emotional extremes gave him, as it gave others, inspiration—and Ovid, witty and passionate by rapid turns, walked swiftly, smoothly where other Augustan poets feared to tread.

It is in the play of emotional extremes, the forces of illogical and conflicting impulses that Ovid offers the richness of psychological detail to the modern reader. His many heroines (and there are over fifty stories in *The Metamorphoses*) are set before us in dramatic moments of their indecision. Actually they do not meditate; they waver between extremes of right and wrong. They live and act within a world of irrational desires which are as vivid to them as things that happen in a dream. They act in heat and are caught up in disaster. One might complain that their motives, however complex and contradictory, are not subtle. The situations which changed tempting, white-skinned Io to a cow, or incestuous Myrrha to a tree are obvious—and Ovid's comments on their fate are those of the half-cynical, half-affectionate observer. His tone is ironic, warm, humorous, mock-moral. We are asked not to forgive them but to see them. It is by their dreams (desires)—and their actions—that we know them.

As he tells a story of a transformation, Ovid frequently remarks, "so it is believed," or presents a story within a story at second hand; these are his warnings that he regarded his truths as truths of fiction, which are often far more convincing than any document or "case history" can hope to be. What he gives us is miraculous rather than "abnormal" psychology, so in reading his excursions into sexual psychology, we are as far from literal truth as we are from the literal, or even scientific recital of mythology and historical legend. What he suggests or what we may be able to read into what he writes are other matters. In his miracles and because he expresses the extremes of passionate desire, there are truths so obvious we tend to overlook them. Are there better "case histories" than those found in his versions of the plights of Orpheus, Hermaphroditus, and Narcissus? Of course not. Does Spenser in his great allegory of *The Faerie Queen* actually excel Ovid's portrait of Minerva and his personification of Envy? I doubt it. Ovid lacks "high seriousness," but not perception.

Because he lacked religious and moral purpose, Ovid's vision of the Olympian gods has less depth than Homer's. But Ovid was not only of another age than Homer's but clearly of a different culture, one that had a broader base, one that contained coarse-textured, material Roman "glory" fused with alloys of Persian, Egyptian, Italian origin, and in *The Metamorphoses* all scenes are coloured by Italian landscape and Ovid's thoroughly Italian imagination. A. E. Housman (that Dr. Jekyll and Mr. Hyde of latter-day English poets, who was both spokesman for a Shropshire lad and a zealous, often angry, Latin scholar) remarked that Ovid, nearing the age of fifty, and completing *The Metamorphoses,* had transformed himself from a carelessly well-educated man into a learned one. His masterpiece demanded that metamorphosis. Certainly the work demanded the resources of a well-stocked library and an active memory. More than that, there was largeness in Ovid's vision. His epic, made up of many stories, extending from the creation of the world to his own day, was very nearly a mock epic; the variety of stories that he chose to remember, retell, or invent, was in itself a distraction from depth of purpose. He ignored Greek unities of time and place. Through his own lack of reverence for their behaviour, he reduced the heroic stature of his gods, demigods, and heroes.

For us as well as for readers of his own day Ovid opened many strange windows into the past, showing scenes of savage action, grotesque images of giants, or of Scylla, monstrously deformed by a girdle of barking dogs around her waist. If we think of things classical as being noted for restraint and in proportion, certain scenes in *The Metamorphoses* may be called less classical than violently baroque. The very theme of metamorphosis depended on violent and rapid transformations, distortions, if you will, of normal law and action. Of these deflections from a "golden mean" surely Ovid's early contemporary Horace would have disapproved. Yet these recitals of miraculous events, the quick changes, the shifts from images of beauty to the grotesque, from fear and terror to deadly evil, the migration of human souls to trees and stones, even to pools and springs, to birds, to wolves, delighted readers

who perceived, not without wit, the psychological significance of these changes. What could be more appropriate than placid, yielding Io changed to a cow? Or matronly, slow-thinking Niobe, still weeping, into monumental stone? Or the charm of frightened Daphne into a quivering laurel tree, or a shrewd, quick-witted girl servant into a red-haired weasel? In all these changes one can almost say that Ovid anticipated the arts of the Italian baroque, but for the meantime he knew how to gratify his own fancy and imagination, and with instinctive wit he placed a heroine in the foreground of more than half his stories. His concern for the psychology of women was no less marked than in the poems of his friend Propertius—or for that matter, than in the novels of such modern writers as Flaubert and Henry James. At the very least, his concern was never petty, but the stress that he placed on the play of feminine emotions in his stories continued the motifs of his earlier books of poems. His *Amores* and his instructions in the art of love brought him into conflict with Augustus. . . . (pp. xi-xv)

[Ovid] liked women. His *Confessions of Women* were briefs written in their defense. Whatever arts he possessed were devoted to their cause. His understanding of their misfortunes, his compassion, his wit, the external polish of his verse made him the fashionable poet of the hour, his verses read aloud at theatres and at public festivals. He did not frequent circles which paid homage to Augustus, but rather those that received his daughter, Julia, and her daughter, Julia, the two Julias whose conduct was the scandal of Augustus's household. Augustus's effort to reform the sexual morality of the Roman matron had its obvious burlesque in the conduct of his daughter and granddaughter, for the younger Julia encouraged the attention of her lovers in the Forum itself in direct answer to her grandfather's disapproval of current sexual morality. Augustus, nearing the age of seventy, began to feel (as his own blood ran cooler) that the dignity of the Roman state could be preserved only by a return to ancient austerities. The office that he held demanded respect as well as lip service to its power. He himself had mounted to power up stairs that streamed with blood. Like Ovid, Augustus had had three wives, and had taken his last, his Livia, while she was pregnant, from an earlier husband. As if to undo his own past, as if to turn back the clock in his old age, his announcement of an Augustan morality showed signs of an approaching senility. He had carried his love of order one step too far beyond a practical solution. His idealism was that of a preternaturally sane yet unimaginative man of action and ruler of his people. Ideally he was right: something should have been done to check the excesses of Augustan Rome, but the Punic Wars (as Toynbee so forcefully reminds us) had already bred the seeds of internal decay. Practical statesman as Augustus was, he could not see or did not wish to see that his effort to enforce the sexual moralities of ancient Rome by law was nonsense. Effective as he was, he shared the blindness of all successful first-rate, second-rate men, who are usually the rulers of things on earth. That ten years after the publication of Ovid's *Amores* Augustus found such literature harmful and immoral should cause no surprise. We scarcely need—nor did Augustus in late middle age—Plato's *Re-*

public to remind us that the ideal tyranny rejects the poet. (pp. xviii-xix)

Augustus's worldliness . . . proved itself far more effective than Ovid's poetic genius. Ovid, like the mythological Irish hero Sweeney, was doomed to humiliating banishment. Sweeney, because of his unruly temperament, his lack of reverence for other heroes and the gods, was forced to sit among high branches of a tree to learn the language of the birds. Ovid was sent to Tomis, where he, as lonely as Sweeney, was forced to learn the language of a barbarous northern people. Ovid's *Tristia,* filled with self-pity, show how deeply his vanity was wounded. He was caught up in Augustus's net as neatly as Vulcan trapped his adulterous wife Venus with her lover Mars, embraced and naked for the gods to laugh at. The gifted poet's cleverness was futile; he delayed his trip to Tomis, making it a roundabout journey seaward as long as he could. His friends, his affectionate wife, talked him out of committing suicide. Meanwhile, before he had left Rome, he had finished his major work, *The Metamorphoses.*

In his *Tristia* Ovid claimed to have burned his poems, including the recently finished work, *The Metamorphoses.* Perhaps he actually destroyed one set of manuscripts—a symbolic act of suicide. Of course there were other copies. Although by Augustus's order Ovid's books were banned from public libraries (how closely that order resembles twentieth-century banning of books in Hitler's Germany and Soviet Russia!), private collectors treasured them. Forbidden books always acquire an attractive immortality of their own, quite apart from whatever merits they contain.

Among Ovid's friends *The Metamorphoses* was secure enough. And for that matter, so were Ovid's claims to an immortality in the last lines of Book XV of *The Metamorphoses.* These were no boast; he knew that his masterpiece would last as long as men could read a book. Twentieth-century readers of *The Metamorphoses* are likely to regard it as an invaluable book of Myths, "myths" spelled with a capital M. But it is doubtful if Ovid regarded his masterpiece in quite the same way that we are permitted to read it. As precedent Ovid had before him Lucretius's great philosophical treatise in verse, *De Rerum Natura,* a showing forth, an epiphany, in verse, of the teachings of Epicurus. Ovid was not however a philosopher; he was a collector, a reteller of stories, and his stories were collected and retold with the purpose of showing a cycle of miraculous changes. However familiar some of the stories were, Ovid's interpretation of them provided a new look at the world in which the Homeric epics were no more than a part of a large Greco-Roman tradition of being. Nor was Ovid under any obligation to accept the literal truth of any story he retold or invented. It was enough if the stories had imaginative and psychological reality and were true in their celebration of the life force in its many changes. The stories were written to entertain, to charm, to shock their readers; to move them toward further understanding of the condition of man- or womankind, to show the mystery of life, its savagery, its splendor, and at times its violent waste of blood. The Romans loved a show of blood, and Ovid gave it to them. Whenever Ovid supplies a moral to

his stories, his moralizings have a false ring (like his overpraise of Augustus in Book XV) or an ironic air. The Age of Virtue belonged to the Golden Age of Book I—but that was very, very long ago. (pp. xxiii-xxiv)

Ovid's re-creation of myths as stories, within a theme of eternal change, liberated him from the necessity of following a Homeric precedent such as Virgil employed in the writing of his great Roman epic. Ovid used his loosely gathered romances and tales to exhibit his imaginative virtuosity. Within his large design, he incorporated stories from all reaches of the Mediterranean world, from Egypt as well as Crete, nor was his interest that of the anthropologist. It was rather that of one who could not resist the retelling of any story, provided it had color and enough action to hold attention. The story of Iphis and Ianthe reflects the worship of Isis in Augustan Rome, the shadow that Cleopatra left behind her—a shadow, by the way, that Augustus did his utmost to dispel. The inclusion of that story would offer further proof of Ovid's *lèsemajesté,* his lack of concern for elder Roman virtues, his irresponsibility. At the very least, Ovid as poet was incorrigible, not to be trusted in choice of worthy subjects and themes—wilful and sometimes at fault in tracing exact mutations of one myth into another. The fifteen books of *The Metamorphoses* contain a number of repetitious details as men and women are turned into trees, birds, or stones. Ovid's battle scenes have an overflow of blood and destruction; his fond listing of names is often tiresome; his flaws of taste are frequent, and his retelling of some Greek stories coarsens the clear lines of the originals. But having said this much in dispraise of Ovid's masterpiece, one feels that one has missed the reasons why it has survived. At his best no writer of his Golden Age in Roman literature has excelled him in the rapid unfolding of a narrative, nor has any surpassed him in the direct revelations of psychological detail. However far-fetched, melodramatic, or strained a few of his situations may seem to the twentieth-century reader, they never fail to create the illusion of life—in its mystery and irony, in its splendour or cruelty; in its affectionate humours and warmth of feeling, in its celebration of earthly beauty. His many mistresses of Jove, his demigoddesses are irresistible carriers of the life-force in nature, and that is why complaints of his carelessness in joining one mythological cycle to another seem an effort at pedantry. As he came to the last of his fifteen books, he felt the need of a philosophy to sustain his device of eternal transformations. An Alexandrian Greek philosopher, a certain Sotion, had recently come to Rome. He was a disciple of Pythagoras, a vegetarian, and a popular lecturer. Ovid incorporated the gist of his lectures into Book XV. The Pythagorean doctrine with its protest against the killing of animals made its appeal to the humane warmth of Ovid's character, and it allowed him to give a semblance of Lucretian seriousness to his entire work. Ovid's nature of things was the nature of transformations. He did his best to make Pythagorean theory support the large design of *The Metamorphoses.* He had rounded out his conception of a world he had promised to reveal in Book I. However shallow many of Ovid's convictions were, he held to his belief that nothing in the world could be destroyed; all things become transformed—and not least, his own poetry into an immortality. (pp. xxv-xxvii)

Horace Gregory, in an introduction to The
Metamorphoses *by Publius Ovidius Naso,
translated by Horace Gregory, Viking Press,
1958, pp. xi-xxix.*

Frank O. Copley (essay date 1969)

[*In the excerpt below, Copley discusses Ovid's oeuvre,
commenting on the nature of his love poetry and praising
the* Metamorphoses *as an "utterly charming tapestry of
stories, and an invaluable source book of ancient Greek
and Roman mythology."*]

[The last] of the Roman elegists was Ovid (Publius Ovidius Naso, 43 B.C.–18 A.D.), a poet of enormous talents, who
eventually became better known for his nonelegiac poems
than for his elegies: his great work, the one that assured
his reputation in his own day and made him in later ages
the most widely read, studied, and imitated of all the
Roman poets, even including Vergil, was his *Metamorphoses,* a sort of mytho-historical epic in fifteen books of
dactylic hexameters. Ovid was born at Sulmo, about 90
miles from Rome, of a family of some standing, although
not of the aristocracy. We are told that Ovid's father intended him to follow a career in the law, the only one, in
fact, that was considered entirely respectable for a well-
born Roman. For most of his preparatory studies in this
field, Ovid had little taste; but for rhetoric, the molding of
speech into interesting and provocative patterns, he felt a
great attraction, so great, we are told, that he even enjoyed
the generally detested school exercise of preparing set
speeches on formal topics.

Ovid's rhetorical studies, together with his witty proclivities, and his quick and facile genius, are no doubt responsible for much of the brilliance of his poetry and for his signal genius as a storyteller. The *Metamorphoses* is one long
series of neatly spun tales, carefully dovetailed one into another. It is no wonder that this was later to become the favorite storybook of the Western world. But stories are
scarcely less prevalent in Ovid's other poetical works; no
matter what he is writing, he cannot resist a good yarn.
(pp. 264-65)

Ovid's first published work, the collection of elegies
known as the *Amores,* earned him immediate popularity.
It was succeeded by a series of such compositions, the
most famous of which was the *Art of Love.* This latter, a
witty and rather cynical discussion of sex, rather than of
love, seems harmless enough to the modern reader, yet it
apparently incurred the displeasure of the emperor for its
immoral teachings, and, at least according to the poet
himself, was the chief reason for his being sent into exile
in the year 8 A.D.

Ovid's exile remains one of the puzzles of ancient biography and history; the excuse that the *Ars amatoria* was a
naughty book seems a very feeble one in view of the anything but puritanical writings of other Roman authors and
of the tolerance of Roman society in general for sexual liberties. All that Ovid himself has to offer beyond his
naughty verses is the mysterious statement that he had
"seen too much." What he saw, he does not say, and we
shall probably never know what it was. In any event, the

upshot of all of this was the banishment of the poet to a
wretched frontier town, Tomi, on the shores of the Black
Sea. Here he spent the remaining ten years of his life,
bored and miserable, writing dull and melancholy poems
of self-pity, and hoping to the last for pardon from the emperor. Augustus died without granting the pardon; his
dour successor, Tiberius, was even less inclined to be forgiving. The weary and homesick poet finally died at Tomi
in 18 A.D.

It is patent that Ovid was a voluminous writer. Even
though much of his verse is lost we still have extant a long
list of works from his hand: the *Amores* in 3 books, the
Heroides, the *Art of Love* in 3 books, the *Remedy of Love,
On Cosmetics,* the *Metamorphoses* in 15 books, the *Fasti*
in 6 books, the *Tristia (Poems of Lament)* in 5 books, the
Ibis, the *Halieutica (On Fishing),* and the *Letters from
Pontus* in 4 books. Of greatest interest to the modern reader are the *Amores,* the *Ars amatoria,* and the *Metamorphoses;* these are in fact the works of Ovid that have had
the most marked and lasting influence on later literature.

It is in the three books of *Amores* that Ovid shows himself
most closely in line with his two predecessors, Propertius
and Tibullus. His attitude, however, toward the literary
love affair is quite different from theirs; while his stance
is as personal as theirs, his involvement with the lady of
whom he writes—a certain Corinna—is of a very different
nature. It is almost wrong to say that Ovid was ever "involved" in the literary love affair at all; even when he
writes in the first person of his amorous escapades, it
sounds more as if he were merely playing a part on the
stage, or even better, were standing in the wings and amusing himself by observing himself in the role of the unhappy
lover. All the clichés of the standard literary love affair are
there; the life of love, as we saw it in the poems of Propertius is represented in Ovid's poems, personality by personality, and scene by scene; yet it is impossible to take the
poet seriously or to think that he would ever have allowed
himself, even on the pages of a poem, to become so deeply
involved with anyone else.

The solemn sorrows of the elegiac lover become in Ovid's
hands the foolish divagations of not very sensible men. In
Amores 1.2, for example, Ovid professes to feel the restlessness brought on by the sting of love, and debates with
himself whether to give in to it or struggle against it:

> What should I say this means? My bed feels so
> hard and my blankets won't stay in place! I've
> not slept a wink all night, and Oh, how long that
> night was! I've tossed and turned till I ache to
> my weary bones. Why! I think I would know if
> it was love that was troubling me. Or has he
> sneaked up on me, cleverly concealed his strate-
> gy, and inflicted his wound? That must be it! His
> little arrows are fixed in my heart; Love, the bar-
> barian, has captured my breast, and now is ruler
> there! Am I to yield, or am I, by struggling, to
> set the whole thing on fire? I'd better yield: a
> burden borne graciously weighs less.

Again, in what looks suspiciously like a daring satirization
of the emperor Augustus's attempts to restore the old
Roman military spirit, Ovid playfully compares the sufferings of the lover with the hardships of the soldier:

Every lover is a soldier, and Cupid has his camp, too. Believe me, Atticus, every lover is a soldier! The years fit for soldiering also go well with love; the old soldier is ugly; the love of an old man is ugly. The heart that generals look for in a brave soldier, a pretty girl also looks for in the man at her side. Both watch through the night; they sleep on the bare ground; the lover stands watch at his lady's door, the soldier at his general's. The long march is the soldier's job; send away the girl, and the lover, bursting with energy, will follow her, world without end.

The poem ends on a note that, with its savagely barbed puns, must have tickled the dissidents of the day and infuriated the Augustan imperialists:

> I myself was a lazy fellow, born to sloth and ease; my hammock in the shade had turned me soft. Then I fell in love with a beautiful girl. That woke me from my lethargy! That sent me to the camp to earn my soldier's pay! That's why you see me so nimble now and so busy at nocturnal battling. You want to stop being a slugabed? Fall in love!

The modern reader may perhaps catch the pun in "nimble" (*agilis*); the even sharper pun involved in "nocturnal battling" (*nocturna bella*) will pass unnoticed unless we recall that one of the Latin words for a "battle" (*rixa*) is also the recognized term for sexual intercourse.

In actuality, Ovid's **Amores,** together with his better known **Art of Love** and its companion piece, the **Remedy of Love,** scarcely deserve the name of love poetry at all. They need only be laid beside the poems of Propertius and Tibullus to show wherein the difference lies: for all their limitations and their colossal egotism Propertius and Tibullus write about love; Ovid writes about sex. The fact that critics have commonly expressed doubts about the reality of the girl, Corinna, whose name figures largely in Ovid's poetry, suggests that, unlike Propertius's Cynthia or Tibullus's Delia—to say nothing of Catullus's Lesbia—Ovid's Corinna had little cogency or reality outside of bed.

The book called the **Heroides** (**Letters of the Heroines**) is of a piece with these earlier works. Ovid has composed a series of fictitious poetic epistles from deserted heroines to their faithless lovers; the characters are largely drawn from Greek tragedy and epic; we have a letter from Penelope to Ulysses, from Medea to Jason, from Ariadne to Theseus, from Phaedra to Hippolytus, and so on. There is also one Roman letter, from Dido to Aeneas. Although these letters may perhaps be said to embody Congreve's famous maxim, "Heaven has no wrath like love to anger turned nor Hell a fury like a woman scorned," they can scarcely be said to express a great deal more than that. Their pleas are little speeches embodying all the tricks and devices of the rhetorical schools, clever and amusing, especially to one who, like any educated Roman, could contrast Ovid's treatment of these famous women with their originals in tragedy and epic. In spite of all the posturing and weeping of these heroines, we feel that they are no more than a bit grieved and hurt, and that in time they will get over it. The women of these letters have lost not a lover, but a bed-companion.

The schoolmaster Quintilian, writing in the second century A.D., tells us that Ovid wrote a tragedy, the **Medea,** in which, says Quintilian, "he showed how great a poet he might have become if he had chosen to regulate rather than to indulge his genius." Quintilian was an earnest man, with little sense of humor; it could be anticipated that he would never appreciate the gaiety and the irony of Ovid's erotic poems, and would have turned with some relief to a work that, at least to him, seemed to be serious in intent.

Unfortunately, Ovid's *Medea* is lost, but one is forced to wonder whether Quintilian had ever read Ovid's greatest and most extensive poetic effort, his **Metamorphoses.** This is indeed a serious poem, not lacking in humor and irony, for Ovid could scarcely have written anything without these notes, but predominantly serious in purpose and executed with a skill, grace, and human understanding that come only to the poet who has let himself become deeply involved in an artistically meaningful project.

The **Metamorphoses** has often wrongfully been regarded simply as a collection of short stories; it is not that, but rather an epic in fifteen books, a kind of mythological history of the development of the world, from its beginning in chaos up to the times of the emperor Augustus. In the poem, Ovid views this history as a series of changes— hence the name **Metamorphoses**—from the first great change of chaos into cosmic order, up to the translation of Julius Caesar into a constellation and the change of Rome from the discord and bloodshed of the civil wars to the ordered, peaceful, and prosperous world of Augustus.

In telling the story of these changes, Ovid manages to introduce into his poem an amazing number of myths, most of which are true "changes," e.g. of Io into a heifer, of Daphne into a tree, of Echo into a rock and voice, of Narcissus into a flower, of Niobe into a waterfall, etc., etc. To anyone at all familiar with ancient mythology, it is a constant delight to read the **Metamorphoses** and to run across these ancient stories here told in a setting that could scarcely have been excelled by any other poet of antiquity.

Originally, these stories had religious significance, sometimes quite profound; as we may imagine, Ovid is little if at all interested in this aspect of his tales, but sees them primarily as stories, as vehicles for a narrative art in which he was unsurpassed. It is sometimes tempting to think that it was his fascination with narrative that prompted him to bring into his poem stories that, strictly speaking, are not changes, e.g. the story of the rape of Proserpina, yet this is probably quibbling; in any event he weaves all these tales so gracefully into the thread of his narrative that we scarcely stop to question their appropriateness.

In the end, Ovid produces a wonderful catalogue of myths, the most complete and most entertaining collection that has survived from antiquity. In the most ingenious fashion, story is woven into story, so that we seem to glide imperceptibly from one to the next, always guided by some titillating device: a contest in song, a description of tapestry, a tale told by a soldier or a returning traveler, bedtime stories told by mothers to their children, stories told by lovers, etc., etc. The mood of the stories also varies; a frivolous tale will be balanced by one on a serious note, the comic by the tragic, the idyllic by the horrible. In every one of the fifteen books these elements are combined in different ways and in different order.

The poem begins on a serious note with a description of the birth of the world from chaos, that reads not unlike the opening of Genesis:

> Before there was sea and land and the heavens
> that cover all things, there was only one face of
> nature in all the world; men have called it Chaos.
> It was a crude and disordered mass; there was
> nothing but lifeless weight and a heap, gathered
> in one place, of the elements of things not joined
> in useful union.

From this beginning Ovid passes on to a description of the creation of the earth out of chaos, the creation of man "in the image of the gods"; we are taken through the four ages, the Golden, the Silver, the Bronze, and the Iron. The real body of the work then begins with the story of the Deluge and of Deucalion and Pyrrha, the pair who, according to ancient pagan mythology, survived the flood, and for their piety were given the right to create a new race of men, "from the bones of their great mother."

It is perhaps characteristic of Ovid that, after this solemn introductory story, he should turn at once to a love escapade, the tale of Apollo and Daphne, Apollo's "first love"; she was saved from his amorous demands by her father, the river-god Peneus, who changed her into a tree, the laurel, forever after sacred to Apollo. Perhaps the most notable thing about this story, apart from the grace and poetic skill with which it is told, is its total lack of religious reverence: in Ovid's hands, the god Apollo—and the same is to be true of virtually every other deity who appears in the poem—becomes no more than a self-centered youth, not many degrees above the fatuous *iuvenis* of the Roman comedy, and showing very few traits of divinity beyond the presumed possession of supernatural powers.

Perhaps best known of the love stories in the *Metamorphoses* is the tale of Pyramus and Thisbe, whom Shakespeare has made doubly famous: their story is in a very real sense the original of the tragedy of *Romeo and Juliet,* and it appears in its own right in broad caricature in *Midsummer Night's Dream.* Nor was Ovid himself above caricature; his account of the love of Polyphemus for Galatea makes great sport of the hopeless passion of the ugly one-eyed Cyclops for the beautiful sea-nymph. In the story of Narcissus, Ovid treats the theme of self-love, and deftly turns this aberration into a lighthearted and playful tale. (pp. 265-71)

It would be impossible in a treatment such as this to examine even any large number of the stories incorporated into the *Metamorphoses.* And although the poem undoubtedly has epic structure, it will certainly always be loved as it has been in the past for the individual stories themselves, which for all the neatness with which they are incorporated into the total structure, can still be extracted and enjoyed one at a time. Not as great in any sense as Vergil's *Aeneid,* the *Metamorphoses* remains a beautiful, graceful,

and utterly charming tapestry of stories, and an invaluable source book of ancient Greek and Roman mythology.

Ovid's other works never enjoyed the popularity of his love poems and his *Metamorphoses.* Most learned of his works, and again a valuable source book for the mythology of Rome, is the *Fasti.* Ovid originally planned twelve books, one for each month of the Roman year, but his work on the poems was interrupted by his exile, and as a result only the first six books were completed. The plan is a simple one; Ovid follows the days of the year in logical order and describes and discusses the ceremonies, stories, and myths that are appropriate to each day. He returns here to the elegiac form, and in fact much of the *Fasti* resembles very closely some of the aetiological poems of Propertius's fourth book. As poetry, the *Fasti* leaves a good deal to be desired; it shows little of Ovid's customary wit and grace and sounds at times suspiciously like a duty performance—a kind of concession to the pressure that no doubt had been placed upon him as it was upon Propertius and Horace, to write "more serious" poems. To the student of ancient religion, the *Fasti* is invaluable for its description of Roman cult and ritual; perhaps it is not too much to say that, at least from time to time, the work reveals a certain degree of true religious feeling.

After Ovid was exiled to Tomi, he gave himself over to lament and self-pity. But we must not blame him too harshly for this; he had certainly lost all that meant anything to him: the life of Rome, his friends, his family, and his ever-loyal wife. The work of his years of exile, as we might expect, is filled with bitterness and sadness; the two collections called the *Tristia (Poems of Lament)* and the *Epistulae ex Ponto (Letters from Pontus)* are collections of elegies more interesting now for the historical and biographical information they give us than as poetry. One of the *Tristia* (4.10) gives us an autobiography of the poet—one of the few such that we have from antiquity. The rest of the poems are mostly pleas for intercession to friends who had remained faithful to him and ill-tempered reproofs to those whose faith and loyalty the poet questioned. There are also a few pitifully hopeful panegyrics on the emperor Augustus, and later on his successor Tiberius, and along defense of Ovid's writings, and a kind of apology for his shortcomings. These two collections make dreary reading and reflect all too accurately the misery of their author.

The influence of Ovid is an enormous subject. It began almost immediately; a popular best seller in his own day, his poems were widespread throughout the Empire, where they continued to be read on down through the Middle Ages. Ovid was the favorite author of the period of chivalry. His works live again in the *Romance of the Rose,* in Chaucer, Boccaccio, Petrarch, and the whole circle of Italian writers and painters—for the *Metamorphoses* in particular provided many a subject for the artists of the Renaissance. Later, Ovid was to influence Ariosto, Erasmus, Goethe, Ronsard, La Fontaine, Molière, Spenser, Shakespeare, Milton, Congreve, Byron; and early American literature has preserved a retelling of some of his stories by Nathaniel Hawthorne (*Tanglewood Tales*). Neither great nor profound, with none of the historical vision or human sympathy of Vergil, he remains one of the most skillful

Venus cannot bear to be parted from her lover Adonis, in this Metamorphoses-*inspired painting by Titian.*

writers of verse and tellers of tales that the Western world has ever known. (pp. 273-75)

> Frank O. Copley, "The Elegists: Tibullus, Propertius, and Ovid," in his Latin Literature: From the Beginnings to the Close of the Second Century A.D., *The University of Michigan, 1969, pp. 241-75.*

A. S. Hollis   (essay date 1973)

[*In the following excerpt, Hollis explores the* Ars amatoria *and the* Remedia amoris, *revealing the "sharpness and detached, ironical sense of humor" present in both works.*]

Until recently the **Ars Amatoria** has been more or less taboo, and conspicuously absent from school and university classical courses. As a result many literate non-specialists consider it a very naughty poem; they cannot be blamed for this opinion when professional scholars [such as S. G. Owen and J. Wight Duff] have thrown out such comments as 'shameless compendium of profligacy' or 'vade mecum in wantonness'. Fulminations of this kind, besides being unfair to Ovid, are liable to distort the un-

derstanding of those who do penetrate to reading the **Ars**—finding it not such a naughty piece after all, they may think it poor stuff and overlook the real qualities of the gayest and wittiest among Ovid's love poems. But since the **Ars Amatoria** is known to have been a partial cause of Ovid's exile and thereafter was removed from the public libraries, perhaps we should examine briefly the charges which might be or actually were brought against it; in the end we may be led on to a truer appreciation of the poem's nature. Most of our information derives from the remarkable 'open letter to Augustus' (*Tristia,* II) composed in exile. We must remember the varying pressures on Ovid, to offer a defence without implying that Augustus had made a fool of himself in condemning him and to plead not so much for restoration to Rome (which would have been unrealistic) as for a more hospitable place of banishment. Personally I think that Ovid's defence of the **Ars** is on the whole well-founded, and that the most striking parts of **Tristia,** II are those where he warms to his task and even says more than prudence would dictate in such circumstances.

First of all we can clear out of the way one possible objection to the **Ars.** No Roman could well have considered it obscene; their tradition, both in oratory and verse, was for considerable frankness in sexual matters. Indeed the future emperor Augustus as a young man had written lines against Antony expressed with what Martial calls 'Roman simplicity'. For the Latin equivalent of four-letter words one must go to Catullus, and for a technical description of sexual intercourse to Lucretius, IV. Ovid does not approach either; certainly his *Ars Amatoria* is not a manual of sexual technique, but rather an 'Art of Courtship'.

A charge that the poem undermined marriage was definitely made. Ovid foresaw this, and tried to forestall it by the statement that he was writing only about *hetaerae* (high-class courtesans who would probably be freedwomen), not about respectable married women:

> este procul, vittae tenues, insigne pudoris,
>   quaeque tegis medios instita longa pedes:
> nos Venerem tutam concessaque furta canemus
>   inque meo nullum carmine crimen erit.

> (Away, away, all who wear narrow head-bands,
> symbols of modesty, and long skirts which cover
> half the feet. Our subject will be safe love-
> making, and amusements allowed by the law, so
> my poem will contain nothing objectionable.)

In defending himself Ovid constantly returns to these lines. One could object that married women still might profit from instruction meant for others, but this takes the *Ars* too seriously. It was not really intended as a practical guide to ensnaring the opposite sex, any more than Virgil really intended his *Georgics* to be a practical handbook of farming which would supplant Varro's prose treatise. The work's didactic form was something of a façade; as for the subject-matter, this rested for the most part upon a background of Greek epigram and Roman love-elegy which itself contained a high degree of convention. So on two counts the *Ars* had only a tenuous and intermittent connexion with real life. Ovid makes both these points in *Tristia,* II, but Augustus either failed to understand, or, more probably, pretended not to understand. Similarly Cicero, when attacking L. Piso, pretended that the erotic epigrams of his protégé Philodemus accurately represented the goings-on in Piso's household, although he must have been aware that the poems were merely conventional. The most one can fairly say is that the general atmosphere of the *Ars* was unhelpful to Augustus' policy of moral reform.

Could it be that Ovid is basically opposed to the Augustan régime, and showed it in his writings, so that the charge against his poetry did not rest on moral grounds alone? This theory has gained a number of adherents among modern scholars and certainly deserves a run for its money. When Ovid advises the girls to arrange their admirers in the same way as the emperor makes his military appointments, the introductory couplet hardly lessens his cool audacity:

> quis vetat a magnis ad res exempla minores
>   sumere nec nomen pertimuisse ducis?
> dux bonus huic centum commisit vite regendos,
>   huic equites, illi signa tuenda dedit:
> vos quoque, de nobis quem quisque erit aptus ad
>   usum,
>   inspicite et certo ponite quemque loco.

munera det dives; ius qui profitebitur, adsit. . . .

> (Why should I not illustrate my trivialities from
> great affairs, and dare to mention the Leader's
> name? Our good Leader makes one man a centu-
> rion, another a commander of cavalry, yet an-
> other a standard-bearer. You too must observe
> what profit you can derive from each of us, and
> arrange each in the appropriate place. Let the
> rich man give you presents, and the lawyer rep-
> resent you in court. . . .)

After a charming digression on the Rape of the Sabine Women, whereby Romulus provided a wife for his soldiers, Ovid adds in conclusion:

> Romule, militibus scisti dare commoda solus:
>   haec mihi si dederis commoda, miles ero

> (Nobody has ever seen to his soldiers' comforts
> like you, Romulus. Offer me comforts like that,
> and even I will join up!)

Now *commoda* was the technical prose term for the 'fringe-benefits' of military life, in addition to regular wages, and at this very time Augustus was having difficulties in filling his legions due to the lowness of these extra rewards. Another respectable Roman profession, the Law, does not escape. . . . There were further pin-pricks: when is a good time to start courting your girl? Answer, the anniversary of a national disaster, because the shops are shut and you will not have to buy her a present. Should the young receive a liberal education? Yes, but not only to protect the innocent and make powerful speeches before the people, the courts or the senate (time-honoured occupations of a public-spirited noble). Oratory will be just as useful for winning a girl-friend. To praise the unequalled variety and quality of native Italian products was a stock theme of patriotic literature at this time, but the compliment becomes two-edged when extended to feminine beauty:

> tot tibi tamque dabit formosas Roma puellas,
>   'haec habet' ut dicas 'quicquid in orbe fuit.'

> (Rome can offer you so many girls of such beau-
> ty that you will say 'The fruits of the whole
> world are here.')

Yet we should not exaggerate the significance of such points (many of which do not touch Augustus directly), and at the same time Ovid will turn his pen to a facile panegyric of the imperial house. Our poet hardly fits into any recognizable category of men who opposed the Augustan régime. Born in 43 B.C. he was not one who, in Tacitus' phrase, had 'seen the Republic', even in its last convulsions, nor would the austere ideals represented by the elder Cato have much appeal to him on the intellectual level. In my opinion the passages mentioned above can be explained by Ovid's unrivalled sense of the ridiculous. He enjoyed nothing more than deflating pomposity, and the Augustan establishment, like other establishments, offered a good measure of that. It has been said that Ovid's attachment was to personal rather than public values. This trait may be discerned in his poetry and supported by his abandonment of a political career; it might make him impatient of any government. But when one considers the régimes which Rome had endured in the past, or any alternative which might have seemed feasible to a contemporary, I doubt whether Ovid should be reckoned as specifically anti-Augustan.

All the same the *Ars Amatoria* clearly upset traditional Roman sentiment, and it is important to discover where exactly it hurt. If the opinions against which Ovid reacted seem a little stuffy and old-fashioned, yet they must still have had force. Perhaps the main irritation lay in the poem's frivolity; several stages of disrepute are involved here. In the first place Romans had strong feelings about what was worthwhile and what was a waste of time. Literary pursuits were still not wholly respectable—it may surprise us that even historians could be represented as 'genus ignavum quod lecto gaudet et umbra' ('an idle breed, given to putting their feet up out of the sun', Juvenal), and Sallust felt it necessary to excuse his withdrawal from practical affairs. For a man of the administrative class (to which Ovid belonged) a public career was expected, with literature confined to spare moments or retirement. Poetry had less obvious use than prose history, and the opening of *Amores,* I. 15 indicates that Ovid was criticized for his passionate belief in poetry as a full-time occupation:

> quid mihi, Livor edax, ignavos obicis annos
>   ingeniique vocas carmen inertis opus,
> non me more patrum, dum strenua sustinet aetas,
>   praemia militiae pulverulenta sequi
> nec me verbosas leges ediscere nec me
>   ingrato vocem prostituisse foro?

> (Why, consuming Jealousy, do you charge me with a life of idleness, and call poetry an occupation for sluggish spirits, complaining that I do not seek the usual hard-won rewards of soldiering, while the prime of life gives me strength, or learn by heart long-winded laws or prostitute my voice in the thankless courts?)

But, if you must write poetry, some types were more worthy than others. Epic and tragedy could be patriotic and morally uplifting. On the other hand Cicero said that not even if his life-span were doubled would he find time to read the lyric poets—this is revealing from a man who could once have been reckoned the leading Roman poet of the day. Place epic and tragedy at the top, and love poetry will rate low in the scale of utility. Furthermore, by the same convention according to which a pastoral poet must himself be a shepherd, the full-time love poet must himself be a full-time lover, which was no way for a Roman to spend his life. And the worst is still to come. In the *Ars Amatoria,* as earlier in the *Amores,* Ovid provocatively reverses the usual moral categories, presenting love as a worthy and strenuous occupation, like farming or hunting, in which all his fellow-citizens should be expert. (pp. 84-9)

I mentioned earlier that the *Ars Amatoria* has the superficial appearance of a didactic or instructional poem, and now is the time to consider this didactic tradition and how it affected the *Ars.* Later poets in this style, both Greek and Roman, looked back to the *Works and Days* of Hesiod as the original of the genre. Hesiod, writing in the eighth

or seventh century B.C. was giving advice on agriculture, interspersed with many moral maxims of a homely and down-to-earth type. But it was not until the third century B.C. that this Hesiodic tradition really flourished and became self-conscious. An important figure was Aratus, with his astronomical poem *Phaenomena* which Callimachus praised as being 'in the manner of Hesiod'. Aratus wrote competently, sometimes even elegantly, although his popularity and influence in later times seem to us excessive. Little can be said in favour of Nicander (c. 135 B.C.), who in addition chose the most unpromising subjects for his verse, such as venomous reptiles (*Theriaca*) or antidotes to poison (*Alexipharmaca*), but even Nicander had his followers. Aratus and Nicander illustrate the characteristics of this genre quite well. Their language is archaic and often obscure beyond the demands of a technical subject; these features show them trying to recreate the style of Hesiod, as well as following the taste of their own age. (pp. 89-90)

Among the Romans didactic poetry found two practitioners whose talent was immeasurably superior to that of Aratus or Nicander—Lucretius with his *De Rerum Natura* and Virgil in the *Georgics.* Lucretius, admittedly, drew on a rather different tradition of philosophical poetry going back to such men as Empedocles, but he exhibits similar features, e.g. in his love of archaism, being a great admirer of Ennius and the old epic and tragic style of Roman poetry, and in his digressions. Both Lucretius and Virgil stood to Ovid in the *Ars Amatoria* in much the same relationship as Hesiod to Aratus and Nicander—they provided for him a fount of dignified and old-fashioned language which gave the colouring appropriate to this genre. One must say, however, that there is no question of our poet mocking Lucretius or Virgil in any hostile spirit; in *Amores,* I. 15 he states his admiration for the pair of them, and shows it in practice elsewhere. Two lesser Roman didactic poems offer some illuminating parallels to Ovid, the *Cynegetica* of Grattius (on hunting), perhaps composed a little before the *Ars,* and the *Astronomica* of Manilius, written soon afterwards. Since Grattius in particular lacks all the genius of Lucretius and Virgil, we can appreciate both the pompous nature of the genre and Ovid's delightful parody. He makes use of didactic language mainly when introducing, closing, or passing from one section to another; here we find formulae like *nunc age, adde quod, principio, praeterea,* familiar from Lucretius and Virgil. Other features belonging to the same tradition are the summary of proposed contents, a recapitulation showing how far we have progressed, and the personal 'seal' which closes both Books II and III, since the work was originally planned in only two books. Of course the joke could easily be overdone, and Ovid avoids that temptation. (pp. 90-1)

The idea of writing a frivolous didactic poem was not new. Ovid himself had composed one on female cosmetics (*Medicamina Faciei Femineae*), from which a hundred lines survive. And, when defending himself at *Tristia,* II. 471ff., he mentions several others, e.g. on indoor and outdoor games, etiquette or the bottling of wine. All these are described as 'amusements for the fireside in December'. But none had the high possibilities of an *Ars Amatoria.* The very title promises a delicious incongruity and tension between form and content. It is not merely a case of pedantry against passion—one might reasonably hold that love, like virtue, is not teachable, not to be governed by rules and prescriptions. This particular tension had never been exploited before, although earlier Latin elegy contains a fair amount of instruction in love, and the background deserves to be mentioned briefly. Among the influences on Roman elegy, Greek New Comedy together with its Latin followers played an important part, and one stock scene in Comedy showed the unsavoury old *lena* advising a girl how to attract men. Both Propertius and Ovid write elegies on this theme which betray their antecedents clearly. A still closer parallel to the *Ars* exists at Tibullus, I. 4. The poet has a conversation with Priapus (in itself a 'learned' touch—compare Hesiod's visit from the Muses and the appearances of Cupid, Venus and Apollo in Ovid) wherein the god gives advice for success in love; his tone is pompous, with an occasional hint of Ovid's mannerisms. At the end Tibullus foresees a time when the eager young will crowd round him for instruction:

> tempus erit cum me Veneris praecepta ferentem
> deducat iuvenum sedula turba senem.
>
> (The day will come in my old age when an attentive crowd of youths follows me about as I impart to them guidance in love.)

Propertius too instructs his readers, not only in the *lena*-poem: 'invenies eadem blandi praecepta Properti' ('You will find that graceful Propertius teaches the same', *Tristia*).

But neither Tibullus nor Propertius allowed the didactic tradition to influence the way they depicted love; that was a masterstroke of Ovid himself. To appreciate it fully we must understand the conception of love which is regular in Roman elegy and which broadly speaking, Ovid followed in the *Amores.* Love appears as an overwhelming force, even a disease or madness, which carries the poet by storm; he has little choice as to whom he falls in love with (the woman may well take the initiative) and little freedom of manœuvre once he has succumbed. Often the painful rather than the pleasurable side of love is uppermost. If this seems too searing a picture, it can easily be exemplified from the very first poem of Propertius—and there are indications that the lost elegies of Cornelius Gallus possessed the same colouring in even greater degree. Consider the opening line of Propertius:

> Cynthia prima suis miserum me cepit ocellis
>
> (Cynthia was the first to trap me helpless with her gaze.)

Propertius himself is no more than a powerless victim, who has no chance of escape once the fateful glance has fallen upon him. And a few lines below:

> et caput impositis pressit Amor pedibus
>
> (Love trod upon my head and bore me down.)

Certain conventional images in love elegy reinforce this attitude. For example, the lover may be spoken of as the captive of Cupid, as at *Amores,* I.2 where Ovid imagines a Roman-type triumphal procession in which he himself is paraded through the streets as a prisoner. Particularly revealing is the figure of *servitium amoris*—the lover is a slave of his girl-friend and forced to perform duties which degrade a free man. Often this is expressed in strongly Roman terms, to make his disgrace feel all the more sharp. . . . (pp. 93-4)

Another notable feature of the *Ars* is the wealth of contemporary Roman colouring. Earlier elegy had for the most part been conducted in a nebulous half-Greek, half-Roman world; a poem like *Amores,* III. 2, set at a race-meeting in the Circus Maximus, is a rarity (and all the more effective for that). But from the first line of the *Ars:*

> si quis *in hoc* artem *populo* non novit amandi . . .
>
> (Any fellow-citizen of mine who has not learnt the art of love . . .)

we are firmly in the capital. To Ovid's young hero, conventionally poor but leisured, it is 'tua Roma'. So there are frequent glimpses of the city which Augustus boasted that he had transformed from brick to marble, its temples and fountains

> . . . subdita qua Veneris facto de marmore templo
> Appias expressis aera pulsat aquis.
>
> (. . . where below Venus' marble temple the Appian fountain sends a jet of water into the air.)

Whether the emperor would approve of his splendid new buildings being recommended for meeting elegant females is another matter. The full round of Roman social activity is here: theatres, festivals, markets, law-courts, race-meetings, gladiatorial displays, a triumph, a naval spectacular, exercises in the Campus Martius. [There is a] section on what the well-dressed man was wearing in 2 B.C., and Ovid offers plenty of corresponding advice to young ladies.

This much sharper definition of a Roman milieu in the *Ars* did, however, bring a problem which eventually proved fatal to its author. His girls must also be set more recognizably in real Roman society, and this was likely to raise moral objections. Orthodox scholarly opinion nowadays holds that the typical heroine of Roman love poetry should be considered a *hetaera,* but in my view Gordon Williams [in his *Tradition and Originality in Roman Poetry*] is basically right in arguing that some of the most famous figures over whose reality we feel we have most grasp (particularly Catullus' Lesbia, also Propertius' Cynthia) were women of some social standing, maybe married, who played fast and loose in the chaotic conditions of the late Republic. Ovid's heroines in the *Amores* often seem to be pale reflections of this type. So there was a real danger that our poet would be accused of undermining marriage. He tried to avoid this by making the women more obviously *hetaerae* of the class of freedwomen. Thereby he adhered more closely to his models in Greek Comedy and epigram, and at the same time ranged himself with a long-standing Roman view (indeed the 'inspired pronouncement of Cato', Horace) that irregular affairs were quite acceptable as long as they did not involve other people's wives. None the less Ovid has retained in the **Ars** a conventional figure of earlier elegy—it might have been advisable to remove him—the girl's 'husband', who is a rival to the hero.

So far we have looked individually at three main elements in the **Ars:** the didactic tradition, material taken from straight love elegy and the added colouring of Roman social life. Now observe [that] Ovid interweaves all of them in a longer passage: he is telling the lover that some times are better than others for starting a courtship (an idea derived ultimately from the *Days* of Hesiod's *Works and Days*). The point in every case is that the young man, conventionally poor, must avoid times when he will be expected to bring a present, and make a move only when the shops are shut. This results in a grim sort of humour—cheerful festivals are out, but days of national mourning excellent. Altogether the lines are unusually intricate and sometimes obscure due to our defective knowledge of the Roman festivals. (pp. 96-8)

Now of course one can enjoy the **Ars** in a simple way without appreciating the background and complexity of themes, as many people have enjoyed this poem in the past. The learning is unobtrusive and never diminishes gaiety. But undoubtedly Ovid wanted and expected his readers to follow him in such an amazing *tour de force,* and I think one has a certain duty to respect the author's intentions. Also the result is surely a gain in pleasure. Writing on more than one level is a constant feature of Ovid's style, but in this poem he surpasses himself.

The **Ars** shows clear signs of having originally been planned in two books, addressed to men only. Before long Ovid decided on a third, for the benefit of young women, but did not obliterate signs of the original two-book scheme. The **Remedia Amoris,** addressed almost solely to men but said to be equally applicable to both sexes, may belong to this second stage; in any case the complete work, **Ars Amatoria** in three books together with its companion piece, must have seen the light of day about A.D. I. Ovid's final conception gave him the chance to handle the stock themes of love poetry in a number of ways: straightforwardly in Books I and II, from another angle for the girls in Book III, and completely in reverse for the **Remedia.** (pp. 100-01)

I have not yet spoken about one of the work's chief delights, its digressions. As mentioned earlier, these derive from the didactic tradition; they appear occasionally in Aratus and Nicander, but with much greater frequency and brilliance in Lucretius and Virgil's *Georgics.* For us, with our knowledge of the poet's later development, there is a tendency to see them as a testing-ground for the **Metamorphoses,** and in fact two stories (Daedalus and Icarus and Cephalus and Procris) recur in the hexameter poem. Ovid overcomes the slight restrictions of the elegiac couplet and for the first time gives free rein to his talent for narrative, a talent fulfilled in the **Fasti** as well as the **Metamorphoses.** Every trait which endeared the poet to later generations is here: economy of means, visual brilliance, simplicity masking sophistication and restrained wit. I can only point to some of my own favourite episodes, and give

the reasons why I like them. First of all, the Rape of the Sabine Women. This is amusingly presented in the learned Hellenistic manner as an aetiological story, explaining why the theatre is still a dangerous place for pretty girls (the formal conclusion). It must surely have aroused conflicting emotions in a traditionally minded Roman; on the one hand the Rape was a firmly established legend of infant Rome, but it does not show the ancestors in too favourable a light. Ovid enthusiastically endorses Romulus' actions, claiming in effect that the great Founder had anticipated his own doctrines! He sets the scene at a theatrical performance rather than a race-meeting, as was usual, perhaps to give extra spice because conservative Roman sentiment had disapproved of the theatre. I have already mentioned the sly hit at contemporary recruiting difficulties in the army. For the rest, Ovid constantly makes fun of the primitive conditions of early Rome—in the theatre itself, the entertainment and even the hairstyles. (pp. 104-05)

The **Remedia Amoris** deserves more than the brief consideration which space will allow here. Nobody nowadays would hold that it was prompted either by an attack of bad conscience for having written the **Ars,** or a desire to avert the wrath of the emperor. But there remains a feeling that poetically it is somewhat inferior to the **Ars,** and I am not sure that this is fair. The title **Remedia Amoris** takes Ovid's didactic joke one stage further: in adding the piece on antidotes he probably had in mind the example of Nicander, whose *Alexipharmaca* (remedies for poisons) was to some extent a companion to his *Theriaca* (on poisonous reptiles). As with the **Ars,** we can find the germ in earlier elegy. I have mentioned that love is often presented as a disease or madness; Propertius may ask his friends for any patent medicines, prescribe a course of treatment for himself, and finally pronounce the patient cured. Sober philosophers too had pondered the best way to deal with such a grave threat to mental stability: 'On occasion he should be diverted to other interests, concerns, pursuits and occupations; often, like invalids who do not respond to medicine, he must be treated by a change of climate. Some authorities believe in driving out an old love with a new one, on the principle of knocking out one nail with another.'

Even if Ovid's heart was not in the **Remedia,** his mind and wit were, as usual, actively engaged. We have already seen some examples of the way he reverses precepts from the **Ars.** Perhaps more entertaining are those passages where he argues against his own, or at least customary elegiac attitudes. One way to free yourself from love, says Cupid, is to concentrate on money problems. . . . (p. 110)

Positively the greatest danger is to have no proper business with which to occupy yourself. Therefore, to avoid love, you should plunge into politics, the law, or the army. Here, for once, Ovid is arguing like a traditionally minded Roman, using the stock terms of abuse like *otium* and *desidia.* This is proved by a famous example from mythology: the anachronistic Roman colouring has a particular spice:

> quaeritis, Aegisthus quare sit factus adulter?
> in promptu causa est: desidiosus erat.
> pugnabant alii tardis apud Ilion armis;

transtulerat vires Graecia tota suas.
sive operam bellis vellet dare, nulla gerebat,
    sive foro, vacuum litibus Argos erat.
quod potuit, ne nil illic ageretur, amavit.
    sic venit ille puer, sic puer ille manet.

(Can you wonder why Aegisthus became an
adulterer? The explanation is obvious—he had
nothing to occupy him! The others were engaged
in a protracted struggle round Troy—in fact the
flower of Greece had gone on service overseas.
Suppose he wished to concentrate on war, Argos
was not waging one; suppose it was the law, the
courts were in vacation. So he seized his only
chance of avoiding complete idleness and played
the lover; that is how Cupid gains a foothold and
cannot be ejected.)

Unlike Tibullus Ovid does not in the **Amores** regularly depict the countryside as an ideal setting for love. So in the
Remedia he suggests that country pursuits are an effective
antidote to love, and shows incidentally that he can write
just as prettily as Tibullus90-1)

The main features of the **Ars** and **Remedia** stressed in this
[essay] have been the sharpness and detached, ironical humour. To pinpoint these might be thought no service to
a poet who has often been condemned for his lack of sincere feelings. Personally I can believe that Ovid was himself a man of genuine humanity, capable both of giving and
inspiring affection; only on rare occasions, however, does
such a quality break through the glittering surface of the
Ars, because this poem, while containing much shrewd
psychological insight, is in every sense the most artificial
of Ovid's creations. But need 'artificial' be nothing but a
term of abuse? If in the last analysis we must admit that
Roman traditionalists who objected to the frivolity of the
Ars had more than a grain of truth on their side, we can
still be grateful for this link across the centuries to the intricate workings of a lively and brilliant mind. (p. 113)

> *A. S. Hollis, "The 'Ars Amatoria' and 'Re-
> media Amoris',' in* Ovid, *edited by J. W.
> Binns, Routledge & Kegan Paul, 1973, pp. 84-
> 115.*

FURTHER READING

GENERAL

Binns, J. W. *Ovid.* London: Routledge & Kegan Paul, 1973,
250 p.
    Collection of seven essays exploring the *Amores,* the
    Heroides, the *Ars amatoria* and *Remedia amoris,* the
    Metamorphoses, the *Tristia,* and Ovid's influence in the
    Middle Ages and in sixteenth-century Europe.

Rand, Edward Kennard. *Ovid and His Influence.* New York:
Longmans, Green and Co., 1925, 184 p.
    Seminal twentieth-century study that stresses the rele-
    vance of Ovidian scholarship to critical assessments.

Thibault, John C. *The Mystery of Ovid's Exile.* Berkeley: University of California Press, 1964, 177 p.
    The critic collects all the theories of Ovid's exile and
    evaluates the cogency of the arguments, finally deter-
    mining that "certainty can never be attained" unless new
    evidence is uncovered or modern scholarship offers an
    acceptable hypothesis.

Wilkinson, L. P. *Ovid Recalled.* Cambridge: Cambridge at
the University Press, 1955, 483 p.
    Balanced study of Ovid and his works for a general audi-
    ence, later published in abridged form as *Ovid Surveyed*
    (1962).

INFLUENCE

Brewer, Wilmon. "Introductory Survey" in his *Ovid's Metamorphoses in European Culture,* pp. 1-42. Boston: The Cornhill Publishing Company, 1933.
    Succinct account of the influence of the *Metamorphoses*
    in Western culture as a source and inspiration to writers
    and artists.

Crosland, Jessie. "Ovid's Contribution to the Conception of
Love Known as 'L'amour Courtois'." *The Modern Language
Review* XLII, No. 2 (April 1947): 199-206.
    Traces the impact of Ovid on early troubador material.

DuRocher, Richard J. *Milton and Ovid.* Ithaca: Cornell University Press, 1985, 241 p.
    Asserts that "Milton's extensive use of the *Metamor-
    phoses* introduces an inventive method of presenting uni-
    versal, mythic change." The critic also claims that "*Par-
    adise Lost* is the high-water mark of Ovidian imitation"
    in English literary history.

Feder, Lillian. "Pound and Ovid." In *Ezra Pound among the
Poets,* edited by George Bornstein, pp. 13-34. Chicago: The
University of Chicago Press, 1985.
    Investigates Pound's use of Ovid, especially in the *Can-
    tos.* Reveals that Pound, while repeatedly praising Ovid,
    found the ancient poet enigmatic.

Fyler, John M. *Chaucer and Ovid.* New Haven: Yale University Press, 1979, 206 p.
    Explores the affinity between the two poets in aims, tone,
    language, wordplay, and use of the obstrusive narrator,
    often counterpointing them with Dante and Vergil.
    Finds that Chaucer and Ovid are "poets who speak for
    the comic pathos of human frailty and human preten-
    sions."

Guyer, Foster E. *The Influence of Ovid on Crestien de Troyes.*
Chicago: The University of Chicago Libraries, 1921, 247 p.
    Examines the effect of Ovid's works on Crestien's con-
    cept of love through the latter's use of Ovidian themes,
    characters, language, and episodes.

Martindale, Charles, ed. *Ovid Renewed.* Cambridge: Cambridge University Press, 1988, 298 p.
    Contains fifteen essays concerning Ovidian influence in
    European art and literature. Concentrates on Ovid's im-
    pact on such English authors as John Gower, Shake-
    speare, Dryden, Spenser, and T. S. Eliot.

Shevill, Rudolph. *Ovid and the Renascence in Spain.* Hildes-
heim: Georg Olms Verlag, 1971, 268 p.
    Considers the inspiration Ovid's works provided to me-
    dieval Italian, French, and Spanish literature, concen-

trating on the effect in Spain. Traces parallels in the works of Cervantes, Lope de Vega, and various anonymous works.

WORKS

Galinsky, G. Karl. *Ovid's Metamorphoses: An Introduction to the Basic Aspects.* Oxford: Basil Blackwell, 1975, 285 p.
> Discusses the variety of tone, style, and subject matter in the *Metamorphoses.*

Jacobson, Howard. *Ovid's Heroides.* Princeton: Princeton University Press, 1974, 437 p.
> Interpretive study of the first fifteen of the *Heroides* focusing on Ovid's original approach to the genre.

Otis, Brooks. *Ovid as an Epic Poet.* Cambridge: Cambridge at the University Press, second edition, 1970, 441 p.
> Attempts to understand Ovid's intention and performance in the *Metamorphoses.* The critic refutes the conclusion of the first edition of the work by asserting that it is intentionally anti-Augustan. The appendix contains an examination of the sources believed to have been used by Ovid.

Verducci, Florence. *Ovid's Toyshop of the Heart: Epistulae Heroidum.* Princeton: Princeton University Press, 1985, 310 p.
> Addresses the issues of wit, parody, and irony to illustrate how the *Heroides* may be read to gain the most pleasure.

Rainer Maria Rilke

1875-1926

(Born René Karl Wilhelm Johann Josef Maria Rilke) German poet, novelist, biographer, and short story writer.

Rilke was a major poet of the twentieth century whose *Duineser Elegien* (*Duino Elegies*) and *Die Sonette an Orpheus* (*Sonnets to Orpheus*) are considered among the most important poetic cycles in modern world literature. Characterized by striking perceptions, rich imagery, and mystical introspection and prophecy, Rilke's work endeavors to capture the essence of inner experience, often through exacting descriptions of physical objects. Throughout his career, according to translator J. B. Leishman, Rilke sought "symbolic or 'external' equivalents for experiences that were becoming ever more 'inward' and incommunicable, and which when he tried to communicate them, were continually bringing him up against the limitations of language." Rilke's commitment to expressing the inner self and exploring the role of art in life has earned him an honored position among modern poets.

Rilke was the only child of a German-speaking family in Prague, then part of the Austro-Hungarian empire. His father was a retired officer in the Austrian army who worked as a railroad official; his mother, a socially ambitious and possessive woman. At age eleven, Rilke began his formal schooling at a military boarding academy, and in 1891, less than a year after transferring to a secondary military school, he was discharged due to health problems that he would suffer throughout his life. He immediately returned to Prague, where in his absence his parents had divorced, and shortly began receiving private instruction toward passing the entrance exams for Prague's Charles-Ferdinand University. In 1894 his first book of verse, *Leben und Lieder: Bilder und Tagebuchblätter,* was published. Regarded by both critics and the mature Rilke as primarily naive and sentimental, these early poems reflect the styles of both nineteenth-century German poet Heinrich Heine and traditional German folk songs.

By 1895 Rilke had enrolled in the philosophy program at Charles-Ferdinand University, but soon became disenchanted with his studies and left Prague for Munich, ostensibly to study art. In Munich Rilke mingled within the city's literary circles, had several of his plays produced, published his poetry collections *Larenopfer* and *Traumgekrönt,* and was introduced to the work of Danish writer Jens Peter Jacobsen, a decisive influence during Rilke's formative years. Visiting Venice in 1897, Rilke met Lou Andreas-Salomé, a married woman fifteen years his senior who stimulated radical personal changes in Rilke, including the gesture of replacing his given name, René, with the masculine form, Rainer. After spending the summer of 1897 with her in the Bavarian Alps, Rilke accompanied Salomé and her husband to Berlin in late 1897 and to Italy the following year. In 1899 Rilke made the first of two pivotal trips to Russia with Salomé, discovering what he

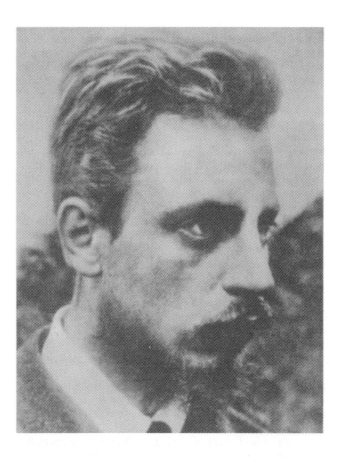

termed his "spiritual fatherland" in both the people and the landscape. There Rilke met Leo Tolstoy, L. O. Pasternak (father of writer Boris Pasternak), and peasant poet Spiridon Droschin, whose work Rilke translated into German. These trips provided Rilke with the poetic material and inspiration essential to his developing philosophy of existential materialism and art as religion. Retaining the delicate, impressionistic style of his earlier poetry, Rilke's work during this period often featured traditional Christian imagery and concepts, and presented art as the sole redeemer of humanity. *Das Buch der Bilder* and *Das Stunden-Buch. Enthaltend die drei Bücher: Vom mönchischen Leben, Von der Pilgerschaft, Von der Armuth und vom Tode* (*The Book of Hours; Comprising the Three Books: Of the Monastic Life, Of Pilgrimage, Of Poverty and Death*) display this mystical tendency; the latter work is considered by many critics to mark the end of Rilke's poetic apprenticeship. Also during this time, Rilke composed the first draft of what would later be published as *Die Weise von Liebe und Tod des Cornets Christoph Rilke* (*The Story of the Love and Death of the Cornet Christopher Rilke*). This work is comprised of twenty-six brief prose poems that detail the last days in the life of an eighteen-year-old officer from Saxony during an Austrian campaign against the Turks in Western Hungary in 1663. It was Rilke's most popular work during his lifetime and gained him a wide audience when it was published in 1906.

Rilke's affair with Salomé ended in 1901, when he married sculptor Clara Westhoff and moved to Westerwede, near the artist colony of Worpswede in Germany. However, within a year after the birth of their only child in late 1901, Rilke and Clara separated. In the summer of 1902 Rilke traveled to Paris to write a book about French sculptor Auguste Rodin, whose work he greatly admired, and soon after traveled through Italy, Scandinavia, and Germany. In 1905 Rilke returned to Paris, which became the focus of his life and work until the start of World War I, and served as Rodin's secretary for eight months. Due largely to Rodin's influence, Rilke strove to endow his writings from this time with the plasticity of the visual arts, to dispense with ideas and treat his poems as carefully crafted objects. His collection *Neue Gedichte* (*New Poems*) displays this transformation of his aesthetic vision and contains what most critics regard as Rilke's first mature verse. Regarding the poetry of this period, W. H. Auden has remarked, "Rilke is almost the first poet since the seventeenth century to find a fresh solution [of how to express abstract ideas in concrete terms]."

Following the publication of *Die Aufzeichnungen des Malte Laurids Brigge* (*The Notebooks of Malte Laurids Brigge*), a loosely autobiographical novel that is widely considered his most accomplished prose work, Rilke did not publish a major work for twelve years, though during this time he was composing segments of his most highly respected verse. In the years 1911-12, after traveling through North Africa and Egypt, Rilke made two visits to the Castle Duino, near the city of Trieste on the Balkan coast of the Adriatic Sea, as the guest of Princess Maria von Thurn und Taxis. Rilke claimed that while there an angel appeared to him, inspiring the first two poems of his ten-poem cycle, *Duino Elegies,* the remainder of which he completed in 1922. During the intervening years Rilke continued to travel extensively, visiting Venice, Spain, Paris, Munich, and, most significantly, Switzerland, where he stayed throughout most of his final years. During a remarkable three week period in early 1922, while residing at the Château de Muzot in the Rhone valley of Switzerland, Rilke completed the final six of his ten *Duino Elegies* and his *Sonnets to Orpheus.* Together, these volumes brought Rilke international recognition as a major artist and constituted the pinnacle of his career. In the years following, Rilke's health declined and he spent long periods of time at health resorts and spas in Switzerland, particularly the sanatorium at Valmont in Montreaux. During 1925 he traveled a final time to Paris, where he was treated with great respect and importance. Rilke's last works were translations of poetry and prose by French writer Paul Valéry and three small volumes of his own French verse. He died of leukemia at Valmont in 1926.

Rilke's poetic career is generally divided into three periods and epitomized by the works *The Book of Hours,* the two volumes of his *New Poems,* and, in the last period, *Duino Elegies* and *Sonnets to Orpheus. The Book of Hours,* written between 1899 and 1903, is closely associated with Rilke's visits to Russia. The three sections of this extended poetic cycle embody Rilke's admiration for what he perceived as the simplicity and piety of Russian people and the beauty of the country's landscape. They also reflect his notion of God as a developing creation of the artist and offer a celebration of self that permeates his later work. Although Christian motifs and themes appear throughout these poems, the whole is a rejection of the traditional Christian God. In the final section, Rilke introduces variations on themes of human misery, which many critics attribute to the suffering and squalor that Rilke observed in Paris in 1902.

The two volumes of *New Poems* were written mainly in the years 1906-08 during Rilke's prolonged residence in Paris, and, according to most critics, represent the height of his development in the short poem. In these poems Rilke employed a precise visual style, inspired by the poetry of German writer Stephan George and the visual art of Rodin and French painter Paul Cézanne, to lend structure to the inward focus of his poetry. These works often feature specific physical objects, including paintings, sculptures, animals, and buildings, as indications of Rilke's admiration for the intrinsic beauty of physical existence and as a means of expressing the inner self in tangible things. As such, these poems are representative of Rilke's contribution to the development of the *dinggedicht,* or "object poem," in which the focus of the work is on an object. By clarifying the object's essence through precise, evocative description, the poet strives to place the object into the realm of symbolic function. This technique is perhaps most readily observed in the well-known poems "Der Panther" ("The Panther"), "Das Karussell" ("Merry-Go-Round"), and the group of "cathedral poems" that center upon the physical attributes of European cathedrals.

Rilke's final period of poetic achievement began in 1911, when he first visited the Castle Duino, and includes two of the most significant works in modern literature: *Duino Elegies* and *Sonnets to Orpheus.* Through these thematically linked works, critics contend that Rilke sought to redefine his perception of the poet's calling from one of using the creative process to analyze and master reality to one of turning the external world inward in order to preserve existence. In the cycle of ten poems that make up *Duino Elegies,* Rilke employed free rhythms, dactylic and iambic forms, questions and exclamations, and moved from lament to praise, exploring the precariousness of human life in an increasingly inhuman world. In the end, Rilke advanced a resolution by suggesting, according to E. L. Stahl, that the earth and its objects are raised again in our souls, "transforming external realities into invisible inward possessions in life as in death" and positing that death resolves the contradictions of human life. The intimate style and inwardness of these poems and their expansive imagery enabled Rilke to establish and maintain a mythical atmosphere throughout, the most notable examples of which are the angels who appear from the initial line of the first elegy: "Who, if I cried, would hear me among the angelic orders?" *Sonnets to Orpheus* has frequently been interpreted as a response to the *Elegies,* voicing affirmation and joy in the acceptance of humanity's situation. Comprising two linked cycles of fifty-five poems, this entire work was composed within three week's time along with six of the *Duino Elegies*. Musical in tone, these sonnets exude an atmosphere of serenity in contrast to an aura of majesty in the *Elegies*. Using the mythical lyrist/singer/poet Orpheus as representative of humanity's potential for change, creativity, and the ability to perceive and interpret reality in consonance, Rilke is concerned in these sonnets with life and the role of art in life. A celebration of poetry and how it functions, *Sonnets to Orpheus* documents Rilke's intention to create a poetic song that transcends all boundaries between internal and external reality, life and death.

Throughout his career, Rilke remained concerned with certain recurring subjects: the importance of the poet's role, the essence of religious faith, and the nature of life and how it should be experienced. His ideas on art and religion, the benefits of solitude and inwardness, and his striking powers of perception and literary technique mark him as an important force in modern poetry. His contributions to literature include the development of the *dinggedicht*, the blending of traditional and modern poetic forms, his unwavering commitment to exploring the role of art, and his belief in art as saviour of humanity. Rilke's career is often considered symbolic of the condition of the modern poet, representing a quest to confirm the need for poetry in an age that seems to deny importance to poetic accomplishments.

(For further discussion of Rilke's life and career, see *Twentieth-Century Literary Criticism*, Vols. 1, 6, 19; *Contemporary Authors*, Vol. 104; and *Dictionary of Literary Biography*, Vol. 81.)

PRINCIPAL WORKS

POETRY

Leben und Lieder: Bilder und Tagebuchblätter   1894
Larenopfer   1896
Traumgekrönt   1897
Das Buch der Bilder   1902; enlarged edition, 1906
Das Stunden-Buch. Enthaltend die drei Bücher: Vom mönchischen Leben, Von der Pilgerschaft, Von der Armuth und vom Tode   1905
    [*The Book of Hours; Comprising the Three Books: Of the Monastic Life, Of Pilgrimage, Of Poverty and Death*, 1961]
Neue Gedichte. 2 vols.   1907-08
    [*New Poems*, 1964]
Duineser Elegien   1923
    [*Duineser Elegien: Elegies from the Castle of Duino*, 1931; also published as *Duino Elegies*, 1939]
Die Sonette an Orpheus: Beschrieben als ein Grab-Mal für Wera Ouckama Knoop   1923
    [*Sonnets to Orpheus: Written as a Monument for Wera Ouckama Knoop*, 1936; also published as *Sonnets to Orpheus*, 1942]
Selected Poems of Rainer Maria Rilke   1981

OTHER MAJOR WORKS

Vom lieben Gott und Anderes: An Große für Kinder erzählt

(short stories)   1900; revised edition, *Geschichten vom lieben Gott*, 1904
    [*Stories of God*, 1932]
Auguste Rodin   (biography)   1903
    [*Auguste Rodin*, 1919]
Die Weise von Liebe und Tod des Cornets Christoph Rilke (prose poem)   1906
    [*The Story of the Love and Death of the Cornet Christopher Rilke*, 1927; also published as *The Lay of Love and Death of Cornet Christopher Rilke*, 1948]
Die Aufzeichnungen des Malte Laurids Brigge   (novel) 1910
    [*The Notebook of Malte Laurids Brigge*, 1930; also published as *The Journal of My Other Self*, 1930]
Briefe an einen jungen Dichter   (letters)   1929
    [*Letters to a Young Poet*, 1934]

Ernst Rose   (essay date 1943)

[*Rose is a German-born, American educator, critic, editor, and translator whose publications include* Contemporary German Literature from Sensuous to Spiritual Poetry, 1880-1930 *(1930) and* A History of German Literature *(1960). In following excerpt, Rose focuses on Rilke's "Fünf Gesänge" and argues that these poems display artistic and thematic unity with Rilke's entire body of work, foreshadowing viewpoints and themes later examined in his masterpieces,* Duineser Elegien *and* Sonette an Orpheus.]

The biographical approach to a work of pure art is seldom the most happy one. We are tempted to trace exclusively the subjective process of its creation and to forego the responsibility of interpreting it objectively. Works of living and of recently deceased authors have frequently suffered most from the personal curiosity of their contemporaries. Thus one is hardly astonished when Rainer Maria Rilke's poetry also has been misinterpreted as a result of the application of a narrow biographical method. The conflict between life and work, which forms part of every poet's biography, in the case of Rilke has been overstressed. One has falsely attributed an aesthetic significance to interruptions in the flow of his poetry, which, in a more correct interpretation, have only a biographical meaning. In the face of these misleading results of a purely biographical approach, the objective unity and the intrinsic meaning of Rilke's poetic work must be reestablished by consistent aesthetic interpretation.

For example, let us take the **"Fünf Gesänge,"** which Rilke wrote during the first weeks of the war in 1914. They have been variously viewed as interruptions or exceptions in Rilke's poetic career, and their meaning has found a most divergent interpretation, which, in the interest of an adequate understanding, must be clarified. Hermann Pongs in recent articles has reviewed these five odes as proof of Rilke's essential individualism and has dogmatically denied to him wider national significance. Others, like Roman Woerner, have attempted to prove Rilke's nationalism and to connect his war poems with the general German trend of the August days of 1914. Miss E. M. Butler in her latest book has made our poet into an effeminate weakling who generally shrank from war, but who could nevertheless for brief moments be swayed by a mass emotion into the opposite attitude. Lastly, Dieter Bassermann and Hugo Kuhn have interpreted Rilke in terms of a spiritual bravery which is not afraid of facing unpleasant as well as pleasant facts of existence and which consciously affirms death and misery as meaningful parts of it. War, from the point of view of these last-mentioned scholars, would have been just one of the ugly realities that had to be given a meaning, and Rilke's facing of it they would describe as a sign of spiritual courage and of unflinching intellectual honesty.

In our own attempt to arrive at a clarification, we shall first confine ourselves strictly to the problem of war, which forms the main theme of Rilke's **"Fünf Gesänge."** His attitude toward his own nation and toward other nations is, to be sure, a related topic. But it is by no means identical with the war theme, and it is too inclusive to be treated in the discussion of just a small number of poems. We shall, secondly, avoid all biographical references, as we intend to proceed on a strictly aesthetic basis. Aside from their doubtful value for criticism in general, the biographical data in this particular case for the most part follow the poetic experiences. These data should therefore not be used even as source material for a biographical study of the **"Fünf Gesänge."** For an aesthetic investigation they possess hardly any meaning at all. (pp. 266-67)

It has to be emphasized that Rilke, as soon as he found himself, immediately embraced existence as an ambiguous, two-faced phenomenon. After he had once overcome the feminine, nervous impressionism of his first poems, he never failed to see life in death as the force releasing it and endowing it with meaning; and he never ceased to perceive death in life as its most natural fruit and consummation. Right from the beginning Rilke frequently expressed these views through images taken from the life of the soldier. Nor was this an accident for a young man who had to endure four years at a military academy, where for the first time he came to realize the darker sides of life. Unlike many of his contemporaries, Rilke did not have to wait for the great war in order to embrace the heroic attitude toward suffering and death. When he was not yet twenty-four years old he was inspired by one of Hans Thoma's paintings to write his poem **"Ritter."** Here the knight's existence is depicted as having two different aspects. The knight enjoys riding out into the bustling world of his everyday life, but he is constantly aware of the presence of death. The knight's everyday world comprises friends and enemies and meals in the castle hall, beautiful May days and maidens and forests, the Holy Grail and the images of God. But behind this everyday world looms up the world of death waiting for his hour, when the hissing blade of a stranger will set him free to sing and play according to his liking. So to the knight here is attributed a matter-of-fact acceptance of death as an indissoluble part of existence, and his way of facing this reality can be described as hardly anything but soldierlike or heroic.

In the same year, 1899, was completed **Die Weise von**

Liebe und Tod des Cornets Christoph Rilke, which, according to Harry Maync's excellent interpretation, can be called a fascinating poetic picture of war. It treats the ever-recurrent tragic fate of the youth who is prematurely hurled into the war and is destroyed by it before he has had time really to ripen into manhood. Rilke's cornet is in no way an outstanding leader, but rather a representative of youth in general. Before taking part in the campaign he is scarcely aware of the existence of the other sex. Then, during the long, uneventful ride to battle, its presence gradually forces itself on his attention, and shortly before his death the youthful cornet tastes the sweetness of womanly love. At the same time he follows stubbornly his call to duty and defends the flag entrusted to him to the very end. In an emotional confusion which, though beautiful, might also be described as unreasonable by a man of more advanced years, Rilke's cornet finally sheds his blood for his flag.

There is no moralistic or nationalistic tendency in Rilke's interpretation of this young life. He simply records it with all its aspects and tells us: so it was. To be sure, this manner of telling it is still somewhat external and impressionistic. The form of **Die Weise von Liebe und Tod** was modeled after the fashion of Jens Peter Jacobsen and clearly represents an impressionistic mixture of lyric, epic, and dramatic elements, unified by musical themes. Rilke's record has a seeming artlessness which, however, must not lead us to underestimate his effort. Already this narrative is the product of a conscious artistic will aimed at an uncompromising picture of existence as a whole. Such a picture by its very nature cannot be superficially optimistic, and thus the gentle, dark undertones seem to dominate. But the poet does not deprive us at all of the intoxicating ecstasies of the young life he describes, the most supreme of which is its sacrificial death. Here death still is something like the most festive moment of life, it does not yet clearly and coolly enter the cornet's consciousness, nor is it achieved by a knowing effort. It reminds one somewhat of Ibsen's *Hedda Gabler* with her ideal of dying in beauty with vine-leaves in her hair. This impressionistic conception was later on revised by the poet in favor of a deeper and more responsible attitude. But certainly that does not make the cornet's death less heroic.

I say nothing new to the reader familiar with Rilke when I emphasize that the theme treated in **Die Weise von Liebe und Tod** reappears again and again in his subsequent poetry. In the **Buch der Bilder** (1898-1906) one finds not only the early poem about the knight, but also the later lines on the Swedish King Charles XII's ride into the Ukraine, which is in more than one way reminiscent of the ride of Cornet Rilke into Hungary. These lines from the autumn of the year 1900 depict impressionistically a king who rides into battle as if he were in love and who sheds blood like a spendthrift. Similar notes are also struck in the second poem of the cycle on the czars.

In the **Neue Gedichte,** composed during the years from 1903 to 1908, the theme of **Die Weise von Liebe und Tod** is, for instance, repeated in the poem about the Count von Brederode who, in an exuberant love of life, jumps into a river in order to escape from Turkish imprisonment.

Death grants him the freedom for which he was striving. Here, already, death is achieved by a conscious effort and is no longer hailed simply as the highest intoxication of all.

In the *Neue Gedichte* we also find the poem about the standard-bearer who is a direct counterpart of Cornet Rilke. He loves his flag as a lover loves a girl, and his comrades call courage and love of glory what really is a self-forgetting love of life.

Then we come across the sonnet, **"Letzter Abend,"** about a youthful hussar who before riding into battle plays on the clavecin for the lady he loves. But on the pier table looms ominously the black shako decorated with a skull. Here the theme of **"Ritter"** is repeated, but in a stricter, more significant form. Or we read the sonnet **"Spätherbst in Venedig,"** where we witness the departure of a navy for battle, gloriously displaying its numerous flags, and at the same time a tool for destruction, "strahlend und fatal."

Among the separately published poems of this time one finds a **"Skizze zu einem Sankt Georg,"** where Rilke depicts the same uncompromising attachment to an ideal that characterized the youthful Cornet Christopher Rilke. One suddenly realizes how little the poet's sympathy with the pure, self-sacrificing heroes has changed during his whole life.

It must be conceded, of course, that all the poems discussed heretofore express the Rilkean conception of an existence which postulates death as a necessary constituent of it; of a life that finds its ultimate consummation in a meaningful death. This idea is one of Rilke's basic ideas, if not *the* basic idea of his poetry, and forms the major theme of both his *Requiem* (written in 1908) and his *Sonette an Orpheus* (written in February, 1922). In the ninth sonnet of the first part of this latter cycle it is said clearly that existence cannot be properly evaluated without an understanding of death. . . . (pp. 267-70)

But this is not the point that the present paper is especially emphasizing. What it rather wants to stress is the fact that the ideal life ending in a meaningful death is frequently envisaged as the life of a soldier, especially the youthful soldier who offers his sacrifice as the crowning achievement of his days. In other words, Rilke's view of life displays a natural and unaffected affinity to the heroic, which, of course, must never be confused with the nationalistic.

Still, up to the August days of the fateful year of 1914, the poet had met the hero only in tales and remembrances. Now he suddenly faced him in reality. Rilke's first immediate reaction to this new experience was exactly the one to be expected on the basis of all his previous development. It was enthusiasm, although not of the blind sort. Already in the later poems of the *Buch der Bilder* heroism had ceased to be a beautiful intoxication and had assumed the sobering aspect of a very conscious effort. Similarly the **"Fünf Gesänge,"** which Rilke composed in August, 1914, express no intoxicated state of mind at all.

The beginning of the first of these hymns shows awe and astonishment over the sudden rising of the incredible God of War. But he is not simply the leader to glory and perfection. He is the fiery reaper come to harvest the field of men still rooted in life, and his gigantic harvest overshadows the mere human harvest of the autumn of the first year of the war. Only children, old men, and women remain behind. But their life, too, is made more meaningful by the leave-taking of the soldiers. The brides-to-be forget their individual loves in a feeling of patriotism. The youths who before were hardly decided about their careers now see a clear path before them. And the whole nation unites. Rilke's lines end in a note of enthusiasm, although even this first hymn is tempered by a glance at the reddish glare of the sky bearing a thunderstorm in its lap. This is a distinct reaction to war as such, as it can be felt by any nation, and there is absent even the slightest reference to any of the specific questions that disturbed Europe in 1914. Neither the causes of the war nor their righteousness are in the least way discussed or even alluded to. Rilke faced war as a purely human, and not as a national or a political phenomenon. Miss Butler is basically wrong in chiding him for having taken a one-sided German stand on the issues involved. Hermann Pongs, in his recent articles, is somewhat more correct in drawing a clear line between Rilke and the nationalistic attitude towards war, but he fails to see that war can be sincerely experienced as a human phenomenon, and that a narrowly tribal reaction to war is not the only valid feeling that can be engendered by it. Rilke's attitude towards war, even in his first hymn, is deeply *religious,* and his religion is not confined by any national or geographical boundaries.

The second hymn also is not a song of the war of 1914, but centers around war as such. If anything specific is stressed at all, it is the modern, total aspect of war, which again is not restricted to any one nation. But even this modern note is deliberately tuned down by our poet. The shadows of the ancient prophets are evoked to describe adequately the unheard-of spectacle of a whole nation marching into battle. Youths and mature men are marching, and even the immature adolescents are bent for the army. But mothers and girls must remain behind and are exhorted to give gladly and to love heroically, either filled with hope as in prehistoric times, or filled with eternal grief like the weeping woman transplanted among the stars. So the second hymn ends surprisingly on a note of weeping after having at first stressed the sublime aspects of the moment. This again is a deeply human and sincerely religious attitude that has nothing at all to do with the specific issues on which the particular war of 1914 to 1918 was fought.

In the third hymn the poet at first expresses the realization that he too has changed and has become a part of the new whole glowingly fused into one. Yet he still cannot quiet his asking whether this will mean the beginning of a new future or not. He realizes primarily the destruction of traditional values. Little is seen as yet of a possible new future. However, his heart feels totally changed, a blazing iron in an iron world. We have a hymn full of questions and doubts.

The fourth hymn ascertains that this iron world is not only new, but is also connected with the oldest times of history. These times apparently have not yet outlived themselves and now have come back to be fulfilled to their utmost satisfaction. There are compensations in this, and Rilke tries hard to lift himself above the feeling of the loss of the past. He is actually able to see that the spirit of a glowing community is more glorious than the self-centered worries of the individual. But still his heart is not completely committed and his attempts at consoling himself are not entirely successful. It is the past rather than the future that has risen. But out of the complaint over this the unknown future will rise. In the last lines of this fourth hymn, Rilke realizes that the war is changing everything, although he does not see clearly the direction. Thus both the complaint and the hope. But the accent is on complaint.

In the beginning of the fifth hymn, it is on grief. But this grief has to be examined to see whether it may not simply be sentimental grief over the loss of a customary style of life. It ought rather to be an active grief, a grim endeavor for the creation of a better future. But we should permanently realize that behind our intellectual endeavors and pleasures there always loom blind national passions. They are not only in the foreign nations, but also in our own national heart, and we should cleanse ourselves and thus rise to the occasion. This end of the fifth hymn endows war with a deeper human meaning in terms of the future. It cannot be emphasized too strongly, however, that this meaning has nothing to do with any of the political or national issues of 1914. Rilke embraces neither nationalism nor anti-nationalism, neither defeatism nor political pacifism. All such descriptions of Rilke's poetic war attitude are basically wrong and fail to understand the essentially religious motivation of his poetry. Just as Job and Christ and Buddha were perturbed by the existence of evil rather than by any particular evils, thus Rilke was perturbed by war rather than by any particular wars, and the attempt to understand this attitude in terms of national politics or of tribal religion is necessarily doomed to failure. Especially would it be wrong to describe this attitude as a running away from facts. The fifth hymn is anything else but that. Just like the rest of Rilke's poetry it is a brave facing of existence in all its aspects. And just as in the *Neue Gedichte,* it is conscious, wide-awake bravery that is the virtue of the best soldiers, an attitude that has little to do with blind, intoxicated fury. The kinship of Rilke's attitude to soldierly heroism is clearly brought out by the use of his old symbol from *Die Weise von Liebe und Tod.* I mean the symbol of the flag, which here again serves to emphasize Rilke's meaning. It is the flag, not of simple glory, but of resolute grief, and of self-sacrificing ire glowing for a better humanity. It is purposely described in words which remind one of St. Veronica's veil and thus assumes an almost metaphysical meaning.

Yet Rilke is clearly aware that the flag is not only this but also a symbol for the customary, national ties of nations. And in a sequel to the five hymns, he gives expression to this thought also: "Dich will ich rühmen, Fahne." He glorifies the banner which he greeted as a child with awe and astonishment and which now flies before the combatants "like a glorious bride." There suddenly rises into the wide realms of the air what before was a hidden secret of the heart. This feeling certainly is not confined to one nation, and thus even in these lines of Rilke the word "German" is significantly absent.

So also this last of Rilke's war poems serves to emphasize that our poet has tried to interpret war as such and not a recent war of specific origin. He has seen it not as a political or historical event, but in terms of a recurrent human experience. And although he could never entirely repress the individual emotions demanded by war, he at least made a valiant effort to understand war as a social phenomenon. This phenomenon he approached from a deeply religious basis, and so the problem of war was finally dissolved into the greater problem of evil and of death. At this point, the discussion was taken up by the *Duineser Elegien* (1912-22) and the *Sonette an Orpheus* (1922).

There was no longer room for any specific treatment of war, but there still was room for general references to heroism as one of the enduring human attitudes towards life. The first elegy (1912) names the hero right next to the deserted lovers as examples of human victory over the tragedy of life. . . . The sixth elegy, the final form of which was established in 1922, ranges the heroes next to the youthful dead who early found the accomplishment of their life. . . . Although these lines represent no longer the somewhat irresponsible impressionism of the youthful Rilke, they do meet it in their enthusiastic response to the heroic form of existence, to the hero's denial of fear born out of the tragic knowledge of human dubiousness. The theme of *Die Weise von Liebe und Tod* has again been sounded, but in a richer key. The "Fünf Gesänge" stand in between and no longer appear as a disturbing accident in Rilke's poetry. After their accomplishment the war theme was not simply forgotten, but merely merged into the larger theme of heroism.

In their form, too, the "Fünf Gesänge" constitute a direct continuation of the trend begun with the first elegies composed at Duino in 1912, and in 1922 successfully concluded at Muzot. In both the *Duineser Elegien* and the *Sonette an Orpheus* one is more than once reminded of Friedrich Hölderlin. And Friedrich Beissner's painstaking article has demonstrated satisfactorily that in the "Fünf Gesänge" Rilke followed consciously the example of his great predecessor. Hölderlin was the one representative of older German poetry who was most devoted to the eternal and who in his lofty idealism was least willing to compromise with actualities. Hölderlin's verses repeatedly passed through Rilke's mind in those first weeks of August, 1914, and the similarity between these two great poets is certainly more than an insignificant accident. Hölderlin's attitude toward life may adequately be summarized as fundamentally dualistic, and the attitude taken in Rilke's war odes can be described in like terms. Rilke is constantly aware of the two poles of the war experience, of war's regenerative as well as of its destructive force. In this dualism, the "Fünf Gesänge" foreshadow distinctly the attitude of the *Duineser Elegien* and the *Sonette an Orpheus.* Thus from every possible angle of consideration Rilke's war hymns are far from representing an interruption in the poet's development and rather actually form a necessary link in its chain.

Consequently, a strictly literary critic should not fail to see

Rilke's poetry as a great unity moving on, in spite of some pauses, to a more and more vigorous expression. Of course, there was also a personal life behind this, but in the case of his **"Fünf Gesänge"** the personal experience is even less pertinent to an aesthetic interpretation than elsewhere. A too personal contact with war could only have made their balanced attitude impossible, and Rilke would have found it hard to assume their detached religious point of view. It was distinctly to the advantage of his war odes that his personal war experience succeeded rather than preceded his poetic war experience. We can therefore safely leave it out of the aesthetic discussion. Rilke's personal war experience belongs to the subjective side of a subsequent creative process. The discussion of this subjective side we gladly leave to the biographers. Objectively speaking, this subsequent process also led to a unified work of art, namely to the final form of the *Duineser Elegien.* A consistently aesthetic discussion of their process of creation would then also confirm what we here have tried to establish by a different example: the essential artistic unity of Rainer Maria Rilke's great poetry. (pp. 271-76)

Ernst Rose, *"Rainer Maria Rilke and the Heroic,"* in The Germanic Review, *Vol. XVIII, No. 4, December, 1943, pp. 266-76.*

Derek Stanford   (essay date 1949)

[*Stanford is an British poet, editor, and critic who has written studies of numerous British authors, including Christopher Fry, Emily and Anne Brontë, Dylan Thomas, and Muriel Spark. In the following excerpt, Stanford offers an appreciative evaluation of Rilke's poetic mythology, labeling it "a religion and morality essentially poetic."*]

More and more mankind will discover that we have to turn to poetry to interpret life for us, to console us, to sustain us. Without poetry, our science will appear incomplete; and most of what now passes with us for religion and philosophy will be replaced by poetry."

So wrote Matthew Arnold in 1880; and if his times and their customs, both good and bad, seemed then to be in the melting-pot that process has met with great acceleration since. In the realm of conventions and collective-beliefs the electric-furnace and the apparatus for splitting the atom have their counterparts—giant psychological engines, so to speak, for the manufacture of nihilism and crude political religions of power.

This being so, it is not surprising that literature and art are largely judged today, not for their formal excellence alone, but in proportion to that degree in which they contain a faith for living. From "The Bible designed to be read as literature" to literature designed to be read as a Bible only a single step was wanting; and that step has now been taken. (p. 401)

For us, in an age where belief is partial (concerning the Vote or Transubstantiation, but never embracing the whole field of life), we come to art for a universal meaning and read its images as a kind of catholic gloss. This mean-

ing, perhaps, is best described by use of the term "mythology"—implying a coherent imaginative word-picture, a non-didactic exegesis of things.

One of the first factors observed in such a study of the German poet Rilke is the private and unadulterated make-up of his myth. Unlike most poets whose verse has held a system of belief in solution, the credo to be found in the work of Rilke evolves from no extra-literary source. For Dante and the later Eliot, Catholicism has been the sure base; for Wordsworth and Shelley respectively, Hartley and Plato were the instructors; for Hölderlin, the gods of Greece and Christ provided the twin foundation-stone; while in the "mad" sonnets of Gerard de Nerval the names of conflicting deities are strewn like the fragments of fallen temples.

Along with William Blake, but even more unremittingly poetic—allowing even less to the claims of logic and the common insistence on an argued system—the mythology of Rilke originates in pure unforced poetic perception. In him we can study a type of revelation utterly untampered by the intellectual will; in no way distorted or made to square with any predestined beliefs. As the reports of intuition came in, as they were newly expressed in his verse, as they were stored and resorted in his mind year after year with an eager trusting patience, so little by little a whole organum grew, value upon value came to emerge, until at the end of his real creative life—after *The Duino Elegies,* that is—a full interpretative gospel stood forth: a religion and morality essentially poetic.

That impersonal analytical machine, patented by the Western mind and christened logic, was an apparatus which Rilke never used to solve his problems. In place of this method of calculation on the scientific margin of the human page—this manner of discarding the affective situation—Rilke substituted an inward-speaking voice. "Have patience," he wrote in his *Letters to a Young Poet,* "with everything that is unsolved in your heart and try to cherish the questions themselves, like closed rooms and like books written in a strange tongue." For him there existed no convenient mental adding-machines to answer life's teasers. There was no ready-reckoner accessible to all. Truth was to be come at in a private fashion; born only from an experiential relation. "Do not search now," he continued to advise, "for the answers which cannot be given you because you could not live them. It is a matter of living everything. Live the question now."

Following from this, it seemed to Rilke that there was no time-limit for any of these questions. Unlike the Schoolmen, who believed that by the correct employment of Reason, the right application of the proper formula, a problem might be solved in so many steps, Rilke placed his faith in patience and time; in the sure working-out of an inner growth of light. "To be an artist," he writes in his "Third Letter," "means not to reckon and count; to ripen like the tree which does not force its sap and stands confident in the storms of Spring without fear lest no Summer might come after. It does come. But it comes only to the patient ones, who are there as if eternity lay in front of them, so unconcernedly still and far."

At first we may wonder how such an approach, abandoning the common instrument of reason, can possibly create a mythology to furnish the needs of a multitude of men. Solipsist, however, as all poets tend to be, through the intense nature of their internal life, their final unrefuted claim upon our ear is the basic human element that leaves us all kin. Just as the demagogue-opportunist addresses his appeal to the lowest common denominator in man, so the poet unconsciously or consciously feels that in answering his own personal problem he likewise provides an articulate answer to the queries of man's highest common denominator. How far this was so in Rilke's case is something we must now decide.

Poetic perception and passive will, a mind both open and obedient in recording the data of intuition: these were the agents which Rilke employed in his pursuit of truth and meaning. The matter, however, does not rest here. Another factor now enters in. Unfalsified as were these dispatches of sensibility by the intellect—by means of a conscious shaping theory, adjusting our first apprehension of things to fit some standardised cosmic account—another force was at work upon them, giving them a uniform direction and dress. Indeed, some collective girdle for our thoughts, some string to bind our separate sensations, to make from our moments of individual living a personal continuum in time and space, is necessary to each of us; and, what is more, inevitable. With Rilke, this unifying power was the instinct which led him to interpret phenomena according to the needs of his own artistic life. Setting the requirements and desires of man—of the natural male in his own make-up—under the heel of the artist in him, he inverted the attitude giving rise to most of our current human values.

The artist, thought Freud, resorts to art in order to readjust the balance which nature and his early years have weighted against his worldly success. Once this balance has been established and approval of women and his fellow-men gained, the need for creation becomes abated; the "productive neurotic" approaches the normal. Such has been the lot of many creators: of Wordsworth, Rossini, and—dare one hazard—Shakespeare. To others, though, this haven is denied. Never can they return at peace to graze with the "satisfied" human herd. Their boundaries must for ever remain outside the pastures of "normality." Here—either because their original neuroses were wells too deep for their art to drain, or because their creative powers were too weak to disperse their complex by its projection—they are doomed to live out their whole existence in a condition of solitude.

This, one cannot doubt, was Rilke's state; which a certain poetic pride, perhaps a certain masochistic arrogance, a certain conscious perversity strengthened. "The artist," wrote Novalis—that great aphorist of Romanticism—"stands on the man, as a statue stands on its pedestal"; and in every single affair of life Rilke so ordered his actions and decisions that this supremacy might be maintained: a selfish martyr who indulged his splendid talents.

Paradoxically enough, it is these mental exiles, these creative pariahs whose works have most enriched and modified our world by the peculiar substance of their message. Whereas the art produced by those figures who finally come to terms with life, accepting the outward conventions of men, paying their respects to popular values, may often charm us with its form—the tranquil perfection of its poise, the harmony, sweetness and peace of its tone—it lacks a dynamic urgency; that grasp on our mind which only conflicts held in tension can produce. Of such a latter kind is the poetry of Rilke.

Every epoch or century, as Drucker and Chakotkin have pointed out, has its dominant concept of the human being. For the Thirteenth Century, man was chiefly a spiritual creature; for the Sixteenth Century, an intellectual creature; for the Eighteenth Century, an economic creature. In what light does man most regard himself today; on what aspect of his nature does he place a premium? On the sexual, answers the critic J. F. Hendry; and from the middle of the last century onwards our literature has given it a heavy underlining. For Baudelaire—along with God (so making up Original Sin)—sex was the central and ramifying theme; for Rimbaud—desiring to reinvent love—sex was the springboard and the gate, the magic passport to ecstatic truth; for Dostoievsky, it meant much more than any critic save Berdyaev in his splendid study of that novelist has shown. It is hardly important to trace the matter further; for the imprint of the satyr's hoof, in some form or other, disguised or apparent, is present in most of our key modern writing: in Lawrence, Kafka, Nietzsche, Gide, Joyce, and Proust. A significant approach to the subject of sex might almost form a criterion, then, for estimating in a ready fashion the claims of a writer upon our age. (A touchstone, in fact, which Lawrence employed in *Classical American Literature*.) Under such a testing Rilke starts off well.

From the beginning, he repudiates all Puritan and Catholic conceptions of sex without adopting the other extreme—a Walpurgis cult of debauchery and whores, somewhat in favour among artists of his time. Against the mortification of the flesh, and its repression, preached by the Church his poem **"A Nun's Complaint"** makes a poignant protestation; while in his "Fourth Letter" he strikes with clarity a sane middle note. "Bodily delight," he writes,

> is a sense experience, just like pure seeing or the pure feeling with which a lovely fruit fills the tongue; it is a great boundless experience which is given us, a knowing of the world, the fullness and splendour of all knowing. Our acceptance of it is not bad; what is bad is that almost all men misuse and squander this experience, and apply it as a stimulus to the weary places of their lives, a dissipation instead of a rallying for the heights.

It is clear, too, from the following, that Rilke deeply understood the profound relation of sex and song, the source of the lyrical in the erotic; the fact that however hidden it may be our life is irrigated by this physical spring. "The thought of being a creator, of begetting and forming," he says,

> is nothing without its continual great confirmation and realization in the world, nothing without the thousandfold assent from things and animals,—and its enjoyment is so indescribably beautiful and rich only because it is full of inher-

ited memories of the begetting and bearing of millions. In one creator's thought a thousand and forgotten nights of love revive again and fill it full of loftiness and grandeur. Those who come together in the nighttime and entwine in swaying delight perform a serious work and gather up sweetness, depth and strength for the song of some poet that is to be, who will rise to tell of unspeakable bliss.

Here, we may notice the de-carnalising touch, and how the description would better fit the nuptials of a tree and a hamadryad than the grosser mating of man and woman. Rilke, for all his pagan "Yea-saying," had not a Dionysian mind. His temperament was Apollonian; and what interested him in Orpheus was not his awful loss but his potent song. He saw the phallus only as a peg for the lyre.

If, indeed, he foresaw without reference to Freud the sexual nature of the subconscious and its sublimation in art, he was no worshipper of Lawrence's "dark gods." For him, they represented chaotic forces, instincts to be tutored by the "will to form." This pre-social undergrowth of the *id,* by means of which the child reaches back to the primitive past, is described by the poet in his **"Third Elegy"**:

> How he gave himself up to it! Loved
> his interior world, his interior jungle,
> that primal forest within, on whose mute over-
>   throwness,
> green-lit, his heart stood. Loved. Left it, contin-
>   ued
> into his own roots and out into violet beginnings
> where his tiny birth was already outlived. De-
>   scended
> lovingly, into the older blood, the ravines
> where Frightfulness lurked, still gorged with his
>   fathers. And every
> terror knew him, and winked, and quite under-
>   stood.

Such, says Rilke, are the elements quickened by contact of the male with woman, whose task is to use her civilising touch (what Remy de Gourmont and Coleridge, respectively, call her "conservative genius" and her "continuating" sense) to mitigate and channelise these wild feelings:

>   you have conjured up
> prehistoric time in your lover. What feelings
> whelmed up from beings gone by! What women
> hated you in him! What sinister men
> you roused in his youthful veins! Dead children
> were trying to reach you. . . . Oh, gently, gent-
>   ly
> show him daily a loving, confident task done,—
>   guide him
> close to the garden, give him those counter—
> balancing nights. . . .
>   Withold him. . . .

Men, maintained Rilke, were careless "botchers" of love; but while the sentiments of the Elegy form an excellent antidote against the modern mystique of lust disseminated by Hollywood its conclusion or remedy is open to doubt. Why, after all, should women be thought exempt from those same chaotic dregs; that primitive residue decried in man?

The reasons for Rilke's belief in this are tortuous and not easily come at. To begin with, Rilke despised and hated all those characteristics of man known as exclusively masculine. Perhaps, too, at the Military Academy, where he had spent his boyhood years and where he had been continuously unhappy, he had also learned to fear and avoid them. In his "Third Letter" he criticised Richard Dehmel—that swashbuckling Bacchus of late nineteenth century German poetry—with a kind of restrained antipathy. There was, he observed, in the spirit of his work "no entirely mature and unmixed sex world, but one which is not human enough, merely masculine, which is heat, intoxication, and restlessness, and loaded with the old prejudices and arrogances with which men have disfigured and burdened love." So he disposes of that Junker of song! Another factor in Rilke's preference was probably the low estimate in which he held the intellect and logic—qualities almost limited to man. Opposed to these he posited female intuition, and the more biological and organic—and less mechanical—methods of thought; and he speaks of the "innermost consciousness," behind which "the understanding" lags in a wondering out-paced fashion. Finally, it is possible that the breaking of his marriage with the sculptress Clara Westhoff after only a six-month's trial—so avoiding the responsibility of a domestic and paternal existence—might have produced a sense of guilt from which he found an escape or release in his generous but far-fetched assessment of woman.

From sex to love is one step, from love to marriage another. Without accepting the common ideas regarding these states, Rilke embraced them and found a place for them in his scheme. As a personal living proposition he soon came to discard the second; but before the experiment had proved a failure he set down his notions of it in a letter. "I hold this to be the highest task," he wrote, "for a union of two people: that one shall guard the other's solitude." Again, in writing to the "Young Poet" of the Letters, he speaks of those couples who have not kept this law of respecting a mutual privacy. The penalty they pay is to lose the expanses and possibilities of communion for "a sterile helplessness out of which nothing more can come; nothing but a little disgust, disillusionment and poverty and deliverance into one of the many conventions which are set up in large numbers as public refuges along this most dangerous of roads."

Before this sense of marital constriction, in his own case, became too intense Rilke made his getaway; and little by little there came to be formed the idea of "love without the beloved." So, in his poem **"The Risen One,"** as C. M. Bowra has pointed out, "Rilke sees the Magdalene as one whom the Crucifixion makes to love Christ without wishing to be loved in return," and after the Resurrection the poet describes her new state of mind:

> She only comprehended later, hidden
> Within her cave, how, fortified by death,
> The gratefulness of oil he had forbidden
> And the presentiment of touch and breath,
>
> Meaning to form for her the lover
> Who hangs no more on a beloved's choice,
> Since, yielding to enormous storms above her,
> She mounts in ecstasy beyond his voice.

On just such a transcendentally dizzy note does the unknown young confessor (the author himself) in Kierkegaard's book "Repetition" close the last letter to his confidant on hearing of the marriage of his (the former's) ex-fiance:

> The chalice of inebriation is again held out to me, already I inhale its fragrance, already I am sensible of its foaming music—but first a libation to her who saved a soul which sat in the solitude of despair. Hail to feminine magnanimity! Long life to the high flight of thought, to moral danger in the service of the idea! Hail to the danger of battle! Hail to the solemn exultation of victory! Hail to the dance in the vortex of the infinite! Hail to the breaking wave which covers me in the abyss! Hail to the breaking wave which hurls me up above the stars!

As the confidant says of his correspondent's passion: "The young girl was not his love, she was the occasion of awakening the primitive poetic talent within him and making him a poet. Therefore he could only love her, could never forget her, never wish to love anyone else; . . . She had meant much to him, she had made him a poet, and thereby she had signed her own death-warrant."

Love, then, as Rilke sees it, is a kind of rocket-platform, whence—by the fuel of unrequited passion—one soars beyond the boundaries of narrow desire; a type of spiritual catapult-act. This amorous self-denial in the name of inspiration (self-denial sprung from creative accident) finds its expression in much of Rilke's writing, especially in *The Notebook of Malte Laurids Brigge*. "It would be difficult," he writes at the end, "to persuade me that the story of the Prodigal Son is not the legend of one who did not want to be loved," and imagines this character thinking of "the troubadours who feared nothing more than to be granted what they asked." Very significantly the book concludes: "He was now terribly difficult to love, and he felt that One alone was capable of loving him. But was not yet willing."

This penultimate quotation is a reference to the rules of the Courts of Love in old Provence, influenced, as Denis de Rougemont has observed, by the Albigensian heresy. Briefly, this rule in question stipulated that the troubadour should praise and adore his lady but never think to possess her person (she was generally married to another). The main contention of de Rougemont is that the beloved woman was viewed by these gnostics as a direct gate-way to God (short-cutting mediation by the Catholic Church). Access, then, was believed possible between the troubadour and Hagia Sophia (the great vision of divine wisdom) only providing the lines of communication—i.e. the beloved woman—was kept free from carnal contact.

The resemblance between the Manichean (whose theories had affected the Albigensian Church) who looked on procreation as a sin—Arnaut Daniel, one of the greatest troubadours, being himself a homosexual though he still made devotional songs to his lady, and the artist whose ultimate mistress is art is seen to be a powerful one. Both of them use woman as an occasion; for both of them love is a kind of transformer, adapting the lower currents of passion to the higher currents of God or art. Neither views love as a social force, as something that generates and rears a family, as something that prolongs and conserves society. The concepts of both of them are specialised and private; alien and remote from the life of everyday.

Perhaps, at this point, one may object that this constant reference to the needs of Everyman as a touchstone to judge the values discovered in a work of art is inapposite; that the greater minds of artists and thinkers invariably sail beyond the requirements of the masses. Here we must make a clear distinction. It is evident that the artist's life must be seen in terms of the value of his art, and that we do not demand from him obedience to the by-laws of social convention if they should prove constrictive to his work—always providing that work in the end is seen to enrich our understanding with values that answer to our deepest needs. In other words, we may judge an author for his ability to provide us with functional answers to our needs: functional, that is, at a high imaginative level; long-range, long-term answers, so to speak.

Now, with regard to the question of love, this is a matter where Rilke fails us. . . . (pp. 401-08)

In his book *Passion and Society* de Rougemount remarks on the close relationship between the idea of mystical passion-love and death, and in his chapter on German Romanticism (which he describes as a "new Albigensian heresy") he quotes Novalis to illustrate this sentiment. "Our vows were not exchanged for this world," the poet remarks in his private diary on the death of his bride-to-be, while in his maxims he observes: "All passions end in tragedy. Whatever is finite ends in death. All poetry has a tragic element in it."

True to this lineage of subjective German thinkers, Rilke, too, makes a cult of death. With him, however, we find modifications of the original Manichean concept. Unlike earlier Romanticists, Rilke established no hard and fast division between the worlds of life and death. He constantly talked of the poet's task of keeping "life open towards death," and regarded himself as dwelling in a kind of twin kingdom—this "now first whole, first hale world" (as he calls it in his *Journal*).

In his earlier verse this idea of death has too often seemed to lend itself to the sentimental mitigation of a dark mystery. There is something precociously make-belief about it; a highly imaginative make-belief, but compensation-thinking none the less, and, what is more, a little dishonest. So, in his poem **"The Death of the Beloved"** it appears that the poet is determined to discover some means or other to mitigate the grief. If not to be discovered, why, then he will invent! . . . This suggestion of a compensating after-thought as being the starting-point of the poem is further strengthened by two factors. Firstly, Rilke's conception of God was one which depended on man's pre-existence. God, he believed, was "built" by man; built daily by the artists, thinkers and saints—a Gothic cathedral of the ideal which every century enriched and transformed. God was therefore co-extensive with man: an attitude little lending itself to a ready belief in an after-life. The second of these factors—by far the more important—was the fear and pity Rilke felt at any occasion of death.

(The great **Requiem,** written for the decease of the painter Paula Mendersohn-Becker, confirms this remark through its deep pathos—more unflinchingly expressed there than in any other of his poems). Long after his mourner's sugar-candy verses for **"The Death of the Beloved,"** he wrote in a letter to a friend: "How is it possible to live, when the very elements of this life are completely incomprehensible to us? When continually we are inadequate in loving, uncertain in resolution, and incapable of facing death, how is it possible to exist?" Hardly the attitude of one much sheltered by the roof-tree of his fantasy!

True enough, in the magnificent **"Tenth Elegy"** a more durable conception of death appears. But again, its main interest is for the artist. Death is seen as the sphere of permanence; a realm of objects, perfected in form and proof against the depredations of time; a kind of "Grecian Urn" universe; a metaphysical museum world for Parnassian minds. In all, allowing for the discount occasioned by his earlier post-mortem Cockaigne, it seems that Rilke contributed less to a widely valid poetic eschatology than such a writer as Wordsworth, say, who offered us the consolation of a sort of stoical pantheism (v. his lovely lyric in the "Lucy" sequence, "A slumber did my spirit seal.").

If Rilke's detached asocial nature left him at a disadvantage when he conceived his myths of love (holding him back from the creation of some universal image applicable to all, instead of seeing it as an elixir, rich in proteins for the artist and the saint), it helped him to avoid several cliché-approaches when he came to write of the Hero. Especially was he fortunate in viewing the hero in non-racial terms—as a kind of national Hercules—in a country where Bismarck and the two Prussian Fredericks had tended to militarise the fire-stealer myth, shadowing forth Prometheus in the dress of Grenadier.

Here, again, it would appear that Rilke, "uncertain in resolution" (as he confessed himself to be), was bent on appeasing his own hesitation by the image of a figure "immovably centred." As this figure of the hero represents the ideal self of the poet there is no question of seeing it shown in the light of patriot or communal martyr. Rilke was always an individualist; and so he portrays the hero as seeking, not to shoulder the burdens of others—to discharge in himself the duties of the group—but rather to follow and achieve those quests peculiarly intended by fate for him alone. Thus we have the picture of hero as Independent: a being of internal integrity whose life is consummated in outward deeds. (pp. 409-11)

Action, says the poet, in some lovely lines of his splendid but still somewhat barren **"Sixth Elegy,"** is life's fruition; and its point of ripeness, death. So we are left perhaps a little incredulous—or depressed—regarding the hero's labours. What has all this epical pother been about? Who is this already half-transformed mortal hunting his quest as a squire hunts a fox? And what is the point to human society, stepping in the foot-prints the hero has left in the spots that were plotted by an unspeaking fate? Possessed as he was of a sense of the past, but with little sense of history—of man's continuation—the poet seems to leave these questions in the air.

If we were pleased to see Rilke eschewing a portrait of the hero as mass-saviour, we are the more surprised and sorry to find him reflecting the mass-hysteria of war. Yet this is just what we discover in the first two of the **"Five Songs"** written in August, 1914. In **"Song I"** he raises popular excitement to the height of the panoplied figure of Mars. "A god at last," he writes.

> . . . . Since the God of Peace so often
> eluded our grasp, the God of Battles has grasped
> us.

This, of course, was the typical reaction which poets all over Europe expressed. Our own Rupert Brooke excelled in it (producing the kind of poetry which might, one feels, well have its roots in a Decadent's late reading of *Henry V*). Just this crude school-boy volte-face from "the lilies and languours of vice" to khaki and cannon-fodder enthusiasm was something unlooked for in the sensitive Rilke. For such a writer as the Hungarian Ady, diseased and surfeited with the pleasures of life, it was easy to imagine the carnage of war as a kind of purifying cure. "Blood, blood, blood," the poet could write,

> Man will be much more beautiful
> once he is cleansed with blood,
> and better too.

Apart from its therapeutic value, war for such a jaded rake would be the ultimate global *frisson;* a kind of final cosmic debauch.

In the case of Rilke's own acclamation none of these factors were operative. Even so, in the **"Second Song"** he goes one better, rivalling Wagner, and we hear the old Teutonic trombone once more desecrating the linden trees:

> . . . . O mothers, the joy of giving!
> Give as though you were infinite! Give! Be a
> bountiful Nature
> to these good-growing days. Send out your sons
> with a blessing.
> And girls, to think that they love you! To think
> of being felt
> in such hearts.

As if this is not already bad enough, we have in addition that unfortunate piece of typical civilian flag-wagging in verse, **"Now it is you I praise, Banner."**

Already, however, by the **"Third Song"** jubilation is exchanged for penitential griefs: which does not altogether cover up a doubt. Pain, not anger, now maintains the poet: sacrifice and not fulfilment—these are the only goodnesses of war.

By the October of 1915, this dark half-mood of doubt had changed to one of frenzied protestation—a type of hysteria, in every way as extreme and unreal as his earlier outburst had been. "Can no one hinder and stop it?" he wrote in a letter to a friend. "Why is it that there are not two, three, five, ten persons gathered together in the market-place and shouting: Enough? They would be shot down; but at least they would have given their lives to end the war; whereas those at the front are dying so that the horror shall go on and on."

In another letter he wrote these self-revealing lines, loaded with a kind of hermetic egoism: ". . . I find it very hard to attain the valid, where possible, the somewhat fruitful attitude to this monstrous universality. Happy are those that are within it, whom it carries away, whose voices it drowns!" The logic of this clumsy implication being that the poet feels his own disturbance is of more consequence than another's loss of life.

In all these reactions, as C. M. Bowra points out, reality was testing the doctrines of Rilke: testing their durability; seeking out the poet's weakest links. "O tell us, poet, what you do," he wrote—in the verses which J. B. Leishman calls "an epitome of Rilke's *Religio Poetae*"—and unwaveringly back comes the answer "I praise":

> But those dark, deadly, devastating ways,
> how do you bear them, suffer them?—I praise.

And later, this faculty for total celebration is taken as proof of the poet's credentials:

> And whence your right in every kind of maze,
> in every mask, to remain true, I praise.

Just this elaborate aesthetic facade it has taken two wars to reveal in its weakness. The point is that one cannot always praise. One must then denounce or learn to be dumb, or turn to praise that to which value still adheres. This was never understood by Rilke, whose power to bless was only matched by his lack of power to truly assess. The most difficult task of the poet; namely, the retention of praise with values was something he did not constantly realize. The first distinction he certainly achieved: he won to that conscious pinnacle from whose tip the spirit is aware of all things, looking reality squarely in the face. This is the state of understanding or acceptance: the realization that such things are. The second step, however, of acclamation, of celebrating all things possessed of value and denouncing or ignoring those things without it, was one which Rilke failed to make. He did not comprehend that acclamation must be preceded by selection; that the poet must sift the things of the world just as he sorts and sifts his words.

Perhaps the factor at the root of this instability of judgment in Rilke was his dependence on sensitivity: his passive over-readiness in the reception of phenomena. "All absolute sensation," said Novalis, "is religious"; so helping us to see how the transcendental aestheticism of Rilke was prone to fall a victim to the powerful impact of events. "O to see men in the grip of something," the poet exalts in his **"Second Song."** "Whatever it is?" one feels like adding. A case of intensity at all costs!

Another recurrent element in the poet's change of heart with regard to war was the dictation of a purely personal need. For some months Rilke was obliged to act in a clerical capacity, far behind the lines, in Army dress. This, much more than external horror, clarified and strengthened his growing disenchantment. "Never," he wrote in 1919, "have I been so far beyond the reach of the wind in the spaces, of the trees, of the stars by night. Ever since I had to stare out at all this from the evil disguise of an infantry uniform, it has been alienated from me. . . ." He, who had so affirmed the individual, was learning the griefs of being anonymous.

Love, death, war (and their sum-total, life): these are the themes of the major poets, and Rilke's responses to them have been shown. In each case we see how his attitude seems to have been compulsorily dictated by the needs and claims of his artistic life. In the name of the poet he sacrificed the man, and on art's high alter he gave himself and others. Here, it would appear, he lacks that double hunger which animated the greatest poets: the twin adoration of poetry and life. So it arises that in his work we look in vain for the full-blooded zest, the thronging reflections of jostling beings, that ant-hill movement of living colours.

This absence, however, is a modern trait. We find it harder to be jolly and kind than Homer, Chaucer, or Shakespeare did. Added to this contemporary "Angst"—this lack of elation about existence—a further defect must be advanced. Rilke had hardly any interest, any affection for the grown-up world. Adult human life meant little to him. As his friend, the philosopher Kassner wrote: "In truth he had not this masculine separation between judgment and feeling that belongs so peculiarly to man. Oh, he took absolutely no cognizance of man. Man remained an intruder in Rilke's world; only children, women, and old people were at home in it."

Locked in his "separate fantasy" more exclusively than most great artists, he fails as a modern mythologist because—as he said—he skipped the human (One cannot, after all, find a full-scale mythos in a system of animals, Angels, and things).

Rilke's mythology is limited, then; and only significant for the few. It is not so broad as that of Hölderlin or de Nerval, or—in our own times—that of T. S. Eliot, though perhaps it is deeper than two of these three. (pp. 411-14)

Just as Eliot interprets man to man only so far as the individual inclines to be a religious solitary like himself, so Rilke explains man to man in so far as he inclines to be a poet. His is an artist's mythology for artists.

Once this limitation has been understood, the treasure which his poetry offers is enormous. It is true that we miss the bovine exultation of such a poet as Apollinaire, the salty immediacy of Lorca, the athletic conjuring of Boris Pasternak. Compared with these poets there is, indeed, something of glorified old maid about him, a kind of exquisite far-flung Platonic shimmer, a rarefied thirst to penetrate the sky.

This, in its own way, of course, is his attraction; a quality reserved exclusively for him. Rilke discovered a new use for the earth; a fresh justification for existence. This was, to furnish the poet's spiritual landscape, which in turn would be the landscape of an earthly future. Here, no phenomena must be admitted; and again and again Rilke took on trust the entire gamut of destructive elements, achieving sometimes those rare poems where the Janus nature of existence is seen like a shield whose one side displays putrefaction while the other is bright as a peacock's tail.

Never was there any question with Rilke of settling down

comfortably with his vision; of putting things ship-shape once and for all. Persistently he felt the need to liberate the clothed heart's Holy Ghost; and in such poems as **"The Harrowing of Hell"** we find him adventuring on the farthest fringe of thought—that stratospherical frontierland, dizzy with the threat of infinite space. To read these verses is like a revelation of beacons, statues, towers, and proclamations seen and heard on the out-posts of the mind. No other poet conveys like him the feel of the vistas of psychic distance.

Another great quality peculiar to Rilke is the way in which his poetry looks ahead. For him the sensibility is continually unlocking the doors of the future. He never allows his daemon to grow fat.

More, too, than any other poet Rilke accomplished the difficult task of painting intangibilities; of describing silence, water, wind, and air. Read, for example, the following poems: **"Shatter me, music"**; **"Soul in Space"**; **"What Stillness round a God"**; and the verses to **"Night"**— sympathetic hand-shakes of the mind with pure dimension. (pp. 414-15)

> *Derek Stanford, "Rilke and His Exclusive Myth," in* Quarterly Review of Literature, *Vol. IV, No. 4, 1949, pp. 401-15.*

"Being an artist means, not reckoning and counting, but ripening like the tree which does not force its sap and stands confident in the storms of spring without the fear that after them may come no summer. It does come. But it comes only to the patient, who are there as though eternity lay before them, so unconcernedly still and wide. I learn it daily, learn it with pain to which I am grateful: *patience* is everything!"

—Rainer Maria Rilke, 1903

Theodore Ziolkowski   (essay date 1959)

[*Ziolkowski is an American educator, critic, and editor who has written extensively on German literature, particularly the life and work of Hermann Hesse. In the following excerpt, Ziolkowski focuses on the three sonnets that Rilke published as a group under the collective title "Das Portal" in his* Neue Gedichte. *According to Ziolkowski, in these works, which are ostensibly mere poetic depictions of the portal of a cathedral in France, Rilke utilized symbolic overtones to express both "the visual, objective harmony of the actual portal, which he had learned through [French sculptor Auguste] Rodin to recognize, and the implicit, subjective harmony that he sought, with every fibre of his being, throughout his entire life."*]

The three sonnets that Rilke published in his *Neue Gedichte* (1907-08) under the collective title "Das Portal"

were written between 8 and 11 July 1906, during the period of intense productivity following the break with Rodin (May 1906). Ever since it has become fashionable to ignore Rilke's *Neue Gedichte* as "intellektuell aufgezwungen," these poems have been overlooked by many scholars and critics; even the most recent and staunchest champion of the *Neue Gedichte,* Hans Berendt, has failed to explore various aspects of these sonnets that would serve to relate them more closely to Rilke's earlier and later work. The reasons for this neglect are obvious. The three sonnets represent a perfect example of the "Dinggedicht" of this period, being apparently nothing more than the poetic depiction of a particular portal of a certain cathedral in France; such an objective attempt to grasp and express the essence of a foreign "thing" is, by common consent, necessarily alien to the singularly subjective flow of the poet's own thoughts and emotions. Furthermore, this new conception of poetry arose under the influence of the sculptor Rodin, whom Rilke was striving to emulate in his efforts always to capture the essential nature of the model and the "modelé" to the exclusion of subjective impressions. Since Rilke learned much about cathedrals under the tutelage of Rodin, his poems on architectural subjects are even more highly suspect of being "intellektuell aufgezwungen" than, say, poems dealing with gazelles or carrousels. Yet in many of the *Neue Gedichte,* as has been demonstrated, there is more to be found than sheer poetic virtuosity, and undeniable thematic connections with the entire body of Rilke's poetic creation have been uncovered. A closer examination of the "Portal" sonnets reveals that even here certain characteristic themes may be found.

The sonnets belong topically to the group of eight cathedral poems that appear early in the *Neue Gedichte,* beginning with **"l'Ange du méridien"** and ending with **"Gott im Mittelalter."** All eight were written in Paris during the months of June and July 1906, and only the first, in a subtitle, refers explicitly to the cathedral at Chartres. Hans Berendt assumes that the entire group was inspired by Chartres alone, but this is an unnecessary (and, as we shall see, misleading) restriction, for Rilke was an ardent admirer of many cathedrals and never limited his enthusiasm to one exclusively. . . . [Composing] his poems in retrospect after a certain interval of time (as he habitually did), Rilke did not necessarily have Chartres specifically in mind for any of the poems except **"l'Ange du méridien."** That cathedral was unquestionably one of his major sources of inspiration, but in the "Portal" group, as well as **"Die Kathedrale"** or **"Das Kapitäl,"** he was depicting a typical ideal rather than a specific prototype.

Auguste Rodin was the vociferous champion of the French cathedral. His book, *Les cathédrales de France,* a collection of loosely organized notes that were jotted down over a period of thirty years, contains a curious potpourri of penetrating technical remarks on architecture and sculpture, dithyrambic paeans, and an old man's fussy scolding of the younger generation. The book was printed seven years after the *Neue Gedichte* appeared, and it was only after his reconciliation with "le Maître" that Rilke was requested to look over the notes and manuscript of the work. . . . Yet the book is of interest in so far as it represents comments of the sort that Rilke surely heard expressed by Rodin on their visits, for instance, to Notre Dame in Paris (which Rodin does not discuss in his book) and Chartres. Rodin must have been especially elegiac and articulate about Chartres, "l'Acropole de la France," when he revisited the cathedral with Rilke on 25 January 1906, roughly half a year before the poems of "Das Portal" were written. In his book he calls attention to the portal . . . . There can be little doubt that the trained eye of the sculptor taught the poet to observe many aspects of the cathedral that might otherwise have escaped his notice. . . . [Based on reports in his letters to Clara from his time in Paris, it would seem] that Rilke's mind, which even before his acquaintance with Rodin had become receptive to the effect of the great cathedrals, was stimulated immensely by the sculptor's superior insight into their structure and nature in principle and detail. When Rilke, in retrospect, set down his impressions in poetic form, he was expressing his own ideas, but these were no doubt colored by the memory of Rodin's eloquent interpretations of the cathedrals they had visited together.

The three sonnets of the "Portal" group become progressively more complex. The first is a relatively simple depiction of the large stone figures that line the portal of the (unspecified) cathedral. The word *Heilige* appears in none of the three poems, but references in the first one to *Nimbus* and *Bischofshut* make it clear that the poet's eye is considering these prominent saints. . . . The objective portrayal is complicated only by the geological metaphor that introduces the poem. The statues are likened to stone formations carved out by the constant washings of a tide that has now receded, taking with it something formerly held in their hands (possibly a reference, on the realistic level, to the time-worn stone of the statues). The flood, in turn, can be interpreted to mean the wave of medieval religious enthusiasm that produced the statues and cathedrals; when this fervor waned, it took away many of the mystical attributes ascribed to the statues, for only faith endows them with their miraculous powers. Through a flashback as it were, this opening metaphor brings a touch of motion into the poem: the remaining verses emphasize the purely static nature of the statues and express the contrast between time past and present. Formerly the saints were the focal point of all activity in times when life was still centered around the cathedral. The church as a place of confession is called metaphorically the ear (scil. of God), and the portal statues, by a logical extension, are visualized as the concha of the ear. Now, however, the statues exist in a state of perpetual peace and rest: a state characterized by the smile that is also such a prominent feature of **"l'Ange du méridien."** The portal is empty and void of men, and the saints have lost their function: they symbolize pure existence.

The second sonnet turns away from the prominent figures of the saints and, introducing the new image of a theater, dwells upon the secondary figures of the columns, consoles, and tympanum. . . . This sonnet is diametrically opposed to the first: there the image was static, here the prevailing mood is dynamic. This feeling is intensified by participles like *handelnd, wallend, verwandelnd,* and by verbs like *tritt* and *entsteht.* In the first poem Rilke kept his eyes focused upon the saints; here he steps back and regards the entire portal from the figure of Christ in the tympanum to all His hypostases in the multifarious reliefs. The portal is considered a tragic theater by virtue of the legendary scenes depicted in its panels and the "Blinden, Fortgeworfenen und Tollen," the models for the anguished figures of the consoles and columns. The word *Fortgeworfenen* is highly characteristic here, for it is the expression used repeatedly in *Malte Laurids Brigge* (1910), which Rilke defines there as "Abfälle, Schalen von Menschen, die das Schicksal ausgespieen hat." They are clearly tragic existences. Yet in reminiscence of the third part of *Stundenbuch* (written in 1903), the poet explains that only from such as these can the Saviour be born. This is a concise recapitulation of "Das Buch von der Armut und vom Tode," which has as its main theme the notion that only the truly poor of humanity will be able to effect the birth of the true Saviour. It is in this way, then, that the portal symbolizes "sehr viel Weite" and affords a suitable background for the protagonist of the poem, "das Dunkel dieses Tores," who like God Himself is boundless and heaving and capable of transforming himself. The second part of the sonnet is so heavily laden with symbolic overtones that it is tempting, in rereading the poem, to ascribe some lofty significance to this "Dunkel," such as death. However, it seems more likely that Rilke is speaking here simply of shadow as an element of architecture, the shadow that Rodin praised so highly in his *Cathédrales.* . . . Rodin writes on and on about the merits of shadow in architecture and sculpture. How well Rilke learned this lesson is apparent as early as 1903 in the first part of his book on Rodin. . . . Rilke perceived that light and shadow are as much a part of the portal and the cathedral as the sculptured figures or the flying buttresses themselves. In this poem he has chosen to dramatize the role of shadow by placing it metaphorically on a stage comprising the various minor figures of the portal. It remains only to be pointed out that the contrast between static and dynamic that we find in the first two poems is intensified by the contrast between light and darkness; but this second contrast is only an implicit one since the sole evidence of light in the first sonnet is the vivid impression produced by the penetrating smiles of the saints.

We come now to the third and most problematic of the poems. . . . In this sonnet Rilke juxtaposes the subjects of the first two poems and brings about in the last three lines a synthesis of the apparent opposites. It is immediately apparent that the natural divisions of the poem correspond in no way to its rigid strophe pattern; rather, the poem falls into natural groups of respectively six, five, and three verses. Verses 1-6 present the statues of the saints. The reader's eye follows this first sentence smoothly, and no syntactical complexity mars the impression of absolute calm. Noteworthy especially is the fourth verse, in which the natural rhythm of the line contrasts sharply with the meter of the verse, drawing the reader's attention forcibly to the archaic rigidity of the frozen attitudes of the various saints. Otherwise the first sentence is nothing but a statement: the saints, their hearts in a state of suspended animation, stand immovably fixed in the attitudes that they have maintained eternally; time overtakes and passes them by.

After this initial statement Rilke turns to the figures of the console. Grammatically the saints remain the subject of the second sentence, but the true object of the poet's eye is the mass of console figures. These five verses (up to the colon) are so complex syntactically that the reader is compelled to analyze the entire period in order to discern its precise structure; the overwhelming impression is one of awkward and anguished contortions, which reflect syntactically the theme of the period. The figures of the console, unlike the saints, live in a state of perpetual agitation. The contrast is brought out especially effectively by Rilke's use, in verse 4, of the noun *Gebärde,* which for him always designates a set attitude such as the act of kneeling, and, in verse 13, the verbal form *gebärden,* which here implies wild gesticulation. Their world is one that the stony saints, whose eyes are focused upon eternity, never see, and one that the saints never stamped out of existence. They go through their weird contortions, yet despite this they do not upset the saints who stand, perfectly poised, above them. The last three verses, finally, bring the surprising synthesis. The state of equilibrium is maintained precisely because the figures of the console, like acrobats attempting to balance some object on the end of a pole upon their foreheads, must execute wild gyrations in order to preserve the balance of the object being supported. This visual image suddenly makes the whole poem come to life, and in itself it is perhaps sufficient to form the substance of a unique "Dinggedicht." Rilke is expressing poetically the verity of Rodin's theories of architecture, for, to the sculptor's mind, the essence of cathedrals is their harmony. His book begins on this note and returns to it constantly throughout the text. . . . In his visual comprehension of the portal Rilke seems greatly influenced by the sculptor. But is this visual depiction actually enough?

If one were content to accept Berendt's contention that the poems refer specifically to the south portal of the cathedral at Chartres, the analysis might end at this point. Berendt is admittedly puzzled by the concluding verses of the poem, and his interpretation amounts to little more than a paraphrase. . . . It seems more fruitful to take another approach and to suppose that Rilke did not have any specific portal group in mind, but was simply depicting a typical archetype that has symbolic potentialities.

The saints "sind im Gleichgewicht auf den Konsolen." *Gleichgewicht* is a key word in Rilke's work; it occurs over a dozen times in his poems, and practically always in a position of significance. In a few poems the word appears in a context where it is possible to construe it with no symbolic meaning. . . . But in almost every other case it is obvious that the poet attaches a special meaning to the expression. (1) It is used to refer to God in the **Stundenbuch:** "Falle nicht, Gott, aus deinem Gleichgewicht," and again in **"Das jüngste Gericht."** (2) It describes man in his perfect state, as in **Stundenbuch:** "Und ihre Menschen dienen in Kulturen / und fallen tief aus Gleichgewicht und Maß. . . . " (3) It is the attribute of things that exist outside the sphere of human turmoil. . . . This aspect is defined most cogently, perhaps, in a letter to Ellen Key (3 April 1903): "O wie ich daran glaube, an das Leben. Nicht das, das die Zeit ausmacht, jenes andere Leben, das Leben der kleinen Dinge, das Leben der Tiere und der großen

Ebenen. Dieses Leben, das durch die Jahrtausende dauert, scheinbar ohne Teilnahme, und doch im Gleichgewicht seiner Kräfte voll Bewegung und Wachstum und Wärme." (4) This extended sense of equilibrium was brought home to Rilke most forcibly by his acquaintance with Rodin, the only living man to whom he applied the term. In the *Briefe aus den Jahren 1892 bis 1904* (Leipzig, 1939) it is to be found repeatedly. . . . The term emerges, then, as a lifelong ideal of the poet: a principal attribute of God, of the world, of things; and the example of Rodin convinces him that this ideal of harmonic balance can be attained. The saints of our sonnet not only rest on their consoles in physical equilibrium as soulless stones; they also partake, as true saints, of the ideal state of being that is summed up for Rilke by this one word.

The saints in their repose are contrasted with the world of the consoles, which they do not deign to look upon. By implication Rilke is referring here to the world of men who have not attained spiritual equilibrium. "Figur und Tier," of course, is merely synecdoche for the whole corps of devils, basilisks, and tormented human beings of the actual portal; but on another level of meaning they stand for mankind. The only problematic word in the second part of the poem, the antithesis, is the verb *zertreten*. This is an extremely rare word in Rilke's vocabulary (although other *zer-* compounds occur in super-abundance): it appears, for instance, twice toward the beginning of *Malte Laurids Brigge,* in the poem **"Aus einer Sturmnacht,"** and later in the **Sonette an Orpheus.** But these passages are of little aid in determining the meaning of the word in our poem. The parallel instance that immediately flashes to mind is rather the Tenth Elegy, in which Rilke portrays with disgust the cheap, gaudy pleasures that men indulge in so as to deaden their senses to life as it actually is. After mentioning the gilded turmoil and the fulsome monument, the poet turns away in revulsion. . . . *Zertreten* is the verb used to signify the complete extermination of false human existence by a higher being, like the angel, who is in possession of spiritual equilibrium. Important, of course, is the conditional form of the verb in the Tenth Elegy, for the angel is too indifferent to inflict the punishment. In the "Portal" sonnet the conditional becomes a simple preterit, for the saints are not true angels; they are frozen in stone and only represent the higher beings. The use of this verb simply implies the potentiality and heightens the contrast between the two worlds depicted here: that of harmonic equilibrium and the other of psychic instability.

The meaning of the synthesis in the last three verses can be interpreted only by reference to the key word *Akrobaten.* Rilke's predilection for acrobats as a symbol for struggling mankind extends from his first years in Paris until the very end of his life. . . . To be sure, allusions to acrobats are sparse in the poems and letters. In a letter written in 1907 Rilke mentions by name a family of acrobats whom he had known personally in Paris for at least two years—that is, prior to the composition of the poem under consideration. His enthusiasm for acrobats made the poet's mind particularly receptive to the magic of Picasso's painting "La Famille des Saltimbanques," and in the summer of 1915 he spent almost four months with the "Saltimbanques" while he was residing in the Munich apartment of Frau Hertha Koenig, the owner of the painting (to whom he subsequently dedicated the Fifth Elegy). During this period he mentioned the painting at least three times in letters—in rapturous tones. A year and a half after the completion of the Fifth Elegy he composed four short prose poems in French under the title **"Saltimbanques"** (7-11 August 1924). It is irrelevant to the purposes of this paper to what extent the Fifth Elegy is indebted to Picasso's painting. What is important is the fact that *acrobats* emerged as an important symbol in Rilke's mind, and some light may be cast upon our poem by inspecting the word in its symbolic contexts. For, as in the case of the words *Gleichgewicht* and *zertreten,* it is highly questionable whether Rilke used the expression simply as an unusual rhyme or merely in order to give a clever twist to an otherwise objective "Dinggedicht."

In the Fifth Elegy it is interesting to find, at one point, that Rilke offers us a visual image that is remarkably similar to the one in "Das Portal": an acrobat balancing, or attempting to balance, an object at the end of a pole (placed upon his forehead?). After describing the skillful acts of the family of acrobats the poet turns away, no longer apostrophizing, and reflects. . . . The poet is searching elegiacally for the moment when the acrobats were still unable to balance the plates on the ends of their poles—that is, when they had not yet acquired such perfect physical control of themselves. The solution to this problematic passage is expressed quite clearly in the fourth of the prose poems entitled **"Saltimbanques,"** where Rilke returns to the same problem. . . . In both passages the poet laments the empty virtuosity of the acrobats and denies that the *Gleichgewicht* of the saint is to be found in the physical balancing feats of the acrobats. Indeed, they approach spiritual harmony most closely in the moments when, forgetting the outside world and the task at hand, they falter and cast a quick inward glance at their souls. Thus the acrobat who is actually engaged in his act (that is, balancing his pole) becomes a symbol for the futile peripheral activities of mankind. It seems reasonable, in view of this interpretation, to assume that the figures of the console are compared to acrobats not because, like the latter, they attempt to balance a staff on their foreheads, but rather because their efforts to balance the saints resemble the acrobats' manipulations of the balancing rod. In other words, the last three verses of the sonnet may be read as an elaborate metaphor in which *Stab* is equivalent to *saint,* and not merely, in line with Berendt, as a simile. (The extended metaphors of the first two sonnets lend credence, through parallelism, to this theory.) A reading of this sort implies a much more dynamic relationship between the saints and the console figures than Berendt's "zarte Berührung" and produces, moreover, a structurally tighter poem.

An interesting link between the late poems and the earlier sonnet is to be found in a fragment dealing with "Notre-Dame de Paris" (August 1907). . . . In this extended wish the poet, as the following fragment makes even more obvious, identifies himself fully with the stone figures of the cathedral. Here Rilke, not concerned with the representation of the visual image confronting him, leads us through the metamorphoses that precede what we have chosen to call equilibrium and then shows us the result:

können in the pregnant sense of the Fifth Elegy. But *können* refers here, of course, not to the physical virtuosity of the acrobats, but rather to the inner balance ultimately achieved by the statues (and mankind). This poem mentions neither acrobats nor *Gleichgewicht,* but it is significant for two reasons. In the first place, Rilke here again employs the stone figures of the cathedral (not Chartres!) as vehicles to express unattained and then attained harmony: the figures of the console and the saints in their niches. By a quick shift of perspective, as it were, the poet depicts the console figures as we have them in "Das Portal" and then switches to the state of their existence in the projected ideal of the elegy and the French poem, when they will have attained spiritual balance. In the second place, these strophes stress the fact that spiritual harmony is indeed an attainable ideal; in this sense they bear out Rilke's use of the word *Gleichgewicht* to refer to a living man like Rodin. In other words, the tension between mankind and the saints is not irreconcilable.

In this fragment as well as in the late French poem we have found the same polarity that is expressed in our sonnet. The saints, in their spiritual balance, are juxtaposed to mankind, which contorts itself wildly in the effort to achieve mere physical equilibrium. It is the irony of the sonnet that mankind upholds the saints precisely through its contortions, thereby precluding the introspection that is necessary to attain true inner harmony. Yet, according to the fragment, the situation is by no means hopeless (as Berendt implies), for there exists the possibility of progression. The tension of the poem is resolved in the final act of balance that endows the futile actions of mankind with a provisional meaning (until they too achieve true equilibrium). Thus Rilke finds harmony and unity on the subjective level as well as in the visual image, for only the saints and console figures together produce a perfect whole. This interpretation is perfectly in accord with his views as expressed in other connections (and these views in turn reflect Rodin once again). . . . It was this harmony through the resolution of tensions that Rilke was trying to express in his poem—a harmony on two levels: the visual, objective harmony of the actual portal, which he had learned through Rodin to recognize, and the implicit, subjective harmony that he sought, with every fibre of his being, throughout his entire life.

This interpretation is at variance in one respect with the accepted view of Rilke's "Dinggedicht. . . ." For the whole essence of the three "Portal" sonnets lies in the contrast, in the first and second, between static and dynamic and, in the third, the restatement of these themes with the ingenious resolution. . . . No one leaves room for the possibility that *both* terms of the polarity might be expressed in the same poem: not only the repose of "things," but also the turmoil of life. This seems to be precisely the case in our poem. It is not, however, the only case of this sort, for in a number of "Dinggedichte" the subject of the poet (and mankind) is placed into a direct, albeit implicit, contrast with the object of the poem. In **"Römische Sarkophage,"** for instance, the opening lines immediately establish the principle of tension between the poet and the sarcophagus: it is not sheer objective portrayal with no dynamics. (This poem, incidentally, also implies the synthesis that we have established in the third "Portal" sonnet.) Or, in the sonnet which opens the group of cathedral poems, the figure of the angel is explicitly contrasted with mankind. Apart from the "Portal" sonnets, however, there is perhaps no other true "Dinggedicht" in which the subjective element of the polarity is so vividly represented.

These observations conflict in no way with the standard definitions of Rilke's conception of "Ding. . . ." They merely suggest that the definition of "Dinggedicht," in Rilke's case, might be broadened so as to include the principle of tension between subject and object: both implicitly and explicitly stated. For this is a principle that obsessed Rilke until the end of his life. . . . (pp. 298-305)

> *Theodore Ziolkowski, "Rilke's 'Portal' Sonnets," in* PMLA, *Vol. LXXIV, No. 3, June, 1959, pp. 298-305.*

Karen Elias   (essay date 1969)

[*In the following excerpt, Elias provides an overview of Rilke's personal and literary development in which she concludes, "It is as if his entire life had been lived in preparation for his greatest work."*]

The development of Rainer Maria Rilke as a poet and as a self is difficult to analyze intellectually because he proceeded in a circular, rather than linear, fashion, his progress was achieved only by traveling backward, and in a real sense his success lay in ending where he had started. Thus his childhood becomes the source of his epitaph:

> Rose, oh pure contradiction, desire,
> to be no one's sleep under so many
> lids.

Some of the contradictions and ambiguities inherent in his poetry can be understood by a discussion of Rilke's early years. He was born in 1875 in Prague and, because his mother had lost a baby girl the year before and wanted another daughter, was christened in the Catholic ceremony René Karl Wilhelm Josef Maria. Not only did his mother inflict a girl's name on him, but she also forced on him feminine sensibilities, turning him out in curls and dresses and playing with him as with a doll. His father, on the other hand, was a frustrated officer who wanted his son to pursue a military career. Soon after his parents separated in 1884 as a result of their obvious incompatibility, Rilke was abruptly forced to leave his mother's world and was placed in a military school at St. Pölten. Here, in order to endure the terrors it held for him, he indulged in dreams of military glory and in the writing of poetry.

And yet, although the complexities of his early years created severe divisions in the man, childhood for the poet came to mean a time of grace which must somehow be recaptured. In a poem called **"Requiem for the Death of a Boy"** written in November 1915, eleven years before his death, Rilke contrasts the divided consciousness of the adult with the pristine consciousness of the child. Speaking of adults he states, "You talked, you laughed, but none of you were ever / Inside the talking or the laughing. No. / The sugar bowl, a glass of milk / Would never waver the way you would waver." And as a solution to this problem

Rilke dressed in girl's clothing, at age four.

of self-division he offers two alternatives. "Sometimes I'd sit against the house for hours / And look up at a bird. If only I could have turned into the looking! / It lifted me, it flew me, how my eyes / Were open up there then!" Here the poet seeks refuge in full conscious awareness, possible only through transformation into something beyond the human, something without contours: the flight of the bird. Rilke offers this as a vital alternative until, in the *Duino Elegies,* he substitutes for the bird an angel who is forbidding and far away, thus indicating that this kind of transformation is impossible. The second alternative expressed in the **"Requiem"** involves the things of the world. . . . By making himself at home with these things, the poet not only gives them some of his life, but also partakes of their thing-ness, of their self-containment. And the sadness of the poem derives from the poet's realization that he has become separated from these things, has grown up. He laments the death of his boyhood. It is, in part, this oneness with the things of the world that he attempts to regain through his poetry.

Rilke realized the close relationship between the consciousness of childhood and his poetry. In his *Tuscan Diary* he stated, "Art is childhood. Art means not knowing that the world already *is* and making one. Not destroying what one finds left but simply finding nothing finished. Nothing but possibilities. Nothing but desires." The body of Rilke's poetry represents this new world in the process of becoming, a paradoxical world both self-contained and without contours.

After leaving the military school Rilke vacillated between business and law, had a love affair with Valery David-Rhonfeld, entered the German University of Prague to study philosophy, literature and the history of art, and edited a literary journal. During this time, in an attempt to convince his relatives that he could earn his living as a writer, he wrote and published a great deal of poetry, including in 1895 his book *An Offering to the Lares* and in 1896 *Crowned with Dreams.* In 1897, because he felt stifled in provincial Prague, he moved to Munich where he met Lou Andreas-Salome, an extremely vital and intelligent woman who was fourteen years his senior and who was to play a most important part in Rilke's life, first as his lover and then as his confidante. In Munich he clung stubbornly to the profession of the poet, publishing *Advent* in 1897 and *In My Honor* in 1899, as well as writing *The Tale of the Love and Death of Cornet Christoph Rilke,* several groups of poems and some plays. Under Lou's influence he changed his name to the more masculine Rainer and also (in 1899 and 1900) traveled with her to Russia where he was awed by the ability of the people to endure suffering. Returning from Russia, Rilke spent some time at Worpswede, an artist's colony near Hamburg, where he met Clara Westhoff, a young artist, whom he married in March of 1901. A daughter, Ruth, was born to them in December and, because of growing financial worries, Rilke began writing reviews, newspaper articles, and finally, commissioned in 1902 to write a monograph on Rodin, left his family for Paris.

Most of the poetry written during these years has a vague, elusive quality and is stocked with such abstract terms as Life, Dream, Heaven, Time. To live outside of time, with no boundaries or contours, and to be able to communicate with eternity: this is the poet's dream. In his *New Poems,* however, written between 1903 and 1907, Rilke turns from the emphasis on the personal to "compression of statement and elimination of subjective states of mind. . . ." These are the Dinggedichte, or thing-poems, in which the poet concentrates on anonymously fulfilling the "willing objects" of the world by perceiving them in his receptive consciousness in all their totality. An explanation for this change in Rilke's poetry lies with the influence Rodin exerted on him during this period. To understand Rilke's conception of art at this time, it is interesting to look briefly at his *Rodin-Book,* the first part of which was written in 1903, the second in 1907, corresponding to the period of the *New Poems.* Much of what Rilke says here may be viewed as a commentary more on himself than on Rodin. In discussing Rodin's group, the *Burgers of Calais,* for example, he states, "Like all Rodin's groups, this one was self-contained, a world within itself, a whole, filled with life which circulated within it and nowhere pressed outside or lost itself." Rodin's work represents the kind of world Rilke is attempting to create.

Even though the concentration on objectivity was necessary to off-set the extreme subjectivity of the earlier poems, however, it was not the final answer. The simple fact that, while Rilke was writing his *New Poems,* he was also working on the introspective *Notebooks of Malte Laurids Brigge* (begun in 1903 and finished in 1910), indicates that the writing of objective poetry involved a self-imposed limitation. In one of his *New Poems* called "The Poet" Rilke wrote:

> I have no earthly spot where I can live,
> I have no love, I have no household fane,
> And all the things to which myself I give
> Impoverish me with richness they attain.

Thus, he was now faced with the problem of establishing a new basis for his art; according to Frank Wood in his book, *Rainer Maria Rilke: The Ring of Forms* [see Further Reading list], the poet's correspondence of this time revealed his dilemma: "He was a hollowed out shell, the constant litany goes, and had stood so long at the service of objective things that his humanity had atrophied. Or, again, he had so exaggerated the material impact of things that he ran the risk of becoming a caricature of his spiritual nature." The objective element was to become, in the new art, the precise contours of the creative consciousness. The 'thing' was finally to merge with the flight of the bird to produce what Rilke called the Innenraum or inner space of the *Elegies* and the *Sonnets.*

The years between 1910 and 1922 were very important, for during this time Rilke prepared himself for his later achievements. He traveled a great deal, journeying back and forth between Paris, Germany, North Africa, Egypt, Italy, and Spain, staying from time to time in various castles as the guest of a succession of princesses and countesses who had decided to appoint themselves as his patrons. It was during the winter of 1911-12, as the guest of Princess Marie von Thurn und Taxis at Castle Duino, that Rilke conceived the cycle of the *Duino Elegies.* When the war broke out, Rilke was drafted and served in the archives of the Austrian War Ministry in Vienna from December 1915 to June 1916, at which time, as the result of a petition drawn up by his friends, he was discharged. Because Duino had been destroyed in the war, he spent the next few years lecturing in Switzerland and looking for a suitable place in which to work. Finally in 1921 his friend Werner Reinhart gave him as a permanent home the Chateau de Muzot sur Sierre where, in February of 1922, Rilke completed the cycle of the *Duino Elegies* and wrote fifty-five *Sonnets to Orpheus,* his major achievements, in a storm of creative inspiration.

Much of Rilke's work in the period prior to the writing of the *Elegies* and *Sonnets* involved preparation for this almost miraculous outburst which he knew, somehow, was going to come. Besides looking for the right place in which to work, he also freed himself from the influence of Rodin and the plastic arts and also from the idea that it was necessary to write purely objective poetry. In a poem called "Turning," written on June 20, 1914, he makes clear the kind of poetry he wishes to write: "Work of sight is finished, do now the heart work / on the pictures within you, those captives: for you / have overpowered them: and in the end you know them not." According to Siegfried Mandel in his book, *Rainer Maria Rilke: The Poetic Instinct* [see Further Reading list], "In a manuscript note to the poem, Rilke expressed the wish to free himself from an interior-based gazing outward and substituting 'a loving preoccupation with inner fullness'. . . ." Rilke states, again in **"Turning,"** "For see, gazing has a limit, / And the much gazed-upon world / wishes to flower in love."

This is Rilke's idea of transformation, that the poet, by allowing the external things of the world to enter him, gives them a new eternal reality, creating thereby a Weltinnenraum or inner world space, a world in which eternity and time, subject and object are one. In the *Duino Elegies* this world is prepared for, and in the *Sonnets to Orpheus* it is finally brought to fruition. The *Elegies* begin with lamentation and end by providing the possibility for praise. The angel has now replaced the flight of the bird as symbol; the fullness of consciousness it represents no longer exists for Rilke in *this* world but resides in what Wood calls "a higher order of reality in the invisible." The angel is, as Wood states, "a mediator too remote from the concerns of man to be more than the unattainable yet constantly sought goal of his longing. . . ." In the **"First Elegy"** the poet has placed himself midway between earth and angel and finds himself unable to embrace either. Here Rilke gives voice at last to the tension which heretofore he had tried to avoid by dealing with each of its poles separately. The question he asks here is, "whom can we use then?" And his answer expresses the human predicament: we long to be whole but are neither spirit nor thing, and this is the source of our sorrow. In spite of the poet's despair, however, he indicates, even in this **"First Elegy,"** where our help might lie. The things of the earth have called to him to respond to them: "All this was assignment," but the poet has always felt too inadequate to respond sufficiently. Nevertheless, he tells himself, "Ever newly begin the praise you cannot accomplish." And at the end of the poem he indicates that an answer might be found in the form of a paradox, for "blessed advancement so often comes from grief," and only after the death of Linos, a figure much like Orpheus, did "the daring first music [pierce] the barren numbness," only then did "the void [begin] to feel that vibration which now enraptures, consoles and helps us."

In the **"Seventh Elegy"** Rilke is able to state, "To be here is glorious." And here he sets forth his idea of transformation, that the things of the world must be transmuted within us, that inner space is the true reality:

> Nowhere, beloved, can world exist but within.
> Our life is spent in changing. And ever-
> lessening,
> the outer world disappears.

The symbols of this process are the structured embodiments of our creative energy, Chartres and Sphinx, which the poet is now able to point out to the angel:

> Was it not miracle? Oh, marvel, angel, because
> it is *we*, O mighty one, we: announce that we did
> it,
> I've not breath enough to hold out for such
> praising.

Thus, at the end of this Elegy, Rilke's yearning for the angel is mixed with defiance: "For my appeal is always full of refusal."

Even more space is devoted to praise of this world in the **"Ninth Elegy."** Here Rilke says that even though the human being is "the most transient," he is glad to be human "because to be here is much, and the transient Here seems to need and concern us strangely. . . . But this having been *once,* although only *once,* to have been of the earth, seems irrevocable." The poet, in accepting his unique humanity, wants to achieve a thereness, a solidity. Moving to earth from the realm of the angel, he decides to bring with him his creative consciousness, the ability to transform the things of the world by means of the word. . . . It is not the "Unutterable world" which we should praise to the angel, for the unutterable is the province of the angel himself. But rather we should "Tell him about the things. . . . Show him how happy a thing can be, how blameless and ours."

> And these things that live,
> slipping away, understand that you praise them;
> transitory themselves, they trust us for rescue,
> us, the most transient of all. They wish us to
> transmute them
> in our invisible heart—oh, infinitely into us!
> Whoever we are.

It is the earth's dream "to be some day invisible," and the earth's commission is transformation. Rilke states that he is won over: "From afar I'm utterly determined to be yours," and is able to end the Elegy on a joyful note: "Behold I'm alive. . . . surplus of existence is welling up in my heart."

In the *Duino Elegies* Rilke moves from a yearning for full consciousness by means of union with the impossible angel, to a joyful acceptance of his own creative consciousness as a means of transforming the world. By limiting his consciousness, giving it contours, he has at the same time opened it to embrace the whole world. In the *Sonnets* he gives this consciousness a name: "We should not take thought about other names. Once and for all, it's Orpheus when there's song." Orpheus, whose body was scattered to become a universal singing, represents openness to experience and, at the same time, the stance of the poet who orders this experience. Thus, the things of the world are transformed into song, while the song becomes an object through the pure and permanent act of singing, of praising, of making poetry. . . . (pp. 78-84)

It is not surprising that many of the *Sonnets to Orpheus* are devoted to things, for here Rilke put into practice the theory he had worked out in the *Elegies:* to *say* the object. Unlike the *New Poems,* however, where objects more or less represented an escape from consciousness, the *Sonnets* present the object as one with consciousness. Body and spirit, object and mind, the 'things' and the flight of the bird are all interrelated; all partake of a constant rejoicing. . . . The poem (perhaps like the haiku) is the place where inner world-space is made concrete; it is not only a song but is also itself a thing. Rilke himself states, "Anything in the nature of 'allusion' in the *Sonnets* contradicts, for my feeling, the poem's indescribable Thereness." And just as the poem takes on contours, so does the poet. . . . Through the figure of Orpheus, who is a name as well as a universal singing, the Poet Rilke has given birth to himself.

Rilke lived only four more years after producing his **Elegies** and **Sonnets.** His last poems, a good many of them written in French, are lighter, more relaxed. It is as if his entire life had been lived in preparation for his greatest work. While gathering roses from his garden one day to present to a young visitor, he pricked his finger on a thorn and, noticing later that it had not healed, sought medical aid and discovered that he was very ill. He died of leukemia on December 29, 1926. (p. 85)

> Karen Elias, "Rainer Maria Rilke: The Pur-
> suit of the Self," in Discourse: A Review of the
> Liberal Arts, *Vol. XII, No. 1, Winter, 1969,*
> *pp. 78-86.*

Egon Schwarz (essay date 1972)

[*Schwarz is an Austrian-born, American educator, editor, and critic who has written, among many other
works,* Das Verschluckte Schluchzen: Poesie und Poli-
tik bei Rainer Maria Rilke *(1972; Poetry and Politics
in the Work of Rainer Maria Rilke). In the following
excerpt, Schwarz presents what he views as Rilke's opinions on the social and political events of his time, as revealed through the poet's writings, and relates the significance of these beliefs to his poetry, specifically the*
Duino Elegies.]

Over the years the hagiographical and critical literature on Rainer Maria Rilke has proliferated to fill whole libraries. Most of it reads as though this poet had spent his life on some remote planet rather than here among us, on an earth visited with catastrophes of all kinds—famine, inflations, wars, and revolutions. Thanks to these efforts, the prophet of Prague's tremendous metaphorical edifice stands before us, clearly profiled and firmly established, like a sort of erratic formation in a world ruled by laws of a completely different nature—a splendid Taj Mahal of poetry, entirely without function, to be gaped at uncomprehendingly by curious spectators. But the younger generation rejects Rilke with a disdain which cannot be fully explained even as a reaction to the frenetic admiration which its elders have accorded him.

Rilke himself is partly to blame for this. Not only did he fail to express himself very clearly on the questions over which his contemporaries were literally fighting each other to death; he actually made a principle of his aloofness from current events. He wrote to the Duchess Gallarati Scotti, a young admirer. "So far as politics goes, I am such an outsider and I feel so incapable of understanding its actions and reactions that it would be ridiculous for me to express an opinion on a political event of any kind."

For this reason I want to follow a course that runs counter to the mainstream of Rilke scholarship in order to bring into view the poet's entanglement in the social conditions of his time. The problem of what position to adopt toward the social tensions and conflicts of one's time is not disposed of simply by proclaiming one's impartiality. Indeed, in the twentieth century the very decision to remain apolitical is a political matter of a high order.

Thus one ought not be much surprised to find Rilke disregarding the apolitical declaration of beliefs he has just made and blithely assuring the young duchess, who is disturbed about political developments, that he approves of the Fascist regime in Italy. He hails Mussolini as "the architect of the Italian will" and "a smith forging a consciousness rekindled at the flames of an ancient fire," and salutes as "happy Italy" the country responsible for the Fascist murder squads and the assassination of the peace-loving member of parliament Matteotti.

With few exceptions, the critics have calmly ignored Rilke's espousal of Fascism in the *Lettres Milanaises,* thus implying that it has nothing to do with defining human existence, which is what the poet was trying to do in the **Duino Elegies,** for instance. My second premise then is: that in the spiritual mastery of life (especially when the one who seeks to master it is as sincere in his endeavor and as creative as Rilke was) everything is interconnected, and an interpretation of social life, once adopted, will be reflected even in the most sublime regions of poetry.

All theoreticians of history and society seem to agree on one point: that Fascism is a reaction to the twin phenomena of the industrial revolution and capitalism. Indeed, the whole history of modern civilization might be said to consist of the sum of all the answers that have been proposed to these and other related phenomena. Rilke's answer has much in common with those of the European Right. This element was oriented toward preindustrialist and precapitalist models and sought the inner renewal of man on a national basis rather than a radical reorganization of the structure of society. It was composed of those who felt themselves threatened or injured by industrialism, so that its range extended from the middle class, crushed between the big capitalist interests and the organized proletariat, to the old aristocracy and the big landholders. Despite its diversity, the Right was held together ideologically by its rejection of the capitalist economic system, of mass democracy and its organizational forms, and, to some extent, of modern technology. It resisted scientific rationalism on which these systems are based by turning toward irrational intellectual trends of all kinds. Its bitter dissatisfaction with existing conditions, combined with an insuperable dislike of real revolution, gave it a certain psychological coherence. Rilke's attitude to a few phenomena which the social historians consider conclusive, such as an aversion to big cities and technology, a conservative view of the social hierarchy, revolution, and nationalism, indicates that he belonged to this group.

Everyone who has read Rilke is familiar with his dislike of big cities. It was only self-discipline that enabled him to bear Paris—his stoic determination to stand a test imposed upon him. A glance at *Malte* suffices, the book he wrote under the impact of Paris, where the city is the ghastly setting of modern reality, stripped of its magic, with its hospitals, old people's homes, morgues, and monstrosities of all kinds. Ancient castles offer a contrast to this, symbolizing a sound pre-revolutionary world. Malte, the typical declassé, lives between the two worlds. His aristocratic society has collapsed, and in Paris he is in constant danger of being classed among the "outcasts."

In Book III of the **Stunden-Buch** this feeling builds up to an impressive invective. The cities, says Rilke, "burn up many nations."

> And those who dwell there are the slaves of cul-
> ture.
> And lose their balance and all sense of scale,
> And take their little snaillike tracks for progress,
> And rush and hurry where they used to saunter,
> And feel and look like whores in garish clothing,
> And make more noise with metal and with glass.

Here again Rilke evokes an anti-world: pastoral tribes tend their sheep in mountain meadows—a natural, patriarchial, biblical world, close to the earth, animals, plants, and God.

Rilke's attitude to technology and the machine can be stated equally briefly. A stanza from one of the **Sonnets to Orpheus** tells us all we need to know. "See the machine turn, / taking its vengeance, / distorting and sapping us." When he seems to praise machines, it is only because he has come to believe that the poet's supreme task is to praise everything indiscriminately—even that which is execrable. In another poem he pays tribute to Baudelaire for "glorifying even what tortures him."

Of course Rilke was not just afraid that beautiful handmade objects would die out. He felt that in general the machine was making it more and more difficult for the sensitive soul to get its bearings in the world. He foresaw the extinction of the elitist poet, supported by distinguished patrons to produce profound, obscure works for a tiny minority of the intelligentsia. He saw a time approaching when the highest value he knew: the individual's cultivation of his inner resources, would no longer be recognized, when "everything would tend toward the expropriation of individual powers," in which case, "what we now call art and spirit would seem to be abolished, together with all inwardness of feeling and the heartfelt arrangement of things." While his terrible vision of "machines supplanting the hand" may be the same nightmare that haunted the German Craftsmen's Union, we should not forget that what he was chiefly concerned about was his own craft.

Rilke's views of society, his peculiar notions of poverty and wealth are evident already in early works such as the *Two Prague Stories*, the *Geschichten vom lieben Gott* and *Von der Armut und dem Tode*. But it is to a questionnaire that Rilke replied in a coherent enough discourse to be called his theory of society. One of the questions it asked was: what was responsible for the strong social slant of *Wegwarten*? Thirty years after the fact Rilke was so upset by the possible implications of the word "social" that he wrote a whole disquisition protesting against them. He asserts that:

> it would be wrong to classify any of my endeav-
> ors under this heading. Of course I have an in-
> voluntary fellow-feeling, a brotherliness, which
> must be inherent in my nature. . . . But what
> distinguishes such a joyful, natural responsive-
> ness from social conscience in the commonly ac-
> cepted sense is my unwillingness—not to say re-
> pugnance—to alter or, as they say, ameliorate,
> anyone's situation. No one's position in the
> world is such that it cannot be of use to his soul

> in its own particular way. If I have sometimes
> succeeded in casting the imaginary voice of a
> dwarf or a beggar in the form of my own heart,
> I did not derive the molten metal from which I
> cast it from the wish that things might be less
> hard for the dwarf or beggar. On the contrary,
> it is only by praising their incomparable lot that
> the poet committed to them can be true and rad-
> ical. The worst thing he could fear—something
> he must reject outright—would be a corrected
> world in which the dwarfs are made taller and
> the beggars richer. The god of completeness sees
> to it that all these varieties do not die out, and
> it would be utterly superficial to take the poet's
> pleasure in their suffering diversity for anaes-
> thetic excuse. So my conscience is clear of any
> charge of escapism when I claim for my poem,
> confronted with concepts of "rich" and "poor,"
> the legitimate impartiality of artistic statement.

Here is the abnegation of any change in society, even the mildest palliatives of a welfare state. This answer to an innocuous questionnaire is actually an unqualified acceptance of the status quo. Rilke's attitude has one factor in common with the medieval reverence for the beggar: both regard poverty as God's will. But the radical solipsism of his position differentiates it from the Christian one. The charitable alleviation of poverty is no longer a way for the more fortunate to get to Heaven. Poverty now merely serves its own end by providing its victims with a certain amount of spiritual uplift. Rilke differs from the Darwinist advocates of laisse-faire in that he does not regard poverty as a well-deserved consequence of excessive stupidity or insufficient zeal. Rilke's formulation is ideal for all those who for some reason decline social responsibility without being willing to give up their awareness of tragic conditions. Poverty is not a phenomenon connected with the outward world whose causes might be investigated and eliminated, but something compounded of religious and aesthetic elements. The god of completeness decrees that all this must exist so that the world may be beautiful and interesting. The expression "varieties" applied to poor people and cripples is especially revealing. In fact it suggests a zoo. It would never occur to anyone that it might be "improved" by removing some rare bird. The cause of all such defects is nothing else than nature itself. This is why dwarfs and beggars are lumped together. To manipulate society—and Rilke obviously believes that this does not normally happen—is to unleash more evil than good.

Rilke sees the aesthetic component of this doctrine in the "impartiality" toward poverty and wealth that the poet can claim "with a clear conscience." But this is not a case of the ethical viewpoint yielding to the artistic one, as Rilke thought. On the contrary, the imagination—the poetic element—simply fails in its task. Self-interest, that is to say, Rilke's fear of certain changes in society, obviously dulled his perception of the disadvantages of poverty and influenced his aesthetic principles. Just as an apolitical stance in our own agitated age necessarily becomes political, to be impartial toward rich and poor means to take the side of the rich. The connection between sheer "praising" and a definable social and political position is already becoming clear.

Such declarations are supplemented by a document in which this same problem is posed, as it were, from the inside: from the viewpoint of the disadvantaged individual. The imaginary young worker, to whom Rilke attributes a fictitious letter (assumed to be Emile Verhaeren, Rilke's poet friend), is a most unexpected mask which Rilke assumes in order to bring up matters of great personal concern. Most of the thoughts expressed in the letter deal with religious questions, but one passage touches upon the problem of secular power. This quite implausible factory worker says that there is only one remedy against it, which is "to go even further than it goes itself."

> If in all power, even if it be evil or malevolent, we could see power as such—I mean that which in the end always comes out with the right to be powerful—would we not then survive, safe and sound as it were, even injustice and arbitrariness? . . . In my inmost heart I know that submission takes one further than revolt. . . . The rebel struggles out of the gravity of a power centre and may perhaps succeed in escaping from its field of force. But once outside it, he finds himself in empty space and must look for another force toward which he may gravitate. And this force is usually even less legitimate than the first one. So why not recognize as supreme the force in whose field we find ourselves, disregarding its weakness and vacillations? Arbitrariness is bound to run up against the law at some point, and we can save energy by letting it take care of its own conversion.

This needs no analysis. It is a divine sanction for every wrong on earth. It means the repudiation of secular justice and law and automatic concurrence in all kinds of human bondage. This essay dating back to 1922, the reply to the questionnaire of 1924, and the letters about Mussolini written in 1926, the year of Rilke's death, constitute his political testament. It is rich in content. Surprisingly, it is a modern counterpart of a strictly orthodox Lutheranism. On the ground of religious convictions concerning the relationships between force and law, every conceivable concession is made to a secular power, no matter how corrupt. However acute one's anguish over the wrongness of outward conditions may be, even the most timid wish for liberation is inexorably relegated to the inward sphere. If we ask what attitude such a quietistic concept of society would take toward Fascism, we realize that not only does it raise no obstacle, but it actually expresses precisely the state of consciousness that the conservatives need if they are to join up with Fascism.

A return to nationalistic values is another rightist characteristic. On this score, however, Rilke seems to have a cast iron alibi. Well traveled, speaking several languages, having friends among the artists and aristocrats of all Europe, familiar with many literatures, alienated forever at an early age from his own German heritage, he seems immune to any kind of nationalistic impulse. Attempts to dissociate himself from Germany and Austria are common. During World War I he wrote: "To realize how distressing these times are to me, you must remember that I do not react as a German . . . I would even go so far as to say that it is unthinkable and emotionally impossible

for me ever to feel at home in the Austrian culture." Ultimately he blamed Germany for the war and thought it had sabotaged all chance of a better world after 1918. "For me there is no doubt that it is Germany that . . . is holding back the world."

Drastic as this proclamation may sound, it is surpassed by Rilke's repeated references to his undoubtedly spurious Slavic origins. Even in his youth, in the *Stories of Prague,* he identifies with the Czech characters and satirizes the German ones. In *Die Geschwister* the Czech heroine Louisa triumphs over all obstacles; in the end a relationship with the only pro-Slav German in the story looms in the offing. "I do wish I could improve my German," she says invitingly. "Perhaps you could use a little Bohemian in exchange." This rudimentary Berlitz Institute symbolizes Rilke's somewhat naive desire for international reconciliation—a desire which is in strong contrast with the chauvinism around him. Twenty years later he is still talking about being "a profoundly Slavic man" and expressing the hope that "the Slavic stream may not be the least important one in the heterogeneity of my blood." All this ended in open conflict with the vigilant guardians of German honor when Rilke added insult to injury by publishing poems written in French.

With Rilke, however, matters are seldom as simple as they appear at first sight. Perhaps the sharpest attack on Germany occurs in the *Lettres Milanaises,* which in the same breath sing a joyful hymn of praise to Mussolini's Italy—a country which could certainly not be called free of nationalistic impulses. "The German example," says Rilke didactically, "is more likely to make any conscious effort to achieve a planned nationalism dubious." He reproves the Germans for their "ambitious grimacing," speaks of the "utterly irresponsible abuse of national sentiment," calls Wilhelm II "the most reprehensible figure in contemporary history," and describes his empire as "unfortunate, pretentious and bombastic, . . . a decoction of vanity and bad taste." He for his part, he says quite truthfully, has always detested German nationalism.

Here the key word is "German." The whole exchange of ideas actually stems from a remark of Rilke's about one of the Duce's speeches: "What a splendid address by Monsieur Mussolini to the Governor of Rome!" he exclaims effusively. The duchess gives her mentor in poetic matters a soft but unmistakably negative answer: "My dear Rilke, I am no admirer of Mr. Mussolini," and declares that it has been "impossible from the outset for me to come to any kind of terms with Fascism." What an admirable woman! (pp. 30-5)

What was it then that Rilke liked so much about the Duce's speech? If we look up its text we find that it dealt with new housing and streets, the improvement of schools and parks, sport stadiums and health services, the restoration of temples and other antiquities—all very laudable subjects but hardly sufficient to arouse such enthusiasm in a great metaphysical poet. In the end our attention is caught by certain peculiar turns of phrase, the characteristic Fascist rhetoric of order, heroism, and discipline. Was Rilke's heart stirred by phrases like *"stile romano"* and *"solenne romanitá,"* by the idea of a return to "the Age of Augustus," or "the liberation of monuments that com-memorate the thousands of years of our history from cen-turies of decadence"? Or by the highflown patriotic final cadence about "the greater Rome that will rise out of our endeavors, our tenacious will, our love," and the *"sacrifiz-io concorde e consapevole,"* the assent and spirit of sacri-fice, of the whole Italian people? This must be it. At that time many minds were obsessed with dreams of "the Latin spirit" or "the Roman spirit." One finds this confirmed when Mussolini's phrases begin to reappear in Rilke's own letters quite naturally—phrases like *"l'idée romaine,"* and *"l'unité sentie et consentie"* (which is no doubt the French translation of *"concorde e consapevole").* He continues in the unmistakable tones of his model: "It is this glorious past, whose gigantic traces your soil still bears, that ren-ders possible this architect of the Italian will, this forger of a new consciousness!"

So it seems that there are two kinds of nationalism, a for-bidden German kind and an acceptable Roman one. "Something that would have been difficult for me else-where I could have done with conviction and enthusiasm in one of those countries, if I had been born there: become an Italian or French soldier. Yes, I could really have done that, fraternally and right up to the ultimate sacrifice"— strange enthusiasm coming from a renegade student of the Imperial Austrian Military Academies who once claimed to be so profoundly distressed by militarism of any kind. Rilke now comes up with this explanation: nationalism is good for some countries but not for others. "The question of nationalism is one of the thorniest that exist. It seems to me that it is not the same for all nations." One passage in particular catches our attention: "I think every nation needs these sudden flare-ups of nationalism to create its own consciousness or simply to recognize itself." (pp. 35-6)

If we re-examine Rilke's statements about Germany with this in mind, we discover a dimension we had previously missed. What Rilke finds lacking in the contemporary Germans is the lost agrarian idyll of bygone days: "the en-chanting, somewhat old-fashioned and provincial qualities of the old German principalities with their slow and pecu-liar customs." He even goes a step further: "To find the true German prototype we must go back to the drawings of Albrecht Dürer. One of their essential characteristics was a tough, enduring and smalltown submissiveness." Here Rilke has succumbed to the illusion cherished by many conservatives that Fascism will turn back the wheel of history, industrialism, and capitalism, and lead the world back to the simple virtues of ancient Rome and the German Middle Ages, the rural village paradise of the *an-cien régime.*

In mentioning Dürer, Rilke is not just invoking an old German master. Dürer's name is a watchword for Ger-man conservatives. We have already encountered it once in Rilke: in the letter in which he accuses Germany of holding back the world. After the war, he says, he had hoped that "the lost trait of submissiveness, which gives Dürer's drawings such a constructive appeal, might be re-stored to—or superimposed upon—the German face, which has become extraordinarily one-sided and willful."

This is what is expected of Germany: "a determined re-nunciation of its falsely developed prosperity."

> Germany has failed to offer its purest, best con-tribution, re-established on the most ancient foundation. It has failed to renew itself radically and change its way of thinking. It has not creat-ed for itself the dignity that is rooted in heartfelt submissiveness. All it was interested in was being saved, in a superficial, quick, mistrustful, and profit-seeking sense. It wanted to achieve, to rise and to escape, instead of following its deep-est nature and suffering, surviving and holding itself in readiness for its miracle (*Briefe an eine junge Frau*).

Rilke reproves Germany for its democratic capitalism. The key word is "profit-seeking." This must be the reason for refusing to Germany, for the moment at least, the "flare-up" of nationalism he allows—or even prescribes for—other countries. If Germany had come up with a re-gime like the Italian one, preaching the Catonian virtues of the simple life, discipline and order, he might well have overcome his *kleindeutsch,* anti-Prussian prejudices and sanctioned a Germanic patriotism along with the Latin one. The necessary elements are all there: a new will for toughness, desire for peace and order at any price, satisfac-tion with freedom, contempt for democratic parliamen-tarianism, detestation of material profit, readiness to serve as a soldier, and an upsurge of mystic enthusiasm for the nation.

There remains little doubt that Rilke was more deeply in-volved in the social and political events of his time than is generally assumed. It remains now to focus upon a work of poetry to see if and how this involvement is reflected in the sublime Rilkean verses seemingly far removed from the everyday strife of political groups and social classes. We have chosen for this purpose the **Duino Elegies** which Rilke himself regarded as central to his endeavors. The El-egies begin with the famous question: "Who, if I cried, would hear me among the angelic orders?" A self is strug-gling to find expression for its loneliness, heightened to un-bearable agony. But the cry of protest remains purely hy-pothetical. A series of conditional clauses resignedly indi-cates that things have progressed beyond the point where a creaturely cry of pain would have any meaning.

The opposite pole, the highest authority confronting the powerless self of the **Elegies,** is the angel, an invented fig-ure which has already transcended that which is responsi-ble for the self's suffering: namely, the world of concrete reality. In the angel, the protest against empiricism, which Rilke was still talking about in the letter to the young worker, has been transformed into unpretending inward-ness. "The angel," he wrote, "is the creature in whom the transformation of the visible into the invisible . . . already appears complete." However, the angel, the sole authority in the **Elegies,** is not concerned, in his perfection, with man but remains infinitely distant from him, unreach-able—not unlike the authorities invented by that other Prague writer, Kafka. The angel is so terrible and so over-whelming that no one would want to come closer to him; indeed, to do so would mean the destruction of the indi-vidual. The self is therefore forced to stifle his barely begun cry. "And so I hold myself in and stifle the call-note / of sobbing protest." The relief that Goethe's sufferer gained from expressing his suffering has no meaning for the twentieth century.

The cry of protest can be stifled, but not the despair. What follows is a moving description of human isolation, a total alienation, which compels the realization that it is no longer related to anything in the world. Even the individual's habits become independent personifications, free to stay on with him or not, at their own discretion. Rilke sums up this misery in the understatement: "We don't feel very securely at home / within our interpreted world" ("First Elegy"). For it is gradually becoming clear that on this one score: the unquestionable meaningfulness of existence, all the creatures that appear in the *Elegies*—the angel, the various plants and animals, even the lifeless doll—are better off than man.

Even men themselves are no help to one another. The poet now presents a series of almost mythical figures which have traditionally represented a particularly meaningful or sublime heightening of the human condition: the child, the hero, the "youthfully dead," the lovers, and questions them about the purpose of life. They are all called upon to disclose how life's rushing futility and oppressive loneliness might be overcome. All this "when?" "who?" and "why?" is the rhetorical counterpart of his questioning and uncertainty. The outcome is always the same: although Rilke never tires of praising the earthly splendor of these figures, not one of them can justify man's existence or break through his absolute exposedness. Even the lover—the figures Rilke most admires, for, after all, a girl in love reaches to an angel's knee ("Seventh Elegy")— merely prevent each other from seeing the lot to which all men are condemned.

This primal melody will be constantly resumed, with subtle changes, modulating through all the major and minor keys. Can this fundamental experience—the isolation and the threatening loss of meaning that hangs over human life—be connected with the anomie of the technological age, a wholly historical concept? Perhaps loneliness is a condition inseparable from man. The modern trend, however, is for him to become ever more acutely aware of it. Odysseus lashed to his plank in the ocean, Robinson Crusoe on his island, did not feel as lonely as Dostoevski's characters in Saint Petersburg or Malte in Paris. But the *Duino Elegies* make the connection between a phenomenon long recognized by the historical disciplines and Rilke's existential despair much more explicit and convincing.

To be sure, the peregrinations through the realm of the laments and across an earth that is, after all, presided over by angels even though they ignore it, the glittering of mystical constellations in the nights "full of cosmic space" ("First Elegy" and "Tenth Elegy"), this whole world inhabited by silent plants and animals, could hardly be presented more timelessly. The representatives of the anthropological order: father, mother, and child, those who died young, heroes and lovers, even the members of certain occupational groups such as acrobats, ropemakers, and potters, could hardly be selected more a-historically. Yet, for all that, the man of the *Elegies* is a historical being; his situation is seen historically. The rhythms flow along, with their esoteric vocabulary—"shields of delight," "state of timeless serenity," ("Second Elegy" and "Tenth Elegy"), etc.—an eternally-human element immune to the passage of time and to all earthly troubles. At certain points, however, this existential, timeless stream drastically changes course. A historical force suddenly breaks in, leaving its stamp upon the whole work. It becomes clear that Rilke is deliberately creating a historical experience.

Certain temporal expressions first arrest our attention. In the "Seventh Elegy", for instance, we find the lines: "and, ever diminishing, / outwardness dwindles" and in the ["Ninth Elegy"] the complaint: "more than ever / things we can live with are falling away." These comparatives point to the progressive deterioration of social conditions and contrast two levels of time: one where life was still fulfilled, and another where it is in danger of becoming meaningless. But this is what we call historical consciousness.

What did Rilke dislike about the present? Among the many allusions scattered throughout the cycle there are three major passages, in the Seventh, Ninth, and Tenth Elegies, where he states his charges. Although they are interrelated, they form the frame of reference of his late poetry. The passage from the "Seventh Elegy" reads:

> Where once was a permanent house, up starts some invented structure across our vision, as fully / at home among concepts as though it still stood in a brain. / Spacious garners of power are formed by the Time Spirit, formless / as that tense urge he's extracting from everything else. / Temples he knows no longer. We're now more secretly saving / such lavish expenses of heart. Nay, even where one survives, / one single thing once prayed or tended or knelt to, / it's reaching, just as it is, into the unseen world. / Many perceive it no more. . . .

Here a power station is presented as a structure characteristic of our time. Various associations are linked with it, but two properties are emphasized: rationality and anti-symbolism. These are the same principles the Romantics denounced in Enlightenment. Modern buildings are arbitrary, "invented," indistinguishable from "concepts," because they have no traditions and only their function determines their appearance. Moreover the modern style of architecture—and architecture is symptomatic of every activity—is formless. The element of human feeling is lacking. The temples that typify earlier, better ages were places of worship. In this happy "once upon a time" the numinous and the aesthetic fused with the human in a beneficent unity. Modern civilization is hostile to the arts, unfeeling, irreverent, and interested in nothing but the utilitarian subjugation of nature.

The two ages correspond to two contrasting human types: modern men have no appreciation of ancient things. They spiritualize nothing and thus fail in man's essential task. Fortunately, though, there is a second type. In the line "This shall not confuse *us*" Rilke clearly singles out the initiated, the conservatives, from the rank of the new masses. The whole conflict between old and new can be subsumed in the opposition of the two powers expressly evoked in this passage: heart and brain.

The **"Tenth Elegy"** opens new perspectives, being less concerned with technology itself than with its effects on society. The City of Pain becomes a place symbolizing all the negative features of the modern age. Again the attributes of the city are alienation and hypocrisy, the noise that drowns out all other sounds, the meretricious monuments, the general spiritual emptiness, the gaudy tinsel. Far from opposing all this, the church is a major contributor to it. Rilke compares it to a government-subsidized post office and describes it as "bought ready-made"—just one more mass-produced article of the mechanized world.

Urban civilization extends outward to the "fair" on the outskirts of the city. There, the efforts of social reformers are derided as "swings of freedom, the presumably radical agitators and revolutionaries as "divers and jugglers of zeal," whereas the "posters for 'Deathless'—that bitter beer" ridicule the common man's publicity-minded ideology which euphemistically evades all tragic sense of life. But the impetus behind everything is money. Curious spectators watch its anatomical, sexual reproductive process in obscene peepshows, typifying the whole scene. The total effect is splendidly satirical.

Perhaps it should be stressed here that it would be foolish to disparage Rilke for sharing these aversions with many European rightists. What makes his attitude politically significant and susceptible of diagnosis is the cumulative effect, the occurrence of a symptom in conjunction with others. The poetic impact derives from two factors: the brilliantly executed comparison of the modern urban scene with a fair, and the truth of the whole statement. Rilke may have seen it one-sidedly, but there is no doubt that our modern civilization has some ugly features. The intellectual content of this indictment is by no means new. One thing, however, is highly significant in the present context: that we find the same ideas in Rilke's pro-Fascist letters, the *Lettres Milanaises*. The *Elegies,* which are visual and synthetical, and the letters, which are intellectual and analytical, stand in the same mutual relationship as historic myth and historic theory. (pp. 36-40)

The Rilke of the *Lettres Milanaises* would like to return to the "rustic and small-town submissiveness" of bygone days. Like many of his contemporaries, he hoped that Mussolini would show him the way, having revived, in his own country, "the gesture, the action—the *visible* example." In 1922, the year of the *Elegies,* Fascism had barely crossed Rilke's horizon, nevertheless his own wishful thinking was already moving in the same direction: toward a return to the simple life. The ultimate wisdom: the justification of this so precarious and threatened earthly life, consists in letting the otherwise indifferent angel see the world in what for the poet was obviously its highest state. "Show him the simple," he says, citing a list of "house, bridge, fountain, gate, jug, fruit tree, window" (**"Ninth Elegy"**), and evoking a bucolic village landscape, a patriarchal world of production and consumption in which man was not yet alienated from things. This much admired catalogue, sublime and estimable as it may be, intrinsically represents no more than escape into a precapi-

talist past, no more than *Blut und Boden.* As a program for the future it is by no means free of a terrifying atavistic element—as we can now say with the shudder of experience.

Is this parallel an example of "clumsy sociologizing" or have we made a contribution to the understanding of Rilke? Theodor Adorno once asked whether any but a person lacking all sense of art could speak about poetry and society. And since he is pleading his own cause, he sets up some guidelines: "Suspicion is allayed only when poetic images are not misused as classroom examples for sociological theses—when, on the contrary, relating them to a sociological context brings out some essential characteristic." It is essential to know how a work of art fits into the contemporary intellectual field of force, to know what position the *Duino Elegies* occupy on the cultural map of the twentieth century, if we are to understand them in all their profundity.

A contempt for current affairs is an old tradition among the German intelligentsia. But in Rilke this haughtily asserted aloofness from politics and history was quite compatible with involvement in the ideological controversies of his time, and apolitical principles could be combined with a political attitude producing a characteristic stance: that of the European Right. By virtue of his background and self-chosen identity Rilke tended to be an "old school conservative" and a "counter-revolutionary," but under the pressure of developments his position became increasingly extreme. We might say that this urbane, highly strung, amiable poet, like most of the conservatives of his time, slipped toward the radical right wing.

Rilke's insights into social mechanisms were very primitive; his political wishes were not oriented toward things as they are. His greatest fault in an age of mass movements and collectivist problems was his extreme individualism. For him the nation reacts like a single individual. He transfers experiences from the life sphere of the individual artist to complex entities such as the state. The poor are not a homogeneous class whose condition derives from a common cause; each of them is poor for himself alone and in his own particular way. For this reason Rilke was blind to the great powers of his time which coerce and overpower the individual. He had little sense of history and did not really understand what was actually going on around him. His strength lay in the spiritual sphere. He intuitively sensed into what psychological correlatives social conditions are transformed within the individual. With a display of rhetoric and a splendid array of images, he lamented what distressed him in modern developments and sang the praises of what he held to be unalterably eternal. In doing so, he enriched that precious store of truths by which we live.

Mountain and valley, river and meadow, desert, sea, and stars are elements of our earthly dwelling place. These, just as much as our inner nature, the needs and impulses of the soul, the effect of love, loneliness, and death, are essential components of our experience and legitimate subjects for the poet. Who if not he is qualified to know and speak about them? What Rilke was seeking was also "that which is most universal, the ultimately valid, the fundamental stuff of life, the drive toward life's basic colors and then finally again the longing for the eternal light to which they all inexhaustibly abandon themselves" (*Briefe an eine junge Frau*). To find a meaning in life beyond the limitations imposed by time and society is one of man's ancient and probably ineradicable dreams. But anyone who, in his longing to find this meaning, neglects the one thing that gives life visible form and makes it comprehensible: history—anyone who would like to leave out society and politics altogether—is in danger of becoming an advocate of inhuman barbarism, no matter how pure his intentions may be.

Rilke's example has at least one thing to teach the historically and the poetically minded: that any interpretation of life and history that precludes protest against what is unworthy of human beings paves the way for the darkest despotism. If we find the times so distressing that we think we ought to protest, then let us at least insist upon a social organization—or to put it quite modestly and realistically, stand up for a social order—in which we do not need to stifle our protest. (pp. 41-2)

Egon Schwarz, "Stifled Protest: Politics and Poetry in the Work of Rainer Maria Rilke," in Boston University Journal, *Vol. XX, No. 3, Autumn, 1972, pp. 30-42.*

AUTHOR'S COMMENTARY

A work of art is good if it has sprung from necessity. In this nature of its origin lies the judgment of it: there is no other. Therefore, my dear sir, I know no advice for you save this: to go into yourself and test the deeps in which your life takes rise; at its source you will find the answer to the question whether you *must* create. Accept it, just as it sounds, without inquiring into it. Perhaps it will turn out that you are called to be an artist. Then take that destiny upon yourself and bear it, its burden and its greatness, without ever asking what recompense might come from outside. For the creator must be a world for himself and find everything in himself and in Nature to whom he has attached himself.

(*letter date 1903*)

Robert Bly (essay date 1981)

[*An American poet and translator, Bly is considered an important influence on contemporary American poetry. A leader in the loosely defined movement called "deep imagism," Bly holds that human intellect forms a barrier between inner and outer realities, and that the poet must create art "which disregards the conscious and the intellectual structure of the mind entirely and by the use of images . . . bring forward another reality from inward experience." In the following excerpt from commentary included in his translation of* Selected Poems of Rainer Maria Rilke, *Bly provides biographical background and critical interpretation of poems collected in* Das Stundenbuch, *which he translated as* A Book for the Hours of Prayer, *and characterizes this work as a book of inner reflection and focus.*]

Rilke's first large book, and the first he had confidence in, was **Das Stundenbuch,** which I have translated as **A Book for the Hours of Prayer.** The German title suggests a medieval monk's or nun's handbook of prayers. *Innigkeit* is the German word associated with such poetry, which becomes "inwardness" in English; but the syllables of the German word have so much more drive and finality than the English sounds. *Innigkeit* has the depth of a well where one finds water. And water is the element of this book, a water whose source Rilke found inside himself.

The first group of poems in the book, called "The Book of Monkish Life," came in a wonderful rush, shortly after Rilke returned home from a trip to Russia with Lou Andreas-Salomé and her husband in 1899. He was twenty-three years old. Until then he had felt his life to be constricted and restrained: the narrow streets of his native Prague seemed stiflingly provincial, and his mother's love and her piety left little space for him. He later said of her:

> In some heart-attic she is tucked away
> and Christ comes there to wash her every day.

The power of Lou Andreas-Salomé's personality and the open spaces of the Russian plains astounded him. He understood Russia's outer space as inner space. It lay east of "Europe":

> Sometimes a man stands up during supper
> and walks outdoors, and keeps on walking,
> because of a church that stands somewhere in
>   the East.
>
> And his children say blessings on him as if he
>   were dead.
>
> And another man, who remains inside his own
>   house,
> stays there, inside the dishes and in the glasses,
> so that his children have to go far out into the
>   world
> toward that same church, which he forgot.

He doesn't mean any orthodox church, but says that if a man walks toward that inner space, he will free his children. It is not too late.

> Because One Man wanted so much to have you,
> I know that we can all want you.

He is astonished to realize that this wanting and having are perfectly possible right now, even for twentieth-century man. Growth is growth into space, as a tree grows through its rings, as the snail grows in spirals and the solar system moves in circles . . . In his surprise he doesn't even identify himself as a man; he could be a falcon or a storm.

Before his Russian trip, Rilke had spent a few months in Italy, and he loved the religious paintings of the early Renaissance, the heavy gold frames, the gold flake: he noticed that the Mediterranean psyche associated gold with religious feeling. But he saw something different when he looked within himself—what we could call a North European unconscious. . . . He then realizes that he may have claimed too much for himself, and he delicately suggests how unformed he is:

I know that my trunk rose from his warmth, but
    that's all,
because my branches hardly move at all
near the ground, and only wave a little in the
    wind.

The language broods; it stays in the moist mood of the North European unconscious. The holy is below us, not above; and a line moves to descend, to dip down, to touch water that lies so near we are astonished our hands haven't dipped into it before. The lines suggest holy depth, always distant, always close. . . . He becomes aware that he has two separate lives.

My life is not this steeply sloping hour,
in which you see me hurrying. . . .
I am only one of my many mouths,
and at that the one that will be still the soonest.

He loves the tension between the poles, hurry and quiet, life and death. Even though death's note wants to dominate, he is the rest between two notes. . . . The problem is not whether the song will continue, but whether a dark space can be found where the notes can resonate. This dark space resembles the hub of a wheel, a pitcher, the hold of a ship that carries us "through the wildest storm of all," the grave earth under the tree, the lower branches of a pine, the darkness at the edge of a bonfire. The dark space is the water in the well. This hub, or hold, or dark space, is not a Pre-Raphaelite preciosity, nor the light of narcissism; the dark space can be rough and dangerous. It is something out there, with the energy of an animal, and at the same instant it is far inside. Once a man or a woman inhabits that space, he or she finds it hidden inside objects, in walnuts or tree roots, in places where people don't ordinarily look for it.

I find you in all these things of the world
that I love calmly, like a brother;
in things no one cares for you brood like a seed;
and to powerful things you give an immense
    power.

Strength plays such a marvelous game—
it moves through the things of the world like a
    servant,
groping out in roots, tapering in trunks,
and in the treetops like a rising from the dead.

How magnificent the last line is! In German: *"und in den Wipfeln wie ein Auferstehn."* This "darkness" or "hub" or "circling power" is a strength best discovered in objects. The word Rilke loves, *Ding,* literally "thing," is difficult. Of course, he means "things" and "objects" by it, but also animals, and even thunder and rocks. "Things of the world" is a attempt to include what he includes in it. He notices that the energy takes the shape and mood of the creature it is in—when it roots, it gropes; when it trunks, it tapers.

A Book for the Hours of Prayer circles, then, with an athletic power inside inner space, among secret things. . . . It can be a shock for readers used to public literature. Most American writers begin proudly, even aggressively, in the outer world: Thoreau, Mark Twain, Howells, Robinson Jeffers, Marianne Moore, Robert Frost, the Eliot who listened to conversations in bars, the William Carlos

Williams who paid attention to back sheds and wheelbarrows. Their start in the outer world is marvelous, but Rilke begins elsewhere. When I first read Rilke, in my twenties, I felt a deep shock upon realizing the amount of introversion he had achieved, and the adult attention he paid to inner states. From the pragmatist or objectivist point of view, Rilke goes too far in this attention; he goes over the line. The American, in Latin America or North America, is willing to accept some introversion, but when it goes this far, he may dismiss the whole thing as solipsism, or as an evasion of political responsibility. Neruda attacked Rilke on precisely this point, in "Poetes Celestes," though late in his life he took back the criticism.

Rilke knows what Tolstoy knows in *The Death of Ivan Ilyich:* that our day-by-day life, with its patterns and familiar objects, can become a husk that blocks anything fresh from coming in. Before the industrial revolution brought its various creature comforts, it is conceivable that the shocks of winter cold, sudden poverties, plague, brutal invasions, abrupt unexplainable deaths, regularly broke the husk. In our time the husk is strong, and Rilke turns to look at it. A man or woman inside the husk, Rilke says, resembles a medieval city that has succeeded—so far—in withstanding or ignoring a siege. . . . The fairy tale called "Sleeping Beauty" describes this situation of invisible siege, where the woman—and perhaps the soul—sleeps undisturbed inside a wall of thorns. No one can get through. In the fairy tale, the "man" or the "suitor" is the awakening force, who fails again and again; the Sufis interpret the last suitor as the spiritual teacher or master. In Rilke's poem the awakening force is a massive energy *out there,* symbolized by an encamped army and the countryside itself.

He lies outside the walls like a countryside. . . .
Climb up on your roofs and look out:
his camp is there, and his morale doesn't falter,
his numbers do not decrease, he will not grow
    weaker,
and he sends no one into the city to threaten
or promise, and no one to negotiate.

When I translated the last few lines, I felt frightened; the lines imply that the awakening force will not make the first move; perhaps no one will come to help, no parents, no gurus, no Christ. When the walls break, Rilke says, they break "in silence."

When the walls are broken, the energy approaches. . . . Realizing that the energy that tapers in trunks and gropes in roots can be met or touched, Rilke begins to speak of that energy as "you." Sometimes the "you" is the dark space I've mentioned, inhabiting the hold or the pitcher:

You darkness, that I come from,
I love you more than all the fires
that fence in the world . . .

Sometimes the "you" is a primitive initiatory force, female in tone:

you are the early dawn, from whom the whole
    morning rose . . .

At other times it is the inner guide, a Khadir or "Faithful John"; at yet other times it is the collective "God" in his more conventional role. . . . When he speaks of it as "deltas," or when he says

> . . . your primitive wind is blowing
> the fragrance of your marvelous power
> to every being and to every creature in need

We sense it is related to the primitive uprushing of non-ego waters that Freud called "the unconscious." Freud published *The Interpretation of Dreams* in 1899, the same year Rilke wrote the first group of these poems. Rilke does not insist on any one identification of the "you," nor does he insist that he is always active. In one energetic and sweet poem, he describes himself as no more active than a watchman in the wine fields, who stays in a shed at night to keep robbers away. . . .

In *A Book for the Hours of Prayer* Rilke included three separate groups of poems, written in different places at different times. The second group, which he called "The Book of Pilgrimage," was written two years after his return from Russia. . . . He had moved to an artists' colony called Worpswede, near Bremen, in a moorlike country, and was living among landscape painters. We notice in Rilke's creative life, as in Yeats's and Mallarmé's, the cross-fertilization between poetry and painting; in Rilke's case, between poetry and sculpture as well. The two painters Heinrich Vogeler and Otto Modersohn became close friends of Rilke's at Worpswede; Rilke was probably in love with both Paula Becker and Clara Westhoff. He loved Paula Becker deeply but she married Otto Modersohn, and it was Clara, a sculptor of great ability, whom Rilke married.

The sense of "the road" continues in "The Book of Pilgrimage"; the sense of danger also increases. Rilke sees that it is possible to "die on the road" if you leave the conventional warmth of collectivized feeling. . . . During this time he wrote "Already the ripening barberries are red," his marvelous poem on fall. In fall Rilke always tried to give himself time alone to look within; in the fall, he found, one can look down long avenues of trees inside, when the vision is not blocked by leaves. . . . The test of whether you owned yourself was this: to close the eyes, and wait to see what sort of images rose up around you in the dark. . . . The danger is greatest for those who have started on the road. If the psychic power is then dissipated by sociability or dishonesty or triviality, the man or woman is in danger.

> Nothing else will come; no more days will open,
> and everything that does happen will cheat him.
> Even you, my God. And you are like a stone
> that draws him daily deeper into the depths.

God himself is dangerous. These lines mark the first appearance of this idea, which will later dominate the Second Elegy.

Rilke named the last group of poems "The Book of Poverty and Death." . . . By that time two more years had passed; Clara and he had married, and their daughter, Ruth, had been born. Supporting a family at Worpswede was impossible, and he and Clara decided he should accept a commission on a prose piece and move to Paris. He wrote the third set of poems in a rush, at Viareggio, but

they came after his first experience of a great modern city, of Paris. . . . Neither writing nor living was easy. . . . Saint Francis, whom he loved, had praised poverty; but the idea didn't seem useful to the poor in Paris.

> And where is he, the clear one, whose tone rings
> to us?
> Why don't the poor feel him, the rejoicing one,
> mastering us, the young one, even though far
> off?
>
> Why doesn't he climb then in their dusk—
> the great evening star of poverty.

Rilke in Paris, then, began to experience a poverty that does not necessarily lead to spirit; and his tremendous energy turned to face that dark. (pp. 3-11)

> *Robert Bly, in an excerpt from his commentary in* Selected Poems of Rainer Maria Rilke, *translated by Robert Bly, Harper & Row, Publishers, 1981, pp. 3-11.*

Carol Keon   (essay date 1982)

[*In the following excerpt, Keon analyzes language, tone, and meaning in the fifth and seventh sonnets of Part Two of* Die Sonette an Orpheus *and examines how Rilke's use of flowers as subjects in these poems manifests his conviction that "by recognizing the essences of existence, namely transformation, simultaneity and infinity, one approaches the totality of pure existence."*]

In *Die Sonette an Orpheus* Rilke views existence as a totality of which life and death are merely different phases. He sees the human being as an integral part of this greater existence which individual existence reflects. The passage of time, inevitable change and loss are construed not as things to be feared and lamented, but rather as things to be embraced and praised. Rilke perceives existence unambiguously as transformation in which we must participate and not become static. We must overcome the consciousness of our mortal condition and the perceptual limitations of time and space. We must recognize, too, the impossibility of participating in pure existence as isolated, limited individuals and the importance of relatedness and interdependence in such existence. In so doing, we transcend the fragmenting barriers between subject and object imposed by those faculties which make us uniquely human, and ironically, with which we sing and praise: speech and reason. In *Die Sonette an Orpheus* Rilke postulates that by recognizing the essence of existence, namely transformation, simultaneity and infinity, one approaches the totality of pure existence. Rilke does not want to halt time or pursue permanence in a transitory world—he embraces and explores transitoriness to the utmost and exults in the evanescence of existence. As an illustration of Rilke's view of existence in this poetic cycle I shall discuss two sonnets, the Fifth and the Seventh of Part Two, which have flowers as their subject. In the temporary and transient nature of the flower Rilke sees manifested the ultimate participation in existence through transformation.

In the Fifth Sonnet of Part Two Rilke praises the anemone's open receptivity and full involvement in life; he questions whether humankind can ever be as open. This motif, explicit in the **"Eighth Duino Elegy,"** is a familiar one and echoes Heidegger's concept that our consciousness of death, time and futurity impinges on our current state of being. Rilke evolves this motif by intermingling time and spatial imagery in praise of the flower and then he poses a straightforward question about humankind. The sonnet begins, as do many of the Orpheus sonnets, as an invocation where the noun of direct address, *Blumenmuskel,* is followed by appositives and relative clauses in the two quatrains and the first tercet. The final tercet deviates from this pattern with a direct statement and a rhetorical question about humanity. The series of clauses and the omission of subject and predicate imitate the convolutions and foldings of the flower petals through pure description, without action, without cause and effect, and thus contrast with the introduction of consciousness in the last lines referring to humankind.

Although the poem is initially directed toward the "muscle" of the anemone and its functions, the resolution of the poem focuses final attention on humanity and through a rhetorical question forces a direct comparison. As in all rhetorical questions the answer is apparent and here it is clearly negative, "never," since the question is couched in a temporal *wann.* However, since Rilke does phrase the question "When are we . . . ?" rather than "Are we . . . ?" he implies that we might sometime achieve this state. The question does not stop with the simple temporal *wann,* it expands the possibilities for achievement by a spatial apposition—"Aber *wann,* in welchem aller Leben, / sind wir endlich offen und Empfänger?" The phrase "in welchem aller Leben," though it is indeed primarily a time reference, is posed as a spatial question as if it were "where" rather than "when." Thus Rilke questions our consciousness of existence more forcefully and effectively with a combination of graphic spatial and temporal terms. Consequently the final question has the force of a statement that we, the conscious beings, are less fortunate than the flower, the unconscious being, because it is open and we are closed. The exhortation, here in physical, spatial terms, is to be like the anemone, receiving existence and life so that death is no threat. Rilke implies here a philosophical stage in the transcendence over fear of death, namely being "endlich offen und Empfänger," although he mentions neither death nor transcendence explicitly.

The sonnet sings the praises of the hard-working *Blumenmuskel,* concentrating attention on the anemone's center of responsiveness rather than on the flower's fragile beauty. This center of power opens the anemone to the morning on the meadows and allows the polyphonic light of the heavens to pour in with such fullness that it is almost impossible for the flower to close. . . . The implicit parallel of light and existence is deliberately emphasized in its contrast with *Untergang,* which in turn implies an association of sunset with death or decline—especially in the lines " . . . der Ruhewink des Untergangs / kaum vermag die weitzurückgeschnellten / Blätterränder dir zurückzugeben." The implied polarity between light and dark forms a basis for Rilke's affirmation of transitoriness and change

as the essentials of existence. The flower is so full of light and existence that dusk and death bring about its closing only with great difficulty, but nevertheless with inevitability.

Implied here is the idea familiar in Rilke's work that, without consciousness of death, the fullness of everchanging life can best be experienced. Fear and anxiety about death play no role in the existence of the flower; its existence without consciousness of death allows its life to be unfragmented; thus *Untergang* effects the closing of the flower only with great effort. The fragility of flowers, which are far more transient than violent humans, is emphasized by the comparison in the first line of the final tercet, "Wir, Gewaltsamen, wir währen länger"—but we never exist as purely as this simple flower. Perhaps we *are* violent because we fear death and perceive our mortality as a fragility more threatening than the flower's.

The highly descriptive series of appositives attributing an unlikely consciousness to these flowers, "du, Entschluß und Kraft von *wie*viel Welten!" indicates that the muscle of the flower performs its functions out of some decision-making process. Through this poetic conceit Rilke gives greater weight to the contrast he wishes to emphasize. Note, too, that this decision and power supposedly come from more than one world, a spatial image which forces an association with the term *Untergang* and at least the two realms of life and death. Rilke uses this metaphor to link the essential points of reference in the poem, just as the muscle both opens the flower to the world of light and morning, that is, to life and existence, and closes it at the beckoning of the evening world of darkness, or death. Once the muscle opens the blossom so completely to life, it relinquishes all control over the flower; only the call of death, as part of life, can return the petals to the muscle. The cycle of life and death, which is the fullness of existence, is here metaphorically completed.

Temporality is implicit in this poem, particularly in the passage from morn till dusk, which is reinforced by Rilke's use of *nach und nach,* indicating a gradual opening. However, the poet contrasts this process with the final state of openness by the fused time-space image, "Muskel des unendlichen Empfangs." Further, the poet continues to intermingle these types of images to illustrate the opposite state of humanity: *wir währen länger; endlich offen; wann, in welchem aller Leben.* In addition the plurality of the noun *Leben* parallels the plurality of *Welten* earlier in the sonnet, emphasizing the disharmony and fragmentation of human conscious existence as opposed to the wholeness of the unconscious existence of flowers. The idea of reception (*Empfang*), as described in this poem, and receiver (*Empfänger*) are also essentially physical and, by context, spatial. Indeed, not only is light poured in but also the morning, *Wiesenmorgen,* another brilliant spatial-temporal image. The act of opening is primarily a spatial configuration, but the flower also opens to receive the temporal glory of the day. Sexual connotations of *Empfang* (conception) and *Schooß* (womb), again physical as well as spatial images, reinforce the notion of the fullness of such an existence. Time and space are again creatively intermingled in *weitzurückgeschnellt(en),* formed by comgining the past participle *zurückgeschnellt* and the adverb *weit,* an idea which is inextricably connected with the total openness of the anemone. (pp. 114-18)

The ultimate point of this sonnet is that the total acceptance of time and existence involves the total opening of one's self to change. A flower, the most transient, the most susceptible to the passage of time because it fully embraces transformation, exists more truly than the sturdier human, who indeed survives longer but only on the periphery of pure existence. The *aber* of the last two lines implies that, though we humans experience more of existence when measured by temporal accumulation of hours and days, we, who are never truly open and receiving, who are the violent aggressors and defenders of our life, enjoy less of existence for we in fact experience it less fully. Wholeness, as enjoyed by the open, receptive and short-lived flower, is indeed greater than the sum of all its fractions as experienced by humankind.

This sonnet raises clearly the questions which preoccupy Rilke in this cycle. He wonders *when* humanity can fully experience existence and concomitantly *how.* The question itself in this sonnet supplies the answer: by being open and receptive to change and thus to existence.

In the other sonnet under consideration, the Seventh of Part Two, Rilke touches subtly on the problem of facing and overcoming the threat of death. His questions as well as his answers are less explicit. The significance of these flowers for the poet lies in the fact that they have been picked, not in their beauty. The flowers have left one life, are confronting death and are on the threshold of a new phase of existence. The human being is not merely a comparison in this sonnet but the agent, the interceder who enables the flowers to embrace their transformation. Yet the artistry of the flower arrangers is not the central focus of the sonnet. The alliance, rather, between flower and arranger is more important as the means for imperfect beings to participate in pure existence.

Rilke fixes the reader's attention on the flowers by the familiar *ihr* of direct address. Thus, the metaphoric confrontation with death becomes essentially an encounter between the reader (or poet) and the plucked blossoms. There are no complete sentences; there is simply a noun of direct address, *Blumen,* and a series of appositives and relative clauses. The descriptive effect is thereby heightened, the description not of flowers in general, but of flowers in that particular state of having been cut. The result, however, is not static, for there are three transformations which these cut flowers undergo: being scattered, collected and revived. Predominantly present and past participles portray these three stages by isolating the uniqueness of the situation and emphasizing the interrelatedness of the three stages as one phenomenon—the essence of cut flowers. Rilke implies here that apparent death (being cut) and life after apparent death (revival) are really indistinguishable. This notion is supported by the fairly even distribution of words with dying or negative connotations and those with living or positive connotations, such as *ermattet, verletzt, begonnener Tod, trübe ermüdende Sünden* and, on the other hand, *erhole, wieder, erhobene, wohlzutun, erkühlend, blühend.* All of this is summed up in the

ambiguous *Gepflücktsein,* the central motif of the poem. The relationship to Rilke's titulary figure, Orpheus, thus becomes clear, for these flowers have also passed through the realm of death and, through change, have returned, in a sense, to life.

It is significant that their new life is different from their former one; it is in fact change *per se* from which the flowers derive their new existence. The transition to a new lifestyle may be regarded as transcendence beyond the flowers' former dependence on the earth and their roots, traditionally an image of stability but at the same time clearly a limitation of their existence. However, this new freedom and independence from a previous life is relative, for it has been brought about by an agent upon which the flowers are equally or perhaps more dependent; namely, those hands which cut them loose must also perform the functions necessary to revive them and grant them this new life. The water of sustenance no longer is supplied by nature but by human beings. Out of this relationship derives the vitality and strength for their new phase of existence. . . . In the Twelfth Sonnet of Part One Rilke clearly states the importance of relationships and configurations as central to the notion of *pure* existence, "Heil dem Geist, der uns verbinden mag; / denn wir leben *wahrhaft* in Figuren" and "(wir) handeln aus *wirklichem* Bezug," (emphasis added). *Verbünden,* the final important word of this sonnet, emphasizes the alliance between the participants and the need for relatedness in approaching perfect existence.

The flower arrangers, *Mädchen,* are well chosen participants in this ritual of death and transformation, for they in their traditional innocence represent one of the least fragmented aspects of the human condition and as such are nearly as fragile and transient as the flowers. Rilke, however, is primarily concerned with them as they interact with and relate to the flowers they have cut. He imposes a distance between the reader and the maidens to ensure that the relationship and the transformation of the flowers remain the center of attention. The first reference to these girls is in terms of *ordnende Hände,* which are then parenthetically attributed to girls. These hands are "ordering," performing the mechanical function of a conscious mind imposing order on its world. The second reference is in terms of fingers—the agents of agents of agents: the fingers of hands of girls (actually the poles of the fingers of the hands of the girls). By thus depersonalizing the image Rilke emphasizes the natural human impulse to bring coherence to a chaotic and incomprehensible existence. The poet also imputes consciousness to the flowers in the line "Finger, die wohlzutun / mehr noch vermögen, als *ihr* ahntet, . . . " (emphasis added). This conceit, much like the personification which begins the poem, shifts attention to the flowers and their dependence on the maidens. The electrical image, "strömende Pole fühlender Finger," exudes a dynamic power from the conscious mind which lends the flowers their new existence. The final line, where the antecedent to *ihnen* is deliberately ambiguous but most likely refers to fingers, again emphasizes the relatedness essential to pure existence. The reader is further inclined to see a relationship, even interdependence, between life and death, which parallels the relationship and interdependence of the maidens and the flowers. The transformation of the flowers clearly implies that death itself is nothing more than transformation.

There is in this sonnet a lesser attempt to form a union *per se* between subject and object, flowers and maidens, than in the other Orpheus sonnets. Metaphors are noticeably missing, as well as grammatical statements of union. The explicit statements of this poem point out the relationship rather than the union between the flowers and the girls, to support the philosophical content of the sonnet. For example, the lines, "ihr schließlich den ordnenden Händen verwandte," and "wieder erhobene zwischen die strömende Pole," and "wieder zu ihnen, die sich euch blühend verbünden," show a clearly defined relationship but not a blending of identities. Only once does the poet indulge in an expression of shared essences, ". . . und Warmes der Mädchen . . . von euch gebend," and this at the precise moment of renewed life granted to the blossoms by the girls, but even this moment is qualified by similes, *wie Beichten, wie trübe ermüdende Sünden.* Sexual implications are also apparent in these lines, in which plucked flowers are so closely related to young maidens. (pp. 118-22)

The peculiar nature of cut flowers, which is the essence of transition to a different phase of existence, is emphasized in this sonnet not only by the extensive use of participles but also by the interweaving of their tenses. The past participles appear in the first two stanzas of the poem indicating the intimacy of flower and cutter, *verwandt(e),* who has brought the blossom close to death. The past participles also heighten the feeling of finality implicit in this proximity to death: *ermattet, verletzt, begonnener Tod.* The final past participle, *erhoben(e),* serves as a transition to the next stage of revival. In addition, among the past participles is the present participle, *wartend,* which thereby reinforces the idea of retaining life while close to death, as well as the anticipation of revival and new life, explicit in the meaning "waiting." The present participles which dominate the final tercets celebrate the restoration to life. They indicate life images implicitly through grammar (ongoing activity), explicitly through meaning (cooling, giving, blooming), and lyrically through the combination of the final letters, *-end,* which are more vibrant and resonant than the final sharp *t* of weak past participles. Rilke has selected for his transitional participles strong ones with highly resonant nasals along with optimistic meanings, *begonnen* and *erhoben.* Present participles appear elsewhere in reference to the hands of the girls, *ordnend* and *strömend,* which are also life-oriented references.

Rilke creates a tone of universality by using an invocation and he further enhances this feeling by employing adverbs of time, for example, *einst, oft, noch einmal, nun wieder,* and *wieder.* This tone makes the sonnet strongly metaphoric, implying that the flowers here described are representatives of one phase of existence: participants in change and metamorphosis. Rilke deliberately uses religious imagery of sins and confession in order to associate the transformation inherent in the absolution of sins through confession with the new phase of existence of the flowers. This use of simile places the poem once again on a more univer-

sal level concerned with metamorphosis in general. The sins which exhaust and burden have been metaphorically caused by the state of being picked, *Gepflücktsein,* that is, by fear of approaching death. This anxiety is, however, alleviated by transformation and by transcendence over the idea of death. This is precisely the same notion which Heidegger, strongly influenced by Rilke, formulated several years later in 1927 as "Being toward Death" (*Sein zum Tode*), which burdens the individual conscious being, whose life is then dominated by the idea of death. Rilke implies in *Die Sonette an Orpheus* that one must overcome the fear of mortality and become aware that life and death are but related phenomena, the realization of which his flowers, without a consciousness, have already achieved. In the **"Eighth Duino Elegy"** Rilke also focuses on the problem of human consciousness, contrasting it with that of animals. His preference for the more philosophical *Bewußtheit* rather than *Bewußtsein . . . ,* pinpoints the distinction he makes between human consciousness, which is an awareness of abstractions, time, death, etc., and creature consciousness, which is an awareness of only the immediate and the tangible—and consequently of pure existence. . . . (pp. 122-24)

Rilke's fascination for the animal in the **"Eighth Duino Elegy"** and for the flowers in the two sonnets treated here reveals in fact his concern with humankind. The poet's praise of pure uncomplicated existence as experienced by less conscious participants proclaims his fervent wish and hope that such pure existence might be possible for humankind. *Die Sonette an Orpheus* resound with this affirmation of human existence. (p. 124)

> Carol Keon, "Flowers as Pure Existence in Rilke's 'Sonette an Orpheus'," in Modern Austrian Literature, *Vol. 15, Nos. 3-4, 1982, pp. 113-26.*

AUTHOR'S COMMENTARY

[Read] as little as possible of aesthetic criticism—such things are either partisan views, petrified and grown senseless in their lifeless induration, or they are clever quibblings in which today one view wins and tomorrow the opposite. Works of art are of an infinite loneliness and with nothing so little to be reached as with criticism. Only love can grasp and hold and be just toward them. Consider *yourself* and your feeling right every time with regard to every such argumentation, discussion or introduction; if you are wrong after all, the natural growth of your inner life will lead you slowly and with time to other insights. Leave to your opinions their own quiet undisturbed development, which, like all progress, must come from deep within and cannot be pressed or hurried by anything. *Everything* is gestation and then bringing forth. To let each impression and each germ of a feeling come to completion wholly in itself, in the dark, in the inexpressible, the unconscious, beyond the reach of one's own intelligence, and await with deep humility and patience the birth-hour of a new clarity: that alone is living the artist's life: in understanding as in creating.

(letter date 1903)

Kathleen L. Komar   (essay date 1989)

[*Komar is an American educator, critic, and translator who has written* Transcending Angels: Rainer Maria Rilke's "Duino Elegies" *(1987)* [*see Further Reading list*]. *In the following excerpt, Komar discusses Rilke's characterization of women and femininity in his writings, concluding that Rilke associates "the highest and most profound roles" in his work with a feminine sensibility, though these roles can be performed by either men or women.*]

Rainer Maria Rilke's attitude toward women has generally been seen by feminist critics as a near miss. Whereas he is certainly benevolent in his view of women, giving them superiority in their capacity to love and to turn their pain into aesthetic accomplishment, he does limit the range of their activities to the traditional pedestal of nonsexual idealization. Feminists have also argued that Rilke confines to women certain "virtues" of self-lessness and mediation that he never attributes to men. Adrienne Rich in *Of Woman Born,* for example, examines Rilke's depiction of mothers and of the female-male relationship in general in the third of his **Duineser Elegien.** Rich rightly points out that "the young woman is to mediate for [the male] in his 'monstrous' inner life, just as the mother mediated in his childhood." She then goes on to conclude:

> The woman, yet again, as healer, helper, bringer of tenderness and security. The roles (or rules) are clear; nowhere in the **Elegies** is it suggested that a man might do the same for a woman. . . .

Although Rich is certainly right in asserting that Rilke does not conceive of a male performing the mediating task for a woman in the **Elegien** (and certainly not in the third elegy, permeated as it is with male sexuality, it is not true that men never take on the "feminine" qualities that Rich describes. In fact, Rilke has a number of "feminine" male figures in his work. And precisely these characters are linked to aesthetic creation and poetic capacity. An examination of the presence of such "feminized" males and the importance of feminine "gender markings" to them might help to recuperate Rilke's seemingly exclusively patriarchal view of women and the feminine. (p. 129)

To understand Rilke's attitudes toward women, one must begin with his most famous and celebrated characterization of women as unrequited lovers. Rilke's pantheon of admired and praised women is made up of those whose intensity of existence depends upon deprivation. Ranging from the unattached Abelone in his *Aufzeichnungen des Malte Laurids Brigge* to Vera Knoop whose early death removed her from both art and love and to the abandoned poetesses Gaspara Stampa and Marianna Alcoforado, Rilke focuses on and values those women for whom renunciation and absence figure prominently.

In a number of his major works and personal letters, Rilke explores the concept and implications of unrequited love, which is exemplified in women such as Gaspara Stampa and Marianna Alcoforado. The women, deserted by their lovers, nevertheless find the strength to turn their objectless passion into more universal aesthetic comprehensions, into literary texts. Rilke gives women a rather privileged position in the love relationship. They seem to be unassailed by sexuality and are "so far beyond man in loving" that they become his teachers. All of Rilke's examples of the virtues of unrequited love are female—and they all transform their deprivation into aesthetic accomplishments. (As noted earlier, for example, Gaspara Stampa (1523-54), the Italian noblewoman abandoned by her lover, transforms her frustrating love relationship into some two hundred sonnets; Marianna Alcoforado (1640-1723), the Portuguese Franciscan nun, transforms hers into letters that Rilke translated into German.) While women may find the privileged image flattering—as, no doubt, Rilke's many patronesses did—it is disturbing that woman's position is defined by absence, deprivation or renunciation, and inescapable limitation.

But in order to understand Rilke's attitude toward women, we must understand the function of absence, renunciation and limitation in his poetics. . . . In one of his typical acts of unification, Rilke bends the poles of the love experience—i.e., fulfillment or renunciation—into a unified circle where deprivation and completion meet. Thus the deprivation provided so typically for women in love can be transformed by the act of perfect renunciation into a fulfillment in another realm, that of the aesthetic. At those times of deprivation—or perhaps of liberation—women become artists, writers, poets. For these women what Rich calls "the cost of doing the 'work of love' for men" is indeed acknowledged by Rilke, but it is counterbalanced by the necessarily independent achievement of poetic creation—which in Rilke's ontology and epistemology is the highest human act.

When the Portuguese Nun is betrayed by her lover, she turns to writing as a means of completion. This gesture is

Lou Andreas-Salomé

seen by Rilke as the greatest opportunity. But he does not limit it to women. He suggests early on in his work that the poet (male or female) must renounce (or even escape) *being loved* personally in order to create on a larger level of existence. This lesson is embodied in the story of the Prodigal Son at the end of Rilke's *Malte.* And in the *Duineser Elegien,* Rilke cites unrequited love as a main strategy for approaching the aesthetic and even the transcendent realm. Renunciation and absence, therefore, take on a positive creative value for Rilke. They are not confined to women alone although they are, for Rilke, a privilege more often granted to women than to men. However much we may disagree with turning unrequited love and deprivation into a positive poetic strategy, we must grant that Rilke does so and that his assignment of renunciation, absence and limitation to women is not, therefore, wholly negative. This role gives women the start over men in striving toward a more profound understanding and expression of existence. Only the poet among men can approach the powers of women.

And this connection of the poetic and the feminine becomes a mainstay in the project of recuperating Rilke's view of women and the feminine. In his poem **"Gegen-Strophen"** (begun in 1912, completed in 1922), which Rilke originally wrote as the fifth of the *Duineser Elegien* but later replaced with the **"Saltimbanque Elegie,"** Rilke gives women the laudatory epithet of "Blumen des tieferen Erdreichs" (stanza 7, line 1). This label is not merely romantic nature imagery for Rilke. His *Duineser Elegien* make it clear that this earthly realm is the productive domain of poetry, art and human accomplishment. Women's ability to participate in this realm at its very roots demonstrates a closeness to the essence of human existence that men, who are always seeking to climb away from the earthly, lack. Like Eurydice (as Rilke presents her in **"Gegen-Strophen"**), women are "immer voll heiliger Umkehr hinter dem steigenden Mann" (stanza 7, lines 4-5). In a rather surprising interpretation of Eurydice's return to the underworld as positive, Rilke suggests that women's strength lies precisely in their connection to the earthly and to the unity of death and birth. He counsels the poet, too, to return to the earthly and to acknowledge positively the presence of death in all life. He thus draws a parallel between women and the class of men he sees as most advanced in the expansion of their consciousness and perceptions—poets. (pp. 129-30)

Whatever the limitations of Rilke's views of women, the identification of women with the poet is an unqualified act of praise (narcissistic perhaps, but genuine nonetheless).

Rilke's vision of women as more proficient at approaching the aesthetic and creative realm than men and at avoiding the ill effects of passion may be an improvement over the views of earlier male poets. Disturbing, however, is Rilke's insistence on a negative role for woman. She must separate the male from the outer and inner worlds he inhabits; she must curb his passions and obsessions; she is productive only in the absence of her own fulfillment as a lover. She creates aesthetic forms primarily as an unrequited lover. In fact, her most positive role is one of absence—as the missing beloved the loss of whom can be turned to productivity in the creation of literary texts.

Rilke thus at least partly creates a femininity of productive deprivation, creative loss and a powerful poetic presence in absence. His poetics as a whole, however, might be described in much the same terms. Rilke offers a problematic and struggling sense of poetic creation that generates new totalities from losses and absences. His unique view of women places them very close to the source of poetic creation itself while Rilke's men in the third elegy have their energies drawn off and expended in life's tributary activities.

Rilke does, however, allow some of his more privileged male characters to participate in the "feminine" roles of mediation, healing and protecting. These exemplary males are, quite pointedly, poets or young men striving to become poets. (p. 130)

[A] compelling example of the poetic male taking on "feminine" qualities is offered in the character of Orpheus in Rilke's *Die Sonette an Orpheus.* While Eurydice is mentioned by name only once in the sonnets, the story of Orpheus and Eurydice informs the poems. And certainly Orpheus must be counted among those men who are helpers, bringers of tenderness, and would-be healers. Orpheus does risk self-sacrifice for his beloved. In his descent to Hades to retrieve Eurydice from the realms of death, Orpheus attempts the ultimate mediation. In a moment of uncertainty, he loses Eurydice again to death, but he clearly plays the role Rich is demanding.

In fact, in an earlier Orpheus poem, **"Orpheus. Eurydike. Hermes"** (1904), Rilke makes it clear that Orpheus is the lover whose dedication is so strong that even the gods relent in the face of his lament over the loss of his wife. Orpheus's error in looking back for Eurydice is coupled with the fact that Eurydice has already begun to dissolve into the reunification and totality of death. . . . Eurydice no longer returns the personal love of Orpheus; she has moved beyond him into the All. No longer even recognizing him, she leaves to Orpheus the role of unrequited lover.

Again, it is for Rilke the special man, the poet, who can fulfill Rich's demands and take on the female role. But in celebrating Orpheus and Eurydice, Rilke also links that role again to the source of poetic creation and prophet power. In Eurydice's absence, Orpheus has only his music. His, too, is ultimately a (physically) unrequited love from which he creates his poetry. This being the case, Orpheus joins Gaspara Stampa and Marianna Alcoforado as poets of deprivation and absence. It is surprising, perhaps, that the young Rilke of 1904 (**"Orpheus. Eurydike. Hermes"**) and 1910 (*Malte*) had already intuited the necessity of participating in the "feminine" as Rilke's early Orpheus and Malte do. The capacity to take on a female persona or feminine characteristics remains an essential ability for the poet who comes fully to realize its importance by the time he writes his late *Sonette an Orpheus.*

In fact, in the one poem of the two series of the *Sonette an Orpheus* that directly acknowledges the feminine by mentioning Eurydice by name (i.e., part 2, Sonnet 13),

Rilke stresses the productive aspect of absence and loss and their connection to the poetic. . . . (pp. 131-32)

Rilke suggests here that the poet must use his loss of Eurydice in order better to understand the realms of death that are the groundsoil of meaning in our living world. Rather than being paralyzed by the absence of the verdant world (in winter) and the loss of the beloved to the realm of Not-being, the poet must turn his deprivation into a more perspicacious and jubilant affirmation of nature as a whole in poetry. Orpheus, and by extension all those who would be poets, is counselled to behave as his female counterparts (Stampa and Alcoforado) have. He must come to understand absence, Nicht-Sein, as the very source of his poetic capacity and of the sympathetic resonance set up in the ground of his being. . . .

The highest and most profound roles in Rilke's poetics, then, can be occupied by either men or women—but they are ineluctably stamped with the feminine. (p. 132)

> *Kathleen L. Komar, "The Mediating Muse: Of Men, Women and the Feminine in the Work of Rainer Maria Rilke," in* The Germanic Review, *Vol. LXIV, No. 3, Summer, 1989, pp. 129-33.*

FURTHER READING

Aiken, Conrad. "Rilke, Rainer Maria," in his *Collected Criticism,* pp. 331-33. New York: Oxford University Press, 1968.
>   Characterizes Rilke as "perhaps the first great poet of the unconscious" and praises his courage to accept the whole of that "dark, fluid, 'private world'." (This article originally appeared under the title "Rilke's Greatness" in the *New Republic,* October 19, 1942.)

Auden, W. H. "Rilke in English." *The New Republic* 100, No. 1292 (6 September 1939): 135-36.
>   Review of an English translation of *Duino Elegies* in which Auden praises Rilke's ability to "express abstract ideas in concrete terms" and likens Rilke's central concerns to those of D. H. Lawrence, particularly "their conception of the writer's real task and the lifelong and humble devotion which they brought to it."

Baron, Frank; Dick, Ernst S.; and Maurer, Warren R., eds. *Rilke: The Alchemy of Alienation.* Lawrence, Kan.: Regents Press of Kansas, 1980, 268 p.
>   Collection of essays, most of which deal with individual works or specific themes of Rilke's. Included are Dana Rothe on the poetic cycle "Die Zaren," Lev Kopelev on Rilke's relationship to Russia, and Erich Simenauer on Rilke's exploration of dream states.

Boney, Elaine E. "Structural Patterns in Rilke's *Duineser Elegien.*" *Modern Austrian Literature* 15, Nos. 3 & 4 (1982): 71-90.
>   Expands upon comments Boney included in her 1975 translation of the *Duinser Elegien* and attempts to establish "integrated structural patterns for the cycle as a whole."

Bowra, C. M. "Rainer Maria Rilke," in his *The Heritage of Symbolism,* pp. 56-97. London: Macmillan, 1943.
>   Technical and thematic discussion of Rilke's elegies and sonnets, which Bowra describes as works characterized by "nervous, excited, discursive thought in which sensibility plays a large part."

Casey, Timothy J. *Rainer Maria Rilke: A Centenary Essay.* London: Macmillan Press, 1976, 118 p.
>   Re-examines Rilke's poetry in view of scepticism among some critics concerning several of Rilke's philosophies. Casey concludes that perhaps a biographical approach to Rilke's poetry is most fruitful.

Closs, August. "Rainer Maria Rilke's Poetic Vision," in his *Medusa's Mirror: Studies in German Literature,* pp. 169-84. London: Cresset Press, 1957.
>   Discusses the development of Rilke's poetic sensibilities, which he characterizes as composed of "transformation and acceptance of life."

de Man, Paul. "Tropes (Rilke)," in his *Allegories of Reading: Figural Language in Rousseau, Nietzsche, Rilke, and Proust,* pp. 20-56. New Haven: Yale University Press, 1979.
>   Overview analysis of Rilke's work with attention to previous criticism, emphasizing elements of theme, style, and language.

Franklin, Ursula. "The Angel in Valèry and Rilke." *Comparative Literature* 35, No. 3 (Summer 1983): 215-46.
>   Attempts to trace, according to Franklin, "some of the significant configurations of the angel image in each of the poets, note how that image conveys for each poet themes essential to his poetic vision, and finally examine and comment on the fundamental differences between the two poets in their understanding and use of the image."

Guardini, Romano. *Rilke's* Duino Elegies: *An Interpretation.* Translated by K. G. Knight. Chicago: Henry Regnery, 1961, 306 p.
>   Detailed reading of the *Duino Elegies.*

Heller, Erich. "The Poet in the Age of Prose: Reflections on Hegel's *Aesthetics* and Rilke's *Duino Elegies,*" in *The Turn of the Century: German Literature and Art, 1890-1915,* edited by Gerald Chapple and Hans H. Schulte, pp. 5-20. Bonn, Germany: Bouvier Verlag Herbert Grundmann, 1981.
>   Text of Heller's 1979 faculty lecture, which was presented in a slightly shortened form to the College of Arts and Sciences of Northwestern University. Discusses similarities between German philosopher Georg Wilhelm Friedrich Hegel's pronouncements on art in his *Aesthetics* and Rilke's views as expressed in his *Duino Elegies,* regarding the "history of the increasing spiritual uncertainty of the arts."

Kellenter, Sigrid. "Rilke's Last Sonnets (1924-1926)." *Modern Austrian Literature* 15, Nos. 3 & 4 (1982): 291-316.
>   Examines technical aspects of Rilke's *Sonnets to Orpheus,* proposing that "in order to make the sonnet a most pliable instrument, Rilke took the liberty to alter various traditional elements such as the division of the stanzas, the rhyme scheme, and the rhythm, if these alterations enhanced and supported what he wanted to express."

Komar, Kathleen L. *Transcending Angels: Rainer Maria Rilke's* Duino Elegies. Lincoln, Neb.: University of Nebraska Press, 1987, 286 p.

Detailed book-length study of Rilke's poem cycle that Komar states adopts a "unified view of the ten poems and attempts to deal with genre and structure as well as lexical meaning and style."

Mandel, Siegfried. *Rainer Maria Rilke: The Poetic Instinct.* Crosscurrents: Modern Critiques, edited by Harry T. Moore. Carbondale and Edwardsville, Ill.: Southern Illinois University Press, 1965, 222 p.

Biographical and critical study that draws heavily from Rilke's abundant letters.

Mason, Eudo C. Introduction to *The Book of Hours: Comprising the Three Books, Of the Monastic Life, Of Pilgrimage, Of Poverty and Death* by Rainer Maria Rilke, translated by A. L. Peck, pp. 21-44. Richmond, England: Hogarth Press, 1961.

Asserts that the "real theme" of the *Book of Hours* is "Rilke's own inner life, the vibrations and oscillations of a hovering, dithyrambic soul, the sinking and soaring of his aspirations and, above all, his sense of his own uniqueness, of that which distinguishes him as a kind of uncrowned king from everybody else, of his vocation, his creative powers and also his perils *as a poet.*"

Olbrich, Marshall. "Rilke and the World of Feeling." *Quarterly Review of Literature* II, No. 1 (Fall 1944): 36-44.

Contends that Rilke's poetry displays an optimism that to Olbrich reveals "something yielding in his temperament and too obliging for these sad days."

Parry, Idris. "Rilke and Orpheus." *The Times Literary Supplement* (12 December 1975): 1494-95.

Introduces many of Rilke's themes in his *Sonnets to Orpheus,* focusing on the figure of Orpheus himself.

Prater, Donald. *A Ringing Glass: The Life of Rainer Maria Rilke.* Oxford: Clarendon Press, 1986, 472 p.

Thorough biography.

Rose, William, and Houston, G. Craig, eds. *Rainer Maria Rilke: Aspects of His Mind and Poetry.* 1938. Reprint. New York: Guardian Press, 1970, 183 p.

Collection of essays on Rilke by C. M. Bowra, E. L. Stahl, G. Craig Houston, and William Rose.

Schwarz, Egon. *Poetry and Politics in the Work of Rainer Maria Rilke.* Translated by David E. Wellbery. New York: Frederick Ungar Publishing Co., 1981, 159 p.

Asserts that Rilke's poetry is "part of the emotional and intellectual system of defenses that serves the individual's need to orient himself in a world of impenetrable complexities." Using Rilke's poetry as example, Schwarz "shows the connections between a consciousness that considered itself hermetic and autarchic and the social-psychological constellations of the world surrounding it."

Slochower, Harry. "Goethe and Rilke: Contemporary Revaluations." *Accent* 2, No. 4 (Summer 1942): 204-13.

Asserts that Rilke's literary and aesthetic influences included Franz Kafka, Leo Tolstoy, and sculptor Auguste Rodin.

Van Heerikhuizen, F. W. *Rainer Maria Rilke: His Life and Work.* Translated by Fernand G. Renier and Anne Cliff. London: Routledge and Kegan Paul, 1951, 396 p.

Biographical and critical study of Rilke, providing specific discussions of influences on Rilke's work, and containing many extracts from his letters. The critic believes that *The Notebooks of Malte Laurids Brigge, Sonnets to Orpheus,* and *Duino Elegies* form a modern *Divine Comedy.*

Warnke, Frank J. "Rilke's *Sonette an Orpheus,* Part 1, Number 6." In *Textual Analysis: Some Readers Reading,* edited by Mary Ann Caws, pp. 45-53. New York: Modern Language Association of America, 1986.

Close textual reading of Rilke's poem in which Warnke contends that "the experience of this lyric, like that of most great lyrics, is of a merging with the godhead, with the divine."

Wood, Frank. "Rilke and D. H. Lawrence." *The Germanic Review* XV, No. 3 (October 1940): 213-23.

Compares ideas, philosophies, and doctrines of these two writers as evidenced in their writings.

————. *Rainer Maria Rilke: The Ring of Form.* Minneapolis: University of Minnesota Press, 1958, 240 p.

Study of Rilke's work that seeks "by analyzing persistent themes and motifs in their original context, to give a broader idea of how a great poet can be, at one and the same time, one of the most 'paradoxical' and yet most 'consistent' personalities of our time."

Carl Sandburg

1878-1967

(Full name: Carl August Sandburg; also wrote under the pseudonyms Charles A. Sandburg, Militant, and Jack Phillips.) American poet, biographer, autobiographer, novelist, journalist, songwriter, editor, and author of children's books.

One of America's most celebrated poets during his lifetime, Sandburg developed a unique and controversial form of free verse that captured the rhythms and color of Midwestern American vernacular. While some critics have dismissed Sandburg for his sentimental depictions of urban and agrarian landscapes and for his simple style, others have lauded his rhapsodic and lyrical technique and his effective patterns of parallelism and repetition. In *Chicago Poems,* his first major collection and one of his most respected works, Sandburg employs images and topics not commonly considered poetical to paint realistic portraits of common people in such environments as the railroad yard, the marketplace, and the factory. Louis D. Rubin affirmed Sandburg's unique approach: "Sandburg's particular talent is that he opens up areas of our experience which are not ordinarily considered objects of aesthetic contemplation, through language that enables him, and us, to recognize such experience in new ways."

Sandburg was one of seven children born to hardworking, conservative Swedish immigrants in Galesburg, Illinois. Although Sandburg's parents were fluent in both English and Swedish, they did not encourage their children's education. Sandburg developed an interest in reading and writing but was forced to leave school at age thirteen to help supplement the family income. Before borrowing his father's railroad pass at age eighteen to visit Chicago for the first time, Sandburg drove a milk wagon, worked in a barber shop, and was an apprentice tinsmith. He would later utilize the images and vernacular he was exposed to during such experiences to create verse reflective of the working class.

After spending three and a half months traveling through Iowa, Missouri, Kansas, and Colorado on the railroad, Sandburg volunteered for service in the Spanish-American War in 1898, and served in Puerto Rico. As a veteran he was offered free tuition for a year at Lombard College in Galesburg. He studied there for four years, but left in 1902 before graduating. It was at Lombard that Sandburg began to develop his talents for writing, encouraged by the scholar Philip Green Wright. On a small hand press in the basement of his home, Wright set the type for Sandburg's first publications: *In Reckless Ecstasy, Incidentals, The Plaint of a Rose,* and *Joseffy.* These four slim volumes contain Sandburg's juvenilia and are stylistically conventional. In retrospect Sandburg declared them "many odd pieces . . . not worth later reprint."

Sandburg gained recognition when Harriet Monroe, editor of the progressive literary periodical *Poetry: A Maga-*

zine of Verse, published six of Sandburg's poems in 1914. During this time Sandburg cultivated literary friendships with, among others, Edgar Lee Masters, Vachel Lindsay, Amy Lowell, and Sherwood Anderson, and gained the attention of Henry Holt and Company, the firm that was to publish his first major volume of poetry, *Chicago Poems.* This collection, with its humanistic renderings of urban life, place descriptions, and casual assemblage of character sketches, provides a stark but idealistic view of the working class. While "Chicago," one of Sandburg's most celebrated poems, depicts the faults of the midwestern metropolis, it also praises what Sandburg considered the joy and vitality integral to life there. "Chicago," along with the poem "Skyscraper," which proclaims that buildings have souls, initiated what was to be called the "Chicago Myth," or the belief that Chicago was somehow tougher than other cities but also more genuine and robust. *Chicago Poems* is generally regarded as one of Sandburg's finest poetic achievements, but initial reaction to the volume was mixed, with many reviewers finding the subject matter startling and the prosaic poetry oddly structured.

While *Chicago Poems* depicts the urban experience, Sandburg's next volume, *Cornhuskers,* explores the realities of agrarian life. In such poems as "Prairie" and "Laughing Corn," Sandburg expresses his fondness for family life and nature. Also included in this collection are a number of war poems with images of soliders who died in conflicts previous to World War I. *Smoke and Steel,* published in 1920, addresses complex postwar issues such as industrialization and urbanization and was less optimistic and idealistic than Sandburg's earlier works. With *Slabs of the Sunburnt West,* Sandburg began using a technique in which a series of images are presented in parallel forms as well as in rough, colloquial language. In 1928 Sandburg published his fifth significant volume of poetry, *Good Morning, America.* This collection begins with his thirty-eight "Tentative (First Model) Definitions of Poetry," but because Sandburg never developed a consistent critical theory of poetry, these definitions are generally considered unenlightening. In this volume Sandburg delves into mythology, history, and universal humanism through extended use of proverbs and folk idioms. His concentration on historical fact foreshadowed the content of Sandburg's epic prose-poem, *The People, Yes.* In this work, which he crafted over a period of eight years, Sandburg fused American colloquialisms with descriptions of historical and contemporary events to create a collection of verbal portraits of the American people. Because Sandburg chose to allow his subjects to speak for themselves, many critics accused him of foregoing the role of poet for folklorist. While considered an important historical and cultural reflection of the American people, *The People, Yes* is not widely regarded as poetry in the traditional sense.

Sandburg won the Pulitzer Prize in 1951 for *Complete Poems,* a cumulation of his six previous volumes of poetry. While numerous critics commented briefly on the occasion of its publication, few took the opportunity to evaluate the whole of Sandburg's poetic career. William Carlos Williams represents the general critical response to this volume: "Carl Sandburg petered out as a poet ten years ago. I imagine he wanted it that way. His poems themselves said what they had to say, piling it up, then just went out like a light. He had no answers, he didn't seek any." However, while many critics spoke nostalgically about the "Chicago Poet" of 1916, they failed to acknowledge or comment upon the seventy-two poems published for the first time in *Complete Poems.* Recent commentators use such poems as "The Fireborn Are at Home in Fire" and "Mr. Longfellow and His Boy" to demonstrate Sandburg's continuing stylistic and thematic development, which was also evident in his last volume, *Honey and Salt.* Despite the fact that some commentators noted a quiet and reflective mastery of the poetic craft in the title poem, "Foxgloves," and "Timesweep," *Honey and Salt* generated little critical attention.

Sandburg was an eminent figure of the "Chicago Renaissance" and the era encompassing World War I and the Great Depression, but his reputation waned in midcentury when his folksy and regional approach was overshadowed by the allusive and cerebral verse of such poets as Ezra Pound and T. S. Eliot. While Sandburg continued to depict ordinary people in their everyday settings, other poets were gaining critical acclaim for internalizing and codifying experiences. Nonetheless, some recent commentators purport that this disfavor was a result of the whims of various critical movements, and not based on the strength or significance of Sandburg's poetic contribution. Dan G. Hoffman asserts: "[Sandburg] was a realistic voice which caught the cacaphonous choruses of 'the mob—the crowd—the mass' and made a new poetry in a new form, from the jangling noises about our ears."

(For further discussion of Sandburg's life and work, see *Contemporary Literary Criticism,* Vols. 1, 4, 10, 15, 35; *Contemporary Authors,* Vols. 5-8, rev. ed., Vols. 25-28, rev. ed. [obituary]; *Something about the Author,* Vol. 8; *Dictionary of Literary Biography,* Vols. 17, 54; and *Concise Dictionary of American Literary Biography: Realism, Naturalism, and Local Color 1865-1917.*)

PRINCIPAL WORKS

POETRY

In Reckless Ecstasy [as Charles A. Sandburg] 1904
Incidentals [as Charles A. Sandburg] 1907
The Plaint of a Rose [as Charles A. Sandburg] 1908
Joseffy [as Charles A. Sandburg] 1910
Chicago Poems 1916
Cornhuskers 1918
Smoke and Steel 1920
Slabs of the Sunburnt West 1922
Selected Poems 1926
Good Morning, America 1928
The People, Yes 1936
Complete Poems 1950
Honey and Salt 1963

OTHER MAJOR WORKS

The Chicago Race Riots (journalism) 1919
Rootabaga Stories (fables) 1922
Rootabaga Pigeons (fables) 1923
Abraham Lincoln: The Prairie Years (biography) 1926
Carl Sandburg (autobiography) 1926
Mary Lincoln: Wife and Widow (biography) 1932
Abraham Lincoln: The War Years (biography) 1939
Home Front Memo (journalism/radio broadcasts) 1943
Remembrance Rock (novel) 1948
Always the Young Strangers (autobiography) 1955
The Letters of Carl Sandburg (letters) 1968

Harriet Monroe   (essay date 1916)

[*Monroe was a central figure in the American "poetry renaissance" of the early twentieth century. As the founder and editor of* Poetry: A Magazine of Verse, *Monroe maintained an editorial policy of printing "the best of English verse which is being written today, regardless of where, by whom, or under what theory of art it is written." Monroe played an integral part in Carl Sandburg's poetic career by being the first to publish six poems later collected in* Chicago Poems *and by actively supporting his verse throughout his lifetime. In a review of* Chicago Poems *excerpted below, Monroe praises Sandburg's unprejudiced eye for beauty and the authenticity of his verse.*]

Carl Sandburg has the unassailable and immovable earthbound strength of a great granite rock which shows a weather-worn surface above the soil. Like such a rock, he has a tender and intimate love of all soft growing things—grasses, lichens, flowers, children, suffering human lives. One would no more question his sincerity than that of the wind and rain. His [*Chicago Poems,*] whether you like it or not, whether you call it poetry or not, is fundamental in the same majestic sense—it is a man speaking with his own voice, authoritatively like any other force of nature.

I remember the emotion with which I first read many of these poems—in type-written sheets sent to *Poetry* over two years ago by some friend of the poet. That first conviction of beauty and power returns to me as I read them again. This is speech torn out of the heart, because the loveliness of "yellow dust on a bumble-bee's wing," of "worn wayfaring men," of ships at night, of a fog coming "on little cat feet,"—the incommunicable loveliness of the earth, of life—is too keen to be borne; or because the pain of "the poor, patient and toiling," of children behind mill-doors, of soldiers bleeding in the trenches—all the unnecessary human anguish—is too bitter for any human being, poet or not, to endure in silence.

Mr. Sandburg knows his Chicago, and the book as a whole gives us the city in a masterpiece of portraiture. The town—its streets and people, its parks and broad lake and the sand-dunes beyond—the whole half-formed metropolis—is painted in broad vital strokes and rich colors by the loving unflattering hand of an artist. . . . (pp. 91-2)

Mr. Sandburg's free-verse rhythms are as personal as his slow speech or his massive gait; always a reverent beating-out of his subject. They are rugged enough at times—as when he salutes Chicago, "stormy, husky, brawling," and sets her high among cities, "with lifted head singing, so proud to be alive and coarse and strong and cunning." In some of the war poems his rhythms pound like guns booming, and when he talks back to the loud-mouthed Billy Sunday the swing of a smashing prose hammer is good enough.

But again, under softer inspiration, this poet's touch becomes exquisitely delicate. Indeed, there is orchestral richness in his music; he plays divers instruments. Such lyrics as **"The Great Hunt," "Under," "Beachy," "At a Window," "The Road and the End,"** have a primal, fundamental beauty, a sound and swing as of tides or bending grain. . . . (pp. 92-3)

The spirit of the book is heroic, both its joy and its sorrow. It says, "Keep away from the little deaths!" (p. 93)

> *Harriet Monroe, "Chicago Granite," in* Poetry, *Vol. VIII, No. 2, May, 1916, pp. 90-3.*

O. W. Firkins (essay date 1916)

[*Firkins was an American educator and critic whose works include studies of Jane Austen and William Dean*

Howells. In the following excerpt, Firkins states that while Sandburg paints an authentic picture of the working class, his style in Chicago Poems *lacks discipline and leads to superfluous phrasing.*]

Mr. Carl Sandburg has two divergent aspirations [in *Chicago Poems*]: he reaches out simultaneously towards the brawny and the lissome, two ideals linked only by the fact that both are fashionable. The brawny section, which includes the "Chicago Poems," paints the distresses and iniquities of a great city with an unsparing plainness which twenty-five years ago would have been courageous. Mr. Carl Sandburg is a good fellow, with an authentic pity for the poor; and I am glad that he should lash the sodden and selfish rich, if the lash be reformatory. But I think in his pictures of misery there is a lesson he might profitably learn from Galsworthy or Hauptmann, or, for that matter, from Hugo or Dickens. The *man* in the man must be clearly visible before his immersion in the mud can be either tragic or pathetic. Too often—not always—in Mr. Sandburg's pictures the man is so like the mud that his submergence produces no effect of tragic incongruity. These poems, which are all in free verse or shackled prose, show a rude power here and there, a power rather forensic or journalistic than strictly poetical, evident sometimes in a quick eye for dramatic juxtapositions.

In his lissome work he shows not poems, but mild poeticisms, little pennons or banderoles of detached and pleasing phrase, sometimes merely decorative, sometimes fluttering from the spear of his polemic. What sense of beauty he has is evoked oftenest by colors and mists.

Mr. Sandburg's error and calamity is the refusal of discipline. Any healthy and spirited boy in a gymnasium will set for himself restrictions and exactions from the sheer pride of endeavor. How can Mr. Sandburg, who values Chicago because Chicago toils and strives, when a choice is offered between the lax and the tense in metre, in description, in logic, content himself with the spineless preference for the easy and supine alternative? His style, he tells us, is his own, like his face. I concede the analogy. His face, if the interesting photograph supplied to me by the forethought of his publishers be veracious, is not left in a state of nature. I suggest a razor for his style.

> *O. W. Firkins, "American Verse," in* The Nation, *New York, Vol. CIII, No. 2668, August 17, 1916, p. 152.*

Francis Hackett (essay date 1916)

[*Hackett was a respected Irish-American biographer, novelist, and literary critic during the first half of the twentieth century. His reviews appeared in the* New Republic, *the* Saturday Review of Literature, *and other prominent periodicals. In the following excerpt, Hackett focuses on the Imagistic aspect of Sandburg's verse. While stating that Sandburg may initially appear overly impressionistic, Hackett concludes that the poet's interpretation of mood is ultimately very effective and beautiful.*]

The free rhythms of Mr. Carl Sandburg are a fine achievement in poetry. No one who reads **Chicago Poems** with rhythm particularly in mind can fail to recognize how much beauty he attains in this regard. But the more arresting aspect of Mr. Sandburg's achievement is, for myself, the so-called imagistic aspect; the aspect, that is to say, which the subject-matter itself reveals. The rhythm, one may insist, is part of the imagism—one may resent having the so-called subject-matter considered separately. Rhythm, however, is far from the dominant novelty in Carl Sandburg, and it is convenient to assume that his rhythms are delectable to many who yet do not admit the beauty or originality of his way of approaching the world.

The originality of the imagist approach can scarcely be long disputed. Never before has there been such firm seizure of the object to be presented. Never before has the impression of the moment been so poignantly dramatized. Make a contrast, for example, between the Anacreon verse on an old man and the Sandburg verse on a baby. One is a brief description, the other a brief characterization. The comparison is not on all fours but at least it is suggestive of just that quality in the modern poet which is making imagism what it is. Take the old man first:

> Gray are my temples long since and snowy my
>   hair:
> Gracious youth is departed; old are my teeth,
> Brief is the space of sweet life that is left to me
>   now.

Mr. Sandburg's verse runs this way:

> The child's wonder
> At the old moon
> Comes back nightly.
> She points her finger
> To the far, silent, yellow thing
> Shining through the branches
> Filtering on the leaves a golden sand,
> Crying with her little tongue, "See the moon!"
> And in her bed fading to sleep
> With babblings of the moon on her little mouth.

Each of these poems is an epigram and each characterizes a special period of life, but the antique epigram is generalized still-life, the modern is particularized life in motion. (pp. 305-07)

The amazing difference, as it strikes me, is the skill of the modern in concentrating attention. The presenting of a figure, a picture, an image, is, as quotation will show, a frequent consequence of the imagist purpose. But Mr. Sandburg illustrates above all the intensity, the momentousness, that is gained by declining to refer each object to some remoter cause, by tending to treat each object as self-contained, purposive in its own measure, dynamic. "I am the Great White Way of the city." "In western fields of corn and northern timber lands, they talk about me, a saloon with a soul." "I am the crumbler: to-morrow." "They offer you many things, I a few." "I am the nigger, Singer of songs." "Here is a tall bold slugger set vivid against the little soft cities." "I am a copper wire slung in the air." This is not a trick. It is simply a pushing of the imagination to the centre of the will. And even where there is no such unity as the will provides another kind of composure is secured, a visual composure. There is none of the laxity

that comes from splitting attention several ways. Consider these envisagements of a commonplace world:

"Fog"

> The fog comes
> on little cat feet.
>
> It sits looking
> over harbor and city
> on silent haunches
> and then moves on.

"Nocturne In A Deserted Brickyard"

> Stuff of the moon
> Runs on the lapping sand
> Out to the longest shadows.
> Under the curving willows,
> And round the creep of the wave line,
> Fluxions of yellow and dusk on the waters.
> Make a wide dreaming pansy of an old pond in
>   the night.

At first these poems may appear too innocent of self-interpretation to mean anything, too impressionistic to compel the name of beauty—to give that completion which has no shadow and knows no end beyond itself. But such exquisite realization of the scenes that gave Mr. Sandburg the mood of beauty is in itself a creation of the beautiful. Mr. Sandburg has such art in representing these scenes and the actors in them that doubt as to his capture of beauty could only occur to a person filled with a wrong expectation. If expectation is unfulfilled, indeed, it can almost certainly be deemed wrong, for these imagist verses are as good as any of their kind. (pp. 307-09)

> *Francis Hackett, "Illuminations," in his* Horizons: A Book of Criticism, *B. W. Huebsch, 1918, pp. 305-10.*

Louis Untermeyer   (essay date 1918)

[*Untermeyer was a contributing editor to the* Liberator *and the* Seven Arts, *and served as a poetry editor of the* American Mercury *from 1934 to 1937. He is best known as an anthologist of poetry and short fiction, including such collections as* Modern American Poetry *(1919) and* The Book of Living Verse *(1931). In the following excerpt, Untermeyer provides a comparison between Sandburg's first two major volumes of poetry,* Chicago Poems *and* Cornhuskers. *While he finds the language of both collections brutal, Untermeyer believes* Cornhuskers *has more depth and dignity and is also less forced.*]

When Carl Sandburg's *Chicago Poems* appeared two years ago, most of the official votaries and vestrymen in the temple of the Muse raised their hands in pious horror at this open violation of their carefully enshrined sanctities. In the name of their belovéd Past, they prepared a bill of particulars that bristled with charges as contradictory as they were varied. They were all united however on one point—Sandburg's brutality. In this they were correct. (p. 263)

As in *Chicago Poems,* the first poem of his new volume—

Cornhuskers—brims with an uplifted coarseness, an almost animal exultation that is none the less an exaltation.

> I was born on the prairie, and the milk of its
>   wheat, the red of its clover, the eyes of its
>   women, gave me a song and a slogan.
> Here the water went down, the icebergs slid with
>   gravel, the gaps and the valleys hissed, and the
>   black loam came.

(pp. 263-64)

These are the opening lines of **"Prairie,"** a wider and more confident rhythm than Sandburg has yet attempted. The gain in power is evident at once and grows with each section of this new collection. The tone in *Cornhuskers* has more depth and dignity; the note is not louder, but it is larger. In *Chicago Poems* there were times when the poet was so determined to worship ruggedness that one could hear his adjectives strain to achieve a physical strength of their own. One occasionally was put in mind of the professional strong man in front of a mirror, of virility basking in the spotlight, of an epithet exhibiting its muscle. Here the accent is less vociferous, more vitalizing; it is a summoning of strong things rather than the mere stereotypes of strength. Observe the unusual athletic beauty of **"Leather Leggings," "Always the Mob," "The Four Brothers,"** and [**"Prayers of Steel"**]. . . .

These and a dozen others seem a direct answer to Whitman's hope of a democratic poetry that would express itself in a democratic and even a distinctively American speech. He maintained that before America could have a powerful poetry our poets would have to learn the use of hard and powerful words; the greatest artists, he insisted, were simple and direct, never merely "polite or obscure." "Words are magic . . . limber, lasting, fierce words," he wrote in an unfinished sketch for a projected lecture. "Do you suppose the liberties and the brawn of These States have to do only with delicate lady-words? with gloved gentlemen-words?" Later he said, "American writers will show far more freedom in the use of names. Ten thousand common and idiomatic words are growing, or are today already grown, out of which vast numbers could be used by American writers—words that would be welcomed by the nation, being of the national blood."

No contemporary is so responsive to these limber and idiomatic phrases as Sandburg. His language lives almost as fervidly as the life from which it is taken. And yet his intensity is not always raucous; it would be a great mistake to believe that Sandburg excels only in verse that is heavy-fisted and stentorian. . . .

This creative use of proper names and slang (which would so have delighted Whitman), this interlarding of cheapness and nobility is Sandburg's most characteristic idiom as well as his greatest gift. And it is this mingling that enriches his heritage of mingled blood; the rude practical voice of the American speaks through a strain of ruder Swedish symbolism. Beneath the slang, one is aware of the mystic; *Cornhuskers* shows a cosmic use of penetrating patois; it is Swedenborg in terms of State Street. This mysticism shines out of **"Caboose Thoughts, Wilderness, Southern Pacific, Old Timers."** And it is always a more extended and musical spirituality than the earlier volume;

the new collection may not be more dynamic, but it is more lyric.

The struggles, the social criticism, the concentrated anger, and the protests are here as prominently as in *Chicago Poems,* but they assert themselves with less effort. The war has temporarily harmonized them; they are still rebellious, but somehow resigned. The chants of revolt are seldom out of tune with Sandburg's purely pictorial pieces. Both are the product of a strength that derives its inspiration from the earth; they are made of tough timber; they have "strong roots in the clay and worms." (p. 264)

Louis Untermeyer, "Strong Timber," in The Dial, *Chicago, Vol. LXV, October 5, 1918, pp. 263-64.*

Conrad Aiken   (essay date 1919)

[*An American poet, critic, and fiction writer, Aiken was deeply influenced by the psychological and literary theories of Sigmund Freud, Havelock Ellis, Edgar Allan Poe, and Henri Bergson, and is considered a master of the stream of consciousness literary technique. In reviews noted for their perceptiveness and barbed wit, Aiken exercises his theory that "criticism is really a branch of psychology." In the following excerpt, Aiken attempts to identify Sandburg's unique poetic characteristics, stating that while Sandburg's verse is vigorous and sensual it is also overly sentimental, simplistic, and clumsy.*]

It is one of the anomalies of the present poetic revival in this country that it is not dominated by any one single group or tendency, but shared in and fought for by many: classicists, romanticists, and realists, of varying degrees of radicalism, all exist simultaneously, so that we have a spectacle to which perhaps no era was ever before treated,—a complete cycle of poetic evolution presented not in the usual span of two centuries, more or less, but in the space of two years. Those who are interested in poetry are today permitted to watch a three-ringed circus, and to distribute their applause as they please; with a fair certainty that they will find something worth applauding. The rivalry is keen. Nobody will hazard a guess as to which ring will dominate the circus. But so long as the competitors are goaded on by the feats of their rivals to new and more astonishing acrobatics, it does not so much matter.

More akin to Mr. Masters, perhaps, than to Mr. Frost, Carl Sandburg nevertheless has character of his own,—whatever we think of his work we cannot deny that it is individual, that it has the raciness of originality. The cumulative effect is one of vigour, a certain harshness bordering on the sadistic, a pleasant quality of sensuousness in unexpected places, ethical irony,—and sentimentality. Mr. Sandburg is a socialist, and consistently preaches socialist morals. Next to his deficiencies as regards form, it is perhaps Mr. Sandburg's greatest fault that he allows the poet to be out-talked by the sociologist. If Tennyson is now regarded as a tiresome moral sentimentalist, who knows whether a future generation, to whom many of Mr. Sandburg's dreams may have become realities, will not so regard Mr. Sandburg? That is the danger, always, of being doctrinaire. Doctrine is interesting only when new.

Mr. Sandburg restricts himself almost entirely to free verse: among free verse writers he is the realist, as the Imagists are the romanticists. But the free verse of the Imagists is a highly complex and formal vehicle by comparison with Mr. Sandburg's free verse: it is comparatively seldom that Mr. Sandburg betrays anything more than a rather rudimentary sense of balance or echo. For the most part, he employs a colloquial, colourful journalese prose, arranged either in successions of sharply periodic sentences, each sentence composing one verse-line, or in very long and often clumsy sentences formed of successive suspended clauses, a suspense which he ultimately relieves by a return to the periodic. In other words, Mr. Sandburg is so intent on saying, without hindrance whatsoever, precisely what he has it in his mind to say, that he will not submit to the restraints of any intricate verse-form, even of his own invention, but spreads out in a sort of gnomic prose. There are exceptions, of course: in such poems as **"Sketch," "Lost," "Fog," "White Shoulders," "Graves," "Monotone," "Follies," "Nocturne in a Deserted Brick-yard," "Poppies,"**—and there are others, too,—there is movement, balance, sometimes a return by repetition, sometimes a return by echo. But even in these the movement, balance and return are often those of a rhetorical and orotund prose rather than of verse. The rhythm is slurred, unaccented, in fact a prose rhythm, with interspersions of single lines or groups of lines which rise to a simple cantabile sometimes a little astonishing in the context. These are Mr. Sandburg's lyric moments—the moments when the sentimental Sandburg masters the ethical or ironic Sandburg. Some of the poems listed above, and others, such as **"Pals," "Gone"** (which has a delightful balance), **"Used Up," "Margaret,"** are almost completely rhythmic, rhythmic in a simple and unsubtle sense, with a regular and easily followed ictus. These are short flights, they suggest,—as indeed all of Mr. Sandburg's work suggests,—the penguin aeroplanes in which novice aviators are trained: at the maximum speed the penguin barely manages to lift from the ground, and to achieve a sort of skipping glide.

Now, if these observations on Mr. Sandburg's technique are in any measure accurate, it becomes important to know whether for his sacrifice of form Mr. Sandburg receives sufficient compensation from the increased freedom of speech thus obtained. Has Mr. Sandburg by sacrifice of those qualities of verse which appeal to the ear, and in some measure to the eye, been enabled to say anything which could not have been said more beautifully, or more forcefully, by a keener use of symmetry? For the present critic the answer must, on the whole, be negative. In a general sense, Mr. Sandburg's material is the material of Frost, Masters, Gibson, Masefield: the dominant characteristic of all five men is the search for colour and pathos in the lives of the commonplace. Mr. Sandburg is less selective, that is all,—he spills in the chaff with the wheat. With much that is clear, hard, colourful, suggestive, there is much also that is muddy, extraneous, and dull. The other members of the realist school use the same material, but, being defter artists, use it better. What Mr. Sandburg

adds is the sociological element, which is the least valuable part of his book. Ethics and art cannot be married.

In this, I think, we get at the whole secret of Mr. Sandburg's weakness: he does not completely synthesize, or crystallize his poems. He always gives too much, goes too far. His poetic conception is not sufficiently sharp, and in consequence his speech cannot always be sufficiently symmetrical or intense to be called poetic speech. Clear thought brings clear expression, and the converse also is true, as Croce says. Something of the sort is true of the writing of poetry. The clearer, the more intense the emotion or idea, the more direct, forceful, beautiful, and rhythmic will be the expression of it. By a graded scale one passes from the more to the less intense, and that is the passage from poetry to prose. Examine carefully even the more rhythmic of Mr. Sandburg's poems, and you will almost invariably find, even in poems of four lines or less, that the poem can be improved by the omission of one or more lines, one or more ideas, which only cloud the mood. It is no use arguing that Mr. Sandburg deliberately adopts this cumulative and arhythmic method, as Whitman did, out of genuine belief that such a method is truer, or subtler, than any other. The fact is that in such cases the temperament comes first, the theory afterwards: we write in such and such a way because it is the only way in which we can write. If we can then persuade others that our way is best, so much the better—for us.

Classification is apt to seem more important than it really is. It has been many times said during the past few years that it does not so much matter whether a work be called poetry or prose, provided it be true, or beautiful. This study might be closed, then, by simply asking a question: is Mr. Sandburg a realistic poet, or a poetic realist? It is of no importance that the question be answered. It is only important, perhaps, that it shall have been asked. (pp. 143-48)

> *Conrad Aiken, "Poetic Realism: Carl Sandburg," in his* Scepticisms: Notes on Contemporary Poetry, *Alfred A. Knopf, 1919, pp. 143-48.*

Amy Lowell   (essay date 1920)

[*Lowell was a leading proponent of Imagism in American poetry. Like the French Symbolists before her, Lowell experimented with free verse forms and, influenced by Ezra Pound, developed a style characterized by clear and precise rhetoric, exact rendering of images, and metrical innovations. Although she was popular in her own time, current evaluations of Lowell accord her more importance as a promoter of new artistic ideas than as a poet in her own right. In the following excerpt, Lowell examines the ways in which Sandburg's socialistic political ideology is manifested in his poetry and questions whether Sandburg's future poetic reputation is dependent upon his willingness to temper the propagandistic elements of his verse.*]

Two men speak in Mr. Sandburg, a poet and a propagandist. His future will depend upon which finally dominates the other. Since a poet must speak by means of suggestion and a propagandist succeeds by virtue of clear presentation, in so far as a propagandist is a poet, just in that ratio is he a failure where his propaganda is concerned. On the other hand, the poet who leaves the proper sphere of his art to preach, even by analogy, must examine the mote in his verse very carefully lest, perchance, it turn out a beam.

In my study of Mr. Sandburg in *Tendencies in Modern American Poetry* I pointed out this danger of his practice. Then I had only one book to go upon, now I have three, [the latest being *Smoke and Steel*], and the danger seems to me to be looming larger with terrific speed. It may be that Mr. Sandburg has determined to stuff all his theories into one book and let it go at that. In which case there cannot be too much objection, but I fear—oh, I fear.

Mr. Sandburg loves people, perhaps I should say the "people." But I believe it is more than that. I think he has a real love for human beings. But evidently, from his books, his experience with people is limited to a few types, and it is a pity that these types should so often be the kind of persons whom only the morbidly sensitive, unhealthily developed, modern mind has ever thought it necessary to single out for prominence—prominence of an engulfing sort, that is. If we admit that the degraded are degraded there is not much danger of losing our perspective; if we hug them to our hearts and turn a cold shoulder to the sober and successful of the world, then we are running fast toward chaos. . . .

In *Cornhuskers* Mr. Sandburg seemed content to let the back alley folk stay in the back alleys. He spoke to us of other things, of the great, wide prairies, for instance, and, in so speaking, achieved a masterpiece. He gave his lyrical gift far more space than he usually allows, and the result was some of the finest poems of the modern movement. For Mr. Sandburg has a remarkable originality. His outlook is his own, his speech meets it, together the two make rarely beautiful poetry, when Mr. Sandburg permits. Then conscience pricks him, the "people" rise and confront him, gibbering like ghouls, he experiences an uneasy sense of betrayal and writes "Galoots" for example. I think these things hurt Mr. Sandburg as much as the things they represent hurt him. If they did not hurt him they would not have become an obsession. Much morbid verse has been written by tortured lovers, and we shall never understand these particular poems of Mr. Sandburg's until we realize that he too is a tortured lover, a lover of humanity in travail. It is seldom that the kind of exaggerated misery which Mr. Sandburg feels produces good poetry, and these poems are seldom successful.

I do not wish to imply that all the poems in [*Smoke and Steel*] are the results of the mood in question. That would be far from the case, but the proportion of such poems is too great for the thorough satisfaction of a reader who is a profound admirer of Mr. Sandburg at his best—and, shall I add, his most lyrical. The book is divided into eight sections, of which only two, "Mist Forms" and "Haze" are frankly lyrical, while another two, "People Who Must" and "Circle of Doors," are as frankly the other

thing, which, for want of a better name, we may call "the obsession." But this obsession creeps into many poems in the sections, "Playthings of the Wind" and "Passports"; even when "it," specifically, is not present, some crude and irrelevant turn of speech, the outgrowth of it, will crop up and ruin an otherwise noble thing. Colloquialisms, downright slang, have their place in poetry as in all literature. My contention here is not that Mr. Sandburg does not often use them with happy effect, but that quite as often he drags them in where (to my ear, at least) they should emphatically not be. A line like "We'll get you, you sbxyzch!" may be perfect realism, but it hurts the reader, as does "stenogs" and "thingamajig." The last appears in a poem in which it is at least in place if we admit the poem itself, "Manual System," to a place anywhere; but "stenogs" is smashed into a serious poem called "Trinity Peace," which is built around a highly poetic thought. "Stenographers" would not have been out of order, because it is a mere description of a calling, and in one stanza Mr. Sandburg is enumerating people by their callings; to shorten the word into "stenogs" brings in an element of cheapness, which in this instance has no dramatic value, and so rivets the attention as to break the force of the poem. One can skip such sheer propaganda as "Alley Rats," "The Mayor of Gary" and "The Liars," if one wants to, but it is hard to have something otherwise beautiful spoiled by a line or a word, which is hopelessly out of key. It dislocates the mood of appreciation, and is, I believe, the chief cause why the general reader does not yet entirely recognize how fine and true a poet Mr. Sandburg is.

Having registered my protest, which is the disagreeable part of the critic's work, let me immediately admit that one of Mr. Sandburg's excellencies is that he sets down the life about him, that very life of the people of which I have been speaking. When he sees it as a poet, he makes it poetically adequate; it is only when he sees it obliquely as a biased sentimentalist that he injures it and himself. He has an inclusive vision, something which gathers up the essences of life and work and relates them to the pulsing fabric which is the whole energy of human existence. His "Prairie" was not only a slice of Mother Earth, it was Mother Earth cherishing her children. So, in "Smoke and Steel," we have not a mere metal being manufactured, not mere men toiling at their work—we have man's impulse to spend himself in creation and the far ramifications of what that creation means. . . .

"Smoke and Steel" is worthy to stand beside "Prairie." There is an epic sweep to this side of Mr. Sandburg's work. Somehow it brings the reader into closer contact with his country, reading these poems gives me more of a patriotic emotion than ever "The Star-Spangled Banner" has been able to do. This is America, and Mr. Sandburg loves her so much that suddenly we realize how much we love her, too. What has become dulled by habit quickens under his really magical touch. Freight cars mean all the prosperity of the country; in the first stanza of "Work Gangs" they become a great chorus of men's hearts building a land to live in, to grow and make homes and happiness in. Because he can do this Mr. Sandburg has a glorious responsibility set on his shoulders.

The seeing eye—Mr. Sandburg has it to a superlative degree, and, wedded to it, an imaginative utterance which owes nothing whatever to literature or tradition. It is a fascinating and baffling study this of examining how Mr. Sandburg does it. The technique of this magic is so unusual that no old knowledge applies. It is, more than anything else, the sharp, surprising rightness of his descriptions which gives Mr. Sandburg his high position in the poetry of today. . . .

Some people have had difficulty in understanding Mr. Sandburg's rhythms, these long, slow cadences, like the breath of air over an open moor. Indeed they are the very gift of the prairies, for where else do we find them? Not in Whitman, not in the Frenchmen, not among his contemporaries. Mr. Sandburg's ear seldom fails, I can recall but one instance of a false notation. In **"How Yesterday Looked,"** occurs this stanza:

> Ask me how the sunset looked on
>   between the wind going
> Down and the moon coming up and
>   I would struggle
> To tell the how of it.

This may be a typographical error, for the beat of the cadence requires the first line to end after "looked on," the second line after "coming up," and the rest of the stanza to be contained in the third line. But, even here, the error occurs merely in the break of the lines and not in the cadence per se.

There is one thing we can say with Mr. Sandburg's three books in front of us. Either this is a very remarkable poet or he is nothing, for which the minors he clearly has no place. He has greatly dared, and I personally believe that posterity, with its pruning hand, will mount him high on the ladder of poetic achievement.

> *Amy Lowell, "Poetry and Propaganda," in*
> The New York Times Book Review, *October*
> *24, 1920, p. 7.*

The Times Literary Supplement   (essay date 1920)

[*The following excerpt represents the initial English response to Sandburg's* Smoke and Steel *and also notes the essential differences between European and American poetry of this time. The review was initially published on December 9, 1920, in the* Times Literary Supplement.]

American poets may be divided into those who stay in America and those who emigrate; a distinction which is equivalent to that applied to modern French poets by M. Georges Duhamel—acceptation or evasion of modern life. Mr. Carl Sandburg is one of those who have accepted Americanism. The book [*Smoke and Steel*] is the third large volume of poetry published by him since 1914. But his work is interesting apart from its bulk and worth some attention to its *milieu,* its tradition, its objects, and its achievements.

In considering realistic poetry like this the *milieu,* the kind of life from which it grows and which it purports to interpret, is of more importance than in other kinds of poetry. Since one of the primary claims of such poetry is that it is "true to life," true to its surroundings, we must know something about that life before we can judge if this object at least has been achieved. Now, the life which Mr. Carl Sandburg wishes to express is, generally speaking, the life of the Middle West, which is different from that of the aristocratic South, ruined in the Civil War, different again from the Puritan New England which found expression in Lowell, Emerson and Hawthorne, and yet again different from the life of the Coast. The distinguishing feature of the Middle West, to quote Mr. J. G. Fletcher is "its immense flatness and monotony"; its population, after achieving a gigantic piece of pioneering, is isolated in farms or concentrated in small provincial towns, in either case with an attitude towards life which renders it indifferent or hostile to the arts. Yet in this monotony of landscape there are great stretches of beauty; in this worship of material success there is a stirring of the ideal; and Mr. Sandburg is, as it were, a mouthpiece for this inarticulate idealism to make itself heard.

One of the best poems in his new book is a description of a Middle Western town, whose sins are "neither scarlet nor crimson" but "a convict gray, a dishwater drab." This town, the poet continues, is

> . . . a spot on the map
> And the passenger trains stop there
> And the factory smokestacks smoke
> And the grocery stores are open Saturday nights
> And the streets are free for citizens who vote
> And inhabitants counted in the census.
> Saturday night is the big night.

and then:—

> Main street there runs through the middle of the
>   town,
> And there is a dirty post office
> And a dirty city hall
> And a dirty railroad station . . .

Not an inspiring home for poetry, one feels. But Mr. Sandburg sends into it a "loafer," who says some harsh things of the town, and concludes:—

> . . . you ain't in a class by yourself,
> I seen you before in a lot of places.
> If you are nuts America is nuts.

To smile over that as quaint or amusing is to miss its significance. This criticism from Mr. Sandburg, who is on the whole too easy-going, too easily satisfied with mere activity, is as significant as Arnold's "By the Ilyssus there was no Wragg." It is a recognition of an essential spiritual truth: mere material prosperity is not enough. "To blaspheme wealth" needs courage in any modern community; it needs especial courage in an Anglo-Saxon country. But the significance of this is not that it comes from an exceptional and educated person—there are plenty such in the United States—but that Mr. Sandburg utters it as a feeling of the people.

No writer is without a literary tradition or literary influences of some sort, because no one writes without previously reading. The tradition of Mr. Sandburg is Whitman, journalism, and to a slighter extent modern *vers libre* poets, just as Whitman's tradition was journalism and prose translations of epic poetry. The value of a tradition is of course invaluable to the artist; at its best it is a sure foundation to build on, at its worst something to rebel against. We Europeans have an immense, an august tradition; even as Englishmen we have a considerable tradition. And since most Americans speak English and are descended from Europeans they also inherit our tradition. But, following Whitman, many American poets choose deliberately to ignore it, to forfeit its great benefits. Why? Whitman has explained his views in his prose works, but we do not need to go to them for an answer. These American poets desire their writings to possess above everything the qualities of vitality, novelty, and Americanism. Above all they wish to produce work which is emphatically American. They argue, like Whitman, that they are not "out" to follow any tradition, however great and splendid, but to create one, the tradition of America. They have therefore a distrust, almost a hatred, of the past and the beauty it created.

Always that irritation with the past, that opposition of the live dog to the dead lion, that flattery of a living mediocrity. But there is the essence of Mr. Sandburg's writing: vitality, novelty, Americanism, at all costs. What does it matter (he seems to say) that the Parthenon is the supreme expression of a supreme wisdom, that Shakespeare is the supreme poet of tragedy and comedy, that anything supremely excellent and beautiful has been created *by the past?* The Parthenon is a ruin; Shakespeare is dust; excellence and beauty—what are they? Cowley said that there was no need to sing new songs but to say the old. These American poets would violently disagree. They are convinced that life, modern life, the "now" alone are important, that vitality, energy, truth to modern life, to the outward phenomena of modern life, are all that is asked of the poet.

How far have they succeeded in this? Have they achieved novelty, vitality and truth to life? In the case of Mr. Sandburg the answer is that to a great extent he has. He has introduced themes which have seldom, perhaps never, been treated before. There is an impressive display of energy in **Smoke and Steel.** His poems are true to a certain kind of life, they are undoubtedly American. They do succeed, then, in doing what they set out to do, but whether this in itself constitutes a high and right art is another question. Yet we ought to be sympathetic, as open-minded as possible to this kind of writing, remembering that one danger to poetry is always that it may become too bookish, preoccupied with formalities and dignities, and too little stirred by the rough energies of life. Mr. Yeats has said that modern poetry has two ways before it, one of increasing refinement and one "among the market carts." Mr. Sandburg has chosen the way "among the market carts," and we are wrong if we refuse to accept what he has to give us. Yet, though European criticism must recognize these experiments and strive to understand them, European poetry may well reject them. . . .

A review of "Smoke and Steel: The Poetry of Carl Sandburg," in The Times Literary Supplement, *No. 2746, September 17, 1954, p. 77.*

Stuart P. Sherman   (essay date 1922)

[*For many years Sherman was considered one of America's most conservative literary critics. During the early twentieth century he was influenced by the New Humanism, a critical movement which subscribed to the belief that the aesthetic quality of any literary work must be subordinate to its support of traditional moral values. During the ten years he served as a literary critic at the* Nation, *Sherman established himself as a champion of the Anglo-Saxon, genteel tradition in American letters and a bitter enemy of Naturalism and its proponents. In the 1920s Sherman became the editor of the* New York Herald Tribune *book review section, a move that coincided with the liberalization of his staunch critical tastes. In the following excerpt, Sherman deprecates Sandburg's failure to individualize his working class people and themes and his tendency to produce poems that were disconcertingly obscure.*]

Many of the things which Carl Sandburg relishes I relish: the jingle of the "American language" in the making; the Great Lakes, prairies, mountains, and the diurnal and seasonal scene-shifting of the elements; all kinds of workmen with their tools in city and country, and the "feel" of an axe or shovel in my own hands; the thunder of overland trains and the cross-fire of banter in a barber shop; eating ham-and-eggs with a Chinese chemist at a wayside lunch-counter at four o'clock in the morning. . . . (p. 239)

All these things I relish and am familiar with; and yet, as I study my fourth volume of Mr. Sandburg's poems, [*Slabs of the Sunburnt West*], I wonder why Mr. Untermeyer and the other fugelmen of the "movement" congratulate the public on the ease with which they may read and enjoy poetry, now that classical allusions and the traditional poetic diction have been banished. It is a sham and a delusion. Mr. Sandburg is not easy to read. He is as difficult in his own fashion as John Donne or Browning. If any of the men in my common smoker should glance over my shoulder at the pages before me, they would see abundance of familiar words: "taxi-drivers," "window-washers," "booze-runners," "hat-cleaners," "delicatessen clerks." Perhaps also "shovel-stiffs," "work-plugs," "hoosegow," and "exhausted eggheads" would be familiar to them. But I think they would gasp and stare at "sneaking scar-faced Nemesis," "miasmic" women, and "macabre" moons. I think they would meditate a long while before they felt any emotion whatever in the presence of such word patterns as:

> Pearl memories in the mist circling the horizon,
> Flick me, sting me, hold me even and smooth.

And I believe they might read the long title-poem, **"Slabs of the Sunburnt West,"** twenty times without suspecting for a moment that it is a meditation on God, civilization, and immortality, conceived on the brink of the Grand Canyon of the Colorado.

Now, the considerable obscurity in Mr. Sandburg's work may be accounted for in two ways.

In the first place, his literary allegiance is mixed. When in his interesting poem on **"The Windy City"** he begins a lucid paragraph thus: "Mention proud things, catalogue them"—he is writing under the formative influence of Whitman; and both his language and his emotion are straightforward and sincere. But in **"Fins,"** for example, and in **"Pearl Horizons,"** where he asks the "pearl memories" to flick him and hold him even and smooth, he is writing under the deformative influence of the most artificial phase of Imagism; and both his language and his emotion are tortured and insincere.

In the second place, Mr. Sandburg thinks that he is really sympathetic with the "working classes" and with the unloved and not altogether lovely portion of humanity which Mr. Masefield has sung as "the scum of the earth"; and he imagines that he is pretty much out of sympathy with "the great ones of the earth" and with all those who speak complacently of "the established order." Robert Burns sympathized with the Scotch peasant and wrote of him and for him, incidentally pleasing the rest of mankind. The late James Whitcomb Riley sympathized with the farmer's boy and wrote of him and for him; and as there were a great many farmers' boys in the land, he pleased a wide audience. But Mr. Sandburg, who sympathizes with the taxi-drivers and delicatessen clerks, does not write for them; he writes for the literary smart set, for the readers of *The Freeman, The Liberator, The Dial, Vanity Fair,* etc.

As a consequence of his confronting this audience, Mr. Sandburg appears to me to lack somewhat the courage of his sympathies. He seldom individualizes his working-man; almost never does the imaginative work of penetrating the consciousness of any definite individual and telling his story coherently with the concrete emotion belonging to it. Instead, he presents a rather vague lyrical sense of the surge of but slightly differentiated "masses"; he gives, as the newspaper does, a collection of accidents to undifferentiated children; he is the voice of the abstract city rather than of the citizen. He chants of dreams, violences, toils, cruelties, and despairs. In his long poem, **"And So To-day,"** commemorating the burial of the Unknown Soldier, he finds, however, an appointed theme; he is in the presence of an almost abstract fate, which he renders piteously concrete by a curious parody of Whitman's threnody on Lincoln in a language of vulgar brutality—a language reflecting, it is to be supposed, the vulgarity and brutality of the civilization for which the Unknown Soldier died, as Mr. Sandburg bitterly suggests, in vain. In the short ironical piece, **"At the Gate of the Tombs,"** adopting once more the most biting lingo of the mob, he expresses powerfully the attitude, let us say, of *The New Republic* towards the government's treatment of political prisoners and conscientious objectors—"gag 'em, lock 'em up, get 'em bumped off."

Radical journals, like *The Nation* and *The New Republic,* radical journalists like Mr. Upton Sinclair, and radical poets like Mr. Sandburg, create for themselves purely artistic problems of very great difficulty, of which they do not always find triumphant solutions. . . . When Mr. Sandburg, in his poem, **"And So To-day,"** presents the official pageant of mourning for the Unknown Soldier as a farcical mummery; the President, the commanding officers, the "honorable orators, buttoning their prinz alberts," as empty puppets; and the people from sea to sea

as stopping for a moment in their business—"with a silence of eggs laid in a row on a pantry shelf"—when Mr. Sandburg presents a great symbolic act of the nation as vacuous and meaningless, he creates for himself the pretty problem of showing where the meaning of the nation lies: till he has shown that, and with at least equal earnestness and power, he is in danger. He is in grave danger of leaving his readers with a sense either that his conception of the nation is illusory or that both he and they inhabit a world of illusions—a world of dreams, violences, toils, cruelties, and despairs, in which nothing really matters, after all. (pp. 240-44)

Stuart P. Sherman, "A Note on Carl Sandburg," in his Americans, *Charles Scribner's Sons, 1922, pp. 239-45.*

Harry Hansen   (essay date 1923)

[*An American critic and editor, Hansen served as a foreign correspondent, and later literary editor, for the Chicago* Daily News *when the city was the center of intense literary activity. During his career Hansen wrote critical commentary for* Harper's Magazine, *introductions and special chapters for numerous books, and authored such works as* Midwest Portraits: A Book of Memories and Friendships *(1923) and* Carl Sandburg: The Man and his Poetry *(1924). In the following excerpt taken from* Midwest Portraits, *Hansen examines the social and lyrical moods recurrent in Sandburg's verse.*]

[There are] two moods that are ever recurrent in Sandburg; the social and the lyrical; the note of protest, of indignation, of grief at the oppressive conditions under which the humbler brethren of this earth live, and the note of exultation that has as its basis love of life, love of laughter, love of beautiful, fantastic and colorful pictures in nature. In his own cadence Sandburg portrays moods, feelings, surface impressions. Sometimes it is the wisp of smoke on the sky that engages his fancy; sometimes it is the great sweep of the virginal prairie; sometimes it is a face that awakens thoughts of laughter that has died down, of an ecstasy that has been crushed by human woes. In taking his work progressively we find first a strong emphasis upon the social note, a desire to place before the eyes of the smug, respectable, sluggish middle-class tradesman and the sleek, swaggering "millionaire" a conception of the drudgery, the pain and the suffering of the under dog in society. With a defiant air he thrusts the picture forward. This in ***Chicago Poems.*** Then strong emphasis upon the pictorial, unrelated to social significance, as in **"Prairie,"** the first poem in ***Cornhuskers,*** his second book, in which the fine exultation of a man in what he sees of his own homeland carries him away into ecstatic renderings of its pictorial values. If there is any social significance at all in his thoughts it is in the inter-relation of historic events, in the feeling of a historical sequence, of a progression, that comes over him when he contemplates first the prairie of the frontier days and now the prairie of the Pioneer Limited. Then ***Smoke and Steel***—again a heavy emphasis upon the pictorial and the lyrical, for the title poem, which men might look to as a social document, proves to have very little in it about oppressed humans who work at the great steel ingots; rather is it a hymn to human achievement, in which all, big and little, high and low, have a part; yes, truly he writes: "In the blood of men and the ink of chimneys, the smoke nights write their oaths," but it is only an observation that comes to the poet as he considers the "curves of fire, the rough scarf women dancing, dancing out of the flues and smoke-stacks— flying hair of fire, flying feet upside down." No bitterness marks the poems, only a note of resignation: "Finders in the dark, you Steve with a dinner bucket . . . wondering where we all end up; Finders in the dark, Steve— I hook my arm in cinder sleeves; we go down the street together; it is all the same to us; you Steve and the rest of us end on the same stars; we all wear a hat in hell together, in hell or heaven. . . ." True, there are social poems in *Smoke and Steel,* but already we find Sandburg moving toward general themes, rather than particularizing one instance. And when we come to *Slabs of the Sunburnt West* we realize how far he has moved from his first moods in *Chicago Poems*—his tone is less bitter, though no less effective; he aims at a general picture, rather than at the pointed portrayal of one or two specific incidents; and although he is still eloquent in the portrayal of a single tragic episode, as in **"Ambassadors of Grief,"** he is dealing for the most part with bigger themes, themes of national significance in **"And So Today,"** philosophies and experiences of a whole city in **"The Windy City,"** and of a whole continent in **"Slabs of the Sunburnt West."** It is a mellowing Sandburg, contemplating the mass rather than the individual, flinging out his arms and finding room therein for all humankind.

His first mood was a vital one, it brought him his name as a fighter, as a propagandist. How deeply he felt, how thoroughly he lived, the hurts that came to humbler men—how defiantly he hurled these gloomy, depressing facts out of the heart of life at the heads of our "best people." No wonder they declared his themes were not of the stuff of poetry; no wonder they stressed his uncouth manner, his uneven lines, his plain words, not yet accepted in the first circles. He was a rebel, a nonconformist, a man using the sacred cows of poetry and yoking them to the lumbering wagon of the barnyard. That he was forceful they were willing to admit; courageous, too, but alas, they made lament, his were not the graceful pirouettings, the cadenced steps of the minuet—how attune his blaring songs to the melodies of the poetic muse? And yet he wrote on.

Chicago Poems is close to earth; there is in it the tang of the soil; you rub elbows with the fish crier, the hunky, the shovel man, the dago, the factory girl, the cash girl; the ice handler, the gang on Halsted Street, "the worn wayfaring men":

> That pigsticker in one corner—his mouth—
> that overall factory girl—her loose cheeks . . .

He sees "tired empty faces, tired of wishes, empty of dreams"; he hears on Clark Street bridge "voices of dollars and a drop of blood." He becomes ironical when he contemplates:

> Tomb of a millionaire,
> A multimillionaire, ladies and gentlemen,

Place of the dead where they spend every year
The usury of twenty-five thousand dollars
For upkeep and flowers. . . .

And then by simple contrast he paints the woes of the oppressed: "A hundred cash girls want nickels to go to the movies. . . ." Similarly he is affected adversely by the contemplation of a fine stone house on the lake front, around which workmen are erecting an iron fence with cruel palings, but he concludes, not regretfully; "Passing through the bars and over the steel points will go nothing except Death and the Rain and To-morrow." He tells how "I drank musty ale at the Illinois Athletic club with the millionaire manufacturer of Green River butter one night. . . ." All of these he uses for contrast. He has a contempt for the misuse of wealth and the millionaire of his poems represents that misuse, that abuse of the poor. He is calm, defiant, contemptuous; but he is never vindictive, nor is there in his philosophy any hint of violence. He is in love with the poor, as when he wrote later on: "And then one day I got a look at the poor, millions of the poor, patient and toiling, more patient than crags, tides, stars; innumerable, patient as the darkness of night. And all broken humble ruins of nations."

Contrasted with this is Sandburg's love for plain things, his glorification of humble occupations. Most notable is the widely quoted example of the fish crier on Maxwell street. "His face is that of a man terribly glad to be selling fish; terribly glad that God made fish." The picture of a group of Hungarians out with their wives and children and beer and an accordian he labels: **"Happiness."** He contemplates the "muckers wiping sweat off their faces with red bandanas" with something of approval and satisfaction. The dago shovel man is a "child of the Romans." He is proud of Jack London and O. Henry because "both were jailbirds; no speechmakers at all . . . who knew the hearts of these booze-fighters?" **"Work Gangs"** have to him a matured philosophy; it runs like this: "A long way we come; a long way to go; long rests and long deep sniffs for our lungs on the way. Sleep is a belonging of all. . . ." And many more.

Best of all he develops a fine irony; he contemplates the foibles of mankind with an appraising eye; he observes incongruities, injustices, oppressions. Has any one surpassed the forcefulness of **"Man, the Man-Hunter"?** with its terrible dénouement:

> In the morning the sun saw
> Two butts of something, a smoking rump
> And a warning in charred wood:
>
> > Well, we got him
> > the sbxyzch.

In that mood he has done any number of poems that depend for their power on contrast. There is **"The Mayor of Gary"** who wore "cool, cream pants and white shoes" pitted against the workmen with leather shoes scruffed with fire and cinders. There is **"The Sins of Kalamazoo,"** an indictment of the small town, a "Main Street" of poetry. There is that powerful little poem entitled **"Knucks"** which relies for its interest on the fact that he finds brass knuckles for sale in a store in "the city of Abraham Lincoln." In his irony he is forceful and direct, but rarely subtle. In only one or two instances does he achieve that bit of sardonic laughter that we can imagine comes from a man contemplating a joke played on him by fate. One of the best instances of it is **"Three Ghosts."** It might be a miniature ballad; it tells that "Three tailors of Tooley street wrote: We the People. The names are forgotten. It is a joke in ghosts." He goes on to tell how they sat cross-legged, working for wages, meeting after work to drink their beer to "the people." They are forgotten. It is a joke in ghosts. They wrote: "We the People." Laughter—the low, ironic laughter of the man who views life as a burlesque, a horrible joke on the frail idealists, runs between the lines.

In his love lyrics, in his sentimental moods, Sandburg reaches the heights. For he is never maudlin, never unbridled, even at his most ecstatic moments. Take the poems about the children—and they run through most of his books—and you will observe a quiet satisfaction, a peace and happiness in the lines that are dedicated to the doings of little folk. When he comes to write the simple love lyrics of which he is capable he dreams in homely metaphor and simile, never in fantastic, outlandish embroidery. He is always of the soil. **"Home Thoughts"** is a lyric of exquisite beauty because of its simple imagery:

> Speak to me of the drag on your heart
> The iron drag of the long days.
> I know hours empty as a beggar's tin cup on
>   a rainy day, empty as a soldier's sleeve
>   with an arm lost
>
> Speak to me . . .

His poems of the streets, his emphatic pounding with hard words, have become so characteristic of him that many persons know no other side of him; when they think of Sandburg they picture the Sandburg of the "hog butcher of the world" forgetting that in him live fantasy and whimsicality, lyricism and lyrical beauty. His delicate images may be found in every book. (pp. 65-71)

> *Harry Hansen, "Carl Sandburg, Poet of the Streets and of the Prairie," in his* Midwest Portraits: A Book of Memories and Friendships, *Harcourt Brace Jovanovich, 1923, pp. 15-92.*

Gorham B. Munson   (essay date 1924)

[*Munson, an American editor, critic, and professor of English, wrote numerous critical studies, including* Destinations: A Canvass of American Literature *(1928) and* New Directions in Prose and Poetry *(1936). In the following excerpt, Munson castigates Sandburg for writing what he calls "a large and undeniable amount of dross," reserving praise only for Sandburg's poem "Slabs of the Sunburnt West."*]

Sandburg is still highly esteemed, but one meets an increasing number of readers who once liked his poetry and now remark that "it does not seem to last." Re-reading his four books of verse, I am convinced that the original enthusiasm for them was somewhat uncritical. In them was

a new idiom, not too difficult for easy comprehension, traceable to Whitman, whose prestige lent Sandburg's admirers courage, yet simpler, less volumned than Whitman, and voicing the emotionalism of revolt so current in the last decade. (p. 17)

The former admirer of Sandburg, who says that his poetry does not seem to last, has doubtless discovered that Sandburg has written a large and undeniable amount of dross. Take such a poem as **"Street Window"** from *Cornhuskers.*

> The pawn-shop man knows hunger,
> And how far hunger has eaten the heart
> Of one who comes with an old keepsake.
> Here are wedding rings and baby bracelets,
> Scarf pins and shoe buckles, jeweled garters,
> Old-fashioned knives with inlaid handles,
> Watches of old gold and silver,
> Old coins worn with finger marks.
> They tell stories

Now every sensitive person has at some time paused in front of a pawn-shop, noted with curiosity and sorrow the surrendered trinkets and articles, speculated on the stories which would account for their presence here, surmised that the dealer knows hunger and many other sad and dispairful things, and shaken his head. The subject matter of this poem is parcel of our common personal experience, and the objection to the poem is that Sandburg has done no more with personal experience of his than we have done with ours. He has not distinguished it from others by a rhythmic or metaphorical achievement, he has not driven his emotion further nor defined it more sharply than anyone else. It is slack and immediate expression.

The trouble is that Sandburg has little faculty for converting or combining his personal emotions into art emotions. Esthetic delight, curiosity, arises from contrasted sources. It may be given by the definition which comes from the acute and accurate perception of an emotion or a related series of emotions and denotes both the essence and the strict boundaries of the emotions. This is an estheticism of shape and arrangement. It is generally called classicism. Or esthetic pleasure may be given by a revelation of unexpected proportions. In this case, the emotion is used as an instrument of knowledge, it is followed through to some passionate apprehension of the significance of life. It gives place, in fact, to some intuitive combustion, a state of ecstasy. This is an estheticism of lyrical evocation or, better, of expansiveness. Romanticism. Carl Sandburg is perhaps too much the poet of the newspaper occasion to take the time for this chemistry of the art emotions. His failure so to do produces on me not "the cumulative effect of vigor" Conrad Aiken felt [see excerpt dated 1919], but a cumulative effect of weakness, a lack of tension, a sense of impurities not burned out. (pp. 17-18)

The technic of Carl Sandburg has improved from book to book. His idiom, in reality, lies in the shadowy region between what is clearly prose and what is clearly poetry. The ictus is not very pronounced, nor do his lines carry enough verbal energy for poetry. On the other hand, the diction is too monotonous and unvaried for prose. The chief claim to be poetry rests on the use of repetition and of echoes woven in and out of the loose pattern. In metaphor he is at times highly successful. . . .

> the pearl-gray haystacks
> in the gloaming
> are cool prayers
> to the harvest hands.

In the way of structure, balance and symmetry he attempts hardly anything. His longer poems—and Sandburg needs space to get his effects—are generally a series of loose associations hung together by repetitive chants. He is, of course, more complex than the anonymous authors of Cotton Belt songs, but, compared to the full organ-toned movements of Whitman, he is single-voiced.

The vocabulary is partly drawn from the American argot on its way perhaps to being the American language. This matter is again a side-issue which might lead us into a long essay, partly philological and partly literary, on the use of Americanisms. Suffice it to raise the question whether Sandburg has made a sufficiently *literary* use of our argot. To me he often uses it with the inexactitude of the man on the street, and on the whole he is less alert to the verb-activity of our vulgar speech than E. E. Cummings is. (p. 19)

The indigenous nature of Sandburg's work pricks our interest, but it is obviously not enough. In our delight at getting a few indigenous writers, we have forgotten briefly that what we need are indigenous artists. Otherwise, we are greeting merely local and contemporary precursors of an emergent culture.

And what of the personality which flavors this work? No one claims intellectual subtlety or depth for Carl Sandburg, but it is justly said that he has a sense of irony. That needs to be qualified by saying that his perception of discrepancies is rudimentary and almost purely on the surface. (p. 20)

More arresting is the theatrical contrast in values between Sandburg and the crude acquisitive welter of Chicago, "Hog Butcher for the World." Sandburg is tender, sympathetic, loving, wayward in his contemplation of flowers and sunsets, yearnful for peace, quiet and sleep. To the impulses of a burly capitalism he opposes the impulses, sometimes sentimentalized, of humanitarianism. But his desire for drowsiness is so often frustrated and interrupted that he rises in anger and snarls. Indeed, his protests against war, against the impinging brutalities of capitalism, the sterility of greed, seem to arise, not so much from a man who loves a more free, active and gracious life of the spirit than these permit, but from a man whose simple dreamy life has been rudely disturbed. Unfortunately, at those moments Sandburg is likely to assume the image of the brute strength he hates.

The vague charge of social propaganda has been aimed at Sandburg, principally in connection with his earlier work, by people who did not like his humanitarian emotions. But propaganda is a rational activity designed to win adherents to one's intellectual or emotional convictions. It is special pleading which may be conducted honestly or with chicanery. However, a poet is entitled to present his own genuine emotions, even though the appearance of rebel-lious feeling may alarm what is customarily referred to as "fat and prosperous gentry." The rationalizing faculty is singularly absent from Sandburg's make-up. What was mistaken for social propaganda was really a failure in the expression of his emotion due to an unclear perception of them or to an insufficient technic to externalize them. The result was not special pleading but sentimentality.

Conrad Aiken closed a paper on Sandburg by asking whether his work is poetic realism or realistic poetry. This question, he said, it is not important to answer; it is only important that it be asked. Aiken showed too great a passion for labels; a writer *does* certain things and it is the critic's business to say just what he does; poetry and realism are highly disputable terms. Sandburg has achieved no general synthesis for himself. A loose temperament and a loose workman, he slips away as soon as the tentacles of any particular label stretch out to grasp him. A realist is a man of imagination. That is, he discovers in the phenomena which relate to him proportions and harmonies so just that, as Poe remarked, the reader exclaims at the obviousness of them, "why was this not seen before?" Inevitability is the test. But Sandburg is more often fanciful than imaginative. He is moderately unexpected and very arbitrary. His metaphors seldom impress one as being the unique metaphorical truth of the object. (pp. 20-1)

To label the quality of Sandburg's work as a whole is impossible beyond saying, as I did at the outset, that it is slack and immediate expression. Undistilled impressions, fancies, angers, desires and sympathies. *Voila tout!* His better poems are, of course, not accidents, but neither are they consciously achieved. It is likely enough that the bulk of his writing will sift away as the clouds over the prairies disappear every few hours. Some fifteen or twenty poems, most of which the anthologists have already netted, may linger. How long depends on other circumstances than esthetic. (p. 21)

It is not pleasant for a patriot to pare down the sort of reputation Carl Sandburg has acquired, and I am, therefore, glad to dwell at last on the one quality which seems to me rare and important, and upon the one poem, **"Slabs of the Sunburnt West"** (titular monstrosity), which presents that quality as flaming rather than smouldering. I refer to Sandburg's mysticism. (p. 22)

The rarity of a genuine mysticism in American writing needs no argument. The importance of its appearance may be briefly indicated. Positivism is in disrepute. The modern era has witnessed an enormous growth in nescience. Skepticism has overthrown or questioned the fundamental assumptions and conventions upon which our inherited culture has rested, such as the supremacy of reason and the tri-dimensionality of the universe. . . .

What is mysticism? It is first the belief, gained intuitively or rationally, that the Kantian formulation of the utter impossibility of knowing a thing in itself is not an impassable frontier, but a problem. It is the belief that this problem can be solved if more of the resources of human consciousness are applied to it, the belief that human consciousness has a power of expansion it is not generally credited with possessing. (p. 23)

Mysticism differs from classical thought by denying the perdurable validity of those conventions and necessities which classicism sees in the external world. It is more akin to religion which is simply a serious attitude toward life and a resolute search for a way of living in accord with one's deepest experience. . . . What mysticism seeks is a higher logic, a logic of intuition and ecstasy; in one word, it seeks simply knowledge. Perhaps it may be termed a higher romanticism, and it may, in its turn, become a new classicism. For its drive is toward an organization of new conventions and assumptions.

It is natural, then, that the mystic should brood much on the nature of time. Sandburg's preoccupation with time is noticeable throughout his work. He sees it as motion, the past disappearing, the present existent for a moment, the future coming on, all things being washed over by time. This is not the mystic's view of time as an imperfectly sensed dimension, on which what we call past, present and future lie side by side. . . . The point is that Sandburg has continually fumbled over the nature of time. And and the next point is that his work is underlaid by a fumbling smouldering sentimental mysticism. I call that mystic sentimental who is content with a feeling of wonder at things and makes no effort to discover causes for his wonderment. In the absence of such discovery, his emotion gushes and runs away. It is, in appearance at least, excessive. This type of sentimental mysticism is particularly prevalent in Scandinavian writings. But in **"Slabs of the Sunburnt West"** the smoulder leaps into a conflagration. It is regrettable that the fire did not quite burn out all the dross. The poem is still somewhat inchoate. And I would not have the reader think that I am introducing it as a document of the high mystical order of Blake or Whitman; my preamble was designed to clear away misconceptions infesting the term, mysticism. (pp. 23-4)

Whether or not Sandburg will use the experience presented in *Slabs of the Sunburnt West* as a basis for his future poetic vision is an open question. To develop it will require a greater cohesiveness, a greater intensity, a greater daring than the rest of his writing displays. Will he undergo the great effort? Perhaps he is destined to be remembered as an author of delightful children's stories, who wrote a remarkable poem entitled **"Slabs of the Sunburnt West."** (p. 26)

> *Gorham B. Munson, "The Single Portent of Carl Sandburg," in* The Double Dealer, *Vol. 7, No. 39, October, 1924, pp. 17-26.*

Carl Van Doren   (essay date 1924)

[*Van Doren is considered one of the most perceptive critics of the first half of the twentieth century. He worked for many years as a professor of English at Columbia University and served as a literary editor and critic of the* Nation *and the* Century *during the 1920s. A founder of the Literary Guild and author or editor of several American literary histories, Van Doren was also a critically acclaimed historian and biographer. In the following excerpt, Van Doren discusses Sandburg's immigrant background and how this effected the style and subject manner of his verse. While admonishing Sandburg for inef-*

fective wording, Van Doren also praises a number of Sandburg's poems as "objects of a strangely authentic beauty and tenderness."]

The older stocks of the United States have in their imaginations one picture of the country and its inhabitants; the newer stocks have another. In the first there is the persistent image of the pioneer advancing from the seaboard, by forest trail and waterway, across rich prairie and naked plain, contending mightily, romantically, victoriously with aboriginal men and beasts, in the end settling peacefully down in farm, village, or thriving city to enjoy the Canaan he has thus won for himself and his children's children. . . . If there are hardships, they are relatively brief, yielding to enterprise and thrift in a decade or two at most. If there are ugly aspects, they are largely unpreventable, like frontier violence or ignorance, and they yield to solid contentment and popular enlightenment. Ultimately these stocks inherit the earth, in the picture, though increasingly their descendants look with irritation and some anger upon the later stocks who are arriving among them and beside them. The new-comers, beginning anew the old process, have other images for it. Their pioneer is set down in shop or mill or mine, herded with others of his race in a slum, exploited at every turn by the lucky older stocks, forced to carry the double burden of making his way in a hostile world and of remaking himself into the pattern of man which that world requires. He breathes air which is black with smoke or smutted with the grime of cities. He finds no welcoming land for his house or garden. Wherever he turns, others have been there before him and erected obstacles more difficult or at least more complicated than the first settlers had to level in their war with stubborn nature. He has not been long enough on the continent to cherish that epic sense of the American past which even the dullest members of the older stocks have picked up in some degree or other from the little history they know; he is sustained, instead, by that sense of a radiant American future which helped draw him from his native soil. He rarely has the easy humor which has arisen in part from the free and open lives of the older stocks; he has, instead, the darker irony which springs from his discovery of the contrast between the vision which drew him hither and the facts which awaited him. By his hopefulness he is made more naïve, by his irony more sophisticated than the average older American.

Carl Sandburg, a genius, not an average man, speaks out of the sentiments of the new order of Americans. The son of a Swedish immigrant, he himself in his youth belonged to the ranks of unskilled labor, drifting about the Middle West at odd jobs and into a volunteer company as a private during the war with Spain. His subsequent career in college and in journalism but gave him words for emotions which had been beating within him in his inarticulate years. He too, like the typical immigrant pioneer, flames with the future, though in Mr. Sandburg the flame leaps higher than it has done in any other poet of his order. With what fervor, in **"Prayers of Steel,"** he voices the aspiration not only of steel but of men to give themselves to a great cause:

> Lay me on an anvil, O God.

Beat me and hammer me into a crowbar.
Let me pry loose old walls.
Let me lift and loosen old foundations.
Lay me on an anvil, O God.
Beat me and hammer me into a steel spike.
Drive me into the girders that hold a skyscraper
  together.
Take red-hot rivets and fasten me into the cen-
  tral girders.
Let me be the great nail holding a skyscraper
  through blue nights into white stars.

A poet of the older order might have put some such prayer into the mouth of a plow or of an ax or of a tree or of a stone, eager each of them to be used at no matter what cost to themselves; for a poet of the new order steel has taken the place of these things among the images of ardor and devotion. The immigrants—how many of them!—live by steel, within sight of it melting in furnaces, within sound of it clanging into place in structures that crowd the earth and shut out the sun. They have found that steel, long symbol for a warrior, may be symbol as well for a martyr or a saint.

Yet Mr. Sandburg, thus close to the world of steel and smoke around him, is not buried in it, but sees it under the

Sandburg shortly after leaving Lombard College.

long light of irony, as in the poem which he slyly calls **"Limited"**:

I am riding on a limited express, one of the crack
  trains of the nation.
Hurtling across the prairie into blue haze and
  dark air go fifteen all-steel coaches holding a
  thousand people.
(All the coaches shall be scrap and rust and all
  the men and women laughing in the diners
  and sleepers shall pass to ashes.)
I ask a man in the smoker where he is going and
  he answers: 'Omaha.'

With infinite destiny ahead of him, the man in the smoker, the poet learns, sees no further than one undistinguished town. The artist in Mr. Sandburg, thus viewing the life of an industrial society around him, employs it passionately for his art; the thinker, no less than in any simpler age, understands that the things which seem most solid among the works of man will flow into other forms, as clouds and mountains do, and that nothing holds the long span of human time together but the flexible links of change running through the generations.

From this irony, mated with this rapture, springs the tenderness which barely misses being Mr. Sandburg's most distinctive trait. He writes exquisitely of children, in the brooding, reverent, whimsical tone of a father speaking to his little daughters, touched by the coolness in them, aware of the fire there, thinking how soon both shall do their work and go. . . .

He [also] writes tenderly of old people remembering, of fragile souls driven into paths too steep for them, of the hulks of broken men, of the pity that lies near the heart of friendship and love, near the sense of beauty, near the willingness to forgive life for being no better than it is because it is as good as it is. Among all the recent American poets, Mr. Sandburg speaks most naturally with the accents of pity.

Pity, indeed, carries him now and then to the point of bathos, as in that often cited line in **Chicago Poems** in which he makes Truth boast:

I dabble in the blood and guts of the terrible.

Or, rather, pity for many things ordinarily unconsidered or trodden under foot carries his sympathy to a point beyond the reach of his imagination, so that, as Whitman did before him, he runs into long lists of objects which he declares are beautiful or moving, but which, if they are so to him, are so to him only, for the reason that he has not an imaginative power over them sufficient to bring them into any universal language. To go back now, however, after seven years to Mr. Sandburg's first book of verse is to observe how much which seemed unassimilated then in his poetry now seems to fit into the general pattern, as it fits into the pattern of the poetic idiom of the century. Not for many years can Chicago occur to the mind of any reader of poetry without some reminiscence, direct or indirect, of the loud words with which its chief poet has saluted or characterized it:

Hog Butcher for the World,
Tool Maker, Stacker of Wheat,

Player with Railroads and the Nation's Freight
   Handler;
Stormy, husky, brawling,
City of the Big Shoulders: . . .
Come and show me another city with lifted head
   singing so proud to be alive and coarse and
   strong and cunning.
Flinging magnetic curses amid the toil of piling
   job on job, here is a tall bold slugger set vivid
   against the little soft cities; . . .
Laughing even as an ignorant fighter laughs who
   has never lost a battle,
Bragging and laughing that under his wrist is the
   pulse, and under his ribs the heart of the people,
            Laughing!

                         (pp. 136-43)

Chicago, the windy, insolent city, was of all themes the
one most likely to excite this poet whom it has helped to
shape. He found in it a spectacle grandiose enough for his
taste, yet not enough in the grand style, since it lacks the
traditional and the ceremonial, to amuse the satirist in
him. He found, as he goes on finding, the city enormous,
unformed, moving in a direction not yet determined, but
obviously started on a long road with momentum sufficient to take it almost any distance. . . . Here common
men and common women and common children swirl as
in Mr. Sandburg's vision of life, modestly attending to
their business, robustly elbowing their way to their desires.
What for another poet might be distasteful in the noise
and disorder of Chicago is for Mr. Sandburg inspiriting,
because it seems to him the symptom of power and freedom. For power and freedom to him are most impressive
in their shirt-sleeves. He is not stirred by the king or the
bishop on his throne, by the premier or the capitalist at
his desk, by the general or the admiral at the head of disciplined forces; these men to him are but pictures of power,
not power itself, because they merely guide, and that at
second hand, concerted energies which have already lost
their prime vigor in the process of being regimented. His
imagination insists on turning to the raw materials of existence, on being lifted by the sight of human elements not
yet civilized. Such materials and elements he has found in
unmatched bulk in his stormy, husky, brawling city.

Mr. Sandburg's language ranges freely from the fine, pure
speech of his too few lyrics to the boisterous vernacular
with which he plays on the trombone and the horse fiddle.
He can write as hauntingly as in these lines from *Cornhuskers:*

   Bees and a honeycomb in the dried head of a
     horse in a pasture corner—a skull in the tall
     grass and a buzz and a buzz of the yellow
     honey-hunters.
   And I ask no better a winding sheet (over the
     earth and under the sun).
   Let the bees go honey-hunting with yellow blur
     of wings in the dome of my head, in the rum-
     bling, singing arch of my skull. . . . .

He can write as curtly and sardonically as in these lines
from *Smoke and Steel:*

   Five geese deploy mysteriously.
   Onward proudly with flagstaffs,

Hearses with silver bugles,
Bushels of plum-blossoms dropping
For ten mystic web-feet—
Each his own drum major,
Each charged with the honor
Of the ancient goose nation,
Each with a nose-length surpassing
The nose-length of rival nations.
Somberly, slowly, unimpeachably,
Five geese deploy, mysteriously.

He can explode in a guffaw of disgust at persons who seem
to him to tangle the skeins of life:

   The work of a bricklayer goes to the blue.
   The knack of a mason outlasts a moon.
   The hand of a plasterer holds a room together.
   The land of a farmer wishes him back again.
     Singers of songs and dreamers of plays
     Build a house no wind blows over
   The lawyers—tell me why a hearse horse snick-
     ers hauling a lawyer's bones.

He was perhaps never more thoroughly himself as a poet
than when, on the occasion of the burial of the Unknown
Soldier, he disturbed the universal chorus of solemn eloquence with his terrible picture, in **"And So To-day,"** of
a skeleton army riding down Pennsylvania Avenue, unseen by the official orators, and yet mocking them as they
go about the rites. . . . To Mr. Sandburg the ceremony
seemed a kind of blasphemy. As he saw it, the "buck private" thus chosen for symbolic honors had not died as a
symbol, but as an actual man, burned by disease or torn
by gunshot, racked by the solitary agony which goes with
death in no matter what cause. Nor was it certain that the
unknown soldier had loved or even approved this cause.
How, then, as long as there was this doubt, could he be
paid in the coin of this show? It meant nothing to Mr.
Sandburg to be told that the survivors had no other coin,
and that they were doing what they could to discharge
their sense of obligation. The dead man had belonged to
the primary material of human life. He had died not while
going about his own affairs of work or love but while doing
what others had commanded him to do for their sake as
well as his. If now, when his senses were stopped, they
were smothering him with words and roses, it was with
roses for them to smell, with words for them to hear. At
such a spectacle Mr. Sandburg could feel no mood but a
brooding, savage irony, and could find no outlet but to
burst forth in his rough, powerful language, hooting lest
he weep, reminding the mourners of the skeleton orator
who stood by, almost silent. . . . (pp. 144-49)

Mr. Sandburg has trouble as well as luck with the raw materials of life which he handles and with the raw materials
of language which he uses in handling them. Both his trouble and his luck come from his unwillingness, possibly his
inability, to accept any help whatever. He will not see with
the majority, and thus take advantage of audiences already prepared to thrill him. He will not touch customary
themes, and thus take advantage of the failures or successes of other poets with those themes. He will not select his
language from among the tried and prosperous words of
poetry, but insists on grabbing up any or all words and
hammering them into the shape he chooses. The consequences of his method are that he often strikes off sparks

of a peculiar vividness and that he often throws off cinders of no vividness at all, much as their weight may be. To go through his books is to stumble again and again upon heaps of slag, ore never quite melted or ore in some way burned past any use, spread about in a large disorder. Yet here and there from these piles of slag emerge objects of a strangely authentic beauty and grace and tenderness. And over the whole field, what hot, what blue flames leap and dance! (pp. 149-50)

> Carl Van Doren, "Flame and Slag," in his Many Minds, *Alfred A. Knopf, 1924, pp. 136-50.*

Rebecca West   (essay date 1926)

[*West is considered one of the foremost English novelists and critics of the twentieth century. Born Cicily Isabel Fairfield, she began her career as an actress—taking the name Rebecca West from the emancipated heroine of Henrik Ibsen's drama* Rosmersholm—*and as a book reviewer for the* Free-woman. *Her early criticism was noted for its militantly feminist stance and its reflection of West's Fabian socialist concerns. The following excerpt, taken from her preface to* Selected Poems of Carl Sandburg, *praises the Middle Western characteristics of Sandburg's poetry.*]

[Sandburg] is, like Robert Burns, a national poet. Just as Robert Burns expresses the whole life of Lowland Scotland of his time, so Carl Sandburg expresses the whole life of the Middle West of to-day. He has learned his country by heart. . . . He has published four books of poems, *Chicago Poems* (1915), *Cornhuskers* (1918), *Smoke and Steel* (1920), and *Slabs of the Sunburnt West* (1922). The qualities of the Middle West are his qualities. The main determinant of his art is the power of his native idiom to deal with the inner life of man. He can describe the inner life, the not too bad life, that lies behind the shapeless sky-scrapers, like so many giant petrol-cans, and the dreary timber houses of an ordinary Middle Western town. He can describe the inner life of the eager little girls who leave those small towns and come to Chicago, but still find no world that makes use of their sweetness. He can describe the inner life of the strong young men who wander about the vast land, proud and yet perplexed; proud because they are lending their strength to the purposes of the new civilization, perplexed because they do not know what it is all about. His idiom shapes him also in making him not so wise in his pictures of the external life. (pp. 24-5)

[Sandburg] is characteristically Middle Western in that his poems have no great sense of melody but a strong sense of rhythm. It will be said of him by Philistines that his poetry has no music in it, particularly by such Philistines as do not, like the lady in the limerick, know 'God Save the Weasel' from 'Pop Goes the Queen.' The same sort of people accuse Cézanne, who was born with a mahl-stick in his hand, of painting like Leader. In point of fact, Carl Sandburg is an accomplished musician, who is famous both for his singing and for his researches into American folk-song, and the music of his poetry is based on the technique of the banjo, very much as Manuel de Falla's music is based on the technique of the guitar. It must be remembered that

his lines will not reveal their music, and indeed have none to reveal, unless they are read with a Middle Western accent. . . . (p. 26)

There is also in Carl Sandburg a full expression of the counter-movements of those who truly love the Middle West against those who love it not so well. This might seem a consideration too purely moral and political to be relevant to one's estimate of a poet; but actually each of these counter-movements implies an aesthetic liberation. It has been the tendency of America to limit its art to the delineation of what is called the Anglo-Saxon element within its territories. This has been to deny the artist the right to use some of the most entrancing brightly-coloured patterns that he saw in the real world before him. Carl Sandburg uses everything he sees that looks to him a good subject. . . . And he writes of the navvy and the hoodlum, not from any 'open road' infantilism, but because they are at any rate men who withdraw themselves from the areas of standardized living and thinking and who can look at reality with their own eyes. . . . It is a curious fact that no writer of Anglo-Saxon descent, no representative of the New England tradition, has described the break between Lincoln's America and modern industrialized America so poignantly as Carl Sandburg has. But his revolutionary passion so often betrays him, for poem after poem is ruined by a coarsely intruding line that turns it from poetry to propaganda. But the effect of this resistance to his environment is sum an aesthetic benefit. It enables him to write of the real America, which one might describe to the present-day, over-prosperous America, in the words of one of its own advertisements, as 'the Venus beneath your fat'. In **"Prairie"** and **"The Windy City"** and **"Slabs of the Sunburnt West"**, he has evoked the essential America which will survive when this phase of commercial expansion is past and the New World is cut down to the quick as the Old World is to-day: a vast continent which by the majesty of its plains and its waters and its mountains, calls forth a response of power in the men who behold it, now that they are white as it did when they were red. His is not a talent that is too easily accepted in this age, which is inclined to regard poetry as necessarily lyric and to demand that the poet shall write brief and perfect verse; but the reason he cannot satisfy such standards is that his art is dominated by an image so vast that it requires as house-room not one but a thousand poems. (pp. 26-8)

> Rebecca West, in a preface to Selected Poems of Carl Sandburg, *edited by Rebecca West, Harcourt Brace Jovanovich, 1926, pp. 15-28.*

Carl Sandburg   (essay date 1928)

[*Sandburg included the following thirty-eight definitions of poetry in the introduction of* Good Morning, America. *While critics attempted to locate a consistent critical theory within the poet's definitions, Sandburg took a whimsical attitude toward his explication on the nature of poetry. In a letter to his longtime friend and fellow poet Archibald MacLeish, Sandburg wrote: "I am sending you . . . 38 definitions of poetry hot off the pan—or rather aged in charred oak casks for several years. I am going to charge some magazine ten dollars a definition. . . . Or I may refuse to print them and continue to proudly publish them orally before audiences who say I am as good as Houdini defying them to bring on handcuffs I can't get out of."]*

TENTATIVE (FIRST MODEL) DEFINITIONS OF POETRY

1 Poetry is a projection across silence of cadences arranged to break that silence with definite intentions of echoes, syllables, wave lengths.

2 Poetry is an art practised with the terribly plastic material of human language.

3 Poetry is the report of a nuance between two moments, when people say, 'Listen!' and 'Did you see it?' 'Did you hear it? What was it?'

4 Poetry is the tracing of the trajectories of a finite sound to the infinite points of its echoes.

5 Poetry is a sequence of dots and dashes, spelling depths, crypts, crosslights, and moon wisps.

6 Poetry is a puppet-show, where riders of skyrockets and divers of sea fathoms gossip about the sixth sense and the fourth dimension.

7 Poetry is a plan for a slit in the face of a bronze fountain goat and the path of fresh drinking water.

8 Poetry is a slipknot tightened around a time-beat of one thought, two thoughts, and a last interweaving thought there is not yet a number for.

9 Poetry is an echo asking a shadow dancer to be a partner.

10 Poetry is the journal of a sea animal living on land, wanting to fly the air.

11 Poetry is a series of explanations of life, fading off into horizons too swift for explanations.

12 Poetry is a fossil rock-print of a fin and a wing, with an illegible oath between.

13 Poetry is an exhibit of one pendulum connecting with other and unseen pendulums inside and outside the one seen.

14 Poetry is a sky dark with a wild-duck migration.

15 Poetry is a search for syllables to shoot at the barriers of the unknown and the unknowable.

16 Poetry is any page from a sketchbook of outlines of a doorknob with thumb-prints of dust, blood, dreams.

17 Poetry is a type-font design for an alphabet of fun, hate, love, death.

18 Poetry is the cipher key to the five mystic wishes packed in a hollow silver bullet fed to a flying fish.

19 Poetry is a theorem of a yellow-silk handkerchief knotted with riddles, sealed in a balloon tied to the tail of a kite flying in a white wind against a blue sky in spring.

20 Poetry is a dance music measuring buck-and-wing follies along with the gravest and stateliest dead-marches.

21 Poetry is a sliver of the moon lost in the belly of a golden frog.

22 Poetry is a mock of a cry at finding a million dollars and a mock of a laugh at losing it.

23 Poetry is the silence and speech between a wet struggling root of a flower and a sunlit blossom of that flower.

24 Poetry is the harnessing of the paradox of earth cradling life and then entombing it.

25 Poetry is the opening and closing of a door, leaving those who look through to guess about what is seen during a moment.

26 Poetry is a fresh morning spider-web telling a story of moonlit hours of weaving and waiting during a night.

27 Poetry is a statement of a series of equations, with numbers and symbols changing like the changes of mirrors, pools, skies, the only never-changing sign being the sign of infinity.

28 Poetry is a packsack of invisible keepsakes.

29 Poetry is a section of river-fog and moving boat-lights, delivered between bridges and whistles, so one says, 'Oh!' and another, 'How?'

30 Poetry is a kinetic arrangement of static syllables.

31 Poetry is the arithmetic of the easiest way and the primrose path, matched up with foam-flanked horses, bloody knuckles, and bones, on the hard ways to the stars.

32 Poetry is a shuffling of boxes of illusions buckled with a strap of facts.

33 Poetry is an enumeration of birds, bees, babies, butterflies, bugs, bambinos, babayagas, and bipeds, beating their way up bewildering bastions.

34 Poetry is a phantom script telling how rainbows are made and why they go away.

35 Poetry is the establishment of a metaphorical link between white butterfly-wings and the scraps of torn-up love-letters.

36 Poetry is the achievement of the synthesis of hyacinths and biscuits.

37 Poetry is a mystic, sensuous mathematics of fire, smoke-stacks, waffles, pansies, people, and purple sunsets.

38 Poetry is the capture of a picture, a song, or a flair, in a deliberate prism of words. (pp. 317-19)

Carl Sandburg, "Tentative (First Model) Defi-

nitions of Poetry," in his Complete Poems, *Harcourt Brace Jovanovich, 1950, pp. 317-19.*

Harriet Monroe   (essay date 1932)

[*In the following excerpt, Monroe provides an overview of Sandburg's first three major volumes of poetry,* Chicago Poems, Cornhuskers, *and* Smoke and Steel.]

Chicago Poems is an urban book—the subjects are a city and its people, including of course the author; also the War, which was killing men over-seas. **Cornhuskers** goes back to the western-Illinois country where the poet was born, and to the railroads he rode on, the taverns he stopped in, and the laborers and hoboes, the children, women, horses, he got acquainted with while earning a living at rough jobs. **Smoke and Steel** carries the tale into the shops and factories, taking for its special motive man-made machines and machine-made men. In a sense all three books are epic—that is, they give us the tale of the tribe in a strongly centralized locale. But the method is lyric rather than epic. The story is presented by flashes; it is revealed by strongly lit details, emotions, episodes, rather than told by chapters which knit together into a shaped and ordered whole. Even the two longest poems—**"Prairie"** in nine pages, and **"Smoke and Steel"** in seven—are series of lyrics following each other with a deliberate and effective irregularity, like a necklace of different-colored beads which harmonize because an artist strung them. And if **"Prairie"** is such a string, from it hangs a jewel of value, for the finale, with that marvelous line,

> I tell you the past is a bucket of ashes,

is one of the imperishable poems of the world's new age.

One gets the very feel of the prairie in such poems—the planted prairie, flowing like a sea with corn; and bearing people of its own kind, simple, faithful to the soil, accustomed to wide horizons. Details fill out the landscape—**"Laughing Corn," "Fall Time," "Prairie Waters by Night," "River Roads"**; and people it with human waifs and workers in such poems as **"Illinois Farmer," "Singing Nigger," "Hits and Runs," "Potato Blossom Songs and Jigs."** **Smoke and Steel** stresses more strongly the gauntness of many human lives, their separation from their rightful human heritage, from all the richness and beauty of nature and art. If **Cornhuskers** dances out in the sun to a devil-may-care jazz tune, **Smoke and Steel** moves usually more slowly, asking bitter questions in queer harsh rhythms full of unexpected glides and dashes.

One feels in all these poems a true and deep emotion of love as the central controlling motive—love of the prairie country, the prairie towns and city, and the people who struggle through toilsome lives there. It is this which gives richness to Sandburg's music. In some of his finest lyrics the love becomes special and personal; his tributes to Nancy Hanks, Inez Milholland, "Chick Lorimer" (whoever she may have been), to Don Magregor, Adelaide Crapsey, Bill Reedy, Ossawatomie Brown, are remarkable for simplicity of style and nobility of mood. The emotion here, and in all his best lyrics, rings absolutely true in a strain of melody fit and beautiful; without a false note or a jarring word.

Granted the theme, and the emotional impulse beneath it, we have still to consider this poet's art: how far does he get the effects he aims at, and what means does he employ to produce them?

In my opinion, his finest lyrics rank, as artistic achievements, among the best in the language. The rhythm of most English lyrics, indeed of most European poetry of the last five hundred years, is an overlay, more or less adroit, of large cadences upon the iambic metrical pattern; as when large waves, swinging in toward the shore, bear the little parallel ripples along. Shakespeare's sonnets—take the twenty-ninth or the seventy-first—show with what mastery he swung his large measures over the three-time iambic pattern of his verse. In a few songs he and other Elizabethans changed magically to a four-time anapaestic pattern in each stanza—a trick used also by Byron in "Stanzas for Music"; and Shelley, Swinburne and others used the anapaestic pattern throughout certain poems as the foundation on which they laid their larger cadences.

What Sandburg does is not, as some students seem to infer, the complete sweeping-away of the metrical pattern. There is an underlying three-time or four-time beat in each poem, his preference leaning, oftener than with most poets, to four-time, which admits that generous use of spondees—sometimes four long syllables in succession—from which he gets some of his most telling effects. But in his underlying pattern Sandburg permits himself more variety than the prosodic laws have allowed for, especially in the number of syllables to a bar, and in a free use of rests. In four-time especially he uses this freedom quite wonderfully, getting rhythms as different as in the quick-stepping **"Gone"** and the slow-moving **"Our Prayer of Thanks;"** while in **"The Great Hunt,"** which begins in a creeping four-time, he tries with magical effect the old but rarely used trick of changing the beat to three-time for the final stanza. And in two poems as different in movement as **"Bringers"** and **"Four Preludes on Playthings of the Wind,"** the underlying pattern is three-time and almost straight iambic. On these patterns Sandburg, like all poets but more skilfully than most of them, swings the larger tides of his cadences.

Certain of these poems may be quoted here to show the intimate response of his method to his feeling:

"Gone"

> Everybody loved Chick Lorimer in our town.
>   Far off
> Everybody loved her.
> So we all love a wild girl keeping a hold
>   On a dream she wants.
> Nobody knows now where Chick Lorimer went.
> Nobody knows why she packed her trunk . . .
>   a few old things
> And is gone,
>   Gone with her little chin
>   Thrust ahead of her,
>   And her soft hair blowing careless
>   From under a wide hat—
> Dancer, singer, a laughing passionate lover.

Were there ten men or a hundred hunting
    Chick?
Were there five men or fifty with aching hearts?
    Everybody loved Chick Lorimer.
        Nobody knows where she's gone.

(pp. 31-5)

"Bringers"

Cover me over
In dusk and dust and dreams.

Cover me over
And leave me alone.

Cover me over,
You tireless, great.

Hear me and cover me,
Bringers of dusk and dust and dreams.

To say that there is less art in such manipulation of rhythms than in following accurately, for example, the exact metrics of a sonnet, is simply to show one's own limitations as a student of poetics. It makes no difference whether the art is conscious or instinctive. With Sandburg it is probably instinctive; he may not know a spondee from a kilowatt, but he has a marvellously sensitive ear—he listens for his rhythms over and over, and beats them out with elaborate care. None of the scholarly imagists, or other free-versifiers of the present period, has so greatly widened the rhythmic range of English poetry; and the prosodists of the future will have to study him in order to make new rules to enslave poets yet to come. (p. 36)

Harriet Monroe, "Carl Sandburg," in her Poets and Their Art, *revised edition, Macmillan Publishing Company, 1932, pp. 29-38.*

Stephen Vincent Benét   (essay date 1936)

[*Benét was an American poet and fiction writer often concerned with examining, understanding, and celebrating American history and culture. The comic short story "The Devil and Daniel Webster" and the Pulitzer Prize-winning Civil War epic* John Brown's Body *are his best-known works. In the following excerpt, Benét praises Sandburg's* The People, Yes *for its celebration and documentation of American life and vernacular.*]

Carl Sandburg occupies a unique position in the contemporary American scene. When he first came before the public, with *Chicago Poems,* he was labeled by the people who love to label things—largely on such poems as **"Chicago"** and **"To a Contemporary Bunk-Shooter"**—as a brutal realist and a smasher of idols. Yet that same book showed a poet who could work with great sensitiveness and grace, and bring to his work not only an interest in live words and live people but a sort of folk fairytale quality that was as far east of automatic realism as it was west of sentimentality. He has always been an American but his Americanism has never been a horse-and-buggy hired for the occasion—he talks United States because that is his language and he talks it with a sure tongue. . . .

[In] *The People, Yes,* he brings us the longest and most sustained piece of work he has yet done in verse. It is a

book that will irritate some; and some will find it meaningless. . . . It deals with people; it deals with these times. But Carl Sandburg has his own way of going about things. He will go back to the Tower of Babel if he feels like it; he will go forward to the wreck of the skyscrapers. . . .

And there is something to be said about the man who was feeding a hatful of doughnuts to a horse, explaining to the curious, "I want to see how many he'll eat before he asks for a cup of coffee." There is something to be said about doctors and restaurant cashiers, about airplane stunters and mine strikers and city editors, about the railroad engineer on the Pennsy, directing in his will that they should burn his body as a piece of rolling stock beyond rehabilitation and repair and scatter the ashes from the cab on the Beverley curve, and about the bottom of the sea which accommodates the mountain ranges. *The People, Yes* is not a dogmatic book and it turns corners and goes around alleys. It is full of proverbs, questions, memoranda, folklore, faces and wonderings. It is a fresco and a field of grass and a man listening quietly to all the commonplace, extraordinary things that people say. Yet it has its own coherence and its own confidence.

It is hard to get all the people into any one book. You forget two martins on the shore of Lake Michigan, you forget the hobo who said, "Give me something to eat. I'm so thirsty I don't know where I'm going to sleep tonight." And then you have to turn around and start over again. Otherwise, you begin to talk about case histories, proletarians, the lower classes, the typical American farmer, the rabble, the intelligent voters. . . . But Carl Sandburg doesn't do that. He knows all that has been said against the people—and said in this country, past and present.

It is unfair to pick bits out of a poem that owes its power to its mass and its cumulative effect, to its rambling diversions, even to its occasional long-windedness and hold them up like dress samples in front of the reader. But Sandburg's attitude is an important one and I have to quote to show how that attitude expresses itself. Though quotations, no matter how selected, will not give the full flavor of this book. For it is the people themselves who are celebrated here—more completely perhaps than by any American poet since Whitman and with as essential a love. The people "so often sleepy, weary, enigmatic," the people so often saying "aw nuts, aw go peddle yer papers," saying, "Men will yez fight or will yez run?" and "The coat and pants do the work but the vest gets the gravy," are yet the rock and the spring and the good ground.

> The people will live on.
> The learning and blundering people will live on,
> They will be tricked and sold and again sold
> And go back to the nourishing earth for
>   rootholds. . . .
>
> . . . This reaching is alive.
> The panderers and liars have violated and smut-
>   ted it.
> Yet this reaching is alive yet for lights and keep-
>   sakes.

And, if Sandburg writes with honesty, he also writes, and with a biting anger, of the rare and suave folk who pay themselves a fat swag of higher salaries while they out wages, of the pay day, patriots that Lincoln called "respectable scoundrels," of all those who deny, debauch, oppress, mock, enslave the people, of all those who say, "Your people, sir, is a great beast," covertly or openly, in past times or now. (p. 1)

This voice does not come from Moscow or Union Square. It comes out of Western America, soil of that soil and wheat of that wheat, and it is the voice of somebody who knows the faces, the folkwords and the tall tales of the people. It is as honest as it is questioning and it speaks its deep convictions in a tongue we know. And there is warning in it as well as hope. Sometimes it goes runabout; not all of it is poetry. But it is the memoranda of the people. And every line of it says "The People—Yes." (p. 2)

> Stephen Vincent Benét, "Carl Sandburg—Poet of the Prairie People," in New York Herald Tribune Books, *August 23, 1936, pp. 1-2.*

Morton Dauwen Zabel   (essay date 1936)

[*Zabel is a poet, critic, and prominent scholar. He became acquainted with Sandburg's mentor, Harriet Monroe, in 1926 when Monroe asked Zabel to become the associate editor of* Poetry. *Zabel assumed editorship of* Poetry *for a year after Monroe's death in 1936, and continued to make frequent contributions thereafter. In the following excerpt, Zabel compares* The People, Yes *to Sandburg's earlier, highly acclaimed collection,* Chicago Poems. *Describing* The People, Yes *as a "manual of words and phrases, episodes and characters, conflicts and forces," he praises Sandburg for being a reporter of contemporary life.*]

Carl Sandburg's new book, **The People, Yes,** is impressive at first sight because in it he speaks with exactly the same voice he used in the **Chicago Poems** of 1914 and yet succeeds in making it as eloquent as any American poem of 1936. He risks two extreme hazards of the contemporary writer. He writes on the social problem, and he writes in popular language. It will be suggested immediately that he has simplified them primarily by stopping short of his full responsibilities as a poet. To this one must agree at once that hardly a fifth of this volume is classifiable by any definition as poetry, although any definition of poetry must include the purpose and imagination that run through its pages, even when they contain nothing but inventories of popular speech or long lists of trades and slogans. But no American poet now living could publish with the same authority and completeness a survey of the specifically American issue in twentieth century poetry—how it has emerged and developed, how it diverges from foreign influence and contacts, and what it may expect, in extension or solution, from the coming talents of the humanitarian front. This long document of 286 pages is not only a guidebook on American themes; it is a manual of words and phrases, episodes and characters, conflicts and forces, and in addition it contains a demonstration of how the social idealism of American poetry may be successfully domesticated in the immediate future.

But its first interest comes from the fact that here Sandburg has summarized his purposes of a quarter-century and handed them as a testament to his inheritors. The book forms a remarkable unity with its predecessors. It is true that such consistency has deprived his work of exact points of interest or decision. His poems as they have appeared in his five volumes have progressively cancelled their predecessors, repeating their themes and dulling their emphasis. Yet Sandburg is one of the few native poets of whom it may be said, with all respect to the priority of Whitman, that he has written no verse, good or bad, but his own. He has sacrificed to his own single-voiced personality—as candidly as Frost or Robinson, but without their irony or close-lipped pessimism—whatever variety or progress might have made him a more forceful character among post-War writers and readers. In this first book since **Good Morning, America** eight years ago he shows a purpose not only more serious than it has ever been before, but a talent tuned to uses and broken to duties which many members of the present generation of humanitarian poets, whatever their superior sophistication or craftsmanship, have hardly begun to understand.

In poetry or prose dealing with human causes it is usually a rule that there are no substitutes for thorough practical acquaintance with the matter in hand. Here brilliant technical advantages may display what they are intended to disguise—the writer's failure in immediate knowledge of his materials, or his substitution of journalism or secondhand study for it. . . . In other words, Sandburg triumphs on all the scores in which experience counts: in his use of speech and lingoes, in the range and authenticity of his folklore, in the scope of his social familiarity, in the reach of his memory, and in the size and variety of the history he has made of the whole age of industrial labor in America during the past half-century. Compared with these resources the younger talents offer a meagre fare. Their phrases are thin and their colloquialisms synthetic, their data specialized and experiences green, their references as often warped as enriched by literary derivation, and the structure of their poems is held up by rhetoric or the false props of borrowed arguments.

On these grounds **The People, Yes** escapes criticism, even when it does so by casting esthetic claims to the winds. It is a vast retrospect of life and labor in America that suggests an obvious comparison—*Leaves of Grass.* It is prefaced by a poem that announces the casual and miscellaneous nature of its scheme:

> Being several stories and psalms nobody
> would want to laugh at
>
> interspersed with memoranda variations
> worth a second look
>
> along with sayings and yarns traveling on
> grief and laughter. . . .

It opens with a spectacle of the "Howdeehow powpow," which is the American nation in its immense dimensions and disorder—a "Tower of Babel job" which now stands

> as a skull and a ghost,
> a memorandum hardly begun,
> swaying and sagging in tall hostile winds,
> held up by slow friendly winds—

and so proceeds through 107 sections that alternate, on no apparent principle of contrast or structure, between personal episodes and mass movements, local anecdotes and epic generalities, lists of scenes, trades, occupations, and causes, passages of vague symbolic imagery, long catalogues of popular phrases, catchwords, clichés, and proverbs, and intervals of gnomic lyricism. Nothing has apparently been left out, but everything that Sandburg has put into his earlier poems is here again, particularly from previous surveys like *Many Hats* and **Good Morning, America.** The prevailing quality of style is "tough and mystical." It derives from the dogged patience of common humanity in being outwitted by keener brains and criminal exploiters, the pathetic endurance of the underdog who waits grimly for the reprisals of time. This style derives from Whitman only in structure. It has as little to do with his rhetorical strain or oracular grandiloquence as it has with Whitman's final lyric and choral mastery. It has even little of the belabored hardboiledness of Hemingway, Dos Passos, or Phelps Putnam. It comes with the laconic ease of talk on streets and farms, from section-gangs, night shifts, pick-and-shovel outfits, and hobo campfires, Union Square soapboxes and grocery-store rag-chewing. From these sources Sandburg has compiled a catalogue of American lore that must astonish anyone. Where he gets it all is beyond telling. Whether all of it is equally authentic or not is beyond present calculation. But it rings true to the American ear far beyond the language of the average "regional" novel or proletarian poem, and one has only to compare any random sample of it with the slang parts of Pound's *Cantos* or MacLeish's *Frescoes* to realize that one is the pure article and the other something like a parody heard from the stage of the London Colosseum.

In other words, Sandburg looks after his facts first, and waits for argument to follow from them. He is empirical in the rough native tradition. If he hears the jeer that "the people is a myth, an abstraction," he asks "What myth would you put in place of the people? And what abstraction would you exchange for this one?" If the cause of social justice has any validity for reformers or poets it must come not from the mind but from "the bowels of that mystic behemoth, the people." The difference between Whitman and Sandburg is primarily a difference between a visionary imagination and a realistic one, between a prophet who deals in the racial and social aspects of humanitarianism and a historian who handles the specific facts of industrial life and labor. Whitman, given his sympathies and cause and with his greater imaginative vision, might have written his book without any immediate contact with its materials, whereas Sandburg, so denied, could have written none of his. The two poets join only at the point which is their common weakness: in the rhapsodic cries and flights that are the diffused and prevalent bane of the one and the merely incidental weakness of the other. Sandburg is saved from this pretension by his plain verbal sanity. He does not discard the lyric imagination; it filters through his pages and produces many short passages of characteristic fancy. . . . But it is seldom allowed to develop into vague apostrophe or inflated allegory, any more than his language is allowed to use the pompous phrases, French or Latin counterfeit, and hollow pedantry of Whitman's

style. In the same way his general tendency is to avoid those vague spectres of human ordeal that make up the panoramic symbolism of Perse's *Anabase,* Aragon's *Front Rouge,* or MacLeish's *Conquistador,* and when such effects do appear they immediately strike the eye with their uneasy falseness, as in parts 29 and 107, to select two examples from opposite ends of the poem. Three lines are enough to show how Sandburg on occasion veers into a pompous phraseology from which his cruder humors must rescue him:

> While the rootholds of the earth nourish the ma-
>   jestic people
> And the new generations with names never
>   heard of
> Plow deep in broken drums and shoot craps for
>   old crowns,

but one also runs into longer passages that come with particular inconclusiveness in the book's last pages, when something more than immortal truisms is wanted for force of thought or art, however such temporizations may agree with the skepticism of history:

> The people will live on.
> The learning and blundering people will live on.
>   They will be tricked and sold and again sold
> And go back to the nourishing earth for root-
>   holds,
>   The people so peculiar in renewal and come-
>   back,
>   You can't laugh off their capacity to take it.
> The mammoth rests between his cyclonic dra-
>   mas.

This kind of writing, coming on top of passages of the most brisk and vivid realism, rings with a special shallowness; another poet, stronger in rhetorical powers or symbolic skill, might make poetry of it, but where the general spirit of the poem casts suspicion on matter or ideas untested by hard fact, these references to dreams and mammoths, "cyclonic dramas," "the strength of the winds" and the "constellations of universal law" . . . show up as evasions of what either social necessity or poetic strength requires.

In other words, Sandburg, taken in the mass and for the general effect of his detail, is a master without rivals, a poetic realist of great range and authority, a folklorist in the best tradition, and easily the finest reporter of contemporary life that the modern poetic revival has produced, as comparison with Masters, Lindsay, Frost, or their younger successors will show. But taken in the specific poem or argument he offers as unsatisfactory a case to social critics as to literary. He eludes argument and dependability; he seems in the end evasive of responsibility; and his loyal purposes and honesty come to much less than they should. His immense knowledge of human ills and fortunes is too immense; it immerses and engulfs him; he is pulled by so many claims on sympathy and forbearance that nothing survives the prodigious outlay of tolerance and compassion but his inexhaustible supply of pure human nature. . . . The answer to the whole urgent problem of human salvation is thrown back on "the folded and quiet yesterdays, put down in the book of the past," or thrown forward by the unanswered question, "Where do we go from here? Where to? What next?" or allowed to hang between unresolved opposites: "The people, yes, out of what is their change from chaos to order and chaos again?"

Obviously these are among the most difficult questions in the world to answer, but neither a poet nor a reformer would ask them if he had no answer to offer. As its title indicates, *The People, Yes* is written as a great affirmation of man's strength and value, but the practical regeneration of the human lot promised throughout the record finally hangs suspended in the void of love and patience. We knew it all before, even if not in this vivid and familiar language, and we are left wanting to know more. No doubt the avoidance of formulated solutions is dictated as much by common sense as by the plain facts of history, but one expects more than common sense or plain facts from a poet or a philosopher. It soon follows that if Sandburg had worked harder at his social or moral philosophy, he would have been a greater poet. In a book of this kind the test of poetic form is almost beside the point; it would apply in so small a fraction of the content. Yet as soon as one understands what it takes to achieve real form in the construction of language, one sees what it takes to arrive at that form through the structure and integration of thought. If one's thought remains undecided among the evidence at hand, inconclusively empirical or superior to proof, it is likely that the force and authority of the verse will remain scattered and confused among its details, words, and phrases, however abundant and authentic these may be. Sandburg's poetic instrument is exactly fitted to his purposes; it simply happens that those purposes are too vaguely poetic to make the instrument become anything more than the loose, amorphous, copious, semi-prose medium that it still remains after twenty-five years of use. (pp. 34-43)

> *Morton Dauwen Zabel, "Sandburg's Testament," in* Poetry, *Vol. XLIX, No. 1, October, 1936, pp. 33-45.*

Newton Arvin   (essay date 1937)

[*An American biographer and critic, Arvin was a professor of English at Smith College. In the following excerpt, which was first published in 1937, Arvin offers a summary of Sandburg's work, concluding: "Of tenderness, of humane feeling, of generous and robust sentiment, there is notoriously a great deal: of strong, sharp and ardent emotion, of the specific passion and intensity of poetry, there is singularly little."*]

A little more than twenty years have gone by since Carl Sandburg became known as a poet to the generality of American readers, and now one looks back over his career with a kind of esteem that only a few of his contemporaries inspire. In the interests of criticism several things may have to be said about his writings in their actual execution, but so long as you have your mind on the main intention of Sandburg's books or the spirit in which they have mostly been written, you are bound—unless that intention and that spirit are too alien to you—to take pleasure in his work and to hope that it will have a long line of offspring. There are cases in which a fine intention patiently and

faithfully adhered to becomes itself a production to estimate and respect, and in that sense Carl Sandburg's continuous effort to find a poetic outlet for the fast, hard, noisy, smoky, machine-ridden experience of Middle Western city people and for the dry, unshaded experience of Middle Western villagers and farmers—his effort, I say, has taken on the dimensions of a literary achievement, and one that no disparagement can minimize. In a generation in which most poets set themselves more manageable and more opportune tasks, he undertook to be the poet of a people among whom the sources of poetry, though by no means exhausted, were untapped, grown over, and all but completely forgotten.

He was not content, unlike most poets of that generation, to explore and exploit the tortuous reaches of a highly private and often abstruse experience, or to work out the forms of expression for a complicated sensibility—aims which, even after more than a century, still promised the most certain results to writers who worked within the romantic-individualist tradition. Sandburg's was the intention of a rhapsode or scop or (with important differences) of a younger political poet; and it led him to the attempt to get into verse the whole disorderly and humid life of the twentieth-century United States, with its violence, its grandiosity, its social tensions, and its waste of human impulse and power. He has described himself officially as an American folk song recitalist, and obviously enough the impetus behind the great bulk of his work has been to provide a minstrelsy for Chicago and Kalamazoo; for the mechanic, the typist and the farmhand. (pp. 67-8)

Under all the circumstances, however—circumstances of time and social condition—there was something honorably quixotic and something paradoxical in his attempting to fill this ancient or anticipatory role. The chances are that Sandburg himself has been well aware of the paradox: he once remarked to an interviewer that "saying 'Chicago' and 'poems' close together like that is like saying 'hell roses' or 'hell lilies.' " At any rate, it is certainly true that he was not very lucky in his milieu and his moment. The relation between a reflective and highly organized modern poet and the great mass of middle-class or working-class Americans could not actually be the relation between a folk-poet and his people; could not be spontaneous, intimate, many-sided and unreserved. The creator of a lay or a ballad is nourished by the life of the community about him because he can share it unselfconsciously on every level; can enter not only into the physical experiences of his people at work and play, into their sentiments and general emotions, but into their thought, their imagination and their spiritual experience. A poet of Sandburg's time and place might share, as he has certainly done, many of the simpler aspects of his people's life; but if he were a man of fine talent and serious purposes, he could not really identify himself, heart and mind, with the social world of which he was a part. There might be, as the proletarian poets have been showing, another relation and a fruitful one into which he might consciously enter; but just that was never Sandburg's clear choice, and the result has been that his environing culture has not nourished him and his poetry as they deserved to be nourished.

Thanks to the genuineness of his gifts and perhaps to some deep resource of health and sanity, he made himself a remarkable writer in spite of Chicago and Kalamazoo. But to reread his books at this hour is to see how little he has owed—how much too little—to a common way of life, a common mortality, a common fund of ideas and convictions. Sandburg has not aimed, needless to say, at being a metaphysical poet, but like all writers he has evidently felt the need to discern some meaning in the welter of things and events, and the need has mainly gone unanswered. Like Dreiser, like Masters, like Anderson, he has been able to mirror—often with startling fidelity—the world about him: he has not been able to focus or integrate it. A troubled skepticism, an enervating indecisiveness, overlie much of what he has written: whenever the raw fact or the strong primitive sentiment is left behind, we are likely to find ourselves in a chartless prairie of bewilderment and doubt, with little to fix our eyes upon but a riddle or a question-mark. "Mist," "fog," "phantoms," "ashes," "dust," these are favorite images, and they are the true emblems of the poet's almost unrelieved uncertainty. Obsessed with the grimly impersonal drift of time, he has often failed to see any understandable tendency in the whole course of human experience:

> History is no sure thing to bet on.
> History is a box of tricks with a lost key.

More than once he has fallen back on a helpless relativism and a philosophy of pure chance:

> God is Luck: Luck is God: we are all bones the
>   High Thrower rolled: some are two spots,
>   some are double sixes.

And in the poem about the Grand Canyon:

> each one makes his own Canyon
> before he comes, each one brings
> and carries away his own Canyon—
> who knows? and how do I know?

Behind so dubious a state of mind as this lie certainly the too easy beliefs or the vulgar unbelief of our harried and leaderless population: out of that state of mind must have sprung the surprisingly harsh despondency that came more and more to prevail in Sandburg's work after the first volume and that led him, in *Good Morning, America,* to speak of "the short miserable pilgrimage of mankind" between an ice age far in the past and an ice age perhaps not so far in the future. Certainly the winds that blow across his city streets and his open prairies seem often to have reached them after passing over some near and menacing glacier. It is extraordinary, considering the warm and genial temperament that the evidence forces us to believe in, how little heat one actually finds in the pages of Sandburg's books. Of tenderness, of humane feeling, of generous and robust sentiment, there is notoriously a great deal: of strong, sharp and ardent emotion, of the specific passion and intensity of poetry, there is singularly little. This verse, you feel, is the work of a man whose emotional nature, like his intellectual life, has never found the earth and air in which it could develop freely and expansively. His strength has lain in his closeness to the people, but they are a people whose impulses and affections have been nipped and stunted like trees in a city park or like wild flowers on a stock farm; and of so cramped an emotional existence this frequently too cool, too inexpansive, too phlegmatic poetry—this poetry of half-lights and understatement and ironic anticlimaxes—is the inevitable expression.

In form and language it has of course reflected the intellectual perplexity and the emotional constraint that have been its setting. Diffused through half a dozen books there is the fruit of much thoughtfulness, much pondering, much sensitive perception and understanding; but, with admirable exceptions, it *is* all diffused, and not concentrated: in a score of poems it is unmistakable; in single poems it is rarely fused and final. The frequent looseness of the form corresponds to the indeterminateness of the mental structure beneath it; and if the rhythms are sometimes broken and prosaic, the images sometimes whimsical or merely customary, the words themselves sometimes naked and inexpressive, it is because they have not passed through the lens of heightened and translucent emotion. Sandburg's words, it is true, have often come to him from the inexhaustible reservoirs of American slang; and, given his purpose, that was just where they should have come from: with no other language could he ever have rendered the surfaces or even the spirit of contemporary life as he has rendered them with his "galoots," his "necktie parties," his "fadeaways" and his "fake passes." But slang is an instrument with a big end and a little end, and if one of its uses is to magnify and clarify perceptions, another is to dwarf and blur and weaken them: it is as often prompted by a distrust of ideas, of strong emotion and of beauty, as by quick intelligence and fresh feeling. It has sometimes been a decoy to Sandburg as to certain other writers: it has led him to fritter away his meanings instead of pointing and pressing them.

He has not, in short, made by any means so full a use of his manifest gifts as under better circumstances he might have made; but in spite of the pedants who prefer the perfect achievement of a modest or trifling intention to the imperfect achievement of an ambitious or difficult one, his qualified success has been far more impressive than the less qualified—and lesser—successes of some of his contemporaries. This son of an immigrant Swede railroad worker, this ex-housepainter, ex-dishwasher, ex-newspaper man, has done more than all but two or three other writers of his time to keep somewhat open and unclogged the channels that ought to flow between the lives at the base of society and the literary consciousness. The substance of his poetic insights and sympathies may be scattered rather loosely through *Chicago Poems* and *Smoke and Steel, Abraham Lincoln: The Prairie Years* and, now, *The People, Yes;* but at least it is ever present in those books, and it is not easy to think of another writer who has perceived more subtly or reproduced more variously that world of towering silos and pregnant-looking cornfields, of band concerts on July evenings and lighted ice-cream parlors, of stockyards and crowded streetcars and night skies lurid over the din of rolling-mills. The eye of a reporter-poet and the ear of a born musician have contributed their large share toward making Sandburg's books what they are.

His eye and his ear, however, have not been deserted by more essential faculties, and *The People, Yes* reminds us that, whatever his confusions and his negations may have been, Carl Sandburg's intuitive grasp of a few basic values, human and social, has never been more than intermittently relaxed. His earliest poetry drew much of its color and its lift from Sandburg's affiliation with the Socialist movement in the Middle West in the years just before the War; and even in the extreme doldrums of the twenties, his wise, homely, tender book on Lincoln showed that his imagination could not wander far from the democratic center of the American folk tradition. How generously the imagination of an American poet can be fed and the art of such a poet mellowed by that tradition, *The People, Yes,* in spite of some air pockets, amply demonstrates. In the midst of sharper and sharper conflicts between the principle of subordination and the principle of equality, this poem is an eloquent and sometimes a passionate reassertion of the dignity, the fortitude, the unweariable creativeness, the historic and unrelinquished hopes of "the laboring many." It is not, after all, as a short and miserable pilgrimage merely that Sandburg now sees the difficult record of the race:

> And man the stumbler and finder, goes on,
> man the dreamer of deep dreams,
> man the shaper and maker,
> man the answerer.

Like one of his own fogs, Sandburg's doubts and apprehensions seem to have burned off at last, and his latest words are again in the strong and sanguine spirit of his inheritance from Whitman:

> And across the bitter years and the howling winters
> the deathless dream will be the stronger,
> the dream of equity will win.

(pp. 68-73)

> *Newton Arvin, "Carl Sandburg," in* After the Genteel Tradition: American Writers (1910-1930), *edited by Malcolm Cowley, Southern Illinois University Press, 1964, pp. 67-73.*

William Carlos Williams (essay date 1948)

[*Williams was one of America's most renowned poets of the twentieth century. Rejecting as overly academic the Modernist poetic style established by T. S. Eliot, he sought a more natural poetic expression, endeavoring to replicate the idiomatic cadences of American speech. Williams sought "a language modified by our environment; the American environment," an aspiration similar to Sandburg's. In the following excerpt, however, Williams offers a negative assessment of Sandburg's free verse and stylistic development.*]

Carl Sandburg has been around a long time. In that period, during which modern art has celebrated some of its greatest triumphs, he has accumulated a mass of poems which have now been published as a single volume [*Complete Poems*]. Because of the man's name, his position and the conclusion forced on us that here summarized is the

work of one of our best known poets, we should give the book major attention.

Search as we will among them we must say at once that technically the poems reveal no initiative whatever other than their formlessness; there is no motivating spirit held in the front of the mind to control them. And without a theory, as Pasteur once said, to unify it, a man's life becomes little more than an aimless series of random and repetitious gestures. In the poem a rebellion against older forms means nothing unless, finally, we have a new form to substitute for that which has become empty from the exhaustion of its means. There never has been any positive value in the form or lack of form known as free verse into which Sandburg's verse is cast.

That drive for new form seemed to be lacking in Sandburg. We must never make the mistake of trying to substitute the materials of a new territory for the great and universal power of the art itself. The vigor of new forms demands its own prerogatives but only to increase the range and break through the restrictions of the old. (p. 272)

There are those all too ready to take the opportunity of Sandburg's comparative failure to reject the whole that he represents—which at least ran synchronously with the upsurge of the modern impetus—ready at any excuse to reject the whole new configuration at sight of any flaw. They're delighted to be able to snigger behind their hands and, throwing him out, profit by the occasion to rush back to their old and respectable deadness. Sandburg may not have known what he was doing, it may never have entered his mind that there was anything significant to do with the structure of the verse itself, but the best of him was touched with fire.

Carl Sandburg petered out as a poet ten years ago. I imagine he wanted it to be that way. His poems themselves said what they had to say, piling up, then just went out, like a light. He had no answers, he didn't seek any. Without any attempt at the solace which the limitations of art (as with a Baudelaire) might bring, the formlessness of his literary figures was the very formlessness of the materials with which he worked. That was his truth. That was what he wanted truthfully to make plain, that was his compulsion. That form he could accept but at a terrible cost: failure deliberately invited, a gradual inevitable slackening off to ultimate defeat.

"**Chicago,**" his first brilliantly successful poem, should have been his last. Between the writing of that and "**Number Man**" . . . , one of his latest, occurs the mass of his work. It is that bulk that makes up the book with which we are dealing, pushing it on our attention. The devotion he has spent on it, the painstaking and voluminous notes he has gathered, the indignation it has caused him—tripped him up. He refused to lie, or was incapable of taking his eyes away from what he saw. Nor could he be neat, or choosy, or selective about it. It overwhelmed him. He couldn't get over it. He let it dictate its own terms, he was willing to go under with it. He must have looked occasionally at some pleasant guys and the way they could train the words to stand on tubs and jump through hoops. He kept wandering off behind the scenes to talk with the hands who set up the props.

There is a lot of talk of "kings who shall no longer be kings, nor the sons of kings become kings." But the language generally is just talk, the sort of reporting that never gets over straight in newspapers and never can. It's always bitched up in the magazine section on Sunday; it's always slanted with maddening implications, made nauseating at the editor's desk, in the slicks and true-stories magazines. This is the subtle censorship which Sandburg tried to avoid. Without art it is a task almost impossible to accomplish.

It goes on and on from the Swede in the flat below, through railroad men, the farmer reaping his acres, the Texas ranger, slum dwellers, women, pimps playing the piano in whorehouses, back to the salesgirls in department stores in the big cities. In the end he sums it up, *The People, Yes,* and lets it go at that.

For twenty years he kept this up with diminishing force, book after book, *Chicago Poems,* 1916, *Cornhuskers,* 1918, *Smoke and Steel,* 1920, *Slabs of the Sunburnt West,* 1922, *Good Morning, America,* 1928, and *The People, Yes,* 1936. In *Cornhuskers* occurs a different sort of poem from his usual wont, it was called **"Ashurnatsirpal III"** . . . and shows a more indirect approach to the theme from that which Sandburg usually exploited. Had he followed that lead the man's natural love of violence, so wonderfully exhibited at the start of his career in the poem **"Chicago,"** might have carried him on to great distinction. But the theme remains neglected. (pp. 273-75)

There is a steady diminution of the poetic charge in his verses from about the period of *Cornhuskers* to *The People, Yes.* He seems to have lost the taste for it. When Picasso became a Communist, convinced that that was his human duty, it did NOT alter his dedication to his task as an artist. And the official Communist blackguards were forced to accept his point of view, not he theirs. They did NOT suppress him.

But Sandburg, convinced that the official democracy he was witnessing was rotten, abandoned his art to expose it. He suffered the inevitable results. He knew what he was doing. To have persisted as a pure poet would have maimed what to him was the outstanding thing: the report of the people, the basis of all art and of everything that is alive with regenerative power.

He didn't see that the terms the people use are so often the very thing that defeats them. It is by his invention of new terms that the artist uniquely serves. The process is much more complex than Sandburg realizes. It is not, as between the mob and supremely sensitive man, a direct process though its incentives are no less simple for that. The most inspired artist is moved by SIMPLE designs dormant in the very "people" of which Sandburg speaks. It doesn't matter how compelled to distortion their inventions may appear on the canvas or the page, in fact it is the very character of distortion which has shaped their truth. (pp. 275-76)

It is shocking for the uninformed to look at a Picasso or

to pick up a poem by Rosalie Moore. He can't understand them. He will never understand them until he has CHANGED within himself. When he does that he will change what he performs. He will no longer be the same man. He will be MOVED by those works of art more than he is by all the piling up of images that Sandburg has ever assembled. Because the instances Sandburg has piled up merely say to them, "somebody" is responsible. But it is never they themselves whom they consider responsible (though they are directly responsible for their own comparable misfortunes). But if they face and are faced by the canvas and the page of which I have spoken they will not be able any longer glibly to accept the facts Sandburg has so assiduously assembled. They will be changed as the facts could never change them, they will have been acted on by a new principle and they will in turn act on their part. (pp. 276-77)

In [*Complete Poems*], covering a period of close to forty years, the poems show no development of the thought, in the technical handling of the material, in the knowledge of the forms, the art of treating the line. The same manner of using the words, of presenting the image is followed in the first poem as in the last. All that can be said is that a horde walks steadily, unhurriedly through its pages, following without affection one behind the other.

It is a monstrous kind of show. It isn't even a pageant, it might be a pilgrimage. It comes off best as a pilgrimage, but look at Chaucer's varied art. That is all the unchanging meaning to be got, a massive pilgrimage: good and bad, male and female, the sheer weight of numbers going in one direction (the same as the sun) they seem unable to turn right or left and never back. Its unchanging burden, unchangeable it seems as we read, is the failure to find happiness. The theme of happiness in Sandburg is always something remembered and lost. Even the hope for it is lost. There is only a pressing forward (without understanding), pressing forward, an unrelenting drive, oxlike you might almost call it. That is the great image Sandburg draws.

It is hopeful, it is massive, it is impressive—but not for itself. Fatigue is the outstanding phenomenon as it affects the characters, they walk as if doped. The ideal for the self seems very nearly that of Eastman, spoken of in one of the poems, a man knowing himself doomed who shoots himself, through a wet towel, in the heart, after carefully putting his will in order so that it may have the exact effect he has planned.

Nowhere among the poems will you find anything that you can speak of as a recurrence: nowhere a rhyme, a stated line, a recognizable stanza, it is one long flight. This could not be different. It is the very formlessness of the material, its failure to affirm anything formal, the drift of aimless life through the six hundred and seventy-six pages that is the form. It had to be shapeless to affirm what was being said: persistence in change.

Of Sandburg himself there seems to emerge more in *Cornhuskers* than the other books. One catches glimpses of a half-hidden figure that looks at you a moment with questioning eyes before disappearing again in the crowd. I was struck by such poems as **"Roses," "Horses," "Joliet," "Knucks," "In Tall Grass," "Mammy Hums"** and **"Bringers."** But they are lost in the drift of all that surrounds them.

For it is formless as a drift of desert sand engulfing the occasional shrub or tree and as formed. The *Complete Poems* make a dunelike mass; no matter where you dig into them it is sand. (Sandburg! I didn't think of that. It seems as if the name itself has gotten into it.) His characters, a drift of people, a nameless people for the most part, are sand, giving the wind form in themselves until they lie piled up filling his pages. (pp. 277-79)

> *William Carlos Williams, "Carl Sandburg's 'Complete Poems'," in his* Selected Essays of William Carlos Williams, *Random House, 1954, pp. 272-79.*

AUTHOR'S COMMENTARY

I am still studying verbs and the mystery of how they connect nouns. I am more suspicious of adjectives than at any other time in all my born days. I have forgotten the meaning of twenty or thirty of my poems written thirty or forty years ago. I still favor several simple poems published long ago which continue to have an appeal for simple people. I have written by different methods and in a wide miscellany of moods and have seldom been afraid to travel in lands and seas where I met fresh scenes and new songs. All my life I have been trying to learn to read, to see and hear, and to write. . . . I should like to think that as I go on writing there will be sentences truly alive, with verbs quivering, with nouns giving color and echoes. It could be, in the grace of God, I shall live to be eighty-nine, as did Hokusai, and speaking my farewell to earthly scenes, I might paraphrase: "If God had let me live five years longer I should have been a writer."

(essay date 1950)

Dan G. Hoffman   (essay date 1950)

[*An American poet, educator, and critic, Hoffman is the author of* An Armada of Thirty Whales *(1933), winner of the Yale Series of Younger Poets Award, and a number of critical works, including* English Literary Criticism: Romantic and Victorian *(1963). Concerning Hoffman's myriad talents, Judith Moffett asserts: "Hoffman is one of the minority of true writer/scholar /teacher hybrids whose intelligence turns as naturally to the crafting of creative scholarship as to poetry. . . ." In the following excerpt, Hoffman examines the limitations involved in Sandburg's attempt to represent communal emotion rather than individual emotion.*]

"The hardest part of being a pioneer is remaining a contemporary," Morton D. Zabel wrote of Sandburg in 1936. It has been Sandburg's misfortune to see his own reputation decline during the dozen years since his most successful poetry was published. Rising to fame in the excitement of the "Little Renaissance," he continued during the '20's and '30's to be popular among readers who take their poetry seriously. When the lyricism of Aiken, Cummings and Millay set the boom decade to music, Carl Sandburg described deserted city brickyards where "Fluxions of yellow and dusk on the waters / Make a wide dreaming pansy of an old pond in the night." When the depression gave poetry of social protest its short-lived hour, Sandburg found his fame greater than it had ever been. He had been protesting for twenty years; the old lines in "Hog butcher for the world" sounded still fresh, while those of Masters and Lindsay, his fellow-rebels of the "Little Renaissance," seemed naive and quaintly dated. From the beginning an accurate observer of the urban scene, Sandburg had made city life the surface as well as the subject of his poetry. His was a realistic voice which caught the cacaphonous choruses of "the mob—the crowd—the mass" and made a new poetry, in a new form, from the jangling noises about our ears.

Sandburg has a following still, but it no longer numbers many of modern poetry's serious readers. The loose, proselike surface, the flat, colloquial diction, and the apparent lack of organization and of intensity in his verse have alienated those who see Eliot, Pound, and Wallace Stevens as the chief poetic spokesmen of the contemporary dilemma. "The age demanded an image / Of its accelerated grimace," Pound told us when the age had scarcely begun; within a few short years Sandburg's image for the age seemed singularly inappropriate. He had made an abstraction of "the people," and his poetry was to represent communal, rather than individual, emotion. This program of literary populism denied the poet access to the dark night of the soul, which must ever be an individual experience. It also limited the range of his language, as well as of his emotions, to the popular, the communal, and only too often, the common. Yet these limitations are exactly the sources of Sandburg's strength. In denying himself the experiences of the more introspective artist and the private diction of the individualistic poet, he became a pioneer in ways of feeling and speaking which most other poets neglect.

Nonetheless, Sandburg is now very much out of favor among the *avant garde,* both as poet and as social thinker. His name is rarely seen in the advanced quarterlies; when it does come up, it is attended by little praise. When *Poetry* recently published its thirty-fifth anniversary issue, the presence of Sandburg among the contributors seemed anachronistic. Indeed, it was almost a matter for wonder, as though a man were to address a memorial service held in his own honor.

Before taking for granted the justice of Sandburg's present eclipse it may be worth while to look into the reasons for his decline. Is the descent of his reputation caused solely by the New Critics' preference for intensity, form, and intellectualized content? Or is it possible that Sandburg has been neglected because most readers have neglected to learn how to read him? Why is it that, while everyone concedes him to be a pioneer in communal expression, so few have followed his lead with any success? Is this because his followers have imitated his faults without understanding his virtues? Or is it because the program to which he has dedicated his career as a poet is an unpromising, even an impossible, basis for art? (pp. 265-66)

Since his favorable critics have been at . . . a loss to understand the form of his verse, it is no surprise that his significant followers are few, though his imitators many. His casual stanzas are so difficult to reconcile with the discipline expected in traditional poetry that the critics are puzzled, and the poet attracts a kind of adulation-by-imitation from those who think that his is an easier way to spread poetry on a page. This opinion is widely held, and has contributed to the decline of Sandburg's prestige.

However, there is more form in Sandburg's verse than meets the eye. I believe a careful reading of **The People, Yes** will show a definite and ingenious organization of the very lists of proverbs and catalogues of popular phrases which seemed to Mr. Zabel to reveal "no apparent principle of contrast or structure." These lists do not, as Professor [Willard] Thorp suggested, "merely assemble the collective wisdom of the people." There is more to Sandburg's art than that; otherwise [critics] would find the files of *The World Almanac* just as satisfying as Sandburg's poems.

The most distinguished portions of **The People, Yes** are those in which the poet succeeds, or nearly succeeds, in imposing form upon his almost intractible materials. Where his scheme can be recognized, those parts of the book assume a power they did not have before that recognition. One such portion includes Sections 36 through 47, which brings to a focus several of Sandburg's major themes. A brief analysis of Sandburg's method here will clarify his intentions for us, and help make evident the direction in which his writings have pioneered. And since his faults are interfused with his virtues, we can also see the limitations of his achievement, and the dangers inherent in making that achievement an example.

In this portion of **The People, Yes,** Sandburg's theme is recovery: recovery from the economic paralysis of the depression, and more immediately, recovery of human dignity from the ravages of want, hopelessness, and fear. The assertion,

> "I am zero, naught, cipher,"
> meditated the symbol preceding the numbers

introduces six verse paragraphs which argue that money brings status, pride, and selfishness. Then,

> Said the scorpions of hate: "The poor hate the rich. The rich hate the poor. The south hates the north. The west hates the east. The workers hate their bosses. The bosses hate their workers. . . . We are a house divided against itself. We are millions of hands raised against each other. We are united in but one aim—getting the dollar. And when we get the dollar we employ it to get more dollars."

The capitalistic economy makes men inhuman. In the next section they wrangle over "what is mine" and "what is yours" and "who says so?" Yet along with the arguing and hating there is joking and laughter, though the humor may be wry indeed.

Sandburg describes the farmers who had overproduced their crops and cattle until they were themselves near starvation. Theirs is the smoldering hatred that verges on violence:

> "I want to shoot somebody but I don't know who.
> "We'll do something. You wait and see.
> "We don't have to stand for this skin game if we're free Americans."

Speaking through the many voices he has chosen to speak for him or to echo in his own words, Sandburg is moved to anger by the greatest of all injustices: the disavowal of human dignity, the crushing of men and of Man by the economic machine.

> Have you seen men handed refusals
> till they began to laugh
> at the notion of ever landing a job
> again— . . .
>
> (pp. 267-69)

The theme of Section 40 is, "We live only once"; we are all played for suckers by one another, but fate in the end makes suckers out of all the players. Meanwhile,

> programs, inventions,
> plans, promises,
> hints, insinuations pour
> from the professional schemers
> into the ears of the people.

But as we learn in Number 41, the people are unpredictable. You can't regulate them. Section 42 presents twenty-seven proverbs and jests which illustrate their diversity and their humor. In 43 people are compared to eggs.

> What sort of an egg are you? . . .
> Under the microscope Agassiz studied one egg:
> chaos, flux, constellations, rainbows:
> "It is a universe in miniature."

Similarly, one man is a paradigm of humanity. There follow twenty-six samples of the jokes and quips of the people. These, like the egg, are microcosms which suggest more than they seem to contain. In Section 45 these jests accumulate with growing intensity:

> They have yarns
> Of a skyscraper so tall they had to put hinges
> On the top two stories so to let the moon go by,
> Of one corncrop in Missouri when the roots
> Went so deep and drew off so much water
> The Mississippi riverbed that year was dry. . . .
> Of the man who drove a swarm of bees across
> the Rocky Mountains and the Desert "and didn't lose a bee," . . .
> Of the boy who climbed a cornstalk growing so fast he would have starved to death if they hadn't shot biscuits up to him, . . .
> Of mosquitoes: one can kill a dog, two of them a man . . .
> Of Paul Bunyan's big blue ox, Babe, measuring between the eyes forty-two ax-handles and a plug of Star tobacco exactly.

From Sandburg's long list of yarns I have abstracted those which point toward the climax of this portion a few pages later. The six motifs quoted above are all taken from the body of comic anecdotes which used to be told by lumber-jacks about their hero, Paul Bunyan. Sandburg has long been familiar with this folklore . . . In their present context these fragments of the Bunyan yarns are piled helter-skelter one upon another; the list includes other folktale motifs, too, from cowboys, engineers, farmers, sailors, sheepherders, and Negro section gangs. A common bond of humor links them in their diversity. These are the incongruities the people laugh at. Sandburg brings the old yarns up to date, too, with jokes about the high-pressure salesman who sold a cop the idea of jumping off the Brooklyn Bridge; the oil man in heaven who succumbs to his own suggestion that there are gushers in hell; and four "fantasies heard at filling stations in the midwest." They are simply old tall tales mechanized. . . . (pp. 269-70)

In these twelve poems (36-47), the scraps of comic folklore have consistently grown in length and continuity from short proverbs and one-line jests to one-paragraph anecdotes, and now, in Number 47, at last to a full poem on a single subject. The increasing length is accompanied by an acceleration of intensity. "Who made Paul Bunyan" is the climax of this development, and the rhapsodic flow of its first paragraph is among the high points of Mr. Sandburg's book and of the Paul Bunyan tales in any form.

Why should Paul Bunyan emerge as the climactic image of the age in this portion of *The People, Yes*? We remember that eleven poems ago the chain of comic links that led to Paul was fastened to the dull weight of despair. The progression from "I am zero" . . . to the ecstatic affirmation of "The people, the bookless people" is a record of the resilience of the human spirit. For Sandburg the Bunyan stories are a major triumph of the collective imagination. They fulfill in this poem the selfsame function that they played in the lives and the art of the hundreds of anonymous raconteurs who told them in the woods, when logging was a folk life which inherited directly the comic traditions of the old frontier. . . . (pp. 271-72)

Whether Sandburg learned them from oral sources or read them watered-down in books, his retelling of these motifs here lacks any distinctive flavor. Only the introductory paragraph has a truly individual tone. The flatness of his diction and the choice of anecdotes combines to defeat the poet's purpose. What was intended as a culmination of his efforts turns out an anticlimax which reveals two endemic weaknesses of Sandburg's art. One is his poetic language, the other his social thinking. A philosophy which appears so full of hope that liberal democracy will in the end prevail contains denials of those very hopes within its own statements of affirmation.

It is Sandburg's personal triumph to have fashioned from the intransigent materials of these dozen poems a form which has the power to invoke our sympathies for the "bottom people," and which invites us to rejoice with them in the imaginative conquests of their hero, Paul Bunyan. But we must also ask whether it was really of moment in 1936 to assume the guise of old Paul Bunyan, so big his footsteps made earthquakes, so strong he turned off water-spouts. The natural elements were not our important enemies then. Neither does it seem especially relevant to thump the expansionist tub with hosannas of a three-mile

table and an ox of fantastic size. Is not this a retreat into the vanished past? The Paul Bunyan tales are not even told any longer among the lumberjacks; how is the poet justified in resurrecting them as a symbol of the contemporary popular imagination?

Sandburg is not using Paul Bunyan narrowly to represent the loggers' hero. Accurately, he saw that these tales of Paul do convey the sense of certain aspects of our national character, and these aspects are not yet extinct simply because bulldozers have displaced ox-teams in the lumber-camps. The concepts of character which such folklore preserves from our past and presents to our future are the tenets of individualism which the pioneers needed to practice in order to survive. Paul Bunyan is the last of a long line of pioneer demigods; his ancestors are Mike Fink and Davy Crockett. Riverboating and hunting died out years ago, but logging continued well into the twentieth century as a way of life which preserved the pioneer's struggles against the hostile wilderness. Hence the yarns of the older heroes were retold about Bunyan, and so survived the passing of the old frontier.

The grip of such comic figures upon the popular imagination continues despite the changing times. The virtues of the pioneers, which the Bunyan tales and other legends keep still fresh in the public mind, derive from their heroic struggle to establish human life where for ages thunderstorms had reigned unchallenged. We admire their indomitable energy; the skills and ingenuity with which they fashioned homes in a hostile wilderness; the persistence with which they seized, held, and populated the resisting earth; and their individualism, forged in the heat of unending adversity, danger, and toil. "The people will live on," Sandburg writes; "You can't laugh off their capacity to take it."

But when civilization overtakes the rugged settlement, how useful are these same virtues? The pioneer ethic of individualism was seldom fitted to deal with interpersonal relationships on other levels than self-assertive violence. The tradition of lawlessness was so cherished on the frontier that such a man as Judge Roy Bean could be celebrated in oral tradition as a hero. Bean was that member of the bench who declared, "I am the law west of the Pecos," held court in a barroom, and said, "The jury will not deliberate; and if it brings a verdict short of hanging' it'll be declared in contempt." Paul Bunyan, too, represents Activity and Will, free from Responsibility, Conscience, or Cooperation. In many ways this frontier individualism is the very antithesis of life in a democratic civilization. While these pioneer virtues may still be admired among "the people," primitive individualism of this sort survives most vigorously in the ethic of old-style business executives, who, in the assertion of their rights of ownership, leave no ground for intelligent analysis in the solution of economic problems.

The depression was the greatest of such problems. Apparently Sandburg proposes to solve its attendant problems of poverty, hopelessness, and fear by exhorting "the people" to remember Paul Bunyan and the virtues of the pioneers. This is really cold comfort for those bottom people who find themselves at the bottom exactly because there is no longer room in America for men to emulate Paul Bunyan. Sandburg's offering is more a testament of his faith in the will of the people to survive than it is even a hint toward any constructive program. He does not suggest the application of rational intelligence in the continual effort to find an equitable balance between the rights and desires of the individual and the institutions with which he lives. In Sandburg's panoramic representation of American life, as Zabel suggests, "he is pulled by so many claims on sympathy and forbearance that nothing survives the prodigious outlay of tolerance and compassion." Like many another native radical he has faith and good intentions, but has not penetrated to the core of those appearances which he records so faithfully. It is hard, too, to reconcile his celebration of rugged individualism with his well-known interest in the Socialist movement.

In resurrecting the dying folklore of a vanished way of life Sandburg resembles his only important literary forbear. Whitman, writing at the moment when industrialization was changing the landscape of the cities and the tempo of the people's lives, saw not the factory and lathe but the teamster, trapper, and Indian squaw. Both poets attempted to create an imaginary portrait of America. Both portrayed the expansive youth of the nation, but missed the maturer visage in which that youthfulness is interfused with other elements. In the modern struggle for survival, energy and resilience and determination—and even a sense of humor—are no longer enough. While these qualities may have helped avert the explosion of baffled anger into senseless violence in the 1930's, they alone did not restore our economy or regenerate our character. To maintain that they did so, or could do so, is a sentimental fiction, romantic but untrue.

A literature employing national myths may well be romantic, but if the romance is a fiction inadequate to the truth, then neither the myths nor the literature they inspire will be living things. Sandburg has performed a remarkable achievement in delineating our comic heritage, and suggesting its possibilities for poetry. But in his emphasis on the resilience and the energy of the people he overlooks many other strands in American culture which should be represented in the epic panorama he has attempted to write. The omission of these strands seriously weakens the validity of his achievement.

The aesthetic of literary populism holds that the people themselves will give language its most interesting forms and thought its most significant development. Such a belief in common speech and popular democracy as the basis for art limits the artist to one or another form of realism. He literally attempts to transcribe from nature, since the diction, structure, and content that he seeks are already expressed in the free intercourse of the common people. Sandburg seems to follow such a program in his verse, which has always reflected his early training in journalism and his highly skilled reportorial eye.

Sandburg has an unusually accurate reportorial ear, too. There is an authenticity about his slang, his yarns, his folklore, that marks him as an accurate historian of the popular imagination. He has chosen to give us his record of that imagination in the words and inflections of the many men

who created its original documents. It is often said that his language is unpoetic; yet who more than Sandburg writes in the spirit of the *Lyrical Ballads?* The language that men actually use, heightened under tension by the faculty of the imagination, is the idiom which he sought in the streets, factories, and farms—the only places where that language may actually be found.

However, he suffers from the same faults which afflicted Wordsworth, and to the degree that Sandburg follows Wordsworth's program further, so he is penalized the more. It is by now clearly evident that the most promising language for poetry is that of the uncommon, rather than the common, man. The variety of common speech which Wordsworth and Coleridge sought was itself uncommon, the supercharging under emotional stress of a limited vocabulary. The result was common words in unusual juxtapositions which suggested thoughts that no amount of aristocratic diction could inspire, unless a similar intensity had produced a similar effect.

The attempt to simplify the diction of poetry is characteristic of the major poets of our time. Eliot, Yeats, and Frost, each in his own fashion, have sought to reinvigorate poetic language by overthrowing the sweet and stuffy vocabularies of the Victorians. Sandburg, too, went to the limit of his premises in his attempt to make the language of poetry come alive. But standing on Chicago street corners to set down verbatim the wry jokes from Skid Row rewarded him more often with urbanality than with the words of power we may presume he sought. Again and again the excitement of Sandburg's concepts dissipates in their conception; the language does not project the intensity of the idea.

From the looseness of his diction it is evident that Sandburg has an unusual notion of the poet's role in producing poetry. Unlike Whitman, from whom his style is usually thought to be derived, Sandburg does not attempt to achieve in the very texture of his language organic forms arising from the tensions of the ideas his images suggest. Whitman's most successful idiom was fresh because he had assimilated many new influences into the language of his poems. The rhythms of the sea, the solemnity of the King James Bible, the incremental repetitions of Biblical verse and nineteenth-century oratory, and the "barbaric yawp" of the backwoods boaster were combined to fashion a new poetic diction. This combination was an act of discipline as well as of the inexplicable processes of creation; it was an operation of intelligence and will, which in time produced an idiom that was the natural expression of the poet's sensibility.

The laxity of Sandburg's style shows that he has not subjected himself to a discipline as forceful as Whitman's. Instead, he strongly relies upon his raw material to suggest or supply the finished forms of his verse. Though he resembles other poets in his colloquial diction and his disregard of traditional forms, it is precisely in these departments that he is most at odds with the main trends in contemporary verse. We may say that "Easter, 1916," "Burnt Norton," "The Death of the Hired Man," and **"Who made Paul Bunyan"** all show a trend away from rhetoric; but Yeats, Eliot, and Frost also show a command of rhythm in the line, tension in the stanza, and compression in language that Sandburg almost never achieves. The ultimate distinction between poetic and prosaic diction is one of intensity. It is here that Sandburg fails. While his craftsmanship is considerable in many other respects, his efforts are denied a power which might be theirs but for his almost complacent reliance upon popular joke and proverb to furnish him finished language to be juggled into poems.

It may well be that what Carl Sandburg attempts to do is not a promising possibility for art. He has tried to record the emotions of a society instead of an individual. His greatest weakness is not even the sagging diction of his stanzas, but the simple fact that "the people" is and remains a faceless abstraction, just as in the people's folklore Paul Bunyan is an abstraction, rather than a personification, of size, strength, cunning, and prowess. In limiting the range of his own sensibilities to experiences which are widely shared the poet of communal emotions cuts himself off from his own deepest resources. He is also likely to underestimate—and even patronize—"the people." No writer has ever portrayed or manipulated communal emotions with the power and assurance of Shakespeare, that relentless prober of the individual soul. Except in patches, Sandburg's work is undramatic, unconcerned with the portrayal or development of character. His "people" are a hive of bees who hum snatches of human speech.

Perhaps Sandburg's major purpose was doomed from the start. In a culture as pre-eminently noncollective as ours, the poet who presents collective emotions divorced from the individual consciousness may have set himself an impossible task. He has explored a peninsula of poetry isolated from the heartland of contemporary writing. MacLeish and Stephen V. Benet have skirted his shores. John Dos Passos made poetic prose in the wake of his prosaic poems; *U.S.A.* is perhaps the only book whose plan at all resembles that of *The People, Yes.* But Carl Sandburg is a lonely figure in modern literature, a pioneer whom few have followed.

And yet *The People, Yes* has an impact, an individual stamp. It demands recognition and refuses to be forgotten. Different as it is from all other poetry produced in our time, unsuccessful as it is when judged by the standards which all other poetry demands, it billows with an imagination widely informed and widely curious which gives it a life within itself. Though its over-all structure fails to sustain it as a single poem, its parts seem more important than the whole. They are the authentic records of a single imagination the popular imagination deeply stirred. Perhaps Carl Sandburg's brighter day is yet to come, when younger writers will find in his virtues a touchstone to the development of their own. Some of them may temper his wide-ranging consciousness with their own introspection, with an intensity and a formal discipline he has failed to achieve. But surely he has much to teach them of the imaginative possession of the American past, as well as of the sensitive observation of the American scene today. (pp. 272-78)

Dan G. Hoffman, "Sandburg and 'The People': His Literary Populism Reappraised," in The Antioch Review, *Vol. X, No. 2, June, 1950, pp. 265-78.*

Henry E. Kolbe   (essay date 1959)

[*An American minister and professor of religion and philosophy, Kolbe wrote* One World Under God *(1963). In the essay excerpted below, Kolbe examines the many allusions to Christ found throughout Sandburg's poetry. While stating that Sandburg displayed much tenderness, love, and sympathy for Christ and Christianity, Kolbe also asserts that Sandburg expressed a great deal of rage toward evangelical exploitation of religion.*]

Carl Sandburg at eighty is not only a great author and artist. He has become a living symbol of the land and the age in which he lives. His historical writings, notably his works on Lincoln, and his poems have made him the most authentic literary voice of twentieth-century America.

On the dust jacket of his *Complete Poems* there is a statement from Irita Van Doren, editor of the *New York Herald Tribune Book Review:* "Always he has written poetry, even when he called it history or biography or fiction." And in his poetry, Sandburg has caught the feel of America as no one else, not even Walt Whitman, has ever done. Whitman, it is true, reflected the mood of lusty expansionist America in the middle of the nineteenth century in a manner unmatched by any of his contemporaries. The last years of his life, however, were spent in the semi-retirement of invalidism, whereas Sandburg has continued to be active well beyond the Scriptural threescore and ten. (p. 248)

Sandburg is the poet of *America* in a manner which is true of no other poet of our time. Vachel Lindsay has never caught the imagination of the people in the manner of Sandburg. The rhythm of Lindsay's poems is haunting but it is not the rhythm of the country. Robert Frost is rather the poet of New England than of the nation, and he has not received the popular reception which has made Sandburg "one of the people" in so distinctive a manner.

For Carl Sandburg "sings America," to borrow a phrase from Whitman—the America of the twentieth century, America come of age. In his hundreds of poems, short and long, early and late, there are caught up the voices and echoes of our time, the words that portray not merely the sounds but also the sights and even the smells and the indefinable feelings of the age in which he lives.

Here are the clanging of Chicago streetcars, the roar of factories, the hissing of hot steel poured forth from a tapped furnace at Gary, the noise of the factory gate at quitting time, the rude language and the dull pain of the poor and the slum-dweller. Here too are the concerns for people, especially the common people, and the strong hatred of cant and hypocrisy, especially that which parades in religious dress—the concern and the hatred which reveal not only the soul of the poet but of the religious and spiritually sensitive man as well.

All of this is part of the familiar story of Carl Sandburg. This is the Sandburg that every one knows. What is perhaps not so familiar is that a strong current of explicitly religious feeling and expression runs throughout his poems—from the earliest ones in the 1916 volume to the previously unpublished ones included in the final section of the *Complete Poems* of 1950. There are direct references or indubitable allusions to religious themes on more than two hundred of the 676 pages of the *Complete Poems.* Many of these references or allusions or words are, as may be expected, of small significance. The name of God or of Christ appears a few times as expletive. Occasionally biblical or other religious allusions are used almost casually to illustrate a particular point. Far more often, however, the explicitly religious passages in the poems are at once profoundly moving and spiritually penetrating. (p. 249)

This does not mean, however, that Sandburg is a theological poet after the same fashion as T. S. Eliot, Gerard Manley Hopkins, or W. H. Auden. For Sandburg does not theologize: he describes, and in his descriptions there are manifested the strong feelings of those whom he describes, whether they be others or himself. He does not argue nor persuade. He does not seek to point the reader toward God nor to moralize about an abstract good. He seeks neither to preach nor to teach. He is neither prophet nor pedagogue but, as in his journalistic days, basically a reporter.

If in fact Sandburg may be said to point the reader toward anything at all, it is simply to the world around him, with its people and their feelings and desires and dreams and cares and hopes. But the poet knows that these people live not simply in relation to their neighbors and their physical environment but in relation to God as well. His native sensitivity to the wholeness of the human person repeatedly brings to explicit expression this Godward aspect of man's experience.

Sandburg's concern for quite ordinary people and for equally ordinary run-of-the-street experience is manifested in his constant emphasis on what has been aptly called "the little picture"—frequently the single, often inconspicuous, person of the crowded sections of the city. This, in turn, is tied up with his thought of God. Indeed, as one reads Sandburg's poems, one is rather naturally drawn to think that in them he is revealing his own awareness of Jesus' concern for the poor and the outcast and the downcast of his own time. This is not, of course, to make a messianic claim for the poet. It is simply to record what is there to be seen and felt. And, in view of Sandburg's own early religious training in the little Swedish Lutheran church at Galesburg, it is surely not too much to expect that his understanding of Jesus should have played a large part in his own concerns for those "little ones" among whom Christ himself found his own most friendly reception. For Jesus, too, we ought never to forget, was a poet!

The references to Christ in Sandburg's poems are, on the affirmative side, such as to suggest not merely the admiration of the poet for the poetic spirit of Jesus. Rather they manifest the authentic devoutness which is reverence mingled with love. The other side of this, the negative aspect, is the hot anger which flames out in denunciation of those who would reduce the living words and the vital sensitivities of Jesus to dead and deadening religious cant, who would turn his prophetic and dynamic teachings and the

inspiration of his nobility of spirit into an opiate. Here the sensitivity of the poet and the strength of the prophet combine to pour out the rage which is the obverse of reverence.

First, let us see some of the affirmative aspects of Sandburg's treatment of Christ. Here we turn to his warm and loving poem about Christ at twelve, entitled simply **"Child."** The poet's picture does not fit in with historic church tradition, it is true, but rather it identifies Christ with the basic beauty and naturalness and grace of all children and, by quite warrantable extension, to all that is "divinely human" in man:

> The young child, Christ, is straight and wise
> And asks questions of the old men, questions
> Found under running water for all children
> And found under shadows thrown on still waters
> By tall trees looking downward, old and gnarled.
> Found to the eyes of children alone, untold,
> Singing a low song in the loneliness.
> And the young child, Christ, goes on asking
> And the old men answer nothing and only know love
> For the young child, Christ, straight and wise.

The same sensitive tenderness is revealed in many other poems. It is suggested in the way in which the poet takes note of small details: In the window of "Jabowsky's (pawnshop) on a side street" in Chicago he notices "a porcelain crucifix with the glaze nicked where the left elbow of Jesus is represented." He records a sentence written by "a pauper"

> To a patch of purple asters at a whitewashed wall:
> "Let every man be his own Jesus—that's enough."

In **"Brass Keys"** the poet draws a picture of joy. . . . Here human love, devoutness, hope, and courage are met together to fill out the poet's conception of what joy means to men. And, quite characteristically, this joy is centered around the image of Christ. (pp. 250-52)

His sensitive appreciation for the genuine and simple faith of the poor is indicated in the sympathetic and even joyous tone of the little poem **"Washerwoman"**:

> The washerwoman is a member of the Salvation Army.
> And over the tub of suds rubbing underwear clean
> She sings that Jesus will wash her sins away
> And the red wrongs she has done God and man
> Shall be white as driven snow.
> Rubbing underwear she sings of the Last Great Washday.

There is exquisite and almost infinite tenderness in the way the poet writes of a bit of carved ivory in **"Loin Cloth"**—a tenderness which beyond doubt reflects Sandburg's identification of himself with the carver in his faith and devotion. (pp. 252-53)

There is, however, another side to Sandburg's poems about Christ. There is not simply tenderness and love and sympathy, but there is also the rage which is the negative counterpart of reverence. The lover of Christ is the hater of pious and empty cant.

Something of this anger is suggested in **"Jaws,"** written at the outbreak of the first world war and reflecting the poet's judgment upon men and nations which refused to heed the words of him whom they all looked to as Savior and Lord:

> Seven nations stood with their hands on the jaws
>   of death.
> It was the first week in August, Nineteen Hun-
>   dred Fourteen.
> I was listening, you were listening, the whole
>   world was listening.
> And all of us heard a Voice murmuring:
>   "I am the way and the light,
>   He that believeth on me
>   Shall not perish
>   But shall have everlasting life."
> Seven nations listening heard the Voice and an-
>   swered:
>   "O Hell!"
> The jaws of death began clicking and they go on
>   clicking:
>   "O Hell!"

The fires of the poet's anger burn perhaps more hotly in the bitter protest of the depression period of the mid-thirties. For this economic debacle was rooted in, and brought to explicit manifestation, a lack of basic human sympathy and concern—of what in the New Testament is called love. The poet's protest against brutalization and hypocrisy is well revealed in this passage from *The People, Yes:*

> When violence is hired
> and murder is paid for
> and tear gas, clubs, automatics,
> and blam blam machine guns
> join in the hoarse mandate,
> "Get the hell out of here,"
> why then reserve a Sabbath
> and call it a holiness day
> for the mention of Jesus Christ
> and why drag in the old quote
> "Thou shalt love thy neighbor
>   as thyself"?

In the light of the tenderness with which he himself deals with Jesus and the sympathy which he manifests toward those whose faith bears the seal of reality, it is not to be wondered at that what is probably Sandburg's angriest poem should have been written in denunciation of one whom he felt to abuse the spirit of Jesus while making free and frequent use of his name. Often the poet's protests against injustice are expressed in irony, but there is no subtlety of literary device in his attack on the revivalist preacher in the poem, **"To a Contemporary Bunk-shooter."**

It would be difficult to match the feeling of prophetic rage which this poem manifests against the evangelist's exploitation of Christ. The poet's rage runs at white heat because of the double betrayal which he senses—the betrayal of Christ by one ostensibly preaching for him, and of the people whom Jesus loved and for whom he poured out his own very life. (pp. 253-55)

Nor is it simply what religious scholars term "the historical Jesus" which is the object of Sandburg's attention. The sense of "the eternal Christ" is present, too, to illuminate and intensify the significance of the man of Galilee. There is no use of the technical theological word, but the idea of incarnation is frequently suggested.

In the following passage from **"Slabs of the Sunburnt West,"** the poet records his musings on riding muleback out of the Grand Canyon. The God of the beauty and grandeur of nature—even the majestic awesome beauty and grandeur of the great Canyon itself—is not adequate to satisfy the needs of the spirit of man. In an obvious allusion to Jesus, Sandburg gives expression to his feelings on the necessity of incarnation:

> Before a ten mile float
> of auburn, gold, and purple,
> footprints on a sunset airpath haze,
>   I ask:
> How can I taste with my tongue a tongueless
>   God?
> How can I touch with my fingers a fingerless
>   God?
> How can I hear with my ears an earless God?
> Or smell of a God gone noseless long ago?
> Or look on a God who never needs eyes for look-
>   ing?

Every one who has stood on the rim of the Grand Canyon can testify to the awesomeness of the spectacle, the sense of religious hush which overcomes the soul and lays the finger of the heart upon the lips. (pp. 255-56)

To this same period of Sandburg's writing there belongs a portion of another poem—the 1928 Phi Beta Kappa poem at Harvard, **"Good Morning, America."** Here, while one does not find—as one does not expect—the ecclesiastical dogma of redemption, one does find the mystic's sense of the reality and the presence of Christ in life, and especially in those dimensions of life where love is expressed, as it was at the crucifixion, in the pouring out of life for life:

> There is a Sleepwalker
> goes walking and talking—
> Go alone and away from all books, go with your
>   own heart into the storm of human hearts and
>   see if somewhere in that storm there are bleed-
>   ing hearts, sacred hearts taking a bitter wages
>   of doom, red-soaked and crimson-plunged
>   hearts of the Redeemer of Men.

Something of this same sense of the identification of Christ with man is probably intended to be suggested in the poem entitled **"Early Lynching."** It is in keeping with Sandburg's trend of thought that the death of Jesus should be referred to as a lynching—not as something which Jesus himself deliberately chose, even though he would not flinch from it when it came. Nor was the death of Jesus foreordained of God, a thought which is doubtless repugnant to the poet's mind. Rather Jesus is the victim of human injustice, the same kind of injustice which injures and destroys man in today's world.

In this poem, however, Christ is not simply the man Jesus, in innocence suffering pain and death because of the wrongs of other men. Rather he is also those other men who are caught up—at least relatively innocent—in the matrix of events. Christ is in a mystic sense identified with the people who are being used by the foes of Jesus to further their own evil ends: the crowd who without knowing why are led to cry for his death; the workmen who fashion the cross and drive the nails through the hands of Jesus; the spectators who look on at the scene of tragedy unaware of the meaning of the events in which they thus participate.

There is in this poem, too, a strong note of irony of judgment. For the Christ who is hated and finally killed because of his concern for the poor and his denunciation of their oppressors is not only the man with "the smell of the slums . . . on him." He is also partaker in or inheritor of the eternity of the world of nature and of the God who is the creator of nature. (pp. 256-57)

It is not without significance that immediately following this poem there is one titled **"Plunger,"** which speaks of what Abraham Lincoln called "the last full measure of devotion." While the name of Jesus does not appear in this poem, its very proximity to the other one makes it impossible to mistake the "plunger" to whom reference is made:

> Empty the last drop.
> Pour out the final clinging heartbeat.
> Great losers look on and smile.
> Great winners look on and smile.
>
> Plunger!
> Take a long breath and let yourself go.

The sense of the ever-living Christ is reflected again in **"Precious Moments,"** which speaks of the poet's conception of the living words which characterize true poetry and which he relates to "the living Word" in a theological sense:

> Bright vocabularies are transient as rainbows.
> Speech requires blood and air to make it.
> Before the word comes off the end of the tongue,
> While the diaphragm of flesh negotiates the word,
> In the moment of doom when the word forms
> It is born, alive, registering an imprint—
> Afterward it is a mummy, a dry fact, done and gone.
> The warning holds yet: Speak now or forever hold your peace.
> *Ecce homo* had meanings: Behold the Man!
> Look at him! Dying he lives and speaks.

The concern for incarnation in Sandburg's poems is manifest not only in the poems referring to Easter and its surrounding events. It is manifested, too, in the sense of wonder which emerges in two poems about Christmas. The first of these comes from the early period of his writing and is entitled **"Rusty Crimson (Christmas Day, 1917)."** In it the wonder of Christmas is brought down to date as the poet pictures Jesus as being born, not long ago in the stable at Bethlehem but today in Sandburg's own prairie state of Illinois: . . .

> "Jesus in an Illinois barn early this morning, the baby Jesus . . . in flannels . . . "

In the final collection within the **Complete Poems**—those previously unpublished—there is another poem, **"Special Starlight,"** which manifests both profound understanding of the meaning of Christmas and sensitive appreciation for what must forever be one of the basic meanings of incarnation. Apart from the direct quotations from the Bible, this poem does not make use of established religious language or symbolism. It does, however, point clearly to a meaning of Christmas which is all too often overlooked—the new sanctifying of all life because the Son of God has shared it.

> The Creator of night and of birth
> was the Maker of the stars.
>
> (pp. 258-59)

In this poem, with its manifestation of the poet's own deep and sensitive devotion, we have a fitting signature to Carl Sandburg's portrayal of Jesus Christ and his meaning for the life of man. (p. 261)

> *Henry E. Kolbe, "Christ and Carl Sandburg,"
> in* Religion in Life, *Vol. XXVIII, No. 2,
> Spring, 1959, pp. 248-61.*

Michael Yatron   (essay date 1959)

[*An American educator, Yatron is the author of the novels* Sappho's Island *(1964) and* In Pink Balloons *(1967). In the following excerpt, Yatron examines the value of using Sandburg's poetry as a model of nonconformity and humanitarianism in the classroom.*]

Carl Sandburg, who wrote simple poetry for simple people . . . is a good poet for the high school English teacher, faced with indifferent students, to begin his poetic chore with. Sandburg devoted his life to translating into poetry the idiom of the people, by whom he meant the majority of native-born and naturalized Americans, who built post-Civil War America with the strength of their hands, the sweat of their brows, and the obstinacy of their spirit into the present-day Colossus. Sandburg was not sure he was writing poetry, but he was sure that what he said had to be meaningful to the average truck driver on Chicago's Wabash Avenue, whose intelligence "the Dark Spirits," Sandburg's epithet for esoteric poets and critics, treated with contempt. . . .

Sandburg's popular appeal can be extended to the classroom, precisely because his diction and content are not likely to arouse the antagonism of anti-poetic students. If anything, he offers the thrill of recognition to the student, particularly since the America Sandburg chants of is an America that, despite jet airplanes and television sets, still exists and conforms to the student's own experience. (p. 524)

Sandburg presents a model of nonconformity and humanitarianism and, it is here, in my opinion, that his true worth for the student lies. In our age of the supremacy of the state and the rationalization of industry the individual has been reduced to a cipher. The Myrmidons of Hitler, Stalin, and Tojo and the American "organization man" are symptomatic of the antlike society toward which twentieth century man is gravitating. . . . (pp. 524-25)

The first requirement for freedom is the recognition that the state is not the master of the individual, but his servant. This requirement of freedom is met by the individual's having a voice in the ultimate power of the state, the power to go to war. In this connection Sandburg's voice has always been the voice of a free man. He has written many anti-war poems, pointing out that wars are often made by despots and fought by and suffered by the people. . . .

Sandburg himself served as a common soldier in the Spanish American War, attended West Point briefly as a "veteran," turned violently pacifistic during World War I, and rejected pacifism in World War II. This completion of the circle shows that Sandburg was not stupidly consistent, and its value for our conformist students lies in sowing the seed in their minds that there is nothing sacred about militarism and rascality, albeit they may wear the cloak of patriotism.

Sandburg was equally scathing as regards big business, which too often has maximized profits while minimizing humanity. (p. 525)

In the area of racial relationships, Sandburg is without prejudice. Hungarians with accordions (**"Happiness"**), Greeks shoveling gravel (**"Near Keokuk"**), Italians working with pick and shovel (**"The Shovel Man"**), and Jews selling fish (**"Fish Crier"**) are presented sympathetically. And what is more to Sandburg's credit is that his tolerance is extended to Asiatics. "My prayers go . . . for the Russian people. If they are merely 'Asiatic hordes,' then I'm a barrel-house bum," he stated. For a man born in the isolationist Middle West, whose mind was formed during the period when the spectre of "the yellow peril" was publicized often, this sanity is reasonableness itself. (pp. 525-26)

Quite consistently, Sandburg was a champion of the Negro. At the close of World War I, some white boys of Chicago stoned a colored youth on a raft with the result that he was drowned. A race riot ensued and Sandburg was sent by the Chicago *Daily News* to report the situation. Out of this reportage grew a book, *The Chicago Race Riots,* which clearly revealed Sandburg's belief that "a man's a man for a' that."

Another ugly thing that Sandburg saw growing in American society is class stratification. . . . Sandburg is not ashamed of unpressed and patched pants, of unshined and worn shoes, of long hair. He detests expensive night clubs and dress suits, and, I suppose, fin-tailed automobiles. Material things and glossy appearances may have their place in brightening life, but they are not the end-all and be-all of existence which our middle class society has made them. And they are certainly not worth the never-ending wage slavery and bill-paying which their possession entails. Our poet in ignoring materialism again provides youth with a needed alternate possibility to the drive for success.

Sandburg is a fine example for the youth who suspects that a mess of pottage isn't worth a soul and a life. Sandburg rode freight trains, washed dishes, worked in a construction camp, threshed wheat, learned the painter's trade, en-

listed in the Army, was a college student, a hobo, a wandering minstrel, a newspaperman, a militant Socialist, a poet, and a man of letters. He was a man trying to find himself but always moving in the direction of his true self. (pp. 526-27)

Another area where our student may profit from Sandburg's voice is the area of work. . . . Sandburg sings praises of honest toil; he calls work a privilege. And he does not think a diploma makes a man. He realizes that many folk with homely virtues and skills are far superior to both lettered and unlettered blockheads, and their society healthier and stabler than a parasitic one where men prey on men.

Sandburg, then, has a basic content which can be summed up in the word Man and which can nourish the mind of the young in the best traditions of Western Civilization. The next question to be raised is, Is what Sandburg writes poetry, and, if so, how good is it?

Sandburg, as I have stated earlier, was not sure that he was writing poetry. He was trying to communicate to an audience which was not sophisticated verbally, to whom the connotations of words are very closely related to their denotations, to whom literary allusion and subtle metaphor are meaningless. He has been an exponent of Wordsworth's "man talking to men." But this use of a *lingua communis* carries with it its own trap, as Coleridge pointed out. The language of prose and the language of metrical composition are two different entities. Thus Sandburg's work quite often degenerates into a pedestrian prosaism summed up by the word "talk." Accordingly, he has been accused, justifiably in this writer's opinion, of being diffuse, clownish, and vulgar.

Sandburg (right) and friend Fred Dickinson.

Such criticism, however, is by no means the final word. (p. 527)

There is no blind spot, however, in my feeling that Sandburg has many limitations. His is not a lyric gift; he neither sings nor can he give expression to deep human emotions. He is not a philosophical poet, nor a dramatic one—rather he is a poet descriptive of the surface, whose eye and ear are keen and who reproduces America as no one else has. He is, as I have stated, a good beginning for the anti-poetic—no mean contribution. He can attract to poetry many of our youth who would normally be repulsed by other poets who seem to say nothing in antiquated and dull language. And once Sandburg has been the initial magnet, and he has given the student the thrill of recognition and of understanding, the next step is to teach the mechanics of traditional poetry and lead the student to the rich veins of English, and ultimately, world poetry. (pp. 527, 539)

> *Michael Yatron, "Carl Sandburg: The Poet as Nonconformist," in* English Journal, *Vol. XLVIII, No. 9, December, 1959, pp. 524-27, 539.*

Gay Wilson Allen (essay date 1960)

[*Allen, an American educator and biographer, is a respected contributor to the scholarship of Walt Whitman. His* The Solitary Singer: A Critical Biography of Walt Whitman *(1955) won the Tamiment Institute Book Award. Allen also contributed to the* Saturday Review of Literature *and the* New York Times Book Review, *as well as other scholarly journals. In his reexamination of Sandburg's literary reputation excerpted below, Wilson finds Sandburg's poetics worthwhile but dismisses his sentimentality.*]

In 1950, at the age of seventy-two, Carl Sandburg published a collected edition of his poetry called **Complete Poems.** It was a heavy volume, running to nearly seven hundred large pages and spanning a generation of poetic output, from **"Chicago,"** first published in Harriet Monroe's *Poetry* in March, 1914, to the great elegy on Franklin Roosevelt, **"When Death Came April Twelve 1945."** In his "Notes for a Preface" Sandburg wrote, "It could be, in the grace of God, I shall live to be eighty-nine, as did Hokusai, and speaking my farewell to earthly scenes, I might paraphrase: 'If God had let me live five years longer I should have been a writer.'"

Sandburg's most severe critics would probably grant that he is a "writer," even a gifted one, but whether he deserves to be called "poet" is still disputed. (p. 315)

The "puzzlement" experienced by critics thirty years ago becomes even more persistent now after Sandburg has completed his fourscore of years. To some extent this is the natural consequence of the shift in sensibility of both poets and critics during the past three decades, but it is also in part the result of the literary role that Sandburg chose for himself at the beginning of his career, as the reception of his **Complete Poems** demonstrated. It was widely and prominently reviewed, but reviewers betrayed by their words that they had not read the book; indeed, had

hardly read Sandburg since the 1920's or 1930's, for the man they wrote about was the theatrical, self-conscious "Chicago poet" and the optimistic affirmer of **The People, Yes.** There was one exception; Louis D. Rubin, Jr., began his perceptive critique in the *Hopkins Review:*

> It seems to me that the critics who most dislike the poetry of Carl Sandburg do so for precisely the wrong reasons, and that those who praise Sandburg's work do so for equally mistaken reasons. What is bad in Sandburg is not his poetics, but his sentimentality. And when he is good, it is not because he sings of the common people, but because he has an extraordinarily fine gift of language and feeling for lyric imagery.

This is an admirably clear statement of the problem. And readers will either learn to distinguish the poetry from the propaganda and sentimentality or Sandburg's name will fade from the history of twentieth-century poetry. In old age he is still one of the most vivid personalities on the American scene, but his reputation has suffered in almost direct ratio to the rise of Eliot's and Pound's, both members of his own generation; and this is unfortunate, for he has written some poetry that deserves to live.

Sandburg's early role as the poet of Chicago and the sunburnt Midwest helped him gain quick recognition. What might now be called the "Midwest myth" was then in formation, and he found it both convenient and congenial. In part this myth was the final phase of American romantic nationalism. Emerson, in his historymaking "American Scholar" address, called for literary independence from Europe; in the twentieth century a group of Midwestern writers adapted this threadbare doctrine to mean liberation from the cultural dominance of the Eastern United States. There were, of course, new experiences and environments in the region demanding newer literary techniques and a retesting of values and standards, and in the novel especially these needs were met with Realism and Naturalism which yielded stimulating and beneficial results. (pp. 316-17)

Here is the myth: other cities are "soft"; Chicago is brutal, wicked, and ugly, but to be young, strong, and proud is more important. In the first place, Chicago was not unique in its brutality or virility. For social and moral degradation, New York, Boston, or San Francisco could equal it, . . . and for business enterprise and physical expansion, Cleveland, Dallas, Seattle, and a dozen other cities were as dynamic. However, for the first three decades of the twentieth century the Midwest did produce more writers (notably, Anderson, Hart Crane, Dreiser, Fitzgerald, Hemingway, Masters, Lindsay, Frank Norris) than any other region of the United States, thus supporting the notion that the East was effete and that cultural vitality was shifting to midcontinent.

A more unfortunate influence on Sandburg's poetry than his acceptance of the Midwest myth was his own private myth, in which only the poor and oppressed have souls, integrity, the right to happiness, and the capability of enjoying life. There are only two classes in Sandburg's **Chicago Poems,** day laborers and "millionaires." He is contemptuous of the millionaire's "perfumed grief" when his daughter dies, but "I shall cry over the dead child of a stockyards hunky." Certainly a poet has a right to his sympathies, perhaps even a few prejudices—in which no poet could rival Pound. What is objectionable in Sandburg's attitudes and choice of subject in his early poems is his use of stereotypes and clichés. In **"The Walking Man of Rodin"** he finds "a regular high poem of legs" and praises the sculptor for leaving "off the head." This is one of Sandburg's worst stereotypes, leaving off the head, "The skull found always crumbling neighbor of the ankles." Consequently, in the 1930's, when proletarian sympathies were valued more than artistry or universal truth, Sandburg's reputation as a poet reached its highest point. . . . In the 1950's, when social protest was less popular or even suspect, most serious critics simply ignored Sandburg. Perhaps, however, this is the most propitious time for a re-evaluation, for discovering exactly what as a poet he is or is not.

Sandburg is not, whatever else he may be, a thinker like Robinson or Eliot; not even a cracker-barrel philosopher like Frost. So far as he has a philosophy it is pluralistic, empirical, positivistic. He loves "facts," and has made a career of collecting them to be used in journalism, speeches, biography, a novel, and poetry. Yet he is in no sense a pedant; his facts (when they are facts and not prejudiced supposition) are alive and pertinent, and he is usually willing to let them speak for themselves. "What is instinct?" he asks in "Notes for a Preface" (and the title itself is characteristic). "What is thought? Where is the absolute line between the two. Nobody knows—as yet." He is still, he says, a "seeker." He might be called a pragmatic humanist. Certainly he is not a Naturalist, who believes that human nature is simply animal nature; or a supernaturalist, who has an equally low opinion of mankind. Among his new poems is a satire on a contemporary poet, probably Eliot, who believes that "The human race is its own Enemy Number One." There is no place for "original sin" in Sandburg's theology.

From first to last, Sandburg writes of man in the physical world, and he still regards the enemies of humanity as either social or political. Man's salvation, he thinks, is his instinctive yearning for a better world; in the practical sense: idealism, the "dream." At the end of World War II he wrote **"The Long Shadow of Lincoln: A Litany,"** in which, remembering the "liberation" of Europe and the battles of the South Pacific, he advised his countrymen to

> Be sad, be kind, be cool,
> remembering, under God, a dreamdust
> hallowed in the ruts and gullies,
> solemn bones under the smooth blue sea,
> faces warblown in a falling rain.

In this role as the conscience of his nation he has written some of his best poems, neither blatantly patriotic nor mawkishly sentimental. He plays this role, in fact, more gracefully than Whitman, whose best poems are usually his least self-consciously nationalistic. (pp. 317-19)

Whitman is the older poet with whom Sandburg is most often compared, and there are superficial resemblances, in their humble origins, their anti-intellectual poses, their seeing beauty and nobility in common objects and simple

people. It is true, too, that Sandburg greatly admires Whitman, and once wrote a preface for an edition of *Leaves of Grass.* Yet despite these affinities, the two poets are different in temperament, in sources of power, and especially in prosody.

Because most of Sandburg's poems are in "free verse" it has often been assumed that he has continued Whitman's verse techniques. Some of his long lines do resemble Whitman's, and achieve the same space empathy, which is one of their chief aesthetic functions. But the big difference is that Whitman composed by line units, making great use of parallelism (a "rhythm of thought"), with almost no enjambment. Sometimes he used true metrical patterns, but freely, organically. Yet regardless of metrics or their absence, his basic unit was the verse, or line—usually a complete predication. . . . This is not Sandburg's structure, or his music. Of course he was influenced by Whitman's freedom, but his versification is usually nearer the experiments of Arno Holz in Germany and the French poets of the late nineteenth century, such as Jules Laforgue, Gustave Kahn, and Francis Vielé-Griffin, who gave currency to the term "vers libre." (p. 319)

In his first volume of poems, *In Reckless Ecstasy,* privately published (1904) and wisely never reprinted, he still used conventional rhyme and meter. . . . At some period between 1904 and 1912 Sandburg adopted the newer phrasal prosody, in which neither number of syllables or counting of accents determined the pattern. The line might be a complete statement . . . or it might be a single word:

> Bareheaded,
> Shoveling,
> Wrecking,
> Planning, etc.

Here the arrangement is mainly typographical to emphasize thought, word, and even rhythm (a kind of grammatical rhyme). But in other poems the line division is by clause or sentence, in prose rhythms, often even without any striking or "poetic" imagery. One of many examples is **"Happiness"**:

> I asked professors who teach the meaning of life
> to tell me what is happiness.
>
> And I went to famous executives who boss the
> work of thousands of men.
>
> They all shook their heads and gave me a smile
> as though I was trying to fool with them.
>
> And then one Sunday afternoon I wandered out
> along the Desplaines river
>
> And I saw a crowd of Hungarians under the
> trees with their women and children and a keg
> of beer and an accordion.

This is essentially prose, but the terse, simple language does heighten the implied definition. It is a poem by Sandburg's own theory, which we should examine before further analysis.

He began, as the title of his first book plainly reveals, with the typical romantic concept that poetry is simply words arranged to evoke emotion. In his preface he agreed with Marie Corelli (from whom he derived his title) in her praise of "reckless ecstasies of language." In his own words, "There are depths of life that logic cannot sound. It takes feeling." (pp. 320-21)

Beginning with the **Chicago Poems** and continuing through to his latest compositions, Sandburg has always created a new form—or at least format—for each poem, not counting the unconscious repetition of trivial mannerisms. He is, in fact, one of the most *formal* of all free-verse poets, with a greater sense of form than many poets who use rhyme and meter. His control of emotion and thought fluctuates, but his architectural instinct and judgment seldom desert him.

The famous **"Chicago"** poem has a clear, logical structure. The introduction contains five short lines of brutal labels for the city—technically, synecdoches: "Hog Butcher . . . , / Tool Maker, Stacker of Wheat, ..." Then comes the logical development in seven long lines, which are banded and subdivided by parallelism, so perfectly balanced that they create a rhythmical pattern of their own: "They tell me . . . ," "Yes, it is true . . . ," but. . . . The poet flings back his answer with new similes, rising to another set of single-word attributes, displayed on the page as separate lines to balance the epithets of the opening lines of the poem: "Bareheaded, / Shouting, / Wrecking, / Planning," and,—with rising tempo,—"Building, breaking, rebuilding, . . . " (Both sense and rhythm are strengthened by placing "breaking" between "Building" and "rebuilding.") Then, more calmly, "Under the smoke . . . ," "Under the terrible burden . . . ," balanced by "Laughing . . . / Bragging . . . ," repeated with variations in the final line, which also completes the circle, returns to the epithets of the introduction, and makes a final logical application of them.

The very next poem in this early collection, **"Sketch,"** has a decidedly different form and structure. Here syntactical and rhetorical patterns have very little to do with the line divisions, which are based on images. In his sketch the poet paints with words, but using words gives him the advantage of movement; his images are dynamic, and this enables one image to charge the contiguous image with its power.

> The shadows of the ships
> Rock on the crest
> In the low blue lustre
> Of the tardy and the soft inrolling tide.
>
> A long brown bar at the dip of the sky
> Puts an arm of sand in the span of salt.
> The lucid and endless wrinkles
> Draw in, lapse and withdraw.
> Wavelets crumble and white spent bubbles
> Wash on the floor of the beach.
>
> Rocking on the crest
> In the low blue lustre
> Are the shadows of the ships.

The ships themselves are not seen, but their presence is felt in the undulating shadows and the rhythms of the waves,

> A long brown bar at the dip of the sky

> Puts an arm of sand in the span of salt.

(pp. 326-27)

The emphasis on blue, brown, and white in the shimmering light gives the poem the form and color of a French impressionistic painting. The picture is complete without the last three lines, but the reiteration of the words and the composite images of the opening stanza (for the lines are spaced and function as a stanza) are typical of Sandburg's structure and demonstrate his sense of form. (pp. 327-28)

No schematic prosody or basic structural pattern can be educed from the study of Sandburg's **Complete Poems.** But he nevertheless has an intuitive sense of equivalence (balance and counterbalance); he likes a closed circuit in sound and sense. In his most ambitious effort to write a whole book on one theme (however general), **The People, Yes,** he made a compendium of folklore, vernacular observations, graphic descriptions of episodes and incidents in American life, and interspersed these with his epigrammatic comments. In appearance it is the most formless book he ever published; yet even in this loose composition his sense of form is apparent on every page. Section 87, for instance, begins in this way:

> The people learn, unlearn, learn,
> a builder, a wrecker, a builder again,
> a juggler of shifting puppets.
> > In so few eyeblinks
> > In transition lightning streaks,
> the people project midgets into giants,
> the people shrink titans into dwarfs.
>
> > Faiths blow on the winds
> > and become shibboleths
> > and deep growths
> > with man ready to die
> for a living word on the tongue,
> for a light alive in the bones,
> for dreams fluttering in the wrists.

The end of this section, however, raises a serious question about Sandburg's diction:

> This free man is a rare bird and when you meet
> > him take a good look at him and try
> > to figure him out because
> Some day when the United States of the Earth
> > gets going and runs smooth and pretty there
> > will be more of him than we have now.

These mixtures of slang and colloquialism ("rare bird," "figure him out," "gets going," "runs . . . pretty," etc.) were deliberately chosen to represent the speech and thinking of common people, but the objections that Coleridge raised to Wordsworth's similar theory of diction are still pertinent. Perhaps it might be argued that such usages in **The People, Yes** serve an aesthetic purpose that Sandburg probably did not consider: they serve to change pace and highlight by contrast the more dignified language that usually follows (as it does in the beginning of section 88). It is doubtful, however, that such contrasts sufficiently compensate for the loss of concentration, the diffusion of emotion, the general arousing of prosaic connotations. Yet it cannot be denied that Sandburg is light on his feet and constantly shifts his weight and stance. And it is on the most elevated plane that the book ends, with the identification of "the people" and cosmic laws:

> The people is a polychrome,
> a spectrum and a prism
> held in a moving monolith. . . .

The People, Yes was written during the great economic depression, and when it appeared in 1936 many critics hailed it as a sociological document and political philosophy. Reading it today we can see that it was neither, and a poem should not be—better, cannot be. It is rather a psalm—or a series of psalms—written out of Sandburg's religion of humanity. This religion is less openly confessed today than it was a generation ago, and the change in religious fashions has affected Sandburg's poetic reputation. It is easy for a high church critic to rationalize his aesthetic objections to a poet who has not yet discovered original sin. (pp. 328-30)

At the age of sixty-seven . . . Sandburg was still learning; but he need not pray, after he reaches eighty-nine, for God to spare him five more years so that he may become a writer. God made him a writer, and by his own efforts he has become a poet. How long he will be read only the future can decide, but certainly he is worthy of respect and deserves to be read—the kind of immortality dearest to every poet. (p. 331)

> *Gay Wilson Allen, "Carl Sandburg: Fire and Smoke," in* South Atlantic Quarterly, *Vol. 59, 1960, pp. 315-31.*

William Stafford   (essay date 1963)

[*An American poet, critic, and biographer, Stafford is the author of* Traveling through the Dark *(1962), winner of a National Book Award, and* Friends to this Ground: A Statement for Readers, Teachers, and Writers of Literature *(1967). In the following excerpt, Stafford praises* Honey and Salt *for its realistic and exciting depictions of the American people.*]

Through some ten collections, beginning with **Chicago Poems** in 1916, Carl Sandburg has established a tradition which exists as part of the consciousness of American readers. [**Honey and Salt**], with almost eighty recent poems, reveals more clearly than before that we should take account of several aspects of what we think we simply understand.

A striking element in the early poems was direct irony—such memorable things as the man swept along in a train described as rushing toward vast destinations, a part of a cosmic movement, and the man's response to inquiry about where he was going: "Omaha." Or the section workers who lean and watch the train go by on a track they have made so smooth that flowers in the vases in the passenger cars do not tremble. Or the mayor with soft hands discussing the slackness of the calloused workmen on strike.

These poems confronted readers with abrupt realizations about themselves: there was the immediate, poster-paint effect of murals to reflect a new land. America was shoveled into books; and for many, particularly in the West,

there was a nouveau-literate exhilaration:—"That man who seemed like a hobo, who came around with the harvest hands in that park by the railroad right there in Sterling, Kansas, he listened and put what happened into a book." With the shock of the man who learned that he had been speaking prose all his life, we learned that we had been living poetry. For readers on the move from farm to town to city Carl Sandburg delivered the word; and his delight in the names and in the encounters full of meaning in our kind of world was one of the natural resources of the country.

A second aspect of the Sandburg tradition derived from the first, but veered from it. This aspect may be identified with the title of the book which most clearly asserted it: **The People, Yes.** Gags, hunches, slang phrases, a kind of cozying up to large groups not differentiated by troublesome particularities—this move in the poems began to dominate the Sandburg tradition. This present book, the new book, is much given over to this kind of experience; an example is the first poem in its first lines: "A bag of tricks—is it? / And a game smoothies play? / If you're good with a deck of cards / or rolling the bones—that helps?" This new book has variety, and it even has the unexpected; but it does line out along the second aspect of the tradition: "Be loose. Be easy. Be ready." "Love is a . . . ".

But there is another aspect, or perhaps it is the quality which has validated both aspects above. The quality is an alertness, a readiness to capture what is implicit in the material. This potential makes any of the poems or the pronouncements a constant or at least a recurrent excitement in Carl Sandburg's books. The new book has that poise and validity. (pp. 388-89)

> *William Stafford, "In the Sandburg Tradition," in* Poetry, *Vol. CII, No. 6, September, 1963, pp. 388-89.*

Archibald MacLeish   (lecture date 1967)

[*A Pulitzer Prize-winning American poet and dramatist, MacLeish also served as a lawyer, university professor, Librarian of Congress, and Assistant Secretary of State. His philosophy of art rejects isolationism in favor of activism; he argues: "To declare, as the American aesthetic seems to do, that the effort to act upon the external world in the making of a work of art is a betrayal of the work of art is a misconception of the nature of art. The nature of art is action, and there is no part of human experience, public or private, on which it cannot act or should not." MacLeish was also a longtime literary and political ally of Sandburg, with correspondence between the two poets spanning more than thirty years. The following excerpt was taken from an address delivered on the steps of the Lincoln Memorial, September 17, 1967, on the occasion of the Carl Sandburg Memorial Ceremony. President Lyndon B. Johnson also spoke.*]

Sandburg had a *subject*—and the subject was belief in man. You find it everywhere. You find it announced in the title of the book in which his Chicago poem appears: **The People, Yes.** You find it in one form or another throughout the hundred odd poems and proses of which that extraordinary book is composed. You find it in other poems. And in other books. Most important of all, you find it in the echo which all these poems and these books leave in the ear—your ear and the ears of others: the echo which has made the body of Sandburg's work a touchstone for two generations of readers—almost, by this time, for three.

A touchstone of what? A touchstone of America. If ever a man wrote for a particular people, however he may have reached in his heart for all people, it was Sandburg. . . . And if ever a man was heard by those he wrote for it was Carl. Europeans, even the nearest in that direction, the English, do not truly understand him but Americans do. There is a raciness in the writing, in the old, strict sense of the word raciness: a tang, a liveliness, a pungency, which is native and natural to the American ear. And underneath the raciness, like the smell of earth under the vividness of rain, there is a seriousness which is native too— the kind of human, even mortal, seriousness you hear in Lincoln.

An American touchstone. But is there not a contradiction here? *Can* a body of work bound together by credulity constitute a touchstone for Americans? For Americans *now?* Once, perhaps, in the generation of Jefferson, or once again in the generation of Lincoln—but *now?* There is a notion around in great parts of the world—in Asia and in certain countries of Europe—that America has changed in recent years: that the last thing one can expect from America or from Americans today is credulity. It is asserted that the American people have now, as the saying goes, grown up. That they have put aside childish things, beliefs which can't be proved. That they have come to see what the world is, to put their trust in the certainties of power. That they have become, in brief, what is favorably known as "realistic": about themselves, about humanity, about the destiny of man.

Listening to contemporary speeches, reading the papers, one can see where these opinions of America may have come from. But are they true? Are they really true? Can we believe, in *this* place, thinking of *this* man, that they are true? Sandburg was an American. He was an American also of our time, of our generation. He died fifty-seven days ago. He was seen and known and talked to by many in this meeting. His struggles were the struggles of the generation to which most of us belong—the struggles of the great depression and the many wars and the gathering racial crisis and all the rest. He was a man of our time who lived in our time, laughed at the jokes our time has laughed at, shed its tears. And yet *Sandburg was a credulous man*—a man credulous about humanity—a man who believed more than he could prove about humanity. And Sandburg, though he listened to those who thought themselves realists, though he was attentive to the hard-headed, was not convinced by them. In *The People, Yes* it is said:

> The strong win against the weak.
> The strong lose against the stronger.
> And across the bitter years and the howling winters
> the deathless dream will be the stronger . . .

> Shall man always go on dog-eat-dog?
> Who says so?
> The stronger?
> And who is the stronger? . . .

What Sandburg knew and said was what America knew from the beginning and said from the beginning and has not yet, no matter what is believed of her, forgotten how to say: that those who are credulous about the destiny of man, who believe more than they can prove of the future of the human race, will *make* that future, *shape* that destiny. This was his great achievement that he found a new way in an incredulous and disbelieving and often cynical time to say what Americans have always known. And beyond that there was another and even greater achievement: that the people listened. They are listening still. (pp. 42-4)

Archibald MacLeish, "A Memorial Tribute to Carl Sandburg," in The Massachusetts Review, *Vol. IX, No. 1, Winter, 1968, pp. 41-4.*

Louis D. Rubin, Jr.   (essay date 1977)

[*Rubin is an American critic and educator who has written and edited numerous studies of Southern literature. In the following excerpt, Rubin provides an overview of Sandburg's work, declaring him the "best of the Chicago Poets."*]

Whatever has happened to the Chicago poets? Their renown is gone from the Republic, and almost even from the academy. Literary history has a way of effacing, in its long-range shifts in sensibility, all but the most durable of reputations. When Carl Sandburg, Edgar Lee Masters, and Vachel Lindsay are recalled nowadays, it is as regional phenomena, untutored midwestern rebels against the late nineteenth century's taste for Ideality, who wrote crude pieces about such subjects as slaughterhouses, skyscrapers, abortions, and transcontinental railroads. They flourished briefly, only to be overwhelmed and ploughed under by the vastly more far-reaching overturning in language and sensibility effected by Eliot, Pound, and the Waste Land generation, revolutionary modernists of far greater innovation and imagination than the naïve and simpleminded Chicagoans.

The anthologies have room for only so many poets, so many poems; hierarchies are drawn up, those who are omitted drop from sight, and the hierarchies become orthodoxies. Very occasionally there is a rediscovery, a revaluation, but not often or importantly: half a century or so and the thing is set for good. The process is silent, ruthless, and we risk losing some good poetry along the way.

I think of Carl Sandburg. He was the best of the Chicago poets, an interesting artist. He is not entirely overlooked, I am thankful to say: three or four of his early lyrics are still tucked into most of the anthologies, as specimens of the upper midwestern revolt from the Genteel Tradition. But it is a far comedown for the onetime Authentic Voice of Inland America, the American Songbag Himself, the self-taught author of *The People, Yes.* (p. 181)

As always in good poetry, it is language that does it. But

Sandburg is very difficult in this respect, because his way of using language can be deceptive. It is much like prose in its syntax, and the colloquial vocabulary adds to an apparent casualness. In his best poetry Sandburg *uses* vernacular language, slang even; by this I mean that in Sandburg's instance it isn't the self-conscious employment of a "low" vocabulary to call attention to commonness, a vaunting of plebeian virtue (though later in his career Sandburg was prone to do just this, ad nauseam). An expression such as "the *crack* trains of the nation" is an organic part of his vocabulary, not an affectation, and he employs the adjective because it is simply the appropriate word to image what he wishes to convey about the train. As such it provides precisely the intensification of language, the heightened awareness of the texture of experience, that the best poetry affords.

I stress this because unless the way in which Sandburg employs vernacular imagery is properly recognized, his way of poetry will be misunderstood. (pp. 182-83)

Of course there is no inherent literary virtue to using vernacular discourse in a poem, or for that matter any other kind of discourse. But given Sandburg's mastery of the vernacular, his ability *as a poet* to think in it without self-consciousness, it should be obvious that he enjoys certain advantages in dealing as poet with the kind of experience that he writes about. If you wish to write a poem about a railroad train, then if you can do so in the kind of documentary denotation that you and others customarily use to think about a train, without having to introduce for your purposes a different convention of language not customarily applied to it, you will be able to come closer to being able to reproduce your personal experience of the train. The same goes for other objects of Sandburg's experience, such as streetcars, a bridge, a fog, the subway, a fish crier, a farmer, a picnic boat, ditchdiggers, railroad-track gangs, an iron fence, factory girls, police reporters, ice handlers, statues in a Chicago park, Billy Sunday, skyscrapers, and so on. And in the poems of Sandburg's best years he is able not only to invest that kind of experience with language that can give it the intensity of poetry but also to achieve the intensification within and through the rhythms, syntax, parallelisms, and imagery of the vernacular reference customarily employed to denote that experience. He is able, in short, to make the ordinary into the extraordinary on its own terms, without violating the everyday authenticity of the documentation.

The result is an enlargement of the range and nature of our poetic experience through his poems. Any good poet provides that; Sandburg's particular talent is that he opens up areas of our experience which are not ordinarily considered objects of aesthetic contemplation, through language that enables him, and us, to recognize such experience in new ways.

A great deal has been made of his work as being, in its subject and its language, essentially midwestern American, and this is quite true. It is not thereby the less general or sophisticated in its relevance, however; and the view of Sandburg as a kind of rude, untutored regional bard whose poetry achieves its effects through its presentation of novel subjects attendant upon the industrialization of

the cities and towns of the Corn Belt hardly bears serious scrutiny. He is, at his best, a poet of much subtlety and sophistication; and it is through the skillful intensification of language, not fresh subjects alone, that he works his art. It is true that his language is much closer to the rhythms and word choices of vernacular discourse than what one normally encounters in verse, but it is precisely *through* that discourse that he works his poetry. Consider the last line of **"Fish Crier"**:

> His face is that of a man terribly glad to be selling
> fish, terribly glad that God made fish, and customers
> to whom he may sell his wares from a pushcart.

The line may resemble prose; it is not prose. It has cadence, parallelism, ironic juxtaposition; it plays skillfully upon the vernacular use of the word *terribly* as against its more formal associations, offering in "terribly glad" an apparent contradiction in terms (an oxymoron, if one will) that illuminates not only the theme of the poem but the face of the fish crier as well. Once again it is not the subject as such, so much as what Sandburg does with the language, that makes the poem. Sandburg's best poetry will survive, where the once popular *Spoon River Anthology* of Edgar Lee Masters has faded, because Masters placed his emphasis on subject, the "thought," while Sandburg at his best achieves it with language.

There is, of course, a built-in psychological hazard in such poetics, and by the early 1920s Sandburg succumbed to it. The best poems in **Chicago Poems** (1916), **Cornhuskers** (1918), and **Smoke and Steel** (1920) succeed because of the tension between the idiom and the subject; their impact lies in the resolution, through language, of that tension. But from using vernacular language to intensify everyday experience into poetry it is an easy, and a fatal, step for one to begin assuming that because the experience is ordinary and the language is of the earth earthy, they are therefore inherently Poetic. To depict in compelling and appropriate language a train moving across the prairie is one thing; it is another and a considerably less interesting matter to assert that because it is a train on the midwestern American prairie, and because the language is avowedly vernacular, the joint appearance within a poem constitutes the poetry. On the contrary the instant that the tension between language and object is slackened, what is produced is not poetry but rhetoric.

This is what begins happening to Sandburg as poet very early in his career; following the **Chicago Poems** his poetry shows an increasing tendency thereafter, in almost a kind of geometric progression, to substitute rhetoric about experience for evocation of his experience. Sandburg began to believe his press notices. He was now the Poet of Mid-America, and thenceforward he sought to live up to the title by cataloguing the everyday scene in the Midwest. His poetry had been likened to Walt Whitman's; now he proceeded to imitate the least attractive aspects of Whitman's verse, producing only hot air and chaff. . . . This is precisely what he was doing, with the process culminating in **The People, Yes** (1936), in which democratic ideology is passed off as being Poetic merely because it is personified and documented. There is no tension, no discovery. There are no people in *The People, Yes;* all is abstract, "typical." The single, terribly glad fish crier of the *Chicago Poems* is more human and credible than all the varieties of abstracted Common Men catalogued in the 107 sections of *The People, Yes.* (pp. 184-86)

It is almost as if there were two Carl Sandburgs, one of them the private, sensitive artist, the other the public performer, self-important and pompous, willing to debase the language for gain. And if so, he would seem himself to have recognized it early; for in *Cornhuskers* (1918) there is a poem, **"Chicago Poet,"** containing these lines:

> Ah, this looking-glass man!
> Liar, fool, dreamer, play-actor,
> Soldier, dusty drinker of dust—
> Ah! he will go with me
> Down the dark stairway
> When nobody else is looking,
> When everybody else is gone.

He proved to be all these things and more.

In 1963, at the age of eighty-five, he brought out a new volume of poetry, *Honey and Salt.* Astoundingly he seemed to have regained his long neglected energy as lyric poet. Here was the old vision of the real world he inhabited, a trifle dimmed perhaps but once again depicting remembered experience in new language. . . . Compared with the best of the early poems, only a few of those in *Honey and Salt* quite manage to hold their own. But the verse in Sandburg's last book is in large part interesting, genuine, alive: once again, after many years, language is being put to work.

Those who chronicle and interpret American letters are bound ultimately to rediscover for themselves the excellence of Carl Sandburg. When that happens, the fine poet . . . will at last reemerge from the dumps. There have been other poets who have written and spoken silly things—things far sillier and sometimes considerably more sinister than ever he wrote or spoke—and who have woven a public image of specious rhetoric and role-playing about their reputations, and yet been remembered finally because at their best they wrote well. (pp. 188-89)

> *Louis D. Rubin, Jr., "Not to Forget Carl Sandburg . . . ," in* The Sewanee Review, *Vol. LXXXV, No. 1, Winter, 1977, pp. 181-89.*

Bernard Duffey (essay date 1979)

[*An American scholar specializing in the literary accomplishments of the "Chicago Renaissance," Duffey is the author of* The Chicago Renaissance in American Letters (1954) *and the co-editor of* Chicago's Public Wits (1982). *In the following excerpt, Duffey suggests that Sandburg actually sought to escape what many critics termed his "easy idealism."*]

No one of the three notable poets spawned by the Chicago literary renaissance of the second decade of this century can be said to have fared very prosperously at the hands of later times. Vachel Lindsay, haunted during his life by a resonantly idealistic vision of possibilities inherent in American life, now seems a proclaimer of apocalypse too unreal for more than rhetoric and gesture. Edgar Lee Masters (the reportorial impulse of *Spoon River Anthology* apart) is surely a failed poet, one lost in a cloud of variously colored romantic posturings, a writer to whom his work was more self-indulgence than either art or expression. Carl Sandburg, in comparison, seems more durable. He is in print. His memory has called forth centenary observance. He has had a special stamp struck off in his honor. He is something, at least, of an institution.

But even this degree of survival presents something of a puzzle. He is, in a predominating view, no more than a schoolroom poet, "populistic," "sentimental," and yet one who affords leads to suggest to the children that poetry may be contemporary in interest and personal in form. His work is visibly there, on the map of American literature, yet it is hard to call to mind any criticism of it that has succeeded in giving it major character. Allowing for all this, and conceding that few feel any pressing need for a Sandburg revival, I want nevertheless to take some exception to our willingness to give his poetry a no more than marginal place in our 1ense of twentieth-century writing. Sandburg certainly stands wide of the major thrusts of both the writing and criticism of poetry in our time. Many of the critical terms which condescend to him are indubitably right in their import. At the same time, I think it fair to suggest that their import is less than adequate to Sandburg's whole poetic achievement. He was engaged in the same pursuit of the native which occupied his two Chicago contemporaries, but I want in fact to argue that unlike them he located a poetically constructive imagination of the land in and for which he wrote. His voice gains authenticity when it is considered across its breadth of utterance, and I would find it difficult to make this claim for either Masters or Lindsay. Unlike the latter, his is only occasionally the effort at poetic beatification, and unlike the former he is largely guiltless of ingrown maundering. Instead, I shall argue, though Sandburg shared a certain tentativeness and openness with his contemporaries, he in fact fashioned and for the most part held fast to a close and living sense of the native, one congruent, finally, with his land's own aspect.

What emerges from the whole poetry, in this view, is a wholeness of perception, one rooted in a consistent feel for a land conditioned by a problematic history and filling a landscape difficult to redeem by transcentental gesture. His scene is peopled with the kind of minor movers and doers who in fact have so largely occupied it, and who have little choice but to take their character from the land's own spatial and temporal indeterminateness. The people and their work, or the poet's perception of the land itself, occasionally prompted him to a sort of overblownness, a raising of cities, the land, or the people to improbably conceived heights (compare for example, **"Chicago," "Prairie,"** or parts of *The People, Yes,*) but such rhetoric, sharing something with Lindsay's or Masters' distention, is more occasional than pervasive. (pp. 295-96)

An early poem observed that "all things human rise from the mob and relapse again as rain to the sea." That theme, of course, was to be written out at length in "**Four Preludes on Playthings of the Wind**:" "Well, what of it?" says the figure of Tomorrow in the poem, "My grandmother, Yesterday, is gone. / What of it? Let the dead be dead." . . . History, time, is an ultimate reality for him and mutability its only fruit. Such perception is ironically aware of the tragi-comic man on the railway smoker in "**Express**" who, as he moves toward a future where his train and all its passengers will "Pass to ashes," calmly announces his own idea of a destination, "Omaha." In the whole of Sandburg's work, as in reality, the ultimate setting for mankind is a time indifferent in itself and endemic in the restless chronology of Midwestern history. Here is where his people live, and while it is possible to see many things in their lives, whatever we see is seen falsely unless it is allowed the color of such time and its openness. The Sandburg world has its first element of being in the transitory. In one sense, everybody's destination is Omaha, but who is to make permanent definition for that terminus?

And such indifference of passage transfers from Sandburg's sense of time to his sense of space also. His landscape is no more a deliverer than his history. At such formative points as the perception of time and space, thus, he is the poet of a tolerable but clear disenchantment. Unlike Masters, however, his is not the disenchantment of self-pity. Landscape for him is setting and stage both, aesthetic presence and practical presence, but it gives mankind only himself in a sometimes dark and nearly always indeterminate world. The *Complete Poems,* from beginning to end, is studded with observations of place that, across their breadth, can best be characterized negatively, as the absence of any romantic power in nature resembling, say, Emerson's feeling for spirit; and the absence also of the historically bred sense of homeland, of place that has been given its character by deep, repeated actions of will. Landscape for Sandburg is most often simply here, or there, and no more. Instead of the rooted place, there is the open Midwestern landscape known to every eye. It appears most often as prairie. The occasional drama of hill, or forest, or river is seen only seldom. Habitation, rather than dwelling, is the rule. Apart from prairie, and unpredictably, an empty and ever shifting waste of water takes a large place in the poet's work; and he is fascinated over and over again by the palpable impalpable presence of mist. All present themselves as what may be called durations of space, something stretching out in undetermined vectors of distance.

Perhaps the commonest humanizer of landscape in Sandburg is that of response to its beauty, but if we are to understand the sense of beauty that moves him we should beware of easy responses. His is perhaps a little nearer to the negative sense of the sublime than to the beautiful itself, to that which confronts observation almost as an alien realm to be tested in a tremor of mind and feeling rather than received in congenial warmth and pleasure. He seems more often to be haunted by the land than at home in it, and his verse becomes that of a man against the sky to whom connections and relations are inapplicable.

> Smoke of autumn is on it all.
> The streamers loosen and travel.
> The red west is stopped with a gray haze.

> They fill the ash trees, they wrap the oaks,
> They make a long-tailed rider
> In the pocket of the first, the earliest,
>   evening star.

The aesthetic in Sandburg is a mode of seeing and feeling that by its nature precludes other participation. It is a mode that asserts itself by negating action or ready involvement, and the poet can be explicit on the point.

> Better the blue silence and the gray west,
> The autumn mist on the river,
> And not any hate and not any love,
> And not anything at all of the keen and the deep:
> Only the peace of a dog head on a barn floor,
> And the new corn shoveled in bushels
> And the pumpkins brought from the corn rows,
> Umber lights of the dark,
> Umber lanterns of the loam dark.

> Here a dog needs dreams,
> Not any hate, not any love,
> Not anything but dreams.
> Brother of dusk and umber.

But it is a third aspect, the problem of action that must engage us especially, a question that in Sandburg and across the breadth of much of what is called "modernist" poetry raises complicated questions stemming from the fact that the poetry of our time, like so much of its fiction and drama as well, has been a literature of what is felt to have have happened to us rather than of what we have done. In this regard, Sandburg seems distinct from his contemporaries most plainly by reason of his own willingness to build whole sections of his poetry upon action in the world. The characteristic of our times, however, has been a contrary one, seeking decision for the poet rather *in* his action as poet. To swing sharply away from the Chicago ambience, we think of Sandburg's contemporaries like Pound, Eliot, Crane Stevens, or Williams as devisers of poetics almost as much as achieved poets. Each of them puts a major effort into the theory of poetry, their deep involvement in what it is to act as a poet.

Sandburg's concerns, to the contrary, flowed almost entirely into practice so that poetry for him became simply expression rather than the act of its definition. It is expression that his own slender essays, "Tentative (First Model) Definitions of Poetry [see excerpt dated 1928]," or the "Notes for a Preface" to the *Complete Poems,* largely insist on. As a result, action in Sandburg has largely to inhere in what he could find to be action outside his poetry, in his own witnessing of action; but such witnessing could only be structured on what were two impediments to active fulfillment and meaning, those of indeterminate time and indeterminate space.

The French critic, George Poulet, has produced some of his own analysis of French writing from a concern that may be a help here, one that he conceives of as the radically subjective nature of literature. "Thought," he notes, "is not make up simply of . . . thoughts; it is made up also, even more perhaps, of all the *interior distance* which separates me from or draws me closer to that which I am able to think." Sandburg, I have suggested, is a poet for whom both time and space may be said to have had a distancing effect, one largely denying to them any great possibility as definers or generators of his action. They tend to frame everything in in the poetry in an "out there" position, a place where it is beheld rather than participated in. Action, it would follow, suffers from the same fate. Farm life, city life, war, labor, suffering, endurance, or happenstance are with rare exceptions events noted rather than responded to. There are exceptions. The "Contemporary Bunkshooter," Billy Sunday, is excoriated by the poet; warmongers are put outside a human pale; the red blood of labor struggle, or it may be the red hue of socialist allegiance, momentarily commands the poet's feeling, but such exceptions are not numerous.

The land of Sandburg's expression is undetermined in time and space alike. It is widely open and calls out for filling. But the actions which the poet seeks in it can only share the fate of the land itself and so share in the indeterminateness of history and landscape.

> A forefinger of stone, dreamed by a sculptor,
>   points to the sky.
> It says: This way! this way!
>
> Four lions snore in stone at the corner of the
>   shaft.
> They too are the dream of a sculptor.
> They too say: This way! this way!
>
> (pp. 296-300)

Rather than action, Sandburg's land is supplied most often with potentialities of action, and often with potentiality that is explicitly arrested. His interior distance, again, is that of standing at some remove, of finding the land which has encompassed him and generated his poems to be itself less than encompassable, a milieu in which he can resume motion only toward his own indeterminate ends.

> I saluted a nobody.
> I saw him in a looking-glass.
>
> (p. 301)

What emerges from all this I want to suggest is a poetic vision seeking escape from easy idealism, from resolution by willed environment. Such direction sets Sandburg apart not only from his Chicago fellows but, if I may risk such generalization, from any of the prevailing poetic imaginations of America. In our national history there have been three reliances or references poetry has chiefly invoked to resolve the scattered picture the land presents. The first may be called resolution by landscape, or, more properly, by a spiritually informing nature. This is the way, most familiarly, of the Emerson of such essays as *Nature* itself or of "Self-Reliance." The second is resolution by time. It is the resolution most fully invoked by Whitman and given its fullest statement in the reliance of "Song of Myself" on the evolution of a self, standing outside of culture in its democratic openness, away from the tentativeness of its beginnings and toward self-reliance and a reliance of selves on each other, but all in turn relied upon through faith in the material thrust of reality, of time's passage toward resolution. The third is that of action, voiced variably across our writing but one presenting great difficulties to the modern. In the poetry of our times, it has most notably found expression in the poet's feeling for his art itself as redemptive act. (pp. 301-02)

Sandburg, I suggest is a fourth case, that of recognizing and instituting the undetermined itself. Nature in him has become simply landscape, and, apart from the distance, the remoteness of its beauty, it is made to suggest no redemption. Equally in Sandburg time is no healer. The redemptive hope on which Whitman rested his vision of evolution has become the reiteration of something that now is felt to be no more than process, action subsumed by time and space, which, in themselves, afford no definition.

It may be thought that something important has been omitted in this drift of judgment, something that can be identified with Sandburg's own affirmation, and booktitle, *The People, Yes.* In the concluding section of that work, certainly, he rises to the hortatory note, to the push of idealistic need.

> The people will live on.
> The learning and blundering people will live on.
>   They will be tricked and sold and again sold
> And go back to the nourishing earth for root-
>   holds,
>   The people so peculiar in renewal and
>   comeback,
>   You can't laugh off their capacity to take it.
> The mammoth rests between his cyclonic dra-
>   mas.
>
> (*The People, Yes*)

But in fact the actual people of his poem is constituted in its detail of a variegated and always uncertain compost of no particular character other than that of recurrence, variety, and the duration of which he speaks. His final lines form—our own final paradigm. "In the night, and overhead a shovel of stars for keeps, the people march," the poet first announces, suggesting an enclosure of the whole at least in sidereal process, but he ends with the question which such generality evokes "Where to? What next"?

Perhaps no one could wish really to classify Sandburg as a naturalistic writer, but I may conclude by suggesting that his sense of time, space, and action, all three, forms a sort of protonaturalistic poetic vision, a landscape in which event and endurance provide the basic parameters of his vision as, he suggests, they provide such parameters for existence in his world. He holds back from willed ideality in favor of shaping that world close to the spectacle it most commonly presents. (p. 302-03)

> *Bernard Duffey, "Carl Sandburg and the Undetermined Land," in* The Centennial Review, *Vol. XXIII, No. 3, Summer, 1979, pp. 295-303.*

FURTHER READING

Adams, Stephen J. "Apovitch in Canto XII." *Paideuma* 15, Nos. 2 & 3 (Fall-Winter 1986): 131-33.

Investigates a possible reference to Sandburg in Ezra

Pound's "Canto XII" and provides an overview of the relationship between the two poets.

Aiken, Conrad. "Carl Sandburg." In his *A Reviewer's ABC: Collected Criticism of Conrad Aiken, From 1919 to the Present,* pp. 349-52. New York: Meridian Books, Inc., 1958.
    Response to Rebecca West's edition of *Selected Poems.* Aiken uses this volume as evidence that Sandburg's poetic talent is minimal and that he is nothing but "a lover of surfaces."

Basler, Roy P. "Your Friend the Poet—Carl Sandburg." *Midway* 10, No. 2 (Autumn 1969): 3-15.
    Overview of critical response to both Sandburg's prose and poetry.

Brenner, Rica. "Carl Sandburg." In her *Ten Modern Poets,* pp. 117-48. New York: Harcourt, Brace and Company, 1930.
    Biographical study focusing on Sandburg's poetical development.

Carneveli, Emanuel. "A Review of *Smoke and Steel.*" *Poetry: A Magazine of Verse* XVII, No. 5 (February 1921): 266-72.
    Praises Sandburg's use of the "language of workers and criminals" in his poetry, but also states that this technique can lead to an emphasis on "turning a quick phrase" instead of genuine poetic expression.

Compton, Charles H. "Who Reads Carl Sandburg?" *The South Atlantic Quarterly* XXVII, No. 2 (April 1929): 190-200.
    Attempts to determine the source of Sandburg's popularity among the general readership.

Gregory, Horace. "Sandburg's Salutation." *Poetry: A Magazine of Verse* XXXIII, No. 4 (January 1929): 214-18.
    Identifies Sandburg as a nationalistic poet who expresses the moods, ideas, and desires of many people.

Jones, Llewellyn. "Carl Sandburg." In his *First Impressions: Essays on Poetry, Criticism and Prosody,* pp. 53-68. New York: Alfred A. Knopf, Inc., 1925.
    Formalist analysis of Sandburg's verse.

Korges, James. "James Dickey and Other Good Poets." *The Minnesota Review* III, No. 4 (Summer 1963): 473-91.
    Negative assessment of what Korges terms Sandburg's "humanitarian yea-saying and superficial cynicism."

Loeber, William. "A Review of *Chicago Poems.*" *The Double Dealer* 3, No. 14 (February 1922): 105-07.
    Attempts to refute the charge made by Dr. Felix E. Schelling that Sandburg is nothing more than an "Intellectual Tough."

Lurye, Frida. "The Bard of Toiling America (On Carl Sandburg's Centenary)." *Soviet Literature* No. 358 (1978): 163-66.
    Examines the Soviet response to Sandburg's poetry, specifically focusing on Sandburg's devotion to the ideals of socialism.

Monroe, Harriet. "His Hometown." *Poetry: A Magazine of Verse* XX, No. 6 (September 1922): 332-38.
    Discusses the strengths and weaknesses of Sandburg's *Slabs of the Sunburnt West.*

——. "Comment." *Poetry: A Magazine of Verse* XXIV, No. 6 (September 1924): 320-26.
    Discusses Sandburg's talent for rhythm, dialogue, and description as displayed in *Chicago Poems, Cornhuskers,* and *Smoke and Steel.*

Nash, J. V. "Carl Sandburg: An American Homer." *The Open Court* 44, No. 893 (October 1930): 633-39.
    Identifies Sandburg as an epic poet of the common people.

Perkins, Agnes Regan. "Carl Sandburg." In *Writers For Children: Critical Studies of Major Authors Since the Seventeenth Century,* edited by Jane E. Bingham, pp. 503-10. New York: Charles Scribner's Sons, 1988.
    Examines Sandburg's two poetry collections for children, *Early Moon* and *Wind Song.*

Rickword, Edgell. "An Early American Poet." *The Calendar* III (April 1926): 75-6.
    Discusses Sandburg's place in American literary history as a regional poet.

Rosenberg, Harold. "Poets of the People." *Partisan Review and Anvil* III, No. 6 (October 1936): 21-6.
    Comparison between the poetry of Sandburg and Walt Whitman, with emphasis on their reliance on conversational dialect.

Anne Sexton

1928-1974

(Born Anne Gray Harvey) American poet, short story writer, dramatist, and author of children's books.

Sexton was among the best-known of the often controversial Confessional poets, a group composed primarily of New England writers who rose to prominence during the 1950s and early 1960s. Like such fellow Confessionalists as Robert Lowell and Sylvia Plath, Sexton wrote highly introspective verse that revealed intimate details of her emotional troubles, including the severe depression from which she suffered for most of her adult life and which led to her suicide. Characterized by vivid imagery and daring metaphors, Sexton's early work deals intensively with her psychic traumas and her attempts to overcome mental illness. While she began her career as a highly methodical poet who wrote within formal metrical and rhyme schemes and reworked her manuscripts through several drafts, Sexton composed her later poems in various experimental forms, often with little or no revision. In addition to focusing upon her emotional life, Sexton's later work includes frequent allusions to mythology, fairy tales, and Christian motifs, and explores such topics as romantic love, motherhood, and relationships between the sexes.

Sexton spent most of her life in the affluent, upper-middle-class suburbs of Boston. She married at age nineteen and attempted to settle into the role of housewife and mother. During her early twenties, however, Sexton began to experience bouts of depression that eventually led to hospitalization. After the birth of her second daughter in 1955, Sexton attempted suicide and was placed under the care of Dr. Martin Orne who encouraged her to write poems as a form of therapy. After her release, Sexton joined John Holmes's writing course at the Boston Center for Adult Education and later won a scholarship to the Antioch Writer's Conference where she studied under W. D. Snodgrass, whose confessional poem "Heart's Needle" she deeply admired and attempted to emulate. At Snodgrass's suggestion, Sexton also enrolled in Robert Lowell's graduate writing seminar at Boston University where she became friends with Sylvia Plath and George Starbuck, among others. Under the auspices of Snodgrass and Lowell, Sexton began writing extremely personal verse concerning her experiences as a mental patient. When she composed enough poems to consider compiling a book, however, Holmes discouraged her from publishing, expressing in a letter to Sexton his fear "that what looks like a brilliant beginning might turn out to be so self-centered and so narrowed a diary that it would be clinical only." Sexton responded to this evaluation by writing "For John Who Begs Me Not to Inquire Further," a poem that expresses the psychological motives underlying Confessionalism. She included this piece in her first collection, *To Bedlam and Part Way Back,* which, along with ensuing volumes, rapidly gained her a reputation as an important new poet. During the 1960s, Sexton gave spirited public

readings accompanied by the musical group Her Kind, and in 1968 composed the play *Mercy Street* with Marian Seldes. She also wrote several highly regarded children's books with Maxine Kumin, her close friend and fellow poet. Yet despite her literary success, Sexton continually battled depression and psychosis. She repeatedly attempted suicide and was committed twice more to mental institutions by her family. In 1974, she ended her life by carbon monoxide poisoning.

Sexton's early belief that complete honesty and self-revelation were essential to her creative work is strongly reflected in *To Bedlam and Part Way Back.* "You, Dr. Martin," for instance, candidly portrays her desolate existence in a psychiatric ward. In "The Double Image," one of her most acclaimed works, Sexton describes the conflict between her desire to be a loving and devoted mother and daughter and her withdrawal into psychosis. "Elizabeth Gone" and "Some Foreign Letters" concern the death of her beloved Great-Aunt Anna, a figure who reappears in numerous works by Sexton, including "The Nana-Hex" and *Mercy Street.* Other poems, while thematically and tonally impersonal, focus on the emotional states of fictional narrators. More than any of her later writings, the poems in *To Bedlam and Part Way Back* conform to traditional structural patterns. In her second collection, *All My Pretty Ones,* Sexton began to experiment with a less formal, more intuitive and spontaneous approach to composition. In many of these poems, particularly the title piece, Sexton confronts her ambivalent feelings toward her parents and expresses grief over their deaths. Sexton's penchant for vivid imagery is evident in "Letter Written on a Ferry While Crossing Long Island Sound," in which a surrealistic vision of floating nuns represents the narrator's yearning for a heavenly blessing and "In the Deep Museum," a vision of Christ's martyrdom in which He is eaten alive by rats.

Sexton received the Pulitzer Prize in poetry for her third collection, *Live or Die,* which many critics consider her finest volume. While her earlier poems are mostly cathartic outpourings of emotion, Sexton's pieces in *Live or Die* evince a more controlled, analytical approach to the Confessional style as she contemplates possible causes for her psychological anguish. In "Those Times . . ." and "Imitations of Drowning," for example, she related some of the traumatic incidents from her childhood. The major theme of this collection involves the choice that Sexton must make between life, with its attendant joys and miseries, and death, through suicide. The final poem in the collection, "Live," affirms her decision to continue living.

Most commentators regard *Love Poems* and *Transformations* as the last accomplished collections of Sexton's career. While the pieces in *Love Poems* chronicle an extramarital love affair, *Transformations* develops a sardonic pastiche of the fairy tales of the Brothers Grimm. In the latter volume, Sexton abandons Confessionalism and adopts the persona of a middle-aged witch who perverts the legends of such archetypal heroines as Rapunzel and Cinderella. Her version of Rapunzel, for instance, involves a love triangle between Rapunzel, the witch who holds her captive, and the prince who rescues her. In "Cinderella," Sexton cynically compares the well-known fairy tale to equally unlikely stories in which the desires of the downtrodden are miraculously gratified.

In *The Book of Folly,* Sexton returned to the Confessional mode, reiterating themes of trauma, anguish, and alienation. Her occasional interest in religious symbolism resurfaces in "The Jesus Papers," a nine-poem sequence depicting the life of Christ through images of birth, death, and sacrifice. The predominate theme in her final collections, *The Death Notebooks* and *The Awful Rowing Toward God,* is the desire for salvation through a transcendent mystical experience. "The Death Baby," a sequence from *The Death Notebooks,* makes use of the image of the title figure to express a complex range of associations, including Sexton's hunger for spiritual fulfillment. The infant also represents her obsession with mortality, a force that impels her toward self-destruction but which paradoxically provides the chief inspiration for creative endeavors that give meaning to her life. In the poems that conclude *The Awful Rowing Toward God,* Sexton envisions a journey by boat to confront her Creator; the last poem in the sequence, "The Rowing Endeth," describes the climax of her spiritual quest, as God challenges her to

a poker game and draws the winning hand. Several additional volumes of Sexton's writings have been issued posthumously, some edited by her daughter, Linda Gray Sexton. *45 Mercy Street* contains "The Divorce Papers," written shortly before Sexton's death, in which she describes her divorce and the failed romances that followed. The title sequence in *Words for Dr. Y,* a collection of poems and short stories, recounts in verse a series of sessions with her psychotherapist.

When Sexton's poems first appeared, a critical debate ensued that continues to dominate evaluations of her work. While several commentators echoed John Holmes's condemnation of them as solipsistic, others perceived in them an honesty and technical control that effectively transcend her narrow subject matter. Comparing her style to that of other Confessionalists, J. D. McClatchy observed: "More than the others, Sexton resisted the temptations to dodge or distort, and the continuity and strength of her achievement remain the primary witness to the ability of confessional art to render a life into poems with all the intimacy and complexity of feeling and response with which that life has been endured." Although generally regarding her work as uneven, critics have increasingly lauded her stylistic innovations and unflinching examination of formerly taboo subjects, including female sexuality and mental illness, as abiding aspects of her art. According to Maxine Kumin, Sexton "delineated the problematic position of women—the neurotic reality of the time—though she was not able to cope in her own life with the personal trouble it created. If it is true that she attracted the worshipful attention of a cult group pruriently interested in her suicidal impulses, her psychotic breakdowns, her frequent hospitalizations, it must equally be acknowledged that her very frankness succored many who clung to her poems as to the Holy Grail. Time will sort out the dross among these poems and burnish the gold. Anne Sexton has earned her place in the canon."

(For further discussion of Sexton's life and career, see *Contemporary Literary Criticism,* Vols. 2, 4, 6, 8, 10, 15, 53; *Contemporary Authors,* Vols. 1-4, rev. ed., Vols. 53-56 [obituary]; *Contemporary Authors New Revision Series,* Vol. 3; *Contemporary Authors Bibliographical Series,* Vol. 2; *Something about the Author,* Vol. 10; *Dictionary of Literary Biography,* Vol. 5; and *Concise Dictionary of American Literary Biography: The New Consciousness, 1941-1968.*)

PRINCIPAL WORKS

POETRY

To Bedlam and Part Way Back 1960
All My Pretty Ones 1962
**Selected Poems* 1964
Live or Die 1966
Love Poems 1969
Transformations 1971
The Book of Folly 1972
The Death Notebooks 1974
The Awful Rowing Toward God 1975
45 Mercy Street 1976

Words for Dr. Y   1978
The Complete Poems   1981

OTHER MAJOR WORKS

Anne Sexton: A Self-Portrait in Letters   (letters)   1978

**Contains poems from *To Bedlam and Part Way Back* and *All My Pretty Ones.*

Louis Simpson   (essay date 1960)

[*The winner of the 1963 Pulitzer Prize for his verse collection* At the End of the Open Road, *Simpson is considered an important figure in post-World War II American poetry. Primarily concerned with the decline of American morality, his diverse oeuvre ranges from tightly structured lyrics to surrealistic free verse. In the following excerpt from his review of* To Bedlam and Part Way Back, *Simpson praises the collection as original and moving.*]

For once the blurbs don't lie. [***To Bedlam and Part Way Back***] . . . is an experience—original, moving, and delightful. Above all, delightful—for though Mrs. Sexton's poems sometimes deal with Bedlam, that is, scenes in a mental hospital, and often with anguish, yet the mind at work is so keen and the technique is so excellent that her book is an uninterrupted joy. It is a *book,* as so few collections of verse are, everywhere infused with the character of the author. From the jacket I learn that she has been writing poems for only three years. This then is a phenomenon, like Rimbaud, to remind us, when we have forgotten in the weariness of literature, that poetry can happen.

The poems are lyrical structures: the movement of the lines and the ease of rhyme provide an impetus, an aesthetic pleasure, that balances the almost, at times, intolerable reality she deals with. But the more poetry succeeds, the less it can be described. . . . (pp. 291-92)

Mrs. Sexton has an eye for ordinary life too, like W. D. Snodgrass, whose *Heart's Needle* was so welcome last year. For example, there is a description in her **"Funnel"** of a house in Maine that seems like all the old seaside houses that ever were:

> It is rented cheap in the summer musted air
> to sneaker-footed families who pad through
> its rooms and sometimes finger the yellow keys
> of an old piano that wheezes bells of mildew.

Yet this descriptive gift does not restrict her imagination. I have read many descriptions of war, yet have seen none truer than this:

> This was the first beach of assault;
> the odor of death hung in the air
> like rotting potatoes; the junkyard
> of landing craft waited open and rusting.
> The bodies were strung out as if they were
> still reaching for each other . . .

The point is, her poetry is much more than a recreation of facts, though apparently it draws largely on experience; it is a power of imagination also. Maybe Mrs. Sexton really *is* a witch. And this imaginative power can be sustained over long stretches, as in her story of a woman who, in 1890, traveled in Europe, and was loved by a man who was already married, and returned to wither in New England—ending with these extraordinary strokes of fiction:

> I tell you, you will come
> here, to the suburbs of Boston, to see the blue-
>   nose
> world go drunk each night, to see the handsome
> children jitterbug, to feel your left ear close
> one Friday at Symphony. And I tell you,
> you will tip your boot feet out of that hall,
> rocking from its sour sound, out onto
> the crowded street, letting your spectacles fall
> and your hair net tangle as you stop passers-by
> to mumble your guilty love while your ears die.

I won't try to predict Mrs. Sexton's future. There is always an air of apology in the forecasts with which reviewers are so free. But she has a present, and it is great. (pp. 292-93)

> Louis Simpson, "A Garland for the Muse," in
> The Hudson Review, *Vol. XIII, No. 2, Summer, 1960, pp. 284-93.*

James Dickey   (essay date 1961)

[*Best known for his novels* Deliverance *(1970) and* Alnilan *(1987), Dickey explores through fiction the primal, irrational, creative, and ordering forces of life. As a poet, he is often classified as a visionary Romantic in the tradition of Walt Whitman, Dylan Thomas, and Theodore Roethke. He rejects formalism, artifice, and confession, favoring instead a narrative mode characterized by energetic rhythms and charged emotions. In the following excerpt from his review of* To Bedlam and Part Way Back, *Dickey voices his disapproval.*]

[The poems of ***To Bedlam and Part Way Back***] so obviously come out of deep, painful sections of the author's life that one's literary opinions scarcely seem to matter; one feels tempted to drop them furtively into the nearest ashcan, rather than be caught with them in the presence of so much naked suffering. The experiences she recounts are among the most harrowing that human beings can undergo: those of madness and near-madness, of the pathetic, well-meaning, necessarily tentative and perilous attempts at cure, and of the patient's slow coming back into the human associations and responsibilities which the old, previous self still demands. In addition to being an extremely painful subject, this is perhaps a major one for poetry, with a sickeningly frightening appropriateness to our time. But I am afraid that in my opinion the poems fail to do their subject the kind of justice which I should like to see done. Perhaps no poems could. Yet I am sure that Mrs. Sexton herself could come closer than she does here, did she not make entirely unnecessary concessions to the conventions of her literary generation and the one just before it. One can gather much of her tone and procedure from quotations like "You, Doctor Martin, walk / from breakfast to madness," and "All day we watched the gulls / striking the top of the sky / and riding the blown roller coaster." "Riding the blown roller coaster" is a kind of writing I dislike to such an extent that I feel, perhaps irrationally, that everyone else including Mrs. Sexton ought to dislike it, too, for its easy, A-student, superficially-exact "differentness" and its straining to make contrivance and artificiality appear natural. One would hope that a writer of Mrs. Sexton's seriousness, and with her terrible story to tell, would avoid this kind of thing at any price. Yet a large part of her book is composed of such figures. In the end, one comes to the conclusion that if there were some way to relieve these poems of the obvious effort of trying to be poems, something very good would emerge. I think they would make far better short stories, and probably in Mrs. Sexton's hands, too, than they do poems. As they are, they lack concentration, and above all the profound, individual linguistic suggestibility and accuracy that poems must have to be good. As D. H. Lawrence once remarked in another connection, they don't "say the real say". But Mrs. Sexton's candor, her courage, and her story are worth anyone's three dollars. (pp. 318-19)

James Dickey, in a review of "To Bedlam and Part Way Back," in Poetry, *Vol. XCVII, No. 5, February, 1961, pp. 318-19.*

May Swenson   (essay date 1963)

[*In the following excerpt, Sexton's* All My Pretty Ones *is praised as a masterful example of the confessional mode.*]

[With ***To Bedlam and Part Way Back***], Anne Sexton threw a startling light over the poetic horizon; discerning poets and critics picked up their telescopes and reported something very like a new planet. Her material was startling and it had been lived through, in her own person or through persons closely around her: mental breakdown, accident, death in war, abortion, suicide and "no special god to refer to." Her handling, in poetic form, of her own exposed and wounded psyche, seemed appalling, but courageous. With a technique apparently fully grown, she transposed her experiences out of their private realm and made them mesh with the instinctive knowledge we all carry of grief, guilt, compulsion, self-disintegration. But ***To Bedlam and Part Way Back,*** though shocking as a laparotomy, was an achievement not on the score of its subject matter, but because of its poetic mastery.

This is also true of Anne Sexton's second book, ***All My Pretty Ones,*** which continues to probe other parts of the same psychological terrain. Her method is as uninhibited as entries in a diary or letter writing (in fact several of the poems have "letters" as part of their titles or are addressed to specific persons); the diction seems effortless, yet when we examine for form we find it solidly there, and its expertness is a pleasurable thing in contrast to the often mercilous *débridement* taking place in the content:

> Concerning your letter in which you ask
> me to call a priest and in which you ask
> me to wear The Cross that you enclose;
> your own cross,
> your dog-bitten cross,
> no larger than a thumb,

small and wooden, no thorns, this rose—

> I pray to its shadow,
> that gray place
> where it lies on your letter . . . deep, deep.
> I detest my sins and I try to believe
> in The Cross. I touch its tender hips, its dark
>   jawed face,
> its solid neck, its brown sleep.

> True. There is
> a beautiful Jesus.
> He is frozen to his bones like a chunk of beef.
> How desperately he wanted to pull his arms in!
> How desperately I touch his vertical and hori-
>   zontal axes!
> But I can't. Need is not quite belief . . .

This poem, **"With Mercy for the Greedy,"** states in the last stanza Mrs. Sexton's impelling impulse behind all her poetry so far: "My friend, my friend, I was born / doing reference work in sin, and born / confessing it. This is what poems are. . . . "

The confessional element, as well as her kind of dexterity, reminds me a good deal of Robert Lowell; she is as savage with herself, as entangled with her New England background, as he. Her new book, however, seems less Lowell-like in its rhythms and pattern schemes than the first, while retaining her stance of the open soul. She says scathing things about her own sex in such poems as **"Housewife"** and **"Woman With Girdle."** And in **"In the Deep Museum"** she conducts us through several kinds of hell and hallucination, which is not to say that she deliberately deals in horror; these true and terrible poems are potential snapshots of any of our lives these days. In the midst of neurotic sadness are charming instances of humor and fantasy. . . . (p. 165)

It seems to me that with the beginning poem in ***All My Pretty Ones,*** called **"The Truth the Dead Know"** (dedicated to her parents), Mrs. Sexton is perhaps laying away her past, to which she has written these remarkable epitaphs, and striding into a sunlight earned through grief. The form of this poem is bare and pure, musical and not tortured. It is a revelatory and healing poem, and quite different in tone from anything else in the book. (p. 166)

May Swenson, "All My Pretty Ones," in The Nation, *New York, Vol. 196, No. 8, February 23, 1963, p. 165-66.*

A. R. Jones   (essay date 1965)

[*Jones examines how Sexton transforms intensely personal experiences into art.*]

Sylvia Plath recorded her debt to Robert Lowell and linked her work to that of Anne Sexton. She acknowledged her excitement at Lowell's "intense breakthrough into very serious, very personal emotional experience", and remarked that these "peculiar private and taboo subjects" had been explored by Anne Sexton, who writes "also about her experiences as a mother; as a mother who's had a nervous breakdown, as an extremely emotional and feeling young woman. And her poems are wonderfully craftsmanlike poems, and yet have a kind of emotional and psychological depth which I think is something perhaps quite new and exciting".

Notice that she relates, almost incidentally, the idea of 'break-through" with the idea of "breakdown", and that she isolates the dualism between the taboo nature of the subject of the poetry and the "wonderfully craftsmanlike" quality of the poetry itself.

Anne Sexton's recently published *Selected Poems* are drawn from her two volumes of poems, *To Bedlam and Part Way Back* (1960), and *All My Pretty Ones* (1962). On the whole the poems of the second volume are richer in texture, more diversified in subject matter and more composed than the poems of the earlier volume, which are often powerful and raw. At her best there is no doubt of her craftsmanship; her control of diction and rhythm is remarkably assured, and commands immediate attention and respect. Her themes are those of love, motherhood and death, of suffering and breakdown, and at their best her poems are both harrowing and compassionate. Like Lowell, her framework of reference is ultimately religious; without being overtly theological, traditional religious values are gently but firmly insisted upon. The world of her poems is intimately personal, and her difficulty is to relate morally a world of physical and mental suffering that can only be diagnosed clinically. She sees evil and suffering as the condition of humankind. . . . She is very conscious of evil and of Original Sin, and if she sees the relation between confession and poetry it is because she believes poetry to be morally directed. In her poetry she transcends imaginatively what she can only otherwise patiently accept as the lot of man. Her best poems are filled with a profound compassion for man as a suffering being and for the human predicament, and often the image of the suffering self tends to merge into the figure of the crucified Christ. Thus far from endorsing or exploiting madness or pain her poetry comes to terms with human suffering in order to redeem it. Poetry is not a way of evading the purgatory of human experience but a means of facing and controlling it. In her poem, **"For John, Who Begs Me Not to Enquire Further"**, she claims on behalf of the poet that courage to face experience which Schopenhauer in a letter to Goethe claimed for the philosopher:

> It is the courage to make a clean breast of it in face of every question that makes the philosopher. He must be like Sophocles's Oedipus, who, seeking enlightenment concerning his terrible fate, pursues his indefatigable enquiry, even when he divines that appalling horror awaits him in the answer. But most of us carry in our heart the Jocasta who begs Oedipus for God's sake not to inquire further . . .

Her poetry describes in images of powerful violence the suffering and terror of life, not for the sake of the suffering or the terror, but for the sake of a different order of reality that she finds through them. Thus her poems achieve something of a tragic dignity, and display an attitude of mind that is neither cynical nor despairing, but which is clearly related to the whole powerful tradition of Christian stoicism, to King's "Exequy" and Johnson's "Vanity of Human Wishes".

Her poems are mostly formally organized as dramatic narratives; set in a particular place at a particular time, they tell a story in an almost old-fashioned way, except that whereas the narrative seems to move longitudinally, so to speak, the meaning of the poem moves latitudinally, across and below the narrative line. At its most direct, in a poem such as **"Flight"**, for instance, the narrative structure is extremely simple and describes a woman driving through Boston to the airport and back again through Boston; but the subject of the poem is revealed through the state of mind of the woman, the sudden and desperate need for love and the despair when that need is frustrated. The description of the drive to the airport is full of anticipation and outward-going images:

> There was rose and violet on the river
> as I drove through the mist into the city.
> I was full of letters I hadn't sent you,
> A red coat over my shoulders
> and new white gloves in my lap.

At the airport, the turning point of the poem and of the journey, there is a terrible note of finality:

> All flights were grounded.
> The planes sat and the gulls sat,
> heavy and rigid in a pool of glue.

The return journey is marked by a sense of almost cosmic desolation and the realisation that there is no escape, that flight from the self and the world that self creates is illusory:

> I drove past the eye and ear infirmaries,
> past the office buildings lined up like dentures,
> and along Storrow Drive the street lights
> sucked in all the insects who
> had nowhere else to go.

Although she drives to the airport through "Sumner Tunnel" and away from it along "Storrow Drive", a happy coincidence of naming, the symbolic level of the narrative is not schematised or insisted upon but allowed to emerge naturally and gradually through the narrative.

She has a remarkable sense of particularities, a fine awareness of the detail that will bring the whole scene vividly before the eyes and that, at the same time, will be psychologically telling and exact. This ability to realize complex landscapes of mind in visually concrete terms is one of the main sources of her poetic strength. Curiously enough, this can be seen as clearly in her unsuccessful poems as in her best work. Because her poems, particularly those concerned with mental breakdown, build such intense and violent conflicts, she sometimes escapes conclusions glibly in the way that the last couplet of the Shakespearean sonnet is occasionally used to distract attention from the fact that the tensions the poem creates have not been fully resolved. Thus what ought to have been dramatic is merely theatrical. In the poem **"The Abortion"**, the *persona* driving back from the abortionist rationalises her sense of guilt and loss and concludes by turning upon herself:

> Yes, woman, such logic will lead
> to loss without death. Or say what you meant,
> you coward . . . this baby that I bleed.

However brilliantly horrible the last image may be in itself, the effect of this last stanza is to turn an already sensational subject into sensationalism, to drop from the reality of drama into the over-simplifications of melodrama. In poems such as this, and it must be said that her **Selected Poems** contains a number of them, it is as if the subject has got out of control, become indeed almost hysterical, and that the poet has asserted herself in an arbitrary way, forcing the poem to a conclusion.

In her best poems, in a poem such as **"The Operation"**, for example, she uses all her imaginative resources to create a statement of disturbing, even terrifying, beauty. The poem is straightforwardly narrative in structure, beginning with a description of her visit to the doctor's and his diagnosis that she is suffering from hereditary cancer of the womb, which killed her mother the previous year:

> I come to this white office, its sterile sheet,
> its hard tablet, its stirrups, to hold my breath
> while I, who must, allow the glove its oily rape,
> to hear the almost mighty doctor over me equate
> my ills with hers
> and decide to operate.

The description is almost horrifyingly precise, and, apart from the image of the glove, almost clinical. The rhythms fall gently, rather hesitantly, into place and the rhyme is regular but unobtrusive. The second and third sections of the poem describe in similar detail the operation and recovery, re-enacting the patient's feelings in the dramatic and vivid present tense:

> I glide down the halls
> and rise in the iron cage towards science and pitfalls.
>
> The great green people stand
> over me; I roll on the table
> under a terrible sun, following their command
> to curl, head touching knee if I am able.
> Next, I am hung up like a saddle and they begin.
> Pale as an angel I float out over my own skin.

In the operating theatre she is commanded to adopt a foetal position, and her recovery, slow and bewilderingly painful, is like the re-enactment of the birth trauma. The association between the evil of disease and birth is established earlier in the poem in the connection between her own birth and her mother's cancer of the womb:

> It grew in her
> as simply as a child would grow
> as simply as she housed me once, fat and female.
> Always my most gentle house before that embryo
> of evil spread in her shelter and she grew frail.

Although the child is in some senses innocence, there is no doubt that the traditionally religious idea of being born into a world of evil and disease is suggested in these images. In so far as the operation is seen as a re-birth, her ultimate discharge from hospital is a re-emergence into childhood; chivied and cajoled, like a child, she is again ready to participate in the bitter and sorrowful game we call life:

> Time now to pack this humpty-dumpty

> back the frightened way she came
> and run along, Anne, and run along now
> my stomach laced up like a football
> for the game.

The humour is sardonic, the attitude stoical compassion. While the patient faces the violent and painful images of suffering, the creative mind uses the operation to establish a complex and comprehensive image of the continuity of human life, evil and suffering, the jest, the glory and the riddle of the world. The poet meaningfully organizes the incoherent and meaningless world of suffering. However startling or gruesome, it is not the quality of the experience itself or the fact of its confession that hold our attention, but the quality of the imaginative energy.

Although she avoids any ready-made theological conclusions she does endorse the traditional idea of redemption through suffering. In several of her poems she associates suffering with the agony of Christ crucified. Sometimes the association is direct as in the poem **"In the Deep Museum"**:

> My God, my God, what queer corner am I in?
> Didn't I die, blood running down the post,
> lungs gagging for air, die there for the sin
> of anyone, my sour mouth giving up the ghost? . . .

But in the poem **"With Mercy for the Greedy"** she examines the crucifixion as both suffering and symbol and relates it directly to her poetry:

> I detest my sins and I try to believe
> in The Cross. I touch its tender hips, its dark jawed face,
> its solid neck, its brown sleep.
>
> True. There is
> a beautiful Jesus.
> He is frozen to his bones like a chunk of beef.
> How desperately he wanted to pull his arms in!
> How desperately I touch his vertical and horizontal axes!
> But I can't. Need is not quite belief.

She rejects the consolations of a "beautiful Jesus", for, however much she would like to believe such an idea, it runs counter to her experience of sin and suffering. The Christ in which she believes is the suffering Christ of the crucifix, whose pain she recreates so physically in the line "How desperately he wanted to pull his arms in!" But the crucifix is not only an image of tortured suffering: it is also a symbol of unselfish love and redemption. Thus the cross is at one and the same time an image of intense agony which can be realized personally, and a geometric symbol of the intersection of the timeless eternity of God and the world of man which is changeless and impersonal. Similarly, the man who suffers in a world of suffering and evil can be transcended by the mind that creates in the unchanging, timeless world of art. Through the world of poetic imagination, man can move from the realm of necessity into the realm of freedom. (pp. 24-9)

A. R. Jones, "Necessity and Freedom: The Poetry of Robert Lowell, Sylvia Plath and Anne Sexton," in Critical Quarterly, *Vol. 7, No. 1, Spring, 1965, pp. 11-30.*

"I began to think that if one life, somehow made into art, were recorded—not all of it, but like the testimony on an old tombstone—wouldn't that be worth something? Just one life—a poor middle-class life, nothing extraordinary (except maybe madness, but that's so common nowadays)—that seems worth putting down. It's the thing I have to do, the thing I want to do—I'm not sure why."

—Anne Sexton, 1973

Robert Phillips (essay date 1973)

[*An American poet, short story writer, critic, and editor, Phillips has been praised for the craftsmanship, wit, and inventiveness of his poetry. Among his critical studies are the volumes* Denton Welch *(1974) and* William Goyen *(1979). In the following excerpt, taken from his book* The Confessional Poets, *Phillips provides an overview of Sexton's career, ending with an evaluation of her collection* Transformations.]

Great poetry, it seems, has often been born of misfortune. (p. 73)

But with Anne Sexton the poetry of misfortune reaches some sort of apogee. So many are her afflictions, we recognize in the poet a female Job. One is able to reconstruct a hellishly unhappy life from her nakedly autobiographical poems: Birth into the well-to-do Harvey family in Newton, Massachusetts, in 1928; her mother's materialism and father's alcoholism; apparently an accident at the age of six, in which the young girl nearly lost an arm in a clothes wringer; the arrival to live with the Harveys of a great-aunt, who later suffered deafness and lapsed into madness; summers on Cape Cod; marriage to an unimaginative man; the deaths of two poet friends, John Holmes and Sylvia Plath; the birth of two daughters, Linda and Joy; the death of both parents within three months of one another, in 1959; her confinements in mental institutions; the temporary loss of a daughter; her search for release through religion, drugs, lovers, art. Her books, as she herself says, "read like a fever chart for a bad case of melancholy" [*Live or Die,* 1966].

These events, whether wholly autobiographical or only partly, all occur and recur in her work—they are the straws with which she weaves her thearapeutic baskets, the terrible threads of her private mythology. Totally frank about each event, Mrs. Sexton renders it as if in a diary. One does not sit down with a volume of her poems to be entertained (though her work is laced with a wicked wit, especially the volume in which she goes most outside herself, *Transformations*). Indeed, her poetry has repelled a good many. Reviewing her early poems, James Dickey conceded their "sickeningly frightening appropriateness to our time," but felt it all had "so obviously come out of deep, painful sections of the author's life that one's literary opinions scarcely seem to matter; one feels tempted to drop them furtively into the nearest ash can, rather than be caught with them in the presence of so much naked suffering" [see excerpt dated 1961]. Another Dickey, this one William, found her fourth book equally repellent. That critic found himself out of sympathy with the world of her imagination: "For while Sexton's world is full of objects, they have no independent validity; they exist as projections of her own indulgent emotional states" [*Hudson Review,* Summer, 1969].

I would suggest both critics have suffered an overreaction to Anne Sexton, as have others too embarrassed to criticize the work because it seemed so much a piece of the life that a criticism of one was a criticism of the other. Despite the autobiographical events cited above, which appear to adhere to the truth, one must be very careful in reading Anne Sexton to separate the truth from the fiction. For instance, she has no brother. Yet two of her fine poems, **"For Johnny Pole on the Forgotten Beach"** (from *To Bedlam and Part Way Back*) and **"The Papa and Mama Dance"** (from *Love Poems*) are addressed to a brother in uniform. This has led astray a number of critics. . . . Others have taken the **"Unknown Girl in the Maternity Ward,"** from her first book, to be Mrs. Sexton herself, thereby endowing her with an illegitimate child she later gave away. (A symbolic act, by her own admission, for the temporary loss of her daughter due to her own madness. [see excerpt dated 1971]. Others have assumed the act in **"The Abortion"** to be factual as well. What is essential to recognize is that, while more acutely autobiographical than most, including Lowell, Mrs. Sexton's work is also populated by a gallery of "real" yet totally fictitious figures, such as the old man, the seamstress, and the young girl in **"Doors, Doors, Doors"** (from *All My Pretty Ones*); and the one-eyed man and the mother of two sons (in *Live or Die*). Indeed as she publishes more books, Mrs. Sexton seems to have exhausted the autobiographical and to be turning increasingly to the fictional. Her fifth book, *Transformations* (1971), is a transmogrification of seventeen of Grimm's fairy tales, with popular mythology displacing the personal. (pp. 73-5)

All these imaginary characters reveal Anne Sexton is very deft at assuming *personae*. Yet her best and most characteristic work invariably is her most autobiographical. This is the form of poetic expression to which she is firmly committed. As she has said in an early interview, "It's very embarrassing for someone to expose their body to you. You don't learn anything from it. But if they expose their soul, you learn something. That's true of great writers: They expose their souls and then suddenly I am moved and I understand my life better" [*New York Times,* November 9, 1969]. Elsewhere she has said, "I think if I had written twenty years ago I'd have written this way, whether it were stylish, whether it were a good thing to do or a bad thing to do. I can just do my own thing and that's the way I do it. I have been quite aware of criticism about this, naturally, because I do it; but I can't seem to change. I don't think I'm aiming at anything from an intellectual standpoint. I didn't make up my mind to write personal poems . . . You might call it an accident" [*Talk with Authors,* 1968]. (pp. 75-6)

I hold back nothing: That could be the motto for all of Anne Sexton's work. Beginning with her first collection, *To Bedlam and Part Way Back* (1960), her work has stunned readers with its realism, its shocking details. That she intends to shock is made manifest by the epigraph which she appends to her second book, *All My Pretty Ones . . . :*

> The books we need are the kind that act upon us like a misfortune, that make us suffer like the death of someone we love more than ourselves, that make us feel as though we were on the verge of suicide, or lost in a forest remote from all human habitation—a book should serve as the ax for the frozen sea within us.

Written after her mother's death, but before her father's, the individual poems of this volume collectively chart the poet's drift toward madness and back to partial recovery, as the title graphically communicates. Mrs. Sexton is even more forthright about her mental illness and frequent institutionalizations than was Lowell, the first to make the subject permissible in such works as **"Waking in the Blue," "Home After Three Months Away,"** and **"Skunk Hour."** (p. 76)

The first poem in Sexton's first book places the reader directly in bedlam without explanation, history, or apology. The first lines, "You, Doctor Martin, walk / from breakfast to madness" make use of apostrophe and halting enjambment for startling effect. The realities of the madhouse inform all the imagery in this collection, even that of nature: "It was the strangled cold of November; / even the stars were strapped in the sky / and that moon too bright / forking through the bars." It is doubtful that any poet never institutionalized would employ straitjacket imagery in relation to the stars.

Therapy and elegy are the book's two concerns. Those mourned are the poet's mother, grandfather, great-aunt, and, most important, the poet's lost self which she hopes to regain. In the poem about the great-aunt, **"Some Foreign Letters,"** the young poet is surprised to discover, through reading the dead woman's correspondence, that she had once been young, had once led a life of her own. The poet can remember only the deaf and dying crone. From this particularization the poet generalizes about the nature of life, and concludes that the promise of youth is a false one. Wars come, lovers die, flesh weakens, and ultimately "life is a trick, life is a kitten in a sack." A most unsettling metaphor, that.

More poems of disillusionment follow. **"The Farmer's Wife"** is a *persona* through whose eyes one sees a marriage in which love has become routine, an unfulfilling pantomime. The protagonist wants the ordinariness of her life transformed, wishes her husband somehow transformed into someone more romantic—a cripple, a poet, perhaps even a dead lover. Another poem of contrasts, **"Funnel,"** compares the largesse and love of life possessed by her grandfather with her current niggardly existence. The title predicts the shape of the poem's subject, the shape of more flowing into less, of dwindling. In **"For Johnny Pole on the Forgotten Beach,"** the fantasy and innocence of children playing with toy boats is contrasted with the horror of war and a soldier's death on a beach front before a junkyard of landing craft.

These explorations of disillusionment are followed by poems in which the human need for rite, the attempt to right one's life, is expressed—such as **"The Lost Ingredient." "Ringing the Bells"** is about a more literal ritual, the games used in therapy, written as a nursery rhyme to enforce the realization of the regressive or restorative infantilism to which the self has been forced. (The childish language is buttressed by images of patients in diapers.) This is one of Mrs. Sexton's greatest gifts—her ability not only visually to present the precise mental state she intends, but to render the lines in the correspondingly correct musical mood as well.

Two of the book's most important poems are **"For John, Who Begs Me Not to Enquire Further"** and **"The Double Image."** The first is Mrs. Sexton's defense of her poetry, addressed to her former teacher John Holmes. Her probing of her mind's recesses, she explains, was done "Not that it was beautiful, / but that, in the end, there was / a certain sense of order there." The poem is related to **"The Lost Ingredient"** in its theme of the search for order. Introspection, however painful, is advantageous, for out of examination comes order and out of order, release. **"The Double Image"** repeats and embellishes upon the topic of the poet's guilt for neglecting her mother in her sickness, which was the theme of the shorter **"The Waiting Head."** Guilt, alienation, the necessity for loving oneself before one can love others, and the gulf between generations are the poem's concerns. Its central image is the pair of portraits of her mother and herself which capture the outward resemblance of the two, but which are symbolically hung on opposite walls. The subject of guilt is explored to include not only her own toward her mother, but also the effects of Sexton's own suicide attempts on her daughter. The double image becomes triple, the guilt multiplied in a hall of mirrors.

All My Pretty Ones (1962) followed the first book by just two years. It is a continuation of the themes of death and ruin, guilt and mortality. It could be called the second volume of Mrs. Sexton's autobiography in verse. In the first book she re-created the experience of madness; the second book explores its causes. At the time of its writing, her father also had died, an event which left the poet tired of being brave. The volume reveals she had reached a reconciliation of sorts with her father just before his death. Many poems (like **"Young"**) contrast the innocence of her girlhood with her present world-weariness.

The imagery in this second collection derives less from institutionalization than from domesticity, a transition perhaps paralleling the poet's own removal from clinic to home. The images are in no way less sharp, however. In **"The Starry Night"** we see "one black-haired tree slips / up like a drowned woman into the hot sky"; in **"Lament,"** a "Canada goose rides up, / spread out like a gray suede shirt"; in **"Ghosts,"** women have "breasts as limp as killed fish"; and in **"Woman with Girdle,"** the subject is seen as having "thighs, thick as young pigs." But when Mrs. Sexton does get clinical, she does so with a vengeance: **"The Operation"** is a poem full of psychological and clinically precise observations, and revolves about the irony that she must have removed from her body the same type of malignancy which killed her mother. The poem concludes with the figure of Humpty-Dumpty, symbol of all which is precarious in life, the difficult balance we all must maintain.

There is a glimmering of optimism in this book, **"A Curse Against Elegies,"** which posits the thesis that one must live for the living and not the dead. But what is really new in this second collection, besides the additional grief for and details of her father's dying, are the poetic evidences of Mrs. Sexton's search for faith. **"From the Garden"** expresses the need for the spiritual in the midst of the secular. In all probability the two deaths, and the attendant guilt which ensued, caused the poet to ruminate on the nature of life and of death and the existence of the soul as never before. In other poems, such as **"With Mercy for the Greedy," "For God While Sleeping,"** and **"In the Deep Museum,"** we experience with her a pull toward death which seems at times stronger than the will for redemption. The final poem of her first book, **"The Division of Parts,"** had pointed the way, inviting comparison as it did between the sorting of her mother's earthly effects on Good Friday and the division of the crucified Christ's possessions. As Ralph J. Mills, Jr., observed,

> Since she is a poet without mystical inclinations, but rather is earthbound, committed to a vision that shocks by its unvarnished realism, it is hardly surprising that she should approach religious belief through the person of Christ, who is, for her, the man claiming to be God and subjecting Himself to the extremes of bodily and spiritual torture as proof of His appointed task. He is the one who reminds her again of the destiny to which all flesh is ordered—death.
>
> (pp. 76-80)

While these "religious" poems are terrible in their detail, with Christ "hung up like a pig on exhibit," elsewhere the volume manages to reveal another neglected aspect of Mrs. Sexton's talent, a rare whimsy which rescues certain poems from bathos. At the conclusion of **"Letter Written on a Ferry While Crossing Long Island Sound,"** a poem about the aftermath of a breakup with a lover, the poet is amazed to see the world going on as before. In need of some sign of the extraordinary, she playfully imagines the four shipboard nuns in a state of miraculous levitation, an imaginative act which predated the television series "The Flying Nun."

The volume concludes with an inconclusive **"Letter Written During a January Northeaster,"** a six-part refusal to mourn "Those dear loudmouths, gone for over a year." Mrs. Sexton sees the dead as lost baggage—gone, beyond recovery, yet stuffed with aspects of the self. As in **"In the Deep Museum,"** the poem expresses "both nostalgia for and denial of absolute love" [Beverly Fields, *Poets in Progress*, 1967].

Live or Die (1966), which won the Pulitzer Prize, continues the poet's search for reconciliations, her obsession with the limits of the body and its failures to be equal to the demands of the spirit. It marks a turning point in her work, a passage from pessimism to optimism. Chronologi-

cally arranged, the poems chart her inner and outer lives between January 1962 and February 1966. The book commences with the first direct account of her father's death, though its event had been accounted for earlier. The need for renewal and therapy is set forth in the second poem, **"The Sun,"** symbol of all that is restorative in life. That poem prefigures a third, **"Flee on Your Donkey,"** in which she proclaims, "Dreams came into the ring / like third string fighters, / each one a bad bet / who might win / because there was no other." (pp. 80-1)

During the time covered by the diarylike book, death ("that old butcher") hacks away at her dear ones again, this time taking her teacher John Holmes and her friend Sylvia Plath. During this stage of her life even nature seems malevolent: the rain "drops down like worms." Weary of the flesh again, she thirsts for the water of the spirit. Yet formal religion continues to fail her, and in its collapse she grows scornful ("Those are the people that sing / when they aren't quite / sure") and she turns from the church to the comforts of drug addiction and attempted suicide.

The book is riddled with guilt. There are more poems on guilt feelings toward her mother ("I did not know that my life, in the end, / would run over my mother's like a truck") and toward her daughter, who as a baby she may or may not have abandoned in a ditch during one of her illnesses. I suspect this is yet another of Mrs. Sexton's "disguised poems," with the fictional act of ditching the baby surplanting the actual act of leaving her to go to the mental hospital.

"Self in 1958" is a strong portrayal of deadened sensibilities. Mrs. Sexton here employs the figure of a plastic doll as symbol of the self (as did Plath in "The Applicant" from *Ariel*). Yet despite the stoicism which develops into negativism, *Live or Die* ends on the strongest note of affirmation found in all three books Mrs. Sexton had published up to that time. After the apparent exploration of pills and suicide, the poet can find in life values worth living for. Between the two alternatives posited in the title, she chooses life. The final poem, **"Live,"** shows life opening up for her. (pp. 81-2)

Just where all this affirmation took Mrs. Sexton, if we are to trust the tales told in her fourth collection, *Love Poems* (1969), is to an unhappy extramarital affair. Anticlimax, oh yes. And not much more therapeutic than drug addiction or attempted suicide, one might say. Except that the poems are considerably less bitter than her early work. In seeking a lover at least one is serving the self. The old brooding over the death of parents has been, if not forgotten, at least put on the back burner and turned down to Low. As the new collection indicates, she has achieved more than the realization of some additional confessional poems. She has grown. She has abandoned her previous preoccupations with ancestry, madness, and partial recovery. Most of these latest pieces are ironic love poems, speaking more of alienation than of conciliation, more of loneliness than togetherness. Yet her rather loveless, unlovely love poems are apropos of our time. Based upon the physical rather than the metaphysical, their depiction of unsatisfactory relationships between lovers reflects the failure to communicate in the modern world. And they do reflect a new attitude, "an awareness of the possibly good as well as the possibly rotten," she herself has commented; "inherent in the process is a rebirth of a sense of self, each time stripping away a dead self " [see excerpt dated 1971].

Mrs. Sexton's fourth book documents the pain as well as the absence of love. There is as much redness from blood as from roses and as many real broken bones as metaphorically broken hearts. Further, it employs the most homely or blatantly commercial images to communicate transcendental truths. Mrs. Sexton has become by this time a master at finding the telling image in domestic detail. . . . "We are a pair of scissors / Who come together to cut," a metaphysical conceit embodying the shape and the psychological effect of the physical contact. It is a figure worthy of comparison with Donne's celebrated compass conceit in "A Valediction Forbidding Mourning." The difference between Donne's stiff-twinned compasses, symbolizing tender married love, and Sexton's mutilating scissors-figure for her adulterer reveals how basically images of juncture have come to be conceived as destructive rather than constructive in the anxious modern mind with pathological tendencies.

Individual pieces in *Love Poems* examine love in its many guises: sensual, filial, adulterous, self—and the impossibility of reciprocal love (there are numerous poems on the struggle against loneliness). Others, some of the best in the collection, fall altogether outside the range of love. These include two powerful war (more correctly, antiwar) poems, **"December 9th"** and **"The Papa and Mama Dance."** Another group recounts the various states of womanhood: **"In Celebration of My Uterus"; "The Nude Swim"; "Song for a Red Night Gown"; "Loving the Killer";** and **"December 18th."** Significantly, Mrs. Sexton's poems on loneliness are among her most fully realized. Especially fine is the volume's initial poem, **"The Touch,"** in which a severed hand serves as synecdoche for the isolated self. . . . **"The Ballad of the Lonely Masturbator"** relates one woman's solitary solution to such intense frustration and loneliness. Its rather startling subject matter (startling even in the post-Portnoy era, and only alluded to guardedly by Roethke in his sequence poems, more openly by Allen Ginsberg and Frederick Seidel) is hammered into the Procrustean bed of the ancient ballad form with the recurring refrain, "At night, alone, I marry the bed."

This is a pathetic vision. So is that conveyed in **"December 12th,"** one of the volume's most difficult poems. Here the lonely poet seeks solace in volunteer hospital work. The unnatural states of body and mind which she sees there parallel the unnatural state in which she finds herself—that of sharing her lover with his wife. The poet-narrator is like the abnormal children in the ward to whom permanent possessions are forbidden. The only thing she is allowed to bring for the children's amusement is—herself; just as the only thing she can share with her lover is her body. The poet's need for love is shown ultimately to be as intense as the need of the hospitalized children whom she visits.

Not all the "loneliness" poems are pathetic, however. **"The Nude Swim,"** yet another of spiritual isolation, cul-

minates in the narrator's triumphant floating on the water, mistress of her element. Another affirmative poem, **"It Is a Spring Afternoon,"** concludes that, as death is the way of the natural world, so time and nature are restorative: "Everything is altogether possible / And the blind men can also see." The collection's second recurring theme, adulterous love, is treated in **"You All Know the Story of the Other Woman,"** a fine firm poem which elaborates upon the irregularity of any affair with a married man: "When it is over he places her, / like a phone, back on the hook." The same subject is treated in **"For My Lover, Returning to His Wife,"** with the permanence of the wife's position (the already-quoted "as real as a cast-iron pot" image) contrasted with the impermanence of the other woman's ("As for me, I am water-color. / I wash off"). A third poem in this category, **"December 16th,"** also deserves attention for its diction, which emphasizes the story-book quality of the lovers' lives.

Among Mrs. Sexton's celebrations of sensual love—the third classification—are the poems **"Us," "Now," "Barefoot,"** and **"Song for a Lady." "Us"** concludes with an almost Biblical sexual metaphor: "And we rose up like wheat, / acre after acre of gold, / And we harvested, we harvested." A *carpe diem* poem, "Now" carries such sexually symbolic freight as bullets and blood, a hammer and balloons. **"Barefoot"** is an ambitious poem in which the predatory nature of lovers is compared to the predatory nature of wildlife. . . . The tenderest of the love lyrics, and the poem containing the most striking sexual metaphor, is **"Song for a Lady,"** one of Mrs. Sexton's few poems "sung" from a male point of view. This male voice is sentimental, in contrast to the strident female voice of **"Mr. Mine."** The poem climaxes in a miraculous image for male virility: "Oh my Swan, my drudge, my dear wooly rose, / even a notary would notarize our bed / As you knead me and I rise like bread."

A fourth group defines the impossibility of fully reciprocal love. Mrs. Sexton registers this conviction in **"The Interrogation of the Man of Many Hearts,"** declaiming: "Every bed has been condemned, not by morality, or law, but by time." As in **"The Breast"** (which employs the nipple as *eye* and *I*, with a woman's physical inadequacy mirroring her emotional instability), she sees the narrator/beloved not only as a surrogate wife, but as a daughter- and mother-figure as well. **"Mr. Mine"** asserts that one reason lasting love is impossible is the egotisim implicit in every sexual act. The lover's selfish conquest of the beloved's body recalls the building of a city, the woman's flesh yet another material thing to be possessed. And the female is shown to be as much the predator as the male in **"December 18th,"** where the vagina is called "my tiny mail." (See also **"Loving the Killer"** for a variation on this theme.) That both parties are responsible for the failure of love is affirmed in "December 10th," the poem yielding the scissors image cited earlier. To effect a cut, blades must oppose one another.

The physical and emotional aftermaths of an affair are conveyed in **"The Break"** where the literal fracture of bones parallels the metaphorical fracture of the heart. The break of the title refers, on a third level, to the severed relationship. The literal fall down the stairs, a reversal of the conventional Freudian metaphor for the sexual act, is rendered with the homely description of her fractures: "I was like a box of dog bones." But the poet immediately gives us a mythic account as well: "What a feat sailing queerly like Icarus / until the tempest undid me and I broke." (pp. 82-5)

"Pro Femina" poems could be seen as constituting a fifth group. The title of **"In Celebration of My Uterus"** tells all: the poet sings of the universality of womanhood and sexuality. **"Song for a Red Night Gown"** details the wildness inherent in all women, the sanguine color of the gown symbolizing their blood allegiance to barbarity. The poem's world in which a rose bleeds and a mouth blooms relates directly to and repeats that of **"The Kiss"** and **"The Break."** One of the most ambitious poems in the volume, **"Loving the Killer,"** explores domestic love in the midst of wilderness and danger. A corollary theme of the eighty-four-line poem, the persistence of the past, relates it also in this respect to the concerns of her first three books. Yet the poem's two themes are organically entwined: though the lovers have escaped their native New England for Africa, the past accompanies them. The big game hunt becomes the larger hunt for selfhood; and the bones and skins of beasts that accompany them back to the States are symbols of what Whitehead has called "the withness of the flesh" (a concept which receives consummate poetic treatment in Delmore Schwartz's "The Heavy Bear"). The final stanza reveals the woman as the ultimate predatory beast, whereas her lover, the hunter, is mere skin and bones like the wildlife he has stalked.

The disparity between appearance and reality is felt or seen in the volume's many uniforms, costumes, and masks. **"You All Know the Story of the Other Woman"** vividly contrasts the comforting illusions of night with the harsher realities of day. **"Again and Again and Again"** features once more the image of the blood clot, only this time analogous to the manner in which the poet wears her *persona:* "It is a mask I try on. / I migrate toward it and its frog / sits on my lips and defecates." The poet's mask is akin to the death mask worn by the animals in "It Is a Spring Afternoon." And in **"December 14th"** we find a circus used as an extended metaphor for the reality behind the illusions of the love affair.

Though only two in number, war poems constitute a final grouping. **"December 9th"** is a strong, ironic statement on the Vietnam War. The irony is implicit in the poem's central action, the unloading of bodies from a Starlifter jet. In death the men are accorded a dignity and consideration denied them in life. Unfortunately, the poem echoes two other well-known ones. "This is the stand / that the world took" sounds uncomfortably like the closing lines of Eliot's "The Hollow Men." Similarly, the hero's being addressed as "carrying / your heart like a football / to the goal" recalls Mrs. Sexton's own, **"The Operation"** from *All My Pretty Ones,* with its notorious line, "My stomach laced up like a football for the game" (which prompted one critic to ask if footballs were laced up just prior to game time). Nevertheless, **"December 9th"** is an important new poem and a strong one, as is **"The Papa and**

Mama Dance," in which a brother in uniform prompt his sister to recall their childhood masquerades, when they played "dress-up" in their father's academic robes as black-clad bride and groom. The color now is seen as prefiguring their ultimate doom. The poem is a companion piece to that other, and even more impressive, Sexton poem about the reminiscences of a woman with a brother in uniform, **"For Johnny Pole on the Forgotten Beach."**

In **"The Papa and Mama Dance,"** the apostrophe to the brother, Mr. Gunman, is but one of many—far too many!—that flood the book's pages and threaten to inundate even the best poems. (pp. 86-7)

Love Poems concludes with a sequence of a dozen and a half short poems under the collective title, "Eighteen Days Without You." I have treated the component pieces as separate poems, because that is how they are best perceived. All of the above mentioned concerns are included in the group, but—except for those designated **"December 9th,"** **"December 12th,"** and **"December 16th"**—the sections are not as strong as the individual poems in the volume. As a whole they add up to considerably less than Snodgrass's "Heart's Needle" sequence, to which the group inevitably invites comparison, since both are confessional cycles on the enforced absence of a loved one. What is unquestionably Sexton's is the superimposition of surreal dream imagery upon the no less horrifying realities of modern life. She writes, for example, of falling in love the day John F. Kennedy was shot, and accuses her lover of having dragged her off by a Nazi hook. The times themselves are justification for such savage imagery, if justification is necessary. The conventional love poem seems anachronistic.

There is less regression in *Love Poems* than in the previous three collections. The book's general effect is one of stoicism and self-reliance rather than of self-pity and dependence. There are of course deliberate regressions in language for special effect, much as Roethke uses them throughout his sequence poems. Mrs. Sexton has used this device effectively in the past, notably in **"Ringing the Bells"** from *To Bedlam and Part Way Back:* "And this is the way they ring / the bells in Bedlam / and this is the bell-lady." She repeats the technique several times in *Love Poems,* however, to the point that it seems now a gimmick rather than a technique, a trick rather than an organic part of the poem. In **"That Day,"** a poem written in schoolgirl nursery rhyme rhetoric ("This is the desk I sit at / And this is the desk where I love you too much"), we become conscious not only of the Mother Goosery of "This Is the House That Jack Built," but also of the other Sexton poems in which she has cribbed from the nursery. (pp. 88-9)

Despite these faults, the achievement of *Love Poems* is considerable. If one counts the parts of "Eighteen Days Without You" as separate poems, as they were originally conceived, the volume contains forty-two new poems written between 1966 and 1969, making Anne Sexton one of our most productive artists. Of that number, more than a quarter deserve to be listed with the indispensable Sexton. And this time she has forsaken the indignities of the body for the more uniquely human dignities of the heart.

Earlier I observed that Mrs. Sexton's body of work evinces a definite progress in personalization. This progress made a giant leap when, in 1971, appeared *Transformations,* a rich collection of seventeen long poems. Each begins with a contemporary observation or application of the "moral" of some fairy tale, then segues into a contemporary recasting of the fairy tale itself. These "transformations" of Grimm's tales into grim parables for our time are deftly done, and in them Mrs. Sexton continues her practice of transforming the dross of commonplace experience into pure poetic gold—and vice versa, for shocking effect. The ancient is remythologized into the modern: Snow White's cheeks are as "fragile as cigarette paper"; the wicked queen's bodice is laced "tight as an Ace bandage"; the dwarf Rumpelstiltskin's body "wasn't Sanforized." And so it goes.

Mrs. Sexton retells the mythological stories, those master keys to the human psyche, in images and metaphors of Hitler and Eichler, Linus and Orphan Annie, Isadora Duncan and Joe DiMaggio, speed and electroshock, Thorazine and Thalidomide. By transforming the stories into the language and symbols of our own time, she has managed to offer us understandable images for the world around us. The tales focus on the psychological crises of living, from childhood dependence through adolescent trauma, adult frustrations through the deathbed. The two most successful are her versions of "Cinderella" and "Sleeping Beauty." The former she takes to be a prototype of the old rags-to-riches theme ("From diapers to Dior. / That story.") Cinderella is said to have slept on the sooty hearth each night and "walked around looking like Al Jolson"—a comparison indicative of the level of invention and humor in the book. At the end, when Cinderella marries the handsome prince to live happily ever after, Mrs. Sexton pulls a double whammy and reveals that that ending, in itself, is another fairy tale within a fairy tale, totally unreal and unlikely. How could anyone live

> like two dolls in a museum case
> never bothered by diapers or dust,
> never arguing over the timing of an egg,
> never telling the same story twice,
> never getting a middle-aged spread,
> their darling smiles pasted on for eternity.
> Regular Bobbsey Twins.
> That story.

The **"Briar Rose (Sleeping Beauty)"** tale is not so rich in imagery, but is fraught with frightening implications evoked by examining, as no poet has done before, what happens to a girl's psyche after she has been disturbed from the sleep of death, her renewed life becoming a life after death and bringing with it fear-induced insomnia. (This sleeping beauty also has an Electra complex, but in the words of Mrs. Sexton, that's another story. . . .)

While technically not "confessional" poetry, these verses of *Transformations* do at times strip the poet bare, as when she uses the wolf's deceptions in **"Red Riding Hood"** as occasion to reveal that she, too, practices such masquerades:

> Quite collected at cocktail parties,
> meanwhile in my head

Photograph from Sexton's modeling portfolio, circa 1949-51.

I'm undergoing open-heart surgery.

In her fifth book then, as in her first, Anne Sexton is domesticating our terrors. With outstanding artistic proficiency, she renders the particular pain of her life into universal truths. (pp. 89-91)

> *Robert Phillips, "Anne Sexton: The Blooming Mouth and the Bleeding Rose," in his* The Confessional Poets, *Southern Illinois University Press, 1973, pp. 73-91.*

"[Poetic inspiration is] something getting in the way, I think, probably magic, the unconscious, and the depths; what I would say calling forth the muse. Evoke her, as she drops down in a little string bag from God; or, as you pull her forth, fork her, and tear her out of your unconscious. Or she just happens to float by like a little butterfly, like a 'given poem,' as we would say. 'This poem just came, that's all: I did nothing to get it'."

—Anne Sexton, 1974

J. D. McClatchy (essay date 1978)

[*The poetry editor for the* Yale Review, *McClatchy is the author of the verse collections* Scenes from Another Life *(1981) and* Stars Principal *(1986). In the following excerpt from his critical anthology* Anne Sexton: The Artist and Her Critics, *McClatchy applies the principles of freudian psychoanalysis to Sexton's poetry.*]

Even the covers of an Anne Sexton book are contradictory. The poet posed demurely on their jackets: a sun-streaked porch, white wicker, the beads and pleated skirt, the casual cigarette. Their tame titles—literary or allusive: **To Bedlam and Part Way Back, All My Pretty Ones, Love Poems, Transformations, The Book of Folly.** And yet beyond, inside, are extraordinary revelations of pain and loss, an intensely private record of a life hungering for madness and stalked by great loves, the getting and spending of privileged moments and suffered years. The terrible urgency of the poems, in fact, seems to invite another sort of contradiction, the kind we feel only with strong poets: disappointments. Occasionally there are poems which frankly misfire for being awkward or repetitious, stilted or prosaic. One critic has caught it:

> So her work veers between good and terrible almost indiscriminately. It is not a question of her writing bad poems from time to time, like everybody else; she also prints them cheek by jowl with her purest work. The reason, I suppose, is that the bad poems are bad in much the same way as her good ones are good: in their head-on intimacy and their persistence in exploring whatever is most painful to the author [A. Alvarez, *Beyond All This Fiddle* (1969)].

The influences on her poetry—ranging from Rilke, Lawrence, Rimbaud and Smart, to Jarrell, Roethke, Lowell, Plath, and C. K. Williams—were easily acquired, obviously displayed, and often quickly discarded, while a few deeper influences—like that of Neruda—were absorbed and recast. She described herself as "a primitive," yet was master of intricate formal techniques. Her voice steadily evolved and varied and, at times, sought to escape speaking of the self, but her strongest poems consistently return to her narrow thematic range and the open voice of familiar feelings. *Do I contradict myself? Very well then I contradict myself.* For the source of her first fame continued as the focus of her work: she was the most persistent and daring of the confessionalists. Her peers have their covers: Lowell's allusiveness, Snodgrass's lyricism, Berryman's dazzle, Plath's expressionism. More than the others, Sexton resisted the temptations to dodge or distort, and the continuity and strength of her achievement remain the primary witness to the ability of confessional art to render a life into poems with all the intimacy and complexity of feeling and response with which that life has been endured.

Endurance was always her concern: why must we? how can we? why we must, how we do: "to endure, / somehow to endure." It is a theme which reenacts not only the sustained source of her poetry but its original impulse as well. At the age of twenty-eight, while recovering from a psychotic breakdown and suicide attempt, she began writing poems on the advice of her psychiatrist: "In the beginning, the doctor said, 'Write down your feelings because someday they might mean something to somebody. No matter how despairing you are, there are other people going through this who can't express it, and if they should read it they would feel less alone.' And so he gave me my little reason to go on; it shifted around, but that was always a driving, driving force." The essentially practical motive here, and the fact of her coming to write so late and unlearned, accounts for her ironic fortune in pursuing a poetry not only then unfashionable but also difficult to achieve without a kind of clumsy innocence: "I couldn't do anything else," she said.

The spur to more serious concentration—the conscious conversion of a means for survival into a necessary art—was her reading of five poems by W. D. Snodgrass from his "Heart's Needle" sequence. . . . Not the influence of his achievement, but the encouragement of his example mattered, and she left to study with him at the 1958 Antioch Writers Conference, where she showed him her poem **"Unknown Girl in the Maternity Ward,"** written in direct response to "Heart's Needle" and dealing too with the loss of a child. Snodgrass sensed that her poem was a disguise and advised her simply, "Tell the real story." The result, written over many months and in obvious imitation of the strategies of "Heart's Needle," became one of her best-known poems, **"The Double Image."** Snodgrass also told her to study with Robert Lowell, which she returned to Boston to do in the fall of 1958. She later evaluated Lowell's influence: "He helped me to distrust the easy musical phrase and to look for the frankness of ordinary speech. If you have enough natural energy he can show you how to chain it in. He didn't teach me what to put in a poem, but what to leave out" [*Harvard Advocate* (November 1961)]. At the same time, she was studying at the Boston Adult Center with John Holmes, who discouraged her confessional impulse and tried to impose a more traditional subject matter on her. "I couldn't do anything else. I tried, but I couldn't do it. I mean, I did a couple. There's a stupid poem called **'Venus and the Ark,'** which should never have been in that first book, that is the sort of thing that was approved of. That's one of the attempts; I do it, and then think, 'No!' " There are a few other false starts among the poems she had gathered by 1959, but **To Bedlam and Part Way Back** (1960) has fewer hollows and sags than betray most beginners because it is the product not only of several years of determined effort but of the longer years which, to paraphrase Shelley, had learned in suffering what they teach in song.

It may be appropriate first to consider the general problem of the confessional aesthetic which Sexton's poetry helped establish. Even if it were possible, any description of the psychogenesis and psychopathology of confessionalism could only be reductive. More general psychoanalytical theories of poetry are either so broad as to be impractical for this special use of poetry, or so vague and unmanageable as to be of no use at all. Freud's sense of poetry as compensatory gratification is not really applicable for confessional poetry, and more recent theories—for instance, art as "restitution" or symbolic recreation of what the artist's aggressive fantasies have already destroyed—still cannot account for a poetry which largely avoids the symbolic approach and instead seeks naked revelation. In fact, surprisingly little has been written with any authority on the subject of confessionalism, which has become, under the rubric of "sincerity," an impulse behind many of the significant social movements and styles since 1960.

One of the few studies available is Theodor Reik's *The Compulsion to Confess,* a work which, while hardly exhaustive, at least opens up a few theoretical approaches toward an understanding of the "compulsion" and its results. Broadly, Reik defines a confession as "a statement about impulses or drives which are felt or recognized as forbidden," and their expression involves both the repressed tendency and the repressing forces. . . . That is to say, confession is at once the process of exorcism and the plea for absolution. And the result, in Reik's view, is that "the disintegrating of the personality is at least temporarily halted by the confession. The communication between the ego and that part of the ego from which it was estranged is restored."

Although Freud recognized the "flexibility of repression" in artists, allowing them greater access to the unconscious and what Ernst Kris calls "functional regression" in service to the ego and its art, Reik's discussion is more directly apt for the poetry by Sexton under discussion in this essay. At the same time, it must be admitted that however much such sequences as **"The Death of the Fathers"** (in *The Book of Folly*) or **"The Divorce Papers"** (in *45 Mercy Street*) may have served Sexton as punishments for sins confessed, such an explanation, if it doubles as evaluation, cannot be finally satisfactory. It is their importance as art, rather than as mere self-expression, that matters. Even with that caution, Reik's explanation can be used to describe the impulses behind the expression that a confessional art then transforms. The repression through which such poems as Sexton's **"The Double Image"** or Sylvia Plath's "Daddy" explode is a part of their compulsive force. In fact, the great poems of madness and loss in Sexton's early books had their deeply personal source in what she once described as "a terrible need to kill myself."

To some extent, then, the poetry is therapeutic; or as D. H. Lawrence said, "One sheds one's sicknesses in books—repeats and presents again one's emotions, to be master of them." Eric Erikson underscores this aspect of the situation by reminding that "the individual's mastery over his neurosis begins where he is put in a position to accept the historical necessity which made him what he is" [*Identity: Youth and Crisis* (1968)]. Acceptance becomes survival. Anne Sexton: "writing, and especially having written, is evidence of survival—the books accumulate ego-strength." And so confessional poets are driven back to their losses, to that alienation—from self and others, from sanity and love—which is the thematic center of their vision and work. The betrayals in childhood, the family romance, the divorces and madnesses, the suicide attempts, the self-defeat and longing—the poets pursue them in their most intimate and painful detail. The pressure of public events, of the world outside the skin, is rarely felt, except perhaps in Robert Lowell's work. But the lives these poets have survived in their poems become emblems of larger forces. (pp. 244-49)

All the contemporary poets central to confessionalism have undergone extensive psychotherapy, and while it would be foolish to account for their poetry by this experience, it would be careless to ignore its influence, especially given the strong similarities between the process of therapy they have needed as individuals and the process of poetry by which they have then sought to express the lives they have come to explore or understand. Psychotherapy and psychoanalysis, abstractly outlined, involve a process during which the patient recounts his or her most intimate experiences, both conscious and unconscious, memories and fantasies. Though these "spots of time" overlap and perhaps even contradict each other, their deeper continuities assume the crucial patterns by which a life was led and sense is made. Both the experiences still painfully central and the unaccountable gaps are endlessly recircled, and those recountings—themselves depending on the same sense of experience-in-time—not only reveal the neuroses that have obscured the real experience and self, but also work toward what Freud once called a *Nacherziehung,* an after-education. We learn what we are by relearning what we have become. But what is important to note now is the essentially narrative structure of the process, of one's experiences recounted in this time as remembered in their own past time. And narrative is likewise the most distinctive structural device in confessional poetry. The importance and integrity of chronology affect both the way in which individual poems are composed and the way they are collected into sequences and volumes, and these arrangements, in turn, are of thematic importance as facts or memories, shifting desires or needs or anxieties or gratifications change the landscape of personality. Sexton's poem **"The Double Image,"** for instance, is a closely written and carefully parted account of her hospitalization and her necessary separation from her mother's shame and her daughter's innocence. The poem opens with the specificity of the achieved present—"I am thirty this November. . . . We stand watching the yellow leaves go queer"—and then drifts back through three yeers of madness and bitter history, to Bedlam and part way back, its larger thematic concerns held in precise details—dates, objects, places, names—among which are studded still smaller stories that memory associates with the main narrative. The destructions that survival implies in the poem are given their haunting force and authenticity by the history which the narrative leads the reader through so that he himself experiences the dramatic life of events and feelings.

In the same way, the poems of the confessionalists—Sexton especially—have a kind of chronicle effect on readers, as one keeps track volume by volume. This pervasive need to follow the contours of time, as if they sanctioned the truth they contain, is most clearly exemplified by *Live or Die,* where the poems are arranged in no particular narrative chronology but rather according to the compositional chronology, with the date carefully added to each poem like a clinching last line—from "January 25, 1962" to "February the last, 1966." Such a dependence on the details of time and place becomes a rhetorical method of definition and discovery, and points finally to the essentially epistemological concern of confessional poetry: since all that can meaningfully be known is my individual self, how is that self to be known and communicated except through the honest precision of its cumulative experience?

The rhetorical importance of confessional subject matter—especially insofar as it involves a characteristically Freudian epistemology—leads, in turn, to another consideration. In his most important gloss on the mediation of art, Freud wrote: "The essential *ars poetica* lies in the technique of overcoming the feeling of repulsion in us which is undoubtedly connected with the barriers that rise between each single ego and the others" [*The Standard Edition of the Complete Psychological Works of Sigmund Freud* (1953-)]. Or between the single ego and its history, he might have added. And among the barriers the self constructs are the familiar defense mechanisms: repression, displacement, suppression, screen memories, condensation, projection, and so on. Such psychological techniques, in turn, have their rhetorical analogues, not surprisingly those most favored by modernist poets and their New Critics: paradox, ambiguity, ellipsis, allusion, wit, and the other "tensions" that correspond to the neurotic symptoms by which the self is obscured. And in order to write with greater directness and honesty about their own experiences, Sexton and the other confessional poets have tended to avoid the poetic strategies of modernism—to derepress poetry, so to speak—and have sought to achieve their effects by other means. Sexton's turn toward open forms, as though in trust, is an example. In general, it can be said of Sexton's poems, as of other confessional poems, that the patterns they assume and by which they manage their meanings are those which more closely follow the actual experiences they are recreating—forms that can include and reflect direct, personal experience; a human, rather than a disembodied voice; the dramatic presentation of the flux of time and personality; and the drive toward sincerity. By this last concept is meant not an ethical imperative, but the willed and willing openness of the poet to her experience and to the character of the language by which her discoveries are revealed and shared. Not that the structures of sincerity abandon every measure of artifice. While she may have associated the imagination so strongly with memory, Sexton realized as well that the self's past experiences are neither provisional nor final, that even as they shape the art that describes them, so too they are modified by that very art. The flux of experience, rather than its absolute truth, determines which concerns or wounds are returned to in poem after poem, either because they have not yet been understood or because the understanding of them has changed. And Sexton is sharply aware, in her work, of the difference between factual truth and poetic truth—of the need to "edit" out, while trying not to distort, redundant or inessential "facts" in the service of cleaner, sharper poems. In a crucial sense, confessional art is a means of *realizing* the poet.

As the poet realizes himself, inevitably he catches up the way we live now: especially the personal life, since our marriages are more difficult than our wars, our private nightmares more terrifying than our public horrors. In addition, then, to our sense of the confessional poet as a survivor, he or she functions as a kind of witness. What may have begun as a strictly private need is transformed, once it is published, into a more inclusive focus—and here one recalls Whitman's "attempt, from first to last, to put a *Person,* a human being (myself, in the latter half of the Nineteenth Century, in America) freely, fully, and truly on record." The more naked and directly emotional nature of confessional poems heightens the integrity and force of their witness to the inner lives of both poets and readers; or, as Sexton has remarked, "poems of the inner life can reach the inner lives of readers in a way that anti-war poems can never stop a war." The final privatism of poetry itself, in other words, affords the confessional poet a certain confidence in using the details of intimate experience in ways that earlier would have been considered either arrogant or obscure. And the ends to which those details are put are not merely self-indulgent or self-therapeutic—or, in Robert Lowell's phrase, "a brave heart drowned on monologue." Of her own work, Anne Sexton once reminisced: "I began to think that if one life, somehow made into art, were recorded—not all of it, but like the testimony on an old tombstone—wouldn't that be worth something? Just one life—a poor middle-class life, nothing extraordinary (except maybe madness, but that's so common nowadays)—that seems worth putting down. It's the thing I have to do, the thing I want to do—I'm not sure why." And she went on to describe a reader's response to this "testimony": "I think, I hope, a reader's response is: 'My God, this has happened. And in some real sense it has happened to me too.' This has been my reaction to other poems, and my readers have responded to my poems in just this way."

Perhaps the most telling evidence of this sort of response are the countless letters that anonymous readers sent to Sexton, explaining how her poetry revealed their own troubled lives to them and often making impossible demands on the poet, so strong was the readers' sense of the real, suffering person in the poetry. It is no wonder that, with bitter wit, Sexton once described herself in a poem as "mother of the insane." But at a deeper level, there is some dark part in any one of us which her work illuminated, often distressingly. Like Wordsworth, who wished to allow his audience "new compositions of feeling," Sexton's response to her own experience becomes a model for a reader's response to his or her own. The poems function as instruments of discovery for the reader as well as for the poet, and the process of discovery—ongoing through poems and collections, as through life—is as important as the products, the poems which the poet has drawn directly out of her experience, often as isolated stays against confusion. (pp. 249-53)

Despite the authority and abundance in *To Bedlam and Part Way Back,* Sexton was careful, perhaps compelled, to include an apologia, a poem called **"For John, Who Begs Me Not to Enquire Further"**—addressed to her discouraging teacher John Holmes, and so finally to the critic in herself. The poem's title echoes the book's epigraph, from a letter of Schopenhauer to Goethe concerning the courage necessary for a philosopher: "He must be like Sophocles's Oedipus, who, seeking enlightenment concerning his terrible fate, pursues his indefatigable enquiry, even when he divines that appalling horror awaits him in the answer. But most of us carry in our heart the Jocasta who begs Oedipus for God's sake not to inquire further. . . . " The sympathy she can afford for Holmes—"although your fear is anyone's fear, / like an invisible veil between us all"—recalls Freud's sense of the repulsion with the self and others which art overcomes. Her cautious justification is modeled on her psychiatrist's plea: "that the worst of anyone / can be, finally, / an accident of hope." And the standard she sets herself is simply making sense:

> Not that it was beautiful,
> but that, in the end, there was
> a certain sense of order there;
> something worth learning
> in that narrow diary of my mind,
> in the commonplaces of the asylum
> where the cracked mirror
> or my own selfish death
> outstared me.

Part of that order is substantive and thematic, the urge to recover and understand the past: "I have this great need somehow to keep that time of my life, that feeling. I want to imprison it in a poem, to keep it. It's almost in a way like keeping a scrapbook to make life mean something as it goes by, to rescue it from chaos—to make 'now' last." But if the ability to extend the past and present into each other further depends upon the orders of art, that art cannot succeed without a prior commitment to honesty—or, to use Sexton's peculiar term, as a confessional poet she must start with a wise passivity, with being "still." That word occurs in her poem about the tradition, **"Portrait of an Old Woman on the College Tavern Wall,"** where the poets sit "singing and lying / around their round table / and around me still." "Why do these poets lie?" the poem goes on to question, and leaves them with mortal irony "singing / around their round table / until they are still." Whether death or silence, this "stillness" is the view of experience, both prior to and beyond language, from which her ordering proceeds. The difficulty, as she knows in another poem, **"Said The Poet to The Analyst,"** is that "My business is words":

> I must always forget how one word is able to pick
> out another, to manner another, until I have got
> something I might have said . . .
> but did not.

The business of the Analyst—again, an internal figure, a sort of artistic conscience—is "watching my words," guarding against the Jocasta who would settle for "something I might have said" instead of what must be revealed.

Sexton's business with words—the ordering of statement and instinct—is the adjustment of their demands to her experience: in her figure, to make a tree out of used furniture. Though her attitudes toward form evolved, from the beginning there was an uneasy ambivalence: the poet insisting on control, the person pleading, "Take out rules and leave the instant," as she said in one interview. Her solution was to use the metaphor of deceit, but to reverse it into a very personally inflected version of form:

> I think all form is a trick to get at the truth.
> Sometimes in my hardest poems, the ones that are difficult to write, I might make an impossible

scheme, a syllabic count that is so involved, that it then allows me to be truthful. It works as a kind of super-ego. It says, "You may now face it, because it will be impossible ever to get out." . . . But you see how I say this not to deceive you, but to deceive me. I deceive myself, saying to myself you can't do it, and then if I can get it, then I have deceived myself, then I can change it and do what I want. I can even change and rearrange it so no one can see my trick. It won't change what's real. It's there on paper [*Hudson Review* (Winter 1965-66)].

Though her early work occasionally forces itself with inversions and stolid High Style, her concern for the precisions of voice and pace reveal her care in indulging a lyric impulse only to heighten the dramatic. What Richard Howard has said of her use of rhyme is indicative of her larger sense of form: "invariably it is Sexton's practice to use rhyme to bind the poem, irregularly invoked, abandoned when inconvenient, psychologically convincing" [*Alone With America* (1971)]. The truth-getting tricks, in other words, serve as a method of conviction for both poet and reader. For the poet, form functions to articulate the details and thrust of her actual experience, while for the reader it guides his dramatic involvement in the recreation: both convictions converging on authenticity, on realization. And so the voice is kept conversational, understated by plain-speech slang or homely detail—its imagery drawn from the same sources it counterpoints, its force centered in the pressure of events it contours, the states of mind it maps. This is clearly the case with the poems of madness in the first section of *To Bedlam and Part Way Back*. . . . True to the several experiences, cut across time, that they describe, the poems vary the means they take to explore the common meaning. They range from expressionistic projections [to the menacing, flat accent of life-in-death]. . . . Together they devise, in Michel Foucault's phrase, "the formulas of exclusion."

M. L. Rosenthal has seen in these poems "the self reduced to almost infantile regression" [*The New Poets* (1967)]. But more often the voice is that of an older child, which implies a consciousness that can experience the arbitrariness of authority and the sufferings of loss without understanding either chance or cause. The inferno of insanity opens, appropriately, with the poet lost in the dark wood of her "night mind":

> And opening my eyes, I am afraid of course
> to look—this inward look that society scorns—
> Still I search in these woods and find nothing worse
> than myself, caught between the grapes and the thorns.
>
>   **("Kind Sir: These Woods")**

The disorientation necessitates the search: here, the descent into her own underworld, as later she will ascend part way back. Likewise, the figure of the child—so important in Part Two, where it subsumes both the poet and her daughter—introduces the themes of growth and discovery, of the growth into self by discovering its extremes, as in the poem addressed to her psychiatrist:

> And we are magic talking to itself,

noisy and alone. I am queen of all my sins
   forgotten. Am I still lost?
   Once I was beautiful. Now I am myself,
counting this row and that row of moccasins
   waiting on the silent shelf.

("You, Dr. Martin")

The "private institution on a hill," like Hamlet's nutshell, is finally the self in which she is confined:

They lock me in this chair at eight a.m.
   and there are no signs to tell the way,
just the radio beating to itself
   and the song that remembers
more than I. Oh, la la la,
   this music swims back to me.
That night I came I danced a circle
   and was not afraid.
Mister?

("Music Swims Back to Me")

The struggle to find "which way is home" involves the dissociation and resumption of different personalities (**"Her Kind," "The Expatriates," "What's That"**), the limits of paranoia and mania (**"Noon Walk on the Asylum Lawn," "Lullaby"**), and the dilemma of memory that drives pain toward exorcism (**"You, Dr. Martin," "Music Swims Back to Me," "The Bells," "Said the Poet to the Analyst"**).

Though, as she says, there is finally "no word for time," the need to restore it is the essential aspect of the ordering process:

Today is made of yesterday, each time I steal
   toward rites I do not know, waiting for the lost
ingredient, as if salt or money or even lust
   would keep us calm and prove us whole at last.

("The Lost Ingredient")

What has been lost, along with sanity, is the meaning of those who made her, and this first book introduces us to the cast she will reassemble and rehearse in all her subsequent work, even through **"Talking to Sheep"** and **"Divorce, Thy Name is Woman"** in *45 Mercy Street:* the hapless boozy father, the helpless cancer-swollen bitch of a mother, the daughters as both victims and purifiers, the shadowy presence of her husband, the analyst as dark daddy and muse, the clutching company of doomed poets—and most touchingly, the great-aunt whom she calls Nana. Sexton's obsession with her Nana—the "Nana-hex" she calls it later—results from both sympathy and guilt. "She was, during the years she lived with us, my best friend, my teacher, my confidante and my comforter. I never thought of her as being young. She was an extension of myself and was my world" [*Poet's Choice* (1962)]. For this very reason, when her great-aunt, after a sudden deafness, had a nervous breakdown from which she never recovered, the poet could find her both an emblem of her own suffering and a source of guilt for fear she had somehow caused it. Nana is brought on tenderly in the lyrical elegy **"Elizabeth Gone,"** but in the next poem, **"Some Foreign Letters,"** her life is used as the focus of the poet's own anxieties as she sits reading the letters her great-aunt had sent to her family as a young woman on her Victorian Grand Tour. The poem proceeds by verse and refrain—Nana's letters of her youth, the poet's images of the same

woman different—to point up the disjunction between memories: Nana's diaried ones, which have trapped her youth in an irretrievable past, and the poet's own memories of Nana trapped in age and lost to death. (pp. 254-59)

The "guilty love" with which the poem ends is the poet's own ambivalent response to her inability to have rescued her Nana—even as she realizes she will not be able to save herself—from the facts that are fate, a life that cannot be unlived or chosen. The last stanza's pathos derives from its prediction of what has already occurred, the proof that guilt is suffered again and again:

Tonight I will learn to love you twice;
   learn your first days, your mid-Victorian face.
Tonight I will speak up and interrupt
   your letters, warning you that wars are coming,
that the Count will die, that you will accept
   your America back to live like a prim thing
on a farm in Maine. I tell you, you will come
   here, to the suburbs of Boston, to see the blue-
      nose
world go drunk each night, to see the handsome
   children jitterbug, to feel your left ear close
one Friday at Symphony. And I tell you,
   you will tip your boot feet out of that hall,
rocking from its sour sound, out onto
   the crowded street, letting your spectacles fall
and your hair net tangle as you stop passers-by
   to mumble your guilty love while your ears die.

The poet speaks her warning here not as a suspicious Jocasta but as a knowing Tiresias, helpless before time, that most visible scar of mortality. And the family to which she resigns Nana is, of course, her own as well, and the self-recovery which the volume's arrangement of poems plots necessarily moves to recover her parents, as so much of her later work too will do.

The book's second section is The Part Way Back, in the sense of both return and history. The painful realizations of adjustment, the lessons of loss and recovery weight the book's two anchor poems—**"The Double Image"** and **"The Division of Parts."** They are long poems, explorations lengthened to accommodate their discoveries and unresolved dilemmas, and extended by subtle modulations of voice and structure to dramatize their privacies. **"The Double Image,"** the book's strongest and most ambitious poem, is actually a sequence of seven poems tracing the terms of Sexton's dispossession—similar to Snodgrass's "Heart's Needle," which was its model. The other poem, which clearly echoes Snodgrass's voice as well, is an independent summary of her losses, and makes the subsequent poems seem to have insisted themselves on her later. If that was the case, there is reason for it, since the jagged lines of the first poem reflect the uncertain hesitancy in naming the guilt that had caused her self-hatred and her suicide attempts and breakdown. It is addressed, in retrospect, to the daughter whose infant illness released the long-held guilt:

. . . a fever rattled
   in your throat and I moved like a pantomime
above your head. Ugly angels spoke to me. The
   blame,
I heard them say, was mine. They tattled

359

like green witches in my head, letting doom
leak like a broken faucet;
as if doom had flooded my belly and filled your
        bassinet,
an old debt I must assume.

She tries to solve her life with death—"I let the witches
take away my guilty soul"—but is forced back from the
"time I did not love / myself " to face the new life she has
made in her child and the old life she had made for herself.
She assumes the old debts in the following narrative of her
recovery. If the first poem turned on her commitment and
the loss of her daughter, the second turns on her release
and the loss of her mother, to whom she returns as "an
angry guest," "an outgrown child." The poet had grown
"well enough to tolerate / myself," but her mother cannot
forgive the suicide attempt and so cannot accept her
daughter: she "had my portrait / done instead," a line that
refrains the tedium and repressed menace that punches
out each stanza. The tension of presence begins to sort the
past; the church is another Bedlam, her parents her
keepers. . . . (pp. 259-61)

The third poem opens up the deaths in and of relationships. Sexton's distance from her own daughter gains its
double reference: "as if it were normal / to be a mother
and be gone." As the poet gathers her strength, her mother sickens, and madness, love-loss, and death are drawn
into a single figure which points again at guilt. Her mother's cancer—"as if my dying had eaten inside of her"—
accuses Sexton with questions that "still I couldn't answer." The fourth poem is centered as an interlude of partial return and acceptance: Sexton back from Bedlam, her
mother from the hospital, her daughter from the exile of
innocence. The fact of survival converts its sterility into
patience: the blank, facing portraits mirror the reversal of
concern:

> During the sea blizzards
> she had her
> own portrait painted.
> A cave of a mirror
> placed on the south wall;
> matching smile, matching contour.
> And you resembled me; unacquainted
> with my face, you wore it. But you were mine
> after all.

The fifth poem begins to draw the women together into a
chorus, their roles merging into a new knowledge. . . .
The sixth is a self-study, the poet finding herself in the distanced image of her mother, as in the next poem she discovers how selfish are the maternal motives of love. But
in this poem, it is the process of life that learns from *la nature morte:*

> And this was the cave of the mirror,
> that double woman who stares
> at herself, as if she were petrified
> in time—two ladies sitting in umber chairs.
> You kissed your grandmother
> and she cried.

The final poem, again addressed to the poet's daughter,
summarizes her learning:

> You learn my name,

wobbling up the sidewalk, calling and crying.
You call me *mother* and I remember my mother
        again,
somewhere in greater Boston, dying.

But the last stanza unwinds into a tentative resumption of
guilt—its last line speaking, with an odd irony, the voice
of Jocasta: "And this was my worst guilt; you could not
cure / nor soothe it. I made you to find me."

In **"The Division of Parts,"** Sexton carries the account
past her mother's death, which has left her, on Good Friday, with "gifts I did not choose." The last hospital days
are retold, and the numbness with which they stun her implies the larger truth of the poem:

> But you turned old,
> all your fifty-eight years sliding
> like masks from your skull;
> and at the end
> I packed your nightgowns in suitcases,
> paid the nurses, came riding
> home as if I'd been told
> I could pretend
> people live in places.

But people live not in space or places, but in time and in
others, and their demands puzzle the poet's guilt: "Time,
that rearranger / of estates, equips / me with your garments, but not with grief." Her inheritance steals on her
"like a debt," and she cannot expiate her loss: "I planned
to suffer / and I cannot." Unlike "Jesus, *my stranger,*"
who assumed "old debts" and knew how and why to suffer, Sexton is emptied of belief by need:

> . . . Fool! I fumble my lost childhood
> for a mother and lounge in sad stuff
> with love to catch and catch as catch can.
>
> And Christ still waits. I have tried
> to exorcise the memory of each event
> and remain still, a mixed child,
> heavy with cloths of you.
> Sweet witch, you are my worried guide.

And she realizes the motive of her subsequent books: "For
all the way I've come / I'll have to go again." Only ever
part way back, she tries her art against her mind—"I
would still curse / you in my rhyming words / and bring
you flapping back, old love"—but her litany of incantatory adjectives cannot lose loss, and if she cannot love it, she
has learned to live it.

The religious note introduced at the end of *To Bedlam and
Part Way Back,* evoked by the death which aligns it with
other needs and losses, is even more apparent in her next
book, *All My Pretty Ones* (1962). Two of its best-known
poems—**"For God While Sleeping"** and **"In the Deep
Museum"**—are really part of a much larger group that
threads through all her collections, on through **"The Jesus
Papers"** in *The Book of Folly* and into **"Jesus Walking"**
in *The Death Notebooks* and the major poems in *The
Awful Rowing Toward God,* whose title best describes the
project. Though she herself referred to these poems as
"mystical," they are more obviously religious since their
concerns are always the human intricacies of need and belief, and their context is Sexton's need for belief and her
inability to believe as that dilemma interacts with her rela-

tionships to herself and others, the dead and dying. This explains too why her religious poetry centers almost exclusively on the person of Jesus, the central figure of belief who himself despaired at the end, who brought love and found none, who gave life and was nailed to a tree. But her relationship to Jesus, as it develops through the books, is an ambivalent one. On the one hand, he serves as a sympathetic emblem of her own experience: "That ragged Christ, that sufferer, performed the greatest act of confession, and I mean with his body. And I try to do that with words" [see excerpt dated 1971]. This is the force of the poems in *All My Pretty Ones.* To touch a crucifix—"I touch its tender hips, its dark jawed face, / its solid neck, its brown sleep"—is to remind herself of poetry's work for salvation. . . . The Christ who is "somebody's fault," like the poet, is "hooked to your own weight, / jolting toward death under your nameplate" (**"For God While Sleeping"**). But at the same time, Sexton is fascinated by another Jesus: "Perhaps it's because he can forgive sins" [*The New York Times* (19 November 1969)]. Like her psychiatrist, Jesus is a man who can take on her guilt, a man who suffers with her and for her. This is the Jesus **"In the Deep Museum,"** where gnawing rats are the "hairy angels who take my gift," as he blesses "this other death": "Far below The Cross, I correct its flaws. Her purest statement of this sense of Christ comes in *The Death Notebooks,* in **"Jesus Walking"**: "To pray, Jesus knew, / is to be a man carrying a man." It is the simplicity of such strength which takes the measure of weaker men in her life, especially her father, whose death brings him into the poetry of *All My Pretty Ones.*

This second book is less an extension than a completion of her first, just as its epigraph—from Kafka—describes the motive and effect of the courage invoked earlier: "the books we need are the kind that act upon us like a misfortune, that make us suffer the death of someone we love more than ourselves, that make us feel as though we were on the verge of suicide, or lost in a forest remote from all human habitation—a book should serve as the ax for the frozen sea within us." But Sexton's own evaluation is misleadingly neat: "Well, in the first book, I was giving the experience of madness; in the second book, the causes of madness" [see excerpt dated 1971]. That account of "causes" is not sustained, and most of this book—whose poems are more expert but less urgent than before—catches the reader up with the poet's life. That is to say, its confessions converge toward the present, and the chronicle begins to include more immediate and intimate events. Previously worked aspects of and approaches to her experience are here retried: **"The Operation"** clearly derives from **"The Double Image," "The House"** expands **"Some Foreign Letters."** The greater assurance of her verse likewise allows Sexton to experiment successfully with open forms and new voices. Besides the religious poems already mentioned, *All My Pretty Ones* includes several distinctive love poems, real and invented, of which **"Flight"** and **"Letter Written on a Ferry While Crossing Long Island Sound"** are most incisive, the latter poem recalling Whitman's **"Crossing Brooklyn Ferry,"** whose "dumb, beautiful ministers" are redressed as nuns who float up in a fantasy of redemption.

But Sexton's burden remains her inward argument: "I cannot promise very much. / I give you the images I know." The effort in these early books remains to get back at herself. The dead haunt like "bad dreams," and the heart loves only "the decay we're made of." The poem addressed to her **"Old Dwarf Heart,"** in lines that echo Roethke and fold back in their rhymes like a trap, sets the stakes for *All My Pretty Ones:*

> Good God, the things she knows!
> And worse, the sores she holds
> in her hands, gathered in like a nest
> from an abandoned field. At her best
> she is all red muscle, humming in and out, cajoled
> by time. Where I go, she goes.
>
> Oh now I lay me down to love,
> how awkwardly her arms undo,
> how patiently I untangle her wrists
> like knots. Old ornament, old naked fist,
> even if I put on seventy coats I could not cover
> you . . .
> mother, father, I'm made of.

The book opens on **"The Truth the Dead Know,"** which is their absolute isolation, against which the poet fights to save both herself and her dead parents. Her father's death, three months after her mother's, intervened not only between the different concerns of these first two books but also between the completed realization of her inheritance: in the fine print of their wills, the poet fears to find her father's alcoholism and her mother's cancer, which would at the same time prove her their daughter and destroy her. The sins of the father are revisited in the title poem, which blends memories and objects like snapshots out of order to invoke the man's loss and, again, her guilt:

> This year, solvent but sick, you meant
> to marry that pretty widow in a one-month rush.
> But before you had that second chance, I cried
> on your fat shoulder. Three days later you died.

The fear that she has somehow killed her father is the familiar origin of guilt for which she seeks both the retribution of punishment and the reconciliation of a forced forgiveness:

> I hold a five-year diary that my mother kept
> for three years, telling all she does not say
> of your alcoholic tendency. You overslept,
> she writes. My God, father, each Christmas Day
> with your blood, will I drink down your glass
> of wine? The diary of your hurly-burly years
> goes to my shelf to wait for my age to pass.
> Only in this hoarded span will love persevere.
> Whether you are pretty or not, I outlive you,
> bend down my strange face to yours and forgive
> you.

The volume's most striking poem, **"The Operation,"** returns to her mother's death, which the poet must now have cut out of herself: "the historic thief / is loose in my house / and must be set upon." Unconscious under the surgeries of survival, her experience is another madness:

> Next, I am hung up like a saddle and they begin.
> Pale as an angel I float out over my own skin.

I soar in hostile air
over the pure women in labor,
over the crowning heads of babies being born.
I plunge down the backstair
calling *mother* at the dying door,
to rush back to my own skin, tied where it was
　　torn.
Its nerves pull like wires
snapping from the leg to the rib.
Strangers, their faces rolling like hoops, require
my arm. I am lifted into my aluminum crib.

Reborn from death, as in **"The Double Image"** she was from insanity, her scarred, scared response to life is inadequate to its new demands, and the poem ends understated, with a child's diction, a deflecting image:

Time now to pack this humpty-dumpty
back the frightened way she came
and run along, Anne, and run along now,
my stomach laced up like a football
for the game.

Much more is faced in **"The House,"** which loosens its regard and drifts back over her childhood, dream-distorted and so clarified. Reruns of "the same bad dream . . . the same dreadful set, / the same family of orange and pink faces" are set spinning to portray the atmosphere in which death was first preferred. These three album photographs, each a collage of hurt and menace—in ways that oddly prefigure *Transformations*—are sufficient example of the poem's force:

Father,
an exact likeness,
his face bloated and pink
with black market scotch,
sits out his monthly bender
in his custom-made pajamas
and shouts, his tongue as quick as galloping
　　horses,
shouts into the long distance telephone call.
His mouth is as wide as his kiss.

Mother,
with just the right gesture,
kicks her shoes off,
but is made all wrong,
impossibly frumpy as she sits there
in her alabaster dressing room
sorting her diamonds like a bank teller
to see if they add up.

The maid
as thin as a popsicle stick,
holds dinner as usual,
rubs her angry knuckles over the porcelain sink
and grumbles at the gun-shy dog.
She knows something is going on.
She pricks a baked potato.

The poet then walks into her own dream, "up another flight into the penthouse, / to slam the door on all the years / she'll have to live through . . . " until she wakes in italics: *"Father, father, I wish I were dead."* She wakes as well into the self she has become, caught between neurosis and nostalgia: "At thirty-five / she'll dream she's dead / or else she'll dream she's back." In the death that poses desire as dream nothing has changed, and it merges

in her awareness with history—again, facts are fate, the infernal machine: "All day long the machine waits: rooms, / stairs, carpets, furniture, people— / those people who stand at the open windows like objects / waiting to topple." What the past has lost cannot be salvaged in the future, and her poem **"The Fortress,"** a meditation over her sleeping daughter Linda, submits to a life other than hers:

Darling, life is not in my hands;
life with its terrible changes
will take you, bombs or glands,
your own child at your
breast, your own house on your own land.
Outside the bittersweet turns orange.
Before she died, my mother and I picked those
　　fat
branches, finding orange nipples
on the gray wire stands.
We weeded the forest, curing trees like cripples.

Time draws on change, and the love she leaves her child seems as fragile as innocence. That too is part of the weary acceptance of this book.

The oneiric organization of **"The House"** looks forward to the important changes that her next and decisive book, *Live or Die* (1966), announces. With its longer poems in open forms which more subtly accommodate a greater range of experience, and with a voice pitched higher to intensify that experience, *Live or Die* represents not a departure from her earlier strengths but the breakthrough into her distinctive style. Perhaps the most immediate aspect of that style is its more extravagant use of imagery:

I sat all day
stuffing my heart into a shoe box,
avoiding the precious window
as if it were an ugly eye
through which birds coughed,
chained to the heaving trees;
avoiding the wallpaper of the room
where tongues bloomed over and over,
bursting from lips like sea flowers. . . .
　　　　　　　　　　　　　　("Those Times . . . ")

This is the sort of imagery that will be even more exploited in later books where "like" becomes the most frequently encountered word. It is a technique that risks arbitrary excesses and embarrassing crudities, that at its best can seem but a slangy American equivalent of Apollinaire's surrealism: *Les nuages coulaient comme un flux menstruel.* But it is crucial to remember, with Gaston Bachelard, that "we live images synthetically in their initial complexity, often giving them our unreasoned allegiance" [*L'Eau et les rêves* (1942)]. And Sexton's use of images is primarily psychotropic—used less for literary effect than as a means to pry deeper into her psychic history, to float her findings and model her experience. As she said, "The poetry is often more advanced, in terms of my unconscious, than I am. Poetry, after all, milks the unconscious" [see excerpt dated 1971]. And so she came increasingly to identify the imagination less with her memory than with her unconscious: "Images are the heart of poetry. And this is not tricks. Images come from the unconscious. Imagination and the unconscious are one and the same." Sexton's commitment to honest realization is thus only carried to a deeper level. And if Rimbaud was right to demand of such associative poetry a *"dérèglement de tous les sens,"* it can be seen as Sexton's necessary road of excess through her experiences of madness and the disorientation of her past, so that her metaphors are a method not to display similarities but to discover identities.

Although *Live or Die* shows, for this reason, the influence of her readings in Roethke and Neruda, a more important factor was the new analyst she began seeing while at work on this book. He was more interested in dreams than her earlier doctors had been, and Sexton found herself dealing more directly with her unconscious: "You taught me / to believe in dreams; / thus I was the dredger" (**"Flee on Your Donkey"**). Several poems in *Live or Die* are direct dream-songs—**"Three Green Windows," "Imitations of Drowning," "Consorting with Angels," "In the Beach House,"** and **"To Lose the Earth."** The latent content in these poems—such as the primal scene of "the royal strapping" in **"In the Beach House"**—is expressive but abandoned to its own independence, unlike more conscious fantasies such as **"Menstruation at Forty,"** in which themes of death and incest are projected onto the imagined birth of a son. The insistence of the unconscious also draws up the poems of her childhood—**"Love Song," "Protestant Easter,"** and especially **"Those Times . . . ,"** one of the book's triumphs. Robert Boyers has described *Live or Die* as "a poetry of victimization, in which she is at once victim and tormentor" [*Salmangundi* (Spring 1967)]. and **"Those Times . . . "** torments the poet with her earliest memories of victimization. . . . But her felt exclusion was assumed and rehearsed in a closet's dark escape, where she sat with her hurts and dreams, as later she would sit in madness and poetry:

> I did not know that my life, in the end,
> would run over my mother's like a truck
> and all that would remain
> from the year I was six
> was a small hole in my heart, a deaf spot,
> so that I might hear
> the unsaid more clearly.

The other crucial influence on *Live or Die* is the play she wrote at the time—first titled *Tell Me Your Answer True* and eventually produced in 1969 as *Mercy Street*—sections of which were carried over as poems into *Live or Die* and lend the book its character of psychodrama. Sexton's description of herself during a poetry reading could apply to her presence in this book as well: "I am an actress in my own autobiographical play" [see excerpt dated 1971]. . . . To match the expansive forms and intense imagery of these poems, the voice that speaks them grows more various in its effects, matching a strident aggression or hovering tenderness with the mood and matter evoked. Above all, there is energy, whether of mania or nostalgia. And it is more expressly vocative here, as her cast is introduced separately and her relationship to each is reworked: her father (**"And One for My Dame"**), mother (**"Christmas Eve"**), daughters (**"Little Girl, My Stringbean, My Lovely Woman," "A Little Uncomplicated Hymn," "Pain for a Daughter"**), husband (**"And One for My Dame," "Man and Wife," "Your Face on the Dog's Neck"**), and Nana (**"Crossing the Atlantic," "Walking in Paris"**).

There is a very conscious sense about these poems of the times since her first book that she has spent with her living and her dead. **"A Little Uncomplicated Hymn,"** for instance, alludes directly to **"The Double Image"** to catch at a perspective for the interval; the new poem, according to Sexton, was the "attempt to master that experience in light of the new experience of her life and how it might have affected her and how it affects me still; she wasn't just an emblem for me any longer. Every book, every poem, is an attempt to master things that aren't ever quite mastered." And so one watches her recircling her experiences to define and refine her understanding of them. Her parents are written of more sharply, and her regret is less for what she has lost than for what she never had. Her great-aunt's account of her youth in Europe, which structures **"Some Foreign Letters,"** was the motive for Sexton's attempt to retrace in person Nana's journey. . . . But the attempt is not only abandoned, it is impossible; she cannot walk off her history, the past cannot be toured, only endured: where I am is hell.

The hell in her head is the subject of **"Flee on Your Donkey,"** whose title and other details are taken from Rimbaud's *Fêtes de la faim.* Begun in a mental hospital and worked over four years, the poem draws the past into the present to realign the poet's perspective on both:

> Recently I noticed in **"Flee on Your Donkey"** that I had used some of the same facts in *To Bedlam and Part Way Back,* but I hadn't realized them in their total ugliness. I'd hidden from them. This time was really raw and really ugly and it was all involved with my own madness. It was all like a great involuted web, and I presented it the way it really was [see excerpt dated 1971].

The madness that in **"The Double Image"** had been an escape from guilt has become a "hunger": "Six years of shuttling in and out of this place! / O my hunger! My hunger!" The hospital scene this time resembles a sort of religious retreat—"Because there was no other place / to flee to, / I came back to the scene of the disordered senses"—and the poet inventories her time, fingers the black beads of loss. Like Rimbaud, she has been "a stranger, / damned and in trance" during the years huddled in her analyst's office. Another poem, **"Cripples and Other Stories,"** makes explicit the connection implied here: this ambivalent love song to her doctor is the pleas to her father, and the self he helps her deliver describes a birth:

> O my hunger! My hunger!
> I was the one
> who opened the war eyelid
> like a surgeon
> and brought forth young girls
> to grunt like fish.
> I told you,
> I said—
> but I was lying—
> that the knife was for my mother . . .
> and then I delivered her.

Similarly, **"For the Year of the Insane"** invokes "Mary, fragile mother," the name of both the Virgin and Sexton's own mother. And again, her prayer for rebirth fantasizes a return: "A beginner, I feel your mouth touch mine." But more striking still is the repetition of the image of the eye as vagina in the call for delivery into light:

> O Mary, open your eyelids.
> I am in the domain of silence,
> the kingdom of the crazy and the sleeper.
> There is blood here
> and I have eaten it.
> O mother of the womb,
> did I come for blood alone?
> O little mother,
> I am in my own mind.
> I am locked in the wrong house.

This demand for release into life, as the title *Live or Die* balances her options, is the counterweight to the measure of death in the book, scaled from suicide attempts (**"Wanting to Die," "The Addict"**) to the deaths of past figures who were part of her—John Holmes (**"Somewhere in Africa"**) and Sylvia Plath (**"Sylvia's Death"**). **"Flee on Your Donkey"** struggles with the ambiguous impatience, introducing it first as weariness with "allowing myself the wasted life": "I have come back / but disorder is not what it was. / I have lost the trick of it! / The innocence of it!" Her desire for communion—"In this place everyone talks to his own mouth"—reverses her earlier escape inward: "Anne, Anne, / flee on your donkey, / flee this sad hotel." And by the time she can write the simple title **"Live"** over the book's last poem, the "mutilation" that previous poems had struck off is renounced. The evidence of survival is enough: "Even so, / I kept right on going, / a sort of human statement" that says finally: "I am not what I expected." If her guilt has not been solved, it has at least been soothed by her acceptance of and by her "dearest three"—her husband and daughters. And if the resolution of **"Live"** sounds unconvinced, unconvincing, it is because of Sexton's dependence on others, lulling the self into a passive tense.

The survival achieved, the rebirth delivered, is then praised in *Love Poems* (1969), in many ways her weakest collection since most of it is sustained by language alone. Its self-celebration tends either to avoid or to invent the experience behind it, or revolves on minimal events: a hip-fracture, a summer safari. Secure in her use of free verse, Sexton crafts these poems with equivalents: litanies of images which are more often additional than accumulative. As before, the book's epigraph—this time from Yeats—defines its intention, and here the concern is with roles: "One should say before sleeping, 'I have lived many lives. I have been a slave and a prince. Many a beloved has sat on my knees and I have sat on the knees of many a beloved. Everything that has been shall be again.'" And so she explores her womanhood (**"The Breast," "In Celebration of My Uterus"**), and her roles as woman, wife and lover. Not surprisingly, she is best when describing how lovers swim "the identical river called Mine": "we are a pair of scissors / who come together to cut, without towels saying His. Hers" (**"December 10th"**). (pp. 261-75)

The masks she wears in *Love Poems* don't hide Sexton's confessional impulse, they avoid it. Her motive may well have been to search out new voices. Certainly this is the case with her next work, *Transformations* (1971). She

began these versions of Grimms' tales on the advice of her daughter after an extended dry spell in her work, and when, five poems later, she had written "Snow White and the Seven Dwarfs," she felt she should continue the experiment into a book which would release a more playful aspect of her personality that her earlier books had neglected. The result—considering its cloyingly "cute" Kurt Vonnegut introduction, its illustrations, and commercial success—seems at most a divertissement and surely a conscious effort to avoid her confessional voice. Like *Love Poems,* it seems content to present women in their roles, from princess to witch, with the poet merely presiding as "Dame Sexton," as the introductory poem, **"The Gold Key,"** explains:

> The speaker in this case
> is a middle-aged witch, me—
> tangled on my two great arms,
> my face in a book
> and my mouth wide,
> ready to tell you a story or two.

And the poem goes on to offer a key to her technique here:

> It opens this book of odd tales
> which transform the Brothers Grimm.
> Transform?
> As if an enlarged paper clip
> could be a piece of sculpture.
> (And it could.)

That is to say, her "transformations" exaggerate and so distort the originals to create contemporary camp. And indeed the tales are blown up like pop-art posters by means of an irreverently zippy style, slangy allusions, and a strongly Freudian slant to her stories. But what draws *Transformations* more centrally into this discussion is Sexton's inability to keep her characteristic concerns from seeping into what would otherwise seem her most distanced work. (pp. 275-76)

The power of fairy tales has always resided in their "changed" dream-landscapes, and Freud discussed them as "screen memories," survivals of persistent human conflicts and desires, narratives whose characters and situations are symbolic of the unconscious dramas in any individual's psyche. With this in mind, the psychoanalytical uses of the word "transformations" bear on Sexton's work. It can refer both to the variations of the same thematic material represented in a patient's dreams of experience and to the process by which unconscious material is brought to consciousness. So too Sexton's poems are variations on themes familiar from her earlier work—at one point she says, "My guilts are what / we catalogue"—transformed into fantasies or dreams discovered in the Grimm tales, which are anyone's first "literature" and become bound up with the child's psyche. The introductions that precede each story—replacing the analogous moral-pointing in the fairy tale—usually isolate her more private concern in each, and the tales which elaborate them include subjects ranging from adultery (**"The Little Peasant"**) to despair (**"Rumpelstiltskin"**) to deception (**"Red Riding Hood"**) to parents' devouring their children (**"Hansel and Gretel"**). Other poems are even more explicit in that their subjects allude directly to earlier poems:

"The Operation" is recalled in **"The Maiden Without Hands"** with its lines "If they have cut out your uterus / I will give you a laurel wreath / to put in its place." **"Rapunzel"** fantasizes on her "Nana-hex," and **"The Frog Prince"** is a daring exploration of her father-feelings: "Frog is my father's genitals. . . . He says: Kiss me. Kiss me. / And the ground soils itself." But a majority of these poems link their dreams with those of madness and with Sexton's strong poem on its asylum. **"The White Snake," "Iron Hans," "One-Eye, Two-Eyes, Three-Eyes," "The Wonderful Musician," "The Twelve Dancing Princesses,"** and **"Briar Rose (Sleeping Beauty)"**—each is set at an outpost of psychosis, the often bizarre details creating a narrative of insanity from the inside. **"Briar Rose (Sleeping Beauty),"** the final and most intense poem in the book, was actually written while Sexton was hospitalized, and loosens its disguise into an identity. Once awake, Briar Rose cannot bear to sleep again, to imprison herself in the dreams that are Sexton's. . . . (pp. 277-78)

The fabular impulse behind *Transformations* is resumed in *The Book of Folly* (1972), both in the three short stories included among the poems and in "The Jesus Papers" sequence, which is a taunting, Black-mass transformation of the salvation story. The entire book, in fact, has a summary quality to it. The forged stylization of *Love Poems* returns in **"Angels of the Love Affair,"** six sonnets on love's seasons. The angel in each is the "gull that grows out of my back in the dreams I prefer," and those dreams are hushed, flamboyant, touching memories of certain sheets, bits of dried blood, lemony woodwork, a peace march—all the abstracted details of moments that are warm only in her darkness. But what is more important is her return to the fully confessional mode: "I struck out memory with an X / but it came back. / I tied down time with a rope / but it came back" **("Killing the Spring")**. On the simplest level, the detritus of time has clustered new collisions or crises: the death of her sister—"her slim neck / snapped like a piece of celery" in a car crash—or the national disasters **("The Firebombers," "The Assassin")**. Generally, the subjects she recircles are familiar, but her angle of attack and attitude is new: more self-conscious, often more strident and defiant, more searching. Like the later Lowell, Sexton's self-consciousness results from the ironies of exposure, the logistics of fame. These permit her both a guilty longing [and an empty pride]. . . . (pp. 278-79)

Both her art and her audience, her fans and family exist beyond their ability to help her, as a poem to her now-grown daughter Linda laments:

> Question you about this
> and you will sew me a shroud
> and hold up Monday's broiler
> and thumb out the chicken gut.
> Question you about this
> and you will see my death
> drooling at these gray lips
> while you, my burglar, will eat
> fruit and pass the time of day.
>   **("Mother and Daughter")**

It is this sense of what still remains to be lost that occasions the tonal shift. In contrast with **"You, Dr. Martin"** or **"Cripples and Other Stories,"** a new poem to her psy-

chiatrist, **"The Doctor of the Heart,"** is scornfully reductive, resentful of the soothing instead of solving, challenging the doctor with her history and her art:

> But take away my mother's carcinoma
> for I have only one cup of fetus tears.
>
> Take away my father's cerebral hemorrhage
> for I have only a jigger of blood in my hand.
>
> Take away my sister's broken neck
> for I have only my schoolroom ruler for a cure.
>
> Is there such a device for my heart?
> I have only a gimmick called magic fingers.

Whether the mind is too strong or not strong enough to adjust to the violent changes that death forces on us no longer seems to matter to the poem's manic finale:

> I am at the ship's prow.
> I am no longer the suicide
>
> with her raft and paddle.
> Herr Doktor! I'll no longer die
>
> to spite you, you wallowing
> seasick grounded man.

This defiance of death demands, first of all, that the tyranny of her own impulse toward suicide be fully evoked: she must "lie down / with them and lift my madness / off like a wig," since "Death is here. There is no / other settlement" **("Oh")**. And for this reason she returns, in **"The Other,"** to what has always terrified her poetry: the alien self she cannot escape, who insanely possesses her and can keep her from the self that makes poems and love and children:

> When the child is soothed and resting on the
>   breast
> it is my other who swallows Lysol.
> When someone kisses someone or flushes the toi-
>   let
> it is my other who sits in a ball and cries.
> My other beats a tin drum in my heart.
> My other hangs up laundry as I try to sleep.
> My other cries and cries and cries
> when I put on a cocktail dress.
> It cries when I prick a potato.
> It cries when I kiss someone hello.
> It cries and cries and cries
> until I put on a painted mask
> and leer at Jesus in His passion.

As in *Live or Die,* these are the dreams that confront endurance. Reformulated, death and madness, which had once seemed her only innocence, come to the silence she is writing against:

> The silence is death.
> It comes each day with its shock
> to sit on my shoulder, a white bird,
> and peck at the black eyes
> and the vibrating muscle
> of my mouth.
>   **("The Silence")**

The *Book of Folly's* remembrance of things past is likewise more direct when it turns to her family. "Anna Who Was Mad"—Anna, the anagram for the Nana whose namesake Sexton is—alternates interrogative and imperative lines to force the guilt of cause and effect: "Am I some sort of infection? / Did I make you go insane?" This paralyzing guilt, itself a form of self-hatred, is "all a matter of history" in **"The Nana-Hex,"** a poem which links her relationship with this same great-aunt to that with The Other: "Every time I get happy / the Nana-hex comes through." This strong poem on how "The dead take aim" to leave her "still the criminal" is an angry pacing off of the past's cage. (pp. 279-82)

But this is a prelude to the book's centering six-poem sequence, **"The Death of the Fathers"**—surely one of Sexton's triumphs, daring in its explorations and revelations, its verse superbly controlled as the voice of each poem is modulated to its experience, now shifting to the declaratives of a child, now heightening to involved regrets and prayers. While watching Sexton trace memories of her father mixed with sexual fantasies, one must recall Freud's sense of the origin of childhood memories:

> Quite unlike conscious memories from the time of maturity, they are not fixed at the moment of being experienced and afterwards repeated, but are only elicited at a later age when childhood is already past; in the process they are altered and falsified, and are put into the service of later trends, so that generally speaking they cannot be sharply distinguished from phantasies [*The Standard Edition of the Complete Psychological Works of Sigmund Freud* (1953-)].

Similarly, since fantasies become memories, it becomes impossible and useless beyond a certain point to distinguish between "events" that happened and fears or desires imagined so strongly that they might as well have happened. And further, Freud writes that the "screen memories" made of childhood traumas "relate to impressions of a sexual and aggressive nature, and no doubt also to early injuries to the ego (narcissistic mortifications). In this connection it should be remarked that such young children make no sharp distinction between sexual and aggressive acts, as they do later."

Sexton's sequence divides naturally into two parts of three poems each, the first set in childhood to evoke her father, and the second set in the present to focus his double death and the "later trends" that have occasioned the fantasies in the first. The opening poem, **"Oysters,"** is her initiation, at once a fantasy of self-begetting and a memory of desire that, once conscious, defeats innocence. She is Daddy's Girl having lunch with her father at a restaurant, and fearfully eats her oysters—"this father-food," his semen: "It was a soft medicine / that came from the sea into my mouth, / moist and plump. / I swallowed." Then they laugh through this "death of childhood"—"the child was defeated. / The woman won." The second poem, **"How We Danced,"** continues the fantasy in an Oedipal round. . . . And the third poem, **"The Boat,"** though it reverts to an earlier time, is a kind of coital coda to her subconscious victory. This time Leda's swan is her godlike captain, out in the same sea from which the oysters came, "out past Cuckold's Light," where "the three of us" ride through a storm that her father masters, but at its height there is the moment which both resolves her fantasies and

predicts their destruction, in a memory of violence both sexual and aggressive:

> Now the waves are higher;
> they are round buildings.
> We start to go through them
> and the boat shudders.
> Father is going faster.
> I am wet.
> I am tumbling on my seat
> like a loose kumquat.
> Suddenly
> a wave that we go under.
> Under. Under. Under.
> We are daring the sea.
> We have parted it.
> We are scissors.
> Here in the green room
> the dead are very close.

The second part narrates the death of the fathers. In **"Santa,"** the child's mythic sense of her father is killed: "Father, / the Santa Claus suit / you bought from Wolff Fording Theatrical Supplies, / back before I was born, / is dead." After describing how her father dressed up her childhood—when "Mother would kiss you / for she was that tall"—she comes to liquor's reality principle: "The year I ceased to believe in you / is the year you were drunk." And by the time her father, in turn, dressed up for her own children, the emptiness of having replaced her mother is apparent: "We were conspirators, / secret actors, / and I kissed you / because I was tall enough. / But that is over." **"Friends"** details another death, as her father is distanced by doubt. The Stranger in her childhood could have been any of the men who would come to steal her from her father, but this family friend is more ominous:

> He was bald as a hump.
> His ears stuck out like teacups
> and his tongue, my God, his tongue,
> like a red worm and when he kissed
> it crawled right in.
>
> Oh Father, Father,
> who was that stranger
> who knew Mother too well?

The question this poem ends on—"Oh God, / he was a stranger, / was he not?"—is answered brutally in the last poem, **"Begat,"** a kind of family romance in reverse:

> Today someone else lurks in the wings
> with your dear lines in his mouth
> and your crown on his head.
> Oh Father, Father-sorrow,
> where has time brought us?
>
> Today someone called.
> "Merry Christmas," said the stranger.
> "I am your real father."
> That was a knife.
> That was a grave.

The father she had called hers dies again—the stranger takes "the *you* out of the *me*"—and the poems end with a pathetic elegy on the distance she has come since childhood and the first poem of this sequence, since the understood desire. The end rises to a last regret with the simple details of intimacy's allowances and sadnesses, and the memory of her father dressed as Santa turns as raw as the blood they no longer share, the "two lonely swans" who danced in fantasy are now fired by betrayal and loss. . . . (pp. 282-85)

The blend of memory and fantasy in **"The Death of the Fathers,"** each sharpening and supporting the effect of the other, is the culmination of Sexton's confessional style. Her next book, *The Death Notebooks* (1974), develops this technique still further, but without any consistency. The reason for this is that the book collects poems she had written over many years without intending to publish them, and as meditations on her own death they tend to fantasize forward rather than remember back. But with their frequent sense of having been written from beyond death, there is a retrospective character to them that continually catches up long memories and fragments of experience. And the exercise itself—especially its eventual publication, which seems reluctant but inevitable, even in its duplication of the smaller deaths she had detailed before—adds a note of shabby self-consciousness to "this last peep show" (**"Making a Living," "For Mr. Death Who Stands with His Door Open," "Faustus and I," "Clothes"**). But the book's powerful confrontation with death—and even its cover schemes in black-and-blue—tries to work its way toward the accommodations of understanding: "For death comes to friends, to parents, to sisters. Death comes with its bagful of pain yet they do not curse the key they were given to hold" (**"Ninth Psalm"**). So Sexton sees herself "knitting her own hair into a baby shawl" because "There is a death baby / for each of us. / We own him" (**"Baby"**), carried for a lifetime, delivered slowly and rocked into darkness. And as she sits "in that dark room putting bones into place" (**"Seventh Psalm"**), she edges "the abyss, / the God spot" (**"The Fury of Sundays"**)—a dilemma first raised in **"The Division of Parts"** back in *To Bedlam and Part Way Back* and left as ambiguous here in several religious poems. That personal paradox reflects the difficulty with the book itself, whose "summing-up" remains too immediate and unresolved.

The title of the book implies excerpts of unfinished spontaneity, and there are two long experiments which, by their very nature, could have been continued or concluded at the poet's will. **"The Furies"** was written while the poet was recuperating in bed from an illness and began associating at the typewriter on suggestive topics. Their antecedent is **"Angels of the Love Affair"** (or even the variations-form in the uneven sequence titled **"Bestiary U. S. A.,"** later included in *45 Mercy Street*), and their energy is their own rather than the poet's. And a sequence of nine psalms called **"O Ye Tongues"** attempts to adapt the patterns of Smart's *Jubilato Agno* and to identify Smart with both herself and The Other, combined into "the mad poet":

> For I am an orphan with two death masks on the
>   mantel
>   and came from the grave of my mama's belly
>   into the
>   commerce of Boston.

> For there were only two windows on the city and
>   the
>   buildings ate me.

> For I was swaddled in grease wool from my fa-
>   ther's
>   company and could not move or ask the time.

> For Anne and Christopher were born in my
>   head as I
>   howled at the grave of the roses, the ninety-
>   four rose
>   crèches of my bedroom.
>   (**"Third Psalm"**)

Her success is variable, but when the excess is simplified the result is the genuine pathos of Smart's own verse: "For in my nature I quested for beauty, but God, God, hath sent me to sea for pearls."

But clearly the most significant and successful poem in *The Death Notebooks* is **"Hurry Up Please It's Time,"** a sort of long, hallucinatory diary-entry: "Today is November 14th, 1972. / I live in Weston, Mass., Middlesex County, / U.S.A., and it rains steadily / in the pond like white puppy eyes." The style is pure pastiche, mixing dialect and dialogue, nursery rhymes and New Testament, references ranging from Goethe to Thurber, attitudes veering between arrogance and abasement. At times she is "Anne," at times "Ms. Dog"—becoming her own mock-God. She can sneer at herself ("Middle-class lady, / you make me smile"), or shiver at what "my heart, that witness" remembers. The recaptured spots of time—say, a quiet summer interlude with her husband and friends—are run into projected blotches spread toward the death to come. And though its expansive free form dilutes all but its cumulative force, the poem is an advance on the way **"The Death of the Fathers"** had whispered its confessions.

Sexton's two posthumously published collections—*The Awful Rowing Toward God* (1975) and *45 Mercy Street* (1976)—are largely disappointing and anticlimactic, except when isolated poems in either book echo earlier successes. The last volume is particularly flat—because, one presumes, the poet did not revise the poems or arrange the selection. Its dominating section is a painful sequence called **"The Divorce Papers,"** an entirely unresolved series of reactions to "the dead city of my marriage" and to the ways in which divorce exhumes it. The ambivalence that informs these seventeen poems—alternating relief and regret, guilt, despair, and exhilaration—is less enriching than enervating. One reason for that is the very immediacy of the work, which is not grounded in an adequate perspective on the history of her marriage, the evolution of her feelings, or the complication of two lives lived together. It is as if the poet—and her poetry—simply resigned themselves to necessary conditions. And that aspect of autopsy is also apparent elsewhere in *45 Mercy Street,* for instance in the title poem, the book's best. Here we are given glimpses of a dream-vision whose burden is the inability to recover what has been lost in and to the past, whose own character shifts from history to hallucination. This can result in bursts of self-disgust or helpless bewilderment, which are combined in the poem's final lines and testify to the blind end these last poems embody:

Next I pull the dream off
and slam into the cement wall
of the clumsy calendar
I live in,
my life,
and its hauled up
notebooks.

The stronger and more fluent book is *The Awful Rowing Toward God,* which consolidates her experiments in *The Book of Folly* and *The Death Notebooks.* Like the latter, it is thematically organized into a series of variations on a religious doubt that swerves between exorcism and exultation. What she calls "my ignorance of God" is figured as a cancerous crab "clutching fast to my heart" (**"The Poet of Ignorance"**), while on the other hand there is an ecstatic, almost murderous release of desire:

I am on the amphetamine of the soul.
I am, each day,
typing out the God
my typewriter believes in.
Very quick. Very intense,
like a wolf at a live heart.
                    (**"Frenzy"**)

Within such a dialectic, "You have a thousand prayers / but God has one," and she repeats her poems as if hoping they accumulate into *His* prayer. But though this may be a God a typewriter can believe in, it seems questionable that Sexton does. At the very least, He is an abstracted presence—perhaps merely an obvious displacement of the father with whom she is attempting to effect a reconciliation. This may be one reason why the religious experience she records in this book is transposed into an almost mythic mode—one which, for instance, projects a version of her asylum life into a vision of an afterlife. As if to underscore this mode, both her voice and her line have the poise and concision of proverbs. There is little interest in elaborate exposition or explanation; instead there is a dialogue with herself, private and associative. The surrealistic and domestic imagery employed have considerable authority, and the book's long—and usually successful—poem **"Is It True?"** is a continuation of the diaristic **"Hurry Up Please It's Time,"** though the later poem has a quiet control that strengthens the free form's urgent sprawl. Though still intensely personal, the book's privatism is of the peculiar variety that renders it accessible, undoubtedly because its subject is one in which the individual personality is less prominent than the character of the quest itself. At its best moments, Sexton's voice swells to assume that character, her rhetoric purified to austere grandeur. The conclusion of **"The Big Heart,"** a poem addressed to her intimate companions, is one such moment:

They hear how
the artery of my soul has been severed
and soul is spurting out upon them,
bleeding on them,
messing up their clothes,
dirtying their shoes.
And God is filling me,
though there are times of doubt
as hollow as the Grand Canyon,
He is giving me the thoughts of dogs,
the spider in its intricate web,

the sun
in all its amazement,
and a slain ram
that is the glory,
the mystery of great cost,
and my heart,
which is very big,
I promise it is very large,
a monster of sorts,
takes it all in—
all in comes the fury of love.

That very fury of love, occasionally so moving in the posthumous books, does tend to distort or diffuse their force. Still, they remain as flawed evidence of Sexton's steady boldness, her readiness to risk new experiments in verse to record renewed perceptions of her experience in life, in the manner Emerson claimed that art is the effort to indemnify ourselves for the wrongs of our condition. There is, as one critic has said of her, "something awesome, even sublime in a woman who is not afraid to sound crude or shrill so long as she is honest, who in her best work sounds neither shrill nor crude precisely because she is honest" [Robert Boyers]. Her courage in coming true not only made Sexton one of the most distinctive voices in this generation's literature, and a figure of permanent importance to the development of American poetry, but has revealed in its art and its honesty a life in which we can discover our own. (pp. 285-90)

ANNE SEXTON, IN A LETTER TO KURT VONNEGUT, JR.

The enclosed manuscript is of my new book of poems. I've taken Grimms' Fairy Tales and "Transformed" them into something all of my own. The better books of fairy tales have introductions telling the value of these old fables. I feel my *Transformations* needs an introduction telling of the value of my (one could say) rape of them. Maybe that's an incorrect phrase. I do something very modern to them (have you ever tried to describe your own work? I find I am tongue-tied). They are small, funny and horrifying. Without quite meaning to I have joined the black humorists. I don't know if you know my other work, but humor was never a very prominent feature . . . terror, deformity, madness and torture were my bag. But this little universe of Grimm is not that far away. I think they end up being as wholly personal as my most intimate poems, in a different language, a different rhythm, but coming strangely, for all their story sound, from as deep a place. To get to the point. I am submitting the book to my publishers this week. I have already discussed with them that I would like an introduction. Is there any chance you would be willing to write it?

The first poem is an introductory one and doesn't give the flavor or have the zest of the others, so I'd skip it to begin with. Perhaps **"Snow White," "The Little Peasant," "Iron Hans," "Rapunzel," "Hansel and Gretel," "Briar Rose"** could give you a feeling of the project. **"Cinderella,"** unfortunately, is not very good despite the aura of your graph. Sending you this seems like a rather forward move on my part, but I thought I'd give it a try. . . . Many thanks.

(letter date 1970)

J. D. McClatchy, "Anne Sexton: Somehow To Endure," in Anne Sexton: The Artist and Her Critics, *edited by J. D. McClatchy, Indiana University Press, 1978, pp. 244-90.*

Lynette McGrath   (essay date 1988)

[*McGrath is a professor of English and Women's Studies at West Chester University. In the following excerpt from* Original Essays on the Poetry of Anne Sexton, *she refutes the common contention that Sexton's poetic abilities declined toward the end of her life, and asserts that her verse grew "away from feelings of confinement and infantilism toward a sense of openness, power, and freedom."*]

In the work of any poet, adjustments in theme and form inevitably occur, sometimes signaling increased control of the poetic craft, sometimes a gradual decline of poetic power. The majority of Anne Sexton's readers, feminist and nonfeminist alike, seem agreed that the changes in her poetic practice are signs of progressive decline rather than increased poetic power. In addition, the sensational details of her life and death have fed the accepted judgment that, because she was losing control of herself, at the end of her career Sexton abandoned the formally controlled style of her early work and took to writing loose, episodic poetry concentrated on themes of death and suicide. This view implies that Sexton's death brought to a tidy close the collapse into madness and despair already evident in her poetry. Alicia Ostriker . . . further suggests that Sexton's failure to edge out of a relationship with an incorrigibly patriarchal God in some sense led to what Ostriker still sees as Sexton's ultimate selfdefeat [*Stealing the Language* (1986)].

All of these critical responses, however, are colored by their partisans' insufficient analysis of two cultural problems affecting women's poetry. In the first place, biographical material is, for a woman writer, especially susceptible to a type of unsympathetic or hasty interpretation which, in Sexton's case, encourages a reading of her life as a psychological failure. Second, such biographical references often determine value judgments about women writers' style and form. The readings of Sexton's life as a personal failure have thus promoted the view that her poetry also was doomed to fail, breaking down into necessarily confused and indeterminate forms of expression. I think that these readings, all emphasizing psychological and poetic failure and conditioned by culturally condoned notions of what a woman might or might not be expected to achieve, need an immediate adjustment. Dominant cultural attitudes toward women and suicide make an understanding of Sexton's biography and especially her view of death very difficult. A patriarchal view that expects in women weakness and loss of control will tend to interpret a woman's suicide not as a heroic act but as a sign of failure, seeing it as "hysterically" interruptive of her more appropriate biological and nurturing functions. On the other hand, even a sympathetically feminist view like Ostriker's may see a suicidal woman like Sexton as victimized by patriarchal pressures and betrayed by a "sex-rejecting mi-

sogynist zealot" hiding behind the image of a "gentle Jesus." . . . [I would] like, insofar as is possible, to move away from a reading context that assumes that a woman's life and work must be interpreted only in terms of a dominant male hegemony and attempt a more independently feminist assessment of the successes Sexton achieved and the freedoms she grasped, however painfully, within her own self-defined contexts.

This admittedly tricky endeavor is further complicated by the commonly adopted critical point of view that considers poetry wholly successful only when it is organically structured, autonomous, whole, and achieving closure through metaphoric and thematic coherence, for these are not conventions that encourage sufficient appreciation of Sexton's unique poetic accomplishments. To understand Sexton's poetic performance, we need to allow for the deconstruction of those principles that insist on poetic authority and packed-up "works of art." A critical approach that does not demand thematic and structural closure may better reveal how Sexton's later poetry, especially, functions.

I intend to develop an argument, just as feminist in sympathy as Ostriker's, to celebrate the remarkable degree to which, against all cultural odds, Sexton challenged the contexts that at first conditioned her writing. Negotiating these contextual circumstances required an ongoing and devastatingly honest self-examination, shifts in theme, an adjustment of the image of her Muse as an inspirational divinity whom Sexton struggled to release from the oppressive role of the traditional patriarchal God, and finally the structural experimentation made possible by these other risky and courageous explorations.

In particular, my argument annotates thematic changes in Sexton's poetry that are significant, not casual, and that indicate a growth away from feelings of confinement and infantilism toward a sense of openness, power, and freedom. These thematic changes are accompanied by a changing poetic style which produces a poem that opens itself to include the reader instead of closing itself around the poet. The shift away from metrically, stanzaically, and syntactically ordered pieces to loose, open-ended forms does not, in my view, represent poetic failure but a brave

Sexton outdoors, Winter 1962. An avid sun bather, she often sat in the sun atop the snowbanks in her backyard, wrapped in the mink coat bequeathed to her by her mother.

choice to involve the reader with the poem and with the poet's experience.

Reading through the codes of Sexton's poetic and personal context, we find that these thematic and structural changes reflect the increased confidence she achieved in mid-life and mid-career. This confidence she based in a Muse-like divinity whose nature she adjusted to fit her poetic and female experience. Under the aegis of this inspiriting image, the once tight, closed statement, centered on self-disclosure, expands toward liberation and draws the reader into the experience the poem describes. As the audience is urged more insistently into the poetic experience, formal polish and subtlety diminish, and the whole poem shifts into a relaxed form, structurally open and latent rather than closed and already realized.

Such a reading of Sexton's work (in the nature of an *apologia*), documents poetic growth instead of failure and perplexity. It implies also a connection between her suicide and the epigraph to the last book of poetry published under her supervision before her death: "There are two ways to victory—to strive bravely, or to yield. How much pain the last will save we have not yet learned." Sexton's last poetry and her death may well represent her brave yielding to a psychological possibility which she had already actualized in overt poetic configuration.

In any case, Sexton wanted, I believe, to develop a poetry based on an interaction among what she called a "storytelling" poet, an open text, and a responsive reader. The success of this interaction depended heavily on Sexton's decision to take conscious risks with the form of her poems—risks that have led to some critical misjudgments, but which, in the long run, will be acknowledged as having successfully extended her poetic range rather than reducing it.

Although major thematic and metaphoric constructs remain constant throughout Sexton's poetry, their range of reference and significance changes. Fundamental in Sexton's poetry is the project of self-exploration. She engages in a prolonged and valiant effort to know herself, while realizing that this kind of self-analytic writing might require of both poet and reader violent and even potentially self-mutilating means: "a book should serve as the ax for the frozen sea within us" (epigraph to *All My Pretty Ones*). Initially, Sexton's poetry sought a means to break up the frozen sea within herself; the later poetry expands its therapeutic goals by attempting to release the reader from the frozen role of passive observer. With regard to the early poetry, there may be some truth in Joyce Carol Oates's observation that "Sexton emphasizes her private sorrows to the exclusion of the rest of the world." . . . (pp. 138-42)

Although Sexton's honest self-confrontations may strike a sympathetic response from the reader, the early poems are not really designed to produce this result. There are no invitations to shared experience, only fortuitous connections between Sexton's perceptions and the reader's. To begin with, Sexton seems to have used the self-revealing poem as a medium of self-discovery. For example, in **"To a Friend Whose Work Has Come To Triumph,"** or **"With Mercy for the Greedy,"** Sexton addresses her early poems outward to a particular person rather than to a general audience. The widely communicating, reaching poems, characteristic in the last books, are exceptional in these early works. In typical early poems, Sexton records her confinement within the "widely" domestic role bounded by the house or kitchen—"Some women marry houses. / It's another kind of skin" (**"Housewife"**)—and within the "womanly" sexual role invaded and possessed by the male body. . . . (pp. 142-43)

Seeking to dramatize her sense of restriction and alienation, Sexton frequently writes of herself as a child, speaking in a child-like voice, confined and dominated by the adult world. The plight of the child parallels the woman's. Neither is free or articulate; both remember—and are directed by—"the song my mother / used to sing" (**"The Fish That Walked"**). This late poem implies that, through poetry, the child grown to womanhood will eventually become freely eloquent, but Sexton does not explicitly draw connections with poetry as a means to freedom until her last work. More typically, in the early poetry, as in **"Those Times,"** Sexton associates her present woman's frustrations with those of her childhood. The voice of a rejected and confined child is heard in the rhythms and language of much of the poetry, although the alienated, unripe personality does occasionally deride itself. This level of ironic self-appraisal, when it occurs, betokens a degree of mature self-understanding that in the later poetry becomes most vivid and emphatic and begins there to include the reader in the ironic transaction.

"Baby Picture" is exemplary of this later style of self-analysis. As the poet gazes at an old, peeling picture of her seven-year-old self, she sees, without nostalgia or self-pity, what she then was and now is. The view of herself as she is now is telescoped into what she was as a child, and the juxtaposed images are appraised with ironic detachment. By the time of *The Death Notebooks,* in which this poem appears, Sexton has substituted self-appraisal for self-pity. She casts herself now in the saving role she has sought all along: she needs to write "real," as she puts it, "because that is the one thing that will save (and I do mean save) other people" [*Anne Sexton: A Self-Portrait in Letters* (1977)]. In her last two books, Sexton emphatically insists on connections between herself and her audience and God. These connections facilitated the self-discovery through affiliation—which feminist theorists now understand to be characteristic of women's experience—more effectively than did her initial attempts to achieve a detached, solipsistic sense of the self. The unexpected "wild card" for Sexton in this eventual arrival at self-recognition is the assisting factor of death.

As Sexton's early poems develop the theme of confinement in its varying aspects, the imagery of death as enclosure also insistently recurs. Death is the extinction of love: "The end of the affair is always death" (**"The Ballad of the Lonely Masturbator"**). One enters into death as into an enclosed space: "Thief!— / how did you crawl into, / crawl down alone / into the death I wanted so badly and for so long" (**"Sylvia's Death"**). . . . (pp. 143-45)

Yet the symbolic weight of death is much more complicated than this for Sexton. Even attached as it is in the early poetry to a sense of restriction, death is still yearned after as a cessation from pain. . . . [Her] early taste for death establishes a foundation for a later treatment of death as the means of freedom instead of the way to confinement.

As with the themes of self-exploration and childhood, the early treatment of death contains an undercurrent of feeling which foreshadows a subsequent change of attitude. The central lines of **"The Starry Night,"**—a crucial poem in Sexton's development—read: "This is how / I want to die: / into that rushing beast of the night, / sucked up by that great dragon, to split / from my life with no flag, / no belly, / no cry." The longing for death is at the same time a longing for release and freedom: "Sexton's death wish is envisioned as a slow diffusion of the self into air, elements, separation. . . . There is the suggestion not of diminishment so much as assimilation into a larger whole" [Mizejewski, *College English* 35 (1973)]. The representation of death as both engulfing and releasing is not usual in the early poetry, but by the time of *The Death Notebooks,* with its ambiguous epigraph—"Look, you con man, make a living out of your death"—death has become a means to life. The last poems see the self as passing through death, whether symbolic or literal, into a more spacious, freer mode of existence within which the personal and poetic self can be defined and affirmed through connections, made at one end of the poetic process with a divine Muse, and at the other with the reader.

The Death Notebooks and *The Awful Rowing Toward God* present this wider, freer prospect in the context of a poetic and personal alliance with God, but revise the traditional aspect of a restrictive and disciplinary patriarchal divinity. What amounts to a redefinition begins most clearly in **"Somewhere in Africa"**:

> Let God be some tribal female who is known but
>   forbidden.
> Let there be this God who is a woman who will
>   place you
> upon her shallow boat, who is a woman naked
>   to the waist,
> moist with palm oil and sweat, a woman of some
>   virtue
> and wild breasts, her limbs excellent, unbruised
>   and chaste.

In **"For Eleanor Boylan Talking With God,"** "God has a brown voice, as soft and full as beer"; "God is as close as the ceiling"; "Now he is large, covering up the sky / like a great resting jellyfish." In **"For God While Sleeping,"** the Christ figure is a "poor old convict"; the relationship between the poet and her God is familiar, equalized, reciprocally intimate. This kind of relationship, which allows for devotion but rejects a hierarchically-based reduction of the worshipping woman, is thoroughly typical in Sexton's late religious verse. God becomes all-inclusive, literally omni-present, Protean, androgynous, non-authoritarian. Sexton discovers that the divine is utterly pervasive and sanctifying, even to the extent that "the gods of the world were shut in the lavatory." . . . And in **"The Rowing Endeth,"** a liberating union with God accompanies the experience of death, which is a crucial component in a unified and equalized creation. The project to eliminate God's oppressive and judgmental aspects enables

Sexton to make spiritual peace with a more expansive divinity. In the context of this new relationship, Sexton thematically welds together her enhanced self knowledge, her willingness to engage with death, her sense of psychological freedom, and her text's connection with the now all-important reader. Unhappy self-absorption and a sense of restriction are replaced by a sense of self-acceptance and of freedom from the harrying demons that pervade the early poetry. Self-critical complaint changes into ironic and even affectionate self-appraisal. . . . Where Sexton now assumes the role of the child, it is to mock kindly and ironically what remains of the child in herself, and also to emphasize the child's need for the connection and support she now finds in divine love. She now sees the domestic role as salvaging and soothing instead of destructively restrictive. Accepted freely, the elements of domestic life may be small means to saving ends, especially to human connections. . . . The creative offices of God may bring to resolution even the contest for power between man and woman: the concluding injunction in **"Two Hands,"** to the two God-created hands, one "man," the other "woman," is: "Unwind hands, / you angel webs, / unwind like the coil of a jumping jack, / cup together and let yourselves fill up with the sun / and applaud, world, applaud." Sex, once seen as invasive, now becomes a divinely blessed connection: "All the cocks of the world are God, blooming, blooming, blooming / into the sweet blood of woman" **("The Fury of Cocks")**.

An analysis that styles itself feminist can hardly pass over in silence this kind of association of masculine sexual virility and divine power, especially in light of Alicia Ostriker's claim that Sexton was engaged in a "grotesque attempt to placate and conciliate a God of our Fathers who is being experienced as atrocious, brutal, a betrayer" [*Writing Like a Woman* (1983)]—a reading which I think should be contextualized differently. Ostriker's "Freudianized" reading of Sexton as caught in the rapacious grasp of a Father-God leads her to clump Sexton with Atwood and Wakoski, none of whom, she says, was able to "synthesize opposites or imagine contexts larger than the ancient text of dualism" [*Stealing the Language* (1986)]. In Sexton's case at least, as I shall show below, I think this conclusion is really not justifiable.

That Sexton did not, and probably could not, dispense with images of masculine sexual influence in her metaphoric store is indisputable. . . . This does not mean, however, that her project to revise the image of a patriarchal God failed. While still incorporating some of the culturally pandemic qualities of masculine power in her image of the divine, Sexton made a serious effort to represent the divine figure as non-dominant, to cut back its aggressive power, to imbue it with the nurturing and sexual qualities of female power, and to weigh her own woman's poetic power in a more equalized relationship with it. In fact, it is not the inevitable imbalance of power that prescribes an antagonistic relation between the divine and the human. On the contrary, the question is whether Sexton is submissive to, and oppressed by, that power, and she is not. She is, rather, assertive and, as Diane Middlebrook says, "impudent."

As enlightened as feminists may have been by all of the theory that has been worked out since Sexton's time, we still struggle to free ourselves from the orbit of male power. To deny Sexton the successes she undoubtedly achieved in beginning to deconstruct the closed poem and the patriarchal God, because she did not also complete a deconstruction of sexual identity, is to layer our own contexts onto Sexton's and to accede to the interminable power of the patriarchal. I prefer to celebrate the movement along the stages of the journey Sexton began to make toward the remolding of the divine as universal and polymorphous. Her poems in quest of this image are more than simply that. They are also communications in which a relationship with the reader is established by analogy with the poet's relationship with God. In other words, even what we may now view as Sexton's limited renegotiation of the nature of her God nevertheless made it possible for her to embark on a major new poetic venture. As a consequence of this newly defined relationship with a revised God, Sexton now found ways to link what she once saw as opposing and dualistic activities: **"Words"** represents the creation of poetry and the creation of an omelet as two aspects of the same large process. Earlier thematic oppositions can also be resolved. Processes, connections, and sequences now define the ultimate nature of human experience. Good and evil are essentially interdependent; in order to pursue good, Sexton now suggests that we must recognize and accept evil as an inevitable part of our lives. . . . In God, the body-soul dichotomy itself can reach a baptismal resolution: "He is all soul / but He would like to house it in a body / and come down / and give it a bath / now and then" (**"The Earth"**). And death follows in natural order as part of the process of life. (pp. 145-50)

Sexton's later poems present death as the savored beginning of a connection, both comically macabre and sexual, for which one prepares as for a wedding; it is no longer a narrow end that opposes and destroys life: "But when it comes to my death / let it be slow, / let it be pantomime, this last peep show, / So that I may squat at the edge trying on / my black necessary trousseau" (**"For Mr. Death Who Stands With His Door Open"**). In *The Death Notebooks,* death becomes a freeing experience, a release into spiritual freedom. "The approaches to death are by illumination," said Christopher Smart, and in the psalms modeled on Smart's *Jubilate Agno,* Sexton concludes: "God was as large as a sunlamp and laughed his heat at us and therefore we did not cringe at the death hole" (**"O Ye Tongues, Tenth Psalm"**). Death is a release of the self into the divine, a speeding up of the rowing toward God, a union which triumphs over life's confining power. In her last books of poetry, Sexton's connection with a Muse-like, inspirational God promotes the changes in theme, tone, and attitude that I have traced above. Most striking, though, is a change of mind that drew Sexton out of the ranks of poets who use the poem as a communication with the self about the self in order to join those who see the poem as potentially enlightening for others. The audience presupposed by her poetry is larger and more eclectic now than before, and the poetic consequences are apparent in the poet's increased awareness of her readers and in her increased sophistication about both overt and covert ways of communication. Overtly, through image, metaphor, and theme, Sexton's poems insistently encourage the reader to participate in or learn from the poet's own experience. The later poems are filled with an assured sense that what has helped the poet reach self-definition and self-affirmation will also help the reader. The poems in *The Awful Rowing Toward God* are neither cries for help nor suicide notes. They are poems of freedom and power that confidently propose an alternative to life and its suffering in the embrace of death and God. These poems teach by example and sometimes by direct insistence on the need for connection: "take off your flesh, unpick the lock of your bones. / In other words / take off the wall / that separates you from God." . . . The idea inspiring this poetry is expressed at the end of **"Welcome Morning"**: "The Joy that isn't shared, I've heard, / dies young." Another version of the same idea concludes **"What The Bird With The Human Head Knew"**: "Abundance is scooped from abundance, / yet abundance remains." And this abundance is shared by Sexton with the readers of her poetry. Reclaimed from a state of despair herself, she passes on a talismanic flower, given her by a friend, to another in need: "My kindred, my brother, I said / and gave the yellow daisy / to the crazy woman in the next bed" (**"The Sickness Unto Death"**).

By covert means, in the structuring of her last poems, Sexton sought to open lines of communication between herself and her audience. Anne Sexton began as a poet of polished, formalist structures like the variable refrain in **"The Starry Night"** or the tight narrative in **"The Double Image."** Her early poems are carefully made and finished: "And we both wrote poems we couldn't write / and cried together the whole long night / and fell in love with a delicate breath / on the eve that great men call for death" (**"December 4th"**). Rhythm and line length in the early poems integrate with and affirm the statement: "avenues of fish that never got back, / all their proud spots and solitudes / sucked out of them" (**"The Sun"**). And, characteristically, these poems conclude tersely: "As for me, I am a watercolor. / I wash off" (**"For My Lover Returning to His Wife."** . . . (pp. 151-53)

In the earlier poems, then, the structure is coherent, and the patterns of rhyme, stanza, and syntax are clear and tight. The poem as a finished object expresses a finished experience; in a sense, Sexton's solipsistically closed view of experience predicts a closed, structured control. The already realized statement discourages any possible response. Here, as elsewhere, a strong connection exists between presentations of the self and evidences of the text; as Sexton's point of view altered, so too did the formal nature of her poetry. Together with the thematic and metaphoric invitations of the text, structural clues begin to entice the reader's participation in the experience revealed in the poem. Adrienne Rich has described the movement that occurred in her own poetry as she grew dissatisfied with traditional poetic structures as ways to promote a sense of process and dialogue; this shift from structured form to a sense of process also occurred with Sexton.

As Sexton's poems become less structurally controlled, they begin to incorporate the loose syntax of conversation. . . . The cataloguing and listing of ideas and images in no ordered, sequential pattern characterizes **"Gods," "The Fury of Sundays," "Faustus and I,"** the psalms of **"O Ye Tongues,"** and **"The Death Baby"** while the structural elements within these poems also fall into relaxed, episodic relationships. Sexton abandons formal control almost entirely in her later poetry, presumably because such restrictions mirror the life-boundaries she wants to overcome. The adoption of looser forms asserts her sense of personal freedom and encourages the reader to an engagement with the text. As Louise Rosenblatt points out, "When we turn from the broader environment of the reading act to the text itself, we need to recognize that a very important aspect of the text is the clues it provides as to what stance the reader adopts." These casually worded poems with their looser structures retain their power even beyond their conclusions. Sexton achieves this movement of the poem beyond itself into the reader's life by employing open-ended forms. The ways in which the poems in the last volumes conclude are highly significant, with questions asked, potentialities left open, and conditional structures remaining incomplete. Covert tactics of communication, established through the poetic structures, invite the reader to participate in the experience of the poem. . . . (pp. 153-54)

More subtly, poems like **"Praying on a 707," "Rowing," "Jesus Walking," "The Witch's Life,"** and **"Riding the Elevator Into the Sky,"** although their syntactic patterns are complete, evoke experiences the reader is urged to emulate. Especially in *The Awful Rowing Toward God,* Sexton typically chooses not to tie off the ends of her poems, insisting instead on opening options for the reader. At the time when this shifting emphasis was occurring in her poetry, Sexton applauded the kind of poem that could induce its readers to an adequate, active response. (p. 155)

[Her] sense of the reader as a creative respondent reduced Sexton's need to control her poetic statements in an ordered form. She gave up using the formal effects which she dismissed as "tricks," rejecting the "kind of short lyric that remains coin of the realm in American poetry" [Middlebrook, *Parnassus* 12-13 (1985)]. The reader was now regularly expected to complete the poem; Sexton absolved herself of the responsibility to do so. . . . Because it accommodates her need to invite the reader to participate in a spiritually illuminating experience like her own, an open-ended form is especially appropriate in Sexton's more emphatically religious verse. Sexton's last poems extend their scope indefinitely into their readers' lives by implying the need to continue beyond the poem's graphemic termination. Finally, her later poems link together the role poetry plays in the writer's life, the consequent forms and functions of the poem, and the role it may play for the reader.

Sexton always acknowledged the difficult and ambiguous relationship of the poet with her art, a relationship specifically complicated when the poet is a woman:

> A woman who writes feels too much,
> Those transports and portents!
> As if cycles and children and islands
> weren't enough; as if mourners and gossips

> and vegetables were never enough.
> She thinks she can warn the stars
> A writer is essentially a spy.
>
> **("The Black Art")**

Such a poem reveals Sexton's awareness that she is trespassing in alien territory both because of the intrinsically uncooperative nature of language, and because of the limited precedence established by other women poets for a "lady of evil luck" who longs to be what she can only visit **("The Fish That Walked").** Even though, at their best, the words of poetry are benignant miracles—"doves falling out of the ceiling" **("Words")**—as it is coming into being, the poem shifts and slips elusively in the poet's grasp: "However, nothing is just what it seems to be. / My objects dream and wear new costumes, / compelled to, it seems, by all the words in my hands" **("The Room of My Life").** **"Words"** deals extensively with the fugitive nature of the poem: Words "can be both daisies and bruises," and "often they fail"; "I have so much I want to say, / so many stories, images, proverbs, etc. / But the words aren't good enough / the wrong ones kiss me." (pp. 156-57)

Sexton sees herself as both "saved and lost," and thus connected with the fallen angels who "come on to my clean / sheet of paper and leave a Rorschach blot," "a sign which they shove . . . around till something comes" **("The Fallen Angels,").** Writing poetry for Sexton is not a neat experience of direct inspiration breathed into the worthy, receptive, and authoritative poet by the gods; it is a messy, human, even gendered process, attractively and acknowledgedly flawed, affirming connections among female poet, open poem, reconstructed God, and participating reader. It is clear that the poetic text was not, for Sexton, an autonomous, organic, unified object—any more than she was herself. Sexton finally does not claim authority over her poem, but passes on to the reader the responsibility of "owning" the text. "Look to your heart," she tells her reader, "that flutters in and out like a moth. / God is not indifferent to your need. / You have a thousand prayers / but God has one" **("Not So, Not So")** Here, if anywhere, we may relevantly link Sexton's life to her poetic practice. Even without benefit of Carol Gilligan, Nancy Chodorow, or Jean Baker Miller, Sexton was able to construct a sense of herself and her poetry as essentially affiliative and defined by connection rather than by autonomy. She seems to have rejected at the same time both the notion of an autonomous, successful self and the model of a unified, organic, closed text. Even without the later feminist and deconstructionist critiques of phallogocentric aesthetic by critics like Gayatri Spivak, Alice Jardine, and Peggy Kamuf, Sexton wrote poetry whose very form embodies a critique of what has, until recently, been accepted as the dominant Western aesthetic, but which we now recognize as only one among many potential cultural and aesthetic constructs. In addition, Sexton's later poetic style seems to affirm the view that "a poem cannot be understood apart from its results. Its 'effects,' psychological or otherwise, are essential to any accurate description of its meaning, since the meaning has no effective existence outside of its realization in the mind of a reader" [Tompkins, *Reader-Response Criticism* (1980)].

As I have been arguing, Sexton's sense of her own and her

poetry's potential came to depend on connections, not drawn in the usual way, detachedly and aesthetically, among elements internal to the poem, but established personally and experientially, among factors which, though external to the poem, nevertheless dictate its theme and form. First, a relationship is established between a polymorphous Muse-God, not detached from the woman poet by conventions of gender, position, or sanctimony, "who owns heaven / but . . . craves the earth, / . . . even its writers digging into their souls" (**"The Earth"**), and the writer, who addresses herself in priestly fashion to "the typewriter that is my church / with an altar of keys always waiting" (**"Is It True?"**). Ultimately, it seems that Sexton came to view death as a way to embrace this particular connection. Second, a relationship is confirmed between poet and reader, with the poem serving as its connective link. At the end of her career, the writing of poetry was for Sexton an activity akin to the holy, a means of earthly salvation for its creator and a means of communicating the possibility of salvation to the reader. As poet-priestess, Sexton was able to see that "Evil is maybe lying to God. / Or better, lying to love" (**"Is It True?"**) and that good is an authentic realization of the consecrating love that connects us all. An auspicious corroboration of my argument concerning Sexton's commitment to the value of connection is found in the poem Linda Gray Sexton chose to conclude **45 Mercy Street.** Appropriating the two roles most metaphorically exemplary of connection in our culture, Sexton presents herself as mother and priest—agents and beneficiaries of the rich and innumerable connections between divine and human, between individual and individual, between generation and generation, between life and death, between Muse and poet, between poet and reader. In **"The Consecrating Mother,"** Sexton dedicates herself to a womanly consecrating role: "I am that clumsy human / on the shore / loving you, coming, coming, / going, / and wish to put my thumb on you like the Song of Solomon." Such a commitment endorses an experience that seems compatible with many recent feminist formulations; it demands no closure, refuses authority, and exemplifies continuous human process. In a comment that syntactically reflects the opened access to herself and to her poetry, Sexton herself said "I have, you know, after all one does grow, change, evolve, and you know, it. . . ." (pp. 157-60)

> Lynette McGrath, *"Anne Sexton's Poetic Connections: Death, God, and Form,"* in Original Essays on the Poetry of Anne Sexton, *edited by Francis Bixler, University of Central Arkansas Press, 1988, pp. 138-63.*

FURTHER READING

Boyers, Robert. "*Live or Die:* The Achievement of Anne Sexton." *Salmangundi* 2, No. 1 (Spring 1967): pp. 61-71.
  Uses the poems of *Live or Die* to illustrate Sexton's strengths and weaknesses as a poet.

Cam, Heather. " 'Daddy': Sylvia Plath's Debt to Anne Sexton." *American Literature* 59, No. 3 (October 1987): 429-32.
  Contends that Plath's poem "Daddy" draws upon Sexton's earlier "My Friend, My Friend."

Fitz Gerald, Gregory. "The Choir from the Soul: A Conversation with Anne Sexton." *MR: The Massachusetts Review* XIX, No. 1 (Spring 1978): 69-88.
  Interview with Sexton that originally took place three months before her suicide.

George, Diana Hume. "Anne Sexton's Suicide Poems." *Journal of Popular Culture* 18, No. 2 (Fall 1984): 17-31.
  Discussion of contemporary attitudes toward suicide that revolves around Sexton's poems "Wanting to Die" and "Suicide Note."

——. *Oedipus Anne: The Poetry of Anne Sexton.* Urbana: University of Illinois Press, 1987, 210 p.
  Biographical and critical study.

——, ed. *Sexton: Selected Criticism.* Urbana: University of Illinois Press, 1988, 326 p.
  Contains previously published essays on Sexton by such critics as Diane Wood Middlebrook, J. D. McClatchy, and Estella Lauter.

Hankins, Liz Porter. "Summoning the Body: Anne Sexton's Body Poems." *The Midwest Quarterly* XXXVII, No. 4 (Summer 1987): 511-24.
  Argues that Sexton "transcends history, rationality, society, and assumes her own unique identity—she *becomes* through her body and its parts."

Howard, Richard. "Anne Sexton: 'Some Tribal Female Who Is Known But Forbidden'." In his *Alone With America: Essays on the Art of Poetry in the United States Since 1950,* pp. 442-50. New York: Atheneum, 1969.
  Evaluation of Sexton's poetry that focuses upon her ability to effectively convey personal and often taboo subjects.

Johnson, Rosemary. "The Woman of Private (But Published) Hungers." *Parnassus* 8, No. 1 (Fall-Winter 1979) 92-107.
  Disparaging evaluation of Sexton's confessionalism.

Juhasz, Suzanne. "Seeking the Exit or the Home: Poetry and Salvation in the Career of Anne Sexton." In *Shakespeare's Sisters,* edited by Sandra M. Gilbert and Susan Gubar, pp. 261-68. Bloomington: University of Indiana Press, 1979.
  Offers a feminist interpretation of Sexton's life and career.

Kumin, Maxine. Introduction to *The Complete Poems* by Anne Sexton, pp. xix-xxxiv. Boston: Houghton Mifflin Company, 1981.
  Personal evaluation of Sexton's work by the poet's close friend and collaborator.

Lauter, Estella. "Anne Sexton's Radical Discontent." In her *Women as Mythmakers: Poetry and Visual Art by Twentieth-Century Women,* pp. 23-46. Bloomington: University of Indiana Press, 1984.
  Examines the psychological significance of Sexton's religious poems.

Middlebrook, Diane. "Poet of Weird Abundance." *Parnassus* 12/13, Nos. 1/2 (Spring-Summer, Fall-Winter 1985): 293-315.

Extensive review of *Anne Sexton: The Complete Poems* that touches upon the major aspects of her verse.

Middlebrook, Diane Wood. " 'I Tapped My Own Head': The Apprenticeship of Anne Sexton." In *Coming to Light: American Women Poets in the Twentieth Century,* edited by Diane Wood Middlebrook and Marilyn Yalom, pp. 195-213. Ann Arbor: The University of Michigan Press, 1985.

Biographical account of Sexton's early career, focusing upon her ambivalent relationship with John Holmes.

Oates, Joyce Carol. "The Rise and Fall of a Poet." *The New York Times Book Review* (18 October 1981): 3, 37.

Review of *Anne Sexton: The Complete Poems,* charting what Oates perceives as Sexton's poetic decline in the late 1960s and early 1970s.

Ostriker, Alicia. "That Story: Anne Sexton and Her Trans-formations." *The American Poetry Review* 11, No. 4 (July-August 1982): 11-16.

Insightful review of *Transformations* that addresses the major elements of Sexton's poetry.

Rosenthal, M. L. "Other Confessional Poets." In his *The New Poets: American and British Poetry Since World War II,* pp. 130-38. New York: Oxford University Press, 1967.

Uses poems from *To Bedlam and Part Way Back* and *All My Pretty Ones* to examine Sexton's confessionalism.

Sharr, William H. "Anne Sexton's *Love Poems:* The Genre and the Differences." *Modern Poetry Studies* X, No. 1 (1980) 58-68.

Posits that Sexton's *Love Poems* "merges the possibilities of the ancient genre of erotic love poetry with the immediacy of modern experience."

Dylan Thomas

1914-1953

(Full name: Dylan Marlais Thomas) Welsh poet, short story writer, dramatist, critic, and novelist.

Thomas is as much remembered for his raucous lifestyle as he is for his complex poetry. Thomas enjoyed great popularity during his lifetime, particularly with the American public, and his rich, lyrical verse, steeped in the lore of his Welsh homeland, became even more celebrated after his premature death. Often focusing on such universal concerns as birth, death, love, and religion, Thomas's poetry remains distinctly personal through a blend of rich metaphorical language, sensuous imagery, and psychological detail. Although Thomas was influenced by the Bible and the writings of James Joyce and Sigmund Freud, the majority of critics do not consider him an intellectual poet; they regard him as a "primitivistic" writer who powerfully asserts ideas without scrutinizing them. While some critics faulted Thomas's works as ambiguous and immoral, most praised the insight and emotional impact of his verse. D. S. Savage commented: "Dylan Thomas is a primary agent in keeping poetry alive among us, and through poetry, a proper sense of life, of values. Whatever may be said of Thomas' limitations must rest upon recognition of his superb qualities—a powerful and compelling imaginative vision held in delicate equipoise, matched by a subtle intelligence, wit and verbal sensitiveness and informed by passionate feeling."

Thomas was born in Swansea, Wales, the second child and only son of a housewife and a grammar school English teacher. His father, a bitter, angry man who nevertheless doted on his son, failed to fulfill his lifelong dream of writing poetry, and many of Thomas's friends believe that it was out of deep love, fear, and respect for his father that Thomas realized his goal for him. Thomas was introduced to the Bible and the works of Shakespeare at a young age, and these literary classics would later inform much of his verse, as would the surrounding Welsh countryside and nearby sea. "Fern Hill," for example, a nostalgic reflection of childhood which many critics consider Thomas's finest poem, was inspired by his boyhood vacations to a farm his uncle owned near Llangain. Thomas's real education took place at home, in his father's vast library. There he read and absorbed such diverse authors as Edgar Allan Poe, the Brothers Grimm, Sir Thomas Browne, and Fyodor Dostoevsky, nurturing a talent for words and writing. An indolent student, his only genuine interest in school was editing the *Swansea Grammar School Magazine,* in which he published comic poems imitative of the era's popular works. Thomas's first serious poems were printed in small literary journals and, when he was nineteen, his first volume of poetry, *18 Poems,* was published.

The critical reception that greeted *18 Poems* was overwhelmingly positive; reviewers sensed in Thomas a highly unique yet traditional poetic voice. Much of the verse

draws upon his childhood and adolescent experiences, or speculates philosophically on the human condition. Often described as incantatory, *18 Poems* records Thomas's experimentations with vibrant imagery and with sound as "verbal music." Thomas's brilliant debut—and subsequent brief career and life—would later prompt comparisons to the short, dazzling, and ultimately tragic career of American poet Hart Crane, who drowned himself in 1932. After the success of *18 Poems,* Thomas moved to London and his already established reputation for outrageous behavior was intensified by ample money, rowdy company, and alcohol. The comical stories of his adventures that emerged during this period helped confirm Thomas as a consummate wit and conversationalist.

Thomas's second book of verse, *Twenty-Five Poems,* was published in 1936 and concerns many of the same themes as his first work. William York Tindall referred to Thomas's first two books as the poet's "womb-tomb" period because of his penchant to focus on the polarity of birth and death. In many of the poems, Thomas questions or comments upon religion, using images and terminology from Christian mythology, history, and doctrine. "And Death Shall Have No Dominion" was considered by many critics to be a breakthrough work in Thomas's career. In it, the poet addresses the Christian ideas of life and death, ultimately defying death and celebrating the possibility of eternal life. Another acclaimed poem, "Altarwise by Owllight," is a sequence of ten sonnets discussing the crucifixion of Christ. Both poignant and comic, the sequence is generally regarded as one of Thomas's best works and Thomas himself viewed it as the most mature verse of his first major period of creativity. It was during this triumphant time that he met his future wife, Caitlin Macnamara. Thomas fell in love at first sight, and they were married in 1937. Their tumultuous marriage, which lasted sixteen years, involved constant financial hardship and numerous affairs on Thomas's part, although friends of the couple never doubted Thomas's intense love and respect for his wife.

The Map of Love, which also includes several short stories, indicates Thomas's attempts with surrealistic techniques. Throughout, the intrinsic world of the poet is contrasted with the exterior world of humanity. The outbreak of World War II and the subsequent plummeting economy hurt the volume's sales, and *The Map of Love* failed to achieve the popular and critical success of Thomas's previous works. However, with his next major book, *Deaths and Entrances,* Thomas reached the pinnacle of his career. Critical reaction to the volume strongly confirmed his reputation as an important twentieth-century poet. In an initial review of *Deaths and Entrances* W. J. Turner asserted: "Dylan Thomas shows himself to be the authentic, magical thing, a true poet—original and traditional, imperfect but outstanding, with the unmistakable fire and power of genius. If anyone is looking for new contemporary poetry worthy of our great—and, I would add, world-supreme— English tradition, here it is." Less introspective than his earlier poetry, this volume centers more on nature and the shared anguish of humanity. Reviewers also noted that Thomas's religious attitude had evolved into one of positive acceptance, particularly in such acclaimed poems as "A Refusal to Mourn the Death, by Fire, of a Child in London" and "Vision and Prayer."

In "A Refusal to Mourn the Death, by Fire, of a Child in London," a sentimental, metaphysical elegy to suffering and war, the speaker will not mourn a child killed in an air raid because the death is too catastrophic for such conventional grief, and because the youth has been spared the disillusionment and corruption of adulthood. "Vision and Prayer" was hailed for its startling, mystic imagery. Emphasizing the passage of time through its hourglass shape, the poem celebrates Thomas's ultimate, triumphant acknowledgment of God's love. Edenic nature, Thomas's other dominant theme in *Deaths and Entrances,* is the subject of several pastoral poems, including "Poem in October" and the aforementioned "Fern Hill." Both works convey the beauty of the Welsh landscape and the simplicity and peace of childhood. Written while Thomas weathered the horrors of wartime London, these poems were considered to be particularly soothing, skillful evocations of a more nostalgic age. Numerous critics contended that Thomas's finest poems were those of a gentle, romantic, and nostalgic nature. Karl Shapiro observed: "It is significant that his joyous poems, which are few, though

among his best, are nearly always his simplest. Where the dominant theme of despair obtrudes, the language dives down into the depths; some of these complex poems are among the most rewarding, the richest in feeling, and the most difficult to hold to. But, beyond question, there are two minds working in Thomas, the joyous, naturally religious mind, and the disturbed, almost pathological mind of the cultural fugitive or clown." Thomas's pastoral concerns extended to his next work, *In Country Sleep,* a collection of poems that received relatively little attention. In this volume, Thomas comes to terms with life while confronting the reality of his own death. Such poems as "In Country Heaven" and "Over St. John's Hill" exude beauty and confidence as the poet affirms the eternal cycle of life, death, and rebirth through rustic settings.

Throughout his writing career, Thomas was a captivating reader of his enigmatic works, and gained public attention as a touring poet. At the height of his popularity in the early 1950s, Thomas agreed to a series of public readings in the United States, bringing about a revival of the oral reading of poetry. Although his fame in America was unsurpassed and he was well-received on tour, Thomas was ill-equipped to handle the constant pressure to perform. An essentially shy man when sober, the public appearances unnerved him and he took to drinking while performing, as well as indulging heavily offstage. His dependency on alcohol during this period, which is documented in several biographies, ended in tragedy. During a tour of New York City in 1953, Thomas disappeared for several hours. Upon his return to his hotel, he allegedly remarked to a friend, "I've had eighteen straight whiskeys. I think that's the record," and fell unconscious. He lapsed into a coma and died several days later of alcohol poisoning. Thomas's brooding, dark persona, scandalous behavior, and pitiable death became legendary. Both critical and popular audiences viewed him as a tragically heroic figure, a romantic artist condemned by the volatile world he exposed in his poetry. After Thomas's death, the poet John Malcolm Brinnin, who had organized the American poetry readings, stated: "[Dylan Thomas] was exciting because his language was brilliantly rich, gaudy, reverberant and lavishly spent." He added: "As a poet, Dylan Thomas was and is available only to those who regard language and the imagination as divine rights to be continually possessed and repossessed and who regard the art of poetry as a profound source of knowledge. He wanted readers, and though in his lifetime he too often gained merely companions . . . , his poems are still an open invitation to all men to share the world he made."

(For further discussion of Thomas's life and career, see *Twentieth-Century Literary Criticism,* Vols. 1, 8; *Short Story Criticism,* Vol. 3; *Contemporary Authors,* Vols. 104, 120; and *Dictionary of Literary Biography,* Vols. 13, 20.)

PRINCIPAL WORKS

POETRY

18 Poems 1934
Twenty-Five Poems 1936
The Map of Love 1939

OTHER MAJOR WORKS

Michael Roberts   (essay date 1935)

[*Roberts is an English poet and critic who has written
extensively on British poets of the early modernist period, including Ezra Pound and T. S. Eliot. His critical
work is generally informed by his interest in philosophy.
In the following review of* 18 Poems, *Roberts examines
Thomas's thematic treatment of psychology and the unconscious mind.*]

Mr. Dylan Thomas is the most striking of the new poets
who have appeared in the last twelve months: he has unravelled some of the relations of a new group of images, and
he can stamp a traditional metre with an honest contemporary accent. [In **18 Poems** he] is consciously exploiting
the subconscious: he sees that the psychological patterns
underlying the sequence of images which come into our
minds when we are not engaged in conscious thought, give
those sequences a unity and impressiveness of their own.
Underlying patterns of that kind can often be found in poetry, though the poet and the reader may not always be
conscious of them: the poetic effect is often greatest when
the latent content is not consciously recognized. Here,
perhaps, the present weakness of the poems of Mr. Thomas lies: he is concerned directly with the dark skeleton of
the unconscious behind the face of poetry; the latent content is often identical with the explicit content; it is not,
in fact, latent at all, and consequently some of the poems
appear to be too consciously arranged. Mr. Thomas has
found what he set out to find; the poem has not found and
surprised the poet. The poems, like some Russian films,
and sham Surrealist poetry, are too *voulu;* the reader sees
through them, and agrees that according to psychoanalytic theory the images are in order, but is disappointed not
to find in the poem a revelation of something which may

well be in his own mind, but which he could not himself
bring to light, and he is not imaginatively convinced as he
is, shall we say, by some of the recent poems of Robert
Graves. The poem is a deduction from psychology, not a
psychological discovery.

Again, some of the symbols which occur most frequently
in these **18 Poems** appear at first, to be private symbols,
which though comprehensible, are not necessarily valid
for the reader. Perhaps Mr. Thomas's mind is more addicted than most to word-inversion: thus the references to
'Death's feather' become clearer, but not necessarily more
evocative, if we associate the word 'wreathe' with 'feather'. Sometimes this first-order remoteness of the image
from one more usual seems to serve the purpose of explicit
content: the method is interesting, but it lacks the effectiveness of a fully-ordered 'explicit meaning' in which the
whole of the explicit meaning is a symbol of the latent content.

But the technical interest, and the present monotony of
Mr. Thomas's work must not blind us to the fact that the
poems are good, some of them very good indeed. His interest in poetic technique, in words, and in those subjective
experiences which can only be expressed through images
of tactile, kinæsthetic, and visceral sensation already produces good poems. The use of religious symbols in some
of his poems seems to show that he realizes that 'religious'
poetry is psychological poetry which uses a symbolism
more effective and profound than his own limited and self-
conscious Freudian images. (pp. 496-97)

> *Michael Roberts, in a review of "18 Poems,"
> in* The Criterion, *Vol. XIV, No. LVI, April,
> 1935, pp. 496-97.*

The Times Literary Supplement   (essay date 1936)

[*In the following review of* Twenty-Five Poems, *the critic contends that Thomas's writing is idiomatic and highly individual.*]

Mr. Thomas's language as a poet is so much his own that
it is often as difficult to interpret as a foreign tongue. One
of his poems [in **Twenty-Five Poems**] for example, opens
with the following stanzas:

> How soon the servant sun
> (Sir morrow mark)
> Can time unriddle, and the cupboard stone
> (Fog has a bone
> He'll trumpet into meat)
> Unshelve that all my gristles have a gown
> And the naked egg stand straight,
>
> Sir morrow at his sponge,
> (The wound records)
> The nurse of giants by the cut sea basin,
> (Fog by his spring
> Soaks up the sewing tides)
> Tells you and you, my masters, as his strange
> Man morrow blows through food.

The rest of the poem is no less obscure and there are many
others of which the meaning is equally hard to unravel,
nor is the reader aided by any explanatory notes in his

struggle with the apparently unintelligible. That Mr. Thomas is essentially a poet is certainly proved by the symbolical quality of his language. He writes in images peculiar to himself, but so intensely conceived that it is only when we cease trying to explain them to the reason that we begin to grasp the quality of experience they communicate. To quote one of his own definitions of this surrender to a new mode of consciousness:

> What's never known is safest in this life.
> Under the skysigns they who have no arms
> Have cleanest hands, and, as the heartless ghost
> Alone's unhurt, so the blind man sees best.

Yet even those who are prepared to adventure into the unknown will find much in these poems that is baffling. And it is in the simpler of them, such as **"This bread I break,"** **"Why east wind chills," "Ears in the turrets hear," "I have longed to move away,"** or in the magnificent triumph song over death beginning **"And death shall have no dominion"** that the highly original quality of his idiom and of his vision may be best appreciated.

> *A review of "Twenty-Five Poems," in* The Times Literary Supplement, *No. 1807, September 19, 1936, p. 750.*

Frederick J. Hoffman   (essay date 1945)

[*Hoffman was an American educator and critic who wrote extensively on twentieth-century American literature. In the excerpt below, Hoffman discusses the influence of Sigmund Freud's theories of dream interpretation upon Thomas's poetry.*]

The poetry and fiction of the young Welsh writer, Dylan Thomas, pay tribute to . . . [one] of Freud's contributions to modern aesthetics. In no other single body of work has the aesthetic interest in the dream-life received such exhaustive treatment. . . . [Francis Scarfe, in "The Poetry of Dylan Thomas"] refers to Thomas' "assimilation of Joyce, Freud, and the Bible." Of his serious study of Freud we have abundant evidence, and this evidence is supported by a frank avowal of his indebtedness: to the question, "Have you been influenced by Freud?" Thomas answered affirmatively and added:

> Whatever is hidden should be made naked. To be stripped of darkness is to be clean, to strip of darkness is to make clean. Poetry, recording the stripping of the individual darkness, must inevitably cast light upon what has been hidden for too long and by so doing, make clean the naked exposure. Freud cast light on a little of the darkness he had exposed. Benefiting by the sight of the light and the knowledge of the hidden nakedness, poetry must drag further into the clean nakedness of light more even of the hidden causes than Freud could realize.

The career of Dylan Thomas begins conservatively enough. His great mastery of sensory detail, suitable for the most excellent of simple poetic description, betrays at first no serious preoccupation with the "individual darkness." Progress toward his ultimate mythical awareness of the Unconscious and of the dream-life can be observed in

his series of autobiographical sketches [*Portrait of the Artist as a Young Dog*]. By some strange alchemic process, his insight into the unconscious self is linked with a maturing sensitivity to the mystery and charm of sex, and a certain paralyzing hesitation to realize it fully. The *Portrait* has its measure of references to a small boy's vulgarities; in fact, these are the common self-conscious acts of schoolboyish scorn for the pomp and circumstance of adult society. In the last of the sketches of the *Portrait,* the direction of his interests is indicated. Physical love is allied with creation in this one respect, that it opens the door to a secret, mysterious, and dark world, the world of "hidden nakedness." It is this world which the artist seems compelled to explore, bring into the light, and creatively re-present. Hence the imagery of this poetic vision of the sexual act is associated closely with Thomas' own theory of poetic imagery: "He and Lou could go down together, one cool body weighted with a boiling stone, on to the falling, blank white, entirely empty sea, and never rise."

Strikingly evident in most of his visions of the "inner darkness" is this image of death: a spiritual anonymity, a blotting out of the single personality in the act of physical and poetic creation. Death stalks his pages; it is linked with life as both are trafficked in the womb:

> A weather in the flesh and bone
> Is damp and dry; the quick and dead
> Move like two ghosts before the eye.

"Death is all metaphors"—a courageous but puzzling slogan, full of the burden of creative grappling with the infinite darkness of unconscious life. This is a poetic view of the Unconscious, assuredly. Freud has in fact given the poet his initial opportunity to explore it; he has provided neither the details nor a suggestion of the end of the search.

Three important clues to the poetry and prose both of Dylan Thomas may give some suggestion of his purpose and direction: the theme of death and life, at times a sexual theme, death being simply the expulsion of seminal force; the recurrence of references to the womb as a thing of great physical and spiritual force, ambiguous and obscure though the poet's use of it is; and, finally, the dream symbols for love and lust, scattered and distorted as they are in Thomas' stories, giving them a strange power and beauty.

Of the first it may be said that it has really two meanings, a superficial one and a profound. Death and dying are obviously enough symbols of detumescence, so that it is through such "dying" that life must come. We give of ourselves so that we may receive ourselves in return. The second meaning is the inevitable linkage, organic and spiritual, of life with decay. Some part of that decay may be called simply "frustration"—a forcible suspension of natural or instinctual impulses, which, though it may insure external or sensory continuity, throws both the poet and the lover back upon certain spiritual resources, most of which reside in the Unconscious. Psychic decay, caused by fundamental misunderstanding and misuse of the human psyche, renews the poet's need for deeper roots, makes him dissatisfied with the trivial and the traditional.

Thomas' use of the womb as a great mother-symbol is, of course, linked with the notion of life and death. Within the limits of physical generation, the womb is the great and only area in which life is cherished and supported during its period of pre-natal helplessness. It is perhaps natural to think of it as a source of renewal when the initial helplessness is duplicated in later social or psychic distress. The womb thus becomes animate and alive, a creative medium in which life and death struggle for domination of the human soul.

The imagery of Thomas' poems and stories is in part derived from these two all-encompassing ideas. But he is also much preoccupied with the dream-life; and some examination of his use of dreams may reward us with a further insight into his work. Within their boundaries one sees the geography of physical love, the dream symbols referring again and again to physical contours given a sexual emphasis. The "map of love," on which dwell the "first beasts of love" is a "square of seas and islands and strange continents with a forest of darkness at each extremity." Here the sea—a persistent image, suggesting birth or a return to the sources of life—is strangely and persistently referred to. We find also the forest and grasses, luxuriant and rich; "the abominations of the swamp, content in the shadow of their own rains and snowings, in the noise of their own sighs, and the pleasures of their own green achings." (pp. 295-97)

Thomas recognizes in Freud's researches a brave attempt to reveal what is hidden within us. But he is not satisfied with a psychologist's description of the Unconscious; he must *begin* there and, by creative means, "drag further into the clean nakedness of light more even of the hidden causes than Freud could realize." (pp. 298-99)

> *Frederick J. Hoffman, "Further Interpretations," in his* Freudianism and the Literary Mind, *Louisiana State University Press, 1945, pp. 277-308.*

W. J. Turner   (essay date 1946)

[*Turner was one of the first critics to realize Thomas's poetic potential. In his review of* Deaths and Entrances *excerpted below, Turner hails Thomas as "a true poet—original and traditional, imperfect but outstanding, with the unmistakable fire and power of genius."*]

It is my long-held opinion that any useful criticism of new poetry can only be of the nature of recognition. The first necessary act is pure, personal divination. Poetry is rare; it is scattered, even among true poems, like the nuggets and veins in a gold-bearing stratum of stiff, ragged, unsparkling rock or half-smothered through broad, spreading bands of dull alluvial soil. Only the poetic nature has an eye to detect it; failing that, the sharpest intelligence of a university wit, the surest trained literary taste will miss it, and pursue in place of the true ore whatever secondary brightness it is accustomed to perceive.

Thus I make just my own personal declaration that in this new book of twenty-four poems [***Deaths and Entrances***], Mr. Dylan Thomas shows himself to be the authentic,

magical thing, a true poet—original and traditional, imperfect but outstanding, with the unmistakable fire and power of genius. If anyone is looking for new contemporary poetry worthy of our great—and, I would add, world-supreme—English tradition, here it is. For I do not find such wealth of poetry elsewhere among the poems of most of our deservedly known and genuinely gifted writers. A fine, thin-worn Georgian coin of gold is tossed up here and there by one of our finer craftsmen; but here we are in an ocean of poetry and there is a spate of immense long rollers, huge-shouldered, transparent-green with magic light and foaming into billows of the purest snow of creation with the energy of an earlier age.

I think that this is all that is really necessary to be said, for anything else can be but of minor importance. And if I add that, for good or ill, Mr. Thomas is not an intellectual poet, I only mean that he does not obtrude his intellectual processes upon us. That there are a powerful mind and a great driving force behind this remarkable poet is implied when I am ready to declare that not only is Mr. Thomas a truly creative writer, but that this book alone, in my opinion, ranks him as a major poet. His poems are difficult because everything flat and prosy is squeezed out and we are often left with nothing more tangible than pure radiance; but here is one simple poem as an easy example of his style:

> In my Craft or Sullen Art
> Exercised in the still night
> When only the moon rages
> And the lovers lie abed
> With all their griefs in their arms,
> I labour by singing light
> Not for ambition or bread
> Or the strut and trade of charms
> On the ivory stages,
> But for the common wages
> Of their most secret heart.
>
> Not for the proud man apart
> From the raging moon I write
> On these spindrift pages
> Nor for the towering dead
> With their nightingales and psalms
> But for the lovers, their arms
> Round the griefs of the ages,
> Who pay no praise or wages
> Nor heed my craft or art.

That is a poem in the best lyrical tradition, yet new in spirit, original in expression and consummate in craft. It is not a great poem, but I am much mistaken if there are not great poems in this book. (pp. 148, 150)

> *W. J. Turner, "A Major Poet," in* The Spectator, *Vol. 176, No. 6137, February 8, 1946, pp. 148, 150.*

D. S. Savage   (essay date 1946)

[*Savage is an English poet, literary scholar, and social reformer devoted to pacifist and human rights causes. In the following excerpt, Savage analyzes the artistic development in Thomas's first four volumes of poetry, noting his treatment of the mundane aspects of human experience.*]

Dylan Thomas' status as a poet is now firmly established; informed opinion both in England and in America is unanimous in its agreement that his work is not only valid and important in its own right, but that, by inference, it provides a positive touchstone for current poetic practice and appreciation. We are fortunate indeed, in these days of deterioration, to possess such a touchstone. Dylan Thomas is a primary agent in keeping poetry alive among us, and through poetry, a proper sense of life, of values. Whatever may be said of Thomas' limitations must rest upon recognition of his superb qualities—a powerful and compelling imaginative vision held in delicate equipoise, matched by a subtle intelligence, wit and verbal sensitiveness and informed by passionate feeling. The recent publication . . . of Thomas' fourth volume of verse, **Deaths and Entrances,** provides the occasion for the following brief survey of his development up to the present.

To the question, what *sort* of a poet is Dylan Thomas, one can best reply that he is first of all a *maker*, that his poems must be apprehended as verbal structures before any attempt is made to torture a series of statements out of them. What Thomas—what any poet—says is precisely what is contained in the exact number and arrangement of words by which he says it. A clear understanding of this obvious truth will prevent a lot of idle talk about "obscurity." Having made this clear, it is possible to pass on to a further definition. Thomas is a poet to whom the overworked epithet "metaphysical" may without unfitness be applied. He is a poet preoccupied, not primarily with human experience as it is commonly apprehended, but with aspects of that experience lifted out of their apparent context and seen in extra-mundane relationship to their absolute, vertical, determining conditions. Central to his work, therefore, is a proto-philosophical, impassioned *questioning* of the ultimates—origins and ends—of existence. The vision which results is not philosophical in the abstract sense, but concrete, imaginative, poetic. The poet is cerebrating, certainly, but in a primordial, mythologizing fashion, dealing, not impersonally with secondary counters of thought, but imaginatively with the primary data of his own particularized existence, in which he is emotionally involved. Therefore the deep seriousness of Thomas' central vision is accompanied by a corresponding intensity of emotion, expressed in the grand, sometimes majestic movement of his powerful and subtle rhythms.

In his poems we have no re-creation (as, *par excellence,* in the early Eliot) of a specific, localized social environment; no projection of separate human figures or dwelling upon particular experiences for their own sake. And this can only be for the reason that the vertical character of Thomas' vision tends to disrelate the components of immediate experiences in their field of local, temporal connectedness, where they are held together in a lateral sequence, in order to draw them into the instantaneous pattern of the poet's perception. His theme is thus that of the human condition itself; not, as I have said, the condition of man in his personal relationships or natural or social environment, nor even, as some have thought, his merely racial and biological origins and ends, but the essential or fundamental "existential" human state, which is also the cosmic state, the condition of being, itself. Taking his stand within concrete, particular existence, Thomas places birth and death at the poles of his vision. His viewpoint is at once individual and universal—"I" is also, and without transition, "man," and man is microcosmic. The individual birth, therefore, abuts immediately upon the cosmic genesis death, upon cosmic catastrophe. Seen thus absolutely, however, birth and death are instantaneous; time is, equally, timeless; so that human life is mortal and immortal, flesh has its ghostly counterpart; though the relationship of each to each is enigmatic. In fact, all Thomas' best poems are erected from the double vision which is the source of his understanding: their coherence and firm structure result from the "androgynous" mating, the counterpoising in equilibrium, of contraries. Add to all these briefly enumerated factors a quasi-mystical, cabalistic perception of the world itself as of a metaphorical nature, intimately related to the articulation of language, and you have a fairly complete picture of Thomas' mind and method of composition. This brief exposition is conveniently illustrated by a short and simple poem from his third book:

> Twenty-four years remind the tears of my eyes.
> (Bury the dead for fear that they walk to the
>   grave in labor.)
> In the groin of the natural doorway I crouched
>   like a tailor
> Sewing a shroud for a journey
> By the light of the meat-eating sun.
> Dressed to die, the sensual strut begun,
> With my red veins full of money,
> In the final direction of the elementary town
> I advance for as long as forever is.
>   (*The Map of Love,* 1939)

In what sense Thomas may legitimately be termed a religious poet is a question which has been too little considered. For Thomas makes central, and not merely peripheral, use of images and terminology drawn from Christian mythology, history and doctrine. And, of course, his perspectives are themselves those of religious insight. But he is a religious poet writing out of the indeterminate, sub-spiritual situation of a Hamlet. Accompanying Thomas' imaginative activity—the very activity of course which makes him so indubitably a poet—there is, one cannot fail to remark, a moral or spiritual passivity. In his poems there is no subjective activity beyond the agonized, suffering or exultant, but always passive, acceptance of that which is given by the inexorable nature of existence; the poet is the victim of his experience. . . . Thomas gains something poetically, perhaps, by his very inclusiveness, his undifferentiating, intoxicated embracing of life and death and the Yeats-like celebration of blind sexual vitality.

The knottiest problem for such a poet as Thomas is that of development. An intense imaginative activity accompanied by a psychological and moral passivity is bound eventually to result in a curbing of the growth to maturity and in consequent artistic repetitiveness and stultification. In this connection we may note the marked shift in emphasis from the earlier poems to the later. In the first, speculation and statement predominate:

In the beginning was the three-pointed star,
One smile of light across the empty face;
One bough of bone across the rooting air,
The substance forked that marrowed the first
    sun;
And, burning ciphers on the round of space,
Heaven and hell mixed as they spun.
                            (*Eighteen Poems,* 1934)

Later there appears a more pronounced note of bewilderment and questioning:

Why east wind chills and south wind cools
Shall not be known till windwell dries
And west's no longer drowned
In winds that bring the fruit and rind
Of many a hundred falls;
Why silk is soft and the stone wounds
The child shall question all his days,
Why night-time rain and the breast's blood
Both quench his thirst he'll have a black reply.
                            (*Twenty-five Poems,* 1936)

And this is succeeded, in the latest phase, by a positive, exulting note of acceptance and praise:

In
The spin
Of the sun
In the spuming
Cyclone of his wing
For I lost was who am
Crying at the man drenched throne
In the first fury of his stream
And the lightnings of adoration
Back to black silence melt and mourn
For I was lost who have come
To dumbfounding haven
And the finding one
And the high noon
Of his wound
Blinds my
Cry.
                            (*Deaths and Entrances,* 1946)

This rapt and exalted note, in the latest volume, as it occurs in the celebration of birth, sexuality and death, predominates in the best and most sustained poems—**"Vision and Prayer," "Ballad of the Long-Legged Bait," "Ceremony After a Fire Raid," "Holy Spring"** and **"A Refusal to Mourn the Death, by Fire, of a Child in London."** It expresses, certainly, a development—but a development which takes the form of an accession of *intensity;* that is, it is an introversion and not an expansion. Simultaneously, in the same volume, however, there are unmistakable signs of an effort, prompted no doubt by the poet's recognition of the danger of repetitiveness, toward the lateral extension of scope. The poems are now for the first time entitled instead of numbered, and attached to specific, recognizable occasions. It is significant, then, that the best poems are still precisely those which directly celebrate birth and death: particular, localized births and deaths, indeed, but seen still in unavoidable relation to the absolute perspectives. Yet not all the poems in this latest collection achieve the same high level. **"Poem in October," "A Winter's Tale"** and **"Fern Hill"** are three of the poems which, as I have said, mark a new venturing toward the comprehension of specific lateral fields of experience. And in these

poems, while the scope is indeed superficially extended, the result, removed from immediate relation to the birth-death polarity, is an unexpected diffusion and prolixity. One is led, furthermore, to wonder to what extent the too simple celebration of childhood, predominantly descriptive and correspondingly devoid of imaginative-metaphysical insight, in the last poem, is permissibly to be termed retrogressive; as indicating, that is, a deliberate avoidance of the complexities (which exist on the active level of moral choice and psychological discrimination) of adult, mature experience.

Faced with a poet of Dylan Thomas' ability, a fitting humility is called for in the critic. Thomas is still developing, and doubtless will do so in accordance with a true poet's fidelity to his own vision. Yet I cannot refrain from recording my strong feeling that authentic development for such a poet as Thomas lies not in a simple, lateral widening of scope, nor of course in a simple intensification of passionate feeling, but in something much more arduous, much more difficult, but also, ultimately, much more rewarding—in a spiritual, moral and intellectual movement toward the clarification and (perhaps, even,) systematization of the primary imaginative-poetical vision, involving struggle, discrimination, choice. This might well involve a bitter period of non-productivity, but if that were endured and overcome, we might yet find that we had in our midst a poet worthy to be classed with Dante, Shakespeare or Milton, and not merely with Hölderlin, Rimbaud or Hart Crane. (pp. 618, 620, 622)

> *D. S. Savage, "The Poetry of Dylan Thomas,"
> in* The New Republic, *Vol. 114, No. 17, April
> 29, 1946, pp. 618, 620, 622.*

AUTHOR'S COMMENTARY

There is torture in words, torture in their linking & spelling, in the snail of their course. . . . . In the beginning was a word I can't spell, not a reversed Dog, or a physical light, but a word as long as Glastonbury and as short as pith. Nor does it lisp like the last word, break wind like Balzac through a calligraphied window, but speaks out sharp & everlastingly with the intonations of death and doom on the magnificent syllables.

(essay date 1934)

M. L. Rosenthal   (essay date 1960)

[*In the essay excerpted below, Rosenthal touches upon various facets of Thomas's poetry, including imagery, metaphorical language, and his common themes of sexuality, religion, and humanity's incommunicability.*]

> . . . I let, perhaps, an image be 'made' emotionally in me and then apply to it what intellectual and critical forces I possess—let it breed another, let that image contradict the first, make, of the third image bred of the other two together, a fourth contradictory image, and let them all, within my imposed formal limits, conflict. . . .

Out of the inevitable conflict of images—inevitable because of the creative, recreative, destructive and contradictory nature of the motivating centre, the womb of war—I try to make that momentary peace which is a poem. . . .

Few poets could be less like Auden than the author of that statement. Dylan Thomas, the Welsh poet who died in 1953 at the age of thirty-nine, is an adept in 'the logic of metaphor,' even more than Hart Crane, with whom he has great affinities. He is Romantic, incantatory, 'bardic,' though not really—any more than Crane—nonintellectual. He is primitivistic but far from primitive. His intellectuality has little in common, however, with the surface cleverness and knowingness, or the existentialist ironies, of Auden and the poets who follow him. Rhapsodic and mystical, he shows us the character of his thought and aims in the poem **"In My Craft or Sullen Art"**:

> In my craft or sullen art
> Exercised in the still night
> When only the moon rages
> And the lovers lie abed
> With all their griefs in their arms,
> I labour by singing light
> Not for ambition or bread
> Or the strut and trade of charms
> On the ivory stages
> But for the common wages
> Of their most secret heart. . . .

The poet sees himself the instrument of that same life force which makes both moon and lovers 'rage' with their separate yet implicitly related ecstasies. He writes by the moon's 'singing light'; and the lovers, like his poetry, carry all human meaning into what they do. They lie, he says, 'with all their griefs in their arms'—griefs because implicit in their embrace is the whole cycle of begetting, bringing to birth, growth, suffering, and death. The tragic character of that cycle is also the poet's own theme, and it is what makes the moon, that symbol of cyclical change and mortality, 'rage' in the sky. An additionally painful aspect of this strange relationship is that only the poet is aware of it. He cannot communicate his knowledge—either to the inhuman moon or to the lovers who, he says, do not 'heed my craft or art.' If one allows oneself to be possessed by this poem, with its chanting intensity and its deeply solemn 'magic' interlacing of rhyme, the incommunicability of the essential kinship of all things (the universal analogy implied in the paralleling of the moon and human beings) becomes unbearable to contemplate.

Both the 'universal analogy' and its incommunicability are themes Thomas immerses himself in again and again, as he immerses himself also in the 'Freudian' theme of the all-pervasive sexuality of existence and the implacable death drive that is the maggot within it. He is preoccupied with the relationship of these themes to one another and to religious faith. **"Twenty-Four Years,"** crammed with paradoxical and lurid figures for the roistering tragedy that any one life must be, is an excellent example:

> Twenty-four years remind the tears of my eyes
> (Bury the dead for fear that they walk to the
>   grave in labour.)

In the groin of the natural doorway I crouched
  like a tailor
Sewing a shroud for a journey
By the light of the meat-eating sun.
Dressed to die, the sensual strut begun,
With my red veins full of money,
In the final direction of the elementary town
I advance for as long as forever is.

This grotesquely powerful little poem reawakens the sense of life behind the old cliché that the moment of conception is also the beginning of death. The hero is the poet himself, looking back to the womb and forward to the grave from the vantage point of his twenty-fourth birthday. His piled-up years 'remind' him of mortality—the embryo building out its own cells until it reaches human form is a tailor sewing his own funeral shroud. When it enters the outside world through the mother's 'natural doorway' it is 'dressed to die'—an obvious, and typical, pun on the familiar 'dressed to kill.' Life is a 'sensual strut' toward death; the flesh-clothed tailor-dandy is also a spendthrift—of his own vital force, his 'red veins full of money.' He struts—actually, is impelled—in the direction of the 'elementary town' of subhuman nature, to whose endless processes and shiftings he must return. This last, suddenly quiet figure has genuine religious implications. It very closely resembles certain key metaphors in **"A Refusal to Mourn the Death, by Fire, of a Child in London."** There Thomas speaks of how, eventually,

> I must enter again the round
> Zion of the water bead
> And the synagogue of the ear of corn. . . .

These latter images bring out, a little more clearly than does the phrase 'elementary town,' the religious aspect of Thomas's somewhat desperate and fatalistic 'philosophy.' The terror behind the grotesque buffoonery of most of **"Twenty-Four Years"** is found in many of his poems; the speaker's hair rises in horror at the irresistible brutality of the life force, which catapults us into birth and consciousness, then exhausts and discards us. Yet there is often the strange, contrasting calm of metaphors such as the ones we have just been contemplating, which seem to be a quiet affirmation of the community, and more, the holy communion, of all being. The Freudian link is obvious between the terror of death's immanence and the longing for the state of existence which preceded birth and personality. These contradictory motifs are present in every mind, but we usually hold them off at a dim distance as morbid and maddening. Thomas tried to possess them fully, for to him they are the real world of subjective awareness, and he must throw the most violently intense light possible on them, must pitch every resource of language into them, if he is to discover the revelation hidden within them and blaze the discovery forth. The poet's task, for him, is to illuminate what Yeats called 'the uncontrollable mystery on the bestial floor.' In Christian terms, that mystery may lie in the relationship between the Virgin Birth and Jesus the man, and between Jesus the Son of God and the crucified Christ who begged to be spared if that should be possible. In artistic terms, it lies in the relationship between the poet as a man, subject to the onrushing fate and 'redemption' through death in the natural sense, and the poet as one who creates out of the common experience and suffering a work that outlasts and transcends them:

> By the sea's side, hearing the noise of birds,
> Hearing the raven cough in winter sticks,
> My busy heart who shudders as she talks
> Sheds the syllabic blood and drains her words.
> **("Especially When the October Wind")**

Thomas's modernity lies particularly in his absorption in these themes and in the way he pours his amazing psychic energy into the manipulation of sound, syntax, and metaphor. At times his exploitation of the resources of language seems reckless or vulgarly sensational, but there is little question of Thomas's right understanding of his task. Indeed, he explicitly describes it in the poem **"Especially When the October Wind"**:

> Shut, too, in a tower of words, I mark
> On the horizon walking like the trees
> The wordy shapes of women, and the rows
> Of the star-gestured children in the park.
> Some let me make you of the vowelled beeches,
> Some of the oaken voices, from the roots
> Of many a thorny shire tell you notes,
> Some let me make you of the water's speeches.

Doubtless this investment of his energies in language—the high emotional and dramatic charge, the magnificent richness of his whole utterance considered as a music of poetic rhetoric—accounts for his public success more than any other single factor. What Lawrence says [in his *Sea and Sardinia and Selections from Twilight in Italy*] of the effect of D'Annunzio on the typical Italian reader is true also of the effect of Thomas on English and American readers:

> . . . It is the movement, the physical effect of
> the language upon the blood which gives him su-
> preme satisfaction. His mind is scarcely engaged
> at all. He is like a child, hearing and feeling with-
> out understanding. It is the sensuous gratifica-
> tion he asks for. Which is why D'Annunzio is a
> god in Italy. He can control the current of the
> blood with his words, and although much of
> what he says is bosh, yet the hearer is satisfied,
> fulfilled.

The difference, of course, is that what Thomas says is not generally 'bosh'—*if* Lawrence was right about D'Annunzio. On the other hand, it is possible to revel in Thomas simply for that same 'sensuous gratification.' Here are some passages from his first book, **18 Poems** (1934), published when Thomas was twenty:

> I see the boys of summer in their ruin
> Lay the gold tithings barren,
> Setting no store by harvest, freeze the soils;
> There in their heat the winter floods
> Of frozen loves they fetch their girls,
> And drown the cargoed apples in their tides.
> **("I See the Boys of Summer")**

> And that's the rub, the only rub that tickles.
> The knobbly ape that swings along his sex
> From damp love-darkness and the nurse's twist
> Can never raise the midnight of a chuckle. . . .
> **("If I Were Tickled by the Rub of Love")**

> Before I knocked and flesh let enter,

> With liquid hands tapped on the womb,
> I who was as shapeless as the water
> That shaped the Jordan near my home
> Was brother to Mnetha's daughter
> And sister to the fathering worm.
> **("Before I Knocked")**

> A candle in the thighs
> Warms youth and seed and burns the seeds of
> age;
> Where no seed stirs,
> The fruit of man unwrinkles in the stars,
> Bright as a fig;
> Where no wax is, the candle shows its hairs.
> **("Light Breaks Where No Sun Shines")**

What is it that gratifies in these passages? Even less than with most poets does the answer lie in their themes. The first passage is from a poem which presents a three-cornered debate on self-love and barren or perverted love. The second is from a poem contrasting the magnetic pull of each phase of the life cycle with its eventual dismal outcome. This poem also seeks to define the symbolic meaning of man as the clue to all truth: 'Man be my metaphor.' The third is from a poem in which Jesus recalls the sense of his state before conception; implicit in it was all his future, and with it all the potentialities for suffering of all men. And the fourth is from a poem which, again, explores the 'universal analogy.' Recognition of these themes is essential to a full grasp of the poems, but it is the intoxication of sound and phrase that engages most of us at once, long before the connection of one phrase with another, or even the meaning of individual phrases, is at all clear. Moreover, there is a bold articulateness, very often sexual, that is startling in itself and stands out in relief from its mysterious context. Thomas, like D'Annunzio, 'can control the current of the blood with his words.' When one is reading Thomas, one wonders how poetry exists in any other fashion.

A great source of power in his work is its primitivistic orientation. There is relatively little overt intellectualizing, and a great deal of sheer assertion. He wills, and chants, primal desires and insights into the foreground of consciousness. He feverishly denies the pointlessness of life, and hurls defiance into the face of death. His insistence on the universal analogy, the incommunicable kinship of all modes of physical being, is really one form this feverish denial takes. The kinship he sees is essentially tragic; yet to affirm it is to affirm meaning, for somehow it is at the heart of the mystery 'on the bestial floor.'

> The force that through the green fuse drives the
> flower
> Drives my green age; that blasts the roots of
> trees
> Is my destroyer.
> And I am dumb to tell the crooked rose
> My youth is bent by the same wintry fever.
> **("The Force That Through the Green Fuse")**

The life force, this first stanza tell us, drives both flowers and human beings through to their full growth, then discards both when it has exhausted them. All living things are thus exploded into birth, maturity, death, and each stage of the cycle implies all the others. The next two stanzas push the same principle down into the world of sub-organic nature:

> And I am dumb to mouth unto my veins
> How at the mountain spring the same mouth
> sucks.

Then the fourth stanza brings in sexual analogy on a cosmic scale:

> The lips of time leech to the fountain head;
> Love drips and gathers, but the fallen blood
> Shall calm her sores.
> And I am dumb to tell a weather's wind
> How time has ticked a heaven round the stars.

The basic thought of these lines departs from the simple propositions advanced hitherto. The proposition of the first stanza we have already seen; the second asserted the obvious identity of the kind of physical force that 'drives the water through the rocks' with that which 'drives my red blood.' The third extended this thought rather mechanically to the realization that this same impersonal force makes a constant death trap for man: whirlpools, quicksand, windstorms. It ended with a subtler if somewhat awkward turn, however, intended to restore the centrality of the *human* image:

> And I am dumb to hell the hanging man
> How of my clay is made the hangman's lime.

Now, in the fourth stanza, there is a projection out of despair that appears at first to break the pattern of all these propositions. In the image of 'the lips of time' that 'leech to the fountain head' is symbolized the powerful yearning of all mortality to clasp and be impregnated by the life force. Out of that yearning, with all its pain, man dreamed of a timeless paradise beyond death to console himself for his limitations of mortality: 'time has ticked a heaven round the stars.' The dream cannot, of course, be communicated to the rest of nature. The poem ends in despair, with a bizarre and deliberately ugly phallic image that, in degrading the symbolism of the fourth stanza, doubly underlines the anguish out of which it has arisen:

> And I am dumb to tell the lover's tomb
> How at my sheet goes the same crooked worm.

"The Force That Through the Green Fuse" is primitivistic, then, in its self-hypnotic incantation that brings chanter and listener face to face with the appalling destructive force with which the unity of all nature is bound up. At the same time, the element of the speaker's helpless 'dumbness' to 'tell' this universal secret is a sophistication upon the primal sense of awe, and the 'lips of time' stanza is a further sophistication bringing into the poem's scheme the entire skeptical bent, and regret for lost certainties, of modern thought. Another poem, **"And Death Shall Have No Dominion,"** is doubtless closer to undiluted primitivism. The central argument is less complicated, and the repeated defiance of death at the beginning and end of each stanza gives it the character of a spell.

> And death shall have no dominion.
> Dead men naked they shall be one
> With the man in the wind and the west moon;

When their bones are picked clean and the clean
> bones gone,
> They shall have stars at elbow and foot. . . .

Granting the worst death can do, the poem proclaims life *will* reassert itself. In some manner the physical limits of the universe will be turned to advantage by the innermost will of life. Only the frenzy of the assertion, a frenzy so extreme that it symbolically destroys the created universe to obtain its demand, betrays the modern sensibility behind it:

> Though they be mad and dead as nails,
> Heads of the characters hammer through dai-
> sies;
> Break in the sun till the sun breaks down,
> And death shall have no dominion.

On the other hand, Thomas was capable of an infinite gentleness of tone, and sometimes his poems descend to whimsey and sentimentality (the great defects of his prose and of his play *Under Milk Wood*). His best works in a gentler mode, however, show him in his essential character as a modern Romantic, entranced in his visions and his recollections. The nostalgic **"Fern Hill"** is such a poem, buoyant and vivid in its memories of childhood but at the same time weaving into its scheme an ever more piercing adult sadness. As we read, we are first taken with the gay and fanciful note of many lines, with the singing, fluent liquids and sibilants:

> Time let me hail and climb
> Golden in the heydays of his eyes,
> And honoured among wagons I was prince of
> the apple towns
> And once below a time I lordly had the trees
> and leaves
> Trail with daisies and barley
> Down the rivers of the windfall light.

There are so many such effects that we hardly notice the casual, deceptive presence of Time in the background. And besides, Time is kind and 'permissive' in this beginning stanza. In the next he shows his power a little more openly:

> Time let me play and be
> Golden in the mercy of his means. . . .

By the last two stanzas, though all is still gentle and melodic, the terror lurking in things has become as overwhelming as death itself:

> And nothing I cared, at my sky blue trades,
> that time allows
> In all his tuneful turning so few and such
> morning songs
> Before the children green and golden
> Follow him out of grace

and, concluding the poem:

> Time held me green and dying
> Though I sang in my chains like the sea.

"A Winter's Tale" has the same tone of gentle, almost naïve simplicity and sadness, though it becomes far more involved than **"Fern Hill."** 'It is a winter's tale,' the poet begins, describing the season in delicate, mysterious pastoral images of cold and stillness. The story unfolds like a fairy tale or myth:

> Once when the world turned old
> On a star of faith pure as the drifting bread,
> As the food and flames of the snow, a man un-
> rolled
> The scrolls of fire that burned in his heart and
> head. . . .

The man of the tale prays for a transcendent, transforming love. He prays with so burning an intensity out of his deep deprivation that nature and time itself are aroused to sing his tale even yet. And eventually a miraculous vision does come to him, annunciation in the form of a bird-woman singing through the mysteriously opened door of his farmhouse. He pursues her, but she is beyond life and descends to him only after his death. The poem ends with a vision of combined sexual and spiritual beatitude reminiscent of the climactic moment in "The Eve of St. Agnes."

> And through the thighs of the engulfing bride,
> The woman breasted and the heaven headed
>
> Bird, he was brought low,
> Burning in the bride bed of love, in the whirl-
> Pool at the wanting centre, in the folds
> Of paradise, in the spun bud of the world.
> And she rose with him flowering in her melting
> snow.

There are other reminiscences of the story of Madeline and Porphyro: the winter landscape and intense imagery of cold and whiteness, the opposition and mingling of sacred and profane themes, the distinction between the continuing present and the long-ago character of the tale, and the ambiguity in which Keats veils the climactic union. Thomas's poem is more pervasively ambiguous, however, for he is not 'simply' telling a romantic tale which brings together holy and fleshly values. In his story of the man who sacrifices himself for love—'the believer lost and the hurled outcast of light'—and then is 'hymned and wedded' in the realm beyond life, there is more than a suggestion of Virgin Birth, Crucifixion, and Resurrection, though the order of events is altered and the roles of the sexes are reversed. The many sacramental figures, such as 'a star of faith as pure as the drifting bread' and the Dantean descriptions of the 'she bird' who is 'rayed like a burning bride,' support this interpretation. Finally, however, it is a symbolic creation out of the very nature of myth and religion that Thomas gives us. The poem has no ultimate literal referent beyond that fact, unless it be the pathos of the human condition.

Looking over his work as a whole, it is clear that this pathos is the emotion on which everything is based: the terror, the mystery, the crucified sexuality . . . , the bawdy Rabelaisian religiosity, the conception of his poetry as 'the record of my individual struggle from darkness toward some measure of light,' the preoccupation with what he called 'the crumbling of dead flesh before the opening of the womb.' Together with the tremendous, impersonal fact of his natural gifts, this dominant pathos is what keeps his poetry of the physiology of conception, with its 'sperm's-eye view' of life, from being repulsively gross and

renders it as magical as the mythopoeia of **"A Winter's Tale."**

> I would not fear the muscling-in of love
> If I were tickled by the urchin hungers
> Rehearsing heat upon a raw-edge nerve.
> I would not fear the devil in the loin
> Nor the outspoken grave. . . .

He would not, says the poet in this poem, **"If I Were Tickled by the Rub of Love,"** refuse the challenge to be brought to birth if he were sperm or ovum, though lust and the 'outspoken grave' are all that lie ahead. It is the pitiful courage of all life which he here contemplates and advocates despite 'the rub' of things as they are. The dialogue between an unborn child and its mother in **"If My Head Hurt a Hair's Foot"** is to the same effect. The poet imagines the compassionate fetus protesting:

> If my bunched, monkey coming is cruel
> Rage me back to the making house. My hand
> unravel
> When you sew the deep door. . . .

But the mother takes the same position of desolate courage as the poet in **"If I Were Tickled."**

> No. Not for Christ's dazzling bed
> Or a nacreous sleep among soft particles and
> charms
> My dear would I change my tears or your iron
> head,
> Thrust, my son or daughter, to escape, there is
> none,
>   none, none,
> Nor when all ponderous heaven's host of waters
> breaks. . . .
>
> The grain that hurries this way from the rim of
> the
>   grave
> Has a voice and a house, and there and here you
> must
>   couch and cry. . . .

A poetry based on elaboration of the self-evident, sad ironies of existence cannot entirely escape the sentimentality of excessive emotionalism, unless concentrated power and formal control dam up this emotionalism and transfer its energy into self-contained image and statement. Thomas took the risk consciously. He kept himself close to the 'ordinary' emotions of day-by-day experience, and yet brought forth also the repressed implication hidden within them. Sometimes, as in **"A Refusal to Mourn the Death, by Fire, of a Child in London,"** he is sentimental, yet something magnificent results. The child's death, this poem argues, is too 'majestic' and destructive an event to be mourned conventionally. But as he presents his argument against the usual ceremonial forms of mourning, the speaker employs the very language and intonations of lamentation in his falling rhythms, his arrangement of lines, and the solemnity of his long, periodic opening sentence (which takes up just over half the poem). The liturgical note, at certain moments resembling that in "The Wreck of the Deutschland," is clear in sequences like

> . . . the mankind making
> Bird beast and flower

Thomas as a child. With him, right to left, are his mother, a family friend, and sister Nancy.

Fathering and all humbling darkness . . .

and the funereal note is inescapable in such phrases as 'sow my salt seed,' 'valley of sackcloth,' 'a grave truth.' The poet's negatives—'Never . . . shall I let pray the shadow of a sound,' 'I shall not murder . . . nor blaspheme . . . with . . . elegy,' and so on—actually support this note, and thus the two long sentences that make up three-fourths of the poem are anything but 'refusals to mourn.' Nor does the last stanza, with its two concentrated assertions that the girl is now with her 'friends' in the mother-earth's womb and that 'after the first death, there is no other,' relieve the tragic tone of the poem. It, too, is of the order of 'desolate courage,' and so is Thomas's allusion to his own death as a reentering of the 'round Zion of the water bead' and the 'synagogue of the ear of corn.' The poem is one of the great funeral sermons, and of the same order of conviction. That is, it says what we wish to hear, says it with the great Negative lying, as it were, there before us so dreadfully and nakedly we cannot bear to credit its unqualified factuality. But to muffle agony is not to undo it.

This aspect of Thomas, this self-consoling, pathetic, 'soft'

alternative voice, diminishes his achievement. There are times when his final effects are not of what he called 'momentary peace,' with the opposed forces tensed in equal balance, but rather there is something spurious or contrived in the final direction the poem takes. If Thomas is superior to Crane in the luxuriant exuberance and daring of his language and in the equal daring of his allusive and tangential symbolic statement, he is below him in courage to renounce this kind of unearned assertion. The uncompromising self-exposure of Crane's "Passage," the yearning in his "Repose of Rivers" for total annihilation of the self unrelieved by any self-indulgence such as Thomas often allows himself, his refusal to be taken in by his own dreams in the *Voyages* are not quite to be matched by anything in Thomas. Not to overstate the case, sometimes Thomas was a little too much the slick professional. 'I am so glad,' he wrote to Vernon Watkins, 'you liked the **"Vision and Prayer"** poem; and that the diamond shape of the first part seems no longer to you to be cramped & artificed. I agree that the second part is, formally, less inevitable, but I cannot alter it, except, perhaps, in detail. . . . Yes, the Hound of Heaven is baying there in the last verse. . . .' (The allusion is to the idiom and thought of Francis Thompson's "The Hound of Heaven," which culminates in the speaker's inevitable capture after a symbolic flight from God.)

Not only is the second part 'less inevitable' than the first; it has no inevitability at all, at least after its first stanza. Even Part I, in fact, hardly sustains the tremendous, awestruck paradoxical vision its two opening stanzas introduce. Those stanzas express fully the keen, sensually conditioned apperceptiveness of mystery which Thomas possessed. He could

> . . . hear the womb
> Opening and the dark run
> Over the ghost and the dropped son
> Behind the wall thin as a wren's bone. . . .

But he lets these stanzas carry the poem, and right after them the Hound of Heaven starts its 'baying.' Echoes from Hopkins mar the poem also, though Thomas denied their presence.

"Vision and Prayer" appeared in 1945, that is, toward the end of a literary career that began when the poet was twenty and virtually ended when he was thirty-two, for he wrote very little poetry after his *Deaths and Entrances* appeared in 1946. We can see a certain mellowing and relaxation of surface tension in his later work (after 1939 or so), but little development. His first two books do show a wilder, fresher fancy than his later ones, and a greater integrity of balance in the 'conflict' of feelings and values. But the 'elder' Thomas can often enough rekindle the early spark and tough-mindedness, and the 'younger' has the sad satyr-wisdom of the latest poems. All his writing seems the result of one single, if unevenly sustained, outpouring.

Probably the ten **"Altarwise by Owl-light"** sonnets printed in 1936, almost a decade before **"A Refusal to Mourn"** and **"Vision and Prayer,"** provide an important clue to the poet's failure to show real progress. Despite their relatively early composition, at least one of his critics has felt that they tower 'perhaps above all his work,' and 'are among the greatest poems of our century.' Certainly they are richly impressive in their originality and multiple symbolism. . . . Yet with all their ingenuity they do not justify the leap into unqualified faith implied in the closing sonnet. Their whole direction has been toward creating a difficult balance based on the *aperçu* of **"Sonnet II"** that 'Death is all metaphors, shape in one history.' From the first sonnet, in which a Christ-like figure is seen lying 'graveward with his furies,' his genitals 'bitten out . . . with tomorrow's scream' by the malevolent spirit of reality, to the ninth sonnet with its ironic comment on the inadequacy of either the ancient Egyptian art of embalming or the writer's art to give us more than a token immortality, this grim thought is the inescapable theme of the sequence. Death is the principle behind the redundant cycles of the seasons (**"Sonnet III"**); in its light the paradoxes of faith are without conviction; it bends the essential symbol of the Christian faith, the Crucifixion, to its merely human meaning: sacrifice without promise of resurrection (**"Sonnet VIII"**). Then, in **"Sonnet X,"** Thomas takes all the wishes for that promise which death has 'defeated' in the preceding poems and says, 'Let them come true'—

> . . . let the garden diving
> Soar, with its two bark towers, to that Day
> When the worm builds with the gold straws of
>   venom
> My nest of mercies in the rude, red tree.

Let these things happen, indeed! Thomas's habit of identifying himself symbolically with Christ has in this instance led him into grandiosity, despite the loveliness of individual lines in this concluding sonnet. At times his very gift for standing back and letting the wonderful phrases soar is self-defeating, an improvised orchestral swelling and flourishing where the poetry demands more depth and discipline. But the wit and elegance of his presentation of a mood of sheer dread in the first sonnet, the heavy music of the third, and the bitter beauty of the climactic eighth make these particular poems stand with his best work. As for the sequence as a whole, the fact that Thomas never carried out his intention to make it longer doubtless has something to do with an unwillingness to face the issues beyond the point of their casual muting in the tenth sonnet. Nor did he ever face them in all their demanding difficulty. Like Rimbaud and Crane, he was one of those poets who exhaust the possibilities of their art fairly early after a dazzling breakthrough.

Dylan Thomas's precocity made him . . . a poet of the 'thirties and, in that purely chronological sense, out of his own generation. . . . [However], he did not fall into the pattern of political poetry that dominated the age. Politics touched his writing mainly through the war, and then in terms purely personal and characteristic of his usual concerns. **"A Refusal to Mourn," "Ceremony After a Fire Raid," "Among Those Killed in the Dawn Raid Was a Man Aged a Hundred"** are hardly even 'war poems' despite their implicit pacifism. A poem like the earlier **"The Hand That Signed the Paper"** (1935) is really a poem against political power itself, rather than one that takes sides. Thomas's poetry is a reaction away from the topical, the 'social,' and the ratiocinative to a realm of introspective personalism which is at the same time inclusively human. It was that reaction, as well as the native genius he revealed, which so surprised and overwhelmed Thomas's first audience and persuaded their affection. He did truly, despite his 'tough' swaggering and the barrier of difficulty he often presented,

> . . . by this blowclock witness of the sun
> Suffer the heaven's children through my
>   heartbeat.
>   (**"Sonnet VIII"**)
>   (pp. 203-19)

M. L. Rosenthal, "Exquisite Chaos: Thomas and Others," in his The Modern Poets: A Critical Introduction, *Oxford University Press, Inc., 1960, pp. 203-72.*

Howard Sergeant   (essay date 1962)

[*In the following excerpt, Sergeant examines Thomas's role as a religious poet.*]

From the time that his work began to appear in [the Welsh newspaper] *The Sunday Referee,* Thomas was preoccupied with spiritual values and the ultimates of existence, related through his peculiar, in some ways almost mystical, vision of sex, which he regarded as the unifying force of all creation:

> And yellow was the multiplying sand,
> Each golden grain spat life into its fellow. . . .
>
> In the beginning was the mounting fire
> That set alight the weathers from a spark,
> A three-eyed, red-eyed spark, blunt as a flower;
> Life rose and spouted from the rolling seas,
> Burst in the roots, pumped from earth and rock
> The secret oils that drive the grass.

Despite the legends of his outrageously bohemian mode of life, and the circumstances surrounding his death, Dylan Thomas was a naturally religious poet. With the Welsh Bethel as its probable source, his religious faith was so firmly implanted and so much a part of his poetic make-up that, unlike those who become Christians by deliberate choice, he was never at pains to declare it; or to attempt to define his beliefs in relation to experience. God, for him, was an established fact, and divine manifestations were to be celebrated rather than examined or questioned. Nevertheless, if he finally admitted, in the preface to his collected volume, that his poems were 'written for the love of Man and in praise of God', the religious element was somewhat obscured in his earliest poetry because he was so engrossed in sexual and prenatal experience, and because he seemed, in such poems as **"I have longed to move away"** to be denying the faith in which he had been brought up:

> I have longed to move away
> From the hissing of the spent lie. . . .

By 'the hissing of the spent lie', Thomas could be referring either to Christianity or to that stultification of spiritual life which institutionalised religion, with its empty platitudes and gestures, and church-attendance as a social habit, so often becomes. The latter construction is supported by the poet's use of the phrases 'from the repetition of salutes' (conventional expressions of fellowship) and 'half convention and half lie'. But even at this point of denial he hesitates in a state of uncertainty and, unable to suppress his religious instincts entirely, almost retracts the statement:

> I have longed to move away but am afraid;
> Some life, yet unspent, might explode
> Out of the old lie burning on the ground,
> And, crackling into the air, leave me half-blind.

Though his early poems were rich in Biblical symbols and allusions, they were used to express his own sexual interpretation of life and death. Yet at the centre of his vision was an awareness of the spiritual nature of man. It is interesting to trace the development of his religious outlook from 1934 when, in reply to a questionnaire, he wrote— 'My poetry is, or should be, useful to me for one reason; it is the record of my individual struggle from darkness towards some measure of light'. In his second volume there are three *inclusions* which have special bearing on this particular aspect of his work, **"This bread I break," "And death shall have no dominion,"** and the sonnet sequence

"Altarwise by owl-light." To take the last first, **"Altarwise by owl-light"** is a series of ten poems dealing with the crucifixion in Thomas's most complicated and obscure language, ranging from the near comic (though serious enough in its context) with its cowboy version of the Annunciation:

> And from the windy West came two-gunned
>   Gabriel,
> From Jesu's sleeve trumped up the king of spots,
> The sheath-decked jacks, queen with a shuffled
>   heart. . . .

to the poignant:

> This was the crucifixion on the mountain,
> Time's nerve in vinegar, the gallow grave
> As tarred with blood as the bright thorns I
>   wept. . . .

Several critics have attempted to decipher the poem, but even when in possession of these elaborate keys, one is left floundering between the actual Biblical account and Thomas's idiosyncratic interpretation of the Scriptures, doctrinally confused as it is with its compressed imagery and sexual implications. But successful as poetry or not, the sequence does indicate the direction in which the poet was moving at the time he wrote it. In **"This bread I break"** Thomas gives a pantheistic emphasis to Christ's words at the Last Supper, on which both the Catholic Mass and the Noncomformist Sacrament of the Lord's Supper are founded:

> This bread I break was once the oat,
> This wine upon a foreign tree
> Plunged in its fruit;
> Man in the day or wind at night
> Laid the crops low, broke the grape's joy.

—and, engaged with his theme of the unity of all life, he comes close to a mystical view of the Catholic doctrine of Transubstantiation; though, if one is to judge by the sexual overtones of the third stanza, where the oat and grape are described as 'born of the sensual root and sap', this was obviously not his intention.

Of the poems in Thomas's second collection **"And death shall have no dominion"** is by far the most significant from a religious point of view, for three principal reasons— firstly, it marks a definite change of the poet's attitude towards death; secondly, it envisages human love as a dynamic force without limiting it to its sexual elements as do most of the earlier poems; and, finally, it celebrates what may reasonably be termed a Christian conception of life, death and resurrection, if not entirely an orthodox one in all its implications. (pp. 59-62)

Most critics of Thomas's work have observed that this poem is concerned with the continuity of life after death, and some have quoted Biblical texts referring to the Christian doctrine of the Resurrection, but few of them have given the poem really close attention (largely, I assume, because it is static and lacks poetic development). In *Vision and Rhetoric* Mr. G. S. Fraser describes it as 'a poem in which the poet faced by the harsh fact of death is not properly confronting it but cheering himself up'. No one, to my knowledge, has related it to the actual passage in the Bible from which the theme is derived, and as this text is the starting-point, so to speak, and important to the understanding of the poem, perhaps we ought to have recourse to it:

> Now if we be dead with Christ, we believe that
>   we shall also live with him:
> Knowing that Christ being raised from the dead
>   dieth no more;
> Death hath no more dominion over him (Romans 6).

In the light of this passage it will be seen that the poem is . . . not an expression of some vaguely held belief in an after-life. . . . Such lines as:

> Though they go mad they shall be sane,

and

> Twisting on racks when sinews give way,
> Strapped to a wheel, yet they shall not
>   break . . .

would surely have little significance in these days of brainwashing and concentration camps if all they were intended to mean was that at death man would merely achieve an impersonal state of oneness with nature. Least of all is the poem a poetic equivalent to the child whistling in the dark to keep up his failing spirits, as Mr. Fraser would have it. On the contrary, it is a poem of affirmation and praise. Because the poet's faith in the Resurrection is so deeply rooted—that is, if I may be excused for putting it in a Christian terminology which Thomas would never have used himself, because he accepts the belief that Christ has triumphed over death—there is no problem of ideological development; it suffices for him to expatiate in his own individual way on the original statement that 'death hath no more dominion over him'. The unity to which he refers is already presented by the text—*Now if we be dead with Christ, we believe that we shall also live with him.* A new feeling of hope is reflected in the poem. To appreciate this change of tone we have only to compare the attitude expressed in **"And death shall have no dominion"** with that of the earlier poems in which death is portrayed as having almost absolute dominion over man, beginning at the very moment of birth—'and the womb / drives in a death as life leaks out'—and extending to all his activities, especially his sexual activities.

In his third book, *The Map of Love,* the poet acknowledges his state of conflict and admits that 'it is the sinners' dust-tongued bell claps me to churches', but, with one important exception, the poems in this collection are of a transitional character. The exception is **"After the Funeral,"** sub-titled "In Memory of Ann Jones." Previously, his poems dealing with birth and death, his favourite subjects, were strictly impersonalised. These were concerned with man in general on his journey from womb to grave—'In the groin of the natural doorway I crouched like a tailor / Sewing a shroud for the journey'—and failed to communicate any feeling for man in particular. In **"After the Funeral,"** however, we find not only that the new attitude to death and to human love is more positively presented, but that Thomas is concerned with a particular individual, the old aunt with whom he often stayed as a child, and all his

natural affection, combined with respect and humility, is communicated to the reader:

> I know her scrubbed and sour humble hands
> Lie with religion in their cramp, her threadbare
> Whisper in a damp word, her wits drilled hollow,
> Her fist of a face died clenched on a round pain;
> And sculptured Ann is seventy years of stone.
> These cloud-sopped, marble hands, this monumental
> Argument of the hewn voice, gesture and psalm,
> Storm me forever over her grave. . . .

This was quite unlike anything he had attempted before, and it seems to me that **"After the Funeral,"** with its intensely human sympathy, continues the line of development from **"And death shall have no dominion"** to the magnificent elegy **"A refusal to Mourn the Death, by Fire, of a Child in London"** in his next book, *Deaths and Entrances* (1946). The child concerned may be any child, for all the reader knows, yet the poignancy and solemn beauty of the poem seem to suggest that it is a particular child, and one for whom the whole intensity of the poet's experience is directed into the channels of majestic sorrow. It is almost a prayer in its effect, and Thomas's use of the phrase 'stations of the breath' carries with it the atmosphere of grief surrounding the Stations of the Cross. And the association here is singularly appropriate. No one could deny the religious depths of the final stanza:

> Deep with the first dead lies London's daughter,
> Robed in the long friends,
> The grains beyond age, the dark veins of her
>   mother,
> Secret by the unmourning water
> Of the riding Thames.
> After the first death, there is no other.

If the foregoing interpretation of **"And death shall have no dominion"** is correct, there can be no difficulty with the last line of the extract above—'After the first death, there is no other'—despite the apparent ambiguity. Thomas is back with Romans 6, the child '. . . being raised from the dead dieth no more. . . .'

Deaths and Entrances can hardly be said to reveal a new Thomas, since many of the features which make it so successful can be traced to his earlier poetry, but it does show that a new integrating force was at work, as if something which had previously been suppressed had suddenly thrust itself forth into the light and taken control. In his study of Dylan Thomas, Mr. Henry Treece has voiced the opinion that this phenomenon indicates that a change of heart had taken place. 'The poet', he says with reference to **"Vision and Prayer,"** 'has openly accepted God's love, and has rejoiced in his acceptance.' We do not know, and perhaps we shall never know, how much truth there is in this observation, but certainly such poems as **"This Side of Truth,"** **"The Conversation of Prayer,"** **"Holy Spring"** and **"There Was a Saviour"** provide evidence of a complete change of outlook. The most skeptical reader could not miss the Christian exaltation of **"Vision and Prayer,"** so reminiscent of Herbert in its hourglass form and of Thompson's "Hound of Heaven" in its mysticism:

I turn the corner of prayer and burn
In a blessing of the sudden
Sun. In the name of the damned
I would turn back and run
To the hidden land
But the loud sun
Christens down
The sky.
I
Am found
O let him
Scald me and drown
Me in his world's wound
His lightning answers my
Cry. My voice burns in his hand.
Now I am lost in the blinding
One. The sun roars at the prayer's end.

Thomas's antipathy towards dogma of any kind makes it extremely difficult to ascertain the real nature of the religious convictions he held towards the end of his life, or to identify them with orthodox Christian beliefs at more than a few isolated points. Even when he appeared to be on the verge of committing himself in his poetry there were inconsistencies and contradictions which can hardly be attributed to poetic license or a colourful imagination; for in his later poems Thomas paid more attention to craftsmanship than ever before, and although it might be a justifiable criticism of his early poetry to say that his words and images were not always used with precision, it would be quite inapplicable to his later work. Again and again he seemed to be saying something acceptable to a Christian frame of mind, only to give the poem a contradictory twist. (pp. 62-6)

Perhaps these ambiguities arose, not from any religious uncertainty or doubt, but out of the poet's method of composition; his manipulation of conflicting images set up in opposition to each other and his partiality for paradox. As the tension at the heart of Thomas's poetry was created by the resolution of such conflicts and paradoxes in the 'struggle from darkness to some measure of light', we can hardly quibble. There is, however, no ambiguity about the conclusion of the poem. Thomas seems to have had a premonition of his early death and referred to it increasingly towards the end of his life. In **"Poem on his birthday,"** one of the last poems he wrote, he counts his blessings:

And this last blessing most,

That the closer I move
To death, one man through his sundered
hulks,
The louder the sun blooms
And the tusked, ramshackling sea exults;
And every wave of the way
And gale I tackle, the whole world then,
With more triumphant faith
Than ever was since the world was said,
Spins its morning of praise. . . . .

. . . As I sail out to die.

(pp. 66-7)

Howard Sergeant, "The Religious Development of Dylan Thomas," in A Review of English Literature, *Vol. 3, No. 2, April, 1962, pp. 59-67.*

Babette Deutsch   (essay date 1963)

[*Deutsch is an internationally renowned American poet, critic, editor, and translator. Some of her most famous works include the prizewinning juvenile biography* Walt Whitman: Builder for America *(1941), and an acclaimed translation of Alexander Pushkin's* Eugene Onegin, *which was published in 1943. In the essay excerpted below, Deutsch discusses Thomas's exuberant poetic style, the sexual and religious aspects of his works, and his use of ambiguity.*]

The revolutionary hopes of the poets of the thirties withered in the fires of the second world war. Their dream of social regeneration exploded, they turned away from the rubble around them and the abyss before them, looking inward, seeking to make peace with themselves, or upward, toward a transcendent vision of a Love that would yet redeem humanity. In the disturbed years that preceded the outbreak of the war in Europe a few young men, among whom George Fraser, J. F. Hendry, and Henry Treece were the moving spirits, banded together as poets of the "Apocalypse". Their dreams had something of the magnitude and the confused splendor, if not the esoteric character, of Revelation. Yet if their program, like their poetry, was disconcertingly vague and evangelistic, it carried a recognition of what was wrong with their world. They believed that human development must be in the direction of an integrity that valued the emotions no less than the intellect, taking account of the realities of dream life as well as of the wakeful consciousness. To poetry they gave a quasi-religious significance. Eager to rediscover personality, they wanted to free men from the domination of the machine, and they exalted myth and imagination. This they took in Coleridge's sense as, in its primary form, "the living Power and prime Agent of all human Perception, and as a repetition in the finite mind of the eternal act of creation in the infinite I AM."—and in its secondary form that which "dissolves, diffuses, dissipates, in order to recreate; . . . or where this process is rendered impossible, . . . it struggles to idealize and unify." Their religiosity, however publicized, was of a private nature, and eventually they turned toward a "Personalism" that might be described as a kind of ethical anarchism, in which a leonine Christianity lay down with a lamblike Freudianism. The significance of the Apocalypse movement was rather symptomatic than intrinsic, though a few notable poems were written by some of its adherents, G. S. Fraser and Vernon Watkins among them. None of its members, however, has achieved the distinction or the vitality of their literary forebears, D. H. Lawrence, Herbert Read, and the wild Welshman, Dylan Thomas.

Thomas . . . is a religious poet, not of the dour company that explored the Waste Land, but possessed, as was Hart Crane, by the revivalist's fervor, and so an exuberant poet, who heaps image on image as prodigally as he chimes rhyme with rhyme. Thomas's work presents even more difficulties than does Crane's because it combines with equally private references both Freudian and Christian symbols and allusions to Welsh mythology with which few outside of Wales are familiar. Further, he was more alive to the music of his meaning than to the meaning of his music.

Poetry has a long and honorable history in Wales. Thomas, though ignorant of Welsh, profited from the literary heritage of his native region even more than from the rough grandeur of its landscape. He was not a visually-minded poet, but one with an extraordinarily keen ear. Among the technical peculiarities of Welsh verse are the elaborate braiding of rhyme, alliteration, and consonance known as "cynghanedd." Traces of this are to be found in the work of [Gerard Manley] Hopkins, to whom the classical Welsh metres with their dependence on stress and the compound words of the Cymric bards were also congenial. The richness of verbal texture that Hopkins rejoiced to discover, were Thomas's birthright. Gifted, moreover, with a remarkably resonant voice, he was the better equipped to compose poetry made to be heard.

Some of his most memorable poems divide their beauties between praise of nature and praise of poetry that is nature's luminous mirror. This, even if, as he assured Vernon Watkins, he was "not a country man" but a suburban provincial, "making his own weathery world inside". Although his imagery derives from astrology as well as from astronomy, from his interest in magic and in the cinema, his private weather is governed by nature's. Witness the lyric in which he enumerates what he sees, shut in his "tower of words", a lyric that gains significance from its reminder that the root meaning of "poet" is "maker":

> Some let me make you of the vowelled beeches,
> Some of the oaken voices, from the roots
> Of many a thorny shire tell you notes,
> Some let me make you of the water's speeches.

Here, too, is one of his few relatively simple images, the October wind that "With fists of turnips punishes the land". This is an autumnal poem, and ends darkly. Another **"Poem in October"**, far more intricately patterned, concludes on a note of exaltation frequent with him. It opens:

> It was my thirtieth year to heaven
> Woke to my hearing from harbour and
> neighbour wood
> And the mussel pooled and the heron
> Priested shore
> The morning beckon
> With water praying and call of seagull and
> rook
> And the knock of sailing boats on the net
> webbed wall
> Myself to set foot
> That second
> In the still sleeping town and set forth.

It is clear that the year woke to his "hearing". The poem proceeds so resonantly that one scarcely sees, for the sound of the calling gulls and knocking boats, the simple fisher scene with its flying birds, rocking masts, and quiet "net webbed wall". The echo in "harbour" and "neighbour" is one of many in the first stanza alone. "Heaven" "heron" "beckon" "second" are woven on one warp of vowels and "wood" "rook" "foot" are woven on another. But the warp is a twist of several threads or, not to push the metaphor too far, there are other repetitive sounds, "woke" alone having five alliterations, and echoing again in the vowels of "shore" and "forth", the consonants of

"rook" and "knock". The pattern is far more elaborate than this and offers delights that no dry sum of vocables can ever suggest. Naturally, the rhymes and half rhymes serve to punctuate the poem meaningfully. (pp. 369-72)

The child of whom Thomas writes in his **"Poem in October"** is spoken of as long dead, but his joy knows resurrection in the poet, who *was* that child. Like **"Fern Hill"**, one of his best-known poems, this lyric is suffused with sensual understanding. **"Fern Hill"** offers another variation on the theme of **"Intimations of Immortality"**.

> Now as I was young and easy under the apple
> boughs
> About the lilting house and happy as the grass
> was green,

it begins gaily, with a glance at an early Eden and only a hint of the advancing shadow of the prison house. Thomas does not tire of repeating what his predecessors, along with the author of the Gospel according to Luke, had to say about "the lamb white days" and their passing. (p. 372)

The motif recurs in Thomas's quasi-sonnet, **"When all my five and country senses see"**. This is to be read not for the novelty of its tenor but for the freshness of its presentation. It tells us once more, but with what packed urgency, that as the youth becomes more self-conscious, his virginal sensuous delight in the world about him decays or is blurred or grows callous, but that the poet's emotional energy will restore and vivify his responsiveness and make him as a little child who needs no pass to paradise. "The heart is sensual, . . . ". Jean Garrigue uses this lyric in her angry "Oration against the Orator's Oration". Her diatribe refers definitely to Thomas's poem at the close, with its plea for fresh winds that will blow away the mechanical verbiage of those who cannot bear the "Unpropped, unbooked, and unreasoned" world, demanding winds that would restore the world

> All naked, maculate and faulty,
> And five green senses then but all the Word.

One of Thomas's most touching lyrics on this theme is about a child killed in an air raid. It is obscure enough at first reading, but illumination comes readily, and indeed, this is one of his few poems that can be roughly translated into prose, however cold and bare. It says that the poet will never mourn the child's death until God, who is named only in a roundabout way as the mankind making, bird, beast, and flower fathering, all humbling darkness, bids *him* die. The last line gives the clue to the poem: "After the first death, there is no other." After this early death, the child will not have to die again, as we who grow up to adulthood repeatedly die: first the child in us, then the young man or woman, one self after another. But this child, dying without much experience of the meanness of life, without having to watch the brightness leak away . . . is not to be mourned.

The lyric is as remarkable for its imagery as for its harmonies and cadences. Thomas speaks of his own death as the time when he will enter again the round

> Zion of the water bead

And the synagogue of the ear of corn,

that is, when he again becomes one with the elements, to which he gives a sacramental character. Declaring that he will not lament the child's death, he speaks of lament, too, in his own strange yet persuasive way. To sigh is to "let pray the shadow of a sound"; to weep is to sow the

> salt seed
> In the least valley of sackcloth . . .

The next stanza, which contains a Shakespearean pun on "a grave truth", says that he will not "blaspheme down the stations of the breath", a reference to the stations of the Cross that reinforces the poem's meaning. For life is passion, and passion is suffering; had the child lived, she would have endured evil that her innocence and youth did not know. Only one who remembers childhood as a time of peculiar radiance could write so. (pp. 373-74)

Thomas will not mourn the child killed in the air raid, because she was prevented from suffering corruption. That she was nevertheless the victim of an unimaginably dirty device, the poet does not say, though he wrote a documentary on the bombing raids so harrowing that it was not released. The fact that, if the child was not to lose her innocence, she was likewise never to know the peculiar joys of maturity, he also ignores. Yet the second part of another poem on a raid, in the course of which an infant was murdered, speaks of little else. The poet wonders what possibility denied was the first to die "in the cinder of the little skull," and laments all that perished with the dead baby. In a prose tale that is like the transcript of a childhood memory, Thomas writes: "There, playing Indians in the evening, I was aware of me myself in the exact middle of a living story, and my body was my adventure and my name." This is the feeling that his poems of childhood and youth convey with the liveliness of a throbbing pulse. The loss of that first intensity of being is more regretted than final dissolution. And this is not solely because the poet sometimes speaks with credence of resurrection, but also because his lament is like that of Wordsworth for the irrecoverable "splendour in the grass" and "glory in the flower", like that of Coleridge for the spent "beautiful and beauty-making power" of imagination.

Thomas once defined poetry as "the rhythmic, inevitably narrative, movement from an over-clothed blindness to a naked vision that depends, in its intensity, on the strength of the labour put into the creation of the poetry." The word "narrative" is misleading. There is no plot, in the ordinary sense, in Thomas's poems, save for his **"Ballad of the Long-legged Bait"**, one of his most demanding performances. Even if one gives the word "narrative" the largest significance, the myth central to his poetry as a whole is nowhere so explicit as was Hart Crane's. The beclouded pantheism of his early work gives place to a more orthodox religiosity, but expressed in the same intensely personal terms. (pp. 375-76)

Thomas courted ambiguity. His account of the way in which he developed his imagery is instructive.

> I let, perhaps, an image be 'made' emotionally
> in me and then apply to it what intellectual and
> critical forces I possess,—let it breed another, let

that image contradict the first, make, of the third image bred of the other two a fourth contradictory image, and let them all, within my imposed formal limits, conflict . . . Out of the inevitable conflict of images—inevitable, because of the creative, recreative, destructive and contradictory nature of the motivating center, the womb of war—I try to make that momentary peace which is a poem . . .

This is . . . [complicated but describes with great] veracity what goes on in our minds. It does not explain all of the obscurities in Thomas's poetry, with its fusion of pagan and Freudian and Christian imagery, but insofar as it indicates their genesis, it is helpful. The poet delivered himself over to "the womb of war" in more ways than one. The conflict was not alone between images but between the ideas and attitudes they represent. The Freudian recognized the generous beauty of sexuality. The Christian poet, shadowed by the sense of sin of his chapel-going forebears, was prodded to destroy the body to liberate the spirit. Nearly every poem moves tempestuously among contradictory themes: birth is an act of violence, but the child is born into a world quick with delight; all living is involved with dying, but he would have it that the death of the body means the first free breath of the spirit.

Seldom does he remark thus quietly upon the repetition of the ancient cycle:

> A process in the eye forewarns
> The bones of blindness; and the womb
> Drives in a death as life leaks out.

Rather he envisages the dusty forefathers coming "Out of the urn the size of a man" and crying out at the pangs of Time, bearing another son, and therewith new deaths. Typical is a dialogue between the unborn infant and its mother, where the embryo, pitying the pain it must inflict, cries out:

> If my bunched, monkey coming is cruel
> Rage me back to the making house. . . .

But the mother replies that there is no escape, for her or for the unborn, from the joy and the anguish, the life and the death that she carries.

One of his early lyrics speaks wryly of his sympathy with all that grows and flourishes: the blowing flower, the flowing stream, the rising wind, and with all that fades and dies: the crooked rose, the dried-up stream, the slackened wind, the man on the gallows, the lover in the grave (do these refer to Christ?). As in less lucid poems, the hammering effect of alliteration is refined by other consonantal echoes and by the chime of rhyme and assonance throughout. Sometimes Thomas seems to seek violence, whether of music or of metaphor, for its own sake, and to a degree that defies the necessary formal limits. Even those images that have a Dantesque clarity are dense with implications.

> In the groin of the natural doorway I crouched
>   like a tailor
> Sewing a shroud for a journey
> By the light of the meat-eating sun.

Only the initiate know that the manifold meanings in the line about "the meat-eating sun" include allusion to a

A melancholy Thomas stands in the ivy-covered cemetery of St. Martin's churchyard in Laugharne, Swansea, South Wales, where he would later be buried.

Welsh fertility ritual. But the reference in the first line to the position of the embryo is obvious, as is the reference to the fact that we are no sooner conceived than we begin to build a body moving towards death. It is less obvious that the tailor represents the world of the flesh as against that of the spirit, the world of time as against that of eternity. The derogatory meanings of this image are clarified by its use elsewhere, as in the allusion to "the clock faced tailors", the line: "Comes, like a scissors stalking, tailor age," or the passage in another poem on his fabulous youth, telling how "up through the lubber crust of Wales" the poet "rocketed to astonish"

> The flashing needle rock of squatters,
> The criers of Shabby and Shorten,
> The famous stitch droppers.

Many of Thomas's lyrics are indecipherable. The fewest have the Yeatsian directness of the poem dealing with his "craft or sullen art". The phrase suggests a sobriety quite foreign to him. He is drunk with the world, with the grape on the vine as well as in the glass, or he is overwhelmed by the sense of loss, often uttered in a thundering darkness, sometimes expressed in clear sexual imagery . . . or

with the sad simplicity of the grown man's lament for "the farm forever fled from the childless land." There are a few poems that speak with an authority both quiet and somber. Among them are **"The Hunchback in the Park"** and the elegy in memory of Ann Jones.

The first begins with a prose statement that the cadence and the vocables render lyrical:

> The hunchback in the park
> A solitary mister
> Propped between trees and water . . .

The second stanza completes the picture of him

> Eating bread from a newspaper
> Drinking water from the chained cup
> That the children filled with gravel
> In the fountain basin where I sailed my ship . . .

The detail work is masterly, having an apparent simplicity that is nevertheless open to interpretation. The fountain basin where a lucky boy sails his ship is the rough answer to the hunchback's animal need. The chained cup there that the children filled with gravel is the only cup he has. This we learn from the concluding lines of the stanza that tell us how he spent the night in a dog kennel, though "nobody chained him up." The repetition of "chained", this time as a verb, is a reminder that the solitary mister needs no constraint, his hunch is his shackle. The poem proceeds with a picture of him chased by the boys and helplessly dodging the park attendant, "With his stick that picked up leaves", as if the hunchback were fearful of being mistaken for trash. His loneliness is italicized by the presence of the nurses and the swans no less than by the boys making "tigers jump out of their eyes" and the groves "blue with sailors". We are told that the hunchback made a "woman figure without fault" in his daydream to stand "Straight as a young elm" in his sight when he returned to the kenneled dark, and the last lines remind us that she is his sole protection when the memories of the day follow to assault him there. The piece is the more poignant because there is in it no word or hint of pity, and the hunchback's tormentors are honestly represented as "wild boys innocent as strawberries". Indeed, as G. S. Fraser has observed, they too are "locked out": debarred from the imaginative richness that his deprivation gives the hunchback, a richness of which they are a part.

The poem composed in memory of Ann Jones is written, at least partially, in Thomas's elliptical idiom. Thus, the mourners at the funeral feast are evoked by such phrases as "Windshake of sailshaped ears", "the teeth in black", the

>   . . . desolate boy who slits his throat
>   In the dark of the coffin and sheds dry
>   leaves, . . .

But suddenly the conjuring verbiage is swept away and we stand with the speaker alone, remembering the dead, "In a room with a stuffed fox and a stale fern." At once the dense imagery resumes, forcing us into the presence of the poor dead woman. . . . But then the poet recalls himself:

> (Though this for her is a monstrous image blind-
>   ly

> Magnified out of praise; her death was a still
>   drop; . . .).

The poem moves back and forth between the monstrous magnifications that are Thomas's signature and a language that without sacrificing its density is yet unmistakably plain. . . . We are caught up into the speaker's grief for the poverty and the dignity of this provincial life, so distantly related to "the ferned and foxy woods", a grief that will not give over until

> The stuffed lung of the fox twitch and cry Love
> And the strutting fern lay seeds on the black sill.

The miracle is real and it seems as though not the poet had wrought it, but "dead humped Ann".

Much more straightforward and equally moving is the poem referred to above on his "craft or sullen art". He says there that he writes "Not for ambition or bread" nor for the proud solitary,

> Nor for the towering dead
> With their nightingales and psalms
> But for the lovers, their arms
> Round the griefs of the ages,
> Who pay no praise or wages
> Nor heed my craft or art.

For those who do heed it, his poetry rewards scrutiny. It also wins immediate response to its rich aural harmonies, to its profound pathos. . . . (pp. 377-82)

At its rare best it offers the most direct kind of apprehension with an immediacy and intimacy foreign to the adult mind. Certain of his lyrics might be called musical epiphanies. Joyce's word for the illuminated moment seized upon by the artist comes to mind in connection with Thomas because of the way in which he manipulates his vocabulary. This Joycean gift for making his words do multiple duty, the acknowledged struggle that engendered his poems, and the conflict within him between the gospel according to Freud and that according to the saints, helped frame the poet's dazzling, crowded idiom. Yet the scenery is the landscape of his childhood, the farms and the fox-haunted hills, the weather and the sea that the fisherman knows. Such Christian and Freudian symbols as fish and cock were as natural to him as the sea and the barnyard. What is novel is the curious mineral associations he had with flesh, and the many references to tailoring: God is "The cloud perched tailors' master with nerves for cotton" and himself "The boy of common thread". (pp. 383-84)

Poetry expressive of . . . [an euphoric] attitude, like that of Crane and Thomas, can perhaps be written in a secular vein, but so savage an assault upon reality as is made by poets of this stripe argues a religious, or at least a metaphysical, urge. Their attack upon language is like a battering-ram set against the mystery of the universe. It yields not the fraction of an inch to such treatment, and sometimes makes the poetry seem ridiculous. But there are occasions when the opposite is true. Then the poem that cannot shake the door, much less broach it, is like a powerful light illumining some of its details, or an impalpable telescope orienting us with regard to unearthly things. It is nevertheless in his poems praising earthly things and the waters that hold the earth, and the lovers who for a little while rejoice in it, rejoicing in each other, that Dylan Thomas speaks most tellingly.

Three years before he died, he held out the promise of a long poem, only a part of which had been written, and which was to be called **"In Country Heaven"**. It was to be about the self-destruction of one of the worlds of God. With his customary prodigality and only one capitalized noun, Thomas called Him "the godhead, the author, the milky-way farmer, the first cause, the architect, lamplighter, quintessence, the beginning Word, the anthropomorphic bowler-out and black-baller, the stuff of all men, scapegoat, martyr, maker, woe-bearer— . . . ". The projected poem was to begin with His weeping on a hill in Heaven because Earth had killed itself: "insanity has blown it rotten;" and on it there was no creature at all. Then, while God weeps, those in Heaven who had been countrymen on Earth, call to one another, remembering the things they had known there. "The poem," said Thomas, "is made of these tellings. . . . It grows into praise of what is and what could be on this lump in the skies. It is a poem about happiness." So are most of the lyrics on which his reputation is likely to rest. Some sense of what the projected work might have been may be gleaned from three poems that were to have a place in it: **"In Country Sleep", "Over St. John's Hill"**, and **"In the White Giant's Thigh"**, the White Giant being a no mythical kinsman of Goliath but a landmark on a Welsh hill. All three lyrics are plainly "in praise of what is" in the natural world.

In an early poem Thomas wrote, cheering himself up: "The insect fable is a certain promise." Uncertain, we turn back to the boy whispering "the truth of his joy"

> To the trees and the stones and the fish in the
>   tide.
>   And the mystery
>   Sang alive
> Still in the water and singing birds.
>
> (pp. 387-88)

Babette Deutsch, "Alchemists of the Word," in her Poetry in Our Time: A Critical Survey of Poetry in the English-Speaking World, 1900 to 1960, *revised edition, Doubleday & Company, Inc., 1963, pp. 349-88.*

"The aim of a poem is the mark that the poem itself makes: it's the bullet and the bull's-eye; the knife, the growth, and the patient. A poem moves only towards its own end, which is the last line. Anything further than that is the problematical stuff of poetry, not of the poem."

—Dylan Thomas, 1938

J. V. Crewe   (lecture date 1971)

[*The following essay originated as a lecture at the University of Natal in Pietermaritzburg, South Africa. In the work, Crewe explores the reasons behind attacks on Thomas by traditionalist critics.*]

The poetry of Dylan Thomas remains a puzzle to critics, and a vivid experience to many readers. What is its value, and where does it stand within twentieth-century literature? These questions may be easier to answer now than they were ten years ago. Thomas does not come to us white-hot and unfamiliar, and if some of the force has gone, so has some of the obscurity. In fact, Thomas has been (if somewhat hesitantly) installed as a 'modern classic,' and it is possible to discuss him with that in mind. Has he anything approaching 'classic' vitality, and if so, how is that vitality to be defined?

My starting point in trying to give a part of the answer to these questions will be a quotation from Yeats's poem "Ego Dominus Tuus:"

> The rhetorician would deceive his neighbour
> The sentimentalist himself: while art
> Is but a vision of reality.

The more one examines these lines, especially in their context, the less simple they are likely to appear, but ignoring some of the complexities for a moment we may say that they are a permanently useful definition of the poet's responsibility, and that as a summary of the assumptions prevailing in the rich creative period following the First World War they can hardly be bettered. . . . No doubt many historical and literary-historical causes lie behind Yeats's formulation. The war itself had shown the lethal aspect of sentimentality and rhetoric in public life, and anything similar in poetry or art was deservedly suspect. It also seemed that the poetry of the late nineteenth and early twentieth centuries amounted to little more than the crumbs from the romantics' table, perhaps chiefly the marzipan icing. After 1918 a civilisation that had been brutally shaken (if nothing worse) needed something other than saccharine consolations.

In criticism 'real' and 'unreal', as distinct from 'true' and 'false', acquired a new importance as evaluative terms, implying new expectations of the poet. Poetry as sincere personal statement, or (much worse) as day-dream or 'self-expression', could not satisfy the communal need for a 'reality' that would withstand the disintegrating forces of twentieth-century life, and that would replace the many shams that the war had exposed. The poet had to be, in the old English sense, a 'maker', not merely a sensitive private citizen: he had acquired responsibilities.

Dylan Thomas began to write poetry in the wake of that post-war generation, but he is in some ways an alien rather than merely an inferior in the company of Yeats, Eliot, and their contemporaries. He has sometimes been dismissed as though he were merely a ludicrous anomaly among serious artists: in fact, though he must surely be considered a minor poet, his art is within its limits a real art, and his historical importance should not be underestimated. (pp. 65-6)

In a manner of speaking a great artist is always more radical, whatever his social or political affiliations, than a lesser one. When we say this we testify to the power of the superior imagination to 'get at the roots of things'. In that sense Yeats or Eliot might be called more 'radical' than Thomas, but in the more common sense of the word, the opposite is true. Thomas was genuinely and wholeheartedly democratic, revolutionary and even anarchistic; his great near-contemporaries were almost to a man élitist, traditionalist and conservative. Their work represents a conscious reinforcement (and perhaps the swan-song) of a 'high bourgeois civilisation'; Thomas's portends the radical democratisation of Western culture, its cutting adrift from time-honoured moorings, and its attempt to 'make it new' without serious reference to the subtle inherited wisdom of the past.

Not unexpectedly, Thomas laid himself open to devastating attack by traditionalist critics, but (unlike some who were given the treatment) he rebounded. I suspect that the reason for that was not merely that readers sensed his 'talent', but that they sensed something even more important—a fresh breeze blowing. The framework of assumptions within which the attack on Thomas was conducted had itself been called in question. (One recalls the penetrating but unavailing attacks of the neo-classical critics upon the romantic poets.)

The charge brought against Thomas . . . is the classic one: he is both rhetorical and sentimental, and is hopelessly unqualified to talk about the nature of reality. At best he had a minor talent for lyrical description; he lacks intellectual and moral passion; is often obscure and psuedo-profound; there is no evidence that he did more than skim the books he is supposed to have read, but he shows, nonetheless, a surprising facility in picking up snippets from the Bible, Donne, Hopkins, Lawrence, Freud, Joyce and various other writers. This formidable attack, in which the word hovers constantly between the lines is 'charlatan,' has been diversified and extended in other directions. Kingsley Amis, for example, implies that there is something obnoxious about a poetic technique in which one need only take a phrase like 'In the beginning was the word,' and invert it to read 'In the word was the beginning' in order to produce a suitably portentous opening line for a poem. And Robert Graves says about Thomas: 'He kept musical control of the reader without troubling about the sense. I do not mean he deliberately aimed off-target as the later Yeats did. He seems to have decided that there was no need to aim at all as long as the explosion sounded loud enough.' Thomas does not escape unscathed from this barrage. It only remains to be explained why he is not wiped out by it.

The first poem I should like to examine is the well-known and well-liked **"Fern Hill"**. . . . I think, without committing myself on whether this poem is 'for an age, or for all time', that it can hardly fail to give immediate pleasure. It sparkles; it is moving; it is full of verbal inventiveness; it vividly evokes certain pictures and sensations of childhood, it is rhythmically seductive, it conveys, in spite of 'time', a magnificent sense of untrammelled life. Though there are greater modern poets than Thomas, none of them could have written this poem, and our first reaction must be one of pleasure and gratitude.

However, first impressions are not everything.

It has sometimes been said that **"Fern Hill"** is sentimental in that it presents, instead of the actuality of childhood, a nostalgically idealised state of being into which the adult may project himself. 'The sentimentalist would deceive himself', you will remember, and the appeal of the poem lies in the fact that it allows a simultaneous indulgence of adult self-pity and romantic self-inflation. This charge has been taken further. The poem describes a visionary childhood. . . . It is not childhood as such that is (in Thomas's words) 'Adam and maiden'. Together with the child's pure and intense apprehension of the world there is from the start a contact with corruption (not merely time) that fairly soon dispels the glory and the dream. In speaking about Thomas's poem **"And death shall have no dominion"** Professor D. G. Gillham asked whether the idea of triumph over death in that poem can have any meaning at all, since Thomas is an agnostic poet, and the poem seems to convey no credible or even intelligible idea of victory over death. Perhaps the question to be asked in this case is whether the visionary, rhapsodic evocation of 'innocent' childhood can have more than sentmental significance, considering that this, too, is an agnostic poem, and one which appeals to our common experience of childhood, enabling us to say 'This simply is not true'.

Let us look at . . . ["**Fern Hill**"] more closely. It begins with a phrase that is like a traditional formula used by storytellers: 'Now as I was . . . ', not 'When I was . . . '. That storyteller's phrase is associated with the larger-than-life, *selective* world of the fable, and the apparent confusion of tenses in it helps to suggest the timeless present of a story, which is also, mysteriously, part of a fabulous past. We should not assume too quickly that Thomas purports to give a naturalistic description of childhood, or that the child's world in the poem is a *sentimentalised* image. I shall return to this point later.

The main tension in the poem is apparently that between past and present; between the eternal 'now' of childhood, and the disillusioning 'then' of the 'farm forever fled from the childless land'. The world of the child is a timeless present, because he has not yet learnt to relate, or to see what is implied in the movement of the heavenly bodies which contribute so much to the beauty of the poem. To the child the sun is pure gold: to the adult the gift of gold carries the penalty both of time and of universal law imposed from without. The child is 'golden in the mercy of his means', a line which plays cleverly on the phrase 'in the meantime', as well as on the idea of 'largesse', and perhaps evokes the antithesis: 'the mercilessness of his ends'. The meantime is merciful; the end of time is cruel, and 'end' can mean both 'object' or 'conclusion'. Both mean and end are experienced simultaneously as we read the poem.

Fern Hill is an actual farm (in the last stanza of the poem the 'swallow thronged loft' is still there, and the 'moon is always rising') but for the child it is a farm transfigured. The 'easiness' (line 1) of the child, which implies a blessed

absence of tragic, or merely prosaic concern, is evoked first in the idyllic calm 'under the apple boughs'. We might notice that they are *boughs,* not *branches.* The word is slightly archaic and 'poetical', and we are already at one remove from circumstantial fact as we read it. It has connotations of peace, security and solidity which are not present in the more neutral word 'branches', and which are connected with the state of being 'easy'. One might compare the use of 'bough' here with Wordsworth's use of 'slumber' in 'a *slumber* did my spirit seal'. There, too, the word suggests idyllic security, retrospectively seen to be false. It implies, not the total oblivion of sleep, but half-oblivion, and because the word is slightly archaic and poetical we are reminded that certain hard, everyday facts are being left out of the reckoning. However, in **"Fern Hill"** the 'boughs' retain much of their power to shelter and give delight, and the suggestion of false security is less drastic than it is in the Wordsworth poem.

In the second line we come to the 'lilting house', the first of those seemingly arbitrary but vividly expressive conjunctions that occur throughout the poem: 'the rivers of the windfall light', the 'happy yard', the 'tunes from the chimneys', the 'sky blue trades', the 'lamb white days'. The house is lilting because the rhythm of the poem is lilting, and because the rhythm of the child's life is lilting—a buoyant, varied, relaxed existence simply assimilates the surroundings into itself. The effect of all these phrases I have mentioned is to make connexions where the logical mind makes distinctions, or simply perceives no connexion. They tend to bring the entire farmyard scene into one harmonious totality, and to suggest the power of the child to embrace and transform his surroundings in whatever way his mood or fantasies dictate. There is no subjective and objective; there is merely an actuality in which the house is a 'lilting house' and has no separate, rationally admitted, existence as a prosaic farmhouse. Throughout the poem no distinction whatever is made between the fantastic or the fabulous, and the real; the child is:

> prince of the apple towns
>
> famous among barns
>
> the calves (sing) to (his) horn
>
> Honoured among foxes and pheasants,

and everywhere the vivid, fresh, sensuous apprehensions are caught up and transfigured in the visionary patterns of his mind. He is the centre of a harmonious universe that exists equally within and beyond his own mind, and the 'within' and 'beyond' are inseparable. Time conspires in allowing that visionary world to exist, and even enhances it by introducing into it the principle of variety. Day and night have their own revelations and sensations, and without time there would be none of those contrasts between the luxuriance of the 'golden heydays' and the sharp brilliance of 'night above the dingle starry' or the freshness of the 'farm like a wanderer white'. It is only in the final stanza that time reveals its power to disenchant as well as to enchant, and where there is a sudden consciousness of the invisible chains which set a limit to human autonomy as surely as they do to the movement of the sea. 'The moon that is always rising' implies the vision of the child, who is unconscious of the moon's setting since he is asleep before that occurs, but it is now also the moon that rises again night after night, and that measures the months, and controls the tides with its invisible chains of gravitational force.

So far I have done little more than give a superficial sketch of the poem, but I want to take this analysis a bit further, and also link this poem more generally with Thomas's other work.

Let me begin by pointing out that, though I don't consider this to be a fault of the poem, it is fundamentally repetitive. Though there is a movement of time, which brings about a continual change of scene, and leads finally to the recognition that there has always been a serpent in the Garden of Eden, there is a very large static element in the poem. In Stanza I the child is 'young and easy', in Stanza II, 'green and carefree', in Stanza III 'it was running it was lovely', in Stanza V, 'ran my heedless ways', in Stanza VI, 'young and easy' again. In Stanza I we find 'happy as the grass was green', in Stanza II, 'green and golden', in Stanza III, 'fire green as grass', in Stanza V, 'green and golden', in Stanza VI, 'green and dying'. Again, in Stanza I, 'honoured among wagons', Stanza II, 'famous among barns', Stanza III, 'blessed among stables', Stanza V, 'honoured among foxes and pheasants'. It would easily be possible to isolate other repetitive elements. The child's world, for all its variety is fundamentally a static one, and there is in the poem no very profound development; rather a horizontal elaboration and diversification. It may be argued that the child's world is necessarily static, since it exists 'below a time' and not in time. That may be, but even allowing for that there is some truth in the view that **"Fern Hill"** is a sixfold repetition of the same general effect; idyllic enchantment given poignancy by the adult consciousness of time. One could imagine two or three more stanzas to similar effect being added to the poem, and there is perhaps not one single stanza in it which is entirely indispensable: the last one probably comes closest to being so, although the outcome is already implied before one reaches it. The vitality of the poem has little to do with dramatic development, or progressive organisation of the kind one might find in a poem by Yeats, for example. Its vitality has something in common with that of a characteristic passage of Thomas's prose:

> There they go, every spring, from New York to Los Angeles: exhibitionists, polemicists, histrionic publicists, theological rhetoricians, historical hoddy-doddies, balletomanes, ulterior decorators, windbags, and bigwigs and humbugs; men in love with stamps, men in love with steaks, men after millionaires' widows, men with elephantiasis of the reputation (huge trunks and teeny minds), authorities on gas, bishops, best sellers, editors looking for dollars, existentialists, serious physicists on nuclear missions, men from the B.B.C. who speak as though they had the Elgin marbles in their mouths, potboiling philosophers, professional Irishmen (very lepricorny), and, I am afraid, fat poets with slim volumes. And see, too in that linguaceous stream, the tall monocled men, smelling of saddle soap and club armchairs, their breath a nice blending of whis-

ky and fox's blood, with big protruding upper-class tusks and county moustaches, presumably invented in England and sent abroad to advertise *Punch.*

Thomas has none of the 'traditional' English respect for understated effects, and there is clearly a connexion between this kind of ebullient virtuoso performance and the art of **"Fern Hill."** One is beguiled, not merely by the frank self-indulgence, but by the fertile recklessness of the prose, which is of a sort that one has to go back to Elizabethan writing to match. (pp. 66-73)

If we say that in Thomas's poems we often find, not the profound development of a theme within a minutely organised totality, but rather an almost improvisatory elaboration of a theme that remains itself fairly rudimentary, then we might go on to say that Thomas's poetry is to that of his immediate predecessor as jazz is to classical music. Arabesque begins to predominate over statement, and at the same time 'expression' acquires a new importance. (Thomas's broadcast or recorded readings of his poems contributed a good deal to their success). The poem is no longer to be regarded only independent, permanent creation on the printed page, but also as a 'live' communication, in the interests of which any or all of the modern media might be utilised. There is a conscious attempt to break down the wall that separates 'mass civilisation' from 'minority culture', and art begins to take on the appearance of a spontaneous 'manifestation' rather than a monument more lasting than bronze.

However, the 'jazz age' view of Thomas is incomplete, and I must move on to another aspect. Let us consider again the improvisatory *tone* of **"Fern Hill."** This tone is suggested by the breathless, elated movement of the lines, the punning, and the apparently wayward use of language in defiance of grammatical and logical relations. All these things appear to be connected with the child's experience of the world, and with the dramatic representation of that experience in poetry. However, one can see how Thomas's diction in this poem might be adapted to other uses: to the symbolic or 'stream of consciousness' representation of the adult psyche; to the achievement of surrealistic compression and association, and to a kind of impressionistic description of the natural scene. These, let me say, are among the healthier possibilities. There are others which critics have not been slow to seize upon, namely, tedious word-spinning, obscurity and pseudo-bardic declamation.

So far, I have spoken only of **"Fern Hill,"** which is principally about childhood, and in which the diction seems, as I have said, to be determined by the need to evoke dramatically the child's state of being. I want to introduce now a poem of purely adult consciousness [**"A Refusal to Mourn the Death, by Fire, of a Child in London"**].

> Never until the mankind making
> Bird beast and flower
> Fathering and all humbling darkness
> Tells with silence the last light breaking
> And the still hour
> Is come of the sea humbling in harness
>
> And I must enter again the round
> Zion of the water bead

And the synagogue of the ear of corn
Shall I let pray the shadow of a sound
Or sow my salt seed
In the least valley of sackcloth to mourn

The majesty and burning of the child's death.
I shall not murder
The mankind of her going with a grave truth
Nor blaspheme down the stations of the breath
with any further
Elegy of innocence and youth.

Deep with the first dead lies London's daughter,
Robed in the long friends,
The grains beyond age, the dark veins of her
    mother,
Secret by the unmourning water
Of the riding Thames.
After the first death, there is other.

I have time only for a brief comment. In the first stanza 'darkness' is both 'making' and 'humbling'. It 'makes' and 'humbles' mankind, in common with 'bird, beast and flower': it is the darkness of death as well as the womb, and of the chaos preceding creation as well as the chaos in which the universe ends with the last light 'breaking'. (Thomas characteristically puns on *breaking,* as he does later on the word *grave* in 'grave truth'.) In the second stanza the continuous movement from dark to dark becomes fully cyclical, as the speaker enters 'the round Zion of the water bead', a tricky phrase. 'Round' implies a cycle, but also the perfect sphere of a drop of water. That drop of water is a microcosm, an infinity of such drops makes up the sea, which is associated with 'darkness' both as source and end of life. It is a Zion by virtue of its brilliant purity, perhaps, but also because Zion, the Holy Land, is present in every particle of creation. It does not lie beyond the universe of created things, but rather within it, and it is in that universe and not beyond it that God has his being. Men come out of darkness and return into darkness, but with the implication of further resurrection. Never will Thomas 'blaspheme down the stations of the breath' with any further 'elegy of innocence of youth', not simply because compassion is out of place, or because there are already too many elegies, but because death is part of a cosmic process, to which there is no beginning, middle, and end, except in infinity. The 'unmourning water' of the Thames symbolises that process: it moves back to the sea, as 'London's daughter' returns to the 'first dead' and the 'dark veins of her mother', which implies at once the womb and the earth itself. 'After the first death, there is no other' implies, among other things, that individual deaths are implicit in the 'first death' and that to mourn them individually is therefore meaningless.

I am aware that I have left many questions unanswered, and perhaps some of them are unanswerable. Furthermore, there are possible critical objections to this poem which I am simply ignoring for the moment. All I want to suggest is that there is a clear affinity between the poetic diction of **"Fern Hill"** and that in this poem, and that further affinities exist between these two poems and the majority of Thomas's other poems. I have already suggested some of the uses to which the diction of **"Fern Hill"** might be, and is in fact, adapted: symbolic expression, free asso-

ciation, surrealistic compression and impressionistic description. Is it possible to link these together in a unified theory of Thomas's diction?

Here I must rely on quotation, from a book of modern literature by the American critic, J. Hillis Miller. He begins by quoting Thomas who said: 'I am lots of people', and then goes on:

. . . It is not a question of a first-person singular 'self' which becomes 'another' and enters into a new state of existence. Thomas from the beginning contains in himself the furtherest star. He is the centre of an adventure which is the total cosmic adventure, and, after the first experience of birth, which is coming into existence of everything, there is no possibility of adding more to the self. What exists for Thomas as soon as anything exists at all is a single, continuous realm which is at once consciousness, body, cosmos and the words which express all three at once.

To give an example, 'in the beginning' describes as identical events the creation of the universe by God, the creation of Adam, the formation of the poet's body in the womb, and his attainment of consciousness. If anything is prior in this series, it is God's all-creating word, but this is identical with the coming to consciousness of the poet.

The overlapping of body, mind and world means that language, which in conventional speech would apply to one of these three realms can be used to describe all three simultaneously. The difficulty of so many of his poems stems from the assertion as literally true of what would usually be thought of as metaphorical relations: e.g. 'The owls are bearing the farm away'.

Miller's explanation is a good attempt, and perhaps as successful as any could be, to state a unified theory of Thomas's diction though, of course, it cannot be used to 'explain' all the poems. He elaborates his arguments in the book from which these quotations are taken, and which has as its title *Poets of Reality.* You will have noticed that word: *'reality'.* Thomas is being credited by implication with the very achievement which is one of the highest aims of the poet, and which he has consistently been denied by his hostile critics.

This explanation makes some of Thomas's linguistic practices clearer, and weakens the charge of arbitrariness that has so often been brought against him. As an organising principle within his work there appears to be a cosmic vision with a logic of its own—perhaps we should add, a vision and a logic that actively repudiate those by which our society ordinarily lives. (pp. 74-8)

However, for readers brought up on 'the great tradition' (and of these I am one) there is a resistance to be overcome before Thomas can be taken really seriously. **"Fern Hill"** is one of Thomas's most easily accessible poems because the kind of cosmic egoism attributed to him by Hillis Miller is easier to take in a child than in an adult. For a child to imagine itself 'the centre of an adventure which is the total cosmic adventure' is one thing: for an adult to do so is another. The child's world of **"Fern Hill"** turns out, perhaps, to be a fairly close representation of adult reality, or at least of adult reality as perceived and communicated by a poet. The child's vision need only be slightly refined by the consciousness of time for it to become the full adult reality. Even then the change is not as fundamental as one might think.

> Time held me green and dying,
> Though I sang in my chains like the sea.

As in **"A Refusal to Mourn the Death"** . . . , green and dying exist almost statically within the same moment; they are not just opposite ends of a scale. Once again the image of the sea is significant, since, although it is time-bound, its movement within time is one of continuous withdrawal and resurgence, and it remains a symbol at once for the beginning and the end of life. Time is both linear and cyclical, as 'time in all its tuneful turnings' suggests. We remember, too, that the poem does not begin with the usual storyteller's formula 'Once upon a time', but with 'Now as I was . . . ', which implies a complex or paradoxical attitude to time. The effect of disillusioning consciousness in the poem is only relative, and we are not presented with a linear progression from childhood fantasy to adult maturity. In one perspective the farm *has* 'forever fled', leaving behind a disenchanted and perhaps envious adult, but in another perspective, also offered by the poem, both child and adult are present together in a single, timeless existence. Historically speaking, the time is lost; poetically speaking, the time is regained in the act of visionary creation.

Perhaps enough has been said for the moment in justification of Thomas's poetry. I have already mentioned a number of criticisms that have been levelled against it, and I should like to return briefly to them. The two most important seem to me to be that the poetry is meaningless, and that it is inhuman. To take the second point first: **"A Refusal to Mourn the Death"** . . . exhibits the potentially dangerous aspect of the visionary mentality. The poet assumes a rôle as interpreter of the universe, and the child's death becomes 'the majesty and burning' which solemnly affirms the visionary world beyond mundane actuality. There is (or perhaps should be) something in us that protests against such a high-handed view of things.

On the second point—namely that Thomas's poetry is generally meaningless—both the attacker and the defender are likely to find themselves stalemated in the end. As far as I can see it is impossible to prove or disprove the validity of Thomas's work in ordinary rational terms. We find ourselves forced to regard it as the social anthropologist might regard primitive myth: it is 'a sacred tale . . . divinely true for those who believe, but a fairy tale for those who do not'. Furthermore, the interpretation of vision or symbol may give us unique access to the human psyche, or to the nature of reality, and it may just as easily be nothing more than what Edmund Leach, in his book on Lévi-Strauss, calls 'clever talk'. Proof, or even consensus, appears to be unattainable. (pp. 79-80)

> *J. V. Crewe, "The Poetry of Dylan Thomas,"*
> in Theoria, *Pietermaritzburg, Vol. XXXVIII,*
> *May, 1972, pp. 65-83.*

AUTHOR'S COMMENTARY

I make one image—though "make" is not the word, I let, perhaps, an image be 'made' emotionally in me and then apply to it what intellectual and critical forces I possess—let it breed another, let that image contradict the first, make, of the third image bred of the other two together, a fourth contradictory image, and let them all, within my imposed formal limits, conflict. . . . Out of the inevitable conflict of images—inevitable because of the creative, recreative, destructive and contradictory nature of the motivating centre, the womb of war—I try to make that momentary peace which is a poem. . . .

(letter date 1938)

J. M. Kertzer (essay date 1979)

[*In the excerpt below, Kertzer analyzes the lyrical and metaphysical qualities of Thomas's early poems.*]

In a letter complaining about the composition of *Under Milk Wood*, Dylan Thomas noted that through "the complicated violence of the words," his comedy was turning into "some savage and devious metaphysical lyric." The phrase more accurately describes his early poetry, which intricately and energetically argues about questions of life and death in a manner which is nevertheless lyrical. Friends and biographers agree that, though he had a perceptive mind, Thomas was no philosopher. But he argued as a poet, not as a philosopher, and there is little value in reducing his poetry to its ideas. The question is neither how intelligent he was nor how extensive his reading nor how sophisticated his ideas, but rather how he wrote poetry: how he *used* ideas, displayed them and dramatized their conflict to persuade his readers. We must consider in what way Thomas regarded poetry as a vehicle of thought, debate, and persuasion; how he set himself within his poetic disputes; and what logic he used to shape his arguments and make them systematic.

Thomas' critics have continually made two rival claims: some insist that he is "the least intellectual poet of the century" because his poetry does not appeal to or depend on reason; others hold that his work displays "rigorous intellectual organization" which provokes a subtle play of thought. The first claim is not just that Thomas' "mind had no metaphysical proclivities," but that his poems do not rely on logic because they are "not intellectual or cerebral, but so spontaneous that the poet himself might well be amazed and bewildered in the face of them." They attempt to "short-cut the reason" in pursuit of "extrarational communication." The second claim accepts Thomas' debt to "the cult of irrationality," but finds that he combines "the irrational bases of poetic power with a rigorous intellectual control" that prompts a metaphysical debate [from Geoffrey Moore in "Dylan Thomas"]: "Central to his work, therefore, is a proto-philosophical, impassioned *questioning* of the ultimates—origins and ends—of existence. The vision which results is not philosophical in the abstract sense, but concrete, imaginative, poetic."

Thomas himself seems to sanction both views. He asserted in an early poem: "The head's vacuity can breed no truth / Out of its sensible tedium." He defended his poems by telling Vernon Watkins that their "form was consistently emotional" and "illogical naturally: except by a process it's too naturally obvious to misexplain." Yet he proclaimed himself a "painstaking, conscientious, involved and devious craftsman in words," and advised Pamela Hansford Johnson to "intellectualize more" and to put her "literary intelligence to work." More importantly, he sought to reconcile the two views by advocating "passionate ideas" that come to life "out of the red heart through the brain." Both thought and feeling must be engaged in "the antagonistic interplay of emotions and ideas . . . brain chords and nerve chords." The song must be devious and thought-provoking; the metaphysic must be lyrical.

Early in his career, Thomas tried to write with "intellectual passion," only to find: "I have been told to reason by the heart / But heart, like head, leads helplessly." His problem was how to reconcile two faculties which are unruly in themselves and antagonistic, a problem which engaged his fundamental notions of what poetry is, how it makes its statements and argues its case. (pp. 293-95)

Thomas felt that a poem must prove itself by engaging the reader in a strenuous emotional and intellectual adventure. [In *Dylan Thomas in America*], John Malcolm Brinnen reports that Thomas

> had picked up somewhere a notion that he liked: poems are hypothetical and theorematic. In this view the hypothesis of a poem would be the emotional experience, the instant of vision or insight, the source of radiance, the minute focal point of impulse and impression. While these make up what is commonly called inspiration, poetic logic should prove the validity of the ephemeral moments they describe. To look at a new poem, then, is to ask: How successfully does it demonstrate its hypothesis?

To be valid, every poem must establish its own "logic" through which it moves towards its own end. A poem has to prove something, though it be nothing but itself: it is "its own question and answer . . . the bullet and the bull's eye." A poem must not state, but demonstrate. Thomas told Pamela Hansford Johnson not simply to assert in her poetry that she is one with nature, but to "prove it" through "the magic of words and images." A poet must make his words "effectively true" if he is to convince the reader and win him over.

The truth of a poetic demonstration must be enforced by language that displays "heart and mind and muscle," for poetry is also an argument in the sense of a brawling dispute. Its passionate ideas require a "passionate wordiness" that comes from "a pen dipped in fire and vinegar." Forcefulness and vitality of language overwhelm the reader and compel belief: hence the immature violence which Thomas wished to control, but not to subdue. He felt that a poet should be "a person of words in action" who makes his writing "an event, a happening, an action perhaps, not a still life." The momentary peace which is a poem comes

only after a battle of words and wits, a prolonged effort which he often called an "adventure."

"All poetical impulses," wrote Thomas, "are towards the creation of adventure. And adventure is movement." The adventure of a poem is the unfolding and enforcing of its hypothesis. As it moves towards its own end, a poem raises questions, explores the unknown, conducts a "brief adventure in the wilderness." That wilderness rests in the self, because poetry is essentially introspective. Here Thomas' concern with how poems work merges with his need to set himself within them, and so gives rise to his characteristic themes. The forms of his arguments—the ways in which he reasons by the heart—arise from the fact that he is the hero of his adventures. (pp. 295-96)

Thomas' devious metaphysical lyric is an argument, hypothesis, or dispute about the adventure of himself, and its forms are determined by the way he conceives of the self. He does not, especially in the early poetry, present an autobiographical self, perhaps because he was aware of the dangers of arrogance and sentimentality that beset the lyric egoist. He disparaged the "saccharine wallowings of near-schoolboys in the bowels of a castrated muse," and the "private masturbatory preoccupation of the compulsive egoist." As a corrective, he created an impersonal, dramatic, fabulous self, set at a safe distance from the author, to serve as hero and victim of an epic adventure. Like other mythical heroes, the self is born to face a great curse and a great destiny. From the instant of sexual conception, it has a powerful potential that it strives to realize. An implicit urgency, which it shares with all life, drives the self on a quest for liberation, self-assertion, and self-possession. There is little sense of peace or repose in Thomas' poetry—even in the later brooding and nostalgic pieces—because of the passionate wordiness that urges the hero through his adventure. . . . In the published poetry the impulse [for liberation] is expressed through the imagery of sun, song, ascent, and, later, grace, joy, glory. When, in **"If I Were Tickled by the Rub of Love,"** Thomas proclaims "Man be my metaphor," he affirms his adventure and proclaims the self, despite its contradictions, the standard of all creation. Many of his arguments aim at, but not all achieve, this conclusion.

Thomas' effort to liberate the self and celebrate its life, so often remarked in the later poems, is present in the early ones as well. Here, however, it is continually thwarted by the grandeur of his enterprise. The hero, identified with all creation, engages in a "total cosmic adventure" so vast that it seems fatal. He is swept through a predestined history by forces beyond his control. Because he cannot even control his own impulses, he must assert himself and seek liberation through powers which he has not mastered. Consequently, he seems to be the "victim of his experience," and is often defeated by his own argument. Life proves to be a "mortal miracle," a double cross, a wound healed only by death. Very early in his career Thomas seized on the paradox that was to provoke, promote, and thwart his arguments: "my everlasting ideas of the importance of death on the living." . . . The early poetry argues whether or not death will have dominion, and questions the nature of its sovereignty and the worth of the self subject to its rule. The debate is endless, marked by temporary victories and defeats: rarely do the poems achieve a clear assertion or denial. The characteristic argument goes astray, and the poem then struggles, with or without success, to set it straight. The poetry subverts the very terms through which it seeks to define and affirm the self. It aims at liberation, but cannot identify its freedom within the "grief of certainty," time. It sings of love, but tastes the poison of sin and sex. The hero discovers that he is his own adversary, and through his arguments may condemn himself.

As soon as the young Thomas sought to give shape to his yearnings for power and freedom, he experimented with techniques that would offer perspective, direction, and momentum. He sought a system to turn them into adventures and arguments. A common theme in the early *Notebook* poems is the difficulty of reasoning by the heart, of expressing in an orderly manner the troubled feelings of adolescence:

> And my thoughts flow so uneasily
> There is no measured sea for them,
> No place in which, wave perched on wave,
> Such energy may gain
> The sense it has to have.

The measured sea he lacks is a poetic which would give coherence and energy to his ideas, and sense to his emotions. It is a principle of order, a logic:

> Tether the first thought if you will,
> And take the second to yourself
> Close for companion, and dissect it, too, . . .

The aim of his analysis is to make sense of and so liberate all aspects of his being. . . . (pp. 297-99)

The first logic that Thomas tried and immediately rejected was narrative. It provides a sequential pattern, the "movement" of a "living story," and a strong narrating voice to give rhetorical power to his adventure. After a few attempts, often in a Yeatsian manner (**"Osiris, Come to Isis," "Hassan's Journey into the World"**), Thomas abandoned this method, but he retained the desire for a narrative principle. He continued to stress the need for a "progressive line, or theme, of movement in every poem," a "thread of action" that ensured a "rhythmic, inevitably narrative, movement." Only in works like **"A Winter's Tale"** and **"Ballad of the Long-Legged Bait"** would narrative in the strict sense return to his poetry, but the progressive line remains in the early poetry. Instead of stories, however, these poems present dramatic situations, moments of insight or conflict. . . . Or they show through temporal clauses that they are parts of a more extensive narrative: **"Before We Sinned (Incarnate Devil)," "Before I knocked," "Before we mothernaked fell," "When once the twilight locks."** (pp. 299-300)

In these instances, it is the narrative shape, the contours of the experience, that Thomas retains. From a comment about a poem in a letter to Vernon Watkins—"I have made such a difficult shape"—it is apparent that Thomas regarded the whole poem as a shape. Poetry is the "sound of shape," or a "rumpus of shapes" using figures of speech which are "wordy shapes." The figure a poem makes as it traces the curves of emotion and thought is its argument:

> A hole in space shall keep the shape of thought,
> The lines of earth, the curving of the heart,
> And from this darkness spin the golden soul.

These lines describe both the impalpable human spirit and the formation of a poem. Because Thomas' argument always concerns himself, because poem, ego, and adventure are identified, their shape must come from the self. His hero is a "merry manshape" formed in the creative "shaping time" in maternal "dens of shape." His shape is, in one sense, his personality as it develops from birth to death. When he speaks of his "wizard shape," he means the magical life of a poet. When he prays, "I would be woven a religious shape," he means a holy life. Several of the "process" poems follow the shape of the hero's life from love's first fever to her plague, and the later birthday poems are stages in the same adventure. But Thomas is not content to trace the hazards of a lifetime; if he were, he would have been satisfied with narrative and autobiography. The shape of his argument corresponds to the shape of the self in another sense.

As we have observed, the adventure is presented as a mythic exploration, a struggle from dark to light, a voyage "into the sea of yourself like a young dog [to] bring out a pearl." The pearl is assertion of both the self and its adventure: the poet-creator must look upon his work and see that it is good. He argues against death in order to make "an affirmation of the beautiful and terrible worth of the Earth." But only poetry offers the means of affirmation. The quest is conducted solely within the poem, not in the life of the writer, and the poem must sustain that effort. It must not narrate, but demonstrate and prove its case. The whole exercise is a verbal one, a contest of images and the ideas and emotions which they express. The development of the poem must dramatize this struggle. . . . [The shape of Thomas' arguments] depends on the disposition of the self in its struggle for understanding and liberation.

Thomas sought to replace narrative with a system that would retain a narrative dynamic, trace the contours of his experience without relying on biography, and dramatize the shaping process of his own awareness. He did not, of course, deliberately set out to discover such a system; he merely followed the example of other poets. [In his *Articulate Energy*] Donald Davie sees this desire to "articulate without asserting," to give "the morphology of the feeling, not its distinctive nature"—or, in our terms, to give the shape of an experience but not its substance—as part of the symbolist legacy of modern poetry, the desire to write poetry that aspires to the condition of music. He gives as characteristic techniques "the invention of a fable or an 'unreal' landscape, or the arrangement of images, not for their own sakes, but to stand as a correlative for the experience that is thus the true subject of a poem in which it is never named." Thomas used all three forms, separately and in combination. (pp. 300-01)

Fables offer Thomas an appeal to both heart and head through their sensuous images (sight) and the hidden significance or moral (trust) which they dramatize. They aid him in what Walford Davies calls [in his essay "The Wanton Starer"] "mythologizing the actual," giving a vivid and noble shape to his experiences. For example, "Today, This Insect," which adapts the lines quoted above, shows the poet in the act of transforming an ordinary insect into the "plague of fables." Fables also offer Thomas the power and elevation he demanded of poetry, contact with other works of literature and, above all, heroes to undertake the quest of self-liberation. His favorite fables are the Biblical adventure, moving from Genesis to the Apocalypse; the "Christian voyage" from annunciation to resurrection; the human pilgrimage from conception to death. Comparable to these, and giving voice to them, is a fable of language, advancing from "rocking alphabet" and first Word to a "world of words," the whole universe made articulate. . . . (pp. 301-02)

The value of these fables lies in their congruent, organic shapes. All are voyages over the "seafaring years" impelled by "the drive of time." Time is the forum and often the antagonist of the early adventures ("But time has set its maggot on their track"), and sometimes seems to be the cruel god whose disfavor the epic hero flees. It is also, paradoxically, the impulse of growth and liberation. Time both sustains and kills us, providing the energy to live and to die. It is thief and surgeon, grief and patient gentleman. The temporal shape of the fables also depends on the continuity of inheritance: the heritage of Biblical sin; of Christian suffering and redemption; of human and family traits; of "All that I owe the fellows of the grave." Inheritance is the ambiguous blessing of time. It comprises both an external force, the curse of "bonebound fortune" imposed on us, and an inner compulsion present in us from the moment of conception. It is a principle of unity and diversity, giving us our distinguishing features, yet joining us to the family of mankind from Adam to the present. . . . It offers a legacy of pleasure and pain, of "all the flesh inherits," including growth and decay, as Thomas suggests through puns on the words wax, sheet, grain:

> All night and day I wander in these same
> Wax clothes that wax upon the ageing ribs;
> All night my fortune slumbers in its sheet,
> Then look, my heart, upon the scarlet trove,
> And look, my grain, upon the falling wheat.

Through such puns and paradoxes, Thomas likes to compress the beginning and end of a fable into a phrase: "the living grave," "the milk of death," "the endless beginning," "My Jack of Christ born thorny on the tree." Their congruent shapes make the fables interchangeable: every man is "Jack Christ," and every baby is "sea-sucked Adam in the hollow hulk." Three fables converge in the phrase "the Christ-cross-row (that is, the alphabet) of death." All the fables merge in the poem **"In the Beginning"**:

> In the beginning was the pale signature,
> Three-syllabled and starry as the smile;
> And after came the imprints on the water,
> Stamp of the minted face upon the moon;
> The blood that touched the crosstree and the
>   grail
> Touched the first cloud and left a sign.

The starry, three-syllabled signature is Jehovah, Jesus Christ, zodiac, *lux fiat,* the poet's work, and all of creation. The imprints on the water are Christ's footsteps, poetry, the face of the waters at creation and at birth. The man in the moon adds another fable to the freshly coined creation, while the grail suggests the quests of Christ, Adam ("the ribbed original of love") and every man through a universe marked with ambivalent signs and portents. Thomas delights in interweaving fables in this way, developing a poem by increasing its range of reference and thereby making its texture increasingly rich. Its logic depends on the discovery of correspondences between adventures. Its argument is the confirmation of the fables and their common shape and, through the Biblical tone, the celebration of the unity, harmony, vitality, and sexuality of creation. Such a poem proves that man is heroic and at home in a universe which is human and passionate.

The culmination of this line of argument is **"Altarwise by Owl-light,"** the most devious of Thomas' metaphysical lyrics and the most strenuous of his adventures. Though filled with passionate and witty dispute, it remains lyrical, a sonnet sequence using imagery of song and music to express the cosmic harmony its hero once again seeks. The "tale's sailor" is Christ, Adam, the poet, Rip Van Winkle, Ishmael, Odysseus, and Pharaoh, all intermingled through a network of cross-references and a deliberate confusion of personal pronouns. Its shape depends on the progression of these adventures and on a series of contests between rival forces: devil and angel, Abaddon and Jack Christ, winter and spring, worm and whale, evil index and Lord's Prayer, furies and ladies, Cancer and Capricorn, crossbones and sawbones, time's joker and time's nerve, hollow and marrow, flood and rainbow, desert and garden. The dispute grows in range and complexity due to a sense of expansion from the microscopic to the cosmic, from "short spark" to "long world," a process of elaboration that accounts for, though it may not always justify, the encyclopedic character of the imagery.

Although the fables contribute patterns of imagery to the poem, they do not make it a linear narrative. All their episodes are present simultaneously, often compressed into a phrase: "the scarecrow word," "The gentleman lay graveward with his furies," "December's thorn screwed in a brow of holly." The dynamic, which Thomas saw as the essence of narrative, derives instead from the proliferation of contrasts and correspondences between and within fables; from the sense of expansion and elaboration; and from a regular rhythm of affirmation and denial that dramatizes the poet's struggle to understand and accept his fate. Each sonnet disputes the central issue—"the importance of death on the living" and of life on the dying—seeking to affirm the validity of the dispute and the worth of the self. If we consider the poem as a whole and avoid the confusion of many of the details, we can see the arguments arranged in paired sonnets, each pair examining one stage of the adventure, but reaching opposite conclusions. The first and last sonnets provide a frame, setting the limits of the fables from genesis in the Christward shelter to the harbor of the Day of Judgment. Corresponding images suggest departure in the first, arrival or completion in the last. We begin in the direction of the beginning, "altarwise," approaching the mystery, hatching heaven's egg;

and end "atlaswise," after seeing the world and its wonders, finding the nest of mercies. We start with the "windy salvage" of creation, and finish with the "ship-racked gospel" of the apocalypse. (pp. 302-05)

Because **"Altarwise by Owl-light"** gradually discovers, confirms and proves the wonder of . . . [the everyday magic of life] through its exploration of the fables and the growing density of their interrelation, the poem as a whole is affirmative. Its argument is conducted with equivocal terms and images, through confidence and doubt, assertion and denial, to a final affirmation which prevails because of the periodic defeats that it subsumes. The sequence ends with a call to "let the garden diving / Soar." The "nest of mercies" is woven with the "gold straws of venom." Death is not negated, but incorporated into the harmonious shape of the whole argument.

The mythical landscape which Thomas uses to give shape to his arguments is an aspect of his interest in fables. It too first appears in the notebooks where he relies on the changing features of a scene to express the development of thought and feeling. The setting is sometimes literal, sometimes metaphorical. . . . The landscape that emerges in the early poetry is general, composed of earth, air, fire, and water, driven by elemental forces of weather, wind, tides, and seasons. It varies little from poem to poem. In the "process" poems, the scene moves inward and becomes the human anatomy, which Thomas called "my solid and fluid world of flesh and blood":

> We see the secret wind behind the brain,
> The sphinx of light sit on the eyes,
> The code of stars translate in heaven.
> A secret night descends between
> The skull, the cells, the cabinned ears
> Holding for ever the dead moon.

Only in later poems such as **"Over St. John's Hill"** and **"In the White Giant's Thigh"** does the landscape reemerge as a recognizable Welsh scene, and even then it retains some of its fabulous qualities. Thomas noted the shift in his use of landscape when he referred to **"Poem in October"** (published in February, 1945) as "a Laugharne poem: the first place poem I've written."

Thomas argues through landscape just as he does through fables. The setting provides images that replace the experience that occurs within it. Poems of this sort give only the lie of the land. . . . They are obscure because they never declare the exact nature of the experience in question; they present a conflict of natural forces or evoke an atmosphere which is never precisely defined. The best example of a poem arguing by exploring its landscape is **"We Lying by Seasand."** . . . Thomas compresses his narrative to one episode of effort and failure. Very little happens to the human figures whose ineffectual desires are indicated by the verbs of the poem: mock, deride, follow, watch, fend off. Instead, Thomas concentrates on the setting and establishes, mainly through nouns and adjectives, a contrast between the grave, yellow seasand and the more colorful red rivers and "Navy blue bellies of the tribes." The first setting is passive and supine; the second, with its suggestion of poetry ("Alcove of words") and sailors is active and adventurous. The "calling for colour," which is the

main desire of the poem, is also expressed through landscape and, in particular, through the wind which will "blow away / The strata of the shore and leave red rock." Feeble though it may be, this is the call to action and self-assertion which Thomas' poems frequently make. But the characters make no real effort ("But wishes breed not"), and their desires are thwarted by the very landscape through which they tried to assert them. The wind proves ambiguous: instead of a breath of life, it is a "sandy smother . . . of death."

Ambiguous and untrustworthy, the landscape subverts the argument of the poem, and the lethargic rhythm undercuts the call to action. The logic is confounded by confused syntax ("mock who deride / Who follow") that makes it uncertain who is doing what, and by misleading connectives. In the lines "For in this yellow grave twixt sea and sand / A calling for colour calls with the wind," the word "For" seems to be announcing a logical connection to advance the argument. But in fact it does not relate the earlier mocking and deriding to the subsequent "calling for colour." . . . [The] mind tries and fails to make sense of its experience. It confounds itself and, through its attempt to reason, dramatizes a state of torpor and confusion. The failure to argue coherently by interpreting the landscape expresses the condition of the characters, whose attempt to rouse themselves is subverted by the very effort of doing so.

Thomas' revisions of the poem, far from clarifying the argument, subvert it further. He expands and complicates the landscape, and so complicates the experience it represents. The additions increase the poem's density and ambiguity by confusing the impulses towards affirmation and dissolution, life and death. They both counter and confirm the torpor which inhibits the poem's development. For example, the line "That's grave and *gray* as grave and sea" becomes "That's grave and *gay* as grave and sea," thereby varying the music of the line and making wind and sea simultaneously deadly and lively (my italics). (pp. 306-09)

Setting, rhythm, and the confusion of syntax, logic, and imagery all serve to portray a divided state of mind, striving but failing to come to terms with its own confusion, asserting itself yet lapsing back into lethargy and anguish. And after all, we still do not know exactly what the experience is. In his *Reader's Guide,* W. Y. Tindall reads love, poetry, T. S. Eliot, politics, Hitler, and war into the poem, an interpretation which seems farfetched because Thomas resolutely argues only through the landscape, finding there the shapes of feeling and desire and of his poetic effort to master them.

From fable and landscape, Thomas draws "warring" images which he links . . . in a "dialectical" sequence of conflicting images. For our purposes, the most telling aspect of his description is not its dialectic, but its insistence on the generative power of language. Thomas wants to account for what he calls the "life in any poem of mine." He speaks in organic terms (breed, central seed, born and die, the womb of war) in order to indicate the vitality or muscle through which poetry enforces its claims and compels belief. On another occasion he declared that poetry must be "orgiastic and organic as copulation, dividing and unifying," as it grows or forces its way "from words, from the substance of words and the rhythm of substantial words set together." The poet works "out of " rather than "towards" words (a distinction Thomas was fond of and used throughout his career) because they are the source of energy, the main weapon in the war of images and ideas. Their power resides in their music and in the various ways they can convey meaning. Sound and rhythm may be enough to animate language: "And what a pleasure of baskets! Trugs, creels, pottles and punnets, heppers, dorsers and mounds, wiskets and whiskets. And if these are not the proper words, they should be." Thomas plays with words to dazzle the reader. Admitting that he has invented some of the terms is itself a tactic, a way of drawing attention to the words, delighting in their sounds, and so endowing them with power. They are coined for the occasion and meaningful only in context, not because they provide more precise definitions, but because they are convincing, or "effectively true." They win the reader's admiration and approval.

Words are generative when they display such vitality or when they expand in significance or implication. In his early work especially, Thomas experimented with various ways of expressing, compressing, and concealing meaning, of saying "two things at once in one word, four in two and one in six." One tactic was to use images of multiplication to insist, sometimes without further proof, on a process of growth and complication:

> In me ten paradoxes make one truth,
> Ten twining roots meet twining in the earth
> To make one root that never strangles light.
>
> From the divorcing sky I learnt the double,
> The two-framed globe that spun into a score;
> A million minds gave suck to such a bud
> As forks my eye.

Thomas also cultivated ambiguities through puns, conflated and rearranged words: manwax, tide-tongued, Bible-leaved, the man in the wind, and the west moon. He stretched metaphors and similes to see how remote such comparisons could be, how far they could tease the imagination:

> She is a lady of high degree,
> Proud and hard, and she wears a coat
> Clinging and strident,
> Like a net or a basket for berries.

He elaborated the contradictions of a paradox to explore its ramifications:

> For welcoming sleep we welcome death,
> And death's an end to sleep,
> And sleep to death, an end to love,
> Ending and sleeping,
> Love sleeps and ends for it cannot last.

These are early, sometimes clumsy efforts to tap the generative power of language by using ambiguity, comparison, and contradiction as principles of elaboration to expand the meanings condensed in imagery. Such expansion acts like the movement of narrative, permitting Thomas to portray "A season's fancy flown into a figure." The progression of images charts his devious, lyrical adventure

and directs his struggle for self-understanding and assertion because it may, as Alastair Fowler says in discussing **"Fern Hill,"** "mime growth of consciousness." Often it actively hinders that growth by disclosing the ambiguities inherent in the imagery. The paradox of time, which at once creates and destroys, is a common source of warring images that generate and complicate Thomas' arguments.

"I Know This Vicious Minute's Hour" is based on a sequence of contrasting images that track the poet's sensibilities and divided impulses in a quest for escape ("Go is my wish") and self-possession ("I want reality to hold / within my palm"). The paradox of time suggested by the "vicious minute's hour"—an hour's anguish compressed into a minute—prompts a contest between head and heart, silver moment and vicious minute, circle and stair, love and lust ("blood"). Because the heart, with its "sour motion in the blood," creates anguish, it is condemned for being offensive and passionate: "Too full with blood to let my love flow in." But here the paradox comes into play: the firm reality sought to oppose the unruly heart is associated with time ("Stop is unreal") and therefore with the "periodic heart" which beats out the vicious minutes of life. To renounce the heart is to renounce the life it gives. Consequently, the argument confounds itself. "I go or die," the poet concludes, showing that he remains "caught in midair" between the contradictions of his nature, unable to stop, yet unable to proceed confidently. (pp. 309-12)

As in the case of fables and landscapes, the tendency of this line of argument with its continual elaboration and contradiction is towards dense, cryptic poems which defy not only the reader's but the poet's attempt to reason out his dilemma. **"Grief Thief of Time"** is a good example of a poem of this sort; it argues through warring, proliferating images whose dispute is prompted and sustained by the paradox of time; and its argument is subverted by the inconsistency of its premises.

Thomas revised the early version of the poem, obscuring its clear statements and increasing the ambiguity of its images in order to render a complex vision of the interdependence of grief, love, life, and death. He made the key words of the argument interchangeable. Time, traditionally the subtle thief of youth, is identified with both life and the aging that leads to death. Grief is the thief robbing us of time, life, and love. Yet grief *is* time, because the passage of time is a process of grieving (as in **"A Grief Ago"**). And grief *is* love with its attendant pain, because lovers lie "loving with the thief," just as in a later poem they will lie "abed / With all their griefs in their arms." Love is the force that defies time ("blew time to his knees") and sustains life; but it is also, as an agent of generation and grief, an ally of time and death. Implicit in the poem is the old sexual pun on the verb "to die": hence "the bone of youth" and "the stallion grave." The argument is conducted with equivocal terms so that all assertions suggest their opposites, adversaries prove to be allies, affirmations prove to be denials.

The first stanza elaborates the setting, a seascape for another fabulous adventure. Its heroes are predecessors of Captain Cat in *Under Milk Wood:* they recall the high tide of passion from their "seafaring years . . . in a time of stories." Robbed of vitality, the old forget the pain, the "lean time," and the shame ("albatross") of their grief, and remember only the lusty adventures ("salt-eyed stumble bedward where she lies") which seemed to defy time. But the images of memory are untrustworthy, indicating that there is no escape from time or grief. The adventurous sea is tomb as well as womb ("moon-drawn grave"); the tide measures the flight of time as well as the height of passion; the "salt-eyed" sailors stumble from tears of grief as well as excitement. Even crueler is the paradox that the remembered woman "timelessly lies loving with the thief"—that is, both grief and time—suggesting that we must embrace our fates even though they prove unkind. Yet the woman lies with the sailor: apparently he himself is the thief, both victim and perpetrator of the crime of life. The next stanza confirms the identity of thief and hero; the old men are called "Jack my fathers," a name which corresponds to the "knave of pain," grief, from the first stanza.

The second stanza elaborates the image of the thief, and in it the poet addresses the old men, speaking with a confidence that the poem does not support and offering advice that, given its ambiguous terms, can only be equivocal. He advises them to let the thief escape because his loot is deadly, sinful, and ghoulish: "These stolen bubbles have the bites of snakes / And the undead eye-teeth." He tells them not to indulge the "third eye" of memory, now reduced to a "eunuch crack," not to recall the rainbow of sexual union and prolong grief throughout one's life "down the weeks' / Dayed peaks." He counsels them to accept their losses and their lives, yet to release grief ("free the twin-boxed grief") is to cry or grieve for bed and coffin, one lost, the other approaching. There is no escape from grief or from time because the hero is identified with his enemy. In the final judgment of the poem, the criminal is condemned to contemplate images of his own condition. He is punished with his own crime: "All shall remain and on the graveward gulf / Shape with my fathers' thieves."

How far this conclusion is from a direct affirmation or from transcendence of the vicious circle of life and death is apparent in comparison with an earlier version of the lines:

When the knave of death arrives,
Yield the lost flesh to him and give your ghost;
All shall remain, and on the cloudy coast
Walk the blithe host
Of god and ghost with you, their newborn son.

Instead of a blithe resurrection of the spirit, the later version presents a recapitulation of the paradoxes that prompted the poem. "All shall remain"; yet all shall be stolen. The "graveward gulf," like the "moon-drawn grave," is the abyss of life, both womb and tomb. The fathers both steal and are stolen by time and grief in the phrase "my fathers' thieves." The newborn son from the notebook is still present, though not as an angel, but as a future thief. The figure taking "shape" (being born and dying) in the last line is the poet himself, since he has acknowledged himself the offspring of the old men ("Jack my fathers"), the son of love, grief, and time. He inherits their crime and their adventure, and finds himself—as in **"Altarwise by Owl-light"**—entrenched in the human condition of time and generation. But the poem does not offer the same affirmative attitude from within that condition. Instead—as in **"Upon Your Held-Out Hand"**—it attempts to offer consoling advice called into question by the very images in which it is expressed. The poem concludes with the self, the point at which all the arguments begin, but with a self which has not been set free because it is defined in terms of its own dissolution.

Given Thomas' mischievous and mistrustful self-consciousness, his reliance on ambiguous premises, equivocal images, and techniques that complicate and contradict, it is not surprising that his early poetry grows increasingly devious until it argues itself into confusion. Neither is it surprising that in subsequent work he began to look for means of simplifying his poems, though in ways that would not rob them of their power and adventurousness. In the best of his early poems, however, the finely crafted confusion dramatizes his effort to understand and free himself or, at least, to affirm a self he has failed to understand. (pp. 313-15)

> *J. M. Kertzer, "'Argument of the Hewn Voice': The Early Poetry of Dylan Thomas," in* Contemporary Literature, *Vol. XX, No. 3, Summer, 1979, pp. 293-315.*

Diane Ackerman   (essay date 1987)

[*In the following excerpt, Ackerman comments upon Thomas's frenzied, unique use of metaphors and linguistics, asserting that "no poet gives a greater sense of the feel of life."*]

It is unfortunate when a poet's personality, indeed his pageant of a private life, gets in the way of his poems, and perhaps even worse, thanks to the human love of spectacle, when his voice itself obtrudes. The trouble with Dylan Thomas is that he played up the bardic role for all it was worth, even to the extent of resorting to vocal melodrama as the redeemer of inferior poems (as well as the perfect embodiment of good ones). Trying to read him plain, on the page, gets one into the grandiosity that includes Yeats's cloak, the eyes Shelley saw in nipples, and Byron's

Thomas at the bar of the White Horse Tavern, his favorite New York City haunt.

moonlit comminations among the ruins upon Sir Samuel Romilly. One has to try, though, and I've done so off and on out of a variety of motives: trying to hear the quieter and more straightforward poems without sideband splash from the turbulent, noisy ones; wondering how much genuine vision lay behind the mumbo jumbo and the sometimes frantic, Klein-bottled imager; trying to relate the knobbly concreteness of his poems about everyday surfaces to the omnipresent madman howling at the moon from the attic. After all, who hasn't puzzled about how to get from that aromatic, audible, by now rather hackneyed, Welsh Christmas to the visceral spirals of gristle, bone, hair, seaweed in his other poems? He doesn't shift from atom to star along logical lines of inference. It's almost an epistemological dyslexia. I think he wants to make the shift, but is kept from managing it by a specialized ignorance that restricts him to myth. I mean that you will find Adam or Gabriel in the way, the one with a rubber ball stolen from a toilet cistern, the other with a pair of six-shooters, and this gives even the best poems an air of facetious interpolation. Not that I assume certain things just can't be put into poems, or have poems made from them; or that the accumulated trivia in an idiosyncratic person's head cannot function as a lightning conductor for the gravest, the most inexplicable, and ravishing matters known. But it makes Thomas quirky when his rhythms announce something majestic in the offing. It makes him elliptical beyond most readers' willingness to make a leap of mind.

What he does provide, though, is a circular continuum in which things lose their identity in the identities of other things ("a rumpus of shapes") until the reader is haunted by an acute sense of how physical life is, and how freely things metamorphose one into another. No poet gives a greater sense of the *feel of life*. One thing in another's context works him into a frenzy of neighborly reverence, provoking metaphors that don't so much combine A and B as trail both A and B through the slush of other phenomena. I don't know when I last saw the word *nympholepsy* used, but I am going to use it now. It means, or meant, "a frenzy induced by having seen nymphs" and is no doubt common. It also means "an obsession for something unobtainable." Thomas gets into this state often enough for it to become a habit, and that other nymph-like sense of things—when the young of any insect undergoes metamorphosis—attracts him too because it suggests both the discrete entities in nature and the quickness of the life process itself. Thomas weds himself to as many forms of life as he can spot, in a frenzy that becomes an act of homage to Creation, and mainly to it in a state of chaos.

For Thomas, nature is a force field, an open-ended experiment. By garbling taxonomy and larding language with a free hand, he seems at times to reproduce in the linguistic medium itself the actual feel of life as it might come to a drunk, or a deer, or a devout astronomer freezing to death at his telescope aimed at the Virgo-Coma region of the galaxies. This primitive, atavistic mania is fairly uncommon, but the communication of it through language—the unlanguaged via language itself—is just about unique. Some readers will not want it, feeling that such poetry makes too many demands of their taxonomic sense, or that the whole

idea is just a pretext for being obscure. Take this random sample:

> Because the pleasure-bird whistles after the hot
>   wires,
> Shall the blind horse sing sweeter?

Successive readings of, or guesses at, this can widen the couplet out until it becomes everything and nothing, not only an emblem of bird-song on telephone wires crammed with information a bird knows nothing about (any more than the horse in the field below which is blinkered like a resting falcon?), but also a dizzy meander among phenomena that don't belong together: wire of the canary's cage, wire in a jew's-harp, electricity flowing along a cable, nonsense through the mis-conductor of a bad syllogism (A bird cannot hear what's in the wires—the horse is minus a dimension too—so do both perform better for their being undistracted?). Admittedly these are not Thomas's most rewarding lines, but they share the speculative disruption of things that elsewhere raises itself to an exponential maximum equivalent to, at least, a vision of Rimbaud's. . . . (pp. 86-7)

Look now at one of the poems Thomas himself discussed: **"If my head hurt a hair's foot,"** a poem similar to the prenatal empathy of Louis MacNeice's "Prayer before Birth," or Beckett's *Texts for Nothing,* which tracks what seems to be the thirteen days between April 1st and Good Friday, April 13th, the day on which Beckett was born in 1906. The first stanza of Thomas's poem goes as follows:

> If my head hurt a hair's foot
> Pack back the downed bone. If the unpricked
>   ball of my breath
> Bump on a spout let the bubbles jump out.
> Sooner drop with the worm of the ropes round
>   my throat
> Than bully ill love in the clouted scene.

Histrionic delicacy is appropriate here. Perhaps we are not far from the day when instruments will give us an exact idea of how the fetus feels during labor (children have already been quizzed for their very first memories). The stanza teems with associations, most of which work into the poem and clarify it by multiplying its impact. The emergent head has hair of its own, so the care for hair is double. The idea of "down" works on several levels, from fleece to downward and as far as fleece-clad bone, which includes skull too. There is no need to follow all the colliding implications of "unpricked ball," "Bump on a spout," and "bubbles"; enough to say we are in a realm of post- and pre-sexual Cartesian diving, with somewhere an unstated image of a child's balloon, which some readers will need more than others. As for "ropes" and "clouted," they are similarly ambivalent, the one oddly evocative of George Herbert's pulley, the other reminding us of an expression Thomas uses: *Don't cast a clout till May is out.* The whole stanza quivers with imminent energy, and what alliteration doesn't do to enact both stealth ("*h*ead *h*urt a *h*air's") and percussion ("*b*all of my *b*reath / *B*ump"), assonance delivers with its jarring, physical insistence. If sound alone can be eloquent, irrespective of what the words mean, the stanza is a bout of fragile whispers and implacable natural force, the point being (when you get into the conditionals the fetus utters) that the baby-to-be can do nothing about what's going on. Therefore the opening of the poem introduces us to an entire mood of helpless altruism, and this is moving: the speech of the infant-to-be reminds us that infants are so called because they cannot speak, never mind alliterate persuasively, and the result of that is a tuning-up of the reader's compassion. You *feel with* what hasn't been much represented in poetry, though grasses have sighed and stones have spoken.

Thomas's own comment on this unusual poem is full of his customary militant modesty.

> It is not a narrative, nor an argument, but a series of conflicting images which move through pity and violence to an unreconciled acceptance of suffering: the mother's *and* the child's. This poem has been called obscure. I refuse to believe that it is obscurer than pity, violence, or suffering. But being a poem, not a lifetime, it is more compressed.

It's a refreshing point of view. Who else has considered the obscurity of pity, violence, or suffering? *Are* they obscure? Their external configurations are not, but their roots—in the ancient areas of the brain, in body chemistry—are, and we might be grateful to a poet who tries to work such concepts into an almost tactile empathy. Notice that Thomas doesn't say the poem is *about* "pity, violence, or suffering"; he *equates* parts of the poem *with* these. The entire thing could have lapsed into foolish ventriloquism (chit-chat during parturition), but it doesn't, partly because the sheer intensity of the images distracts us from the patent contraption of two speakers, partly because the poem exceeds his original intention and turns into an affirmation on a grander level than the immediate scenery implies. It's life addressing life about dangerous business. It's a racial impulse made vocal. And this is one of the ways in which Thomas, for all his skimpy knowledge of how nature works, waxes metaphysical; he makes the ineffable sayable, and he enacts a life process intricately through a whole register of discernible, almost palpable physical events. In other words, he creates more than most poets a physics to match his idea, so much so that in his best work (of which this poem is a sample) the mechanics of enunciation seem closer than we thought they could be to the behavior of the subject-matter cells.

Thomas achieves this startling effect in a variety of ways, willing to vary a sensation endlessly, to let it overlap with others. His handling of language implies a nod to denotation, an all-out welcome for connotation, a sign of his almost neurotic sensitivity to the flux that underlies our verbal concepts. He isn't often as prescient (accidentally so) as in "a nacreous sleep among soft particles and charms": particle physics had not evolved its fetchingly whimsical vocabulary when Thomas wrote this poem, but it's significant that, without knowing it, he had overreached into the terrain of the charm quark. That's a bonus over and above what the line tells about his attitude to phenomena. A Heisenberg couldn't be cagier about the very uncertainty of things, or a gypsy about the magic implied in "charms." And to say this is only to indicate in diffident fashion his uncanny openness to experience of all kinds, including the uncouth and the visceral, the electrostatic and the photo-

synthetical, the peptic and the congenital. He really does nibble the oat in the bread he breaks, intuit the monkey in the emergent baby, and, if you add myth to nature, the parting of the Red Sea in the breaking of the waters, the shroudmaker in the surgeon who sews after the Caesarian birth.

If we cast a wider net, assembling his least decipherable utterances ("Foster the light nor veil the manshaped moon") and those of Thomas the clear-eyed reporter ("the mousing cat stepping shy, / The puffed birds hopping and hunting"), as well as Thomas the near-arguer who can sustain something like musical variations on one vivid concept ("The hand that signed the paper felled a city") alongside Thomas the celebrant of suburban Swansea, Thomas the interceptor of political ricochet ("Cry Eloi to the guns"), Thomas the lyrical birthday poet, and—we always run out of breath before he does!—we have a conspectus of the miscellaneous seer. I do not think it has been sufficiently recognized how ramshackle, how flea-market his fund of ideas was. He creates his ritual out of the most unceremonious attitude to things, and he extracts his scapegrace reverence from an almost grotesque jumble of schoolboy comics, dirty jokes, bible-pounding provincialism, beer-garden shibboleths, snippets of all kinds of superstitions, rumors and hokum and balderdash. He just about personifies the voracious Metaphysical sensibility of which Eliot wrote, the bizarre thing being that he was able to transform the Saturday-afternoon reputation of the planet—a couple of imposing-sounding tropics, its being called a "star," the Pyramids, Jesus, Adam, radium, birth, death, masturbation—into something almost sacramental. Not neat. Not demure. Not explicit. Not argued or even structured. But bold, wild, and tenderly voluptuous.

This is not the place to rehearse the misdemeanors he has been charged with by exegetes straying off the reservation. Whether or not he commits pseudo-syntax is beside the point, which is much more complicated. Through his almost preternatural sensitivity to the interactions of juxtaposed words, he manages to write poems that feel indistinguishable from their subject matter, or (more alarming to a certain kind of reader) have no subject matter at all, but just *are,* transcribing nothing, modifying nothing, but (as if he had undertaken a dare) showing how far language can take us toward the nonverbal. This is why a case must be made for what are supposed his obscurest poems, which among other things provide feverish exercise, celebrate play and inventiveness and, above all, mimic the motion of life. Certain poems of his—**"The spire cranes"** and **"A Saint About to Fall,"** say—are as much exercises in calisthenics as they're anything else. It is no accident that he rarely uses the vocative: he doesn't feel apart enough from things or other people to muster the autonomies underlying a form of address; he is, in his invasive way, already at the heart of whatever he deals with. Listen to him in the act of turning into a bird, oddly graced with vocabulary:

> The spire cranes. Its statue is an aviary.
> From the stone nest it does not let the feathery
> Carved birds blunt their striking throats on the
>   salt gravel,
> Pierce the spilt sky with diving wing in weed and
>   heel

An inch in froth. . . .

He grows more and more avian with each syllable. We have just witnessed a metamorphosis, although one not half so demanding as the almost sculptural rendering in **"A Saint About to Fall"** of the sensations attending moral and spiritual collapse:

> On the angelic etna of the last whirring feather-
> lands,
> Wind-heeled foot in the hole of a fireball,
> Hymned his shrivelling flock,
> On the last rick's tip by spilled wine-wells. . . .

My point is that he doesn't intend such lines as these to correspond to anything else; they correspond only to themselves. Such language isn't referential, it's a sample of energy likely to sweep the reader along with it, even if "the angelic etna of the last whirring featherlands" never 'makes sense.' When Etna becomes 'etna' we are among the generic, but the specific connotation never gets lost, and it helps more than it hinders. Not one of his metaphors isn't a metaphor for the act of being metaphorical, which means that what often seems the superplus in his combinations—what doesn't need to be there—is present as a note to the activity itself, reminding us blatantly of what is going on, as when a clown falls once too often or a gymnast insists on virtuosity by doing something reckless. Not that we need to be warned: he overdoes things out of sheer natural abundance, in parallel with the Creation he hymns with ebullient lushness. What's abidingly uncommon about him is his untechnical command of what goes on in veins, capillaries, tissues, sinuses, and cells: the unseen physical, yet next door to the physical we see. In that sense he is the maestro of the fleshly neighborhood, the reluctant Canute of his own head's tides. He rides that rare, gorgeous flux like one appointed and sure of keeping his unique job. (pp. 88-92)

> Diane Ackerman, *"Among Soft Particles and Charms," in* Parnassus: Poetry in Review, *Vol. 14, No. 1, 1987, pp. 86-92.*

FURTHER READING

Adams, Robert M. "Metaphysical Poets, Ancient and Modern: Donne and Eliot." In his *Strains of Discord,* pp. 105-45. Ithaca, N.Y.: Cornell University Press, 1958.
    Compares Thomas's religious sonnets to the seventeenth-century metaphysical school of poetry characterized by elaborate effects of language and imagery.

Bayley, John. "Dylan Thomas." In his *The Romantic Survival: A Study in Poetic Revolution,* pp. 186-227. London: Constable and Co., 1957.
    Examines the complex relationship between Thomas's style and his subjects.

Blackburn, Thomas. "Dylan Thomas." In his *The Price of an Eye,* pp. 111-23. New York: William Morrow and Company, 1961.
    Illuminates the tragic vision and the polarity between death and life in Thomas's verse.

Bloom, Edward A. "Dylan Thomas' 'Naked Vision'." *Western Humanities Review* XIV, No. 4 (Autumn 1960): 389-400.
    Asserts that poetry itself is often the subject of Thomas's poetry and explores the "ars poetica" (statements about personal poetic aims) throughout his works.

Brinnin, John Malcolm. *Dylan Thomas in America: An Intimate Journal.* Boston: Little, Brown and Company, 1955, 303 p.
    Candid, controversial discussion of Thomas's public life in the United States from February, 1950 to November, 1953. (Brinnin, an American poet, initially arranged Thomas's poetry readings in the United States).

Davies, Aneirin Talfan. *Dylan: Druid of the Broken Body.* Swansea, Wales: Christopher Davies, 1977, 124 p.
    Classifies Thomas as a religious poet, viewing his works as "decidedly Christian."

Day Lewis, Cecil. "The Living Image." In his *The Poetic Image,* pp. 111-34. New York: Oxford University Press, 1948.
    Examines Thomas's writing methods and the contradictory images in "After the Funeral," which Day Lewis labels "a most brilliant, beautiful poem."

Ferris, Paul. *Dylan Thomas: A Biography.* New York: Dial Press, 1977, 399 p.
    This meticulously detailed book is the result of interviews with over 200 people and first-time availability of records in the British Broadcasting Corporation's archives. Includes photographs, index, bibliography.

Gingerich, Martin. "Dylan Thomas: Curse-Bless." *The Anglo-Welsh Review* 22, No. 49 (Spring 1973): 178-82.
    Addresses the alternately constructive and destructive forces of Thomas's poetic imagery.

Grubb, Frederick. "Worm's Eye: Dylan Thomas." In his *A Vision of Reality: A Study of Liberalism in Twentieth-Century Verse,* pp. 179-87. New York: Barnes & Noble, Inc., 1965.
    Maintains that the difficulties in Thomas's verse stem from his narcissistic style and overindulgence in myth.

Hardwick, Elizabeth. "America and Dylan Thomas." *Partisan Review* XXIII, No. 2 (Spring 1956): 258-64.
    Concerns the frenzied reception which greeted Thomas's United States poetry tour in the last several years of his life.

Holroyd, Stuart. "Dylan Thomas and the Religion of the Instinctive Life." In his *Emergence from Chaos,* pp. 77-94. Boston: Houghton Mifflin Company, 1957.
    Examines the metaphysical qualities of Thomas's poetry and his thematic treatment of the human psyche.

Jones, Richard. "The Dylan Thomas Country." *The Texas Quarterly* IV, No. 4 (Winter 1961): 34-42.
    Illuminates the pervasive influence of the Welsh countryside on Thomas's writing.

Killingley, Siew-yue. "Lexical, Semantic and Grammatical Patterning in Dylan Thomas." *Orbis* XXIII, No. 2 (1974): 285-99.
    Highly academic study of the stylistics of Thomas's verse.

Leech, Geoffrey. " 'This Bread I Break': Language and Interpretation." *A Review of English Literature* 6, No. 2 (April 1965): 66-75.

Linguistic study of Thomas's poem "This Bread I Break."

Loesch, Katharine T. "The Shape of Sound: Configurational Rime in the Poetry of Dylan Thomas." In *Studies in Interpretation,* pp. 33-66. Edited by Esther M. Doyle and Virginia Hastings Floyd, Amsterdam: Rodopi, 1972.

Detailed, academic examination of the configurational rhyme schemes in "After the Funeral."

Melchiori, Giorgio. "Dylan Thomas: The Poetry of Vision." In his *The Tightrope Walkers: Studies of Mannerism in Modern English Literature,* pp. 213-42. London: Routledge & Kegan Paul, 1956.

Discusses the ubiquitous, organic imagery of nature in Thomas's works.

Read, Bill. *The Days of Dylan Thomas.* New York & London: McGraw-Hill Book Company, 1964, 184 p.

Chronological treatment of Thomas's life and writings. Includes photographs, maps, index, bibliography.

Rolph, J. Alexander. *Dylan Thomas: A Bibliography.* London: J. M. Dent & Sons, Ltd., 1956, 108 p.

Primary bibliography with a foreword by Edith Sitwell.

Scarfe, Francis. "The Poetry of Dylan Thomas." *Horizon* II, No. 11 (November 1940): 226-39.

Explores the linguistic, mythological, and psychological influences of James Joyce, the Bible, and Sigmund Freud in Thomas's work.

Smith, A. J. "Ambiguity as Poetic Shift." *The Critical Quarterly* 4, No. 1 (Spring 1962): 68-74.

Academic analysis of the rhythmic language of Thomas's verse and his "exploitation of ambiguities" to heighten poetic effect.

Spender, Stephen. "Poetry for Poetry's Sake and Poetry beyond Poetry." *Horizon* XIII, No. 76 (April 1946): 221-38.

Focuses on Thomas's "opaque" use of language and the enormous range of experiences and impressions in his poems.

Stearns, Marshall W. "Unsex the Skeleton: Notes on the Poetry of Dylan Thomas." *The Sewanee Review* LII, No. 3 (July-September 1944): 424-40.

Examines Thomas's idiomatic tendencies and his influence upon other poets of his time.

Theisen, Lois. "Dylan Thomas: A Bibliography of Secondary Criticism." *Bulletin of Bibliography and Magazine Notes* 26, No. 1 (January-March 1969): 9-28, 32.

Comprehensive list includes reviews, essays, and books spanning the years 1935-1965.

Thomas, Caitlin, and Tremlett, George. *Caitlin: Life with Dylan Thomas.* New York: Henry Holt and Company, 1986, 212 p.

Candid, highly personal work by Thomas's wife of sixteen years. Keen insight into his equally tumultuous creative and personal lives.

Thomas, R. George. "Dylan Thomas: A Poet of Wales?" *English* XIV, No. 82 (Spring 1963): 140-45.

Explores Thomas's peculiar role as a Welsh poet, contrasting him with his English colleagues.

Young, A. "Radical Tradition: Thomas Hardy and Dylan Thomas." *The Thomas Hardy Yearbook,* No. 7 (1977): 39-47.

Compares and contrasts the two poets, finding them alike in their style, subject matter, and radical beliefs.

Young, Alan. "Image as Structure: Dylan Thomas and Poetic Meaning." *Critical Quarterly* 17, No. 4 (Winter 1975): 333-45.

Focuses on the metaphysical and poetic questions posed in Thomas's verse.

Paul Verlaine

1844-1896

(Full name: Paul Marie Verlaine; also wrote under the pseudonym Pablo de Herlagñez) French poet, essayist, autobiographer, and short story writer.

A poet renowned for the fluidity and impressionistic imagery of his verse, Verlaine succeeded in liberating the musicality of the French language from the restrictions of its classical, formal structure. Highly influenced by the French painter Antoine Watteau, Verlaine was fascinated by the visual aspects of form and color and attempted to capture in his poems the symbolic elements of language by transposing emotion into subtle suggestions. As a contributor to the French Symbolists, who believed the function of poetry was to evoke and not describe, Verlaine created poetry that was both aesthetic and intuitive. Although his verse has often been overshadowed by his scandalous bohemian lifestyle, Verlaine's literary achievement was integral to the development of French poetry. Arthur Symons purports that Verlaine's place in literary history rests on the fact that he "made something new of French—something more pliable, more exquisitely delicate and sensitive, than the language ever before has been capable of."

Born in Metz to religious middle-class parents, Verlaine's youth was guarded and conventional until he became a student at the Lycée Bonaparte (now Condorcet). While he never truly excelled in his studies, Verlaine did enjoy a certain success in rhetoric and Latin. Despite winning a number of prizes in these areas, however, Verlaine was not a highly respected student—one of his instructors claimed he looked like a criminal and was the filthiest and most slovenly pupil in school—and he barely managed to obtain the baccalaureate. Upon graduation Verlaine enrolled in law school, but because of his tendency to frequent bars and to associate with women of questionable morals, he was quickly withdrawn from his academic pursuits. His father was able to secure a clerical position for his son at a local insurance company and while the work was mundane, it did allow Verlaine time to patronize the Café du Gaz, then the rendezvous of the literary and artistic community, and develop his poetic talents.

Verlaine made his literary debut with the publication of *Poèmes saturniens* in 1866. At this time Verlaine began to associate with a group of young poets known as La Parnasse, or the Parnassians. This poetic movement, which had adopted Théophile Gautier's doctrine of "Art for Art's Sake," included François Coppée, Charles Leconte de Lisle, and Charles Baudelaire. While Verlaine's *Poèmes saturniens,* a volume true to the Parnassian ideals of detached severity, impeccable form, and stoic objectivity, was well-received by his fellow poets, it took twenty years to sell five hundred copies, leaving Verlaine virtually unknown to general readers following its publication. Verlaine began to move away from the tenets of the Parnassians with his third volume, *Fêtes galantes.* In this collec-

tion, Verlaine used visual and spatial imagery to create poetry that has been described as "impressionistic music." According to many critics, this volume first revealed Verlaine's poetic talents in their pure form and later established Verlaine as a precursor to the Symbolist movement.

While Verlaine's poetic style was taking shape and setting precedents, his personal life was slowly dissipating due to his increasing consumption of absinthe, a liqueur flavored with wormwood. Despite his growing addiction and sometimes violent temperament, Verlaine's family encouraged him to marry, believing it could stabilize his raucous life. Verlaine sought out a young girl, Mathilde Mauté, who was sixteen in 1869, the year of their engagement. Following their marriage in 1870, Verlaine published *La bonne chanson,* a volume that contains verse inspired by his young wife. This was Verlaine at his happiest; he seemed to truly believe that love and marriage would save him from his dangerous lifestyle. Verlaine's hopes and good intentions, however, were shattered when he received a letter from the then unknown poet Arthur Rimbaud in 1871. Verlaine urged Rimbaud, a precocious and unpredictable seventeen-year-old genius, to visit him in Paris. Tempted by the anarchic and bohemian lifestyle the young poet represented, Verlaine abandoned his wife, home, and employment for Rimbaud. The two poets traveled throughout Europe, a journey punctuated by drunken quarrels, until Verlaine shot and wounded Rimbaud during an argument in 1873. Verlaine was arrested and later sentenced to serve two years at Mons, a Belgian prison. During this time he wrote *Romances sans paroles,* a collection of verse strongly influenced by his affair with Rimbaud. Verlaine's masterful use of ambiguities, the smoothness and economy of his verse, and his usage of "half-light," or vague but deeply suggestive visual imagery, led Arthur Symons to speak for many when he called this volume "Verlaine's masterpiece of sheer poetry."

While in prison, Verlaine turned from atheism to a fervent acceptance of the Roman Catholic faith in which he had been born. While some observers have questioned the sincerity of Verlaine's conversion, others have pointed to *Sagesse,* a volume of poems which depicts his religious crisis, as evidence of his depth of feeling and moral commitment. Critical response to *Sagesse* was somewhat mixed, with some reviewers castigating its long, grave lines as nothing more than religious pretense, and others, Arthur Symons among them, claiming that "this book of religious poetry . . . is second scarcely to any religious poetry in the world." Following *Sagesse,* Verlaine produced a trilogy exemplifying his religious genesis: *Amour* was to represent religious perseverance, *Parallèlement* moral relapse, and *Bonheur* repentance and consolation. In all three collections, Verlaine continued to develop his personal voice and to progress toward simple and graceful accentuations.

After being released from Mons, Verlaine traveled to Stickney and Bournemouth in England to become a teacher of French, Latin and drawing. Although he called his stay in Stickney an *enchantement,* Verlaine decided in 1878 to take up a rustic life in the Ardennes with one of his former students, Lucien Létinois, whom he termed his *fils adoptif* (adoptive son). Many of the elegies of *Amour* refer to Létinois, who died in 1886 of typhoid, two years after the death of Verlaine's mother. For the remainder of his life, Verlaine lived in poverty and reverted to drink. Although he managed to publish a few works during this time, among them the tragic and brutal *Chansons pour elle,* most critics contend that Verlaine's best and most original work can be found in his earlier volumes. After a number of hospital stays which allowed him to recuperate from his excesses, Verlaine died in humble lodgings in 1896.

While many critics consider Verlaine one of the harbingers of the French Symbolists due to the impressionistic and evocative nature of his poetry, he denied belonging to any particular poetic movement. Instead of labeling himself a Décadent or Symbolist, Verlaine preferred to call himself a "degenerate," indicating his individualistic and anarchic tendencies. Much attention has been given to Verlaine's use of familiar language in a musical and visual manner and his ability to evoke rather than demand a response from his readers. Stéphane Mallarmé declared that "to name an object is to suppress three-fourths of the enjoyment of the poem . . . to suggest it, there is the dream." This statement, often considered the credo for the Symbolist movement, can be used to describe much of Verlaine's poetry. As C. F. Keary purports: "If there is one note which occurs more frequently than any other in [Verlaine's] poems, it is the longing for repose, a love of half-lights and the minor key."

Verlaine's well-documented personal life has often overshadowed discussion of the merits of his numerous volumes of verse and his poetic genius. In Verlaine's work, as in his life, there was a constant struggle between the soul and the senses; between debauchery and repentance. This prompted critics to call him everything from a "propagator of moral cowardice" to "a victim of his own genius." Despite the many attacks on his character, Verlaine is considered a consummate poet whose extraordinary talents for fluid verse, figurative and suggestive language, and impressionistic imagery have assumed legendary stature. It was Verlaine, most critics agree, who was responsible for releasing French poetry from its technical severity and for bringing out the musicality inherent in the French language. "Remember," Anatole France wrote as early as 1891, "this lunatic has created a new art, and there is a chance that some day it will be said of him . . . : 'He was the greatest poet of his time.' "

(For further discussion of Verlaine's life and career, see *Nineteenth-Century Literature Criticism,* Vol. 2.)

PRINCIPAL WORKS

POETRY

Poèmes saturniens 1866
Les Amies [as Pablo de Herlagñez] 1868
Fêtes galantes 1870
La bonne chanson 1870
Romances sans paroles 1874
Sagesse 1881
Jadis et naguère 1884
Amour 1888
Parallèlement 1889
Bonheur 1891
Chansons pour elle 1891
Hombres 1891
Liturgies intimes 1892
Elégies 1893
Odes en son honeur 1893
Dans les limbres 1894
Poems of Paul Verlaine 1895
Chair 1896
Invectives 1896

OTHER MAJOR WORKS

Les poètes maudits (essays) 1884
Les Uns et les autres (one-act play in *Jadis et naguère*) 1884
Mes hôpitaux (essays) 1891
Mes prisons (essays) 1892
Confessions (autobiography) 1895
Oeuvres complètes. 5 vols. (short stories, essays, autobiography) 1898-1903
Oeuvres posthumes. 3 vols. (essays and letters) 1911-1929

Anatole France   (essay date 1891?)

[*France was a French novelist, essayist, and critic of the late nineteenth and early twentieth centuries. According to contemporary literary historians, France's best work was characterized by clarity, control, perceptive judgement of world affairs, and traits typical of the Enlightenment: tolerance and justice. In the following excerpt, France discusses Verlaine's spirituality, specifically his fluctuations between repentence and moral relapse, and its effects on the style and subject matter of his verse.*]

Poèmes saturniens, published in 1867 . . . , certainly never foreshadowed the most singular, monstrous, mystical, complicated, simple, nervous, eccentric, and undoubtedly most inspired and truest of contemporary poets. Still, through these manufactured poems, and in spite of the manner of the school, one divined a kind of strange, unhappy and tormented genius. (p. 297)

Fêtes galantes appeared in the following year. It was only a slim volume. But Paul Verlaine had already shown himself therein in his perturbing candour, and something of his slight, awkward and inexpressible charm. What are these *fêtes galantes?* They were held in Watteau's Cythera. But though folk still go in couples to the woods in the evening, the laurels are cut, as the song says, and the magic grasses which have grown in their place exhale a mortal languor.

Verlaine, who is one of those musicians who play false by refinement, has put many discords in these minuet airs, and his violin sometimes scrapes horribly; but all at once some note tugs at your heart-strings. The wicked fiddler has stolen your soul. He steals it, for instance, in playing **"Clair de lune"**:

[Your soul is a favourite landscape
Where pass charming masks and bergamasks
Playing the lute, and dancing, and half
Sad beneath their fantastic disguises.

While they sing in a minor key,
Of Love the victor, and fortunate life,
They do not seem to believe in their good fortune,
And their song mingles with the light of the moon,

With the light of the moon, sad and lovely,
Which sets the birds dreaming in the trees
And makes the fountains sob with ecstasy,
The tall fountains amid the marble statues.]

The accent is new, peculiar, and profound.

Our poet was heard once more, but this time barely heard, when, on the eve of the war, too near those terrible days, he issued **La bonne chanson**—some very simple, obscure, and infinitely sweet verses. He was then engaged, and the most tender and chaste of fiancés. Satyrs and fauns must sing thus when they are very young, when they have drunk milk, and the forest wakes in dawn and dew.

Suddenly Paul Verlaine disappeared. There happened to the poet of **Fêtes galantes** what happened to the companion of Vau-de-Vire, of whom the plaint tells. Nothing further was heard of him. For fifteen years he kept silence; after which it was learnt that the penitent Verlaine was publishing a volume of religious poetry with a Catholic publishing-house. What had happened in these fifteen years? I know not, and what does anybody know? The true history of François Villon is ill known. And Verlaine much resembles Villon: they are two "bad hats," to whom it was granted to say the sweetest things in the world. As for those fifteen years, we must adhere to the legend which states that our poet was a great sinner, and, to speak in the manner of the greatly regretted Jules Tellier, "one of those whom dreams have led to sensual folly." Legend speaks. It further says that the "bad hat" was punished for his misdemeanours, and that he expiated them painfully. It has been sought to give some verisimilitude to the legend by quoting these penitent stanzas, full of delightful candour:

[The sky is up above the roof
So blue, so calm!
A tree, above the roof,
Waves its boughs.

The bell in the sky one sees
Gently strikes;
A bird on the tree one sees
Sings his song.

My God, my God, Life is there
Simple and calm!
That peaceful hum
Comes from the town.

What have you done, O you who are there,
Weeping unceasingly?
What have you done, O you who are there,
With your youth?]

Doubtless it is but a legend, but it will prevail. It must. This detestable and charming poet's verses would lose their value and meaning if they came not from the dense atmosphere "lacking all light" where the Florentine saw carnal sinners who subordinated reason to lust.

Moreover, the fault must be real for the repentance to be genuine. In his repentance Paul Verlaine returned to the God of his baptism and of his first communion with the completest candour. He was entirely sentimental. He never reflected nor argued.

No human thought, no intelligence ever troubled his idea of God. We have seen that he was a faun. Those who have read the Lives of the Saints know how easily the fauns, who are very simple, allowed themselves to be converted to Christianity by the Apostles to the Gentiles. Paul Verlaine wrote the most Christian verses we have in France. I am not the first to make that discovery. M. Jules Lemaître used to say that a certain strophe in **Sagesse** recalled in its accent a verse of the *Imitation.* The seventeenth century, to be sure, left us some beautiful spiritual poetry. Corneille, Brébeuf, and Godeau were inspired by the *Imitation* and the Psalms. But they wrote in the Louis XIII style, which was too proud, and even rather swaggering and hectoring. Like Polyeuctus in the time of the Cardinal, these painted poems wore a feathered hat, gloves with ruffles, and a long cape raised by a rapier like a cock's tail.

Verlaine was naturally humble; mystical poetry surged up from his heart, and he found once again the accents of a St. Francis, a St. Theresa. . . .

> [I wish to love none other now than my mother Mary
>
>   . . . . .
>
> For when I was feeble, and still very wicked,
> With idle hands, and eyes dazzled by the road,
> She lowered my eyes, and joined my hands,
> And taught me the words by which to adore.]
>   (pp. 298-302)

This conversion was truly sincere, but not enduring. Like the dog of Holy Scripture, he returned to his vomit. Once more his relapse inspired him with exquisite candour. What, then, did he do? As sincere in sin as in repentance, he accepted the alternatives with cynical innocence. He resigned himself to taste in turn the pleasures of crime and the horrors of despair. Even more, he so to speak tasted them together: he kept the affairs of his soul in two separate compartments. Hence the curious collection of verse entitled *Parallèlement.* It is doubtless perverse, but of such artless perversity that it almost seems pardonable.

And then, this poet must not be judged like an ordinary man. He has rights which we have not, for he is at once greater and smaller than we are. He has no conscience, and is a poet such as is not met with once in a hundred years. M. Jules Lemaître judged him well when he said: "He is a barbarian, a savage, a child . . . only this child has music in his soul, and on certain days he hears voices heard by none before him."

You say he is mad? I agree. And if I did not think so, I should not have written what I have. He is certainly mad. But remember that this lunatic has created a new art, and there is a chance that some day it will be said of him, as it is now said of François Villon, with whom he may be well compared: "He was the greatest poet of his time." (pp. 303-04)

> *Anatole France, "Paul Verlaine," in his* On Life & Letters, *third series, translated by D. B. Stewart, John Lane, The Bodley Head Ltd., 1922, pp. 295-304.*

Arthur Symons   (essay date 1892)

[*An English critic, poet, dramatist, short story writer, and editor, Symons was one of the most important critics of the modern era. While his sensitive translations of Paul Verlaine and Stéphane Mallarmé proved he was a gifted linguist, it was as a critic that Symons made his most important contribution to literature. His* The Symbolist Movement in Literature *(1899) provided his English contemporaries with an appropriate vocabulary with which to define their new aesthetic—one that communicated their concern with dreamlike states, imagination, and a reality that exists beyond the boundaries of the senses. Symons also laid the foundation of modern poetic theory by stating the symbol was a vehicle by which a "hitherto unknown reality [is] suddenly revealed." In the following excerpt, Symons attempts to* define the revolutionary nature of Verlaine's verse by identifying the unique stylistic and thematic devices found throughout his poetic canon.]

The art of Paul Verlaine is something new, absolutely new, to poetry. *Romances sans Paroles*—songs without words—is the name of one of his volumes, and his poetry at its best might almost be called disembodied song. It is an art of impressionism—sometimes as delicate, as pastoral, as Watteau, sometimes as sensitively modern as Whistler, sometimes as brutally modern as Degas. It is all suggestion, evocation . . . the suggestion and evocation of sensations, a restless, insistent search for the last fine shade of expression. . . . Verlaine has gone farther than any other poet in the direction of an art which suggests, with close-lipped, pausing reticence, "things too *subtle* and too sweet for words." But, having done this, having perfected an art in which the tinge of personal feeling was only a glow of richer colour in the verse, he has gone on, he has modified or developed his art, unconsciously, inevitably, as the years had their way with him.

Verlaine's first volume, published in 1867, when he was twenty-three, the *Poèmes Saturniens,* is a book of charming Parnassian verse, not without touches of personal originality, but, both in form and substance, very definitely under the influence of Baudelaire and of Leconte de Lisle. In the *Fêtes Galantes,* two years later, there is nothing but Verlaine—Verlaine in his first and purely decorative stage. This lovely little book of fifty pages is well-nigh perfect from first line to last. Parnassian it is, in a sense; but it is more than Parnassian—this diaphanous little comedy of masks in a park *à la Watteau.* It is the very soul of the eighteenth century—the art of Watteau in words and cadences, with that tone as of old rose-leaves, that same evanescent charm, that same happy sense of exquisite moments; and, also, the dainty melancholy, the consciousness of fleeting time and passing beauty and the death of roses—that haste to gather the rose-buds while we may. . . . Next year came *La Bonne Chanson,* a wedding-bouquet of songs for a young wife. It is delicate, sweet, pure; it is very pretty, but one sees too clearly that the poems were written to please a woman. The emotion is too near nature, not being poignant enough to support poetic treatment. The verse reminds one of Coppée. It is an episode, a step in life. The tone is so gay, tuneful, and happy, that one instinctively forsees storms. Nor were they long in coming. One need only see Verlaine for a moment to realize that no long continued tranquillity could be possible for a man with so radically disharmonized a face—a face in which so much of the brute waits the bidding of so fitful and furious a power for good or evil. I have heard Verlaine talk of that period—in the most simple and matter-of-fact way. The details are not all clear. The marriage, certainly, was an unhappy one; nor is that wonderful, for the disorder of Verlaine's life passed all bounds. He defied civilization, started on a mad vagabondage with his friend, the "marvellous boy" Arthur Rimbaud; and after two years' wanderings, now in England, now in Belgium, there was a quarrel, a happily ill-directed pistol-shot, and Verlaine was condemned to eighteen months' imprisonment at Mons. It was during this tumultuous time . . . that *Romances sans Paroles* appeared: Verlaine's masterpiece, as

I think, of sheer poetry. There is all the magic of the *Fêtes Galantes,* and how much deeper a personal note, how individual a grasp of the whole art of poetry! There is a new directness, a rhythm which is more surely the rhythm of heartbeats. . . . Then there are the **"Aquarelles,"** with their English names (**"Green," "Spleen," "Streets"**), where the rhythm undulates in a vague, dreamy dance, like the very spirit of the hour and place in certain twilight moods. Then there are the **"Paysages Belges,"** marvellous little silhouettes struck off during those wanderings with the boy-poet Rimbaud—impressionist studies of railways, of the wooden horses at the fair of St. Gilles, . . . of Walcourt, where the Kobolds dance in the darkness of the grass. And then there is that pitifully personal poem, **"Birds in the Night,"** in which the heart speaks straight out—and so strangely! He addresses his wife; but it is not in tones of remorse—in a sort of childlike astonishment. . . . He complains like a child—Verlaine, all his life, has been a big, unmanageable child—that he has not been understood—his good intentions, his helplessness. There is the same half-piteous, half-defiant protest that looks out of his suffering and exultant face. He is conscious that he has done wrong; but he is conscious, too, that it is nature which has been too much for him. *Homo duplex,* he feels himself condemned to oscillate eternally between the poles of good and evil. Well, he accepts the fact, he proclaims his unworthiness; but it surprises him, it distresses him, if you do not see the "simplicity," as he calls it, which lies at the root of his nature. Something of this comes out in the poem I have named; but it is in the volume published after a seven years' silence, *Sagesse,* which appeared in 1881, that these personal confessions are mainly to be found.

Sketch of Verlaine and Arthur Rimbaud in London by F. Regamey.

The conversion of Paul Verlaine—a most important fact in his life—took place while he was in prison. The circumstance was quite natural. He had gone as far in one direction as it was possible to go, and then came these solitary eighteen months in company with his thoughts, an enforced physical inactivity which could but concentrate all the energies of the man on the only kind of sensation then within his capacity—the sensation of the mind and the conscience. The question of religion—which can be so subtly distinguished from the question of conduct—naturally forced itself upon him. Probably it had never occurred to him before. (pp. 501-04)

The conversion, and that long solitude in the prison, alone with his thoughts, had a very considerable effect upon Verlaine's art. For seven years he published nothing. During all this time he was wandering from country to country, from city to city, teaching French in England . . . ; teaching English in France. . . . (p. 504)

Sagesse, the book of religious poems, came out in the midst of this lamentable Odyssey, with its profession of faith, its declaration: "The author published at an early age, that is to say ten or twelve years ago, sceptical and sadly trifling verses. He dares rely that in those he now publishes there is no dissonance that can shock the delicacy of a Catholic ear: that would be his highest reward, as it is his proudest hope." And, indeed, the book is full of religious poetry which is second to scarcely any religious poetry in the world. With this change of mood there is a corresponding change of style. Sincere to himself Verlaine was from the beginning. But from this point he had convictions to be sincere to. He had a new feeling of duty, of religious obligation—the obligation of confession. In the *Fêtes Galantes* he had to express a troubled, exquisite beauty; in *Romances sans Paroles,* a beauty which was still more troubled, which was poignant, perverse, but still able to be expressed by an art of delicately depraved æsthetic charm. *Sagesse* is written mainly in long lines, with a graver, more measured note—certainly not so fascinating. The language is not so choice, so carefully selected; it has not the flickering, luminous quality of the earlier work. The words used seem often to be the first words that come: there is a strenuous quest after extreme sincerity of speech, sincerity being now a religious duty. "Sincerity, and the impression of the moment followed to the letter,"—that is how Verlaine defines his rule of preference . . . in a criticism on the *Poèmes Saturniens* published a year or two ago in the *Revue d'Aujourd'hui.* The result of this new attempt has a naturally varying success. There are poems in *Sagesse* which are merely dull arguments, where simplicity is tiresome, where the language of everyday speech has no sort of poetic effect. There are other poems where this simple, intense language becomes sublime. Perhaps the finest thing that Verlaine has written is the series of ten sonnets beginning **"Mon Dieu m' a dit."** It is a dialogue between God, claiming the tribute of love, and the Sinner, refusing out of very humbleness. (p. 505)

Only in Christina Rosetti is there such abasement of spirit, such elevation of imagination, as in these marvellous sonnets—a scalding heat of sincerity, and a personal passion wholly fused in art. Nor are these sonnets alone. There is the solemn litany of penitence: **"O mon Dieu, vous m'avez blessé d'amour"**—as fine, as simple, as Villon's ballad for his mother. Throughout the book—not unaccompanied, as I have said, by dull treatises, like that which proves that **"Le seul savant, c'est encore Moïse"**—there are poems in the same note of passionate humility. Often the note is less intense, but with a wonderful penetrating quality in its charm. **"Beauté de femmes, leur faiblesse, et ces mains pâles," "Les chères mains qui furent miennes," "L'espoir luit comme un brin de paille dans l'étable," "Ecoutez la chanson bien douce"**—need one quote more than the first lines to show the charm there is in these sensuous, perverse, troubled evocations of hours and impressions? Appendage or antithesis to the religious feeling, a strangely perverse strain of emotion comes into Verlaine's poetry. It is the voice of the flesh, repressed, but crying out against the spirit: the voice of bewitching temptations, which could never have been possible—in just that savour of deadly delight—without the consciousness of sin, the desire to repent, the desire of salvation. (p. 506)

[In 1884] Verlaine published a new collection of poems, *Jadis et Naguère,* a volume, as the title indicates, made up of early and recent work. It makes no pretence to unity, but has something in it of every variety of his style, with certain poems, here and there, which rank among his special triumphs. Thus, the first section, "Sonnets et Autres Vers," is the dying echo of the Parnasse—exquisite pieces of decorative work, some of them subtly evocative. . . . Others presage the loose later manner, in which the sensation of the moment, and the imperious need to express it, anyhow, are the poet's only considerations. Here are some lines which should interest an English public.—

> Tout l'affreux passé saute, piaule, miaule et
>   glapit
> Dans le brouillard rose et jaune et sale des *sohos*
> Avec des *indeeds* et des *all rights* et des *hâos.*

That is most expressive; but it is scarcely poetry. It reminds one of the astonishing American which Walt Whitman occasionally used. But turn from this to the triumphantly and terribly beautiful sonnet **"Luxures,"** which chants the flesh with all the mystic fervour of the Christian. Turn to **"L'Art Poétique,"** that confession of faith which is only a song, and so all the more a confession of faith. A little comedy, *Les Uns et les Autres,* fills forty pages, fills them deliciously—though indeed the dramatic form is only an acquirement with Verlaine. Beautiful shadows pass in a twilight: it is a company out of Watteau, under his trees: there is some delicate entanglement and disentanglement, resolved into song. In the section called "A la Manière de Plusieurs"—I suppose because it is so characteristic of Verlaine—there is some of his most finely chiselled "Byzantine" work, such as that languid sonnet, with its "contour subtil," **"Je suis l'Empire à la fin de la Décadence."** (p. 508)

Jadis et Naguère is a step aside in Verlaine's progress. In *Amour* (1888) he resumes his course, and the poet of *Sagesse* re-appears, the personal note still further developed. **"Lucien Létinois,"** a poem in twenty-four sections, in varying metres, can be compared only with "In Memoriam,"

which, as Verlaine has an immense admiration for Tennyson, probably suggested it. It is a poem written to the memory of a young friend; and it tells, in broken snatches, the idyl of their friendship, and the sad and sordid way in which death came and turned the idyl into a tragedy. It is singularly fine in its extreme simplicity and closeness to life—the direct, unadorned, yet poetic way in which little details are brought back out of the past, just in the simple, naked way in which they really recur to the mind—the walks they took together, the meals in little inns, the meetings at railway-stations. . . .

Just these things, just such thoughts as these, without any sort of remoteness, or the veil of an elaborately chosen language, Verlaine has strung together, as if casually, yet with how certain, how immediate an effect! (p. 509)

Besides the elegy to Lucien Létinois, there is a whole crowd of sonnets and poems addressed to friends and companions, some of them not very interesting for any but personal reasons. One of the most pleasing is that addressed to Fernand Langlois—a young artist with a somewhat womanish charm and appeal—in which a note of gracious and passionate friendship is very frankly and simply struck. Among the sonnets there are some which triumph by an amazing virtuosity—the sonnet on Parsifal, for example, to which Mr. George Moore has given such just and eloquent praise—and a **"Sonnet Héroïque,"** which is like the music of gongs and cymbals. A cluster of poems at the beginning of the volume, mainly in long lines, might have found their place in *Sagesse,* of which they have the simple, naïve piety, the personal preoccupation, the graver, more measured verse. There is a **"Prière du Matin,"** . . . a hymn to the Virgin, confessions and aspirations. Then there are English sketches—**"Bournemouth," "There,"** etc.—in which one misses, as one could not but miss, the iridescent charm, the evanescent delicacy, of the earlier work in that kind. The gaiety of life has become more sordid, the charm more severe, the grace of things has been soiled; and for these things, which happen in life, there is no redemption in art. . . . This loss of illusions, with its inevitable effect upon art, we have seen in *Sagesse,* more distinctly still in *Amour,* and we see it nakedly—naked and hideous—in *Parallèlement,* which followed *Amour* in the subsequent year, 1889.

"Parallèlement," Verlaine explains, to *Sagesse, Amour,* and *Bonheur.* In these others he has interpreted the spiritual side of his nature; here, with the same frankness, and in the spirit of that dialectic of **"Pauvre Lélian"** . . . , he gives us the flesh. Few poets have ever been so direct and sincere in the expression of religious emotions as Verlaine; but certainly no poet ever gave such sincere and direct expression to "the lust of the flesh, the lust of the eye, the pride of life," as he has done in *Parallèlement.* The book is full of a gross hilarity, a frantic impetuosity, a wild and conscious perversity. It is as perverse as Baudelaire; but it has none of Baudelaire's subtlety, a corruption less intricate and comprehensive—more naïve, spontaneous, explosive. The style undergoes the same depravation as the ideas; it becomes almost as unintelligible as the thieves' argot in Villon. Slang swamps the precise and exquisite poetic language of the earlier work; the rhythms, still marvellously agile, are handled with dexterity rather than charm.

But Verlaine would tell us that he did not intend to be charming: that he intended to give voice to certain instincts, which his determined sincerity forbade him to silence. The question is whether many of these pieces come within any possible limits of art. A poem like **"Laeti et Er-rabundi"**—the story of that strange vagabondage with Rimbaud—is most certainly a work of art. A piece like **"L'Impenitent"** seems to me simply disagreeable without justifying its existence by any artistic quality. Psychologically, pathologically, the whole volume is of immense interest; artistically, of much less. Yet the book is not without delicious touches, turned obstinately perverse, of the poet who can still write lines that sing themselves. . . . (pp. 510-11)

Two years after *Parallèlement,* in 1891, came *Bonheur,* the third part of the trilogy. Written very much in the style of *Sagesse,* part of it might have been assigned, on internal evidence, to a period anterior to *Amour* and *Parallèlement.* It has none of the perversity, moral and artistic, of the latter book, despite a few experiments upon metre and rhyme. Nor is space devoted as occasionally in *Amour,* to the mere courtesies of literary friendship. The verse has an exquisite simplicity, a limpid clearness; there is a strenuous rejection of every sort of literary "dandyism"—the word is Verlaine's:

> et que cet arsénal,
> Chics fougueux et froids, mots secs, phrase re-
> dondante,
> Et cætera, se rende à l'émeute grondante
> Des sentiments enfin naturels et réels.

I take these lines from a poem which may be considered a new **"Art Poétique."** In that delicate and magical poem—itself the ideal of the art it sang—Verlaine said nothing about sincerity, except, inferentially, to the fleeting impression of something almost too vague for words. Music first of all and before all; and then, not colour, but the *nuance,* the last fine shade. Poetry is to be something intangible, a winged soul in flight "towards other skies and other loves." To express the inexpressible, he speaks of beautiful eyes behind a veil, of the full palpitating sunlight of noon, of the blue swarm of clear stars in a cool autumn sky; and the verse in which he makes this confession of faith has the exquisite troubled beauty . . . which he commends as the essential poetry. Now in this new poem of poetical counsel, he tells us that art should, first of all, be absolutely clear and sincere; it is the law of necessity, hard, no doubt, but the law.

> L'art, mes enfants, c'est d'être absolument soi-
> meme.
> Foin! d'un art qui blasphéme et fi! d'un art qui
> pose,
> Et vive un vers *bien* simple, autrement c'est la
> prose.
>
> (pp. 511-12)

Almost all the poems in *Bonheur* are closely personal—confessions of weakness, confessions of "l'ennui de vivre avec les gens et dans les choses," confessions of good attempts foiled, of unachieved resolutions. One of the finest

pieces tells the story of that endeavour to rebuild the ruined house of life which Verlaine made at the time of his conversion, after those calm and salutary eighteen months of seclusion. Elsewhere he writes of his life in hospital— "last home, perhaps, and best, the hospital;"—of his child-wife, for whose memory he has so strange a mixture of regretful complaint and unassuaged self-reproach. . . . Here, as in *Sagesse,* there are times when confession becomes analysis, not to the advantage of the poetry. But here, as in *Sagesse,* the really distinguishing work is an outpouring of desires that speak the language of desire, of prayers that go up to God as prayers, not as literature; of confessions that have no reticences.

In *Chansons pour Elle,* which followed *Bonheur* in the same year, almost simultaneously with a book of unimportant prose sketches, *Mes Hôpitaux,* Verlaine has relapsed into the mood of *Parallèlement.* It represents, indeed, a lower depth—a dead level of animal contentment which has never, perhaps, been expressed in literature since the "Grosse Margot" of Villon. . . . There is a sort of tragic brutality in this record of a life which has come to accept so sordid a condition of things, simply, without disguise, without revolt, gratefully even. No matter, he says to the casual heroine of his verses, what the past of both of us may have been: let us unite our two miseries: let us be happy, after the only manner that is left to us, together. In these naïve, often trivial, poems we touch the bottom of Bohemia. There is not even the distinction of perversity. The singing-voice is somewhat thickened: it comes to us from the tavern, from the dubious garret, in the turbulent hours after midnight. It is the end of all. . . . (pp. 513-14)

Absolute as this is, there is still the sigh, the sigh coming unawares, after that other life, that other side of life; and it is, after all, not surprising—when one has realized the extraordinary simplicity of Verlaine's nature, its sincerity of alternations, of temporary exclusions—to find that *Chansons pour Elle* has already been followed by a tiny pamphlet, privately printed in a "Bibliothèque du Saint Graal," of *Liturgies Intimes,* a collection of devotional pieces addressed solely to Catholics. "This quite small book," says the preface, "is intended for a quite small and select public, and is indeed the complement—dare I say the crown?—of a work of some extent, which the author believes to be correct in regard to the Faith. This work is in four volumes: *Sagesse,* the conversion; *Amour,* the perseverance; a backsliding deliberately confessed, *Parallèlement;* and *Bonheur,* conclusion sorrowfully calm in the supreme consolation." *Chansons pour Elle* is not referred to: no doubt that, too, is to be regarded as "a backsliding deliberately confessed." In these *Liturgies Intimes* Verlaine has endeavoured to recapture the note of *Sagesse*— not altogether with success. Simplicity there is indeed, a simplicity sometimes verging on childishness; but some lack of that distinction which Verlaine's simplicity has rarely lacked. The metrical experiments are not always quite fortunate: the naïveté not always quite convincing. But there is an evident sincerity in . . . curious humbleness. . . . (p. 514)

With what Verlaine has made of his life we are concerned only so far as the life has made or modified the artistic work; and in him the two are one, as surely as the two are one in Villon. From the date of **Romances sans Paroles** to the date of **Liturgies Intimes,** every stage of the "fever called living" has been chronicled and characterized in verse. The verse has changed as the life has changed, remaining true to certain fundamental characteristics, as the man, through all, has remained true to his strange and self-contradictory temperament. Verlaine has made something new of French verse—something more pliable, more exquisitely delicate and sensitive, than the language has ever before been capable of. He has invented this new kind of impressionist poetry—"la nuance, la nuance encor"—which seems to correspond so subtly with the latest tendencies in the other arts: the painting of Whistler, the music of Wagner. Himself a creature of passions and sensations, tossed to and fro by every wind, he has given voice to all the vague desires, the tumultuous impressions, of that feeble and ravenous creature, the modern man of cities. He has set them to music that is now exquisite, as the mood is exquisite, now dissonant, as the mood is dissonant, always an acute, a floating music, that had never been heard before. So modern, so typical, is this singer who has sung only of himself—of his sorrows, his faults, his distresses; of the times when he has been glad and believed himself happy; of the hours when the flesh has triumphed, and the hours of mystical communion with the spirit; of the colours, the sounds, that have delighted him, the hands that he has kissed, the tears that he has wept. (p. 515)

> *Arthur Symons, "Paul Verlaine," in* The National Review, *London, Vol. XIX, 1892, pp. 501-15.*

Augustus Manston   (essay date 1896)

[*In the following excerpt, Manston underscores the importance of Verlaine's contribution to French verse. Although the critic finds Verlaine's use of language limited, he states that "Verlaine excels . . . in the beauty of his musical efforts."*]

If the author of **Sagesse** did not bring much art to bear on the conduct of life, he nevertheless put a great deal into the fabrication of his verse. Matthew Arnold had a theory that the French metrical system is incapable of the finest effects of poetry. It is incapable of the deep poetic sentiment of

> Charmed magic casements, opening on the foam
> Of perilous seas, in faery lands forlorn

Perhaps a critic is more capable of appreciating the finest *nuances* of effect in his own language than in another. Certainly, however, there is something over-drilled and mechanical about the stately ordered march of the Alexandrine double file through the pages of French poetry. We miss the breadth, fluidity, flight of the unrhymed English measure. But in France the moderns are showing the variety, movement, melody of which their lyre is capable. And Verlaine excels them all in the beauty of his musical effects, the organ-richness of his vowel-chords, the linked liquidity of his consonants, the sonority of his assonances. In many of his lyrics there is a Wagnerian fulness of or-

chestration, an unfathomable ground-swell of melody. (pp. 505-06)

Melody, with Verlaine, is always the first consideration. We need be in no doubt, for the poet has stated his intention in his literary testament to his favorite disciple, M. Charles Morice. This consists of nine stanzas ambitiously named **"Art Poétique."** The first line is the important one—

> De la musique avant toute chose.

It is repeated later—

> De la musique encore et toujours!

Minor precepts are: to choose *l'Impair* with its fugitive dissolving effects, void of everything "qui pèse ou pose;" to select your words with easy indifference, for nothing is more enchanting than a tipsy stave . . . ; to prefer *nuance* to color and to avoid *la Pointe* like an assassin; not less, cruel *Esprit* and impure Laughter "wring the neck of Eloquence. Let Rhyme learn wisdom. Melody always, and again I say, melody. Everything else is—literature."

Of course the prescription contains too much of the poet's favorite ingredient. Melodious verbiage will never form a real substitute for poetical sentiment handled with intellectual strength. Perhaps Verlaine felt . . . that it is always necessary to overstate the case a little when you really want to drive home an idea. The remaining precepts poets will follow on their own responsibility. They may, however, be recommended to avoid *la chanson grise,* where the words are chosen a little scornfully, and follow the laborious Flaubert in his quest of the one only right word. (p. 506)

Perhaps it is too figurative an expression to say that Verlaine has added a new string to the French lyre: but at least it cannot be denied that he has made the old ones capable of new effects. True, the vocabulary is limited, and there is a great deal of "rabâchage," a great deal of repetition of favorite phrases and mannerisms. The affectations of the school over which he presided are not entirely absent. Into the vexed sea of symbolist controversy we do not propose to enter, but we may quote, with an eye to Verlaine's defect, M. Stéphane Mallarmé's definition of its aim:

> To name an object means to suppress three-quarters of the pleasure of a poem, *i.e.,* of the happiness which consists in gradually divining it. Our dream should be to suggest the object. The symbol is the perfected use of this mystery, viz., to conjure up an object gradually in order to show the condition of a soul; or, conversely, to choose an object, and out of it to reveal a state of the soul by a series of interpretations.

The result of this suggestion-process is that, for a foreigner at any rate, it is sometimes a little difficult to seize the meaning. Puzzle-verses, even nonsense-verses appear, in which the poet seems to be indulging his own caprice at the reader's expense—verses that seem to have more rhyme than reason, and more assonance than common sense.

I have spoken of the art in treatment: what shall I say of it in the choice of subject? Verlaine is so various, so unexpected and surprising. He will depict one of the great familiar themes, Paris at sunset for example, until you see the towers of Notre Dame darkly expressed on the luminous background, as in an etching by Méryon. Or, passing to the other extreme, he will set the barrel-organ grinding for you until you want to shut your ears to the harsh cacophony, only keeping open eyes for the gutter-ball, surpassing in gravity and precision the march along the smoothest floors to the divinest music. Then the magician shifts the scene, and a whole series of delicately tinted "chromo-lithographs" in Louis Quinze frames is presented to you in metres as dainty as the subject—such tripping, tricksy metres as would have made Racine's wig stand on end. Perhaps there are not many new thoughts, but there are many new pictures, new rendering of old effects, above all new tunes! A train, a "merry-go-round," a steamboat—prosaic, unpromising subjects enough—are made to yield more poetry than anybody before suspected them to contain. Corot-landscapes abound—grey-green spaces with their silent pools and nodding poplars. The aristocratic pride of old château-parks, the impish spirit of the harlequinade, the dreaming life of trees, the animation of Paris streets, the Belgium levels dotted with kine, are a few of the subjects Verlaine sets to music. Of such materials he has built a rhyme which cannot perhaps, in Miltonic phrase, be called "lofty," but which has a character and music of its own. (p. 507)

> *Augustus Manston, "Verlaine," in* Littell's Living Age, *Vol. XI, No. 2720, August 22, 1896, pp. 501-07.*

The Spectator   (essay date 1896)

[*In the following excerpt, the anonymous critic provides an analysis of Verlaine's posthumous volume of poetry,* Invectives. *While stating that this collection is marred by the scathing treatment of its subject, namely the complexities of modern literature, the critic also purports that Verlaine's literary reputation, founded on the strength of his previous volumes, will remain secure.*]

Féroce et doux,"—in these words Paul Verlaine once described his own character, and while he was always anxious . . . to proclaim his ferocity, his verses still attested the serenity of the artist. But the folly of his friends, added to his own extravagance, persisted in creating a misunderstanding; for twenty years the man has been confused with the poet; and his posthumous book, *Invectives* is not altogether designed to correct a false impression.

In the first place, the book must be judged not as poetry, but as a confidence. Written in a loose, familiar style, it is essentially prosaic, and reveals merely the bitter, if justified, hatreds of the man. To appreciate its acridity one must recall the poet's sinister career. Born with an exquisite talent for verse—a talent which neither poverty nor misfortune has impaired—Verlaine was also born into a modern, logical world with the careless habit of the gipsy. He found it perpetually impossible to square his temper with his surroundings; his books were an example and a delight to a whole generation, but he remains the feckless beggar of the Middle Ages. Though he gave far more than

his contemporaries could repay, his life was a long experience of poverty and neglect; and, worse than all, the ungenerous curiosity of his friends, combined with his own imperturbable candour, convinced the ignorant that he was a monster, to whom all the vices were familiar. (p. 237-38)

To the ignorant his name is a synonym for impropriety, but, if you put aside a single volume—*Parallèlement*—there is not one of his works which could offer the slightest affront to a proper modesty. And where in modern literature shall you find a daintier set of impressions than *Romances sans Paroles,* a more delicate expression of love than *La Bonne Chanson,* or a nobler piece of devotion than *Sagesse*? That he resented the misappreciation, in which his own recklessness had helped to involve him, there was no proof until to-day. But in his *Invectives* he makes clear his own sensitiveness, and attacks all those who have patronised his poetry and defamed his life. The book is packed with material of offence, and perhaps it would have been better to publish it before death had made reparation impossible. None the less, it completes the character of the poet, and shows that for all his simplicity he fiercely resented the infamy of his enemies and the lamentable indiscretion of his pretended friends. Among the victims of his invective are journalists, critics, doctors, magistrates, and anarchists. His hatred of professional literature is dignified in its sincerity. "I hate," says he, "all that savours of literature." . . . Strangely enough, slipped in amidst the abuse of publishers, critics, and magistrates, are half a dozen poems of pure patriotism. And these in themselves will be recognised as "invectives" by those who have followed the tortuous movement of modern French literature. For the last ten years poetry and anarchy have been inextricably confused, until the middle-class mind might have believed that the writing of verses and the throwing of bombs were one and the same action. Now, no poet has suffered so bitterly from this lamentable confusion as Verlaine. He has been surrounded by a mob of illiterate youths, for whom literature was a pastime, and the throwing of bombs a *beau geste.* These illiterates have proclaimed themselves everywhere the friends and patrons of the poet, and have involved him, obliquely, in complicity with crime. And now he comes forth with a denunciation of all those who love anarchy, and for whom anti-patriotism is a constant pose. . . . *Invectives,* in brief, will not affect the reputation of Verlaine the poet. It is rather a pamphlet than a work of art. Moreover, it is marred by grave faults of taste and temper. But now it is plain that Verlaine from the first felt and resented the constant aspersions that were cast upon his character. He did not, as the foolish man believed, pocket the insult with a silent shrug. (p. 238)

> *"The Posthumous Verlaine," in* The Spectator, *Vol. 77, No. 3556, August 22, 1896, pp. 237-38.*

Harold Nicolson   (essay date 1921)

[*An English diplomat, critic, and academic, Nicolson is the author of numerous books, including* Tennyson *(1923) and* The Age of Reason, 1700-1789 *(1960). In the following excerpt, Nicolson documents Verlaine's literary relationship with the French Symbolists, provides an in-depth explication concerning the various forms of intimacy Verlaine employed in his verse, and underscores Verlaine's contribution to the extenuation of French syntax.*]

The Symbolist movement stands . . . in a vital relation to the French literature of to-day and of to-morrow, and the reason for this abiding influence is to be found in the scope and pliability of the Symbolist method, in the exploitation of suggestion and intimacy. By the year 1885 the Symbolist temperament was already in existence, already tremulous. It needed only a nucleus of coherence, and this nucleus was provided by Paul Verlaine. Verlaine did not invent Symbolism; he certainly did not direct its future development. But he was able at the psychological moment to catch and reflect the floating aspiration, and to give to it a definite cadence and a form.

Even a cursory reading, even the most exclusive anthology of Verlaine's poems, must give a very vivid sense of intimacy, a feeling of a definite and immensely human personality. The methods by which this impression is conveyed are perfectly obvious; they require no very detailed analysis. The intimacy of Verlaine's better poems is no idle exhibitionism. . . . Its effect resides firstly in the sparing and skilful use of attributes, in an apparently incidental but vivid reference to minor objects which for him radiate with emotional significance. It is not that such objects are of themselves of any interest to us, it is not that we are really affected by their relation to Verlaine's emotions; it is simply that our sentiment of association is set vibrating by these references, that a pleasurable chord is struck by the thought of other objects, intimate to us, which have precisely such a connexion in our own experience. The device is one which can be effective only if used with the most skilful precision, if introduced with consummate musical tact. And it is in this that Verlaine is, at least in his earlier poems, so complete a master.

The instances in which Verlaine employs association, this first device of intimacy, are without number, and in his later poems they multiply and coarsen into triviality. In the verses of his early youth and manhood, however, the device is used but sparingly and with great discretion, and it was through these early poems that he influenced the Symbolists. Sometimes this throb of association will come with a sudden pang in the first line of a poem, sometimes it will be allowed to beat gently through the whole, sometimes, even, its effect will continue in soft pulsations after the poem has been concluded. In all cases Verlaine avoids the trivial by setting the association to some wistful cadence, modulating his line to the exact semitone required. (pp. 238-40)

The device of association is not, however, the only method by which Verlaine attains to the peculiar intimacy of his manner. He secures a similar effect by the garrulous confidences of his poems, by the way in which he renders the casual moods and habits of his life interesting and emotional. The troubles and pleasures of his daily experience, the rain and the sunshine, some trees shivering in a January wind, the warm feel of a south wall, the rattle of a train at night-time, the flare of gas-jets at street corners, the music of a merry-go-round, the silence of white walls, the drip of raindrops upon the tiles;—all these are set to plaintive music, are made to become an emotional reality. With the frankness of a child babbling to some stranger of its toys and its relations, Verlaine is convinced that the most trivial events of his experience are tremendously interesting, are of almost cosmic significance. Like Walt Whitman he is imbued with the interest of things, "even the least particle," with the spirituality of things. For him the value of an emotion is not its depth, not even its intensity, but its truth. He knew full well that his peculiar poetic quality was not attuned to the grandiose, he knew that the deeper emotions would always elude him, and he preferred, therefore, to deal with the more incidental sensations, and to reflect in them the passions and tragedies in which his life was involved. In this he was abundantly right: the minor key can convey its message only by the indirect method; in order to be wistful one must above all be elusive. Where Verlaine was to go wrong was in the exaggeration of this manner, and in his later poems he loses all selective faculty; he becomes too garrulous: he becomes a bore. (pp. 241-42)

But these faults occur in a rush towards the end of his life, and detract but little from his general and more scrupulous handling of the intimate. At moments he uses the direct method with a definite literary effect. In such cases he obtains the impression of intimacy by adopting the tone almost of conversation while being careful to retain the melody of verse. (p. 243)

The methods by which [Verlaine] enriched the element of suggestion and rendered it the main weapon of the Symbolist movement are equally recognisable.

In one of Ruskin's books there is a passage (so far as I recollect, he is discussing the Dutch school of genre pictures) in which he contends that no picture can be really effective without some glimpse of infinity, without some casement opening upon the illimitable, or at least the reflection in mirror or in polished brass of the sky and the open country. The criticism is illuminating in itself and useful as an analogy to the Symbolist conception. Their aim, indeed, was to reveal the infinite, to construct a synthesis which should suggest the whole of man by the whole of art; for them the fatal thing in creation was a sense of finality: the masterpiece should begin only where it appeared to end; it should not merely describe, it should suggest; it should leave behind it some unexpressed vibration. It is this sense of suggestion, this indication of the unattained, which constitutes Verlaine's chief contribution to the new theory.

He has achieved this effect by different methods. In some poems he reaches it deliberately and with conspicuous craftmanship, by placing the glimpse of infinity in the last line. An obvious instance is the effect of continuity secured by the last verse and especially the last line of the **"Clair de lune"**:

> Au calme clair de lune triste et beau,
> Qui fait rêver les oiseaux dans les arbres
> Et sangloter d'extase les jets d'eau,
> Les grands jets d'eau sveltes parmi les marbres.
>
> (pp. 244-45)

[Verlaine] was aware of his own virtues as of his limitations: he knew that he was a master of the elusive, he knew that, with one stroke of the violin, he could render tremulous what would otherwise have been incidental. He knew better than any other man how to make the most fragile poem vibrate with the unattained. But he knew also, at least in his days of complete mastery he knew, that the arrows of his quiver were but few in number. He felt instinctively that in each poem one arrow alone should soar to the empyrean. And hence his economy, hence the supreme certainty of his method. There are many instances of this. One has only to read the last lines of his published poems in order to see how often he kept his violin for the conclusion. He liked to leave his listeners strung by the echoing pulsation of his final resonance: he liked them to gaze at the arrow climbing to the stars. And in this he was triumphant. (p. 246)

Such, therefore, was the manner in which Verlaine was able to voice the twin elements of intimacy and suggestion which were to play so large a part in the machinery of Symbolism. His contribution in this respect was vital to the new school, the coherence which he gave to these two doctrines was definitely constructive in quality. His influence, however, was to go further. He was to succeed more than any other man in enfranchising the French speech, and in rendering French prosody the servant of the poet rather than his master.

Monsieur Jean Cocteau, borrowing brilliantly from André Gide, has in one of his more recent publications defined the French language as a piano without pedals. There is some basis for this assertion. The speech of our so serious neighbours is in truth a chilly mechanism, a machine at once dignified and precise. For generations the French have placed lucidity in the forefront of literary virtues; for them precision has become at once an art and a science. In extreme cases, and in France quite mild cases are terribly apt to become extreme, this fetish of precision has played havoc with their intelligence. . . . [For] many bright and charming people over there in France it does not matter so much what one says so long as one says it lucidly. In serious or simple matters this ideal is not disadvantageous; but in poetry it hampers and it disconcerts, it leads either to a cold reserve or to a turgid rhetoric; it leads either to sterilisation or unreality. Neither of the so Parisian movements of the Romanticists or the Parnassiens had availed to any permanent extent in overturning this oligarchy of words. It was left to the alien immigration of the Symbolists to achieve the final revolution. It was left largely to Verlaine really to vulgarise the poetic diction of the French. And they, for their part, were never wholly to forgive him.

It must be admitted, indeed, that the vocabulary, the syntax and the versification of Verlaine were the "enfants terribles" of the Parnassien movement. He would insist on using expressions which were often affected, sometimes vulgar and sometimes merely odd: he would insist on twisting his grammar into the most derogatory convolutions: he would insist in playing disrespectfully with the Alexandrine, in wallowing shamelessly in shattered caesura and gaping hiatus: he would insist in treating the

French language as a cheery contemporary and not as an aged and unassailable tradition. His choice of expressions is undoubtedly one of Verlaine's minor assets. Sometimes, but not often, he uses isolated words which are strange and arresting in themselves, and we find "bergamasques" and "Ecbatane" incidentally, as well as the following more deliberate jingle:

> Richepin
> N'est pas le nom d'un turlupin
> Ni d'un marchand de poudre de perlinpinpin,
> C'est le nom d'un bon bougre et d'un gentil co-
> pain.

But such instances are not characteristic. Verlaine, who was far from being precious, preferred on the whole to use ordinary and current words and to give them personality by strange attributes or still stranger tricks of syntax and phraseology. (pp. 250-52)

A more personal trick is perhaps his inveterate use of adverbs, which, in violation of the fundamental principle of French versification, he sometimes places at the end of his line. That he resorts to this with great effect can be shown as follows:

> Le piano que baise une main frêle
> Luit dans le soir rose et gris vaguement,

or again:

> L'allée est sans fin
> Sous le ciel, divin
> D'être pâle ainsi!
> . . .

There is a further linguistic habit of Verlaine's which seriously perturbed his contemporaries, namely, his predilection for using foreign words in the midst of his verses. This trick is not always successful, as in his more fluid poems it breaks the flow of the music, but on occasions and when he desires a syncopated effect he can use it well enough:

> Tout l'affreux passé saute, piaule, miaule et
>   glapit
> Dans le brouillard rose et jaune et sale des *Sohos*
> Avec des *indeeds* et des *all rights* et des *haôs*.

All this, to his contemporaries, was to prove infinitely disconcerting, but it must be confessed that one can exaggerate the extent and importance of Verlaine's own innovations in the mere diction of French poetry. In this direction he was to be equalled and outdistanced by most of the new generation of writers. He figures, indeed, rather as the executant of the new diction than as its inventor, and even in this capacity his function was rather to reconcile the public to the audacities of others than to be particularly audacious himself. . . . He treated the French language as an equal, but he did not, as the others, treat it as an inferior. His originality was to manifest itself less in his diction than in his prosody. And here at least he was to be apocalyptic; here at least he was to become, and to remain, enormously unpopular.

I have explained how Verlaine, more than any artist of his period, had exploited the doctrines of intimacy and suggestion: I have explained how he had been able, by giving a new suppleness to French poetic diction, to reconcile the reading public to much that was to follow, and I have qualified his contribution under the latter head by the reservation that in this field he was to be outdistanced by others. He was not as great a man as Mallarmé, his influence to-day is less than that of Rimbaud. He was not as intensely literary as [Jules] Laforgue, he had not the energy of [Maurice] Barrès, nor the intellect of André Gide. He was above all personal, and for this reason he stands to some extent in an isolated position. His influence is all-pervading rather than concentrated. He left behind him an atmosphere rather than a doctrine. He is universal rather than particular.

There is one field, however, in which he was quite consciously to innovate. There is one direction in which his place in literary history will, whatever his intrinsic value, be permanently assured. He was the first to restore to French poetry that wide gamut of melody which it had so unfortunately relinquished.

It is perhaps necessary to explain or at least to indicate the basis on which French prosody is constructed. . . .

In French the stress of the spoken word is almost entirely absent, and their verse is for this reason obliged to fall back upon balance and rhyme. In other words, the rhythm of verse is attained not by the ebb and sway of the spoken language, but by the artificial orchestration of prosody. It is merely the intrinsic beauty of the French language which has prevented this system from becoming gravely defective: it had not, however, until Verlaine's arrival, prevented it from becoming monotonous. (pp. 252-56)

Verlaine, with his sensitive ear for music, felt these limitations instinctively. He determined to free French verse from the distressing monotony which menaced it, and he was able, while not denaturalising the essential quality of the language, to introduce a new and sensitive method by which the slightest tremor of feeling could be registered and expressed. (pp. 259-60)

The prosody of Verlaine is indeed an interesting subject, but it is one which a foreigner can only approach with diffidence. To a foreign ear the poetry of Verlaine is without a doubt the most musical in the French language. It is not so for all his compatriots. . . . Even, however, if we discount much of this apparent obtuseness of the French ear by attributing it to the inherent conventionality of the French character, to the unfortunate extent to which they are taught their own literature at school, the fact must remain that the French language after all is their business and not ours. An Englishman, however well he may know French, is apt to read Verlaine's poems with a more decided lilt than would a Frenchman. . . . Does it mean that the foreign ear catches a deliberate intonation in Verlaine's poems to which the French ear is not attuned? Or does it mean, simply, that we, with our habit of a tonic accent, actually mispronounce the verses, and that we read into them a melody which Verlaine himself had not intended? The truth lies probably between the two. (pp. 261-63)

All this is important, and indeed vital, as explaining Verlaine's influence upon his contemporaries and his successors, but it does not explain why, even to a foreign ear, his

poetry has so personal a cadence, or why it is that his melody is so exactly suited to his own temperament and to the whole range of secondary lyricism. To a large extent, of course, the intense personality of Verlaine's style is due to elements which must escape analysis as they have . . . eluded imitation. But in some minor details of style and prosody it is possible to add to what has already been said by giving certain supplementary suggestions. The essence of Verlaine's style is its gentleness, or, as his detractors would say, its effeminacy. He secures this effect by the profuse employment of labial consonants, and broad vowels, and by the avoidance of all dentals, sibilants or closed vowel-sounds. Verlaine, to a greater degree than other lyric poets, had a predilection for the alliteration or alternation of "l," "m," "n" and "r," and the tune of his most characteristic poems is based on the interchange of these weak and fluid consonants. . . . There was another and even more obvious method by which Verlaine secured the characteristic gentleness of his verse, namely, by his use of feminine rhymes. The rules of French prosody divide, as is well known, all rhymes into either "masculine" or "feminine." Masculine rhymes are those which end with the syllable which contains the tonic vowel: feminine rhymes are those in which the rhyme-syllable is followed by another containing an "e muet." The rule is that the masculine and feminine rhymes should alternate throughout the verse, and this rule, until Verlaine's day, was rarely violated. In some of his more plaintive poems, however, Verlaine has deliberately omitted the masculine couplets and based the whole structure on a feminine sequence, as in the following:

> Je devine, à travers un murmure,
> Le contour subtil des voix anciennes
> Et dans les lueurs musiciennes,
> Amour pâle, une aurore future?

Nor is this all. Even in those poems where he abides by the rule and alternates his masculine with his feminine couplets he is able, by the unsparing use of labials, to render his masculine rhymes as epicene as possible, to render them indeed almost hermaphroditic. The effect obtained is one of fluid simplicity and of plaintive impotence, and that, after all, was the effect which he himself desired. (pp. 265-68)

Verlaine's verses, in their shrouded music, can be appreciated instinctively and without elaboration. Some technical dissection is necessary, of course, if only to disprove the school of criticism which accuses him of ignorance and clumsiness; but the vital essence of his lyrical powers will inevitably elude analysis. It will always remain intuitive in that it was so sincere.

Such was the work and such the life of Paul Verlaine. I have come to a conclusion, and yet I hesitate to conclude. I have endeavoured to furnish a definite, it may be merely a particular, aspect of the works and life of Paul Verlaine. I have endeavoured to do this with sympathy and with that degree of reverence which he would himself have desired. And at the end I am left with one impression only: an impression of disquiet. Is it the elusiveness of the man which leaves behind it this vibration? Is it merely his wistfulness which disconcerts? There are some, of course, who will be privileged readily to dismiss Verlaine as a degenerate whose antics can have but little relation to the complexities of normal life. Many will read into his life-story a warning against the palpable consequences of moral frailty. To many the thing will appear as little more than a reflexion of what they have always, with no little hostility, conceived as being the artistic temperament. Others again will welcome his life and works as constituting a peculiarly vivid specimen for the indulgence of sexual psychology. A few, and to these I render sincere apology, will healthily resent this tampering with an idealised if scarcely apprehended poet. (pp. 269-70)

The quality of Paul Verlaine is not a noble quality; it is not, perhaps, very inspiring. Affable always, courageous sometimes, and so feebly human, he reflects little that is not transitory, he represents much that will always be condemned. The new generation which is now arising in France, a generation dumb as yet, hard and mysterious, but undeniably different, may render little honour to Paul Verlaine. They are less intellectual than their predecessors. It may be that they will be more intelligent. It is quite possible that they will give no thought to poetry.

But for those who have lived before the war the spirit of Paul Verlaine will for long be merged with that of the fair city which he loved so fatally. For them his spirit will still limp and linger in boulevard and alley, in book shop and in tavern: or along those quays whose jumbled outlines glitter in the gay and gentle river as it slides with garbaged waters past church, past prison and past charnelhouse; and so, through soft French meadows, to the sea. (pp. 270-71)

Harold Nicolson, in his Paul Verlaine, *Constable & Company Limited, 1921, 271 p.*

Jean Carrère   (essay date 1922)

[*In the following excerpt, Carrère provides a moralistic analysis of Verlaine's poetic canon. While he acknowledges that Verlaine had the potential to be a great poetical genius, Carrère castigates Verlaine's bohemian lifestyle and dismisses him as a "propagator of moral cowardice."*]

> Am I not born too soon, or late?
>   In all the world what can I do?
> And so profound my pains become;
>   Pray for poor Gaspard, all of you.

These four verses, as moving as a sob, these popular verses which leave a haunting refrain in the heart even more than in the head, and will, like Villon's ballads, live as long as our literature in the memory of men, with their mournful avowal of helplessness, are an admirable summary of the whole of Paul Verlaine's work. They express in a few words, with a radiant simplicity, the whole native nobleness and final decay of this poet of lost genius. (p. 171)

A marvellous and virile genius he was when he made his way at the beginning of his career, resplendent with grace and strength, in the flower-crowned procession of the new poets. He was a genuine, an indisputable, an irresistible master. What would this son of destiny become? A stirrer

of ideas, a guide of souls, a renovator of civilisation? Were we to have a new Vergil, a Dante, an Orpheus? (p. 173)

The very genius of Verlaine, his lyric gifts, the spontaneity of his mind, the frankness of his character, the limpidity of his ingenuous heart—every quality marked him out plainly to write sincere work; and his work is, in fact, verse by verse, the mirror of his own life. . . . [His life] was the most deplorable fall of a being equipped for beauty, strength, and creativeness, who, from lack of will and courage, allowed himself to drift into intellectual weakness, moral cowardice, the defiling of human dignity, until he ended miserably in a useless regret of the time he had lost, a maddening horror of himself, and all the impotence of remorse.

As he was and lived, so he sang and expressed his soul. And this sickly soul lingers in his work. It continues to spread the unwholesome influence with which Verlaine was infected. (p. 181)

When an ordinary man, of poor heart and mediocre mind, with no greatness and no mission, sinks under the burden of misfortune, and drifts from fall to fall into a state of helpless resignation, the unhappy man will, after all, do no harm to any but himself, or, at the most, only to those immediately round him. But if the man is a poet, a great poet, a marvellous inventor of rhythm, one of those privileged beings whose every sensation is transmuted into a figure, and every vision translated into imperishable language, then, by the irresistible prestige of genius, the ideas, the dreams, the desires of this predestined mortal infiltrate stealthily into the mind of all who feel his charm, and they provoke there the same mood.

Suppose Verlaine, with all his gifts, had lived the heroic life of an Æschylus, a Dante, or a Cervantes—suppose he had had the calm majesty of a Petrarch or a Goethe, his work would have been suffused with a noble enthusiasm, or would have held the strength of a robust serenity; and we, the readers and admirers, carried away by his lyricism, would have felt in ourselves the happy radiation of his sunlike genius. Instead of that, the gifts being the same, but the courage of the man having failed, it is the nocturnal and pestilential vapours of a vanquished soul that have gradually spread to our deluded souls.

To deny the influence of Verlaine would be to ignore fifteen or twenty years of the literary history of France, to ignore the frame of mind of many of the young even of our own time. Verlaine was, in all the strength of the word, "a master." He is still. He dominated and guided a whole generation; and the prestige of his work continues to act upon minds that are not well prepared to resist it.

But he is a "bad master"; his work is noxious. Like Musset and Baudelaire, he is a "propagator of moral cowardice." He saps energy, kills hope, annihilates virility. In respect of helplessness and evil he completes the work begun by Musset and continued by Baudelaire. The one resigned all heroism to bury himself wholly in love; the other feared life, and sought refuge in dreaming. . . . [Verlaine] is the last step of the ladder by which a man descends when he refuses to do manly work. In him the last spring of the enfeebled will was broken. Poetic individualism, the great blunder of sickly ages, the exaggerated individualism which in the case of his two predecessors still issued in the fumes of an illusory intoxication, reached a sort of comatose condition in his case. It is the refusal to make any kind of struggle, the spirit of indifference to all external dignity—in a word, absolute *decay*—which Verlaine invests in his work with a magical and pernicious beauty.

Perhaps it would be superfluous to give here a few examples of Verlaine's poetry. We should have to quote, one after the other, every verse of the dozen collections. His work has, in fact, in spite of apparent contrasts, a desolating unity. It is the sad drama of his own life; and in his life, even in the days when he seems to be making an effort, he is "the poor Gaspard," who knows no longer "what he came into the world to do." Never was the distress of helplessness, the paralysis of moral weakness, more consistently expressed.

This comedy—or, rather, this lamentable drama of his life—may be divided into five acts, corresponding with five chief moral situations:

1. Fear of struggle, submission to fate, "saturnism."
2. Stupor and oblivion in pleasure and love.
3. Sadness without cause, despair.
4. Attempt to rise, prayer, morbid mysticism.
5. Final fall, renunciation of all effort, definitive abdication.

Did he not from the very outset of his career and his work place himself under the influence of the planet Saturn?

> The yellow orb which necromancers love.

Did he not speak of the futility of effort and invoke the higher power of fate?

> This plan of life was drafted line by line
> By all the logic of a power malign.

Why struggle, then, if one feels oneself the irresponsible toy of a destiny which one cannot control?

> Away I roam
> On the wicked storm,
>   When it blows.
> First here, then there,
> On the whirling air,
>   Like the straws.

Later, in his most sinister hours, the poet will again plead in excuse this servitude to fate, this futility of struggling against a fore-ordained destiny:

> My life I have squandered; 'tis gone;
> And to all cries of shame and abuse
> I can plead the sufficient excuse
> That 'neath Saturn's dark eye I was born.

It goes so far that in his most cruel trials, in his Belgian prison, he has no cry of revolt either against others or himself. He merely murmurs these lines of tired resignation:

> Of joy in this world I've despaired—
>   Yet am patient still
>   And quite prepared
> For every ill.

But such abandonment of oneself leaves too large a void in the heart, and a man must seek oblivion and numbness elsewhere. Where shall he find them, these entertainments of a feeble soul, if not in love, pleasure, and debauch? . . . So Verlaine, fleeing in his turn the truth that summons him with its daily appeals, asks of love the "drunkenness of the soul" which seems to the dreamers in search of oblivion the great soporific for all our sufferings:

> Hail, sonorous and beautiful kiss! Divine kiss!
> Delight without peer, drunkenness of the soul!
> For the man who puts lip to thy adorable bowl
> Soaks his being in thy deep, inexhaustible bliss.

This "delight without peer," this "soaking in bliss," begins, in Verlaine's work, with a delicious picture which, in its grace and its luminous frame, has an illusive appearance of strength. It is in the **Fêtes galantes,** where we learn that

> The swains that give the serenade,
>   And the fair listeners too,
> Exchange some ponderous conceits
>   Beneath the murmuring bough.

But already, here and there, in this scene of festivity and sweet visions, where we hear the

> . . . thrill of mandolines that down
> The shivering breezes goes,

we see trembling in the poet's avowals that perturbation of heart and sense which follows the inebriation of artificial paradises:

> Dusk fell, Autumn dusk so dubious;
> Dreaming on our arms so low,
> Beauty whispered things that set
> *My soul a-tremble even now.*
>   . . .

But, alas! who can exorcise what Baudelaire calls "the knowing Ideal"? Neither the "drunkenness of the soul" in kisses, nor the "ponderous conceits of the fair listeners," nor the "dark woods" in which they seek refuge from the world, can prevent what the other great poet of the dream called "the operation of avenging mystery." And the "good song" soon gives place to the mournful air of the **Romances sans paroles:**

> This little soul which doth lament
> Itself in such a sleepy plaint,
>   It is our own, is it not so?
>   . . .

And in that mood of despair sadness invades the heart, and the poet knows no longer what the cause of all his trouble is:

> He weeps for no reason
> In his disheartened heart.
> What, was there no treason?
> The tears have no reason.
>
> 'Tis the worst kind of fate
> When one knows not even why,
> Without love, without hate,
> The heart finds not its mate.

This bitter lament over the difficulty of finding joy poor

Verlaine was to repeat all his life, on every possible note. It is a sort of *leit motiv* of his work:

> A sleep black and deep
> Dully falls on my life.
> Dear hope, do thou sleep;
> Desire, cease thy strife.
>   . . .

And at last he breaks out against everything—against himself, fate, and woman:

> Of a truth I have suffered enough,
> Ever spurred by the hounds like a wolf
> That must fly every day to new place,
>   With no den and no rest,
>   Ever haunted and pressed,
> Driven on by the whole human race.

Will he never find the refuge that he seeks, this "hunted wolf," "driven on" by sadness and remorse?

Yes. He finds it for a moment. At least, he thinks that he has found it—in mysticism.

Much has been said about Verlaine's mysticism. Many have spoken highly of the supposed evolution of the poet, raising himself to "the pure light of the Christian faith" after the trials and errors of his youth. I have heard devout Catholics say that the author of *Sagesse* was a great Christian poet; if not the greatest, the only, Christian poet. Others saw in him the restorer of mysticism in France. I have been present at very learned lectures in psychic science, at which some of Verlaine's sonnets were read as models of spiritual purity. I am incompetent, I admit, to discuss questions of religious doctrine with theologians and *magi;* yet I think that these learned critics are mistaken. In default of special light, I have for my guidance in this study, as a basis of comparison, some knowledge of other poets and writers whose Christian faith was indisputable, such as Dante, Bossuet, and Lamartine; and I am certainly not wrong in thinking that in their prayers and invocations there is an entirely different accent from that of poor Verlaine. In any case, we are quite certain of one thing—that books like *Sagesse* and *Amour* do not mean either a change or an exception in Verlaine's work. They are completely bound up with all the others. They are a logical outcome of the others. They have the same general tone. They round off the lamentable unity of this lost life. They are simply one act, along with others, of this painful drama. It is the attempt of a despairing man to find salvation: a useless attempt, moreover, because the poet will show just the same moral inertia here as elsewhere.

Certainly there is no doubt about the sincerity of his conversion. His faith is profound. The prayers issue from his heart. Verlaine is incapable of hypocrisy, either in good or evil. But there is no force in his faith. It does nothing. It consists only in weeping over himself, in unceasing repentance, without the least attempt to rise.

> God of the lowly! Save this child of wrath
>   (pp. 181-89)

One feels that, even in the sincerity of prayer, Verlaine has no will. His mysticism is merely a refuge from life. He casts himself into the arms of the Church much as vaga-

bonds and swashbucklers once sought protection in monasteries. It is not with an idea of bettering his life; it is to escape the punishment that threatens.

The whole "wisdom" of the poet may be summed up in these words—Catholic, I admit, but far from heroically Catholic: "Lord, I am a very wicked child, and I fear I am unable to change. But I love You so much, Lord, and I feel so humble a contrition, that, surely, You will let me off." (p. 190)

In spite of this movement toward the light, the last act of [Verlaine's] life and his work was even more deplorable than the rest. He went from fall to fall, finally abdicating all moral beauty, defiling even the flower of his poetic genius in the degradations of *Jadis et naguère* and the insanities of *Parallèlement.* No doubt, we occasionally still find the admirable lyric note of *Sagesse,* the marvellous picturesqueness of the *Fêtes galantes;* but the soul becomes weaker and weaker, the poetry poorer and poorer, until at last we get these painful confessions of depravation:

> Prince or princess, slave of virtue or vice.
> Whoever doth chide me, be he high or low,
> Poet of fame or announcer of bliss,
> Know that I am the peer of the fiery Sappho.

We will go no farther. Had he not in his hidden soul the naïveness of a savage child? He knew not the evil that he did to himself and others. But he did it. Let us, all the same, pity him and love him. Let us recall with deferential compassion the "dolorous way" of this failure. Let us pray for the poor Gaspard. But we have a right to defend ourselves against the contagion: to say that the great poet Verlaine, born to realise a high destiny, endowed to accomplish a work of beauty and strength, stopped at the first inns on his journey and failed in his mission. (pp. 192-93)

> *Jean Carrère, "Paul Verlaine," in his* Degeneration in the Great French Masters, *translated by Joseph McCabe, T. Fisher Unwin, Limited, 1922, pp. 169-96.*

Havelock Ellis   (essay date 1935)

[Ellis was a pioneering psychologist and a respected contributor to English letters as both an editor and critic. His most famous work, the seven-volume Studies in the Psychology of Sex *(1897-1928), was greatly responsible for changing British and American attitudes toward human sexuality. In addition to his scientific writings, Ellis retained an active interest in literature throughout his life, editing the highly respected Mermaid Series and authoring such critical works as* Affirmations *(1898) and* From Marlowe to Shaw: The Studies, 1876-1936, in English Literature *(1950). In the following excerpt, Ellis provides a psychological analysis of Verlaine, stating that the poet was "the world's absolute victim, [representing] genius naked and helpless."]*

If I were asked to say which among the persons of distinction I had met seemed to possess most of the primitive emotional temperament of genius I should reply: 'Verlaine.' There were some, possibly less rare, whose genius was primarily the expression of intellectual constitution; others in whom intellect seemed to conceal a highly organised emotional temperament; still others, more numerous, in whom an element of genius seemed inhibited or disguised by some foreign mask, a man of the world's, a moralist's, and so forth. But here genius was reduced to its simplest terms, naked and helpless to all the winds of heaven, all compact of imagination, the prey of its impulses. In all genius there is the child; Verlaine was a child on a colossal scale, with the child's eternal freshness, and the full endowment of those less innocent instincts which in some degree psychologists find to mark even the healthy normal child. A mass of living sensitive protoplasm open to every influence of Nature and humanity, he remained unconfined by that tough restricting hide which gives to most of us adults a certain stolid rigidity, a factitious indifference to our environment. He stood at the furthest remove from the pachyderms, more like those primitive molluscous creatures of the sea which zoologists have shown to be permeated all through by as yet undifferentiated and unprotected senses.

Thus Verlaine represents genius naked and helpless. All, or nearly all, the eminent French men of letters who were his contemporaries had some breastplate against the arrows of the world. Victor Hugo was saved, amply saved, by his colossal superiority-complex; Edmond de Goncourt held fast by the tastes and traditions, as well as the income, of a gentleman; Zola always cultivated the industrious habits of an accomplished journalist; Huysmans devoted much of the energy of his acute intellect to warding off the shocks of the world against his exquisitely sensitive organism; Rimbaud possessed a tough virile energy which more than balanced his genius; Villiers de l'Isle Adam, alone almost as helpless as Verlaine, was in some degree protected by his ability to merge the practical world in an ideal world. Verlaine, throughout, was by native constitution the world's absolute victim. (pp. 268-69)

Verlaine was a pilgrim throughout life, the victim of all the Fates, severely shunned by all respectable people, libelled as the head of a ridiculous coterie, twice the inmate of a prison, many times the inmate of hospitals; and at the end his death was recorded in a few lines of small type, among which one caught the words 'dissipation,' 'vice,' 'crime,' 'failure.' Certainly from the ephemeral point of view Verlaine was a failure. Even for his publisher, who would, however, occasionally advance a few francs, he can have been little better than a failure, and when I have seen the poet draw a two-franc piece from his purse, it seemed with a proud and joyful surprise. For the Church he was a failure, a depressing failure, for when he seemed at the point of becoming a miracle of saving grace he relapsed. From whatever worldly or social viewpoint we look at his life, it was a failure. But from another standpoint it has been possible to consider him as the greatest success in French literature on his own lines since Villon. (pp. 269-70)

Verlaine's periods of religious adoration and humility were as spontaneous and genuine as his more vicious impulses. The priest who received Verlaine's last confession is still living, and it is reported that, when directly questioned about Verlaine, his only reply is: 'C'était un Chrétien, Monsieur,' though Lepelletier states that he was not a believer, and that *Sagesse* was the expression of a pass-

ing mood, even that associated with *Parallèlement.* 'On our side,' concludes Thibaudet, 'we may settle the matter, with Mallarmé in his *Divagations,* by saying: "He was a poet." And a fine English critic, with the facts of Verlaine's life before him, Earle Welby, asks: 'Where else shall we find so complete an illustration of the qualities, personal and literary, which go to the making of the purest poetry? We see here the most completely poetical life lived by any modern poet.' (pp. 270-71)

When approaching Verlaine, we . . . encounter aspects seemingly in conflict, each of which we have to come to terms with before we can see him truly. Even if they may not seem so disastrous as to his contemporaries, we must recognise them in order to comprehend his significance.

In the first place, we have to realise that here is not the kind of poet we have learnt to expect in France. He was not even a poet the French expected. . . . Even the genius of Baudelaire had remained more in touch with those accepted masters than this rebel, who yet owed something of his first inspiration to Baudelaire and others. He broke the traditional moulds of verse, he violated conventional modes of sentiment. His forms of verse and his ways of feeling were alike new. Several critics and poets of distinction, indeed, spoke words of admiration. Only, however, in 1888—about a year before I met him and when most of his best work had already appeared—was there any clear and decisive recognition of Verlaine's genius or any attempt to analyse it. Even then it came not from any critic of acknowledged authority, but from one of the new men, Charles Morice, a critic of singular receptivity for new influences and able to enter into the spirit of Verlaine, though he was himself a child of Provence and Verlaine characteristically a Northerner. (p. 272)

It was Morice who first emphasised the conflicting elements of character—often dwelt on since—so well expressed in Verlaine's extraordinary face. Never was a human face, he remarks, more violently expressive of irreconcilable enjoyments than in the contradictory formation of this strange head: 'the high and broad brows which serve as the dome of powerful jaws—the forehead of a dreamy cenobite and the jaws of a voracious barbarian—in a struggle left to chance, an irregular head, without grace and yet of almost terrifying beauty,' the head of an immortal child.

It is pleasant to me to pay a tribute to the insight of Charles Morice who thus clearly set forth a critical estimate which was a daring novelty at the time, though now we take it for granted; it was Morice who first clearly grasped the genius of Verlaine, and his analysis of it has never been excelled. For an Englishman, however, it was perhaps easier than for a Frenchman to recognise the genius of Verlaine. And that not only because in our own island we have had poetic manifestations of allied character; in Burns, for instance, alike in his genius and his personality, we have, less extravagantly presented, those two conflicting elements. More deeply, Verlaine had a real affinity to the genius of England not to be found in any other French poet of the same eminence. (p. 273)

We frequently see Verlaine's face described, usually by

people who never met him, as 'hideous.' It may be possible to say the same of the traditional image of Socrates (whom Verlaine somewhat resembled), though its irregularity was interesting and redeemed by its expressiveness. His mother, whom he is said to have resembled in features, was good-looking. In later years Verlaine's features in real life, while far from regular or handsome, could not fairly be called hideous, nor—putting aside caricatures—do they so appear in his portraits. But there is no doubt that an inborn irregularity and disharmony of feature was present—evidently associated with defective heredity—and that this was pronounced in early life. Verlaine's first and most sympathetic biographer, Lepelletier, a friend and early school-fellow, states that in youth he showed 'grotesque ugliness,' and mentions that when he first brought the boy Verlaine to his own home, his mother remarked afterwards that he looked like 'an orang-utang escaped from the Zoo.'

It is thus that the approach to Verlaine has been rendered difficult. Even for some early admirers 'decadence' seemed 'really a new and beautiful and interesting disease,' while more robust English critics, brushing aside these fantasies, were content to regard Verlaine as 'one of the chiefs of the Fleshly school,' and even in the same breath—with equal

Reproduction of a Verlaine poem addressed to Edmond Lepelletier, the poet's friend and biographer.

incongruity and absurdity—'the hierophant of the Art for Art dogma.' So hard has been the approach to Verlaine! (pp. 276-77)

Even before [Verlaine] had an interest in poetry, he showed taste in drawing with ink, pencil, and colours. His sense of the music of speech, of which he says nothing, evidently came later and might even be regarded as a transformation of his visual concentration, a love of *nuances* in language. With it there was a curious love for the plastic moulding of speech. Sometimes, I well recall, one would hear him mouthing some strange new word over and over on his tongue, shouting it in different tones, emitting it with sudden explosive energy as though to catch unaware its spirit, not resting until he had gained a mastery of its vocal value. So a dog will sometimes lick round and round some morsel of dubious value until at last it gains a sweetness, not its own, which he has imparted to it, and he swallows it with gusto. It was thus, I am sure, that Verlaine had dealt with the various English words he has used as titles for poems, finding in them a beauty and expressiveness which for our ears they mostly lack. But to this habit of patiently testing the precise value of words in sound and their exact *nuance,* Verlaine owed his miraculous mastery of verbal enchantment, which seems so artless and instinctive.

By origin, as well as by the quality of his art, Verlaine singularly recalls Watteau, who also was of Walloon origin, and also born in France to come under French influences. There was the same kind of inspiration, the same style of genius, in both, and in both it was that of the Ardennes. The critic of Watteau insists on his delicate and sensitive realism, his love of *nuance,* the almost musical quality of his rhythms, his partiality for detached studies. We seem to be hearing about Verlaine in terms of a closely related art. And for both of them alike it is the *Fête Galante*—the title each chose—which expresses the ideal of life. (pp. 280-81)

Verlaine was a child, a dreamer, who walked in his own remote world, putting together words that seem to be made of sighs, yet when they came from this magician's lips turned to music which haunts us for ever. He was not a good citizen, not an effective man in any relationship; it was possible to consider him vicious, and on one occasion even to treat him as a criminal; it was scarcely respectable to be seen walking down the boulevard with him. Yet of such is the Kingdom of Heaven, and it is not only in the New Testament that they are met.

He died in humble lodgings in the Rue Descartes. . . . And again an English journalist ended up a supercilious obituary notice with 'another sample of a certain kind of unsuccess which is the halo of the modern French poet.'

The halo has become more radiant even to the journalists now. Less than twenty years later the sale of a single volume of Verlaine's poems had passed one hundred thousand copies. He has exchanged his worn-out garments for more dignified raiment and looks down more imposingly than he was wont to in life from his monument in the Luxembourg Gardens, amid the roses and rhododendrons, and the chestnuts on the outskirts. Not too far away, yet not too indiscreetly near, he is accompanied by the indolent Silenus in bronze, riding among fauns and supported by naked nymphs. No spot in Paris could be more fittingly devoted to the memory of Verlaine, and here in autumn the mists that he loved and the purifying rain envelop him in their beneficent gloom. (pp. 282-83)

> *Havelock Ellis, "The Approach to Verlaine," in his* From Rousseau to Proust, *Houghton Mifflin Company, 1935, pp. 268-283.*

Mary M. Colum (essay date 1937)

[*Colum, who regularly contributed criticism to such periodicals as* The New Republic *and* The Saturday Review of Literature, *was called "the best woman critic in America" by William Rose Benét in 1933. In the following excerpt, which was originally published in 1937, Colum investigates Verlaine's role in the revolt against realism by emphasizing the influence of Arthur Rimbaud on Verlaine's literary accomplishments. The translations in the text are provided by the critic.*]

In the inner courts of literature, for over fifty years there has been a struggle against the doctrine, the technique, the content, and the language of realism. It began in France, for it was there that the doctrine and the practice had ripened fastest, and the revolt was in full blast before the original doctrine had reached some of the other literatures. The revolters made little headway as far as the novel and drama went, for it was to the interest, not only of the real writers in these forms, but especially of a large group of the new trade writers, to hold the novel and the drama bound to the fact, the document, the observation of external and everyday life. (p. 312)

[Therefore, the] first clear indication of a strong revolt against realism was given in poetry. Of the two who began the revolt, Paul Verlaine and Arthur Rimbaud, both were in descent from Baudelaire, though they started with a leaning towards the Parnassians. (p. 315)

Verlaine, before his meeting with Rimbaud, was a fine poet; after this meeting, he became a great one, for all the potentialities that were in him, of original thought, of emotion, of musical utterance, all his latent sense of revolt against the nullity towards which literature was heading, came to the surface under the influence of this prophetic and penetrating mind and this disrupting personality. All that Verlaine did not of himself understand of the necessity for renewal in literature, this young man made him aware of. Rimbaud was an example of precocious intellect and poetical intuition unparalleled in literature, with perhaps the exception of Chatterton. He was a sort of elemental creative force, bursting to reform everything he touched. In his "L'Alchimie du Verbe"— "Transfiguration of the Word"—he tells us how he wanted to invent not only new poetical forms but a new world with new stars, new flowers, new flesh; he wanted especially to invent a new language, for, as he said, it was impossible to write poetry in words and sentences that had been weighed down by the leaden meanings of practical life. (pp. 322-23)

Whatever has to be said against their relationship, it was,

while it lasted, a period of intense intellectual, poetical, and emotional activity for both Rimbaud and Verlaine. Under the influence of Rimbaud, Verlaine wrote his **"Art Poétique,"** which crystallized the new attitudes towards poetry and which later became a sort of gospel with the Mallarméan symbolists. Most of the theories of this poem were derived from Rimbaud and from English poetry. To write poetry like English poetry in a language like French, which had been developed logically with the avowed intention of becoming an instrument of expression of the greatest clarity, was immensely difficult. To express under-tones and over-tones, hidden meanings, to attain the half-said thing, to make an appeal directly from one sensibility to another, was, in the language and in the existent metres, if not exactly an impossibility, at least a perplexing task. Consequently Verlaine's **"Art of Poetry,"** which, though written during his relation with Rimbaud, became generally known only a decade later, was accepted as a liberation; Verlaine, following Poe and Baudelaire, demanded in poetry *de la musique avant toute chose*— music above all—and he marched haughtily past the great French sign-posts demanding the *mot juste*. The latest of these, it will be remembered, had been set up by Gautier and Flaubert. Verlaine asked the poet to choose his words somewhat carelessly, unprecisely, to join the precise to the unprecise—in short, to achieve, not the exact, but the nuanced. This was more in accordance with Rimbaud's practice than with Verlaine's.

> Car nous voulons la nuance encor,
> Pas la couleur, rien que la nuance!
> Oh! la nuance seule fiance
> Le rêve au rêve et la flûte au cor!
>
> . . . .
>
> For we want the nuance,
> Nothing of color, only the nuance!
> Oh! the nuance alone weds
> The dream to the dream and the flute to the horn.

In a succeeding stanza he tenders that since often-quoted advice—"Prends l'éloquence et tords-lui son cou!"— "Take eloquence and wring its neck." This manifesto has been taken very seriously by the poets in English since the 1890's, the line about twisting the neck of eloquence being put forward as a poetical principle, though, as a matter of fact, it has very little application for an English poet, for what Verlaine meant by "eloquence" was that deliberate study of rhetoric so usual in France and which had played such havoc with French literature after the great classical period. But eloquence had been a glory in English poetry, especially with the great dramatic poets, and still remains a glory when it does not sink to mere declamation. Verlaine recommended the break-up of the French line into unequal lines, and after a mocking attack on rhyme and a praise of assonance, he summed up the modern Art of Poetry in two stanzas that have passed into the literatures of the world.

> De la musique encore et toujours!
> Que tons vers soit la chose envolée,
> Qu'on sent qui fuit d'une âme en allée
> Vers d'autres cieux à d'autres amours.

Que ton vers soit la bonne aventure
Éparse au vent crispé du matin
Qui va fleurant la menthe et le thym . . .
Et tout le reste est littérature!

. . . .

Music again and ever!
Let your verse be a thing on wings,
Which visibly came from a soul in flight
Towards other skies and other loves.

Let your verse be the gay adventure
Scattered on the crisp wind of morning
Which snares the scents of mint and thyme . . .
And all the rest is literature.

(pp. 323-26)

Mary M. Colum, "The Revolt," in her From These Roots: The Ideas That Have Made Modern Literature, 1937. Reprint by Columbia University Press, 1944, pp. 312-60.

Ruth Z. Temple   (essay date 1944)

[*Temple is an American critic and educator specializing in English literature of the late-Victorian and Edwardian periods. Her critical history,* The Critic's Alchemy: A Study of the Introduction of French Symbolism into England, *(1953) is among the most informative and illuminating works on fin-de-siècle writing. In this excerpt, taken from an essay read at the meeting of the Modern Language Association in December, 1944, Temple examines Verlaine's laudable reputation among the English critics of his day and suggests that the poet's popularity among English readers was due to the fact that "Verlaine's verse lends itself with comparatively little distortion of the French prosodic cadence to scansion according to English meters."*]

For centuries English critics have been disposing of French poetry as un-English and therefore not poetry, or, on rare and mellow occasions, paying it the doubtful compliment that George Saintsbury paid Baudelaire: Baudelaire may really be called a poet for his poetry is un-French. Not essentially different from this was the conclusion of so supposedly sympathetic a critic as Mr. Harold Nicolson, writing as recently as 1921, on Verlaine [see excerpt dated 1921].

There have been various attempts to account for this stubborn English prejudice, and indeed a thorough-going explanation must precede the formulation of an adequate theory of "western" poetry. I propose to consider here one small aspect of the large problem, namely, why of all 19th century French poets Verlaine is the one who has most nearly disarmed English critics and charmed English readers. (p. 63)

One quality conceded to Verlaine's poetry by his English admirers is among those which English critics generally deny to French poetry as a whole and indeed to the French language. In 1899, that is, when Verlaine had been before the English public for about ten years, a discussion of the French language in the correspondence columns of the *Saturday Review* was able to generate enough interest to last through the issues from June 17 to September 2. Max

Beerbohm initiated the controversy. . . . The French language, commented Max, as so many Englishmen before him had done, though a perfect instrument of expression, lacks mystery. "It casts none of those purple shadows which do follow and move with the moving phrases of our great poets."

Maurice Baring rose to defend the French language. French words, he said, are no less suggestive than English words to one who has learned them in childhood, and, since he was of that privileged group, he cited lines of French poetry which to him were as evocative as the lines of *Hamlet*—lines from Racine, from Hugo, from Baudelaire, and from a Verlaine poem which has tempted several translators, **"Clair de lune."** . . . One gathers, however, that the majority of correspondents . . . were no less groundlessly convinced of the inferiority of the French language both in general and as a vehicle for poetic suggestion.

Yet the power of "suggestion of the infinite" is one of the qualities which English critics unanimously find in Verlaine. Mr. Nicolson (in his *Verlaine*) called it Verlaine's chief contribution to the new poetic theory, that is, symbolism. And, of course, once it is found in a poet—a single poet—it can no longer be denied to the language in which he writes. The wonder is that if it can be discerned in one poet, it cannot be discerned in another. (p. 64)

[How] is it that Verlaine, who uses the language which so many of the English have condemned as unevocative, incapable of infinite suggestion, nevertheless enchants the English reader by those very qualities.

It is not that Verlaine exploits as few French poets have done the *sound* effects of language to the end of establishing a mood, or creating an impression, of "infinite" vagueness and mystery. If it really were infinite suggestion of associative meaning that the English reader was susceptible to,—associative meaning achieved through the rare epithet, the startling metaphor, the stark juxtaposition of concrete and abstract—this he would find in Rimbaud, in Mallarmé, in Baudelaire. . . . But may it not be that the kind of verbal magic to which the foreigner is most responsive is that of sound. The associative meanings of a word are a function of its use in living and in literature and therefore are not readily accessible except to one who has known a language fully in both these ways. The suggestions of sound do not depend to the same extent on daily familiarity and literary sophistication. (One need only point out, if this seems paradoxical, that music is a more nearly universal art than poetry.) Sound effects of this order in language must indeed be fairly *obvious* to be perceptible to the foreigner—the texture of Racine's poetry is no more easily appreciated than the texture of Pope's, and some of our most famous poets have been insensitive to the latter. But these magical effects of sound in Verlaine's poetry *are* fairly obvious: It is certain that they were admired by the English critics, who extolled, together with the "infinity" of Verlaine's verse, its melodies, though not, I think, perceiving the connection between the two. (p. 65)

Effects of sound, then, lingering, plaintive, infinitely suggestive and thus even on occasion suggestive of the infinite, were certainly a primary cause of Verlaine's popularity with English readers. But these were not *wholly* new in French verse. Was there not something else that predisposed the English reader to listen more sympathetically to Verlaine than to other French poets? The critics said that it was the simple rhythms of his verse and praised him (quite inaccurately) for having broken the back of the alexandrine and for defying all the rules of French prosody. One or two of them even spoke of his rhythms as *English*—and this, of course, they meant as the highest tribute. I think it may be—though not the virtue it seemed to them—quite literally true, and even more important than they realized.

I suspect that the extraordinary popularity the little song from *Sagesse* has enjoyed (one of those Nicolson mentioned and the one chosen for the *Academy* contest) is owing in part to the fact that it scans almost perfectly as iambic verse—the most common English metre. . . . [The] frequent occurrence of familiar English *cadences* in Verlaine's poetry—which has not, I think, been pointed out—quite certainly supplements the English metres of his verse in attracting English readers.

It would seem, then, that much of Verlaine's verse lends itself with comparatively little distortion of the French prosodic cadence to scansion according to English metres and rings to English ears familiar strains. Thus one of the major stumbling blocks for the English in reading French verse intelligently is removed, and it is not surprising that Verlaine's English readers were—and are—predisposed to hear the music of his words and so to find in his poetry that other excellence of English poetry, suggestions of the infinite. (p. 66)

Ruth Z. Temple, "Verlaine and his English Readers," in Comparative Literature Newsletter, *Vol. III, No. 8, May, 1945, pp. 63-6.*

Philip Stephan   (essay date 1961)

[*An American educator noted for his scholarship of French literature, Stephan is the author of a number of critical essays, including "The Poetry of Tristan Corbière" (1961) and "Naturalist Influences on Symbolist Poetry, 1882-1886" (1972). In the following excerpt, Stephan focuses on the humor evident, but often ignored, throughout Verlaine's verse, using the dictate that "[the] esthetic basis of humor is the spectator's dissociation from the comic character" as the foundation of his argument.*]

While the numerous commentaries on Verlaine's **"Art poétique"** have placed understandable emphasis on the questions of music and rime, they have ignored the fact that Verlaine devotes almost as much space to wit, or humor, as he does to rime and music. Why does Verlaine attack wit so vehemently, when we are not aware that he wrote humorous verse? That is a question which this article proposes to take under consideration. . . .

[The] esthetic basis of humor is the spectator's dissociation from the comic character. Thus, we laugh at the players in a comedy because we feel they are different from us

and we suffer with the protagonist of a tragedy because we identify ourselves with him. While not all Verlaine's impassive poetry is humorous, all his humorous poetry springs from the same sense of personal detachment that we find both in the Parnassian poems of *Poèmes saturniens* and in the eighteenth-century poems of *Fêtes galantes.* (p. 196)

Even in Verlaine's early Parnassian poems, one can see that two types of impassivity are present. In one type appears the young poet's debt to his poetic predecessors, such as Gautier and Baudelaire. In the poem, **"Une Grande Dame"** . . . , the emphasis on the tactile, enduring qualities of the lady's beauty, the use of artistic terms like *sertir* and *bleu de Prusse,* the clever *pointe* and Baudelairian sadism of the conclusion, all suggest imitation of older, established poets. (p. 197)

In a second type of impassivity, Verlaine's treatment of prostitutes and beautiful women reveals, we feel, something more than his desire to imitate the Parnassians. While Spain, the sea, and medieval scenes are typically Parnassian subjects, the courtesan is a less frequent theme of the *Parnasse*. On the contrary, we believe that Verlaine has chosen a subject emotionally near to him—biographically, we know that he was already frequenting *filles de joie* at the time *Poèmes saturniens* were composed—and that the impassivity of these poems is a mask for his personal anxieties. . . . Although he often describes women and love, he keeps them distant by impassive description or by consigning them to the unreal world of dream and memory.

Such distant emotions occur on a wider and more complex scale in *Fêtes galantes,* where the poet is separated from emotion, not by his own impassivity, but by his use of "dramatic space" to isolate both the characters of his poems and the emotions they undergo. (pp. 197-98)

A noteworthy trait of [**"Sur L'Herbe"**] is that it consists almost entirely of dialogue, which establishes mood and expresses ideas as in a play. The theatrical analogy is heightened by the title and the opening sentence, "L'Abbé divague," which can be construed as stage direction. . . . A poem composed as a play suggests a spectator-actor relationship between the reader and the characters of the poem. While the reader is open to the characters' emotions and even shares them to a certain degree, still those emotions tend to remain distant; they belong to the actors, not to the reader, not even to the poet. . . . The reader is an onlooker and not a party to the situation and, as an onlooker, he is separated not only by psychological distance, but also by physical distance. The spectator relationship suggests, at least by implication, that the reader is as far from the scene as the audience is from the players on a stage. (pp. 198-99)

Furthermore, the pictorial quality of the term "dramatic space" is exemplified by the poems **"Pantomime"** and **"Fantoches,"** where the visual description of the characters and of their actions suggests, indeed, a painting. . . .

This is not to say that Verlaine expresses himself with diminished effectiveness in the dramatic poems of *Fêtes galantes,* but we do mean to assert that there is not the same intimacy, the same immediacy of feeling for the reader that we find in poems where the poet speaks directly, expressing himself without the intermediary of dramatic characters.

As with the reader, so with the poet. Verlaine places his emotions in other persons, away from himself, entrusting them with the expression of his own feelings. . . . Instead of talking to the reader, he has his characters speak to the reader for him. . . . In his use of dramatic space, Verlaine writes emotion-filled verses, if not coldly, at least with the dispassionate craft of a dramatist.

Verlaine's humor and irony serve to alienate him from the emotional situations of his poetry; this statement is especially true, in *Fêtes galantes,* of love. By treating amorous relationships humorously, Verlaine dissociates himself from them, implying that he, too, is remote and unmoved. . . . (p. 199)

That Verlaine uses humor consciously in order to establish a distance between himself and the emotion of love is apparent, we feel, in poems where wit disintegrates and a more authentic expression of emotion emerges. Such a poem is **"La Chanson des ingénues,"** where, in the initial stanzas, Verlaine presents, again in somewhat theatrical fashion, the reaction of a group of innocent girls, the *ingénues,* who ridicule love because they fail to understand it. (p. 200)

In his comic portrayal of lovers, Verlaine emphasizes their exaggerated poses and sighs, their complete failure with the frivolous girls, who, in their innocence, cannot understand why the men act as they do. Here is a fitting example of humor as detachment, for it is only in their ignorance of an emotion they have not yet experienced that the girls are able to take such a humorous view. In contrast to this is the last stanza, suddenly serious, where the girls' prescience destroys the comic aspect and causes their hearts to beat harder. . . . Thus, in a poignant ending, Verlaine abandons the distance which he has established between himself and emotion, to bring it closer to himself and to the reader in a moment of intimacy and empathy. (p. 201)

Verlaine develops the idea of psychologically distant emotion further by emphasizing the superficiality of characters in *Fêtes galantes.* Just as the girls of **"Ingénues"** ridicule the love which they do not yet understand . . . , so the persons in **"Sur L'Herbe"** and **"En Bateau"** . . . give themselves over to a mood of reckless and irresponsible gaiety. Love is the subject of their witty remarks, yet we know that love for them is not a sincere affection, but a gay farce; indeed, in spite of the sensuous tenor of *Fêtes galantes,* in some of these poems one is inclined to wonder if the characters carry their feelings as far as physical gratification. On the contrary, the hilarity of such poems seems suspended at an indefinite point in time, with no tomorrow to reckon with, without even the possibility of further development of the emotions which Verlaine sketches deftly and almost, it seems, hastily. (p. 202)

By their façade of inane gaiety, by their failure to understand personal sentiment, Verlaine's *personnages* show the distance that separates them from genuine pathos or joy. (p. 203)

While Verlaine's emotions are distant from him in many poems of his first two collections of verse, in subsequent volumes the poet is closely identified with his emotions, locating them within himself. In *La Bonne Chanson* he expresses his feelings directly and without reservation. If the enthusiastic lyricism of that collection appears poetically less sophisticated than *Poèmes saturniens* or *Fêtes galantes,* a new refinement of method appears in *Romances sans paroles,* which represent another effort to express emotions in an intimate, subtle fashion.

A distinction should be made between distant emotions and those which, while close to the poet, are expressed in restrained and indirect language. Particularly in *Romances sans paroles* Verlaine expresses close emotions indirectly, often by fusing physical sensation and personal sentiment in a description of landscape, as in a poem of the **"Ariettes oubliées"** series:

> O bruit doux de la pluie
> Par terre et sur les toits!
> Pour un coeur qui s'ennuie,
> O le chant de la pluie! . . .

Here the poet's sadness is stated impersonally, by the figure of "a heart" and by the suggestion that the "gentle sound of the rain" comforts his heart. . . . Verlaine does not commit the pathetic fallacy of projecting his emotions into the landscape; rather, physical sensation serves as a meeting point between man and nature, and by comparing his emotions to the sensations he feels, the poet is able to ascribe his emotions to the scene before him in "an intimate interpenetration of man and nature." Thus the landscapes of *Romances sans paroles* do not remove the poet's sentiments from him, as do the dramatic poems of *Fêtes galantes;* neither do these careful, Impressionist descriptions represent the objectivity of Parnassian descriptions like **"Une Grande Dame"** or **"Un Dahlia."**

Furthermore, it should be pointed out that both in *Poèmes saturniens* and in *Fêtes galantes* poems where emotions are close to the poet exist along with poems of distant emotion. . . . The poems representing distant emotions are, then, one current among several. It is important to note, however, that this attitude of emotional distance, or detachment, forms an audibly distinct note on Verlaine's many-toned lyre, and that, beginning with a few poems of Parnassian impassivity, it is highly developed in *Fêtes galantes,* only to die out with that volume.

It is only five years later, in [*Romances sans paroles*], that Verlaine returns to the idea of distant emotions, and this time it is to condemn humor in his **"Art poétique"**. . . . The target at which this attack is aimed would be unclear, were it not for the extensive use of humor in Verlaine's own poetry. It is not likely that Verlaine would attack so explicitly a few humorous poems such as **"L'Enterrement"** . . . or **"Femme et chatte"** . . . , or that he would comment on the work of other poets when most of **"Art poétique"** deals with trends in his own work. Rather, the stanza refers, we feel, to his humorous, ironic treatment of love in *Fêtes galantes.* By extension, we may infer that Verlaine here is also turning his back on all his poetry where emotions are dealt with distantly. (pp. 204-05)

[The] assertion "Car nous voulons la Nuance encor, / Pas la coleur, rien que la nuance!" indicates a particular method of expressing emotions, that of suggesting nice distinctions of feeling. Verlaine's use of nuance reaches a high level of achievement in the landscape poems of *Romances sans paroles,* in which physical description suggests, rather than states, his mood with remarkable precision. . . . [In] 1874, date of composition of **"Art poétique"** and of many poems of *Romances sans paroles,* Verlaine . . . decided to concentrate on this method of treating emotion, to the exclusion of others.

It is appropriate, therefore, to consider why, having developed such an efficacious expression of distant emotions, Verlaine returns to a position of emotional immediacy. (p. 206)

At the period of *Poèmes saturniens* . . . and *Fêtes galantes* . . . , Verlaine was single, unhappy, and desperately searching for the great love that would, he hoped, bring him happiness. . . . Although he engaged in the more sordid aspects of love, as is seen in the clandestine, pornographic volume, *Les Amies,* . . . these activities did not satisfy his desire for a sincere, noble affection leading to marriage. On the contrary, love seemed to him, in real life as well as poetically, a distant and inaccessible ideal. . . .

After the publication of *Fêtes galantes,* the situation was radically changed by Verlaine's marriage in 1870 to Mathilde Mauté; and while the marriage did not last very long, it was followed immediately by his affair with Arthur Rimbaud in 1872-74. These two events are reproduced poetically by *La Bonne Chanson* . . . and *Romances sans paroles.* . . . If he was disillusioned by marriage, at least love was no longer a distant ideal, it was a close, immediate experience, something he had lived through and seen from the inside. To have attained his ideal, even though it proved to be a disillusionment, altered his poetic treatment of the ideal by bringing it closer to him, so that he no longer treats the emotions connected with it distantly. (p. 207)

If biographically we find a maturation of personal experience in Verlaine's amorous adventures, then poetically there is a parallel growth in the development of his style. As a beginning poet he is subject to several outside influences—hence the eclecticism apparent in *Poèmes saturniens*—as well as to divergent but original tendencies from within himself. Not only is Verlaine open to outside influences—more so, perhaps, than other poets—but he has a particular flair for adopting divergent styles; hence, his numerous *pastiches,* in which he mimics not only other poets but even, in his later years, his own poems. . . .

Poetically, Verlaine's situation in 1874, when he wrote **"Art poétique,"** was as different from that of 1866 as was his private life. The company of Rimbaud was a very real stimulus to his poetic creativity, and discussions with Rimbaud led him to reflect on poetic problems. Not only did Rimbaud's influence lead him to freer and bolder techniques, but the very act of reflecting on poetic theory led him to analyze his own methods more incisively than he had ever, perhaps, done before. Certainly **"Art poétique"**

is a much deeper and more methodical outline of artistic principles than the random, *Parnasse*-inspired suggestions of the **"Prologue"** and **"Epilogue"** of *Poèmes saturniens.* Verlaine was, of course, a much maturer and more experienced poet, too. (p. 208)

Intent on perfecting his new system of poetry, more experienced in life itself, Verlaine abandons some of his earlier styles of writing. A more efficacious way of presenting emotion supplants the idea of placing emotion in the distance; similarly, a more complete experience of life renders unnecessary the view of love as a distant ideal. Verlaine has progressed beyond questions of impassivity and of distantly expressed emotions, to reach a new fusion of emotion and symbol, with the poet discreetly involved in both. (p. 209)

> *Philip Stephan, "Verlaine's Distant Emotions," in* The Romanic Review, *Vol. LII, No. 3, October, 1961, pp. 196-209.*

A. W. Raitt   (essay date 1965)

[*An English writer specializing in French literature, Raitt is the author of* French Life and Letters: The Nineteenth Century *(1965) and* Prosper Mérimée *(1970). In the following excerpt, Raitt presents Verlaine's "Art Poétique" as a poetic document protesting the classical traditions of rhetoric and pictorial descriptions.*]

When Paul Verlaine wrote his **"Art poétique"** in 1874, he was protesting against two traditions firmly rooted in the poetry of the time: the tradition of pictorial description and the tradition of rhetoric. 'De la musique avant toute chose' ['You must have music first of all'] is, in the first instance, a precept intended to prevent poetry from being either verbal painting or a consciously elaborated, heightened form of prose, both of which things it had tended to be in and before Verlaine's own lifetime.

The connection between poetry and painting had begun to grow close about 1830, when the Romantic predilection for *couleur locale* had necessitated a liberal use of colour in general. The innumerable representations of exotic scenes, beautiful landscapes, strange costumes which help to set the mood of Romantic escapism give rise to a descriptive technique which, with increasing mastery, reproduces the effect of brilliant and variegated painting. In particular, Hugo shows the utmost skill from *Les Orientales* onwards in creating the illusion of something physically visible to the reader. This tendency was reinforced in the later stages of Romanticism both by the insistence of upholders of the doctrine of *l'art pour l'art* that only beautiful forms were worthy of an artist's interest, and by the mid-century scepticism about the existence of anything outside the observable world of shapes and colours. (p. 154)

The manifestations of this convergence are multiple. The Bohemian artistic groups of the Romantic and post-Romantic era seem usually to have been compounded of equal proportions of writers and painters. Many of the writers of the time were either painters themselves or else closely associated with painters. . . . Painters figure prominently in the fiction of the period, for instance in Balzac's *Le Chef-d'œuvre inconnu,* Mürger's *Scènes de la vie de Bohème,* the Goncourts' *Manette Salomon* and Zola's *L'Œuvre.* The Parnassians in general, sceptical about Romantic emotionalism, doubtful of the existence of any kind of spiritual ideal, found themselves with few poetic subjects except the evocation of visual beauty (and positivist philosophy), since that alone appeared to offer some guarantee of material reality. As a result the poetry of Leconte de Lisle and Hérédia contains a high proportion of descriptive writing, often of excellent quality. (p. 155)

There is a similar tendency in prose fiction, where the growth of Realist doctrines implied the depiction of scenes easily visualised by the reader; and if the writer is concerned with stylistic elegance, the depiction often takes the form of a transposition on to an imaginary canvas. Gautier's tales and novels are full of such passages. . . . It is against this unending flow of description, with its implications of a solid material world devoid of any spiritual background, that Verlaine is reacting when he proclaims:

> . . . nous voulons la Nuance encor,
> Pas la Couleur, rien que la nuance!
>
>   . . . . .
>
> [. . . the Color, always the Shade,
> always the nuance is supreme!]

The second *bête noire* which Verlaine attacks is rhetoric—everything which tends to make poetry into an oratorical and intellectual exercise. The Romantics, it is true, had tried to break with the classical concept of rigid formal diction in poetry. . . . But in reality the Romantic revolution in poetry, if it overthrew the classical idea of an elevated poetic vocabulary, did little to touch the rhetorical basis of verse. It changed the rules, admittedly; the rhetoric became personal, emotive, torrential; but rhetoric it remained. (pp. 155-57)

[Verlaine's] own way of avoiding rhetoric is demonstrated here by the informality of the second person singular imperatives, by the casual omission of verbs, by imprecise turns of phrase ['It is the veiled and lovely eye'], by familiar locutions ['You would do well, by force and care'], by apparently artless repetitions (the unexpected recurrence of 'de la musique' in the eighth stanza) and by loose grammatical constructions ['or she's off, if you don't watch, God knows where?']. The result is a note of spontaneity and intimacy characteristic of almost all Verlaine's poetry and as far removed as can well be imagined from the grand style of much Romantic and Parnassian poetry.

It is likewise as a mark of disrespect for Parnassian ideas on poetic composition as something accomplished in accordance with strict rules and regulations, that Verlaine departs from the traditional laws of prosody. If he advises the use of metres with an odd number of syllables in each line, it is because the standard 'official' metres are mostly even-numbered, and because the consistent use of, for instance, nine-syllabled lines . . . creates an impression of mild irregularity, of a rhythm slightly syncopated and hence less obtrusive than the too-familiar beat of the alexandrine. . . . Verlaine's preference for weak rhymes or even mere assonance helps to prevent his poetry from having the stiff, contrived air of much Parnassian verse, and it paves the way for the inauguration of the Symbolist *vers libre,* with its optional rhymes and its indefinite number of syllables. (Not that Verlaine approved of such revolutionary extremities. Even Banville envisages the nine-syllabled line of **"Art poétique,"** with the caesura after the fourth syllable, as a curious but perfectly legitimate possibility, and the Symbolists could never induce Verlaine to lend his name to their audacities.)

But while Verlaine's **"Art poétique"** is provoked by and directed at some of the excesses of Parnassianism, it is far from being a purely negative document. 'De la musique avant toute chose' marks a radically new departure in French poetry, and one which was full of consequences for the future: the move from poetry as painting to poetry as music is almost as fundamental as the move from Classicism to Romanticism. Certain of the Romantics and Parnassians had shown an interest in music; it plays a large part in Balzac's *Massimilla Doni* and *Gambara,* in George Sand's *Consuelo* and in Nerval's *Sylvie,* Stendhal wrote lives of Rossini and Mozart, and Gautier was a music critic as well as an art critic. But for most of them the main attraction tended to be opera, where the purely musical experience was diluted by the theatrical element. Even George Sand, whose sensitivity to music was unusually high, reacted to it in such a personal and emotional way that the original aesthetic impression was almost invariably submerged by the waves of feeling which it aroused. It is only with Baudelaire (and possibly with Nerval) that one finds writers appreciating music for its own sake and in its own right, and it is significant that they were among the first people in France to recognise the greatness of Wagner, whose music was to mean so much to two generations of men of letters in France. From Baudelaire's time onwards, there is a growing acknowledgment of the fact that music as an art is far more than just an accompaniment to plays, songs or private musings, that it has its own powerful modes of expression, and that these, in certain respects, may even be superior to those of the other arts.

Verlaine, for instance, has clearly realised that music can never evoke visual impressions with any clarity (even if, for some people, sounds and colours are vaguely associated) and that poetry which creates vivid scenes and sights is always far removed from the condition of music; hence the substitution of nuances for colours. Similarly, however coherent the pattern of a piece of music may be, it can never translate the logical processes of the intellect; hence Verlaine's antipathy for the more intellectual forms of diction. What music can do, because it is nonrepresentational, is to elicit a direct response of the hearer's whole being, without having to enlist incidental auxiliaries from the world around us (like the nominal subject of a painting). So when Verlaine tries to make poetry partake of the essence of music, he is (consciously or unconsciously) aiming at a purer form of art. The same ambition, sharpened by the prestige of Wagner's music and by Schopenhauer's contention that music stood at the top of the hierarchy of the arts, dominated much of the writing and theorising of the Symbolist school ten years after Verlaine's **"Art poétique"**.. . . . (pp. 157-60)

Some poets followed Verlaine in creating melodious verse in which the logical and intellectual content was reduced to a minimum and in which the outside world was used simply as a means of expressing by analogy the poet's inner world (the first three lines of the last stanza are a good example of this kind of allusive imagery, in which the two terms of the comparison—'le vers' and 'la bonne aventure'—are equated, while the reason for the equation is left unspoken). Others, with Mallarmé chief among them, took a more complex and more abstract view of music as a system of interlocking relationships of sound, on which poetry could superimpose a system of relationships of sense and imagery. A few, led by René Ghil, attempted to construct a theory of 'instrumentism' which postulated rigorous correspondences between instrumental timbres, vowel sounds and colours. Almost all of them would have agreed with Verlaine in shunning clear, direct statement and proceeding instead by allusion, suggestion or symbol. . . . Verlaine's **"Art poétique"** is one of the most significant landmarks in this change and one of the most interesting poetic documents of the second half of the century. (pp. 160-61)

> *A. W. Raitt, "Paul Verlaine: Art Poetique," in his* Life and Letters in France: The Nineteenth Century, *Charles Scribner's Sons, 1965, pp. 153-61.*

FURTHER READING

Cohn, Robert Greer. "Rescuing a Sonnet of Verlaine: 'L'espoir luit . . .'." *Romantic Review* LXXVII, No. 2 (March 1986): 125-30.

> Examines the religious and stylistic elements in Verlaine's sonnet.

Gosse, Edmund. "A First Sight of Verlaine." In his *French Profiles,* pp. 177-84. London: William Heinemann, 1904.

> Personal account of Gosse's first meeting with Verlaine in 1893.

King, Russell S. "Verlaine's Verbal Sensation." *Studies in Philology* 72, No. 2 (April 1975): 226-36.

> Linguistic study of Verlaine's poetry with a concentration on Verlaine's unique use of verbs and adjectives.

Leventhal, A. J. "Paul Verlaine or the Foolish Virgin." *The Dublin Magazine* XVIII, No. 1 (January-March 1943): 38-45.

> Discusses Verlaine's relationship with Arthur Rimbaud, noting that Verlaine's influence on Rimbaud and his work is generally underestimated.

Rifelj, Carol de Dobay. "Verlaine: Wringing the Neck of Eloquence." In her *Word and Figure: The Language of Nineteenth Century French Poetry,* pp. 100-31.

> Examines Verlaine's use of colloquial diction, metaphor, and figurative language in his verse.

Sonnenfeld, Albert. "The Forgotten Verlaine." *The Bucknell Review* XI, No. 1 (December 1962): 73-80.

> Investigates the anti-lyrical strain often found in Verlaine's verse, attributing it to the poet's need for irony and his feelings of inadequacy.

Walker, Hallam. "Visual and Spatial Imagery in Verlaine's 'Fêtes galantes.'" *Publications of the Modern Language Association of America* 87, No. 5 (October 1972): 1007-1015.

> Analyzes the visual and spatial elements of Verlaine's poetry which elicit intense intellectual and emotional responses.

Poetry Criticism
INDEXES

Literary Criticism Series
Cumulative Author Index

Cumulative Nationality Index

Cumulative Title Index

This Index Includes References to Entries in These Gale Series

Contemporary Literary Criticism

Presents excerpts of criticism on the works of novelists, poets, dramatists, short story writers, scriptwriters, and other creative writers who are now living or who have died since 1960.

Twentieth-Century Literary Criticism

Contains critical excerpts by the most significant commentators on poets, novelists, short story writers, dramatists, and philosophers who died between 1900 and 1960.

Nineteenth-Century Literature Criticism

Offers significant passages from criticism on authors who died between 1800 and 1899.

Literature Criticism from 1400 to 1800

Compiles significant passages from the most noteworthy criticism on authors of the fifteenth through eighteenth centuries.

Classical and Medieval Literature Criticism

Offers excerpts of criticism on the works of world authors from classical antiquity through the fourteenth century.

Short Story Criticism

Compiles excerpts of criticism on short fiction by writers of all eras and nationalities.

Poetry Criticism

Presents excerpts of criticism on the works of poets from all eras, movements, and nationalities.

Children's Literature Review

Includes excerpts from reviews, criticism, and commentary on works of authors and illustrators who create books for children.

Contemporary Authors Series

Contemporary Authors provides biographical and bibliographical information on more than 97,000 writers of fiction and nonfiction. *Contemporary Authors New Revision Series* provides completely updated information on active authors covered in *CA*. *Contemporary Authors Permanent Series* consists of listings for deceased and inactive authors. *Contemporary Authors Autobiography Series* presents specially commissioned autobiographies by leading contemporary writers. *Contemporary Authors Bibliographical Series* contains primary and secondary bibliographies as well as analytical bibliographical essays by authorities on major modern authors.

Dictionary of Literary Biography

Encompasses four related series. *Dictionary of Literary Biography* furnishes illustrated overviews of authors' lives and works. *Dictionary of Literary Biography Documentary Series* illuminates the careers of major figures through a selection of literary documents, including letters, interviews, and photographs. *Dictionary of Literary Biography Yearbook* summarizes the past year's literary activity and includes updated entries on individual authors. *Concise Dictionary of American Literary Biography* comprises six volumes of revised and updated sketches on major American authors that were originally presented in *Dictionary of Literary Biography*.

Something about the Author Series

Encompasses three related series. *Something about the Author* contains well-illustrated biographical sketches on juvenile and young adult authors and illustrators from all eras. *Something about the Author Autobiography Series* presents specially commissioned autobiographies by prominent authors and illustrators of books for children and young adults. *Authors of Artists for Young Adults* provides high school and junior high school students with profiles of their favorite creative artists.

Yesterday's Authors of Books for Children

Contains heavily illustrated entries on children's writers who died before 1961. Complete in two volumes.

Literary Criticism Series
Cumulative Author Index

This index lists all author entries in the Gale Literary Criticism Series and includes cross-references to other Gale sources. References in the index are identified as follows:

AAYA:	*Authors & Artists for Young Adults,* Volumes 1-3
CAAS:	*Contemporary Authors Autobiography Series,* Volumes 1-11
CA:	*Contemporary Authors* (original series), Volumes 1-131
CABS:	*Contemporary Authors Bibliographical Series,* Volumes 1-3
CANR:	*Contemporary Authors New Revision Series,* Volumes 1-31
CAP:	*Contemporary Authors Permanent Series,* Volumes 1-2
CA-R:	*Contemporary Authors* (revised editions), Volumes 1-44
CDALB:	*Concise Dictionary of American Literary Biography,* Volumes 1-6
CLC:	*Contemporary Literary Criticism,* Volumes 1-63
CLR:	*Children's Literature Review,* Volumes 1-23
CMLC:	*Classical and Medieval Literature Criticism,* Volumes 1-6
DC:	*Drama Criticism,* Volume 1
DLB:	*Dictionary of Literary Biography,* Volumes 1-101
DLB-DS:	*Dictionary of Literary Biography Documentary Series,* Volumes 1-7
DLB-Y:	*Dictionary of Literary Biography Yearbook,* Volumes 1980-1988
LC:	*Literature Criticism from 1400 to 1800,* Volumes 1-15
NCLC:	*Nineteenth-Century Literature Criticism,* Volumes 1-30
PC:	*Poetry Criticism,* Volumes 1-2
SAAS:	*Something about the Author Autobiography Series,* Volumes 1-11
SATA:	*Something about the Author,* Volumes 1-62
SSC:	*Short Story Criticism,* Volumes 1-7
TCLC:	*Twentieth-Century Literary Criticism,* Volumes 1-40
YABC:	*Yesterday's Authors of Books for Children,* Volumes 1-2

Aiken, Conrad (Potter)
1889-1973 .... **CLC 1, 3, 5, 10, 52**
See also CANR 4; CA 5-8R;
obituary CA 45-48; SATA 3, 30; DLB 9,
45

Aiken, Joan (Delano) 1924- .... **CLC 35**
See also CLR 1; CANR 4; CA 9-12R;
SAAS 1; SATA 2, 30

Ainsworth, William Harrison
1805-1882 .... **NCLC 13**
See also SATA 24; DLB 21

Ajar, Emile 1914-1980
See Gary, Romain

Akhmadulina, Bella (Akhatovna)
1937- .... **CLC 53**
See also CA 65-68

Akhmatova, Anna
1888-1966 .... **CLC 11, 25; PC 2**
See also CAP 1; CA 19-20;
obituary CA 25-28R

Aksakov, Sergei Timofeyvich
1791-1859 .... **NCLC 2**

Aksenov, Vassily (Pavlovich) 1932-
See Aksyonov, Vasily (Pavlovich)

Aksyonov, Vasily (Pavlovich)
1932- .... **CLC 22, 37**
See also CANR 12; CA 53-56

Akutagawa Ryunosuke
1892-1927 .... **TCLC 16**
See also CA 117

Alain-Fournier 1886-1914 .... **TCLC 6**
See Fournier, Henri Alban
See also DLB 65

Alarcon, Pedro Antonio de
1833-1891 .... **NCLC 1**

Alas (y Urena), Leopoldo (Enrique Garcia)
1852-1901 .... **TCLC 29**
See also CA 113

Albee, Edward (Franklin III)
1928- ... **CLC 1, 2, 3, 5, 9, 11, 13, 25, 53**
See also CANR 8; CA 5-8R; DLB 7;
CDALB 1941-1968

Alberti, Rafael 1902- .... **CLC 7**
See also CA 85-88

Alcott, Amos Bronson 1799-1888 .. **NCLC 1**
See also DLB 1

Alcott, Louisa May 1832-1888 .... **NCLC 6**
See also CLR 1; YABC 1; DLB 1, 42;
CDALB 1865-1917

Aldanov, Mark 1887-1957 .... **TCLC 23**
See also CA 118

Aldington, Richard 1892-1962 ...... **CLC 49**
See also CA 85-88; DLB 20, 36

Aldiss, Brian W(ilson)
1925- .... **CLC 5, 14, 40**
See also CAAS 2; CANR 5; CA 5-8R;
SATA 34; DLB 14

Alegria, Fernando 1918- .... **CLC 57**
See also CANR 5; CA 11-12R

Aleixandre, Vicente 1898-1984 ... **CLC 9, 36**
See also CANR 26; CA 85-88;
obituary CA 114

Alepoudelis, Odysseus 1911-
See Elytis, Odysseus

Aleshkovsky, Yuz 1929- .... **CLC 44**
See also CA 121

Alexander, Lloyd (Chudley) 1924- .. **CLC 35**
See also CLR 1, 5; CANR 1; CA 1-4R;
SATA 3, 49; DLB 52

Alger, Horatio, Jr. 1832-1899 ..... **NCLC 8**
See also SATA 16; DLB 42

Algren, Nelson 1909-1981 .... **CLC 4, 10, 33**
See also CANR 20; CA 13-16R;
obituary CA 103; DLB 9; DLB-Y 81, 82;
CDALB 1941-1968

Alighieri, Dante 1265-1321 .... **CMLC 3**

Allard, Janet 1975- .... **CLC 59**

Allen, Edward 1948- .... **CLC 59**

Allen, Roland 1939-
See Ayckbourn, Alan

Allen, Woody 1935- .... **CLC 16, 52**
See also CANR 27; CA 33-36R; DLB 44

Allende, Isabel 1942- .... **CLC 39, 57**
See also CA 125

Allingham, Margery (Louise)
1904-1966 .... **CLC 19**
See also CANR 4; CA 5-8R;
obituary CA 25-28R

Allingham, William 1824-1889 ... **NCLC 25**
See also DLB 35

Allston, Washington 1779-1843 .... **NCLC 2**
See also DLB 1

Almedingen, E. M. 1898-1971 ...... **CLC 12**
See also Almedingen, Martha Edith von
See also SATA 3

Almedingen, Martha Edith von 1898-1971
See Almedingen, E. M.
See also CANR 1; CA 1-4R

Alonso, Damaso 1898- .... **CLC 14**
See also CA 110

Alta 1942- .... **CLC 19**
See also CA 57-60

Alter, Robert B(ernard) 1935- ...... **CLC 34**
See also CANR 1; CA 49-52

Alther, Lisa 1944- .... **CLC 7, 41**
See also CANR 12; CA 65-68

Altman, Robert 1925- .... **CLC 16**
See also CA 73-76

Alvarez, A(lfred) 1929- .... **CLC 5, 13**
See also CANR 3; CA 1-4R; DLB 14, 40

Alvarez, Alejandro Rodriguez 1903-1965
See Casona, Alejandro
See also obituary CA 93-96

Amado, Jorge 1912- .... **CLC 13, 40**
See also CA 77-80

Ambler, Eric 1909- .... **CLC 4, 6, 9**
See also CANR 7; CA 9-12R

Amichai, Yehuda 1924- ...... **CLC 9, 22, 57**
See also CA 85-88

Amiel, Henri Frederic 1821-1881 .. **NCLC 4**

Amis, Kingsley (William)
1922- ...... **CLC 1, 2, 3, 5, 8, 13, 40, 44**
See also CANR 8; CA 9-12R; DLB 15, 27

Amis, Martin 1949- .... **CLC 4, 9, 38, 62**
See also CANR 8, 28; CA 65-68; DLB 14

Ammons, A(rchie) R(andolph)
1926- .... **CLC 2, 3, 5, 8, 9, 25, 57**
See also CANR 6; CA 9-12R; DLB 5

Anand, Mulk Raj 1905- .... **CLC 23**
See also CA 65-68

Anaya, Rudolfo A(lfonso) 1937- .... **CLC 23**
See also CAAS 4; CANR 1; CA 45-48

Andersen, Hans Christian
1805-1875 .... **NCLC 7; SSC 6**
See also CLR 6; YABC 1, 1

Anderson, Jessica (Margaret Queale)
19??- .... **CLC 37**
See also CANR 4; CA 9-12R

Anderson, Jon (Victor) 1940- ...... **CLC 9**
See also CANR 20; CA 25-28R

Anderson, Lindsay 1923- .... **CLC 20**

Anderson, Maxwell 1888-1959 ..... **TCLC 2**
See also CA 105; DLB 7

Anderson, Poul (William) 1926- .... **CLC 15**
See also CAAS 2; CANR 2, 15; CA 1-4R;
SATA 39; DLB 8

Anderson, Robert (Woodruff)
1917- .... **CLC 23**
See also CA 21-24R; DLB 7

Anderson, Roberta Joan 1943-
See Mitchell, Joni

Anderson, Sherwood
1876-1941 ...... **TCLC 1, 10, 24; SSC 1**
See also CAAS 3; CA 104, 121; DLB 4, 9;
DLB-DS 1

Andrade, Carlos Drummond de
1902-1987 .... **CLC 18**
See also CA 123

Andrewes, Lancelot 1555-1626 .... **LC 5**

Andrews, Cicily Fairfield 1892-1983
See West, Rebecca

Andreyev, Leonid (Nikolaevich)
1871-1919 .... **TCLC 3**
See also CA 104

Andrezel, Pierre 1885-1962
See Dinesen, Isak; Blixen, Karen
(Christentze Dinesen)

Andric, Ivo 1892-1975 .... **CLC 8**
See also CA 81-84; obituary CA 57-60

Angelique, Pierre 1897-1962
See Bataille, Georges

Angell, Roger 1920- .... **CLC 26**
See also CANR 13; CA 57-60

Angelou, Maya 1928- .... **CLC 12, 35**
See also CANR 19; CA 65-68; SATA 49;
DLB 38

Annensky, Innokenty 1856-1909 ... **TCLC 14**
See also CA 110

Anouilh, Jean (Marie Lucien Pierre)
1910-1987 ...... **CLC 1, 3, 8, 13, 40, 50**
See also CA 17-20R; obituary CA 123

Anthony, Florence 1947-
See Ai

Anthony (Jacob), Piers 1934- ...... **CLC 35**
See also Jacob, Piers A(nthony)
D(illingham)
See also DLB 8

Antoninus, Brother 1912-
See Everson, William (Oliver)

Bell, Madison Smartt 1957-........ **CLC 41**
See also CA 111

Bell, Marvin (Hartley) 1937-..... **CLC 8, 31**
See also CA 21-24R; DLB 5

Bellamy, Edward 1850-1898 ...... **NCLC 4**
See also DLB 12

Belloc, (Joseph) Hilaire (Pierre Sebastien
    Rene Swanton)
    1870-1953 .... **TCLC 7, 18**
See also YABC 1; CA 106; DLB 19

Bellow, Saul
    1915- ..... **CLC 1, 2, 3, 6, 8, 10, 13, 15,
                   25, 33, 34, 63**
See also CA 5-8R; CABS 1; DLB 2, 28;
    DLB-Y 82; DLB-DS 3;
    CDALB 1941-1968

Belser, Reimond Karel Maria de 1929-
See Ruyslinck, Ward

Bely, Andrey 1880-1934.......... **TCLC 7**
See also CA 104

Benary-Isbert, Margot 1889-1979... **CLC 12**
See also CLR 12; CANR 4; CA 5-8R;
    obituary CA 89-92; SATA 2;
    obituary SATA 21

Benavente (y Martinez), Jacinto
    1866-1954 .... **TCLC 3**
See also CA 106

Benchley, Peter (Bradford)
    1940- .... **CLC 4, 8**
See also CANR 12; CA 17-20R; SATA 3

Benchley, Robert 1889-1945 .... **TCLC 1**
See also CA 105; DLB 11

Benedikt, Michael 1935- .... **CLC 4, 14**
See also CANR 7; CA 13-16R; DLB 5

Benet, Juan 1927-................ **CLC 28**

Benet, Stephen Vincent
    1898-1943 .... **TCLC 7**
See also YABC 1; CA 104; DLB 4, 48

Benet, William Rose 1886-1950 ... **TCLC 28**
See also CA 118; DLB 45

Benford, Gregory (Albert) 1941-.... **CLC 52**
See also CANR 12, 24; CA 69-72;
    DLB-Y 82

Benjamin, Walter 1892-1940..... **TCLC 39**

Benn, Gottfried 1886-1956........ **TCLC 3**
See also CA 106; DLB 56

Bennett, Alan 1934-.............. **CLC 45**
See also CA 103

Bennett, (Enoch) Arnold
    1867-1931 .... **TCLC 5, 20**
See also CA 106; DLB 10, 34

Bennett, George Harold 1930-
See Bennett, Hal
See also CA 97-100

Bennett, Hal 1930-................ **CLC 5**
See also Bennett, George Harold
See also DLB 33

Bennett, Jay 1912-............... **CLC 35**
See also CANR 11; CA 69-72; SAAS 4;
    SATA 27, 41

Bennett, Louise (Simone) 1919-..... **CLC 28**
See also Bennett-Coverly, Louise Simone

Bennett-Coverly, Louise Simone 1919-
See Bennett, Louise (Simone)
See also CA 97-100

Benson, E(dward) F(rederic)
    1867-1940 .... **TCLC 27**
See also CA 114

Benson, Jackson J. 1930-.......... **CLC 34**
See also CA 25-28R

Benson, Sally 1900-1972 .... **CLC 17**
See also CAP 1; CA 19-20;
    obituary CA 37-40R; SATA 1, 35;
    obituary SATA 27

Benson, Stella 1892-1933........ **TCLC 17**
See also CA 117; DLB 36

Bentley, E(dmund) C(lerihew)
    1875-1956 .... **TCLC 12**
See also CA 108; DLB 70

Bentley, Eric (Russell) 1916-...... **CLC 24**
See also CANR 6; CA 5-8R

Berger, John (Peter) 1926- ...... **CLC 2, 19**
See also CA 81-84; DLB 14

Berger, Melvin (H.) 1927-........ **CLC 12**
See also CANR 4; CA 5-8R; SAAS 2;
    SATA 5

Berger, Thomas (Louis)
    1924- .... **CLC 3, 5, 8, 11, 18, 38**
See also CANR 5; CA 1-4R; DLB 2;
    DLB-Y 80

Bergman, (Ernst) Ingmar 1918-..... **CLC 16**
See also CA 81-84

Bergson, Henri 1859-1941 .... **TCLC 32**

Bergstein, Eleanor 1938-.......... **CLC 4**
See also CANR 5; CA 53-56

Berkoff, Steven 1937-............. **CLC 56**
See also CA 104

Bermant, Chaim 1929-............ **CLC 40**
See also CANR 6; CA 57-60

Bernanos, (Paul Louis) Georges
    1888-1948 .... **TCLC 3**
See also CA 104; DLB 72

Bernard, April 19??-.............. **CLC 59**

Bernhard, Thomas
    1931-1989 .... **CLC 3, 32, 61**
See also CA 85-88,; obituary CA 127;
    DLB 85

Berriault, Gina 1926-............. **CLC 54**
See also CA 116

Berrigan, Daniel J. 1921-........... **CLC 4**
See also CAAS 1; CANR 11; CA 33-36R;
    DLB 5

Berrigan, Edmund Joseph Michael, Jr.
    1934-1983
See Berrigan, Ted
See also CANR 14; CA 61-64;
    obituary CA 110

Berrigan, Ted 1934-1983 .... **CLC 37**
See also Berrigan, Edmund Joseph Michael,
    Jr.
See also DLB 5

Berry, Chuck 1926- .... **CLC 17**

Berry, Wendell (Erdman)
    1934- .... **CLC 4, 6, 8, 27, 46**
See also CA 73-76; DLB 5, 6

Berryman, John
    1914-1972 ..... **CLC 1, 2, 3, 4, 6, 8, 10,
                  13, 25, 62**
See also CAP 1; CA 15-16;
    obituary CA 33-36R; CABS 2; DLB 48;
    CDALB 1941-1968

Bertolucci, Bernardo 1940- .... **CLC 16**
See also CA 106

Bertran de Born c. 1140-1215 ..... **CMLC 5**

Besant, Annie (Wood) 1847-1933 ... **TCLC 9**
See also CA 105

Bessie, Alvah 1904-1985.......... **CLC 23**
See also CANR 2; CA 5-8R;
    obituary CA 116; DLB 26

Beti, Mongo 1932-.............. **CLC 27**
See also Beyidi, Alexandre

Betjeman, (Sir) John
    1906-1984 .... **CLC 2, 6, 10, 34, 43**
See also CA 9-12R; obituary CA 112;
    DLB 20; DLB-Y 84

Betti, Ugo 1892-1953 .... **TCLC 5**
See also CA 104

Betts, Doris (Waugh) 1932-.... **CLC 3, 6, 28**
See also CANR 9; CA 13-16R; DLB-Y 82

Bialik, Chaim Nachman
    1873-1934 .... **TCLC 25**

Bidart, Frank 19??-.............. **CLC 33**

Bienek, Horst 1930-............ **CLC 7, 11**
See also CA 73-76; DLB 75

Bierce, Ambrose (Gwinett)
    1842-1914? .... **TCLC 1, 7**
See also CA 104; DLB 11, 12, 23, 71, 74;
    CDALB 1865-1917

Billington, Rachel 1942-........... **CLC 43**
See also CA 33-36R

Binyon, T(imothy) J(ohn) 1936- .... **CLC 34**
See also CA 111

Bioy Casares, Adolfo 1914-.... **CLC 4, 8, 13**
See also CANR 19; CA 29-32R

Bird, Robert Montgomery
    1806-1854 .... **NCLC 1**

Birdwell, Cleo 1936-
See DeLillo, Don

Birney (Alfred) Earle
    1904- .... **CLC 1, 4, 6, 11**
See also CANR 5, 20; CA 1-4R

Bishop, Elizabeth
    1911-1979 ...... **CLC 1, 4, 9, 13, 15, 32**
See also CANR 26; CA 5-8R;
    obituary CA 89-92; CABS 2;
    obituary SATA 24; DLB 5

Bishop, John 1935-.............. **CLC 10**
See also CA 105

Bissett, Bill 1939-................ **CLC 18**
See also CANR 15; CA 69-72; DLB 53

Bitov, Andrei (Georgievich) 1937-... **CLC 57**

Biyidi, Alexandre 1932-
See Beti, Mongo
See also CA 114, 124

Bjornson, Bjornstjerne (Martinius)
    1832-1910 .... **TCLC 7, 37**
See also CA 104

Bradbury, Ray(mond Douglas)
    1920- . . . . **CLC 1, 3, 10, 15, 42**
    See also CANR 2; CA 1-4R; SATA 11;
    DLB 2, 8

Bradford, Gamaliel 1863-1932. . . . . **TCLC 36**
    See also DLB 17

Bradley, David (Henry), Jr. 1950- . . **CLC 23**
    See also CANR 26; CA 104; DLB 33

Bradley, John Ed 1959- . . . . **CLC 55**

Bradley, Marion Zimmer 1930-. . . . . **CLC 30**
    See also CANR 7; CA 57-60; DLB 8

Bradstreet, Anne 1612-1672. . . . . **LC 4**
    See also DLB 24; CDALB 1640-1865

Bragg, Melvyn 1939- . . . . **CLC 10**
    See also CANR 10; CA 57-60; DLB 14

Braine, John (Gerard)
    1922-1986 . . . . **CLC 1, 3, 41**
    See also CANR 1; CA 1-4R;
    obituary CA 120; DLB 15; DLB-Y 86

Brammer, Billy Lee 1930?-1978
    See Brammer, William

Brammer, William 1930?-1978 . . . . . **CLC 31**
    See also obituary CA 77-80

Brancati, Vitaliano 1907-1954. . . . . **TCLC 12**
    See also CA 109

Brancato, Robin F(idler) 1936-. . . . . **CLC 35**
    See also CANR 11; CA 69-72; SATA 23

Brand, Millen 1906-1980. . . . . **CLC 7**
    See also CA 21-24R; obituary CA 97-100

Branden, Barbara 19??- . . . . **CLC 44**

Brandes, Georg (Morris Cohen)
    1842-1927 . . . . **TCLC 10**
    See also CA 105

Brandys, Kazimierz 1916- . . . . **CLC 62**

Branley, Franklyn M(ansfield)
    1915- . . . . **CLC 21**
    See also CLR 13; CANR 14; CA 33-36R;
    SATA 4

Brathwaite, Edward 1930- . . . . **CLC 11**
    See also CANR 11; CA 25-28R; DLB 53

Brautigan, Richard (Gary)
    1935-1984 . . . . **CLC 1, 3, 5, 9, 12, 34, 42**
    See also CA 53-56; obituary CA 113;
    DLB 2, 5; DLB-Y 80, 84

Brecht, (Eugen) Bertolt (Friedrich)
    1898-1956 . . . . **TCLC 1, 6, 13, 35**
    See also CA 104; DLB 56

Bremer, Fredrika 1801-1865 . . . . . **NCLC 11**

Brennan, Christopher John
    1870-1932 . . . . **TCLC 17**
    See also CA 117

Brennan, Maeve 1917- . . . . **CLC 5**
    See also CA 81-84

Brentano, Clemens (Maria)
    1778-1842 . . . . **NCLC 1**

Brenton, Howard 1942- . . . . **CLC 31**
    See also CA 69-72; DLB 13

Breslin, James 1930-
    See Breslin, Jimmy
    See also CA 73-76

Breslin, Jimmy 1930-. . . . . **CLC 4, 43**
    See also Breslin, James

Bresson, Robert 1907- . . . . **CLC 16**
    See also CA 110

Breton, Andre 1896-1966. . . **CLC 2, 9, 15, 54**
    See also CAP 2; CA 19-20;
    obituary CA 25-28R; DLB 65

Breytenbach, Breyten 1939-. . . . . **CLC 23, 37**
    See also CA 113

Bridgers, Sue Ellen 1942- . . . . **CLC 26**
    See also CANR 11; CA 65-68; SAAS 1;
    SATA 22; DLB 52

Bridges, Robert 1844-1930. . . . . **TCLC 1**
    See also CA 104; DLB 19

Bridie, James 1888-1951 . . . . **TCLC 3**
    See also Mavor, Osborne Henry
    See also DLB 10

Brin, David 1950-. . . . . **CLC 34**
    See also CANR 24; CA 102

Brink, Andre (Philippus)
    1935- . . . . **CLC 18, 36**
    See also CA 104

Brinsmead, H(esba) F(ay) 1922- . . . . **CLC 21**
    See also CANR 10; CA 21-24R; SAAS 5;
    SATA 18

Brittain, Vera (Mary) 1893?-1970. . . **CLC 23**
    See also CAP 1; CA 15-16;
    obituary CA 25-28R

Broch, Hermann 1886-1951. . . . . . . **TCLC 20**
    See also CA 117

Brock, Rose 1923-
    See Hansen, Joseph

Brodkey, Harold 1930-. . . . . **CLC 56**
    See also CA 111

Brodsky, Iosif Alexandrovich 1940-
    See Brodsky, Joseph (Alexandrovich)
    See also CA 41-44R

Brodsky, Joseph (Alexandrovich)
    1940- . . . . **CLC 4, 6, 13, 36, 50**
    See also Brodsky, Iosif Alexandrovich

Brodsky, Michael (Mark) 1948- . . . . **CLC 19**
    See also CANR 18; CA 102

Bromell, Henry 1947-. . . . . **CLC 5**
    See also CANR 9; CA 53-56

Bromfield, Louis (Brucker)
    1896-1956 . . . . **TCLC 11**
    See also CA 107; DLB 4, 9

Broner, E(sther) M(asserman)
    1930- . . . . **CLC 19**
    See also CANR 8, 25; CA 17-20R; DLB 28

Bronk, William 1918-. . . . . **CLC 10**
    See also CANR 23; CA 89-92

Bronte, Anne 1820-1849. . . . . **NCLC 4**
    See also DLB 21

Bronte, Charlotte 1816-1855 . . . . **NCLC 3, 8**
    See also DLB 21

Bronte, (Jane) Emily 1818-1848 . . **NCLC 16**
    See also DLB 21, 32

Brooke, Frances 1724-1789 . . . . **LC 6**
    See also DLB 39

Brooke, Henry 1703?-1783 . . . . **LC 1**
    See also DLB 39

Brooke, Rupert (Chawner)
    1887-1915 . . . . **TCLC 2, 7**
    See also CA 104; DLB 19

Brooke-Rose, Christine 1926- . . . . . . **CLC 40**
    See also CA 13-16R; DLB 14

Brookner, Anita 1928-. . . . . . . **CLC 32, 34, 51**
    See also CA 114, 120; DLB-Y 87

Brooks, Cleanth 1906- . . . . **CLC 24**
    See also CA 17-20R; DLB 63

Brooks, Gwendolyn
    1917- . . . . **CLC 1, 2, 4, 5, 15, 49**
    See also CANR 1; CA 1-4R; SATA 6;
    DLB 5, 76; CDALB 1941-1968

Brooks, Mel 1926- . . . . **CLC 12**
    See also Kaminsky, Melvin
    See also CA 65-68; DLB 26

Brooks, Peter 1938-. . . . . **CLC 34**
    See also CANR 1; CA 45-48

Brooks, Van Wyck 1886-1963. . . . . . **CLC 29**
    See also CANR 6; CA 1-4R; DLB 45, 63

Brophy, Brigid (Antonia)
    1929- . . . . **CLC 6, 11, 29**
    See also CAAS 4; CANR 25; CA 5-8R;
    DLB 14

Brosman, Catharine Savage 1934-. . . . **CLC 9**
    See also CANR 21; CA 61-64

Broughton, T(homas) Alan 1936- . . . **CLC 19**
    See also CANR 2, 23; CA 45-48

Broumas, Olga 1949-. . . . . **CLC 10**
    See also CANR 20; CA 85-88

Brown, Charles Brockden
    1771-1810 . . . . **NCLC 22**
    See also DLB 37, 59, 73;
    CDALB 1640-1865

Brown, Christy 1932-1981. . . . . **CLC 63**
    See also CA 105; obituary CA 104

Brown, Claude 1937- . . . . **CLC 30**
    See also CA 73-76

Brown, Dee (Alexander) 1908- . . **CLC 18, 47**
    See also CAAS 6; CANR 11; CA 13-16R;
    SATA 5; DLB-Y 80

Brown, George Douglas 1869-1902
    See Douglas, George

Brown, George Mackay 1921-. . . . **CLC 5, 28**
    See also CAAS 6; CANR 12; CA 21-24R;
    SATA 35; DLB 14, 27

Brown, Rita Mae 1944-. . . . . **CLC 18, 43**
    See also CANR 2, 11; CA 45-48

Brown, Rosellen 1939-. . . . . **CLC 32**
    See also CANR 14; CA 77-80

Brown, Sterling A(llen)
    1901-1989 . . . . **CLC 1, 23, 59**
    See also CANR 26; CA 85-88;
    obituary CA 27; DLB 48, 51, 63

Brown, William Wells
    1816?-1884. . . . . **NCLC 2; DC 1**
    See also DLB 3, 50

Browne, Jackson 1950- . . . . **CLC 21**
    See also CA 120

Browning, Elizabeth Barrett
    1806-1861 . . . . **NCLC 1, 16**
    See also DLB 32

Browning, Robert
    1812-1889 . . . . **NCLC 19; PC 2**
    See also YABC 1; DLB 32

Browning, Tod 1882-1962 . . . . **CLC 16**
    See also obituary CA 117

Capra, Frank 1897-............... **CLC 16**
See also CA 61-64

Caputo, Philip 1941-.............. **CLC 32**
See also CA 73-76

Card, Orson Scott 1951- .... **CLC 44, 47, 50**
See also CA 102

Cardenal, Ernesto 1925-.......... **CLC 31**
See also CANR 2; CA 49-52

Carducci, Giosue 1835-1907...... **TCLC 32**

Carew, Thomas 1595?-1640 .... **LC 13**

Carey, Ernestine Gilbreth 1908-.... **CLC 17**
See also CA 5-8R; SATA 2

Carey, Peter 1943-............ **CLC 40, 55**
See also CA 123, 127

Carleton, William 1794-1869...... **NCLC 3**

Carlisle, Henry (Coffin) 1926-...... **CLC 33**
See also CANR 15; CA 13-16R

Carlson, Ron(ald F.) 1947-......... **CLC 54**
See also CA 105

Carlyle, Thomas 1795-1881 ...... **NCLC 22**
See also DLB 55

Carman, (William) Bliss
1861-1929 .... **TCLC 7**
See also CA 104

Carpenter, Don(ald Richard)
1931- .... **CLC 41**
See also CANR 1; CA 45-48

Carpentier (y Valmont), Alejo
1904-1980 .... **CLC 8, 11, 38**
See also CANR 11; CA 65-68;
obituary CA 97-100

Carr, Emily 1871-1945........... **TCLC 32**
See also DLB 68

Carr, John Dickson 1906-1977 ...... **CLC 3**
See also CANR 3; CA 49-52;
obituary CA 69-72

Carr, Virginia Spencer 1929-....... **CLC 34**
See also CA 61-64

Carrier, Roch 1937-.............. **CLC 13**
See also DLB 53

Carroll, James (P.) 1943-.......... **CLC 38**
See also CA 81-84

Carroll, Jim 1951- .... **CLC 35**
See also CA 45-48

Carroll, Lewis 1832-1898........ **NCLC 2**
See also Dodgson, Charles Lutwidge
See also CLR 2; DLB 18

Carroll, Paul Vincent 1900-1968.... **CLC 10**
See also CA 9-12R; obituary CA 25-28R;
DLB 10

Carruth, Hayden 1921- .... **CLC 4, 7, 10, 18**
See also CANR 4; CA 9-12R; SATA 47;
DLB 5

Carter, Angela (Olive) 1940-..... **CLC 5, 41**
See also CANR 12; CA 53-56; DLB 14

Carver, Raymond
1938-1988 .... **CLC 22, 36, 53, 55**
See also CANR 17; CA 33-36R;
obituary CA 126; DLB-Y 84, 88

Cary, (Arthur) Joyce (Lunel)
1888-1957 .... **TCLC 1, 29**
See also CA 104; DLB 15

Casanova de Seingalt, Giovanni Jacopo
1725-1798 .... **LC 13**

Casares, Adolfo Bioy 1914-
See Bioy Casares, Adolfo

Casely-Hayford, J(oseph) E(phraim)
1866-1930 .... **TCLC 24**
See also CA 123

Casey, John 1880-1964
See O'Casey, Sean

Casey, John 1939- .... **CLC 59**
See also CANR 23; CA 69-72

Casey, Michael 1947-.............. **CLC 2**
See also CA 65-68; DLB 5

Casey, Warren 1935- .... **CLC 12**
See also Jacobs, Jim and Casey, Warren
See also CA 101

Casona, Alejandro 1903-1965 ...... **CLC 49**
See also Alvarez, Alejandro Rodriguez

Cassavetes, John 1929-........... **CLC 20**
See also CA 85-88

Cassill, R(onald) V(erlin) 1919-... **CLC 4, 23**
See also CAAS 1; CANR 7; CA 9-12R;
DLB 6

Cassity, (Allen) Turner 1929- .... **CLC 6, 42**
See also CANR 11; CA 17-20R

Castaneda, Carlos 1935?-.......... **CLC 12**
See also CA 25-28R

Castelvetro, Lodovico 1505-1571..... **LC 12**

Castiglione, Baldassare 1478-1529 ... **LC 12**

Castro, Rosalia de 1837-1885 ..... **NCLC 3**

Cather, Willa (Sibert)
1873-1947 ...... **TCLC 1, 11, 31; SSC 2**
See also CA 104; SATA 30; DLB 9, 54;
DLB-DS 1; CDALB 1865-1917

Catton, (Charles) Bruce
1899-1978 .... **CLC 35**
See also CANR 7; CA 5-8R;
obituary CA 81-84; SATA 2;
obituary SATA 24; DLB 17

Cauldwell, Frank 1923-
See King, Francis (Henry)

Caunitz, William 1935- .... **CLC 34**

Causley, Charles (Stanley) 1917-..... **CLC 7**
See also CANR 5; CA 9-12R; SATA 3;
DLB 27

Caute, (John) David 1936-........ **CLC 29**
See also CAAS 4; CANR 1; CA 1-4R;
DLB 14

Cavafy, C(onstantine) P(eter)
1863-1933 .... **TCLC 2, 7**
See also CA 104

Cavanna, Betty 1909-............. **CLC 12**
See also CANR 6; CA 9-12R; SATA 1, 30

Cayrol, Jean 1911-.............. **CLC 11**
See also CA 89-92

Cela, Camilo Jose 1916-...... **CLC 4, 13, 59**
See also CAAS 10; CANR 21; CA 21-24R

Celan, Paul 1920-1970 ...... **CLC 10, 19, 53**
See also Antschel, Paul
See also DLB 69

Celine, Louis-Ferdinand
1894-1961 ..... **CLC 1, 3, 4, 7, 9, 15, 47**
See also Destouches,
Louis-Ferdinand-Auguste
See also DLB 72

Cellini, Benvenuto 1500-1571 .... **LC 7**

Cendrars, Blaise 1887-1961........ **CLC 18**
See also Sauser-Hall, Frederic

Cernuda, Luis (y Bidon)
1902-1963 .... **CLC 54**
See also CA 89-92

Cervantes (Saavedra), Miguel de
1547-1616 .... **LC 6**

Cesaire, Aime (Fernand) 1913- .. **CLC 19, 32**
See also CANR 24; CA 65-68

Chabon, Michael 1965?-........... **CLC 55**

Chabrol, Claude 1930-............ **CLC 16**
See also CA 110

Challans, Mary 1905-1983
See Renault, Mary
See also CA 81-84; obituary CA 111;
SATA 23; obituary SATA 36

Chambers, Aidan 1934- .... **CLC 35**
See also CANR 12; CA 25-28R; SATA 1

Chambers, James 1948-
See Cliff, Jimmy

Chandler, Raymond 1888-1959 ... **TCLC 1, 7**
See also CA 104

Channing, William Ellery
1780-1842 .... **NCLC 17**
See also DLB 1, 59

Chaplin, Charles (Spencer)
1889-1977 .... **CLC 16**
See also CA 81-84; obituary CA 73-76;
DLB 44

Chapman, Graham 1941?- .... **CLC 21**
See also Monty Python
See also CA 116

Chapman, John Jay 1862-1933 ..... **TCLC 7**
See also CA 104

Chappell, Fred 1936- .... **CLC 40**
See also CAAS 4; CANR 8; CA 5-8R;
DLB 6

Char, Rene (Emile)
1907-1988 .... **CLC 9, 11, 14, 55**
See also CA 13-16R; obituary CA 124

Charles I 1600-1649 .... **LC 13**

Charyn, Jerome 1937- .... **CLC 5, 8, 18**
See also CAAS 1; CANR 7; CA 5-8R;
DLB-Y 83

Chase, Mary (Coyle) 1907-1981
See also CA 77-80, 105; SATA 17, 29; DC 1

Chase, Mary Ellen 1887-1973....... **CLC 2**
See also CAP 1; CA 15-16;
obituary CA 41-44R; SATA 10

Chateaubriand, Francois Rene de
1768-1848 .... **NCLC 3**

Chatterji, Bankim Chandra
1838-1894 .... **NCLC 19**

Chatterji, Saratchandra
1876-1938 .... **TCLC 13**
See also CA 109

Chatterton, Thomas 1752-1770 .... **LC 3**

Chatwin, (Charles) Bruce
1940-1989 . . . . CLC 28, 57, 59
See also CA 85-88,; obituary CA 127

Chayefsky, Paddy 1923-1981 . . . . . . CLC 23
See also CA 9-12R; obituary CA 104;
DLB 7, 44; DLB-Y 81

Chayefsky, Sidney 1923-1981
See Chayefsky, Paddy
See also CANR 18

Chedid, Andree 1920- . . . . CLC 47

Cheever, John
1912-1982 . . . . . CLC 3, 7, 8, 11, 15, 25;
SSC 1
See also CANR 5; CA 5-8R;
obituary CA 106; CABS 1; DLB 2;
DLB-Y 80, 82; CDALB 1941-1968

Cheever, Susan 1943- . . . . CLC 18, 48
See also CA 103; DLB-Y 82

Chekhov, Anton (Pavlovich)
1860-1904 . . . . . . TCLC 3, 10, 31; SSC 2
See also CA 104, 124

Chernyshevsky, Nikolay Gavrilovich
1828-1889 . . . . NCLC 1

Cherry, Caroline Janice 1942-
See Cherryh, C. J.

Cherryh, C. J. 1942- . . . . CLC 35
See also CANR 10; CA 65-68; DLB-Y 80

Chesnutt, Charles Waddell
1858-1932 . . . . TCLC 5, 39; SSC 7
See also CA 106, 125; DLB 12, 50, 78

Chester, Alfred 1929?-1971 . . . . CLC 49
See also obituary CA 33-36R

Chesterton, G(ilbert) K(eith)
1874-1936 . . . . TCLC 1, 6; SSC 1
See also CA 104; SATA 27; DLB 10, 19,
34, 70

Ch'ien Chung-shu 1910- . . . . CLC 22

Child, Lydia Maria 1802-1880 . . . . NCLC 6
See also DLB 1, 74

Child, Philip 1898-1978 . . . . CLC 19
See also CAP 1; CA 13-14; SATA 47

Childress, Alice 1920- . . . . CLC 12, 15
See also CLR 14; CANR 3; CA 45-48;
SATA 7, 48; DLB 7, 38

Chislett, (Margaret) Anne 1943?- . . . CLC 34

Chitty, (Sir) Thomas Willes 1926- . . CLC 11
See also Hinde, Thomas
See also CA 5-8R

Chomette, Rene 1898-1981
See Clair, Rene
See also obituary CA 103

Chopin, Kate (O'Flaherty)
1851-1904 . . . . TCLC 5, 14
See also CA 104, 122; DLB 12;
CDALB 1865-1917

Christie, (Dame) Agatha (Mary Clarissa)
1890-1976 . . . . . . CLC 1, 6, 8, 12, 39, 48
See also CANR 10; CA 17-20R;
obituary CA 61-64; SATA 36; DLB 13

Christie, (Ann) Philippa 1920-
See Pearce, (Ann) Philippa
See also CANR 4; CA 7-8

Christine de Pizan 1365?-1431? . . . . . . LC 9

Chulkov, Mikhail Dmitrievich
1743-1792 . . . . LC 2

Churchill, Caryl 1938- . . . . CLC 31, 55
See also CANR 22; CA 102; DLB 13

Churchill, Charles 1731?-1764 . . . . LC 3

Chute, Carolyn 1947- . . . . CLC 39
See also CA 123

Ciardi, John (Anthony)
1916-1986 . . . . CLC 10, 40, 44
See also CAAS 2; CANR 5; CA 5-8R;
obituary CA 118; SATA 1, 46; DLB 5;
DLB-Y 86

Cicero, Marcus Tullius
106 B.C.-43 B.C. . . . . CMLC 3

Cimino, Michael 1943?- . . . . CLC 16
See also CA 105

Clair, Rene 1898-1981 . . . . CLC 20
See also Chomette, Rene

Clampitt, Amy 19??- . . . . CLC 32
See also CA 110

Clancy, Tom 1947- . . . . CLC 45
See also CA 125

Clare, John 1793-1864 . . . . NCLC 9
See also DLB 55

Clark, (Robert) Brian 1932- . . . . CLC 29
See also CA 41-44R

Clark, Eleanor 1913- . . . . CLC 5, 19
See also CA 9-12R; DLB 6

Clark, John Pepper 1935- . . . . CLC 38
See also CANR 16; CA 65-68

Clark, Mavis Thorpe 1912?- . . . . CLC 12
See also CANR 8; CA 57-60; SAAS 5;
SATA 8

Clark, Walter Van Tilburg
1909-1971 . . . . CLC 28
See also CA 9-12R; obituary CA 33-36R;
SATA 8; DLB 9

Clarke, Arthur C(harles)
1917- . . . . . . CLC 1, 4, 13, 18, 35; SSC 3
See also CANR 2; CA 1-4R; SATA 13

Clarke, Austin 1896-1974 . . . . CLC 6, 9
See also CANR 14; CAP 2; CA 29-32;
obituary CA 49-52; DLB 10, 20, 53

Clarke, Austin (Ardinel) C(hesterfield)
1934- . . . . CLC 8, 53
See also CANR 14; CA 25-28R; DLB 53

Clarke, Gillian 1937- . . . . CLC 61
See also CA 106; DLB 40

Clarke, Marcus (Andrew Hislop)
1846-1881 . . . . NCLC 19

Clarke, Shirley 1925- . . . . CLC 16

Clash, The . . . . CLC 30

Claudel, Paul (Louis Charles Marie)
1868-1955 . . . . TCLC 2, 10
See also CA 104

Clavell, James (duMaresq)
1924- . . . . CLC 6, 25
See also CANR 26; CA 25-28R

Cleaver, (Leroy) Eldridge 1935- . . . . CLC 30
See also CANR 16; CA 21-24R

Cleese, John 1939- . . . . CLC 21
See also Monty Python
See also CA 112, 116

Cleland, John 1709-1789 . . . . LC 2
See also DLB 39

Clemens, Samuel Langhorne
1835-1910 . . . . . . TCLC 6, 12, 19; SSC 6
See also Twain, Mark
See also YABC 2; CA 104; DLB 11, 12, 23,
64, 74; CDALB 1865-1917

Cliff, Jimmy 1948- . . . . CLC 21

Clifton, Lucille 1936- . . . . CLC 19
See also CLR 5; CANR 2, 24; CA 49-52;
SATA 20; DLB 5, 41

Clough, Arthur Hugh 1819-1861 . . NCLC 27
See also DLB 32

Clutha, Janet Paterson Frame 1924-
See Frame (Clutha), Janet (Paterson)
See also CANR 2; CA 1-4R

Coburn, D(onald) L(ee) 1938- . . . . . . CLC 10
See also CA 89-92

Cocteau, Jean (Maurice Eugene Clement)
1889-1963 . . . . CLC 1, 8, 15, 16, 43
See also CAP 2; CA 25-28; DLB 65

Codrescu, Andrei 1946- . . . . CLC 46
See also CANR 13; CA 33-36R

Coetzee, J(ohn) M. 1940- . . . . CLC 23, 33
See also CA 77-80

Cohen, Arthur A(llen)
1928-1986 . . . . CLC 7, 31
See also CANR 1, 17; CA 1-4R;
obituary CA 120; DLB 28

Cohen, Leonard (Norman)
1934- . . . . CLC 3, 38
See also CANR 14; CA 21-24R; DLB 53

Cohen, Matt 1942- . . . . CLC 19
See also CA 61-64; DLB 53

Cohen-Solal, Annie 19??- . . . . CLC 50

Colegate, Isabel 1931- . . . . CLC 36
See also CANR 8, 22; CA 17-20R; DLB 14

Coleridge, Samuel Taylor
1772-1834 . . . . NCLC 9

Coles, Don 1928- . . . . CLC 46
See also CA 115

Colette (Sidonie-Gabrielle)
1873-1954 . . . . TCLC 1, 5, 16
See also CA 104; DLB 65

Collett, (Jacobine) Camilla (Wergeland)
1813-1895 . . . . NCLC 22

Collier, Christopher 1930- . . . . CLC 30
See also CANR 13; CA 33-36R; SATA 16

Collier, James L(incoln) 1928- . . . . . CLC 30
See also CLR 3; CANR 4; CA 9-12R;
SATA 8

Collier, Jeremy 1650-1726 . . . . LC 6

Collins, Hunt 1926-
See Hunter, Evan

Collins, Linda 19??- . . . . CLC 44
See also CA 125

Collins, Tom 1843-1912
See Furphy, Joseph

Collins, (William) Wilkie
1824-1889 . . . . NCLC 1, 18
See also DLB 18, 70

Collins, William 1721-1759 . . . . LC 4

Colman, George   1909-1981
See Glassco, John

Colter, Cyrus   1910- .... CLC 58
See also CANR 10; CA 65-68; DLB 33

Colton, James   1923-
See Hansen, Joseph

Colum, Padraic   1881-1972........ CLC 28
See also CA 73-76; obituary CA 33-36R;
SATA 15; DLB 19

Colvin, James   1939-
See Moorcock, Michael

Colwin, Laurie   1945- .... CLC 5, 13, 23
See also CANR 20; CA 89-92; DLB-Y 80

Comfort, Alex(ander)   1920-........ CLC 7
See also CANR 1; CA 1-4R

Compton-Burnett, Ivy
1892-1969 .... CLC 1, 3, 10, 15, 34
See also CANR 4; CA 1-4R;
obituary CA 25-28R; DLB 36

Comstock, Anthony   1844-1915 .... TCLC 13
See also CA 110

Conde, Maryse   1937-............. CLC 52
See also Boucolon, Maryse

Condon, Richard (Thomas)
1915- .... CLC 4, 6, 8, 10, 45
See also CAAS 1; CANR 2, 23; CA 1-4R

Congreve, William   1670-1729 .... LC 5
See also DLB 39

Connell, Evan S(helby), Jr.
1924- .... CLC 4, 6, 45
See also CAAS 2; CANR 2; CA 1-4R;
DLB 2; DLB-Y 81

Connelly, Marc(us Cook)
1890-1980 .... CLC 7
See also CA 85-88; obituary CA 102;
obituary SATA 25; DLB 7; DLB-Y 80

Conner, Ralph   1860-1937........ TCLC 31

Conrad, Joseph
1857-1924 .... TCLC 1, 6, 13, 25
See also CA 104; SATA 27; DLB 10, 34

Conroy, Pat   1945-................ CLC 30
See also CANR 24; CA 85-88; DLB 6

Constant (de Rebecque), (Henri) Benjamin
1767-1830 .... NCLC 6

Cook, Michael   1933- .... CLC 58
See also CA 93-96; DLB 53

Cook, Robin   1940-............... CLC 14
See also CA 108, 111

Cooke, Elizabeth   1948- .... CLC 55

Cooke, John Esten   1830-1886 ..... NCLC 5
See also DLB 3

Cooney, Ray   19??-............... CLC 62

Cooper, J. California   19??- .... CLC 56
See also CA 125

Cooper, James Fenimore
1789-1851 .... NCLC 1, 27
See also SATA 19; DLB 3;
CDALB 1640-1865

Coover, Robert (Lowell)
1932- .... CLC 3, 7, 15, 32, 46
See also CANR 3; CA 45-48; DLB 2;
DLB-Y 81

Copeland, Stewart (Armstrong)
1952- .... CLC 26
See also The Police

Coppard, A(lfred) E(dgar)
1878-1957 .... TCLC 5
See also YABC 1; CA 114

Coppee, Francois   1842-1908 ..... TCLC 25

Coppola, Francis Ford   1939-....... CLC 16
See also CA 77-80; DLB 44

Corcoran, Barbara   1911-.......... CLC 17
See also CAAS 2; CANR 11; CA 21-24R;
SATA 3; DLB 52

Corman, Cid   1924-................ CLC 9
See also Corman, Sidney
See also CAAS 2; DLB 5

Corman, Sidney   1924-
See Corman, Cid
See also CA 85-88

Cormier, Robert (Edmund)
1925- .... CLC 12, 30
See also CLR 12; CANR 5, 23; CA 1-4R;
SATA 10, 45; DLB 52

Corn, Alfred (Dewitt III)   1943-..... CLC 33
See also CA 104; DLB-Y 80

Cornwell, David (John Moore)
1931- .... CLC 9, 15
See also le Carre, John
See also CANR 13; CA 5-8R

Corso, (Nunzio) Gregory   1930-... CLC 1, 11
See also CA 5-8R; DLB 5, 16

Cortazar, Julio
1914-1984 ..... CLC 2, 3, 5, 10, 13, 15,
33, 34; SSC 7
See also CANR 12; CA 21-24R

Corvo, Baron   1860-1913
See Rolfe, Frederick (William Serafino
Austin Lewis Mary)

Cosic, Dobrica   1921- .... CLC 14
See also CA 122

Costain, Thomas B(ertram)
1885-1965 .... CLC 30
See also CA 5-8R; obituary CA 25-28R;
DLB 9

Costantini, Humberto   1924?-1987... CLC 49
See also obituary CA 122

Costello, Elvis   1955-.............. CLC 21

Cotter, Joseph Seamon, Sr.
1861-1949 .... TCLC 28
See also DLB 50

Couperus, Louis (Marie Anne)
1863-1923 .... TCLC 15
See also CA 115

Courtenay, Bryce   1933-........... CLC 59

Cousteau, Jacques-Yves   1910-...... CLC 30
See also CANR 15; CA 65-68; SATA 38

Coward, (Sir) Noel (Pierce)
1899-1973 .... CLC 1, 9, 29, 51
See also CAP 2; CA 17-18;
obituary CA 41-44R; DLB 10

Cowley, Malcolm   1898-1989 .... CLC 39
See also CANR 3; CA 5-6R; DLB 4, 48;
DLB-Y 81

Cowper, William   1731-1800....... NCLC 8

Cox, William Trevor   1928- ...... CLC 9, 14
See also Trevor, William
See also CANR 4; CA 9-12R

Cozzens, James Gould
1903-1978 .... CLC 1, 4, 11
See also CANR 19; CA 9-12R;
obituary CA 81-84; DLB 9; DLB-Y 84;
DLB-DS 2; CDALB 1941-1968

Crabbe, George   1754-1832....... NCLC 26

Crace, Douglas   1944-............. CLC 58

Crane, (Harold) Hart
1899-1932.................TCLC 2, 5
See also CA 104; DLB 4, 48

Crane, R(onald) S(almon)
1886-1967 .... CLC 27
See also CA 85-88; DLB 63

Crane, Stephen
1871-1900 ..... TCLC 11, 17, 32; SSC 7
See also YABC 2; CA 109; DLB 12, 54, 78;
CDALB 1865-1917

Craven, Margaret   1901-1980....... CLC 17
See also CA 103

Crawford, F(rancis) Marion
1854-1909 .... TCLC 10
See also CA 107; DLB 71

Crawford, Isabella Valancy
1850-1887 .... NCLC 12

Crayencour, Marguerite de   1903-1987
See Yourcenar, Marguerite

Creasey, John   1908-1973.......... CLC 11
See also CANR 8; CA 5-8R;
obituary CA 41-44R

Crebillon, Claude Prosper Jolyot de (fils)
1707-1777 .... LC 1

Creeley, Robert (White)
1926- .... CLC 1, 2, 4, 8, 11, 15, 36
See also CANR 23; CA 1-4R; DLB 5, 16

Crews, Harry (Eugene)
1935-............. CLC 6, 23, 49
See also CANR 20; CA 25-28R; DLB 6

Crichton, (John) Michael
1942-.................. CLC 2, 6, 54
See also CANR 13; CA 25-28R; SATA 9;
DLB-Y 81

Crispin, Edmund   1921-1978........ CLC 22
See also Montgomery, Robert Bruce

Cristofer, Michael   1946-.......... CLC 28
See also CA 110; DLB 7

Croce, Benedetto   1866-1952 ...... TCLC 37
See also CA 120

Crockett, David (Davy)
1786-1836 .... NCLC 8
See also DLB 3, 11

Croker, John Wilson   1780-1857 .. NCLC 10

Cronin, A(rchibald) J(oseph)
1896-1981 .... CLC 32
See also CANR 5; CA 1-4R;
obituary CA 102; obituary SATA 25, 47

Cross, Amanda   1926-
See Heilbrun, Carolyn G(old)

Crothers, Rachel   1878-1953....... TCLC 19
See also CA 113; DLB 7

Crowley, Aleister   1875-1947 .... TCLC 7
See also CA 104

Crowley, John   1942-
    See also CA 61-64; DLB-Y 82

Crumb, Robert   1943- . . . . **CLC 17**
    See also CA 106

Cryer, Gretchen   1936?- . . . . **CLC 21**
    See also CA 114, 123

Csath, Geza   1887-1919. . . . . **TCLC 13**
    See also CA 111

Cudlip, David   1933- . . . . **CLC 34**

Cullen, Countee   1903-1946 . . . . . **TCLC 4, 37**
    See also CA 108, 124; SATA 18; DLB 4,
    48, 51; CDALB 1917-1929

Cummings, E(dward) E(stlin)
    1894-1962 . . . . **CLC 1, 3, 8, 12, 15**
    See also CA 73-76; DLB 4, 48

Cunha, Euclides (Rodrigues) da
    1866-1909 . . . . **TCLC 24**
    See also CA 123

Cunningham, J(ames) V(incent)
    1911-1985 . . . . **CLC 3, 31**
    See also CANR 1; CA 1-4R;
    obituary CA 115; DLB 5

Cunningham, Julia (Woolfolk)
    1916- . . . . **CLC 12**
    See also CANR 4, 19; CA 9-12R; SAAS 2;
    SATA 1, 26

Cunningham, Michael   1952- . . . . **CLC 34**

Currie, Ellen   19??- . . . . **CLC 44**

Dabrowska, Maria (Szumska)
    1889-1965 . . . . **CLC 15**
    See also CA 106

Dabydeen, David   1956?- . . . . **CLC 34**
    See also CA 106

Dacey, Philip   1939- . . . . **CLC 51**
    See also CANR 14; CA 37-40R

Dagerman, Stig (Halvard)
    1923-1954 . . . . **TCLC 17**
    See also CA 117

Dahl, Roald   1916- . . . . **CLC 1, 6, 18**
    See also CLR 1, 7; CANR 6; CA 1-4R;
    SATA 1, 26

Dahlberg, Edward   1900-1977. . . **CLC 1, 7, 14**
    See also CA 9-12R; obituary CA 69-72;
    DLB 48

Daly, Elizabeth   1878-1967. . . . . **CLC 52**
    See also CAP 2; CA 23-24;
    obituary CA 25-28R

Daly, Maureen   1921- . . . . **CLC 17**
    See also McGivern, Maureen Daly
    See also SAAS 1; SATA 2

Daniken, Erich von   1935-
    See Von Daniken, Erich

Dannay, Frederic   1905-1982
    See Queen, Ellery
    See also CANR 1; CA 1-4R;
    obituary CA 107

D'Annunzio, Gabriele
    1863-1938 . . . . **TCLC 6, 40**
    See also CA 104

Dante (Alighieri)
    See Alighieri, Dante

Danziger, Paula   1944- . . . . **CLC 21**
    See also CLR 20; CA 112, 115; SATA 30,
    36

Dario, Ruben   1867-1916 . . . . **TCLC 4**
    See also Sarmiento, Felix Ruben Garcia
    See also CA 104

Darley, George   1795-1846 . . . . **NCLC 2**

Daryush, Elizabeth   1887-1977. . . . **CLC 6, 19**
    See also CANR 3; CA 49-52; DLB 20

Daudet, (Louis Marie) Alphonse
    1840-1897 . . . . **NCLC 1**

Daumal, Rene   1908-1944 . . . . **TCLC 14**
    See also CA 114

Davenport, Guy (Mattison, Jr.)
    1927- . . . . **CLC 6, 14, 38**
    See also CANR 23; CA 33-36R

Davidson, Donald (Grady)
    1893-1968 . . . . **CLC 2, 13, 19**
    See also CANR 4; CA 5-8R;
    obituary CA 25-28R; DLB 45

Davidson, John   1857-1909 . . . . **TCLC 24**
    See also CA 118; DLB 19

Davidson, Sara   1943- . . . . **CLC 9**
    See also CA 81-84

Davie, Donald (Alfred)
    1922- . . . . **CLC 5, 8, 10, 31**
    See also CAAS 3; CANR 1; CA 1-4R;
    DLB 27

Davies, Ray(mond Douglas)   1944- . . **CLC 21**
    See also CA 116

Davies, Rhys   1903-1978. . . . . **CLC 23**
    See also CANR 4; CA 9-12R;
    obituary CA 81-84

Davies, (William) Robertson
    1913- . . . . **CLC 2, 7, 13, 25, 42**
    See also CANR 17; CA 33-36R; DLB 68

Davies, W(illiam) H(enry)
    1871-1940 . . . . **TCLC 5**
    See also CA 104; DLB 19

Davis, H(arold) L(enoir)
    1896-1960 . . . . **CLC 49**
    See also obituary CA 89-92; DLB 9

Davis, Rebecca (Blaine) Harding
    1831-1910 . . . . **TCLC 6**
    See also CA 104; DLB 74

Davis, Richard Harding
    1864-1916 . . . . **TCLC 24**
    See also CA 114; DLB 12, 23

Davison, Frank Dalby   1893-1970 . . . **CLC 15**
    See also obituary CA 116

Davison, Peter   1928- . . . . **CLC 28**
    See also CAAS 4; CANR 3; CA 9-12R;
    DLB 5

Davys, Mary   1674-1732. . . . . **LC 1**
    See also DLB 39

Dawson, Fielding   1930- . . . . **CLC 6**
    See also CA 85-88

Day, Clarence (Shepard, Jr.)
    1874-1935 . . . . **TCLC 25**
    See also CA 108; DLB 11

Day, Thomas   1748-1789. . . . . **LC 1**
    See also YABC 1; DLB 39

Day Lewis, C(ecil)
    1904-1972 . . . . **CLC 1, 6, 10**
    See also CAP 1; CA 15-16;
    obituary CA 33-36R; DLB 15, 20

Dazai Osamu   1909-1948 . . . . **TCLC 11**
    See also Tsushima Shuji

De Crayencour, Marguerite   1903-1987
    See Yourcenar, Marguerite

Deer, Sandra   1940- . . . . **CLC 45**

Defoe, Daniel   1660?-1731 . . . . **LC 1**
    See also SATA 22; DLB 39

De Hartog, Jan   1914- . . . . **CLC 19**
    See also CANR 1; CA 1-4R

Deighton, Len   1929- . . . . **CLC 4, 7, 22, 46**
    See also Deighton, Leonard Cyril

Deighton, Leonard Cyril   1929-
    See Deighton, Len
    See also CANR 19; CA 9-12R

De la Mare, Walter (John)
    1873-1956 . . . . **TCLC 4**
    See also CLR 23; CA 110; SATA 16;
    DLB 19

Delaney, Shelagh   1939- . . . . **CLC 29**
    See also CA 17-20R; DLB 13

Delany, Mary (Granville Pendarves)
    1700-1788 . . . . **LC 12**

Delany, Samuel R(ay, Jr.)
    1942- . . . . **CLC 8, 14, 38**
    See also CA 81-84; DLB 8, 33

De la Roche, Mazo   1885-1961 . . . . . **CLC 14**
    See also CA 85-88; DLB 68

Delbanco, Nicholas (Franklin)
    1942- . . . . **CLC 6, 13**
    See also CAAS 2; CA 17-20R; DLB 6

del Castillo, Michel   1933- . . . . **CLC 38**
    See also CA 109

Deledda, Grazia   1871-1936 . . . . **TCLC 23**
    See also CA 123

Delibes (Setien), Miguel   1920- . . . **CLC 8, 18**
    See also CANR 1; CA 45-48

DeLillo, Don
    1936- . . . . **CLC 8, 10, 13, 27, 39, 54**
    See also CANR 21; CA 81-84; DLB 6

De Lisser, H(erbert) G(eorge)
    1878-1944 . . . . **TCLC 12**
    See also CA 109

Deloria, Vine (Victor), Jr.   1933- . . . . **CLC 21**
    See also CANR 5, 20; CA 53-56; SATA 21

Del Vecchio, John M(ichael)
    1947- . . . . **CLC 29**
    See also CA 110

de Man, Paul   1919-1983 . . . . **CLC 55**
    See also obituary CA 111; DLB 67

De Marinis, Rick   1934- . . . . **CLC 54**
    See also CANR 9, 25; CA 57-60

Demby, William   1922- . . . . **CLC 53**
    See also CA 81-84; DLB 33

Denby, Edwin (Orr)   1903-1983 . . . . . **CLC 48**
    See also obituary CA 110

Dennis, John   1657-1734. . . . . **LC 11**

Dennis, Nigel (Forbes)   1912- . . . . **CLC 8**
    See also CA 25-28R; DLB 13, 15

De Palma, Brian   1940- . . . . **CLC 20**
    See also CA 109

De Quincey, Thomas   1785-1859 . . . **NCLC 4**

Author Index

Dubus, Andre 1936- .... CLC 13, 36
See also CANR 17; CA 21-24R

Ducasse, Isidore Lucien 1846-1870
See Lautreamont, Comte de

Duclos, Charles Pinot 1704-1772 ..... LC 1

Dudek, Louis 1918- .... CLC 11, 19
See also CANR 1; CA 45-48

Dudevant, Amandine Aurore Lucile Dupin
1804-1876
See Sand, George

Duerrenmatt, Friedrich
1921- .... CLC 1, 4, 8, 11, 15, 43
See also CA 17-20R; DLB 69

Duffy, Bruce 19??- .... CLC 50

Duffy, Maureen 1933- .... CLC 37
See also CA 25-28R; DLB 14

Dugan, Alan 1923- .... CLC 2, 6
See also CA 81-84; DLB 5

Duhamel, Georges 1884-1966 .... CLC 8
See also CA 81-84; obituary CA 25-28R

Dujardin, Edouard (Emile Louis)
1861-1949 .... TCLC 13
See also CA 109

Duke, Raoul 1939-
See Thompson, Hunter S(tockton)

Dumas, Alexandre (Davy de la Pailleterie)
(pere) 1802-1870.......... NCLC 11
See also SATA 18

Dumas, Alexandre (fils)
1824-1895 .... NCLC 9; DC 1

Dumas, Henry 1918-1968 .... CLC 62

Dumas, Henry (L.) 1934-1968...... CLC 6
See also CA 85-88; DLB 41

Du Maurier, Daphne 1907- ... CLC 6, 11, 59
See also CANR 6; CA 5-8R;
obituary CA 128; SATA 27

Dunbar, Paul Laurence
1872-1906 .... TCLC 2, 12
See also CA 104, 124; SATA 34; DLB 50,
54; CDALB 1865-1917

Duncan (Steinmetz Arquette), Lois
1934- .... CLC 26
See also Arquette, Lois S(teinmetz)
See also CANR 2; CA 1-4R; SAAS 2;
SATA 1, 36

Duncan, Robert (Edward)
1919-1988 ... CLC 1, 2, 4, 7, 15, 41, 55;
PC 2
See also CANR 28; CA 9-12R;
obituary CA 124; DLB 5, 16

Dunlap, William 1766-1839 ...... NCLC 2
See also DLB 30, 37, 59

Dunn, Douglas (Eaglesham)
1942- .... CLC 6, 40
See also CANR 2; CA 45-48; DLB 40

Dunn, Elsie 1893-1963
See Scott, Evelyn

Dunn, Stephen 1939- .... CLC 36
See also CANR 12; CA 33-36R

Dunne, Finley Peter 1867-1936.... TCLC 28
See also CA 108; DLB 11, 23

Dunne, John Gregory 1932-........ CLC 28
See also CANR 14; CA 25-28R; DLB-Y 80

Dunsany, Lord (Edward John Moreton Drax
Plunkett) 1878-1957......... TCLC 2
See also CA 104; DLB 10

Durang, Christopher (Ferdinand)
1949-.................... CLC 27, 38
See also CA 105

Duras, Marguerite
1914- .... CLC 3, 6, 11, 20, 34, 40
See also CA 25-28R

Durban, Pam 1947-.............. CLC 39
See also CA 123

Durcan, Paul 1944-.............. CLC 43

Durrell, Lawrence (George)
1912-1990 .... CLC 1, 4, 6, 8, 13, 27, 41
See also CA 9-12R; DLB 15, 27

Durrenmatt, Friedrich
1921- .... CLC 1, 4, 8, 11, 15, 43
See also Duerrenmatt, Friedrich
See also DLB 69

Dutt, Toru 1856-1877.......... NCLC 29

Dwight, Timothy 1752-1817...... NCLC 13
See also DLB 37

Dworkin, Andrea 1946- .... CLC 43
See also CANR 16; CA 77-80

Dylan, Bob 1941-.......... CLC 3, 4, 6, 12
See also CA 41-44R; DLB 16

Eagleton, Terry 1943-............ CLC 63

East, Michael 1916-
See West, Morris L.

Eastlake, William (Derry) 1917-..... CLC 8
See also CAAS 1; CANR 5; CA 5-8R;
DLB 6

Eberhart, Richard 1904-... CLC 3, 11, 19, 56
See also CANR 2; CA 1-4R; DLB 48;
CDALB 1941-1968

Eberstadt, Fernanda 1960-........ CLC 39

Echegaray (y Eizaguirre), Jose (Maria Waldo)
1832-1916 .... TCLC 4
See also CA 104

Echeverria, (Jose) Esteban (Antonino)
1805-1851 .... NCLC 18

Eckert, Allan W. 1931- .... CLC 17
See also CANR 14; CA 13-16R; SATA 27,
29

Eco, Umberto 1932-........... CLC 28, 60
See also CANR 12; CA 77-80

Eddison, E(ric) R(ucker)
1882-1945 .... TCLC 15
See also CA 109

Edel, Leon (Joseph) 1907-...... CLC 29, 34
See also CANR 1, 22; CA 1-4R

Eden, Emily 1797-1869 .... NCLC 10

Edgar, David 1948-.............. CLC 42
See also CANR 12; CA 57-60; DLB 13

Edgerton, Clyde 1944-........... CLC 39
See also CA 118

Edgeworth, Maria 1767-1849...... NCLC 1
See also SATA 21

Edmonds, Helen (Woods) 1904-1968
See Kavan, Anna
See also CA 5-8R; obituary CA 25-28R

Edmonds, Walter D(umaux) 1903-.. CLC 35
See also CANR 2; CA 5-8R; SAAS 4;
SATA 1, 27; DLB 9

Edson, Russell 1905- .... CLC 13
See also CA 33-36R

Edwards, G(erald) B(asil)
1899-1976 .... CLC 25
See also obituary CA 110

Edwards, Gus 1939-.............. CLC 43
See also CA 108

Edwards, Jonathan 1703-1758........ LC 7
See also DLB 24

Ehle, John (Marsden, Jr.) 1925-.... CLC 27
See also CA 9-12R

Ehrenburg, Ilya (Grigoryevich)
1891-1967.......... CLC 18, 34, 62
See also CA 102; obituary CA 25-28R

Eich, Guenter 1907-1971
See also CA 111; obituary CA 93-96

Eich, Gunter 1907-1971.......... CLC 15
See also Eich, Guenter
See also DLB 69

Eichendorff, Joseph Freiherr von
1788-1857 .... NCLC 8

Eigner, Larry 1927- .... CLC 9
See also Eigner, Laurence (Joel)
See also DLB 5

Eigner, Laurence (Joel) 1927-
See Eigner, Larry
See also CANR 6; CA 9-12R

Eiseley, Loren (Corey) 1907-1977.... CLC 7
See also CANR 6; CA 1-4R;
obituary CA 73-76

Eisenstadt, Jill 1963-............. CLC 50

Ekeloef, Gunnar (Bengt) 1907-1968
See Ekelof, Gunnar (Bengt)
See also obituary CA 25-28R

Ekelof, Gunnar (Bengt) 1907-1968 .. CLC 27
See also Ekeloef, Gunnar (Bengt)

Ekwensi, Cyprian (Odiatu Duaka)
1921-...................... CLC 4
See also CANR 18; CA 29-32R

Eliade, Mircea 1907-1986 .... CLC 19
See also CA 65-68; obituary CA 119

Eliot, George 1819-1880.... NCLC 4, 13, 23
See also DLB 21, 35, 55

Eliot, John 1604-1690 .... LC 5
See also DLB 24

Eliot, T(homas) S(tearns)
1888-1965 .... CLC 1, 2, 3, 6, 9, 10, 13,
15, 24, 34, 41, 55, 57
See also CA 5-8R; obituary CA 25-28R;
DLB 7, 10, 45, 63; DLB-Y 88

Elkin, Stanley (Lawrence)
1930-........ CLC 4, 6, 9, 14, 27, 51
See also CANR 8; CA 9-12R; DLB 2, 28;
DLB-Y 80

Elledge, Scott 19??- .... CLC 34

Elliott, George P(aul) 1918-1980..... CLC 2
See also CANR 2; CA 1-4R;
obituary CA 97-100

Elliott, Janice 1931-.............. CLC 47
See also CANR 8; CA 13-16R; DLB 14

Elliott, Sumner Locke 1917-....... **CLC 38**
　　See also CANR 2, 21; CA 5-8R

Ellis, A. E. 19??-................ **CLC 7**

Ellis, Alice Thomas 19??-......... **CLC 40**

Ellis, Bret Easton 1964-........... **CLC 39**
　　See also CA 118, 123

Ellis, (Henry) Havelock
　　1859-1939 .... **TCLC 14**
　　See also CA 109

Ellis, Trey 1964-................ **CLC 55**

Ellison, Harlan (Jay) 1934-... **CLC 1, 13, 42**
　　See also CANR 5; CA 5-8R; DLB 8

Ellison, Ralph (Waldo)
　　1914- ....**CLC 1, 3, 11, 54**
　　See also CANR 24; CA 9-12R; DLB 2;
　　CDALB 1941-1968

Ellmann, Lucy 1956- .... **CLC 61**
　　See also CA 128

Ellmann, Richard (David)
　　1918-1987 .... **CLC 50**
　　See also CANR 2; CA 1-4R;
　　obituary CA 122; DLB-Y 87

Elman, Richard 1934-............ **CLC 19**
　　See also CAAS 3; CA 17-20R

Eluard, Paul 1895-1952 .... **TCLC 7**
　　See also Grindel, Eugene

Elyot, (Sir) Thomas 1490?-1546 ..... **LC 11**

Elytis, Odysseus 1911-........ **CLC 15, 49**
　　See also CA 102

Emecheta, (Florence Onye) Buchi
　　1944- .... **CLC 14, 48**
　　See also CA 81-84

Emerson, Ralph Waldo
　　1803-1882 .... **NCLC 1**
　　See also DLB 1, 59, 73; CDALB 1640-1865

Empson, William
　　1906-1984 .... **CLC 3, 8, 19, 33, 34**
　　See also CA 17-20R; obituary CA 112;
　　DLB 20

Enchi, Fumiko (Veda) 1905-1986 ... **CLC 31**
　　See also obituary CA 121

Ende, Michael 1930-............. **CLC 31**
　　See also CLR 14; CA 118, 124; SATA 42;
　　DLB 75

Endo, Shusaku 1923-..... **CLC 7, 14, 19, 54**
　　See also CANR 21; CA 29-32R

Engel, Marian 1933-1985......... **CLC 36**
　　See also CANR 12; CA 25-28R; DLB 53

Engelhardt, Frederick 1911-1986
　　See Hubbard, L(afayette) Ron(ald)

Enright, D(ennis) J(oseph)
　　1920- ....**CLC 4, 8, 31**
　　See also CANR 1; CA 1-4R; SATA 25;
　　DLB 27

Enzensberger, Hans Magnus
　　1929- .... **CLC 43**
　　See also CA 116, 119

Ephron, Nora 1941- .... **CLC 17, 31**
　　See also CANR 12; CA 65-68

Epstein, Daniel Mark 1948- .... **CLC 7**
　　See also CANR 2; CA 49-52

Epstein, Jacob 1956- .... **CLC 19**
　　See also CA 114

Epstein, Joseph 1937-............. **CLC 39**
　　See also CA 112, 119

Epstein, Leslie 1938- .... **CLC 27**
　　See also CANR 23; CA 73-76

Erdman, Paul E(mil) 1932- .... **CLC 25**
　　See also CANR 13; CA 61-64

Erdrich, Louise 1954-........ **CLC 39, 54**
　　See also CA 114

Erenburg, Ilya (Grigoryevich) 1891-1967
　　See Ehrenburg, Ilya (Grigoryevich)

Eseki, Bruno 1919-
　　See Mphahlele, Ezekiel

Esenin, Sergei (Aleksandrovich)
　　1895-1925 .... **TCLC 4**
　　See also CA 104

Eshleman, Clayton 1935-........... **CLC 7**
　　See also CAAS 6; CA 33-36R; DLB 5

Espriu, Salvador 1913-1985........ **CLC 9**
　　See also obituary CA 115

Estleman, Loren D. 1952- .... **CLC 48**
　　See also CA 85-88

Evans, Marian 1819-1880
　　See Eliot, George

Evans, Mary Ann 1819-1880
　　See Eliot, George

Evarts, Esther 1900-1972
　　See Benson, Sally

Everett, Percival L. 1957?- .... **CLC 57**
　　See also CA 129

Everson, Ronald G(ilmour) 1903-... **CLC 27**
　　See also CA 17-20R

Everson, William (Oliver)
　　1912- .... **CLC 1, 5, 14**
　　See also CANR 20; CA 9-12R; DLB 5, 16

Evtushenko, Evgenii (Aleksandrovich) 1933-
　　See Yevtushenko, Yevgeny

Ewart, Gavin (Buchanan)
　　1916- .... **CLC 13, 46**
　　See also CANR 17; CA 89-92; DLB 40

Ewers, Hanns Heinz 1871-1943 ... **TCLC 12**
　　See also CA 109

Ewing, Frederick R. 1918-
　　See Sturgeon, Theodore (Hamilton)

Exley, Frederick (Earl) 1929-.... **CLC 6, 11**
　　See also CA 81-84; DLB-Y 81

Ezekiel, Nissim 1924-............. **CLC 61**
　　See also CA 61-64

Ezekiel, Tish O'Dowd 1943-....... **CLC 34**

Fagen, Donald 1948-............. **CLC 26**

Fair, Ronald L. 1932-............. **CLC 18**
　　See also CANR 25; CA 69-72; DLB 33

Fairbairns, Zoe (Ann) 1948- .... **CLC 32**
　　See also CANR 21; CA 103

Fairfield, Cicily Isabel 1892-1983
　　See West, Rebecca

Fallaci, Oriana 1930-............. **CLC 11**
　　See also CANR 15; CA 77-80

Faludy, George 1913-............. **CLC 42**
　　See also CA 21-24R

Fante, John 1909-1983............ **CLC 60**
　　See also CANR 23; CA 69-72;
　　obituary CA 109; DLB-Y 83

Farah, Nuruddin 1945-............ **CLC 53**
　　See also CA 106

Fargue, Leon-Paul 1876-1947 ..... **TCLC 11**
　　See also CA 109

Farigoule, Louis 1885-1972
　　See Romains, Jules

Farina, Richard 1937?-1966........ **CLC 9**
　　See also CA 81-84; obituary CA 25-28R

Farley, Walter 1920- .... **CLC 17**
　　See also CANR 8; CA 17-20R; SATA 2, 43;
　　DLB 22

Farmer, Philip Jose 1918-....... **CLC 1, 19**
　　See also CANR 4; CA 1-4R; DLB 8

Farrell, J(ames) G(ordon)
　　1935-1979 .... **CLC 6**
　　See also CA 73-76; obituary CA 89-92;
　　DLB 14

Farrell, James T(homas)
　　1904-1979 ....**CLC 1, 4, 8, 11**
　　See also CANR 9; CA 5-8R;
　　obituary CA 89-92; DLB 4, 9; DLB-DS 2

Farrell, M. J. 1904-
　　See Keane, Molly

Fassbinder, Rainer Werner
　　1946-1982 .... **CLC 20**
　　See also CA 93-96; obituary CA 106

Fast, Howard (Melvin) 1914- ...... **CLC 23**
　　See also CANR 1; CA 1-4R; SATA 7;
　　DLB 9

Faulkner, William (Cuthbert)
　　1897-1962 .... **CLC 1, 3, 6, 8, 9, 11, 14,
　　18, 28, 52; SSC 1**
　　See also CA 81-84; DLB 9, 11, 44;
　　DLB-Y 86; DLB-DS 2

Fauset, Jessie Redmon
　　1884?-1961 .... **CLC 19, 54**
　　See also CA 109; DLB 51

Faust, Irvin 1924-................ **CLC 8**
　　See also CA 33-36R; DLB 2, 28; DLB-Y 80

Fearing, Kenneth (Flexner)
　　1902-1961 .... **CLC 51**
　　See also CA 93-96; DLB 9

Federman, Raymond 1928- ...... **CLC 6, 47**
　　See also CANR 10; CA 17-20R; DLB-Y 80

Federspiel, J(urg) F. 1931-........ **CLC 42**

Feiffer, Jules 1929-.............. **CLC 2, 8**
　　See also CA 17-20R; SATA 8; DLB 7, 44

Feinberg, David B. 1956-........... **CLC 59**

Feinstein, Elaine 1930-............ **CLC 36**
　　See also CAAS 1; CA 69-72; DLB 14, 40

Feldman, Irving (Mordecai) 1928-.... **CLC 7**
　　See also CANR 1; CA 1-4R

Fellini, Federico 1920-............ **CLC 16**
　　See also CA 65-68

Felsen, Gregor 1916-
　　See Felsen, Henry Gregor

Felsen, Henry Gregor 1916- .... **CLC 17**
　　See also CANR 1; CA 1-4R; SAAS 2;
　　SATA 1

Fenton, James (Martin) 1949-...... **CLC 32**
　　See also CA 102; DLB 40

Ferber, Edna 1887-1968............ **CLC 18**
　　See also CA 5-8R; obituary CA 25-28R;
　　SATA 7; DLB 9, 28

Ferlinghetti, Lawrence (Monsanto)
1919?- .... **CLC 2, 6, 10, 27; PC 1**
See also CANR 3; CA 5-8R; DLB 5, 16;
CDALB 1941-1968

Ferrier, Susan (Edmonstone)
1782-1854 .... **NCLC 8**

Feuchtwanger, Lion 1884-1958 ..... **TCLC 3**
See also CA 104; DLB 66

Feydeau, Georges 1862-1921 ...... **TCLC 22**
See also CA 113

Ficino, Marsilio 1433-1499 .... **LC 12**

Fiedler, Leslie A(aron)
1917- .... **CLC 4, 13, 24**
See also CANR 7; CA 9-12R; DLB 28, 67

Field, Andrew 1938- .... **CLC 44**
See also CANR 25; CA 97-100

Field, Eugene 1850-1895 .... **NCLC 3**
See also SATA 16; DLB 21, 23, 42

Fielding, Henry 1707-1754 .... **LC 1**
See also DLB 39

Fielding, Sarah 1710-1768 .... **LC 1**
See also DLB 39

Fierstein, Harvey 1954- .... **CLC 33**
See also CA 123

Figes, Eva 1932- .... **CLC 31**
See also CANR 4; CA 53-56; DLB 14

Finch, Robert (Duer Claydon)
1900- .... **CLC 18**
See also CANR 9, 24; CA 57-60

Findley, Timothy 1930- .... **CLC 27**
See also CANR 12; CA 25-28R; DLB 53

Fink, Janis 1951-
See Ian, Janis

Firbank, Louis 1944-
See Reed, Lou
See also CA 117

Firbank, (Arthur Annesley) Ronald
1886-1926 .... **TCLC 1**
See also CA 104; DLB 36

Fisher, Roy 1930- .... **CLC 25**
See also CANR 16; CA 81-84; DLB 40

Fisher, Rudolph 1897-1934 .... **TCLC 11**
See also CA 107; DLB 51

Fisher, Vardis (Alvero) 1895-1968. ... **CLC 7**
See also CA 5-8R; obituary CA 25-28R;
DLB 9

FitzGerald, Edward 1809-1883 .... **NCLC 9**
See also DLB 32

Fitzgerald, F(rancis) Scott (Key)
1896-1940 .... **TCLC 1, 6, 14, 28; SSC 6**
See also CA 110, 123; DLB 4, 9, 86;
DLB-Y 81; DLB-DS 1;
CDALB 1917-1929

Fitzgerald, Penelope 1916- ... **CLC 19, 51, 61**
See also CAAS 10; CA 85-88,; DLB 14

Fitzgerald, Robert (Stuart)
1910-1985 .... **CLC 39**
See also CANR 1; CA 2R;
obituary CA 114; DLB-Y 80

FitzGerald, Robert D(avid) 1902- ... **CLC 19**
See also CA 17-20R

Flanagan, Thomas (James Bonner)
1923- .... **CLC 25, 52**
See also CA 108; DLB-Y 80

Flaubert, Gustave
1821-1880 .... **NCLC 2, 10, 19**

Fleming, Ian (Lancaster)
1908-1964 .... **CLC 3, 30**
See also CA 5-8R; SATA 9

Fleming, Thomas J(ames) 1927- .... **CLC 37**
See also CANR 10; CA 5-8R; SATA 8

Fletcher, John Gould 1886-1950 ... **TCLC 35**
See also CA 107; DLB 4, 45

Flieg, Hellmuth
See Heym, Stefan

Flying Officer X 1905-1974
See Bates, H(erbert) E(rnest)

Fo, Dario 1929- .... **CLC 32**
See also CA 116

Follett, Ken(neth Martin) 1949- .... **CLC 18**
See also CANR 13; CA 81-84; DLB-Y 81

Fontane, Theodor 1819-1898 ..... **NCLC 26**

Foote, Horton 1916- .... **CLC 51**
See also CA 73-76; DLB 26

Forbes, Esther 1891-1967 .... **CLC 12**
See also CAP 1; CA 13-14;
obituary CA 25-28R; SATA 2; DLB 22

Forche, Carolyn 1950- .... **CLC 25**
See also CA 109, 117; DLB 5

Ford, Ford Madox
1873-1939 .... **TCLC 1, 15, 39**
See also CA 104; DLB 34

Ford, John 1895-1973 .... **CLC 16**
See also obituary CA 45-48

Ford, Richard 1944- .... **CLC 46**
See also CANR 11; CA 69-72

Foreman, Richard 1937- .... **CLC 50**
See also CA 65-68

Forester, C(ecil) S(cott)
1899-1966 .... **CLC 35**
See also CA 73-76; obituary CA 25-28R;
SATA 13

Forman, James D(ouglas) 1932- .... **CLC 21**
See also CANR 4, 19; CA 9-12R; SATA 8,
21

Fornes, Maria Irene 1930- ...... **CLC 39, 61**
See also CANR 28; CA 25-28R; DLB 7

Forrest, Leon 1937- .... **CLC 4**
See also CAAS 7; CA 89-92; DLB 33

Forster, E(dward) M(organ)
1879-1970 .... **CLC 1, 2, 3, 4, 9, 10, 13,
15, 22, 45**
See also CAP 1; CA 13-14;
obituary CA 25-28R; DLB 34

Forster, John 1812-1876 .... **NCLC 11**

Forsyth, Frederick 1938- ...... **CLC 2, 5, 36**
See also CA 85-88

Forten (Grimke), Charlotte L(ottie)
1837-1914 .... **TCLC 16**
See also Grimke, Charlotte L(ottie) Forten
See also DLB 50

Foscolo, Ugo 1778-1827 .... **NCLC 8**

Fosse, Bob 1925-1987 .... **CLC 20**
See also Fosse, Robert Louis

Fosse, Robert Louis 1925-1987
See Bob Fosse
See also CA 110, 123

Foster, Stephen Collins
1826-1864 .... **NCLC 26**

Foucault, Michel 1926-1984 .... **CLC 31, 34**
See also CANR 23; CA 105;
obituary CA 113

Fouque, Friedrich (Heinrich Karl) de La
Motte 1777-1843 .... **NCLC 2**

Fournier, Henri Alban 1886-1914
See Alain-Fournier
See also CA 104

Fournier, Pierre 1916- .... **CLC 11**
See also Gascar, Pierre
See also CANR 16; CA 89-92

Fowles, John (Robert)
1926- .... **CLC 1, 2, 3, 4, 6, 9, 10, 15, 33**
See also CANR 25; CA 5-8R; SATA 22;
DLB 14

Fox, Paula 1923- .... **CLC 2, 8**
See also CLR 1; CANR 20; CA 73-76;
SATA 17; DLB 52

Fox, William Price (Jr.) 1926- ..... **CLC 22**
See also CANR 11; CA 17-20R; DLB 2;
DLB-Y 81

Foxe, John 1516?-1587 .... **LC 14**

Frame (Clutha), Janet (Paterson)
1924- .... **CLC 2, 3, 6, 22**
See also Clutha, Janet Paterson Frame

France, Anatole 1844-1924 .... **TCLC 9**
See also Thibault, Jacques Anatole Francois

Francis, Claude 19??- .... **CLC 50**

Francis, Dick 1920- .... **CLC 2, 22, 42**
See also CANR 9; CA 5-8R

Francis, Robert (Churchill)
1901-1987 .... **CLC 15**
See also CANR 1; CA 1-4R;
obituary CA 123

Frank, Anne 1929-1945 .... **TCLC 17**
See also CA 113; SATA 42

Frank, Elizabeth 1945- .... **CLC 39**
See also CA 121, 126

Franklin, (Stella Maria Sarah) Miles
1879-1954 .... **TCLC 7**
See also CA 104

Fraser, Antonia (Pakenham)
1932- .... **CLC 32**
See also CA 85-88; SATA 32

Fraser, George MacDonald 1925- .... **CLC 7**
See also CANR 2; CA 45-48

Frayn, Michael 1933- ...... **CLC 3, 7, 31, 47**
See also CA 5-8R; DLB 13, 14

Fraze, Candida 19??- .... **CLC 50**
See also CA 125

Frazer, Sir James George
1854-1941 .... **TCLC 32**
See also CA 118

Frazier, Ian 1951- .... **CLC 46**

Frederic, Harold 1856-1898 ...... **NCLC 10**
See also DLB 12, 23

Frederick the Great 1712-1786 ...... **LC 14**

Fredman, Russell (Bruce) 1929-
See also CLR 20

Fredro, Aleksander 1793-1876 ..... **NCLC 8**

Freeling, Nicolas   1927- . . . .   **CLC 38**
  See also CANR 1, 17; CA 49-52

Freeman, Douglas Southall
  1886-1953 . . . .   **TCLC 11**
  See also CA 109; DLB 17

Freeman, Judith   1946- . . . .   **CLC 55**

Freeman, Mary (Eleanor) Wilkins
  1852-1930 . . . .   **TCLC 9; SSC 1**
  See also CA 106; DLB 12

Freeman, R(ichard) Austin
  1862-1943 . . . .   **TCLC 21**
  See also CA 113; DLB 70

French, Marilyn   1929- . . . . . .   **CLC 10, 18, 60**
  See also CANR 3; CA 69-72

Freneau, Philip Morin   1752-1832 . .   **NCLC 1**
  See also DLB 37, 43

Friedman, B(ernard) H(arper)
  1926- . . . .   **CLC 7**
  See also CANR 3; CA 1-4R

Friedman, Bruce Jay   1930- . . . .   **CLC 3, 5, 56**
  See also CANR 25; CA 9-12R; DLB 2, 28

Friel, Brian   1929- . . . .   **CLC 5, 42, 59**
  See also CA 21-24R; DLB 13

Friis-Baastad, Babbis (Ellinor)
  1921-1970 . . . .   **CLC 12**
  See also CA 17-20R; SATA 7

Frisch, Max (Rudolf)
  1911- . . . .   **CLC 3, 9, 14, 18, 32, 44**
  See also CA 85-88; DLB 69

Fromentin, Eugene (Samuel Auguste)
  1820-1876 . . . .   **NCLC 10**

Frost, Robert (Lee)
  1874-1963 . . .   **CLC 1, 3, 4, 9, 10, 13, 15,**
                          26, 34, 44; PC 1
  See also CA 89-92; SATA 14; DLB 54;
    DLB-DS 7; CDALB 1917-1929

Fry, Christopher   1907- . . . .   **CLC 2, 10, 14**
  See also CANR 9; CA 17-20R; DLB 13

Frye, (Herman) Northrop   1912- . . . .   **CLC 24**
  See also CANR 8; CA 5-8R

Fuchs, Daniel   1909- . . . .   **CLC 8, 22**
  See also CAAS 5; CA 81-84; DLB 9, 26, 28

Fuchs, Daniel   1934- . . . .   **CLC 34**
  See also CANR 14; CA 37-40R

Fuentes, Carlos
  1928- . . . . . .   **CLC 3, 8, 10, 13, 22, 41, 60**
  See also CANR 10; CA 69-72

Fugard, Athol   1932- . . .   **CLC 5, 9, 14, 25, 40**
  See also CA 85-88

Fugard, Sheila   1932- . . . .   **CLC 48**
  See also CA 125

Fuller, Charles (H., Jr.)
  1939- . . . .   **CLC 25; DC 1**
  See also CA 108, 112; DLB 38

Fuller, John (Leopold)   1937- . . . .   **CLC 62**
  See also CANR 9; CA 21-22R; DLB 40

Fuller, (Sarah) Margaret
  1810-1850 . . . .   **NCLC 5**
  See also Ossoli, Sarah Margaret (Fuller
    marchesa d')
  See also DLB 1, 59, 73; CDALB 1640-1865

Fuller, Roy (Broadbent)   1912- . . . .   **CLC 4, 28**
  See also CA 5-8R; DLB 15, 20

Fulton, Alice   1952- . . . .   **CLC 52**
  See also CA 116

Furphy, Joseph   1843-1912 . . . .   **TCLC 25**

Futrelle, Jacques   1875-1912 . . . . . .   **TCLC 19**
  See also CA 113

Gaboriau, Emile   1835-1873 . . . . . .   **NCLC 14**

Gadda, Carlo Emilio   1893-1973 . . . .   **CLC 11**
  See also CA 89-92

Gaddis, William
  1922- . . . .   **CLC 1, 3, 6, 8, 10, 19, 43**
  See also CAAS 4; CANR 21; CA 17-20R;
    DLB 2

Gaines, Ernest J.   1933- . . . . . .   **CLC 3, 11, 18**
  See also CANR 6, 24; CA 9-12R; DLB 2,
    33; DLB-Y 80

Gale, Zona   1874-1938 . . . .   **TCLC 7**
  See also CA 105; DLB 9

Gallagher, Tess   1943- . . . .   **CLC 18, 63**
  See also CA 106

Gallant, Mavis
  1922- . . . .   **CLC 7, 18, 38; SSC 5**
  See also CA 69-72; DLB 53

Gallant, Roy A(rthur)   1924- . . . .   **CLC 17**
  See also CANR 4; CA 5-8R; SATA 4

Gallico, Paul (William)   1897-1976 . . .   **CLC 2**
  See also CA 5-8R; obituary CA 69-72;
    SATA 13; DLB 9

Galsworthy, John   1867-1933 . . . .   **TCLC 1**
  See also CA 104; DLB 10, 34

Galt, John   1779-1839 . . . .   **NCLC 1**

Galvin, James   1951- . . . .   **CLC 38**
  See also CANR 26; CA 108

Gamboa, Frederico   1864-1939 . . . . .   **TCLC 36**

Gann, Ernest K(ellogg)   1910- . . . . . .   **CLC 23**
  See also CANR 1; CA 1-4R

Garcia Lorca, Federico
  1899-1936 . . . .   **TCLC 1, 7**
  See also CA 104

Garcia Marquez, Gabriel (Jose)
  1928- . . . .   **CLC 2, 3, 8, 10, 15, 27, 47, 55**
  See also CANR 10; CA 33-36R

Gardam, Jane   1928- . . . .   **CLC 43**
  See also CLR 12; CANR 2, 18; CA 49-52;
    SATA 28, 39; DLB 14

Gardner, Herb   1934- . . . .   **CLC 44**

Gardner, John (Champlin, Jr.)
  1933-1982 . . . .   **CLC 2, 3, 5, 7, 8, 10, 18,**
                          28, 34; SSC 7
  See also CA 65-68; obituary CA 107;
    obituary SATA 31, 40; DLB 2; DLB-Y 82

Gardner, John (Edmund)   1926- . . . . .   **CLC 30**
  See also CANR 15; CA 103

Garfield, Leon   1921- . . . .   **CLC 12**
  See also CA 17-20R; SATA 1, 32

Garland, (Hannibal) Hamlin
  1860-1940 . . . .   **TCLC 3**
  See also CA 104; DLB 12, 71

Garneau, Hector (de) Saint Denys
  1912-1943 . . . .   **TCLC 13**
  See also CA 111

Garner, Alan   1935- . . . .   **CLC 17**
  See also CLR 20; CANR 15; CA 73-76;
    SATA 18

Garner, Hugh   1913-1979 . . . .   **CLC 13**
  See also CA 69-72; DLB 68

Garnett, David   1892-1981 . . . .   **CLC 3**
  See also CANR 17; CA 5-8R;
    obituary CA 103; DLB 34

Garrett, George (Palmer, Jr.)
  1929- . . . .   **CLC 3, 11, 51**
  See also CAAS 5; CANR 1; CA 1-4R;
    DLB 2, 5; DLB-Y 83

Garrick, David   1717-1779 . . . .   **LC 15**
  See also DLB 84

Garrigue, Jean   1914-1972 . . . .   **CLC 2, 8**
  See also CANR 20; CA 5-8R;
    obituary CA 37-40R

Gary, Romain   1914-1980 . . . .   **CLC 25**
  See also Kacew, Romain

Gascar, Pierre   1916- . . . .   **CLC 11**
  See also Fournier, Pierre

Gascoyne, David (Emery)   1916- . . . .   **CLC 45**
  See also CANR 10; CA 65-68; DLB 20

Gaskell, Elizabeth Cleghorn
  1810-1865 . . . .   **NCLC 5**
  See also DLB 21

Gass, William H(oward)
  1924- . . . .   **CLC 1, 2, 8, 11, 15, 39**
  See also CA 17-20R; DLB 2

Gautier, Theophile   1811-1872 . . . . .   **NCLC 1**

Gaye, Marvin (Pentz)   1939-1984 . . .   **CLC 26**
  See also obituary CA 112

Gebler, Carlo (Ernest)   1954- . . . .   **CLC 39**
  See also CA 119

Gee, Maggie   19??- . . . .   **CLC 57**

Gee, Maurice (Gough)   1931- . . . .   **CLC 29**
  See also CA 97-100; SATA 46

Gelbart, Larry   1923?- . . . .   **CLC 21, 61**
  See also CA 73-76

Gelber, Jack   1932- . . . .   **CLC 1, 6, 14, 60**
  See also CANR 2; CA 1-4R; DLB 7

Gellhorn, Martha (Ellis)   1908- . .   **CLC 14, 60**
  See also CA 77-80; DLB-Y 82

Genet, Jean
  1910-1986 . . .   **CLC 1, 2, 5, 10, 14, 44, 46**
  See also CANR 18; CA 13-16R; DLB 72;
    DLB-Y 86

Gent, Peter   1942- . . . .   **CLC 29**
  See also CA 89-92; DLB 72; DLB-Y 82

George, Jean Craighead   1919- . . . . . .   **CLC 35**
  See also CLR 1; CA 5-8R; SATA 2;
    DLB 52

George, Stefan (Anton)
  1868-1933 . . . .   **TCLC 2, 14**
  See also CA 104

Gerhardi, William (Alexander)   1895-1977
  See Gerhardie, William (Alexander)

Gerhardie, William (Alexander)
  1895-1977 . . . .   **CLC 5**
  See also CANR 18; CA 25-28R;
    obituary CA 73-76; DLB 36

Gertler, T(rudy)   1946?- . . . .   **CLC 34**
  See also CA 116

Gessner, Friedrike Victoria   1910-1980
  See Adamson, Joy(-Friederike Victoria)

Ghelderode, Michel de
1898-1962 .... CLC **6, 11**
See also CA 85-88

Ghiselin, Brewster 1903- .... CLC **23**
See also CANR 13; CA 13-16R

Ghose, Zulfikar 1935-............. CLC **42**
See also CA 65-68

Ghosh, Amitav 1943- .... CLC **44**

Giacosa, Giuseppe 1847-1906 ...... TCLC **7**
See also CA 104

Gibbon, Lewis Grassic 1901-1935... TCLC **4**
See also Mitchell, James Leslie

Gibbons, Kaye 1960- .... CLC **50**

Gibran, (Gibran) Kahlil
1883-1931 .... TCLC **1, 9**
See also CA 104

Gibson, William 1914- .... CLC **23**
See also CANR 9; CA 9-12R; DLB 7

Gibson, William 1948- .... CLC **39, 63**
See also CA 126

Gide, Andre (Paul Guillaume)
1869-1951 .... TCLC **5, 12, 36**
See also CA 104, 124; DLB 65

Gifford, Barry (Colby) 1946-....... CLC **34**
See also CANR 9; CA 65-68

Gilbert, (Sir) W(illiam) S(chwenck)
1836-1911 .... TCLC **3**
See also CA 104; SATA 36

Gilbreth, Ernestine 1908-
See Carey, Ernestine Gilbreth

Gilbreth, Frank B(unker), Jr.
1911- .... CLC **17**
See also CA 9-12R; SATA 2

Gilchrist, Ellen 1935-......... CLC **34, 48**
See also CA 113, 116

Giles, Molly 1942- .... CLC **39**
See also CA 126

Gilliam, Terry (Vance) 1940-
See Monty Python
See also CA 108, 113

Gilliatt, Penelope (Ann Douglass)
1932-.............. CLC **2, 10, 13, 53**
See also CA 13-16R; DLB 14

Gilman, Charlotte (Anna) Perkins (Stetson)
1860-1935 .... TCLC **9, 37**
See also CA 106

Gilmour, David 1944-
See Pink Floyd

Gilpin, William 1724-1804 .... NCLC **30**

Gilroy, Frank D(aniel) 1925-........ CLC **2**
See also CA 81-84; DLB 7

Ginsberg, Allen
1926- .... CLC **1, 2, 3, 4, 6, 13, 36**
See also CANR 2; CA 1-4R; DLB 5, 16;
CDALB 1941-1968

Ginzburg, Natalia 1916-...... CLC **5, 11, 54**
See also CA 85-88

Giono, Jean 1895-1970......... CLC **4, 11**
See also CANR 2; CA 45-48;
obituary CA 29-32R; DLB 72

Giovanni, Nikki 1943- .... CLC **2, 4, 19**
See also CLR 6; CAAS 6; CANR 18;
CA 29-32R; SATA 24; DLB 5, 41

Giovene, Andrea 1904-............. CLC **7**
See also CA 85-88

Gippius, Zinaida (Nikolayevna) 1869-1945
See Hippius, Zinaida
See also CA 106

Giraudoux, (Hippolyte) Jean
1882-1944 .... TCLC **2, 7**
See also CA 104; DLB 65

Gironella, Jose Maria 1917-....... CLC **11**
See also CA 101

Gissing, George (Robert)
1857-1903 .... TCLC **3, 24**
See also CA 105; DLB 18

Gladkov, Fyodor (Vasilyevich)
1883-1958 .... TCLC **27**

Glanville, Brian (Lester) 1931- ...... CLC **6**
See also CANR 3; CA 5-8R; SATA 42;
DLB 15

Glasgow, Ellen (Anderson Gholson)
1873?-1945............... TCLC **2, 7**
See also CA 104; DLB 9, 12

Glassco, John 1909-1981 .... CLC **9**
See also CANR 15; CA 13-16R;
obituary CA 102; DLB 68

Glasser, Ronald J. 1940?- .... CLC **37**

Glendinning, Victoria 1937-....... CLC **50**
See also CA 120

Glissant, Edouard 1928-.......... CLC **10**

Gloag, Julian 1930- .... CLC **40**
See also CANR 10; CA 65-68

Gluck, Louise (Elisabeth)
1943- .... CLC **7, 22, 44**
See also CA 33-36R; DLB 5

Gobineau, Joseph Arthur (Comte) de
1816-1882 .... NCLC **17**

Godard, Jean-Luc 1930-.......... CLC **20**
See also CA 93-96

Godden, (Margaret) Rumer 1907-... CLC **53**
See also CLR 20; CANR 4, 27; CA 7-8R;
SATA 3, 36

Godwin, Gail 1937-........ CLC **5, 8, 22, 31**
See also CANR 15; CA 29-32R; DLB 6

Godwin, William 1756-1836...... NCLC **14**
See also DLB 39

Goethe, Johann Wolfgang von
1749-1832 .... NCLC **4, 22**

Gogarty, Oliver St. John
1878-1957 .... TCLC **15**
See also CA 109; DLB 15, 19

Gogol, Nikolai (Vasilyevich)
1809-1852 ... NCLC **5, 15; DC 1; SSC 4**
See also CAAS 1, 4

Gokceli, Yasar Kemal 1923-
See Kemal, Yashar

Gold, Herbert 1924-........ CLC **4, 7, 14, 42**
See also CANR 17; CA 9-12R; DLB 2;
DLB-Y 81

Goldbarth, Albert 1948-........ CLC **5, 38**
See also CANR 6; CA 53-56

Goldberg, Anatol 1910-1982 .... CLC **34**
See also obituary CA 117

Goldemberg, Isaac 1945-.......... CLC **52**
See also CANR 11; CA 69-72

Golding, William (Gerald)
1911- ..... CLC **1, 2, 3, 8, 10, 17, 27, 58**
See also CANR 13; CA 5-8R; DLB 15

Goldman, Emma 1869-1940....... TCLC **13**
See also CA 110

Goldman, William (W.) 1931-.... CLC **1, 48**
See also CA 9-12R; DLB 44

Goldmann, Lucien 1913-1970 ...... CLC **24**
See also CAP 2; CA 25-28

Goldoni, Carlo 1707-1793 .... LC **4**

Goldsberry, Steven 1949-......... CLC **34**

Goldsmith, Oliver 1728?-1774........ LC **2**
See also SATA 26; DLB 39

Gombrowicz, Witold
1904-1969 .... CLC **4, 7, 11, 49**
See also CAP 2; CA 19-20;
obituary CA 25-28R

Gomez de la Serna, Ramon
1888-1963 .... CLC **9**
See also obituary CA 116

Goncharov, Ivan Alexandrovich
1812-1891 .... NCLC **1**

Goncourt, Edmond (Louis Antoine Huot) de
1822-1896 .... NCLC **7**

Goncourt, Jules (Alfred Huot) de
1830-1870 .... NCLC **7**

Gontier, Fernande 19??-........... CLC **50**

Goodman, Paul 1911-1972.... CLC **1, 2, 4, 7**
See also CAP 2; CA 19-20;
obituary CA 37-40R

Gordimer, Nadine
1923- .... CLC **3, 5, 7, 10, 18, 33, 51**
See also CANR 3; CA 5-8R

Gordon, Adam Lindsay
1833-1870 .... NCLC **21**

Gordon, Caroline
1895-1981 .... CLC **6, 13, 29**
See also CAP 1; CA 11-12;
obituary CA 103; DLB 4, 9; DLB-Y 81

Gordon, Charles William 1860-1937
See Conner, Ralph
See also CA 109

Gordon, Mary (Catherine)
1949- .... CLC **13, 22**
See also CA 102; DLB 6; DLB-Y 81

Gordon, Sol 1923-................. CLC **26**
See also CANR 4; CA 53-56; SATA 11

Gordone, Charles 1925- .... CLC **1, 4**
See also CA 93-96; DLB 7

Gorenko, Anna Andreyevna 1889?-1966
See Akhmatova, Anna

Gorky, Maxim 1868-1936 .... TCLC **8**
See also Peshkov, Alexei Maximovich

Goryan, Sirak 1908-1981
See Saroyan, William

Gosse, Edmund (William)
1849-1928 .... TCLC **28**
See also CA 117; DLB 57

Gotlieb, Phyllis (Fay Bloom)
1926- .... CLC **18**
See also CANR 7; CA 13-16R

Gould, Lois 1938?- .... CLC **4, 10**
See also CA 77-80

Gourmont, Remy de 1858-1915.... **TCLC 17**
See also CA 109

Govier, Katherine 1948-.......... **CLC 51**
See also CANR 18; CA 101

Goyen, (Charles) William
1915-1983 ....**CLC 5, 8, 14, 40**
See also CANR 6; CA 5-8R;
obituary CA 110; DLB 2; DLB-Y 83

Goytisolo, Juan 1931- .... **CLC 5, 10, 23**
See also CA 85-88

Gozzi, (Conte) Carlo 1720-1806 .. **NCLC 23**

Grabbe, Christian Dietrich
1801-1836 .... **NCLC 2**

Grace, Patricia 1937-............ **CLC 56**

Gracian y Morales, Baltasar
1601-1658 .... **LC 15**

Gracq, Julien 1910- .... **CLC 11, 48**
See also Poirier, Louis

Grade, Chaim 1910-1982 .... **CLC 10**
See also CA 93-96; obituary CA 107

Graham, Jorie 1951-............. **CLC 48**
See also CA 111

Graham, R(obert) B(ontine) Cunninghame
1852-1936 .... **TCLC 19**

Graham, W(illiam) S(ydney)
1918-1986 .... **CLC 29**
See also CA 73-76; obituary CA 118;
DLB 20

Graham, Winston (Mawdsley)
1910- .... **CLC 23**
See also CANR 2, 22; CA 49-52;
obituary CA 118

Granville-Barker, Harley
1877-1946 .... **TCLC 2**
See also CA 104

Grass, Gunter (Wilhelm)
1927- .. **CLC 1, 2, 4, 6, 11, 15, 22, 32, 49**
See also CANR 20; CA 13-16R; DLB 75

Grau, Shirley Ann 1929- .... **CLC 4, 9**
See also CANR 22; CA 89-92; DLB 2

Graves, Richard Perceval 1945- .... **CLC 44**
See also CANR 9, 26; CA 65-68

Graves, Robert (von Ranke)
1895-1985 ... **CLC 1, 2, 6, 11, 39, 44, 45**
See also CANR 5; CA 5-8R;
obituary CA 117; SATA 45; DLB 20;
DLB-Y 85

Gray, Alasdair 1934- .... **CLC 41**
See also CA 123

Gray, Amlin 1946- .... **CLC 29**

Gray, Francine du Plessix 1930-.... **CLC 22**
See also CAAS 2; CANR 11; CA 61-64

Gray, John (Henry) 1866-1934 .... **TCLC 19**
See also CA 119

Gray, Simon (James Holliday)
1936- .... **CLC 9, 14, 36**
See also CAAS 3; CA 21-24R; DLB 13

Gray, Spalding 1941- .... **CLC 49**

Gray, Thomas 1716-1771 .... **LC 4; PC 2**

Grayson, Richard (A.) 1951- .... **CLC 38**
See also CANR 14; CA 85-88

Greeley, Andrew M(oran) 1928- .... **CLC 28**
See also CAAS 7; CANR 7; CA 5-8R

Green, Hannah 1932-......... **CLC 3, 7, 30**
See also Greenberg, Joanne
See also CA 73-76

Green, Henry 1905-1974 .... **CLC 2, 13**
See also Yorke, Henry Vincent
See also DLB 15

Green, Julien (Hartridge) 1900- .. **CLC 3, 11**
See also CA 21-24R; DLB 4, 72

Green, Paul (Eliot) 1894-1981...... **CLC 25**
See also CANR 3; CA 5-8R;
obituary CA 103; DLB 7, 9; DLB-Y 81

Greenberg, Ivan 1908-1973
See Rahv, Philip
See also CA 85-88

Greenberg, Joanne (Goldenberg)
1932-.................. **CLC 3, 7, 30**
See also Green, Hannah
See also CANR 14; CA 5-8R; SATA 25

Greenberg, Richard 1959?- .... **CLC 57**

Greene, Bette 1934- .... **CLC 30**
See also CLR 2; CANR 4; CA 53-56;
SATA 8

Greene, Gael 19??-................ **CLC 8**
See also CANR 10; CA 13-16R

Greene, Graham (Henry)
1904- ..... **CLC 1, 3, 6, 9, 14, 18, 27, 37**
See also CA 13-16R; SATA 20; DLB 13, 15;
DLB-Y 85

Gregor, Arthur 1923-.............. **CLC 9**
See also CANR 11; CA 25-28R; SATA 36

Gregory, Lady (Isabella Augusta Persse)
1852-1932 .... **TCLC 1**
See also CA 104; DLB 10

Grendon, Stephen 1909-1971
See Derleth, August (William)

Grenville, Kate 1950- .... **CLC 61**
See also CA 118

Greve, Felix Paul Berthold Friedrich
1879-1948
See Grove, Frederick Philip
See also CA 104

Grey, (Pearl) Zane 1872?-1939 ..... **TCLC 6**
See also CA 104; DLB 9

Grieg, (Johan) Nordahl (Brun)
1902-1943 .... **TCLC 10**
See also CA 107

Grieve, C(hristopher) M(urray) 1892-1978
See MacDiarmid, Hugh
See also CA 5-8R; obituary CA 85-88

Griffin, Gerald 1803-1840 .... **NCLC 7**

Griffin, Peter 1942- .... **CLC 39**

Griffiths, Trevor 1935-......... **CLC 13, 52**
See also CA 97-100; DLB 13

Grigson, Geoffrey (Edward Harvey)
1905-1985 .... **CLC 7, 39**
See also CANR 20; CA 25-28R;
obituary CA 118; DLB 27

Grillparzer, Franz 1791-1872...... **NCLC 1**

Grimke, Charlotte L(ottie) Forten 1837-1914
See Forten (Grimke), Charlotte L(ottie)
See also CA 117, 124

Grimm, Jakob (Ludwig) Karl
1785-1863 .... **NCLC 3**
See also SATA 22

Grimm, Wilhelm Karl 1786-1859 .. **NCLC 3**
See also SATA 22

Grimmelshausen, Johann Jakob Christoffel
von 1621-1676 .... **LC 6**

Grindel, Eugene 1895-1952
See also CA 104

Grossman, Vasily (Semenovich)
1905-1964 .... **CLC 41**
See also CA 124

Grove, Frederick Philip
1879-1948 .... **TCLC 4**
See also Greve, Felix Paul Berthold
Friedrich

Grumbach, Doris (Isaac)
1918-.................. **CLC 13, 22**
See also CAAS 2; CANR 9; CA 5-8R

Grundtvig, Nicolai Frederik Severin
1783-1872 .... **NCLC 1**

Grunwald, Lisa 1959-............. **CLC 44**
See also CA 120

Guare, John 1938- .... **CLC 8, 14, 29**
See also CANR 21; CA 73-76; DLB 7

Gudjonsson, Halldor Kiljan 1902-
See Laxness, Halldor (Kiljan)
See also CA 103

Guest, Barbara 1920-............. **CLC 34**
See also CANR 11; CA 25-28R; DLB 5

Guest, Judith (Ann) 1936-....... **CLC 8, 30**
See also CANR 15; CA 77-80

Guild, Nicholas M. 1944-......... **CLC 33**
See also CA 93-96

Guillen, Jorge 1893-1984.......... **CLC 11**
See also CA 89-92; obituary CA 112

Guillen, Nicolas 1902-1989 .... **CLC 48**
See also CA 116, 125

Guillevic, (Eugene) 1907-......... **CLC 33**
See also CA 93-96

Guiraldes, Ricardo 1886-1927..... **TCLC 39**

Gunn, Bill 1934-1989 .... **CLC 5**
See also Gunn, William Harrison
See also DLB 38

Gunn, Thom(son William)
1929-................ **CLC 3, 6, 18, 32**
See also CANR 9; CA 17-20R; DLB 27

Gunn, William Harrison 1934-1989
See Gunn, Bill
See also CANR 12, 25; CA 13-16R

Gurney, A(lbert) R(amsdell), Jr.
1930-................ **CLC 32, 50, 54**
See also CA 77-80

Gurney, Ivor (Bertie) 1890-1937... **TCLC 33**

Gustafson, Ralph (Barker) 1909-.... **CLC 36**
See also CANR 8; CA 21-24R

Guthrie, A(lfred) B(ertram), Jr.
1901-................... **CLC 23**
See also CA 57-60; DLB 6

Guthrie, Woodrow Wilson 1912-1967
See Guthrie, Woody
See also CA 113; obituary CA 93-96

Guthrie, Woody 1912-1967 .... **CLC 35**
See also Guthrie, Woodrow Wilson

Guy, Rosa (Cuthbert) 1928-..... **CLC 26 13**
See also CANR 14; CA 17-20R; SATA 14;
DLB 33

Haavikko, Paavo (Juhani)
1931- . . . . **CLC 18, 34**
See also CA 106

Hacker, Marilyn 1942- . . . . . . **CLC 5, 9, 23**
See also CA 77-80

Haggard, (Sir) H(enry) Rider
1856-1925 . . . . **TCLC 11**
See also CA 108; SATA 16; DLB 70

Haig-Brown, Roderick L(angmere)
1908-1976 . . . . **CLC 21**
See also CANR 4; CA 5-8R;
obituary CA 69-72; SATA 12

Hailey, Arthur 1920- . . . . **CLC 5**
See also CANR 2; CA 1-4R; DLB-Y 82

Hailey, Elizabeth Forsythe 1938- . . . **CLC 40**
See also CAAS 1; CANR 15; CA 93-96

Haines, John 1924- . . . . **CLC 58**
See also CANR 13; CA 19-20R; DLB 5

Haldeman, Joe 1943- . . . . **CLC 61**
See also CA 53-56; DLB 8

Haley, Alex (Palmer) 1921- . . . . . . **CLC 8, 12**
See also CA 77-80; DLB 38

Haliburton, Thomas Chandler
1796-1865 . . . . **NCLC 15**
See also DLB 11

Hall, Donald (Andrew, Jr.)
1928- . . . . **CLC 1, 13, 37, 59**
See also CAAS 7; CANR 2; CA 5-8R;
SATA 23; DLB 5

Hall, James Norman 1887-1951 . . . **TCLC 23**
See also CA 123; SATA 21

Hall, (Marguerite) Radclyffe
1886-1943 . . . . **TCLC 12**
See also CA 110

Hall, Rodney 1935- . . . . **CLC 51**
See also CA 109

Halpern, Daniel 1945- . . . . **CLC 14**
See also CA 33-36R

Hamburger, Michael (Peter Leopold)
1924- . . . . **CLC 5, 14**
See also CAAS 4; CANR 2; CA 5-8R;
DLB 27

Hamill, Pete 1935- . . . . **CLC 10**
See also CANR 18; CA 25-28R

Hamilton, Edmond 1904-1977 . . . . **CLC 1**
See also CANR 3; CA 1-4R; DLB 8

Hamilton, Gail 1911-
See Corcoran, Barbara

Hamilton, Ian 1938- . . . . **CLC 55**
See also CA 106; DLB 40

Hamilton, Mollie 1909?-
See Kaye, M(ary) M(argaret)

Hamilton, (Anthony Walter) Patrick
1904-1962 . . . . **CLC 51**
See also obituary CA 113; DLB 10

Hamilton, Virginia (Esther) 1936- . . . **CLC 26**
See also CLR 1, 11; CANR 20; CA 25-28R;
SATA 4; DLB 33, 52

Hammett, (Samuel) Dashiell
1894-1961 . . . . **CLC 3, 5, 10, 19, 47**
See also CA 81-84

Hammon, Jupiter 1711?-1800? . . . . **NCLC 5**
See also DLB 31, 50

Hamner, Earl (Henry), Jr. 1923- . . . **CLC 12**
See also CA 73-76; DLB 6

Hampton, Christopher (James)
1946- . . . . **CLC 4**
See also CA 25-28R; DLB 13

Hamsun, Knut 1859-1952 . . . . . . **TCLC 2, 14**
See also Pedersen, Knut

Handke, Peter 1942- . . **CLC 5, 8, 10, 15, 38**
See also CA 77-80

Hanley, James 1901-1985 . . . **CLC 3, 5, 8, 13**
See also CA 73-76; obituary CA 117

Hannah, Barry 1942- . . . . **CLC 23, 38**
See also CA 108, 110; DLB 6

Hansberry, Lorraine (Vivian)
1930-1965 . . . . **CLC 17, 62**
See also CA 109; obituary CA 25-28R;
CABS 3; DLB 7, 38; CDALB 1941-1968

Hansen, Joseph 1923- . . . . **CLC 38**
See also CANR 16; CA 29-32R

Hansen, Martin 1909-1955 . . . . **TCLC 32**

Hanson, Kenneth O(stlin) 1922- . . . . **CLC 13**
See also CANR 7; CA 53-56

Hardenberg, Friedrich (Leopold Freiherr) von
1772-1801
See Novalis

Hardwick, Elizabeth 1916- . . . . **CLC 13**
See also CANR 3; CA 5-8R; DLB 6

Hardy, Thomas
1840-1928 . . . **TCLC 4, 10, 18, 32; SSC 2**
See also CA 104, 123; SATA 25; DLB 18,
19

Hare, David 1947- . . . . **CLC 29, 58**
See also CA 97-100; DLB 13

Harlan, Louis R(udolph) 1922- . . . . . **CLC 34**
See also CANR 25; CA 21-24R

Harling, Robert 1951?- . . . . **CLC 53**

Harmon, William (Ruth) 1938- . . . . . **CLC 38**
See also CANR 14; CA 33-36R

Harper, Frances Ellen Watkins
1825-1911 . . . . **TCLC 14**
See also CA 111, 125; DLB 50

Harper, Michael S(teven) 1938- . . **CLC 7, 22**
See also CANR 24; CA 33-36R; DLB 41

Harris, Christie (Lucy Irwin)
1907- . . . . **CLC 12**
See also CANR 6; CA 5-8R; SATA 6

Harris, Frank 1856-1931 . . . . **TCLC 24**
See also CAAS 1; CA 109

Harris, George Washington
1814-1869 . . . . **NCLC 23**
See also DLB 3, 11

Harris, Joel Chandler 1848-1908 . . . **TCLC 2**
See also YABC 1; CA 104; DLB 11, 23, 42

Harris, John (Wyndham Parkes Lucas)
Beynon 1903-1969
See Wyndham, John
See also CA 102; obituary CA 89-92

Harris, MacDonald 1921- . . . . **CLC 9**
See also Heiney, Donald (William)

Harris, Mark 1922- . . . . **CLC 19**
See also CAAS 3; CANR 2; CA 5-8R;
DLB 2; DLB-Y 80

Harris, (Theodore) Wilson 1921- . . . **CLC 25**
See also CANR 11; CA 65-68

Harrison, Harry (Max) 1925- . . . . . . **CLC 42**
See also CANR 5, 21; CA 1-4R; SATA 4;
DLB 8

Harrison, James (Thomas) 1937-
See Harrison, Jim
See also CANR 8; CA 13-16R

Harrison, Jim 1937- . . . . **CLC 6, 14, 33**
See also Harrison, James (Thomas)
See also DLB-Y 82

Harrison, Tony 1937- . . . . **CLC 43**
See also CA 65-68; DLB 40

Harriss, Will(ard Irvin) 1922- . . . . . . **CLC 34**
See also CA 111

Harte, (Francis) Bret(t)
1836?-1902 . . . . **TCLC 1, 25**
See also CA 104; SATA 26; DLB 12, 64,
74; CDALB 1865-1917

Hartley, L(eslie) P(oles)
1895-1972 . . . . **CLC 2, 22**
See also CA 45-48; obituary CA 37-40R;
DLB 15

Hartman, Geoffrey H. 1929- . . . . **CLC 27**
See also CA 117, 125; DLB 67

Haruf, Kent 19??- . . . . **CLC 34**

Harwood, Ronald 1934- . . . . **CLC 32**
See also CANR 4; CA 1-4R; DLB 13

Hasek, Jaroslav (Matej Frantisek)
1883-1923 . . . . **TCLC 4**
See also CA 104

Hass, Robert 1941- . . . . **CLC 18, 39**
See also CA 111

Hastings, Selina 19??- . . . . **CLC 44**

Hauptmann, Gerhart (Johann Robert)
1862-1946 . . . . **TCLC 4**
See also CA 104; DLB 66

Havel, Vaclav 1936- . . . . **CLC 25, 58**
See also CA 104

Haviaras, Stratis 1935- . . . . **CLC 33**
See also CA 105

Hawkes, John (Clendennin Burne, Jr.)
1925- . . . . . . **CLC 1, 2, 3, 4, 7, 9, 14, 15,
27, 49**
See also CANR 2; CA 1-4R; DLB 2, 7;
DLB-Y 80

Hawking, Stephen (William)
1948- . . . . **CLC 63**
See also CA 126, 129

Hawthorne, Julian 1846-1934 . . . . . **TCLC 25**

Hawthorne, Nathaniel
1804-1864 . . . **NCLC 2, 10, 17, 23; SSC 3**
See also YABC 2; DLB 1, 74;
CDALB 1640-1865

Hayashi Fumiko 1904-1951 . . . . **TCLC 27**

Haycraft, Anna 19??-
See Ellis, Alice Thomas

Hayden, Robert (Earl)
1913-1980 . . . . **CLC 5, 9, 14, 37**
See also CANR 24; CA 69-72;
obituary CA 97-100; CABS 2; SATA 19;
obituary SATA 26; DLB 5, 76;
CDALB 1941-1968

Hayman, Ronald 1932- . . . . **CLC 44**
See also CANR 18; CA 25-28R

Haywood, Eliza (Fowler) 1693?-1756 . . **LC 1**
See also DLB 39

Hazlitt, William 1778-1830 . . . . . . **NCLC 29**

Hazzard, Shirley 1931- . . . . **CLC 18**
See also CANR 4; CA 9-12R; DLB-Y 82

H(ilda) D(oolittle)
1886-1961 . . . . **CLC 3, 8, 14, 31, 34**
See also Doolittle, Hilda

Head, Bessie 1937-1986 . . . . **CLC 25**
See also CANR 25; CA 29-32R;
obituary CA 109

Headon, (Nicky) Topper 1956?-
See The Clash

Heaney, Seamus (Justin)
1939- . . . . **CLC 5, 7, 14, 25, 37**
See also CANR 25; CA 85-88; DLB 40

Hearn, (Patricio) Lafcadio (Tessima Carlos)
1850-1904 . . . . **TCLC 9**
See also CA 105; DLB 12

Hearne, Vicki 1946- . . . . **CLC 56**

Hearon, Shelby 1931- . . . . **CLC 63**
See also CANR 18; CA 25-28

Heat Moon, William Least 1939- . . . **CLC 29**

Hebert, Anne 1916- . . . . **CLC 4, 13, 29**
See also CA 85-88; DLB 68

Hecht, Anthony (Evan)
1923- . . . . **CLC 8, 13, 19**
See also CANR 6; CA 9-12R; DLB 5

Hecht, Ben 1894-1964 . . . . **CLC 8**
See also CA 85-88; DLB 7, 9, 25, 26, 28

Hedayat, Sadeq 1903-1951 . . . . **TCLC 21**
See also CA 120

Heidegger, Martin 1889-1976 . . . . . . **CLC 24**
See also CA 81-84; obituary CA 65-68

Heidenstam, (Karl Gustaf) Verner von
1859-1940 . . . . **TCLC 5**
See also CA 104

Heifner, Jack 1946- . . . . **CLC 11**
See also CA 105

Heijermans, Herman 1864-1924 . . . **TCLC 24**
See also CA 123

Heilbrun, Carolyn G(old) 1926- . . . . . **CLC 25**
See also CANR 1; CA 45-48

Heine, Harry 1797-1856
See Heine, Heinrich

Heine, Heinrich 1797-1856 . . . . **NCLC 4**

Heinemann, Larry C(urtiss) 1944- . . **CLC 50**
See also CA 110

Heiney, Donald (William) 1921-
See Harris, MacDonald
See also CANR 3; CA 1-4R

Heinlein, Robert A(nson)
1907-1988 . . . . . . **CLC 1, 3, 8, 14, 26, 55**
See also CANR 1, 20; CA 1-4R;
obituary CA 125; SATA 9; DLB 8

Heller, Joseph
1923- . . . . **CLC 1, 3, 5, 8, 11, 36, 63**
See also CANR 8; CA 5-8R; CABS 1;
DLB 2, 28; DLB-Y 80

Hellman, Lillian (Florence)
1905?-1984 . . . . . **CLC 2, 4, 8, 14, 18, 34,
44, 52; DC 1**
See also CA 13-16R; obituary CA 112;
DLB 7; DLB-Y 84

Helprin, Mark 1947- . . . . . **CLC 7, 10, 22, 32**
See also CA 81-84; DLB-Y 85

Hemans, Felicia 1793-1835 . . . . . . **NCLC 29**

Hemingway, Ernest (Miller)
1899-1961 . . . **CLC 1, 3, 6, 8, 10, 13, 19,
30, 34, 39, 41, 44, 50, 61; SSC 1**
See also CA 77-80; DLB 4, 9; DLB-Y 81,
87; DLB-DS 1

Hempel, Amy 1951- . . . . **CLC 39**
See also CA 118

Henley, Beth 1952- . . . . **CLC 23**
See also Henley, Elizabeth Becker
See also DLB-Y 86

Henley, Elizabeth Becker 1952-
See Henley, Beth
See also CA 107

Henley, William Ernest
1849-1903 . . . . **TCLC 8**
See also CA 105; DLB 19

Hennissart, Martha
See Lathen, Emma
See also CA 85-88

Henry, O. 1862-1910 . . . **TCLC 1, 19; SSC 5**
See also Porter, William Sydney
See also YABC 2; CA 104; DLB 12, 78, 79;
CDALB 1865-1917

Henry VIII 1491-1547 . . . . **LC 10**

Hentoff, Nat(han Irving) 1925- . . . . . **CLC 26**
See also CLR 1; CAAS 6; CANR 5;
CA 1-4R; SATA 27, 42

Heppenstall, (John) Rayner
1911-1981 . . . . **CLC 10**
See also CA 1-4R; obituary CA 103

Herbert, Frank (Patrick)
1920-1986 . . . . **CLC 12, 23, 35, 44**
See also CANR 5; CA 53-56;
obituary CA 118; SATA 9, 37, 47; DLB 8

Herbert, Zbigniew 1924- . . . . **CLC 9, 43**
See also CA 89-92

Herbst, Josephine 1897-1969 . . . . **CLC 34**
See also CA 5-8R; obituary CA 25-28R;
DLB 9

Herder, Johann Gottfried von
1744-1803 . . . . **NCLC 8**

Hergesheimer, Joseph
1880-1954 . . . . **TCLC 11**
See also CA 109; DLB 9

Herlagnez, Pablo de 1844-1896
See Verlaine, Paul (Marie)

Herlihy, James Leo 1927- . . . . **CLC 6**
See also CANR 2; CA 1-4R

Hermogenes fl.c. 175- . . . . **CMLC 6**

Hernandez, Jose 1834-1886 . . . . . . **NCLC 17**

Herrick, Robert 1591-1674 . . . . **LC 13**

Herriot, James 1916- . . . . **CLC 12**
See also Wight, James Alfred

Herrmann, Dorothy 1941- . . . . **CLC 44**
See also CA 107

Hersey, John (Richard)
1914- . . . . **CLC 1, 2, 7, 9, 40**
See also CA 17-20R; SATA 25; DLB 6

Herzen, Aleksandr Ivanovich
1812-1870 . . . . **NCLC 10**

Herzl, Theodor 1860-1904 . . . . **TCLC 36**

Herzog, Werner 1942- . . . . **CLC 16**
See also CA 89-92

Hesiod c. 8th Century B.C.- . . . . . . **CMLC 5**

Hesse, Hermann
1877-1962 . . . . **CLC 1, 2, 3, 6, 11, 17, 25**
See also CAP 2; CA 17-18; SATA 50;
DLB 66

Heyen, William 1940- . . . . **CLC 13, 18**
See also CA 33-36R; DLB 5

Heyerdahl, Thor 1914- . . . . **CLC 26**
See also CANR 5, 22; CA 5-8R; SATA 2,
52

Heym, Georg (Theodor Franz Arthur)
1887-1912 . . . . **TCLC 9**
See also CA 106

Heym, Stefan 1913- . . . . **CLC 41**
See also CANR 4; CA 9-12R; DLB 69

Heyse, Paul (Johann Ludwig von)
1830-1914 . . . . **TCLC 8**
See also CA 104

Hibbert, Eleanor (Burford) 1906- . . . . **CLC 7**
See also CANR 9; CA 17-20R; SATA 2

Higgins, George V(incent)
1939- . . . . **CLC 4, 7, 10, 18**
See also CAAS 5; CANR 17; CA 77-80;
DLB 2; DLB-Y 81

Higginson, Thomas Wentworth
1823-1911 . . . . **TCLC 36**
See also DLB 1, 64

Highsmith, (Mary) Patricia
1921- . . . . **CLC 2, 4, 14, 42**
See also CANR 1, 20; CA 1-4R

Highwater, Jamake 1942- . . . . **CLC 12**
See also CAAS 7; CANR 10; CA 65-68;
SATA 30, 32; DLB 52; DLB-Y 85

Hikmet (Ran), Nazim 1902-1963 . . . . **CLC 40**
See also obituary CA 93-96

Hildesheimer, Wolfgang 1916- . . . . . **CLC 49**
See also CA 101; DLB 69

Hill, Geoffrey (William)
1932- . . . . **CLC 5, 8, 18, 45**
See also CANR 21; CA 81-84; DLB 40

Hill, George Roy 1922- . . . . **CLC 26**
See also CA 110

Hill, Susan B. 1942- . . . . **CLC 4**
See also CA 33-36R; DLB 14

Hillerman, Tony 1925- . . . . **CLC 62**
See also CANR 21; CA 29-32R; SATA 6

Hilliard, Noel (Harvey) 1929- . . . . . . **CLC 15**
See also CANR 7; CA 9-12R

Hilton, James 1900-1954 . . . . **TCLC 21**
See also CA 108; SATA 34; DLB 34

Himes, Chester (Bomar)
1909-1984 . . . . **CLC 2, 4, 7, 18, 58**
See also CANR 22; CA 25-28R;
obituary CA 114; DLB 2, 76

Hinde, Thomas 1926- . . . . **CLC 6, 11**
See also Chitty, (Sir) Thomas Willes

Hine, (William) Daryl 1936- . . . . **CLC 15**
See also CANR 1, 20; CA 1-4R; DLB 60

Hinton, S(usan) E(loise) 1950- . . . . . **CLC 30**
See also CLR 3, 23; CA 81-84; SATA 19

Hippius (Merezhkovsky), Zinaida
(Nikolayevna) 1869-1945...... **TCLC 9**
See also Gippius, Zinaida (Nikolayevna)

Hiraoka, Kimitake 1925-1970
See Mishima, Yukio
See also CA 97-100; obituary CA 29-32R

Hirsch, Edward (Mark) 1950-... **CLC 31, 50**
See also CANR 20; CA 104

Hitchcock, (Sir) Alfred (Joseph)
1899-1980 .... **CLC 16**
See also obituary CA 97-100; SATA 27;
obituary SATA 24

Hoagland, Edward 1932-.......... **CLC 28**
See also CANR 2; CA 1-4R; SATA 51;
DLB 6

Hoban, Russell C(onwell) 1925-.. **CLC 7, 25**
See also CLR 3; CANR 23; CA 5-8R;
SATA 1, 40; DLB 52

Hobson, Laura Z(ametkin)
1900-1986 .... **CLC 7, 25**
See also CA 17-20R; obituary CA 118;
SATA 52; DLB 28

Hochhuth, Rolf 1931-........ **CLC 4, 11, 18**
See also CA 5-8R

Hochman, Sandra 1936-.......... **CLC 3, 8**
See also CA 5-8R; DLB 5

Hochwalder, Fritz 1911-1986 ...... **CLC 36**
See also CA 29-32R; obituary CA 120

Hocking, Mary (Eunice) 1921-..... **CLC 13**
See also CANR 18; CA 101

Hodgins, Jack 1938-.............. **CLC 23**
See also CA 93-96; DLB 60

Hodgson, William Hope
1877-1918 .... **TCLC 13**
See also CA 111; DLB 70

Hoffman, Alice 1952-.............. **CLC 51**
See also CA 77-80

Hoffman, Daniel (Gerard)
1923- .... **CLC 6, 13, 23**
See also CANR 4; CA 1-4R; DLB 5

Hoffman, Stanley 1944-............ **CLC 5**
See also CA 77-80

Hoffman, William M(oses) 1939-... **CLC 40**
See also CANR 11; CA 57-60

Hoffmann, Ernst Theodor Amadeus
1776-1822 .... **NCLC 2**
See also SATA 27

Hoffmann, Gert 1932- .... **CLC 54**

Hofmannsthal, Hugo (Laurenz August
Hofmann Edler) von
1874-1929 .... **TCLC 11**
See also CA 106

Hogg, James 1770-1835.......... **NCLC 4**

Holbach, Paul Henri Thiry, Baron d'
1723-1789 .... **LC 14**

Holberg, Ludvig 1684-1754......... **LC 6**

Holden, Ursula 1921-............. **CLC 18**
See also CANR 22; CA 101

Holderlin, (Johann Christian) Friedrich
1770-1843 .... **NCLC 16**

Holdstock, Robert (P.) 1948-....... **CLC 39**

Holland, Isabelle 1920- .... **CLC 21**
See also CANR 10, 25; CA 21-24R;
SATA 8

Holland, Marcus 1900-1985
See Caldwell, (Janet Miriam) Taylor
(Holland)

Hollander, John 1929-...... **CLC 2, 5, 8, 14**
See also CANR 1; CA 1-4R; SATA 13;
DLB 5

Holleran, Andrew 1943?-.......... **CLC 38**

Hollinghurst, Alan 1954-.......... **CLC 55**
See also CA 114

Hollis, Jim 1916-
See Summers, Hollis (Spurgeon, Jr.)

Holmes, John Clellon 1926-1988.... **CLC 56**
See also CANR 4; CA 9-10R;
obituary CA 125; DLB 16

Holmes, Oliver Wendell
1809-1894 .... **NCLC 14**
See also SATA 34; DLB 1;
CDALB 1640-1865

Holt, Victoria 1906-
See Hibbert, Eleanor (Burford)

Holub, Miroslav 1923-............. **CLC 4**
See also CANR 10; CA 21-24R

Homer c. 8th century B.C.-........ **CMLC 1**

Honig, Edwin 1919-............... **CLC 33**
See also CANR 4; CA 5-8R; DLB 5

Hood, Hugh (John Blagdon)
1928- .... **CLC 15, 28**
See also CANR 1; CA 49-52; DLB 53

Hood, Thomas 1799-1845........ **NCLC 16**

Hooker, (Peter) Jeremy 1941-...... **CLC 43**
See also CANR 22; CA 77-80; DLB 40

Hope, A(lec) D(erwent) 1907-.... **CLC 3, 51**
See also CA 21-24R

Hope, Christopher (David Tully)
1944- .... **CLC 52**
See also CA 106

Hopkins, Gerard Manley
1844-1889 .... **NCLC 17**
See also DLB 35, 57

Hopkins, John (Richard) 1931-...... **CLC 4**
See also CA 85-88

Hopkins, Pauline Elizabeth
1859-1930 .... **TCLC 28**
See also DLB 50

Horgan, Paul 1903- .... **CLC 9, 53**
See also CANR 9; CA 13-16R; SATA 13;
DLB-Y 85

Horovitz, Israel 1939-............ **CLC 56**
See also CA 33-36R; DLB 7

Horwitz, Julius 1920-1986......... **CLC 14**
See also CANR 12; CA 9-12R;
obituary CA 119

Hospital, Janette Turner 1942-..... **CLC 42**
See also CA 108

Hostos (y Bonilla), Eugenio Maria de
1893-1903 .... **TCLC 24**
See also CA 123

Hougan, Carolyn 19??-........... **CLC 34**

Household, Geoffrey (Edward West)
1900-1988 .... **CLC 11**
See also CA 77-80; obituary CA 126;
SATA 14

Housman, A(lfred) E(dward)
1859-1936 .... **TCLC 1, 10; PC 2**
See also CA 104, 125; DLB 19

Housman, Laurence 1865-1959..... **TCLC 7**
See also CA 106; SATA 25; DLB 10

Howard, Elizabeth Jane 1923-... **CLC 7, 29**
See also CANR 8; CA 5-8R

Howard, Maureen 1930-..... **CLC 5, 14, 46**
See also CA 53-56; DLB-Y 83

Howard, Richard 1929-..... **CLC 7, 10, 47**
See also CANR 25; CA 85-88; DLB 5

Howard, Robert E(rvin)
1906-1936 .... **TCLC 8**
See also CA 105

Howe, Fanny 1940- .... **CLC 47**
See also CA 117; SATA 52

Howe, Julia Ward 1819-1910 ..... **TCLC 21**
See also CA 117; DLB 1

Howe, Tina 1937-................ **CLC 48**
See also CA 109

Howell, James 1594?-1666......... **LC 13**

Howells, William Dean
1837-1920 .... **TCLC 7, 17**
See also CA 104; DLB 12, 64, 74;
CDALB 1865-1917

Howes, Barbara 1914-............ **CLC 15**
See also CAAS 3; CA 9-12R; SATA 5

Hrabal, Bohumil 1914-............ **CLC 13**
See also CA 106

Hubbard, L(afayette) Ron(ald)
1911-1986 .... **CLC 43**
See also CANR 22; CA 77-80;
obituary CA 118

Huch, Ricarda (Octavia)
1864-1947 .... **TCLC 13**
See also CA 111; DLB 66

Huddle, David 1942- .... **CLC 49**
See also CA 57-60

Hudson, W(illiam) H(enry)
1841-1922 .... **TCLC 29**
See also CA 115; SATA 35

Hueffer, Ford Madox 1873-1939
See Ford, Ford Madox

Hughart, Barry 1934-............. **CLC 39**

Hughes, David (John) 1930-....... **CLC 48**
See also CA 116; DLB 14

Hughes, Edward James 1930-
See Hughes, Ted

Hughes, (James) Langston
1902-1967 .... **CLC 1, 5, 10, 15, 35, 44;**
PC 1; SSC 6
See also CLR 17; CANR 1; CA 1-4R;
obituary CA 25-28R; SATA 4, 33;
DLB 4, 7, 48, 51, 86; CDALB 1929-1941

Hughes, Richard (Arthur Warren)
1900-1976 .... **CLC 1, 11**
See also CANR 4; CA 5-8R;
obituary CA 65-68; SATA 8;
obituary SATA 25; DLB 15

Hughes, Ted 1930-..... **CLC 2, 4, 9, 14, 37**
See also CLR 3; CANR 1; CA 1-4R;
SATA 27, 49; DLB 40

Hugo, Richard F(ranklin)
1923-1982 .... **CLC 6, 18, 32**
See also CANR 3; CA 49-52;
obituary CA 108; DLB 5

Hugo, Victor Marie
1802-1885 .... **NCLC 3, 10, 21**
See also SATA 47

Huidobro, Vicente 1893-1948 ..... **TCLC 31**

Hulme, Keri 1947- .... **CLC 39**
See also CA 123

Hulme, T(homas) E(rnest)
1883-1917 .... **TCLC 21**
See also CA 117; DLB 19

Hume, David 1711-1776............ **LC 7**

Humphrey, William 1924-........ **CLC 45**
See also CA 77-80; DLB 6

Humphreys, Emyr (Owen) 1919-.... **CLC 47**
See also CANR 3, 24; CA 5-8R; DLB 15

Humphreys, Josephine 1945-.... **CLC 34, 57**
See also CA 121, 127

Hunt, E(verette) Howard (Jr.)
1918- .... **CLC 3**
See also CANR 2; CA 45-48

Hunt, (James Henry) Leigh
1784-1859 .... **NCLC 1**

Hunter, Evan 1926- .... **CLC 11, 31**
See also CANR 5; CA 5-8R; SATA 25;
DLB-Y 82

Hunter, Kristin (Eggleston) 1931-... **CLC 35**
See also CLR 3; CANR 13; CA 13-16R;
SATA 12; DLB 33

Hunter, Mollie (Maureen McIlwraith)
1922- .... **CLC 21**
See also McIlwraith, Maureen Mollie
Hunter

Hunter, Robert ?-1734............. **LC 7**

Hurston, Zora Neale
1891-1960 .... **CLC 7, 30, 61; SSC 4**
See also CA 85-88; DLB 51, 86

Huston, John (Marcellus)
1906-1987 .... **CLC 20**
See also CA 73-76; obituary CA 123;
DLB 26

Huxley, Aldous (Leonard)
1894-1963 .. **CLC 1, 3, 4, 5, 8, 11, 18, 35**
See also CA 85-88; DLB 36

Huysmans, Charles Marie Georges
1848-1907
See Huysmans, Joris-Karl
See also CA 104

Huysmans, Joris-Karl 1848-1907 ... **TCLC 7**
See also Huysmans, Charles Marie Georges

Hwang, David Henry 1957-........ **CLC 55**
See also CA 127

Hyde, Anthony 1946?-............ **CLC 42**

Hyde, Margaret O(ldroyd) 1917-... **CLC 21**
See also CLR 23; CANR 1; CA 1-4R;
SATA 1, 42

Ian, Janis 1951- .... **CLC 21**
See also CA 105

Ibarguengoitia, Jorge 1928-1983.... **CLC 37**
See also obituary CA 113, 124

Ibsen, Henrik (Johan)
1828-1906 .... **TCLC 2, 8, 16, 37**
See also CA 104

Ibuse, Masuji 1898- .... **CLC 22**

Ichikawa, Kon 1915-.............. **CLC 20**
See also CA 121

Idle, Eric 1943-
See Monty Python
See also CA 116

Ignatow, David 1914-...... **CLC 4, 7, 14, 40**
See also CAAS 3; CA 9-12R; DLB 5

Ihimaera, Witi (Tame) 1944-....... **CLC 46**
See also CA 77-80

Ilf, Ilya 1897-1937 .... **TCLC 21**

Immermann, Karl (Lebrecht)
1796-1840 .... **NCLC 4**

Ingalls, Rachel 19??-.............. **CLC 42**
See also CA 123

Ingamells, Rex 1913-1955 .... **TCLC 35**

Inge, William (Motter)
1913-1973 .... **CLC 1, 8, 19**
See also CA 9-12R; DLB 7;
CDALB 1941-1968

Innaurato, Albert 1948-........ **CLC 21, 60**
See also CA 115, 122

Innes, Michael 1906-
See Stewart, J(ohn) I(nnes) M(ackintosh)

Ionesco, Eugene
1912-........ **CLC 1, 4, 6, 9, 11, 15, 41**
See also CA 9-12R; SATA 7

Iqbal, Muhammad 1877-1938 ..... **TCLC 28**

Irving, John (Winslow)
1942- .... **CLC 13, 23, 38**
See also CA 25-28R; DLB 6; DLB-Y 82

Irving, Washington
1783-1859 .... **NCLC 2, 19; SSC 2**
See also YABC 2; DLB 3, 11, 30, 59, 73,
74; CDALB 1640-1865

Isaacs, Susan 1943- .... **CLC 32**
See also CANR 20; CA 89-92

Isherwood, Christopher (William Bradshaw)
1904-1986 .... **CLC 1, 9, 11, 14, 44**
See also CA 13-16R; obituary CA 117;
DLB 15; DLB-Y 86

Ishiguro, Kazuo 1954- ...... **CLC 27, 56, 59**
See also CA 120

Ishikawa Takuboku 1885-1912 ... **TCLC 15**
See also CA 113

Iskander, Fazil (Abdulovich)
1929- .... **CLC 47**
See also CA 102

Ivanov, Vyacheslav (Ivanovich)
1866-1949 .... **TCLC 33**
See also CA 122

Ivask, Ivar (Vidrik) 1927- .... **CLC 14**
See also CANR 24; CA 37-40R

Jackson, Jesse 1908-1983 .... **CLC 12**
See also CA 25-28R; obituary CA 109;
SATA 2, 29, 48

Jackson, Laura (Riding) 1901-
See Riding, Laura
See also CA 65-68; DLB 48

Jackson, Shirley 1919-1965..... **CLC 11, 60**
See also CANR 4; CA 1-4R;
obituary CA 25-28R; SATA 2; DLB 6;
CDALB 1941-1968

Jacob, (Cyprien) Max 1876-1944 ... **TCLC 6**
See also CA 104

Jacob, Piers A(nthony) D(illingham) 1934-
See Anthony (Jacob), Piers
See also CA 21-24R

Jacobs, Jim 1942- and Casey, Warren
1942- .... **CLC 12**

Jacobs, Jim 1942-
See Jacobs, Jim and Casey, Warren
See also CA 97-100

Jacobs, W(illiam) W(ymark)
1863-1943 .... **TCLC 22**
See also CA 121

Jacobsen, Josephine 1908-........ **CLC 48**
See also CANR 23; CA 33-36R

Jacobson, Dan 1929- .... **CLC 4, 14**
See also CANR 2, 25; CA 1-4R; DLB 14

Jagger, Mick 1944-.............. **CLC 17**

Jakes, John (William) 1932-....... **CLC 29**
See also CANR 10; CA 57-60; DLB-Y 83

James, C(yril) L(ionel) R(obert)
1901-1989 .... **CLC 33**
See also CA 117, 125

James, Daniel 1911-1988
See Santiago, Danny
See also obituary CA 125

James, Henry (Jr.)
1843-1916 .... **TCLC 2, 11, 24, 40**
See also CA 104, 132; DLB 12, 71, 74;
CDALB 1865-1917

James, M(ontague) R(hodes)
1862-1936 .... **TCLC 6**
See also CA 104

James, P(hyllis) D(orothy)
1920-.................... **CLC 18, 46**
See also CANR 17; CA 21-24R

James, William 1842-1910..... **TCLC 15, 32**
See also CA 109

Jami, Nur al-Din 'Abd al-Rahman
1414-1492 .... **LC 9**

Jandl, Ernst 1925- .... **CLC 34**

Janowitz, Tama 1957- .... **CLC 43**
See also CA 106

Jarrell, Randall
1914-1965 .... **CLC 1, 2, 6, 9, 13, 49**
See also CLR 6; CANR 6; CA 5-8R;
obituary CA 25-28R; CABS 2; SATA 7;
DLB 48, 52; CDALB 1941-1968

Jarry, Alfred 1873-1907........ **TCLC 2, 14**
See also CA 104

Jeake, Samuel, Jr. 1889-1973
See Aiken, Conrad

Jean Paul 1763-1825 .... **NCLC 7**

Jeffers, (John) Robinson
1887-1962 .... **CLC 2, 3, 11, 15, 54**
See also CA 85-88; DLB 45

Jefferson, Thomas 1743-1826 .... **NCLC 11**
See also DLB 31; CDALB 1640-1865

Jellicoe, (Patricia) Ann 1927- ...... **CLC 27**
See also CA 85-88; DLB 13

Jenkins, (John) Robin 1912- .... **CLC 52**
See also CANR 1; CA 4Rk; DLB 14

Jennings, Elizabeth (Joan)
1926- .... **CLC 5, 14**
See also CAAS 5; CANR 8; CA 61-64;
DLB 27

Jennings, Waylon 1937- .... **CLC 21**

Jensen, Laura (Linnea) 1948- ...... **CLC 37**
See also CA 103

Jerome, Jerome K. 1859-1927..... **TCLC 23**
See also CA 119; DLB 10, 34

Jerrold, Douglas William
1803-1857 .... **NCLC 2**

Jewett, (Theodora) Sarah Orne
1849-1909 .... **TCLC 1, 22; SSC 6**
See also CA 108, 127; SATA 15; DLB 12,
74

Jewsbury, Geraldine (Endsor)
1812-1880 .... **NCLC 22**
See also DLB 21

Jhabvala, Ruth Prawer
1927- .... **CLC 4, 8, 29**
See also CANR 2; CA 1-4R

Jiles, Paulette 1943- .... **CLC 13, 58**
See also CA 101

Jimenez (Mantecon), Juan Ramon
1881-1958 .... **TCLC 4**
See also CA 104

Joel, Billy 1949- .... **CLC 26**
See also Joel, William Martin

Joel, William Martin 1949-
See Joel, Billy
See also CA 108

Johnson, B(ryan) S(tanley William)
1933-1973 .... **CLC 6, 9**
See also CANR 9; CA 9-12R;
obituary CA 53-56; DLB 14, 40

Johnson, Charles (Richard)
1948- .... **CLC 7, 51**
See also CA 116; DLB 33

Johnson, Denis 1949- .... **CLC 52**
See also CA 117, 121

Johnson, Diane 1934- .... **CLC 5, 13, 48**
See also CANR 17; CA 41-44R; DLB-Y 80

Johnson, Eyvind (Olof Verner)
1900-1976 .... **CLC 14**
See also CA 73-76; obituary CA 69-72

Johnson, James Weldon
1871-1938 .... **TCLC 3, 19**
See also Johnson, James William
See also CA 104, 125; DLB 51

Johnson, James William 1871-1938
See Johnson, James Weldon
See also SATA 31

Johnson, Joyce 1935- .... **CLC 58**
See also CA 125

Johnson, Lionel (Pigot)
1867-1902 .... **TCLC 19**
See also CA 117; DLB 19

Johnson, Marguerita 1928-
See Angelou, Maya

Johnson, Pamela Hansford
1912-1981 .... **CLC 1, 7, 27**
See also CANR 2; CA 1-4R;
obituary CA 104; DLB 15

Johnson, Samuel 1709-1784........ **LC 15**
See also DLB 39, 95

Johnson, Uwe
1934-1984 .... **CLC 5, 10, 15, 40**
See also CANR 1; CA 1-4R;
obituary CA 112; DLB 75

Johnston, George (Benson) 1913- ... **CLC 51**
See also CANR 5, 20; CA 1-4R

Johnston, Jennifer 1930- .... **CLC 7**
See also CA 85-88; DLB 14

Jolley, Elizabeth 1923-............ **CLC 46**

Jones, D(ouglas) G(ordon) 1929-.... **CLC 10**
See also CANR 13; CA 113; DLB 53

Jones, David
1895-1974 .... **CLC 2, 4, 7, 13, 42**
See also CA 9-12R; obituary CA 53-56;
DLB 20

Jones, David Robert 1947-
See Bowie, David
See also CA 103

Jones, Diana Wynne 1934- .... **CLC 26**
See also CLR 23; CANR 4; CA 49-52;
SATA 9

Jones, Gayl 1949-................ **CLC 6, 9**
See also CA 77-80; DLB 33

Jones, James 1921-1977.... **CLC 1, 3, 10, 39**
See also CANR 6; CA 1-4R;
obituary CA 69-72; DLB 2

Jones, (Everett) LeRoi
1934- .... **CLC 1, 2, 3, 5, 10, 14, 33**
See also Baraka, Amiri; Baraka, Imamu
Amiri
See also CA 21-24R

Jones, Madison (Percy, Jr.) 1925- ... **CLC 4**
See also CANR 7; CA 13-16R

Jones, Mervyn 1922- .... **CLC 10, 52**
See also CAAS 5; CANR 1; CA 45-48

Jones, Mick 1956?-
See The Clash

Jones, Nettie 19??-............... **CLC 34**

Jones, Preston 1936-1979 .... **CLC 10**
See also CA 73-76; obituary CA 89-92;
DLB 7

Jones, Robert F(rancis) 1934- .... **CLC 7**
See also CANR 2; CA 49-52

Jones, Rod 1953- .... **CLC 50**

Jones, Terry 1942?-
See Monty Python
See also CA 112, 116; SATA 51

Jong, Erica 1942-.......... **CLC 4, 6, 8, 18**
See also CANR 26; CA 73-76; DLB 2, 5, 28

Jonson, Ben(jamin) 1572-1637....... **LC 6**
See also DLB 62

Jordan, June 1936-......... **CLC 5, 11, 23**
See also CLR 10; CANR 25; CA 33-36R;
SATA 4; DLB 38

Jordan, Pat(rick M.) 1941- .... **CLC 37**
See also CANR 25; CA 33-36R

Josipovici, Gabriel (David)
1940- .... **CLC 6, 43**
See also CA 37-40R; DLB 14

Joubert, Joseph 1754-1824 .... **NCLC 9**

Jouve, Pierre Jean 1887-1976...... **CLC 47**
See also obituary CA 65-68

Joyce, James (Augustine Aloysius)
1882-1941 ...... **TCLC 3, 8, 16, 26, 35;**
SSC 3
See also CA 104, 126; DLB 10, 19, 36

Jozsef, Attila 1905-1937......... **TCLC 22**
See also CA 116

Juana Ines de la Cruz 1651?-1695 .... **LC 5**

Julian of Norwich 1342?-1416? .... **LC 6**

Just, Ward S(wift) 1935- .... **CLC 4, 27**
See also CA 25-28R

Justice, Donald (Rodney) 1925- .. **CLC 6, 19**
See also CANR 26; CA 5-8R; DLB-Y 83

Kacew, Romain 1914-1980
See Gary, Romain
See also CA 108; obituary CA 102

Kacewgary, Romain 1914-1980
See Gary, Romain

Kadare, Ismail 1936- .... **CLC 52**

Kadohata, Cynthia 19??- .... **CLC 59**

Kafka, Franz
1883-1924 .... **TCLC 2, 6, 13, 29; SSC 5**
See also CA 105, 126; DLB 81

Kahn, Roger 1927- .... **CLC 30**
See also CA 25-28R; SATA 37

Kaiser, (Friedrich Karl) Georg
1878-1945 .... **TCLC 9**
See also CA 106

Kaletski, Alexander 1946- .... **CLC 39**
See also CA 118

Kallman, Chester (Simon)
1921-1975 .... **CLC 2**
See also CANR 3; CA 45-48;
obituary CA 53-56

Kaminsky, Melvin 1926-
See Brooks, Mel
See also CANR 16; CA 65-68

Kaminsky, Stuart 1934-........... **CLC 59**
See also CA 73-76

Kane, Paul 1941-
See Simon, Paul

Kanin, Garson 1912-.............. **CLC 22**
See also CANR 7; CA 5-8R; DLB 7

Kaniuk, Yoram 1930-............. **CLC 19**

Kant, Immanuel 1724-1804 ...... **NCLC 27**

Kantor, MacKinlay 1904-1977 ...... **CLC 7**
See also CA 61-64; obituary CA 73-76;
DLB 9

Kaplan, David Michael 1946- ...... **CLC 50**

Kaplan, James 19??-.............. **CLC 59**

Karamzin, Nikolai Mikhailovich
1766-1826 .... **NCLC 3**

Karapanou, Margarita 1946-....... **CLC 13**
See also CA 101

Karl, Frederick R(obert) 1927- ..... **CLC 34**
See also CANR 3; CA 5-8R

Kassef, Romain 1914-1980
See Gary, Romain

Katz, Steve 1935- .... **CLC 47**
See also CANR 12; CA 25-28R; DLB-Y 83

Kauffman, Janet 1945-........... **CLC 42**
See also CA 117; DLB-Y 86

Kaufman, Bob (Garnell)
        1925-1986 .... **CLC 49**
    See also CANR 22; CA 41-44R;
        obituary CA 118; DLB 16, 41

Kaufman, George S(imon)
        1889-1961 .... **CLC 38**
    See also CA 108; obituary CA 93-96; DLB 7

Kaufman, Sue 1926-1977 .... **CLC 3, 8**
    See also Barondess, Sue K(aufman)

Kavan, Anna 1904-1968 .... **CLC 5, 13**
    See also Edmonds, Helen (Woods)
    See also CANR 6; CA 5-8R

Kavanagh, Patrick (Joseph Gregory)
        1905-1967 .... **CLC 22**
    See also CA 123; obituary CA 25-28R;
        DLB 15, 20

Kawabata, Yasunari
        1899-1972 .... **CLC 2, 5, 9, 18**
    See also CA 93-96; obituary CA 33-36R

Kaye, M(ary) M(argaret) 1909?-.... **CLC 28**
    See also CANR 24; CA 89-92

Kaye, Mollie 1909?-
    See Kaye, M(ary) M(argaret)

Kaye-Smith, Sheila 1887-1956..... **TCLC 20**
    See also CA 118; DLB 36

Kazan, Elia 1909- .... **CLC 6, 16, 63**
    See also CA 21-24R

Kazantzakis, Nikos
        1885?-1957............. **TCLC 2, 5, 33**
    See also CA 105

Kazin, Alfred 1915- .... **CLC 34, 38**
    See also CAAS 7; CANR 1; CA 1-4R

Keane, Mary Nesta (Skrine) 1904-
    See Keane, Molly
    See also CA 108, 114

Keane, Molly 1904- .... **CLC 31**
    See also Keane, Mary Nesta (Skrine)

Keates, Jonathan 19??-............ **CLC 34**

Keaton, Buster 1895-1966 .... **CLC 20**

Keaton, Joseph Francis 1895-1966
    See Keaton, Buster

Keats, John 1795-1821...... **NCLC 8; PC 1**

Keene, Donald 1922- .... **CLC 34**
    See also CANR 5; CA 1-4R

Keillor, Garrison 1942- .... **CLC 40**
    See also Keillor, Gary (Edward)
    See also CA 111; DLB 87

Keillor, Gary (Edward)
    See Keillor, Garrison
    See also CA 111, 117

Kell, Joseph 1917-
    See Burgess (Wilson, John) Anthony

Keller, Gottfried 1819-1890 ...... **NCLC 2**

Kellerman, Jonathan (S.) 1949-..... **CLC 44**
    See also CA 106

Kelley, William Melvin 1937-...... **CLC 22**
    See also CA 77-80; DLB 33

Kellogg, Marjorie 1922-........... **CLC 2**
    See also CA 81-84

Kelly, M. T. 1947- .... **CLC 55**
    See also CANR 19; CA 97-100

Kelman, James 1946-............. **CLC 58**

Kemal, Yashar 1922- .... **CLC 14, 29**
    See also CA 89-92

Kemble, Fanny 1809-1893 .... **NCLC 18**
    See also DLB 32

Kemelman, Harry 1908-............ **CLC 2**
    See also CANR 6; CA 9-12R; DLB 28

Kempe, Margery 1373?-1440? .... **LC 6**

Kempis, Thomas á 1380-1471 ...... **LC 11**

Kendall, Henry 1839-1882 .... **NCLC 12**

Keneally, Thomas (Michael)
        1935- ...... **CLC 5, 8, 10, 14, 19, 27, 43**
    See also CANR 10; CA 85-88

Kennedy, John Pendleton
        1795-1870 .... **NCLC 2**
    See also DLB 3

Kennedy, Joseph Charles 1929-...... **CLC 8**
    See also Kennedy, X. J.
    See also CANR 4; CA 1-4R; SATA 14

Kennedy, William (Joseph)
        1928- .... **CLC 6, 28, 34, 53**
    See also CANR 14; CA 85-88; DLB-Y 85;
        AAYA 1

Kennedy, X. J. 1929- .... **CLC 8, 42**
    See also Kennedy, Joseph Charles
    See also DLB 5

Kerouac, Jack
        1922-1969 .... **CLC 1, 2, 3, 5, 14, 29, 61**
    See also Kerouac, Jean-Louis Lebris de
    See also DLB 2, 16; DLB-DS 3;
        CDALB 1941-1968

Kerouac, Jean-Louis Lebris de 1922-1969
    See Kerouac, Jack
    See also CA 5-8R; obituary CA 25-28R;
        CDALB 1941-1968

Kerr, Jean 1923-................. **CLC 22**
    See also CANR 7; CA 5-8R

Kerr, M. E. 1927-............. **CLC 12, 35**
    See also Meaker, Marijane
    See also SAAS 1

Kerr, Robert 1970?-........... **CLC 55, 59**

Kerrigan, (Thomas) Anthony
        1918- .... **CLC 4, 6**
    See also CANR 4; CA 49-52

Kesey, Ken (Elton)
        1935- .... **CLC 1, 3, 6, 11, 46**
    See also CANR 22; CA 1-4R; DLB 2, 16

Kesselring, Joseph (Otto)
        1902-1967 .... **CLC 45**

Kessler, Jascha (Frederick) 1929-.... **CLC 4**
    See also CANR 8; CA 17-20R

Kettelkamp, Larry 1933-.......... **CLC 12**
    See also CANR 16; CA 29-32R; SAAS 3;
        SATA 2

Kherdian, David 1931-........... **CLC 6, 9**
    See also CAAS 2; CA 21-24R; SATA 16

Khlebnikov, Velimir (Vladimirovich)
        1885-1922 .... **TCLC 20**
    See also CA 117

Khodasevich, Vladislav (Felitsianovich)
        1886-1939 .... **TCLC 15**
    See also CA 115

Kielland, Alexander (Lange)
        1849-1906 .... **TCLC 5**
    See also CA 104

Kiely, Benedict 1919-.......... **CLC 23, 43**
    See also CANR 2; CA 1-4R; DLB 15

Kienzle, William X(avier) 1928- .... **CLC 25**
    See also CAAS 1; CANR 9; CA 93-96

Killens, John Oliver 1916-......... **CLC 10**
    See also CAAS 2; CANR 26; CA 77-80,
        123; DLB 33

Killigrew, Anne 1660-1685........... **LC 4**

Kincaid, Jamaica 1949?- .... **CLC 43**
    See also CA 125

King, Francis (Henry) 1923- ..... **CLC 8, 53**
    See also CANR 1; CA 1-4R; DLB 15

King, Stephen (Edwin)
        1947- .... **CLC 12, 26, 37, 61**
    See also CANR 1; CA 61-64; SATA 9, 55;
        DLB-Y 80

Kingman, (Mary) Lee 1919-....... **CLC 17**
    See also Natti, (Mary) Lee
    See also CA 5-8R; SAAS 3; SATA 1

Kingsley, Sidney 1906-............ **CLC 44**
    See also CA 85-88; DLB 7

Kingsolver, Barbara 1955-......... **CLC 55**

Kingston, Maxine Hong
        1940- .... **CLC 12, 19, 58**
    See also CANR 13; CA 69-72; SATA 53;
        DLB-Y 80

Kinnell, Galway
        1927- .... **CLC 1, 2, 3, 5, 13, 29**
    See also CANR 10; CA 9-12R; DLB 5;
        DLB-Y 87

Kinsella, Thomas 1928- ...... **CLC 4, 19, 43**
    See also CANR 15; CA 17-20R; DLB 27

Kinsella, W(illiam) P(atrick)
        1935- .... **CLC 27, 43**
    See also CAAS 7; CANR 21; CA 97-100

Kipling, (Joseph) Rudyard
        1865-1936 .... **TCLC 8, 17; SSC 5**
    See also YABC 2; CA 105, 120; DLB 19, 34

Kirkup, James 1918- .... **CLC 1**
    See also CAAS 4; CANR 2; CA 1-4R;
        SATA 12; DLB 27

Kirkwood, James 1930-1989 .... **CLC 9**
    See also CANR 6; CA 1-4R

Kis, Danilo 1935-1989 .... **CLC 57**
    See also CA 118, 129; brief entry CA 109

Kivi, Aleksis 1834-1872 .... **NCLC 30**

Kizer, Carolyn (Ashley) 1925-... **CLC 15, 39**
    See also CAAS 5; CANR 24; CA 65-68;
        DLB 5

Klappert, Peter 1942-............. **CLC 57**
    See also CA 33-36R; DLB 5

Klausner, Amos 1939-
    See Oz, Amos

Klein, A(braham) M(oses)
        1909-1972 .... **CLC 19**
    See also CA 101; obituary CA 37-40R;
        DLB 68

Klein, Norma 1938-1989 .... **CLC 30**
    See also CLR 2; CANR 15; CA 41-44R;
        SAAS 1; SATA 7

Klein, T.E.D. 19??-.............. **CLC 34**
    See also CA 119

Kleist, Heinrich von 1777-1811.... **NCLC 2**

Lucas, George 1944- . . . . **CLC 16**
See also CA 77-80

Lucas, Victoria 1932-1963
See Plath, Sylvia

Ludlam, Charles 1943-1987 . . . . . **CLC 46, 50**
See also CA 85-88; obituary CA 122

Ludlum, Robert 1927- . . . . **CLC 22, 43**
See also CANR 25; CA 33-36R; DLB-Y 82

Ludwig, Ken 19??- . . . . **CLC 60**

Ludwig, Otto 1813-1865. . . . . **NCLC 4**

Lugones, Leopoldo 1874-1938 . . . . . **TCLC 15**
See also CA 116

Lu Hsun 1881-1936 . . . . **TCLC 3**

Lukacs, Georg 1885-1971. . . . . **CLC 24**
See also Lukacs, Gyorgy

Lukacs, Gyorgy 1885-1971
See Lukacs, Georg
See also CA 101; obituary CA 29-32R

Luke, Peter (Ambrose Cyprian)
1919- . . . . **CLC 38**
See also CA 81-84; DLB 13

Lurie (Bishop), Alison
1926- . . . . **CLC 4, 5, 18, 39**
See also CANR 2, 17; CA 1-4R; SATA 46;
DLB 2

Lustig, Arnost 1926- . . . . **CLC 56**
See also CA 69-72; SATA 56

Luther, Martin 1483-1546 . . . . **LC 9**

Luzi, Mario 1914- . . . . **CLC 13**
See also CANR 9; CA 61-64

Lynn, Kenneth S(chuyler) 1923- . . . . **CLC 50**
See also CANR 3; CA 1-4R

Lytle, Andrew (Nelson) 1902- . . . . . . **CLC 22**
See also CA 9-12R; DLB 6

Lyttelton, George 1709-1773 . . . . **LC 10**

Lytton, Edward Bulwer 1803-1873
See Bulwer-Lytton, (Lord) Edward (George
Earle Lytton)
See also SATA 23

Maas, Peter 1929- . . . . **CLC 29**
See also CA 93-96

Macaulay, (Dame Emile) Rose
1881-1958 . . . . **TCLC 7**
See also CA 104; DLB 36

MacBeth, George (Mann)
1932- . . . . **CLC 2, 5, 9**
See also CA 25-28R; SATA 4; DLB 40

MacCaig, Norman (Alexander)
1910- . . . . **CLC 36**
See also CANR 3; CA 9-12R; DLB 27

MacCarthy, Desmond 1877-1952 . . **TCLC 36**

MacDermot, Thomas H. 1870-1933
See Redcam, Tom

MacDiarmid, Hugh
1892-1978 . . . . **CLC 2, 4, 11, 19, 63**
See also Grieve, C(hristopher) M(urray)
See also DLB 20

Macdonald, Cynthia 1928- . . . . . . **CLC 13, 19**
See also CANR 4; CA 49-52

MacDonald, George 1824-1905 . . . . . **TCLC 9**
See also CA 106; SATA 33; DLB 18

MacDonald, John D(ann)
1916-1986 . . . . **CLC 3, 27, 44**
See also CANR 1, 19; CA 1-4R;
obituary CA 121; DLB 8; DLB-Y 86

Macdonald, (John) Ross
1915-1983 . . . . . . **CLC 1, 2, 3, 14, 34, 41**
See also Millar, Kenneth

MacEwen, Gwendolyn (Margaret)
1941-1987 . . . . **CLC 13, 55**
See also CANR 7, 22; CA 9-12R;
obituary CA 124; SATA 50; DLB 53

Machado (y Ruiz), Antonio
1875-1939 . . . . **TCLC 3**
See also CA 104

Machado de Assis, (Joaquim Maria)
1839-1908 . . . . **TCLC 10**
See also CA 107

Machen, Arthur (Llewellyn Jones)
1863-1947 . . . . **TCLC 4**
See also CA 104; DLB 36

Machiavelli, Niccolo 1469-1527 . . . . . . **LC 8**

MacInnes, Colin 1914-1976 . . . . . **CLC 4, 23**
See also CA 69-72; obituary CA 65-68;
DLB 14

MacInnes, Helen (Clark)
1907-1985 . . . . **CLC 27, 39**
See also CANR 1; CA 1-4R;
obituary CA 65-68, 117; SATA 22, 44

Macintosh, Elizabeth 1897-1952
See Tey, Josephine
See also CA 110

Mackenzie, (Edward Montague) Compton
1883-1972 . . . . **CLC 18**
See also CAP 2; CA 21-22;
obituary CA 37-40R; DLB 34

Mac Laverty, Bernard 1942- . . . . **CLC 31**
See also CA 116, 118

MacLean, Alistair (Stuart)
1922-1987 . . . . **CLC 3, 13, 50, 63**
See also CANR 28; CA 57-60;
obituary CA 121; SATA 23, 50

MacLeish, Archibald
1892-1982 . . . . **CLC 3, 8, 14**
See also CA 9-12R; obituary CA 106;
DLB 4, 7, 45; DLB-Y 82

MacLennan, (John) Hugh
1907- . . . . **CLC 2, 14**
See also CA 5-8R

MacLeod, Alistair 1936- . . . . **CLC 56**
See also CA 123; DLB 60

Macleod, Fiona 1855-1905
See Sharp, William

MacNeice, (Frederick) Louis
1907-1963 . . . . **CLC 1, 4, 10, 53**
See also CA 85-88; DLB 10, 20

Macpherson, (Jean) Jay 1931- . . . . . . **CLC 14**
See also CA 5-8R; DLB 53

MacShane, Frank 1927- . . . . **CLC 39**
See also CANR 3; CA 11-12R

Macumber, Mari 1896-1966
See Sandoz, Mari (Susette)

Madach, Imre 1823-1864 . . . . **NCLC 19**

Madden, (Jerry) David 1933- . . . . **CLC 5, 15**
See also CAAS 3; CANR 4; CA 1-4R;
DLB 6

Madhubuti, Haki R. 1942- . . . . **CLC 6**
See also Lee, Don L.
See also CANR 24; CA 73-76; DLB 5, 41

Maeterlinck, Maurice 1862-1949 . . . **TCLC 3**
See also CA 104

Mafouz, Naguib 1912-
See Mahfuz, Najib

Maginn, William 1794-1842 . . . . . . **NCLC 8**

Mahapatra, Jayanta 1928- . . . . **CLC 33**
See also CANR 15; CA 73-76

Mahfuz Najib 1912- . . . . **CLC 52, 55**
See also DLB-Y 88

Mahon, Derek 1941- . . . . **CLC 27**
See also CA 113; DLB 40

Mailer, Norman
1923- . . . . . . **CLC 1, 2, 3, 4, 5, 8, 11, 14,
28, 39**
See also CA 9-12R; CABS 1; DLB 2, 16,
28; DLB-Y 80, 83; DLB-DS 3

Maillet, Antonine 1929- . . . . **CLC 54**
See also CA 115, 120; DLB 60

Mais, Roger 1905-1955 . . . . **TCLC 8**
See also CA 105

Maitland, Sara (Louise) 1950- . . . . . . **CLC 49**
See also CANR 13; CA 69-72

Major, Clarence 1936- . . . . **CLC 3, 19, 48**
See also CAAS 6; CANR 13; CA 21-24R;
DLB 33

Major, Kevin 1949- . . . . **CLC 26**
See also CLR 11; CANR 21; CA 97-100;
SATA 32; DLB 60

Malamud, Bernard
1914-1986 . . . . . **CLC 1, 2, 3, 5, 8, 9, 11,
18, 27, 44**
See also CA 5-8R; obituary CA 118;
CABS 1; DLB 2, 28; DLB-Y 80, 86;
CDALB 1941-1968

Malherbe, Francois de 1555-1628 . . . . . **LC 5**

Mallarme, Stephane 1842-1898 . . . . **NCLC 4**

Mallet-Joris, Francoise 1930- . . . . . . **CLC 11**
See also CANR 17; CA 65-68

Maloff, Saul 1922- . . . . **CLC 5**
See also CA 33-36R

Malone, Louis 1907-1963
See MacNeice, (Frederick) Louis

Malone, Michael (Christopher)
1942- . . . . **CLC 43**
See also CANR 14; CA 77-80

Malory, (Sir) Thomas ?-1471 . . . . **LC 11**
See also SATA 33

Malouf, David 1934- . . . . **CLC 28**

Malraux, (Georges-) Andre
1901-1976 . . . . . **CLC 1, 4, 9, 13, 15, 57**
See also CAP 2; CA 21-24;
obituary CA 69-72; DLB 72

Malzberg, Barry N. 1939- . . . . **CLC 7**
See also CAAS 4; CANR 16; CA 61-64;
DLB 8

Mamet, David (Alan)
1947-1987 . . . . **CLC 9, 15, 34, 46**
See also CANR 15; CA 81-84, 124; DLB 7

Mamoulian, Rouben 1898- . . . . **CLC 16**
See also CA 25-28R

McBrien, William 1930- .... **CLC 44**
See also CA 107

McCaffrey, Anne 1926- .... **CLC 17**
See also CANR 15; CA 25-28R; SATA 8;
DLB 8

McCarthy, Cormac 1933-........ **CLC 4, 57**
See also CANR 10; CA 13-16R; DLB 6

McCarthy, Mary (Therese)
1912-1989-... **CLC 1, 3, 5, 14, 24, 39, 59**
See also CANR 16; CA 5-8R; DLB 2;
DLB-Y 81

McCartney, (James) Paul
1942- .... **CLC 12, 35**

McCauley, Stephen 19??-.......... **CLC 50**

McClure, Michael 1932- .... **CLC 6, 10**
See also CANR 17; CA 21-24R; DLB 16

McCorkle, Jill (Collins) 1958-...... **CLC 51**
See also CA 121; DLB-Y 87

McCourt, James 1941-............. **CLC 5**
See also CA 57-60

McCoy, Horace 1897-1955 .... **TCLC 28**
See also CA 108; DLB 9

McCrae, John 1872-1918........ **TCLC 12**
See also CA 109

McCullers, (Lula) Carson (Smith)
1917-1967 .... **CLC 1, 4, 10, 12, 48**
See also CANR 18; CA 5-8R;
obituary CA 25-28R; CABS 1; SATA 27;
DLB 2, 7; CDALB 1941-1968

McCullough, Colleen 1938?-....... **CLC 27**
See also CANR 17; CA 81-84

McElroy, Joseph (Prince)
1930- .... **CLC 5, 47**
See also CA 17-20R

McEwan, Ian (Russell) 1948- ...... **CLC 13**
See also CANR 14; CA 61-64; DLB 14

McFadden, David 1940-.......... **CLC 48**
See also CA 104; DLB 60

McGahern, John 1934-........ **CLC 5, 9, 48**
See also CA 17-20R; DLB 14

McGinley, Patrick 1937-.......... **CLC 41**
See also CA 120

McGinley, Phyllis 1905-1978 ...... **CLC 14**
See also CANR 19; CA 9-12R;
obituary CA 77-80; SATA 2, 44;
obituary SATA 24; DLB 11, 48

McGinniss, Joe 1942-............. **CLC 32**
See also CA 25-28R

McGivern, Maureen Daly 1921-
See Daly, Maureen
See also CA 9-12R

McGrath, Patrick 1950-.......... **CLC 55**

McGrath, Thomas 1916- .... **CLC 28, 59**
See also CANR 6; CA 9-12R, 130;
SATA 41

McGuane, Thomas (Francis III)
1939- .... **CLC 3, 7, 18**
See also CANR 5; CA 49-52; DLB 2;
DLB-Y 80

McGuckian, Medbh 1950-........ **CLC 48**
See also DLB 40

McHale, Tom 1941-1982........ **CLC 3, 5**
See also CA 77-80; obituary CA 106

McIlvanney, William 1936-...... **CLC 42**
See also CA 25-28R; DLB 14

McIlwraith, Maureen Mollie Hunter 1922-
See Hunter, Mollie
See also CA 29-32R; SATA 2

McInerney, Jay 1955- .... **CLC 34**
See also CA 116, 123

McIntyre, Vonda N(eel) 1948- ..... **CLC 18**
See also CANR 17; CA 81-84

McKay, Claude 1889-1948... **TCLC 7; PC 2**
See also CA 104, 124; DLB 4, 45, 51

McKuen, Rod 1933-............. **CLC 1, 3**
See also CA 41-44R

McLuhan, (Herbert) Marshall
1911-1980 .... **CLC 37**
See also CANR 12; CA 9-12R;
obituary CA 102

McManus, Declan Patrick 1955-
See Costello, Elvis

McMillan, Terry 1951- .... **CLC 50, 61**

McMurtry, Larry (Jeff)
1936- .... **CLC 2, 3, 7, 11, 27, 44**
See also CANR 19; CA 5-8R; DLB 2;
DLB-Y 80, 87

McNally, Terrence 1939-...... **CLC 4, 7, 41**
See also CANR 2; CA 45-48; DLB 7

McPhee, John 1931-.............. **CLC 36**
See also CANR 20; CA 65-68

McPherson, James Alan 1943-..... **CLC 19**
See also CANR 24; CA 25-28R; DLB 38

McPherson, William 1939- .... **CLC 34**
See also CA 57-60

McSweeney, Kerry 19??-.......... **CLC 34**

Mead, Margaret 1901-1978 .... **CLC 37**
See also CANR 4; CA 1-4R;
obituary CA 81-84; SATA 20

Meaker, M. J. 1927-
See Kerr, M. E.; Meaker, Marijane

Meaker, Marijane 1927-
See Kerr, M. E.
See also CA 107; SATA 20

Medoff, Mark (Howard) 1940-... **CLC 6, 23**
See also CANR 5; CA 53-56; DLB 7

Megged, Aharon 1920-............ **CLC 9**
See also CANR 1; CA 49-52

Mehta, Ved (Parkash) 1934-....... **CLC 37**
See also CANR 2, 23; CA 1-4R

Mellor, John 1953?-
See The Clash

Meltzer, Milton 1915- .... **CLC 26 13**
See also CA 13-16R; SAAS 1; SATA 1, 50;
DLB 61

Melville, Herman
1819-1891 ...... **NCLC 3, 12, 29; SSC 1**
See also SATA 59; DLB 3, 74;
CDALB 1640-1865

Membreno, Alejandro 1972- .... **CLC 59**

Mencken, H(enry) L(ouis)
1880-1956 .... **TCLC 13**
See also CA 105; DLB 11, 29, 63

Mercer, David 1928-1980.......... **CLC 5**
See also CA 9-12R; obituary CA 102;
DLB 13

Meredith, George 1828-1909...... **TCLC 17**
See also CA 117; DLB 18, 35, 57

Meredith, William (Morris)
1919- .... **CLC 4, 13, 22, 55**
See also CANR 6; CA 9-12R; DLB 5

Merezhkovsky, Dmitri
1865-1941 .... **TCLC 29**

Merimee, Prosper
1803-1870 .... **NCLC 6; SSC 7**

Merkin, Daphne 1954-............ **CLC 44**
See also CANR 123

Merrill, James (Ingram)
1926- .... **CLC 2, 3, 6, 8, 13, 18, 34**
See also CANR 10; CA 13-16R; DLB 5;
DLB-Y 85

Merton, Thomas (James)
1915-1968 .... **CLC 1, 3, 11, 34**
See also CANR 22; CA 5-8R;
obituary CA 25-28R; DLB 48; DLB-Y 81

Merwin, W(illiam) S(tanley)
1927- ...... **CLC 1, 2, 3, 5, 8, 13, 18, 45**
See also CANR 15; CA 13-16R; DLB 5

Metcalf, John 1938-.............. **CLC 37**
See also CA 113; DLB 60

Mew, Charlotte (Mary)
1870-1928 .... **TCLC 8**
See also CA 105; DLB 19

Mewshaw, Michael 1943-........... **CLC 9**
See also CANR 7; CA 53-56; DLB-Y 80

Meyer-Meyrink, Gustav 1868-1932
See Meyrink, Gustav
See also CA 117

Meyers, Jeffrey 1939- .... **CLC 39**
See also CA 73-76

Meynell, Alice (Christiana Gertrude
Thompson) 1847-1922 .... **TCLC 6**
See also CA 104; DLB 19

Meyrink, Gustav 1868-1932... **TCLC 21**
See also Meyer-Meyrink, Gustav

Michaels, Leonard 1933-....... **CLC 6, 25**
See also CANR 21; CA 61-64

Michaux, Henri 1899-1984 ...... **CLC 8, 19**
See also CA 85-88; obituary CA 114

Michelangelo 1475-1564............ **LC 12**

Michener, James A(lbert)
1907- .... **CLC 1, 5, 11, 29, 60**
See also CANR 21; CA 5-8R; DLB 6

Mickiewicz, Adam 1798-1855 ..... **NCLC 3**

Middleton, Christopher 1926-...... **CLC 13**
See also CA 13-16R; DLB 40

Middleton, Stanley 1919-........ **CLC 7, 38**
See also CANR 21; CA 25-28R; DLB 14

Migueis, Jose Rodrigues 1901-..... **CLC 10**

Mikszath, Kalman 1847-1910 ..... **TCLC 31**

Miles, Josephine (Louise)
1911-1985 .... **CLC 1, 2, 14, 34, 39**
See also CANR 2; CA 1-4R;
obituary CA 116; DLB 48

Mill, John Stuart 1806-1873 ..... **NCLC 11**

Millar, Kenneth 1915-1983 ...... **CLC 14**
See also Macdonald, Ross
See also CANR 16; CA 9-12R;
obituary CA 110; DLB 2; DLB-Y 83

Millay, Edna St. Vincent
1892-1950 .... **TCLC 4**
See also CA 104; DLB 45

Miller, Arthur
1915- ...... **CLC 1, 2, 6, 10, 15, 26, 47;
DC 1**
See also CANR 2, 30; CA 1-4R; CABS 3;
DLB 7; CDALB 1941-1968

Miller, Henry (Valentine)
1891-1980 .... **CLC 1, 2, 4, 9, 14, 43**
See also CA 9-12R; obituary CA 97-100;
DLB 4, 9; DLB-Y 80

Miller, Jason 1939?- .... **CLC 2**
See also CA 73-76; DLB 7

Miller, Sue 19??- .... **CLC 44**

Miller, Walter M(ichael), Jr.
1923- .... **CLC 4, 30**
See also CA 85-88; DLB 8

Millhauser, Steven 1943- ...... **CLC 21, 54**
See also CA 108, 110, 111; DLB 2

Millin, Sarah Gertrude 1889-1968 .. **CLC 49**
See also CA 102; obituary CA 93-96

Milne, A(lan) A(lexander)
1882-1956 .... **TCLC 6**
See also CLR 1; YABC 1; CA 104; DLB 10

Milner, Ron(ald) 1938- .... **CLC 56**
See also CANR 24; CA 73-76; DLB 38

Milosz Czeslaw
1911- .... **CLC 5, 11, 22, 31, 56**
See also CANR 23; CA 81-84

Milton, John 1608-1674 .... **LC 9**

Miner, Valerie (Jane) 1947- .... **CLC 40**
See also CA 97-100

Minot, Susan 1956- .... **CLC 44**

Minus, Ed 1938- .... **CLC 39**

Miro (Ferrer), Gabriel (Francisco Victor)
1879-1930 .... **TCLC 5**
See also CA 104

Mishima, Yukio
1925-1970 .... **CLC 2, 4, 6, 9, 27; DC 1;
SSC 4**
See also Hiraoka, Kimitake

Mistral, Gabriela 1889-1957 ...... **TCLC 2**
See also CA 104

Mitchell, James Leslie 1901-1935
See Gibbon, Lewis Grassic
See also CA 104; DLB 15

Mitchell, Joni 1943- .... **CLC 12**
See also CA 112

Mitchell (Marsh), Margaret (Munnerlyn)
1900-1949 .... **TCLC 11**
See also CA 109; DLB 9

Mitchell, S. Weir 1829-1914 ..... **TCLC 36**

Mitchell, W(illiam) O(rmond)
1914- .... **CLC 25**
See also CANR 15; CA 77-80

Mitford, Mary Russell 1787-1855 .. **NCLC 4**

Mitford, Nancy 1904-1973 .... **CLC 44**
See also CA 9-12R

Miyamoto Yuriko 1899-1951 ...... **TCLC 37**

Mo, Timothy 1950- .... **CLC 46**
See also CA 117

Modarressi, Taghi 1931- .... **CLC 44**
See also CA 121

Modiano, Patrick (Jean) 1945- ..... **CLC 18**
See also CANR 17; CA 85-88

Mofolo, Thomas (Mokopu)
1876-1948 .... **TCLC 22**
See also CA 121

Mohr, Nicholasa 1935- .... **CLC 12**
See also CLR 22; CANR 1; CA 49-52;
SATA 8

Mojtabai, A(nn) G(race)
1938- .... **CLC 5, 9, 15, 29**
See also CA 85-88

Moliere 1622-1673 .... **LC 10**

Molnar, Ferenc 1878-1952 .... **TCLC 20**
See also CA 109

Momaday, N(avarre) Scott
1934- .... **CLC 2, 19**
See also CANR 14; CA 25-28R; SATA 30,
48

Monroe, Harriet 1860-1936 ...... **TCLC 12**
See also CA 109; DLB 54

Montagu, Elizabeth 1720-1800 .... **NCLC 7**

Montagu, Lady Mary (Pierrepont) Wortley
1689-1762 .... **LC 9**

Montague, John (Patrick)
1929- .... **CLC 13, 46**
See also CANR 9; CA 9-12R; DLB 40

Montaigne, Michel (Eyquem) de
1533-1592 .... **LC 8**

Montale, Eugenio 1896-1981 ... **CLC 7, 9, 18**
See also CA 17-20R; obituary CA 104

Montgomery, Marion (H., Jr.)
1925- .... **CLC 7**
See also CANR 3; CA 1-4R; DLB 6

Montgomery, Robert Bruce 1921-1978
See Crispin, Edmund
See also CA 104

Montherlant, Henri (Milon) de
1896-1972 .... **CLC 8, 19**
See also CA 85-88; obituary CA 37-40R;
DLB 72

Montisquieu, Charles-Louis de Secondat
1689-1755 .... **LC 7**

Monty Python .... **CLC 21**

Moodie, Susanna (Strickland)
1803-1885 .... **NCLC 14**

Mooney, Ted 1951- .... **CLC 25**

Moorcock, Michael (John)
1939- .... **CLC 5, 27, 58**
See also CAAS 5; CANR 2, 17; CA 45-48;
DLB 14

Moore, Brian
1921- .... **CLC 1, 3, 5, 7, 8, 19, 32**
See also CANR 1; CA 1-4R

Moore, George (Augustus)
1852-1933 .... **TCLC 7**
See also CA 104; DLB 10, 18, 57

Moore, Lorrie 1957- .... **CLC 39, 45**
See also Moore, Marie Lorena

Moore, Marianne (Craig)
1887-1972 ... **CLC 1, 2, 4, 8, 10, 13, 19,
47**
See also CANR 3; CA 1-4R;
obituary CA 33-36R; SATA 20; DLB 45

Moore, Marie Lorena 1957-
See Moore, Lorrie
See also CA 116

Moore, Thomas 1779-1852 .... **NCLC 6**

Morand, Paul 1888-1976 .... **CLC 41**
See also obituary CA 69-72; DLB 65

Morante, Elsa 1918-1985 .... **CLC 8, 47**
See also CA 85-88; obituary CA 117

Moravia, Alberto
1907- .... **CLC 2, 7, 11, 18, 27, 46**
See also Pincherle, Alberto

More, Hannah 1745-1833 .... **NCLC 27**

More, Henry 1614-1687 .... **LC 9**

More, (Sir) Thomas 1478-1535 ...... **LC 10**

Moreas, Jean 1856-1910 .... **TCLC 18**

Morgan, Berry 1919- .... **CLC 6**
See also CA 49-52; DLB 6

Morgan, Edwin (George) 1920- ..... **CLC 31**
See also CANR 3; CA 7-8R; DLB 27

Morgan, (George) Frederick
1922- .... **CLC 23**
See also CANR 21; CA 17-20R

Morgan, Janet 1945- .... **CLC 39**
See also CA 65-68

Morgan, Lady 1776?-1859 .... **NCLC 29**

Morgan, Robin 1941- .... **CLC 2**
See also CA 69-72

Morgenstern, Christian (Otto Josef Wolfgang)
1871-1914 .... **TCLC 8**
See also CA 105

Moricz, Zsigmond 1879-1942 ..... **TCLC 33**

Morike, Eduard (Friedrich)
1804-1875 .... **NCLC 10**

Mori Ogai 1862-1922 .... **TCLC 14**
See also Mori Rintaro

Mori Rintaro 1862-1922
See Mori Ogai
See also CA 110

Moritz, Karl Philipp 1756-1793 ...... **LC 2**

Morris, Julian 1916-
See West, Morris L.

Morris, Steveland Judkins 1950-
See Wonder, Stevie
See also CA 111

Morris, William 1834-1896 .... **NCLC 4**
See also DLB 18, 35, 57

Morris, Wright (Marion)
1910- .... **CLC 1, 3, 7, 18, 37**
See also CA 9-12R; DLB 2; DLB-Y 81

Morrison, James Douglas 1943-1971
See Morrison, Jim
See also CA 73-76

Morrison, Jim 1943-1971 .... **CLC 17**
See also Morrison, James Douglas

Morrison, Toni 1931- ..... **CLC 4, 10, 22, 55**
See also CA 29-32R; DLB 6, 33; DLB-Y 81;
AAYA 1

Morrison, Van 1945- .... CLC 21
See also CA 116

Mortimer, John (Clifford)
1923- .... CLC 28, 43
See also CANR 21; CA 13-16R; DLB 13

Mortimer, Penelope (Ruth) 1918- .... CLC 5
See also CA 57-60

Mosher, Howard Frank 19??- ...... CLC 62

Mosley, Nicholas 1923- .... CLC 43
See also CA 69-72; DLB 14

Moss, Howard
1922-1987 .... CLC 7, 14, 45, 50
See also CANR 1; CA 1-4R; DLB 5

Motion, Andrew (Peter) 1952- ...... CLC 47
See also DLB 40

Motley, Willard (Francis)
1912-1965 .... CLC 18
See also CA 117; obituary CA 106

Mott, Michael (Charles Alston)
1930- .... CLC 15, 34
See also CAAS 7; CANR 7; CA 5-8R

Mowat, Farley (McGill) 1921- ..... CLC 26
See also CLR 20; CANR 4; CA 1-4R;
SATA 3; DLB 68

Mphahlele, Es'kia 1919-
See Mphahlele, Ezekiel

Mphahlele, Ezekiel 1919-.......... CLC 25
See also CA 81-84

Mqhayi, S(amuel) E(dward) K(rune Loliwe)
1875-1945 .... TCLC 25

Mrozek, Slawomir 1930- .... CLC 3, 13
See also CA 13-16R

Mtwa, Percy 19??- .... CLC 47

Mueller, Lisel 1924-........... CLC 13, 51
See also CA 93-96

Muir, Edwin 1887-1959 .... TCLC 2
See also CA 104; DLB 20

Muir, John 1838-1914 .... TCLC 28

Mujica Lainez, Manuel
1910-1984 .... CLC 31
See also CA 81-84; obituary CA 112

Mukherjee, Bharati 1940- .... CLC 53
See also CA 107; DLB 60

Muldoon, Paul 1951- .... CLC 32
See also CA 113; DLB 40

Mulisch, Harry (Kurt Victor)
1927- .... CLC 42
See also CANR 6; CA 9-12R

Mull, Martin 1943-............... CLC 17
See also CA 105

Munford, Robert 1737?-1783........ LC 5
See also DLB 31

Munro, Alice (Laidlaw)
1931- .... CLC 6, 10, 19, 50; SSC 3
See also CA 33-36R; SATA 29; DLB 53

Munro, H(ector) H(ugh) 1870-1916
See Saki
See also CA 104; DLB 34

Murasaki, Lady c. 11th century-... CMLC 1

Murdoch, (Jean) Iris
1919- ...... CLC 1, 2, 3, 4, 6, 8, 11, 15,
22, 31, 51
See also CANR 8; CA 13-16R; DLB 14

Murphy, Richard 1927- .... CLC 41
See also CA 29-32R; DLB 40

Murphy, Sylvia 19??-............. CLC 34

Murphy, Thomas (Bernard) 1935-... CLC 51
See also CA 101

Murray, Les(lie) A(llan) 1938- ..... CLC 40
See also CANR 11; CA 21-24R

Murry, John Middleton
1889-1957 .... TCLC 16
See also CA 118

Musgrave, Susan 1951- .... CLC 13, 54
See also CA 69-72

Musil, Robert (Edler von)
1880-1942 .... TCLC 12
See also CA 109

Musset, (Louis Charles) Alfred de
1810-1857 .... NCLC 7

Myers, Walter Dean 1937- .... CLC 35
See also CLR 4, 16; CANR 20; CA 33-36R;
SAAS 2; SATA 27, 41; DLB 33

Nabokov, Vladimir (Vladimirovich)
1899-1977 .... CLC 1, 2, 3, 6, 8, 11, 15,
23, 44, 46
See also CANR 20; CA 5-8R;
obituary CA 69-72; DLB 2; DLB-Y 80;
DLB-DS 3; CDALB 1941-1968

Nagy, Laszlo 1925-1978........... CLC 7
See also obituary CA 112

Naipaul, Shiva(dhar Srinivasa)
1945-1985 .... CLC 32, 39
See also CA 110, 112; obituary CA 116;
DLB-Y 85

Naipaul, V(idiadhar) S(urajprasad)
1932-........ CLC 4, 7, 9, 13, 18, 37
See also CANR 1; CA 1-4R; DLB-Y 85

Nakos, Ioulia 1899?-
See Nakos, Lilika

Nakos, Lilika 1899?- .... CLC 29

Nakou, Lilika 1899?-
See Nakos, Lilika

Narayan, R(asipuram) K(rishnaswami)
1906- .... CLC 7, 28, 47
See also CA 81-84

Nash, (Frediric) Ogden 1902-1971 .. CLC 23
See also CAP 1; CA 13-14;
obituary CA 29-32R; SATA 2, 46;
DLB 11

Nathan, George Jean 1882-1958 ... TCLC 18
See also CA 114

Natsume, Kinnosuke 1867-1916
See Natsume, Soseki
See also CA 104

Natsume, Soseki 1867-1916..... TCLC 2, 10
See also Natsume, Kinnosuke

Natti, (Mary) Lee 1919-
See Kingman, (Mary) Lee
See also CANR 2; CA 7-8R

Naylor, Gloria 1950- .... CLC 28, 52
See also CANR 27; CA 107

Neff, Debra 1972-............... CLC 59

Neihardt, John G(neisenau)
1881-1973 .... CLC 32
See also CAP 1; CA 13-14; DLB 9, 54

Nekrasov, Nikolai Alekseevich
1821-1878 .... NCLC 11

Nelligan, Emile 1879-1941....... TCLC 14
See also CA 114

Nelson, Willie 1933-............. CLC 17
See also CA 107

Nemerov, Howard 1920- .... CLC 2, 6, 9, 36
See also CANR 1; CA 1-4R; CABS 2;
DLB 5, 6; DLB-Y 83

Neruda, Pablo
1904-1973 ..... CLC 1, 2, 5, 7, 9, 28, 62
See also CAP 2; CA 19-20;
obituary CA 45-48

Nerval, Gerard de 1808-1855...... NCLC 1

Nervo, (Jose) Amado (Ruiz de)
1870-1919 .... TCLC 11
See also CA 109

Neufeld, John (Arthur) 1938- ...... CLC 17
See also CANR 11; CA 25-28R; SAAS 3;
SATA 6

Neville, Emily Cheney 1919-....... CLC 12
See also CANR 3; CA 5-8R; SAAS 2;
SATA 1

Newbound, Bernard Slade 1930-
See Slade, Bernard
See also CA 81-84

Newby, P(ercy) H(oward)
1918- .... CLC 2, 13
See also CA 5-8R; DLB 15

Newlove, Donald 1928- .... CLC 6
See also CANR 25; CA 29-32R

Newlove, John (Herbert) 1938-..... CLC 14
See also CANR 9, 25; CA 21-24R

Newman, Charles 1938-.......... CLC 2, 8
See also CA 21-24R

Newman, Edwin (Harold) 1919- .... CLC 14
See also CANR 5; CA 69-72

Newton, Suzanne 1936-........... CLC 35
See also CANR 14; CA 41-44R; SATA 5

Ngema, Mbongeni 1955- .... CLC 57

Ngugi, James (Thiong'o)
1938-................ CLC 3, 7, 13, 36
See also Ngugi wa Thiong'o; Wa Thiong'o,
Ngugi
See also CA 81-84

Ngugi wa Thiong'o 1938-... CLC 3, 7, 13, 36
See also Ngugi, James (Thiong'o); Wa
Thiong'o, Ngugi

Nichol, B(arrie) P(hillip) 1944-..... CLC 18
See also CA 53-56; DLB 53

Nichols, John (Treadwell) 1940-.... CLC 38
See also CAAS 2; CANR 6; CA 9-12R;
DLB-Y 82

Nichols, Peter (Richard) 1927- ... CLC 5, 36
See also CA 104; DLB 13

Nicolas, F.R.E. 1927-
See Freeling, Nicolas

Niedecker, Lorine 1903-1970.... CLC 10, 42
See also CAP 2; CA 25-28; DLB 48

Nietzsche, Friedrich (Wilhelm)
1844-1900 .... TCLC 10, 18
See also CA 107

Nievo, Ippolito 1831-1861 .... NCLC 22

Nightingale, Anne Redmon 1943-
See Redmon (Nightingale), Anne
See also CA 103

Nin, Anais
1903-1977 ...... **CLC 1, 4, 8, 11, 14, 60**
See also CANR 22; CA 13-16R;
obituary CA 69-72; DLB 2, 4

Nissenson, Hugh 1933-.......... **CLC 4, 9**
See also CA 17-20R; DLB 28

Niven, Larry 1938-.............. **CLC 8**
See also Niven, Laurence Van Cott
See also DLB 8

Niven, Laurence Van Cott 1938-
See Niven, Larry
See also CANR 14; CA 21-24R

Nixon, Agnes Eckhardt 1927-...... **CLC 21**
See also CA 110

Nizan, Paul 1905-1940.......... **TCLC 40**
See also DLB 72

Nkosi, Lewis 1936-.............. **CLC 45**
See also CA 65-68

Nodier, (Jean) Charles (Emmanuel)
1780-1844 .... **NCLC 19**

Nolan, Christopher 1965-........ **CLC 58**
See also CA 111

Nordhoff, Charles 1887-1947..... **TCLC 23**
See also CA 108; SATA 23; DLB 9

Norman, Marsha 1947- .... **CLC 28**
See also CA 105; DLB-Y 84

Norris, (Benjamin) Frank(lin)
1870-1902 .... **TCLC 24**
See also CA 110; DLB 12, 71;
CDALB 1865-1917

Norris, Leslie 1921-.............. **CLC 14**
See also CANR 14; CAP 1; CA 11-12;
DLB 27

North, Andrew 1912-
See Norton, Andre

North, Christopher 1785-1854
See Wilson, John

Norton, Alice Mary 1912-
See Norton, Andre
See also CANR 2; CA 1-4R; SATA 1, 43

Norton, Andre 1912- .... **CLC 12**
See also Norton, Mary Alice
See also DLB 8, 52

Norway, Nevil Shute 1899-1960
See Shute (Norway), Nevil
See also CA 102; obituary CA 93-96

Norwid, Cyprian Kamil
1821-1883 .... **NCLC 17**

Nossack, Hans Erich 1901-1978..... **CLC 6**
See also CA 93-96; obituary CA 85-88;
DLB 69

Nova, Craig 1945-.............. **CLC 7, 31**
See also CANR 2; CA 45-48

Novak, Joseph 1933-
See Kosinski, Jerzy (Nikodem)

Novalis 1772-1801 .... **NCLC 13**

Nowlan, Alden (Albert) 1933-...... **CLC 15**
See also CANR 5; CA 9-12R; DLB 53

Noyes, Alfred 1880-1958 .... **TCLC 7**
See also CA 104; DLB 20

Nunn, Kem 19??-................ **CLC 34**

Nye, Robert 1939-........... **CLC 13, 42**
See also CA 33-36R; SATA 6; DLB 14

Nyro, Laura 1947-.............. **CLC 17**

Oates, Joyce Carol
1938-..... **CLC 1, 2, 3, 6, 9, 11, 15, 19,**
33, 52; SSC 6
See also CANR 25; CA 5-8R; DLB 2, 5;
DLB-Y 81; CDALB 1968-1987

O'Brien, Darcy 1939-............ **CLC 11**
See also CANR 8; CA 21-24R

O'Brien, Edna 1932-.... **CLC 3, 5, 8, 13, 36**
See also CANR 6; CA 1-4R; DLB 14

O'Brien, Fitz-James 1828?-1862.. **NCLC 21**
See also DLB 74

O'Brien, Flann
1911-1966 .... **CLC 1, 4, 5, 7, 10, 47**
See also O Nuallain, Brian

O'Brien, Richard 19??-........... **CLC 17**
See also CA 124

O'Brien, (William) Tim(othy)
1946-................ **CLC 7, 19, 40**
See also CA 85-88; DLB-Y 80

Obstfelder, Sigbjorn 1866-1900.... **TCLC 23**
See also CA 123

O'Casey, Sean
1880-1964 .... **CLC 1, 5, 9, 11, 15**
See also CA 89-92; DLB 10

Ochs, Phil 1940-1976............ **CLC 17**
See also obituary CA 65-68

O'Connor, Edwin (Greene)
1918-1968 .... **CLC 14**
See also CA 93-96; obituary CA 25-28R

O'Connor, (Mary) Flannery
1925-1964 ... **CLC 1, 2, 3, 6, 10, 13, 15,**
21; SSC 1
See also CANR 3; CA 1-4R; DLB 2;
DLB-Y 80; CDALB 1941-1968

O'Connor, Frank
1903-1966 .... **CLC 14, 23; SSC 5**
See also O'Donovan, Michael (John)
See also CA 93-96

O'Dell, Scott 1903-.............. **CLC 30**
See also CLR 1, 16; CANR 12; CA 61-64;
SATA 12; DLB 52

Odets, Clifford 1906-1963 .... **CLC 2, 28**
See also CA 85-88; DLB 7, 26

O'Donovan, Michael (John) 1903-1966
See O'Connor, Frank
See also CA 93-96

Oe, Kenzaburo 1935-.......... **CLC 10, 36**
See also CA 97-100

O'Faolain, Julia 1932-....... **CLC 6, 19, 47**
See also CAAS 2; CANR 12; CA 81-84;
DLB 14

O'Faolain, Sean 1900-..... **CLC 1, 7, 14, 32**
See also CANR 12; CA 61-64; DLB 15

O'Flaherty, Liam
1896-1984 .... **CLC 5, 34; SSC 6**
See also CA 101; obituary CA 113; DLB 36;
DLB-Y 84

O'Grady, Standish (James)
1846-1928 .... **TCLC 5**
See also CA 104

O'Grady, Timothy 1951-.......... **CLC 59**

O'Hara, Frank 1926-1966 ..... **CLC 2, 5, 13**
See also CA 9-12R; obituary CA 25-28R;
DLB 5, 16

O'Hara, John (Henry)
1905-1970 ...... **CLC 1, 2, 3, 6, 11, 42**
See also CA 5-8R; obituary CA 25-28R;
DLB 9; DLB-DS 2

O'Hara Family
See Banim, John and Banim, Michael

O'Hehir, Diana 1922-............ **CLC 41**
See also CA 93-96

Okigbo, Christopher (Ifenayichukwu)
1932-1967 .... **CLC 25**
See also CA 77-80

Olds, Sharon 1942-............ **CLC 32, 39**
See also CANR 18; CA 101

Olesha, Yuri (Karlovich)
1899-1960 .... **CLC 8**
See also CA 85-88

Oliphant, Margaret (Oliphant Wilson)
1828-1897 .... **NCLC 11**
See also DLB 18

Oliver, Mary 1935-............ **CLC 19, 34**
See also CANR 9; CA 21-24R; DLB 5

Olivier, (Baron) Laurence (Kerr)
1907-...................... **CLC 20**
See also CA 111

Olsen, Tillie 1913- .... **CLC 4, 13**
See also CANR 1; CA 1-4R; DLB 28;
DLB-Y 80

Olson, Charles (John)
1910-1970 ..... **CLC 1, 2, 5, 6, 9, 11, 29**
See also CAP 1; CA 15-16;
obituary CA 25-28R; CABS 2; DLB 5, 16

Olson, Theodore 1937-
See Olson, Toby

Olson, Toby 1937- .... **CLC 28**
See also CANR 9; CA 65-68

Ondaatje, (Philip) Michael
1943-................ **CLC 14, 29, 51**
See also CA 77-80; DLB 60

Oneal, Elizabeth 1934-
See Oneal, Zibby
See also CA 106; SATA 30

Oneal, Zibby 1934-.............. **CLC 30**
See also Oneal, Elizabeth

O'Neill, Eugene (Gladstone)
1888-1953 .... **TCLC 1, 6, 27**
See also CA 110; DLB 7

Onetti, Juan Carlos 1909-....... **CLC 7, 10**
See also CA 85-88

O'Nolan, Brian 1911-1966
See O'Brien, Flann

O Nuallain, Brian 1911-1966
See O'Brien, Flann
See also CAP 2; CA 21-22;
obituary CA 25-28R

Oppen, George 1908-1984 .... **CLC 7, 13, 34**
See also CANR 8; CA 13-16R;
obituary CA 113; DLB 5

Orlovitz, Gil 1918-1973.......... **CLC 22**
See also CA 77-80; obituary CA 45-48;
DLB 2, 5

Ortega y Gasset, Jose 1883-1955 ... **TCLC 9**
See also CA 106

Ortiz, Simon J. 1941-............ CLC 45

Orton, Joe 1933?-1967...... CLC 4, 13, 43
  See also Orton, John Kingsley
  See also DLB 13

Orton, John Kingsley 1933?-1967
  See Orton, Joe
  See also CA 85-88

Orwell, George
  1903-1950......... TCLC 2, 6, 15, 31
  See also Blair, Eric Arthur
  See also DLB 15

Osborne, John (James)
  1929-............ CLC 1, 2, 5, 11, 45
  See also CANR 21; CA 13-16R; DLB 13

Osborne, Lawrence 1958-......... CLC 50

Osceola 1885-1962
  See Dinesen, Isak; Blixen, Karen
  (Christentze Dinesen)

Oshima, Nagisa 1932-............ CLC 20
  See also CA 116

Oskison, John M. 1874-1947...... TCLC 35

Ossoli, Sarah Margaret (Fuller marchesa d')
  1810-1850
  See Fuller, (Sarah) Margaret
  See also SATA 25

Ostrovsky, Alexander
  1823-1886................. NCLC 30

Otero, Blas de 1916-............. CLC 11
  See also CA 89-92

Ovid 43 B.C.-c. 18 A.D.............. PC 2

Owen, Wilfred (Edward Salter)
  1893-1918............... TCLC 5, 27
  See also CA 104; DLB 20

Owens, Rochelle 1936-............ CLC 8
  See also CAAS 2; CA 17-20R

Owl, Sebastian 1939-
  See Thompson, Hunter S(tockton)

Oz, Amos 1939-... CLC 5, 8, 11, 27, 33, 54
  See also CA 53-56

Ozick, Cynthia 1928-...... CLC 3, 7, 28, 62
  See also CANR 28; CA 17-20R; DLB 28;
  DLB-Y 82

Ozu, Yasujiro 1903-1963.......... CLC 16
  See also CA 112

Pa Chin 1904-................... CLC 18
  See also Li Fei-kan

Pack, Robert 1929-............... CLC 13
  See also CANR 3; CA 1-4R; DLB 5

Padgett, Lewis 1915-1958
  See Kuttner, Henry

Padilla, Heberto 1932-........... CLC 38
  See also CA 123

Page, Jimmy 1944-............... CLC 12

Page, Louise 1955-.............. CLC 40

Page, P(atricia) K(athleen)
  1916-..................... CLC 7, 18
  See also CANR 4, 22; CA 53-56; DLB 68

Paget, Violet 1856-1935
  See Lee, Vernon
  See also CA 104

Palamas, Kostes 1859-1943....... TCLC 5
  See also CA 105

Palazzeschi, Aldo 1885-1974....... CLC 11
  See also CA 89-92; obituary CA 53-56

Paley, Grace 1922-........... CLC 4, 6, 37
  See also CANR 13; CA 25-28R; DLB 28

Palin, Michael 1943-............. CLC 21
  See also Monty Python
  See also CA 107

Palma, Ricardo 1833-1919........ TCLC 29
  See also CANR 123

Pancake, Breece Dexter 1952-1979
  See Pancake, Breece D'J

Pancake, Breece D'J 1952-1979.... CLC 29
  See also obituary CA 109

Papadiamantis, Alexandros
  1851-1911.................. TCLC 29

Papini, Giovanni 1881-1956...... TCLC 22
  See also CA 121

Paracelsus 1493-1541............. LC 14

Parini, Jay (Lee) 1948-.......... CLC 54
  See also CA 97-100

Parker, Dorothy (Rothschild)
  1893-1967............ CLC 15; SSC 2
  See also CAP 2; CA 19-20;
  obituary CA 25-28R; DLB 11, 45

Parker, Robert B(rown) 1932-...... CLC 27
  See also CANR 1, 26; CA 49-52

Parkin, Frank 1940-.............. CLC 43

Parkman, Francis 1823-1893..... NCLC 12
  See also DLB 1, 30

Parks, Gordon (Alexander Buchanan)
  1912-.................... CLC 1, 16
  See also CANR 26; CA 41-44R; SATA 8;
  DLB 33

Parnell, Thomas 1679-1718.......... LC 3

Parra, Nicanor 1914-.............. CLC 2
  See also CA 85-88

Pasolini, Pier Paolo
  1922-1975................ CLC 20, 37
  See also CA 93-96; obituary CA 61-64

Pastan, Linda (Olenik) 1932-...... CLC 27
  See also CANR 18; CA 61-64; DLB 5

Pasternak, Boris
  1890-1960.......... CLC 7, 10, 18, 63
  See also CA 127; obituary CA 116

Patchen, Kenneth 1911-1972... CLC 1, 2, 18
  See also CANR 3; CA 1-4R;
  obituary CA 33-36R; DLB 16, 48

Pater, Walter (Horatio)
  1839-1894.................. NCLC 7
  See also DLB 57

Paterson, Andrew Barton
  1864-1941.................. TCLC 32

Paterson, Katherine (Womeldorf)
  1932-................... CLC 12, 30
  See also CLR 7; CA 21-24R; SATA 13, 53;
  DLB 52

Patmore, Coventry Kersey Dighton
  1823-1896.................. NCLC 9
  See also DLB 35

Paton, Alan (Stewart)
  1903-1988.......... CLC 4, 10, 25, 55
  See also CANR 22; CAP 1; CA 15-16;
  obituary CA 125; SATA 11

Paulding, James Kirke 1778-1860.. NCLC 2
  See also DLB 3, 59, 74

Paulin, Tom 1949-............... CLC 37
  See also CA 123; DLB 40

Paustovsky, Konstantin (Georgievich)
  1892-1968................... CLC 40
  See also CA 93-96; obituary CA 25-28R

Paustowsky, Konstantin (Georgievich)
  1892-1968
  See Paustovsky, Konstantin (Georgievich)

Pavese, Cesare 1908-1950......... TCLC 3
  See also CA 104

Pavic, Milorad 1929-............. CLC 60

Payne, Alan 1932-
  See Jakes, John (William)

Paz, Octavio
  1914-..... CLC 3, 4, 6, 10, 19, 51; PC 1
  See also CA 73-76

Peacock, Molly 1947-............. CLC 60
  See also CA 103

Peacock, Thomas Love
  1785-1886................. NCLC 22

Peake, Mervyn 1911-1968....... CLC 7, 54
  See also CANR 3; CA 5-8R;
  obituary CA 25-28R; SATA 23; DLB 15

Pearce, (Ann) Philippa 1920-...... CLC 21
  See also Christie, (Ann) Philippa
  See also CLR 9; CA 5-8R; SATA 1

Pearl, Eric 1934-
  See Elman, Richard

Pearson, T(homas) R(eid) 1956-.... CLC 39
  See also CA 120

Peck, John 1941-................. CLC 3
  See also CANR 3; CA 49-52

Peck, Richard 1934-.............. CLC 21
  See also CLR 15; CANR 19; CA 85-88;
  SAAS 2; SATA 18

Peck, Robert Newton 1928-........ CLC 17
  See also CA 81-84; SAAS 1; SATA 21

Peckinpah, (David) Sam(uel)
  1925-1984................... CLC 20
  See also CA 109; obituary CA 114

Pedersen, Knut 1859-1952
  See Hamsun, Knut
  See also CA 104, 109

Peguy, Charles (Pierre)
  1873-1914................. TCLC 10
  See also CA 107

Pepys, Samuel 1633-1703.......... LC 11

Percy, Walker
  1916-........ CLC 2, 3, 6, 8, 14, 18, 47
  See also CANR 1; CA 1-4R; DLB 2;
  DLB-Y 80

Perec, Georges 1936-1982......... CLC 56

Pereda, Jose Maria de
  1833-1906................. TCLC 16

Perelman, S(idney) J(oseph)
  1904-1979... CLC 3, 5, 9, 15, 23, 44, 49
  See also CANR 18; CA 73-76;
  obituary CA 89-92; DLB 11, 44

Peret, Benjamin 1899-1959....... TCLC 20
  See also CA 117

Peretz, Isaac Leib 1852?-1915..... TCLC 16
  See also CA 109

Rodgers, W(illiam) R(obert)
1909-1969 . . . . **CLC 7**
See also CA 85-88; DLB 20

Rodriguez, Claudio 1934- . . . . **CLC 10**

Roethke, Theodore (Huebner)
1908-1963 . . . . . . **CLC 1, 3, 8, 11, 19, 46**
See also CA 81-84; CABS 2; SAAS 1;
DLB 5; CDALB 1941-1968

Rogers, Sam 1943-
See Shepard, Sam

Rogers, Thomas (Hunton) 1931- . . . . **CLC 57**
See also CA 89-92

Rogers, Will(iam Penn Adair)
1879-1935 . . . . **TCLC 8**
See also CA 105; DLB 11

Rogin, Gilbert 1929- . . . . **CLC 18**
See also CANR 15; CA 65-68

Rohan, Koda 1867-1947 . . . . **TCLC 22**
See also CA 121

Rohmer, Eric 1920- . . . . **CLC 16**
See also Scherer, Jean-Marie Maurice

Rohmer, Sax 1883-1959 . . . . **TCLC 28**
See also Ward, Arthur Henry Sarsfield
See also CA 108; DLB 70

Roiphe, Anne (Richardson)
1935- . . . . **CLC 3, 9**
See also CA 89-92; DLB-Y 80

Rolfe, Frederick (William Serafino Austin
Lewis Mary) 1860-1913 . . . . . **TCLC 12**
See also CA 107; DLB 34

Rolland, Romain 1866-1944 . . . . . . **TCLC 23**
See also CA 118

Rolvaag, O(le) E(dvart)
1876-1931 . . . . **TCLC 17**
See also CA 117; DLB 9

Romains, Jules 1885-1972 . . . . **CLC 7**
See also CA 85-88

Romero, Jose Ruben 1890-1952 . . . **TCLC 14**
See also CA 114

Ronsard, Pierre de 1524-1585 . . . . **LC 6**

Rooke, Leon 1934- . . . . **CLC 25, 34**
See also CANR 23; CA 25-28R

Roper, William 1498-1578 . . . . **LC 10**

Rosa, Joao Guimaraes 1908-1967 . . . **CLC 23**
See also obituary CA 89-92

Rosen, Richard (Dean) 1949- . . . . **CLC 39**
See also CA 77-80

Rosenberg, Isaac 1890-1918 . . . . . . **TCLC 12**
See also CA 107; DLB 20

Rosenblatt, Joe 1933- . . . . **CLC 15**
See also Rosenblatt, Joseph

Rosenblatt, Joseph 1933-
See Rosenblatt, Joe
See also CA 89-92

Rosenfeld, Samuel 1896-1963
See Tzara, Tristan
See also obituary CA 89-92

Rosenthal, M(acha) L(ouis) 1917- . . . **CLC 28**
See also CAAS 6; CANR 4; CA 1-4R;
DLB 5

Ross, (James) Sinclair 1908- . . . . **CLC 13**
See also CA 73-76

Rossetti, Christina Georgina
1830-1894 . . . . **NCLC 2**
See also SATA 20; DLB 35

Rossetti, Dante Gabriel
1828-1882 . . . . **NCLC 4**
See also DLB 35

Rossetti, Gabriel Charles Dante 1828-1882
See Rossetti, Dante Gabriel

Rossner, Judith (Perelman)
1935- . . . . **CLC 6, 9, 29**
See also CANR 18; CA 17-20R; DLB 6

Rostand, Edmond (Eugene Alexis)
1868-1918 . . . . **TCLC 6, 37**
See also CA 104, 126

Roth, Henry 1906- . . . . **CLC 2, 6, 11**
See also CAP 1; CA 11-12; DLB 28

Roth, Joseph 1894-1939 . . . . **TCLC 33**

Roth, Philip (Milton)
1933- . . . . . . **CLC 1, 2, 3, 4, 6, 9, 15, 22,
31, 47**
See also CANR 1, 22; CA 1-4R; DLB 2, 28;
DLB-Y 82

Rothenberg, James 1931- . . . . **CLC 57**

Rothenberg, Jerome 1931- . . . . **CLC 6**
See also CANR 1; CA 45-48; DLB 5

Roumain, Jacques 1907-1944 . . . . . **TCLC 19**
See also CA 117

Rourke, Constance (Mayfield)
1885-1941 . . . . **TCLC 12**
See also YABC 1; CA 107

Rousseau, Jean-Baptiste 1671-1741 . . . **LC 9**

Rousseau, Jean-Jacques 1712-1778 . . . **LC 14**

Roussel, Raymond 1877-1933 . . . . . **TCLC 20**
See also CA 117

Rovit, Earl (Herbert) 1927- . . . . **CLC 7**
See also CANR 12; CA 5-8R

Rowe, Nicholas 1674-1718 . . . . **LC 8**

Rowson, Susanna Haswell
1762-1824 . . . . **NCLC 5**
See also DLB 37

Roy, Gabrielle 1909-1983 . . . . . . **CLC 10, 14**
See also CANR 5; CA 53-56;
obituary CA 110; DLB 68

Rozewicz, Tadeusz 1921- . . . . **CLC 9, 23**
See also CA 108

Ruark, Gibbons 1941- . . . . **CLC 3**
See also CANR 14; CA 33-36R

Rubens, Bernice 192?- . . . . **CLC 19, 31**
See also CA 25-28R; DLB 14

Rudkin, (James) David 1936- . . . . . . **CLC 14**
See also CA 89-92; DLB 13

Rudnik, Raphael 1933- . . . . **CLC 7**
See also CA 29-32R

Ruiz, Jose Martinez 1874-1967
See Azorin

Rukeyser, Muriel
1913-1980 . . . . **CLC 6, 10, 15, 27**
See also CANR 26; CA 5-8R;
obituary CA 93-96; obituary SATA 22;
DLB 48

Rule, Jane (Vance) 1931- . . . . **CLC 27**
See also CANR 12; CA 25-28R; DLB 60

Rulfo, Juan 1918-1986 . . . . **CLC 8**
See also CANR 26; CA 85-88;
obituary CA 118

Runyon, (Alfred) Damon
1880-1946 . . . . **TCLC 10**
See also CA 107; DLB 11

Rush, Norman 1933- . . . . **CLC 44**
See also CA 121, 126

Rushdie, (Ahmed) Salman
1947- . . . . **CLC 23, 31, 55, 59**
See also CA 108, 111

Rushforth, Peter (Scott) 1945- . . . . . **CLC 19**
See also CA 101

Ruskin, John 1819-1900 . . . . **TCLC 20**
See also CA 114; SATA 24; DLB 55

Russ, Joanna 1937- . . . . **CLC 15**
See also CANR 11; CA 25-28R; DLB 8

Russell, George William 1867-1935
See A. E.
See also CA 104

Russell, (Henry) Ken(neth Alfred)
1927- . . . . **CLC 16**
See also CA 105

Russell, Willy 1947- . . . . **CLC 60**

Rutherford, Mark 1831-1913 . . . . . . **TCLC 25**
See also CA 121; DLB 18

Ruyslinck, Ward 1929- . . . . **CLC 14**

Ryan, Cornelius (John) 1920-1974 . . . **CLC 7**
See also CA 69-72; obituary CA 53-56

Rybakov, Anatoli 1911?- . . . . **CLC 23, 53**
See also CA 126

Ryder, Jonathan 1927-
See Ludlum, Robert

Ryga, George 1932- . . . . **CLC 14**
See also CA 101; obituary CA 124; DLB 60

Séviné, Marquise de Marie de
Rabutin-Chantal 1626-1696 . . . . . **LC 11**

Saba, Umberto 1883-1957 . . . . **TCLC 33**

Sabato, Ernesto 1911- . . . . **CLC 10, 23**
See also CA 97-100

Sachs, Marilyn (Stickle) 1927- . . . . . **CLC 35**
See also CLR 2; CANR 13; CA 17-20R;
SAAS 2; SATA 3, 52

Sachs, Nelly 1891-1970 . . . . **CLC 14**
See also CAP 2; CA 17-18;
obituary CA 25-28R

Sackler, Howard (Oliver)
1929-1982 . . . . **CLC 14**
See also CA 61-64; obituary CA 108; DLB 7

Sade, Donatien Alphonse Francois, Comte de
1740-1814 . . . . **NCLC 3**

Sadoff, Ira 1945- . . . . **CLC 9**
See also CANR 5, 21; CA 53-56

Safire, William 1929- . . . . **CLC 10**
See also CA 17-20R

Sagan, Carl (Edward) 1934- . . . . **CLC 30**
See also CANR 11; CA 25-28R

Sagan, Francoise
1935- . . . . **CLC 3, 6, 9, 17, 36**
See also Quoirez, Francoise
See also CANR 6

Sahgal, Nayantara (Pandit) 1927- . . . **CLC 41**
See also CANR 11; CA 9-12R

Sciascia, Leonardo
1921-1989 .... **CLC 8, 9, 41**
See also CA 85-88

Scoppettone, Sandra 1936-........ **CLC 26**
See also CA 5-8R; SATA 9

Scorsese, Martin 1942- .... **CLC 20**
See also CA 110, 114

Scotland, Jay 1932-
See Jakes, John (William)

Scott, Duncan Campbell
1862-1947 .... **TCLC 6**
See also CA 104

Scott, Evelyn 1893-1963.......... **CLC 43**
See also CA 104; obituary CA 112; DLB 9, 48

Scott, F(rancis) R(eginald)
1899-1985 .... **CLC 22**
See also CA 101; obituary CA 114

Scott, Joanna 19??-.............. **CLC 50**
See also CA 126

Scott, Paul (Mark) 1920-1978.... **CLC 9, 60**
See also CA 81-84; obituary CA 77-80; DLB 14

Scott, Sir Walter 1771-1832 ..... **NCLC 15**
See also YABC 2

Scribe, (Augustin) Eugene
1791-1861 .... **NCLC 16**

Scudery, Madeleine de 1607-1701..... **LC 2**

Sealy, I. Allan 1951- .... **CLC 55**

Seare, Nicholas 1925-
See Trevanian; Whitaker, Rodney

Sebestyen, Igen 1924-
See Sebestyen, Ouida

Sebestyen, Ouida 1924-........... **CLC 30**
See also CA 107; SATA 39

Sedgwick, Catharine Maria
1789-1867 .... **NCLC 19**
See also DLB 1

Seelye, John 1931-................ **CLC 7**
See also CA 97-100

Seferiades, Giorgos Stylianou 1900-1971
See Seferis, George
See also CANR 5; CA 5-8R; obituary CA 33-36R

Seferis, George 1900-1971 .... **CLC 5, 11**
See also Seferiades, Giorgos Stylianou

Segal, Erich (Wolf) 1937- .... **CLC 3, 10**
See also CANR 20; CA 25-28R; DLB-Y 86

Seger, Bob 1945-................ **CLC 35**

Seger, Robert Clark 1945-
See Seger, Bob

Seghers, Anna 1900-1983....... **CLC 7, 110**
See also Radvanyi, Netty Reiling
See also DLB 69

Seidel, Frederick (Lewis) 1936-..... **CLC 18**
See also CANR 8; CA 13-16R; DLB-Y 84

Seifert, Jaroslav 1901-1986 ..... **CLC 34, 44**

Sei Shonagon c. 966-1017?....... **CMLC 6**

Selby, Hubert, Jr. 1928-....**CLC 1, 2, 4, 8**
See also CA 13-16R; DLB 2

Senacour, Etienne Pivert de
1770-1846 .... **NCLC 16**

Sender, Ramon (Jose) 1902-1982 .... **CLC 8**
See also CANR 8; CA 5-8R; obituary CA 105

Seneca, Lucius Annaeus
4 B.C.-65 A.D. .... **CMLC 6**

Senghor, Léopold Sédar 1906-...... **CLC 54**
See also CA 116

Serling, (Edward) Rod(man)
1924-1975 .... **CLC 30**
See also CA 65-68; obituary CA 57-60; DLB 26

Serpieres 1907-
See Guillevic, (Eugene)

Service, Robert W(illiam)
1874-1958 .... **TCLC 15**
See also CA 115; SATA 20

Seth, Vikram 1952-.............. **CLC 43**
See also CA 121

Seton, Cynthia Propper
1926-1982 .... **CLC 27**
See also CANR 7; CA 5-8R; obituary CA 108

Seton, Ernest (Evan) Thompson
1860-1946 .... **TCLC 31**
See also CA 109; SATA 18

Settle, Mary Lee 1918-........ **CLC 19, 61**
See also CAAS 1; CA 89-92; DLB 6

Sevigne, Marquise de Marie de
Rabutin-Chantal 1626-1696..... **LC 11**

Sexton, Anne (Harvey)
1928-1974 ... **CLC 2, 4, 6, 8, 10, 15, 53; PC 2**
See also CANR 3; CA 1-4R; obituary CA 53-56; CABS 2; SATA 10; DLB 5; CDALB 1941-1968

Shaara, Michael (Joseph) 1929- .... **CLC 15**
See also CA 102; obituary CA 125; DLB-Y 83

Shackleton, C. C. 1925-
See Aldiss, Brian W(ilson)

Shacochis, Bob 1951-............. **CLC 39**
See also CA 119, 124

Shaffer, Anthony 1926- .... **CLC 19**
See also CA 110, 116; DLB 13

Shaffer, Peter (Levin)
1926- .... **CLC 5, 14, 18, 37, 60**
See also CANR 25; CA 25-28R; DLB 13

Shalamov, Varlam (Tikhonovich)
1907?-1982.................. **CLC 18**
See also obituary CA 105

Shamlu, Ahmad 1925- .... **CLC 10**

Shammas, Anton 1951-........... **CLC 55**

Shange, Ntozake 1948-....... **CLC 8, 25, 38**
See also CA 85-88; DLB 38

Shapcott, Thomas W(illiam) 1935- .. **CLC 38**
See also CA 69-72

Shapiro, Karl (Jay) 1913- .. **CLC 4, 8, 15, 53**
See also CAAS 6; CANR 1; CA 1-4R; DLB 48

Sharp, William 1855-1905 .... **TCLC 39**

Sharpe, Tom 1928-.............. **CLC 36**
See also CA 114; DLB 14

Shaw, (George) Bernard
1856-1950 .... **TCLC 3, 9, 21**
See also CA 104, 109, 119; DLB 10, 57

Shaw, Henry Wheeler
1818-1885 .... **NCLC 15**
See also DLB 11

Shaw, Irwin 1913-1984...... **CLC 7, 23, 34**
See also CANR 21; CA 13-16R; obituary CA 112; DLB 6; DLB-Y 84; CDALB 1941-1968

Shaw, Robert 1927-1978 .... **CLC 5**
See also CANR 4; CA 1-4R; obituary CA 81-84; DLB 13, 14

Shawn, Wallace 1943- .... **CLC 41**
See also CA 112

Sheed, Wilfrid (John Joseph)
1930- .... **CLC 2, 4, 10, 53**
See also CA 65-68; DLB 6

Sheffey, Asa 1913-1980
See Hayden, Robert (Earl)

Sheldon, Alice (Hastings) B(radley)
1915-1987
See Tiptree, James, Jr.
See also CA 108; obituary CA 122

Shelley, Mary Wollstonecraft Godwin
1797-1851 .... **NCLC 14**
See also SATA 29

Shelley, Percy Bysshe
1792-1822 .... **NCLC 18**

Shepard, Jim 19??-.............. **CLC 36**

Shepard, Lucius 19??-............. **CLC 34**

Shepard, Sam
1943- .... **CLC 4, 6, 17, 34, 41, 44**
See also CANR 22; CA 69-72; DLB 7

Shepherd, Michael 1927-
See Ludlum, Robert

Sherburne, Zoa (Morin) 1912-...... **CLC 30**
See also CANR 3; CA 1-4R; SATA 3

Sheridan, Frances 1724-1766........ **LC 7**
See also DLB 39

Sheridan, Richard Brinsley
1751-1816 .... **NCLC 5; DC 1**
See also DLB 89

Sherman, Jonathan Marc 1970?-.... **CLC 55**

Sherman, Martin 19??-............ **CLC 19**
See also CA 116

Sherwin, Judith Johnson 1936-... **CLC 7, 15**
See also CA 25-28R

Sherwood, Robert E(mmet)
1896-1955 .... **TCLC 3**
See also CA 104; DLB 7, 26

Shiel, M(atthew) P(hipps)
1865-1947 .... **TCLC 8**
See also CA 106

Shiga, Naoya 1883-1971.......... **CLC 33**
See also CA 101; obituary CA 33-36R

Shimazaki, Haruki 1872-1943
See Shimazaki, Toson
See also CA 105

Shimazaki, Toson 1872-1943....... **TCLC 5**
See also Shimazaki, Haruki

Smith, David (Jeddie) 1942-
See Smith, Dave
See also CANR 1; CA 49-52

Smith, Florence Margaret 1902-1971
See Smith, Stevie
See also CAP 2; CA 17-18;
   obituary CA 29-32R

Smith, John 1580?-1631 . . . . LC 9
See also DLB 24, 30

Smith, Lee 1944- . . . . CLC 25
See also CA 114, 119; DLB-Y 83

Smith, Martin Cruz 1942- . . . . CLC 25
See also CANR 6; CA 85-88

Smith, Martin William 1942-
See Smith, Martin Cruz

Smith, Mary-Ann Tirone 1944- . . . . . CLC 39
See also CA 118

Smith, Patti 1946- . . . . CLC 12
See also CA 93-96

Smith, Pauline (Urmson)
1882-1959 . . . . TCLC 25
See also CA 29-32R; SATA 27

Smith, Rosamond 1938-
See Oates, Joyce Carol

Smith, Sara Mahala Redway 1900-1972
See Benson, Sally

Smith, Stevie 1902-1971 . . . . CLC 3, 8, 25, 44
See also Smith, Florence Margaret
See also DLB 20

Smith, Wilbur (Addison) 1933- . . . . . CLC 33
See also CANR 7; CA 13-16R

Smith, William Jay 1918- . . . . CLC 6
See also CA 5-8R; SATA 2; DLB 5

Smolenskin, Peretz 1842-1885 . . . . NCLC 30

Smollett, Tobias (George) 1721-1771 . . LC 2
See also DLB 39

Snodgrass, W(illiam) D(e Witt)
1926- . . . . CLC 2, 6, 10, 18
See also CANR 6; CA 1-4R; DLB 5

Snow, C(harles) P(ercy)
1905-1980 . . . . CLC 1, 4, 6, 9, 13, 19
See also CA 5-8R; obituary CA 101;
   DLB 15

Snyder, Gary (Sherman)
1930- . . . . CLC 1, 2, 5, 9, 32
See also CA 17-20R; DLB 5, 16

Snyder, Zilpha Keatley 1927- . . . . . . CLC 17
See also CA 9-12R; SAAS 2; SATA 1, 28

Sobol, Joshua 19??- . . . . CLC 60

Soderberg. Hjalmar 1869-1941 . . . . TCLC 39

Sodergran, Edith 1892-1923 . . . . . . TCLC 31

Sokolov, Raymond 1941- . . . . CLC 7
See also CA 85-88

Sologub, Fyodor 1863-1927 . . . . TCLC 9
See also Teternikov, Fyodor Kuzmich
See also CA 104

Solomos, Dionysios 1798-1857 . . . NCLC 15

Solwoska, Mara 1929-
See French, Marilyn
See also CANR 3; CA 69-72

Solzhenitsyn, Aleksandr I(sayevich)
1918- . . . CLC 1, 2, 4, 7, 9, 10, 18, 26, 34
See also CA 69-72

Somers, Jane 1919-
See Lessing, Doris (May)

Sommer, Scott 1951- . . . . CLC 25
See also CA 106

Sondheim, Stephen (Joshua)
1930- . . . . CLC 30, 39
See also CA 103

Sontag, Susan 1933- . . . CLC 1, 2, 10, 13, 31
See also CA 17-20R; DLB 2

Sophocles
c. 496? B.C.-c. 406? B.C. . . . . . CMLC 2;
                                          DC 1

Sorrentino, Gilbert
1929- . . . . CLC 3, 7, 14, 22, 40
See also CANR 14; CA 77-80; DLB 5;
   DLB-Y 80

Soto, Gary 1952- . . . . CLC 32
See also CA 119

Souster, (Holmes) Raymond
1921- . . . . CLC 5, 14
See also CANR 13; CA 13-16R

Southern, Terry 1926- . . . . CLC 7
See also CANR 1; CA 1-4R; DLB 2

Southey, Robert 1774-1843 . . . . NCLC 8

Southworth, Emma Dorothy Eliza Nevitte
1819-1899 . . . . NCLC 26

Soyinka, Akinwande Oluwole 1934-
See Soyinka, Wole

Soyinka, Wole 1934- . . CLC 3, 5, 14, 36, 44
See also CA 13-16R; DLB-Y 86

Spackman, W(illiam) M(ode)
1905- . . . . CLC 46
See also CA 81-84

Spacks, Barry 1931- . . . . CLC 14
See also CA 29-32R

Spanidou, Irini 1946- . . . . CLC 44

Spark, Muriel (Sarah)
1918- . . . . CLC 2, 3, 5, 8, 13, 18, 40
See also CANR 12; CA 5-8R; DLB 15

Spencer, Elizabeth 1921- . . . . CLC 22
See also CA 13-16R; SATA 14; DLB 6

Spencer, Scott 1945- . . . . CLC 30
See also CA 113; DLB-Y 86

Spender, Stephen (Harold)
1909- . . . . CLC 1, 2, 5, 10, 41
See also CA 9-12R; DLB 20

Spengler, Oswald 1880-1936 . . . . . . TCLC 25
See also CA 118

Spenser, Edmund 1552?-1599 . . . . LC 5

Spicer, Jack 1925-1965 . . . . CLC 8, 18
See also CA 85-88; DLB 5, 16

Spielberg, Peter 1929- . . . . CLC 6
See also CANR 4; CA 5-8R; DLB-Y 81

Spielberg, Steven 1947- . . . . CLC 20
See also CA 77-80; SATA 32

Spillane, Frank Morrison 1918-
See Spillane, Mickey
See also CA 25-28R

Spillane, Mickey 1918- . . . . CLC 3, 13
See also Spillane, Frank Morrison

Spinoza, Benedictus de 1632-1677 . . . . LC 9

Spinrad, Norman (Richard) 1940- . . . CLC 46
See also CANR 20; CA 37-40R; DLB 8

Spitteler, Carl (Friedrich Georg)
1845-1924 . . . . TCLC 12
See also CA 109

Spivack, Kathleen (Romola Drucker)
1938- . . . . CLC 6
See also CA 49-52

Spoto, Donald 1941- . . . . CLC 39
See also CANR 11; CA 65-68

Springsteen, Bruce 1949- . . . . CLC 17
See also CA 111

Spurling, Hilary 1940- . . . . CLC 34
See also CANR 25; CA 104

Squires, (James) Radcliffe 1917- . . . . CLC 51
See also CANR 6, 21; CA 1-4R

Stael-Holstein, Anne Louise Germaine Necker,
   Baronne de 1766-1817 . . . . NCLC 3

Stafford, Jean 1915-1979 . . . . . . CLC 4, 7, 19
See also CANR 3; CA 1-4R;
   obituary CA 85-88; obituary SATA 22;
   DLB 2

Stafford, William (Edgar)
1914- . . . . CLC 4, 7, 29
See also CAAS 3; CANR 5, 22; CA 5-8R;
   DLB 5

Stannard, Martin 1947- . . . . CLC 44

Stanton, Maura 1946- . . . . CLC 9
See also CANR 15; CA 89-92

Stapledon, (William) Olaf
1886-1950 . . . . TCLC 22
See also CA 111; DLB 15

Starbuck, George (Edwin) 1931- . . . . CLC 53
See also CANR 23; CA 21-22R

Stark, Richard 1933-
See Westlake, Donald E(dwin)

Stead, Christina (Ellen)
1902-1983 . . . . CLC 2, 5, 8, 32
See also CA 13-16R; obituary CA 109

Steele, Timothy (Reid) 1948- . . . . CLC 45
See also CANR 16; CA 93-96

Steffens, (Joseph) Lincoln
1866-1936 . . . . TCLC 20
See also CA 117; SAAS 1

Stegner, Wallace (Earle) 1909- . . . CLC 9, 49
See also CANR 1, 21; CA 1-4R; DLB 9

Stein, Gertrude 1874-1946 . . . TCLC 1, 6, 28
See also CA 104; DLB 4, 54

Steinbeck, John (Ernst)
1902-1968 . . . . . CLC 1, 5, 9, 13, 21, 34,
                                       45, 59
See also CANR 1; CA 1-4R;
   obituary CA 25-28R; SATA 9; DLB 7, 9;
   DLB-DS 2

Steinem, Gloria 1934- . . . . CLC 63
See also CANR 28; CA 53-56

Steiner, George 1929- . . . . CLC 24
See also CA 73-76

Steiner, Rudolf(us Josephus Laurentius)
1861-1925 . . . . TCLC 13
See also CA 107

Stendhal 1783-1842 . . . . NCLC 23

Stephen, Leslie 1832-1904 . . . . TCLC 23
See also CANR 9; CA 21-24R, 123;
   DLB 57

Stephens, James   1882?-1950 . . . . TCLC 4
  See also CA 104; DLB 19

Stephens, Reed
  See Donaldson, Stephen R.

Steptoe, Lydia   1892-1982
  See Barnes, Djuna

Sterling, George   1869-1926 . . . . TCLC 20
  See also CA 117; DLB 54

Stern, Gerald   1925- . . . . CLC 40
  See also CA 81-84

Stern, Richard G(ustave)   1928-. . . CLC 4, 39
  See also CANR 1, 25; CA 1-4R

Sternberg, Jonas   1894-1969
  See Sternberg, Josef von

Sternberg, Josef von   1894-1969. . . . . CLC 20
  See also CA 81-84

Sterne, Laurence   1713-1768. . . . . LC 2
  See also DLB 39

Sternheim, (William Adolf) Carl
  1878-1942 . . . . TCLC 8
  See also CA 105

Stevens, Mark   19??-. . . . . CLC 34

Stevens, Wallace   1879-1955. . . . . TCLC 3, 12
  See also CA 104, 124; DLB 54

Stevenson, Anne (Katharine)
  1933- . . . . CLC 7, 33
  See also Elvin, Anne Katharine Stevenson
  See also CANR 9; CA 17-18R; DLB 40

Stevenson, Robert Louis
  1850-1894 . . . . NCLC 5, 14
  See also CLR 10, 11; YABC 2; DLB 18, 57

Stewart, J(ohn) I(nnes) M(ackintosh)
  1906- . . . . CLC 7, 14, 32
  See also CAAS 3; CA 85-88

Stewart, Mary (Florence Elinor)
  1916- . . . . CLC 7, 35
  See also CANR 1; CA 1-4R; SATA 12

Stewart, Will   1908-
  See Williamson, Jack
  See also CANR 23; CA 17-18R

Still, James   1906-. . . . . CLC 49
  See also CANR 10; CA 65-68; SATA 29;
  DLB 9

Sting   1951-
  See The Police

Stitt, Milan   1941-. . . . . CLC 29
  See also CA 69-72

Stoker, Abraham
  See Stoker, Bram
  See also CA 105

Stoker, Bram   1847-1912 . . . . TCLC 8
  See also Stoker, Abraham
  See also SATA 29; DLB 36, 70

Stolz, Mary (Slattery)   1920-. . . . . . . CLC 12
  See also CANR 13; CA 5-8R; SAAS 3;
  SATA 10

Stone, Irving   1903-1989. . . . . CLC 7
  See also CAAS 3; CANR 1; CA 1-4R;
  SATA 3

Stone, Robert (Anthony)
  1937?- . . . . CLC 5, 23, 42
  See also CANR 23; CA 85-88

Stoppard, Tom
  1937- . . . CLC 1, 3, 4, 5, 8, 15, 29, 34, 63
  See also CA 81-84; DLB 13; DLB-Y 85

Storey, David (Malcolm)
  1933-. . . . . CLC 2, 4, 5, 8
  See also CA 81-84; DLB 13, 14

Storm, Hyemeyohsts   1935-. . . . . CLC 3
  See also CA 81-84

Storm, (Hans) Theodor (Woldsen)
  1817-1888 . . . . NCLC 1

Storni, Alfonsina   1892-1938 . . . . . . TCLC 5
  See also CA 104

Stout, Rex (Todhunter)   1886-1975 . . . CLC 3
  See also CA 61-64

Stow, (Julian) Randolph   1935- . . CLC 23, 48
  See also CA 13-16R

Stowe, Harriet (Elizabeth) Beecher
  1811-1896 . . . . NCLC 3
  See also YABC 1; DLB 1, 12, 42;
  CDALB 1865-1917

Strachey, (Giles) Lytton
  1880-1932 . . . . TCLC 12
  See also CA 110

Strand, Mark   1934-. . . . . CLC 6, 18, 41
  See also CA 21-24R; SATA 41; DLB 5

Straub, Peter (Francis)   1943- . . . . . . CLC 28
  See also CA 85-88; DLB-Y 84

Strauss, Botho   1944- . . . . CLC 22

Straussler, Tomas   1937-
  See Stoppard, Tom

Streatfeild, (Mary) Noel   1897- . . . . . CLC 21
  See also CA 81-84; obituary CA 120;
  SATA 20, 48

Stribling, T(homas) S(igismund)
  1881-1965 . . . . CLC 23
  See also obituary CA 107; DLB 9

Strindberg, (Johan) August
  1849-1912 . . . . TCLC 1, 8, 21
  See also CA 104

Stringer, Arthur   1874-1950 . . . . . . TCLC 37
  See also DLB 92

Strugatskii, Arkadii (Natanovich)
  1925- . . . . CLC 27
  See also CA 106

Strugatskii, Boris (Natanovich)
  1933- . . . . CLC 27
  See also CA 106

Strummer, Joe   1953?-
  See The Clash

Stuart, (Hilton) Jesse
  1906-1984 . . . . CLC 1, 8, 11, 14, 34
  See also CA 5-8R; obituary CA 112;
  SATA 2; obituary SATA 36; DLB 9, 48;
  DLB-Y 84

Sturgeon, Theodore (Hamilton)
  1918-1985 . . . . CLC 22, 39
  See also CA 81-84; obituary CA 116;
  DLB 8; DLB-Y 85

Styron, William
  1925- . . . . CLC 1, 3, 5, 11, 15, 60
  See also CANR 6; CA 5-8R; DLB 2;
  DLB-Y 80; CDALB 1968-1987

Sudermann, Hermann   1857-1928 . . TCLC 15
  See also CA 107

Sue, Eugene   1804-1857 . . . . NCLC 1

Sukenick, Ronald   1932-. . . . . CLC 3, 4, 6, 48
  See also CA 25-28R; DLB-Y 81

Suknaski, Andrew   1942- . . . . CLC 19
  See also CA 101; DLB 53

Sully Prudhomme, Rene
  1839-1907 . . . . TCLC 31

Su Man-shu   1884-1918. . . . . TCLC 24
  See also CA 123

Summers, Andrew James   1942-
  See The Police

Summers, Andy   1942-
  See The Police

Summers, Hollis (Spurgeon, Jr.)
  1916- . . . . CLC 10
  See also CANR 3; CA 5-8R; DLB 6

Summers, (Alphonsus Joseph-Mary Augustus)
  Montague   1880-1948 . . . . TCLC 16
  See also CA 118

Sumner, Gordon Matthew   1951-
  See The Police

Surtees, Robert Smith
  1805-1864 . . . . NCLC 14
  See also DLB 21

Susann, Jacqueline   1921-1974. . . . . . CLC 3
  See also CA 65-68; obituary CA 53-56

Suskind, Patrick   1949-. . . . . CLC 44

Sutcliff, Rosemary   1920-. . . . . CLC 26
  See also CLR 1; CA 5-8R; SATA 6, 44

Sutro, Alfred   1863-1933. . . . . TCLC 6
  See also CA 105; DLB 10

Sutton, Henry   1935-
  See Slavitt, David (R.)

Svevo, Italo   1861-1928. . . . . TCLC 2, 35
  See also Schmitz, Ettore

Swados, Elizabeth   1951- . . . . CLC 12
  See also CA 97-100

Swados, Harvey   1920-1972 . . . . CLC 5
  See also CANR 6; CA 5-8R;
  obituary CA 37-40R; DLB 2

Swarthout, Glendon (Fred)   1918- . . . CLC 35
  See also CANR 1; CA 1-4R; SATA 26

Swenson, May   1919-1989. . . . . CLC 4, 14, 61
  See also CA 5-8R; SATA 15; DLB 5

Swift, Graham   1949- . . . . CLC 41
  See also CA 117, 122

Swift, Jonathan   1667-1745. . . . . LC 1
  See also SATA 19; DLB 39

Swinburne, Algernon Charles
  1837-1909 . . . . TCLC 8, 36
  See also CA 105; DLB 35, 57

Swinfen, Ann   19??-. . . . . CLC 34

Swinnerton, Frank (Arthur)
  1884-1982 . . . . TCLC 31
  See also obituary CA 108; DLB 34

Symons, Arthur (William)
  1865-1945 . . . . TCLC 11
  See also CA 107; DLB 19, 57

Symons, Julian (Gustave)
  1912-. . . . . CLC 2, 14, 32
  See also CAAS 3; CANR 3; CA 49-52

Synge, (Edmund) John Millington
　　1871-1909 . . . . TCLC 6, 37
　　See also CA 104; DLB 10, 19

Syruc, J.　1911-
　　See Milosz, Czeslaw

Szirtes, George　1948- . . . . CLC 46
　　See also CA 109

Tabori, George　1914- . . . . CLC 19
　　See also CANR 4; CA 49-52

Tagore, (Sir) Rabindranath
　　1861-1941 . . . . TCLC 3
　　See also Thakura, Ravindranatha
　　See also CA 120

Taine, Hippolyte Adolphe
　　1828-1893 . . . . NCLC 15

Talese, Gaetano　1932-
　　See Talese, Gay

Talese, Gay　1932- . . . . CLC 37
　　See also CANR 9; CA 1-4R

Tallent, Elizabeth (Ann)　1954- . . . . . CLC 45
　　See also CA 117

Tally, Ted　1952- . . . . CLC 42
　　See also CA 120, 124

Tamayo y Baus, Manuel
　　1829-1898 . . . . NCLC 1

Tammsaare, A(nton) H(ansen)
　　1878-1940 . . . . TCLC 27

Tan, Amy　1952- . . . . CLC 59

Tanizaki, Jun'ichiro
　　1886-1965 . . . . CLC 8, 14, 28
　　See also CA 93-96; obituary CA 25-28R

Tarbell, Ida　1857-1944 . . . . TCLC 40
　　See also CA 122; DLB 47

Tarkington, (Newton) Booth
　　1869-1946 . . . . TCLC 9
　　See also CA 110; SATA 17; DLB 9

Tasso, Torquato　1544-1595 . . . . LC 5

Tate, (John Orley) Allen
　　1899-1979 . . . . CLC 2, 4, 6, 9, 11, 14, 24
　　See also CA 5-8R; obituary CA 85-88;
　　DLB 4, 45, 63

Tate, James　1943- . . . . CLC 2, 6, 25
　　See also CA 21-24R; DLB 5

Tavel, Ronald　1940- . . . . CLC 6
　　See also CA 21-24R

Taylor, C(ecil) P(hillip)　1929-1981 . . CLC 27
　　See also CA 25-28R; obituary CA 105

Taylor, Edward　1644?-1729 . . . . LC 11
　　See also DLB 24

Taylor, Eleanor Ross　1920- . . . . CLC 5
　　See also CA 81-84

Taylor, Elizabeth　1912-1975 . . . CLC 2, 4, 29
　　See also CANR 9; CA 13-16R; SATA 13

Taylor, Henry (Splawn)　1917- . . . . . . CLC 44
　　See also CAAS 7; CA 33-36R; DLB 5

Taylor, Kamala (Purnaiya)　1924-
　　See Markandaya, Kamala
　　See also CA 77-80

Taylor, Mildred D(elois)　1943- . . . . . CLC 21
　　See also CLR 9; CANR 25; CA 85-88;
　　SAAS 5; SATA 15; DLB 52

Taylor, Peter (Hillsman)
　　1917- . . . . CLC 1, 4, 18, 37, 44, 50
　　See also CANR 9; CA 13-16R; DLB-Y 81

Taylor, Robert Lewis　1912- . . . . CLC 14
　　See also CANR 3; CA 1-4R; SATA 10

Teasdale, Sara　1884-1933 . . . . TCLC 4
　　See also CA 104; SATA 32; DLB 45

Tegner, Esaias　1782-1846 . . . . NCLC 2

Teilhard de Chardin, (Marie Joseph) Pierre
　　1881-1955 . . . . TCLC 9
　　See also CA 105

Tennant, Emma　1937- . . . . CLC 13, 52
　　See also CAAS 9; CANR 10; CA 65-68;
　　DLB 14

Tennyson, Alfred　1809-1892 . . . . . NCLC 30
　　See also DLB 32

Teran, Lisa St. Aubin de　19??- . . . . . CLC 36

Terkel, Louis　1912-
　　See Terkel, Studs
　　See also CANR 18; CA 57-60

Terkel, Studs　1912- . . . . CLC 38
　　See also Terkel, Louis

Terry, Megan　1932- . . . . CLC 19
　　See also CA 77-80; DLB 7

Tertz, Abram　1925-
　　See Sinyavsky, Andrei (Donatevich)

Tesich, Steve　1943?- . . . . CLC 40
　　See also CA 105; DLB-Y 83

Tesich, Stoyan　1943?-
　　See Tesich, Steve

Teternikov, Fyodor Kuzmich　1863-1927
　　See Sologub, Fyodor
　　See also CA 104

Tevis, Walter　1928-1984 . . . . CLC 42
　　See also CA 113

Tey, Josephine　1897-1952 . . . . TCLC 14
　　See also Mackintosh, Elizabeth

Thackeray, William Makepeace
　　1811-1863 . . . . NCLC 5, 14, 22
　　See also SATA 23; DLB 21, 55

Thakura, Ravindranatha　1861-1941
　　See Tagore, (Sir) Rabindranath
　　See also CA 104

Thelwell, Michael (Miles)　1939- . . . . CLC 22
　　See also CA 101

Theroux, Alexander (Louis)
　　1939- . . . . CLC 2, 25
　　See also CANR 20; CA 85-88

Theroux, Paul
　　1941- . . . . CLC 5, 8, 11, 15, 28, 46
　　See also CANR 20; CA 33-36R; SATA 44;
　　DLB 2

Thesen, Sharon　1946- . . . . CLC 56

Thibault, Jacques Anatole Francois
　　1844-1924
　　See France, Anatole
　　See also CA 106

Thiele, Colin (Milton)　1920- . . . . CLC 17
　　See also CANR 12; CA 29-32R; SAAS 2;
　　SATA 14

Thomas, Audrey (Grace)
　　1935- . . . . CLC 7, 13, 37
　　See also CA 21-24R; DLB 60

Thomas, D(onald) M(ichael)
　　1935- . . . . CLC 13, 22, 31
　　See also CANR 17; CA 61-64; DLB 40

Thomas, Dylan (Marlais)
　　1914-1953 . . . . . TCLC 1, 8; PC 2; SSC 3
　　See also CA 104, 120; SATA 60; DLB 13,
　　20

Thomas, Edward (Philip)
　　1878-1917 . . . . TCLC 10
　　See also CA 106; DLB 19

Thomas, John Peter　1928-
　　See Thomas, Piri

Thomas, Joyce Carol　1938- . . . . CLC 35
　　See also CA 113, 116; SATA 40; DLB 33

Thomas, Lewis　1913- . . . . CLC 35
　　See also CA 85-88

Thomas, Piri　1928- . . . . CLC 17
　　See also CA 73-76

Thomas, R(onald) S(tuart)
　　1913- . . . . CLC 6, 13, 48
　　See also CAAS 4; CA 89-92; DLB 27

Thomas, Ross (Elmore)　1926- . . . . . . CLC 39
　　See also CANR 22; CA 33-36R

Thompson, Ernest　1860-1946
　　See Seton, Ernest (Evan) Thompson

Thompson, Francis (Joseph)
　　1859-1907 . . . . TCLC 4
　　See also CA 104; DLB 19

Thompson, Hunter S(tockton)
　　1939- . . . . CLC 9, 17, 40
　　See also CANR 23; CA 17-20R

Thompson, Judith　1954- . . . . CLC 39

Thomson, James　1834-1882 . . . . . . NCLC 18
　　See also DLB 35

Thoreau, Henry David
　　1817-1862 . . . . NCLC 7, 21
　　See also DLB 1; CDALB 1640-1865

Thurber, James (Grover)
　　1894-1961 . . . . CLC 5, 11, 25; SSC 1
　　See also CANR 17; CA 73-76; SATA 13;
　　DLB 4, 11, 22

Thurman, Wallace　1902-1934 . . . . . . TCLC 6
　　See also CA 104, 124; DLB 51

Tieck, (Johann) Ludwig
　　1773-1853 . . . . NCLC 5

Tillinghast, Richard　1940- . . . . CLC 29
　　See also CANR 26; CA 29-32R

Timrod, Henry　1828-1867 . . . . NCLC 25

Tindall, Gillian　1938- . . . . CLC 7
　　See also CANR 11; CA 21-24R

Tiptree, James, Jr.　1915-1987 . . . CLC 48, 50
　　See Sheldon, Alice (Hastings) B(radley)
　　See also DLB 8

Tocqueville, Alexis (Charles Henri Maurice
　　Clerel, Comte) de　1805-1859 . . NCLC 7

Tolkien, J(ohn) R(onald) R(euel)
　　1892-1973 . . . . . CLC 1, 2, 3, 8, 12, 38
　　See also CAP 2; CA 17-18;
　　obituary CA 45-48; SATA 2, 32;
　　obituary SATA 24; DLB 15

Toller, Ernst　1893-1939 . . . . TCLC 10
　　See also CA 107

Van Doren, Mark 1894-1972..... **CLC 6, 10**
See also CANR 3; CA 1-4R;
obituary CA 37-40R; DLB 45

Van Druten, John (William)
1901-1957 .... **TCLC 2**
See also CA 104; DLB 10

Van Duyn, Mona 1921-....... **CLC 3, 7, 63**
See also CANR 7; CA 9-12R; DLB 5

Van Itallie, Jean-Claude 1936- ...... **CLC 3**
See also CAAS 2; CANR 1; CA 45-48;
DLB 7

Van Ostaijen, Paul 1896-1928..... **TCLC 33**

Van Peebles, Melvin 1932- ...... **CLC 2, 20**
See also CA 85-88

Vansittart, Peter 1920-............ **CLC 42**
See also CANR 3; CA 1-4R

Van Vechten, Carl 1880-1964 ...... **CLC 33**
See also obituary CA 89-92; DLB 4, 9, 51

Van Vogt, A(lfred) E(lton) 1912-..... **CLC 1**
See also CA 21-24R; SATA 14; DLB 8

Varda, Agnes 1928- .... **CLC 16**
See also CA 116, 122

Vargas Llosa, (Jorge) Mario (Pedro)
1936- .... **CLC 3, 6, 9, 10, 15, 31, 42**
See also CANR 18; CA 73-76

Vassilikos, Vassilis 1933-......... **CLC 4, 8**
See also CA 81-84

Vaughn, Stephanie 19??- .... **CLC 62**

Vazov, Ivan 1850-1921.......... **TCLC 25**
See also CA 121

Veblen, Thorstein Bunde
1857-1929 .... **TCLC 31**
See also CA 115

Verga, Giovanni 1840-1922 .... **TCLC 3**
See also CA 104, 123

Verhaeren, Emile (Adolphe Gustave)
1855-1916 .... **TCLC 12**
See also CA 109

Verlaine, Paul (Marie)
1844-1896 .... **NCLC 2; PC 2**

Verne, Jules (Gabriel) 1828-1905 ... **TCLC 6**
See also CA 110; SATA 21

Very, Jones 1813-1880........... **NCLC 9**
See also DLB 1

Vesaas, Tarjei 1897-1970......... **CLC 48**
See also obituary CA 29-32R

Vian, Boris 1920-1959 .... **TCLC 9**
See also CA 106; DLB 72

Viaud, (Louis Marie) Julien 1850-1923
See Loti, Pierre
See also CA 107

Vicker, Angus 1916-
See Felsen, Henry Gregor

Vidal, Eugene Luther, Jr. 1925-
See Vidal, Gore

Vidal, Gore
1925- .... **CLC 2, 4, 6, 8, 10, 22, 33**
See also CANR 13; CA 5-8R; DLB 6

Viereck, Peter (Robert Edwin)
1916- .... **CLC 4**
See also CANR 1; CA 1-4R; DLB 5

Vigny, Alfred (Victor) de
1797-1863 .... **NCLC 7**

Vilakazi, Benedict Wallet
1905-1947 .... **TCLC 37**

**Villiers de l'Isle Adam, Jean Marie Mathias
Philippe Auguste, Comte de,**
1838-1889 .... **NCLC 3**

Vinci, Leonardo da 1452-1519...... **LC 12**

Vine, Barbara 1930-............. **CLC 50**
See also Rendell, Ruth

Vinge, Joan (Carol) D(ennison)
1948- .... **CLC 30**
See also CA 93-96; SATA 36

Visconti, Luchino 1906-1976 .... **CLC 16**
See also CA 81-84; obituary CA 65-68

Vittorini, Elio 1908-1966...... **CLC 6, 9, 14**
See also obituary CA 25-28R

Vizinczey, Stephen 1933-.......... **CLC 40**

Vliet, R(ussell) G(ordon)
1929-1984 .... **CLC 22**
See also CANR 18; CA 37-40R;
obituary CA 112

Voight, Ellen Bryant 1943-........ **CLC 54**
See also CANR 11; CA 69-72

Voigt, Cynthia 1942- .... **CLC 30**
See also CANR 18; CA 106; SATA 33, 48

Voinovich, Vladimir (Nikolaevich)
1932- .... **CLC 10, 49**
See also CA 81-84

Voltaire 1694-1778 .... **LC 14**

Von Daeniken, Erich 1935-
See Von Daniken, Erich
See also CANR 17; CA 37-40R

Von Daniken, Erich 1935-......... **CLC 30**
See also Von Daeniken, Erich

Vonnegut, Kurt, Jr.
1922- ...... **CLC 1, 2, 3, 4, 5, 8, 12, 22,
40, 60**
See also CANR 1; CA 1-4R; DLB 2, 8;
DLB-Y 80; DLB-DS 3;
CDALB 1968-1987

Vorster, Gordon 1924-............ **CLC 34**

Voznesensky, Andrei 1933- ... **CLC 1, 15, 57**
See also CA 89-92

Waddington, Miriam 1917- .... **CLC 28**
See also CANR 12; CA 21-24R

Wagman, Fredrica 1937- .... **CLC 7**
See also CA 97-100

Wagner, Richard 1813-1883....... **NCLC 9**

Wagner-Martin, Linda 1936-....... **CLC 50**

Wagoner, David (Russell)
1926- .... **CLC 3, 5, 15**
See also CAAS 3; CANR 2; CA 1-4R;
SATA 14; DLB 5

Wah, Fred(erick James) 1939-...... **CLC 44**
See also CA 107; DLB 60

Wahloo, Per 1926-1975 .... **CLC 7**
See also CA 61-64

Wahloo, Peter 1926-1975
See Wahloo, Per

Wain, John (Barrington)
1925- .... **CLC 2, 11, 15, 46**
See also CAAS 4; CANR 23; CA 5-8R;
DLB 15, 27

Wajda, Andrzej 1926-............. **CLC 16**
See also CA 102

Wakefield, Dan 1932-............. **CLC 7**
See also CAAS 7; CA 21-24R

Wakoski, Diane
1937- .... **CLC 2, 4, 7, 9, 11, 40**
See also CAAS 1; CANR 9; CA 13-16R;
DLB 5

Walcott, Derek (Alton)
1930- .... **CLC 2, 4, 9, 14, 25, 42**
See also CANR 26; CA 89-92; DLB-Y 81

Waldman, Anne 1945- .... **CLC 7**
See also CA 37-40R; DLB 16

Waldo, Edward Hamilton 1918-
See Sturgeon, Theodore (Hamilton)

Walker, Alice
1944- ...... **CLC 5, 6, 9, 19, 27, 46, 58;
SSC 5**
See also CANR 9, 27; CA 37-40R;
SATA 31; DLB 6, 33; CDALB 1968-1988

Walker, David Harry 1911-........ **CLC 14**
See also CANR 1; CA 1-4R; SATA 8

Walker, Edward Joseph 1934-
See Walker, Ted
See also CANR 12; CA 21-24R

Walker, George F. 1947-....... **CLC 44, 61**
See also CANR 21; CA 103; DLB 60

Walker, Joseph A. 1935-.......... **CLC 19**
See also CANR 26; CA 89-92; DLB 38

Walker, Margaret (Abigail)
1915- .... **CLC 1, 6**
See also CANR 26; CA 73-76; DLB 76

Walker, Ted 1934- .... **CLC 13**
See also Walker, Edward Joseph
See also DLB 40

Wallace, David Foster 1962-....... **CLC 50**

Wallace, Irving 1916-.......... **CLC 7, 13**
See also CAAS 1; CANR 1; CA 1-4R

Wallant, Edward Lewis
1926-1962 .... **CLC 5, 10**
See also CANR 22; CA 1-4R; DLB 2, 28

Walpole, Horace 1717-1797.......... **LC 2**
See also DLB 39

Walpole, (Sir) Hugh (Seymour)
1884-1941 .... **TCLC 5**
See also CA 104; DLB 34

Walser, Martin 1927-............ **CLC 27**
See also CANR 8; CA 57-60; DLB 75

Walser, Robert 1878-1956........ **TCLC 18**
See also CA 118; DLB 66

Walsh, Gillian Paton 1939-
See Walsh, Jill Paton
See also CA 37-40R; SATA 4

Walsh, Jill Paton 1939-.......... **CLC 35**
See also CLR 2; SAAS 3

Wambaugh, Joseph (Aloysius, Jr.)
1937- .... **CLC 3, 18**
See also CA 33-36R; DLB 6; DLB-Y 83

Ward, Arthur Henry Sarsfield 1883-1959
See Rohmer, Sax
See also CA 108

Ward, Douglas Turner 1930-....... **CLC 19**
See also CA 81-84; DLB 7, 38

White, E(lwyn) B(rooks)
1899-1985 .... **CLC 10, 34, 39**
See also CLR 1; CANR 16; CA 13-16R;
obituary CA 116; SATA 2, 29;
obituary SATA 44; DLB 11, 22

White, Edmund III 1940- .... **CLC 27**
See also CANR 3, 19; CA 45-48

White, Patrick (Victor Martindale)
1912- .... **CLC 3, 4, 5, 7, 9, 18**
See also CA 81-84

White, T(erence) H(anbury)
1906-1964 .... **CLC 30**
See also CA 73-76; SATA 12

White, Terence de Vere 1912- ...... **CLC 49**
See also CANR 3; CA 49-52

White, Walter (Francis)
1893-1955 .... **TCLC 15**
See also CA 115, 124; DLB 51

White, William Hale 1831-1913
See Rutherford, Mark
See also CA 121

Whitehead, E(dward) A(nthony)
1933- .... **CLC 5**
See also CA 65-68

Whitemore, Hugh 1936- .... **CLC 37**

Whitman, Sarah Helen
1803-1878 .... **NCLC 19**
See also DLB 1

Whitman, Walt 1819-1892 .... **NCLC 4**
See also SATA 20; DLB 3, 64;
CDALB 1640-1865

Whitney, Phyllis A(yame) 1903- .... **CLC 42**
See also CANR 3, 25; CA 1-4R; SATA 1,
30

Whittemore, (Edward) Reed (Jr.)
1919- .... **CLC 4**
See also CANR 4; CA 9-12R; DLB 5

Whittier, John Greenleaf
1807-1892 .... **NCLC 8**
See also DLB 1; CDALB 1640-1865

Wicker, Thomas Grey 1926-
See Wicker, Tom
See also CANR 21; CA 65-68

Wicker, Tom 1926- .... **CLC 7**
See also Wicker, Thomas Grey

Wideman, John Edgar
1941- .... **CLC 5, 34, 36**
See also CANR 14; CA 85-88; DLB 33

Wiebe, Rudy (H.) 1934- ...... **CLC 6, 11, 14**
See also CA 37-40R; DLB 60

Wieland, Christoph Martin
1733-1813 .... **NCLC 17**

Wieners, John 1934- .... **CLC 7**
See also CA 13-16R; DLB 16

Wiesel, Elie(zer) 1928- ... **CLC 3, 5, 11, 37**
See also CAAS 4; CANR 8; CA 5-8R;
DLB-Y 87

Wiggins, Marianne 1948- .... **CLC 57**

Wight, James Alfred 1916-
See Herriot, James
See also CA 77-80; SATA 44

Wilbur, Richard (Purdy)
1921- .... **CLC 3, 6, 9, 14, 53**
See also CANR 2; CA 1-4R; CABS 2;
SATA 9; DLB 5

Wild, Peter 1940- .... **CLC 14**
See also CA 37-40R; DLB 5

Wilde, Oscar (Fingal O'Flahertie Wills)
1854-1900 .... **TCLC 1, 8, 23**
See also CA 104; SATA 24; DLB 10, 19,
34, 57

Wilder, Billy 1906- .... **CLC 20**
See also Wilder, Samuel
See also DLB 26

Wilder, Samuel 1906-
See Wilder, Billy
See also CA 89-92

Wilder, Thornton (Niven)
1897-1975 ..... **CLC 1, 5, 6, 10, 15, 35;**
DC 1
See also CA 13-16R; obituary CA 61-64;
DLB 4, 7, 9

Wiley, Richard 1944- .... **CLC 44**
See also CA 121

Wilhelm, Kate 1928- .... **CLC 7**
See also CAAS 5; CANR 17; CA 37-40R;
DLB 8

Willard, Nancy 1936- .... **CLC 7, 37**
See also CLR 5; CANR 10; CA 89-92;
SATA 30, 37; DLB 5, 52

Williams, C(harles) K(enneth)
1936- .... **CLC 33, 56**
See also CA 37-40R; DLB 5

Williams, Charles (Walter Stansby)
1886-1945 .... **TCLC 1, 11**
See also CA 104

Williams, Ella Gwendolen Rees 1890-1979
See Rhys, Jean

Williams, (George) Emlyn
1905-1987 .... **CLC 15**
See also CA 104, 123; DLB 10

Williams, Hugo 1942- .... **CLC 42**
See also CA 17-20R; DLB 40

Williams, John A(lfred) 1925- .... **CLC 5, 13**
See also CAAS 3; CANR 6, 26; CA 53-56;
DLB 2, 33

Williams, Jonathan (Chamberlain)
1929- .... **CLC 13**
See also CANR 8; CA 9-12R; DLB 5

Williams, Joy 1944- .... **CLC 31**
See also CANR 22; CA 41-44R

Williams, Norman 1952- .... **CLC 39**
See also CA 118

Williams, Paulette 1948-
See Shange, Ntozake

Williams, Tennessee
1911-1983 .... **CLC 1, 2, 5, 7, 8, 11, 15,**
19, 30, 39, 45
See also CA 5-8R; obituary CA 108; DLB 7;
DLB-Y 83; DLB-DS 4;
CDALB 1941-1968

Williams, Thomas (Alonzo) 1926- ... **CLC 14**
See also CANR 2; CA 1-4R

Williams, Thomas Lanier 1911-1983
See Williams, Tennessee

Williams, William Carlos
1883-1963 .... **CLC 1, 2, 5, 9, 13, 22, 42**
See also CA 89-92; DLB 4, 16, 54

Williamson, David 1932- .... **CLC 56**

Williamson, Jack 1908- .... **CLC 29**
See also Williamson, John Stewart
See also DLB 8

Williamson, John Stewart 1908-
See Williamson, Jack
See also CANR 123; CA 17-20R

Willingham, Calder (Baynard, Jr.)
1922- .... **CLC 5, 51**
See also CANR 3; CA 5-8R; DLB 2, 44

Wilson, A(ndrew) N(orman) 1950- .. **CLC 33**
See also CA 112; DLB 14

Wilson, Andrew 1948-
See Wilson, Snoo

Wilson, Angus (Frank Johnstone)
1913- .... **CLC 2, 3, 5, 25, 34**
See also CANR 21; CA 5-8R; DLB 15

Wilson, August 1945- .... **CLC 39, 50, 63**
See also CA 115, 122

Wilson, Brian 1942- .... **CLC 12**

Wilson, Colin 1931- .... **CLC 3, 14**
See also CAAS 5; CANR 1, 122; CA 1-4R;
DLB 14

Wilson, Edmund
1895-1972 .... **CLC 1, 2, 3, 8, 24**
See also CANR 1; CA 1-4R;
obituary CA 37-40R; DLB 63

Wilson, Ethel Davis (Bryant)
1888-1980 .... **CLC 13**
See also CA 102; DLB 68

Wilson, John 1785-1854 .... **NCLC 5**

Wilson, John (Anthony) Burgess 1917-
See Burgess, Anthony
See also CANR 2; CA 1-4R

Wilson, Lanford 1937- .... **CLC 7, 14, 36**
See also CA 17-20R; DLB 7

Wilson, Robert (M.) 1944- .... **CLC 7, 9**
See also CANR 2; CA 49-52

Wilson, Sloan 1920- .... **CLC 32**
See also CANR 1; CA 1-4R

Wilson, Snoo 1948- .... **CLC 33**
See also CA 69-72

Wilson, William S(mith) 1932- ..... **CLC 49**
See also CA 81-84

**Winchilsea, Anne (Kingsmill) Finch, Countess
of** 1661-1720 .... **LC 3**

Winters, Janet Lewis 1899-
See Lewis (Winters), Janet
See also CAP 1; CA 9-10

Winters, (Arthur) Yvor
1900-1968 .... **CLC 4, 8, 32**
See also CAP 1; CA 11-12;
obituary CA 25-28R; DLB 48

Wiseman, Frederick 1930- .... **CLC 20**

Wister, Owen 1860-1938 .... **TCLC 21**
See also CA 108; DLB 9

Witkiewicz, Stanislaw Ignacy
1885-1939 .... **TCLC 8**
See also CA 105

Wittig, Monique 1935?- .... **CLC 22**
See also CA 116

Wittlin, Joseph 1896-1976 .... **CLC 25**
See also Wittlin, Jozef

PC Cumulative Nationality Index

PC Cumulative Title Index

Title Index